CRITICAL THEORY

CRITICAL THEORY

A READER FOR LITERARY AND CULTURAL STUDIES

Robert Dale Parker

UNIVERSITY OF ILLINOIS
AT URBANA-CHAMPAIGN

NEW YORK   OXFORD
OXFORD UNIVERSITY PRESS

Oxford University Press, Inc., publishes works that further Oxford University's
objective of excellence in research, scholarship, and education.

Oxford New York
Auckland Cape Town Dar es Salaam Hong Kong Karachi
Kuala Lumpur Madrid Melbourne Mexico City Nairobi
New Delhi Shanghai Taipei Toronto

with offices in
Argentina Austria Brazil Chile Czech Republic France Greece
Guatemala Hungary Italy Japan Poland Portugal Singapore
South Korea Switzerland Thailand Turkey Ukraine Vietnam

For titles covered by Section 112 of the US Higher Education
Opportunity Act, please visit www.oup.com/us/he for the latest
information about pricing and alternate formats.

Published by Oxford University Press, Inc.
198 Madison Avenue, New York, NY 10016
http://www.oup.com

Library of Congress Cataloging-in-Publication Data
Parker, Robert Dale, 1953–
Critical theory : a reader for literary and cultural studies / [selected and
edited by] Robert Dale Parker.
p. cm.
Includes bibliographical references and index.
ISBN 978–0–19–979777–6
1. Literature—History and criticism—Theory, etc. 2. Criticism. I. Title.
PN441.C75 2012
801'.95—dc23   2011044294

Printing number: 9 8 7 6 5 4 3 2 1

CONTENTS

v

Psychoanalysis *181*

Feminism *231*

Queer Studies *283*

PREFACE

For a good many years now, debates and controversies in critical theory have driven literary and cultural studies. Through those debates, critical theory and literary and cultural interpretation keep reinventing themselves. As they reinvent themselves, they remain in dialogue with earlier thinking, producing an ongoing conversation across different models of reading and interpretation. This book invites readers into that conversation. It presents an ample (but not overwhelming) selection of the most influential works in critical and literary theory since roughly 1925, along with a selection from key antecedent figures (Marx, Nietzsche, and Freud) and from more recent variations and developments. It is therefore a large book and yet not so large as the books that try to be most things to most readers. Perhaps the moderately smaller size of this still large volume can make the materials more accessible. It can help readers enjoy and think about the histories, controversies, and consequences of critical theory. Then anyone who finds the readings habit forming can go beyond this volume to read more.

The essays are gathered into ten groups representing ten different but often related and overlapping movements that offer a rough narrative of modern literary and cultural criticism: new criticism, structuralism, deconstruction, psychoanalysis, feminism, queer studies, Marxism, historicism and cultural studies, postcolonial studies and race studies, and reader response. The ten groups fall into a loose sequence that matches the sequence that organizes this book's companion volume, *How to Interpret Literature: Critical Theory for Literary and Cultural Studies*. Rather than ordering the various movements according to when they first emerged, they are ordered here, with a few exceptions, according to when they first achieved widespread influence in critical theory and literary studies. Thus new criticism comes first in the sequence. Feminism, Marxism, and psychoanalysis each began before new criticism, but they did not take on their current high prominence as movements in literary criticism until after the arrival of new criticism. The sequence loops a little toward the end of the collection, as more movements began to emerge and overlap in a shorter span of time. Queer studies shows up a little early in the book, so as to set it next to its cousin, feminism, because feminism and queer studies often lead to or respond to each other. Reader response comes last because it has less of a place as a distinct movement at a distinct time, for in many ways all the other movements after new criticism participate in reader response. Of course, there are many ways to slice the same critical pie. Some readers will prefer to group feminism and queer studies under the rubric of gender studies, and some will prefer to separate postcolonial studies and race studies. Readers and teachers should—and of course will—approach the essays in any sequence and grouping that suits their interests and interpretations. Indeed, most essays fit into more than one category, lending a certain arbitrariness to any decision to put them under one heading. Rather than pretend that the headings tell the full story, therefore, I have embraced the multiplicity of possibilities by listing additional essays from elsewhere in the book at the bottom of each section in the table of contents. By that compromise, I try to suggest flexibility without the confusion of multiple listings and alternative tables of contents. I encourage readers to cross categories, as critics and theorists cross them routinely. In particular, most of the feminist essays cross categories and therefore, for readers interested in feminism, the cross-references deserve special attention.

While conciseness and accessibility have sometimes led me to use excerpts and abridgments, I have tried to minimize the surgery or use it to concentrate the selections on ideas and arguments that are most likely to resonate with readers. I also indicate what is left out. Trying to keep the needs of readers uppermost in mind, I have not provided editorial footnotes, because in a book like this, footnotes often magnify the trees and distract readers from the forest. Readers do not need to know every term an essay uses, especially when, in the Internet age, they can easily look things up. And without footnotes, it is easier for readers to decide what (if anything) they want to look up, which varies with different readers and different readings. In most cases, the context of an essay gets across what readers need to know about key terms. In the remaining cases, I have included explanations in the headnotes. The volume also includes a modest glossary, which allows readers to peruse and review key terms that reappear in multiple readings.

The headnotes introducing the essays vary in length and approach because the selections range from densely allusive to more or less self-explanatory. Especially for the denser selections, the headnotes review the key arguments, what the essay responds to or what responds to it, and explain key concepts or terms that readers may not know. They also refer readers to other, related essays elsewhere in the volume. The headnotes aim to provide a ramp into the selections, not to compete with them. They can guide readers through the challenges and help them see the excitement that many readers have found in some of the most provocative critical thinking of our era.

ACKNOWLEDGMENTS

I am grateful to the teacher-scholars who reviewed the proposal for this book: David Ben-Merre, Buffalo State College; Barry Faulk, Florida State University; John Maynard, New York University; Elsie B. Michie, Louisiana State University; and Steven J. Venturino, Loyola University Chicago. Their suggestions proved invaluable. At Oxford University Press, it was my good fortune to work with Janet M. Beatty, my first editor, and her associate editor, Cory Schneider, and then with my current editor, Frederick Speers, and his assistant, Talia Benamy. Their imagination and patience made putting this book together a pleasure. I am also grateful for the patience and perseverance of Marianne Paul and the rest of the production staff at Oxford. As always, I dedicate this book to Janice N. Harrington.

CREDITS

The editor and publisher gratefully acknowledge the permission to reproduce the copyrighted material in this book.

Louis Althusser: Althusser, Louis. "Ideology and Ideological State Apparatuses (Notes towards an Investigation)." *Lenin and Philosophy and Other Essays.* Trans. Ben Brewster. New York: Monthly Review Press, 1971. 162–183.

Gloria Anzaldúa: Anzaldúa, Gloria. "Movimientos de rebeldía y las culturas que traicionan." *Borderlands / La Frontera: The New Mestiza.* 2nd ed. San Francisco: Aunt Lute Books, 1999. 37–45, 115.

Roland Barthes: From "The Death of the Author" from IMAGE/MUSIC/TEXT by Roland Barthes, translated by Stephen Heath. English translation copyright © 1977 by Stephen Heath. Reprinted by permission of Hill and Wang, a division of Farrar, Straus and Giroux, LLC.

Roland Barthes: From "From Work to Text" from IMAGE/MUSIC/TEXT by Roland Barthes, translated by Stephen Heath. English translation copyright © 1977 by Stephen Heath. Reprinted by permission of Hill and Wang, a division of Farrar, Straus and Giroux, LLC.

H-Dirksen L. Bauman: Bauman, H-Dirksen L. "Towards a Poetics of Vision, Space, and the Body: Sign Language and Literary Theory." *The Disability Studies Reader.* Ed. Lennard J. Davis. New York: Routledge, 2nd ed., 2006. 355–66.

Walter Benjamin: "The Work of Art in the Age of Its Technological Reproducibility: Third version," reprinted by permission of the publisher from *Walter Benjamin: Selected Writing, Volume 4, 1938–1940,* edited by Howard Eiland and Michael W. Jennings, translated by Edmund Jephcott and Others, pp. 251–283, Cambridge, Mass: The Belknap Press of Harvard University Press, Copyright © 2003 by the President and Fellows of Harvard College.

Wolfson and Marshall Brown. Seattle: University of Washington Press, 2006. 1–14. Reprinted by permission of the University of Washington Press.

Slavoj Žižek: Žižek, Slavoj. "Why Does a *Letter* Always Arrive at Its Destination?: Imaginary, Symbolic, Real." *Enjoy Your Symptom!: Jacques Lacan in Hollywood and Out.* Rev. ed. New York: Routledge, 2001. 9–23, 25–28.

Lisa Zunshine: Zunshine, Lisa. "Theory of Mind and Experimental Representations of Fictional Consciousness." *Narrative* 11.3 (2003): 270–91.

INTRODUCTION

Why read critical theory? Why not let literature speak directly for itself? As soon as we ask those questions, we have sworn allegiance to the very thing we question, because such questions are themselves theoretical. If we think about literature, if we think about thinking, then we think about critical theory.

Critical theory has the potential to influence our thinking about literature and about everything that literature connects to and parallels, which is to say about almost anything at all. The materials in this book can propel us into new ways of understanding how we already read and propel us as well into new ways of reading—of reading novels, poems, movies, plays, the culture around us, ourselves, and each other.

I came to critical theory because I read literature for pleasure, and that meant wanting to learn more about literature, and because I wanted to understand the world around us, a desire that weaves into the desire to read literature. After all, literature is driven by and helps drive our understanding of other people, as well as our understanding of politics, philosophy, and art. Through studying literature, criticism, and critical theory, I learned that ignorance does not lead to originality, that not to know what others think condemns us to lose what we have the potential to think ourselves. Moreover, I learned that our best thinking is collaborative. Our best thoughts come through engagement with the thoughts of others we can think against and think with.

Although we sometimes suppose that our thoughts are entirely our own, most of our thoughts are made possible by the history of those who have thought before us. This book can connect its readers to some of that thinking, and I hope that such connections, in turn, can provoke and unsettle our own thoughts in unexpected ways. I hope that readers can approach each reading in this book, and—if they read for a class—each class meeting that discusses readings in the book, by asking what the reading changes, what it reveals about how we have and have not thought, and what it provokes about how we can think, whether as we think about theory itself, think about interpreting the works that fascinate, burden, or attract us in literature and culture, or think about all those things together.

Over the past forty years, the study of critical theory has dramatically reinvented the study of literature. Sometimes the changes left screaming, kicking, and controversy in their wake. Even now, in some quarters, skepticism about theory hangs on in talk about a new age of "posttheory," but from the beginning, the skepticism has itself been theoretical and has mirrored the continuing ability of critical theory to provoke and energize the interpretation of literature.

While the focus of this volume remains on the theory and interpretation of literature, I take it as a given that those tasks include the interpretation of culture more largely. This volume therefore includes key pieces from cultural studies that many literary scholars are less familiar with but that have exerted a wide influence and can appeal to students, including the selections on youth culture by Dick Hebdige, Angela McRobbie, and Tricia Rose.

Theory continues to grow and change. The pace of change may have slowed since the heady days of the 1970s, when structuralism and deconstruction first gained force in Anglo-American criticism, and especially since the 1980s, when Anglo-American critics processed a largely formalist structuralism and deconstruction and reinvented them as a poststructuralism that took account of the social movements that the structuralists and especially the deconstructionists often seemed to underestimate. But the change continues, and critical theory remains both thought provoking and central to the contemporary study and interpretation of literature and culture. Across the many different specialties of the humanities and often the social sciences, critical theory offers a common language and set of questions and concerns that allow people of different interests to talk with each other and read and debate each other's writing. Whether we point our interest to literature, music, new media, film, painting, architecture, or—within literary studies, for example—to writings medieval or modern, to poetry or prose, to a time period, an issue, a genre, a style, or an individual writer or work of writing, critical theory provides the hub and spokes that organize the continually turning and traveling variety of contemporary literary and cultural studies.

As a collection of influential works in critical and literary theory since roughly 1925, this book is designed to stand on its own or to go together with *How to Interpret Literature: Critical Theory for Literary and Cultural Studies,* now available in its second edition from Oxford University Press. *How to Interpret Literature* provides a context for the works collected in this anthology, but some instructors who assign the anthology will prefer to do their own contextualizing.

In the study of literature, critical theory emerged as central in the 1970s. While *How to Interpret Literature* discusses the main movements in recent and contemporary critical theory at some length and provides examples of how we can work with critical theory—including many of the ideas in this volume—to interpret literature and culture, this introduction summarizes the history of the most influential movements in recent critical theory and offers a context for the wide range of essays reprinted in this volume. But this introduction is brief. As the editor, I see part of my task here as simply to get out of the way quickly and encourage readers to move on to the essays.

New criticism was the first influential and more or less systematic movement in English-language literary criticism. The new critics called for interpreting literary works primarily as intrinsic objects. They encouraged critics to focus on literary form more than on history, culture, and politics, which they saw as background information. Structuralism, by contrast, was born outside literary criticism, in the structuralist linguistics of Ferdinand de Saussure. Later, encouraged by the linguist Roman Jakobson, the anthropologist Claude Lévi-Strauss drew on Saussurean structuralist linguistics, and the many-faceted cultural critic Roland Barthes then picked up on structuralism and brought it to literary criticism and to cultural interpretation beyond anthropology. The structuralists were formalists, like the new critics, but they had different goals. Where the new critics focused on the interpretation of individual texts, the structuralists focused on the interpretations of larger systems of texts, whether literary texts (lyric poems, detective novels, narratives in general) or what they saw as the *texts* of other cultural phenomena (fashion, sports, and so on). Meanwhile, the Russian formalists, who began earlier in the twentieth century before the new critics and are represented here by Victor Shklovsky, Jakobson, and V. Propp, started to reach a Western audience that was prepared for them in part by the influence of new critical formalism and then especially of structuralist formalism, which shared the Russian formalists' interest in linguistics. Although Russian formalism has its own history, parts of it were in effect absorbed into structuralism.

But before structuralists had much time to enjoy their ascendancy, a reaction against structuralism emerged in deconstruction, inaugurating what is also sometimes called poststructuralism. Where structuralists, inspired by Saussurean linguistics, found rigorous systems, deconstructionists found that systematic interpretation is tempting, and even inevitable, and yet they believed that it oversimplifies. Where structuralists organized their systems through an array of binary oppositions (pairs of opposites that structure and provide stability to systems), deconstructionists saw everything as multiple. They thought that structuralists erred by trying to see stability in processes that deconstructionists saw as endlessly mobile and unstable. Two is never enough to describe what deconstructionists see. Instead of the structuralists' twos or groups or systems of twos, deconstructionists see proliferations of continuously circulating multiples that defy the systems we may turn to in our efforts to understand and describe.

Deconstruction helped give new life to psychoanalysis in literary and cultural criticism. Freudian psychoanalysis had already proposed a system, to be sure. But influenced by the sense of continuous process observed by deconstructionists, psychoanalysis came to seem more like a way of describing the uncertain and continuous process that shapes desires, identifications, and fears, rather than like a rigid system that describes people in static terms. In particular, under the influence of feminism and then queer studies, critics gave considerable attention to how psychoanalysis, influenced by deconstruction, can describe the processes of gender, femininity, masculinity, and sexual desire. Together, feminism, deconstruction, psychoanalysis, queer studies, and gender studies came to see gender and sexual identity as unstable processes in continuous production, as multiple rather than as rigid or stable.

At the same time, some critics worried that the legacy of new critical formalism, with its focus on literary texts as relatively independent of their history and culture, lingered on in the structuralist sense of systems and patterns and the deconstructionist sense of continuously playful language. Such critics turned to Marxism for its interest in the social world and its commitment to social change. Marxist theorists, in the meantime, were also learning from structuralism and psychoanalysis. The influence of structuralism and psychoanalysis on Marxism helped literary critics, in turn, see what they could learn from Marxism. Cultural studies scholars also brought Marxism into the study of contemporary popular culture, which then contributed to Marxism's influence on the study of literature. Similarly, new historicists sought to bring Marxism and the more socially oriented work in poststructuralism, such as the work of Michel Foucault, into the study of literature. They wanted to bring history out from the background that new criticism and some other formalist criticism had relegated it to. Thus, instead of seeing literary texts merely as reflecting history, they saw history and literature as influencing each other in a continuous cycle. Instead of an active history shaping a passive literature that merely reflects history, they saw history and literature as shaping each other.

Thus the new interest in the social world for the study of literature came to change the practice of critics who were still interested in structuralism and deconstruction. The new interest in the social world went hand in hand with queer studies and feminism as socially committed and not exclusively formalist approaches.

The intensified interest in the social world also provided an opening for and a point of dialogue with the belatedly emerging recognition that literary studies, just as it had once focused too narrowly on the work of men and not on the work of women, also needed to take into account the rest of the world beyond Britain, the United States, and Europe. And to do so it needed to understand the inequities of power that shaped literary and other relations between the colonizing powers and the rest of the world. Moreover, literary studies also needed to recognize how the colonizing nations, including Britain and the United States, depend on the peoples they have conquered or dominated militarily or economically. Amid such dependence, deconstruction can help us see that colonizing peoples and colonized peoples and their descendants partly sustain their distinct identities and, at the same time, partly merge or cross with each other, both in culture and in physical spaces, whether in colonized and formerly colonized lands, in metropolitan cities like London and New York, or in the increasingly globalized exurbs, suburbs, and rural spaces.

Thus to raise postcolonial questions, including the question of how much the world is postcolonial and how much it is still colonial, also meant to address questions of race and race relations, which had already emerged as powerful forces first in the broader culture and then in literary studies as scholars found it increasingly false to continue to focus on the work of white writers and readers to the exclusion of the vast number and variety of writers and readers of other races. The social questions generated by the expanding interest in race and race relations fed into and fed off the socially focused and often overlapping interests of gender studies, queer studies, Marxism, feminism, and postcolonialism, as well as the emerging, if still less established, movements of disability studies and ecocriticism (represented in this volume through essays by H-Dirksen L. Bauman, Robert McRuer, and Lisa Zunshine for disability studies and Lawrence Buell for ecocriticism).

Through these many methods of thinking, reading, and interpreting, questions about readers loomed large. The new critics sometimes proposed that the interpretation of literature was about what was *in* the text independently of how readers might respond to it. They considered readers' responses as outside the text and thus outside the interest of literary criticism. In that sense, reader response criticism saw itself as opposed to new criticism. Meanwhile, structuralists studied the structure of responses to literary texts, and deconstructionists and psychoanalytic critics studied the multiplicity of responses. Socially oriented critics, influenced by race studies and postcolonial studies, feminism, queer studies, Marxism, historicism, and cultural studies, looked at or speculated about the social settings, influences, and consequences of readers' responses for the interpretation of literature and culture, and critics interested in cognitive science—the study of how people think—compared how we read each others' thoughts with how we read the thoughts of fictional characters. The essays in this volume provide a series of examples and windows that can open up the brief history of literary and cultural criticism recounted here. I hope that in these essays readers will find an invitation to the ongoing excitements of critical discussion, reading, writing, and interpretation.

NEW CRITICISM

THE LANGUAGE OF PARADOX (1942)
THE FORMALIST CRITICS (1951)

CLEANTH BROOKS

As readers and interpreters, the new critics often focused on paradox, ambiguity, tension, and irony in literary language, and in "The Language of Paradox," Brooks established paradox as a key concept for reading and interpreting poetry. Brooks's essay also models the new critical call for "close readings" of literature. For that reason, readers will do best to read the poems that Brooks discusses before reading his essay, specifically, to read John Donne's "The Canonization" and perhaps William Wordsworth's "It is a beauteous evening" and "Composed upon Westminster Bridge." By focusing on the language of the poem, the new critics focus on its form, versus the social and historical, which Brooks brushes aside as merely "biological, sociological, and economic." New critics are often accused, unfairly, of ignoring history. Brooks does not ignore history. He notes, for example, the history of words, especially the sexual meaning of the word die in Donne's time, and he notes that London is "a pulsating heart of empire" and that Londoners have "disciplined" the Thames "into a rigid and mechanical pattern." But Brooks argues that Wordsworth does not dwell on such gritty things as history and economics. At the same time that new critics, including Brooks in particular, focused on sources of conflict like paradox, ambiguity, tension, and irony, they also focused on unity in the work of literature, seeing unity as essential for great art. Unity may not seem to fit with the conflicts Brooks finds in poetic language. The new critics resolved that contradiction by finding a balance among the competing paradoxes, ambiguities, tensions, and ironies, allowing Brooks to claim in "The Language of Paradox" that unity "welds together the discordant and the contradictory." (Two footnotes that Brooks cut from later reprintings are not included here.)

In "The Formalist Critics," Brooks argues that critics may address such topics as moral problems, social history, and politics but should concentrate on the work of literature itself, including its form and unity. He echoes W. K. Wimsatt and Monroe Beardsley's argument about the intentional and affective fallacies (see the headnote to Wimsatt's essay in this volume), arguing that the only intent that matters is the intent that is realized in the literary work, and that we determine that intent by studying the work itself, not the responses of readers.

THE LANGUAGE OF PARADOX (1942)

CLEANTH BROOKS

Few of us are prepared to accept the statement that the language of poetry is the language of paradox. Paradox is the language of sophistry, hard, bright, witty; it is hardly the language of the soul. We are willing to allow that paradox is a permissible weapon which a Chesterton may on occasion exploit. We may permit it in epigram, a special subvariety of poetry; and in satire, which though useful, we are hardly willing to allow to be poetry at all. Our prejudices force us to regard paradox as intellectual rather than emotional, clever rather than profound, rational rather than divinely irrational.

Yet there is a sense in which paradox is the language appropriate and inevitable to poetry. It is the scientist whose truth requires a language purged of every trace of paradox; apparently the truth which the poet utters can be approached only in terms of paradox. I overstate the case, to be sure; it is possible that the title of this paper is itself to be treated as merely a paradox. Certainly, the paper itself will appear to many people as merely a piece of special case-making, specious rather than convincing. But there are reasons for thinking that the overstatement which I propose may light up some elements in the nature of poetry which tend to be overlooked.

The case of William Wordsworth, for instance, is instructive on this point. His poetry would not appear to promise many examples of the language of paradox. He usually prefers the direct attack. He insists on simplicity; he distrusts whatever seems sophistical. And yet the typical Wordsworth poem is based upon a paradoxical situation. Consider his celebrated

> It is a beauteous evening, calm and free,
> The holy time is quiet as a Nun
> Breathless with adoration....

The poet is filled with worship, but the girl who walks beside him is not worshipping. The implication is that she should respond to the holy time, and become like the evening itself, nun-like; but she seems less worshipful than inanimate nature itself. Yet

> If thou appear untouched by solemn thought,
> Thy nature is not therefore less divine:
> Thou liest in Abraham's bosom all the year,
> And worship'st at the temple's inner shrine,
> God being with thee when we know it not.

The underlying paradox (of which the enthusiastic reader may well be unconscious) is nevertheless thoroughly necessary, even for that reader. Why does the innocent girl worship more deeply than the self-conscious poet who walks beside her? Because she is filled with an unconscious sympathy for *all* of nature, not merely the grandiose and solemn. One remembers the lines from Wordsworth's friend, Coleridge:

> He prayeth best, who loveth best
> All things both great and small.

Her unconscious sympathy is the unconscious worship. She is in communion with nature "all the year," and her devotion is continual whereas that of the poet is sporadic and momentary. But we have not done with the paradox yet. It not only underlies the poem, but something of the paradox informs the poem, though, since this is Wordsworth, rather timidly. The comparison of the evening to the nun actually has more than one dimension. The calm of the evening obviously means "worship," even to the dull-witted and insensitive. It corresponds to the trappings of the nun, visible to everyone. Thus, it suggests not merely holiness, but, in the total poem, even a hint of pharisaical holiness, with which the girl's careless innocence, itself a symbol of her continual secret worship, stands in contrast.

Or consider Wordsworth's sonnet, "Composed upon Westminster Bridge." I believe that most of us will agree that it is one of Wordsworth's most successful poems; yet most students have the greatest difficulty in accounting for its goodness. The attempt to account for it on the grounds of nobility of sentiment soon breaks down. On this level, the poem merely says: that the city in the morning light presents a picture which is majestic and touching to all but the most dull of soul; but the poem says very little more about the sight: the city is beautiful in the morning light and it is awfully still. The attempt to make a case for the poem in terms of the brilliance of its images also quickly breaks down: the student searches for graphic details in vain; there are next to no realistic touches. In fact, the poet simply huddles the details together:

> ... silent, bare
> Ships, towers, domes, theatres, and temples lie
> Open unto the fields....

We get a blurred impression—points of roofs and pinnacles along the skyline, all twinkling in the morning light. More than that, the sonnet as a whole contains some very flat writing and some well-worn comparisons.

The reader may ask: where, then, does the poem get its power? It gets it, it seems to me, from the paradoxical situation out of which the poem arises. Wordsworth is honestly surprised, and he manages to get some sense of awed surprise into the poem. It is odd to the poet that the city should be able to "wear the beauty of the morning" at all. Mount Snowden, Skiddaw, Mont Blanc—these wear it by natural right, but surely not grimy, feverish London. This is the point of the almost shocked exclamation

> Never did sun more beautifully steep
> In his first splendour, *valley, rock,* or *hill* ...

The "smokeless air" reveals a city which the poet did not know existed: man-made London is a part of nature too, is lighted by the sun of nature, and lighted to as beautiful effect.

> The river glideth at his own sweet will ...

A river is the most "natural" thing that one can imagine; it has the elasticity, the curved line of nature itself. The poet had never been able to regard this one as a real river—now, uncluttered by barges, the river reveals itself as a natural thing, not at all disciplined into a rigid and mechanical pattern: it is like the daffodils, or the mountain brooks, artless, and whimsical, and "natural" as they. The poem closes, you will remember, as follows:

> Dear God! the very houses seem asleep;
> And all that mighty heart is lying still!

The city, in the poet's insight of the morning, has earned its right to be considered organic, not merely mechanical. That is why the stale metaphor of the sleeping houses is strangely renewed. The most exciting thing that the poet can say about the houses is that they are *asleep*. He has been in the habit of counting them dead—as just mechanical and inanimate; to say they are "asleep" is to say that they are alive, that they participate in the life of nature. In the same way, the tired old metaphor which sees a great city as a pulsating heart of empire becomes revivi- fied. It is only when the poet sees the city under the semblance of death that he can see it as actually alive—quick with the only life which he can accept, the organic life of "nature."

It is not my intention to exaggerate Wordsworth's own consciousness of the paradox involved. In this poem, he prefers, as is usual with him, the frontal attack. But the situation is paradoxical here as in so many of his poems. In his preface to the second edition of the *Lyrical Ballads* Wordsworth stated that his general purpose was "to choose incidents and situations from common life" but so to treat them that "ordinary things should be pre- sented to the mind in an unusual aspect." Coleridge was to state the purpose for him later, in terms which make even more evident Wordsworth's exploitation of the paradoxical: "Mr. Wordsworth...was to propose to himself as his object, to give the charm of novelty to things of every day, and to excite a feeling analogous to the supernatural, by awakening the mind's attention to the lethargy of custom, and directing it to the loveliness and the won- ders of the world before us...." Wordsworth in short was consciously attempting to show his audience that the common was really uncommon, the prosaic was really poetic.

Coleridge's terms, "the charm of novelty to things of every day," "awakening the mind," suggest the Romantic preoccupation with wonder—the surprise, the revelation which puts the tarnished familiar world in a new light. This may well be the *raison d'etre* of most Romantic paradoxes; and yet the neoclassic poets use paradox for much the same reason. Consider Pope's lines from "The Essay on Man":

> In doubt his Mind or Body to prefer;
> Born but to die, and reas'ning but to err;
> Alike in ignorance, his Reason such,
> Whether he thinks too little, or too much....
>
> Created half to rise, and half to fall;
> Great Lord of all things, yet a Prey to all;
> Sole Judge of Truth, in endless Error hurl'd;
> The Glory, Jest, and Riddle of the world!

Here, it is true, the paradoxes insist on the irony, rather than on the wonder. But Pope too might have claimed that he was treating the things of every day, man himself, and awaken- ing his mind so that he would view himself in a new and blinding light. Thus, there is a cer- tain awed wonder in Pope just as there is a certain trace of irony implicit in the Wordsworth sonnets. There is, of course, no reason why they should not occur together; and they do. Wonder and irony merge in many of the lyrics of Blake; they merge in Coleridge's *Ancient*

Mariner. The variations in emphasis are numerous. Gray's "Elegy" uses a typical Wordsworth "situation" with the rural scene and with peasants contemplated in the light of their "betters." But in the "Elegy" the balance is heavily tilted in the direction of irony, the revelation an ironic rather than a startling one:

> Can storied urn or animated bust
> Back to its mansion call the fleeting breath?
> Can Honour's voice provoke the silent dust,
> Or Flatt'ry sooth the dull cold ear of Death?

But I am not here interested in the possible variations ; I am interested rather in our seeing that the paradoxes spring from the very nature of the poet's language: it is a language in which the connotations play as great a part as the denotations. And I do not mean that the connotations are important as supplying some sort of frill or trimming, something external to the real matter in hand. I mean that the poet does not use a notation at all—as the scientist may properly be said to do so. The poet, within limits, has to make up his language as he goes.

T. S. Eliot somewhere refers to "that perpetual slight alteration of language, words perpetually juxtaposed in new and sudden combinations," which occurs in poetry. It *is* perpetual; it cannot be kept out of the poem; it can only be directed and controlled. The tendency of science is necessarily to stabilize terms to freeze them into strict denotations; the poet's tendency is by contrast disruptive. His terms are continually modifying each other, and thus violating their dictionary meanings. To take a very simple example, consider the adjectives in the first line of Wordsworth's evening sonnet: *beauteous, calm, free, holy, quiet, breathless*. The juxtapositions are hardly startling; and yet notice this: the evening is like a nun breathless with adoration. The adjective "breathless" suggests tremendous excitement; and yet the evening is not only quiet but *calm*. There is no final contradiction, to be sure: it is *that* kind of calm and *that* kind of excitement, and the two states may well occur together. But the poet has no one term. Even if he had a polysyllabic technical term, the term would not provide the solution for his problem. He must work by contradiction and qualification.

We may approach the problem in this way: the poet has to work by analogies. All of the subtler states of emotion, as I. A. Richards has pointed out, necessarily demand metaphor for their expression. The poet must work by analogies, but the metaphors do not lie in the same plane or fit neatly edge to edge. There is a continual tilting of the planes; necessary overlappings, discrepancies, contradictions. Even the most direct and simple poet is forced into paradoxes far more often than we think, if we are sufficiently alive to what he is doing.

But in dilating on the difficulties of the poet's task, I do not want to leave the impression that it is a task which necessarily defeats him, or even that with his method he may not win to a fine precision. To use Shakespeare's figure, he can

> with assays of bias
> By indirections find directions out.

Shakespeare had in mind the game of lawnbowls in which the bowl is distorted, a circumstance which allows the skilful player to bowl a curve. To elaborate the figure, science makes use of the perfect sphere and its attack can be direct. The method of art can, I believe, never be direct—is always indirect. But that does not mean that the master of the game cannot place the bowl where he wants it. The serious difficulties will occur only when he confuses his game with that of science and mistakes the nature of his appropriate instrument. Mr. Stuart Chase a few years ago, with a touching naïveté, urged us to take the distortion out of the bowl—to treat language like notation.

I have said that even the apparently simple and straightforward poet is forced into paradoxes by the nature of his instrument. Seeing this, we should not be surprised to find poets who consciously employ it to gain a compression and precision otherwise unobtainable. Such a method, like any other, carries with it its own perils. But the dangers are not overpowering; the poem is not predetermined to a shallow and glittering sophistry. The method is an extension of the normal language of poetry, not a perversion of it.

I should like to refer you to a concrete case. Donne's "Canonization" ought to provide a sufficiently extreme instance.

> For Godsake hold your tongue, and let me love,
> Or chide my palsie, or my gout,
> My five gray haires, or ruin'd fortune flout,
> With wealth your state, your minde with Arts improve,
> Take you a course, get you a place,
> Observe his honour, or his grace,
> Or the Kings reall, or his stamped face
> Contemplate, what you will, approve,
> So you will let me love.
>
> Alas, alas, who's injur'd by my love?
> What merchants ships have my sighs drown'd?
> Who saies my teares have overflow'd his ground?
> When did my colds a forward spring remove?
> When did the heats which my veines fill
> Adde one more to the plaguie Bill?
> Soldiers finde warres, and Lawyers finde out still
> Litigious men, which quarrels move,
> Though she and I do love.
>
> Call us what you will, wee are made such by love;
> Call her one, mee another flye,
> We'are Tapers too, and at our owne cost die,
> And wee in us finde the'Eagle and the Dove.
> The Phoenix ridle hath more wit
> By us, we two being one, are it.
> So to one neutrall thing both sexes fit,
> We dye and rise the same, and prove
> Mysterious by this love.

Wee can dye by it, if not live by love,
And if unfit for tombes and hearse
Our legend bee, it will be fit for verse;
And if no peece of Chronicle wee prove,
We'll build in sonnets pretty roomes;
As well a well wrought urne becomes
The greatest ashes, as halfe-acre tombes,
And by these hymnes, all shall approve
Us Canoniz'd for Love:

And thus invoke us; You whom reverend love
Made one anothers hermitage:
You, to whom love was peace, that now is rage;
Who did the whole worlds soule contract, and drove
Into the glasses of your eyes
(So made such mirrors, and such spies,
That they did all to you epitomize,)
Countries, Townes, Courts: Beg from above
A patterne of your love!

The basic metaphor which underlies the poem (and which is reflected in the title) involves a sort of paradox. For the poet daringly treats profane love as if it were divine love. The canonization is not that of a pair of holy anchorites who have renounced the world and the flesh. The hermitage of each is the other's body; but they do renounce the world, and so their title to sainthood is cunningly argued. The poem then is a parody of Christian sainthood; but it is an intensely serious parody of a sort that modern man, habituated as he is to an easy yes or no, can hardly understand. He refuses to accept the paradox as a serious rhetorical device; and since he is able to accept it only as a cheap trick, he is forced into this dilemma. Either: Donne does not take love seriously; here he is merely sharpening his wit as a sort of mechanical exercise. Or: Donne does not take sainthood seriously; here he is merely indulging in a cynical and bawdy parody.

Neither account is true; a reading of the poem will show that Donne takes both love and religion seriously; it will show, further, that the paradox is here his inevitable instrument. But to see this plainly will require a closer reading than most of us give to poetry.

The poem opens dramatically on a note of exasperation. The "you" whom the speaker addresses is not identified. We can imagine that it is a person, perhaps a friend, who is objecting to the speaker's love affair. At any rate, the person represents the practical world which regards love as a silly affectation. To use the metaphor on which the poem is built, the friend represents the secular world which the lovers have renounced.

Donne begins to suggest this metaphor in the first stanza by the contemptuous alternatives which he suggests to the friend

...chide my palsy, or my gout,
My five gray haires, or ruin'd fortune flout...

The implications are: (1) All right, consider my love as an infirmity, as a disease, if you will, but confine yourself to my other infirmities, my palsy, my approaching old age, my ruined fortune. You stand a better chance of curing those; in chiding me for this one, you are simply wasting your time as well as mine. (2) Why don't you pay attention to your own welfare—go on and get wealth and honor for yourself. What should you care if I do give these up in pursuing my love?

The two main categories of secular success are neatly, and contemptuously epitomized in the line

Or the Kings reall, or his stamped face.

Cultivate the court and gaze at the king's face there, or, if you prefer, get into business and look at his face stamped on coins. But let me alone.

This conflict between the "real" world and the lover absorbed in the world of love runs through the poem; it dominates the second stanza in which the torments of love, so vivid to the lover, affect the real world not at all—

What merchants ships have my sighs drown'd?

It is touched on in the fourth stanza in the contrast between the word "Chronicle" which suggests secular history with its pomp and magnificence, the history of kings and princes, and the word "sonnets" with its suggestions of trivial and precious intricacy. The conflict appears again in the last stanza, only to be resolved when the unworldly lovers, love's saints who have given up the world, paradoxically achieve a more intense world. But here the paradox is still contained in, and supported by, the dominant metaphor: so does the holy anchorite win a better world by giving up this one.

But before going on to discuss this development of the theme, it is important to see what else the second stanza does. For it is in this second stanza and the third, that the poet shifts the tone of the poem, modulating from the note of irritation with which the poem opens into the quite different tone with which it closes.

Donne accomplishes the modulation of tone by what may be called an analysis of love-metaphor. Here, as in many of his poems, he shows that he is thoroughly self-conscious about what he is doing. This second stanza he fills with the conventionalized figures of the Petrarchan tradition: the wind of lovers' sighs, the floods of lovers' tears, etc.—extravagant figures with which the contemptuous secular friend might be expected to tease the lover. The implication is that the poet himself recognizes the absurdity of the Petrarchan love metaphors. But what of it? The very absurdity of the jargon which lovers are expected to talk makes for his argument; their love, however, absurd it may appear to the world, does no harm to the world. The practical friend need have no fears: there will still be wars to fight and lawsuits to argue.

The opening of the third stanza suggests that this vein of irony is to be maintained. The poet points out to his friend the infinite fund of such absurdities which can be applied to lovers:

Call her one, mee another flye,
We'are Tapers too, and at our owne cost die...

For that matter, the lovers can conjure up for themselves plenty of such fantastic comparisons: *they* know what the world thinks of them. But these figures of the third stanza are no longer the threadbare Petrarchan conventionalities; they have sharpness and bite. The last one, the likening of the lovers to the phoenix, is fully serious, and with it, the tone has shifted from ironic banter into a defiant but controlled tenderness.

The effect of this implied awareness of the lovers' apparent madness is to cleanse and revivify metaphor; to indicate the sense in which the poet accepts it, and thus to prepare us for accepting seriously the fine and seriously intended metaphors which dominate the last two stanzas of the poem.

The opening line of the fourth stanza,

Wee can dye by it, if not live by love,

achieves an effect of tenderness and deliberate resolution. The lovers are ready to die to the world; they are committed; they are not callow but confident. (The basic metaphor of the saint, one notices, is being carried on; the lovers in their renunciation of the world, have something of the confident resolution of the saint. By the bye, the word "legend"—

... if unfit for tombes and hearse
Our legend bee—

in Donne's time meant "the life of a saint.") The lovers are willing to forego the ponderous and stately chronicle and to accept the trifling and insubstantial "sonnet" instead; but then if the urn be well-wrought it provides a finer memorial for one's ashes than does the pompous and grotesque monument. With the finely contemptuous, yet quiet phrase, "half-acre tombes," the world which the lovers reject expands into something gross and vulgar. But the figure works further; the pretty sonnets will not merely hold their ashes as a decent earthly memorial. Their legend, their story, will gain them canonization; and approved as love's saints, other lovers will invoke them.

In this last stanza, the theme receives a final complication. The lovers in rejecting life actually win to the most intense life. This paradox has been hinted at earlier in the phoenix metaphor. Here it receives a powerful dramatization. The lovers in becoming hermits, find that they have not lost the world, but have gained the world in each other, now a more intense, more meaningful world. Donne is not content to treat the lovers' discovery as something which comes to them passively, but rather as something which they actively achieve. They are like the saint, God's athlete:

Who did the whole worlds soule *contract*, and *drove*
Into the glasses of your eyes. . . .

The image is that of a violent squeezing as of a powerful hand. And what do the lovers "drive" into each other's eyes? The "Countries, Townes," and "Courts," which they renounced in the first stanza of the poem. The unworldly lovers thus become the most "worldly" of all.

The tone with which the poem closes is one of triumphant achievement, but the tone is a development contributed to by various earlier elements. One of the more important elements which works toward our acceptance of the final paradox is the figure of the phoenix, which will bear a little further analysis.

The comparison of the lovers to the phoenix is very skilfully related to the two earlier comparisons, that in which the lovers are like burning tapers, and that in which they are like the eagle and the dove. The phoenix comparison gathers up both: the phoenix is a bird, and like the tapers, it burns. We have a selected series of items: the phoenix figure seems to come in a natural stream of association. "Call us what you will," the lover says, and rattles off in his desperation the first comparisons that occur to him. The comparison to the phoenix seems thus merely another outlandish one, the most outrageous of all. But it is this most fantastic one, stumbled over apparently in his haste, that the poet goes on to develop. It really describes the lovers best and justifies their renunciation. For the phoenix is not two but one, "we two being one, are it"; and it burns, not like the taper at its own cost, but to live again. Its death is life: "Wee dye and rise the same...." The poet literally justifies the fantastic assertion. In the sixteenth and seventeenth centuries to "die" means to experience the consummation of the act of love. The lovers after the act are the same. Their love is not exhausted in mere lust. This is their title to canonization. Their love is like the phoenix.

I hope that I do not seem to juggle the meaning of *die*. The meaning that I have cited can be abundantly justified in the literature of the period; Shakespeare uses "die" in this sense; so does Dryden. Moreover, I do not think that I give it undue emphasis. The word is in a crucial position. On it is pivoted the transition to the next stanza,

> Wee can dye by it, if not live by love,
> And if unfit for tombes....

Most important of all, the sexual submeaning of "die" does not contradict the other meanings: the poet is saying: "Our death is really a more intense life"; "We can afford to trade life (the world) for death (love), for that death is the consummation of life"; "After all, one does not expect to live *by* love, one expects, and wants, to die *by* it." But in the total passage he is also saying "Because our love is not mundane, we can give up the world"; "because our love is not merely lust, we can give up the other lusts, the lust for wealth and power"; "because," and this is said with a little vein of irony as by one who knows the world too well, "because our love can outlast its consummation, we are a minor miracle; we are love's saints." This passage with its ironical tenderness and its realism feeds and supports the brilliant paradox with which the poem closes.

There is one more factor in developing and sustaining the final effect. The poem is an instance of the doctrine which it asserts; it is both the assertion and the realization of the assertion. The poet has actually before our eyes built within the song the "pretty room" with which he says the lovers can be content. The poem itself is the well-wrought urn which can hold the lovers' ashes and which will not suffer in comparison with the prince's "half-acre tomb."

And how necessary are the paradoxes? Donne might have said directly, "Love in a cottage is enough." "The Canonization" contains this admirable thesis, but it contains a great deal more. He might have been as forthright as a later lyricist who wrote, "We'll build a sweet little nest, / Somewhere out in the West, / And let the rest of the world go by." He might even have imitated that more metaphysical lyric, which maintains, "You're the cream in my coffee." "The Canonization" touches on all these observations, but it goes beyond them, not merely in dignity, but in precision.

I submit that the only way by which the poet could say what "The Canonization" says is by paradox. More direct methods may be tempting, but all of them enfeeble and distort what is to be said. This statement may seem the less surprising when we reflect on how many of the important things which the poet has to say have to be said by means of paradox:—most of the language of lovers is such; "The Canonization" is a good example; most of the language of religion: "He who would save his life, must lose it"; "The last shall be first." Indeed, almost any insight important enough to warrant a great poem apparently has to be stated in such terms. Deprived of the character of paradox with its twin concomitants of irony and wonder, the matter of Donne's poem unravels into "facts," biological, sociological, and economic. What happens to Donne's lovers if we consider them "scientifically," without benefit of the supernaturalism which the poet confers upon them? Well, what happens to Shakespeare's lovers, for Shakespeare uses the basic metaphor of "The Canonization" in his *Romeo and Juliet*? In their first conversation, you remember, the lovers play with the analogy between the lover and the pilgrim to the Holy Land. Juliet says:

> For saints have hands that pilgrims' hands do touch
> And palm to palm is holy palmers' kiss.

Considered scientifically, the lovers become Mr. Aldous Huxley's animals, "quietly sweating, palm to palm."

For us today, Donne's imagination seems obsessed with the problem of unity; the sense in which the lovers become one—the sense in which the soul is united with God. Frequently, as we have seen, one type of union becomes a metaphor for the other. It may not be too far-fetched to see both as instances of, and metaphors for, the union which the creative imagination itself effects. For that fusion is not logical; it apparently violates science and commonsense; it welds together the discordant and the contradictory. Coleridge has of course given us the classic description of its nature and power. It "reveals itself in the balance or reconcilement of opposite or discordant qualities: of sameness, with difference; of the general, with the concrete; the idea, with the image; the individual, with the representative; the sense of novelty and freshness, with old and familiar objects; a more than usual state of emotion, with more than usual order...." It is a great and illuminating statement, but it is a series of paradoxes. Apparently Coleridge could describe the effect of the imagination in no other way.

Shakespeare, in one of his poems, has given a description that oddly parallels that of Coleridge.

> Reason in itself confounded,
> Saw Division grow together,
> To themselves yet either neither,
> Simple were so well compounded.

I do not know what his "The Phoenix and the Turtle" celebrates. Perhaps it *was* written to honor the marriage of Sir John Salisbury and Ursula Stanley; or perhaps the phoenix is Lucy, Countess of Bedford; or perhaps the poem is merely an essay on Platonic love. But the scholars themselves are so uncertain, that I think we will do little violence to established habits of thinking, if we boldly preempt the poem for our own purposes. Certainly the poem is an instance of that magic power which Coleridge sought to describe. I propose that we take it for a moment as a poem about that power:

> So they loved as love in twaine,
> Had the essence but in one,
> Two distincts, Division none,
> Number there in love was slaine.
>
> Hearts remote, yet not asunder;
> Distance and no space was seene,
> Twixt the *Turtle* and his Queene;
> But in them it were a wonder....
>
> Propertie was thus appalled,
> That the selfe was not the same;
> Single Natures double name,
> Neither two nor one was called.

Precisely! The nature is single, one, unified. But the name is double, and today with our multiplication of sciences, it is multiple. If the poet is to be true to his poetry, he must call it neither two nor one: the paradox is his only solution. The difficulty has intensified since Shakespeare's day: the timid poet, when confronted with the problem of "Single Natures double name," has too often funked it. A history of poetry from Dryden's time to our own might bear as its subtitle "The Half-Hearted Phoenix."

In Shakespeare's poem, you will remember that at the union of the phoenix and the turtle, Reason is "in itselfe confounded"; but it recovers to admit its own bankruptcy,

> Love hath Reason, Reason none,
> If what parts, can so remaine....

and it is Reason which goes on to utter the beautiful threnos with which the poem concludes:

> Beautie, Truth, and Raritie,
> Grace in all simplicitie,
> Here enclosede, in cinders lie....
>
> Truth may seem, but cannot be;
> Beauty brag, but 'tis not she;
> Truth and beauty buried be.
>
> To this urne let those repaire,
> That are either true or faire,
> For these dead Birds, sigh a prayer.

Having preempted the poem for our own purposes, it may not be too outrageous to go on to deduce one further observation. The urn to which we are summoned, the urn which holds the ashes of the phoenix, is like the well-wrought urn of Donne's "Canonization" which holds the phoenix-lovers' ashes; it is the poem itself. One is reminded of still another urn, Keats's Grecian urn, which contained for Keats, Truth and Beauty as Shakespeare's urn encloses "Beautie, Truth, and Raritie." But there is a sense in which all such well-wrought urns contain the ashes of a phoenix. The urns are not meant for memorial purposes only, though that often seems to be their chief significance to the professors of literature. The phoenix rises from its ashes; or ought to rise; but it will not arise merely for our sifting and measuring the ashes, or testing them for their chemical content. We must be prepared to accept the paradox of the imagination itself; else "Beautie, Truth, and Raritie" remain enclosed in their cinders and we shall end with essential cinders, for all our pains.

THE FORMALIST CRITICS (1951)

CLEANTH BROOKS

Here are some articles of faith I could subscribe to:

That literary criticism is a description and an evaluation of its object.

That the primary concern of criticism is with the problem of unity—the kind of whole which the literary work forms or fails to form, and the relation of the various parts to each other in building up this whole.

That the formal relations in a work of literature may include, but certainly exceed, those of logic.

That in a successful work, form and content cannot be separated.

That form is meaning.

That literature is ultimately metaphorical and symbolic.

That the general and the universal are not seized upon by abstraction, but got at through the concrete and the particular.

That literature is not a surrogate for religion.

That, as Allen Tate says, "specific moral problems" are the subject matter of literature, but that the purpose of literature is not to point a moral.

That the principles of criticism define the area relevant to literary criticism; they do not constitute a method for carrying out the criticism.

Such statements as these would not, however, even though greatly elaborated, serve any useful purpose here. The interested reader already knows the general nature of the critical position adumbrated—or, if he does not, he can find it set forth in writings of mine or of other critics of like sympathy. Moreover, a condensed restatement of the position here would probably beget as many misunderstandings as have past attempts to set it forth. It seems much more profitable to use the present occasion for dealing with some persistent misunderstandings and objections.

In the first place, to make the poem or the novel the central concern of criticism has appeared to mean cutting it loose from its author and from his life as a man, with his own particular hopes, fears, interests, conflicts, etc. A criticism so limited may seem bloodless and hollow. It will seem so to the typical professor of literature in the graduate school, where the study of literature is still primarily a study of the ideas and personality of the author as revealed in his letters, his diaries, and the recorded conversations of his friends. It will certainly seem so to literary gossip columnists who purvey literary chitchat. It may also seem so to the young poet or novelist, beset with his own problems of composition and with his struggles to find a subject and a style and to get a hearing for himself.

In the second place, to emphasize the work seems to involve severing it from those who actually read it, and this severance may seem drastic and therefore disastrous. After all, literature is written to be read. Wordsworth's poet was a man speaking to men. In each Sunday *Times,* Mr. J. Donald Adams points out that the hungry sheep look up and are not fed; and less strenuous moralists than Mr. Adams are bound to feel a proper revulsion against "mere aestheticism." Moreover, if we neglect the audience which reads the work, including that for which it was presumably written, the literary historian is prompt to point out that the kind of audience that Pope had did condition the kind of poetry that he wrote. The poem has its roots in history, past or present. Its place in the historical context simply cannot be ignored.

I have stated these objections as sharply as I can because I am sympathetic with the state of mind which is prone to voice them. Man's experience is indeed a seamless garment, no part of which can be separated from the rest. Yet if we urge this fact of inseparability against the drawing of distinctions, then there is no point in talking about criticism at all. I am assuming that distinctions are necessary and useful and indeed inevitable.

The formalist critic knows as well as anyone that poems and plays and novels are written by men—that they do not somehow happen—and that they are written as expressions of particular personalities and are written from all sorts of motives—for money, from a desire to express oneself, for the sake of a cause, etc. Moreover, the formalist critic knows as well as anyone that literary works are merely potential until they are read—that is, that they are recreated in the minds of actual readers, who vary enormously in their capabilities, their interests, their prejudices, their ideas. But the formalist critic is concerned primarily with the work itself. Speculation on the mental processes of the author takes the critic away from the work into biography and psychology. There is no reason, of course, why he should not turn away into biography and psychology. Such explorations are very much worth making. But they should not be confused with an account of the work. Such studies describe the process of composition, not the structure of the thing composed, and they may be performed quite as validly for the poor work as for the good one. They may be validly performed for any kind of expression—non-literary as well as literary.

On the other hand, exploration of the various readings which the work has received also takes the critic away from the work into psychology and the history of taste. The various imports of a given work may well be worth studying. I. A. Richards has put us all in his debt by demonstrating what different experiences may be derived from the same poem by an apparently homogeneous group of readers; and the scholars have pointed out, all along, how different Shakespeare appeared to an 18th Century as compared with a 19th Century audience; or how sharply divergent are the estimates of John Donne's lyrics from historical period to historical period. But such work, valuable and necessary as it may be, is to be distinguished from a criticism of the work itself. The formalist critic, because he wants to criticize the work itself, makes two assumptions: (1) he assumes that the relevant part of the author's intention is what he got actually into his work; that is, he assumes that the author's intention *as realized* is the "intention" that counts, not necessarily what he was conscious of trying to do, or what he now remembers he was then trying to do. And (2) the formalist critic assumes an ideal reader: that is, instead of focusing on the varying spectrum of possible readings, he attempts to find a central point of reference from which he can focus upon the structure of the poem or novel.

But there *is* no ideal reader, someone is prompt to point out, and he will probably add that it is sheer arrogance that allows the critic, with his own blindsides and prejudices, to put himself in the position of that ideal reader. There is no ideal reader, of course, and I suppose that the practising critic can never be too often reminded of the gap between his reading and the "true" reading of the poem. But for the purpose of focusing upon the poem rather than upon his own reactions, it is a defensible strategy. Finally, of course, it is the strategy that all critics of whatever persuasion are forced to adopt. (The alternatives are desperate: either we say that one person's reading is as good as another's and equate those readings on a basis of absolute equality and thus deny the possibility of any standard reading. Or else we take a lowest common denominator of the various readings that have been made; that is, we frankly move from literary criticism into socio-psychology. To propose taking a consensus of the opinions of "qualified" readers is simply to split the ideal reader into a group of ideal readers.) As consequences of the distinction just referred to, the formalist critic rejects two popular tests for literary value. The first proves the value of the work from the author's "sincerity" (or the intensity of the author's feelings as he composed it). If we heard that Mr. Guest testified that he put his heart and soul into his poems, we would not be very much impressed, though I should see no reason to doubt such a statement from Mr. Guest. It would simply be critically irrelevant. Ernest Hemingway's statement in a recent issue of *Time* magazine that he counts his last novel his best is of interest for Hemingway's biography, but most readers of *Across the River and Into the Trees* would agree that it proves nothing at all about the value of the novel—that in this case the judgment is simply pathetically inept. We discount also such tests for poetry as that proposed by A. E. Housman—the bristling of his beard at the reading of a good poem. The intensity of his reaction has critical significance only in proportion as we have already learned to trust him as a reader. Even so, what it tells us is something about Housman—nothing decisive about the poem.

It is unfortunate if this playing down of such responses seems to deny humanity to either writer or reader. The critic may enjoy certain works very much and may be indeed intensely moved by them. I am, and I have no embarrassment in admitting the fact; but a detailed description of my emotional state on reading certain works has little to do with indicating to an interested reader what the work is and how the parts of it are related.

Should all criticism, then, be self-effacing and analytic? I hope that the answer is implicit in what I have already written, but I shall go on to spell it out. Of course not. That will depend upon the occasion and the audience. In practice, the critic's job is rarely a purely critical one. He is much more likely to be involved in dozens of more or less related tasks, some of them trivial, some of them important. He may be trying to get a hearing for a new author, or to get the attention of the freshman sitting in the back row. He may be comparing two authors, or editing a text; writing a brief newspaper review or reading a paper before the Modern Language Association. He may even be simply talking with a friend, talking about literature for the hell of it. Parable, anecdote, epigram, metaphor—these and a hundred other devices may be thoroughly legitimate for his varying purposes. He is certainly not to be asked to suppress his personal enthusiasms or his interest in social history or in politics. Least of all is he being asked to *present* his criticisms as the close reading of a text. Tact, common sense, and uncommon sense if he has it, are all requisite if the practising critic is to do his various jobs well.

But it will do the critic no harm to have a clear idea of what his specific job as a critic is. I can sympathize with writers who are tired of reading rather drab "critical analyses," and who recommend brighter, more amateur, and more "human" criticism. As ideals, these are excellent; as recipes for improving criticism, I have my doubts. Appropriate vulgarizations of these ideals are already flourishing, and have long flourished—in the class room presided over by the college lecturer of infectious enthusiasm, in the gossipy Book-of-the-Month Club bulletins, and in the columns of the *Saturday Review of Literature.*

I have assigned the critic a modest, though I think an important, role. With reference to the help which the critic can give to the practising artist, the role is even more modest. As critic, he can give only negative help. Literature is not written by formula: he can have no formula to offer. Perhaps he can do little more than indicate whether in his opinion the work has succeeded or failed. Healthy criticism and healthy creation do tend to go hand in hand. Everything else being equal, the creative artist is better off for being in touch with a vigorous criticism. But the other considerations are never equal, the case is always special, and in a given case the proper advice *could* be: quit reading criticism altogether, or read political science or history or philosophy—or join the army, or join the church.

There is certainly no doubt that the kind of specific and positive help that someone like Ezra Pound was able to give to several writers of our time is in one sense the most important kind of criticism that there can be. I think that it is not unrelated to the kind of criticism that I have described: there is the same intense concern with the text which is being built up, the same concern with "technical problems." But many other things are involved—matters which lie outside the specific ambit of criticism altogether, among them a knowledge of the personality of the particular writer, the ability to stimulate, to make positive suggestions.

A literary work is a document and as a document can be analysed in terms of the forces that have produced it, or it may be manipulated as a force in its own right. It mirrors the past, it may influence the future. These facts it would be futile to deny, and I know of no critic who does deny them. But the reduction of a work of literature to its causes does not constitute literary criticism; nor does an estimate of its effects. Good literature is more than effective rhetoric applied to true ideas—even if we could agree upon a philosophical yardstick for measuring the truth of ideas and even if we could find some way that transcended nose-counting for determining the effectiveness of the rhetoric.

A recent essay by Lionel Trilling bears very emphatically upon this point. (I refer to him the more readily because Trilling has registered some of his objections to the critical position that I maintain.) In the essay entitled "The Meaning of a Literary Idea," Trilling discusses the debt to Freud and Spengler of four American writers, O'Neill, Dos Passos, Wolfe, and Faulkner. Very justly, as it seems to me, he chooses Faulkner as the contemporary writer who, along with Ernest Hemingway, best illustrates the power and importance of ideas in literature. Trilling is thoroughly aware that his choice will seem shocking and perhaps perverse, "because," as he writes, "Hemingway and Faulkner have insisted on their indifference to the conscious intellectual tradition of our time and have acquired the reputation of achieving their effects by means that have the least possible connection with any sort of intellectuality or even with intelligence."

Here Trilling shows not only acute discernment but an admirable honesty in electing to deal with the hard cases—with the writers who do not clearly and easily make the case for the importance of ideas. I applaud the discernment and the honesty, but I wonder whether the whole discussion in his essay does not indicate that Trilling is really much closer to the so-called "new critics" than perhaps he is aware. For Trilling, one notices, rejects any simple one-to-one relation between the truth of the idea and the value of the literary work in which it is embodied. Moreover, he does not claim that "recognizable ideas of a force or weight are 'used' in the work," or "new ideas of a certain force and weight are 'produced' by the work." He praises rather the fact that we feel that Hemingway and Faulkner are "intensely at work upon the recalcitrant stuff of life." The last point is made the matter of real importance. Whereas Dos Passos, O'Neill, and Wolfe make us "feel that *they* feel that they have said the last word," "we seldom have the sense that [Hemingway and Faulkner] . . . have misrepresented to themselves the nature and the difficulty of the matter they work on."

Trilling has chosen to state the situation in terms of the writer's activity (Faulkner is intensely at work, etc.). But this judgment is plainly an inference from the quality of Faulkner's novels—Trilling has not simply heard Faulkner say that he has had to struggle with his work. (I take it Mr. Hemingway's declaration about the effort he put into the last novel impresses Trilling as little as it impresses the rest of us.)

Suppose, then, that we tried to state Mr. Trilling's point, not in terms of the effort of the artist, but in terms of the structure of the work itself. Should we not get something very like the terms used by the formalist critics? A description in terms of "tensions," of symbolic development, of ironies and their resolution? In short, is not the formalist critic trying to describe in terms of the dynamic form of the work itself how the recalcitrancy of the material is acknowledged and dealt with?

Trilling's definition of "ideas" makes it still easier to accommodate my position to his. I have already quoted a passage in which he repudiates the notion that one has to show how recognizable ideas are "used" in the work, or new ideas are "produced" by the work. He goes on to write: "All that we need to do is account for a certain aesthetic effect as being in some important part achieved by a mental process which is not different from the process by which discursive ideas are conceived, and which is to be judged by some of the criteria by which an idea is judged." One would have to look far to find a critic "formal" enough to object to this. What some of us have been at pains to insist upon is that literature does not simply "exemplify" ideas or "produce" ideas—as Trilling acknowledges. But no one claims that the writer is an inspired idiot. He uses his mind and his reader ought to use his, in processes "not different from the process by which discursive ideas are conceived." Literature is not inimical to ideas. It thrives upon ideas, but it does not present ideas patly and neatly. It involves them with the "recalcitrant stuff of life." The literary critic's job is to deal with that involvement.

The mention of Faulkner invites a closing comment upon the critic's specific job. As I have described it, it may seem so modest that one could take its performance for granted. But consider the misreadings of Faulkner now current, some of them the work of the most brilliant critics that we have, some of them quite wrong-headed, and demonstrably so. What is true of Faulkner is only less true of many another author, including many writers of the past. Literature has many "uses"—and critics propose new uses, some of them exciting and spectacular. But all the multiform uses to which literature can be put rest finally upon our knowing what a given work "means." That knowledge is basic.

THE CONCRETE UNIVERSAL (1947, 1954)

W. K. WIMSATT

W. K. Wimsatt is best known for two essays cowritten with Monroe Beardsley, "The Intentional Fallacy" and "The Affective Fallacy." The first essay argued against the idea (which Wimsatt and Beardsley call a fallacy, a false belief) that the best way to interpret literature is to discover the author's intention and make that intention equal our interpretation. The second essay argues against the idea that the best way to interpret literature is to discover its emotional force (affect) on readers and make our understanding of that force equal our interpretation. In both cases, Wimsatt and Beardsley see the meaning of a work of literature intrinsically in the literature itself rather than in what the author might have intended or in the response of readers. Either of those essays could have appeared in this volume, but the essay about the intentional fallacy has not worn the years nearly so well as the basic concept that it provoked other critics to continue thinking about and, often, believing in, and the essay about the affective fallacy has never attracted many adherents, though it has provoked opposition. Reader response criticism defines itself in opposition to the idea that it is unwise (a fallacy) to take readers' affect into account as we interpret literature.

In the long run, Wimsatt's less famous though still well-known essay "The Concrete Universal" may provide more insight from and into new critical thinking. Against the common misconception that the new critics' desire to focus on the literary text itself made them reject history, Wimsatt's essay, like the work of many new critics, is deeply historical, but its history centers on literary history without much conscious sense of cultural history. Wimsatt writes about earlier writing, including works of literature, literary theory, and the theory of art. Like a characteristic new critic, Wimsatt focuses on literary language. He especially focuses on the harmony and completeness of expression that he finds in literature, at least in good or great literature. The essay ranges widely through a traditional set of references that for many contemporary students may not be as familiar as Wimsatt perhaps too easily supposes, but readers do not need to know much about many of the previous writers and philosophers Wimsatt alludes to, and readers who want to know more can easily look them up. Readers may gain, for example, from perusing or reperusing a few of the poems that Wimsatt mentions, such as John Keats's "On First Looking into Chapman's Homer" and "La Belle Dame sans Merci" and William Wordsworth's "Solitary Reaper."

Once Wimsatt passes through the balanced and reasonable exposition that shapes the bulk of his essay, he finally reaches his argument, which calls for interpreting literature by studying its complexity and unity, another characteristically new critical approach. He objects to the Roman poet Horace's preference, in Horace's poem "Ars Poetica" ("The Art of Poetry"), for merging simplicity and unity. For Wimsatt and the new critics, unity in great literature comes through complexity. Wimsatt sees the process of uncovering complexity and unity as an objective and even absolute process versus the more subjective process that relies on the psychology of the author (as in the intentional fallacy) or the psychology of the reader (as in the affective fallacy). In a typically new critical way, Wimsatt favors a focus on a poem's form, not its ideas. Thus he quotes with approval the famous closing lines from Archibald MacLeish's "Ars Poetica," "A poem should not mean / But be," and the related famous claim from Sir Philip Sidney's "A Defence of Poesie": "the poet, he nothing affirmeth, and therefore never lieth."

In a later critical environment, the objectivity Wimsatt believes he has found may not come across as objectively as he supposes. His unity, for example, seems to envision poets and readers as men who share Wimsatt's class or education, including his points of reference to the history of literature and philosophy. To later critics, that suggests actual unity less than it suggests imposed and fantasized unity. Even so, defenders of Wimsatt and new criticism would likely find convincing the claim that criticism can focus its attention on literature's being and not its meaning and, at the same time, discover such being in the literature itself, rather than letting their own sense of meaning determine their sense of the literature's being.

The central argument of this essay, concerning what I shall call the "concrete universal," proceeds from the observation that literary theorists have from early times to the present persisted in making statements which in their contexts seem to mean that a work of literary art is in some peculiar sense a very individual thing or a very universal thing or both. What that paradox can mean, or what important fact behind the paradox has been discerned by such various critics as Aristotle, Plotinus, Hegel, and Ransom, it will be the purpose of the essay to inquire, and by the inquiry to discuss not only a significant feature of metaphysical poetics from Aristotle to the present day but the relation between metaphysical poetics and more practical and specific rhetorical analysis. In the brief historical survey which forms one part of this essay it will not be my purpose to suggest that any of these writers meant exactly what I shall mean in later parts where I describe the structure of poetry. Yet throughout the essay I shall proceed on the theory not only that men have at different times used the same terms and have meant differently, but that they have sometimes used different terms and have meant the same or somewhat the same. In other words, I assume that there is continuity in the problems of criticism, and that a person who studies poetry today has a legitimate interest in what Plato said about poetry.

The view of common terms and their relations to classes of things from which I shall start is roughly that which one may read in the logic of J. S. Mill, a view which is not much different from the semantic view of today and for most purposes not much different from the Aristotelian and scholastic view. Mill speaks of the word and its denotation and connotation (the term, referent and reference, the sign, denotatum and designatum[1] of more recent terminologies). The denotation is the *it*, the individual thing or the aggregate of things to which the term may refer; the connotation is the *what*, the quality or classification inferred for the it, or implicitly predicated by the application of the term or the giving of the name.* One main difference between all modern positivistic, nominalistic, and semantic systems and the scholastic and classical systems is that the older ones stress the similarity of the individuals denoted by the common term and hence the real universality of meaning, while the modem systems stress the differences in the individuals, the constant flux even of each individual in time and space and its kinetic structure, and hence infer only an approximate or nominal universality of meaning and a convenience rather than a truth in the use of general terms. A further difference lies in the view of how the individual is related to the various connotations of terms which may be applied to it. That is, to the question: What is it? the older writers seem to hold there is but one (essentially right) answer, while the moderns accept as many answers as there are classes to which the individual may be assigned (an indefinite number). The older writers speak of a proper essence or whatness of the individual, a quality which in some cases at least is that designated by the class name most commonly applied to the individual: a bench is a bench, essentially a bench, accidentally a heavy wooden object or something covered with green paint. "When we say *what* it is," observes Aristotle, "we do not say 'white' or 'hot' or 'three cubits long' but 'a man' or 'a god.' "[2] And this view is also a habit scarcely avoidable in our own daily thinking, especially when we think of living things or of artifacts, things made by us or our fellows for a purpose. What is it? Bench, we think, is an adequate answer. An assemblage of sticks painted green, we consider freakish.

---

*   The terms "denotation" and "connotation" are commonly and loosely used by literary critics to distinguish the dictionary meaning of a term (denotation) from the vaguer aura of suggestion (connotation). Both these are parts of the connotation in the logical sense.

II

Whether or not one believes in universals, one may see the persistence in literary criticism of a theory that poetry presents the concrete and the universal, or the individual and the universal, or an object which in a mysterious and special way is both highly general and highly particular. The doctrine is implicit in Aristotle's two statements that poetry imitates action and that poetry tends to express the universal. It is implicit again at the end of the classic period in the mystic doctrine of Plotinus, who in his later writing on beauty reverses the Platonic objection that art does not know the ultimate reality of the forms. Plotinus arrives at the view that the artist by a kind of bypass of the inferior natural productions of the world soul reaches straight to the forms that lie behind in the divine intelligence.[3] Another version of the classic theory, with affinities for Plotinus, lies in the scholastic phrase *resplendentia formae*.

Cicero's account of how Zeuxis painted an ideal Helen from the five most beautiful virgins of Crotona is a typical development of Aristotelian theory, in effect the familiar neo-classic theory found in Du Fresnoy's *Art of Painting*, in the writings of Johnson, especially in the tulip passage in *Rasselas*, and in the *Discourses* and *Idlers* of Reynolds. The business of the poet is not to number the streaks of the tulip; it is to give us not the individual, but the species. The same thing is stated in a more complicated way by Kant in telling how the imagination constructs the "aesthetical normal Idea":

> It is the image for the whole race, which floats among all the variously different intuitions of individuals, which nature takes as archetype in her productions of the same species, but which seems not to be fully reached in any individual case.[4]

And Hegel's account is as follows:

> The work of art is not only for the sensuous apprehension as sensuous object, but its position is of such a kind that as sensuous it is at the same time essentially addressed to the *mind*.[5]

> In comparison with the show or semblance of immediate sensuous existence or of historical narrative, the artistic semblance has the advantage that in itself it points beyond self, and refers us away, from itself to something spiritual which it is meant to bring before the mind's eye.... The hard rind of nature and the common world give the mind more trouble in breaking through to the idea than do the products of art.[6]

The excellence of Shakespeare, says Coleridge, consists in a "union and interpenetration of the universal and particular." In one terminology or another this idea of a concrete universal is found in most metaphysical aesthetic of the eighteenth and nineteenth centuries.

A modern literary critic, John Crowe Ransom, speaks of the argument of a poem (the universal) and a local texture or tissue of concrete irrelevance. Another literary critic, Allen Tate, manipulating the logical terms "extension" and "intension," has arrived at the concept of "tension" in poetry. "Extension," as logicians use the word, is the range of individuals denoted by a term (denotation); "intension" is the total of qualities connoted (connotation). In the ordinary or logical use of the terms, extension and intension are of inverse relationship—the wider the one, the shallower the other. A poem, says Tate, as I interpret him, is a verbal structure which in some peculiar way has both a wide extension and a deep intension.

Not all these theories of the concrete universal lay equal stress on the two sides of the paradox, and it seems indicative of the vitality of the theory and of the truth implicit in it that the two sides have been capable of exaggeration into antithetic schools and theories of poetry. For Du Fresnoy, Johnson, and Reynolds poetry and painting give the universal; the less said about the particulars the better. This is the neoclassic theory, the illustrations of which we seek in Pope's *Essay on Man* or in Johnson's *Ramblers,* where the ideas are moral and general and concerned with "nature," "one clear, unchanged, and universal light." The opposite theory had notable expression in England, a few years before Johnson wrote *Rasselas,* in Joseph Warton's *Essay on Pope:*

> A minute and particular enumeration of circumstances judiciously selected, is what chiefly discriminates poetry from history, and renders the former, for that reason, a more close and faithful representation of nature than the latter.

And Blake's marginal criticism of Reynolds was: "THIS Man was Hired to Depress art." "To Generalize is to be an Idiot. To Particularize is the Alone Distinction of Merit. General Knowledges are those Knowledges that Idiots possess." "Sacrifice the Parts: What becomes of the whole?" The line from Warton's *Essay* to Croce's *Aesthetic* seems a straight and obvious one, from Thomson's specific descriptions of flowers to the individual act of intuition-expression which is art—its opposite and enemy being the concept or generality.[7] The two views of art (two that can be held by different theorists about the same works of art) may be startlingly contrasted in the following passages about fictitious character—one a well known statement by Johnson, the other by the philosopher of the *élan vital.*

> [Shakespeare's] characters are not modified by the customs of particular places, unpractised by the rest of the world; by the peculiarities of studies or professions, which can operate but upon small numbers; or by the accidents of transient fashions or temporary opinions: they are the genuine progeny of common humanity, such as the world will always supply, and observation will always find. His persons act and speak by the influence of those general passions and principles by which all minds are agitated, and the whole system of life is continued in motion. In the writings of other poets a character is too often an individual; in those of Shakespeare it is commonly a species.
>
> Hence it follows that art always aims at what is *individual.* "What the artist fixes on his canvas is something he has seen at a certain spot, on a certain day, at a certain hour, with a colouring that will never be seen again. "What the poet sings of is a certain mood which was his, and his alone, and which will never return.... Nothing could be more unique than the character of Hamlet. Though he may resemble other men in some respects, it is clearly not on that account that he interests us most.[8]

Other critics, notably the most ancient and the most modern have tried to hold the extremes together. Neither of the extremes gives a good account of art and each leads out of art. The theory of particularity leads to individuality and originality (Edward Young was another eighteenth century Crocean), then to the idiosyncratic and the unintelligible and to the psychology of the author, which is not in the work of art and is not a standard for judgment. The theory of universality as it appears in Johnson and Reynolds leads to platitude and to a standard of material objectivity, the average tulip, the average human form, some sort of average.[9]

III

"Just representations of general nature," said Johnson, and it ought to be noted, though it perhaps rarely is, that two kinds of generality are involved, as indeed they are in the whole neoclassic theory of generality. There is the generality of logic or classification, of the more general as opposed to the more specific, "essential" generality, one might say. And there is the generality of literal truth to nature, "existential" generality. The assumption of neoclassic theory seems to be that these two must coincide. As a matter of fact they may and often do, but need not. Thus: "purple cow" is a more general (less specific) term and concept than "tan cow with a broken horn," yet the latter is more general or true to nature. We have, in short, realism or fantasy, and in either there may be various degrees of the specific or the general. We have A *Journal of the Plague year* and *The Rambler, Gulliver's Travels* and *Rasselas*. The fact that there are a greater number of "vicissitudes" and "miscarriages" (favorite *Rambler* events) in human experience than plagues at London, that there are more tan cows than tan cows with broken horns, makes it true in a sense that a greater degree of essential generality involves a greater degree of existential. But in this sense the most generally reliable concept is simply that of "being."

The question is how a work of literature can be either more individual (unique) or more universal than other kinds of writing, or how it can combine the individual and the universal more than other kinds. Every description in words, so far as it is a direct description (The barn is red and square) is a generalization. That is the nature of words. There are no individuals conveyed in words but only more or less specific generalizations, so that Johnson is right, though we have to ask him what degree of verbal generality makes art, and whether "tulip" is a better or more important generality than "tulip with ten streaks," or whether "beauty" is not in fact a much more impressive generality than "tulip." On the other hand, one cannot deny that in some sense there are more tulips in poetry than pure abstracted beauty. So that Bergson is right too; only we shall have to ask him what degree of specificity in verbal description makes art. And he can never claim complete verbal specificity or individuality, even for Hamlet.

If he could, if a work of literary art could be looked on as an artifact or concrete physical work, the paradox for the student of universals would return from the opposite direction even more forcibly—as it does in fact for theorists of graphic art. If Reynolds' picture "The Age of Innocence" presents a species or universal, what species does it present? Not an Aristotelian essence—"man," or "humanity," nor even a more specific kind of being such as "womanhood." For then the picture would present the same universal as Reynolds' portrait of Mrs. Siddons as "The Tragic Muse," and all differences between "The Age of Innocence" and "The Tragic Muse" would be aesthetically irrelevant. Does the picture then present girl-hood, or barefoot girlhood, or barefoot girlhood in a white dress against a gloomy back-ground? All three are equally valid universals (despite the fact that makeshift phrases are required to express two of them), and all three are presented by the picture. Or is it the title which tells us what universal is presented, "The Age of Innocence," and without the title should we not know the universal? The question will be: What in the individual work of art demands that we attribute to it one universal rather than another?

We may answer that for poetry it is the generalizing power of words already mentioned, and go on to decide that what distinguishes poetry from scientific or logical discourse is a degree of irrelevant concreteness in descriptive details. This is in effect what Ransom says in his doctrine of argument and local irrelevance, but it seems doubtful if the doctrine is not a version of the theory of ornamental metaphor. The argument, says Ransom, is the prose or scientific meaning, what the poem has in common with other kinds of writing. The irrel-evance is a texture of concreteness which does not contribute anything to the argument but is somehow enjoyable or valuable for its own sake, the vehicle of a metaphor which one boards heedless of where it runs, whether crosstown or downtown—just for the ride. So Ransom nurses and refines the argument, and on one page he makes the remark that the poet searches for "suitability" in his particular phrases, and by suitability Ransom means "the propriety which consists in their denoting the particularity which really belongs to the logical object."[10] But the difference between "propriety" and relevance in such a context is not easy to see. And relevance is logic. The fact is that all concrete illustration has about it something of the irrelevant. An apple falling from a tree illustrates gravity, but apple and tree are irrelevant to the pure theory of gravity. It may be that what happens in a poem is that the apple and the tree are somehow made more than usually relevant.

Such a theory, not that of Johnson and Reynolds, not that of Warton and Bergson, not quite that of Ransom, is what I would suggest—yet less as a novelty than as something already widely implicit in recent poetical analyses and exegeses, in those of Empson, for instance, Tate, Blackmur, or Brooks. If a work of literature is not in a simple sense either more individual or more universal than other kinds of writing, it may yet be such an indi-vidual or such a complex of meaning that it has a special relation to the world of universals. Some acute remarks on this subject were made by Ruskin in a chapter of *Modern Painters* neglected today perhaps because of its distasteful ingredient of "noble emotion." Poetry, says Ruskin in criticizing Reynolds' *Idlers*, is not distinguished from history by the omission of details, nor for that matter by the mere addition of details. "There must be something either in the nature of the details themselves, or the method of using them, which invests them with poetical power." Their nature, one may add, as assumed through their relation to one another, a relation which may also be called the method of using them. The poetic char-acter of details consists not in what they say directly and explicitly (as if roses and moon-light were poetic) but in what by their arrangement they *show* implicitly.

IV

"One," observes Ben Jonson, thinking of literature, "is considerable two waies: either, as it is only separate, and by it self: or as being compos'd of many parts it beginnes to be one as those parts grow or are wrought together."[11] A literary work of art is a complex of detail (an artifact, if we may be allowed that metaphor for what is only a verbal object), a composition so complicated of human values that its interpretation is dictated by the understanding of it, and so complicated as to seem in the highest degree individual—a concrete universal. We are accustomed to being told, for example, that what makes a character in fiction or drama vital is a certain fullness or rotundity: that the character has many sides. Thus E. M. Forster:

> We may divide characters into flat and round. Flat characters were called "humours" in the seventeenth century, and are sometimes called types, and sometimes caricatures. In their purest form, they are constructed round a single idea or quality: when there is morethan one factor in them, we get the beginning of the curve towards the round. The really flat character can be expressed in one sentence such as "I never will desert Mr. Micawber."

It remains to be said, however, that the many traits of the round character (if indeed it is one character and not a hodgepodge) are harmonized or unified, and that if this is so, then all the traits are chosen by a principle, just as are the traits of the flat character. Yet it cannot be that the difference between the round and flat character is simply numerical; the difference cannot be merely that the presiding principle is illustrated by more examples in the round character. Something further must be supposed—a special interrelation in the traits of the round character. Bobadil is an example of the *miles gloriosus,* a flat humour. He swears by "The foot of Pharaoh," takes tobacco, borrows money from his landlady, is found lying on a bench fully dressed with a hangover, brags about his feats at the siege of Strigonium, beats Cob a poor water carrier, and so on. It is possible that he has numerically as many traits as Falstaff, one of the most vital of all characters. But one of the differences between Falstaff and Bobadil is that the things Falstaff says are funny; the things Bobadil says are not. Compared to Falstaff, Bobadil is unconscious, an opaque butt. There is the vitality of consciousness in Falstaff. And further there is the crowning complexity of self-consciousness. The fact that Morgann could devote a book to arguing that Falstaff is not a coward, that lately Professor Wilson has argued that at Gadshill Falstaff may exhibit " 'all the common symptoms of the malady' of cowardice" and at the same time persuade the audience that he has " 'never once lost his self-possession,' " the fact that one can conceive that Falstaff in the Gadshill running-away scene really knows that his assailants are the Prince and Poins—all this shows that in Falstaff there is a kind of interrelation among his attributes, his cowardice, his wit, his debauchery, his presumption, that makes them in a special way an organic harmony. He is a rounded character not only in the sense that he is gross (a fact which may have tempted critics to speak of a rounded character) or in the sense that he is a bigger bundle of attributes, stuffed more full, than Bobadil or Ralph Roister Doister; but in the sense that his attributes make a circuit and connection. A kind of awareness of self (a high and human characteristic), with a pleasure in the fact, is perhaps the central principle which instead of simplifying the attributes gives each one a special function in the whole, a double or reflex value. Falstaff or such a character of self-conscious "infinite variety"* as Cleopatra are concrete universals because they have no class names,

---

*   I do not mean that self-consciousness is the only principle of complexity in character, yet a considerable degree of it would appear to be a requisite for poetic interest.

only their own proper ones, yet are structures of such precise variety and centrality that each demands a special interpretation in the realm of human values.

Character is one type of concrete universal; there are other types, as many perhaps as the central terms of criticism; but most can be learned I believe by examination of metaphor—the structure most characteristic of concentrated poetry. The language of poets, said Shelley, "is vitally metaphorical: that is, it marks the before unapprehended relations of things and perpetuates their apprehension." Wordsworth spoke of the abstracting and modifying powers of the imagination. Aristotle said that the greatest thing was the use of metaphor, because it meant an eye for resemblances. Even the simplest form of metaphor or simile ("My love is like a red, red rose") presents us with a special and creative, in fact a concrete, kind of abstraction different from that of science. For behind a metaphor lies a resemblance between two classes, and hence a more general third class. This class is unnamed and most likely remains unnamed and is apprehended only through the metaphor. It is a new conception for which there is no other expression. Keats discovering Homer is like a traveler in the realms of gold, like an astronomer who discovers a planet, like Cortez gazing at the Pacific. The title of the sonnet, "On First Looking into Chapman's Homer," seems to furnish not so much the subject of the poem as a fourth member of a central metaphor, the real subject of the poem being an abstraction, a certain kind of thrill in discovering, for which there is no name and no other description, only the four members of the metaphor pointing, as to the center of their pattern. The point of the poem seems to lie outside both vehicle and tenor.

To take a more complicated instance, Wordsworth's "Solitary Reaper" has the same basic metaphorical structure, the girl alone reaping and singing, and the two bird images, the nightingale in Arabian sands and the cuckoo among the Hebrides, the three figures serving the parallel or metaphorical function of bringing out the abstraction of loneliness, remoteness, mysterious charm in the singing. But there is also a kind of third-dimensional significance, in the fact that one bird is far out in the northern sea, the other far off in southern sands, a fact which is not part of the comparison between the birds and the girl. By an implication cutting across the plane of logic of the metaphor, the girl and the two birds suggest extension in space, universality, and world communion—an effect supported by other details of the poem such as the overflowing of the vale profound, the mystery of the Erse song, the bearing of the song away in the witness' heart, the past and future themes which the girl may be singing. Thus a central abstraction is created, of communion, telepathy in solitude, the prophetic soul of the wide world dreaming on things to come—an abstraction which is the effect not wholly of the metaphor elaborated logically (in a metaphysical way) but of a working on two axes, by association rather than by logic, by a three-dimensional complexity of structure.

To take yet a third instance, metaphoric structure may appear where we are less likely to realize it explicitly—in poetic narratives, for example, elliptically concealed in the more obvious narrative outlines. "I can bring you," writes Max Eastman, "examples of diction that is metrical but not metaphoric—a great part of the popular ballads, for example—and you can hardly deny that they too are poetic." But the best story poems may be analyzed, I believe, as metaphors without expressed tenors, as symbols which speak for themselves. "La Belle Dame Sans Merci," for example (if a literary ballad may be taken), is about a knight, by profession a man of action, but sensitive, like the lily and the rose, and about a faery lady with wild, wild eyes. At a more abstract level, it is about the loss of self in the mysterious lure of beauty—whether woman, poetry, or poppy. It sings the irretrievable departure from practical normality (the squirrel's granary is full), the wan isolation after ecstasy. Each reader will experience the poem at his own level of experience or at several. A good story poem is like a stone thrown into a pond, into our minds, where ever widening concentric circles of meaning go out—and this because of the structure of the story.

"A poem should not mean but be." It is an epigram worth quoting in every essay on poetry. And the poet "nothing affirmeth, and therefore never lieth." "Sit quidvis," said Horace, "simplex dumtaxat et unum." It seems almost the reverse of the truth. "Complex dumtaxat et unum" would be better. Every real poem is a complex poem, and only in virtue of its complexity does it have artistic unity. A newspaper poem by Edgar Guest[*] does not have this kind of unity, but only the unity of an abstractly stated sentiment.

The principle is expressed by Aristotle when he says that beauty is based on unity in variety, and by Coleridge when he says that "The Beautiful, contemplated in its essentials, that is, in *kind* and not in *degree,* is that in which the *many,* still seen as many becomes one," and that a work of art is "rich in proportion to the variety of parts which it holds in unity."

V

It is usually easier to show how poetry works than to show why anyone should want it to work in a given way. Rhetorical analysis of poetry has always tended to separate from evaluation, technique from worth. The structure of poems as concrete and universal is the principle by which the critic can try to keep the two together. If it be granted that the "subject matter" of poetry is in a broad sense the moral realm, human actions as good or bad, with all their associated feelings, all the thought and imagination that goes with happiness and suffering (if poetry submits "the shews of things to the desires of the Mind"), then the rhetorical structure of the concrete universal, the complexity and unity of the poem, is also its maturity or sophistication or richness or depth, and hence its value. Complexity of form is sophistication of content. The unity and maturity of good poems are two sides of the same thing. The kind of unity which we look for and find in poetry is attained only through a degree of complexity in design which itself involves maturity and richness. For a visual diagram of the metaphysics of poetry one might write vertically the word complexity, a column,

---

[*]   A reader whose judgment I esteem tells me that such a name appears in a serious discussion of poetics anomalously and in bad taste. I have allowed it to remain (in preference to some more dignified name of mediocrity) precisely because I wish to insist on the existence of badness in poetry and so to establish an antithetic point of reference for the discussion of goodness. Relativistic argument often creates an illusion in its own favor by moving steadily in a realm of great and nearly great art. See, for example, George Boas, *A Primer for Critics* (Baltimore, 1937), where a cartoon by Daumier appears toward the end as a startling approach to the vulgar. The purpose of my essay is not judicial but theoretical, that is, not to exhibit original discoveries in taste, but to show the relationship between examples acknowledged to lie in the realms of the good and the bad.

and give it a head with Janus faces, one looking in the rhetorical direction, unity, and the other in the axiological, maturity.

A final point to be made is that a criticism of structure and of value is an objective criticism. It rests on facts of human psychology (as that a man may love a woman so well as to give up empires), facts, which though psychological, yet are so well acknowledged as to lie in the realm of what may be called public psychology—a realm which one should distinguish from the private realm of the author's psychology and from the equally private realm of the individual reader's psychology (the vivid pictures which poetry or stories are supposed to create in the imagination, or the venerable action of catharsis—all that poetry is said to *do* rather than to *be*). Such a criticism, again, is objective and absolute, as distinguished from the relative criticism of idiom and period. I mean that this criticism will notice that Pope is different from Shakespeare, but will notice even more attentively that Shakespeare is different from Taylor the Water Poet and Pope different from Sir Richard Blackmore. Such a criticism will be interested to analyze the latter two differences and see what these differences have in common and what Shakespeare and Pope have in common, and it will not despair of describing that similarity (that formula or character of great poetry) even though the terms be abstract and difficult. Or, if we are told that there is no universal agreement about what is good—that Pope has not been steadily held in esteem, that Shakespeare has been considered a barbarian, the objective analyst of structures can at least say (and it seems much to say) that he is describing a class of poems, those which through a peculiar complexity possess unity and maturity and in a special way can be called both individual and universal. Among all recorded "poems," this class is of a relative rarity, and further this class will be found in an impressive way to coincide with those poems which have by some body of critics, some age of educated readers, been called great.

The function of the objective critic is by approximate descriptions of poems, or multiple restatements of their meaning, to aid other readers to come to an intuitive and full realization of poems themselves and hence to know good poems and distinguish them from bad ones. It is of course impossible to tell all about a poem in other words. Croce tells us, as we should expect him to, of the "impossibility of ever rendering in logical terms the full effect of any poetry or of other artistic work." "Criticism, nevertheless," he tells us, "performs its own office, which is to discern and to point out exactly where lies the poetical motive and to formulate the divisions which aid in distinguishing what is proper to every work."[12] The situation is something like this: In each poem there is something (an individual intuition—or a concept) which can never be expressed in other terms. It is like the square root of two or like pi, which cannot be expressed by rational numbers, but only as their *limit*. Criticism of poetry is like 1.414... or 3.1416..., not all it would be, yet all that can be had and very useful.

NOTES

1. Charles W. Morris, "Esthetics and the Theory of Signs," in *Journal of Unified Science*, VIII (1939), 131–50.
2. *Metaphysics*, VII (Z), 1 (1028). Cp. Mortimer J. Adler, *The Problem of Species* (New York, 1940), 24–25.
3. "The arts are not to be slighted on the ground that they create by imitation of natural objects; for, to begin with, these natural objects are themselves imitations; then, we must recognize that they give no bare reproduction of the thing seen but go back to the ideas from which Nature itself derives." *Enneads*, V, viii, 1, *Plotinus—The Fifth Ennead*, Stephen MacKenna, tr. (London, 1926), 74.
4. *Kant's Critique of Judgment*, J. H. Bernard, tr. (London, 1931), 88–89.
5. *The Introduction to Hegel's Philosophy of Fine Art*, Bernard Bosanquet, tr. (London, 1886), 67. Cp. Walter T. Stace, *The Meaning of Beauty* (London, 1929), 41.
6. *The Introduction to Hegel's Philosophy of Fine Art*, 16. Cp. pp. 72–78, 133–37.
7. It is true that Croce has protested: "Ce qu'on démontre comme inconciliable avec le principe de la pure intuition, ce n'est pas l'universalité, mais la valeur intellectualiste et transcendante donnée dans l'art á l'universalité, sous la forme de l'allegorie ou du symbole." "Le Caractère de Totalité de l'Expression Artistique," in *Bréviaire d'Esthétique*, Georges Bourgin, tr. (Paris, 1923), 170. But the main drift of Croce's aesthetic, in being against conceptualization, is radically against the universal.
8. Henri Bergson, *Laughter, An Essay on the Meaning of the Comic* (New York, 1928), 161–62.
9. Roger Fry in his Introduction to Reynolds' *Third Discourse* argues that the species presented in painting are not those of the natural, but those of the social world, as king, knight, beggar. *Discourses*, Roger Fry, ed. (London, 1905), 46. And a modern critic of sculpture, R. H. Wilenski, offers what is perhaps the last retreat of the doctrine of universals in visual art: not man, flower, or animal but the forms of life analogous in (that is, common to) man, flower, and animal are abstracted and presented pure in sculptural art. R. H. Wilenski, *The Meaning of Modern Sculpture* (London, 1939), 159–60.
10. *The New Criticism* (Norfolk, 1941), 315. Maritain, coming from a different direction, arrives at somewhat the same poser. "If it pleases a futurist to paint a lady with only one eye, or a quarter of an eye, nobody denies him such a right: all one is entitled to require—and here is the whole problem—is that the quarter eye is all the lady needs *in the given case*." *Art and Scholasticism* (New York, 1937), 28. Here indeed is the whole problem. Aristotle said, "Not to know that a hind has no horns is a less serious matter than to paint it inartistically." *Poetics*, XXV, 5.
11. *Discoveries*, Maurice Castelain, ed. (Paris, 1908), 139. Jonson translates from Heinsius.
12. *Ariosto, Shakespeare and Corneille* (London, 1920), 146–47.

STRUCTURALISM

COURSE IN GENERAL LINGUISTICS (1916)

FERDINAND DE SAUSSURE

Translated from the French by Wade Baskin

Saussure was the founder of structuralist linguistics, but he died before he could write up his most influential ideas. After Saussure's death, several of his colleagues put together a book, Course in General Linguistics, *based on students' notes from his lectures, but it took several decades before Saussurean linguistics gathered its wide influence. Eventually, Saussure's work led to the broader intellectual and interpretive movement known as structuralism and also helped provoke the poststructuralist deconstruction associated with Jacques Derrida. Today, a wide variety of critical thinking continues to work with Saussure's ideas as part of our fundamental way of conceptualizing and interpreting language, literature, and culture.*

Saussure distinguished between what he called language (in Saussure's French, langue) *and speech (in Saussure's French,* parole). *The langue represents the overall system of language, the rules of grammar that apply to all uses of a given language. The parole, by contrast, represents an individual utterance, a particular instance of language. The langue thus represents the overall system, like the rules for playing chess or setting up a Facebook page, while parole refers to an individual instance, like a particular game or move of chess or a particular person's page on Facebook. Saussure turned the attention of linguistics from the individual instances to the overall system and proposed an overall system or structure for language, based on what he called the arbitrary nature of the sign. For Saussure, structuralist linguistics made possible "a science that studies the life of signs within society," which he called semiology. He also proposed that language is the "master-pattern for all branches of semiology," the system, in effect, that can represent the workings of all systems across the various forms of culture. Literary critics picked up on Sausurrean, structuralist linguistics to study the overall systems of literature or the overall system of specific genres of literature (such as the novel, the sonnet, the comedy), and other cultural critics drew on structuralist linguistics to study the systems of many different forms of popular and elite culture (such as TV sitcoms, music videos, classroom behavior, dating, and so on).*

The excerpts included here describe Saussure's ideas about the arbitrary nature of the sign and the difference between syntagmatic and associative relations.

(Sometimes the translator indicates Saussure's French terms in brackets. Saussure also draws on the Latin term for tree, arbor, *and uses the term* equos, *a variant of the more*

usual Latin term for horse, equus. *The translator's and editor's notes are not included; nor are most of the crossreferences to other pages in the* Course in General Linguistics.*)*

NATURE OF THE LINGUISTIC SIGN

SIGN, SIGNIFIED, SIGNIFIER

Some people regard language, when reduced to its elements, as a naming-process only—a list of words, each corresponding to the thing that it names. For example:

This conception is open to criticism at several points. It assumes that ready-made ideas exist before words...; it does not tell us whether a name is vocal or psychological in nature (*arbor,* for instance, can be considered from either viewpoint); finally, it lets us assume that the linking of a name and a thing is a very simple operation—an assumption that is anything but true. But this rather naive approach can bring us near the truth by showing us that the linguistic unit is a double entity, one formed by the associating of two terms.

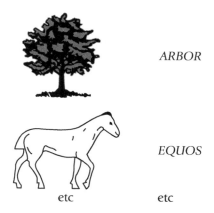

ARBOR

EQUOS

etc   etc

We have seen in considering the speaking-circuit...that both terms involved in the linguistic sign are psychological and are united in the brain by an associative bond. This point must be emphasized.

The linguistic sign unites, not a thing and a name, but a concept and a sound-image. The latter is not the material sound, a purely physical thing, but the psychological imprint of the sound, the impression that it makes on our senses. The sound-image is sensory, and if I happen to call it "material," it is only in that sense, and by way of opposing it to the other term of the association, the concept, which is generally more abstract.

The psychological character of our sound-images becomes apparent when we observe our own speech. Without moving our lips or tongue, we can talk to ourselves or recite mentally a selection of verse. Because we regard the words of our language as sound-images, we must avoid speaking of the "phonemes" that make up the words. This term, which suggests vocal activity, is applicable to the spoken word only, to the realization of the inner image in discourse. We can avoid that misunderstanding by speaking of the *sounds* and *syllables* of a word provided we remember that the names refer to the sound-image.

The linguistic sign is then a two-sided psychological entity that can be represented by the drawing:

The two elements are intimately united, and each recalls the other. Whether we try to find the meaning of the Latin word *arbor* or the word that Latin uses to designate the concept "tree," it is clear that only the associations sanctioned by that language appeal to us to conform to reality, and we disregard whatever others might be imagined.

Our definition of the linguistic sign poses an important question of terminology. I call the combination of a concept and a sounds-image a *sign,* but in current usage the term generally designates only a sound-image, a word, for example (*arbor,* etc.). One tends to forget that *arbor* is called a sign only because it carries the concept "tree," with the result that the idea of the sensory part implies the idea of the whole.

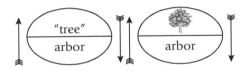

Ambiguity would disappear if the three notions involved here were designated by three names, each suggesting and opposing the others. I propose to retain the word *sign* [*signe*] to designate the. whole and to replace *concept* and *sound-image* respectively by *signified* [*signifié*] and *signifier* [*signifiant*]; the last two terms have the advantage of indicating the opposition that separates them from each other and from the whole of which they are parts. As regards *sign,* if I am satisfied with it, this is simply because I do not know of any word to replace it, the ordinary language suggesting no other.

The linguistic sign, as defined, has two primordial characteristics. In enunciating them I am also positing the basic principles of any study of this type.

PRINCIPLE I: THE ARBITRARY NATURE OF THE SIGN

The bond between the signifier and the signified is arbitrary. Since I mean by sign the whole that results from the associating of the signifier with the signified, I can simply say: *the linguistic sign is arbitrary.*

The idea of "sister" is not linked by any inner relationship to the succession of sounds s-ö-r which serves as its signifier in French; that it could be represented equally by just any other sequence is proved by differences among languages and by the very existence of different languages: the signified "ox" has as its signifier *b-ö-f* on one side of the border and *o-k-s* (*Ochs*) on the other.

No one disputes the principle of the arbitrary nature of the sign, but it is often easier to discover a truth than to assign to it its proper place. Principle I dominates all the linguistics of language; its consequences are numberless. It is true that not all of them are equally obvious at first glance; only after many detours does one discover them, and with them the primordial importance of the principle.

One remark in passing: when semiology becomes organized as a science, the question will arise whether or not it properly includes modes of expression based on completely natural signs, such as pantomime. Supposing that the new science welcomes them, its main concern will still be the whole group of systems grounded on the arbitrariness of the sign. In fact, every means of expression used in society is based, in principle, on collective behavior or—what amounts to the same thing—on convention. Polite formulas, for instance, though often imbued with a certain natural expressiveness (as in the case of a Chinese who greets his emperor by bowing down to the ground nine times), are nonetheless fixed by rule; it is this rule and not the intrinsic value of the gestures that obliges one to use them. Signs that are wholly arbitrary realize better than the others the ideal of the semiological process; that is why language, the most complex and universal of all systems of expression, is also the most characteristic; in this sense linguistics can become the master-pattern for all branches of semiology although language is only one particular semiological system.

The word *symbol* has been used to designate the linguistic sign, or more specifically, what is here called the signifier. Principle I in particular weighs against the use of this term. One characteristic of the symbol is that it is never wholly arbitrary; it is not empty, for there is the rudiment of a natural bond between the signifier and the signified. The symbol of justice, a pair of scales, could not be replaced by just any other symbol, such as a chariot.

The word *arbitrary* also calls for comment. The term should not imply that the choice of the signifier is left entirely to the speaker (we shall see later that the individual does not have the power to change a sign in any way once it has become established in the linguistic community); I mean that it is unmotivated, i.e. 'arbitrary' in that it actually has no natural connection with the signified.

In concluding let us consider two objections that might be raised to the establishment of Principle I:

1) *Onomatopoeia* might be used to prove that the choice of the signifier is not always arbitrary. But onomatopoeic formations are never organic elements of a linguistic system. Besides, their number is much smaller than is generally supposed. Words like French *fouet* "whip" or *glas* "knell" may strike certain ears with suggestive sonority, but to see that they have not always had this property we need only examine their Latin forms (*fouet* is derived from *fāgus* "beech-tree," *glas* from *classicum* "sound of a trumpet"). The quality of their present sounds, or rather the quality that is attributed to them, is a fortuitous result of phonetic evolution.

As for authentic onomatopoeic words (e.g. *glug-glug*, *tick-tock*, etc.), not only are they limited in number, but also they are chosen somewhat arbitrarily, for they are only approximate and more or less conventional imitations of certain sounds (cf. English *bow-wow* and

French *ouaoua*). In addition, once these words have been introduced into the language, they are to a certain extent subjected to the same evolution—phonetic, morphological, etc.—that other words undergo (cf. *pigeon*, ultimately from Vulgar Latin *pīpiō*, derived in turn from an onomatopoeic formation): obvious proof that they lose something of their original character in order to assume that of the linguistic sign in general, which is unmotivated.

2) *Interjections,* closely related to onomatopoeia, can be attacked on the same grounds and come no closer to refuting our thesis. One is tempted to see in them spontaneous expressions of reality dictated, so to speak, by natural forces. But for most interjections we can show that there is no fixed bond between their signified and their signifier. We need only compare two languages on this point to see how much such expressions differ from one language to the next (e.g., the English equivalent of French *aïe!* is *ouch*!). We know, moreover, that many interjections were once words with specific meanings (cf. French *diable!* "darn!" *mordieu!* "golly!" from *mort Dieu* "God's death," etc).

Onomatopoeic formations and interjections are of secondary importance, and their symbolic origin is in part open to dispute.

PRINCIPLE II: THE LINEAR NATURE OF THE SIGNIFIER

The signifier, being auditory, is unfolded solely in time from which it gets the following characteristics: (a) it represents a span, and (b) the span is measurable in a single dimension; it is a line.

While Principle II is obvious, apparently linguists have always neglected to state it, doubtless because they found it too simple; nevertheless, it is fundamental, and its consequences are incalculable. Its importance equals that of Principle I; the whole mechanism of language depends upon it…. In contrast to visual signifiers (nautical signals, etc.) which can offer simultaneous groupings in several dimensions, auditory signifiers have at their command only the dimension of time. Their elements are presented in succession; they form a chain. This feature becomes readily apparent when they are represented in writing and the spatial line of graphic marks is substituted for succession in time.

Sometimes the linear nature of the signifier is not obvious. When I accent a syllable, for instance, it seems that I am concentrating more than one significant element on the same point. But this is an illusion; the syllable and its accent constitute only one phonational act. There is no duality within the act but only different oppositions to what precedes and what follows….

LINGUISTIC VALUE

LANGUAGE AS THOUGHT COUPLED WITH SOUND

Language can also be compared with a sheet of paper: thought is the front and the sound the back; one cannot cut the front without cutting the back at the same time; likewise in language, one can neither divide sound from thought nor thought from sound; the division could be accomplished only abstractedly, and the result would be either pure psychology or pure phonology.

Linguistics then works in the borderland where the elements of sound and thought combine; *their combination produces a form, not a substance.*

These views give a better understanding of what was said before (see pp. 39 ff.) about the arbitrariness of signs. Not only are the two domains that are linked by the linguistic fact shapeless and confused, but the choice of a given slice of sound to name a given idea is completely arbitrary. If this were not true, the notion of value would be compromised, for it would include an externally imposed element. But actually values remain entirely relative, and that is why the bond between the sound and the idea is radically arbitrary.

The arbitrary nature of the sign explains in turn why the social fact alone can create a linguistic system. The community is necessary if values that owe their existence solely to usage and general acceptance are to be set up; by himself the individual is incapable of fixing a single value.

In addition, the idea of value, as defined, shows that to consider a term as simply the union of a certain sound with a certain concept is grossly misleading. To define it in this way would isolate the term from its system; it would mean assuming that one can start from the terms and construct the system by adding them together when, on the contrary, it is from the interdependent whole that one must start and through analysis obtain its elements.

To develop this thesis, we shall study value successively from the viewpoint of the signified or concept (Section 2), the signifier (Section 3), and the complete sign (Section 4).

Being unable to seize the concrete entities or units of language directly, we shall work with words. While the word does not conform exactly to the definition of the linguistic unit…, it at least bears a rough resemblance to the unit and has the advantage of being concrete; consequently, we shall use words as specimens equivalent to real terms in a synchronic system, and the principles that we evolve with respect to words will be valid for entities in general.

LINGUISTIC VALUE FROM A CONCEPTUAL VIEWPOINT

When we speak of the value of a word, we generally think first of its property of standing for an idea, and this is in fact one side of linguistic value. But if this is true, how does *value* differ from *signification*? Might the two words be synonyms? I think not, although it is easy to confuse them, since the confusion results not so much from their similarity as from the subtlety of the distinction that they mark.

From a conceptual viewpoint, value is doubtless one element in signification, and it is difficult to see how signification can be dependent upon value and still be distinct from it. But we must clear up the issue or risk reducing language to a simple naming-process….

Let us first take signification, as it is generally understood…. As the arrows in the drawing show, it is only the counterpart of the sound-image. Everything that occurs concerns only the sound-image and the concept when we look upon the word as independent and self-contained.

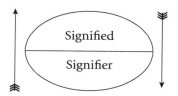

But here is the paradox: on the one hand the concept seems to be the counterpart of the sound-image, and on the other hand the sign itself is in turn the counterpart of the other signs of language.

Language is a system of interdependent terms in which the value of each term results solely from the simultaneous presence of the others, as in the diagram:

How, then, can value be confused with signification, i.e., the counterpart of the sound-image? It seems impossible to liken the relations represented here by horizontal arrows to those represented here ... by vertical arrows. Putting it another way—and again taking up the example of the sheet of paper that is cut in two...—it is clear that the observable relation between the different pieces A, B, C, D, etc. is distinct from the relation between the front and back of the same piece as in A/A′, B/B′, etc.

To resolve the issue, let us observe from the outset that even outside language all values are apparently governed by the same paradoxical principle. They are always composed:

(1) of a *dissimilar* thing that can be *exchanged* for the thing of which the value is to be determined; and

(2) of *similar* things that can be *compared* with the thing of which the value is to be determined.

Both factors are necessary for the existence of a value. To determine what a five-franc piece is worth one must therefore know: (1) that it can be exchanged for a fixed quantity of a different thing, e.g. bread; and (2) that it can be compared with a similar value of the same system, e.g. a one-franc piece, or with coins of another system (a dollar, etc.). In the same way a word can be exchanged for something dissimilar, an idea; besides, it can be compared with something of the same nature, another word. Its value is therefore not fixed so long as one simply states that it can be "exchanged" for a given concept, i.e. that it has this or that signification: one must also compare it with similar values, with other words that stand in opposition to it. Its content is really fixed only by the concurrence of everything that exists outside it. Being part of a system, it is endowed not only with a signification but also and especially with a value, and this is something quite different.

A few examples will show clearly that this is true. Modern French *mouton* can have the same signification as English *sheep* but not the same value, and this for several reasons, particularly because in speaking of a piece of meat ready to be served on the table, English uses *mutton* and not *sheep*. The difference in value between *sheep* and *mouton* is due to the fact that *sheep* has beside it a second term while the French word does not.

Within the same language, all words used to express related ideas limit each other reciprocally; synonyms like French *redouter* "dread," *craindre* "fear," and *avoir peur* "be afraid" have value only through their opposition: if *redouter* did not exist, all its content would go to its competitors. Conversely, some words are enriched through contact with others: e.g., the new element introduced in *décrépit* (un vieillard *décrépit*... results from the coexistence of *décrépi* (un mur *décrépi*). The value of just any term is accordingly determined by its environment; it is impossible to fix even the value of the word signifying "sun" without first considering its surroundings: in some languages it is not possible to say "sit in the *sun*."

Everything said about words applies to any term of language, e.g., to grammatical entities. The value of a French plural does not coincide with that of a Sanskrit plural even though their signification is usually identical; Sanskrit has three numbers instead of two (*my eyes, my ears, my arms, my legs,* etc. are dual); it would be wrong to attribute the same value to the plural in Sanskrit and in French; its value clearly depends on what is outside and around it.

If words stood for pre-existing concepts, they would all have exact equivalents in meaning from one language to the next; but this is not true. French uses *louer* (*une maison*) "let (a house)" indifferently to mean both "pay for" and "receive payment for," whereas German uses two words, *mieten* and *vermieten*; there is obviously no exact correspondence of values. The German verbs *schätzen* and *urteilen* share a number of significations, but that correspondence does not hold at several points.

Inflection offers some particularly striking examples. Distinctions of time, which are so familiar to us, are unknown in certain languages. Hebrew does not recognize even the fundamental distinctions between the past, present, and future. Proto-Germanic has no special form for the future; to say that the future is expressed by the present is wrong, for the value of the present is not the same in Germanic as in languages that have a future along with the present. The Slavic languages regularly single out two aspects of the verb: the perfective represents action as a point, complete in its totality; the imperfective represents it as taking place, and on the line of time. The categories are difficult for a Frenchman to understand, for they are unknown in French; if they were predetermined, this would not be true. Instead of pre-existing ideas then, we find in all the foregoing examples *values* emanating from the system. When they are said to correspond to concepts, it is understood that the concepts are purely differential and defined not by their positive content but negatively by their relations with the other terms of the system. Their most precise characteristic is in being what the others are not.

Now the real interpretation of the diagram of the signal becomes apparent. Thus

means that in French the concept "to judge" is linked to the sound-image *juger*; in short, it symbolizes signification. But it is quite clear that initially the concept is nothing, that is only a value determined by its relations with other similar values, and that without them the signification would not exist. If I state simply that a word signifies something when I have in mind the associating of a sound-image with a concept, I am making a statement that may suggest what actually happens, but by no means am I expressing the linguistic fact in its essence and fullness.

LINGUISTIC VALUE FROM A MATERIAL VIEWPOINT

The conceptual side of value is made up solely of relations and differences with respect to the other terms of language, and the same can be said of its material side. The important thing in the word is not the sound alone but the phonic differences that make it possible to distinguish this word from all others, for differences carry signification.

This may seem surprising, but how indeed could the reverse be possible? Since one vocal image is no better suited than the next for what it is commissioned to express, it is evident, even *a priori*, that a segment of language can never in the final analysis be based on anything except its noncoincidence with the rest. *Arbitrary* and *differential* are two correlative qualities.

The alteration of linguistic signs clearly illustrates this. It is precisely because the terms *a* and *b* as such are radically incapable of reaching the level of consciousness—one is always conscious of only the *a/b* difference—that each term is free to change according to laws that are unrelated to its signifying function.... Signs function, then, not through their intrinsic value but through their relative position.

In addition, it is impossible for sound alone, a material element, to belong to language. It is only a secondary thing, substance to be put to use. All our conventional values have the characteristic of not being confused with the tangible element which supports them. For instance, it is not the metal in a piece of money that fixes its value. A coin nominally worth five francs may contain less than half its worth of silver. Its value will vary according to the amount stamped upon it and according to its use inside or outside a political boundary. This is even more true of the linguistic signifier, which is not phonic but incorporeal—constituted not by its material substance but by the differences that separate its sound-image from all others.

The foregoing principle is so basic that it applies to all the material elements of language, including phonemes. Every language forms its words on the basis of a system of sonorous elements, each element being a clearly delimited unit and one of a fixed number of units. Phonemes are characterized not, as one might think, by their own positive quality but simply by the fact that they are distinct. Phonemes are above all else opposing, relative, and negative entities.

Proof of this is the latitude that speakers have between points of convergence in the pronunciation of distinct sounds. In French, for instance, general use of a dorsal *r* does not prevent many speakers from using a tongue-tip trill; language is not in the least disturbed by it; language requires only that the sound be different and not, as one might imagine, that it have an invariable quality. I can even pronounce the French *r* like German *ch* in *Bach, doch,* etc., but in German I could not use *r* instead of *ch,* for German gives recognition to both elements and must keep them apart. Similarly, in Russian there is no latitude for *t* in the direction of *t'* (palatalized *t*), for the result would be the confusing of two sounds differentiated by the language (cf. *govorit'* "speak" and *goverit* "he speaks"), but more freedom may be taken with respect to *th* (aspirated *t*) since this sound does not figure in the Russian system of phonemes.

Since an identical state of affairs is observable in writing, another system of signs, we shall use writing to draw some comparisons that will clarify the whole issue. In fact:

1. The signs used in writing are arbitrary; there is no connection, for example, between the letter *t* and the sound that it designates.
2. The value of letters is purely negative and differential. The same person can write *t*, for instance, in different ways:

The only requirement is that the sign for *t* not be confused in his script with the signs used for *l*, *d*, etc.

3. Values in writing function only through reciprocal opposition within a fixed system that consists of a set number of letters. This third characteristic, though not identical to the second, is closely related to it, for both depend on the first. Since the graphic sign is arbitrary, its form matters little or rather matters only within the limitations imposed by the system.
4. The means by which the sign is produced is completely unimportant, for it does not affect the system (this also follows from characteristic 1). Whether I make the letters in white or black, raised or engraved with pen or chisel—all this is of no importance with respect to their signification.

THE SIGN CONSIDERED IN ITS TOTALITY

Everything that has been said up to this point boils down to this: in language there are only differences. Even more important: a difference generally implies positive terms between which the difference is set up; but in language there are only differences *without positive terms*. Whether we take the signified or the signifier, language has neither ideas nor sounds that existed before the linguistic system, but only conceptual and phonic differences that have issued from the system. The idea or phonic substance that a sign contains is of less importance than the other signs that surround it. Proof of this is that the value of a term may be modified without either its meaning or its sound being affected, solely because a neighboring term has been modified....

But the statement that everything in language is negative is true only if the signified and the signifier are considered separately; when we consider the sign in its totality, we have something that is positive in its own class. A linguistic system is a series of differences of sound combined with a series of differences of ideas; but the pairing of a certain number of acoustical signs with as many cuts made from the mass of thought engenders a system of values; and this system serves as the effective link between the phonic and psychological elements within each sign. Although both the signified and the signifier are purely differential and negative when considered separately, their combination is a positive fact; it is even the sole type of facts that language has, for maintaining the parallelism between the two classes of differences is the distinctive function of the linguistic institution....

Putting it another way, *language is a form and not a substance....* This truth could not be overstressed, for all the mistakes in our terminology, all our incorrect ways of naming things that pertain to language, stem from the involuntary supposition that the linguistic phenomenon must have substance.

SYNTAGMATIC AND ASSOCIATIVE RELATIONS

DEFINITIONS

In a language-state everything is based on relations. How do they function?

Relations and differences between linguistic terms fall into two distinct groups, each of which generates a certain class of values. The opposition between the two classes gives a better understanding of the nature of each class. They correspond to two forms of our mental activity, both indispensable to the life of language.

In discourse, on the one hand, words acquire relations based on the linear nature of language because they are chained together. This rules out the possibility of pronouncing two elements simultaneously.... The elements are arranged in sequence on the chain of speaking. Combinations supported by linearity are *syntagms*. The syntagm is always composed of two or more consecutive units (e.g. French *re-lire* "re-read," *contre tous* "against everyone," *la vie humaine* "human life," *Dieu est bon* "God is good," *s'il fait beau temps, nous sortirons* "if the weather is nice, we'll go out," etc.). In the syntagm a term acquires its value only because it stands in opposition to everything that precedes or follows it, or to both.

Outside discourse, on the other hand, words acquire relations of a different kind. Those that have something in common are associated in the memory, resulting in groups marked by diverse relations. For instance, the French word *enseignement* "teaching" will unconsciously call to mind a host of other words (*enseigner* "teach," *renseigner* "acquaint," etc.; or *armement* "armament," *changement* "amendment," etc.; or *éducation* "education," *apprentissage* "apprenticeship," etc.). All those words are related in some way.

We see that the co-ordinations formed outside discourse differ strikingly from those formed inside discourse. Those formed outside discourse are not supported by linearity. Their seat is in the brain; they are a part of the inner storehouse that makes up the language of each speaker. They are *associative relations*.

The syntagmatic relation is *in praesentia*. It is based on two or more terms that occur in an effective series. Against this, the associative relation unites terms *in absentia* in a potential mnemonic series.

From the associative and syntagmatic viewpoint a linguistic unit is like a fixed part of a building, e.g. a column. On the one hand, the column has a certain relation to the architrave that it supports; the arrangement of the two units in space suggests the syntagmatic relation. On the other hand, if the column is Doric, it suggests a mental comparison of this style with others (Ionic, Corinthian, etc.) although none of these elements is present in space: the relation is associative.

ART AS TECHNIQUE (1917)

VICTOR SHKLOVKSY

Translated from the Russian by Lee T. Lemon and Marion J. Reis

A leading Russian formalist, Shklovsky argues that the defining feature of literary art comes in its technique, in its form, not in whether it uses language associated with literature, such as images, and not in what it addresses, for "the object," he says, "is not important." In particular, Shklovsky describes the technique of defamiliarization, *sometimes translated more literally as* making strange *or* estrangement. *Instead of seeing literary art as describing unusual objects through a literary vocabulary, Shklovsky believes that literary art rests on techniques that make the familiar seem unusual.*

Readers may compare Shklovsky's notion of defamiliarization to the notion of an alienation effect in Bertolt Brecht's essay in this volume.

(Shklovsky's essay is moderately abridged, mainly by trimming multiple instances of similar examples. Notes attributed to the editors come from the translators, not from the editor of this volume.)

"Art is thinking in images." This maxim, which even high school students parrot, is nevertheless the starting point for the erudite philologist who is beginning to put together some kind of systematic literary theory. The idea, originated in part by Potebnya, has spread. "Without imagery there is no art, and in particular no poetry," Potebnya writes.[1] And elsewhere, "Poetry, as well as prose, is first and foremost a special way of thinking and knowing."[2]

Poetry is a special way of thinking; it is, precisely, a way of thinking in images, a way which permits what is generally called "economy of mental effort," a way which makes for "a sensation of the relative ease of the process." Aesthetic feeling is the reaction to this economy. This is how the academician Ovsyaniko-Kulikovsky,[3] who undoubtedly read the works of Potebnya attentively, almost certainly understood and faithfully summarized the ideas of his teacher. Potebnya and his numerous disciples consider poetry a special kind of thinking—thinking by means of images; they feel that the purpose of imagery is to help channel various objects and activities into groups and to clarify the unknown by means of the known. Or, as Potebnya wrote:

> The relationship of the image to what is being clarified is that: (a) the image is the fixed predicate of that which undergoes change—the unchanging means of attracting what is perceived as changeable.... (b) the image is far clearer and simpler than what it clarifies.[4]

In other words:

> Since the purpose of imagery is to remind us, by approximation, of those meanings for which the image stands, and since, apart from this, imagery is unnecessary for thought, we must be more familiar with the image than with what it clarifies.[5]

It would be instructive to try to apply this principle to Tyutchev's comparison of summer lightning to deaf and dumb demons or to Gogol's comparison of the sky to the garment of God.[6]

"Without imagery there is no art"—"Art is thinking in images."... the definition "Art is thinking in images," which means (I omit the usual middle terms of the argument) that art is the making of symbols, has survived the downfall of the theory which supported it. It survives chiefly in the wake of Symbolism, especially among the theorists of the Symbolist movement.

Many still believe, then, that thinking in images—thinking in specific scenes of "roads and landscape" and "furrows and boundaries"[7]—is the chief characteristic of poetry. Consequently, they should have expected the history of "imagistic art," as they call it, to consist of a history of changes in imagery. But we find that images change little; from century to century, from nation to nation, from poet to poet, they flow on without changing. Images belong to no one: they are "the Lord's." The more you understand an age, the more convinced you become that the images a given poet used and which you thought his own were taken almost unchanged from another poet. The works of poets are classified or grouped according to the new techniques that poets discover and share, and according to their arrangement and development of the resources of language; poets are much more concerned with arranging images than with creating them. Images are given to poets; the ability to remember them is far more important than the ability to create them.

Imagistic thought does not, in any case, include all the aspects of art nor even all the aspects of verbal art. A change in imagery is not essential to the development of poetry. We know that frequently an expression is thought to be poetic, to be created for aesthetic pleasure, although actually it was created without such intent—e.g., Annensky's opinion that the Slavic languages are especially poetic and Andrey Bely's ecstasy over the technique of placing adjectives after nouns, a technique used by eighteenth-century Russian poets. Bely joyfully accepts the technique as something artistic, or more exactly, as intended, if we consider intention as art. Actually, this reversal of the usual adjective-noun order is a peculiarity of the language (which had been influenced by Church Slavonic). Thus a work may be (1) intended as prosaic and accepted as poetic, or (2) intended as poetic and accepted as prosaic. This suggests that the artistry attributed to a given work results from the way we perceive it. By "works of art," in the narrow sense, we mean works created by special techniques designed to make the works as obviously artistic as possible.

Potebnya's conclusion, which can be formulated "poetry equals imagery," gave rise to the whole theory that "imagery equals symbolism," that the image may serve as the invariable predicate of various subjects. (This conclusion, because it expressed ideas similar to the theories of the Symbolists, intrigued some of their leading representatives—Andrey Bely, Merezhkovsky and his "eternal companions" and, in fact, formed the basis of the theory of Symbolism.) The conclusion stems partly from the fact that Potebnya did not distinguish between the language of poetry and the language of prose. Consequently, he ignored the fact that there are two aspects of imagery: imagery as a practical means of thinking, as a means of placing objects within categories; and imagery as poetic, as a means of reinforcing an impression. I shall clarify with an example. I want to attract the attention of a young child who is eating bread and butter and getting the butter on her fingers. I call, "Hey, butterfingers!" This is a figure of speech, a clearly prosaic trope. Now a different example. The child is playing with my glasses and drops them. I call, "Hey, butterfingers!"[8] This figure of speech is a poetic trope. (In the first example, "butterfingers" is metonymic; in the second, metaphoric—but this is not what I want to stress.)

Poetic imagery is a means of creating the strongest possible impression. As a method it is, depending upon its purpose, neither more nor less effective than other poetic techniques; it is neither more nor less effective than ordinary or negative parallelism, comparison, repetition, balanced structure, hyperbole, the commonly accepted rhetorical figures, and all those methods which emphasize the emotional effect of an expression (including words or even articulated sounds).[9] But poetic imagery only externally resembles either the stock imagery of fables and ballads or thinking in images—e.g., the example in Ovsyaniko-Kulikovsky's *Language and Art* in which a little girl calls a ball a little watermelon. Poetic imagery is but one of the devices of poetic language. Prose imagery is a means of abstraction: a little watermelon instead of a lampshade, or a little watermelon instead of a head, is only the abstraction of one of the object's characteristics, that of roundness. It is no different from saying that the head and the melon are both round. This is what is meant, but it has nothing to do with poetry.

The law of the economy of creative effort is also generally accepted. [Herbert] Spencer wrote:

> On seeking for some clue to the law underlying these current maxims, we may see shadowed forth in many of them, the importance of economizing the reader's or the hearer's attention. To so present ideas that they may be apprehended with the least possible mental effort, is the desideratum towards which most of the rules above quoted point.... Hence, carrying out the metaphor that language is the vehicle of thought, there seems reason to think that in all cases the friction and inertia of the vehicle deduct from its efficiency; and that in composition, the chief, if not the sole thing to be done, is to reduce this friction and inertia to the smallest possible amount.[10]

And R[ichard] Avenarius:

> If a soul possess inexhaustible strength, then, of course, it would be indifferent to how much
> might be spent from this inexhaustible source; only the necessarily expended time would
> be important. But since its forces are limited, one is led to "expect that the soul hastens to
> carry out the apperceptive process as expediently as possible—that is, with comparatively
> the least expenditure of energy, and, hence, with comparatively the best result.

Petrazhitsky, with only one reference to the general law of mental effort, rejects [William] James's
theory of the physical basis of emotion, a theory which contradicts his own. Even Alexander
Veselovsky acknowledged the principle of the economy of creative effort, a theory especially
appealing in the study of rhythm, and agreed with Spencer: "A satisfactory style is precisely
that style which delivers the greatest amount of thought in the fewest words." And Andrey Bely,
despite the fact that in his better pages he gave numerous examples of "roughened" rhythm[11]
and (particularly in the examples from Baratynsky) showed the difficulties inherent in poetic
epithets, also thought it necessary to speak of the law of the economy of creative effort....

These ideas about the economy of energy, as well as about the law and aim of creativity,
are perhaps true in their application to "practical" language; they were, however, extended
to poetic language. Hence they do not distinguish properly between the laws of practical language and the laws of poetic language. The fact that Japanese poetry has sounds not found
in conversational Japanese was hardly the first factual indication of the differences between
poetic and everyday language. Leo Jakubinsky has observed that the law of the dissimila-
tion of liquid sounds does not apply to poetic language.[12] This suggested to him that poetic
language tolerated the admission of hard-to-pronounce conglomerations of similar sounds.
In his article, one of the first examples of scientific criticism, he indicates inductively, the
contrast (I shall say more about this point later) between the laws of poetic language and
the laws of practical language.[13]

We must, then, speak about the laws of expenditure and economy in poetic language not
on the basis of an analogy with prose, but on the basis of the laws of poetic language.

If we start to examine the general laws of perception, we see that as perception becomes
habitual, it becomes automatic. Thus, for example, all of our habits retreat into the area
of the unconsciously automatic; if one remembers the sensations of holding a pen or of
speaking in a foreign language for the first time and compares that with his feeling at performing the action for the ten thousandth time, he will agree with us. Such habituation
explains the principles by which, in ordinary speech, we leave phrases unfinished and words
half expressed. In this process, ideally realized in algebra, things are replaced by symbols.
Complete words are not expressed in rapid speech; their initial sounds are barely perceived.
Alexander Pogodin offers the example of a boy considering the sentence "The Swiss mountains are beautiful" in the form of a series of letters: *T, S, m, a, b.*[14]

This characteristic of thought not only suggests the method of algebra, but even prompts
the choice of symbols (letters, especially initial letters). By this "algebraic" method of
thought we apprehend objects only as shapes with imprecise extensions; we do not see
them in their entirety but rather recognize them by their main characteristics. We see the

object as though it were enveloped in a sack. We know what it is by its configuration, but we see only its silhouette. The object, perceived thus in the manner of prose perception, fades and does not leave even a first impression; ultimately even the essence of what it was is forgotten. Such perception explains why we fail to hear the prose word in its entirety (see Leo Jakubinsky's article[15]) and, hence, why (along with other slips of the tongue) we fail to pronounce it. The process of "algebrization," the over-automatization of an object, permits the greatest economy of perceptive effort. Either objects are assigned only one proper feature—a number, for example—or else they function as though by formula and do not even appear in cognition:

> I was cleaning a room and, meandering about, approached the divan and couldn't remember whether or not I had dusted it. Since these movements are habitual and unconscious, I could not remember and felt that it was impossible to remember—so that if I had dusted it and forgot—that is, had acted unconsciously, then it was the same as if I had not. If some conscious person had been watching, then the fact could be established. If, however, no one was looking, or looking on unconsciously, if the whole complex lives of many people go on unconsciously, then such lives are as if they had never been.[16]

And so life is reckoned as nothing. Habitualization devours works, clothes, furniture, one's wife, and the fear of war. "If the whole complex lives of many people go on unconsciously, then such lives are as if they had never been." And art exists that one may recover the sensation of life; it exists to make one feel things, to make the stone *stony*. The purpose of art is to impart the sensation of things as they are perceived and not as they are known. The technique of art is to make objects "unfamiliar," to make forms difficult, to increase the difficulty and length of perception because the process of perception is an aesthetic end in itself and must be prolonged. *Art is a way of experiencing the artfulness of an object; the object is not important.*

The range of poetic (artistic) work extends from the sensory to the cognitive, from poetry to prose, from the concrete to the abstract: from Cervantes' Don Quixote—scholastic and poor nobleman, half consciously bearing his humiliation in the court of the duke—to the broad but empty Don Quixote of Turgenev; from Charlemagne to the name "king" [in Russian "Charles" and "king" obviously derive from the same root, *korol*]. The meaning of a work broadens to the extent that artfulness and artistry diminish; thus a fable symbolizes more than a poem, and a proverb more than a fable. Consequently, the least self-contradictory part of Potebnya's theory is his treatment of the fable, which, from his point of view, he investigated thoroughly. But since his theory did not provide for "expressive" works of art, he could not finish his book. As we know, *Notes on the Theory of Literature* was published in 1905, thirteen years after Potebnya's death. Potebnya himself completed only the section on the fable.[17]

After we see an object several times, we begin to recognize it. The object is in front of us and we know about it, but we do not see it[18]—hence we cannot say anything significant about it. Art removes objects from the automatism of perception in several ways. Here I want to illustrate a way used repeatedly by Leo Tolstoy, that writer who, for Merezhkovsky at least, seems to present things as if he himself saw them, saw them in their entirety, and did not alter them.

Tolstoy makes the familiar seem strange by not naming the familiar object. He describes an object as if he were seeing it for the first time, an event as if it were happening for the first time. In describing something he avoids the accepted names of its parts and instead names corresponding parts of other objects. For example, in "Shame" Tolstoy "defamiliarizes" the idea of flogging in this way: "to strip people who have broken the law, to hurl them to the floor, and to rap on their bottoms with switches," and, after a few lines, "to lash about on the naked buttocks." Then he remarks:

> Just why precisely this stupid, savage means of causing pain and not any other—why not prick the shoulders or any part of the body with needles, squeeze the hands or the feet in a vise, or anything like that?

I apologize for this harsh example, but it is typical of Tolstoy's way of pricking the conscience. The familiar act of flogging is made unfamiliar both by the description and by the proposal to change its form without changing its nature. Tolstoy uses this technique of "defamiliarization" constantly. The narrator of "Kholstomer," for example, is a horse, and it is the horse's point of view (rather than a person's) that makes the content of the story seem unfamiliar. Here is how the horse regards the institution or private property:

> I understood well what they said about whipping and Christianity. But then I was absolutely in the dark. What's the meaning of "his own," "his colt"? From these phrases I saw that people thought there was some sort of connection between me and the stable. At the time I simply could not understand the connection. Only much later, when they separated me from the other horses, did I begin to understand. But even then I simply could not see what it meant when they called me "man's property." The words "my horse" referred to me, a living horse, and seemed as strange to me as the words "my land," "my air," "my water."
>
> But the words made a strong impression on me. I thought about them constantly, and only after the most diverse experiences with people did I understand, finally, what they meant. They meant this: In life people are guided by words, not by deeds. It's not so much that they love the possibility of doing or not doing something as it is the possibility of speaking with words, agreed on among themselves, about various topics. Such are the words "my" and "mine," which they apply to different things, creatures, objects, and even to land, people, and horses. They agree that only one may say "mine" about this, that, or the other thing. And the one who says "mine" about the greatest number of things is, according to the game which they've agreed to among themselves, the one they consider the most happy. I don't know the point of all this, but it's true. For a long time I tried to explain it to myself in terms of some kind of real gain, but I had to reject that explanation because it was wrong.
>
> Many of those, for instance, who called me their own never rode on me—although others did. And so with those who fed me. Then again, the coachman, the veterinarians, and the outsiders in general treated me kindly, yet those who called me their own did not. In due time, having widened the scope of my observations, I satisfied myself that the notion "my," not only in relation to us horses, has no other basis than a narrow human instinct which is called a sense of or right to private property. A man says "this house is mine" and

never lives in it; he only worries about its construction and upkeep. A merchant says "my shop," "my dry goods shop," for instance, and does not even wear clothes made from the better cloth he keeps in his own shop.

There are people who call a tract of land their own, but they never set eyes on it and never take a stroll on it. There are people who call others their own, yet never see them. And the whole relationship between them is that the so-called "owners" treat the others unjustly.

There are people who call women their own, or their "wives," but their women live with other men. And people strive not for the good in life, but for goods they can call their own.

I am now convinced that this is the essential difference between people and ourselves. And therefore, not even considering the other ways in which we are superior, but considering just this one virtue, we can bravely claim to stand higher than men on the ladder of living creatures. The actions of men, at least those with whom I have had dealings, are guided by *words*—ours, by deeds.

...Anyone who knows Tolstoy can find several hundred such passages in his work. His method of seeing things out of their normal context is also apparent in his last works. Tolstoy described the dogmas and rituals he attacked as if they were unfamiliar, substituting everyday meanings for the customarily religious meanings of the words common in church ritual. Many persons were painfully wounded; they considered it blasphemy to present as strange and monstrous what they accepted as sacred. Their reaction was due chiefly to the technique through which Tolstoy perceived and reported his environment. And after turning to what he had long avoided, Tolstoy found that his perceptions had unsettled his faith.

The technique of defamiliarization is not Tolstoy's alone. I cited Tolstoy because his work is generally known.

Now, having explained the nature of this technique, let us try to determine the approximate limits of its application. I personally feel that defamiliarization is found almost everywhere form is found. In other words, the.difference between Potebnya's point of view and ours is this: An image is not a permanent referent for those mutable complexities of life which are revealed through it; its purpose is not to make us perceive meaning, but to create a special perception of the object—*it creates a "vision" of the object instead of serving as a means for knowing it.*

The purpose of imagery in erotic art can be studied even more accurately; an erotic object is usually presented as if it were seen for the first time. Gogol, in "Christmas Eve," provides the following example:

Here he approached her more closely, coughed, smiled at her, touched her plump, bare arm with his fingers, and expressed himself in a way that showed both his cunning and his conceit.

"And what is this you have, magnificent Solokha?" and having said this, he jumped back a little.

"What? An arm, Osip Nikiforovich!" she answered.

"Hmm, an arm! *He, he, he!*" said the secretary cordially, satisfied with his beginning. He wandered about the room.

"And what is this you have, dearest Solokha?" he said in the same way, having approached her again and grasped her lightly by the neck, and in the very same way he jumped back.

"As if you don't see, Osip Nikiforovich!" answered Solokha, "a neck, and on my neck a necklace."

"Hmm! On the neck a necklace! *He, he, he!*" and the secretary again wandered about the room, rubbing his hands.

"And what is this you have, incomparable Solokha?" … It is not known to what the secretary would stretch his long fingers now.

And Knut Hamsun has the following in "Hunger": "two white prodigies appeared from beneath her blouse."

Erotic subjects may also be presented figuratively with the obvious purpose of leading us away from their "recognition." Hence sexual organs are referred to in terms of lock and key,[19] or quilting tools,[20] or bow and arrow, or rings and marlinspikes....

In studying poetic speech in its phonetic and lexical structure as well as in its characteristic distribution of words and in the characteristic thought structures compounded from the words, we find everywhere the artistic trademark—that is, we find material obviously created to remove the automatism of perception; the author's purpose is to create the vision which results from that deautomatized perception. A work is created "artistically" so that its perception is impeded and the greatest possible effect is produced through the slowness of the perception. As a result of this lingering, the object is perceived not in its extension in space, but, so to speak, in its continuity. Thus "poetic language" gives satisfaction. According to Aristotle, poetic language must appear strange and wonderful; asnd, in fact, it is often actually foreign: the Sumerian used by the Assyrians, the Latin of Europe during the Middle Ages, the Arabisms of the Persians, the Old Bulgarian of Russian literature, or the elevated, almost literary language of folk songs. The common archaisms of poetic language, the intricacy of the sweet new style [*dolce stil nuovo*],[21] the obscure style of the language of Arnaut Daniel with the "roughened" [*harte*] forms *which make pronunciation difficult*—these are used in much the same way. Leo Jakubinsky has demonstrated the principle of phonetic "roughening" of poetic language in the particular case of the repetition of identical sounds. The language of poetry is, then, a difficult, roughened, impeded language. In a few special instances the language of poetry approximates the language of prose, but this does not violate the principle of "roughened" form.

> Her sister was called Tatyana.
> For the first time we shall
> Wilfully brighten the delicate
> Pages of a novel with such a name.

wrote Pushkin. The usual poetic language for Pushkin's contemporaries was the elegant style of Derzhavin; but Pushkin's style, because it seemed trivial then, was unexpectedly difficult for them. We should remember the consternation of Pushkin's contemporaries over the vulgarity of his expressions. He used the popular language as a special device for prolonging attention, just as his contemporaries generally used Russian words in their usually French speech (see Tolstoy's examples in *War and Peace*).

Just now a still more characteristic phenomenon is under way. Russian literary language, which was originally foreign to Russia, has so permeated the language of the people that it has blended with their conversation. On the other hand, literature has now begun to show a tendency towards the use of dialects (Remizov, Klyuyev, Essenin, and others,[22] so unequal in talent and so alike in language, are intentionally provincial) and of barbarisms (which gave rise to the Severyanin group[23]). And currently Maxim Gorky is changing his diction from the old literary language to the new literary colloquialism of Leskov.[24] Ordinary speech and literary language have thereby changed places (see the work of Vyacheslav Ivanov and many others). And finally, a strong tendency, led by Khlebnikov, to create a new and properly poetic language has emerged. In the light of these developments we can define poetry as *attenuated, tortuous* speech. Poetic speech is *formed speech*. Prose is ordinary speech—economical, easy, proper, the goddess of prose [*dea prosae*] is a goddess of the accurate, facile type, of the "direct" expression of a child. I shall discuss roughened form and retardation as the general *law* of art at greater length in an article on plot construction.[25]

Nevertheless, the position of those who urge the idea of the economy of artistic energy as something which exists in and even distinguishes poetic language seems, at first glance, tenable for the problem of rhythm. Spencer's description of rhythm would seem to be absolutely incontestable:

> Just as the body in receiving a series of varying concussions, must keep the muscles ready to meet the most violent of them, as not knowing when such may come: so, the mind in receiving unarranged articulations, must keep its perspectives active enough to recognize the least easily caught sounds. And as, if the concussions recur in definite order, the body may husband its forces by adjusting the resistance needful for each concussion; so, if the syllables be rhythmically arranged, the mind may economize its energies by anticipating the attention required for each syllable.[26]

This apparently conclusive observation suffers from the common fallacy, the confusion of the laws of poetic and prosaic language. In *The Philosophy of Style* Spencer failed utterly to distinguish between them. But rhythm may have two functions. The rhythm of prose, or of a work song like "Dubinushka," permits the members of the work crew to do their necessary "groaning together" and also eases the work by making it automatic. And, in fact, it is easier to march with music than without it, and to march during an animated conversation is even easier, for the walking is done unconsciously. Thus the rhythm of prose is an important automatizing element; the rhythm of poetry is not. There is "order" in art, yet not a single column of a Greek temple stands exactly in its proper order; poetic rhythm is similarly disordered rhythm. Attempts to systematize the irregularities have been made, and such attempts are part of the current problem in the theory of rhythm. It is obvious that the systematization will not work, for in reality the problem is not one of complicating the rhythm but of disordering the rhythm—a disordering which cannot be predicted. Should the disordering of rhythm become a convention, it would be ineffective as a device for the roughening of language. But I will not discuss rhythm in more detail since I intend to write a book about it.[27]

NOTES

1. Alexander Potebnya, *Iz zapisok po teorii slovesnosti* [*Notes on the Theory of Language*] (Kharkov, 1905), p. 83.
2. *Ibid.,* p. 97.
3. Dmitry Ovsyaniko-Kulikovsky (1835–1920), a leading Russian scholar, was an early contributor to Marxist periodicals and a literary conservative, antagonistic towards the deliberately meaningless poems of the Futurists. *Ed. note.*
4. Potebnya, *Iz zapisok po teorii slovesnosti*, p. 314.
5. *Ibid.,* p. 291.
6. Fyodor Tyutchev (1803–1873), a poet, and Nicholas Gogol (1809–1852), a master of prose fiction and satire, are mentioned here because their bold use of imagery cannot be accounted for by Potebnya's theory. Shklovsky is arguing that writers frequently gain their effects by comparing the commonplace to the exceptional rather than vice versa. *Ed. note.*
7. This is an allusion to Vyacheslav Ivanov's *Borozdy i mezhi* [*Furrows and Boundaries*] (Moscow, 1916), a major statement of Symbolist theory. *Ed. note.*
8. The Russian text involves a play on the word for "hat," colloquial for "clod," "duffer," etc. *Ed. note.*
9. Shklovsky is here doing two things of major theoretical importance: (1) he argues that different techniques serve a single function, and that (2) no single technique is all-important. The second permits the Formalists to be concerned with any and all literary devices; the first permits them to discuss the devices from a single consistent theoretical position. *Ed. note*
10. Herbert Spencer, *The Philosophy of Style* [(Humboldt Library, Vol. XXXIV; New York, 1882), pp. 2–3. Shklovsky's quoted reference, in Russian, preserves the idea of the original but shortens it].
11. The Russian *zatrudyonny* means "made difficult." The suggestion is that poems with "easy" or smooth rhythms slip by unnoticed; poems that are difficult or "roughened" force the reader to attend to them. *Ed. note.*
12. Leo Jakubinsky, "O zvukakh poeticheskovo yazyka" ["On the Sounds of Poetic Language"], *Sborniki,* I (1916), p. 38.
13. Leo Jakubinsky, "Skopleniye odinakovykh plavnykh v praktcheskom i poeticheskom yazykakh" ["The Accumulation of Identical Liquids in Practical and Poetic Language"], *Sborniki,* II (1917), pp. 13–21.
14. Alexander Pogodin, *Yazyk, kak tvorchestvo* [*Language as Art*] (Kharkov, 1913), p. 42. [The original sentence was in French, "*Les montaignes de la Suisse sont belles,*" with the appropriate initials.]
15. Jakubinsky, *Sborniki,* I (1916).
16. Leo Tolstoy's *Diary,* entry dated February 29, 1897. [The date is transcribed incorrectly; it should read March 1, 1897.]
17. Alexander Potebnya, *Iz lektsy po teorii slovesnosti* [*Lectures on the Theory of Language*] (Kharkov, 1914).

18. Victor Shklovsky, *Voskresheniye slova* [*The Resurrection of the Word*] (Petersburg, 1914).

19. [Dimitry] Savodnikov, *Zagadki russkovo naroda* [*Riddles of the Russian People*] (St. Petersburg, 1901), Nos. 102–107.

20. *Ibid.*, Nos. 588–591.

21. Dante, *Purgatorio*, 24:56. Dante refers to the new lyric style of his contemporaries. *Ed. note.*

22. Alexy Remizov (1877–1957) is best known as a novelist and satirist; Nicholas Klyuyev (1885–1937) and Sergey Essenin (1895–1925) were "peasant poets." All three were noted for their faithful reproduction of Russian dialects and colloquial language. *Ed. note.*

23. A group noted for its opulent and sensuous verse style. *Ed. note.*

24. Nicholas Leskov (1831–1895), novelist and short story writer, helped popularize the *skaz*, or yarn, and hence, because of the part dialect peculiarities play in the *skaz*, also altered Russian literary language. *Ed. note.*

25. Shklovsky is probably referring to his *Razvyortyvaniye syuzheta* [*Plot Development*] (Petrograd, 1921). *Ed. note.*

26. Victor Shklovsky, "Iskusstvo, kak priyom," *Sborniki*, II (1917).

27. We have been unable to discover the book Shklovsky promised. *Ed. note.*

MORPHOLOGY OF THE FOLKTALE (1928)

V. PROPP

Translated from the Russian by Laurence Scott

In this short chapter from a classic of Russian formalism, Propp lays out the conclusions of his influential study of Russian fairy tales. While in the strictest sense his conclusions apply only to fairy tales, or to Russian fairy tales, or to the particular Russian fairy tales he studied, in a loose sense they prove suggestive about larger bodies of stories, novels, and films and about narrative and storytelling at large. After this chapter, Propp lists 31 "functions" that he found in the fairy tales in the order they appear after what he calls the "initial situation," which precedes the first function. Samples include number 2, "an interdiction is addressed to the hero"; number 3, "the interdiction is violated"; number 4, "the villain makes an attempt at reconnaissance"; and number 5, "the villain receives information about his victim." While not all the functions appear in any one story, Propp's idea that the functions come in the same order in each story is one of his most provocative claims.

THE METHOD AND MATERIAL

Let us first of all attempt to formulate our task. As already stated in the foreword, this work is dedicated to the study of *fairy* tales. The existence of fairy tales as a special class is assumed as an essential working hypothesis. By "fairy tales" are meant at present those tales classified by Aarne under numbers 300 to 749. This definition is artificial, but the occasion will subsequently arise to give a more precise determination on the basis of resultant conclusions. We are undertaking a comparison of the themes of these tales. For the sake of comparison we shall separate the component parts of fairy tales by special methods; and then, we shall make a comparison of tales according to their components. The result will be a morphology (i.e., a description of the tale according to its component parts and the relationship of these components to each other and to the whole).

What methods can achieve an accurate description of the tale? Let us compare the following events:

1. A tsar gives an eagle to a hero. The eagle carries the hero away to another kingdom.
2. An old man gives Súčenko a horse. The horse carries Súčenko away to another kingdom.
3. A sorcerer gives Iván a little boat. The boat takes Iván to another kingdom.
4. A princess gives Iván a ring. Young men appearing from out of the ring carry Iván away into another kingdom, and so forth.[1]

Both constants and variables are present in the preceding instances. The names of the dramatis personae change (as well as the attributes of each), but neither their actions nor functions change. From this we can draw the inference that a tale often attributes identical actions to various personages. This makes possible the study of the tale *according to the functions of its dramatis personae.*

We shall have to determine to what extent these functions actually represent recurrent constants of the tale. The formulation of all other questions will depend upon the solution of this primary question: how many functions are known to the tale?

Investigation will reveal that the recurrence of functions is astounding. Thus Bába Jagá, Morózko, the bear, the forest spirit, and the mare's head test and reward the stepdaughter. Going further, it is possible to establish that characters of a tale, however varied they may be, often perform the same actions. The actual means of the realization of functions can vary, and as such, it is a variable. Morózko behaves differently than Bába Jagá. But the function, as such, is a constant. The question of *what* a tale's dramatis personae do is an important one for the study of the tale, but the questions of *who* does it and *how* it is done already fall within the province of accessory study. The functions of characters are those components which could replace Veselóvskij's "motifs," or Bédier's "elements." We are aware of the fact that the repetition of functions by various characters was long ago observed in myths and beliefs by historians of religion, but it was not observed by historians of the tale (cf. Wundt and Negelein[2]). Just as the characteristics and functions of deities are transferred from one to another, and, finally, are even carried over to Christian saints, the functions of certain tale personages are likewise transferred to other personages. Running ahead, one may say that the number of functions is extremely small, whereas the number of personages is extremely large. This explains the two-fold quality of a tale: its amazing multiformity, picturesqueness, and color, and on the other hand, its no less striking uniformity, its repetition.

Thus the functions of the dramatis personae are basic components of the tale, and we must first of all extract them. In order to extract the functions we must define them. Definition must proceed from two points of view. First of all, definition should in no case depend on the personage who carries out the function. Definition of a function will most often be given in the form of a noun expressing an action (interdiction, interrogation, flight, etc.). Secondly, an action cannot be defined apart from its place in the course of narration. The meaning which a given function has in the course of action must be considered. For example, if Iván marries a tsar's daughter, this is something entirely different than the marriage of a father to a widow with two daughters. A second example: if, in one instance, a hero receives money from his father in the form of 100 rubles and subsequently buys a wise cat with this money, whereas in a second case, the hero is rewarded with a sum of money for an accomplished act of bravery (at which point the tale ends), we have before us two morphologically different elements—in spite of the identical action (the transference of money) in both cases. Thus, identical acts can have different meanings, and vice versa. *Function is understood as an act of a character, defined from the point of view of its significance for the course of the action.*

The observations cited may be briefly formulated in the following manner:

1. *Functions of characters serve as stable, constant elements in a tale, independent of how and by whom they are fulfilled. They constitute the fundamental components of a tale.*
2. *The number of functions known to the fairy tale is limited.*

If functions are delineated, a second question arises: in what classification and in what sequence are these functions encountered?

A word, first, about sequence. The opinion exists that this sequence is accidental. Veselóvskij writes, "The selection and *order* of tasks and encounters (examples of motifs) already presupposes a certain *freedom.*" Šklóvskij stated this idea in even sharper terms: "It is quite impossible to understand why, in the act of adoption, the *accidental* sequence [Šklóvskij's italics] of motifs must be retained. In the testimony of witnesses, it is precisely the sequence of events which is distorted most of all." This reference to the evidence of witnesses is unconvincing. If witnesses distort the sequence of events, their narration is meaningless. The sequence of events has its own laws. The short story too has similar laws, as do organic formations. Theft cannot take place before the door is forced. Insofar as the tale is concerned, it has its own entirely particular and specific laws. The sequence of elements, as we shall see later on, is strictly *uniform.* Freedom within this sequence is restricted by very narrow limits which can be exactly formulated. We thus obtain the third basic thesis of this work, subject to further development and verification:

3. *The sequence of functions is always identical.*

As for groupings, it is necessary to say first of all that by no means do all tales give evidence of all functions. But this in no way changes the law of sequence. The absence of certain functions does not change the order of the rest. We shall dwell on this phenomenon later. For the present we shall deal with groupings in the proper sense of the word. The presentation of the question itself evokes the following assumption: if functions are singled out, then it will be possible to trace those tales which present identical functions. Tales with identical functions can be considered as belonging to one type. On this foundation, an index of types can then be created, based not upon theme features, which are somewhat vague and diffuse, but upon exact structural features. Indeed, this will be possible. If we further compare structural types among themselves, we are led to the following completely unexpected phenomenon: functions cannot be distributed around mutually exclusive axes. This phenomenon, in all its concreteness, will become apparent to us in the succeeding and final chapters of this book. For the time being, it can be interpreted in the following manner: if we designate with the letter A a function encountered everywhere in first position, and similarly designate with the letter B the function which (if it is at all present) *always follows A*, then all functions known to the tale will arrange themselves, within a *single* tale, and none will fall out of order, nor will any one exclude or contradict any other. This is, of course, a completely unexpected result. Naturally, we would have expected that where there is a function A, there cannot be certain functions belonging to other tales. Supposedly we would obtain several axes, but only a single axis is obtained for all fairy tales. They are of the same type, while the combinations spoken of previously are subtypes. At first glance, this conclusion may appear absurd or perhaps even wild, yet it can be verified in a most exact manner. Such a typological unity represents a very complex problem on which it will be necessary to dwell further. This phenomenon will raise a whole series of questions.

In this manner, we arrive at the fourth basic thesis of our work:

4. *All fairy tales are of one type in regard to their structure.*

We shall now set about the task of proving, developing, and elaborating these theses in detail. Here it should be recalled that the study of the tale must be carried on strictly deductively, i.e., proceeding from the material at hand to the consequences (and in effect it is so carried on in this work). But the *presentation* may have a reversed order, since it is easier to follow the development if the general bases are known to the reader beforehand.

Before starting the elaboration, however, it is necessary to decide what material can serve as the subject of this study. First glance would seem to indicate that it is necessary to cover all extant material. In fact, this is not so. Since we are studying tales according to the functions of their dramatis personae, the accumulation of material can be suspended as soon as it becomes apparent that the new tales considered present no new functions. Of course, the investigator must look through an enormous amount of reference material. But there is no need to inject the entire body of this material into the study. We have found that 100 tales constitute more than enough material. Having discovered that no new functions can be found, the morphologist can put a stop to his work, and further study will follow different directions (the formation of indices, the complete systemization, historical study). But just because material can be limited in quantity, that does not mean that it can be selected at one's own discretion. It should be dictated from without. We shall use the collection by Afanás'ev, starting the study of tales with No. 50 (according to his plan, this is the first fairy tale of the collection), and finishing it with No. 151.[†] Such a limitation of material will undoubtedly call forth many objections, but it is theoretically justified. To justify it further, it would be necessary to take into account the degree of repetition of tale phenomena. If repetition is great, then one may take a limited amount of material. If repetition is small, this is impossible. The repetition of fundamental components, as we shall see later, exceeds all expectations. Consequently, it is theoretically possible to limit oneself to a small body of material. Practically, this limitation justifies itself by the fact that the inclusion of a great quantity of material would have excessively increased the size of this work. We are not interested in the quantity of material, but in the quality of its analysis. Our working material consists of 100 tales. The rest is reference material, of great interest to the investigator, but lacking a broader interest.

NOTES

1. See Afanás'ev, Nos. 171, 139, 138, 156.
2. W. Wundt, "Mythus und Religion," *Völkerpsychologie*, II, Section I; Negelein, *Germanische Mythologie*. Negelein creates an exceptionally apt term, *Depossedierte Gottheiten*.

THE METAPHORIC AND METONYMIC POLES (1956) LINGUISTICS AND POETICS (1960)

ROMAN JAKOBSON

Jakobson wrote widely about linguistics, structuralism, literature, and their relation to each other. He played a leading role in introducing Saussurean linguistics to scholars of linguistics, anthropology, and literary studies.

What is the first word that comes to your mind when I say spaghetti? *Remember that word, and we will come back to it soon. "The Metaphoric and Metonymic Poles" is the last section of a longer essay, "Two Aspects of Language and Two Types of Aphasic Disturbances." As the first two paragraphs in this section indicate, the earlier parts of the longer essay discuss the language patterns of people who suffer from aphasia (acquired language disorders) and connect them to patterns that Jakobson finds in language more generally. The two aspects of language are the tropes (rhetorical figures) of metaphor and metonymy. In the sense that Jakobson uses these terms, a metaphor substitutes for a term that is not connected to or next to it, as when we call a brave person a* lion *or a timid person a* mouse. *A metonymy substitutes for a term that is connected to or next to it, as*

---

† Tales numbered 50 to 151 refer to enumeration according to the older editions of Afanás'ev. In the new system of enumeration, adopted for the fifth and sixth editions and utilized in this translation (cf. the Preface to the Second Edition, and Appendix V), the corresponding numbers are 93 to 270. [L.A.W.]

when we call soldiers boots on the ground *or call a train a* choo-choo. *Synecdoche (using a part to refer to a whole) is a kind of metonymy, as when people call a person with red hair* Red *or call a detective a* private eye. *According to Jakobson, some aphasics have a similarity disorder; they rely on metonymy (connection) even when we would expect metaphor (substitution). For example, aphasics with a similarity disorder might describe objects by their sequence, that is, by what they are next to, but cannot group them by class, that is, by color, shape, or size. If they see a picture of an object, they cannot think of the word for it. They can respond to someone else's talking about a topic, but they cannot begin the discussion. They cannot come up with the term* knife *by itself, but they can come up with connections like* butter knife *or* paring knife. *By contrast, some aphasics have a contiguity disorder; they rely on metaphor even when we would expect metonymy. They sometimes speak in a telegraphic, text-message style, skipping connective terms like conjunctions (and, but), prepositions (in, on, by, to), pronouns, and articles (a, the). They depend on short, sometimes even one-word, sentences.*

If the word you thought of when you saw the word spaghetti *was something like* lasagna, fettucini, *or* noodles, *then you responded through metaphor, by substitution. If the word you thought of, however, was something like* Italian, sauce, *or* meatballs, *then you responded through metonymy, by connection. In "The Metaphoric and Metonymic Poles," Jakobson compares a predilection for metaphor to a predilection for metonymy, associating each pole with different styles and genres of painting and literature.*

The excerpt from "Linguistics and Poetics" begins after several pages lamenting that some linguists exclude poetics, poetry, and emotions from the study of linguistics. In the course of defining the linguistic characteristics of poetic or literary language, Jakobson proposes an influential overall description of the communication exchange in general. Readers will see, for example, how Stuart Hall's "Encoding/Decoding," included in this volume, builds on Jakobson's model, even though it does not address poetry.

A few of Jakobson's eclectic contexts may bear explanation. As a linguist, Jakobson sometimes indicates the pronunciation of words by using the International Phonetic Alphabet, but readers who are unfamiliar with that alphabet can still follow it roughly by drawing on the context and on Jakobson's explanations. When Jakobson mentions interjections, he refers to expressions like Oh!, Wow!, *or* Ouch! *(His example is* Tut! Tut!*) Paronamasia refers to play with words, often (though not here) through puns. "I like Ike" was a popular slogan among the supporters of Dwight Eisenhower, president of the United States, when Jakobson wrote his essay.*

When Jakobson concludes, in a famous but not always readily clear formula, that "The poetic function projects the principle of equivalence from the axis of selection into the axis of combination," he means, in effect, that poetry bends a reliance on selection into a reliance on combination. That is, it feeds metaphor (often individual words) into metonymy (juxtapositions of words), rolling the metaphors into extended poetic lines through connection, sequence, and contiguity. Building on "The Metaphoric and Metonymic Poles," Jakobson associates selection with metaphor and combination (connection, sequence, continuity) with metonymy.

The remainder of "Linguistics and Poetics," not included here, applies Jakobson's description of the poetic function to a technical linguistic discussion of versification, rhyme, folk poetry, and the sound texture of poetry (paronomasia, echoes between the sound and sense of poetic vocabulary) and then to poetic metonymy itself, which Jakobson sees as prominent in such lines as these from Antony in Shakespeare's Antony and Cleopatra: *"My heart is in the coffin there with Caesar, / And I must pause till it come back to me."*

THE METAPHORIC AND METONYMIC POLES (1956)

ROMAN JAKOBSON

The varieties of aphasia are numerous and diverse, but all of them oscillate between the two polar types just described. Every form of aphasic disturbance consists in some impairment, more or less severe, either of the faculty for selection and substitution or for combination and contexture. The former affliction involves a deterioration of metalinguistic operations, while the latter damages the capacity for maintaining the hierarchy of linguistic units. The relation of similarity is suppressed in the former, the relation of contiguity in the latter type of aphasia. Metaphor is alien to the similarity disorder, and metonymy to the contiguity disorder.

The development of a discourse may take place along two different semantic lines: one topic may lead to another either through their similarity or through their contiguity. The metaphoric way would be the most appropriate term for the first case and the metonymic way for the second, since they find their most condensed expression in metaphor and metonymy respectively. In aphasia one or the other of these two processes is restricted or totally blocked—an effect which makes the study of aphasia particularly illuminating for the linguist. In normal verbal behavior both processes are continually operative, but careful observation will reveal that under the influence of a cultural pattern, personality, and verbal style, preference is given to one of the two processes over the other.

In a well-known psychological test, children are confronted with some noun and told to utter the first verbal response that comes into their heads. In this experiment two opposite linguistic predilections are invariably exhibited: the response is intended either as a substitute for, or as a complement to the stimulus. In the latter case the stimulus and the response together form a proper syntactic construction, most usually a sentence. These two types of reaction have been labeled substitutive and predicative.

To the stimulus *hut* one response was *burnt out*; another, *is a poor little house*. Both reactions are predicative; but the first creates a purely narrative context, while in the second there is a double connection with the subject *hut*: on the one hand, a positional (namely, syntactic) contiguity, and on the other a semantic similarity.

The same stimulus produced the following substitutive reactions: the tautology *hut;* the synonyms *cabin* and *hovel;* the antonym *palace,* and the metaphors *den* and *burrow.* The capacity of two words to replace one another is an instance of positional similarity, and, in addition, all these responses are linked to the stimulus by semantic similarity (or contrast). Metonymical responses to the same stimulus, such as *thatch, litter,* or *poverty,* combine and contrast the positional similarity with semantic contiguity.

In manipulating these two kinds of connection (similarity and contiguity) in both their aspects (positional and semantic)—selecting, combining, and ranking them—an individual exhibits his personal style, his verbal predilections and preferences.

In verbal art the interaction of these two elements is especially pronounced. Rich material for the study of this relationship is to be found in verse patterns which require a compulsory parallelism between adjacent lines, for example in Biblical poetry or in the West Finnic and, to some extent, the Russian oral traditions. This provides an objective criterion of what in the given speech community acts as a correspondence. Since on any verbal level—morphemic, lexical, syntactic, and phraseological—either of these two relations (similarity and contiguity) can appear—and each in either of two aspects—an impressive range of possible configurations is created. Either of the two gravitational poles may prevail. In Russian lyrical songs, for example, metaphoric constructions predominate, while in the heroic epics the metonymic way is preponderant.

In poetry there are various motives which determine the choice between these alternants. The primacy of the metaphoric process in the literary schools of romanticism and symbolism has been repeatedly acknowledged, but it is still insufficiently realized that it is the predominance of metonymy which underlies and actually predetermines the so-called "realistic" trend, which belongs to an intermediary stage between the decline of romanticism and the rise of symbolism and is opposed to both. Following the path of contiguous relationships, the realistic author metonymically digresses from the plot to the atmosphere and from the characters to the setting in space and time. He is fond of synecdochic details. In the scene of Anna Karenina's suicide Tolstoj's artistic attention is focused on the heroine's handbag; and in *War and Peace* the synecdoches "hair on the upper lip" or "bare shoulders" are used by the same writer to stand for the female characters to whom these features belong.

The alternative predominance of one or the other of these two processes is by no means confined to verbal art. The same oscillation occurs in sign systems other than language.[1] A salient example from the history of painting is the manifestly metonymical orientation of cubism, where the object is transformed into a set of synecdoches; the surrealist painters responded with a patently metaphorical attitude. Ever since the productions of D. W. Griffith, the art of the cinema, with its highly developed capacity for changing the angle, perspective and focus of "shots," has broken with the tradition of the theater and ranged an unprecedented variety of synecdochic "close-ups" and metonymic "set-ups" in general. In such pictures as those of Charlie Chaplin, these devices in turn were superseded by a novel, metaphoric "montage" with its "lap dissolves"—the filmic similes.[2]

The bipolar structure of language (or other semiotic systems) and, in aphasia, the fixation on one of these poles to the exclusion of the other require systematic comparative study. The retention of either of these alternatives in the two types of aphasia must be confronted with the predominance of the same pole in certain styles, personal habits, current fashions, etc. A careful analysis and comparison of these phenomena with the whole syndrome of the corresponding type of aphasia is an imperative task for joint research by experts in psychopathology, psychology, linguistics, poetics, and semiotics, the general science of signs. The dichotomy here discussed appears to be of primal significance and consequence for all verbal behavior and for human behavior in general.[3]

To indicate the possibilities of the projected comparative research, we choose an example from a Russian folktale which employs parallelism as a comic device: "Thomas is a bachelor; Jeremiah is unmarried" (*Fomá xólost; Erjóma neženát*). Here the predicates in the two parallel clauses are associated by similarity: they are in fact synonymous. The subjects of both clauses are masculine proper names and hence morphologically similar, while on the other hand they denote two contiguous heroes of the same tale, created to perform identical actions and thus to justify the use of synonymous pairs of predicates. A somewhat modified version of the same construction occurs in a familiar wedding song in which each of the wedding guests is addressed in turn by his first name and patronymic: "Gleb is a bachelor; Ivanovič is unmarried." While both predicates here are again synonyms, the relationship between the two subjects is changed: both are proper names denoting the same man and are normally used contiguously as a mode of polite address.

In the quotation from the folk tale the two parallel clauses refer to two separate facts, the marital status of Thomas and the similar status of Jeremiah. In the verse from the wedding song, however, the two clauses are synonymous: they redundantly reiterate the celibacy of the same hero, splitting him into two verbal hypostases.

The Russian novelist Gleb Ivanovič Uspenskij (1840–1902) in the last years of his life suffered from a mental illness involving a speech disorder. His first name and patronymic, *Gleb Ivanovič*, traditionally combined in polite intercourse, for him split into two distinct names designating two separate beings: Gleb was endowed with all his virtues, while Ivanovič, the name relating the son to the father, became the incarnation of all Uspenskij's vices. The linguistic aspect of this split personality is the patient's inability to use two symbols for the same thing, and it is thus a similarity disorder. Since the similarity disorder is bound up with the metonymical bent, an examination of the literary manner Uspenskij had employed as a young writer takes on particular interest. And the study of Anatolij Kamegulov, who analyzed Uspenskij's style, bears out our theoretical expectations. He shows that Uspenskij had a particular penchant for metonymy, and especially for synecdoche, and that he carried it so far that "the reader is crushed by the multiplicity of detail unloaded on him in a limited verbal space, and is physically unable to grasp the whole, so that the portrait is often lost."[4]

To be sure, the metonymical style in Uspenskij is obviously prompted by the prevailing literary canon of his time, late nineteeth-century "realism"; but the personal stamp of Gleb Ivanovič made his pen particularly suitable for this artistic trend in its extreme manifestations and finally left its mark upon the verbal aspect of his mental illness.

A competition between both devices, metonymic and metaphoric, is manifest in any symbolic process, either intrapersonal or social. Thus in an inquiry into the structure of dreams, the decisive question is whether the symbols and the temporal sequences used are based on contiguity (Freud's metonymic "displacement" and synecdochic "condensation") or on similarity (Freud's "identification and symbolism").[5] The principles underlying magic rites have been resolved by Frazer into two types: charms based on the law of similarity and those founded on association by contiguity. The first of these two great branches of sympathetic magic has been called "homoeopathic" or "imitative," and the second, "contagious magic."[6] This bipartition is indeed illuminating. Nonetheless, for the most part, the question of the two poles is still neglected, despite its wide scope and importance for the study of any symbolic behavior, especially verbal, and of its impairments. What is the main reason for this neglect?

Similarity in meaning connects the symbols of a metalanguage with the symbols of the language referred to. Similarity connects a metaphorical term with the term for which it is substituted. Consequently, when constructing a metalanguage to interpret tropes, the researcher possesses more homogeneous means to handle metaphor, whereas metonymy, based on a different principle, easily defies interpretation. Therefore nothing comparable to the rich literature on metaphor[7] can be cited for the theory of metonymy. For the same reason, it is generally realized that romanticism is closely linked with metaphor, whereas the equally intimate ties of realism with metonymy usually remain unnoticed. Not only the tool of the observer but also the object of observation is responsible for the preponderance of metaphor over metonymy in scholarship. Since poetry is focused upon sign, and pragmatical prose primarily upon referent, tropes and figures were studied mainly as poetical devices. The principle of similarity underlies poetry; the metrical parallelism of lines or the phonic equivalence of rhyming words prompts the question of semantic similarity and contrast; there exist, for instance, grammatical and anti-grammatical but never agrammatical rhymes. Prose, on the contrary, is forwarded essentially by contiguity. Thus, for poetry, metaphor, and for prose, metonymy is the line of least resistance and, consequently, the study of poetical tropes is directed chiefly toward metaphor. The actual bipolarity has been artificially replaced in these studies by an amputated, unipolar scheme which, strikingly enough, coincides with one of the two aphasic patterns, namely with the contiguity disorder.[8]

NOTES

1. I ventured a few sketchy remarks on the metonymical turn in verbal art ('Pro realizm u mystectvi,' *Vaplite*, Kharkov, 1927, No. 2; 'Randbemer-kungen zur Prosa des Dichters Pasternak,' *Slavische Rundschau*, VII, 1935), in painting ('Futurizm,' *Iskusstvo*, Moscow, Aug. 2, 1919) and in motion pictures ('Úpadek filmu,' *Listy pro umění a kritiku*, I, Prague, 1933), but the crucial problem of the two polar processes awaits a detailed investigation.
2. Cf. B. Balazs, *Theory of the film* (London, 1952).
3. For the psychological and sociological aspects of this dichotomy see Bateson's views on "progressional" and "selective integration" and Parsons' on the "conjunction-disjunction dichotomy" in children's development: J. Ruesch and G. Bateson, *Communication, the social matrix of psychiatry* (New York, 1951), pp. I83ff.; T. Parsons and R. F. Bales, *Family, socialization and interaction process* (Glencoe, 1955), pp. I19f.
4. A. Kamegulov, *Stil' Gleba Uspenskogo* (Leningrad, 1930), pp. 65, 145. One of such disintegrated portraits cited by the monograph: "From underneath an ancient straw cap with a black spot on its shield, there peeked two braids resembling the tusks of a wild boar; a chin grown fat and pendulous definitively spread over the greasy collars of the calico dicky and in thick layer lay on the coarse collar of the canvas coat, firmly buttoned on the neck. From below this coat to the eyes of the observer there protruded massive hands with a ring, which had eaten

into the fat finger, a cane with a copper top, a significant bulge of the stomach and the presence of very broad pants, almost of muslin quality, in the broad ends of which hid the toes
of the boots."

5. S. Freud, *Die Traumdeutung,* 9th ed. (Vienna, 1950).
6. J. G. Frazer, *The golden bough: A study in magic and religion,* Part I, 3rd ed. (Vienna, 1950),
   chapter III.
7. C. F. P. Stutterheim, *Het begrip metaphoor* (Amsterdam, 1941).
8. Thanks are due to Hugh McLean for his valuable assistance and to Justinia Besharov for her original observations on tropes and figures.

LINGUISTICS AND POETICS (1960)

ROMAN JAKOBSON

Language must be investigated in all the variety of its functions. Before discussing the poetic
function we must define its place among the other functions of language. An outline of
these functions demands a concise survey of the constitutive factors in any speech event,
in any act of verbal communication. The ADDRESSER sends a MESSAGE to the ADDRESSEE. To
be operative the message requires a CONTEXT referred to ("referent" in another, somewhat
ambiguous, nomenclature), seizable by the addressee, and either verbal or capable of being
verbalized; a CODE fully, or at least partially, common to the addresser and addressee (or in
other words, to the encoder and decoder of the message); and, finally, a CONTACT, a physical
channel and psychological connection between the addresser and the addressee, enabling
both of them to enter and stay in communication. All these factors inalienably involved in
verbal communication may be schematized as follows:

CONTEXT

ADDRESSER . . . . MESSAGE . . . . ADDRESSEE

CONTACT

CODE

Each of these six factors determines a different function of language. Although we distinguish six basic aspects of language, we could, however, hardly find verbal messages that would fulfill only one function. The diversity lies not in a monopoly of some one of these several functions but in a different hierarchical order of functions. The verbal structure of a message depends primarily on the predominant function. But even though a set (*Einstellung*) toward the referent, an orientation toward the CONTEXT—briefly the so-called REFERENTIAL, "denotative," "cognitive" function—is the leading task of numerous messages, the accessory participation of the other functions in such messages must be taken into account by the observant linguist.

The so-called EMOTIVE or "expressive" function, focused on the ADDRESSER, aims a direct expression of the speaker's attitude toward what he is speaking about. It tends to produce an impression of a certain emotion whether true or feigned; therefore, the term "emotive," launched and advocated by Marty (**269**) has proved to be preferable to "emotional." The purely emotive stratum in language is presented by the interjections. They differ from the means of referential language both by their sound pattern (peculiar sound sequences or even sounds elsewhere unusual) and by their syntactic role (they are not components but equivalents of sentences). *"Tut! Tut!* said McGinty"*: the complete utterance of Conan Doyle's character consists of two suction clicks. The emotive function, laid bare in the interjections, flavors to some extent all our utterances, on their phonic, grammatical, and lexical level. If we analyze language from the standpoint of the information it carries, we cannot restrict the notion of information to the cognitive aspect of language. A man, using expressive features to indicate his angry or ironic attitude, conveys ostensible information, and evidently this verbal behavior cannot be likened to such nonsemiotic, nutritive activities as "eating grapefruit" (despite Chatman's bold simile). The difference between [big] and the emphatic prolongation of the vowel [bi:g] is a conventional, coded linguistic feature like the difference between the short and long vowel in such Czech pairs as [vi] "you" and [vi:] "knows," but in the latter pair the differential information is phonemic and in the former emotive. As long as we are interested in phonemic invariants, the English /I/ and /i:/ appear to be mere variants of one and the same phoneme, but if we are concerned with emotive units, the relation between the invariant and variants is reversed: length and shortness are invariants implemented by variable phonemes. Saporta's surmise that emotive difference is a nonlinguistic feature, "attributable to the delivery of the message and not to the message," arbitrarily reduces the informational capacity of messages.

A former actor of Stanislavskij's Moscow Theater told me how at his audition he was asked by the famous director to make forty different messages from the phrase *Segodnja večerom* "This evening" by diversifying its expressive tint. He made a list of some forty emotional situations, then emitted the given phrase in accordance with each of these situations, which his audience had to recognize only from the changes in the sound shape of the same two words. For our research work in the description and analysis of contemporary Standard Russian (under the auspices of the Rockefeller Foundation) this actor was asked to repeat Stanislavskij's test. He wrote down some fifty situations framing the same elliptic sentence and made of it fifty corresponding messages for a tape record. Most of the messages were correctly and circumstantially decoded by Moscovite listeners. May I add that all such emotive cues easily undergo linguistic analysis.

Orientation toward the ADDRESSEE, the CONATIVE function, finds its purest grammatical expression in the vocative and imperative, which syntactically, morphologically, and often even phonemically deviate from other nominal and verbal categories. The imperative sentences cardinally differ from declarative sentences: the latter are and the former are not liable to a truth test. When in O'Neill's play *The Fountain*, Nano, "(in a fierce tone of command)," says "Drink!"—the imperative cannot be challenged by the question "is it true or not?" which may be, however, perfectly well asked after such sentences as "one drank," "one will drink," "one would drink." In contradistinction to the imperative sentences, the declarative sentences are convertible into interrogative sentences: "did one drink?" "will one drink?" "would one drink?"

The traditional model of language as elucidated particularly by Bühler (**51**) was confined to these three functions—emotive, conative, and referential—and the three apexes of this model—the first person of the addresser, the second person of the addressee, and the "third person," properly—someone or something spoken of. Certain additional verbal functions can be easily inferred from this triadic model. Thus the magic, incantatory function is chiefly some kind of conversion of an absent or inanimate "third person" into an addressee of a conative message. "May this sty dry up, *tfu, tfu, tfu, tfu*" (Lithuanian spell: **266**, p, 69). "Water, queen river, daybreak! Send grief beyond the blue sea, to the sea-bottom, like a grey stone never to rise from the sea-bottom, may grief never come to burden the light heart of God's servant, may grief be removed and sink away." (North Russian incantation: **343**, p. 2I7f.). "Sun, stand thou still upon Gibeon; and thou, Moon, in the valley of Aj-a-lon. And the sun stood still, and the moon stayed ... " (Josh. 10.12). We observe, however, three further constitutive factors of verbal communication and three corresponding functions of language.

There are messages primarily serving to establish, to prolong, or to discontinue communication, to check whether the channel works ("Hello, do you hear me?"), to attract the attention of the interlocutor or to confirm his continued attention ("Are you listening?" or in Shakespearean diction, "Lend me your ears!"—and on the other end of the wire "Um-hum!"). This set for CONTACT, or in Malinowski's terms PHATIC function (**264**), may be displayed by a profuse exchange of ritualized formulas, by entire dialogues with the mere purport of prolonging communication. Dorothy Parker caught eloquent examples: " 'Well!' the young man said. 'Well!' she said. 'Well, here we are,' he said. 'Here we are,' she said, 'Aren't we?' 'I should say we were,' he said, 'Eeyop! Here we are.' 'Well!' she said. 'Well!' he said, 'well.' " The endeavor to start and sustain communication is typical of talking birds; thus the phatic function of language is the only one they share with human beings. It is also the first verbal function acquired by infants; they are prone to communicate before being able to send or receive informative communication.

A distinction has been made in modern logic between two levels of language, "object language" speaking of objects and "metalanguage" speaking of language. But metalanguage is not only a necessary scientific tool utilized by logicians and linguists; it plays also an important role in our everyday language. Like Molière's Jourdain who used prose without knowing it, we practice metalanguage without realizing the metalingual character of our operations. Whenever the addresser and/or the addressee need to check up whether they use the same code, speech is focused on the CODE: it performs a METALINGUAL (i.e., glossing) function. "I don't follow you—what do you mean?" asks the addressee, or in Shakespearean diction, "What is't thou say'st?" And the addresser in anticipation of such recapturing questions inquires: "Do you know what I mean?" Imagine, such an exasperating dialogue: "The sophomore was plucked." "But what is *plucked?*" "*Plucked* means the same as *flunked.*" "And *flunked?*" "*To be flunked* is *to fail in an exam.*" "And what is *sophomore?*" persists the interrogator innocent of school vocabulary. "*A sophomore* is (or means) a *second-year student.*" All these equational sentences convey information merely about the lexical code of English; their function is strictly metalingual. Any process of language learning, in particular child acquisition of the mother tongue, makes wide use of such metalingual operations; and aphasia may often be defined as a loss of ability for metalingual operations.

We have brought up all the six factors involved in verbal communication except the message itself. The set (*Einstellung*) toward the MESSAGE as such, focus on the message for its own sake, is the POETIC function of language. This function cannot be productively studied out of touch with the general problems of language, and, on the other hand, the scrutiny of language requires a thorough consideration of its poetic function. Any attempt to reduce the sphere of poetic function to poetry or to confine poetry to poetic function would be a delusive oversimplification. Poetic function is not the sole function of verbal art but only its dominant, determining function, whereas in all other verbal activities it acts as a subsidiary, accessory constituent. This function, by promoting the palpability of signs, deepens the fundamental dichotomy of signs and objects. Hence, when dealing with poetic function, linguistics cannot limit itself to the field of poetry.

"Why do you always say *Joan and Margery*, yet never *Margery and Joan*? Do you prefer Joan to her twin sister?" "Not at all, it just sounds smoother." In a sequence of two coordinate names, as far as no rank problems interfere, the precedence of the shorter name suits the speaker, unaccountably for him, as a well-ordered shape of the message.

A girl used to talk about "the horrible Harry." "Why horrible?" "Because I hate him." "But why not *dreadful, terrible, frightful, disgusting?*" "I don't know why, but *horrible* fits him better." Without realizing it, she clung to the poetic device of paronomasia.

The political slogan "I like Ike" /ay layk ayk/, succinctly structured, consists of three monosyllables and counts three diphthongs /ay/, each of them symmetrically followed by one consonantal phoneme, /. .1. .k. .k/. The make-up of the three words presents a variation: no consonantal phonemes in the first word, two around the diphthong in the second, and one final consonant in the third. A similar dominant nucleus /ay/ was noticed by Hymes in some of the sonnets of Keats. Both cola of the trisyllabic formula "I like / Ike" rhyme with each other, and the second of the two rhyming words is fully included in the first one (echo rhyme), /layk/—/ayk/, a paronomastic image of a feeling which totally envelops its object. Both cola alliterate with each other, and the first of the two alliterating words is included in the second: /ay/—/ayk/, a paronomastic image of the loving subject enveloped by the beloved object. The secondary, poetic function of this electional catch phrase reinforces its impressiveness and efficacy.

As we said, the linguistic study of the poetic function must overstep the limits of poetry, and, on the other hand, the linguistic scrutiny of poetry cannot limit itself to the poetic function. The particularities of diverse poetic genres imply a differently ranked participation of the other verbal functions along with the dominant poetic function. Epic poetry, focused on the third person, strongly involves the referential function of language; the lyric, oriented toward the first person, is intimately linked with the emotive function; poetry of the second person is imbued with the conative function and is either supplicatory or exhortative, depending on whether the first person is subordinated to the second one or the second to the first.

Now that our cursory description of the six basic functions of verbal communication is more or less complete, we may complement our scheme of the fundamental factors by a corresponding scheme of the functions:

REFERENTIAL

EMOTIVE   POETIC   CONATIVE
                            PHATIC

METALINGUAL

What is the empirical linguistic criterion of the poetic function? In particular, what is the indispensable feature inherent in any piece of poetry? To answer this question we must recall the two basic modes of arrangement used in verbal behavior, *selection* and *combination*. If "child" is the topic of the message, the speaker selects one among the extant, more or less similar, nouns like child, kid, youngster, tot, all of them equivalent in a certain respect, and then, to comment on this topic, he may select one of the semantically cognate verbs— sleeps, dozes, nods, naps. Both chosen words combine in the speech chain. The selection is produced on the base of equivalence, similarity and dissimilarity, synonymity and antonymity, while the combination, the build up of the sequence, is based on contiguity. *The poetic function projects the principle of equivalence from the axis of selection into the axis of combination.* Equivalence is promoted to the constitutive device of the sequence. In poetry one syllable is equalized with any other syllable of the same sequence; word stress is assumed to equal word stress, as unstress equals unstress; prosodic long is matched with long, and short with short; word boundary equals word boundary, no boundary equals no boundary; syntactic pause equals syntactic pause, no pause equals no pause. Syllables are converted into units of measure, and so are morae or stresses.

It may be objected that metalanguage also makes a sequential use of equivalent units when combining synonymic expressions into an equational sentence: $A = A$ (*"Mare is the female of the horse"*). Poetry and metalanguage, however, are in diametrical opposition to each other: in metalanguage the sequence is used to build an equation, whereas in poetry the equation is used to build a sequence.

In poetry, and to a certain extent in latent manifestations of poetic function, sequences delimited by word boundaries become commensurable whether they are sensed as isochronic or graded. "Joan and Margery" showed us the poetic principle of syllable gradation, the same principle which in the closes of Serbian folk epics has been raised to a compulsory law (cf. **268**). Without its two dactylic words the combination "*innocent* by*stande*r" would hardly have become a hackneyed phrase. The symmetry of three disyllabic verbs with an identical initial consonant and identical final vowel added splendor to the laconic victory message of Caesar: "*Veni, vidi, vici.*"

Measure of sequences is a device which, outside of poetic function, finds no application in language. Only in poetry with its regular reiteration of equivalent units is the time of the speech flow experienced, as it is—to cite another semiotic pattern—with musical time. Gerard Manley Hopkins, an outstanding searcher in the science of poetic language, defined verse as "speech wholly or partially repeating the same figure of sound" (**179**). Hopkins' subsequent question, "but is all verse poetry?" can be definitely answered as soon as poetic function ceases to be arbitrarily confined to the domain of poetry. Mnemonic lines cited by Hopkins (like "Thirty days hath September"), modern advertising jingles, and versified medieval laws, mentioned by Lotz, or finally Sanscrit scientific treatises in verse which in Indic tradition are strictly distinguished from true poetry (*kāvya*)—all these metrical texts make use of poetic function without, however, assigning to this function the coercing, determining role it carries in poetry. Thus verse actually exceeds the limits of poetry, but at the same time verse always implies poetic function. And apparently no human culture ignores versemaking, whereas there are many cultural patterns without "applied" verse; and even in such cultures which possess both pure and applied verses, the latter appear to be a secondary, unquestionably derived phenomenon. The adaptation of poetic means for some heterogeneous purpose does not conceal their primary essence, just as elements of emotive language, when utilized in poetry, still maintain their emotive tinge. A filibusterer may recite *Hiawatha* because it is long, yet poeticalness still remains the primary intent of this text itself. Self-evidently, the existence of versified, musical, and pictorial commercials does not separate the questions of verse or of musical and pictorial form from the study of poetry, music, and fine arts.

To sum up, the analysis of verse is entirely within the competence of poetics, and the latter may be defined as that part of linguistics which treats the poetic function in its relationship to the other functions of language. Poetics in the wider sense of the word deals with the poetic function not only in poetry, where this function is superimposed upon the other functions of language, but also outside of poetry, when some other function is superimposed upon the poetic function.

REFERENCES

Bühler, K. "Die Axiomatik der Sprachwissenschaft," *Kant-Studien* 38. 19–90 (Berlin, 1933).

Hopkins, G. M. *The journals and papers,* H. House, ed. London, 1959.

Malinowski, B. "The problem of meaning in primitive languages," in C. K. Ogden and I. A. Richards, *The meaning of meaning,* pp. 296–336. New York and London, ninth edition, 1953.

Mansikka, V. T. *Litauische Zaubersprüche. Folklore Fellows communications* 87 (1929).

Maretić, T. "Metrika narodnih naših pjesama," *Rad Yugoslavenske Akademije* 168, 170 (Zagreb, 1907).

Marty, A. *Untersuchungen zur Grundlegung der allgemeinen Grammatik und Sprachphilosophie*, Vol. 1. Halle, 1908.

Rybnikov, P. N. *Pesni*, Vol. 3. Moscow, 1910.

THE STRUCTURAL STUDY OF MYTH (1955)

CLAUDE LÉVI-STRAUSS

Translated from the French by Claire Jacobson and Brooke Grundfest Schoepf

Lévi-Strauss's "The Structural Study of Myth" offered an influential model for ways to use Saussure's ideas about language to understand other cultural phenomena. Because myths (traditional stories that seem foundational to a culture's heritage) come in narrative form, Lévi-Strauss's study of myth proved influential for the study of literary and other narratives. Lévi-Strauss takes his key example from the story of Oedipus. Readers who are unfamiliar with the story might may want to review it before reading Lévi-Strauss's essay, but even then they may hardly recognize the story in Lévi-Strauss's idiosyncratic description of it, which draws especially on the concept of the chthonic (which means emerging from the earth) and the autochthonous (which means self-generated rather than caused by exterior forces). If you find Lévi-Strauss's reading of the Oedipus story farfetched or unconvincing, it can help to keep in mind that he begins by conceding that he may be wrong about the Oedipus story. He says that his point is not so much to interpret the Oedipus story as to use his interpretation as a model for how we can interpret other myths or, we might say, other stories. In the same vein, the binary oppositions he sees structuring the Oedipus myth are not the same binary oppositions that might structure most other stories. Interpreters of other stories can see them as structured by other binary oppositions. The point is not which binary oppositions structure stories or myths. The point is simply that stories and myths—and culture in general—are structured by binary oppositions.

(The selection here begins with the third paragraph and then includes about half the essay before skipping to the concluding paragraph.)

Of all the chapters of religious anthropology probably none has tarried to the same extent as studies in the field of mythology. From a theoretical point of view the situation remains very much the same as it was fifty years ago, namely, a picture of chaos. Myths are still widely interpreted in conflicting ways: collective dreams, the outcome of a kind of esthetic play, the foundation of ritual.... Mythological figures are considered as personified abstractions, divinized heroes or decayed gods. Whatever the hypothesis, the choice amounts to reducing mythology either to an idle play or to a coarse kind of speculation.

In order to understand what a myth really is, are we compelled to choose between platitude and sophism? Some claim that human societies merely express, through their mythology, fundamental feelings common to the whole of mankind, such as love, hate, revenge; or that they try to provide some kind of explanations for phenomena which they cannot understand otherwise: astronomical, meteorological, and the like. But why should these societies do it in such elaborate and devious ways, since all of them are also acquainted with positive explanations?

On the other hand, psychoanalysts and many anthropologists have shifted the problems to be explained away from the natural or cosmological towards the sociological and psychological fields. But then the interpretation becomes too easy: if a given mythology confers prominence to a certain character, let us say an evil grandmother, it will be claimed that in such a society grandmothers are actually evil and that mythology reflects the social structure and the social relations; but should the actual data be conflicting, it would be readily claimed that the purpose of mythology is to provide an outlet for repressed feelings. Whatever the situation may be, a clever dialectic will always find a way to pretend that a meaning has been unravelled.

Mythology confronts the student with a situation which at first sight could be looked upon as contradictory. On the one hand, it would seem that in the course of a myth anything is likely to happen. There is no logic, no continuity. Any characteristic can be attributed to any subject; every conceivable relation can be met. With myth, everything becomes possible. But on the other hand, this apparent arbitrariness is belied by the astounding similarity between myths collected in widely different regions. Therefore the problem: if the content of a myth is contingent, how are we going to explain that throughout the world myths do resemble one another so much?

It is precisely this awareness of a basic antinomy pertaining to the nature of myth that may lead us towards its solution. For the contradiction which we face is very similar to that which in earlier times brought considerable worry to the first philosophers concerned with linguistic problems; linguistics could only begin to evolve as a science after this contradiction had been overcome. Ancient philosophers were reasoning about language the way we are about mythology. On the one hand, they did notice that in a given language certain sequences of sounds were associated with definite meanings, and they earnestly aimed at discovering a reason for the linkage between those sounds and that meaning. Their attempt, however, was thwarted from the very beginning by the fact that the same sounds were equally present in other languages though the meaning they conveyed was entirely different. The contradiction was surmounted only by the discovery that it is the combination of sounds, not the sounds in themselves, which provides the significant data.

Now, it is easy to see that some of the more recent interpretations of mythological thought originated from the same kind of misconception under which those early linguists were laboring. Let us consider, for instance, Jung's idea that a given mythological pattern—the so-called archetype—possesses a certain signification. This is comparable to the long supported error that a sound may possess a certain affinity with a meaning: for instance, the "liquid" semivowels with water, the open vowels with things that are big, large, loud, or heavy, etc., a kind of theory which still has its supporters.[1] Whatever emendations the original formulation may now call for, everybody will agree that the Saussurean principle of the arbitrary character of the linguistic signs was a prerequisite for the acceding of linguistics to the scientific level.

To invite the mythologist to compare his precarious situation with that of the linguist in the prescientific stage is not enough. As a matter of fact we may thus be led only from one difficulty to another. There is a very good reason why myth cannot simply be treated as language if its specific problems are to be solved; myth *is* language: to be known, myth has to be told; it is a part of human speech. In order to preserve its specificity we should thus put ourselves in a position to show that it is both the same thing as language, and also something different from it. Here, too, the past experience of linguists may help us. For language itself can be analyzed into things which are at the same time similar and different. This is precisely what is expressed in Saussure's distinction between *langue* and *parole,* one being the structural side of language, the other the statistical aspect of it, *langue* belonging to a revertible time, whereas *parole* is non-revertible. If those two levels already exist in language, then a third one can conceivably be isolated.

We have just distinguished *langue* and *parole* by the different time referents which they use. Keeping this in mind, we may notice that myth uses a third referent which combines the properties of the first two. On the one hand, a myth always refers to events alleged to have taken place in time: before the world was created, or during its first stages—anyway, long ago. But what gives the myth an operative value is that the specific pattern described is everlasting; it explains the present and the past as well as the future. This can be made clear through a comparison between myth and what appears to have largely replaced it in modern societies, namely, politics. When the historian refers to the French Revolution it is always as a sequence of past happenings, a non-revertible series of events the remote consequences of which may still be felt at present. But to the French politician, as well as to his followers, the French Revolution is both a sequence belonging to the past—as to the historian—and an everlasting pattern which can be detected in the present French social structure and which provides a clue for its interpretation, a lead from which to infer the future developments. See, for instance, Michelet who was a politically-minded historian. He describes the French Revolution thus: "This day...everything was possible....Future became present...that is, no more time, a glimpse of eternity." It is that double structure, altogether historical and anhistorical, which explains that myth, while pertaining to the realm of the *parole* and calling for an explanation as such, as well as to that of the *langue* in which it is expressed, can also be an absolute object on a third level which, though it remains linguistic by nature, is nevertheless distinct from the other two.

A remark can be introduced at this point which will help to show the singularity of myth among other linguistic phenomena. Myth is the part of language where the formula *traduttore, traditore* reaches its lowest truth-value. From that point of view it should be put in the whole gamut of linguistic expressions at the end opposite to that of poetry, in spite of all the claims which have been made to prove the contrary. Poetry is a kind of speech which cannot be translated except at the cost of serious distortions; whereas the mythical value of the myth remains preserved, even through the worst translation. Whatever our ignorance of the language and the culture of the people where it originated, a myth is still felt as a myth by any reader throughout the world. Its substance does not lie in its style, its original music, or its syntax, but in the *story* which it tells. It is language, functioning on an especially high level where meaning succeeds practically at "taking off" from the linguistic ground on which it keeps on rolling.

To sum up the discussion at this point, we have so far made the following claims: 1. If there is a meaning to be found in mythology, this cannot reside in the isolated elements which enter into the composition of a myth, but only in the way those elements are combined. 2. Although myth belongs to the same category as language, being, as a matter of fact, only part of it, language in myth unveils specific properties. 3. Those properties are only to be found *above* the ordinary linguistic level; that is, they exhibit more complex features beside those which are to be found in any kind of linguistic expression.

If the above three points are granted, at least as a working hypothesis, two consequences will follow: 1. Myth, like the rest of language, is made up of constituent units. 2. These constituent units presuppose the constituent units present in language when analyzed on other levels, namely, phonemes, morphemes, and semantemes, but they, nevertheless, differ from the latter in the same way as they themselves differ from morphemes, and these from phonemes; they belong to a higher order, a more complex one. For this reason, we will call them *gross constituent units*.

How shall we proceed in order to identify and isolate these gross constituent units? We know that they cannot be found among phonemes, morphemes, or semantemes, but only on a higher level; otherwise myth would become confused with any other kind of speech. Therefore, we should look for them on the sentence level. The only method we can suggest at this stage is to proceed tentatively, by trial and error, using as a check the principles which serve as a basis for any kind of structural analysis: economy of explanation; unity of solution; and ability to reconstruct the whole from a fragment, as well as further stages from previous ones.

The technique which has been applied so far by this writer consists in analyzing each myth individually, breaking down its story into the shortest possible sentences, and writing each such sentence on an index card bearing a number corresponding to the unfolding of the story.

Practically each card will thus show that a certain function is, at a given time, predicated to a given subject. Or, to put it otherwise, each gross constituent unit will consist in a relation.

However, the above definition remains highly unsatisfactory for two different reasons. In the first place, it is well known to structural linguists that constituent units on all levels are made up of relations and the true difference between our gross units and the others stays unexplained; moreover, we still find ourselves in the realm of a non-revertible time since the numbers of the cards correspond to the unfolding of the informant's speech. Thus, the specific character of mythological time, which as we have seen is both revertible and non-revertible, synchronic and diachronic, remains unaccounted for. Therefrom comes a new hypothesis which constitutes the very core of our argument: the true constituent units of a myth are not the isolated relations but *bundles of such relations* and it is only as bundles that these relations can be put to use and combined so as to produce a meaning. Relations pertaining to the same bundle may appear diachronically at remote intervals, but when we have succeeded in grouping them together, we have reorganized our myth according to a time referent of a new nature corresponding to the prerequisite of the initial hypothesis, namely, a two-dimensional time referent which is simultaneously diachronic and synchronic and which accordingly integrates the characteristics of the *langue* on one hand, and those of the *parole* on the other. To put it in even more linguistic terms, it is as though a phoneme were always made up of all its variants.

Two comparisons may help to explain what we have in mind.

Let us first suppose that archaeologists of the future coming from another planet would one day, when all human life had disappeared from the earth, excavate one of our libraries.

Even if they were at first ignorant of our writing, they might succeed in deciphering it—an undertaking which would require, at some early stage, the discovery that the alphabet, as we are in the habit of printing it, should be read from left to right and from top to bottom. However, they would soon find out that a whole category of books did not fit the usual pattern: these would be the orchestra scores on the shelves of the music division. But after trying, without success, to decipher staffs one after the other, from the upper down to the lower, they would probably notice that the same patterns of notes recurred at intervals, either in full or in part, or that some patterns were strongly reminiscent of earlier ones. Hence the hypothesis: what if patterns showing affinity, instead of being considered in succession, were to be treated as one complex pattern and read globally? By getting at what we call *harmony*, they would then find out that an orchestra score, in order to become meaningful, has to be read diachronically along one axis—that is, page after page, and from left to right—and also synchronically along the other axis, all the notes which are written vertically making up one gross constituent unit, i.e. one bundle of relations.

The other comparison is somewhat different. Let us take an observer ignorant of our playing cards, sitting for a long time with a fortune-teller. He would know something of the visitors: sex, age, look, social situation, etc. in the same way as we know something of the different cultures whose myths we try to study. He would also listen to the séances and keep them recorded so as to be able to go over them and make comparisons—as we do when we listen to myth telling and record it. Mathematicians to whom I have put the problem agree that if the man is bright and if the material available to him is sufficient, he may be able to reconstruct the nature of the deck of cards being used, that is: fifty-two or thirty-two cards according to case, made up of four homologous series consisting of the same units (the individual cards) with only one varying feature, the suit.

The time has come to give a concrete example of the method we propose. We will use the Oedipus myth which has the advantage of being well-known to everybody and for which no preliminary explanation is therefore needed. By doing so, I am well aware that the Oedipus myth has only reached us under late forms and through literary transfigurations concerned more with esthetic and moral preoccupations than with religious or ritual ones, whatever these may have been. But as will be shown later, this apparently unsatisfactory situation will strengthen our demonstration rather than weaken it.

The myth will be treated as would be an orchestra score perversely presented as a unilinear series and where our task is to re-establish the correct disposition. As if, for instance, we were confronted with a sequence of the type: 1,2,4,7,8,2,3,4,6,8,1,4,5,7, 8,1,2,5,7,3,4,5,6,8 ..., the assignment being to put all the 1's together, all the 2's, the 3's, etc.; the result is a chart:

1	2		4			7	8
	2	3	4		6		8
1			4	5		7	8
1	2			5		7	
		3	4	5			
					6		8

We will attempt to perform the same kind of operation on the Oedipus myth, trying out several dispositions until we find one which is in harmony with the principles enumerated above. Let us suppose, for the sake of argument, that the best arrangement is the following (although it might certainly be improved by the help of a specialist in Greek mythology):

Kadmos seeks his sister Europa ravished by Zeus		Kadmos kills the dragon	
	The Spartoi kill each other		Labdacos (Laios' father) = *lame* (?)
	Oedipus kills his father Laios		Laios (Oedipus' father)= *left-sided* (?)
		Oedipus kills the Sphinx	
Oedipus marries his mother Jocasta	Eteocles kills his brother Polynices		Oedipus = *swollen-foot* (?)
Antigone buries her brother Polynices despite prohibition			

Thus, we find ourselves confronted with four vertical columns each of which include several relations belonging to the same bundle. Were we to *tell* the myth, we would disregard the columns and read the rows from left to right and from top to bottom. But if we want to *understand* the myth, then we will have to disregard one half of the diachronic dimension (top to bottom) and read from left to right, column after column, each one being considered as a unit.

All the relations belonging to the same column exhibit one common feature which it is our task to unravel. For instance, all the events grouped in the first column on the left have something to do with blood relations which are over-emphasized, i.e. are subject to a more intimate treatment than they should be. Let us say, then, that the first column has as its common feature the *overrating of blood relations*. It is obvious that the second column expresses the same thing, but inverted: *underrating of blood relations*. The third column refers to monsters being slain. As to the fourth, a word of clarification is needed. The remarkable connotation of the surnames in Oedipus' father-line has often been noticed. However, linguists usually disregard it, since to them the only way to define the meaning of a term is to investigate all the contexts in which it appears, and personal names, precisely because they are used as such, are not accompanied by any context. With the method we propose to follow the objection disappears since the myth itself provides its own context. The meaningful fact is no longer to be looked for in the eventual sense of each name, but in the fact that all the names have a common feature: i.e. that they may eventually mean something and that all these hypothetical meanings (which may well remain hypothetical) exhibit a common feature, namely they refer to *difficulties to walk and to behave straight*.

What is then the relationship between the two columns on the right? Column three refers to monsters. The dragon is a chthonian being which has to be killed in order that mankind be born from the earth; the Sphinx is a monster unwilling to permit men to live. The last unit reproduces the first one which has to do with the *autochthonous origin* of mankind. Since the monsters are overcome by men, we may thus say that the common feature of the third column is *the denial of the autochthonous origin of man*.

This immediately helps us to understand the meaning of the fourth column. In mythology it is a universal character of men born from the earth that at the moment they emerge from the depth, they either cannot walk or do it clumsily. This is the case of the chthonian beings in the mythology of the Pueblo: Masauwu, who leads the emergence, and the chthonian Shumaikoli are lame ("bleeding-foot," "sore-foot"). The same happens to the Koskimo of the Kwakiutl after they have been swallowed by the chthonian monster, Tsiakish: when they returned to the surface of the earth "they limped forward or tripped sideways." Then the common feature of the fourth column is: *the persistence of the autochthonous origin of man*. It follows that column four is to column three as column one is to column two. The inability to connect two kinds of relationships is overcome (or rather replaced) by the positive statement that contradictory relationships are identical inasmuch as they are both self-contradictory in a similar way. Although this is still a provisional formulation of the structure of mythical thought, it is sufficient at this stage.

Turning back to the Oedipus myth, we may now see what it means. The myth has to do with the inability, for a culture which holds the belief that mankind is autochthonous (see, for instance, Pausanias, VIII, xxix, 4: vegetals provide a *model* for humans), to find a satisfactory transition between this theory and the knowledge that human beings are actually born from the union of man and woman. Although the problem obviously cannot be solved, the Oedipus myth provides a kind of logical tool which, to phrase it coarsely, replaces the original problem: born from one or born from two? born from different or born from same? By a correlation of this type, the overrating of blood relations is to the underrating of blood relations as the attempt to escape autochthony is to the impossibility to succeed in it. Although experience contradicts theory, social life verifies the cosmology by its similarity of structure. Hence cosmology is true.

Two remarks should be made at this stage.

In order to interpret the myth, we were able to leave aside a point which has until now worried the specialists, namely, that in the earlier (Homeric) versions of the Oedipus myth, some basic elements are lacking, such as Jocasta killing herself and Oedipus piercing his own eyes. These events do not alter the substance of the myth although they can easily be integrated, the first one as a new case of auto-destruction (column three) while the second is another case of crippledness (column four). At the same time there is something significant in these additions since the shift from foot to head is to be correlated with the shift from: autochthonous origin negated to: self-destruction.

Thus, our method eliminates a problem which has been so far one of the main obstacles to the progress of mythological studies, namely, the quest for the *true* version, or the *earlier* one. On the contrary, we define the myth as consisting of all its versions; to put it otherwise: a myth remains the same as long as it is felt as such. A striking example is offered by the fact that our interpretation may take into account, and is certainly applicable to, the Freudian use of the Oedipus myth. Although the Freudian problem has ceased to be that of autochthony *versus* bisexual reproduction, it is still the problem of understanding how *one* can be born from *two:* how is it that we do not have only one procreator, but a mother plus a father? Therefore, not only Sophocles, but Freud himself, should be included among the recorded versions of the Oedipus myth on a par with earlier or seemingly more "authentic" versions.

An important consequence follows. If a myth is made up of all its variants, structural analysis should take all of them into account. Thus, after analyzing all the known variants of the Theban version, we should treat the others in the same way: first, the tales about Labdacos' collateral line including Agavé, Pentheus, and Jocasta herself; the Theban variant about Lycos with Amphion and Zetos as the city founders; more remote variants concerning Dionysos (Oedipus' matrilateral cousin), and Athenian legends where Cecrops takes the place of Kadmos, etc. For each of them a similar chart should be drawn, and then compared and reorganized according to the findings: Cecrops killing the serpent with the parallel episode of Kadmos; abandonment of Dionysos with abandonment of Oedipus; "Swollen Foot" with Dionysos *loxias,* i.e. walking obliquely; Europa's quest with Antiope's; the foundation of Thebes by the Spartoi or by the brothers Amphion and Zetos; Zeus kidnapping Europa and Antiope and the same with Semele; the Theban Oedipus and the Argian Perseus, etc. We will then have several two-dimensional charts, each dealing with a variant, to be organized in a three-dimensional order

Fig. 1.

so that three different readings become possible: left to right, top to bottom, front to back. All of these charts cannot be expected to be identical; but experience shows that any difference to be observed may be correlated with other differences, so that a logical treatment of the whole will allow simplifications, the final outcome being the structural law of the myth.

One may object at this point that the task is impossible to perform since we can only work with known versions. Is it not possible that a new version might alter the picture? This is true enough if only one or two versions are available, but the objection becomes theoretical as soon as a reasonably large number has been recorded (a number which experience will progressively tell, at least as an approximation). Let us make this point clear by a comparison. If the furniture of a room and the way it is arranged in the room were known to us only through its reflection in two mirrors placed on opposite walls, we would theoretically dispose of an almost infinite number of mirror-images which would provide us with a complete knowledge. However, should the two mirrors be obliquely set, the number of mirror-images would become very small; nevertheless, four or five such images would very likely give us, if not complete information, at least a sufficient coverage so that we would feel sure that no large piece of furniture is missing in our description.

On the other hand, it cannot be too strongly emphasized that all available variants should be taken into account. If Freudian comments on the Oedipus complex are a part of the Oedipus myth, then questions such as whether Cushing's version of the Zuni origin myth should be retained or discarded become irrelevant. There is no one true version of which all the others are but copies or distortions. Every version belongs to the myth.

Finally it can be understood why works on general mythology have given discouraging results. This comes from two reasons. First, comparative mythologists have picked up preferred versions instead of using them all. Second, we have seen that the structural analysis of *one* variant of *one* myth belonging to *one* tribe (in some cases, even *one* village) already requires two dimensions. When we use several variants of the same myth for the same tribe or village, the frame of reference becomes three-dimensional and as soon as we try to enlarge the comparison, the number of dimensions required increases to such an extent that it appears quite impossible to handle them intuitively. The confusions and platitudes which are the outcome of comparative mythology can be explained by the fact that multi-dimensional frames of reference cannot be ignored, or naively replaced by two- or three-dimensional ones. Indeed, progress in comparative mythology depends largely on the cooperation of mathematicians who would undertake to express in symbols multi-dimensional relations which cannot be handled otherwise....

Prevalent attempts to explain alleged differences between the so-called "primitive" mind and scientific thought have resorted to qualitative differences between the working processes of the mind in both cases while assuming that the objects to which they were applying themselves remained very much the same. If our interpretation is correct, we are led toward a completely different view, namely, that the kind of logic which is used by mythical thought is as rigorous as that of modern science, and that the difference lies not in the quality of the intellectual process, but in the nature of the things to which it is applied. This is well in agreement with the situation known to prevail in the field of technology: what makes a steel ax superior to a stone one is not that the first one is better made than the second. They are equally well made, but steel is a different thing than stone. In the same way we may be able to show that the same logical processes are put to use in myth as in science, and that man has always been thinking equally well; the improvement lies, not in an alleged progress of man's conscience, but in the discovery of new things to which it may apply its unchangeable abilities.

NOTES

1. See, for instance, Sir R. A. Paget, "The Origin of Language…," *Journal of World History,* 1, No. 2 (UNESCO, 1953).

THE DEATH OF THE AUTHOR (1968)

ROLAND BARTHES

Translated from the French by Stephen Heath

The title of Barthes's essay plays off Friedrich Nietzsche's famous phrase "the death of god." Barthes argues that we would do better not to romanticize individual authorship. For Barthes, literature is written by the overall system of writing, not by individual authors. No writers make up, all by themselves, the system of writing or the system of any particular kind of writing (novels, plays, poems, screenplays, and so on). They inherit a repertoire of vocabulary, syntax, genre, and convention, and we might say that they do little more than rearrange the materials they find around them. Indeed, Barthes argues that readers and critics typically focus too much on romanticizing the lives and personalities of authors. As part of our larger culture's romanticization of individuality, we romanticize authorship partly to keep ourselves from seeing how repetitive it is. By contrast, Barthes believes that once the words are written, they take on a momentum of their own and trump the now irrelevant author. Drawing on Marxism as well as structuralism, Barthes sees the fascination with individual agents as a means of concealing the overall economic system's powerful way of reproducing itself. In the wake of Barthes's argument, criticism has often focused less on individual authors—or, to put it less romantically, on individual writers—and more on the social forces engaged in many writers' production of literature.

Barthes's interest in the agency of language gradually led him beyond structuralism and to a deconstructive poststructuralism. See his essay in this volume from a few years later, "From Work to Text," which follows the momentum of the ideas in "The Death of the Author" to their poststructuralist consequences.

In his story *Sarrasine* Balzac, describing a castrato disguised as a woman, writes the following sentence: "*This was woman herself, with her sudden fears, her irrational whims, her instinctive worries, her impetuous boldness, her fussings, and her delicious sensibility.*" Who is speaking thus? Is it the hero of the story bent on remaining ignorant of the castrato hidden beneath the woman? Is it Balzac the individual, furnished by his personal experience with a philosophy of Woman? Is it Balzac the author professing "literary" ideas on femininity? Is it universal wisdom? Romantic psychology? We shall never know, for the good reason that writing is the destruction of every voice, of every point of origin. Writing is that neutral, composite, oblique space where our subject slips away, the negative where all identity is lost, starting with the very identity of the body writing.

No doubt it has always been that way. As soon as a fact is *narrated* no longer with a view to acting directly on reality but intransitively, that is to say, finally outside of any function other than that of the very practice of the symbol itself, this disconnection occurs, the voice loses its origin, the author enters into his own death, writing begins. The sense of this phenomenon, however, has varied; in ethnographic societies the responsibility for a narrative is never assumed by a person but by a mediator, shaman or relator whose "performance"—the mastery of the narrative code—may possibly be admired but never his 'genius.' The author is a modern figure, a product of our society insofar as, emerging from the Middle Ages with English empiricism, French rationalism and the personal faith of the Reformation, it discovered the prestige of the individual, of, as it is more nobly put, the "human person." It is thus logical that in literature it should be this positivism, the epitome and culmination of capitalist ideology, which has attached the greatest importance to the "person" of the author. The *author* still reigns in histories of literature, biographies of writers, interviews, magazines, as in the very consciousness of men of letters anxious to unite their person and their work through diaries and memoirs. The image of literature to be found in ordinary culture is tyrannically centred on the author, his person, his life, his tastes, his passions, while criticism still consists for the most part in saying that Baudelaire's work is the failure of Baudelaire the man, Van Gogh's his madness, Tchaikovsky's his vice. The *explanation* of a work is always sought in the man or woman who produced it, as if it were always in the end, through the more or less transparent allegory of the fiction, the voice of a single person, the *author* "confiding" in us.

Though the sway of the Author remains powerful (the new criticism has often done no more than consolidate it), it goes without saying that certain writers have long since attempted to loosen it. In France, Mallarmé was doubtless the first to see and to foresee in its full extent the necessity to substitute language itself for the person who until then had been supposed to be its owner. For him, for us too, it is language which speaks, not the author; to write is, through a prerequisite impersonality (not at all to be confused with the castrating objectivity of the realist novelist), to reach that point where only language acts, "performs" and not "me". Mallarmé's entire poetics consists in suppressing the author in the interests of writing (which is, as will be seen, to restore the place of the reader). Valéry, encumbered by a psychology of the Ego, considerably diluted Mallarmé's theory but, his taste for classicism leading him to turn to the lessons of rhetoric, he never stopped calling into question and deriding the Author; he stressed the linguistic and, as it were, "hazardous" nature of his activity, and throughout his prose works he militated in favour of the essentially verbal condition of literature, in the face of which all recourse to the writer's interiority seemed to him pure superstition. Proust himself, despite the apparently psychological character of what are called his *analyses* was visibly concerned with the task of inexorably blurring, by an extreme subtilization, the relation between the writer and his characters; by making of the narrator not he who has seen and felt nor even he who is writing, but he who *is going to write* (the young man in the novel—but, in fact, how old is he and who is he?—wants to write but cannot; the novel ends when writing at last becomes possible), Proust gave modern writing its epic. By a radical reversal, instead of putting his life into his novel, as is so often maintained, he made of his very life a work for which his own book was the model; so that it is clear to us that Charlus does not imitate Montesquiou but that Montesquiou—his anecdotal, historical reality—is no more than a secondary fragment, derived from Charlus. Lastly, to go no further than this prehistory of modernity, Surrealism, though unable to accord language a supreme place (language being system and the aim of the movement being, romantically, a direct subversion of code—itself moreover illusory: a code cannot be destroyed, only "played off"), contributed to the desacrilization of the image of the Author by ceaselessly recommending the abrupt disappointment of expectations of meaning (the famous surrealist "jolt"), by entrusting the hand with the task of writing as quickly as possible what the head itself is unaware of (automatic writing), by accepting the principle and the experience of several people writing together. Leaving aside literature itself (such distinctions really becoming invalid), linguistics has recently provided the destruction of the Author with a valuable analytical tool by showing that the whole of the enunciation is an empty process, functioning perfectly without there being any need for it to be filled with the person of the interlocutors. Linguistically, the author is never more than the instance writing, just as *I* is nothing other than the instance saying *I:* language knows a "subject," not a "person," and this subject, empty outside of the very enunciation which defines it, suffices to make language "hold together," suffices, that is to say, to exhaust it.

The removal of the Author (one could talk here with Brecht of a veritable "distancing," the Author diminishing like a figurine at the far end or the literary stage) is not merely an historical fact or an act of writing; it utterly transforms the modern text (or—which is the same thing—the text is henceforth made and read in such a way that at all its levels the author is absent). The temporality is different. The Author, when believed in, is always conceived of as the past of his own book: book and author stand automatically on a single line divided into a *before* and an *after*. The Author is thought to *nourish* the book, which is to say that he exists before it, thinks, suffers, lives for it, is in the same relation of antecedence to his work as a father to his child. In complete contrast, the modern scriptor is born simultaneously with the text, is in no way equipped with a being preceding or exceeding the writing, is not the subject with the book as predicate; there is no other time than that of the enunciation and every text is eternally written *here and now*. The fact is (or, it follows) that *writing* can no longer designate an operation of recording, notation, representation, "depiction" (as the Classics would say); rather, it designates exactly what linguists, referring to Oxford philosophy, call a performative, a rare verbal form (exclusively given in the first person and in the present tense) in which the enunciation has no other content (contains no other proposition) than the act by which it is uttered—something like the *I declare* of kings or the *I sing* of very ancient poets. Having buried the Author, the modern scriptor can thus no longer believe, as according to the pathetic view of his predecessors, that this hand is too slow for his thought or passion and that consequently, making a law of necessity, he must emphasize this delay and indefinitely "polish" his form. For him, on the contrary, the hand, cut off from any voice, borne by a pure gesture of inscription (and not of expression), traces a field without origin—or which, at least, has no other origin than language itself, language which ceaselessly calls into question all origins.

We know now that a text is not a line of words releasing a single "theological" meaning (the "message" of the Author-God) but a multi-dimensional space in which a variety of writings, none of them original, blend and clash. The text is a tissue of quotations drawn from the innumerable centres of culture. Similar to Bouvard and Pécuchet, those eternal copyists, at once sublime and comic and whose profound ridiculousness indicates precisely the truth of writing, the writer can only imitate a gesture that is always anterior, never original. His only power is to mix writings, to counter the ones with the others, in such a way as never to rest on any one of them. Did he wish to *express himself*, he ought at least to know that the inner "thing" he thinks to "translate" is itself only a ready-formed dictionary, its words only explainable through other words, and so on indefinitely; something experienced in exemplary fashion by the young Thomas de Quincey, he who was so good at Greek that in order to translate absolutely modern ideas and images into that dead language, he had, so Baudelaire tells us (in *Paradis Artificiels*), "created for himself an unfailing dictionary, vastly more extensive and complex than those resulting from the ordinary patience of purely literary themes." Succeeding the Author, the scriptor no longer bears within him passions, humours, feelings, impressions, but rather this immense dictionary from which he draws a writing that can know no halt: life never does more than imitate the book, and the book itself is only a tissue of signs, an imitation that is lost, infinitely deferred.

Once the Author is removed, the claim to decipher a text becomes quite futile. To give a text an Author is to impose a limit on that text, to furnish it with a final signified, to close the writing. Such a conception suits criticism very well, the latter then allotting itself the important task of discovering the Author (or its hypostases: society, history, psyché, liberty) beneath the work: when the Author has been found, the text is "explained"—victory to the critic. Hence there is no surprise in the fact that, historically, the reign of the Author has also been that of the Critic, nor again in the fact that criticism (be it new) is today undermined, along with the Author. In the multiplicity of writing, everything is to be *disentangled*, nothing *deciphered*; the structure can be followed, "run" (like the thread of a stocking) at every point and at every level, but there is nothing beneath: the space of writing is to be ranged over, not pierced; writing ceaselessly posits meaning ceaselessly to evaporate it, carrying out a systematic exemption of meaning. In precisely this way literature (it would be better from now on to say *writing*), by refusing to assign a "secret," an ultimate meaning, to the text (and to the world as text), liberates what may be called an anti-theological activity, an activity that is truly revolutionary since to refuse to fix meaning is, in the end, to refuse God and his hypostases—reason, science, law.

Let us come back to the Balzac sentence. No one, no "person," says it: its source, its voice, is not the true place of the writing, which is reading. Another—very precise—example will help to make this clear: recent research (J.-P. Vernant[1]) has demonstrated the constitutively ambiguous nature of Greek tragedy, its texts being woven from words with double meanings that each character understands unilaterally (this perpetual misunderstanding is exactly the "tragic"); there is, however, someone who understands each word in its duplicity and who, in addition, hears the very deafness of the characters speaking in front of him—this someone being precisely the reader (or here, the listener). Thus is revealed the total existence of writing: a text is made of multiple writings, drawn from many cultures and entering into mutual relations of dialogue, parody, contestation, but there is one place where this multiplicity is focused and that place is the reader, not, as was hitherto said, the author. The reader is the space on which all the quotations that make up a writing are inscribed without any of them being lost; a text's unity lies not in its origin but in its destination. Yet this destination cannot any longer be personal: the reader is without history, biography, psychology; he is simply that *someone* who holds together in a single field all the traces by which the written text is constituted. Which is why it is derisory to condemn the new writing in the name of a humanism hypocritically turned champion of the reader's rights. Classic criticism has never paid any attention to the reader; for it, the writer is the only person in literature. We are now beginning to let ourselves be fooled no longer by the arrogant antiphrastical recriminations of good society in favour of the very thing it sets aside, ignores, smothers, or destroys; we know that to give writing its future, it is necessary to overthrow the myth: the birth of the reader must be at the cost of the death of the Author.

NOTES

1. [Cf. Jean-Pierre Vernant (with Pierre Vidal-Naquet), *Myths et tragédie en Grèce ancienne*, Paris 1972, esp. pp. 19–40, 99–131.]

DECONSTRUCTION

ON TRUTH AND LYING IN A NON-MORAL SENSE (1873)

FRIEDRICH NIETZSCHE

Translated from the German by Ronald Speirs

To Nietzsche, there is no match between words and the things they designate, between language and the "cause outside." Language is inadequate. Metaphors stay distant from what they represent. Thus when we classify the world around us, dividing it into individuals and species (single instances and larger groups of instances, such as one specific tulip versus tulips or flowers or plants in general), we project human ideas onto a natural world that does not require that way of thinking. We think anthropomorphically, that is, through human biases. We build our thoughts through metaphors and figurative language, not through things in themselves. Yet people come to mistake their own creations—language and art—for truth. Instead of truth, essences, we have appearances, our own creations in language and art. Because Nietzsche's way of thinking sees us as relying on human ideas, not on empirically observed truths and essences, he refers to his way of thinking as idealism.

Nietzsche's thinking in this essay anticipates the way that Jacques Derrida, working with the linguistics of Ferdinand de Saussure (both included in this volume), sees our world as made by how we think about it. In the same vein, Nietzsche anticipates Derrida's view of a continuous difference and deferral between signifiers and the signifieds they represent, that is, between language and what we use it to signify.

(Nietzsche's essay, written in 1873, was not published during his lifetime. The selection here includes all but the brief second part of the essay.)

In some remote corner of the universe, flickering in the light of the countless solar systems into which it had been poured, there was once a planet on which clever animals invented cognition. It was the most arrogant and most mendacious minute in the "history of the world"; but a minute was all it was. After nature had drawn just a few more breaths the planet froze and the clever animals had to die. Someone could invent a fable like this and yet they would still not have given a satisfactory illustration of just how pitiful, how insubstantial and transitory, how purposeless and arbitrary the human intellect looks within nature; there were eternities during which it did not exist; and when it has disappeared again, nothing will have happened. For this intellect has no further mission that might extend beyond the bounds of human life. Rather, the intellect is human, and only its own possessor and progenitor regards it with such pathos, as if it housed the axis around which the entire world revolved. But if we could communicate with a midge we would hear that it too floats through the air with the very same pathos, feeling that it too contains within itself the fly-ing centre of this world. There is nothing in nature so despicable and mean that would not immediately swell up like a balloon from just one little puff of that force of cognition; and just as every bearer of burdens wants to be admired, so the proudest man of all, the philoso-pher, wants to see, on all sides, the eyes of the universe trained, as through telescopes, on his thoughts and deeds.

It is odd that the intellect can produce this effect, since it is nothing other than an aid supplied to the most unfortunate, most delicate and most transient of beings so as to detain them for a minute within existence; otherwise, without this supplement, they would have every reason to flee existence as quickly as did Lessing's infant son.[1] The arrogance inherent in cognition and feeling casts a blinding fog over the eyes and senses of human beings, and because it contains within itself the most flattering evaluation of cognition it deceives them about the value of existence. Its most general effect is deception—but each of its separate effects also has something of the same character.

As a means for the preservation of the individual, the intellect shows its greatest strengths in dissimulation, since this is the means to preserve those weaker, less robust individuals who, by nature, are denied horns or the sharp fangs of a beast of prey with which to wage the struggle for existence. This art of dissimulation reaches its peak in humankind, where deception, flattery, lying and cheating, speaking behind the backs of others, keeping up appearances,[2] living in borrowed finery, wearing masks, the drapery of convention, play-acting for the benefit of others and oneself—in short, the constant fluttering of human beings around the one flame of vanity is so much the rule and the law that there is virtually nothing which defies understanding so much as the fact that an honest and pure drive towards truth should ever have emerged in them. They are deeply immersed in illusions and dream-images; their eyes merely glide across the surface of things and see "forms"; nowhere does their perception lead into truth; instead it is con-tent to receive stimuli and, as it were, to play with its fingers on the back of things. What is more, human beings allow themselves to be lied to in dreams every night of their lives, without their moral sense ever seeking to prevent this happening, whereas it is said that some people have even eliminated snoring by will-power. What do human beings really know about themselves? Are they even capable of perceiving themselves in their entirety just once, stretched out as in an illuminated glass case? Does nature not remain silent about almost everything, even about our bodies, banishing and enclosing us within a proud, illusory consciousness, far away from the twists and turns of the bowels, the rapid flow of the blood stream and the complicated tremblings of the nerve-fibres? Nature has thrown away the key, and woe betide fateful curiosity should it ever succeed in peering through a crack in the chamber of consciousness, out and down into the depths, and thus gain an intimation of the fact that humanity, in the indifference of its ignorance, rests on the pitiless, the greedy, the insatiable, the murderous—clinging in dreams, as it were, to the back of a tiger. Given this constellation, where on earth can the drive to truth possibly have come from?

Insofar as the individual wishes to preserve himself in relation to other individuals, in the state of nature he mostly used his intellect for concealment and dissimulation; however, because necessity and boredom also lead men to want to live in societies and herds, they need a peace treaty, and so they endeavour to eliminate from their world at least the crudest forms of the *bellum omnium contra omnes.*[3] In the wake of this peace treaty, however, comes something which looks like the first step towards the acquisition of that mysterious drive for truth. For that which is to count as "truth" from this point onwards now becomes fixed, i.e., a way of designating things is invented which has the same validity and force everywhere, and the legislation of language also produces the first laws of truth, for the contrast between truth and lying comes into existence here for the first time: the liar uses the valid tokens of designation—words—to make the unreal appear to be real; he says, for example "I am rich," whereas the correct designation for this condition would be, precisely, "poor." He misuses the established conventions by arbitrarily switching or even inverting the names for things. If he does this in a manner that is selfish and otherwise harmful, society will no longer trust him and therefore exclude him from its ranks. Human beings do not so much flee from being tricked as from being harmed by being tricked. Even on this level they do not hate deception but rather the damaging, inimical consequences of certain species of deception. Truth, too, is only desired by human beings in a similarly limited sense. They desire the pleasant, life-preserving consequences of truth; they are indifferent to pure knowledge if it has no consequences, but they are actually hostile towards truths which may be harmful and destructive. And, besides, what is the status of those conventions of language? Are they perhaps products of knowledge, of the sense of truth? Is there a perfect match between things and their designations? Is language the full and adequate expression of all realities?

Only through forgetfulness could human beings ever entertain the illusion that they possess truth to the degree described above. If they will not content themselves with truth in the form of tautology, i.e. with empty husks, they will for ever exchange illusions for truth. What is a word? The copy of a nervous stimulation in sounds. To infer from the fact of the nervous stimulation that there exists a cause outside us is already the result of applying the principle of sufficient reason wrongly. If truth alone had been decisive in the genesis of language, if the viewpoint of certainty had been decisive in creating designations, how could we possibly be permitted to say, "The stone is hard" as if "hard," were something known to us in some other way, and not merely as an entirely subjective stimulus? We divide things up by gender, describing a tree as masculine and a plant as feminine[4]—how arbitrary these translations are! How far they have flown beyond the canon of certainty! We speak of a snake; the designation captures only its twisting movements; and thus could equally well apply to a worm. How arbitrarily these borders are drawn, how one-sided the preference for this or that property of a thing! When different languages are set alongside one another it becomes clear that, where words are concerned, what matters is never truth, never the full and adequate expression;[5] otherwise there would not be so many languages. The "thing-in-itself" (which would be, precisely, pure truth, truth without consequences) is impossible for even the creator of language to grasp, and indeed this is not at all desirable. He designates only the relations of things to human beings, and in order to express them he avails himself of the boldest metaphors. The stimulation of a nerve is first translated into an image: first metaphor! The image is then imitated by a sound: second metaphor! And each time there is a complete leap from one sphere into the heart of another, new sphere. One can conceive of a profoundly deaf human being who has never experienced sound or music; just as such a person will gaze in astonishment at the Chladnian sound-figures in sand,[6] find their cause in the vibration of a string, and swear that he must now know what men call sound—this is precisely what happens to all of us with language. We believe that when we speak of trees, colours, snow, and flowers, we have knowledge of the things themselves, and yet we possess only metaphors of things which in no way correspond to the original entities. Just as the musical sound appears as a figure in the sand, so the mysterious "X" of the thing-in-itself appears first as a nervous stimulus, then as an image, and finally as an articulated sound. At all events, things do not proceed logically when language comes into being, and the entire material in and with which the man of truth, the researcher, the philosopher, works and builds, stems, if not from cloud-cuckoo land, then certainly not from the essence of things.

Let us consider in particular how concepts are formed; each word immediately becomes a concept, not by virtue of the fact that it is intended to serve as a memory (say) of the unique, utterly individualized, primary experience to which it owes its existence, but because at the same time it must fit countless other, more or less similar cases, i.e., cases which, strictly speaking, are never equivalent, and thus nothing other than non-equivalent cases. Every concept comes into being by making equivalent that which is non-equivalent. Just as it is certain that no leaf is ever exactly the same as any other leaf, it is equally certain that the concept "leaf" is formed by dropping these individual differences arbitrarily, by forgetting those features which differentiate one thing from another, so that the concept then gives rise to the notion that something other than leaves exists in nature, something which would be "leaf" a primal form, say, from which all leaves were woven, drawn, delineated, dyed, curled, painted—but by a clumsy pair of hands, so that no single example turned out to be a faithful, correct, and reliable copy of the primal form. We call a man honest; we ask, "Why did he act so honestly today?" Our answer is usually: "Because of his honesty." Honesty!—yet again, this means that the leaf is the cause of the leaves. We have no knowledge of an essential quality which might be called honesty, but we do know of numerous individualized and hence non-equivalent actions which we equate with each other by omitting what is unlike, and which we now designate as honest actions; finally we formulate from them a *qualitas occulta*[7] with the name "honesty."

Like form, a concept is produced by overlooking what is individual and real, whereas nature knows neither forms nor concepts and hence no species, but only an "X" which is inaccessible to us and indefinable by us. For the opposition we make between individual and species is also anthropomorphic and does not stem from the essence of things, although we equally do not dare to say that it does *not* correspond to the essence of things, since that would be a dogmatic assertion and, as such, just as incapable of being proved as its opposite.

What, then, is truth? A mobile army of metaphors, metonymies, anthropomorphisms, in short a sum of human relations which have been subjected to poetic and rhetorical intensification, translation, and decoration, and which, after they have been in use for a long time, strike a people as firmly established, canonical, and binding; truths are illusions of which we have forgotten that they are illusions, metaphors which have become worn by frequent use and have lost all sensuous vigour, coins which, having lost their stamp, are now regarded as metal and no longer as coins. Yet we still do not know where the drive to truth comes from, for so far we have only heard about the obligation to be truthful which society imposes in order to exist, i.e. the obligation to use the customary metaphors, or, to put it in moral terms, the obligation to lie in accordance with firmly established convention, to lie *en masse* and in a style that is binding for all. Now, it is true that human beings forget that this is how things are; thus they lie unconsciously in the way we have described, and in accordance with centuries-old habits—and precisely *because of this unconsciousness*, precisely because of this forgetting, they arrive at the feeling of truth. The feeling that one is obliged to describe one thing as red, another as cold, and a third as dumb, prompts a moral impulse which pertains to truth; from its opposite, the liar whom no one trusts and all exclude, human beings demonstrate to themselves just how honourable, confidence-inspiring and useful truth is. As creatures of *reason*, human beings now make their actions subject to the rule of abstractions; they no longer tolerate being swept away by sudden impressions and sensuous perceptions; they now generalize all these impressions first, turning them into cooler, less colourful concepts in order to harness the vehicle of their lives and actions to them. Everything which distinguishes human beings from animals depends on this ability to sublimate sensuous metaphors into a schema, in other words, to dissolve an image into a concept. This is because something becomes possible in the realm of these schemata which could never be achieved in the realm of those sensuous first impressions, namely the construction of a pyramidal order based on castes and degrees, the creation of a new world of laws, privileges, subordinations, definitions of borders, which now confronts the other, sensuously perceived world as something firmer, more general, more familiar, more human, and hence as something regulatory and imperative. Whereas every metaphor standing for a sensuous perception is individual and unique and is therefore always able to escape classification, the great edifice of concepts exhibits the rigid regularity of a Roman *columbarium,*[8] while logic breathes out that air of severity and coolness which is peculiar to mathematics. Anyone who has been touched by that cool breath will scarcely believe that concepts too, which are as bony and eight-cornered as a dice and just as capable of being shifted around, are only the left-over *residue of a metaphor,* and that the illusion produced by the artistic translation of a nervous stimulus into images is, if not the mother, then at least the grandmother of each and every concept. Within this conceptual game of dice, however, "truth" means using each die in accordance with its designation, counting its spots precisely, forming correct classifications, and never offending against the order of castes nor against the sequence of classes of rank. Just as the Romans and the Etruscans divided up the sky with rigid mathematical lines and confined a god in a space which they had thus delimited as in a *templum,* all peoples have just such a mathematically divided firmament of concepts above them, and they understand the demand of truth to mean that the god of every concept is to be sought only in *his* sphere. Here one can certainly admire humanity as a mighty architectural genius who succeeds in erecting the infinitely complicated cathedral of concepts on moving foundations, or even, one might say, on flowing water; admittedly, in order to rest on such foundations, it has to be like a thing constructed from cobwebs, so delicate that it can be carried off on the waves and yet so firm as not to be blown apart by the wind. By these standards the human being is an architectural genius who is far superior to the bee; the latter builds with wax which she gathers from nature, whereas the human being builds with the far more delicate material of concepts which he must first manufacture from himself. In this he is to be much admired—but just not for his impulse to truth, to the pure cognition of things. If someone hides something behind a bush, looks for it in the same place and then finds it there, his seeking and finding is nothing much to boast about; but this is exactly how things are as far as the seeking and finding of "truth" within the territory of reason is concerned. If I create the definition of a mammal and then, having inspected a camel, declare, "Behold, a mammal," then a truth has certainly been bought to light, but it is of limited value, by which I mean that it is anthropormorphic through and through and contains not a single point which could be said to be "true in itself," really and in a generally valid sense, regardless of mankind. Anyone who researches for truths of that kind is basically only seeking the metamorphosis of the world in human beings; he strives for an understanding of the world as something which is similar in kind to humanity, and what he gains by his efforts is at best a feeling of assimilation. Rather as the astrologer studies the stars in the service of human beings and in relation to humanity's happiness and suffering, this type of researcher regards the whole world as linked to humankind, as the infinitely refracted echo of an original sound, that of humanity, and as the multiple copy of a single, original image, that of humanity. His procedure is to measure all things against man, and in doing so he takes as his point of departure the erroneous belief that he has these things directly before him, as pure objects. Thus, forgetting that the original metaphors of perception were indeed metaphors, he takes them for the things themselves.

Only by forgetting this primitive world of metaphor, only by virtue of the fact that a mass of images, which originally flowed in a hot, liquid stream from the primal power of the human imagination, has become hard and rigid, only because of the invincible faith that *this* sun, *this* window, this table is a truth in itself—in short only because man forgets himself as a subject, and indeed as *an artistically creative* subject, does he live with some degree of peace, security, and consistency; if he could escape for just a moment from the prison walls of this faith, it would mean the end of his "consciousness of self."[9] He even has to make an effort to admit to himself that insects or birds perceive a quite different world from that of human beings, and that the question as to which of these two perceptions of the world is the more correct is quite meaningless, since this would require them to be measured by the criterion of the *correct perception,* i.e, by a *nonexistent* criterion. But generally it seems to me that the correct perception—which would mean the full and adequate expression of an object in the subject—is something contradictory and impossible; for between two absolutely different spheres, such as subject and object are, there is no causality, no correctness, no expression, but at most an *aesthetic* way of relating, by which I mean an allusive transference, a stammering translation into a quite different language. For which purpose a middle sphere and mediating force is certainly required which can freely invent and freely create poetry. The word appearance (*Erscheinung*) contains many seductions, and for this reason I avoid using it as far as possible; for it is not true that the essence of things appears in the empirical world. A painter who has no hands and who wished to express in song the image hovering before him will still reveal more through this substitution of one sphere for another than the empirical world betrays of the essence of things. Even the relation of a nervous stimulus to the image produced thereby is inherently not a necessary relationship; but when that same image has been produced millions of times and has been passed down through many generations of humanity, indeed eventually appears in the whole of humanity as a consequence of the same occasion, it finally acquires the same significance for all human beings, as if it were the only necessary image and as if that relation of the original nervous stimulus to the image produced were a relation of strict causality—in exactly the same way as a dream, if repeated eternally, would be felt and judged entirely as reality. But the fact that a metaphor becomes hard and rigid is absolutely no guarantee of the necessity and exclusive justification of that metaphor.

Anyone who is at home in such considerations will certainly have felt a deep mistrust of this kind of idealism when once he has become clearly convinced of the eternal consistency, ubiquitousness and infallibility of the laws of nature; he will then conclude that everything, as far as we can penetrate, whether to the heights of the telescopic world or the depths of the microscopic world, is so sure, so elaborated, so endless, so much in conformity to laws, and so free of lacunae, that science will be able to mine these shafts successfully for ever, and that everything found there will be in agreement and without self-contradiction. How little all of this resembles a product of the imagination, for if it were such a thing, the illusion and the unreality would be bound to be detectable somewhere. The first thing to be said against this view is this: if each of us still had a different kind of sensuous perception, if we ourselves could only perceive things as, variously, a bird, a worm, or a plant does, or if one of us were to see a stimulus as red, a second person were to see the same stimulus as blue, while a third were even to hear it as a sound, nobody would ever speak of nature as something conforming to laws; rather they would take it to be nothing other than a highly subjective formation. Consequently, what is a law of nature for us at all? It is not known to us in itself but only in its effects, i.e., in its relations to other laws of nature which are in turn known to us only as relations. Thus, all these relations refer only to one another, and they are utterly incomprehensible to us in their essential nature; the only things we really know about them are things which we bring to bear on them: time and space, in other words, relations of succession and number. But everything which is wonderful and which elicits our astonishment at precisely these laws of nature, everything which demands explanation of us and could seduce us into being suspicious of idealism, is attributable precisely and exclusively to the rigour and universal validity of the representations of time and space. But these we produce within ourselves and from ourselves with the same necessity as a spider spins; if we are forced to comprehend all things under these forms alone, then it is no longer wonderful that what we comprehend in all these things is actually nothing other than these very forms; for all of them must exhibit the laws of number, and number is precisely that which is most astonishing about things. All the conformity to laws which we find so imposing in the orbits of the stars and chemical processes is basically identical with those qualities which we ourselves bring to bear on things, so that what we find imposing is our own activity. Of course the consequence of this is that the artistic production of metaphor, with which every sensation begins within us, already presupposes those forms, and is thus executed in them; only from the stability of these original forms can one explain how it is possible for an edifice of concepts to be constituted in its turn from the metaphors themselves. For this conceptual edifice is an imitation of the relations of time, space, and number on the foundations of metaphor.

NOTES

1. Lessing's first and only son died immediately after birth, followed soon after by his mother. This drew from Lessing the comment: "Was it good sense that they had to pull him into the world with iron tongs, or that he noticed the filth so quickly? Was it not good sense that he took the first opportunity to leave it again?" (Letter to Eschenburg, 10 January 1778).
2. The verb Nietzsche uses is *repräsentieren*. This means keeping up a show in public, representing one's family, country, or social group before the eyes of the world.
3. "War of all against all": phrase associated with Thomas Hobbes' description of the state of nature before the institution of political authority (*cf.* Hobbes, *De cive* 1.12 and *Leviathan,* chapter XIII).
4. "Tree" is masculine in German (*der Baum)* and "plant" (*die Pflanze)* is feminine.
5. Nietzsche uses the term *adäquat* which indicates that the meaning of something is fully conveyed by a word or expression; English "adequate" alone does not convey this sense completely.
6. The vibration of a string can create figures in the sand (in an appropriately constructed sand-box) which give a visual representation of that which the human ear perceives as a tone. The term comes from the name of the physicist Ernst Chladni, whose experiments demonstrated the effect.
7. Hidden property.
8. Original a dovecot, then a catacomb with niches at regular intervals for urns containing the ashes of the dead.
9. The word Nietzsche uses here—*Selbstbewußtsein*—could also mean "self-confidence."

THE END OF THE BOOK AND THE BEGINNING OF WRITING (1967)

JACQUES DERRIDA

Translated from the French by Gayatri Chakravorty Spivak

Derrida was a philosopher, not a literary critic. His references and vocabulary may seem arcane to readers accustomed to a different set of reference points. But such readers should not let Derrida's indifference to explaining his contexts intimidate them. Derrida's references and ideas fit into a set of repeated patterns, so that once readers get the general idea and context, then they can follow the argument without needing immersion in, for example, Plato, or the French philosopher and novelist Jean-Jacques Rousseau, or the German philosopher Martin Heidegger, and so on.

"The End of the Book and the Beginning of Writing" is the opening chapter (wittily called "the end") of Of Grammatology, *Derrida's most influential work. It lays out the ideas that came to be called deconstruction. Derrida argues that Western thinking favors speech over writing. According to the traditional line of thinking, which Derrida will both recognize and dispute, speech seems one and the same with the person who speaks it. It seems to evoke the true, inner essence of the speaker. Writing, by contrast, introduces difference and deferral because the word differs from what it represents and can never reach what it represents. Derrida even coins his own word for the difference and deferral between writing and what it represents:* différance. *In French,* différance *sounds just like* difference *but expresses its difference and deferral with a different spelling, so that there is always a gap, partly expressible and partly inexpressible, between the two versions of the same, between* difference *and* différance, *like the gap that* différance *describes between the signifier and the signified.*

Derrida goes so far as to undermine the privileging of speech that he believes Western thinking has taken for granted. He finds the difference and deferral, the différance, *of writing always already within speech, so that he sees the valorization of speech as an effort to repress and deny a more fundamental inefficiency in the system, a gap in the structuralist, Saussurean concept of the sign. Saussure supposed that the sign consists of a signified linked tightly to a signifier (see the selection from Saussure in this volume), but Derrida sees a gap, a* différance, *loosening, wobbling, or deferring the link between the signified and the signifier. In that way, and counterintuitively, Derrida sees writing—in the broad sense of systems of representation, not in the narrow sense of alphabetic representation—as preceding speech. He sees language and structure as always already including their own imperfection, inefficiency, self-undermining,* différance. *Writing, therefore, for Derrida, is not secondary to a primary speech, as we usually suppose. He looks skeptically on what he calls phonocentrism, the worship of speech, the idea that speech genuinely evokes, as we traditionally suppose, true presence, substance, essence, the cogito (René Descartes' famous formula "I think therefore I am"), ego, and intention.*

Thus for Derrida and deconstruction, such notions as origin, ground (in the sense of the base or origin), voice, essence, self, and presence seem like strategies for denying the continuous movement, flux, and instability of all language and representation. Although Derrida does not believe in such concepts, he believes that we cannot do without them. He does not reject them, for he needs them even to argue against them. His readiness to work with the thinking that he also works against is itself an example of his larger argument that all systems of representation always already contain their opposites. They are rife with internal contradictions. And therefore all systems of representation (a novel, a song, a website, a style of clothing, gesture, or behavior) always already suggest the continuous movement and instability of writing, language, and representation. Since deconstruction characterizes all representation, we do not deconstruct something (such as a novel, song, website, or style) so much as we uncover how it always already deconstructs itself.

(Derrida's notes have been abridged for this reprinting, mainly by cutting discursive notes and retaining notes that cite sources.)

Socrates, he who does not write*

——NIETZSCHE

However the topic is considered, the *problem of language* has never been simply one problem among others. But never as much as at present has it invaded, *as such,* the global horizon of the most diverse researches and the most heterogeneous discourses, diverse and heterogeneous in their intention, method, and ideology. The devaluation of the word "language" itself, and how, in the very hold it has upon us, it betrays a loose vocabulary, the temptation of a cheap seduction, the passive yielding to fashion, the consciousness of the avant-garde, in other words—ignorance—are evidences of this effect. This inflation of the sign "language" is the inflation of the sign itself, absolute inflation, inflation itself. Yet, by one of its aspects or shadows, it is itself still a sign: this crisis is also a symptom. It indicates, as if in spite of itself, that a historico-metaphysical epoch *must* finally determine as language the totality of its problematic horizon. It must do so not only because all that desire had wished to wrest from the play of language finds itself recaptured within that play but also because, for the same reason, language itself is menaced in its very life, helpless, adrift in the threat of limitlessness, brought back to its own finitude at the very moment when its limits seem to disappear, when it ceases to be self-assured, contained, and *guaranteed* by the infinite signified which seemed to exceed it.

THE PROGRAM

By a slow movement whose necessity is hardly perceptible, everything that for at least some twenty centuries tended toward and finally succeeded in being gathered under the name of language is beginning to let itself be transferred to, or at least summarized under, the name of writing. By a hardly perceptible necessity, it seems as though the concept of writing—no longer indicating a particular, derivative, auxiliary form of language in general (whether understood as communication, relation, expression, signification, constitution of meaning or thought, etc.), no longer designating the texterior surface, the insubstantial double of a major signifier, *the signifier of the signifier*—is beginning to go beyond the extension of language. In all senses of the word, writing thus *comprehends* language. Not that the word "writing" has ceased to designate the signifier of the signifier, but it appears, strange as it may seem, that "signifier of the signifier" no longer defines accidental doubling and fallen secondary. "Signifier of the signifier" describes on the contrary the movement of language: in its origin, to be sure, but one can already suspect that an origin whose structure can be expressed as "signifier of the signifier" conceals and erases itself in its own production. There the signified always already functions as a signifier. The secondary that it seemed possible to ascribe to writing alone affects all signifieds in general, affects them always already, the

---

* "Aus dem Gedankenkreise der Geburt der Tragödie," I. 3. *Nietzsche Werke* (Leipzig, 1903), vol. 9, part 2, i, p. 66.

moment they *enter the game.* There is not a single signified that escapes, even if recaptured, the play of signifying references that constitute language. The advent of writing is the advent of this play; today such a play is coming into its own, effacing the limit starting from which one had thought to regulate the circulation of signs, drawing along with it all the reassuring signifieds, reducing all the strongholds, all the out-of-bounds shelters that watched over the field of language. This, strictly speaking, amounts to destroying the concept of "sign" and its entire logic. Undoubtedly it is not by chance that this *overwhelming* supervenes at the moment when the extension of the concept of language effaces all its limits. We shall see that this overwhelming and this effacement have the same meaning, are one and the same phenomenon. It is as if the Western concept of language (in terms of what, beyond its plurivocity and beyond the strict and problematic opposition of speech [*parole*] and language [*langue*], attaches it *in general* to phonematic or glossematic production, to language, to voice, to hearing, to sound and breadth, to speech) were revealed today as the guise or disguise of a primary writing; more fundamental than that which, before this conversion, passed for the simple "supplement to the spoken word" (Rousseau). Either writing was never a simple "supplement," or it is urgently necessary to construct a new logic of the "supplement." It is this urgency which will guide us further in reading Rousseau.

These disguises are not historical contingencies that one might admire or regret. Their movement was absolutely necessary, with a necessity which cannot be judged by any other tribunal. The privilege of the *phonè* does not depend upon a choice that could have been avoided. It responds to a moment of *economy* (let us say of the "life" of "history" or of "being as self-relationship"). The system of "hearing (understanding) -oneself-speak" through the phonic substance—which *presents itself* as the nonexterior, nonmundane, therefore nonempirical or noncontingent signifier—has necessarily dominated the history of the world during an entire epoch, and has even produced the idea of the world, the idea of world-origin, that arises from the difference between the worldly and the non-worldly, the outside and the inside, ideality and nonideality, universal and nonuniversal, transcendental and empirical, etc.

With an irregular and essentially precarious success, this movement would apparently have tended, as toward its *telos,* to confine writing to a secondary and instrumental function: translator of a full speech that was fully *present* (present to itself, to its signified, to the other, the very condition of the theme of presence in general), technics in the service of language, *spokesman,* interpreter of an originary speech itself shielded from interpretation.

Technics in the service of language: I am not invoking a general essence of technics which would be already familiar to us and would help us in *understanding* the narrow and historically determined concept of writing as an example. I believe on the contrary that a certain sort of question about the meaning and origin of writing precedes, or at least merges with, a certain type of question about the meaning and origin of technics. That is why the notion of technique can never simply clarify the notion of writing.

It is therefore as if what we call language could have been in its origin and in its end only a moment, an essential but determined mode, a phenomenon, an aspect, a species of writing. And as if it had succeeded in making us forget this, and *in wilfully misleading us,* only in the course of an adventure: as that adventure itself. All in all a short enough adventure. It merges with the history that has associated technics and logocentric metaphysics for nearly three millennia. And it now seems to be approaching what is really its own *exhaustion;* under the circumstances—and this is no more than one example among others—of this death of the civilization of the book, of which so much is said and which manifests itself particularly through a convulsive proliferation of libraries. All appearances to the contrary, this death of the book undoubtedly announces (and in a certain sense always has announced) nothing but a death of speech (of a *so-called* full speech) and a new mutation in the history of writing, in history as writing. Announces it at a distance of a few centuries. It is on that scale that we must reckon it here, being careful not to neglect the quality of a very heterogeneous historical duration: the acceleration is such, and such its qualitative meaning, that one would be equally wrong in making a careful evaluation according to past rhythms. "Death of speech" is of course a metaphor here: before we speak of disappearance, we must think of a new situation for speech, of its subordination within a structure of which it will no longer be the archon.

To affirm in this way that the concept of writing exceeds and comprehends that of language, presupposes of course a certain definition of language and of writing. If we do not attempt to justify it, we shall be giving in to the movement of inflation that we have just mentioned, which has also taken over the word "writing," and that not fortuitously. For some time now, as a matter of fact, here and there, by a gesture and for motives that are profoundly necessary, whose degradation is easier to denounce than it is to disclose their origin, one says "language" for action, movement, thought, reflection, consciousness, unconsciousness, experience, affectivity, etc. Now we tend to say "writing" for all that and more: to designate not only the physical gestures of literal pictographic or ideographic inscription, but also the totality of what makes it possible; and also, beyond the signifying face, the signified face itself. And thus we say "writing" for all that gives rise to an inscription in general, whether it is literal or not and even if what it distributes in space is alien to the order of the voice: cinematography, choreography, of course, but also pictorial, musical, sculptural "writing." One might also speak of athletic writing, and with even greater certainty of military or political writing in view of the techniques that govern those domains today. All this to describe not only the system of notation secondarily connected with these activities but the essence and the content of these activities themselves. It is also in this sense that the contemporary biologist speaks of writing and *program* in relation to the most elementary processes of information within the living cell. And, finally, whether it has essential limits or not, the entire field covered by the cybernetic *program* will be the field of writing. If the theory of cybernetics is by itself to oust all metaphysical concepts—including the concepts of soul, of life, of value, of choice, of memory—which until recently served to separate the machine from man, it must conserve the notion of writing, trace, grammè [written mark], or grapheme, until its own historico-metaphysical character is also exposed. Even before being determined as human (with all the distinctive characteristics that have always been attributed to man and the entire system of significations that they imply) or nonhuman, the *grammè*—or the *grapheme*—would thus name the element. An element without simplicity. An element, whether it is understood as the medium or as the irreducible atom, of the arche-synthesis in general, of what one must forbid oneself to define within the system of oppositions of metaphysics, of what consequently one should not even call *experience* in general, that is to say the origin of *meaning* in general.

This situation has always already been announced. Why is it today in the process of making itself known *as such* and *after the fact?* This question would call forth an interminable analysis. Let us simply choose some points of departure in order to introduce the limited remarks to which I shall confine myself. I have already alluded to *theoretical* mathematics; its writing—whether understood as a sensible *graphic* [manner of writing] (and that already presupposes an identity, therefore an ideality, of its form, which in principle renders absurd the so easily admitted notion of the "sensible signifier"), or understood as the ideal synthesis of signifieds or a trace operative on another level, or whether it is understood, more profoundly, as the *passage* of the one to the other—has never been absolutely linked with a phonetic production. Within cultures practicing so-called phonetic writing, mathematics is not just an enclave. That is mentioned by all historians of writing; they recall at the same time the imperfections of alphabetic writing, which passed for so long as the most convenient and "the most intelligent" writing. This enclave is also the place where the practice of scientific language challenges intrinsically and with increasing profundity the ideal of phonetic writing and all its implicit metaphysics (metaphysics *itself*), particularly, that is, the philosophical idea of the *epistémè;* also of *istoria,* a concept profoundly related to it in spite of the dissociation or opposition which has distinguished one from the other during one phase of their common progress. History and knowledge, *istoria* and *epistémè* have always been determined (and not only etymologically or philosophically) as detours *for the purpose of* the reappropriaton of presence.

But beyond theoretical mathematics, the development of the *practical methods* of information retrieval extends the possibilities of the "message" vastly, to the point where it is no longer the "written" translation of a language, the transporting of a signified which could remain spoken in its integrity. It goes hand in hand with an extension of phonography and of all the means of conserving the spoken language, of making it function without the presence of the speaking subject. This development, coupled with that of anthropology and of the history of writing, teaches us that phonetic writing, the medium of the great metaphysical, scientific, technical, and economic adventure of the West, is limited in space and time and limits itself even as it is in the process of imposing its laws upon the cultural areas that had escaped it. But this nonfortuitous conjunction of cybernetics and the "human sciences" of writing leads to a more profound reversal.

THE SIGNIFIER AND TRUTH

The "rationality"—but perhaps that word should be abandoned for reasons that will appear at the end of this sentence—which governs a writing thus enlarged and radicalized, no longer issues from a logos. Further, it inaugurates the destruction, not the demolition but the de-sedimentation, the de-construction, of all the significations that have their source in that of the logos. Particularly the signification of *truth.* All the metaphysical determinations of truth, and even the one beyond metaphysical onto-theology that Heidegger reminds us of, are more or less immediately inseparable from the instance of the logos, or of a reason thought within the lineage of the logos, in whatever sense it is understood: in the pre-Socratic or the philosophical sense, in the sense of God's infinite understanding or in the anthropological sense, in the pre-Hegelian or the post-Hegelian sense. Within this logos, the original and essential link to the *phonè* has never been broken. It would be easy to demonstrate this and I shall attempt such a demonstration later. As has been more or less implicitly determined, the essence of the *phonè* would be immediately proximate to that which within "thought" as logos relates to "meaning," produces it, receives it, speaks it, "composes" it. If, for Aristotle, for example, "spoken words (ta en tē phonē) are the symbols of mental experience (pathēmata tes psychēs) and written words are the symbols of spoken words" (*De interpretatione*, 1, 16a 3) it is because the voice, producer of *the first symbols*, has a relationship of essential and immediate proximity with the mind. Producer of the first signifier, it is not just a simple signifier among others. It signifies "mental experiences" which themselves reflect or mirror things by natural resemblance. Between being and mind, things and feelings, there would be a relationship of translation or natural signification; between mind and logos, a relationship of conventional symbolization. And the *first* convention, which would relate immediately to the order of natural and universal signification, would be produced as spoken language. Written language would establish the conventions, interlinking other conventions with them.

> Just as all men have not the same writing so all men have not the same speech sounds, but mental experiences, of which these are the *primary symbols* (*semeïa prótos*), are the same for all, as also are those things of which our experiences are the images (*De interpretatione*, 1, 16a. Italics added).

The feelings of the mind, expressing things naturally, constitute a sort of universal language which can then efface itself. It is the stage of transparence. Aristotle can sometimes omit it without risk. In every case, the voice is closest to the signified, whether it is determined strictly as sense (thought or lived) or more loosely as thing. All signifiers, and first and foremost the written signifier, are derivative with regard to what would wed the voice indissolubly to the mind or to the thought of the signified sense, indeed to the thing itself (whether it is done in the Aristotelian manner that we have just indicated or in the manner of medieval theology, determining the *res* as a thing created from its *eidos*, from its sense thought in the logos or in the infinite understanding of God). The written signifier is always technical and representative. It has no constitutive meaning. This derivation is the very origin of the notion of the "signifier." The notion of the sign always implies within itself the distinction between signifier and signified, even if, as Saussure argues, they are distinguished simply as the two faces of one and the same leaf. This notion remains therefore within the heritage of that logocentrism which is also a phonocentrism: absolute proximity of voice and being, of voice and the meaning of being, of voice and the ideality of meaning. Hegel demonstrates very clearly the strange privilege of sound in idealization, the production of the concept and the self-presence of the subject.

> This ideal motion, in which through the sound what is as it were the simple subjectivity [*Subjektivität*], the soul of the material thing expresses itself, the ear receives also in a theoretical [*theoretisch*] way, just as the eye shape and colour, thus allowing the interiority of the object to become inferiority itself [*läßt dadurch das Innere der Gegenstände für das Innere selbst werden*] [*Esthétique*, III. I tr. fr. p. 16).* . . .The ear, on the contrary, perceives [*vernimmt*] the

---

* Georg Wilhelm Friedrich Hegel, *Werke*, Suhrkamp edition (Frankfurt am Main, 1970), vol. 14, p. 256; translated as *The Philosophy of Fine Art* by F. P. Osmaston (London, 1920), vol. 3, pp. 15–16.

result of that interior vibration of material substance without placing itself in a practical relation toward the objects, a result by means of which it is no longer the material form [*Gestalt*] in its repose, but the first, more ideal activity of the soul itself which is manifested [*zum Vorschein kommt*] (p 296) .*

What is said of sound in general is a fortiori valid for the *phonè* by which, by virtue of hearing (understanding) -oneself-speak—an indissociable system—the subject affects itself and is related to itself in the element of ideality.

We already have a foreboding that phonocentrism merges with the historical determination of the meaning of being in general as *presence,* with all the subdeterminations which depend on this general form and which organize within it their system and their historical sequence (presence of the thing to the sight as *eidos,* presence as substance/essence/existence [*ousia*], temporal presence as point [*stigmè*] of the now or of the moment [*nun*], the self-presence of the cogito, consciousness, subjectivity, the co-presence of the other and of the self, intersubjectivity as the intentional phenomenon of the ego, and so forth). Logocentrism would thus support the determination of the being of the entity as presence. To the extent that such a logocentrism is not totally absent from Heidegger's thought, perhaps it still holds that thought within the epoch of onto-theology, within the philosophy of presence, that is to say within philosophy *itself.* This would perhaps mean that one does not leave the epoch whose closure one can outline. The movements of belonging or not belonging to the epoch are too subtle, the illusions in that regard are too easy, for us to make a definite judgment.

The epoch of the logos thus debases writing considered as mediation of mediation and as a fall into the exteriority of meaning. To this epoch belongs the difference between signified and signifier, or at least the strange separation of their "parallelism," and the exteriority, however extenuated, of the one to the other. This appurtenance is organized and hierarchized in a history. The difference between signified and signifier belongs in a profound and implicit way to the totality of the great epoch covered by the history of metaphysics, and in a more explicit and more systematically articulated way to the narrower epoch of Christian creationism and infinitism when these appropriate the resources of Greek conceptuality. This appurtenance is essential and irreducible; one cannot retain the convenience or the "scientific truth" of the Stoic and later medieval opposition between *signans* and *signatum* without also bringing with it all its metaphysico-theological roots. To these roots adheres not only the distinction between the sensible and the intelligible—already a great deal—with all that it controls, namely, metaphysics in its totality. And this distinction is generally accepted as self-evident by the most careful linguists and semiologists, even by those who believe that the scientificity of their work begins where metaphysics ends. Thus, for example:

> As modern structural thought has clearly realized, language is a system of signs and linguistics is part and parcel of the science of signs, or semiotics (Saussure's *sémiologie*). The mediaeval definition of sign—"*aliquid stat pro aliquo*"—has been resurrected and put forward as still valid and productive. Thus the constitutive mark of any sign in general and of any linguistic sign in particular is its twofold character: every linguistic unit is bipartite and involves both aspects—one sensible and the other intelligible, or in other words, both

---

* Hegel, p. 134; Osmaston, p. 341.

the *signans* "signifier" (Saussure's *signifiant*) and the *signatum* "signified" (*signifié*). These two constituents of a linguistic sign (and of sign in general) necessarily suppose and require each other.*

But to these metaphysico-theological roots many other hidden sediments cling. The semiological or, more specifically, linguistic "science" cannot therefore hold on to the difference between signifier and signified—the very idea of the sign—without the difference between sensible and intelligible, certainly, but also not without retaining, more profoundly and more implicitly, and by the same token the reference to a signified able to "take place" in its intelligibility, before its "fall," before any expulsion into the exteriority of the sensible here below. As the face of pure intelligibility, it refers to an absolute logos to which it is immediately united. This absolute logos was an infinite creative subjectivity in medieval theology: the intelligible face of the sign remains turned toward the word and the face of God.

Of course, it is not a question of "rejecting" these notions; they are necessary and, at least at present, nothing is conceivable for us without them. It is a question at first of demonstrating the systematic and historical solidarity of the concepts and gestures of thought that one often believes can be innocently separated. The sign and divinity have the same place and time of birth. The age of the sign is essentially theological. Perhaps it will never *end*. Its historical *closure* is, however, outlined.

Since these concepts are indispensable for unsettling the heritage to which they belong, we should be even less prone to renounce them. Within the closure, by an oblique and always perilous movement, constantly risking falling back within what is being deconstructed, it is necessary to surround the critical concepts with a careful and thorough discourse—to mark the conditions, the medium, and the limits of their effectiveness and to designate rigorously their intimate relationship to the machine whose deconstruction they permit; and, in the same process, designate the crevice through which the yet unnameable glimmer beyond the closure can be glimpsed. The concept of the sign is here exemplary. We have just marked its metaphysical appurtenance. We know, however, that the thematics of the sign have been for about a century the agonized labor of a tradition that professed to withdraw meaning, truth, presence, being, etc., from the movement of signification. Treating as suspect, as I just have, the difference between signified and signifier, or the idea of the sign in general, I must state explicitly that it is not a question of doing so in terms of the instance of the present truth, anterior, exterior or superior to the sign, or in terms of the place of the effaced difference. Quite the contrary. We are disturbed by that which, in the concept of the sign—which has never existed or functioned outside the history of (the) philosophy (of presence)—remains systematically and genealogically determined by that history. It is there that the concept and above all the work of deconstruction, its "style," remain by nature exposed to misunderstanding and nonrecognition.

The exteriority of the signifier is the exteriority of writing in general, and I shall try to show later that there is no linguistic sign before writing. Without that exteriority, the very idea of the sign falls into decay. Since our entire world and language would collapse with it, and since its

---

* Roman Jakobson, *Essais de linguistigue générale*, tr. fr. p. 162

evidence and its value keep, to a certain point of derivation, an indestructible solidity, it would be silly to conclude from its placement within an epoch that it is necessary to "move on to something else," to dispose of the sign, of the term and the notion. For a proper understanding of the gesture that we are sketching here, one must understand the expressions "epoch," "closure of an epoch," "historical genealogy" in a new way; and must first remove them from all relativism.

Thus, within this epoch, reading and writing, the production or interpretation of signs, the text in general as fabric of signs, allow themselves to be confined within secondariness. They are preceded by a truth, or a meaning already constituted by and within the element of the logos. Even when the thing, the "referent," is not immediately related to the logos of a creator God where it began by being the spoken/thought sense, the signified has at any rate an immediate relationship with the logos in general (finite or infinite), and a mediated one with the signifier, that is to say with the exteriority of writing. When it seems to go otherwise, it is because a metaphoric mediation has insinuated itself into the relationship and has simulated immediacy; the writing of truth in the soul, opposed by *Phaedrus* (278a) to bad writing (writing in the "literal" [*propre*] and ordinary sense, "sensible" writing, "in space"), the book of Nature and God's writing, especially in the Middle Ages; all that functions as *metaphor* in these discourses confirms the privilege of the logos and founds the "literal" meaning then given to writing: a sign signifying a signifier itself signifying an eternal verity, eternally thought and spoken in the proximity of a present logos. The paradox to which attention must be paid is this: natural and universal writing, intelligible and nontemporal writing, is thus named by metaphor. A writing that is sensible, finite, and so on, is designated as writing in the literal sense; it is thus thought on the side of culture, technique, and artifice; a human procedure, the ruse of a being accidentally incarnated or of a finite creature. Of course, this metaphor remains enigmatic and refers to a "literal" meaning of writing as the first metaphor. This "literal" meaning is yet unthought by the adherents of this discourse. It is not, therefore, a matter of inverting the literal meaning and the figurative meaning but of determining the "literal" meaning of writing as metaphoricity itself,

In "The Symbolism of the Book," that excellent chapter of *European Literature and the Latin Middle Ages*, E. R. Curtius describes with great wealth of examples the evolution that led from the *Phaedrus* to Calderon, until it seemed to be "precisely the reverse" (tr. fr. p. 372)* by the "newly attained position of the book" (p. 374) [p. 306]. But it seems that this modification, however important in fact it might be, conceals a fundamental continuity. As was the case with the Platonic writing of the truth in the soul, in the Middle Ages too it is a writing understood in the metaphoric sense, that is to say a *natural*, eternal, and universal writing, the system of signified truth, which is recognized in its dignity. As in the *Phaedrus*, a certain fallen writing continues to be opposed to it. There remains to be written a history of this metaphor, a metaphor that systematically contrasts divine or natural writing and the human and laborious, finite and artificial inscription. It remains to articulate rigorously the stages of that history, as marked by the quotations below, and to follow the theme of God's book (nature or law, indeed natural law) through all its modifications.

---

* Ernst Robert Curtius, "Das Buch als Symbol," *Europäische Literatur und lateinisches Mittelalter* (Bern, 1948), p. 307. French translation by Jean Bréjoux (Paris, 1956): translated as *European Literature and the Latin Middle Ages*, by Willard R. Trask, Harper Torchbooks edition (New York, 1963), pp. 305, 306.

Rabbi Eliezer said: "If all the seas were of ink, and all ponds planted with reeds, if the sky and the earth were parchments and if all human beings practised the art of writing—they would not exhaust the Torah I have learned, just as the Torah itself would not be diminished any more than is the sea by the water removed by a paint brush dipped in it."

Galileo: "It [the book of Nature] is written in a mathematical language."*

Descartes: "... to read in the great book of Nature ..."†

Demea, in the name of natural religion, in the *Dialogues*, ... of Hume: "And this volume of nature contains a great and inexplicable riddle, more than any intelligible discourse or reasoning."††

Bonnet: "It would seem more philosophical to me to presume that our earth is a book that God has given to intelligences far superior to ours to read, and where they study in depth the infinitely multiplied and varied characters of His adorable wisdom."

G. H. von Schubert: "This language made of images and hieroglyphs, which supreme Wisdom uses in all its revelations to humanity—which is found in the inferior [*nieder*] language of poetry—and which, in the most inferior and imperfect way [*auf der allerniedrigsten und unvollkommensten*], is more like the metaphorical expression of the dream than the prose of wakefulness, ...we may wonder if this language is not the true and wakeful language of the superior regions. If, when we consider ourselves awakened, we are not plunged in a millennial slumber, or at least in the echo of its dreams, where we only perceive a few isolated and obscure words of God's language, as a sleeper perceives the conversation of the people around him."ʃ

Jaspers: "The world is the manuscript of an other, inaccessible to a universal reading, which only existence deciphers."‖

Above all, the profound differences distinguishing all these treatments of the same metaphor must not be ignored. In the history of this treatment, the most decisive separation appears at the moment when, at the same time as the science of nature, the determination of absolute presence is constituted as self-presence, as subjectivity. It is the moment of the great rationalisms of the seventeenth century. From then on, the condemnation of fallen and finite writing will take another form, within which we still live: it is non-self-presence that will be denounced. Thus the exemplariness of the "Rousseauist" moment, which we shall deal with later, begins to be explained. Rousseau repeats the Platonic

---

* Quoted in Curtius, op. cit. (German), p. 326, (English), p. 324; Galileo's word is "philosophy" rather than "nature."
† Ibid. (German) p. 324, (English) p. 322.
†† David Hume, *Dialogues Concerning Natural Religion*, ed. Norman Kemp Smith (Oxford, 1935), p. 193.
ʃ Gotthilf Heinrich von Schubert, *Die Symbolik des Traumes* (Leipzig, 1862), pp. 23–24.
‖ Quoted in Paul Ricoeur, *Gabriel Marcel et Karl Jaspers* (Paris, 1947), p 45.

gesture by referring to another model of presence: self-presence in the senses, in the sensible cogito, which simultaneously carries in itself the inscription of divine law. On the one hand, *representative*, fallen, secondary, instituted writing, writing in the literal and strict sense, is condemned in *The Essay on the Origin of Languages* (it "enervates" speech; to "judge genius" from books is like "painting a man's portrait from his corpse," etc.). Writing in the common sense is the dead letter, it is the carrier of death. It exhausts life. On the other hand, on the other face of the same proposition, writing in the metaphoric sense, natural, divine, and living writing, is venerated; it is equal in dignity to the origin of value, to the voice of conscience as divine law, to the heart, to sentiment, and so forth.

> The Bible is the most sublime of all books, … but it is after all a book.…It is not at all in a few sparse pages that one should look for God's law, but in the human heart where His hand deigned to write (*Lettre de Vernes*). *

> If the natural law had been written only in the human reason, it would be little capable of directing most of our actions. But it is also engraved in the heart of man in ineffacable characters.…There it cries to him *(L'état de guerre.)*†

Natural writing is immediately united to the voice and to breath. Its nature is not grammatological but pneumatological. It is hieratic, very close to the interior holy voice of the *Profession of Faith*, to the voice one hears upon retreating into oneself: full and truthful presence of the divine voice to our inner sense: "The more I retreat into myself, the more I consult myself, the more plainly do I read these words written in my soul: be just and you will be happy. … I do not derive these rules from the principles of the higher philosophy, I find them in the depths of my heart written by nature in characters which nothing can efface." ††

There is much to say about the fact that the native unity of the voice and writing is *prescriptive*. Arche-speech is writing because it is a law. A natural law. The beginning word is understood, in the intimacy of self-presence, as the voice of the other and as commandment.

There is therefore a good and a bad writing: the good and natural is the divine inscription in the heart and the soul; the perverse and artful is technique, exiled in the exteriority of the body. A modification well within the Platonic diagram: writing of the soul and of the body, writing of the interior and of the exterior, writing of conscience and of the passions, as there is a voice of the soul and a voice of the body. "Conscience is the voice of the soul, the passions are the voice of the body" [p. 249]. One must constantly go back toward the "voice of nature," the "holy voice of nature," that merges with the divine inscription and prescription; one must encounter oneself within it, enter into a dialogue within its signs, speak and respond to oneself in its pages.

---

* *Correspondance complète de Jean Jacques Rousseau*, ed. R. A. Leigh (Geneva, 1967), vol. V, pp. 65–66. The original reads "l'évangile" rather than "la Bible."

† Rousseau, *Oeuvres complétes*, Pléiade edition, vol. Ill, p. 602.

†† Derrida's reference is *Emile*, Pléiade edition, vol. 4, pp. 589, 594. My reference is *Emile*, tr. Barbara Foxley London, 1911), pp. 245, 249. Subsequent references to this translation are placed within brackets.

It was as if nature had spread out all her magnificence in front of our eyes to offer its text for our consideration. ... I have therefore closed all the books. Only one is open to all eyes. It is the book of Nature. In this great and sublime book I learn to serve and adore its author.

The good writing has therefore always been *comprehended*. Comprehended as that which had to be comprehended: within a nature or a natural law, created or not, but first thought within an eternal presence. Comprehended, therefore, within a totality, and enveloped in a volume or a book. The idea of the book is the idea of a totality, finite or infinite, of the signifier; this totality of the signifier cannot be a totality, unless a totality constituted by the signified preexists it, supervises its inscriptions and its signs, and is independent of it in its ideality. The idea of the book, which always refers to a natural totality, is profoundly alien to the sense of writing. It is the encyclopedic protection of theology and of logocentrism against the disruption of writing, against its aphoristic energy, and, as I shall specify later, against difference in general. If I distinguish the text from the book, I shall say that the destruction of the book, as it is now under way in all domains, denudes the surface of the text. That necessary violence responds to a violence that was no less necessary.

THE WRITTEN BEING/THE BEING WRITTEN

The reassuring evidence within which Western tradition had to organize itself and must continue to live would therefore be as follows: the order of the signified is never contemporary, is at best the subtly discrepant inverse or parallel—discrepant by the time of a breath—from the order of the signifier. And the sign must be the unity of a heterogeneity, since the signified (sense or thing, noeme or reality) is not in itself a signifier, a *trace:* in any case is not constituted in its sense by its relationship with a possible trace. The formal essence of the signified is *presence,* and the privilege of its proximity to the logos as *phonè* is the privilege of presence. This is the inevitable response as soon as one asks: "what is the sign?," that is to say, when one submits the sign to the question of essence, to the "ti esti." The "formal essence" of the sign can only be determined in terms of presence. One cannot get around that response, except by challenging the very form of the question and beginning to think that the sign that ill-named the only one, that escapes the instituting question of philosophy: "what is. . .?"

Radicalizing the concepts of *interpretation, perspective, evaluation, difference,* and all the "empiricist" or nonphilosophical motifs that have constantly tormented philosophy throughout the history of the West, and besides, have had nothing but the inevitable weakness of being produced in the field of philosophy, Nietzsche, far from remaining *simply* (with Hegel and as Heidegger wished) within metaphysics, contributed a great deal to the liberation of the signifier from its dependence or derivation with respect to the logos and the related concept of truth or the primary signified, in whatever sense that is understood. Reading, and therefore writing, the text were for Nietzsche "originary" operations (I put that word within quotation marks for reasons to appear later) with regard to a sense that they do not first have to transcribe or discover, which would not therefore be a truth signified in the original element and presence of the logos, as *topos noetos,* divine understanding, or the structure of a priori necessity. To save Nietzsche from a reading of the Heideggerian type, it seems that we must above all not attempt to restore or make explicit a less naive "ontology," "composed of profound ontological intuitions acceding to some originary truth, an entire fundamentality hidden under the appearance of an empiricist or metaphysical text. The virulence of Nietzschean thought could not be more competely misunderstood. On the contrary, one must *accentuate* the "naiveté" of a breakthrough which cannot attempt a step outside of metaphysics, which cannot *criticize* metaphysics radically without still utilizing in a certain way, in a certain type or a certain style of *text,* propositions that, read within the philosophic corpus, that is to say according to Nietzsche ill-read or unread, have always been and will always be "naivetés," incoherent signs of an absolute appurtenance. Therefore, rather than protect Nietzsche from the Heideggerian reading, we should perhaps offer him up to it completely, underwriting that interpretation without reserve; in a *certain way* and up to the point where, the content of the Nietzschean discourse being almost lost for the question of being, its form regains its absolute strangeness, where his text finally invokes a different type of reading, more faithful to his type of writing: Nietzsche has *written what* he has written. He has written that writing—and first of all his own—is not originally subordinate to the logos and to truth. And that this subordination has *come into being* during an epoch whose meaning we must deconstruct. Now in this direction (but only in this direction, for read otherwise, the Nietzschean demolition remains dogmatic and, like all reversals, a captive of that metaphysical edifice which it professes to overthrow. On that point and in that *order of reading,* the conclusions of Heidegger and Fink are irrefutable), Heideggerian thought would reinstate rather than destroy the instance of the logos and of the truth of being as "primum signatum:" the "transcendental" signified ("transcendental" in a certain sense, as in the Middle Ages the transcendental—*ens, unum, verum, bonum*—was said to be the "primum cognitum") implied by all categories or all determined significations, by all lexicons and all syntax, and therefore by all linguistic signifiers, though not to be identified simply with any one of those signifiers, allowing itself to be precomprehended through each of them, remaining irreducible to all the epochal determinations that it nonetheless makes possible, thus opening the history of the logos, yet itself being only through the logos; that is, *being nothing* before the logos and outside of it. The logos *of* being, "Thought obeying the Voice of Being," is the first and the last resource of the sign, of the difference between *signans* and *signatum.* There has to be a transcendental signified for the difference between signifier and signified to be somewhere absolute and irreducible. It is not by chance that the thought of being, as the thought of this transcendental signified, is manifested above all in the voice: in a language of words [*mots*]. The voice *is heard* (understood)—that undoubtedly is what is called conscience—closest to the self as the absolute effacement of the signifier: pure auto-affection that necessarily has the form of time and which does not borrow from outside of itself, in the world or in "reality," any accessory signifier, any substance of expression foreign to its own spontaneity. It is the unique experience of the signified producing itself spontaneously, from within the self, and nevertheless, as signified concept, in the element of ideality or universality. The unworldly character of this substance of expression is constitutive of this ideality. This experience of the effacement of the signifier in the voice is not merely one illusion among many—since it is the condition of the very idea of truth— but I shall elsewhere show in what it does delude itself. This illusion is the history of truth and it cannot be dissipated so quickly. Within the closure of this experience, the word [*mot*] is lived as the elementary and undecomposable unity of the signified and the voice, of the concept and a transparent substance of expression. This experience is considered in its greatest purity—and at the same time in the condition of its possibility— as the experience of "being." The word "being," or at any rate the words designating the sense of being in different languages, is, with some others, an "originary word" ("*Urwort*"), the transcendental word assuring the possibility of being-word to all other words. As such, it is precomprehended in all language and—this is the opening of *Being and Time*—only this precomprehension would permit the opening of the question of the sense of being in general, beyond all regional ontologies and all metaphysics: a question that broaches philosophy (for example, in the *Sophist*) and lets itself be taken over by philosophy, a question that Heidegger repeats by submitting the history of metaphysics to it. Heidegger reminds us constantly that the sense of being is neither the word "being" nor the concept of being. But as that sense is nothing outside of language and the language of words, it is tied, if not to a particular word or to a particular system of language (concesso non dato), at least to the possibility of the word in general. And to the possibility of its irreducible simplicity. One could thus think that it remains only to choose between two possibilities. (1) Does a modem linguistics, a science of signification breaking the unity of the word and breaking with its alleged irreducibility, still have anything to do with "language?" Heidegger would probably doubt it. (2) Conversely, is not all that is profoundly meditated as the thought or the question of being enclosed within an old linguistics of the word which one practices here unknowingly? Unknowingly because such a linguistics, whether spontaneous or systematic, has always had to share the presuppositions of metaphysics. The two operate on the same grounds.

It goes without saying that the alternatives cannot be so simple.

On the one hand, if modern linguistics remains completely enclosed within a classical conceptuality, if especially it naively uses the word *being* and all that it presupposes, that which, within this linguistics, deconstructs the unity of the word in general can no longer, according to the model of the Heideggerian question, as it functions powerfully from the very opening of *Being and Time,* be circumscribed as ontic science or regional ontology. In as much as the question of being unites indissolubly with the precomprehension of the *word being,* without being reduced to it, the linguistics that works for the deconstruction of the constituted unity of that word has only, in fact or in principle, to have the question of being posed in order to define its field and the order of its dependence.

Not only is its field no longer simply ontic, but the limits of ontology that correspond to it no longer have anything regional about them. And can what I say here of linguistics, or at least of a certain work that may be undertaken within it and thanks to it, not be said of all research *in as much as and to the strict extent that* it would finally deconstitute the founding concept-words of ontology, of being in its privilege? Outside of linguistics, it is in psychoanalytic research that this breakthrough seems at present to have the greatest likelihood of being expanded.

Within the strictly limited space of this breakthrough, these "sciences" are no longer *dominated* by the questions of a transcendental phenomenology or a fundamental ontology.

One may perhaps say, following the order of questions inaugurated by *Being and Time* and radicalizing the questions of Husserlian phenomenology, that this breakthrough does not belong to science itself, that what thus seems to be produced within an ontic field or within a regional ontology, does not belong to them by rights and leads back to the question of being itself.

Because it is indeed the *question* of being that Heidegger asks metaphysics. And with it the question of truth, of sense, of the logos. The incessant meditation upon that question does not restore confidence. On the contrary, it dislodges the confidence at its own depth, which, being a matter of the meaning of being, is more difficult than is often believed. In examining the state just before all determinations of being, destroying the securities of onto-theology, such a meditation contributes, quite as much as the most contemporary linguistics, to the dislocation of the unity of the sense of being, that is, in the last instance, the unity of the word.

It is thus that, after evoking the "voice of being," Heidegger recalls that it is silent, mute, insonorous, wordless, originarily *a-phonic* [*die Gewähr der lautlosen Stimme verborgener Quellen...*]. The voice of the sources is not heard. A rupture between the originary meaning of being and the word, between meaning and the voice, between "the voice of being" and the "*phonè,*" between "the call of being," and articulated sound; such a rupture, which at once confirms a fundamental metaphor, and renders it suspect by accentuating its metaphoric discrepancy, translates the ambiguity of the Heideggerian situation with respect to the metaphysics of presence and logocentrism. It is at once contained within it and transgresses it. But it is impossible to separate the two. The very movement of transgression sometimes holds it back short of the limit. In opposition to what we suggested above, it must "be remembered that, for Heidegger, the sense of being is never simply and rigorously a "signified." It is not by chance that that word is not used; that means that being escapes the movement of the sign, a proposition that can equally well be understood as a repetition of the classical tradition and as a caution with respect to a technical or metaphysical theory of signification. On the other hand, the sense of being is literally neither "primary," nor "fundamental," nor "transcendental," whether understood in the scholastic, Kantian, or Husserlian sense. The restoration of being as "transcending" the categories of the entity, the opening of the fundamental ontology, are nothing but necessary yet provisional moments. From *The Introduction to Metaphysics* onward, Heidegger renounces the project of and the word ontology. The necessary, originary, and irreducible dissimulation of the meaning of being, its occultation within the very blossoming forth of presence, that retreat without which there would be no history of being which was completely *history* and history of *being,* Heidegger's insistence on noting that being is produced as history only through the logos, and is nothing outside of it, the difference between being and the entity—all this clearly indicates that fundamentally nothing escapes the movement of the signifier and that, in the last instance, the difference between signified and signifier *is nothing.* This proposition of transgression, not yet integrated into a careful discourse, runs the risk of formulating regression itself. One must therefore *go by way of* the question of being as it is directed by Heidegger and by him alone, at and beyond onto-theology, in order to reach the rigorous thought of that strange nondifference and in order to determine it correctly. Heidegger occasionally reminds us that "being," as it is fixed in its general syntactic and lexicological forms within linguistics and Western philosophy, is not a primary and absolutely irreducible signified, that it is still rooted in a system of languages and an historically determined "significance," although strangely privileged as the virtue of disclosure and dissimulation; particularly when he invites us to meditate on the "privilege" of the "third person singular of the present indicative" and the "infinitive." Western metaphysics, as the limitation of the sense of being within the field of presence, is produced as the domination of a linguistic form. To question the origin of that domination does not amount to hypostatizing a transcendental signified, but to a questioning of what constitutes our history and what produced transcendentality itself. Heidegger brings it up also when in *Zur Seinsfrage,* for the same reason, he lets the word "being" be read only if it is crossed out (*kreuzweise Durchstreichung*). That mark of deletion is not, however, a "merely negative symbol" (p. 31) [p. 83]. That deletion is the final writing of an epoch. Under its strokes the presence of a transcendental signified is effaced while still remaining legible. Is effaced while still remaining legible, is destroyed while making visible the very idea of the sign. In as much as it de-limits onto-theology, the metaphysics of presence and logocentrism, this last writing is also the first writing.

To come to recognize, not within but on the horizon of the Heideggerian paths, and yet in them, that the sense of being is not a transcendental or trans-epochal signified (even if it was always dissimulated within the epoch) but already, in a truly *unheard of* sense, a determined signifying trace, is to affirm that within the decisive concept of ontico-ontological difference, *all is not to be thought at one go*; entity and being, ontic and ontological, "ontico-ontological," are, in an original style, *derivative* with regard to difference; and with respect to what I shall later call *differance*, an economic concept designating the production of differing/deferring. The ontico-ontological difference and its ground (*Grund*) in the "transcendence of Dasein" (*Vom Wesen des Grundes* [Frankfurt am Main, 1955], p. 16 [p. 29]) are not absolutely originary. Differance by itself would be more "originary," but one would no longer be able to call it "origin" or "ground," those notions belonging essentially to the history of onto-theology, to the system functioning as the effacing of difference. It can, however, be thought of in the closest proximity to itself only on one condition: that one begins by determining it as the ontico-ontological difference before erasing that determination. The necessity of passing through that erased determination, the necessity of that *trick of writing* is irreducible. An unemphatic and difficult thought that, through much unperceived mediation, must carry the entire burden of our question, a question that I shall provisionally call *historial* [*historiale*]. It is with its help that I shall later be able to attempt to relate differance and writing.

The hestitation of these thoughts (here Nietzsche's and Heidegger's) is not an "incoherence": it is a trembling proper to all post-Hegelian attempts and to this passage between two epochs. The movements of deconstruction do not destroy structures from the outside. They are not possible and effective, nor can they take accurate aim, except by inhabiting those structures. Inhabiting them *in a certain way*, because one always inhabits, and all the more when one does not suspect it. Operating necessarily from the inside, borrowing all the strategic and economic resources of subversion from the old structure, borrowing them structurally, that is to say without being able to isolate their elements and atoms, the enterprise of deconstruction always in a certain way falls prey to its own work. This is what the person who has begun the same work in another area of the same habitation does not fail to point out with zeal. No exercise is more widespread today and one should be able to formalize its rules.

Hegel was already caught up in this game. *On the one hand*, he undoubtedly *summed up* the entire philosophy of the logos. He determined ontology as absolute logic; he assembled all the delimitations of philosophy as presence; he assigned to presence the eschatology of parousia, of the self-proximity of infinite subjectivity. And for the same reason he had to debate or subordinate writing. When he criticizes the Leibnizian characteristic, the formalism of the understanding, and mathematical symbolism, he makes the same gesture: denouncing the being-outside-of-itself of the logos in the sensible or the intellectual abstraction. Writing is that forgetting of the self, that exteriorization, the contrary of the interiorizing memory, of the *Erinnerung* that opens the history of the spirit. It is this that the *Phaedrus* said: writing is at once mnemotechnique and the power of forgetting. Naturally, the Hegelian critique of writing stops at the alphabet. As phonetic writing, the alphabet is at the same time more servile, more contemptible, more secondary ("alphabetic writing expresses *sounds* which are themselves signs. It consists therefore of the signs of signs ['*aus Zeichen der Zeichen,*'" *Enzyklopädie,* ∫ 459])* but it is also the best writing, the mind's writing; its effacement before the voice, that in it which respects the ideal interiority of phonic signifiers, all that by which it sublimates space and sight, all that makes of it the writing of history, the writing, that is, of the infinite spirit relating to itself in its discourse and its culture:

> It follows that to learn to read and write an alphabetic writing should be regarded as a means to infinite culture (*unendliches Bildungsmittel*) that is not enough appreciated; because thus the mind, distancing itself from the concrete sense-perceptible, directs its attention on the more formal moment, the sonorous word and its abstract elements, and contributes essentially to the founding and purifying of the ground of interiority within the subject.

In that sense it is the *Aufhebung* of other writings, particularly of hieroglyphic script and of the Leibnizian characteristic that had been criticized previously through one and the same gesture. (*Aufhebung* is, more or less implicitly, the dominant concept of nearly all histories of writing, even today. It is *the* concept of history and of teleology.) In fact, Hegel continues: "Acquired habit later also suppresses the specificity of alphabetic writing, which consists in seeming to be, in the interest of sight, a detour [*Umweg*] through hearing to arrive at representations, and makes it into a hieroglyphic script for us, such that in using it, we do not need to have present to our consciousness the mediation of sounds."

---

* *Enzyklopädie der philosophischen Wissenschaftern in Grundrisse,* Suhrkamp edition (Frankfurt am Main, 1970), pp. 273–76.

It is on this condition that Hegel subscribes to the Leibnizian praise of nonphonetic writing. It can be produced by deaf mutes, Leibniz had said. Hegel:

> Beside the fact that, by the practice which transforms this alphabetic script into hieroglyph-
> ics, the aptitude for abstraction acquired through such an exercise *is conserved* [italics added],
> the reading of hieroglyphs is for itself a deaf reading and a mute writing (*ein taubes Lesen und
> ein stummes Schreiben*). What is audible or temporal, visible or spatial, has each its proper
> basis and in the first place they are of equal value; but in alphabetic script there is only *one*
> basis and that following a specific relation, namely, that the visible language is related only
> as a sign to the audible language; intelligence expresses itself immediately and uncondition-
> ally through speech (ibid.).

What writing itself, in its nonphonetic moment, betrays, is life. It menaces at once the breath, the spirit, and history as the spirit's relationship with itself. It is their end, their finitude, their paralysis. Cutting breath short, sterilizing or immobilizing spiritual creation in the repetition of the letter, in the commentary or the *exegesis*, confined in a narrow space, reserved for a minority, it is the principle of death and of difference in the becoming of being. It is to speech what China is to Europe: "It is only to the exegeticism of Chinese spiritual culture that their hieroglyphic writing is suited. This type of writing is, besides, the part reserved for a very small section of a people, the section that possesses the exclu-sive domain of spiritual culture. … A hieroglyphic script would require a philosophy as exegetical as Chinese culture generally is" (ibid.).

If the nonphonetic moment menaces the history and the life of the spirit as self-presence in the breath it is because it menaces substantiality, that other metaphysical name of presence and of *ousia*. First in the form of the substantive. Nonphonetic writing breaks the noun apart. It describes relations and not apellations. The noun and the word, those unities of breath and concept, are effaced within pure writing. In that regard, Leibniz is as disturbing as the Chinese in Europe: "This situation, the analytic notation of representations in hieroglyphic script, which seduced Leibniz to the point of wrongly preferring this script to the alphabetic, rather contradicts the fundamental exigency of language in general, namely the noun. … All differ-ence [*Abweichung*] in analysis would produce another formation of the written substantive."

The horizon of absolute knowledge is the effacement of writing in the logos, the retrieval of the trace in parousia, the reappropriation of difference, the accomplishment of what I have elsewhere called the *metaphysics of the proper* [*le propre*—self-possession, propriety, prop-erty, cleanliness].

Yet, all that Hegel thought within this horizon, all, that is, except eschatology, may be reread as a meditation on writing. Hegel is *also* the thinker of irreducible difference. He rehabilitated thought as the *memory productive* of signs. And he reintroduced, as I shall try to show elsewhere, the essential necessity of the written trace in a philosophical—that is to say Socratic—discourse that had always believed it possible to do without it; the last philoso-pher of the book and the first thinker of writing.

FROM WORK TO TEXT (1971)

ROLAND BARTHES

Translated from the French by Stephen Heath

In this essay, you can see the lingo and legacy of Barthes's structuralism (the Sausurrean language of signified, signifier, and so on). But by the time Barthes wrote this essay, he had moved through structuralism to a poststructuralist language and way of thinking in the vein of Derridean deconstruction. Barthes is at pains here to distinguish between what he calls the work and the text, much like a distinction he makes elsewhere between the readerly (the work), writing that focuses on getting across its story, and the writerly (the text), writing that focuses on getting across its own role as writing. As time went on, however, deconstructive interpreters began to see the textuality of any instance of representation. They saw textuality even in such readerly works as the novels of Anthony Trollope or Balzac, for example, and not only in writing that advertises its textuality, its undecideable and plural signifying, such as Gertrude Stein's Tender Buttons *or James Joyce's* Finnegans Wake.*

For an earlier version of Barthes's ideas, see "The Death of the Author," also in this volume.

It is a fact that over the last few years a certain change has taken place (or is taking place) in our conception of language and, consequently, of the literary work which owes at least its phenomenal existence to this same language. The change is clearly connected with the current development of (amongst other disciplines) linguistics, anthropology, Marxism and psychoanalysis (the term "connection" is used here in a deliberately neutral way: one does not decide a determination, be it multiple and dialectical). What is new and which affects the idea of the work comes not necessarily from the internal recasting of each of these disciplines, but rather from their encounter in relation to an object which traditionally is the province of none of them. It is indeed as though the *interdisciplinarity* which is today held up as a prime value in research cannot be accomplished by the simple confrontation of specialist branches of knowledge. Interdisciplinarity is not the calm of an easy security; it begins *effectively* (as opposed to the mere expression of a pious wish) when the solidarity of the old disciplines breaks down—perhaps even violently, via the jolts of fashion—in the interests of a new object and a new language neither of which has a place in the field of the sciences that were to be brought peacefully together, this unease in classification being precisely the point from which it is possible to diagnose a certain mutation. The mutation in which the idea of the work seems to be gripped must not, however, be over-estimated: it is more in the nature of an epistemological slide than of a real break. The break, as is frequently stressed, is seen to have taken place in the last century with the appearance of Marxism and Freudianism;

since then there has been no further break, so that in a way it can be said that for the last hundred years we have been living in repetition. What History, our History, allows us today is merely to slide, to vary, to exceed, to repudiate. Just as Einsteinian science demands that *the relativity of the frames of reference* be included in the object studied, so the combined action of Marxism, Freudianism and structuralism demands, in literature, the relativization of the relations of writer, reader and observer (critic). Over against the traditional notion of the *work*, for long—and still—conceived of in a, so to speak, Newtonian way, there is now the requirement of a new object, obtained by the sliding or overturning of former categories. That object is the *Text*. I know the word is fashionable (I am myself often led to use it) and therefore regarded by some with suspicion, but that is exactly why I should like to remind myself of the principal propositions at the intersection of which I see the Text as standing. The word "proposition" is to be understood more in a grammatical than in a logical sense: the following are not argumentations but enunciations, "touches," approaches that consent to remain metaphorical. Here then are these propositions; they concern method, genres, signs, plurality, filiation, reading and pleasure.

1. The Text is not to be thought of as an object that can be computed. It would be futile to try to separate out materially works from texts. In particular, the tendency must be avoided to say that the work is classic, the text avant-garde; it is not a question of drawing up a crude honours list in the name of modernity and declaring certain literary productions "in" and others "out" by virtue of their chronological situation: there may be "text" in a very ancient work, while many products of contemporary literature are in no way texts. The difference is this: the work is a fragment of substance, occupying a part of the space of books (in a library for example), the Text is a methodological field. The opposition may recall (without at all reproducing term for term) Lacan's distinction between "reality" and "the real": the one is displayed, the other demonstrated; likewise, the work can be seen (in bookshops, in catalogues, in exam syllabuses), the text is a process of demonstration, speaks according to certain rules (or against certain rules); the work can be held in the hand, the text is held in language, only exists in the movement of a discourse (or rather, it is Text for the very reason that it knows itself as text); the Text is not the decomposition of the work, it is the work that is the imaginary tail of the Text; or again, *the Text is experienced only in an activity of production.* It follows that the Text cannot stop (for example on a library shelf); its constitutive movement is that of cutting across (in particular, it can cut across the work, several works).

2. In the same way, the Text does not stop at (good) Literature; it cannot be contained in a hierarchy, even in a simple division of genres. What constitutes the Text is, on the contrary (or precisely), its subversive force in respect of the old classifications. How do you classify a writer like Georges Bataille? Novelist, poet, essayist, economist, philosopher, mystic? The answer is so difficult that the literary manuals generally prefer to forget about Bataille who, in fact, wrote texts, perhaps continuously one single text. If the Text poses problems of classification (which is furthermore one of its "social" functions), this is because it always involves a certain experience of limits (to take up an expression from Philippe Sollers). Thibaudet used already to talk—but in a very restricted sense—of limit-works (such as Chateaubriand's *Vie de Rancé,* which does indeed come through to us today as a "text"); the Text is that which goes to the limit of the rules of enunciation (rationality, readability, etc.).

Nor is this a rhetorical idea, resorted to for some "heroic" effect: the Text tries to place itself very exactly *behind* the limit of the *doxa* (is not general opinion—constitutive of our democratic societies and powerfully aided by mass communications—defined by its limits, the energy with which it excludes, its *censorship*?). Taking the word literally, it may be said that the Text is always *paradoxical.*

3. The Text can be approached, experienced, in reaction to the sign. The work closes on a signified. There are two modes of signification which can be attributed to this signified: either it is claimed to be evident and the work is then the object of a literal science, of philology, or else it is considered to be secret, ultimate, something to be sought out, and the work then falls under the scope of a hermeneutics, of an interpretation (Marxist, psychoanalytic, thematic, etc.); in short, the work itself functions as a general sign and it is normal that it should represent an institutional category of the civilization of the Sign. The Text, on the contrary, practises the infinite deferment of the signified, is dilatory; its field is that of the signifier and the signifier must not be conceived of as "the first stage of meaning," its material vestibule, but, in complete opposition to this, as its *deferred action.* Similarly, the *infinity* of the signifier refers not to some idea of the ineffable (the unnameable signified) but to that of a *playing;* the generation of the perpetual signifier (after the fashion of a perpetual calendar) in the field of the text (better, of which the text is the field) is realized not according to an organic progress of maturation or a hermeneutic course of deepening investigation, but, rather, according to a serial movement of disconnections, overlappings, variations. The logic regulating the Text is not comprehensive (define "what the work means") but metonymic; the activity of associations, contiguities, carryings-over coincides with a liberation of symbolic energy (lacking it, man would die); the work—in the best of cases—is *moderately* symbolic (its symbolic runs out, comes to a halt); the Text is *radically* symbolic: *a work conceived, perceived and received in its integrally symbolic nature is a text.* Thus is the Text restored to language; like language, it is structured but off-centred, without closure (note, in reply to the contemptuous suspicion of the "fashionable" sometimes directed at structuralism, that the epistemological privilege currently accorded to language stems precisely from the discovery there of a paradoxical idea of structure: a system with neither close nor centre).

4. The Text is plural. Which is not simply to say that it has several meanings, but that it accomplishes the very plural of meaning: an *irreducible* (and not merely an acceptable) plural. The Text is not a co-existence of meanings but a passage, an overcrossing; thus it answers not to an interpretation, even a liberal one, but to an explosion, a dissemination. The plural of the Text depends, that is, not on the ambiguity of its contents but on what might be called the *stereographic plurality* of its weave of signifiers (etymologically, the text is a tissue, a woven fabric). The reader of the Text may be compared to someone at a loose end (someone slackened off from any imaginary); this passably empty subject strolls—it is what happened to the author of these lines, then it was that he had a vivid idea of the Text—on the side of a valley, a *oued* flowing, down below (*oued* is there to bear witness to a certain feeling of unfamiliarity); what he perceives is multiple, irreducible, coming from a disconnected, heterogeneous variety of substances and perspectives: lights, colours, vegetation, heat, air, slender explosions of noises, scant cries of birds, children's

voices from over on the other side, passages, gestures, clothes of inhabitants near or far away. All these *incidents* are half-identifiable: they come from codes which are known but their combination is unique, founds the stroll in a difference repeatable only as difference. So the Text: it can be it only in its difference (which does not mean its individuality), its reading is semelfactive (this rendering illusory any inductive-deductive science of texts—no "grammar" of the text) and nevertheless woven entirely with citations, references, echoes, cultural languages (what language is not?), antecedent or contemporary, which cut across it through and through in a vast stereophony. The intertextual in which every text is held, it itself being the text-between of another text, is not to be confused with some origin of the text: to try to find the "sources," the "influences" of a work, is to fall in with the myth of filiation; the citations which go to make up a text are anonymous, untraceable, and yet *already read:* they are quotations without inverted commas. The work has nothing disturbing for any monistic philosophy (we know that there are opposing examples of these); for such a philosophy, plural is the Evil. Against the work, therefore, the text could well take as its motto the words of the man possessed by demons (*Mark* 5: 9): "My name is Legion: for we are many." The plural of demoniacal texture which opposes text to work can bring with it fundamental changes in reading, and precisely in areas where monologism appears to be the Law: certain of the "texts" of Holy Scripture traditionally recuperated by theological monism (historical or anagogical) will perhaps offer themselves to a diffraction of meanings (finally, that is to say, to a materialist reading), while the Marxist interpretation of works, so far resolutely monistic, will be able to materialize itself more by pluralizing itself (if, however, the Marxist "institutions" allow it).

5. The work is caught up in a process of filiation. Are postulated: a *determination* of the work by the world (by race, then by History), a *consecution* of works amongst themselves, and a *conformity* of the work to the author. The author is reputed the father and the owner of his work: literary science therefore teaches *respect* for the manuscript and the author's declared intentions, while society asserts the legality of the relation of author to work (the *"droit d'auteur"* or "copyright," in fact of recent date since it was only really legalized at the time of the French Revolution). As for the Text, it reads without the inscription of the Father. Here again, the metaphor of the Text separates from that of the work: the latter refers to the image of an *organism* which grows by vital expansion, by "development" (a word which is significantly ambiguous, at once biological and rhetorical); the metaphor of the Text is that of the *network*; if the Text extends itself, it is as a result of a combinatory systematic (an image, moreover, close to current biological conceptions of the living being). Hence no vital "respect" is due to the Text: it can be *broken* (which is just what the Middle Ages did with two nevertheless authoritative texts—Holy Scripture and Aristotle); it can be read without the guarantee of its father, the restitution of the intertext paradoxically abolishing any legacy. It is not that the Author may not "come back" in the Text, in his text, but he then does so as a "guest." If he is a novelist, he is inscribed in the novel like one of his characters, figured in the carpet; no longer privileged, paternal, aletheological, his inscription is ludic. He becomes, as it were, a paper-author: his life is no longer the origin of his fictions but a fiction contributing to his work; there is a

reversion of the work on to the life (and no longer the contrary); it is the work of Proust, of Genet which allows their lives to be read as a text. The word "biography" re-acquires a strong, etymological sense, at the same time as the sincerity of the enunciation—veritable "cross" borne by literary morality—becomes a false problem: the *I* which writes the text, it too, is never more than a paper-*I*.

6. The work is normally the object of a consumption; no demagogy is intended here in referring to the so-called consumer culture but it has to be recognized that today it is the "quality" of the work (which supposes finally an appreciation of "taste") and not the operation of reading itself which can differentiate between books: structurally, there is no difference between "cultured" reading and casual reading in trains. The Text (if only by its frequent "unreadability") decants the work (the work permitting) from its consumption and gathers it up as play, activity, production, practice. This means that the Text requires that one try to abolish (or at the very least to diminish) the distance between writing and reading, in no way by intensifying the projection of the reader into the work but by joining them in a single signifying practice. The distance separating reading from writing is historical. In the times of the greatest social division (before the setting up of democratic cultures), reading and writing were equally privileges of class. Rhetoric, the great literary code of those times, taught one to *write* (even if what was then normally produced were speeches, not texts). Significantly, the coming of democracy reversed the word of command: what the (secondary) School prides itself on is teaching to *read* (well) and no longer to write (consciousness of the deficiency is becoming fashionable again today: the teacher is called upon to teach pupils to "express themselves," which is a little like replacing a form of repression by a misconception). In fact, *reading*, is the sense of consuming, is far from *playing* with the text. "Playing" must be understood here in all its polysemy: the text itself *plays* (like a door, like a machine with "play") and the reader plays twice over, playing the Text as one plays a game, looking for a practice which re-produces *it*, but, in order that that practice not be reduced to a passive, inner *mimesis* (the Text is precisely that which resists such a reduction), also playing the Text in the musical sense of the term. The history of music (as a practice, not as an "art") does indeed parallel that of the Text fairly closely: there was a period when practising amateurs were numerous (at least within the confines of a certain class) and "playing" and "listening" formed a scarcely differentiated activity; then two roles appeared in succession, first that of the performer, the interpreter to whom the bourgeois public (though still itself able to play a little—the whole history of the piano) delegated its playing, then that of the (passive) amateur, who listens to music without being able to play (the gramophone record takes the place of the piano). We know that today post-serial music has radically altered the role of the "interpreter" who is called on to be in some sort the co-author of the score, completing it rather than giving it "expression." The Text is very much a score of this new kind: it asks of the reader a practical collaboration. Which is an important change, for who executes the work? (Mallarmé posed the question, wanting the audience to *produce* the book). Nowadays only the critic executes the work (accepting the play on words). The reduction of reading to a consumption is clearly responsible for the "boredom" experienced by many in the face of the modern ("unreadable") text,

the avant-garde film or painting: to be bored means that one cannot produce the text, open it out, *set it going.*

7. This leads us to pose (to propose) a final approach to the Text, that of pleasure. I do not know whether there has ever been a hedonistic aesthetics (eudaemonist philosophies are themselves rare). Certainly there exists a pleasure of the work (of certain works); I can delight in reading and re-reading Proust, Flaubert, Balzac, even—why not?—Alexandre Dumas. But this pleasure, no matter how keen and even when free from all prejudice, remains in part (unless by some exceptional critical effort) a pleasure of consumption; for if I can read these authors, I also know that I cannot *re-write* them (that it is impossible today to write "like that") and this knowledge, depressing enough, suffices to cut me off from the production of these works, in the very moment their remoteness establishes my modernity (is not to be modern to know clearly what cannot be started over again?). As for the Text, it is bound to *jouissance,* that is to a pleasure without separation. Order of the signifier, the Text participates in its own way in a social Utopia; before History (supposing the latter does not opt for barbarism), the Text achieves, if not the transparence of social relations, that at least of language relations: the Text is that space where no language has a hold over any other, where languages circulate (keeping the circular sense of the term).

These few propositions, inevitably, do not constitute the articulations of a Theory of the Text and this is not simply the result of the failings of the person here presenting them (who in many respects has anyway done no more than pick up what is being developed round about him). It stems from the fact that a Theory of the Text cannot be satisfied by a meta-linguistic exposition: the destruction of meta-language, or at least (since it may be necessary provisionally to resort to meta-language) its calling into doubt, is part of the theory itself: the discourse on the Text should itself be nothing other than text, research, textual activity, since the Text is that *social* space which leaves no language safe, outside, nor any subject of the enunciation in position as judge, master, analyst, confessor, decoder. The theory of the Text can coincide only with a practice of writing.

STEVENS' ROCK AND CRITICISM AS CURE, II (1976)

J. HILLIS MILLER

Miller's influential essay introduces a circle of critics at Yale University whose members, during the heyday of American deconstruction, were perhaps the most influential literary critics in the United States. Following the lead of Jacques Derrida, the so-called Yale School—Paul de Man, Geoffrey Hartman, and Miller—brought deconstruction to literary criticism, especially to English-language criticism. Sometimes, including in this essay, the Yale School stretched to include Harold Bloom, whose methods differed in many ways from their own. Bloom's once influential theory of literary influence argued that every poem is a misreading of an earlier poem. Near the beginning of his essay, Miller includes the deconstructionist critics among the structuralist critics, but this essay and others like it by members of the Yale School were part of the thinking that separated Derridean or deconstructive thought from structuralist thought and helped establish the concept and term poststructuralism.

Along the way, Miller structures and destructures his essay with a bevy of allusions. Mise en abyme, *putting into the abyss, refers to the dizzying effect of seeing an image of one thing in another, whether a small part of a literary work that represents the whole, or a mirror image reflected and endlessly rereflected in another mirror. In Greek mythology, Theseus slew the half-bull half-man Minotaur, ensconced in the Labyrinth, from which no one could escape. But Theseus escaped because Ariadne gave him a thread to drop behind him and mark the way out. For Miller, in this essay and others, the trail of Ariadne's thread through the maze is a figure for the defining loops and knots of narrative itself. Deconstructionists sometimes call a knot in logic an "aporia," meaning an undecidable moment of logical impasse. Miller also draws on Roman Jakobson's structuralist opposition between metaphor and metonymy. (See Jakobson's essay on "The Metaphoric and Metonymic Poles" in this volume.)*

Fitting his title, Miller begins by referring to Wallace Stevens's poem "The Rock" and other poems by Stevens, including "An Ordinary Evening in New Haven" (a jocular reference, since Yale is in New Haven), but his essay soon leaves Stevens and follows the classic deconstructionist pattern of setting up a reassuring, clarifying structure, even a structuralist binary, and then—in the second step of what deconstructionists often call a double reading—"exploding" the binary by showing that what might seem binary and stable is always already dizzyingly multiple and unstable. In this case, the binary is between structuralist criticism and the deconstructionist criticism (the Yale School). Drawing on Nietzsche's binary opposition in The Birth of Tragedy *between the Apollonian and the Dionysian, Miller casts structuralists as Apollonian (rational, orderly, bounded, representational) and deconstructionists as Dionysian (intoxicated, nonrational, nonrepresentational, self-dissolving). Like a good (and Dionysian) deconstructionist, he eventually goes on to explode his own binary, arguing that the structuralists inevitably slide into deconstruction and that the deconstructionists risk too much structure, risk undermining their own deconstructiveness if, as perhaps he does in his own essay, they give in to the temptation to present their argument in rational and clearly argued terms.*

O Socrates, make music and work at it.

PHAEDO, 60E

As readers drown under the ever-accumulating flood of criticism, they are justified in asking, why is there criticism rather than silent admiration? If every literary text performs already its own self-interpretation, which means its own self-dismantling, why is there any need for criticism? A poem, for example Stevens' "The Rock," is entirely self-sufficient. It does not need to have one word added to it. Why does it nevertheless call forth so many supplementary words? The publication, in any given year, of an apparently ungovernable multiplicity of critical texts raises the question of the validity of the whole enterprise. Why must there be literary criticism at all, or at any rate more literary criticism? Don't we have enough already? What ineluctable necessity in literature makes it generate unending oceans of commentary, wave after wave covering the primary textual rocks, hiding them, washing them, uncovering them again, but leaving them, after all, just as they were?

The answer to these questions, insofar as there is an answer, is provided by the formulation of the questions themselves, as well as by what can be seen in such a poem as "The Rock." If that poem is a continuous *mise en abyme*, forming and re-forming itself around words or images—"icon," "rock," "cure," and so on—which both name the "alogical" and cover it over, criticism is a continuation of that activity of the poem. If the poem is a cure of the ground which never succeeds, criticism is a yielding to the temptation to try once more for the "cure beyond forgetfulness," and then once more, and once beyond that, in an ever-renewed, ever-unsuccessful attempt to "get it right," to name things by their right names. As Stevens says, "They will get it straight one day at the Sorbonne," and when "I call you by name, my green, my fluent mundo,/You will have stopped revolving except in crystal" ("Notes Toward a Supreme Fiction"). They never get it right, however, neither in poetry nor in the criticism of poetry, neither at the Sorbonne nor in generations of ordinary evenings in New Haven. The work continues, and the world keeps fluently turning, never called by name, never fixed in a definitive formulation. The critic cannot by any means get outside the text, escape from the blind alleys of language he finds in the work. He can only rephrase them in other, allotropic terms. The critical text prolongs, extends, reveals, covers, in short, cures, the literary text in the same way that the literary text attempts to cure the ground. If poetry is the impossible possible cure of the ground, criticism is the impossible possible cure of literature.

A recognition of the incorporation of the work of criticism into the unending activity of poetry itself seems especially to characterize criticism today. Literature, however, has always performed its own *mise en abyme*, though it has usually been misunderstood as doing the opposite. It has often been interpreted as establishing a ground in consciousness, in the poem as self-contained object, in nature, or in some metaphysical base. Literature therefore needs to be prolonged in criticism. The activity of deconstruction already performed and then hidden in the work must be performed again in criticism. It can be performed, however, only in such a way as to be misunderstood in its turn, like the work itself, so that it has to be done over, and then again. If a work of literature must be read in order to come into existence as a work of literature, and if, as Charles Sanders Peirce said, the only interpretation of one sign is another sign, then criticism is the allegory or putting otherwise of the act of reading. This response of new sign generated by old sign continues interminably as long as the work is read.

What, then, can be said to be special in the present moment in criticism? Each such moment tends to feel itself to be a turning point, an instant of crisis, a crossroads, a time when important new developments are taking place or are about to take place. A recent announcement of a new institute of criticism and theory speaks of our time as "a period of crisis for the humanistic disciplines and of concurrent excitement (and attendant confusion) in the area of critical theory." No doubt this is true, though the odds are strongly against 1976 being as important in literary criticism as, say, 1798. Moreover, it can always be demonstrated that the apparent novelty of any new development in criticism is the renewal of an insight which has been found and lost and found again repeatedly through all the centuries of literary study since the first Homeric and Biblical commentaries. The novelty of any "new criticism" is not in its intrinsic insights or techniques but rather in the "accidents" of its expression, though how can "accident" here be distinguished from "substance"? The novelty of an innovative criticism, nevertheless, is in large part in its institutionalization, in the mode of its insertion into the teaching or reading of literature at a given historical moment, rather than in any absolute originality of terminology or insight.

A distinctive feature of English and American literary criticism today is its progressive naturalization, appropriation, or accommodation of recent continental criticism. Much, though by no means all, of our current criticism in English would be impossible without the continental "influence," meaning primarily, at the moment, so-called structuralism. Structuralism, however, can in no way be described in a single coherent paradigm. It divides and subdivides into warring sects, Saussurians, Barthesians, Marxists, Foucaultians, Lacanians, Lévi-Straussians, Derridians, and so on. No critic would accept a lumping of his work with that of the others. Nevertheless, some paths in this labyrinth may be mapped.

The "new turn" in criticism, which is a return of the old, is characterized by a focus on language as the central problematic of literary study. This focus determines a breaking down of barriers and a putting in question of grounds, even of the apparently solid basis of new linguistic theory. This rediscovery of an often hidden center of gravity in literature might be called the linguistic moment. This moment may have such moment or momentum that it prolongs and expands itself to attract into orbit around its mass all the other themes and features of a given work. These become planets around its solar focus, the other focus being that nameless *abyme* with which language can never coincide. This breaking of barriers and questioning of grounds involves a return to the explicit study of rhetoric. Rhetoric means in this case the investigation of figures of speech rather than the study of the art of persuasion, though the notion of persuasion is still present in a more ambiguous displaced form, as the idea of production, or of function, or of performance. The new turn in criticism involves an interrogation of the notion of the self-enclosed literary work and of the idea that any work has a fixed identifiable meaning. The literary work is seen in various ways as open and unpredictably productive. The reading of a poem is part of the poem. This reading is productive in its turn. It produces multiple interpretations, further language about the poem's language, in an interminable activity without necessary closure.

The boundaries between literature and criticism are broken down in this activity, not because the critic arrogates to himself some vague right to be "poetical" in his writing, but because he recognizes it as his doom not to be able to be anything else. The critic is not able by any "method" or strategy of analysis to "reduce" the language of the work to clear and distinct ideas. He is forced at best to repeat the work's contradictions in a different form. The work is seen as heterogeneous, dialogical rather than monological. It has at least two apparent grounds, centers, foci, or *logoi,* and is therefore incapable of being encompassed in any single coherent or homogeneous interpretation. Any reading can be shown to be a misreading on evidence drawn from the text itself. Moreover, any literary text, with more or less explicitness or clarity, already reads or misreads itself. The "deconstruction" which the text performs on itself and which the critic repeats is not of the superstructure of the work but of the ground on which it stands, whether that ground is history, or the social world, or the solid, extra-linguistic world of "objects," or the givenness of the generative self of the writer, his "consciousness."

If the literary work is within itself open, heterogeneous, a dialogue of conflicting voices, it is also seen as open to other texts, permeable to them, permeated by them. A literary text is not a thing in itself, "organically unified," but a relation to other texts which are relations in their turn. The study of literature is therefore a study of intertextuality, as in the recent work of Harold Bloom, or, in a different way, in that of Geoffrey Hartman. The relation between text and precursor text is devious, problematic, never a matter of direct cause and effect. For this, as for other reasons, such criticism puts in question the traditional notions of literary history as a sequence of self-enclosed "periods," each with its intrinsic characteristics: motifs, genres, ideologies, and so on. It also brings into question the traditional study of "sources."

The boundaries, finally, between literary texts and other kinds of texts are also perforated or dismantled. If insights or methods developed in psychology, anthropology, philosophy, and linguistics are appropriated by literary criticism, linguistics, on the other hand, broadens out imperialistically to redefine all of those disciplines. The founding or fathering texts of these disciplines are reinterpreted according to new notions about language, as Freud is reread in the light of modern linguistics by the school of Jacques Lacan. Lacanian psychoanalysis becomes in its turn the basis of a kind of literary criticism. From the point of view of literary criticism, this blurring of traditional boundaries means that a "philosophical" or "psychological" text, a work by Hegel, say, or one by Freud, is to be read in the same way as a "literary" text. This is done, for example, by Jacques Derrida in his reading of Plato in "La pharmacie de Platon" or in his reading of Hegel in *Glas.* It is done in Edward Said's interpretation, in *Beginnings,* of Freud's *Die Traumdeutung* as a narrative text like a novel.

These assumptions about literature are sufficiently different from the traditional assumptions of much literary study in England and America as to take some time to be assimilated. In time they will be naturalized, tested, challenged, refuted, and perhaps ultimately in some form institutionalized in courses, curricula, and the programs of "departments" in our colleges and universities. This give and take will no doubt characterize literary study, in the United States at least, during the coming years, though with how much giving and how much taking remains to be seen.

Already a clear distinction can be drawn, among critics influenced by these new developments, between what might be called, to conflate two terminologies, Socratic, theoretical, or canny critics, on the one hand, and Apollonian/Dionysian, tragic, or uncanny critics, on the other. Socratic critics are those who are lulled by the promise of a rational ordering of literary study on the basis of solid advances in scientific knowledge about language. They are likely to speak of themselves as "scientists" and to group their collective enterprise under some term like "the human sciences." The human sciences—it has a reassuringly logical, progressive, quantifiable sound, "canny" in the sense of shrewd or practical. Such an enterprise is represented by the discipline called "semiotics," or by new work in the exploration and exploitation of rhetorical terms. Included would be aspects of the work of Gerard Genette, Roland Barthes, and Roman Jakobson, as well as that of scholars like A. J. Greimas, Tzvetan Todorov, Cesare Brandi, and Jean-Claude Coquet. Jonathan Culler's *Structuralist Poetics* is a canny and wholesomely sceptical introduction to the work of such critics.

For the most part these critics share the Socratic penchant, what Nietzsche defined as "the unshakable faith that thought, using the thread of logic (*an den Leitfaden der Kausalität*), can penetrate the deepest abysses of being, and that thought is capable not only of knowing but even of correcting (*corrigiren*) it" (*The Birth of Tragedy*, 15). Here is another meaning for "cure." Socratic or scientific criticism, criticism by what Nietzsche calls *theoretischen Menschen*, criticism as cure, would be not only a penetration of the ground but also its correction, its straightening out. The inheritors today of the Socratic faith would believe in the possibility of a structuralist-inspired criticism as a rational and rationalizable activity, with agreed-upon rules of procedure, given facts, and measurable results. This would be a discipline bringing literature out into the sunlight in a "happy positivism." Such an appropriation of the recent turn in criticism would have the attractive quality of easily leading to institutionalizing in textbooks, courses, curricula, all the paraphernalia of an established academic discipline.

Opposed to these are the critics who might be called "uncanny." Though they have been inspired by the same climate of thought as the Socratic critics and though their work would also be impossible without modern linguistics, the "feel" or atmosphere of their writing is quite different from that of a critic like Culler, with his brisk common sense and his reassuring notions of "literary competence" and the acquisition of "conventions," his hope that all right-thinking people might agree on the meaning of a lyric or a novel, or at any rate share a "universe of discourse" in which they could talk about it. "Uncanny" critics would include, each in his own way, a new group of critics gathered at Yale: Harold Bloom, Paul de Man, and Geoffrey Hartman. Jacques Derrida teaches a seminar early each fall at Yale and so may be included among the Yale group. These critics may be taken by a convenient synecdoche as "examples" of criticism as the uncanny, but there are of course others, for example Derrida's associates in France, Sarah Kofman, Philippe Lacoue-Labarthe, Jean-Luc Nancy, Bernard Pautrat (essays by all of whom are gathered in their new book, *Mimesis.*) The American critic Edward Said admirably explores an uncanny topic in *Beginnings*.

These critics are not tragic or Dionysian in the sense that their work is wildly orgiastic or irrational. No critic could be more rigorously sane and rational, Apollonian, in his procedure, for example, than Paul de Man. One feature of Derrida's criticism is a patient and minutely philological "explication de texte." Nevertheless, the thread of logic leads in both cases into regions which are alogical, absurd. This might find a fit emblem not only in the *polemos* of Apollo and Dionysus but also in the marriage of Dionysus to Ariadne. The work of these critics is in one way or another a labyrinthine attempt to escape from the labyrinth of words, an attempt guided not only by the Apollonian thread of logic but by Ariadne's thread as she might be imagined to have rescued it from the too rational and betraying Theseus, or to have incarnated it in herself as the clue to an escape from the abyss by a cure of the ground. As Ruskin says, in *Fors Clavigera*, "The question seems not at all to have been about getting in; but getting *out* again. The clue, at all events, could be helpful only after you had carried it in; and if the spider, or other monster in midweb, ate you, the help in your clue, for return, would be insignificant. So that this thread of Ariadne's implied that even victory over the monster would be vain, unless you could disentangle yourself from his web also."

Ariadne's thread, then, is another *mise en abyme*, both a mapping of the abyss and an attempted escape from it, criticism as cure. This escape can never succeed, since the thread is itself the interminable production of more labyrinth. What would be outside the labyrinth? More labyrinth, the labyrinth, for example, of the story of Ariadne, which is by no means over with the triumphant escape of Theseus from the maze. According to Ruskin, the traditional labyrinth is "composed of a single path or track, coiled, and recoiled, on itself," and "the word 'Labyrinth' properly means 'rope walk,' or 'coil-of-rope-walk,' its first syllable being probably also the same as our English name 'Laura,' 'the path.'" This is, apparently, a false, but suggestively false, etymology. At the center, "midweb," of Ruskin's image is no male minotaur, but a female spider. The labyrinth is spun from the spider's belly, and Arachne is here conflated with Ariadne. Far from providing a benign escape from the maze, Ariadne's thread makes the labyrinth, is the labyrinth. The interpretation or solving of the puzzles of the textual web only adds more filaments to the web. One can never escape from the labyrinth because the activity of escaping makes more labyrinth, the thread of a linear narrative or story. Criticism is the production of more thread to embroider the texture or textile already there. This thread is like the filament of ink which flows from the pen of the writer, keeping him in the web but suspending him also over the chasm, the blank page that thin line hides. In one version of Ariadne's story she is said to have hanged herself with her thread in despair after being abandoned by Theseus.

In a different way in each case, the work of the uncanny critics, however reasonable or sane their apparent procedure, reaches a point where it resists the intelligence almost successfully. At this point it no longer quite makes rational sense, and the reader has the uncomfortable feeling that she cannot quite hold what is being said in her mind or make it all fit. Sooner or later there is the encounter with an "aporia" or impasse. The bottom drops out, or there is an "abyssing," an insight one can almost grasp or recognize as part of the familiar landscape of the mind, but not quite, as though the mental eye could not quite bring the material into lucid focus. This "abyssmal" discomfort is no doubt the reason why the work of these critics sometimes encounters such hostility from Socratic reviewers and readers. In fact the moment when logic fails in their work is the moment of their deepest penetration into the actual nature of literary language, or of language as such. It is also the place where Socratic procedures will ultimately lead, if they are carried far enough. The center of the work of the uncanny critics is in one way or another a formulation of this experience which momentarily and not wholly successfully rationalizes it, puts it in an image, a figure, a narrative, or a myth. Here, however, the distinction between story, concept, and image breaks down, at the vanishing point where each turns into something other than itself, concept into the alogical, figure into catachresis, narrative into ironical allegory.

In Paul de Man's essays, for example (example in what sense?), there is a sober and painstaking movement through a given text or set of citations. This leads rather suddenly, usually at the end of the essay, to an aporia, a formulation which is itself, necessarily, paradoxical or self-contradictory. The Apollonian here reaches its limits and becomes uncanny, without ceasing for all that to be coolly rational in its tone, keeping its balance over the abyss. De Man might be called "the master of the aporia," though this would be an oxymoron, since the aporia, like the chasm it opens, cannot, in fact, be mastered. "This complication," to give one example of this, in de Man's analysis of Nietzsche's deconstruction of the principle of identity,

> is characteristic for all deconstructive discourse: the deconstruction states the fallacy of reference in a necessarily referential mode....The differentiation between performative and constative language (which Nietzsche anticipates) is undecidable; the deconstruction leading from one model to the other is irreversible, but it always remains suspended, regardless of how often it is repeated....The aporia between performative and constative language is merely a version of the aporia between trope and persuasion that both generates and paralyzes rhetoric and thus gives it the appearance of a history.

In Harold Bloom's case, for example in *Kabbalah and Criticism*, there is the lucid, learned, patient presentation of a systematic terminology, or rather a terminology drawn simultaneously from three or four different language systems, that of somewhat esoteric Greek philosophy (*clinamen, tessera*, etc.), that of Freudian psychology (anxiety, repression, etc.), that of Kabbalah (*tikkun, Zimzum*, etc.), and that of classical rhetoric (synecdoche, hyperbole, metalepsis, etc.). The presentation is so reasonable, so genuinely learned, and so sane in tone, that it is with something of a start that the reader wakes up to realize what outrageous demands are being made on him. Can he adopt such a wildly eclectic vocabulary? *Tikkun? Zimzum? Clinamen?* Transumption? *Nachträglichkeit? Sefirot?* Can he really be expected to make practical use of such terms? Moreover, if the central insight of Bloom's new work is into the rhetorical and figurative relations of intertextuality, into the way each sign or text is a misreading or verbal swerving from a previous sign or text and calls forth new signs or texts which are misinterpretations in their turn, this insight is with difficulty reconciled with his repeatedly affirmed Emersonian desire to maintain the "bedrock" priority of the strong self as the motivating momentum in this dynamic play of sign with sign, text with text. The conflicting demands of sign and self in his criticism form a blind alley, a bifurcated root in his thinking. This double source cannot be synthesized into a logical or dialectical totality. Bloom's self-contradiction is generative rather than paralyzing, however, as is proven by the admirable essays on the major poets of the Romantic tradition in *Poetry and Repression: Revisionism from Blake to Stevens*. The cogs and levers in Bloom's "machine for criticism" proliferate inexhaustibly, six terms becoming twenty-four, the six original ratios becoming in his most recent work doubled again in twelve *topoi* or crossings. The machine, nevertheless, works. It keeps working perhaps through its own constant autodestruction and triumphant hyperbolic replication. It works to produce splendid essays of interpretation (or misinterpretation, misprision, since all strong reading, for Bloom, must be misreading). After Bloom's work we shall never be able to read Shelley or Browning, Tennyson or Stevens, in the same way again. They are changed by being shown to have made their poetry out of changes, anamorphoses, of their precursors.

In Geoffrey Hartman's case there is an increasing tendency to puns and to wordplayfulness. As he says in his essay on Derrida's *Glas,* "I must pun as I must sneeze." This wordplay is carried on, in all Hartman's books from *The Unmediated Vision* to *The Fate of Reading,* for the sake of an interrogation of the *logos,* the ground or *Grund* at the base of all wordplay. The question, for him, is not so much of the fate of reading as of the fate of poetry. It is a question of the vitality of words, their rootedness, the question whether poetry can survive in a post-enlightenment culture. The danger, for Hartman, as he puts it in "False Themes and Gentle Minds," one of the key essays in *Beyond Formalism,* is an uprooting of poetry such as that of "eighteenth century topographical fancies with their personification mania": "Romance loses its shadow, its genuine darkness: nothing remains of the drama of liberation whereby ingenium is born from genius, psyche from persona, and the spirit of poetry from the grave clothes of Romance." True poetry must be like Milton's *L'Allegro* and *Il Penseroso,* which "show a mind moving from one position to another and projecting an image of its freedom against a darker, demonic ground. Poetry, like religion, purifies that ground: it cannot leave it." On the other hand, the danger is that this return from differentiation, which leads from one word to another in endless punning permutation, will reach not a vital source, the ground of puns, but an undifferentiated blur, a meaningless Blouaugh!, like the roar of William Carlos Williams' sea-elephant. Hartman's essay on Gerard Manley Hopkins in *Beyond Formalism* argues that Hopkins' ways with words "evoke the tendency of semantic distinctions to fall back into a phonemic ground of identity. There is, in other words, a linguistic indifference against which language contends, and contends successfully, by diacritical or differential means." Hartman is caught in the aporia of these two irreconcilable models, whose incompatibility both motivates his criticism and prevents it from becoming clear, wholly enlightened. Hovering between a need for the clarifying distinctions of wordplay and a need for the "rich, dark nothing" of the chthonic ground, a ground which may or may not (such uncertainty is the curse of enlightenment) be a vital source, a source in any case both desired and feared, stretched in this double bind, Hartman's criticism conducts its testing of the ground and its covering of the ground, its mode of criticism as cure.

If Paul de Man is the master of the unmasterable aporia, Jacques Derrida is, as Geoffrey Hartman calls him, a "boa-deconstructor." His prodigious effort in the disarticulation of the major texts of Western metaphysics, philosophical and literary, might, however, be more aptly figured in the sinuous emblem of some slenderer and more insinuating serpent than a snake that crushes. Deconstruction as a mode of interpretation works by a careful and circumspect entering of each textual labyrinth. The critic feels his way from figure to figure, from concept to concept, from mythical motif to mythical motif, in a repetition which is in no sense a parody. It employs, nevertheless, the subversive power present in even the most exact and unironical doubling. The deconstructive critic seeks to find, by this process of retracing, the element in the system studied which is alogical, the thread in the text in question which will unravel it all, or the loose stone which will pull down the whole building. The deconstruction, rather, annihilates the ground on which the building stands by showing that the text has already annihilated that ground, knowingly and unknowingly. Deconstruction is not a dismantling of the structure of a text but a demonstration that it has already dismantled itself. Its apparently solid ground is no rock but thin air.

The uncanny moment in Derrida's criticism, the vacant place at the non-center around which all his work is organized, is the formulation and reformulation of this non-existence of the ground out of which the whole textual structure seems to rise like the pleasure dome of Kubla Khan. Derrida has shown marvelous fecundity in finding or inventing new terms to express this generative non-source, absence, forking, or scattering beneath all appearances of presence: *le supplément, le pharmakon, la différance, l'hymen, la dissémination, la marge, le cadre, la signature,* and so on. Each of these both is and is not concept, figure, and infolded narrative. No one of them may be made the ground of its own textual structure, for example, of a discipline of critical studies. Each is eccentric, like all genuine terms, for example those bizarre terms used by Bloom. Of all these critical terms in Derrida's work one could say what he says of *la dissémination* in "La double séance," his essay on Mallarmé:

> In spite of appearances, the endless work of condensation and displacement does not lead us finally back to dissemination as its ultimate signification, or to its initial truth....According to a scheme which we have experienced with the word "between" (*entre*), the quasi "meaning" of dissemination is the impossible return to the rejoined, reattached unity of a meaning, the closed-off way to such a *reflection* [in the sense of veering back]. Is dissemination nevertheless the *loss* of such a truth, the *negative* interdict against reaching such a signification? Far from allowing in this way the supposition that a virgin substance preceded or surveys it from above, dispersing or obstructing itself in a secondary negativity, dissemination *affirms* the always already divided generation of meaning....No more than castration can dissemination, which entails, "inscribes," reprojects it, become an original, central, or ultimate signification, the proper place of the truth. It represents on the contrary the affirmation of that non-origin, the empty and remarkable place of a hundred blanks to which one cannot give meaning, multiplying to infinity supplementary marks and games of substitution.

In *Positions,* Derrida provides a commentary on "hundred blanks" (*cent blancs*) by making it one link in a chain generating a complicated multiple pun. It is a phrase, like the word "cure" in Stevens' poem, which is a node or knot of irreconcilable or undecidable meanings: *sens blanc, sang blanc, sans blanc, cent blancs, semblant.* Such words, says Derrida, "are not *atoms,* but points of economic condensation, necessary stations along the way for a large number of marks, for somewhat more effervescent crucibles. Then their effects not only turn back on themselves through a sort of closed self-excitation, they spread themselves in a chain over the theoretical and practical whole of a text, each time in a different way." These proliferating supplements and substitutions are the other possible words, none equivalents of one another, which may express the chasm of the alogical, each time in a different way. Each term has its own systematic play of concepts and figures folded into it, incompatible with the self-excitation of any other word.

De Man, Bloom, Hartman, and Derrida, then, come together in the way their criticism is an interrogation of the ground of literature, not just of its intrinsic structure. They come together also in the way the criticism of each, in a different manner each time, is uncanny, cannot be encompassed in a rational or logical formulation, and resists the intelligence of its readers. They differ greatly, however, in their modes of uncanniness and in their attitudes toward their own insights. Even so, their criticism seems at the opposite pole from that of the canny critics, the semioticians or structuralists, diagram- and system-makers, seekers for a sound scientific base for literary study.

The most uncanny moment of all, however, in this developing polarity among critics today, is the moment when the apparent opposites reverse themselves, the Socratic becoming uncanny, the uncanny, canny, sometimes all too shrewdly rational. Recognition of this movement of reversal or exchange is the second climax of *The Birth of Tragedy,* the first being the insight into the interchangeability of the Apollonian and the Dionysian in tragic art, according to the formulation that, in tragedy, "Dionysus speaks the language of Apollo; and Apollo, finally, the language of Dionysus" (*Dionysus redet die Sprache des Apollo, Apollo aber schliesslich die Sprache Dionysus*). If tragedy is this fraternal union (*Bruderbund*), a union which is also a constant brother-murder, Socratic or scientific thought seems at first the escape from all such paradoxes into the clear light of logical insight. Insight, however, becomes blindness when it reaches its limits, and science turns back into tragic art, the art of the abyss, the alogical. "This sublime metaphysical illusion," says Nietzsche, the illusion, that is, that science can penetrate and correct or "cure" the deepest abysses of being, "accompanies science as an instinct, and leads science again and again to its limits (*zu ihren Grenzen*), at which it must turn into art—*which is really the aim of this mechanism*" (*aufwelche es eigentlich, bei diesem Mechanismus, abgesehen ist*).

Such a reversal is occurring or has already occurred in a number of ways within the Socratic penchant of contemporary criticism. It has occurred most strikingly, perhaps, in the way the rational and reassuringly "scientific" study of tropes by present-day rhetoricians—though it depends fundamentally on an initially clear distinction between literal and figurative uses of language, and on clear distinctions among the tropes—ends by putting these distinctions in question and so undermines its own ground. This movement is clear in the best of such critics, for example in Gerard Genette's three volumes of *Figures.* His admirable "Métonymie chez Proust," in *Figures III,* aims to build itself on Roman Jakobson's firm distinction between metonymy and metaphor and even to show them working harmoniously to make *A la recherche du temps perdu* possible: "For it is metaphor which recovers lost time, but it is metonymy which reanimates it, and puts it in motion again: which returns it to itself and to its true 'essence', which is its proper fleeting away and its proper Research. Here then, here alone—by metaphor, but *in* metonymy—here begins Narrative." But, as Genette's essay has shown, almost in spite of itself, if metaphor is so dependent on the accidental contiguities of metonymy, then the apparent continuity both of the text of *A la recherche* and of Marcel's life fragment irreparably and become mere juxtapositions of broken shards. The "true" insight of Genette's essay, skirted, avoided, circled around with averted eyes, but unmistakably brought to the surface nevertheless, is the exact opposite of its happy claim that metonymy can be a form of cohesion and therefore a support of metaphor, as Paul de Man has obliquely demonstrated, in "Proust et l'allégorie de la lecture," in *Mouvements premiers.* In fact the same contamination of the substantial similarities of metaphor by the external contingencies of metonymy had already undone the clear distinction between metaphor and metonymy in the precursor texts for Genette's essay, Roman Jakobson's brilliant and influential "Two Aspects of Language and Two Types of Aphasic Disturbances," in *Fundamentals of Language,* and "Linguistics and Poetics,"'in *Style in Language*. A flash of self-subverting genius in the later essay, aided by an aphorism from Goethe, *Alles Vergängliche ist nur ein Gleichnis* ("Anything transient is but a likeness"), breaks down the polarity between the two figures on which the genuinely productive insights (for example into the role of metonymy in realistic fiction) were based: "In poetry where similarity is superinduced upon contiguity, any metonymy is slightly metaphorical and any metaphor has a metonymical tint." The word "slightly" here has the same force as in the phrase "slighty pregnant." It echoes backward to unravel the whole theoretical basis of the essay on aphasia.

If the uncanny turn of current criticism is partly the moment when "the human sciences" reach their limits and become absurd, the fact that this moment recurs is also uncanny. Criticism repeats or reformulates again and again "the same" blind alley, like Freud in "Das Unheimliche" finding himself repeatedly coming back to the bordello section of that Italian town, however hard he tried to escape it. Any "Socratic" method in criticism, if carried far enough (not very far, actually), reaches its limits and subverts itself. The emblem for this might be that recurrent dream Socrates describes in the *Phaedo*. The dream brought an injunction which implictly challenged Socrates' lifelong commitment to reason and logical thought. "'O Socrates,' it said, 'make music and work at it'" (*O Sokrates, ephe, mouskien poiei kai ergathon*).

Examples of this reversal abound in modern criticism. The New Criticism discovered irony and the irresolvable ambiguities of figure. These discoveries subverted, at least implicitly, its presupposition that a poem is a self-contained "object," an organic unity. The criticism of Georges Poulet, basing itself on the assumption of the irreducible priority and "givenness" of the self, of the presence of consciousness to itself, ends by recognizing in consciousness a fathomless chasm. It ends also in recognizing that any stability or coherence in the self is an effect of language. The self is a linguistic construction rather than being the given, the rock, a solid *point de départ*. A similar self-subversion occurs from the other direction in structuralism. In this case, however, it is not the symmetrically opposite discovery that consciousness is the base of language, but rather the discovery that language is not a base. This is the moment of the self-deconstruction of rhetoric. The study of tropes looks at first like a safely scientific, rational, or logical discipline, but it still leads to the abyss, as it did for the old rhetoricians in the endless baroque, though entirely justifiable, proliferation of names for different figures of speech. More fundamentally, the study of rhetoric leads to the abyss by destroying, through its own theoretical procedures, its own basic axiom. Broadening itself imperialistically to take in other disciplines (philosophy, anthropology, literary criticism, psychology), rhetoric ultimately encounters, within itself, the problems it was meant to solve. Nietzsche expressed this aporia of Socratism or scientism in a brilliant passage in the fifteenth section of *The Birth of Tragedy*. The passage matches the double structure of the "cure of the ground" in Stevens' "The Rock":

But science [*Wissenschaft*], spurred by its powerful illusion, speeds irresistibly towards its-limits [*bis zu ihren Grenzen*], where its optimism, concealed in the essence of logic, suffers shipwreck [*scheitert*]. For the periphery of the circle of science [*des Kreises der Wissenschaft*] has an infinite number of points; and while there is no telling how this circle could ever be surveyed completely, noble and gifted men nevertheless reach, e'er half their time [*noch vor der Mitte seines Daseins*] and inevitably, such boundary points [*Grenzpunkte*] on the periphery from which one gazes at what defies illumination. When they see to their horror how logic coils up at these boundaries and finally bites its own tail—suddenly the new form of insight breaks through, *tragic insight,* which, merely to be endured, needs art as a protection and remedy [*als Schutz und Heilmittel*].

If the canny becomes the uncanny and deconstructs itself, the uncanny is also in perpetual danger of becoming Apollonian in a bad sense. Nietzsche also anticipated this moment of reversal. *The Birth of Tragedy* is often erroneously read as granting superior authenticity to the Dionysian, to music, to the irrational, to the formless, which are supposed to be closer to the eternal stream of the underlying universal will. There are passages which seem unequivocally to support such a reading. In fact, however, this error is at crucial moments deconstructed by the text itself. If science is the illusion that seeks to "correct" the abyss, straighten it out, make it solid or rigid, or if science attempts to heal the wound of the abyss, with the suggestion of a sexual absence that must be repaired or filled by some prosthesis, the Apollonian art which intervenes when science fails and recoils in horror from its glimpse of an unfillable, incurable, incorrigible abyss, is no less an illusion than science itself. No less an illusion too is that image of a formless will flowing beneath the forms of both science and of Apollonian beauty. In one extraordinary passage of *The Birth of Tragedy,* the book expresses its own aporia. The terminology of the underlying chaos, of the universal will, "the eternal life beyond all phenomena," on which the book as a whole has been based, the source of the validation of "unconscious Dionysiac wisdom," is rejected as being as much an illusion as the "lies from the features of nature" which are the basis of Apollonian healing and "triumph over the suffering inherent in life." Socratic logic, Apollonian plastic form, and Dionysian music—all three are illusions, and Nietzsche's book becomes itself a *mise en abyme,* the self-subversion of the distinctions on which it seems to be solidly founded. If all three of these "panaceas" are illusions, what then is the will, the "insatiable will" which the passage posits in order to define all veils of the will as illusions? Is it not an illusion too, the third or Buddhistic illusion that the stream flows on beneath all phenomena? The passage, one can see, destroys its own terminology:

It is an eternal phenomenon: the insatiable will always finds a way [*ein Mittel*] to detain its creatures in life and compel them to live on, by means of an illusion spread over things. One is chained by the Socratic love of knowledge and the delusion of being able thereby to heal the eternal wound of existence [*die ewige Wunde des Daseins heilen zu können*]; another is ensnared by art's seductive veil of beauty fluttering before his eyes; still another by the metaphysical comfort that beneath the whirl of phenomena eternal life flows on indestructibly—to say nothing of the more vulgar and almost more powerful illusions which the will always has at hand. These three stages of illusion are actually designed only for the more nobly formed natures, who actually feel profoundly the weight and burden of existence, and must be deluded by exquisite stimulants [*ausgesuchte Reizmittel*] into forgetfulness of their displeasure [*Unlust*]. All that we call culture is made up of these stimulants: and, according to the proportion of the ingredients, we have either a dominantly *Socratic* or *artistic* or *tragic* culture; or, if historical exemplifications are permitted, there is either an Alexandrian or a Hellenic or a Buddhistic culture.

The *mise en abyme* of uncanny criticism, for example in the passage by Nietzsche just cited or in those present-day critics of the uncanny I have discussed, is not the abyss itself in the sense of some direct representation of the truth of things, as Dionysian music may seem to be in *The Birth of Tragedy*. There is no "truth of things," as such, to be represented. The *mise en abyme* of uncanny criticism is rather the ordering of the abyss, the blank, *cent blancs*, its formulation in one or another terminology or figure. Any such formulation, whether it is called "the Dionysian," "the uncanny," "allegory," "*la dissémination*," "the aporia," "*la différance*," "decentering," "deconstruction," "double bind," "cure," "*mise en abyme*," "transumption," "the voice of the shuttle," "signature," or whatever, can quickly become, like any other critical word, a dead terminology able to be coldly manipulated by epigones, mere leaves covering the ground rather than a means of insight into it. The critics of the uncanny must be exceedingly nimble, as de Man, Hartman, Derrida, and Bloom in their different ways conspicuously are, in order to keep their insights from becoming pseudo-scientific machines for the unfolding (explication), or dismantling (deconstruction), of literary texts. This uncanny and yet wholly inevitable reversal of the Apollonian into the Dionysian and of the tragic into the Socratic, the Socratic into the tragic again, like a Möbius strip which has two sides but only one side, is the inner drama or warfare of current literary criticism. The task of criticism in the immediate future should be the further exploration, as much by practical essays of interpretation as by theoretical speculation, of this coming and going in quest and in questioning of the ground.

SEMIOLOGY AND RHETORIC (1979)

PAUL DE MAN

In this classic example of deconstructive thinking, de Man performs a series of characteristically deconstructionist double readings. That is, he poses what seem like secure interpretations, and then he shows, deconstructively, that such interpretations are not so secure after all. He sets up the first readings—of an episode in the popular TV sitcom All in the Family *(with its central characters the bigoted Archie Bunker and his kind but dimwitted wife Edith), of a poem by W. B. Yeats, and of a passage from Marcel Proust's* Remembrance of Things Past—*by finding a structuralist binary opposition. The binary oppositions seem to settle all questions by seeing any possibility as one of two opposites defined by their relation to each other. Then, in a series of second readings, he unsettles the secure binary by displacing it with deconstructive multiplicity. He pits the rigors of grammar against the more freely floating artfulness of rhetoric, with grammar corresponding to the thinking of structuralists, and rhetoric—perhaps more loosely—to the thinking of deconstructionists like de Man himself. For example, de Man finds the structuralist opposition between metaphor and metonymy, proposed by Roman Jakobson (see Jakobson's essay on "The Metaphoric and*

Metonymic Poles" in this volume), a binary that cannot hold up through the playfulness of Proust's rhetoric. More largely, de Man is interested not just in questions of rhetoric or, in this case, rhetorical questions, so much as in the way that deconstructive interpretation can lead beyond what deconstructionists see as the oversimplification, the too rigid structure, of binary oppositions, including the binary oppositions that ground structuralist understandings of language, literature, and culture. For de Man, the systematicity of structuralist binary oppositions eventually gives way to the multiplicitous and almost joyous vertigo of rhetoric, tropes, and figurative language.

To judge from various recent publications, the spirit of the times is not blowing in the direction of formalist and intrinsic criticism. We may no longer be hearing too much about relevance but we keep hearing a great deal about reference, about the nonverbal "outside" to which language refers, by which it is conditioned and upon which it acts. The stress falls not so much on the fictional status of literature—a property now perhaps somewhat too easily taken for granted—but on the interplay between these fictions and categories that are said to partake of reality, such as the self, man, society, "the artist, his culture and the human community," as one critic puts it. Hence the emphasis on hybrid texts considered to be partly literary and partly referential, on popular fictions deliberately aimed towards social and psychological gratification, on literary autobiography as a key to the understanding of the self, and so on. We speak as if, with the problems of literary form resolved once and forever, and with the techniques of structural analysis refined to near-perfection, we could now move "beyond formalism" towards the questions that really interest us and reap, at last, the fruits of the ascetic concentration on techniques that prepared us for this decisive step. With the internal law and order of literature well policed, we can now confidently devote ourselves to the foreign affairs, the external politics of literature. Not only do we feel able to do so, but we owe it to ourselves to take this step: our moral conscience would not allow us to do otherwise. Behind the assurance that valid interpretation is possible, behind the recent interest in writing and reading as potentially effective public speech acts, stands a highly respectable moral imperative that strives to reconcile the internal, formal, private structures of literary language with their external, referential, and public effects.

I want, for the moment, to consider briefly this tendency in itself, as an undeniable and recurrent historical fact, without regard for its truth or falseness or for its value as desirable or pernicious. It is a fact that this sort of thing happens, again and again, in literary studies. On the one hand, literature cannot merely be received as a definite unit of referential meaning that can be decoded without leaving a residue. The code is unusually conspicuous, complex, and enigmatic; it attracts an inordinate amount of attention to itself, and this attention has to acquire the rigor of a method. The structural moment of concentration on the code for its own sake cannot be avoided, and literature necessarily breeds its own formalism. Technical innovations in the methodical study of literature only occur when this kind of attention predominates. It can legitimately be said, for example, that, from a technical point of view, very little has happened in American criticism since the innovative works of New Criticism. There certainly have been numerous excellent books of criticism since, but in none of them have the techniques of description and interpretation evolved beyond the techniques of close reading established in the thirties and the forties. Formalism, it seems, is an all-absorbing and tyrannical muse; the hope that one can be at the same time technically original and discursively eloquent is not borne out by the history of literary criticism.

On the other hand—and this is the real mystery—no literary formalism, no matter how accurate and enriching in its analytic powers, is ever allowed to come into being without seeming reductive. When form is considered to be the external trappings of literary meaning or content, it seems superficial and expendable. The development of intrinsic, formalist criticism in the twentieth century has changed this model: form is now a solipsistic category of self-reflection, and the referential meaning is said to be extrinsic. The polarities of inside and outside have been reversed, but they are still the same polarities that are at play: internal meaning has become outside reference, and the outer form has become the intrinsic structure. A new version of reductiveness at once follows this reversal: formalism nowadays is mostly described in an imagery of imprisonment and claustrophobia: the "prison house of language," "the impasse of formalist criticism," etc. Like the grandmother in Proust's novel ceaselessly driving the young Marcel out into the garden, away from the unhealthy inwardness of his closeted reading, critics cry out for the fresh air of referential meaning. Thus, with the structure of the code so opaque, but the meaning so anxious to blot out the obstacle of form, no wonder that the reconciliation of form and meaning would be so attractive. The attraction of reconciliation is the elective breeding-ground of false models and metaphors; it accounts for the metaphorical model of literature as a kind of box that separates an inside from an outside, and the reader or critic as the person who opens the lid in order to release in the open what was secreted but inaccessible inside. It matters little whether we call the inside of the box the content or the form, the outside the meaning or the appearance. The recurrent debate opposing intrinsic to extrinsic criticism stands under the aegis of an inside/ outside metaphor that is never being seriously questioned.

Metaphors are much more tenacious than facts, and I certainly don't expect to dislodge this age-old model in one short try. I merely wish to speculate on a different set of terms, perhaps less simple in their differential relationships than the strictly polar, binary opposition between inside and outside and therefore less likely to enter into the easy play of chiasmic reversals. I derive these terms (which are as old as the hills) pragmatically from the observation of developments and debates in recent critical methodology.

One of the most controversial among these developments coincides with a new approach to poetics or, as it is called in Germany, poetology, as a branch of general semiotics. In France, a semiology of literature comes about as the outcome of the long-deferred but all the more explosive encounter of the nimble French literary mind with the category of form. Semiology, as opposed to semantics, is the science or study of signs as signifiers; it does not ask what words mean but how they mean. Unlike American New Criticism, which derived the internalization of form from the practice of highly self-conscious modern writers, French semiology turned to linguistics for its model and adopted Saussure and Jakobson rather than Valéry or Proust for its masters. By an awareness of the arbitrariness of the sign (Saussure) and of literature as an autotelic statement "focused on the way it is expressed" (Jakobson) the entire question of meaning can be bracketed, thus freeing the critical discourse from the debilitating burden of paraphrase. The demystifying power of semiology, within the context of French historical and thematic criticism, has been considerable. It demonstrated that the perception of the literary dimensions of language is largely obscured if one submits uncritically to the authority of reference. It also revealed how tenaciously this authority continues to assert itself in a variety of disguises, ranging from the crudest ideology to the most refined forms of aesthetic and ethical judgment. It especially explodes the myth of semantic correspondence between sign and referent, the wishful hope of having it both ways, of being, to paraphrase Marx in the German Ideology, a formalist critic in the morning and a communal moralist in the afternoon, of serving both the technique of form and the substance of meaning. The results, in the practice of French criticism, have been as fruitful as they are irreversible. Perhaps for the first time since the late eighteenth century, French critics can come at least somewhat closer to the kind of linguistic awareness that never ceased to be operative in its poets and novelists and that forced all of them, including Sainte Beuve, to write their main works "contre Sainte Beuve." The distance was never so considerable in England and the United States, which does not mean, however, that we may be able, in this country, to dispense altogether with some preventative semiological hygiene.

One of the most striking characteristics of literary semiology as it is practiced today, in France and elsewhere, is the use of grammatical (especially syntactical) structures conjointly with rhetorical structures, without apparent awareness of a possible discrepancy between them. In their literary analyses, Barthes, Genette, Todorov, Greimas, and their disciples all simplify and regress from Jakobson in letting grammar and rhetoric function in perfect continuity, and in passing from grammatical to rhetorical structures without difficulty or interruption. Indeed, as the study of grammatical structures is refined in contemporary theories of generative, transformational, and distributive grammar, the study of tropes and of figures (which is how the term *rhetoric* is used here, and not in the derived sense of comment or of eloquence or persuasion) becomes a mere extension of grammatical models, a particular subset of syntactical relations. In the recent *Dictionnaire encyclopédique des sciences du langage*, Ducrot and Todorov write that rhetoric has always been satisfied with a paradigmatic view over words (words substituting for each other), without questioning their syntagmatic relationship (the contiguity of words to each other). There ought to be another perspective, complementary to the first, in which metaphor, for example, would not be defined as a substitution but as a particular type of combination. Research inspired by linguistics or, more narrowly, by syntactical studies, has begun to reveal this possibility—but it remains to be explored. Todorov, who calls one of his books a *Grammar of the Decameron*, rightly thinks of his own work and that of his associates as first explorations in the elaboration of a systematic grammar of literary modes, genres, and also of literary figures. Perhaps the most perceptive work to come out of this school, Genette's studies of figural modes, can be shown to be assimilations of rhetorical transformations or combinations to syntactical, grammatical patterns. Thus a recent study, now printed in *Figures III* and entitled *Metaphor and Metonymy in Proust*, shows the combined presence, in a wide and astute selection of passages, of paradigmatic, metaphorical figures with syntagmatic, metonymic structures. The combination of both is treated descriptively and nondialectically without considering the possibility of logical tensions.

One can ask whether this reduction of figure to grammar is legitimate. The existence of grammatical structures, within and beyond the unit of the sentence, in literary texts is undeniable, and their description and classification are indispensable. The question remains if and how figures of rhetoric can be included in such a taxonomy. This question is at the core of the debate going on, in a wide variety of apparently unrelated forms, in contemporary poetics. But the historical picture of contemporary criticism is too confused to make the mapping out of such a topography a useful exercise. Not only are these questions mixed in and mixed up within particular groups or local trends, but they are often co-present, without apparent contradiction, within the work of a single author.

Neither is the theory of the question suitable for quick expository treatment. To distinguish the epistemology of grammar from the epistemology of rhetoric is a redoubtable task. On an entirely naïve level, we tend to conceive of grammatical systems as tending towards universality and as simply generative, i.e., as capable of deriving an infinity of versions from a single model (that may govern transformations as well as derivations) without the intervention of another model that would upset the first. We therefore think of the relationship between grammar and logic, the passage from grammar to propositions, as being relatively unproblematic: no true propositions are conceivable in the absence of grammatical consistency or of controlled deviation from a system of consistency no matter how complex. Grammar and logic stand to each other in a dyadic relationship of unsubverted support. In a logic of acts rather than of statements, as in Austin's theory of speech acts, that has had such a strong influence on recent American work in literary semiology, it is also possible to move between speech acts and grammar without difficulty. The performance of what is called illocutionary acts such as ordering, questioning, denying, assuming, etc., within the language is congruent with the grammatical structures of syntax in the corresponding imperative, interrogative, negative, optative sentences. "The rules for illocutionary acts," writes Richard Ohman in a recent paper, "determine whether performance of a given act is well-executed, in just the same way as *grammatical* rules determine whether the product of a locutionary act—a sentence—is well formed. . . . But whereas the rules of grammar concern the relationships among sound, syntax, and meaning, the rules of illocutionary acts concern relationships among people."[1] And since rhetoric is then conceived exclusively as persuasion, as actual action upon others (and not as an intralinguistic figure or trope), the continuity between the illocutionary realm of grammar and the perlocutionary realm of rhetoric is self-evident. It becomes the basis for a new rhetoric that, exactly as is the case for Todorov and Genette, would also be a new grammar.

Without engaging the substance of the question, it can be pointed out, without having to go beyond recent and American examples, and without calling upon the strength of an age-old tradition, that the continuity here assumed between grammar and rhetoric is not borne out by theoretical and philosophical speculation. Kenneth Burke mentions *deflection* (which he compares structurally to Freudian displacement), defined as "any slight bias or even unintended error," as the rhetorical basis of language, and deflection is then conceived as a dialectical subversion of the consistent link between sign and meaning that operates within grammatical patterns; hence Burke's well-known insistence on the distinction between grammar and rhetoric. Charles Sanders Peirce, who, with Nietzsche and Saussure, laid the philosophical foundation for modern semiology, stressed the distinction between grammar and rhetoric in his celebrated and so suggestively unfathomable definition of the sign. He insists, as is well known, on the necessary presence of a third element, called the interpretant, within any relationship that the sign entertains with its object. The sign is to be interpreted if we are to understand the idea it is to convey, and this is so because the sign is not the thing but a meaning derived from the thing by a process here called representation that is not simply generative, i.e., dependent on a univocal origin. The interpretation of the sign is not, for Peirce, a meaning but another sign; it is a reading, not a decodage, and this reading has, in its turn, to be interpreted into another sign, and so on *ad infinitum*. Peirce calls this process by means of which "one sign gives birth to another" pure rhetoric, as distinguished from pure grammar, which postulates the possibility of unproblematic, dyadic meaning, and pure logic, which postulates the possibility of the universal truth of meanings. Only if the sign engendered meaning in the same way that the object engenders the sign, that is, by representation, would there be no need to distinguish between grammar and rhetoric.

These remarks should indicate at least the existence and the difficulty of the question, a difficulty which puts its concise theoretical exposition beyond my powers. I must retreat therefore into a pragmatic discourse and try to illustrate the tension between grammar and rhetoric in a few specific textual examples. Let me begin by considering what is perhaps the most commonly known instance of an apparent symbiosis between a grammatical and a rhetorical structure, the so-called rhetorical question, in which the figure is conveyed directly by means of a syntactical device. I take the first example from the sub-literature of the mass media: asked by his wife whether he wants to have his bowling shoes laced over or laced under, Archie Bunker answers with a question: "What's the difference?" Being a reader of sublime simplicity, his wife replies by patiently explaining the difference between lacing over and lacing under, whatever this may be, but provokes only ire. "What's the difference" did not ask for difference but means instead "I don't give a damn what the difference is." The same grammatical pattern engenders two meanings that are mutually exclusive: the literal meaning asks for the concept (difference) whose existence is denied by the figurative meaning. As long as we are talking about bowling shoes, the consequences are relatively trivial; Archie Bunker, who is a great believer in the authority of origins (as long, of course, as they are the right origins) muddles along in a world where literal and figurative meaning get in each other's way, though not without discomforts. But suppose that it is a *de*-bunker rather than a "Bunker," and a de-bunker of the arche (or origin), an archie De-bunker such as Nietzsche or Jacques Derrida for instance, who asks the question "What is the Difference"—and we cannot even tell from his grammar whether he "really" wants to know "what" difference is or is just telling us that we shouldn't even try to find out. Confronted with the question of the difference between grammar and rhetoric, grammar allows us to ask the question, but the sentence by means of which we ask it may deny the very possibility of asking. For what is the use of asking, I ask, when we cannot even authoritatively decide whether a question asks or doesn't ask?

The point is as follows. A perfectly clear syntactical paradigm (the question) engenders a sentence that has at least two meanings, of which the one asserts and the other denies its own illocutionary mode. It is not so that there are simply two meanings, one literal and the other figural, and that we have to decide which one of these meanings is the right one in this particular situation. The confusion can only be cleared up by the intervention of an extra-textual intention, such as Archie Bunker putting his wife straight; but the very anger he displays is indicative of more than impatience; it reveals his despair when confronted with a structure of linguistic meaning that he cannot control and that holds the discouraging prospect of an infinity of similar future confusions, all of them potentially catastrophic in their consequences. Nor is this intervention really a part of the mini-text constituted by the figure which holds our attention only as long as it remains suspended and unresolved. I follow the usage of common speech in calling this semiological enigma "rhetorical." The grammatical model of the question becomes rhetorical not when we have, on the one hand, a literal meaning and on the other hand a figural meaning, but when it is impossible to decide by grammatical or other linguistic devices which of the two meanings (that can be entirely incompatible)prevails. Rhetoric radically suspends logic and opens up vertiginous possibilities of referential aberration. And although it would perhaps be somewhat more remote from common usage, I would not hesitate to equate the rhetorical, figural potentiality of language with literature itself. I could point to a great number of antecedents to this equation of literature with figure; the most recent reference would be to Monroe Beardsley's insistence in his contribution to the *Essays* to honor William Wimsatt, that literary language is characterized by being "distinctly above the norm in ratio of implicit [or, I would say rhetorical] to explicit meaning."[2]

Let me pursue the matter of the rhetorical question through one more example. Yeats's poem "Among School Children" ends with the famous line: "How can we know the dancer from the dance?" Although there are some revealing inconsistencies within the commentaries, the line is usually interpreted as stating, with the increased emphasis of a rhetorical device, the potential unity between form and experience, between creator and creation. It could be said that it denies the discrepancy between the sign and the referent from which we started out. Many elements in the imagery and the dramatic development of the poem strengthen this traditional reading; without having to look any further than the immediately preceding lines, one finds powerful and consecrated images of the continuity from part to whole that makes synecdoche into the most seductive of metaphors: the organic beauty of the tree, stated in the parallel syntax of a similar rhetorical question, or the convergence, in the dance, of erotic desire with musical form:

> O chestnut-tree, great-rooted blossomer,
> Are you the leaf, the blossom or the bole?
> O body swayed to music, O brightening glance,
> How can we know the dancer from the dance?

A more extended reading, always assuming that the final line is to be read as a rhetorical question, reveals that the thematic and rhetorical grammar of the poem yields a consistent reading that extends from the first line to the last and that can account for all the details in the text. It is equally possible, however, to read the last line literally rather than figuratively, as asking with some urgency the question we asked earlier within the context of contemporary criticism: *not* that sign and referent are so exquisitely fitted to each other that all difference between them is at times blotted out but, rather, since the two essentially different elements, sign and meaning, are so intricately intertwined in the imagined "presence" that the poem addresses, how can we possibly make the distinctions that would shelter us from the error of identifying what cannot be identified? The clumsiness of the paraphrase reveals that it is not necessarily the literal reading which is simpler than the figurative one, as was the case in our first example; here, the figural reading, which assumes the question to be rhetorical, is perhaps naïve, whereas the literal reading leads to greater complication of theme and statement. For it turns out that the entire scheme set up by the first reading can be undermined, or deconstructed, in the terms of the second, in which the final line is read literally as meaning that, since the dancer and the dance are not the same, it might be useful, perhaps even desperately necessary—for the question can be given a ring of urgency, "Please tell me, how *can* I know the dancer from the dance"—to tell them apart. But this will replace the reading of each symbolic detail by a divergent interpretation. The oneness of trunk, leaf, and blossom, for example, that would have appealed to Goethe, would find itself replaced by the much less reassuring Tree of Life from the Mabinogion that appears in the poem "Vacillation," in which the fiery blossom and the earthly leaf are held together, as well as apart, by the crucified and castrated God Attis, of whose body it can hardly be said that it is "not bruised to pleasure soul." This hint should suffice to suggest that two entirely coherent but entirely incompatible readings can be made to hinge on one line, whose grammatical structure is devoid of ambiguity, but whose rhetorical mode turns the mood as well as the mode of the entire poem upside down. Neither can we say, as was already the case in the first example, that the poem simply has two meanings that exist side by side. The two readings have to engage each other in direct confrontation, for the one reading is precisely the error denounced by the other and has to be undone by it. Nor can we in any way make a valid decision as to which of the readings can be given priority over the other; none can exist in the other's absence. There can be no dance without a dancer, no sign without a referent. On the other hand, the authority of the meaning engendered by the grammatical structure is fully obscured by the duplicity of a figure that cries out for the differentiation that it conceals.

Yeats's poem is not explicitly "about" rhetorical questions but about images or metaphors, and about the possibility of convergence between experiences of consciousness such as memory or emotions—what the poem calls passion, piety, and affection—and entities accessible to the senses such as bodies, persons, or icons. We return to the inside/outside model from which we started out and which the poem puts into question by means of a syntactical device (the question) made to operate on a grammatical as well as on a rhetorical level. The couple grammar/rhetoric, certainly not a binary opposition since they in no way exclude each other, disrupts and confuses the neat antithesis of the inside/outside pattern. We can transfer this scheme to the act of reading and interpretation. By reading we get, as we say, *inside* a text that was first something alien to us and which we now make our own by an act of understanding. But this understanding becomes at once the representation of an extra-textual meaning; in Austin's terms, the illocutionary speech act becomes a perlocutionary actual act—in Frege's terms, *Bedeutung* becomes *Sinn*. Our recurrent question is whether this transformation is semantically controlled along grammatical or along rhetorical lines. Does the metaphor of reading really unite outer meaning with inner understanding, action with reflection, into one single totality? The assertion is powerfully and suggestively made in a passage from Proust that describes the experience of reading as such a union. It describes the young Marcel, near the beginning of Combray, hiding in the closed space of his room in order to read. The example differs from the earlier ones in that we are not dealing with a grammatical structure that also functions rhetorically but have instead the representation, the dramatization, in terms of the experience of a subject, of a rhetorical structure—just as, in many other passages, Proust dramatizes tropes by means of landscapes or descriptions of objects. The figure here dramatized is that of metaphor, an inside/outside correspondence as represented by the act of reading. The reading scene is the culmination of a series of actions taking place in enclosed spaces and leading up to the "dark coolness" of Marcel's room.

> I had stretched out on my bed, with a book, in my room which sheltered, tremblingly, its transparent and fragile coolness from the afternoon sun, behind the almost closed blinds through which a glimmer of daylight had nevertheless managed to push its yellow wings, remaining motionless between the wood and the glass, in a corner, poised like a butterfly. It was hardly light enough to read, and the sensation of the light's splendor was given me only by the noise of Camus...hammering dusty crates; resounding in the sonorous atmosphere that is peculiar to hot weather, they seemed to spark off scarlet stars; and also by the flies executing their little concert, the chamber music of summer: evocative not in the manner of a human tune that, heard perchance during the summer, afterwards reminds you of it but connected to summer by a more necessary link; born from beautiful days, resurrecting only when they return, containing some of their essence, it does not only awaken their image in our memory; it guarantees their return, their actual, persistent, unmediated presence.
>
> The dark coolness of my room related to the full sunlight of the street as the shadow relates to the ray of light, that is to say it was just as luminous and it gave my imagination the total spectacle of the summer, whereas my senses, if I had been on a walk, could only have enjoyed it by fragments; it matched my repose which (thanks to the adventures told by my book and stirring my tranquility) supported, like the quiet of a motionless hand in the middle of a running brook the shock and the motion of a torrent of activity. [*Swann's Way.* Paris: Pléiade, 1954, p. 83.]

For our present purpose, the most striking aspect of this passage is the juxtaposition of figural and metafigural language. It contains seductive metaphors that bring into play a variety of irresistible objects: chamber music, butterflies, stars, books, running brooks, etc., and it inscribes these objects within dazzling fire- and water-works of figuration. But the passage also comments normatively on the best way to achieve such effects; in this sense, it is metafigural: it writes figuratively about figures. It contrasts two ways of evoking the natural experience of summer and unambiguously states its preference for one of these ways over the other: the "necessary link" that unites the buzzing of the flies to the summer makes it a much more effective symbol than the tune heard "perchance" during the summer. The preference is expressed by means of a distinction that corresponds to the difference between metaphor and metonymy, necessity and chance being a legitimate way to distinguish between analogy and contiguity. The inference of identity and totality that is constitutive of metaphor is lacking in the purely relational metonymic contact: an element of truth is involved in taking Achilles for a lion but none in taking Mr. Ford for a motor car. The passage is *about* the aesthetic superiority of metaphor over metonymy, but this aesthetic claim is made by means of categories that are the ontological ground of the metaphysical system that allows for the aesthetic to come into being as a category. The metaphor for summer (in this case, the synesthesia set off by the "chamber music" of the flies) guarantees a presence which, far from being contingent, is said to be essential, permanently recurrent and unmediated by linguistic representations or figurations. Finally, in the second part of the passage, the metaphor of presence not only appears as the ground of cognition but as the performance of an action, thus promising the reconciliation of the most disruptive of contradictions. By then, the investment in the power of metaphor is such that it may seem sacrilegious to put it in question.

Yet, it takes little perspicacity to show that the text does not practice what it preaches. A rhetorical reading of the passage reveals that the figural praxis and the metafigural theory do not converge and that the assertion of the mastery of metaphor over metonymy owes its persuasive power to the use of metonymic structures. I have carried out such an analysis in a somewhat more extended context (pp. 59–67, below); at this point, we are more concerned with the results than with the procedure. For the metaphysical categories of presence, essence, action, truth, and beauty do not remain unaffected by such a reading. This would become clear from an inclusive reading of Proust's novel or would become even more explicit in a language-conscious philosopher such as Nietzsche who, as a philosopher, has to be concerned with the epistemological consequences of the kind of rhetorical seductions exemplified by the Proust passage. It can be shown that the systematic critique of the main categories of metaphysics undertaken by Nietzsche in his late work, the critique of the concepts of causality, of the subject, of identity, of referential and revealed truth, etc., occurs along the same pattern of deconstruction that was operative in Proust's text; and it can also be shown that this pattern exactly corresponds to Nietzsche's description, in texts that precede *The Will to Power* by more than fifteen years, of the structure of the main rhetorical tropes. The key to this critique of metaphysics, which is itself a recurrent gesture throughout the history of thought, is the rhetorical model of the trope or, if one prefers to call it that, literature. It turns out that in these innocent-looking didactic exercises we are in fact playing for very sizeable stakes.

It is therefore all the more necessary to know what is linguistically involved in a rhetorically conscious reading of the type here undertaken on a brief fragment from a novel and extended by Nietzsche to the entire text of post-Hellenic thought. Our first examples dealing with the rhetorical questions were rhetorizations of grammar, figures generated by syntactical paradigms, whereas the Proust example could be better described as a grammatization of rhetoric. By passing from a paradigmatic structure based on substitution, such as metaphor, to a syntagmatic structure based on contingent association such as metonymy, the mechanical, repetitive aspect of grammatical forms is shown to be operative in a passage that seemed at first sight to celebrate the self-willed and autonomous inventiveness of a subject. Figures are assumed to be inventions, the products of a highly particularized individual talent, whereas no one can claim credit for the programmed pattern of grammar. Yet, our reading of the Proust passage shows that precisely when the highest claims are being made for the unifying power of metaphor, these very images rely in fact on the deceptive use of semi-automatic grammatical patterns. The deconstruction of metaphor and of all rhetorical patterns such as mimesis, paranomasis, or personification that use resemblance as a way to disguise differences, takes us back to the impersonal precision of grammar and of a semiology derived from grammatical patterns. Such a reading puts into question a whole series of concepts that underlie the value judgments of our critical discourse: the metaphors of primacy, of genetic history, and, most notably, of the autonomous power to will of the self.

There seems to be a difference, then, between what I called the rhetorization of grammar (as in the rhetorical question) and the grammatization of rhetoric, as in the readings of the type sketched out in the passage from Proust. The former end up in indetermination, in a suspended uncertainty that was unable to choose between two modes of reading, whereas the latter seems to reach a truth, albeit by the negative road of exposing an error, a false pretense. After the rhetorical reading of the Proust passage, we can no longer believe the assertion made in this passage about the intrinsic, metaphysical superiority of metaphor over metonymy. We seem to end up in a mood of negative assurance that is highly productive of critical discourse. The further text of Proust's novel, for example, responds perfectly to an extended application of this pattern: not only can similar gestures be repeated throughout the novel, at all the crucial articulations or all passages where large aesthetic and metaphysical claims are being made—the scenes of involuntary memory, the workshop of Elstir, the septette of Vinteuil, the convergence of author and narrator at the end of the novel—but a vast thematic and semiotic network is revealed that structures the entire narrative and that remained invisible to a reader caught in naïve metaphorical mystification. The whole of literature would respond in similar fashion, although the techniques and the patterns would have to vary considerably, of course, from author to author. But there is absolutely no reason why analyses of the kind here suggested for Proust would not be applicable, with proper modifications of technique, to Milton or to Dante or to Hölderlin. This will in fact be the task of literary criticism in the coming years.

It would seem that we are saying that criticism is the deconstruction of literature, the reduction to the rigors of grammar of rhetorical mystifications. And if we hold up Nietzsche as the philosopher of such a critical deconstruction, then the literary critic would become the philosopher's ally in his struggle with the poets. Criticism and literature would separate around the epistemological axis that distinguishes grammar from rhetoric. It is easy enough to see that this apparent glorification of the critic-philosopher in the name of truth is in fact a glorification of the poet as the primary source of this truth; if truth is the recognition of the systematic character of a certain kind of error, then it would be fully dependent on the prior existence of this error. Philosophers of science like Bachelard or Wittgenstein are notoriously dependent on the aberrations of the poets. We are back at our unanswered question: does the grammatization of rhetoric end up in negative certainty or does it, like the rhetorization of grammar, remain suspended in the ignorance of its own truth or falsehood?

Two concluding remarks should suffice to answer the question. First of all, it is not true that Proust's text can simply be reduced to the mystified assertion (the superiority of metaphor over metonymy) that our reading deconstructs. The reading is not "our" reading, since it uses only the linguistic elements provided by the text itself; the distinction between author and reader is one of the false distinctions that the reading makes evident. The deconstruction is not something we have added to the text but it constituted the text in the first place. A literary text simultaneously asserts and denies the authority of its own rhetorical mode, and by reading the text as we did we were only trying to come closer to being as rigorous a reader as the author had to be in order to write the sentence in the first place. Poetic writing is the most advanced and refined mode of deconstruction; it may differ from critical or discursive writing in the economy of its articulation, but not in kind.

But if we recognize the existence of such a moment as constitutive of all literary language, we have surreptitiously reintroduced the categories that this deconstruction was supposed to eliminate and that have merely been displaced. We have, for example, displaced the question of the self from the referent into the figure of the narrator, who then becomes the *signifié* of the passage. It becomes again possible to ask such naïve questions as what Proust's, or Marcel's, motives may have been in thus manipulating language: was he fooling himself, or was he represented as fooling himself and fooling us into believing that fiction and action are as easy to unite, by reading, as the passage asserts? The pathos of the entire section, which would have been more noticeable if the quotation had been a little more extended, the constant vacillation of the narrator between guilt and well-being, invites such questions. They are absurd questions, of course, since the reconciliation of fact and fiction occurs itself as a mere assertion made in a text, and is thus productive of more text at the moment when it asserts its decision to escape from textual confinement. But even if we free ourselves of all false questions of intent and rightfully reduce the narrator to the status of a mere grammatical pronoun, without which the narrative could not come into being, this subject remains endowed with a function that is not grammatical but rhetorical, in that it gives voice, so to speak, to a grammatical syntagm. The term *voice*, even when used in a grammatical terminology as when we speak of the passive or interrogative voice, is, of course, a metaphor inferring by analogy the intent of the subject from the structure of the predicate. In the case of the deconstructive discourse that we call literary, or rhetorical, or poetic, this creates a distinctive complication illustrated by the Proust passage. The reading revealed a first paradox: the passage valorizes metaphor as being the "right" literary figure, but then proceeds to constitute itself by means of the epistemologically incompatible figure of metonymy. The critical discourse reveals the presence of this delusion and affirms it as the irreversible mode of its truth. It cannot pause there however. For if we then ask the obvious and simple next question, whether the rhetorical mode of the text in question is that of metaphor or metonymy, it is impossible to give an answer. Individual metaphors, such as the chiaroscuro effect or the butterfly, are shown to be subordinate figures in a general clause whose syntax is metonymic; from this point of view, it seems that the rhetoric is superseded by a grammar that deconstructs it. But this metonymic clause has as its subject a voice whose relationship to this clause is again metaphorical. The narrator who tells us about the impossibility of metaphor is himself, or itself, a metaphor, the metaphor of a grammatical syntagm whose meaning is the denial of metaphor stated, by antiphrasis, as its priority. And this subject-metaphor is, in its turn, open to the kind of deconstruction to the second degree, the rhetorical deconstruction of psycholinguistics, in which the more advanced investigations of literature are presently engaged, against considerable resistance.

We end up therefore, in the case of the rhetorical grammatization of semiology, just as in the grammatical rhetorization of illocutionary phrases, in the same state of suspended ignorance. Any question about the rhetorical mode of a literary text is always a rhetorical question which does not even know whether it is really questioning. The resulting pathos is an anxiety (or bliss, depending on one's momentary mood or individual temperament) of ignorance, not an anxiety of reference—as becomes thematically clear in Proust's novel when reading is dramatized, in the relationship between Marcel and Albertine, not as an emotive reaction to what language does, but as an emotive reaction to the impossibility of knowing what it might be up to. Literature as well as criticism—the difference between them being delusive—is condemned (or privileged) to be forever the most rigorous and, consequently, the most unreliable language in terms of which man names and transforms himself.

NOTES

1. "Speech, Literature, and the Space in Between," *New Literary History* 4 (Autumn 1972): 50.
2. "The Concept of Literature," in *Literary Theory and Structure: Essays in Honor of William K. Wimsatt*, ed. Frank Brady, John Palmer, and Martin Price (New Haven, 1973), p. 37.

ESSENTIALISM IN THE CLASSROOM (1989)

DIANA FUSS

In this essay, the final chapter of her Essentially Speaking: Feminism, Nature and Difference, *Fuss considers the conflict between essentialism and constructionism. To essentialists, we experience the world and then apply language to describe what we find. To constructionists, we construct the world through language, and we cannot conceptualize experience apart from the way our language shapes it. Thus to essentialists, our experience of certain objects, ideas, or identities (race, gender, sexual orientation, ethnicity, nationality, and so on) has an essence, an underlying truth that remains consistent across time. But to constructionists, sometimes called anti-essentialists, our experience of such things changes across times and perspectives; it is a construction, not an essence. To essentialists, facts are sure things, consistent and stable, while to constructionists, we construct variables as facts and suppose they are stable only if we overlook how they change according to the way we see them. Like many poststructuralists, Fuss looks with suspicion on arguments based on experience, such as arguments that begin with a phrase like "As a woman, I think" this or "As a Latina, I think" that, because she sees the experience of women or Latinas as varying from one woman and Latina to another, rather than as consistent for all women and Latinas.*

For a related discussion, see the selection in this volume by Toril Moi. For a response to Fuss, see bell hooks, "Essentialism and Experience," also in this volume.

(When Fuss uses the term normative *in her last paragraph, it does not mean* normal. *It means based on standards, also called norms.)*

Nowhere are the related issues of essence, identity, and experience so highly charged and so deeply politicized as they are in the classroom. Personal consciousness, individual oppressions, lived experience—in short, identity politics—operate in the classroom both to authorize and to de-authorize speech. "Experience" emerges as the essential truth of the individual subject, and personal "identity" metamorphoses into knowledge. Who we are becomes what we know; ontology shades into epistemology. In this final chapter I am primarily concerned with the way in which essence circulates as a privileged signifier in the classroom, usually under the guise of "the authority of experience." Exactly what counts as "experience," and should we defer to it in pedagogical situations? Does experience of oppression confer special jurisdiction over the right to speak about that oppression? Can we only speak, ultimately, from the so-called "truth" of our experiences, or are all empirical ways of knowing analytically suspect? Finally, what is the pedagogical status of empiricism in the age of what Alice Jardine labels "the demise of Experience"? (1985, 145–55) How are we to handle our students' (and perhaps our own) daily appeals to experiential knowledge when, with the advent of poststructuralist thought, experience has been placed so convincingly under erasure?

These questions often appear particularly irresolvable and especially frustrating to the feminist scholar and teacher who has invested much of her career in the battle to validate "female experience"—in university classrooms, in academic textbooks, in curricular offerings, and even in institutional infrastructures. The category of "female experience" holds a particularly sacrosanct position in Women's Studies programs, programs which often draw on the very notion of a hitherto repressed and devalued female experience to form the basis of a new feminist epistemology. Virtually all the essays in one of the few volumes devoted entirely to questions of feminist pedagogy, *Gendered Subjects: The Dynamics of Feminist Teaching* (Culley and Portuges 1985), uphold experience as the essential difference of the Women's Studies classroom.[1] But the problem with positing the category of experience as the basis of a feminist pedagogy is that the very object of our inquiry, "female experience," is never as unified, as knowable, as universal, and as stable as we presume it to be. This is why some feminist philosophers recommend resisting the temptation to reduce "women's experiences (plural) to women's experience (singular)" (Griffiths and Whitford 1988, 6). Certainly, Derrida is right to suggest that "egoity is the absolute form of experience" ("Violence and Metaphysics" 1978, 133), but while experience may be underwritten by a metaphysics of presence, this does not mean experience is necessarily present to us—in the form of an unmediated real. The appeal to experience, as the ultimate test of all knowledge, merely subtends the subject in its fantasy of autonomy and control. Belief in the truth of Experience is as much an ideological production as belief in the experience of Truth.

In theories of feminist pedagogy, the category of natural female experience is often held against (and posited as a corrective to) the category of imposed masculinist ideology. The experience/ideology opposition, however, simply masks the way in which experience itself is ideologically cast. One thinks immediately of Louis Althusser:

> When we speak of ideology we should know that ideology slides into all human activity, that it is identical with the "lived" experience of human existence itself.... This "lived experience" is not a *given,* given by a pure "reality", but the spontaneous "lived experience" of ideology in its peculiar relationship to the real. ("A Letter on Art in Reply to André Daspre" 1971, 223)

In the classical, Aristotelian view, experience is the doorway to the apprehension of essence; experience is understood as a real and immediate presence and therefore as a reliable means of knowing. In the poststructuralist, Althusserian view, experience is a product of ideology. It is a sign mediated by other signs. To Jonathan Culler, experience is fundamentally unreliable because it maintains a duplicitous standing: "it has always already occurred and yet is still to be produced—an indispensable point of reference, yet never simply there" (1982, 63). Though it is the latter view of experience which this book explicitly endorses, it is the former view, the "common-sense" Aristotelian understanding of experience, which we all carry into the classroom with us and which constitutes the grounds of a "politics of experience." While it may not always be the case that identity politics is reactionary,[2] arguments based on the authority of experience can often have surprisingly de-politicizing effects. The ideology and effects of the politics of experience are therefore particularly important to confront in the institutional classroom setting, where identities can often seem more rigidified, politics more personalized, and past histories more intensified. This final chapter is concerned with some of the unwelcome effects of essentialism in the classroom, and with the pedagogy and politics of "essentially speaking."

Problems often begin in the classroom when those "in the know" commerce only with others "in the know," excluding and marginalizing those perceived to be outside the magic circle. The circle metaphor is Edward Said's: "inside the circle stand the blameless, the just, the omnicompetent, those who know the truth about themselves as well as the others: outside the circle stand a miscellaneous bunch of querulous whining complainers" ("Intellectuals in the Post-Colonial World" 1986, 50). Said provides the most incisive and compelling critique that I know of the phenomenon which I sometimes call "inside trading." (The economic metaphor is, of course, a calculated one; in the classroom identities are nothing if not commodities.) For Said it is both dangerous and misleading to base an identity politics upon rigid theories of exclusions, "exclusions that stipulate, for instance, only women can understand feminine experience, only Jews can understand Jewish suffering, only formerly colonial subjects can understand colonial experience" (55). The artificial boundary between insider and outsider necessarily contains rather than disseminates knowledge:

> the difficulties with theories of exclusiveness or with barriers and sides is that once admitted these polarities absolve and forgive a great deal more ignorance and demagogy than they enable knowledge.... If you know in advance that the black or Jewish or

German experience is fundamentally comprehensible only to Jews or Blacks or Germans you first of all posit as essential something which, I believe, is both historical and the result of interpretation—namely the existence of Jewishness, Blackness, or Germanness, or for that matter of Orientalism and Occidentalism. Secondly you are pretty likely to construct defenses of the experience rather than promote knowledge of it. And, as a result, you will demote the different experience of others to a lesser status. (55–56)

Experience, then, while providing some students with a platform from which to speak can also relegate other students to the sidelines. Exclusions of this sort often breed exclusivity.

The politics of experience sometimes takes the form of a tendency amongst both individuals and groups to "one down" each other on the oppression scale. Identities are itemized, appreciated, and ranked on the basis of which identity holds the greatest currency at a particular historical moment and in a particular institutional setting. Thus, in an Afro-American Studies classroom, race and ethnicity are likely to emerge as the privileged items of intellectual exchange, or, in a Gay Studies classroom, sexual "preference" may hold the top notch on the scale of oppressions. This delimiting of boundaries or mapping out of critical terrains is not a problem in and of itself (especially if it allows us to devote serious attention to previously ignored or trivialized issues); however, it becomes a problem when the central category of difference under consideration blinds us to other modes of difference and implicitly delegitimates them. Let me pose an example. Recently a student in a class on postcolonialism objected to another student's interest in the social and structural forms of non-Western homosexual relations; "what on earth does sexual preference have to do with imperialism?" the angry student charged. The class as a whole had no immediate response to the indictment and so we returned to the "real" issue at hand (race and ethnicity); the gay student was effectively silenced. Another common version of this phenomenon is the synecdochical tendency to see only one part of a subject's identity (usually the most visible part) and to make that part stand for the whole. A male professor, for example, is typically reduced to his "maleness,"an Asian professor to his or her "Asianness," a lesbian professor to her "lesbianness," and so on. A hierarchy of identities is set up *within* each speaking subject (not just between subjects), and it is this ranking of identities which is often used either to authorize an individual to speak on the basis of the truth of her lived experience (as in the case of a female professor in a Women's Studies classroom) or to de-authorize an individual from speaking on the basis of his *lack* of experience (as in the case of a male professor in a Women's Studies classroom). Identities are treated as fixed, accessible, and determinative, conferring upon the subject's speech an aura of predictability ("Male professors *always* say such things" or "*No* Third World writer would ever make such a claim" are often common refrains). What we see in this ordering of identities is none other than the paradoxical and questionable assumption that some essences are more *essential* than others.

It is the unspoken law of the classroom not to trust those who cannot cite experience as the indisputable grounds of their knowledge. Such unwritten laws pose perhaps the most serious threat to classroom dynamics in that they breed suspicion amongst those inside the circle and guilt (sometimes anger) amongst those outside the circle. In its most extreme incarnation, the guilt of the outsiders is exploited by the insiders to keep everyone in line—that is, to regulate and to police group behavior. "Provoking guilt is a tactic not so much for informing as it is for controlling others," Anne Koedt has written in challenging the notion of "lesbians-as-the-vanguard-of-feminism" ("Lesbianism and Feminism," Koedt et al. 1973, 256). When provoking guilt in "the enemy" becomes the prime motivation for one's politics, we have to begin to question what negative effects such a project might possibly have, especially in the classroom. The tendency to psychologize and to personalize questions of oppression, *at the expense of* strong materialist analyses of the structural and institutional bases of exploitation, poses one such undesirable effect. As we have seen, contrary to the well-worn feminist dictum, "the personal is political," personalizing exploitation can often amount to de-politicizing it:

> Power then becomes primarily a personal issue between individuals—men and women, white and black, gentile and Jew, heterosexual and gay—and not the way an exploitative system is hierarchically structured so as to get maximum differentiation. (Bourne 1987, 14)

We have to be willing to acknowledge, along with Simon Watney, that "the politics of provocation are comprehensible only to the provocateurs" (1980, 72). We have to be willing to recognize that when identity politics is used to monitor who can and cannot speak in the classroom, its effects can be counterproductive. Rather than automatically interjecting a political note, arguments based on the authority of experience can just as often be radically de-politicizing.

Though I remain convinced that appeals to the authority of experience rarely advance discussion and frequently provoke confusion (I am always struck by the way in which introjections of experiential truths into classroom debates dead-end the discussion), I also remain wary of any attempts to prohibit the introduction of personal histories into such discussions on the grounds that they have yet to be adequately "theorized." The anti-essentialist displacement of experience must not be used as a convenient means of silencing students, no matter how shaky experience has proven to be as a basis of episte-mology. It is certainly true that there is no such thing as "the female experience" or "the Black experience" or "the Jewish experience".... And it seems likely that simply *being* a woman, or a Black, or a Jew (as if "being" were ever "simple") is not enough to qualify one as an official spokesperson for an entire community. But while truth clearly does not equate with experience, it cannot be denied that it is precisely the fiction that they *are* the same which prompts many students, who would not perhaps speak otherwise, to enter energetically into those debates they perceive as pertaining directly to them. The authority of experience, in other words, not only works to silence students, it also works to empower them. How are we to negotiate the gap between the conservative fiction of experience as the ground of all truth-knowledge and the immense power of this fiction to enable and encourage student participation?

While experience can never be a reliable guide to the real, this is not to preclude any role at all for experience in the realm of knowledge production. If experience is itself a product of ideological practices, as Althusser insists, then perhaps it might function as a window onto the complicated workings of ideology. Experience would itself then become "evidence" of a sort for the productions of ideology, but evidence which is obviously constructed and clearly knowledge-dependent. What I mean by this is simply that experience is not the raw material knowledge seeks to understand, but rather knowledge is the active process which produces its own objects of investigation, including empirical facts. The theory of experience I have in mind here is, of course, a constructionist one, and is articulated best by two post-Althusserians, Barry Hindess and Paul Hirst:

> Empiricism represents knowledge as constructed out of "given" elements, the elements of experience, the "facts" of history, etc. Unfortunately for these positions facts are never "given" to knowledge. They are always the product of definite practices, theoretical or ideological, conducted under definite real conditions.... Facts are never *given;* they are always produced. (1975, 2–3)

The idea that empirical facts are always ideological productions can itself be a useful fact to introduce to students. And, in terms of pedagogical theory, such a position permits the introduction of narratives of lived experience into the classroom while at the same time challenging us to examine collectively the central role social and historical practices play in shaping and producing these narratives. "Essentially speaking," we need both to theorize essentialist spaces from which to speak and, simultaneously, to deconstruct these spaces to keep them from solidifying. Such a double gesture involves once again the responsibility to historicize, to examine each deployment of essence, each appeal to experience, each claim to identity in the complicated contextual frame in which it is made.

It may well be that the best way to counteract the negative, often hidden effects of essentialism in the classroom is to bring essentialism to the fore as an explicit topic of debate. This book aims to contribute to the renewed interest in rethinking essentialism by laying out the terms of the essentialist/constructionist opposition while also providing the critical lever to displace what, in my mind, is a largely artificial (albeit powerful) antagonism. I have argued from the start that essentialism underwrites theories of constructionism and that constructionism operates as a more sophisticated form of essentialism. This is simply another way of saying that constructionism may be more normative, and essentialism more variable, than those of us who call ourselves poststructuralists hitherto have been willing to acknowledge. Any attempt to intervene in the stalemate produced by the essentialist/constructionist stand-off must therefore involve a recognition of each position's internal contradictions and political investments. While the essentialist/constructionist polemic may continue to cast its shadow over our critical discussions, it is the final contention of this book that reliance on an admittedly overvalued binarism need not be paralyzing.

NOTES

1. See especially Frances Maher's "Classroom Pedagogy and the New Scholarship on Women," and Janet Rifkin's "Teaching Mediation: A Feminist Perspective on the Study of Law." Maher calls for new "appropriate teaching styles to recover the female experience" since "the dominant pedagogical style of most classrooms discriminate against women's experience" (29 and 31), and Janet Rifkin echoes the call for "a pedagogy in which personal experience is viewed as a legitimate and important reference-point for scholarly work" (104).
2. I am here taking issue with a prevalent strain of feminist poststructuralist thinking, represented by Jane Gallop, which holds that "the politics of experience is inevitably a conservative politics" (1983, 83). Could we not rephrase this question to read: *"In my experience,* the politics of experience is inevitably a conservative politics"?

REFERENCES

Althusser, Louis. 1971. *Lenin and Philosophy.* Trans. Ben Brewster. New York and London: Monthly Review Press.

Bourne, Jenny. 1987. "Homelands of the Mind: Jewish Feminism and Identity Politics. "*Race & Class* 29:1 (Summer) 1–24.

Culler, Jonathan. 1982. *On Deconstruction: Theory and Criticism after Structuralism.* Ithaca: Cornell University Press.

Culley, Margo, and Catherine Portuges (eds). 1985. *Gendered Subjects: The Dynamics of Feminist Teaching.* Boston: Routledge & Kegan Paul.

Derrida, Jacques. 1967. *L'Ecriture et la différence.* Paris: Seuil. Trans. Alan Bass (1978). *Writing and Difference.* Chicago: University of Chicago Press.

Gallop, Jane. 1983. "Quand nos lèvres s'écrivent: Irigaray's Body Politic." *Romanic Review* 74:1 (January): 77–83.

Griffiths, Morwenna, and Margaret Whitford. 1988. *Feminist Perspectives in Philosophy.* Bloomington and Indianapolis: Indiana University Press.

Hindess, Barry, and Paul Hirst. 1975. *Pre-capitalist Modes of Production.* London and Boston: Routledge & Kegan Paul.

Koedt, Anne, Ellen Levine, and Anita Rapone (eds.). 1973. *Radical Feminism.* New York: Quadrangle Books.

Said, Edward. 1986. "Intellectuals in the Post-Colonial World." *Salmagundi* 70–71 (Spring-Summer): 44–81.

Watney, Simon. 1980."*The Ideology of GLF.*" In Gay Left Collective (eds). *Homosexuality: Power & Politics.* London and New York: Allison and Busby.

ESSENTIALISM AND EXPERIENCE (1994)

BELL HOOKS

hooks's essay responds to Diana Fuss's "Essentially Speaking," also in this volume. While hooks may exaggerate when she says that all Fuss's examples of students who use essentialism to silence other students come from historically oppressed groups, she notices a tendency in Fuss's argument and in many arguments like Fuss's. Here, as in other essays, hooks often draws on her experience and at the same time theorizes the role of experience. She argues that although Fuss looks on experience with suspicion, Fuss draws on her experience to shape her argument.

Readers may ponder how to compare Fuss's and hooks's views. How might Fuss respond to hooks's thoughts about the race of teachers of African American critical thinking? hooks also refers to the autobiography of Rigoberta Menchú, called I, Rigoberta Menchú, as an example of the authority of experience. Since hooks's essay, some of the details of Menchú's autobiography have been questioned. If some of those details are inaccurate, readers may ask whether or how that helps them think through the issues that Fuss and hooks pose for us. Readers may also ask whether—and if so, how—it is possible to interpret culture and literature without drawing on experience. Readers can also the compare different ways of drawing on experience in Fuss's and hooks's arguments and styles.

For a related discussion, see the selection in this volume by Toril Moi. (The selection here leaves out the beginning of hooks's essay.)

In the concluding chapter to her book, Fuss particularly criticizes using experience in the classroom as a base from which to espouse totalizing truths. Many of the limitations she points out could be easily applied to the way experience informs not only what we write about, but how we write about it, the judgments we make.

More than any other chapter in *Essentially Speaking,* this concluding essay is profoundly disturbing. It also undermines Fuss's previous insightful discussion of essentialism. Just as my experience of critical writing by black feminist thinkers would lead me to make different and certainly more complex assessments from those Fuss makes, my response to the chapter "Essentialism in the Classroom" is to some extent informed by my different pedagogical experiences. This chapter provided me with a text I could engage dialectically; it served as a catalyst for clarifying my thoughts on essentialism in the classroom.

According to Fuss, issues of "essence, identity, and experience" erupt in the classroom primarily because of the critical input from marginalized groups. Throughout her chapter, whenever she offers an example of individuals who use essentialist standpoints to dominate discussion, to silence others via their invocation of the "authority of experience," they are members of groups who historically have been and are oppressed and exploited in this society. Fuss does not address how systems of domination already at work in the academy and the classroom silence the voices of individuals from marginalized groups and give space only when on the basis of experience it is demanded. She does not suggest that the very discursive practices that allow for the assertion of the "authority of experience" have already been determined by a politics of race, sex, and class domination. Fuss does not aggressively suggest that dominant groups—men, white people, heterosexuals—perpetuate essentialism. In her narrative it is always a marginal "other" who is essentialist. Yet the politics of essentialist exclusion as a means of asserting presence, identity, is a cultural practice that does not emerge solely from marginalized groups. And when those groups do employ essentialism as a way to dominate in institutional settings, they are often imitating paradigms for asserting subjectivity that are part of the controlling apparatus in structures of domination. Certainly many white male students have brought to my classroom an insistence on the authority of experience, one that enables them to feel that anything they have to say is worth hearing, that indeed their ideas and experience should be the central focus of classroom discussion. The politics of race and gender within white supremacist patriarchy grants them this "authority" without their having to name the desire for it. They do not attend class and say, "I think that I am superior intellectually to my classmates because I am white and male and that my experiences are much more important than any other group's." And yet their behavior often announces this way of thinking about identity, essence, subjectivity.

Why does Fuss's chapter ignore the subtle and overt ways essentialism is expressed from a location of privilege? Why does she primarily critique the misuses of essentialism by centering her analysis on marginalized groups? Doing so makes them the culprits for disrupting the classroom and making it an "unsafe" place. Is this not a conventional way the colonizer speaks of the colonized, the oppressor of the oppressed? Fuss asserts, "Problems often begin in the classroom when those 'in the know' commerce only with others 'in the know,' excluding and marginalizing those perceived to be outside the magic circle." This observation, which could certainly apply to any group, prefaces a focus on critical commentary by Edward Said that reinforces her critique of the dangers of essentialism. He appears in the text as resident "Third World authority" legitimating her argument. Critically echoing Said, Fuss comments: "For Said it is both dangerous and misleading to base an identity politics upon rigid theories of exclusions, 'exclusions that stipulate, for instance, only women can understand feminine experience, only Jews can understand Jewish suffering, only formerly colonial subjects can understand colonial experience.'" I agree with Said's critique, but I reiterate that while I, too, critique the use of essentialism and identity politics as a strategy for exclusion or domination, I am suspicious when theories call this practice harmful as a way of suggesting that it is a strategy only marginalized groups employ. My suspicion is rooted in the awareness that a critique of essentialism that challenges only marginalized groups to interrogate their use of identity politics or an essentialist standpoint as a means of exerting coercive power leaves unquestioned the critical practices of other groups who employ the same strategies in different ways and whose exclusionary behavior may be firmly buttressed by institutionalized structures of domination that do not critique or check it. At the same time, I am concerned that critiques of identity politics not serve as the new, chic way to silence students from marginal groups.

Fuss makes the point that "the artificial boundary between insider and outsider necessarily contains rather than disseminates knowledge." While I share this perception, I am disturbed that she never acknowledges that racism, sexism, and class elitism shape the structure of classrooms, creating a lived reality of insider versus outsider that is predetermined, often in place before any class discussion begins. There is rarely any need for marginalized groups to bring this binary opposition into the classroom because it is usually already operating. They may simply use it in the service of their concerns. Looked at from a sympathetic standpoint, the assertion of an excluding essentialism on the part of students from marginalized groups can be a strategic response to domination and to colonization, a survival strategy that may indeed inhibit discussion even as it rescues those students from negation. Fuss argues that "it is the unspoken law of the classroom not to trust those who cannot cite experience as the indisputable grounds of their knowledge. Such unwritten laws pose perhaps the most serious threat to classroom dynamics in that they breed suspicion amongst those inside the circle and guilt (sometimes anger) amongst those outside the circle." Yet she does not discuss who makes these laws, who determines classroom dynamics. Does she perhaps assert her authority in a manner that unwittingly sets up a competitive dynamic by suggesting that the classroom *belongs* more to the professor than to the students, to some students more than others?

As a teacher, I recognize that students from marginalized groups enter classrooms within institutions where their voices have been neither heard nor welcomed, whether these students discuss facts—those which any of us might know—or personal experience. My pedagogy has been shaped to respond to this reality. If I do not wish to see these students use the "authority of experience" as a means of asserting voice, I can circumvent this possible misuse of power by bringing to the classroom pedagogical strategies that affirm their presence, their right to speak, in multiple ways on diverse topics. This pedagogical strategy is rooted in the assumption that we all bring to the classroom experiential knowledge, that this knowledge can indeed enhance our learning experience. If experience is already invoked in the classroom as a way of knowing that coexists in a nonhierarchical way with other ways of knowing, then it lessens the possibility that it can be used to silence. When I teach Toni Morrison's *The Bluest Eye* in introductory courses on black women writers, I assign students to write an autobiographical paragraph about an early racial memory. Each person reads that paragraph aloud to the class. Our collective listening to one another affirms the value and uniqueness of each voice. This exercise highlights experience without privileging the voices of students from any particular group. It helps create a communal awareness of the diversity of our experiences and provides a limited sense of the experiences that may inform how we think and what we say. Since this exercise makes the classroom a space where experience is valued, not negated or deemed meaningless, students seem less inclined to make the telling of experience that site where they compete for voice, if indeed such a competition is taking place. In our classroom, students do not usually feel the need to compete because the concept of a privileged voice of authority is deconstructed by our collective critical practice.

In the chapter "Essentialism in the Classroom" Fuss centers her discussion on locating a particular voice of authority. Here it is her voice. When she raises the question "how are we to handle" students, her use of the word "handle" suggests images of manipulation. And her use of a collective "we" implies a sense of a unified pedagogical practice shared by other professors. In the institutions where I have taught, the prevailing pedagogical model is authoritarian, hierarchical in a coercive and often dominating way, and certainly one where the voice of the professor is the "privileged" transmitter of knowledge. Usually these professors devalue including personal experience in classroom discussion. Fuss admits to being wary of attempts to censor the telling of personal histories in the classroom on the basis that they have not been "adequately 'theorized,'" but she indicates throughout this chapter that on a fundamental level she does not believe that the sharing of personal experience can be a meaningful addition to classroom discussions. If this bias informs her pedagogy, it is not surprising that invocations of experience are used aggressively to assert a privileged way of knowing, whether against her or other students. If a professor's pedagogy is liberatory, then students will probably not compete for value and voice in the classroom. That essentialist standpoints are used competitively does not mean that the taking of those positions creates the situation of conflict.

Fuss's experiences in the classroom may reflect the way in which "competition for voice" is an integral part of her pedagogical practice. Most of the comments and observations she makes about essentialism in the classroom are based on her experience (and perhaps that of her colleagues, though this is not explicit). Based on that experience she can confidently assert that she "remain[s] convinced that appeals to the authority of experience rarely advance discussion and frequently provoke confusion." To emphasize this point further she says, "I am always struck by the way in which introjections of experiential truths into classroom debates dead-end the discussion." Fuss draws on her particular experience to make totalizing generalizations. Like her, I have seen the way essentialist standpoints can be used to silence or assert authority over the opposition, but I most often see and experience the way the telling of personal experience is incorporated into classrooms in ways that deepen discussion. And I am most thrilled when the telling of experience links discussions of facts or more abstract constructs to concrete reality. My experience in the classroom may be different from Fuss's because I speak as an institutionally marginalized other, and here I do not mean to assume an essentialist position. There are many black women professors who would not claim this location. The majority of students who enter our classrooms have never been taught by black women professors. My pedagogy is informed by this knowledge, because I know from experience that this unfamiliarity can overdetermine what takes place in the classroom. Also, knowing from personal experience as a student in predominantly white institutions how easy it is to feel shut out or closed down, I am particularly eager to help create a learning process in the classroom that engages everyone. Therefore, biases imposed by essentialist standpoints or identity politics, alongside those perspectives that insist that experience has no place in the classroom (both stances can create an atmosphere of coercion and exclusion), must be interrogated by pedagogical practices. Pedagogical strategies can determine the extent to which all students learn to engage more fully the ideas and issues that seem to have no direct relation to their experience.

Fuss does not suggest that teachers who are aware of the multiple ways essentialist standpoints can be used to shut down discussion can construct a pedagogy that critically intervenes before one group attempts to silence another. Professors, especially those from dominant groups, may themselves employ essentialist notions to constrain the voices of particular students; hence we must all be ever-vigilant in our pedagogical practices. Whenever students share with me the sense that my pedagogical practices are silencing them, I have to examine that process critically. Even though Fuss grudgingly acknowledges that the telling of experience in the classroom may have some positive implications, her admission is quite patronizing:

> while truth clearly does not equate with experience, it cannot be denied that it is precisely the fiction that they are the same which prompts many students, who would not perhaps speak otherwise, to enter energetically into those debates they perceive as pertaining directly to them. The authority of experience, in other words, not only works to silence students, it also works to empower them. How are we to negotiate the gap between the conservative fiction of experience as the ground of all truth-knowledge and the immense power of this fiction to enable and encourage student participation?

All students, not just those from marginalized groups, seem more eager to enter energetically into classroom discussion when they perceive it as pertaining directly to them (when non-white students talk in class only when they feel connected via experience it is not aberrant behavior). Students may be well versed in a particular subject and yet be more inclined to speak confidently if that subject directly relates to their experience. Again, it must be remembered that there are students who may not feel the need to acknowledge that their enthusiastic participation is sparked by the connection of that discussion to personal experience.

In the introductory paragraph to "Essentialism in the Classroom" Fuss asks, "Exactly what counts as 'experience,' and should we defer to it in pedagogical situations?" Framing the question in this way makes it appear that comments about experiences necessarily disrupt the classroom, engaging the professor and students in a struggle for authority that can be mediated if the professor defers. This question, however, could be posed in a manner that would not imply a condescending devaluation of experience. We might ask: How can professors and students who want to share personal experience in the classroom do so without promoting essentialist standpoints that exclude? Often when professors affirm the importance of experience students feel less need to insist that it is a privileged way of knowing. Henry Giroux, in his writing on critigal pedagogy, suggests that the notion of experience has to be situated within a theory of learning. Giroux suggests that professors must learn to respect the way students feel about their experiences as well as their need to speak about them in classroom settings: "You can't deny that students have experiences and you can't deny that these experiences are relevant to the learning process even though you might say these experiences are limited, raw, unfruitful or whatever. Students have memories, families, religions, feelings, languages and cultures that give them a distinctive voice. We can critically engage that experience and we can move beyond it. But we can't deny it." Usually it is in a context where the experiential knowledge of students is being denied or negated that they may feel most determined to impress upon listeners both its value and its superiority to other ways of knowing.

Unlike Fuss, I have not been in classrooms where students find "empirical ways of knowing analytically suspect." I have taught feminist theory classes where students express rage against work that does not clarify its relationship to concrete experience, that does not engage feminist praxis in an intelligible way. Student frustration is directed against the inability of methodology, analysis, and abstract writing (usually blamed on the material and often justifiably so) to make the work connect to their efforts to live more fully, to transform society, to live a politics of feminism.

Identity politics emerges out of the struggles of oppressed or exploited groups to have a standpoint on which to critique dominant structures, a position that gives purpose and meaning to struggle. Critical pedagogies of liberation respond to these concerns and necessarily embrace experience, confessions and testimony as relevant ways of knowing, as important, vital dimensions of any learning process. Skeptically, Fusks asks, "Does experience of oppression confer special jurisdiction over the right to speak about that oppression?" This is a question that she does not answer. Were it posed to me by students in the classroom, I would ask them to consider whether there is any "special" knowledge to be acquired by hearing oppressed individuals speak from their experience—whether it be of victimization or resistance—that might make one want to create a privileged space for such discussion. Then we might explore ways individuals acquire knowledge about an experience they have not lived, asking ourselves what moral questions are raised when they speak for or about a reality that they do not know experientially, especially if they are speaking about an oppressed group. In classrooms that have been extremely diverse, where I have endeavored to teach material about exploited groups who are not black, I have suggested that if I bring to the class only analytical ways of knowing and someone else brings personal experience, I welcome that knowledge because it will enhance our learning. Also, I share with the class my conviction that if my knowledge is limited, and if someone else brings a combination of facts and experience, then I humble myself and respectfully learn from those who bring this great gift. I can do this without negating the position of authority professors have, since fundamentally I believe that combining the analytical and experiential is a richer way of knowing.

Years ago, I was thankful to discover the phrase "the authority of experience" in feminist writing because it gave me a name for what I brought to feminist classrooms that I thought was not present but believed was valuable. As an undergraduate in feminist classrooms where woman's experience was universalized, I knew from my experience as a black female that black women's reality was being excluded. I spoke from that knowledge. There was no body of theory to invoke that would substantiate this truth claim. No one really wanted to hear about the deconstruction of woman as a category of analysis then. Insisting on the value of my experience was crucial to gaining a hearing. Certainly, the need to understand my experience motivated me as an undergraduate to write *Ain't I a Woman: Black Women and Feminism*.

Now I am troubled by the term "authority of experience," acutely aware of the way it is used to silence and exclude. Yet I want to have a phrase that affirms the specialness of those ways of knowing rooted in experience. I know that experience can be a way to know and can inform how we know what we know. Though opposed to any essentialist practice that constructs identity in a monolithic, exclusionary way, I do not want to relinquish the power of experience as a standpoint on which to base analysis or formulate theory. For example, I am disturbed when all the courses on black history or literature at some colleges and universities are taught solely by white people, not because I think that they cannot know these realities but that they know them differently. Truthfully, if I had been given the opportunity to study African American critical thought from a progressive black professor instead of the progressive white woman with whom I studied as a first-year student, I would have chosen the black person. Although I learned a great deal from this white woman professor, I sincerely believe that I would have learned even more from a progressive black professor, because this individual would have brought to the class that unique mixture of experiential and analytical ways of knowing—that is, a privileged standpoint. It cannot be acquired through books or even distanced observation and study of a particular reality. To me this privileged standpoint does not emerge from the "authority of experience" but rather from the passion of experience, the passion of remembrance.

Often experience enters the classroom from the location of memory. Usually narratives of experience are told retrospectively. In the testimony of Guatemalan peasant and activist Rigoberta Menchú, I hear the passion of remembrance in her words:

> My mother used to say that through her life, through her living testimony, she tried to tell women that they too had to participate, so that when the repression comes and with it a lot of suffering, it's not only the men who suffer. Women must join the struggle in their own way. My mother's words told them that any evolution, any change, in which women had not participated, would not be change, and there would be no victory. She was as clear about this as if she were a woman with all sorts of theories and a lot of practice.

I know that I can take this knowledge and transmit the message of her words. Their meaning could be easily conveyed. What would be lost in the transmission is the spirit that orders those words, that testifies that, behind them—underneath, everywhere—there is a lived reality. When I use the phrase "passion of experience," it encompasses many feelings but particularly suffering, for there is a particular knowledge that comes from suffering. It is a way of knowing that is often expressed through the body, what it knows, what has been deeply inscribed on it through experience. This complexity of experience can rarely be voiced and named from a distance. It is a privileged location, even as it is not the only or even always the most important location from which one can know. In the classroom, I share as much as possible the need for critical thinkers to engage multiple locations, to address diverse standpoints, to allow us to gather knowledge fully and inclusively. Sometimes, I tell students, it is like a recipe. I tell them to imagine we are baking bread that needs flour. And we have all the other ingredients but no flour. Suddenly, the flour becomes most important even though it alone will not do. This is a way to think about experience in the classroom.

On another day, I might ask students to ponder what we want to make happen in the class, to name what we hope to know, what might be most useful. I ask them what standpoint is a personal experience. Then there are times when personal experience keeps us from reaching the mountain top and so we let it go because the weight of it is too heavy. And sometimes the mountaintop is difficult to reach with all our resources, factual and confessional, so we are just there collectively grasping, feeling the limitations of knowledge, longing together, yearning for a way to reach that highest point. Even this yearning is a way to know.

SPEECH, WRITING, CODE: THREE WORLDVIEWS (2005)

N. KATHERINE HAYLES

In this chapter from her My Mother Was a Computer: Digital Subjects and Literary Texts, *Hayles compares Ferdinand de Saussure's interpretation of language, which privileges speech over writing; Jacques Derrida's interpretation of language, which revises Saussure to privilege writing over speech; and her own proposed reading of the language of computer code. Computer code is based on binary code. Binary code is based on the binary numeral system, also called the base-2 number system. In the binary numeral system, the symbols 0 and 1 are sufficient to represent all numeric values. Because so simple a system can easily be represented electronically, it has made computer code possible. In our contemporary, computer-driven culture, Hayles argues, code is a form of language worthy of the same serious interpretation that we already bring to speech and writing.*

THE LOCUS OF COMPLEXITY

Speech, writing, code: these three major systems for creating signification interact with each other in millions of encounters every day. Each, as it has been theorized, comes with its own worldview, associated technologies, and user feedback loops. In the progression from speech to writing to code, each successor regime reinterprets the system(s) that came before, inscribing prior values into its own dynamics. Now that the information age is well advanced, we urgently need nuanced analyses of the overlaps and discontinuities of code with the legacy systems of speech and writing, so that we can understand how processes of signification change when speech and writing are coded into binary digits. Although speech and writing issuing from programmed media may still be recognizable as spoken utterances and print documents, they do not emerge unchanged by the encounter with code. Nor is the effect of code limited to individual texts. In a broader sense, our understanding of speech and writing in general is deeply influenced by the pervasive use of code (my deliberate situating of them as legacy systems above is intended as a provocation to suggest the perceptual shifts underway). This chapter will show how the worldview of computation sketched in chapter 1 manifests itself in the specific case of the digital computer. It will also indicate ways in which commonly accepted ideas about signification need to be reevaluated in the context of coding technologies. Finally, it will suggest terms for analysis that, although not absent in speech and writing, assume new importance with code and therefore lead to new theoretical emphases and foci of attention.

In drawing comparisons of code with speech and writing, one is faced with an embarrassment of riches. One thinks, for example, of the embodied views of speech explored by practitioners and theorists as diverse as Walter Ong and Oliver Sacks; of such preeminent theorists of writing as Paul de Man and J. Hillis Miller. Out of many possibilities, I have chosen to focus on Ferdinand de Saussure's view of speech and Jacques Derrida's grammatological view of writing partly because these theorists take systemic approaches to their subjects that make clear the larger conceptual issues. Like them, I want to take a systemic approach by focusing on the conceptual system in which code is embedded, a perspective that immediately concerns programming for digital computers but also includes the metaphysical implications of the Regime of Computation. In addition, both Saussure and Derrida have been extremely influential in shaping contemporary views of speech and writing. By addressing their work in detail, I can by implication address the large number of related projects these two theorists have inspired. An additional advantage is Derrida's engagement with Saussure's theories of the speech system; Derrida's work has an intimate relation with Saussure's, which is richly documented in Derrida's writings, especially his early work. Moreover, one of Derrida's critical points is that writing exceeds speech and cannot simply be conceptualized as speech's written form. Similarly, I will argue that code exceeds both writing and speech, having characteristics that appear in neither of these legacy systems. This project, then, is not meant as a general comparison of code with structuralism and deconstruction but as a more narrowly focused inquiry that takes up specifically Saussure and Derrida.

Before turning to a systematic comparison of code with Saussure's speech system and Derrida's grammatology, I want to establish a general framework for my remarks. Derrida's remarkably supple and complex writing notwithstanding, much of his analysis derives from a characteristic of writing that would likely spring to mind if we were asked to identify the principal way in which writing differs from speech. Writing, unlike speech (before recording technologies), is not confined to the event of its making. It can be stored and transmitted, published in dozens of countries and hundreds of different editions, read immediately after its creation or a thousand years hence. In a sense it is no surprise that Derrida summarizes this difference between writing and speech by fusing "difference" with "defer," for the ability to defer indefinitely our encounter with writing leaps out as perhaps the most salient way in which it differs from speech. Derrida, of course, complicates and extends this common-sense idea by linking it with a powerful critique of the metaphysics of presence—but these complexities have their root in something most people would identify as a constitutive difference between speech and writing.

If we were to ask about the parallel characteristic that leaps to mind to distinguish code from speech and writing, an obvious contender would be the fact that code is addressed both to humans and intelligent machines. A further distinction is implied when we note that computers, although capable of performing diverse and complicated tasks, have at the base level of machine language only two symbols and a small number of logical operations with which to work. As Stephen Wolfram eloquently testifies in relation to his cellular automata, the amazing thing about them is that starting from an extremely simple base they can nevertheless produce complex patterns and behaviors.

This train of thought suggests the following question: Where does the complexity reside that makes code (or computers, or cellular automata) seem adequate to represent a complex world? In his critique of speech and the metaphysics of presence, Derrida makes clear that complexity was vested traditionally in the Logos, the originary point conceptualized as necessarily exceeding the world's complexity, since in this view the world derived from the Logos. For Derrida's grammatology, complexity is conceptually invested in the trace and by implication in the subtle analysis that detects the movement of the trace, which can never be found as a thing-in-itself. For code, complexity inheres neither in the origin nor in the operation of difference as such but in the labor of computation that again and again calculates differences to create complexity as an emergent property of computation. Humans, who have limited access to their own computational machinery (assuming that cognition includes computational elements, a proposition explored in chapter 9), create intelligent machines whose operations can be known in comprehensive detail (at least in theory). In turn, the existence of these machines, as many researchers have noted, suggests that the complexities we perceive and generate likewise emerge from a simple underlying base; these researchers hope that computers might show us, in Brian Cantwell Smith's phrase, "how a structured lump of clay can sit up and think."[1] The advantages of the computational view, for those who espouse it, is that emergence can be studied as a knowable and quantifiable phenomena, freed both from the mysteries of the Logos and the complexities of discursive explanations dense with ambiguities. One might observe, of course, that these characteristics also mark the limitations of a computational perspective.

It is not an accident that my analysis starts by inquiring about the locus of complexity, for the different strategies through which Saussurean linguistics, Derridean grammatology, and the Regime of Computation situate complexity have extensive implications for their respective worldviews. From this starting point I will develop several ways, not all of them obvious, in which code differs from speech and writing. My purpose is not to supplant these legacy systems and especially not to subordinate speech and writing to code (an important point, given Saussure's historic claim that writing must be subordinate to speech, and Derrida's insistence that, on the contrary, speech is subordinate to writing). Rather, for me the "juice" (as Rodney Brooks calls it) comes from the complex dynamics generated when code interacts with speech and writing, interactions that include their mundane daily transactions and also the larger stakes implicit in the conflict and cooperation of their worldviews.

SAUSSUREAN SIGNS AND MATERIAL MATTERS

Let us begin, then, where Saussure began, with his assertion that the sign has no "natural" or inevitable relation to that which it refers; "the linguistic sign is arbitrary," he writes in *Course in General Linguistics*.[2] Partly for this reason, he excludes from consideration hieroglyphic and idiomatic writing. As he makes clear in a number of places, he regards speech as the true locus of the language system (*la langue*) and writing as merely derivative of speech. "A language and its written form constitute two separate systems of signs. The sole reason for the existence of the latter is to present the former. The object of study in linguistics is not a combination of the written word and the spoken word. The spoken word alone constitutes that object"(24–25). Objecting to the primacy Saussure accords to speech, Derrida sees in this hierarchy indications that Saussure remains bound to a metaphysics of presence and to the Logos with which speech has traditionally been associated; in an interview with Julia Kristeva, he remarks that "the concept of the sign belongs to metaphysics."[3]

Derrida marshals numerous arguments to insist that writing, far from being derivative as Saussure claims, in fact precedes speech; "the linguistic sign implies an original writing."[4] This counterintuitive idea, to which we will return, depends on his special understanding of writing as grammatology. In addition, he critiques Saussure's notion of the arbitrariness of the sign, asking if the "ultimate function" of this premise is to obscure "the rights of history, production, institutions etc., except in the form of the arbitrary and in the substance of naturalism" (*Of Grammatology*, 33). Of course he recognizes that the arbitrariness of the sign as Saussure posits it refers to the absence of a necessary connection between sign and referent, but his critique implies that Saussure's formulation tends to suppress the recognition that constraints of any kind might encumber the choice of sign. The productive role that constraints play in the Regime of Computation, functioning to eliminate possible choices until only a few remain, is conspicuously absent in Saussure's theory. Instead, meaning emerges and is stabilized by differential relations between signs. Jonathan Culler, writing his influential book on Saussure just as Saussure was becoming well known in the United States, makes explicit this implication: "The fact that the relation between signifier and signified is arbitrary means, then, that since there are no fixed universal concepts or fixed universal signifiers, the signified itself is arbitrary, and so is the signifier.... Both signifier and signified are purely relational or differential entities."[5]

Culler's interpretation helps explain why material constraints tend to drop out of Saussure's theory as appropriated by American poststructuralism, with a corresponding emphasis on differential relations and shifting uncertain ties to reference and, indeed, to the material conditions of production altogether (interpretations that have been contested by later commentators seeking to recuperate Saussure for various purposes).[6] Although Derrida's suggestion that Saussure had erased "the rights of history, production, institutions, etc." remains underdeveloped in his writing, the recognition that materiality imposes significant constraints becomes crucially important in code, and arguably in speech and writing as well. Why, for example, are there no words in English (and so far as I know, in any other language) that have one hundred or more syllables? Obviously, we have no such words because they would take too long to pronounce. In contrast to the erasure of materiality in Saussure, material constraints have historically been recognized as crucial in the development of computers, from John von Neumann in the 1950s agonizing over how to dissipate heat produced by vacuum tubes to present-day concerns that the limits of miniaturization are being approached with silicon-based chips. Moreover, material constraints have played a central role in favoring the shift to digital computers over analog.

To understand why digital computers have been favored, consider Transistor to Transistor Logic (TTL) chips, where the binary digit zero is represented by zero volts and the binary digit one by five volts. If a voltage fluctuation creates a signal of .5 volts, it is relatively easy to correct this voltage to zero, since .5 is much closer to zero than to five. Error control is much more complex with analog computers, where voltages vary continuously. For code, then, the assumption that the sign is arbitrary must be qualified by material constraints that limit the ranges within which signs can operate meaningfully and acquire significance. As we shall see, these qualifications are part of a larger picture that tie code more intimately to material conditions than is the case either for Saussure's speech system or Derrida's grammatological view of writing. In the worldview of code, materiality matters.

Culler was not wrong in emphasizing differential relations rather than material constraints, for it is clear that Saussure's view of the sign tended toward dematerialization. "The physical part of the [speech] circuit can be dismissed from consideration straight away," he says (13). Although he later acknowledges that "linguistic signs, although essentially psychological, are not abstractions," he sees their materiality as "realities localized in the brain" and distinguishes this mediated materiality from linguistic structure, where "there is only the sound pattern" (15). He argues that differences in pronunciation should be excluded because they "affect only the material substance of words" (18). Considering the sign to consist of signifier and signified, he insists that the signifier is not the acoustic sound itself but the "sound pattern" or "sound image," that is, an idealized version of the sound, whereas the signified is the concept associated with this image. The advantage of defining an immaterial pattern as the signifier is obvious; through this move, he dispenses with having to deal with variations in pronunciation, dialects, and so on (although he does recognize differences in inflection, a point that Johanna Drucker uses to excavate from his theory a more robust sense of the materiality of the sign).[7]

This is Saussure's way of coping with the noise of the world, whereby idealization plays a role similar to the function performed by discreteness in digital systems. It is worth reflecting on the differences between these two strategies. Rectifying voltage fluctuations could be compared to Saussure's "rectification" of actual sounds into idealized sound images. Importantly, however, rectification with code happens in the electronics rather than in the (idealized) system created by a human theorist. Thus it is a physical operation rather than a mental one, and it happens while the code is running rather than retrospectively in a theoretical model. These differences again illustrate that code is more intrinsically bound to materiality than Saussure's conception of *la langue*.

The disjunctions between Saussure's theory and the materially determined practices of code raise the question of whether it makes sense to use such legacy terms as "signifier" and "signified" with code. Many theorists concerned with electronic textuality are starting from new frameworks that do not rely on these traditional terms. In chapter 1, for example, I introduced Espen Aarseth's "textonomy," which sweeps the board clean and works from fundamental considerations to create a taxonomic scheme for analyzing ergodic literature. Similarly, a group of German researchers at the University of Siegen are working together in a project they call "Medienumbrüche" (Media Upheavals). They "regard the semiotic difference between strings and nets of signifiers as the foundation of a theory of 'net literature' which calls basic concepts such as 'author,' 'work,' and 'reader' into question."[8] Although valuing these new theoretical frameworks as necessary interventions, I think it is important also to undertake a nuanced analysis of where code does and does not fit with traditional terms, especially for this project with its focus on intermediation. The exchanges, conflicts, and cooperations between the embedded assumptions of speech and writing in relation to code would be likely to slip unnoticed through a framework based solely on networked and programmable media, for the shift over to the new assumptions would tend to obscure the ways in which the older worldviews engage in continuing negotiations and intermediations with the new. For my purposes, then, the comparison is vital. Later I will perform the reverse operation of trying to fit the speech and writing systems into the worldview of code, and here too I expect the discontinuities to be as revealing as the continuities.

In the context of code, then, what would count as signifier and signified? Given the importance of the binary base, I suggest that the signifiers be considered as voltages—a suggestion already implicit in Friedrich Kittler's argument that ultimately everything in a digital computer reduces to changes in voltages.[9] The signifieds are then the interpretations that other layers of code give these voltages. Programming languages operating at higher levels translate this basic mechanic level of signification into commands that more closely resemble natural language. The translation from binary code into high-level languages, and from high-level languages back into binary code, must happen every time commands are compiled or interpreted, for voltages and the bit stream formed from them are all the machine can understand.[10] Thus voltages at the machine level function as signifiers for a higher level that interprets them, and these interpretations in turn become signifiers for a still higher level interfacing with them. Hence the different levels of code consist of interlocking chains of signifiers and signifieds, with signifieds on one level becoming signifiers on another. Because all these operations depend on the ability of the machine to recognize the difference between one and zero, Saussure's premise that differences between signs make signification possible fits well with computer architecture.

DERRIDA'S *DIFFÉRANCE* AND THE CLARITY OF CODE

This continuity between computer architecture and Saussure's understanding of signification becomes a discontinuity, however, when Derrida transforms difference into *différance,* a neologism suggesting that meanings generated by differential relations are endlessly deferred. Speaking metaphorically, we may say that whereas Saussure focuses on two (or more) linguistic signs and infers a relationship connecting them, Derrida focuses on the gap as the important element, thus converting Saussure's presumption of presence into a generative force of absence: *"différance is not,* does not exist, is not a present-being (*on*) in any form.... It has neither existence nor essence. It derives from no category of being, whether present or absent."[11] To name this generative force, Derrida coins any number of terms in addition to *différance:* "trace," "arche-writing" "non-originary origin," and so on. Whatever the name, the important point is that the trace has no positive existence in itself and thus cannot be reified or recuperated back into a metaphysics of presence. "*Différance* is not only irreducible to any ontological or theological—ontotheological—reappropriation, but as the very opening of the space in which ontotheology—philosophy—produces its system and its history, it includes ontotheology, inscribing it and exceeding it without return" (*Margins,* 6). Always on the move, the trace resides everywhere and nowhere, functioning as the elusive and fecund force that makes possible all subsequent meaning. In this sense the trace, as the arche-writing that enables signification, precedes speech and also writing in the ordinary sense. The notoriously slippery nature of the trace has authorized the widely accepted idea, reinforced by thousands of deconstructive readings performed by those who followed in Derrida's footsteps, that meaning is always indeterminate and deferred.

Let us now consider how this claim for difference/deferral looks from the point of view of code. In the worldview of code, the generation of meaning happens in ways that scholars trained in the traditional humanities sometimes find difficult to understand and even more difficult to accept. At the level of binary code, the system can tolerate little if any ambiguity. For any physically embodied system, some noise and, therefore, possible ambiguities are always present. In the case of digital computers, noise enters the system (among other places) in the voltage trail-off errors discussed earlier, but these are rectified into unambiguous signals of one and zero before they enter the bit stream.[12] As the system builds up levels of programming languages such as compilers, interpreters, scripting languages, and so forth, they develop functionalities that permit increasingly greater ambiguities in the choices permitted or tolerated. The Microsoft Word spell checker is a good example. Given a letter string not in the program's dictionary, it looks for the closest matches and offers them as possibilities. No matter how sophisticated the program, however, all commands must be parsed as binary code to be intelligible to the machine.

In the context of digital computers, even less tenable than ambiguity is the proposition that a signifier could be meaningful without reference to a signified. In Derrida's view, Saussure's definition of the sign undercuts the metaphysics of presence in one sense and reinforces it in another. He argues that the very idea of a signified as conceptually distinct from the signifier (although for Saussure, indissoluble from it) gives credence to a transcendental signified, and to this extent reinscribes classical metaphysics. The distinction between signifier and signified, Derrida writes, "leaves open the possibility of thinking a *concept signified in and of itself,* a concept simply present for thought, independent of a relationship to language, that is of a relationship to a system of signifiers" (*Positions,* 19). At the same time, the distinction also opens the possibility that any signified, extracted from one context and embedded in another, could slide into the position of the signifier (for example, when one concept entails another). Since the idea of a transcendental signified implies that there is nothing above or beyond this originary point, the dynamic of signified-becoming-signifier threatens to undermine the absolute authority given to the transcendental signified. In this sense, Saussure's theory (as interpreted by Derrida) can be seen as working against the metaphysics of presence in which it otherwise remains complicit. This background helps to explain why, in deconstructive criticism, the focus tends to fall on the signifier rather than the signified. Indeed, I venture to guess that in contemporary critical theory, "signifier" is used thousands of times for every time "signified" appears.

In the worldview of code, it makes no sense to talk about signifiers without signifieds. Every voltage change must have a precise meaning in order to affect the behavior of the machine; without signifieds, code would have no efficacy. Similarly, it makes no sense to talk about floating signifiers (Lacan's adaptation of Derrida's sliding signifier) because every change in voltage must be given an unambiguous interpretation, or the program is likely not to function as intended.[13] Moreover, changes on one level of programming code must be exactly correlated with what is happening at all the other levels. If one tries to run a program designed for an older operating system on a newer one that no longer recognizes the code, the machine simply finds it unreadable, that is, unintelligible. For the machine, obsolete code is no longer a competent utterance.

Because it is a frequent point of confusion, I emphasize that these dynamics happen before (or after) any human interpretation of these messages. Whatever messages on screen may say or imply, they are themselves generated through a machine dynamics that has little tolerance for ambiguity, floating signifiers, or signifiers without corresponding signifieds. Although the computational worldview is similar to grammatology in not presuming the transcendental signified that Derrida detects in Saussure's speech system, it also does not tolerate the slippages Derrida sees as intrinsic to grammatology. Nor does code allow the infinite iterability and citation that Derrida associates with inscriptions, whereby any phrase, sentence, or paragraph can be lifted from one context and embedded in another. "A written sign carries with it a force that breaks with its context, that is, with the collectivity of presences organizing the moment of its inscription. This breaking force [*force de rupture*] is not an accidental predicate but the very structure of the written text."[14] Although Derrida asserts that this iterability is not limited to written language but "is to be found in all language" (*Limited Inc*, 10), this assertion does not hold true literally for code, where the contexts are precisely determined by the level and nature of the code. Code may be rendered unintelligible if transported into a different context—for example, into a different programming language or a different syntactic structure within the same language. Only at the high level of object-oriented languages such as C++ does code recuperate the advantages of citability and iterability (i.e., inheritance and polymorphism, in the discourse of programming language) and in this sense become "grammatological."[15]

Ellen Ullman, a software engineer who has been a pioneer in a field largely dominated by men, has written movingly about the different worldviews of code and natural language as they relate to ambiguity and slippage.[16] Asked in an interview with Scott Rosenberg if code is a language, she replied, "We can use English to invent poetry, to try to express things that are very hard to express. In programming you really can't. Finally, a computer program has only one meaning: what it does. It isn't a text for an academic to read. Its entire meaning is its function."[17] Emphasizing the unforgivingness of code, Ullman underscores its functionality. Code has become an important actor in the contemporary world because it has the power to change the behavior of digital computers, which in turn permeate nearly every kind of advanced technology. Code can set off missiles or regulate air traffic; control medical equipment or generate PET scans; model turbulent flow or help design innovative architecture. All of these tasks are built ultimately on a base of binary code and logic gates that are intolerant to error. Above all else, the digital computer is a logic machine, as Martin Davis shows elegantly in *The Universal Computer*, where he discusses the history of the logic on which the digital computer is based.

In *Close to the Machine,* Ullman illustrates vividly the contrast between the worldviews of code and human language when she discusses a software system she was commissioned to create that would help deliver information to AIDS patients. She recounts working in her San Francisco loft with a small group of programmers she had hired. They worked around the clock to meet the deadline, speaking in rapid-fire phrases about the structure of the program, the work-arounds they could devise, the flow charts that showed how the code would be processed. Junk food abounded, dress was disheveled, courtesy was a waste of precious minutes, and sleep became a distant memory as they subordinated all other concerns to the logic of the machine (1–17). Then, as the independent contractor responsible for the system, she met with the staff whose clients would be using the software. Suddenly the clear logic dissolved into an amorphous mass of half-articulated thoughts, messy needs and desires, fears and hopes of desperately ill people. Even as she tried to deal with the cloud of language in which these concerns were expressed, her mind raced to translate the concerns into a list of logical requirements to which her programmers could respond. Acting as the bridge arcing between the floating signifiers of natural language and the rigidity of machine code, she felt acutely the strain of trying to reconcile these two very different views of the world. "I had reduced the users' objections to a set of five system changes. I would like to use the word 'reduce' like a cook: something boiled down to its essence. But I was aware that the real human essence was already absent from the list I'd prepared. An item like 'How will we know if the clients have TB?'—the fear of sitting in a small, poorly ventilated room with someone who has medication-resistant TB, the normal and complicated biological urgency of that question—became a list of data elements to be added to the screens and database" (13–14).

One of the book's poignant scenes comes when Ullman, emotionally stressed by events in her life, decides to take her computer apart and put it back together, in a kind of somatic therapy that soothed by putting her physically in touch with the parts that functioned in such perfectly logical fashion (65–94). The scene illustrates another way in which the worldview of code differs from Saussure's dematerialized view of speech and Derrida's emphasis on linguistic indeterminacy. Although it is possible to view computer algorithms as logical structures that do not need to be instantiated to have meaning (the received view of many computer science departments), in practice any logical or formal system must run on some kind of platform to acquire meaning, whether a human brain or a digital computer. Without the ability to change the behavior of machines, code would remain a relatively esoteric interest of mathematicians working in areas such as the lambda calculus (where algorithms were used for research purposes in the 1930s, prior to the invention of the digital computer).[18] Code has become arguably as important as natural language because it causes things to happen, which requires that it be executed as commands the machine can run.

Code that runs on a machine is performative in a much stronger sense than that attributed to language. When language is said to be performative, the kinds of actions it "performs" happen in the minds of humans, as when someone says "I declare this legislative session open" or "I pronounce you husband and wife." Granted, these changes in minds can and do result in behavioral effects, but the performative force of language is nonetheless tied to the external changes through complex chains of mediation. By contrast, code running in a digital computer causes changes in machine behavior and, through networked ports and other interfaces, may initiate other changes, all implemented through transmission and execution of code. Although code originates with human writers and readers, once entered into the machine it has as its primary reader the machine itself. Before any screen display accessible to humans can be generated, the machine must first read the code and use its instructions to write messages humans can read. Regardless of what humans think of a piece of code, the machine is the final arbiter of whether the code is intelligible. If the machine cannot read the code or if the program does not work properly, then the code must be changed and corrected before the machine can make things happen. In *Protocol*, Alexander R. Galloway makes this point forcefully when he defines code as executable language. "But how can code be so different from mere writing?" he asks. "The answer to this lies in the unique nature of computer code.... Code is a language, but a very special kind of language. *Code is the only language that is executable.*"[19]

This character of code stands in striking contrast to the communities that decide whether an act of speech or a piece of writing constitutes a legible and competent utterance. As Saussure observes, no one person can change the spoken language system. "A language, as a collective phenomenon, takes the form of a totality of imprints in everyone's brain....Thus it is something which is in each individual, but is none the less common to all. At the same time it is out of reach of any deliberate interference by individuals" (*Course*, 19). It takes many individual adopters of a change and a (relatively) long time for changes in the speech system to occur. (To some extent this claim requires modification in light of mass media such as television and newspapers, where a single speaker or small group of speakers can change the system if given enough press coverage. Saussure's point remains valid, however, in the sense that only if the speech acts of such privileged speakers are widely adopted can they actually change the system.) For Derrida, writing differs from Saussure's view of the speech system because inscriptions can endure over centuries or millennia, and thus can be cited, and therefore embedded, in a potentially infinite number of different contexts. Moreover, Derrida reads the qualities of iterability and citation back into speech, instancing precisely the phenomena (e.g., quotations and speeches performed by actors in a theatrical performance) that Austin excluded from his speech act theory because he viewed them as anomalous.[20] In Derrida's grammatology, the more or less coherent community of speakers that Saussure presumes fractures into historically and geographically diverse contexts of different writing (and speaking) practices, different communities of general or expert readers, and different criteria for what constitutes competence and legibility. As William R. Paulson, among others, has observed, Derrida's complex writing style itself performs this diversity, insofar as it creates a class of "priestly" interpreters who can understand his writing, in contrast to many nonspecialist readers who have found it unintelligible.[21]

Like esoteric theoretical writing, code is intelligible only to a specialized community of experts who understand its complexities and can read and write it with fluency. There is, however, a significant difference between the worldview of code, on one hand, and, on the other, the community of speakers Saussure presumes and the infinitely diverse inscription contexts Derrida invokes. With code, a (relatively) few experts can initiate changes in the system that are often so significant they render previous systems illegible, as when Microsoft creates a new operating system such as Windows XP, which is not backward compatible with Windows 95 and earlier versions. Moreover, in code the breaks are much sharper and more complete than with either speech or writing. Occasionally I meet people who are using hardware and software that have been obsolete for years. Although they can still produce documents using these versions, they are increasingly marooned on an island in time, unable to send readable files or to read files from anyone else. Whereas undergraduates can understand (with some help) the Middle English of Chaucer's *Canterbury Tales* or the Elizabethan English of Shakespeare, thus making a connection over the hundreds of years that separate them from these works, no such bridges can be built between Windows 95 and Windows XP (separated by a mere seven or eight years), without both massive recoding and fluency in the nastily complex code of Windows programming.

Although code may inherit little or no baggage from classical metaphysics, it is permeated throughout with the politics and economics of capitalism, along with the embedded assumptions, resistant practices, and hegemonic reinscriptions associated with them. The open source movement testifies eloquently to the centrality of capitalist dynamics in the marketplace of code, even as it works to create an intellectual commons that operates according to the very different dynamics of a gift economy.[22]

THE HIERARCHY OF CODE

As we have seen, code differs from speech and writing in that it exists in clearly differentiated versions that are executable in a process that includes hardware and software and that makes obsolete programs literally unplayable unless an emulator or archival machine is used. Moreover, the historical strata of code do not involve a troublesome metaphysical inheritance but a troublesome deep layer of assembler code that can be understood and reverse engineered only with great difficulty, as demonstrated by attempts to excavate it and correct the problems associated with the Y2K crisis. The ways in which the historical character of code influence its alterations is a subject that requires understanding the difference between change within a given slice of time (synchrony) and change across time (diachrony).

For Saussure, the proper object of study for the semiotics of the speech system is the synchronic orientation. He points out in the introduction to *Course in General Linguistics* that his analysis reorients the field of study from the historicist and philological emphasis it had in previous generations to an understanding that regards the language system as a (more or less) coherent synchronous structure (1–8).[23] For Derrida, the diachronic manifests itself as the (allegedly) inescapable influence of classical metaphysics, whereas the synchronic ceases to have the force it does for Saussure because inscriptions, unlike speech prior to the invention of recording technologies, can be transported into historically disparate contexts, and so exist as rock does: in historically stratified formations that stretch back for thousands of years. Derrida writes, "This citationality, this duplication or duplicity, this iterability of the mark is neither an accident nor an anomaly, it is that (normal/abnormal) without which a mark could not even have a function called 'normal.' What would a mark be that could not be cited? Or one whose origins would not get lost along the way?" (*Limited Inc*, 12).[24]

Along with these differences in conceptualizing the sign and delineating its operations across and through time go related differences in how signs work together to comprise a semiotic system. When Saussure argues that differential relations between signs constitute the engine that drives signification, he identifies two vectors along which these relations operate, working at multiple levels within the speech system. The syntagmatic vector points horizontally, for example, along the syntax of a sentence. By contrast, the paradigmatic vector operates vertically, for example, in the synonyms that might be used in place of a given word in an utterance. Derrida makes little use of these terms in his grammatology, focusing instead on the hierarchical relations between concepts by which a privileged term posits a stigmatized term as the "outside" to its "inside." For Derrida, perhaps the primary instance of this hierarchical relation, in the context of Saussure's theory, is Saussure's attempt to relegate writing to a purely derivative role. Derrida's deconstruction of this hierarchical arrangement is typical of his treatment of hierarchical dichotomies in general, for he shows that the privileged term must in fact contain and depend on what it tries to exclude. "The exteriority of the signifier is the exteriority of writing in general, and I shall try to show ... that there is no linguistic sign before writing. Without that exteriority, the very idea of the sign falls into decay" (*Of Grammatology*, 14).

Like speech, coding structures make use of what might be called the syntagmatic and paradigmatic, but in inverse relation to how they operate in speech systems. As Lev Manovich observes in *The Language of New Media*, in speech or writing the syntagmatic is what appears on the page (or as patterned sound), whereas the paradigmatic (the alternative choices that could have been made) is virtually rather than actually present (229–33). In digital media using dynamic databases, this relationship is reversed. The paradigmatic alternatives are encoded into the database and in this sense actually exist, whereas the syntagmatic is dynamically generated on the fly as choices are made that determine which items in the database will be used. In this sense, the syntagmatic is virtual rather than actual. This insight opens onto further explorations of how databases and narratives interface together, especially in electronic literature and the more general question of literariness.

In *Reading Voices*, Garrett Stewart argues that literary language is literary in part because of its ability to mobilize "virtual" words—related by sound, sense, or usage to those actually on the page—that surround the printed text with a "blooming buzz" of variants enriching and extending the text's meanings. Although operating according to a different dynamic than envisioned by Saussure, the luminous fog created by these variants resembles the paradigmatic vector that Saussure theorized for the speech system. When electronic literature offers the user hypertextual choices that lead to multiple narrative pathways, the strategy of evoking "virtual" possibilities happens not only on the level of the individual word but at the narrative level where different strands, outcomes, and interpretations mutually resonate with one another. This richness is possible, of course, only because all these possibilities are stored in the computer, available to be rearranged, interpolated, followed or not. Somewhat paradoxically, then, the more data that are stored in computer memory, all of which are ordered according to specified addresses and called by executable commands, the more ambiguities are possible. Flexibility and the resulting mobilization of narrative ambiguities at a high level depend upon rigidity and precision at a low level. The lower the level, the closer the language comes to the reductive simplicity of ones and zeros, and yet it is precisely the ability to build up from this reductive base that enables high-level literariness to be achieved. In this sense, the interplay between the virtual syntagmatic sequences and the actual paradigmatic database resembles the dynamic that Wolfram, Fredkin, and Harold Morowitz envision for computer simulations, with high-level complexity emerging out of the brute simplicity of binary distinctions and a few logical relationships. Literariness, as it is manifested in the panoply of choices characteristic of hypertext literature, here converges with the Regime of Computation in using the "simple rules, complex behavior" characteristic of code to achieve complexity.

Along with the hierarchical nature of code goes a dynamic of concealing and revealing that operates in ways that have no parallels in speech and writing. Because computer languages become more English-like as they move higher in the "tower of languages" (Rita Raley's phrase),[25] concealing the "brute" lower levels carries considerable advantage. Knowing how to conceal code with which one is not immediately concerned is an essential practice in computer programming. One of the advantages of object-oriented languages is bundling code within an object, so that the object becomes a more or less autonomous unit that can be changed without affecting other objects in that domain. At the same time, revealing code when it is appropriate or desired also bestows significant advantage. The "reveal code" command in HTML documents, for example, allows users to see comments, formatting instructions, and other material that may illuminate the construction and intent of the work under study, a point Loss Pequeño Glazier makes effectively in *Dig[iT]al Poet(I)(c)s*. With programs such as Dreamweaver that make layers easy to construct, additional dynamics of concealing and revealing come into play through rollovers and the like, re-creating on the screen dynamics that both depend on and reflect the "tower of languages" essential to code.[26]

These practices of concealing and revealing offer fertile ground for aesthetic and artistic exploration. Layers that reveal themselves according to timed sequences, cursor movements, and other criteria have become an important technique for writers seeking to create richly dense works with multiple pathways for interaction. One such work is Talan Memmott's *Lexia to Perplexia*, a notoriously "nervous" digital production that responds to even minute cursor movements in ways a user typically does not expect and finds difficult to control. Layering in this work is arguably the principal way by which complex screen design, text, animation, and movement interact with one another. Another example is M. D. Coverley's *The Book of Going Forth by Day*, where the visual tropes of revealing and concealing resonate with the multiple personae, patterned after ancient Egyptian beliefs, that cohabit in one body. The layers are instrumental in creating a visual/verbal/sonic narrative in which the deep past and the present, modern skepticism and ancient rituals, hieroglyphs and electronic writing merge and blend with one another.

The "reveal code" dynamic helps to create expectations (conscious and preconscious) in which the layered hierarchical structure of the tower of languages reinforces and is reinforced by the worldview of computation. The more the concealing/revealing dynamic becomes an everyday part of life and a ubiquitous strategy in everything from commercial Web pages to digital artworks, the more plausible it makes the view that the universe generates reality though a similar hierarchical structure of correlated levels ceaselessly and forever processing code. Similarly, the more the worldview of code is accepted, the more "natural" the layered dynamics of revealing and concealing code seem. Since these dynamics do not exist in anything like the same way with speech and writing, the overall effect—no doubt subtle at first but growing in importance as digital cultures and technologies become increasingly pervasive and indispensable—is to validate code as the lingua franca of nature. Speech and writing then appear as evolutionary stepping stones necessary to ratchet up Homo sapiens to the point where humans can understand the computational nature of reality and use its principles to create technologies that simulate the simulations running on the Universal Computer. This, in effect, is the worldview Morowitz envisions when he writes about the fourth stage (after the evolution of the cosmos, life, and mind) as mind reflecting on mind.[27] The more "natural" code comes to seem, the more plausible it is to conceptualize human thought as emerging from a machinic base of computational processes, a proposition explored in chapter 7.

As I argue throughout, however, human cognition, although it may have computational elements, includes analog consciousness that cannot be understood simply or even primarily as digital computation. Speech and writing, in my view, should not be seen as predecessors to code that will wither away but as vital partners on many levels of scale in the evolution of complexity. As I said in chapter 1, not Wolfram *or* his cellular automata alone, but *both* together—hence my emphasis on narrative and subjectivity as these are intermediated with computation. It is not the triumph of the Regime of Computation that can best explain the complexities of the world and, especially, of human cultures but its interactions with the stories we tell and the media technologies instrumental in making, storing, and transmitting.

MAKING DISCRETE AND THE INTERPENETRATION OF CODE AND LANGUAGE

Let us now shift from interpreting code through the worldviews of speech and writing to the inverse approach of interpreting speech and writing through the worldview of code. An operation scarcely mentioned by Saussure and Derrida but central to code is digitization, which I interpret here as the act of making something discrete rather than continuous, that is, digital rather than analog. The act of making discrete extends through multiple levels of scale, from the physical process of forming bit patterns up through a complex hierarchy in which programs are written to compile other programs. Understanding the practices through which this hierarchy is constructed, as well as the empowerments and limitations the hierarchy entails, is an important step in theorizing code in relation to speech and writing.

Let me make a claim that, in the interest of space, I will assert rather than substantiate: the world as we sense it on a human scale is basically analog. Over millennia, humans have developed biological modifications and technological prostheses to impose digitization on these analog processes, from the physiological evolution needed to produce speech to sophisticated digital computers. From a continuous stream of breath, speech introduces the discreteness of phonemes; writing carries digitization farther by adding artifacts to this physiological process, developing inscription technologies that represent phonemes with alphabetic letters. At every point, analog processes interpenetrate and cooperate with these digitizations. Experienced readers, for example, perceive words not as individual letters but as patterns perceived in a single glance. The synergy between the analog and digital capitalizes on the strengths distinctive to each. As we have seen, digitization allows fine-tuned error control and depth of coding, whereas analog processes tie in with highly evolved human capabilities of pattern processing. In addition, the analog function of morphological resemblance, that is, similarity of form, is the principal and indeed (so far as I know) the only way to convey information from one instantiated entity to a differently instantiated entity.

How do practices of making discrete work in the digital computer? We have already heard about the formation of the bit stream from changing voltages channeled through logic gates, a process that utilizes morphological resemblance. From the bit pattern bytes are formed, usually with each byte composed of eight bits—seven bits to represent the ASCII code, and an empty one that can be assigned special significance. At each of these stages, the technology can embody features that were once useful but have since become obsolete. For example, the ASCII code contains a seven-bit pattern corresponding to a bell ringing on a teletype. Although teletypes are no longer in use, the bit pattern remains because retrofitting the ASCII code to delete it would require far more labor than would be justified by the benefit. To some extent, then, the technology functions like a rock strata, with the lower layers bearing the fossilized marks of technologies now extinct.

In the progression from speech to writing to code, each successor regime introduces features not present in its predecessors. In *Of Grammatology*, Derrida repeatedly refers to the space between words in alphabetic writing to demonstrate his point that writing cannot be adequately understood simply as the transcription of speech patterns (39, passim). Writing, he argues, exceeds speech and thus cannot be encapsulated within this predecessor regime; "writing is at the same time more exterior to speech, not being its 'image' or its 'symbol,' and more interior to speech, which is already in itself a writing" (46). Not coincidentally, spaces play an important role in the digitization of writing by making the separation of one word from another visually clear, thus contributing to the evolution of the codex book as it increasingly realized its potential as a medium distinct from speech. Similarly, code has characteristics that occur neither in speech nor in writing—processes that, by exceeding these legacy systems, mark a disjunction.

To explore these characteristics, let us now jump to a high level in the hierarchy of code and consider object-oriented programming languages, such as the ubiquitous C++. (I leave out of this discussion the newer languages of Java and C#, for which similar arguments could be made). C++ commands are written in ASCII and then converted into machine language, so this high-level programming language, like everything that happens in the computer, builds on a binary base. Nevertheless, C++ instantiates a profound shift of perspective from machine language and also from the procedural languages like FORTRAN and BASIC that preceded it. Whereas procedural languages conceptualize the program as a flow of modularized procedures (often diagrammed with a flowchart) that function as commands to the machine, object-oriented languages are modeled after natural languages and create a syntax using the equivalent of nouns (that is, objects) and verbs (processes in the system design).

A significant advantage to this mode of conceptualization, as Bruce Eckel explains in *Thinking in* C++, is that it allows programmers to conceptualize the solution in the same terms used to describe the problem. In procedural languages, by contrast, the problem would be stated in real-world terms (Eckel's example is "put the grommet in the bin"), whereas the solution would have to be expressed in terms of behaviors the machine could execute ("set the bit in the chip that means that the relay will close"; 43). C++ reduces the conceptual overhead by allowing both the solution and the problem to be expressed in equivalent terms, with the language's structure performing the work of translating between machine behaviors and human perceptions.

The heart of this innovation is allowing the programmer to express her understanding of the problem by defining classes, or abstract data types, that have both characteristics (data elements) and behaviors (functionalities). From a class, a set of objects instantiate the general idea in specific variations—the nouns referred to above. For example, if a class is defined as "shape," then objects in that class might be triangle, circle, square, and so on (37–38). Moreover, an object contains not only data but also functions that operate on the data—that is, it contains constraints that define it as a unit, and it also has encapsulated within it behaviors appropriate to that unit. For example, each object in "shape" might inherit the capability to be moved, to be erased, to be made different sizes, and so on, but each object would give these class characteristics its own interpretation. This method allows maximum flexibility in the initial design and in the inevitable revisions, modifications, and maintenance that large systems demand. The "verbs" then become the processes through which objects can interact with each other and the system design.

New objects can be added to a class without requiring that previous objects be changed, and new classes and metaclasses can also be added. Moreover, new objects can be created through inheritance, using a preexisting object as a base and then adding additional behaviors or characteristics. Since the way the classes are defined in effect describes the problem, the need for documentation external to the program is reduced; to a much greater extent than with procedural languages, the program serves as its own description. Another significant advantage of C++ is its ability to "hide" data and functions within an object, allowing the object to be treated as a unit without concern for these elements. "Abstraction is selective ignorance," Andrew Koenig and Barbara E. Moo write in *Accelerated* C++, a potent aphorism that speaks to the importance in large systems of hiding details until they need to be known.[28] Abstraction (defining classes), encapsulation (hiding details within objects and, on a metalevel, within classes), and inheritance (deriving new objects by building on preexisting objects) are the strategies that give object-oriented programs their superior flexibility and ease of design.

We can now see that object-oriented programs achieve their usefulness principally through the ways they anatomize the problems they are created to solve—that is, the ways in which they cut up the world. Obviously a great deal of skill and intuition goes into the selection of the appropriate classes and objects; the trick is to state the problem so it achieves abstraction in an appropriate way. This often requires multiple revisions to get it right, so ease of revision is crucial.

Some of the strategies C++ uses to achieve its language-like flexibility illustrate how it makes use of properties that do not appear in speech or writing and are specific to coding systems. Procedural languages work by what is called "early binding," a process in which the compiler (the part of the code hierarchy that translates higher-level commands into the machine language) works with the linker to direct a function call (a message calling for a particular function to be run) to the absolute address of the code to be executed. At the time of compiling, early binding thus activates a direct link between the program, compiler, and address, joining these elements before the program is actually run. C++, by contrast, uses "late binding," in which the compiler ensures that the function exists and checks its form for accuracy, but the actual address of the code is not used until the program is run.[29] Late binding is part of what allows the objects to be self-contained with minimum interference with other objects.

The point of this rather technical discussion is simple: there is no parallel to compiling in speech or writing, much less a distinction between compiling and run-time. The closest analogy, perhaps, is the translation of speech sounds or graphic letter forms into synapses in the human brain, but even to suggest this analogy risks confusing the *production* of speech and writing with its *interpretation* by a human user. Like speech and writing, computer behaviors can be interpreted by human users at multiple levels and in diverse ways, but this activity comes after (or before) the computer activity of compiling code and running programs.

Compiling (and interpreting, for which similar arguments can be made) is part of the complex web of processes, events, and interfaces that mediate between humans and machines, and its structure bespeaks the needs of both parties involved in the transaction. The importance of compiling (and interpreting) to digital technologies underscores the fact that new emphases emerge with code that, although not unknown in speech and writing, operate in ways specific to networked and programmable media. At the heart of this difference is the need to mediate between the natural languages native to human intelligence and the binary code native to intelligent machines. As a consequence, code implies a partnership between humans and intelligent machines in which the linguistic practices of each influence and interpenetrate the other.[30]

The evolution of C++ grew from precisely this kind of interpenetration. C++ is consciously modeled after natural language; once it came into wide use, it also affected how natural language is understood. We can see this two-way flow at work in the following observation by Bruce Eckel, in which he constructs the computer as an extension of the human mind. He writes, "The genesis of the computer revolution was in a machine. The genesis of our programming languages thus tends to look like that machine. But the computer is not so much a machine as it is a mind amplification tool and a different kind of expressive medium. As a result, the tools are beginning to look less like machines and more like parts of our minds, and more like other expressive mediums like writing, painting, sculpture, animation or filmmaking. Object-oriented programming is part of this movement toward the computer as an expressive medium" (*Thinking in* C++, 35). As computers are increasingly understood (and modeled after) "expressive mediums" like writing, they begin to acquire the familiar and potent capability of writing not merely to express thought but actively to constitute it. As high-level computer languages move closer to natural languages, the processes of intermediation by which each affects the other accelerate and intensify. Rita Raley has written on the relation between the spread of Global English and the interpenetration of programming languages with English syntax, grammar, and lexicon.[31] In addition, the creative writing practices of "codework," practiced by such artists as MEZ, Talan Memmott, Alan Sondheim, and others, mingle code and English in a pastiche that, by analogy with two natural languages that similarly intermingle, might be called a creole.[32]

The vectors associated with these processes do not all point in the same direction. As explored in chapter 8, (mis)recognizing visualizations of computational simulations as creatures like us both anthropomorphizes the simulations and "computationalizes" the humans. Knowing that binary code underlies complex emergent processes reinforces the view that human consciousness emerges from similar machinic processes, as explored in chapter 7. Anxieties can arise when the operations of the computer are mystified to the extent that users lose sight of (or never know) how the software actually works, thus putting themselves at the mercy of predatory companies like Microsoft, which makes it easy (or inevitable) for users to accept at face value the metaphors the corporation spoon-feeds them, a concern explored in chapter 6. These dynamics make unmistakably clear that computers are no longer merely tools (if they ever were) but are complex systems that increasingly produce the conditions, ideologies, assumptions, and practices that help to constitute what we call reality.

The operations of "making discrete" highlighted by digital computers clearly have ideological implications. Indeed, Wendy Hui Kyong Chun goes so far as to say that *software is ideology,* instancing Althusser's definition of ideology as "the representation of the subject's imaginary relationship to his or her real conditions of existence."[33] As she points out, desktop metaphors such as folders, trash cans, and so on create an imaginary relationship of the user to the actual command core of the machine, that is, to the "real conditions of existence" that in fact determine the parameters within which the user's actions can be understood as legible. As is true for other forms of ideology, the interpolation of the user into the machinic system does not require his or her conscious recognition of how he or she is being disciplined by the machine to become a certain kind of subject. As we know, interpolation is most effective when it is largely unconscious.

This conclusion makes abundantly clear why we cannot afford to ignore code or allow it to remain the exclusive concern of computer programmers and engineers. Strategies can emerge from a deep understanding of code that can be used to resist and subvert hegemonic control by megacorporations;[34] ideological critiques can explore the implications of code for cultural processes, a project already evident in Matthew Fuller's call, seconded by Matthew Kirschenbaum, for critical software studies;[35] readings of seminal literary texts can explore the implications of code for human thought and agency, among other concerns. Code is not the enemy, any more than it is the savior. Rather code is increasingly positioned as language's pervasive partner. Implicit in the juxtaposition is the intermediation of human thought and machine intelligence, with all the dangers, possibilities, liberations, and complexities this implies.

NOTES

1. Brian Cantwell Smith, *On the Origin of Objects*, 76.
2. Ferdinand de Saussure, *Course in General Linguistics*, 67.
3. Jacques Derrida, *Positions*, 17.
4. Jacques Derrida, *Of Grammatology*, 52.
5. Jonathan Culler, *Ferdinand de Saussure*, 33.
6. Working against these interpretations of Saussure are a number of critics who have argued that his theories were misinterpreted in poststructuralism. Among them are Raymond Tallis, *Not Saussure*, a work that argues in favor of restoring the notion of reference, and Paul J. Thibault, *Re-reading Saussure*, a study that emphasizes Saussure's theory as a model of social/semiological interactions. In *The Visible Word*, a careful analysis of Saussure's theory in historical context, Johanna Drucker seeks to recuperate from Saussure a revitalized role for the materiality of the sign.
7. In *The Visible Word*, Johanna Drucker concludes that "there would seem to be no possibility of generating a concept of materiality out of Saussure's theory of the sign." She notes, however, that "there is one loophole in his argument, namely his view of inflection as altering the value of the sign" (23).
8. Peter Gendolla, Jörgen Schäfer, and Maik Pluschke, e-mail message, February 3, 2004. See also, Peter Gendolla, Jörgen Schäfer, and Maik Pluschke, "Literatur in Netzen/Netz-literatur."
9. Friedrich Kittler, "There Is No Software," in *Essays*, 147–55.
10. Languages that are compiled perform the translation into binary code as a batch run, whereas interpreted languages perform translation into binary code command by command. The advantage of interpreted languages, although they eat up more run time, is increased flexibility and error control.
11. Jacques Derrida, "Différence," in *Margins of Philosophy*, 1–28, esp. 6.
12. A trail-off error denotes a voltage packet that instead of looking like a step function ⌐⌐ trails off at the end of the packet ⌐⌐.
13. Jacques Lacan, *Le Séminaire XX: Encore*, 22, 35. "Function as intended" should be interpreted in context of the program's structure and design. A virus, worm, or Trojan horse, for example, may be intended to crash the system.
14. Jacques Derrida, "Signature Event Context," in *Limited Inc*, 1–24, esp. 9.
15. It is true that bits can be put in any context whatever, but their order signifies a specific meaning that is in general nontransferable. To take Derrida's observation to this level (or for language, to the level of the individual letter) would reduce iterability to a trivial proposition, so I assume this is not what he means.
16. Ellen Ullman, *Close to the Machine*.
17. Ellen Ullman, "Elegance and Entropy."
18. For a brief introduction to the lambda calculus, see Don Blaheta, "The Lambda Calculus."
19. Alexander R. Galloway, *Protocol*, 165.
20. J. L. Austin, *How to Do Things with Words*. Jacques Derrida, "Limited Inc a b c …," in *Limited Inc*, 29–110. This famous response to John R. Searle's "Reiterating the Differences: A Reply to Derrida" demonstrated with acerbic wit why writing cannot, in Derrida's view, be assimilated into speech. Indeed, Derrida's response to Searle's "Reply" launched a brilliant counterattack by assimilating speech into writing.
21. William R. Paulson, *Literary Culture in a World Transformed*. Paulson decries the esoteric nature of much of literary theory, especially deconstruction, and calls for a return to language that ordinary people can understand.
22. See the Open Source Initiative for a statement of principles: "The *basic idea behind open source* is very simple: When programmers can read, redistribute, and modify the source code for a piece of software, the software evolves. People improve it, people adapt it, people fix bugs. And this can

happen at a speed that, if one is used to the slow pace of conventional software development, seems astonishing. We in the open source community have learned that this rapid evolutionary process produces better software than the traditional closed model, in which only a very few programmers can see the source and everybody else must blindly use an opaque block of bits. Open Source Initiative exists to make this case to the commercial world." The success of this and related initiatives can be seen in the movement of Macintosh to a Unix platform.

23. Jonathan Culler briefly reviews this history in *Ferdinand de Saussure,* 45–56. Johanna Drucker in *The Visible Word* also reviews the historical context to evaluate the role of materiality in pre-Saussurean linguistics as well as in Saussure's own theory (9–47).

24. There seems to be slippage here between the elementary unit of a language, such as a letter, and larger units such as words, phrases, sentences, and so on. As indicated in note 15 above, it is trivial to observe that letters are iterable, for this is the nature of alphabetic language. For Derrida's observation to have force, it must apply to larger units, and the larger the unit, the less the observation applies to content-bound code at the binary level.

25. Rita Raley, "Machine Translation and Global English."

26. The importance of this aesthetic to electronic literature is discussed in Rita Raley, "Reveal Codes."

27. Harold J. Morowitz, *The Emergence of Everything.*

28. Andrew Koenig and Barbara E. Moo, "Preface."

29. Bruce Eckel discusses the distinction between early and late binding in *Thinking in C++,* 40.

30. For a discussion of this interpenetration, see Raley, "Machine Translation and Global English."

31. Ibid.

32. For discussions of these practices, see Rita Raley, "Reveal Codes" and "Interferences." A discussion can also be found in N. Katherine Hayles, "From Object to Process." For a carefully nuanced analysis of works using "broken code" versus code that will actually run, see John Cayley, "The Code Is Not the Text (Unless It Is the Text)."

33. Wendy Hui Kyong Chun, "On the Persistence of Visual Knowledge."

34. A playful example of such subversion was the hack into the Google home page that, for a brief time, answered the Google search "Evil as the devil himself" by directing the user to the Microsoft home page. Alexander R. Galloway has an illuminating discussion of hacking as a social good in *Protocol,* 146–207.

35. Matthew Fuller, *Behind the Blip;* Matthew G. Kirschenbaum, "Virtuality and VRML."

REFERENCES

Austin, J. L. *How to Do Things with Words.* 2nd ed. Edited by Marina Sbisa and J. O. Urmsson. Cambridge, MA: Harvard University Press, 1975.

Blaheta, Don. "The Lambda Calculus." http://www.cs.brown.edu/courses/cs173/2003/Textbook/lc.pdf.

Cayley, John. "The Code Is Not the Text (Unless It Is the Text)." *Electronic Book Review* (September 2002). http://www.electronicbookreview.com/v3/servlet/ebr?command=view_essay&essay_id=cayleyele.

Chun, Wendy Hui Kyong. "On the Persistence of Visual Knowledge." Paper presented at the annual convention of the Modern Language Association, San Diego, CA, December 28, 2003.

Coverley, M. D. *The Book of Going Forth by Day.* http://califia.hispeed.com/Egypt/.

Cramer, Florian. "Digital Code and Literary Text." *Beehive* 4, no. 3 (November 2001). http://beehive.temporalimage.com/archive/43arc.html.

Culler, Jonathan. *Ferdínand de Saussure.* Rev. ed. Ithaca, NY: Cornell University Press, 1986.

Davis, Martin. *The Universal Computer: From Leibniz to Turing.* New York: W. W. Norton, 2000.

Derrida, Jacques. *Limited Inc.* Translated by Samuel Weber. Evanston, IL: Northwestern University Press, 1998.

———. *Margins of Philosophy.* Translated by Alan Bass. Chicago: University of Chicago Press, 1984.

———. *Of Grammatology.* Translated by Gayatri C. Spivak. Baltimore: Johns Hopkins University Press, 1977.

———. *Positions.* Translated by Alan Bass. Chicago: University of Chicago Press, 1982.

Drucker, Johanna. *The Visible Word: Experimental Typography and Modern Art, 1909–1923.* Chicago: University of Chicago Press, 1994.

Eckel, Bruce. *Thinking in C++.* Englewood Cliffs, NJ: Prentice Hall, 1995.

Fuller, Matthew. *Behind the Blip: Essays on the Culture of Software.* New York: Autonomedia, 2003.

Galloway, Alexander R. *Protocol: How Control Exists after Decentralization.* Cambridge, MA: MIT Press, 2004.

Gendolla, Peter, Jörgen Schäfer, and Maik Pluschke. "Literatur in Netzen/Netzliteratur." http://www.litnet.uni-siegen.de/Literatur %20in%20 Netzten %20-%20Netzliteratur.pdf.

Glazier, Loss Pequeño. *Dig[iT]al Poet(I)(c)s: The Making of E-Poetries.* Tuscaloosa: University of Alabama Press, 2002.

Hayles, N. Katherine. "From Object to Process: Cinematic Implications of New Media Poetry." *Future Cinema: The Cinematic Imaginary after Film,* edited by Peter Weibel and Jeffrey Shaw, 316–23. Cambridge MA: MIT Press, 2003.

Kittler, Friedrich A. *Essays: Literature, Media, Information Systems.* Edited by John Johnston. Amsterdam: G+B Arts, 1997.

Koenig, Andrew, and Barbara E. Moo. "Preface." In *Accelerated* C++. Redwood City, CA: Addison-Wesley, 2000. http://www.acceleratedcpp.com/details/preface.html.

Manovich, Lev. *The Language of New Media.* Cambridge, MA: MIT Press, 2002.

Memmott, Talan. *Lexia to Perplexia.* http://www.uiowa.edu/~iareview/tirweb/hypermedia/talan_memmott/.

Morowitz, Harold. *The Emergence of Everything: How the World Became Complex.* New York: Oxford University Press, 2002.

Open Source Initiative. Open Source. http://www.opensource.org/.

Paulson, William R. *Literary Culture in a World Transformed.* Ithaca, NY: Cornell University Press, 2001.

Raley, Rita. "Machine Translation and Global English." *Yale Journal of Criticism* 16, no. 2 (Fall 2003): 291–313.

———."Reveal Codes: Hypertext and Performance." *Postmodern Culture* 12, no. 1 (September 2001). http://muse.jhu.edu/journals/postmodern_culture/toc/pmc12.1.html.

Saussure, Ferdinand de. *Course in General Linguistics.* Translated by Roy Harris. Peru, IL: Open Course Publishing Co., 1988.

Searle, John R. "Reiterating the Differences: A Reply to Derrida." *Glyph* 1 (1977): 198–208

Smith, Brian Cantwell. *On the Origin of Objects.* Cambridge, MA: Bradford Books, 1996.

Stewart, Garrett. *Reading Voices: Literature and the Phonotext.* Berkeley: University of California Press, 1990.

Tallis. Raymond. *Not Saussure: A Critique of post-Saussurean Literary Theory.* London: Macmillan Press, 1988.

Thibault, Paul J. *Re-Reading Saussure: The Dynamics of Signs in Social Life.* London: Routledge, 1997.

Ullman, Ellen. *Close to the Machine: Technophilia and Its Discontents.* San Francisco: City Lights Books, 1997.

———"Elegance and Entropy." Interview with Scott Rosenberg. *Salon 21st* (October 9, 1997). http://archive.salon.com/21st/feature/1997/10/09interview.html.

PSYCHOANALYSIS

PSYCHO-ANALYSIS (1922)

SIGMUND FREUD

Translated from the German by James Strachey

Freud's essay "Psycho-analysis" summarizes the history, methods, and ideas of psychoanalysis. Since Freud does not use this essay to introduce new ideas, it is not one of his most famous works. But its clarity and comprehensiveness make it useful as an introduction to Freud's thinking and writing.

Psycho-analysis is the name (1) of a procedure for the investigation of mental processes which are almost inaccessible in any other way, (2) of a method (based upon that investigation) for the treatment of neurotic disorders and (3) of a collection of psychological information obtained along those lines, which is gradually being accumulated into a new scientific discipline.

History.—The best way of understanding psycho-analysis is still by tracing its origin and development. In 1880 and 1881 Dr. Josef Breuer of Vienna, a well-known physician and experimental physiologist, was occupied in the treatment of a girl who had fallen ill of a severe hysteria while she was nursing her sick father. The clinical picture was made up of motor paralyses, inhibitions, and disturbances of consciousness. Following a hint given him by the patient herself, who was a person of great intelligence, he put her into a state of hypnosis and contrived that, by describing to him the moods and thoughts that were uppermost in her mind, she returned on each particular occasion to a normal mental condition. By consistently repeating the same laborious process, he succeeded in freeing her from all her inhibitions and paralyses, so that in the end he found his trouble rewarded by a great therapeutic success as well as by an unexpected insight into the nature of the puzzling neurosis. Nevertheless, Breuer refrained from following up his discovery or from publishing anything about the case until some ten years later, when the personal influence of the present writer (Freud, who had returned to Vienna in 1886 after studying in the school of Charcot) prevailed on him to take up the subject afresh and embark upon a joint study of it. These two, Breuer and Freud, published a preliminary paper "On the Psychical Mechanism of Hysterical Phenomena" in 1893, and in 1895 a volume entitled *Studies on Hysteria* (which reached its fourth edition in 1922), in which they described their therapeutic procedure as "cathartic."

Catharsis.—The investigations which lay at the root of Breuer and Freud's studies led to two chief results, and these have not been shaken by subsequent experience: first, that hysterical symptoms have sense and meaning, being substitutes for normal mental acts; and secondly, that the uncovering of this unknown meaning is accompanied by the removal of the symptoms—so that in this case scientific research and therapeutic effort coincide. The observations were carried out upon a series of patients who were treated in the same manner as Breuer's first patient, that is to say, put into a state of deep hypnosis; and the results seemed brilliant, until later their weak side became evident. The theoretical ideas put forward at that time by Breuer and Freud were influenced by Charcot's theories on traumatic hysteria and could find support in the finding of his pupil Pierre Janet, which, though they were published earlier than the *Studies,* were in fact subsequent to Breuer's first case. From the very beginning the factor of *affect* was brought into the foreground: hysterical symptoms, the authors maintained, came into existence when a mental process with a heavy charge of affect was in any way prevented from being levelled out along the normal path leading to consciousness and movement (i.e., was prevented from being "*abreacted*"); as a result of this the affect, which was in a sense "*strangulated,*" was diverted along wrong paths and flowed off into the somatic innervation (a process named "*conversion*"). The occasions upon which "pathogenic ideas" of this kind arose were described by Breuer and Freud as "*psychical traumas,*" and, since these often dated back to the very remote past, it was possible for the authors to say that hysterics suffered mainly from reminiscences (which had not been dealt with). Under the treatment, therefore, "*catharsis*" came about when the path to consciousness was opened and there was a normal discharge of affect. It will be seen that an essential part of this theory was the assumption of the existence of *unconscious* mental processes. Janet too had made use of unconscious acts in mental life; but, as he insisted in his later polemics against psycho-analysis, to him the phrase was no more than a make-shift expression, a "*manière de parler,*" and he intended to suggest no new point of view by it.

In a theoretical section of the *Studies* Breuer brought forward some speculative ideas about the processes of excitation in the mind. These ideas determined the direction of future lines of thought and even to-day have not received sufficient appreciation. But they brought his contributions to this branch of science to an end, and soon afterwards he withdrew from the common work.

The Transition to Psycho-Analysis.—Contrasts between the views of the two authors had been visible even in the *Studies.* Breuer supposed that the pathogenic ideas produced their traumatic effect because they arose during "*hypnoid states,*" in which mental functioning was subject to special limitations. The present writer rejected this explanation and inclined to the belief that an idea became pathogenic if its content was in opposition to the predominant trend of the subject's mental life so that it provoked him into "*defence.*" (Janet had attributed to hysterical patients a constitutional incapacity for holding together the contents of their minds; and it was at this point that his path diverged from that of Breuer and Freud.) Moreover, the two innovations which led the present writer to move away from the cathartic method had already been mentioned in the *Studies.* After Breuer's withdrawal they became the starting-point of fresh developments.

Abandonment of Hypnosis.—The first of these innovations was based on practical experience and led to a change in technique. The second consisted in an advance in the clinical understanding of neuroses. It soon appeared that the therapeutic hopes which had been placed upon cathartic treatment in hypnosis were to some extent unfulfilled. It was true that the disappearance of the symptoms went hand-in-hand with the catharsis, but total success turned out to be entirely dependent upon the patient's relation to the physician and thus resembled the effect of "suggestion." If that relation was disturbed, all the symptoms reappeared, just as though they had never been cleared up. In addition to this, the small number of people who could be put into a deep state of hypnosis involved a very considerable limitation, from the medical standpoint, of the applicability of the cathartic procedure. For these reasons the present writer decided to give up the use of hypnosis. But at the same time the impressions he had derived from hypnosis afforded him the means of replacing it.

Free Association.—The effect of the hypnotic condition upon the patient had been so greatly to increase his ability to make associations that he was able straight away to find the path—inaccessible to his conscious reflection—which led from the symptom to the thoughts and memories connected with it. The abandonment of hypnosis seemed to make the situation hopeless, until the writer recalled a remark of Bernheim's to the effect that things that had been experienced in a state of somnambulism were only *apparently* forgotten and that they could be brought into recollection at any time if the physician insisted forcibly enough that the patient knew them. The writer therefore endeavoured to insist on his *unhypnotized* patients giving him their associations, so that from the material thus provided he might find the path leading to what had been forgotten or fended off. He noticed later that the insistence was unnecessary and that copious ideas almost always arose in the patient's mind, but that they were held back from being communicated and even from becoming conscious by certain objections put by the patient in his own way. It was to be expected—though this was still unproved and not until later confirmed by wide experience—that everything that occurred to a patient setting out from a particular starting-point must also stand in an internal connection with that starting-point; hence arose the technique of educating the patient to give up the whole of his critical attitude and of making use of the material which was thus brought to light for the purpose of uncovering the connections that were being sought. A strong belief in the strict determination of mental events certainly played a part in the choice of this technique as a substitute for hypnosis.

The "Fundamental Technical Rule" of this procedure of "free association" has from that time on been maintained in psycho-analytic work. The treatment is begun by the patient being required to put himself in the position of an attentive and dispassionate self-observer, merely to read off all the time the surface of his consciousness, and on the one hand to make a duty of the most complete honesty while on the other not to hold back any idea from communication, even if (1) he feels that it is too disagreeable or if (2) he judges that it is nonsensical or (3) too unimportant or (4) irrelevant to what is being looked for. It is uniformly found that precisely those ideas which provoke these last-mentioned reactions are of particular value in discovering the forgotten material.

Psycho-Analysis as an Interpretative Art.—The new technique altered the picture of the treatment so greatly, brought the physician into such a new relation to the patient and produced so many surprising results that it seemed justifiable to distinguish the procedure from the cathartic method by giving it a new name. The present writer gave this method of treatment, which could now be extended to many other forms of neurotic disorder, the name *of psycho-analysis*. Now, in the first resort, this psycho-analysis was an art of *interpretation* and it set itself the task of carrying deeper the first of Breuer's great discoveries—namely, that neurotic symptoms are significant substitutes for other mental acts which have been omitted. It was now a question of regarding the material produced by the patients' associations as though it hinted at a hidden meaning and of discovering that meaning from it. Experience soon showed that the attitude which the analytic physician could most advantageously adopt was to surrender himself to his own unconscious mental activity, in a state of *evenly suspended attention*, to avoid so far as possible reflection and the construction of conscious expectations, not to try to fix anything that he heard particularly in his memory, and by these means to catch the drift of the patient's unconscious with his own unconscious. It was then found that, except under conditions that were too unfavourable, the patient's associations emerged like allusions, as it were, to one particular theme and that it was only necessary for the physician to go a step further in order to guess the material which was concealed from the patient himself and to be able to communicate it to him. It is true that this work of interpretation was not to be brought under strict rules and left a great deal of play to the physician's tact and skill; but, with impartiality and practice, it was usually possible to obtain trustworthy results—that is to say, results which were confirmed by being repeated in similar cases. At a time when so little was as yet known of the unconscious, the structure of the neuroses and the pathological processes underlying them, it was a matter for satisfaction that a technique of this kind should be available, even if it had no better theoretical basis. Moreover it is still employed in analyses at the present day in the same manner, though with a sense of greater assurance and with a better understanding of its limitations.

The Interpretation of Parapraxes and Haphazard Acts.—It was a triumph for the interpretative art of psycho-analysis when it succeeded in demonstrating that certain common mental acts of normal people, for which no one had hitherto attempted to put forward a psychological explanation, were to be regarded in the same light as the symptoms of neurotics: that is to say, they had a *meaning*, which was unknown to the subject but which could easily be discovered by analytic means. The phenomena in question were such events as the temporary forgetting of familiar words and names, forgetting to carry out prescribed tasks, everyday slips of the tongue and of the pen, misreadings losses and mislayings of objects, certain errors, instances of apparently accidental self-injury, and finally habitual movements carried out seemingly without intention or in play, tunes hummed "thoughtlessly" and so on. All of these were shorn of their physiological explanation, if any such had ever been attempted, were shown to be strictly determined and were revealed as an expression of the subject's suppressed intentions or as a result of a clash between two intentions one of which was permanently or temporarily unconscious. The importance of this contribution to psychology was of many kinds. The range of mental determinism was extended by it in an unforeseen manner; the supposed gulf between normal and pathological mental events was narrowed; in many cases a useful insight was afforded into the play of mental forces that must be suspected to lie behind the phenomena. Finally, a class of material was brought to light which is calculated better than any other to stimulate a belief in the existence of unconscious mental acts even in people to whom the hypothesis of something at once mental and unconscious seems strange and even absurd. The study of one's own parapraxes and haphazard acts, for which most people have ample opportunities, is even to-day the best preparation for an approach to psycho-analysis. In analytic treatment, the interpretation of parapraxes retains a place as a means of uncovering the unconscious, alongside the immeasurably more important interpretation of associations.

The Interpretation of Dreams.—A new approach to the depths of mental life was opened when the technique of free association was applied to dreams, whether one's own or those of patients in analysis. In fact, the greater and better part of what we know of the processes in the unconscious levels of the mind is derived from the interpretation of dreams. Psycho-analysis has restored to dreams the importance which was generally ascribed to them in ancient times, but it treats them differently. It does not rely upon the cleverness of the dream-interpreter but for the most part hands the task over to the dreamer himself by asking him for his associations to the separate elements of the dream. By pursuing these associations further we obtain knowledge of thoughts which coincide entirely with the dream but which can be recognized—up to a certain point—as genuine and completely intelligible portions of waking mental activity. Thus the recollected dream emerges as the *manifest dream-content,* in contrast to the *latent dream-thoughts* discovered by interpretation. The process which has transformed the latter into the former, that is to say into "the dream," and which is undone by the work of interpretation, may be called the *"dream-work."*

We also describe the latent dream-thoughts, on account of their connection with waking life, as *"residues of the [previous] day."* By the operation of the dream-work (to which it would be quite incorrect to ascribe any "creative" character) the latent dream-thoughts are *condensed* in a remarkable way, are *distorted* by the *displacement* of psychical intensities and are arranged with a view to being *represented in visual pictures;* and, besides all this, before the manifest dream is arrived at, they are submitted to a process *of secondary revision* which seeks to give the new product something in the nature of sense and coherence. Strictly speaking, this last process does not form a part of the dream-work.

The Dynamic Theory of Dream-Formation.—An understanding of the dynamics of dream-formation did not involve any very great difficulties. The motive power for the formation of dreams is not provided by the latent dream-thoughts or day's residues, but by an unconscious impulse, repressed during the day, with which the day's residues have been able to establish contact and which contrives to make a *wish-fulfilment* for itself out of the material of the latent thoughts. Thus every dream is on the one hand the fulfilment of a wish on the part of the unconscious and on the other hand (in so far as it succeeds in guarding the state of sleep against being disturbed) the fulfilment of the normal wish to sleep which set the sleep going. If we disregard the unconscious contribution to the formation of the dream and limit the dream to its latent thoughts, it can represent anything with which waking life has been concerned—a reflection, a warning, an intention, a preparation for the immediate future or, once again, the satisfaction of an unfulfilled wish. The unrecognizability, strangeness and absurdity of the manifest dream are partly the result of the translation of the thoughts into a different, so to say *archaic,* method of expression, but partly the effect of a restrictive, critically disapproving agency in the mind, which does not entirely cease to function during sleep. It is plausible to suppose that the *"dream-censorship,"* which we regard as being responsible in the first instance for the distortion of the dream-thoughts into the manifest dream, is an expression of the same mental forces which during the day-time had held back or *repressed* the unconscious wishful impulse.

It has been worth while to enter in some detail into the explanation of dreams, since analytic work has shown that the dynamics of the formation of dreams are the same as those of the formation of symptoms. In both cases we find a struggle between two trends, of which one is unconscious and ordinarily repressed and strives towards satisfaction—that is, wish-fulfilment—while the other, belonging probably to the conscious ego, is disapproving and repressive. The outcome of this conflict is a *compromise-formation* (the dream or the symptom) in which both trends have found an incomplete expression. The theoretical importance of this conformity between dreams and symptoms is illuminating. Since dreams are not pathological phenomena, the fact shows that the mental mechanisms which produce the symptoms of illness are equally present in normal mental life, that the same uniform law embraces both the normal and the abnormal and that the findings of research into neurotics or psychotics cannot be without significance for our understanding of the healthy mind.

Symbolism.—In the course of investigating the form of expression brought about by the dream-work, the surprising fact emerged that certain objects, arrangements and relations are represented, in a sense indirectly, by "symbols," which are used by the dreamer without his understanding them and to which as a rule he offers no associations. Their translation has to be provided by the analyst, who can himself only discover it empirically by experimentally fitting it into the context. It was later found that linguistic usage, mythology and folklore afford the most ample analogies to dream-symbols. Symbols, which raise the most interesting and hitherto unsolved problems, seem to be a fragment of extremely ancient inherited mental equipment. The use of a common symbolism extends far beyond the use of a common language.

The Aetiological Significance of Sexual Life.—The second novelty which emerged after the hypnotic technique had been replaced by free associations was of a clinical nature. It was discovered in the course of the prolonged search for the traumatic experiences from which hysterical symptoms appeared to be derived. The more carefully the search was pursued the more extensive seemed to be the network of aetiologically significant impressions, but the further back, too, did they reach into the patient's puberty or childhood. At the same time they assumed a uniform character and eventually it became inevitable to bow before the evidence and recognize that at the root of the formation of every symptom there were to be found traumatic experiences from early sexual life. Thus a sexual trauma stepped into the place of an ordinary trauma and the latter was seen to owe its aetiological significance to an associative or symbolic connection with the former, which had preceded it. An investigation of cases of common nervousness (falling into the two classes of *neurasthenia* and *anxiety neurosis*) which was simultaneously undertaken led to the conclusion that these disorders could be traced to *contemporary* abuses in the patients' sexual life and could be removed if these were brought to an end. It was thus easy to infer that neuroses in general are an expression of disturbances in sexual life, the so-called *actual-neuroses* being the consequences (by chemical agency) of *contemporary* injuries and the *psycho-neuroses* the consequences (by psychical modification) of *bygone* injuries to a biological function which had hitherto been gravely neglected by science. None of the theses of psycho-analysis has met with such tenacious scepticism or such embittered resistance as this assertion of the preponderating aetiological significance of sexual life in the neuroses. It should, however, be expressly remarked that, in its development up to the present day, psycho-analysis has found no reason to retreat from this opinion.

Infantile Sexuality.—As a result of its aetiological researches, psycho-analysis found itself in the position of dealing with a subject the very existence of which had scarcely been suspected previously. Science had become accustomed to consider sexual life as beginning with puberty and regarded manifestations of sexuality in children as rare signs of abnormal precocity and degeneracy. But now psycho-analysis revealed a wealth of phenomena, remarkable, yet of regular occurrence, which made it necessary to date back the beginning of the sexual function in children almost to the commencement of extrauterine existence; and it was asked with astonishment how all this could have come to be overlooked. The first glimpses of sexuality in children had indeed been obtained through the analytic examination of adults and were consequently saddled with all the doubts and sources of error that could be attributed to such a belated retrospect; but subsequently (from 1908 onwards) a beginning was made with the analysis of children themselves and with the unembarrassed observation of their behaviour, and in this way direct confirmation was reached for the whole factual basis of the new view.

Sexuality in children showed a different picture in many respects from that in adults, and, surprisingly enough, it exhibited numerous traces of what, in adults, were condemned as *"perversions."* It became necessary to enlarge the concept of what was sexual, till it covered more than the impulsion towards the union of the two sexes in the sexual act or towards provoking particular pleasurable sensations in the genitals. But this enlargement was rewarded by the new possibility of grasping infantile, normal and perverse sexual life as a single whole.

The analytic researches carried out by the writer fell, to begin with, into the error of greatly overestimating the importance of *seduction* as a source of sexual manifestations in children and as a root for the formation of neurotic symptoms. This misapprehension was corrected when it became possible to appreciate the extraordinarily large part played in the mental life of neurotics by the activities of *phantasy,* which clearly carried more weight in neurosis than did external reality. Behind these phantasies there came to light the material which allows us to draw the picture which follows of the development of the sexual function.

The Development of the Libido.—The sexual instinct, the dynamic manifestation of which in mental life we shall call *"libido,"* is made up of component instincts into which it may once more break up and which are only gradually united into well-defined organizations. The sources of these component instincts are the organs of the body and in particular certain specially marked *erotogenic zones;* but contributions are made to libido from every important functional process in the body. At first the individual component instincts strive for satisfaction independently of one another, but in the course of development they become more and more convergent and concentrated. The first (pregenital) stage of organization to be discerned is the *oral* one, in which—in conformity with the suckling's predominant interest—the oral zone plays the leading part. This is followed by the *sadistic-anal* organization, in which the *anal* zone and the component instinct of *sadism* are particularly prominent; at this stage the difference between the sexes is represented by the contrast between active and passive. The third and final stage of organization is that in which the majority of the component instincts converge under the *primacy of the genital zones.* As a rule this development is passed through swiftly and unobtrusively; but some individual portions of the instincts remain behind at the prodromal stages of the process and thus give rise to *fixations* of libido, which are important as constituting predispositions for subsequent irruptions of repressed impulses and which stand in a definite relation to the later development of neuroses and perversions. (See the article on "The Libido Theory.")

The Process of Finding an Object, and the Oedipus Complex.—In the first instance the oral component instinct finds satisfaction by attaching itself to the sating of the desire for nourishment; and its object is the mother's breast. It then detaches itself, becomes independent and at the same time *auto-erotic,* that is, it finds an object in the child's own body. Others of the component instincts also start by being auto-erotic and are not until later diverted on to an external object. It is a particularly important fact that the component instincts belonging to the genital zone habitually pass through a period of intense auto-erotic satisfaction. The component instincts are not all equally serviceable in the final genital organization of libido; some of them (for instance, the anal components) are consequently left aside and suppressed, or undergo complicated transformations.

In the very earliest years of childhood (approximately between the ages of two and five) a convergence of the sexual impulses occurs of which, in the case of boys, the object is the mother. This choice of an object, in conjunction with a corresponding attitude of rivalry and hostility towards the father, provides the content of what is known as the *Oedipus complex,* which in every human being is of the greatest importance in determining the final shape of his erotic life. It has been found to be characteristic of a normal individual that he learns to master his Oedipus complex, whereas the neurotic subject remains involved in it.

The Diphasic Onset of Sexual Development.—Towards the end of the fifth year this early period of sexual life normally comes to an end. It is succeeded by a period of more or less complete *latency,* during which ethical restraints are built up, to act as defences against the desires of the Oedipus complex. In the subsequent period of *puberty,* the Oedipus complex is revivified in the unconscious and embarks upon further modifications. It is only at puberty that the sexual instincts develop to their full intensity; but the direction of that development, as well as all the predispositions for it, have already been determined by the early efflorescence of sexuality during childhood which preceded it. This diphasic development of the sexual function—in two stages, interrupted by the latency period—appears to be a biological peculiarity of the human species and to contain the determining factor for the origin of neuroses.

The Theory of Repression.—These theoretical considerations, taken together with the immediate impressions derived from analytic work, lead to a view of the neuroses which may be described in the roughest outline as follows. The neuroses are the expression of conflicts between the ego and such of the sexual impulses as seem to the ego incompatible with its integrity or with its ethical standards. Since these impulses are not *ego-syntonic,* the ego has *repressed* them: that is to say, it has withdrawn its interest from them and has shut them off from becoming conscious as well as from obtaining satisfaction by motor discharge. If in the course of analytic work one attempts to make these repressed impulses conscious, one becomes aware of the repressive forces in the form of *resistance.* But the achievement of repression fails particularly readily in the case of the sexual instincts. Their dammed-up libido finds other ways out from the unconscious: for it *regresses* to earlier phases of development and earlier attitudes towards objects, and, at weak points in the libidinal development where there are infantile fixations, it breaks through into consciousness and obtains discharge. What results is a *symptom* and consequently in its essence a substitutive sexual satisfaction. Nevertheless the symptom cannot entirely escape from the repressive forces of the ego and must therefore submit to modifications and displacements—exactly as happens with dreams—by means of which its characteristic of being a sexual satisfaction becomes unrecognizable. Consequently symptoms are in the nature of compromises between the repressed sexual instincts and the repressing ego instincts; they represent a wish-fulfilment for both partners to the conflict simultaneously, but one which is incomplete for each of them. This is quite strictly true of the symptoms of hysteria, while in the symptoms of obsessional neurosis there is often a stronger emphasis upon the side of the repressing function owing to the erection of reaction-formations, which are assurances against sexual satisfaction.

Transference.—If further proof were needed of the truth that the motive forces behind the formation of neurotic symptoms are of a sexual nature, it would be found in the fact that in the course of analytic treatment a special emotional relation is regularly formed between the patient and the physician. This goes far beyond rational limits. It varies between the most affectionate devotion and the most obstinate enmity and derives all of its characteristics from earlier erotic attitudes of the patient's which have become unconscious. This *transference* alike in its positive and in its negative form is used as a weapon by the resistance; but in the hands of the physician it becomes the most powerful therapeutic instrument and it plays a part scarcely to be over-estimated in the dynamics of the process of cure.

The Corner-Stones of Psycho-Analytic Theory.—The assumption that there are unconscious mental processes, the recognition of the theory of resistance and repression, the appreciation of the importance of sexuality and of the Oedipus complex—these constitute the principal subject-matter of psycho-analysis and the foundations of its theory. No one who cannot accept them all should count himself a psycho-analyst.

Later History of Psycho-Analysis.—Psycho-analysis was carried approximately thus far by the work of the writer of this article, who for more than ten years was its sole representative. In 1906 the Swiss psychiatrists Bleuler and C. G. Jung began to play a lively part in analysis; in 1907 a first conference of its supporters took place at Salzburg; and the young science soon found itself the centre of interest both among psychiatrists and laymen. Its reception in Germany, with her morbid craving for authority, was not precisely to the credit of German science and moved even so cool a partisan as Bleuler to an energetic protest. Yet no condemnation or dismissal at official congresses served to hold up the internal growth or external expansion of psycho-analysis. In the course of the next ten years it extended far beyond the frontiers of Europe and became especially popular in the United States of America, and this was due in no small degree to the advocacy and collaboration of Putnam (Boston), Ernest Jones (Toronto; later London), Flournoy (Geneva), Ferenczi (Budapest), Abraham (Berlin), and many others besides. The anathema which was imposed upon psycho-analysis led its supporters to combine in an international organization which in the present year (1922) is holding its eighth private Congress in Berlin and now includes local groups in Vienna, Budapest, Berlin, Holland, Zurich, London, New York, Calcutta and Moscow. This development was not interrupted even by the World War. In 1918–19 Dr. Anton von Freund of Budapest founded the Internationaler Psychoanalytischer Verlag, which publishes journals and books concerned with psycho-analysis, and in 1920 Dr. M. Eitingon opened in Berlin the first psycho-analytic clinic for the treatment of neurotics without private means. Translations of the writer's principal works, which are now in preparation, into French, Italian and Spanish, testify to a growing interest in psycho-analysis in the Latin world as well.

Between 1911 and 1913 two movements of divergence from psycho-analysis took place, evidently with the object of mitigating its repellent features. One of these (sponsored by C. G. Jung), in an endeavour to conform to ethical standards, divested the Oedipus complex of its real significance by giving it only a *symbolic* value, and in practice neglected the uncovering of the forgotten and, as we may call it, "prehistoric" period of childhood. The other (originated by Alfred Adler in Vienna) reproduced many factors from psycho-analysis under other names—repression, for instance, appeared in a sexualized version as the "masculine protest." But in other respects it turned away from the unconscious and the sexual instincts, and endeavoured to trace back the development of character and of the neuroses to the "will to power," which by means of overcompensation strives to check the dangers arising from "organ inferiority." Neither of these movements, with their systematic structures, had any permanent influence on psycho-analysis. In the case of Adler's theories it soon became clear that they had very little in common with psycho-analysis, which they were designed to replace.

More Recent Advances in Psycho-Analysis.—Since psycho-analysis has become the field of work for such a large number of observers it has made advances, both in extent and depth; but unfortunately these can receive only the briefest mention in the present article.

Narcissism.—The most important theoretical advance has certainly been the application of the libido theory to the repressing ego. The ego itself came to be regarded as a reservoir of what was described as narcissistic libido, from which the libidinal cathexes of objects flowed out and into which they could be once more withdrawn. By the help of this conception it became possible to embark upon the analysis of the ego and to make a clinical distinction of the psychoneuroses into *transference neuroses* and *narcissistic* disorders. In the former (hysteria and obsessional neurosis) the subject has at his disposal a quantity of libido striving to be transferred on to extraneous objects, and use is made of this in carrying out analytic treatment; on the other hand, the narcissistic disorders (dementia praecox, paranoia, melancholia) are characterized by a withdrawal of the libido from objects and they are therefore scarcely accessible to analytic therapy. But their therapeutic inaccessibility has not prevented analysis from making the most fruitful beginnings in the deeper study of these illnesses, which are counted among the psychoses.

Development of Technique.—After the analyst's curiosity had, as it were, been gratified by the elaboration of the technique of interpretation, it was inevitable that interest should turn to the problem of discovering the most effective way of influencing the patient. It soon became evident that the physician's immediate task was to assist the patient in getting to know, and afterwards in overcoming, the resistances which emerged in him during treatment and of which, to begin with, he himself was unaware. And it was found at the same time that the essential part of the process of cure lay in the overcoming of these resistances and that unless this was achieved no permanent mental change could be brought about in the patient. Since the analyst's efforts have in this way been directed upon the patient's resistance, analytic technique has attained a certainty and delicacy rivalling that of surgery. Consequently, everyone is strongly advised against undertaking psycho-analytic treatments without a strict training, and a physician who ventures upon them on the strength of his medical qualification is in no respect better than a layman.

Psycho-Analysis as a Therapeutic Procedure.—Psycho-analysis has never set itself up as a panacea and has never claimed to perform miracles. In one of the most difficult spheres of medical activity it is the only possible method of treatment for certain illnesses and for others it is the method which yields the best or the most permanent results—though never without a corresponding expenditure of time and trouble. A physician who is not wholly absorbed in the work of giving help will find his labours amply repaid by obtaining an unhoped-for insight into the complications of mental life and the interrelations between the mental and the physical. Where at present it cannot offer help but only theoretical understanding, it may perhaps be preparing the way for some later, more direct means of influencing neurotic disorders. Its province is above all the two transference neuroses, hysteria and obsessional neurosis, in which it has contributed to the discovery of their internal structure and operative mechanisms; and, beyond them, all kinds of phobias, inhibitions, deformities of character, sexual perversions and difficulties in erotic life. Some analysts (Jelliffe, Groddeck, Felix Deutsch) have reported too that the analytic treatment of gross organic diseases is not unpromising, since a mental factor not infrequently contributes to the origin and continuance of such illnesses. Since psycho-analysis demands a certain amount of physical plasticity from its patients, some kind of age-limit must be laid down in their selection; and since it necessitates the devotion of long and intense attention to the individual patient, it would be uneconomical to squander such expenditure upon completely worthless persons who happen to be neurotic. Experience upon material in clinics can alone show what modifications may be necessary in order to make psycho-analytic treatment accessible to wider strata of the population or to adapt it to weaker intelligences.

Comparison between Psycho-Analysis and Hypnotic and Suggestive Methods.—Psycho-analytic procedure differs from all methods making use of suggestion, persuasion, etc., in that it does not seek to suppress by means of authority any mental phenomenon that may occur in the patient. It endeavours to trace the causation of the phenomenon and to remove it by bringing about a permanent modification in the conditions that led to it. In psycho-analysis the suggestive influence which is inevitably exercised by the physician is diverted on to the task assigned to the patient of overcoming his resistances, that is, of carrying forward the curative process. Any danger of falsifying the products of a patient's memory by sugges-tion can be avoided by prudent handling of the technique; but in general the arousing of resistances is a guarantee against the misleading effects of suggestive influence. It may be laid down that the aim of the treatment is to remove the patient's resistances and to pass his repressions in review and thus to bring about the most far-reaching unification and strengthening of his ego, to enable him to save the mental energy which he is expending upon internal conflicts, to make the best of him that his inherited capacities will allow and so to make him as efficient and as capable of enjoyment as is possible. The removal of the symptoms of the illness is not specifically aimed at, but is achieved, as it were, as a by-product if the analysis is properly carried through. The analyst respects the patient's indi-viduality and does not seek to remould him in accordance with his own—that is, according to the physician's—personal ideals; he is glad to avoid giving advice and instead to arouse the patient's power of initiative.

Its Relation to Psychiatry.—Psychiatry is at present essentially a descriptive and classifica-tory science whose orientation is still towards the somatic rather than the psychological and which is without the possibility of giving explanations of the phenomena which it observes. Psycho-analysis does not, however, stand in opposition to it, as the almost unanimous behav-iour of the psychiatrists might lead one to believe. On the contrary, as a *depth-psychology,* a psychology of those processes in mental life which are withdrawn from consciousness, it is called upon to provide psychiatry with an indispensable groundwork and to free it from its present limitations. We can foresee that the future will give birth to a scientific psychiatry, to which psycho-analysis has served as an introduction.

Criticisms and Misunderstandings of Psycho-Analysis.—Most of what is brought up against psycho-analysis, even in scientific works, is based upon insufficient information which in its turn seems to be determined by emotional resistances. Thus it is a mistake to accuse psycho-analysis of "pan-sexualism" and to allege that it derives all mental occurrences from sexuality and traces them all back to it. On the contrary, psycho-analysis has from the very first distinguished the sexual instincts from others which it has provisionally termed "ego instincts." It has never dreamt of trying to explain "everything," and even the neuroses it has traced back not to sexuality alone but to the conflict between the sexual impulses and the ego. In psycho-analysis (unlike the works of C. G. Jung) the term *"libido"* does not mean psy-chical energy in general but the motive force of the sexual instincts. Some assertions, such as that every dream is the fulfilment of a sexual wish, have never been maintained by it at all. The charge of one-sidedness made against psycho-analysis, which, as *the science of the uncon-scious mind,* has its own definite and restricted field of work, is as inapplicable as it would be if it were made against chemistry. To believe that psycho-analysis seeks a cure for neurotic disorders by giving a free rein to sexuality is a serious misunderstanding which can only be excused by ignorance. The making conscious of repressed sexual desires in analysis makes it possible, on the contrary, to obtain a mastery over them which the previous repression had been unable to achieve. It can more truly be said that analysis sets the neurotic free from the chains of his sexuality. Moreover, it is quite unscientific to judge analysis by whether it is calculated to undermine religion, authority and morals; for, like all sciences, it is entirely non-tendentious and has only a single aim—namely to arrive at a consistent view of one portion of reality. Finally, one can only characterize as simple-minded the fear which is sometimes expressed that all the highest goods of humanity, as they are called—research, art, love, ethical and social sense—will lose their value or their dignity because psycho-analysis is in a position to demonstrate their origin in elementary and animal instinctual impulses.

The Non-Medical Applications and Correlations of Psycho-Analysis.—Any estimate of psycho-analysis would be incomplete if it failed to make clear that, alone among the medical disciplines, it has the most extensive relations with the mental sciences, and that it is in a position to play a part of the same importance in the studies of religious and cultural history and in the sciences of mythology and literature as it is in psychiatry. This may seem strange when we reflect that originally its only object was the understanding and improvement of neurotic symptoms. But it is easy to indicate the starting-point of the bridge that leads over to the mental sciences. The analysis of dreams gave us an insight into the unconscious processes of the mind and showed us that the mechanisms which produce pathological symptoms are also operative in the normal mind. Thus psycho-analysis became a *depth-psychology* and capable as such of being applied to the mental sciences, and it was able to answer a good number of questions with which the academic psychology of consciousness was helpless to deal. At quite an early stage problems of human *phylogenesis* arose. It became clear that pathological function was often nothing more than a *regression* to an earlier stage in the development of normal function. C. G. Jung was the first to draw explicit attention to the striking similarity between the disordered phantasies of sufferers from dementia praecox and the myths of primitive peoples; while the present writer pointed out that the two wishes which combine to form the Oedipus complex coincide precisely with the two principal prohibitions imposed by *totemism* (not to kill the tribal ancestor and not to marry any woman belonging to one's own clan) and drew far-reaching conclusions from this fact. The significance of the Oedipus complex began to grow to gigantic proportions and it looked as though social order, morals, justice and religion had arisen together in the primaeval ages of mankind as reaction-formations against the Oedipus complex. Otto Rank threw a brilliant light upon mythology and the history of literature by the application of psycho-analytic views, as did Theodor Reik upon the history of morals and religions, while Dr. Pfister, of Zurich, aroused the interest of religious and secular teachers and demonstrated the importance of the psycho-analytic standpoint for education. Further discussion of these applications of psycho-analysis would be out of place here, and it is enough to say that the limits of their influence are not yet in sight.

Psycho-Analysis an Empirical Science.—Psycho-analysis is not, like philosophies, a system starting out from a few sharply defined basic concepts, seeking to grasp the whole universe with the help of these and, once it is completed, having no room for fresh discoveries or better understanding. On the contrary, it keeps close to the facts in its field of study, seeks to solve the immediate problems of observation, gropes its way forward by the help of experience, is always incomplete and always ready to correct or modify its theories. There is no incongruity (any more than in the case of physics or chemistry) if its most general concepts lack clarity and if its postulates are provisional; it leaves their more precise definition to the results of future work.

SEMINAR ON "THE PURLOINED LETTER" (1956)

JACQUES LACAN

Translated from the French by Bruce Fink

Lacan saw his essay on Edgar Allan Poe's story "The Purloined Letter" as the best place to begin reading his writing, as an "entryway" to his style, a sometimes surprisingly literary style for psycho-analytic writing. Lacan's intense focus on language has contributed to his writing's appeal for literary critics. Readers will get more from Lacan's essay if they read Poe's story first. Lacan argued that the unconscious—one of the key concepts for psychoanalysis—is structured like a language. He based that argument on Saussure's description of the linguistic sign as the signifier bonded to a signified, with signifiers gaining meaning not in themselves but instead through their links to other signifiers. (See the selection from Saussure in this volume.) Thus the unconscious, as revealed through the sig-nifiers of dreams and symptoms, is structured through representation, like a language. Lacan reads the repetitions of Poe's story as dramatizing the centrality of language and signifiers, the repetitions that make the signifying chain and what Lacan calls the symbolic.

The symbolic is part of a triad of three orders that organize Lacan's interpretation of the human psyche: the imaginary, the symbolic, and the real. The three orders can hardly be reduced to pithy summary, but summary can introduce them and help lead readers to Lacan's own writing. For Lacan, as he describes in his essay on "The Mirror Stage," the infant misrecognizes itself in its mirror image, supposing that the logic of a complete reflection reveals a wholeness of the "I" or ego, which therefore leads the infant to live its psychic life in the imaginary. In the imaginary there is no differ-ence and no absence. Instead, there is fullness and immediacy. In the imaginary, therefore, there is no self versus other, no sense of distance or incompleteness.

But the imaginary cannot last in its unquestioned fullness. The Oedipus complex described by Freud disrupts the imaginary through the threat of castration, thus casting the infant out of the imaginary and into the symbolic, that is, into language. While in the imaginary there is no differ-ence and no absence, in the symbolic difference and absence take over. Instead of the fullness and immediacy of the imaginary, in the symbolic there is incompleteness and distance, characteristics inherent to language and representation, where, as Saussure argues, the signifier gains its meaning by a relation to but not by a full identity with other signifiers.

Through most of Lacan's career, including in his essay on "The Purloined Letter," he paid little heed to the real, the underlying intransigent that resists definition. For that reason, as Lacan's influ-ence gathered force in cultural and literary criticism, the imaginary and the symbolic received most of the attention. Later in his career, Lacan wrote more about the real, and some recent Lacanian critics, notably Slavoj Žižek, give it special attention, as readers can see in Žižek's essay included in this volume. While dedicated Lacanians like Žižek now often focus on the real, on what cannot be explained, most other critics continue to focus on the imaginary and the symbolic, and they continue to address the symbolic as Lacan describes it in his "Seminar on 'The Purloined Letter,'" where he argues for "the signifier's priority over the signified" and concludes, in the famous final words of his essay, that "a letter"—that is, the linguistic signifier itself—"always arrives at its destination."

(Lacan later added additional material after the end of the essay that does not address Poe's story and is not included here. His epigraph at the beginning of the essay comes from Goethe's Faust. *In English, it reads: "And if we score hits / And everything fits, / It's thoughts that we feel" (translation by Walter Kaufman [Garden City, NY: Doubleday, 1961], 245). Asterisks indicate words that Lacan wrote in English.)*

> *Und wenn es uns glückt,*
> *Und wenn es sich schickt,*
> *So sind es Gedanken.*

My research has led me to the realization that repetition automatism (*Wieder-holungszwang*) has its basis in what I have called the *insistence* of the signifying chain. I have isolated this notion as a correlate of the *ex-sistence* (that is, of the eccentric place) in which we must necessarily locate the subject of the unconscious, if we are to take Freud's discovery seriously. As we know, it is in the experience inaugurated by psycho-analysis that we can grasp by what oblique imaginary means the *symbolic* takes hold in even the deepest recesses of the human organism.

The teaching of this seminar is designed to maintain that imaginary effects, far from representing the core of analytic experience, give us nothing of any consistency unless they are related to the symbolic chain that binds and orients them.

I am, of course, aware of the importance of imaginary impregnations (*Prägung*) in the partializations of the symbolic alternative that give the signifying chain its appearance. Nevertheless, I posit that it is the law specific to this chain which governs the psycho-analytic effects that are determinant for the subject—effects such as foreclosure (*Verwerfung*), repression (*Verdrängung*), and negation (*Verneinung*) itself—and I add with the appropriate emphasis that these effects follow the displacement (*Entstellwig*) of the signifier so faithfully that imaginary factors, despite their inertia, figure only as shadows and reflections therein.

But this emphasis would be lavished in vain if it merely served, in your view, to abstract a general form from phenomena whose particularity in analytic experience would remain the core thing to you and whose original composite nature could be broken down only through artifice.

This is why I have decided to illustrate for you today a truth which may be drawn from the moment in Freud's thought we have been studying—namely, that it is the symbolic order which is constitutive for the subject—by demonstrating in a story the major determination the subject receives from the itinerary of a signifier.

It is this truth, let us note, that makes the very existence of fiction possible. Thus a fable is as appropriate as any other story for shedding light on it—provided we are willing to put the fable's coherence to the test. With this proviso, a fable even has the advantage of manifesting symbolic necessity all more purely in that we might be inclined to believe it is governed by the arbitrary.

This is why, without looking any further, I have taken my example from the very story in which we find the dialectic of the game of "even or odd," from which we very recently gleaned something of importance. It is probably no accident that this story proved propitious for the continuation of a line of research which had already relied upon it.

As you know, I am referring to the tale Baudelaire translated into French as "La lettre volée." In it we must immediately distinguish between a drama and its narration as well as the conditions of that narration.

We quickly perceive, moreover, what makes these components necessary and realize that their composer could not have created them unintentionally.

For the narration effectively doubles the drama with a commentary without which no *mise-en-scène* would be possible. Let us say that the action would remain, strictly speaking, invisible to the audience—aside from the fact that the dialogue would be expressly and by dramatic necessity devoid of whatever meaning it might have for a listener. In other words, nothing of the drama could appear, either in the framing of the images or the sampling of the sounds, without the oblique light shed, so to speak, on each scene by the narration from the point of view that one of the actors had while playing his role in it.

There are two such scenes, the first of which I shall immediately designate as the primal scene, and by no means inattentively, since the second may be considered its repetition in the sense of the latter term that I have been articulating in this very seminar.

The primal scene is thus performed, we are told, in the royal boudoir, such that we suspect that the "personage of most exalted station," also referred to as the "illustrious personage," who is alone there when she receives a letter, is the Queen. This sense is confirmed by the awkward situation she is put in "by the entrance of the other exalted personage," of whom we have already been told prior to this account that, were he to come to know of the letter in question, it would jeopardize for the lady nothing less than her "honor and peace." Any doubt that he is in fact the King is promptly dissipated in the course of the scene which begins with the entrance of Minister D—. For at that moment the Queen can do no better than to take advantage of the King's inattentiveness by leaving the letter on the table turned face down, "address uppermost." This does not, however, escape the Minister's lynx eye, nor does he fail to notice the Queen's distress and thus to fathom her secret. From then on everything proceeds like clockwork. After dealing with the business of the day with his customary speed and intelligence, the Minister draws from his pocket a letter similar in appearance to the one before his eyes and, after pretending to read it, places it next to the other. A bit more conversation to pull the wool over the royal eyes, whereupon he picks up the embarrassing letter without flinching and decamps, while the Queen, on whom none of his maneuver has been lost, remains unable to intervene for fear of attracting the attention of her royal spouse, who is standing at her elbow at that very moment.

An ideal spectator might have noticed nothing of this operation in which no one batted an eye, and whose *quotient* is that the Minister has filched from the Queen her letter and, even more important, that the Queen knows that he now has it, and by no means innocently.

A *remainder* that no analyst will neglect, trained as he is to remember everything having to do with the signifier even if he does not always know what to do with it: the letter, left on hand by the Minister, which the Queen is now free to crumple up.

Second scene: in the Minister's office at the Ministerial hotel. We know from the account the Prefect of Police has given Dupin, whose genius for solving enigmas Poe mentions here for the second time, that the police have searched the hotel and its surroundings from top to bottom for the last three months, returning there as often as the Minister's regular absences at night allow them to. In vain, however, although anyone can deduce from the situation that the Minister keeps the letter within easy reach.

Dupin calls on the Minister. The latter greets him with a show of nonchalance, affecting in his conversation romantic ennui. Meanwhile Dupin, who is not taken in by this feigning, inspects the premises his eyes protected by green spectacles. When his gaze alights upon a very chafed letter—which seems to have been abandoned in a compartment of a wretched, eye-catching, trumpery card-rack of pasteboard, hanging right smack in the middle of the mantelpiece—he already knows that he has found what he was looking for. His conviction is reinforced by the very details which seem designed to contradict the description he has been given of the stolen letter, with the exception of the size, which fits.

Whereupon he has but to take his leave, after having "forgotten" his snuffbox on the table, in order to return the following day to reclaim it—armed with a facsimile of the letter in its present state. When an incident out in the street, prepared for the right moment, draws the Minister to the window, Dupin seizes the opportunity to snatch, in his turn, the letter while replacing it with an imitation [*semblant*], and need but maintain the appearances of a normal exit thereafter.

Here too all has transpired, if not without any sound, at least without any din. The quotient of the operation is that the Minister no longer has the letter, but he knows nothing of it and is far from suspecting that it is Dupin who ravished it from him. Moreover, what he is left with here is far from insignificant for what follows. I shall return later to what led Dupin to jot something down on his factitious letter. In any case, when the Minister tries to make use of it, he will be able to read the following words, whose source, Dupin tells us, is Crébillon's *Atrée*, written so that he may recognize Dupin's hand:

> *Un dessein si funeste*
> *S'il n'est digne d'Atrée, est digne de Thyeste.*

Need I emphasize the resemblance between these two actions? Yes, for the similarity I have in mind is not made up of the simple union of traits chosen only in order to prepare [*appareiller*] their difference. And it would not suffice to retain the traits of resemblance at the expense of the others for any truth whatsoever to result therefrom. It is, rather, the intersubjectivity by which the two actions are motivated that I wish to highlight, as well as the three terms with which that intersubjectivity structures them.

These terms derive their privileged status from the fact that they correspond both to the three logical moments through which decision is precipitated and to the three places which this decision assigns to the subjects that it separates out.

This decision is reached in the moment of a glance [*regard*].[1] For the maneuvers that follow, however stealthily that moment is prolonged in them, add nothing to it, no more than their deferral of the opportunity in the second scene disrupts the unity of that moment.

This glance presupposes two others, which it assembles to provide a view of the opening left in their fallacious complementarity, anticipating there the plunder afforded by that uncovering. Thus three moments, ordering three glances, sustained by three subjects, incarnated in each case by different people.

The first is based on a glance that sees nothing: the King and then the police.

The second is based on a glance which sees that the first sees nothing and deceives itself into thereby believing to be covered what it hides: the Queen and then the Minister.

The third is based on a glance which sees that the first two glances leave what must be hidden uncovered to whomever would seize it: the Minister and finally Dupin.

In order to get you to grasp in its unity the intersubjective complex thus described, I would willingly seek patronage for it in the technique legendarily attributed to the ostrich [*autruche*] when it seeks shelter from danger. For this technique might finally be qualified as political, distributed as it is here among three partners, the second believing himself invisible because the first has his head stuck in the sand, all the while letting the third calmly pluck his rear. We need but enrich its proverbial denomination by a letter, producing *la politique de l'autruiche,* for this technique in itself to finally take on a new everlasting meaning.

Having thus established the intersubjective module of the action that repeats, we must now indicate in it a *repetition automatism* in the sense that interests us in Freud's work.

The fact that we have here a plurality of subjects can, of course, in no way constitute an objection to those who are long accustomed to the perspectives summarized by my formulation: *the unconscious is the Other's discourse.* I will not remind you now what the notion of the *inmixing of subjects,* recently introduced in my reanalysis of the dream of Irma's injection, adds here.

What interests me today is the way in which the subjects, owing to their displacement, relay each other in the course of the intersubjective repetition.

We shall see that their displacement is determined by the place that a pure signifier—the purloined letter—comes to occupy in their trio. This is what will confirm for us that it is repetition automatism.

It does not, however, seem superfluous, before pursuing this line of inquiry, to ask whether the aim of the tale and the interest we take in it—inasmuch as they coincide—do not lie elsewhere.

Can we consider the fact that the tale is told to us as a mystery story to be a simple "rationalization," as we say in our crude jargon?

In truth, we would be justified in considering this to be highly dubious, noting as we do that everything about a crime or offense that creates such a mystery—its nature and motives, instruments and execution, the procedure used to discover its author, and the means employed to convict him for it—is carefully eliminated here at the beginning of each episode.

Indeed, the act of deceit is as clearly known from the outset as the plotting of the culprit and its effects on his victim. The problem, as it is exposed to us, is limited to the search for the deceitfully acquired object, for the purposes of restitution; and it seems quite intentional that the solution is already known when it is explained to us. Is that how we are kept in suspense? However much credit we may give the conventions of a genre for arousing a specific interest in the reader, we should not forget that the "Dupin tale"—this being the second to come out—is a prototype, and that since it receives its genre only from the first, it is a little too early for the author to play on a convention.

It would, however, be equally excessive to reduce the whole thing to a fable whose moral would be that, in order to shelter from inquisitive eyes correspondence whose secrecy is sometimes necessary to conjugal peace, it suffices to leave the letters lying around on one's table, even if one turns them signifying face down. For that would be a lure which, personally, I would never recommend anyone try, lest he be disappointed at having trusted in it.

Is there then no other mystery here than incompetence resulting in failure on the part of the Prefect of Police? Is there not a certain discordance on Dupin's part, which we are loath to admit, between the assuredly penetrating remarks (which are not, however, always absolutely relevant when generalized) with which he introduces us to his method and the way in which he in fact intervenes?

Were we to pursue a bit further our sense that we are being hoodwinked, we might soon begin to wonder whether—from the inaugural scene, which only the rank of the protagonists saves from degenerating into vaudeville, to the descent into ridicule that seems to await the Minister at the story's conclusion—it is not, indeed, the fact that everyone is duped which gives us such pleasure here.

I would be all the more inclined to think so in that, along with my readers, I would find anew here the definition I once gave, somewhere in passing, of the modern hero, "represented by ridiculous feats in situations of confusion."[2]

But are we ourselves not taken with the imposing bearing of the amateur detective, prototype of a new kind of braggart, as yet safe from the insipidity of our contemporary superman?

That was a joke, yet it makes us note, by way of contrast, so perfect a verisimilitude in this tale that it may be said that truth here reveals its fictional ordering.

For this is certainly the pathway along which the reasons for this verisimilitude lead us. Entering first into its procedure, we perceive, in effect, a new drama that I would call complementary to the first, since the first was what is termed a silent drama whereas the interest of the second plays on the properties of discourse.[3]

Indeed, while it is obvious that each of the two scenes of the real drama is narrated in the course of a different dialogue, one must be provided with certain notions brought out in my teaching to realize that this is not done simply to make the exposition more pleasing, but that the dialogues themselves, in the opposite use they make of the virtues of speech, take on a tension that makes them into a different drama, one which my terminology will distinguish from the first as sustaining itself in the symbolic order.

The first dialogue—between the Prefect of Police and Dupin—is played out as if it were between a deaf man and one who hears. That is, it represents the veritable complexity of what is ordinarily simplified, with the most confused of results, in the notion of communication.

This example demonstrates how communication can give the impression, at which theorists too often stop, of conveying in its transmission but one meaning, as though the highly significant commentary into which he who hears integrates it could be considered neutralized because it is unperceived by he who does not hear.

The fact remains that if we only retain the dialogue's meaning as a report, its verisimilitude appears to depend on a guarantee of accuracy. But the report then turns out to be more fruitful than it seems, provided we demonstrate its procedure, as we shall see by confining our attention to the recounting of the first scene.

For the double and even triple subjective filter through which that scene comes to us—a narration by Dupin's close friend (whom I will refer to henceforth as the story's general narrator) of the account by which the Prefect reveals to Dupin the version the Queen gave him of it—is not merely the consequence of a fortuitous arrangement.

If, indeed, the extremity to which the original narrator is reduced precludes her altering any of the events, we would be wrong to believe that the Prefect is authorized to lend her his voice here only owing to the lack of imagination for which he holds, as it were, the patent.

The fact that the message is retransmitted in this way assures us of something that is absolutely not self-evident: that the message truly belongs to the dimension of language.

Those who are here are familiar with my remarks on the subject, specifically those illustrated by the counterexample of the supposed language of bees, in which a linguist[4] can see nothing more than a signaling of the location of objects—in other words, an imaginary function that is simply more differentiated than the others.

Let me emphasize here that such a form of communication is not absent in man, however evanescent the natural pregivenness [donné naturel] of objects may be for him due to the disintegration they undergo through his use of symbols.

Something equivalent may, in effect, be grasped in the communion established between two people in their hatred directed at a common object, with the proviso that this can never occur except in the case of one single object, an object defined by the characteristics of (the) being that each of the two refuses to accept.

But such communication is not transmittable in symbolic form. It can only be sustained in relation to this object. This is why it can bring together an indefinite number of subjects in a common "ideal"; the communication of one subject with another within the group thus constituted will nonetheless remain irreducibly mediated by an ineffable relation.

This excursion is not merely a reminder here of principles distantly addressed to those who tax me with neglecting nonverbal communication; in determining the scope of what discourse repeats, it prepares the question of what symptoms repeat.

Thus the indirect relating [of the first scene] clarifies the dimension of language, and the general narrator, by redoubling it, "hypothetically" adds nothing to it. But this is not at all true of his role in the second dialogue.

For the latter is opposed to the first like the poles in language that I have distinguished elsewhere and that are opposed to each other like word to speech.

Which is to say that we shift here from the field of accuracy to the register of truth. Now this register—I dare think I need not go back over this—is situated somewhere else altogether: at the very foundation of intersubjectivity. It is situated where the subject can grasp nothing but the very subjectivity that constitutes an Other as an absolute. I shall confine my attention, in order to indicate its place here, to evoking the dialogue which seems to me to warrant its attribution as a Jewish joke due to the nakedness with which the relation between the signifier and speech appears in the entreaty which brings it to a head: "Why are you lying to me?" one character exclaims exasperatedly, "Yes, why are you lying to me by saying you're going to Cracow in order to make me believe you're going to Lemberg, when in reality you *are* going to Cracow?"

A similar question might be raised in our minds by the torrent of aporias, eristic enigmas, paradoxes, and even quips presented to us as an introduction to Dupin's method if the fact that they were confided to us by a would-be disciple did not add some virtue to them, owing to the act of delegation. Such is the unmistakable prestige of legacies: the witness' faithfulness is the wool pulled over the eyes of those who might criticize his testimony.

What could be more convincing, moreover, than the gesture of turning one's cards face up on the table? It is so convincing that we are momentarily persuaded that the prestidigitator has in fact demonstrated, as he promised he would, how his trick was performed, whereas he has only performed it anew in a purer form; this moment makes us appreciate the supremacy of the signifier in the subject.

This is how Dupin operates when he starts with the story of the child prodigy who takes in all his classmates at the game of even or odd with his trick of identifying with his opponent, concerning which I have shown that he cannot reach the first level of its mental elaboration—namely, the notion of intersubjective alternation—without immediately being tripped up by the stop of its recurrence.[5]

This does not stop us from being treated—in order to dazzle us—to the names of La Rochefoucauld, La Bruyère, Machiavelli, and Campanella, whose reputations now seem trivial compared to the child's prowess.

And then to Chamfort, whose maxim that "the odds are that every idea embraced by the public, every accepted convention, is foolish, since it suits the greatest number" will indubitably satisfy all those who think they escape its law, that is, precisely, the greatest number. The fact that Dupin taxes the French with dishonesty when they apply the word "analysis" to algebra has little chance of threatening our pride when, moreover, the freeing of that term for other ends implies nothing that should stop a psychoanalyst from considering himself in a position to assert his rights to it. And off he goes making philological remarks which should positively delight lovers of Latin; when he recalls without deigning to say any more about it that '*ambitus*' [doesn't imply] 'ambition,' '*religio*' 'religion,' '*homines honesti*' a set of *honorable* men," who among you would not take pleasure in remembering . . . what these words mean to assiduous readers of Cicero and Lucretius. No doubt Poe is having a good time . . .

But a suspicion dawns on us: isn't this display of erudition designed to make us hear the magic words of our drama?[6] Isn't the prestidigitator repeating his trick before our eyes, without deluding us into thinking that he is divulging his secret to us this time, but taking his gamble even further by really shedding light on it for us without us seeing a thing? That would be the height of the illusionist's art: to have one of his fictional beings *truly fool us.*

And isn't it such effects which justify our harmless way of referring to many imaginary heroes as real personages?

Thus, when we are open to hearing the way in which Martin Heidegger uncovers for us in the word *alethes* the play of truth, we merely rediscover a secret to which truth has always initiated her lovers, and through which they have learned that it is in hiding that she offers herself to them *most truly.*

Thus, even if Dupin's comments did not defy us so blatantly to lend credence to them [*y fier*], we would still have to make this attempt against the opposite temptation.

Let us thus detect his track [*dépistons sa foulée*] where it throws us off track [*dépiste*].[7] And first of all in the criticism by which he explains the Prefect's lack of success. We already saw it surface in those furtive gibes the Prefect, in the first conversation with Dupin, paid no mind, finding in them only a pretext for hilarity. The fact that it is, as Dupin insinuates, because a problem is too simple, indeed too self-evident, that it may appear obscure, will never have any more impact on him than a somewhat vigorous rub of the ribcage.

Everything is done to make us believe he is an imbecile. This is powerfully articulated in the claim that he and his henchmen will never conceive of anything beyond what an ordinary rascal might imagine for hiding an object—that is, precisely the all-too-well-known series of extraordinary hiding places, running the gamut from hidden desk drawers to removable tabletops, from the unstitched upholstery of chairs to their hollowed-out legs, and from the back side of the quicksilvering of mirrors to the thickness of book bindings.

This gives way to making fun of the Prefect's error when he deduces that because the Minister is a poet, he is only one remove from a fool, an error, it is argued, that simply consists, although this is hardly negligible, in a *non distributio medii*, since it is far from following from the fact that all fools are poets.

Yes indeed. But we ourselves are left to err regarding what constitutes the poet's superiority in the art of concealment—even if he turns out to be a mathematician to boot—since we suddenly lose whatever momentum we had when we are dragged into a thicket of unprovoked arguments directed against the reasoning of mathematicians, who have never, to my knowledge, showed such devotion to their formulas as to identify them with reasoning reason. At least, let me bear witness to the fact that, unlike what seems to be Poe's experience, I occasionally hazard such serious mischief (virtual blasphemy, according to Poe) before my friend Riguet—whose presence here guarantees you that my incursions into combinatorial analysis do not lead us astray—as to question whether perhaps "$x^2 + px$ is *not* altogether equal to q," without ever (here I refute Poe) having to fend off any unexpected attack.

Isn't so much intelligence being expended then simply to divert our attention from what had been indicated earlier as given, namely, that the police have looked *everywhere?* We were to understand this—regarding the field in which the police, not without reason, assumed the letter must be found—in the sense of an exhaustion of space, which is no doubt theoretical but which we are expected to take literally if the story is to have its piquancy. The division of the entire surface into numbered "compartments," which was the principle governing the operation, is presented to us as so accurate that "the fiftieth part of a line," it is said, could not escape the probing of the investigators. Are we not then within our rights to ask how it happened that the letter was not found *anywhere,* or rather to observe that nothing we are told about a higher-caliber conception of concealment ultimately explains how the letter managed to escape detection, since the field exhaustively combed did in fact contain it, as Dupin's discovery eventually proved?

Must the letter then, of all objects, have been endowed with the property of "nullibiety," to use a term which the well-known *Roget's Thesaurus* picks up from the semiological utopia of Bishop Wilkins?[8]

It is evident ("a little *too* self-evident")[9] that the letter has, in effect, relations with location [*le lieu*] for which no French word has the entire import of the English adjective "odd." *Bizarre,* by which Baudelaire regularly translates it into French, is only approximate. Let us say that these relations are *singuliers* (singular), for they are the very same ones that the signifier maintains with location.

You realize that my intention is not to turn them into "subtle" relations, that my aim is not to confuse letter with spirit [*esprit*] even when we receive the former by pneumatic dispatch, and that I readily admit that one kills if the other gives life, insofar as the signifier—you are perhaps beginning to catch my drift—materializes the instance of death. But whereas it is first of all the materiality of the signifier that I have emphasized, that materiality is *singular* in many ways, the first of which is not to allow of partition. Cut a letter into small pieces, and it remains the letter that it is—and this in a completely different sense than *Gestalttheorie* can account for with the latent vitalism in its notion of the whole.[10]

Language hands down its sentence to those who know how to hear it: through the use of the article employed as a partitive particle. Indeed, it is here that spirit—if spirit be living signification—seems, no less singularly, to allow for quantification more than the letter does. To begin with, through the very signification that allows us to say, "this discourse full *of* meaning" [*plein de signification*], just as it allows us to recognize *some* intentionality [*de l'intention*] in an act, to deplore that there is no longer *any* love [*plus d'amour*], to store up hatred [*de la haine*] and expend devotion [*du dévouement*], and to note that so much infatuation [*tant d'infatuation*) can be reconciled with the fact that there will always be plenty *of* ass [de la *cuisse*] to go around and brawling among men [du *rififi chez les hommes*].

But as for the letter itself, whether we take it in the sense of a typographical element, of an epistle, or of what constitutes a man of letters, we commonly say that what people say must be understood *à la lettre* (to the letter or literally), that *a letter* is being held for you at the post office, or even that you are well versed in *letters*—never that there is (some amount of) *letter* [de la lettre] anywhere, whatever the context, even to designate late mail.

For the signifier is a unique unit of being which, by its very nature, is the symbol of but an absence. This is why we cannot say of the purloined letter that, like other objects, it must be *or* not be somewhere but rather that, unlike them, it will be *and* will not be where it is wherever it goes.

Let us, in fact, look more closely at what happens to the police. We are spared none of the details concerning the procedures used in searching the space subjected to their investigation: from the division of that space into volumes from which the slightest bulk cannot escape detection, to needles probing soft cushions, and, given that they cannot simply sound the hard wood [for cavities], to an examination with a microscope to detect gimlet-dust from any holes drilled in it, and even the slightest gaping in the joints [of the furniture]. As their network tightens to the point that, not satisfied with shaking the pages of books, the police take to counting them, don't we see space itself shed its leaves like the letter?

But the seekers have such an immutable notion of reality [*réel*] that they fail to notice that their search tends to transform it into its object—a trait by which they might be able to distinguish that object from all others.

This would no doubt be too much to ask them, not because of their lack of insight but rather because of ours. For their imbecility is of neither the individual nor the corporate variety; its source is subjective. It is the imbecility of the realist who does not pause to observe that nothing, however deep into the bowels of the world a hand may shove it, will ever be hidden there, since another hand can retrieve it, and that what is hidden is never but what is *not in its place* [manque à sa place], as a call slip says of a volume mislaid in a library. And even if the book were on an adjacent shelf or in the next slot, it would be hidden there, however visible it may seem there. For it can *literally* [à la lettre] be said that something is not in its place only of what can change places—that is, of the symbolic. For the real, whatever upheaval we subject it to, is always and in every case in its place; it carries its place stuck to the sole of its shoe, there being nothing that can exile it from it.

Now, to return to our policemen, how could they have grasped the letter when they took it from the place where it was hidden? What were they turning over with their fingers but something that *did not fit* the description they had been given of it? "A letter, a litter": in Joyce's circle, they played on the homophony of the two words in English.[11] The seeming scrap of waste paper [*déchet*] the police were handling at that moment did not reveal its other nature by being only half torn in two. A different cipher on a seal [*cachet*] of another color and the distinctive mark [*cachet*] of a different handwriting in the superscription served as the most inviolable of hiding places [*cachettes*] here. And if they stopped at the reverse side of the letter, on which, as we know, the recipient's address was written at that time, it was because the letter had for them no other side but this reverse side.

What might they have detected on the basis of its obverse? Its message, as it is often said, an answer pleasing to our amateur cybernetic streak? … But does it not occur to us that this message has already reached its addressee and has even been left behind along with the insignificant scrap of paper, which now represents it no less well than the original note?

If we could say that a letter has fulfilled its destiny after having served its function, the ceremony of returning letters would be a less commonly accepted way to bring to a close the extinguishing of the fires of Cupid's festivities. The signifier is not functional. And the mobilization of the elegant society, whose frolics we are following, would have no meaning if the letter limited itself to having but one. Announcing that meaning to a squad of cops would hardly be an adequate means of keeping it secret.

We could even admit that the letter has an entirely different (if not a more consuming) meaning to the Queen than the one it offers up to the Minister's ken. The sequence of events would not be appreciably affected, not even if the letter were strictly incomprehensible to a reader not in the know.

For the letter is certainly not incomprehensible to everybody, since, as the Prefect emphatically assures us, eliciting everyone's mockery, "the disclosure of the document to a third person, who shall be nameless" (his name leaping to mind like a pig's tail twixt the teeth of Father Ubu) "would bring in question the honor of a personage of most exalted station"—indeed, the illustrious personage's very "honor and peace [would be] so jeopardized."

Hence it would be dangerous to let circulate not only the meaning but also the text of the message, and it would be all the more dangerous the more harmless it might appear to be, since the risks of an unwitting indiscretion by one of the letter's trustees would thus be increased.

Nothing then can save the police's position, and nothing would be changed by making them more "cultured." *Scripta manent:* in vain would they learn from a deluxe-edition humanism the proverbial lesson which the words *verba volant* conclude. Would that it were the case that writings remain, as is true, rather, of spoken words [*paroles*]: for the indelible debt of those words at least enriches our acts with its transfers.

Writings scatter to the four winds the blank checks of a mad charge of the cavalry. And were there no loose sheets, there would be no purloined letters.

But what of it? For there to be purloined letters, we wonder, to whom does a letter belong? I stressed a moment ago the oddity implicit in returning a letter to the person who had formerly let ardently fly its pledge. And we generally deem unworthy the method of such premature publications, as the one by which the Knight of Eon put several of his correspondents in a rather pitiful position.

Might a letter to which the sender retains certain rights then not belong altogether to the person to whom it is addressed? Or might it be that the latter was never the true addressee?

What will enlighten us is what may at first obscure the matter—namely, the fact that the story tells us virtually nothing about the sender or about the contents of the letter. We are merely informed that the Minister immediately recognized the hand that wrote the Queen's address on it and it is only incidentally mentioned, in a discussion of the camouflaging of the letter by the Minister, that the original cipher is that of the Duke of S—. As for the letter's import, we know only the dangers it would bring with it were it to fall into the hands of a certain third party, and that its possession has allowed the Minister to wield, "for political purposes, to a very dangerous extent," the power it assures him over the person concerned. But this tells us nothing about the message it carries.

Love letter or conspiratorial letter, informant's letter or directive, demanding letter or letter of distress, we can rest assured of but one thing: the Queen cannot let her lord and master know of it.

Now these terms, far from allowing for the disparaging tone they have in bourgeois comedy, take on an eminent meaning since they designate her sovereign, to whom she is bound by pledge of loyalty, and doubly so, since her role as spouse does not relieve her of her duties as a subject, but rather elevates her to the role of guardian of the power that royalty by law incarnates, which is called legitimacy.

Thus, whatever action the Queen has decided to take regarding the letter, the fact remains that this letter is the symbol of a pact and that, even if its addressee does not assume responsibility for this pact, the existence of the letter situates her in a symbolic chain foreign to the one which constitutes her loyalty. Its incompatibility with her loyalty is proven by the fact that possession of the letter is impossible to bring forward publicly as legitimate, and that in order to have this possession respected, the Queen can only invoke her right to privacy, whose privilege is based on the very honor that this possession violates.

For she who incarnates the graceful figure of sovereignty cannot welcome even a private communication without power being concerned, and she cannot lay claim to secrecy in relation to the sovereign without her actions becoming clandestine.

Hence, the responsibility of the letter's author takes a back seat to that of its holder: for the offense to majesty is compounded by *high treason*.

I say the "holder" and not the "owner." For it becomes clear thus that the addressee's ownership of the letter is no less questionable than that of anyone else into whose hands it may fall, since nothing concerning the existence of the letter can fall back into place without the person whose prerogatives it infringes on having pronounced judgment on it.

However, none of this implies that, even though the letter's secrecy is indefensible, it would in any way be honorable to denounce that secret. *Honesti homines*, decent people, cannot get off the hook so easily. There is more than one *religio*, and sacred ties shall not cease to pull us in opposite directions any time soon. As for *ambitus*, a detour, as we see, is not always inspired by ambition. For although I am taking a detour here, I have not stolen [*volé*] it—that's the word for it—since, to be quite frank, I have adopted the title Baudelaire gave the story only in order to stress, not the signifier's "conventional" nature, as it is incorrectly put, but rather its priority over the signified. Despite his devotion, Baudelaire nevertheless betrayed Poe by translating his title "The Purloined Letter" as "La lettre volée" (the stolen letter), the English title containing a word rare enough for us to find it easier to define its etymology than its usage.

To *purloin*, says the Oxford English Dictionary, is an Anglo-French word—that is, it is composed of the prefix *pur-*, found in *purpose, purchase,* and *purport,* and of the Old French word *loing, loinger, longé.* We recognize in the first element the Latin *pro-*, as opposed to *ante*, insofar as it presupposes a back in front of which it stands, possibly to guarantee it or even to stand in as its guarantor (whereas *ante* goes forth to meet what comes to meet it). As for the second, the Old French word *loigner* is a verb that attributes place *au loing* (or *longé*), which does not mean *au loin* (far off), but *au long de* (alongside). To purloin is thus *mettre de côté* (to set aside) or, to resort to a colloquialism which plays off the two meanings, *mettre à gauche* (to put to the left side [literally] and to tuck away).

Our detour is thus validated by the very object which leads us into it: for we are quite simply dealing with a *letter* which has been *detoured*, one whose trajectory has been *prolonged* (this is literally the English word in the title), or, to resort to the language of the post office, a letter *en souffrance* (awaiting delivery or unclaimed).

Here then, the letter's singularity, reduced to its simplest expression, is "simple and odd," as we are told on the very first page of the story; and the letter is, as the title indicates, the *true subject* of the tale. Since it can be made to take a detour, it must have a trajectory *which is proper to it*—a feature in which its impact as a signifier is apparent here. For we have learned to conceive of the signifier as sustaining itself only in a displacement comparable to that found in electronic news strips or in the rotating memories of our machines-that-think-like-men,[12] this because of the alternating operation at its core that requires it to leave its place, if only to return to it by a circular path.

This is what happens in repetition automatism. What Freud teaches us in the text I have been commenting on is that the subject follows the channels of the symbolic. But what is illustrated here is more gripping still: It is not only the subject, but the subjects, caught in their intersubjectivity, who line up—in other words, they are our ostriches, to whom we thus return here, and who, more docile than sheep, model their very being on the moment of the signifying chain that runs through them.

If what Freud discovered, and rediscovers ever more abruptly, has a meaning, it is that the signifier's displacement determines subjects' acts, destiny, refusals, blindnesses, success, and fate, regardless of their innate gifts and instruction, and irregardless of their character or sex; and that everything pertaining to the psychological pregiven follows willy-nilly the signifier's train, like weapons and baggage.

Here we are, in fact, once again at the crossroads at which we had left our drama and its round with the question of the way in which the subjects relay each other in it. My apologue is designed to show that it is the letter and its detour which governs their entrances and roles. While the letter may be *en souffrance,* they are the ones who shall suffer from it. By passing beneath its shadow, they become its reflection. By coming into the letter's possession—an admirably ambiguous bit of language—its meaning possesses them.

This is what is demonstrated to us by the hero of the drama that is recounted to us here, when the very situation his daring triumphantly crafted the first time around repeats itself. If he now succumbs to it, it is because he has shifted to the second position in the triad where he was initially in the third position and was simultaneously the thief—this by virtue of the object of his theft.

For if, now as before, the point is to protect the letter from inquisitive eyes, he cannot help but employ the same technique he himself already foiled: that of leaving it out in the open. And we may legitimately doubt that he thus knows what he is doing when we see him suddenly captivated by a dyadic relationship, in which we find all the features of a mimetic lure or of an animal playing dead, and caught in the trap of the typically imaginary situation of seeing that he is not seen, leading him to misconstrue the real situation in which he is seen not seeing. And what does he fail to see? The very symbolic situation which he himself was so able to see, and in which he is now seen seeing himself not being seen.

The Minister acts like a man who realizes that the police's search is his own defense, since we are told he deliberately gives the police total access to his hotel by his absences; he nevertheless overlooks the fact that he has no defense against anything beyond that form of search.

This is the very *autruicherie*—if I may be allowed to multiply my monster by layering—he himself crafted, but it cannot be by some imbecility that he now comes to be its dupe.

For in playing the game of the one who hides, he is obliged to don the role of the Queen, including even the attributes of woman and shadow, so propitious for the act of concealment.

I do not mean to reduce the veteran couple of Yin and Yang to the primal opposition of dark and light. For its precise handling involves what is blinding in a flash of light, no less than the shimmering that shadows exploit in order not to release their prey.

Here the sign and being, marvelously disjoin, reveal which wins out when they are opposed. A man who is man enough to brave, and even scorn, a woman's dreaded ire suffers the curse of the sign of which he has dispossessed her so greatly as to undergo metamorphosis.

For this sign is clearly that of woman, because she brings out her very being therein by founding it outside the law, which ever contains her—due to the effect of origins—in a position as signifier, nay, as fetish. In order to be worthy of the power of this sign she need but remain immobile in its shadow, managing thereby, moreover, like the Queen, to simulate mastery of nonaction that the Minister's "lynx eye" alone was able to see through.

The man is now thus in this ravished sign's possession, and this possession is harmful in that it can be maintained only thanks to the very honor it defies, and it is accursed for inciting him who maintains it to punishment or crime, both of which breach his vassalage to the Law.

There must be a very odd *noli me tangere* in this sign for its possession to, like the Socratic stingray, make its man so numb that he falls into what unequivocally appears in his case to be a state of inaction.

For in remarking, as the narrator does already in the first meeting, that the letter's power departs when used, we perceive that this remark concerns only its use for ends of power—and simultaneously that the Minister will be forced to use it in this way.

For him to be unable to rid himself of it, the Minister must not know what else to do with the letter. For this use places him in so total a dependence on the letter as such, that in the long run this use no longer concerns the letter at all.

I mean that, for this use to truly concern the letter, the Minister—who, after all, would be authorized to do so by his service to the King, his master—could present respectful reproaches to the Queen, even if he had to ensure their desired effects by appropriate guarantees; or he could initiate a suit against the author of the letter (the fact that its author remains on the sidelines reveals the extent to which guilt and blame are not at stake here, but rather the sign of contradiction and scandal constituted by the letter, in the sense in which the Gospel says that the sign must come regardless of the misfortune of he who serves as its bearer); or he could even submit the letter as an exhibit in a case to the "third personage" who is qualified to decide whether he will institute a Chambre Ardente for the Queen or bring disgrace upon the Minister.

We will not know why the Minister does not use the letter in any of these ways, and it is fitting that we do not, since the effect of this non-use alone concerns us; all we need to know is that the manner in which the letter was acquired would pose no obstacle to any of them.

For it is clear that while the Minister will be forced to make use of the letter in a non-significant way, its use for ends of power can only be potential, since it cannot become actual [*passer à l'acte*] without immediately vanishing. Hence the letter exists as a means of power only through the final summons of the pure signifier—either by prolonging its detour, making it reach he whom it may concern through an extra transit (that is, through another betrayal whose repercussions the letter's gravity makes it difficult to prevent), or by destroying the letter, which would be the only sure way, as Dupin proffers at the outset, to be done with what is destined by nature to signify the canceling out [*annulation*] of what it signifies.

The ascendancy which the Minister derives from the situation is thus not drawn from the letter but, whether he knows it or not, from the personage it constitutes for him. The Prefect's remarks thus present him as someone "who dares all things," which is commented upon significantly: "those unbecoming as well as those becoming a man," words whose thrust escapes Baudelaire when he translates: "ce qui est indigne d'un homme aussi bien que ce qui est digne de lui" (those unbecoming a man as well as those becoming him). For in its original form, the appraisal is far more appropriate to what concerns a woman.

This allows us to see the imaginary import of the personage, that is, the narcissistic relationship in which the Minister is engaged, this time certainly without knowing it. It is also indicated right on the second page of the English text by one of the narrator's remarks, whose form is worth savoring: the Minister's ascendancy, we are told, "would depend upon the robber's knowledge of the loser's knowledge of the robber." Words whose importance the author underscores by having Dupin repeat them word for word right after the Prefect's account of the scene of the theft of the letter, when the conversation resumes. Here again we might say that Baudelaire is imprecise in his language in having one ask and the other confirm in the following terms: "Le voleur sait-il? ..." (Does the robber know?), then: "Le voleur sait..." (The robber knows). What? "que la personne volée connaît son voleur" (that the loser knows her robber).

For what matters to the robber is not only that the said person know who robbed her, but that she know what kind of robber she is dealing with; the fact is that she believes him capable of anything, which should be understood as follows: she confers upon him a position that no one can really assume, because it is imaginary, that of absolute master.

In truth, it is a position of absolute weakness, but not for the person we lead to believe in it. The proof is not merely that the Queen takes the audacious step of calling upon the police. For the police merely conform to their displacement to the next slot in the array constituted by the initial triad, accepting the very blindness that is required to occupy that place: "No more sagacious agent could, I suppose," Dupin notes ironically, "be desired, or even imagined." No, if the Queen has taken this step, it is less because she has been "driven to despair," as we are told, than because she takes on the burden [*charge*] of an impatience that should rather be attributed to a specular mirage.

For the Minister has a hard time confining himself to the inaction which is presently his lot. The Minister, in point of fact, is "not *altogether* a fool." This remark is made by the Prefect, whose every word is golden: it is true that the gold of his words flows only for Dupin and does not stop flowing until it reaches the fifty thousand francs' worth it will cost him by the metal standard of the day, though not without leaving him a tidy profit. The Minister then is not *altogether* a fool in his foolish stagnation, and this is why he must behave according to the mode of neurosis. Like the man who withdrew to an island to forget—to forget what? he forgot—so the Minister, by not making use of the letter, comes to forget it. This is expressed by the persistence of his conduct. But the letter, no more than the neurotic's unconscious, does not forget him. It forgets him so little that it transforms him more and more in the image of her who offered it up to his discovery, and that he now will surrender it, following her example, to a similar discovery.

The features of this transformation are noted, and in a form characteristic enough in their apparent gratuitousness that they might legitimately be compared to the return of the repressed.

Thus we first learn that the Minister in turn has *turned* the letter *over*, not, of course, as in the Queen's hasty gesture, but more assiduously, as one turns a garment inside out. This is, in effect, how he must proceed, according to the methods of the day for folding and sealing a letter, in order to free the virgin space in which to write a new address.[13]

This address becomes his own. Whether it be in his handwriting or another's, it appears in a diminutive female script, and, the seal changing from the red of passion to the black of its mirrors, he stamps his own cipher upon it. The oddity of a letter marked with the cipher of its addressee is all the more worth noting as an invention because, although it is powerfully articulated in the text, it is not even mentioned thereafter by Dupin in the discussion he devotes to his identification of the letter.

Whether this omission is intentional or involuntary, it is surprising in the organization of a creation whose meticulous rigor is evident. But in either case it is significant that the letter which the Minister addresses to himself, ultimately, is a letter from a woman: as though this were a phase he had to go through owing to one of the signifier's natural affinities.

And everything—from the aura of nonchalance, that goes as far as an affectation of listlessness, to the display of an ennui verging on disgust in his conversation, to the ambiance that the author of the "Philosophy of Furniture"[14] knows how to elicit from virtually impalpable details (like that of the musical instrument on the table)—seems to conspire to make a personage, whose every remark has surrounded him with the most virile of traits, exude the oddest *odor di femina* when he appears.

Dupin does not fail to emphasize that this is indeed an artifice, describing behind the spurious appearance the vigilance of a beast of prey ready to spring. But how could we find a more beautiful image of the fact that this is the very effect of the unconscious, in the precise sense in which I teach that the unconscious is the fact that man is inhabited by the signifier, than the one Poe himself forges to help us understand Dupin's feat? For, to do so, Poe refers to those toponymic inscriptions which a map, in order not to be silent, superimposes on its outline, and which may become the object of "a game of puzzles" in which one has to find the name chosen by another player. He then notes that the name most likely to foil a novice will be one which the eye often overlooks, but which provides, in large letters spaced out widely across the field of the map, the name of an entire country ...

Just so does the purloined letter, like an immense female body, sprawl across the space of the Minister's office when Dupin enters it. But just so does he already expect to find it there, having only to undress that huge body, with his eyes veiled by green spectacles.

This is why, without any need (nor any opportunity either, for obvious reasons) to listen in at Professor Freud's door, he goes straight to the spot where lies and lodges what that body is designed to hide, in some lovely middle toward which one's gaze slips, nay, to the very place seducers call Sant'Angelo's Castle in their innocent illusion of being able to control the City from the castle. Lo! Between the jambs of the fireplace, there is the object already in reach of the hand the ravisher has but to extend … Whether he seizes it above the mantelpiece, as Baudelaire translates it, or beneath it, as in the original text, is a question that may be abandoned without harm to inferences emanating from the kitchen.[15]

Now if the effectiveness of symbols stopped there, would it mean that the symbolic debt is extinguished there too? If we could believe so, we would be advised of the contrary by two episodes which we must be all the more careful not to dismiss as accessory in that they seem, at first blush, to be at odds with the rest of the work.

First of all, there is the business of Dupin's remuneration, which, far from being one last game, has been present from the outset in the rather offhanded question Dupin asks the Prefect about the amount of the reward promised him, and whose enormousness the Prefect, however reticent he may be about citing the exact figure, does not dream of hiding from him, even returning to the subject later in mentioning its having been doubled.

The fact that Dupin was previously presented to us as a virtual pauper taking refuge in ethereal pursuits ought rather to lead us to reflect on the deal he cuts for delivery of the letter, promptly assured as it is by the checkbook he produces. I do not regard it as negligible that the direct hint by which he broaches the matter is a "story attributed to the personage, as famous as he was eccentric," Baudelaire tells us, of an English doctor named Abernethy; this doctor replied to a rich miser, who was hoping to sponge a free medical opinion off him, not to take medicine, but rather to take advice.

Are we not, in fact, justified in feeling implicated when Dupin is perhaps about to withdraw from the letter's symbolic circuit—we who make ourselves the emissaries of all the purloined letters which, at least for a while, remain *en souffrance* with us in the transference? And is it not the responsibility their transference entails that we neutralize by equating it with the signifier that most thoroughly annihilates every signification—namely, money?

But that's not all here. The profit Dupin so blithely extracts from this feat, assuming its purpose is to allow him to withdraw his ante from the game before it is too late, merely renders all the more paradoxical, even shocking, the rebuke and underhanded blow he suddenly permits himself to deal the Minister, whose insolent prestige would, after all, seem to have been sufficiently deflated by the trick Dupin has just played on him.

I have already quoted the atrocious lines Dupin claims he could not stop himself from dedicating, in his counterfeit letter, to the moment at which the Minister, flying off the handle at the Queen's inevitable acts of defiance, will think of bringing her down and will fling himself into the abyss—*facilis descensus Averni*,[16] he says, waxing sententious—adding that the Minister will not fail to recognize his handwriting. Leaving behind a merciless opprobrium, at the cost of no peril to himself, would seem to be a triumph without glory over a figure who is not without merit, and the resentment Dupin invokes, stemming from "an evil turn" done him in Vienna (at the Congress?), merely adds an extra touch of darkness to it.

Let us consider this explosion of feeling more closely, however, and more specifically the moment at which it occurs in an act whose success depends on so cool a head.

It comes just after the moment at which it may be said that Dupin already holds the letter as securely as if he had seized it, the decisive act of identifying the letter having been accomplished, even though he is not yet in a position to rid himself of it.

He is thus clearly a participant in the intersubjective triad and, as such, finds himself in the median position previously occupied by the Queen and the Minister. In showing himself to be superior here, will he simultaneously reveal to us the author's intentions?

While he has succeeded in putting the letter back on its proper course, it has yet to be made to reach its address. And that address is the place previously occupied by the King, since it is there that it must fall back into the order based on the Law.

As we have seen, neither the King nor the police who replaced Him in that position were capable of reading the letter because that *place entailed blindness.*

Rex et augur—the legendary archaism of the words seems to resound only to make us realize how derisive it is to call upon a man to live up to them. And history's figures have hardly encouraged us to do so for some time now. It is not natural for man to bear the weight of the highest of signifiers all alone. And the place he comes to occupy when he dons it may be equally apt to become the symbol of the most enormous imbecility.[17]

Let us say that the King here is invested—thanks to the amphibology natural to the sacred—with the imbecility that is based precisely on the Subject.

This is what will give meaning to the personages who succeed him in his place. Not that the police can be regarded as constitutionally illiterate, and we are aware of the role played by pikes planted around the university in the birth of the State. But the police who exercise their functions here are plainly marked by liberal forms, that is, by forms imposed on them by masters who are not very interested in enduring their indiscreet tendencies. This is why words are not minced, at times, regarding what is expected of them: "*Sutor ne ultra crepidam*, just take care of your crooks. We'll even give you the scientific means with which to do so. That will help you not to think of truths you'd be better off leaving in the dark."[18]

We know that the relief that results from such sensible principles shall have lasted but a morning's time in history, and that everywhere the march of destiny is already bringing back, after a just aspiration to the reign of freedom, an interest in those who trouble it with their crimes, an interest that occasionally goes so far as to forge its own evidence. It may even be observed that this practice, which has always been accepted as long as it was engaged in only for the benefit of the greatest number, is in fact authenticated through public confessions of its forgeries by the very people who might well object to it: the most recent manifestation of the preeminence of the signifier over the subject.

The fact remains that police files have always been treated with a certain reserve, a reserve which goes well beyond the circle of historians, for some odd reason.

Dupin's intended delivery of the letter to the Prefect of Police will diminish the magnitude of this evanescent credit. What now remains of the signifier when, having already been relieved of its message for the Queen, its text is invalidated as soon as it leaves the Minister's hands?

The only thing left for it to do is to answer this very question: what remains of a signifier when it no longer has any signification? This is the very question asked of it by the person Dupin now finds in the place marked by blindness.

For this is clearly the question that has led the Minister there, assuming he is the gambler we are told he is, as his act suffices to indicate. For the gambler's passion is no other than the question asked of the signifier, which is figured by the *automaton* of chance.

"What are you, figure of the dice I roll in your chance encounter (*tyche*)[19] with my fortune? Nothing, if not the presence of death that makes human life into a reprieve obtained from morning to morning in the name of significations of which your sign is the shepherd's crook. Thus did Scheherazade for a thousand and one nights, and thus have I done for eighteen months, experiencing the ascendancy of this sign at the cost of a dizzying series of loaded tosses in the game of even or odd."

This is why Dupin, *from the place where he is* [*il est*] cannot help but feel rage of a manifestly feminine nature at he who questions in this manner. The high-caliber image, in which the poet's inventiveness and the mathematician's rigor were married to the impassivity of the dandy and the elegance of the cheat, suddenly becomes, for the very person who gave us a taste of it, the true *monstrum horrendum*, to borrow his own words, "an unprincipled man of genius."

It is here that the origin of the horror shows itself, and he who experiences it has no need to declare himself, most unexpectedly at that, "a partisan of the lady" in order to reveal it to us: ladies, as we know, detest it when principles are called into question, for their charms owe much to the mystery of the signifier.

This is why Dupin will at last turn toward us the dumbfounding [*médusante*] face of this signifier of which no one but the Queen has been able to read anything but the other face. The commonplace practice of supplying a quotation is fitting for the oracle that this face bears in its grimace, as is the fact that it is borrowed from tragedy:

> *Un destin si funeste,*
> *S'il n'est digne d'Atrée, est digne de Thyeste.*

Such is the signifier's answer, beyond all significations: "You believe you are taking action when I am the one making you stir at the bidding of the bonds with which I weave your desires. Thus do the latter grow in strength and multiply in objects, bringing you back to the fragmentation of your rent childhood. That will be your feast until the return of the stone guest whom I shall be for you since you call me forth."

To return to a more temperate tone, let us say—as goes the joke with which some of you who followed me to the Congress in Zurich last year and I rendered homage to the local password—that the signifier's answer to whomever questions it is: "Eat your Dasein."

Is that then what awaits the Minister at his appointment with fate? Dupin assures us that it is, but we have also learned not to be overly credulous of his diversions.

The audacious creature is, of course, reduced here to the state of imbecilic blindness in which man finds himself in relation to the wall-like letters that dictate his destiny. But, in summoning him to confront them, what effect can we expect the sole provocations of the Queen to have on a man like him? Love or hatred. The one is blind and will make him lay down his arms. The other is lucid, but will awaken his suspicions. But provided he is truly the gambler we are told he is, he will consult his cards one final time before laying them on the table and, upon seeing his hand, will leave the table in time to avoid disgrace.

Is that all, and must we believe we have deciphered Dupin's true strategy beyond the imaginary tricks with which he was obliged to deceive us? Yes, no doubt, for if "any point requiring reflection," as Dupin states at the start, is examined "to better purpose in the dark," we may now easily read its solution in broad daylight. It was already contained in and easy to bring out of the title of our tale, according to the very formulation of intersubjective communication that I have long since offered up to your discernment, in which the sender, as I tell you, receives from the receiver his own message in an inverted form. This is why what the "purloined letter," nay, the "letter *en souffrance,*" means is that a letter always arrives at its destination.

NOTES

1. The necessary reference here may be found in my essay, "Logical Time and the Assertion of Anticipated Certainty," in *Écrits* 1966, 197–213.
2. See "The Function and Field of Speech and Language in Psychoanalysis," in *Écrits* 1966, 244.
3. To completely understand what follows one must reread the short and readily available text of "The Purloined Letter."
4. See Émile Benveniste, "Communication animale et langage humain," *Diogène* I, and my Rome Report ["The Function and Field of Speech and Language"], *Écrits* 1966, 297. [In English, see Émile Benveniste, *Problems in General Linguistics,* trans. M. Meek (Coral Gables: University of Miami Press, 1971), 49–54.]
5. See *Écrits* 1966, 58.
6. [Added in 1968:] I had at first added a note on the meaning these three [Latin] words would provide by way of commentary on this story if the structure did not suffice, although it aspires to do so.

   I am eliminating that indication, which was overly imperfect, because in rereading my text for this reprinting someone has confirmed to me that, after the era of those who are selling me out (even today, December 9, 1968), another era is coming in which people read my work to explicate it further.

   The latter shall take place elsewhere than on this page.
7. I would like to pose again to Benveniste the question of the antithetical meaning of certain words, whether primal or not, after the masterful correction he made to the erroneous path Freud took in studying the question on the philogical ground (see *"La Psychanalyse"* 1 [1956]: 5–16). For I think that the question remains unanswered once the instance of the signifier has been rigorously formulated. Bloch and Von Wartburg date back to 1875 the first appearance of the signification of the verb *dépister* as I used it the second time in this sentence. [In English, see Émile Benveniste, *Problems in General Linguistics,* 65—75. See also Freud's article "The Antithetical Meaning of Primal Words," *SE* XI, 155–61.]
8. The very utopia to which Jorge Luis Borges, in his work which harmonizes so well with the phylum of my subject matter, has accorded an importance which others reduce to its proper proportions. See *Les Temps Modernes* 113–14 (June–July 1955): 2135–36 and 118 (October 1955): 574–75.

 9. Poe's emphasis.

10. This is so true that philosophers, in those hackneyed examples with which they argue on the basis of the one and the many, will not put to the same purposes a simple sheet of white paper ripped down the middle and a broken circle, or even a shattered vase, not to mention a cut worm.

11. See *Our Exagmination Round His Factification for Incamination of "Work in Progress"* (Paris: Shakespeare & Co., 12 rue de l'Odéon, 1929).

12. See *Écrits* 1966, 59.

13. I felt obliged at this point to demonstrate the procedure to the audience using a letter from that period which concerned Chateaubriand and his search for a secretary. I was amused to find that Chateaubriand had completed the first version of his memoirs (recently published in its original form) in the very month of November 1841 in which "The Purloined Letter" appeared in *Chambers' Journal.* Will Chateaubriand's devotion to the power he decries, and the honor which that devotion does him ("the gift" had not yet been invented), place him in the category to which we will later see the Minister assigned: among men of genius with or without principles?

14. Poe is the author of an essay by this title.

15. [Added in 1966:] And even from the cook herself.

16. Virgil's line reads: *facilis descensus Averno* ["The descent to Hades is easy"; see Virgil's *Aeneid,* book 6, line 126.]

17. Let us recall the witty distich attributed before his fall to the most recent person to have rejoined Candide's meeting in Venice. *"Il n'est plus aujourd'hui que cinq rois sur la terre, / Les quatre rois des cartes et le roi d'Angleterre."* (There are only five kings left on earth today: / The four kings of cards and the King of England.)

18. This statement was openly made by a noble Lord speaking to the Upper House in which his dignity earned him a seat.

19. I am referring to the fundamental opposition Aristotle makes between these two terms [*automaton* and *tyche*] in the conceptual analysis of chance he provides in his *Physics.* Many discussions would be clarified if it were not overlooked.

WHY DOES A *LETTER* ALWAYS ARRIVE AT ITS DESTINATION? IMAGINARY, SYMBOLIC, REAL (1992)

SLAVOJ ŽIŽEK

Here, as in much of his writing, Žižek interprets popular culture, especially movies, through the ideas of Jacques Lacan, especially Lacan's later writings, which tend to give more attention to his concept of the real, the third and incomprehensibly mysterious order in Lacan's triad of the imaginary, the symbolic, and the real. (See the headnote for Lacan.) At the same time, Žižek shapes this essay as a meditation on one of Lacan's earlier essays, his seminar on Edgar Allan Poe's story "The Purloined Letter," included in this volume.

Lacan's essay concludes that "the letter always arrives at its destination." Jacques Derrida contested Lacan's assertion, arguing—deconstructively—that the letter never arrives at its destination. In both cases, the "letter" means far more than the document purloined in Poe's story. It means writing; it means representation itself as represented by writing and by "the letter."

Žižek relies on bold assertions that achieve their power through the drama of the claims they assert and through their connection to Lacanian concepts more than through detailed argument. Cumulatively, however, the bold claims help give a feel for Lacan's way of interpreting, as well as for Žižek's way of interpreting Lacan and of interpreting popular culture through Lacan. Characteristically, as the bold assertions fly forth one after another, so do the allusions to technical Lacanian ideas and to popular culture, but Žižek generally provides enough context for readers to follow the point whether or not they are familiar with or care to look up his allusions. It may help, nevertheless, to note that a "metalanguage" is a language about language, implicitly a language exterior to language. For Žižek, the misrecognition in the Lacanian imaginary includes Louis Althusser's sense of how people misrecognize themselves in the dominant ideas of the culture around them, as Althusser argues in the essay included in this volume. The imaginary is a complete system, identification, or recognition, versus the incomplete system, identification, or recognition of the symbolic. The imaginary supposes connection where the symbolic supposes disconnection through the distancing realm of signifiers and interpretation. But both the imaginary and the symbolic eventually give way to the real. Not even the proliferation of language and signifiers can adequately represent the real. The real cannot be explained, but only inferred, and so Žižek tries to contemplate its mysteries in this essay.

(The first part of Žižek's essay offers a reading of Charlie Chaplin's City Lights, *but the section included here, the majority of the overall essay, stands on its own.)*

So why *does* the letter always arrive at its destination? Why could it not—sometimes, at least—also *fail* to reach it?[1] Far from attesting to a refined theoretical sensitivity, this Derridean reaction to the famous closing statement of Lacan's "Seminar on 'The Purloined Letter'"[2] rather exhibits what we could call a primordial response of common sense: what if a letter does *not* reach its destination? Isn't it always possible for a letter to go astray?[3] If, however, the Lacanian theory insists categorically that a letter *does* always arrive at its destination, it is not because of an unshakable belief in teleology, in the power of a message to reach its preordained goal: Lacan's exposition of the way a letter arrives at its destination *lays bare the very mechanism of teleological illusion.* In other words, the very reproach that "a letter can also miss its destination" misses its own destination: it misreads the Lacanian thesis, reducing it to the traditional teleological circular movement, i.e., to what is precisely called in question and subverted by Lacan. A letter always arrives at its destination—especially when we have the limit case of a letter *without* addressee, of what is called in German *Flaschenpost,* a message in a bottle thrown into the sea from an island after shipwreck. This case displays at its purest and clearest how a letter reaches its true destination the moment it is delivered, thrown into the water—its true addressee is namely not the empirical other which may receive it or not, but the big Other, the symbolic order itself, which receives it *the moment the letter is put into circulation,* i.e., the moment the sender "externalizes" his message, delivers it to the Other, the moment the Other takes cognizance of the letter and thus disburdens the sender of responsibility for it.[4] How, then, *specifically,* does a letter arrive at its destination? How should we conceive this thesis of Lacan which usually serves as the crowning evidence for his alleged "logocentrism"? The proposition "a letter always arrives at its destination" is far from being univocal: it offers itself to a series of possible readings[5] which could be ordered by means of reference to the triad Imaginary, Symbolic, Real.

IMAGINARY (MIS)RECOGNITION

In a first approach, a letter which "always arrives at its destination" points to the logic of recognition/misrecognition (*reconnaissance/méconnaissance*) elaborated in detail by Louis Althusser and his followers (Michel Pêcheux):[6] the logic by means of which one (mis) recognizes oneself as the addressee of ideological interpellation. This illusion constitutive of the ideological order could be succintly rendered by paraphrasing a formula of Barbara Johnson:[7] "A letter always arrives at its destination *since its destination is wherever it arrives.*" Its underlying mechanism was elaborated by Pêcheux apropos of jokes of the type: "Daddy was born in Manchester, Mummy in Bristol and I in London: strange that the three of us should have met!"[8] In short, if we look at the process backward, from its (contingent) result, the fact that "events took precisely this turn" couldn't but appear as uncanny, concealing some fateful meaning—as if some mysterious hand had taken care that "the letter arrived at its destination," i.e., that my father and my mother met … What we have here is, however, more than a shallow joke, as is attested by contemporary physics, where we encounter precisely the same mechanism under the name of the "anthropocentric principle": life emerged on Earth due to numerous contingencies which created the appropriate conditions (if, for example, in Earth's primeval time the composition of soil and air had differed by a small percentage, no life would have been possible); so, when physicists endeavor to reconstruct the process culminating in the appearance of intelligent living beings on Earth, they either presuppose that universe was created in order to render possible the formation of intelligent beings (the "strong," overtly teleological anthropocentric principle) or accept a "circular" methodological rule requiring us to always posit such hypotheses about the primeval state of universe as to enable us to deduce its further development toward the conditions for the emergence of life (the "weak" version).

The same logic is also at work in the well-known accident from the *Arabian Nights:* the hero, lost in the desert, quite by chance enters a cave; there he finds three old wise men, awoken by his entry, who say to him: "Finally, you have arrived! We have been waiting for you for the last three hundred years," as if, behind the contingencies of his life, there was a hidden hand of fate which directed him toward the cave in the desert. This illusion is produced by a kind of "short circuit" between a place in the symbolic network and the contingent element which occupies it: *whosoever* finds himself at this place is the addressee since the addressee is not defined by his positive qualities but by the very contingent fact of finding himself at this place. Although the religious idea of *predestination* seems to be the very exemplar of the delusive "short circuit," it simultaneously intimates a foreboding of radical contingency: if God has decided in advance who will be saved and who will be damned, then my salvation or perdition do not depend on my determinate qualities and acts but on the place in which—*independently of my qualities, that is to say: totally by chance, in so far as I'm concerned*—I find myself within the network of God's plan. This contingency manifests itself in a paradoxical inversion: I'm not damned because I act sinfully, trespassing His Commandments, I act sinfully because I'm damned. ... So, we can easily imagine God easing His mind when some big sinner commits his crime: "Finally, you did it! I have been waiting for it for the whole of your miserable life!" And to convince oneself of how this problematic bears on psychoanalysis, one has only to remember the crucial role of contingent encounters in triggering a traumatic crackup of our psychic balance: overhearing a passing remark by a friend, witnessing a small unpleasant scene, and so forth, can awaken long-forgotten memories and shatter our daily life—as Lacan put it, the unconscious trauma repeats itself *by means of* some small, contingent bit of reality. "Fate" in psycho-analysis always asserts itself through such contingent encounters, giving rise to the question: "What if I had missed that remark? What if I had taken another route and avoided that scene?" Such questioning is, of course, deceitful since "a letter *always* arrives at its destination": it waits for its moment with patience—if not this, then another contingent little bit of reality will sooner or later find itself at this place that awaits it and fire off the trauma. This is, ultimately, what Lacan called "the arbitrariness of the signifier."[9]

To refer to the terms of speech-act theory, the illusion proper to the process of interpellation consists in the overlooking of its *performative* dimension: when I recognize myself as the addressee of the call of the ideological big Other (Nation, Democracy, Party, God, and so forth), when this call "arrives at its destination" in me, I automatically misrecognize that it is this very act of recognition which *makes me* what I have recognized myself as—I don't recognize myself in it because I'm its addressee, I become its addressee the moment I recognize myself in it. *This* is the reason why a letter always reaches its addressee: because one becomes its addressee when one is reached. The Derridean reproach that a letter can also miss its addressee is therefore simply beside the point: it makes sense only insofar as I presuppose that I can be its addressee *before* the letter reaches me—in other words, it presupposes the traditional teleological trajectory with a preordained goal. Translated into the terms of the joke about my father from Manchester, my mother from Bristol, and me from London, the Derridean proposition that a letter can also go astray and miss its destination discloses a typical obsessional apprehension of what would happen if my father and mother had *not* come across each other—all would have gone wrong, I would not exist... So, far from implying any kind of teleological circle, "a letter always arrives at its destination" exposes the very mechanism which brings about the amazement of "Why me? Why was *I* chosen?" and thus sets in motion the search for a hidden fate that regulates my path.

SYMBOLIC CIRCUIT I: "THERE IS NO METALANGUAGE"

On a symbolic level, "a letter always arrives at its destination" condenses an entire chain (a "family" in the Wittgensteinian sense) of propositions: "the sender always receives from the receiver his own message in reverse form," "the repressed always returns," "the frame itself is always being framed by part of its content," "we cannot escape the symbolic debt, it always has to be settled," which are all ultimately variations on the same basic premise that "there is no metalanguage." So let us begin by explaining the impossibility of metalanguage apropos of the Hegelian figure of the "Beautiful Soul," deploring the wicked ways of the world from the position of an innocent, impassive victim. The "Beautiful Soul" pretends to speak a pure metalanguage, exempted from the corruption of the world, thereby concealing the way its own moans and groans *partake actively* in the corruption it denounces. In his "Intervention on Transference,"[10] Lacan relies on the dialectic of the "Beautiful Soul" to designate the falsity of the hysterical subjective position: "Dora," Freud's famous analysand, complains of being reduced to a pure object in a play of intersubjective exchanges (her father is allegedly offering her to Mister K. as if in compensation for his own flirtation with Miss K.), i.e., she presents this exchange as an objective state of things in the face of which she is utterly helpless; Freud's answer is that the function of this stance of passive victimization by cruel circumstances is just to conceal her complicity and collusion—the square of intersubjective exchanges can only sustain itself insofar as Dora *assumes actively* her role of victim, of an object of exchange, in other words, insofar as she finds libidinal satisfaction in it, insofar as this very renunciation procures for her a kind of perverse surplus enjoyment. A hysteric continually complains of how he cannot adapt himself to the reality of cruel manipulation, and the psychoanalytic answer to it is not "give up your empty dreams, life is cruel, accept it as it is" but quite the contrary "your moans and groans are false since, by means of them, you are *only too well adapted* to the reality of manipulation and exploitation": by playing the role of helpless victim, the hysteric assumes the subjective position which enables him to "blackmail emotionally his environs," as we would put it in today's jargon.[11]

This answer, in which the "Beautiful Soul" is confronted with how it actually partakes of the wicked ways of the world, closes the circuit of communication: in it, the subject/sender receives from the addressee his own message in its true form, i.e., the true meaning of his moans and groans. In other words, in it, the letter that the subject put into circulation "arrives at its destination," which was from the very beginning the sender himself: the letter arrives at its destination when the subject is finally forced to assume the true consequences of his activity. This is how Lacan, in the early 1950s, interpreted the Hegelian *dictum* about the rationality of the real ("What is rational is actual and what is actual is rational"):[12] the true meaning of the subject's words or deeds—their *reason*—is disclosed by their actual consequences, so the subject has no right to shrink back from them and say "But I didn't mean it!" In this sense, we may say that Hitchcock's *Rope* is an inherently Hegelian film: the homosexual couple strangles their best friend to win recognition from professor Caddell, their teacher who preaches the right of Supermen to dispose of the useless and weak; when Caddell is confronted with the verbatim realization of his doctrine—when, in other words, he gets back from the other his own message in its inverted, true form, i.e., when the true dimension of his own "letter" (teaching) reaches its proper addressee, namely himself—he is shaken and shrinks back from the consequence of his words, unprepared to recognize in them his own truth. Lacan defines "hero" as the subject who (unlike Caddell and like Oedipus, for example) fully assumes the consequences of his act, that is to say, who does not step aside when the arrow that he shot makes its full circle and flies back at him—unlike the rest of us who endeavor to realize our desire without paying the price for it: revolutionaries who want Revolution without revolution (its bloody reverse). Hitchcock's benevolent-sadistic playing with the spectator takes into account precisely this halfway nature of our desiring: he makes the spectator shrink back by confronting him with the full consequence of the realization of his desire ("you want this evil person killed? OK, you will have it—with all the nauseating details you wanted to pass over in silence..."). In short, Hitchcock's "sadism" corresponds exactly to the superego's "malevolent neutrality": he is nothing but a neutral "purveyor of truth," giving us only what we wanted, but including in the package the part of it that we prefer to ignore.

This reverse of the subject's message is its *repressed*; so it is not difficult to see how the impossibility of metalanguage is linked to the return of the repressed. "There is no metalanguage" insofar as the speaking subject is always already spoken, i.e., insofar as he cannot master the effects of what he is saying: he always says more than he "intended to say," and this surplus of what is effectively said over the intended meaning puts into words the repressed content—in it, "the repressed returns."[13] What are symptoms *qua* "returns of the repressed" if not such slips of the tongue by means of which "the letter arrives at its destination," i.e., by means of which the big Other returns to the subject his own message in its true form? If, instead of saying "Thereby I proclaim the session open," I say "Thereby I proclaim the session closed," do I not get, in the most literal sense, my own message back in its true, inverted form? So what could, at this level, the Derridean notion that a letter can also *miss* its destination mean? That the repressed can also *not* return—yet by claiming this, we entangle ourselves in a naive substantialist notion of the unconscious as a positive entity ontologically preceding its "returns," i.e., symptoms *qua* compromise formations, a notion competently called in question by Derrida himself.[14] Here, we cannot but repeat after Lacan: there is no repression previous to the return of the repressed; the repressed content does not precede its return in symptoms, there is no way to conceive it in its purity undistorted by "compromises" that characterize the formation of the symptoms.[15]

This brings us to the third variation, that of the frame always being framed by part of its content; this formula[16] is crucial insofar as it enables us to oppose the "logic of the signifier" to hermeneutics. The aim of the hermeneutical endeavor is to render visible the contours of a "frame," a "horizon" that, precisely by staying invisible, by eluding the subject's grasp, in advance determines its field of vision: what we can see, as well as what we cannot see, is always given to us through a historically mediated frame of preconceits. There is of course nothing pejorative in the use of the term "preconceit" here: its status is transcendental, i.e., it organizes our experience into a meaningful totality. True, it involves an irreducible limitation of our vision, but this finitude is in itself ontologically constitutive: the world is open to us only within radical finitude. At this level, the impossibility of metalanguage equals the impossibility of a neutral point of view enabling us to see things "objectively," "impartially": there is no view that is not framed by a historically determined horizon of "preunderstanding." Today, for example, we can ruthlessly exploit nature only because nature itself is disclosed to us within a horizon that gives it to be seen as raw material at our disposal, in contrast to the Greek or medieval notion of nature. The Lacanian "logic of the signifier" supplements this hermeneutical thesis with an unheard-of inversion: the "horizon of meaning" is always linked, as if by a kind of umbilical cord, to a point *within* the field disclosed by it; the frame of our view is always already framed (re-marked) by a part of its content. We can easily recognize here the topology of the Moebius band where, as in a kind of abyssal inversion, the envelope itself is encased by its interior.[17]

The best way to exemplify this inversion is via the dialectic of view and gaze: in what I see, in what is open to my view, there is always a point where "I see nothing," a point which "makes no sense," i.e., which functions as the picture's stain—this is the point from which the very picture returns the gaze, looks back at me. "A letter arrives at its destination" precisely in this point of the picture: here I encounter myself, my own objective correlative— here I am, so to speak, inscribed in the picture; this ontic "umbilical cord" of the ontological horizon is what is unthinkable for the entire philosophical tradition, Heidegger included. Therein lies the reason of the uncanny power of psychoanalytical interpretation: the subject pursues his everyday life within its closed horizon of meaning, safe in his distance with respect to the world of objects, assured of their meaning (or their insignificance), when, all of a sudden, the psychoanalyst pinpoints some tiny detail of no significance whatsoever to the subject, a stain in which the subject "sees nothing"—a small, compulsive gesture or tic, a slip of the tongue or something of that order— and says: "You see, this detail is a knot which condenses all you had to forget so that you can swim in your everyday certainty, it enframes the very frame which confers meaning on your life, it structures the horizon within which things make sense to you; if we unknot it, you will lose the ground from under your very feet!" It is an experience not unlike that rendered in the old Oriental formula: "Thou art that!"—"Your entire fate is decided in this idiotic detail!" Or, if we keep ourselves to a more formal level of the set theory: among the elements of a given set, there is always One which overdetermines the specific weight and color of the set as such; among the species of a genus, there is always One which overdetermines the very universality of the genus. Apropos of the relationship of different kinds of production within its articulated totality, Marx wrote:

> In all forms of society there is one specific kind of production which predominates over the rest, whose relations thus assign rank and influence to the others. It is a general illumination which bathes all the other colours and modifies their particularity. It is a particular ether which determines the specific gravity of every being which has materialized within it.[18]

Do not these propositions amount to the fact that the very frame of production (its totality) is always enframed by a part of its content (by one specific kind of production)?

SYMBOLIC CIRCUIT II: FATE AND REPETITION

The encounter with "Thou art that!" is of course experienced as an encounter with the knot which condenses one's fate; this brings us to the last variation on the theme "a letter always arrives at its destination": one can never escape one's fate, or, to replace this rather obscurantist formulation with a more appropriate psychoanalytic one, the symbolic debt has to be repaid. The letter which "arrives at its destination" is also a letter of request for outstanding debts; what propels a letter on its symbolic circuit is always some outstanding debt. This dimension of fate is at work in the very formal structure of Poe's "The Purloined Letter": isn't there something distinctly "fateful" in the way the self-experience of the main characters in Poe's story is determined by the simple "mechanical" shift of their positions within the intersubjective triad of the three glances (the first which sees nothing; the second which sees that the first sees nothing and deludes itself as to the secrecy of what it hides; the third which sees that the two first glances leave what should be hidden exposed to whomever would seize it)? In the way, for example, the minister's fate is sealed not because of his personal miscalculation or oversight but because the simple shift of his position from the third to the second glance in the repetition of the initial triad causes his structural blindness? Here, we encounter again the mechanism of imaginary (mis)recognition: the participants in the play automatically perceive their fate as something that pertains to the letter as such in its immediate materiality ("This letter is damned, whosoever comes into possession of it is brought to ruin!")—what they misrecognize is that the "curse" is not in the letter as such but in the intersubjective network organized around it. However, to avoid repeating the played-out analysis of Poe's story, let us address a formally similar case, the classical Bette Davis melodrama *Now, Voyager,* the story of Charlotte Vale, a frustrated spinster, the "ugly duckling" of the family, who is pushed into a nervous breakdown by her domineering mother, a rich widow.[19] Under the guidance of the benevolent Doctor Jacquith, she is cured to emerge as a poised and beautiful woman; following his advice, she decides to see life and takes a trip to South America. There, she has an affair with a charming married man; he is, however, unable to leave his family for her because of his daughter who is on the brink of madness, so Charlotte returns home alone. Soon afterward, she falls into depression and is hospitalized again; in the mental asylum, she encounters the daughter of her lover who immediately develops a traumatic dependence on her. Dr. Jacquith informs Charlotte that her lover's wife died recently, so that they are now free to marry; yet he is quick to add that this marriage would be an unbearable shock for the daughter—Charlotte is her only support, the only thing standing between her and the final slip into madness. Charlotte decides to sacrifice her love and to dedicate her life to mothering the unfortunate child; when, at the end of the film, her lover asks her for her hand, she promises him just deep friendship, refusing his offer with the phrase: "Why reach for the moon, when we can have the stars?"—one of the purest and therefore most efficient nonsenses in the history of cinema.

When her lover shows to Charlotte a picture of his family, her attention is drawn to a girl sitting aside and staring sadly into camera; this figure arouses her immediate compassion and Charlotte wants to know all about her. Why? She identifies with her because she recognizes in her her own position, that of the neglected "ugly duckling." So when, at the film's end, Charlotte sacrifices her love life for the poor girl's rescue, she does not do it out of an abstract sense of duty: the point is rather that she conceives the girl's present situation, when her very survival depends on Charlotte, as *the exact repetition of her own situation* years ago when she was at her mother's mercy. Therein consists the structural homology between this film and "The Purloined Letter": in the course of the story, the same intersubjective network is repeated, with the subjects shifting to different positions—in both cases, an omnipotent mother holds in her hands the daughter's fate, with the one difference that in the first scene it was an evil mother driving the daughter to madness, while in the second scene a good mother is given a chance to redeem herself by pulling the daughter from the brink. The film displays poetic *finesse* by conferring a double role on Doctor Jacquith: the same person who, in the first scene, "sets free" Charlotte, i.e., opens up to her the perspective of an unchained sexual life, appears in the second scene as the bearer of prohibition who prevents her marriage by reminding her of her debt. Here, we have the "compulsion to repeat" at its purest: Charlotte cannot afford marriage since she must *honor her debt*. When, finally, she seems freed from the nightmare, "fate" (the big Other) confronts her with the price of this freedom by putting her into a situation where she herself can destroy the young girl's life. If Charlotte would not sacrifice herself, she would be persecuted by the "demons of the past": her happy marital life would be spoiled forever by the memory of the unfortunate child in the asylum paying the price, a reminder of how she betrayed *her own* past. In other words, Charlotte does not "sacrifice herself for the other's happiness": by sacrificing herself, she honors her debt to *herself*. So, when she finds herself face to face with a broken girl who can be saved only by means of her sacrifice, we could again say that "a letter arrives at its destination."[20]

Within this dimension of the outstanding debt, the role of the letter is assumed by an object that circulates among the subjects and, by its very circulation, makes out of them a closed intersubjective community. Such is the function of the Hitchcockian object: not the decried MacGuffin but the tiny "piece of the real" which keeps the story in motion by finding itself "out of place" (stolen, etc.): from the ring in *Shadow of a Doubt*, the cigarette lighter in *Strangers on a Train*, up to the child in *The Man Who Knew Too Much* who circulates between the two couples. The story ends the moment this object "arrives at its destination," i.e., returns to its rightful owner: the moment Guy gets back the lighter (the last shot of *Strangers on a Train* where the lighter falls out of dead Bruno's unclasped hand), the moment the abducted child returns to the American couple (in *The Man Who Knew Too Much*), etc. This object embodies, gives material existence to the lack in the Other, to the constitutive inconsistency of the symbolic order: Claude Lévi-Strauss pointed out how the very fact of exchange attests a certain structural flaw, an imbalance that pertains to the Symbolic, which is why the Lacanian mathem for this object is S(Ⱥ), the signifier of the barred Other. The supreme exemplar of such an object is the ring from Richard Wagner's *Ring des Nibelungen*, this gigantic drama of the unbalanced symbolic exchange. The story opens with Alberich stealing the ring from the Rhine maidens, whereby it becomes the source of a curse for its possessors; it ends when the ring is thrown back into the Rhine to its rightful owners—the Gods, however, pay for this reestablishment of the balance with their twilight, since their very existence was founded upon an unsettled debt.

The imaginary and the symbolic dimension of "a letter always reaching its destination" are thus in their very opposition closely connected: the first is defined by the imaginary (mis)recognition (a letter arrives at its destination insofar as I recognize myself as its addressee, i.e., insofar as I find *myself* in it), whereas the second comprises the concealed truth that emerges in the "blind spots" and flaws of the imaginary circle. Let us just recall so-called "applied psychoanalysis," the standard "psychoanalytic interpretation" of works of art: this procedure always "finds itself," and the propositions on Oedipus complex, on sublimation, etc., are again and again confirmed since the search moves in an imaginary closed circle and finds only what it is already looking for—what, in a sense, it already has (the network 'of its theoretical preconceits). A letter traversing the symbolic circuit "arrives at its destination" when we experience the utmost futility of this procedure, its utmost failure to touch the inherent logic of its object. The way "a letter arrives at its destination" within the symbolic circuit therefore implies the structure of a slip, of "success through failure": it reaches us unbeknowst to us. In Agatha Christie's *Why Didn't They Ask Evans?*, the young hero and his girl friend find a mortally wounded man on the links who, seconds before his death, raises his head and says "Why didn't they ask Evans?" They set out to investigate the murder and, long afterward, when the dead man's mysterious phrase is completely forgotten, they concern themselves with the somewhat peculiar circumstances of the certification of a dying country gentleman's will: the relatives called as a witness a distant neighbor instead of using the servant Evans who was present in the house, so... "Why didn't they ask Evans?" Instantaneously, the hero and his girl friend realize that their question reproduces verbatim the phrase of the man who died on the links—therein consists the clue for his murder. What we have here is an exemplary case of how "a letter arrives at its destination": when, in a totally contingent way, it finds its proper place.

This reference to the letter and its itinerary enables us to distinguish between the two modalities of the crowd. When, apropos of his interpretation of the Freudian dream of Irma's injection, Lacan speaks of "l'immixion des sujets," "the inmixing of subjects," of the moment when the subjects lose their individuality by being reduced to little wheels in a nonsubjective machinery (in the dream itself, the moment of this reversal is the appearance of the three professors who exculpate Freud by enumerating mutually exclusive reasons for the failure of Irma's treatment), this machine is of course synonymous with the *symbolic order*. This mode of the crowd is exemplarily depicted in the paintings of Pieter Brueghel from the years 1559 and 1560 (*Dutch Proverbs, Fight between Carnival and Lent, Child Games*): the subject is here "beheaded," "lost in the crowd," yet the transsubjective mechanism which regulates the process (games, proverbs, carnivals) is clearly of a symbolic nature: it can be unearthed by means of the act of interpretation. In other words, it is the signifier which runs the show—through this very confusion and blind automatism, the letter nevertheless "arrives at its destination." How? Let us recall Eric Ambler's spy novel *Passage of Arms*, the story of a poor Chinese in Malaya in the early 1950s, after the breakdown of the Communist insurgency: upon discovering a forgotten hideout of Communist arms in the jungle, he plans to sell them in order to buy an old bus and thus become a small-scale capitalist. He thereby sets in motion an unforeseen chain of events which exceed by far his original intent: the rich Chinese who buys the arms resells them to an Indonesian pro-Communist guerilla, the transaction involves an "innocent" American tourist couple, the story moves from Malaya to Bangkok, then to Sumatra, yet all this improvisatory texture of accidental encounters brings us back to our starting point: at the end, the Chinese becomes the owner of an old, ramshackle bus, "the letter arrives at its destination," as if some hidden "cunning of Reason" regulated the chaotic flow of events. Something not dissimilar to this is at work in the quartets and quintets of Mozart's great operas; it suffices to mention the finale of *Le Nozze di Figaro:* the persons speak and sing over one another, there is an entire network of misapprehensions and false identifications, yet this chaos of comic encounters seems to be run by the hidden hand of a benevolent destiny which provides for the final reconciliation. An abyss separates this "immixture" from, say, the quintet in the third act of Wagner's *Meistersinger von Nürnberg* where all the voices efface their differences and yield to the same pacifying flow—not to mention the brutal irruption of the crowd that follows Hagen's "call to men (*Männerruf)*" in the second act of *Die Götterdämmerung.* The point here is the link between this crowd and the prelude to the opera with the sibyls no longer able to decipher the future course of events, since the cord of destiny is cut—the crowd enters the stage when history is no longer regulated by the texture of symbolic destiny, i.e., when the father's phallic authority is broken (one should remember that, the previous evening, Siegfried broke Wotan's spear). This crowd, the *modern* crowd, appeared for the first time in Edgar Allan Poe's "The Man of the Crowd": the anonymous observer watches through the windowpane of a cafe (this frame that introduces the distance between "inside" and "outside" is crucial here) the turmoil of the London evening crowd and decides to follow an old man; at dawn, after long hours of walking, it becomes clear that there is nothing to discover: "It will be in vain to follow; I shall learn no more of him, nor of his deeds." The old man is thus exposed as the "man of the crowd," the epitome of evil, precisely insofar as he embodies something that "doesn't allow itself to be read"—*es lässt sich nicht lesen,* as Poe himself puts it in German. This "resistance to being read" of the crowd designates of course the passage from the symbolic register to that of the Real.[21]

THE REAL ENCOUNTER

The motif of fate has brought us to the very brink of the third level, that of the Real; here, "a letter always arrives at its destination" equals what "meeting one's fate" means: "we will all die." A common pretheoretical sensitivity enables us to detect the ominous undertone that sticks to the proposition "a letter always arrives at its destination": the only letter that nobody can evade, that sooner or later reaches us, i.e., the letter which has each of us as its infallible addressee, is death. We can say that we live only in so far as a certain letter (the letter containing our death warrant) still wanders around, looking for us. Let us recall the ill-famed "poetic" statement of the Iranian president Ali Hamnei apropos of the sentence of death pronounced on Salman Rushdie: nothing can stop its execution, the bullet is already on its way, sooner or later, it will hit its mark—such is the fate of all and each of us, the bullet with our name on it is already shot. Derrida himself emphasizes the lethal dimension of writing: every trace is condemned to its ultimate effacement. Note the fundamental ambiguity of the very word "end": "aim" and "annihilation"—the closing of the letter's circuit equals its consumption. The crucial point here is that the imaginary, the symbolic, and the real dimension of "a letter always arrives at its destination" are not external to each other: at the end of the imaginary as well as the symbolic itinerary, we encounter the Real. As was demonstrated by Lacan apropos of Freud's dream of Irma's injection, the dual mirror relationship culminates in the horrifying confrontation with the abyss of the Real, exemplified by the flesh of Irma's throat:

> the flesh one never sees, the foundation of things, the other side of the head, of the face, the secretory glands *par excellence*, the flesh from which everything exudes, at the very heart of the mystery, the flesh in as much as it is suffering, is formless, in as much as its form in itself is something which provokes anxiety.[22]

The fascinating image of a double is therefore ultimately nothing but a mask of horror, its delusive front: when we encounter ourselves, we encounter death. The same horror emerges with the fulfillment of symbolic "destiny," as is attested by Oedipus: when, at Colonnus, he closed the circuit and paid all his debts, he found himself reduced to a kind of soap bubble burst asunder—a scrap of the real, the leftover of a formless slime without any support in the symbolic order. Oedipus realized his destiny

> to that final point which is nothing more than something strictly identical to a striking down, a tearing apart, a laceration of himself—he is no longer, no longer anything, at all. And it is at that moment that he says the phrase I evoked last time—*Am I made man in the hour when I cease to be?*[23]

The unpaid symbolic debt is therefore in a way constitutive of our existence: our very symbolic existence is a "compromise formation," the delaying of an encounter. In Max Ophuls's melodrama *Letter from an Unknown Woman*, this link connecting the symbolic circuit with the encounter of the Real is perfectly exemplified. At the very beginning of the film "a letter arrives at its destination," confronting the hero with the disavowed truth: what was for him a series of unconnected, ephemeral love affairs that he only vaguely remembered destroyed a woman's life. He assumes responsibility for this by means of a suicidal gesture: by deciding not to escape and to attend the duel he is certain to lose.

However, as is indicated in Lacan's above-quoted reading of the dream of Irma's injection, the Real is not only death but also life: not only the pale, frozen, lifeless immobility but also "the flesh from which everything exudes," the life substance in its mucous palpitation. In other words, the Freudian duality of life and death drives is *not* a symbolic opposition but a tension, and antagonism, inherent to the presymbolic Real. As Lacan points out again and again, the very notion of life is alien to the symbolic order. And the name of this life substance that proves a traumatic shock for the symbolic universe is of course *enjoyment*. The ultimate variation on the theme of a letter that always arrives at its destination reads therefore: "you can never get rid of the stain of enjoyment"—the very gesture of renouncing enjoyment produces inevitably a surplus enjoyment that Lacan writes down as the "object small a." Examples offer themselves in abundance, from the ascetic who can never be sure he does not repudiate all worldly goods because of the ostentatious and vain satisfaction procured by this very act of sacrifice, to the "sense of fulfillment" that overwhelms us when we submit to the totalitarian appeal: "Enough of decadent enjoyment! It's time for sacrifice and renunciation!" This dialectic of enjoyment and surplus enjoyment—i.e., the fact that there is no "substantial" enjoyment preceding the excess of surplus enjoyment, that enjoyment itself is a kind of surplus produced by renunciation—is perhaps what gives a clue to so-called "primal masochism."[24]

Such a reading, however, leads beyond Lacan's "Seminar on 'The Purloined Letter,'" which stays within the confines of the "structuralist" problematic of a senseless, "mechanical" symbolic order regulating the subject's innermost self-experience. From the perspective of the last years of Lacan's teaching, the letter which circulates among the subjects in Poe's story, determining their position in the intersubjective network, is no longer the materialized agency of the *signifier* but rather an *object* in the strict sense of materialized enjoyment—the stain, the uncanny excess that the subjects snatch away from each other, forgetful of how its very possession will mark them with a passive, "feminine" stance that bears witness to the confrontation with the object-cause of desire. What ultimately interrupts the continuous flow of words, what hinders the smooth running of the symbolic circuit, is the traumatic presence of the Real: when the words suddenly stay out, we have to look not for imaginary resistances but for the object that came too close.

NOTES

1. Cf. Jacques Derrida, "The Purveyor of Truth," in *The Post Card: From Socrates to Freud and Beyond* (Chicago: University of Chicago Press, 1987).
2. Cf. Jacques Lacan, "Seminar on 'The Purloined Letter,'" p. 53.
3. Since this recourse to common sense takes place more often than one might suspect, *systematically* even, within the "deconstruction," one is tempted to put forward the thesis that the very fundamental gesture of "deconstruction" is in a radical sense *commonsensical*. There is namely an unmistakable ring of common sense in the "deconstructionist" insistence upon the impossibility of establishing a clear cut difference between empirical and transcendental, outside and inside, representation and presence, writing and voice; in its compulsive demonstration of how the outside always already smears over the inside, of how writing is constitutive of voice, etc. etc.—as if "deconstructionism" is ultimately wrapping up commonsensical insights into an intricate jargon. Therein consists perhaps one of the hitherto overlooked reasons for its unforeseen success in the USA, the land of common sense *par excellence*.
4. What is crucial here is the difference between the letter's symbolic circuit and its itinerary in what we call "reality": a letter always arrives at its destination on the symbolic level, whereas in reality, it can of course fail to reach it. This difference is strictly homologous to that established by Lacan apropos of the two possible readings of the phrase "You are the one that will follow me" (Jacques Lacan, *Le Séminaire, livre III: Les Psychoses* (Paris: Editions du Seuil, 1981), pp. 315–19):

    1) read as a statement ascertaining a positive state of things, it can of course be falsified if it proves inaccurate, i.e., if you do *not* follow me;

    2) read as a bestowal of a symbolic mandate, or designation, i.e., as the establishment of a pact giving birth to a new intersubjective relation, it cannot simply be falsified by your factual behavior: you *remain* "the one that will follow me" even if, in reality, you do *not* do it—in this case, you simply do not live up to your symbolic title which nevertheless determines your place in the symbolic

network. In other words, read in this second sense, the determination "the one that will follow me" functions as a "rigid designator" in the Kripkeian sense: it remains true "in all possible worlds," irrespective of your factual behavior.

5. As to these readings, cf. Barbara Johnson's "The Frame of Reference: Poe, Lacan, Derrida," in *The Purloined Poe.*

6. Cf. Michel Pêcheux, *Language, Semantics and Ideology* (London: MacMillan, 1982).

7. Cf. Barbara Johnson, op. cit., p. 248.

8. Michel Pêcheux, op. cit., p. 107.

9. An exemplary case of such a (mis)recognition is found in Joseph Mankiewicz's *Letter to Three Wives* where each of the three wives on a Sunday trip recognizes herself as addressee of the letter sent to them by the local *femme fatale* announcing that she has run away with one of their husbands: the letter stirs up the trauma of each of them, each of them becomes aware of the failure of her marriage.

10. Cf. Jacques Lacan, "Intervention on Transference," in Charles Bernheimer and Claire Cahane, eds., *In Dora's Case* (London: Virago Press, 1985).

11. As for the paradoxes of the "Beautiful Soul," cf. Slavoj Žižek, *The Sublime Object of Ideology* (London: Verso Books, 1989), pp. 215–17.

12. G. W. F. Hegel, *Philosophy of Right* (Oxford: Clarendon Press, 1942), p. 8.

13. Therein consists the elementary Hegelian procedure; Hegel demonstrates the "nontruth" of some proposition not by comparing it with the thing as it is "in itself" and thus ascertaining the proposition's inaccuracy, but by comparing the proposition *with itself,* i.e., with its own process of enunciation: by comparing the intended meaning of the proposition with what the subject effectively said. This discord is the very impetus of the dialectical process, as is attested at the very beginning of the *Phenomenology of Spirit* where "sense certainty" is refuted by means of a reference to the universal dimension contained in is own act of enunciation.

14. Cf. Jacques Derrida, "Freud and the Scene of Writing," in *Writing and Difference* (Chicago: University of Chicago Press, 1978), where it is demonstrated by rigorous analysis how it is not possible to differentiate in a clear-cut way between "primary" and "secondary" processes: the "primary" process (subjected to the logic of the unconscious: condensations, displacements, etc.) is always already (re)marked by the "secondary" process that characterizes the system of consciousness/preconscious.

15. *Stricto sensu,* there *is* a subjective position within which a letter does *not* arrive at its destination, within which the repressed does *not* return in the shape of symptoms, within which the subject does *not* receive from the Other his own message in its true form: that of a *psychotic.* "A letter arrives at its destination" only with the subject entering the circuit of communication, i.e., capable of assuming the dialectical relationship toward the Other *qua* locus of truth. However, according to Lacan's famous formula of the psychotic forclusion ("what was foreclosed from the Symbolic returns in the Real"), even in psychosis the letter *does* ultimately reach the subject, namely in the form of psychotic "answers of the Real" (hallucinations, etc.).

16. Elaborated in Jacques Derrida, *La Vérité en peinture* (Paris: Flammarion, 1978).

17. As for this topology, cf. Jacques-Alain Miller, "Théorie de la langue," *Ornicar?* 1 (1975).

18. Karl Marx, *Grundrisse* (Harmondsworth: Penguin Books, 1972), p. 107.

19. We rely here on the perspicacious analysis by Elizabeth Cowie, "Fantasia," *m/f* 9 (1984).

20. There is, however, another side to this story: Charlotte's act of renunciation can also be read as an attempt to elude the inherent impossibility of the sexual relationship by positing an external hindrance to it, thus preserving the illusion that without this hindrance, she would be able to enjoy it fully. In short, the trick is here the same as that of "courtly love": "A very refined manner to supplant the absence of the sexual relationship by feigning that it is us who put the obstacle in its way"(Jacques Lacan, *Le Séminaire, livre XX: Encore* (Paris: Editions du Seuil, 1975) p. 65).

21. When, with the advent of capitalism, the symbolically structured "community" was replaced by the "crowd," community became in a radical sense *imagined*: our "sense of belonging" does not refer anymore to a community we experience as "actual," but becomes a performative effect brought about by the "abstract" media (press, radio, etc.) (cf. Benedict Anderson, *Imagined Communities,* London and New York: Verso Books, 1983). Every community, from the most "primitive" tribes onward, was of course always already "staged" by symbolic rituals; yet it was only with capitalism that the community became "imagined" in the precise sense of being dialectically opposed to the atomized, "actual" economic life. What we have in mind here is not only the fact that, in contrast to the precapitalist ethnic communities, the concept Nation is a product of the expansion of the media (the role of the press in eighteenth and nineteenth centuries, Hitler and radio, Moral Majority's TV evangelism, etc.), but that a more refined logic is at work from political identification up to TV quiz shows and sexuality. Let us recall Stuart Hall's analysis of Thatcherism's political appeal (cf. his *Hard Road to Renewal* (London and New York: Verso Books, 1988)): the Thatcherite interpellation succeeded insofar as the individual recognized himself/herself not as a member of some actual community but as a member of the imagined community of those who may be "lucky in the next round" by way of their individual entrepreneurship. The hope of success the recognition of oneself as the one who *may* succeed, overshadows the actual success and already functions as a success, the same as in a TV quiz show where, in a sense, "taking part in it" already is to win: what really matters is not the actual gains but being identified as part of the community of those who *may* win. Today, such a logic has penetrated even the most intimate domain of sexuality, as attested by the success of "minitel" (the network of personal computers connected by phone) in France: upon entering the circuit of minitel communication, I choose a pseudonym for myself and then exchange the most obscene sexual fantasies with others whom I also know only by their pseudonyms... The point of it, of course, is that, within this imagined community of anonymous participants, everybody knows that these fantasies will never be "realized": gratification is procured by the flow of signifier itself—it is as if "minitel" were made to exemplify Lacan's thesis according to which enjoyment is primarily enjoyment in the signifiers. It seems therefore that today's predominant economy of enjoyment repeats the paradox of quantum physics where possibility (the possible trajectories of a particle) as such possesses a kind of actuality: to imagine a possible gratification of desire equals its actual gratification.
22. *The Seminar of Jacques Lacan, Book II: The Ego in Freud's Theory and in the Technique of Psychoanalysis* (Cambridge: Cambridge University Press, 1988), pp. 154–55.
23. Ibid, p. 226.
24. In other words, if we subtract from enjoyment its surplus, we are left with nothing at all; the closest scientific analogy to it is perhaps the notion of *photon* in physics. When physicists refer to the mass of a particle, they usually refer to its mass when it is at rest. Any mass other than a rest mass is called relativistic mass; since the mass of a particle increases with velocity, a particle can have any number of relativistic masses—the size of its relativistic mass depends upon its velocity. The total mass is thus composed of the rest mass plus the surplus added by the velocity of its movement. The paradox of photons is, however, that *they don't have any rest mass:* their rest mass equals zero. The photon is thus an object which exists only as a surplus, as the acceleration due to its velocity; in a way, it is "without substance"—if we subtract the relativistic mass that depends upon its velocity, i.e., if we "quiet it down" and attempt to seize it in its state of rest, "as it really is," it dissolves. And it is the same with the "object small a" *qua* surplus enjoyment: it exists only in its distorted state (visually, for example, only insofar as it is viewed from aside, anamorphotically extended or contracted)—if we view it "straight," "as it really is," there is nothing to see.

FEMINISM

VISUAL PLEASURE AND NARRATIVE CINEMA (1975)

LAURA MULVEY

Drawing on feminism, Freudian and Lacanian psychoanalysis, and narrative theory, Mulvey writes about how the camera work and editing of classical Hollywood films reduce filmed women to objects of a gaze. She argues that conventional patterns of camera work and film editing position the audience to identify with the men in the films who gaze at the women as little more than erotic objects. She thus sees the structure of the film narrative as steering spectators, regardless of their predilections, into the position of heterosexual masculine spectators, and not as any heterosexual masculine spectators, but more specifically as those who abuse the look, the gaze. Rather than seeing such a process as inevitable or natural, Mulvey sees it as constructed by specific traditions of film narrative. She calls for alternative models of film that would reconstruct gender relations. She recognizes the sexist assumptions of the psychoanalytic thinking that she sees driving classic film, but she sees those assumptions as accurately characterizing sexist cultural patterns that, as a feminist, she asks us to change.

For Mulvey's psychoanalytic terms, see the headnote on Jacques Lacan. Other key terms include ideology *(unconscious and often oppressive social assumptions—see the essay in this volume by Louis Althusser),* diegesis *(narrative progression),* Renaissance space, *and* deep focus. *Before the Renaissance, European paintings showed little sense of depth. People and objects in the distance were not necessarily painted as smaller. In the Renaissance, artists began to draw and paint in ways that suggest more depth and space, so that figures in the distance are smaller and objects that cross from the foreground to the background get smaller as they move back into the illusory depth of the flat surface of paint. In a photograph or film with deep focus, objects far away and objects close up are both in focus. In a photograph or film with shallow focus, objects at one distance from the camera are in focus while objects at other distances are out of focus.*

Mulvey's article has generated extensive discussion and debate. Some critics agree with her. Some blame her for not addressing spectators who resist the steering she describes. Some want her to address the gaze of actresses as well as the gaze of actors. Mulvey's model has often set the terms of discussion both for those who admire her essay and for those who object to it. For a response to Mulvey in this volume, see bell hooks, "The Oppositional Gaze: Black Female Spectators."

I INTRODUCTION

A POLITICAL USE OF PSYCHOANALYSIS

This paper intends to use psychoanalysis to discover where and how the fascination of film is reinforced by pre-existing patterns of fascination already at work within the individual subject and the social formations that have moulded him. It takes as its starting-point the way film reflects, reveals and even plays on the straight, socially established interpretation of sexual difference which controls images, erotic ways of looking and spectacle. It is helpful to understand what the cinema has been, how its magic has worked in the past, while attempting a theory and a practice which will challenge this cinema of the past. Psychoanalytic theory is thus appropriated here as a political weapon, demonstrating the way the unconscious of patriarchal society has structured film form.

The paradox of phallocentrism in all its manifestations is that it depends on the image of the castrated women to give order and meaning to its world. An idea of woman stands as linchpin to the system: it is her lack that produces the phallus as a symbolic presence, it is her desire to make good the lack that the phallus signifies. Recent writing in *Screen* about psychoanalysis and the cinema has not sufficiently brought out the importance of the representation of the female form in a symbolic order in which, in the last resort, it speaks castration and nothing else. To summarise briefly: the function of woman in forming the patriarchal unconscious is twofold: she firstly symbolises the castration threat by her real lack of a penis and secondly thereby raises her child into the symbolic. Once this has been achieved, her meaning in the process is at an end. It does not last into the world of law and language except as a memory, which oscillates between memory of maternal plenitude and memory of lack. Both are posited on nature (or on anatomy in Freud's famous phrase). Woman's desire is subjugated to her image as bearer of the bleeding wound; she can exist only in relation to castration and cannot transcend it. She turns her child into the signifier of her own desire to possess a penis (the condition, she imagines, of entry into the symbolic). Either she must gracefully give way to the word, the name of the father and the law, or else struggle to keep her child down with her in the half-light of the imaginary. Woman then stands in patriarchal culture as a signifier for the male other, bound by a symbolic order in which man can live out his fantasies and obsessions through linguistic command by imposing them on the silent image of woman still tied to her place as bearer, not maker, of meaning.

There is an obvious interest in this analysis for feminists, a beauty in its exact rendering of the frustration experienced under the phallocentric order. It gets us nearer to the roots of our oppression, it brings closer an articulation of the problem, it faces us with the ultimate challenge: how to fight the unconscious structured like a language (formed critically at the moment of arrival of language) while still caught within the language of the patriarchy? There is no way in which we can produce an alternative out of the blue, but we can begin to make a break by examining patriarchy with the tools it provides, of which psychoanalysis is not the only but an important one. We are still separated by a great gap from important issues for the female unconscious which are scarcely relevant to phallocentric theory: the sexing of the female infant and her relationship to the symbolic, the sexually mature woman as non-mother, maternity outside the signification of the phallus, the vagina. But, at this point, psychoanalytic theory as it now stands can at least advance our understanding of the *status quo*, of the patriarchal order in which we are caught.

DESTRUCTION OF PLEASURE AS A RADICAL WEAPON

As an advanced representation system, the cinema poses questions about the ways the unconscious (formed by the dominant order) structures ways of seeing and pleasure in looking. Cinema has changed over the last few decades. It is no longer the monolithic system based on large capital investment exemplified at its best by Hollywood in the 1930s, 1940s and 1950s. Technological advances (16mm and so on) have changed the economic conditions of cinematic production, which can now be artisanal as well as capitalist. Thus it has been possible for an alternative cinema to develop. However self-conscious and ironic Hollywood managed to be, it always restricted itself to a formal *mise en scène* reflecting the dominant ideological concept of the cinema. The alternative cinema provides a space for the birth of a cinema which is radical in both a political and an aesthetic sense and challenges the basic assumptions of the mainstream film. This is not to reject the latter moralistically, but to highlight the ways in which its preocuptions reflect the psychical obsessions of the society which produced it and, further, to stress that the alternative cinema must start specifically by reacting against these obsessions and assumptions. A politically and aesthetically avant-garde cinema is now possible, but it can still only exist as a counterpoint.

The magic of the Hollywood style at its best (and of all the cinema which fell within its sphere of influence) arose, not exclusively, but in one important aspect, from its skilled and satisfying manipulation of visual pleasure. Unchallenged, mainstream film coded the erotic into the language of the dominant patriarchal order. In the highly developed Hollywood cinema it was only through these codes that the alienated subject, torn in his imaginary memory by a sense of loss, by the terror of potential lack in fantasy, came near to finding a glimpse of satisfaction: through its formal beauty and its play on his own formative obsessions. This article will discuss the interweaving of that erotic pleasure in film, its meaning and, in particular, the central place of the image of woman. It is said that analysing pleasure, or beauty, destroys it. That is the intention of this article. The satisfaction and reinforcement of the ego that represent the high point of film history hitherto must be attacked. Not in favour of a reconstructed new pleasure, which cannot exist in the abstract, nor of intellectualised unpleasure, but to make way for a total negation of the ease and plenitude of the narrative fiction film. The alternative is the thrill that comes from leaving the past behind without simply rejecting it, transcending outworn or oppressive forms, and daring to break with normal pleasurable expectations in order to conceive a new language of desire.

II PLEASURE IN LOOKING/FASCINATION WITH THE HUMAN FORM

A   The cinema offers a number of possible pleasures. One is scopophilia (pleasure in looking). There are circumstances in which looking itself is a source of pleasure, just as, in the reverse formation, there is pleasure in being looked at. Originally, in his *Three Essays on Sexuality*, Freud isolated scopophilia as one of the component instincts of sexuality which exist as drives quite independently of the erotogenic zones. At this point he associated scopophilia with taking other people as objects, subjecting them to a controlling and curious gaze. His particular examples centre on the voyeuristic activities of children, their desire to see and make sure of the private and forbidden (curiosity about other people's genital and bodily functions, about the presence or absence of the penis and, retrospectively, about the primal scene). In this analysis scopophilia is essentially active. (Later, in "Instincts and Their Vicissitudes," Freud developed his theory of scopophilia further, attaching it initially to pregenital auto-eroticism, after which, by analogy, the pleasure of the look is transferred to others. There is a close working here of the relationship between the active instinct and its further development in a narcissistic form.) Although the instinct is modified by other factors, in particular the constitution of the ego, it continues to exist as the erotic basis for pleasure in looking at another person as object. At the extreme, it can become fixated into a perversion, producing obsessive voyeurs and Peeping Toms whose only sexual satisfaction can come from watching, in an active controlling sense, an objectified other.

At first glance, the cinema would seem to be remote from the undercover world of the surreptitious observation of an unknowing and unwilling victim. What is seen on the screen is so manifestly shown. But the mass of mainstream film, and the conventions within which it has consciously evolved, portray a hermetically sealed world which unwinds magically, indifferent to the presence of the audience, producing for them a sense of separation and playing on their voyeuristic fantasy. Moreover the extreme contrast between the darkness in the auditorium (which also isolates the spectators from one another) and the brilliance of the shifting patterns of light and shade on the screen helps to promote the illusion of voyeuristic separation. Although the film is really being shown, is there to be seen, conditions of screening and narrative conventions give the spectator an illusion of looking in on a private world. Among other things, the position of the spectators in the cinema is blatantly one of repression of their exhibitionism and projection of the repressed desire onto the performer.

B   The cinema satisfies a primordial wish for pleasurable looking, but it also goes further, developing scopophilia in its narcissistic aspect. The conventions of mainstream film focus attention on the human form. Scale, space, stories are all anthropomorphic. Here, curiosity and the wish to look intermingle with a fascination with likeness and recognition: the human face, the human body, the relationship between the human form and its surroundings, the visible presence of the person in the world. Jacques Lacan has described how the moment when a child recognises its own image in the mirror is crucial for the constitution of the ego. Several aspects of this analysis are relevant here. The mirror phase occurs at a time when children's physical ambitions outstrip their motor capacity, with the result that their recognition of themselves is joyous in that they imagine their mirror image to be more complete, more perfect than they experience in their own body. Recognition is thus overlaid with misrecognition: the image recognised is conceived as the reflected body of the self, but its misrecognition as superior projects this body outside itself as an ideal ego, the alienated subject which, reintrojected as an ego ideal, prepares the way for identification with others in the future. This mirror moment predates language for the child.

Important for this article is the fact that it is an image that constitutes the matrix of the imaginary, of recognition/misrecognition and identification, and hence of the first articulation of the I, of subjectivity. This is a moment when an older fascination with looking (at the mother's face, for an obvious example) collides with the initial inklings of self-awareness. Hence it is the birth of the long love affair/despair between image and self-image which has found such intensity of expression in film and such joyous recognition in the cinema audience. Quite apart from the extraneous similarities between screen and mirror (the framing of the human form in its surroundings, for instance), the cinema has structures of fascination strong enough to allow temporary loss of ego while simultaneously reinforcing it. The sense of forgetting the world as the ego has come to perceive it (I forgot who I am and where I was) is nostalgically reminiscent of that pre-subjective moment of image recognition. While at the same time, the cinema has distinguished itself in the production of ego ideals, through the star system for instance. Stars provide a focus or centre both to screen space and screen story where they act out a complex process of likeness and difference (the glamorous impersonates the ordinary).

C   Sections A and B have set out two contradictory aspects of the pleasurable structures of looking in the conventional cinematic situation. The first, scopophilic, arises from pleasure in using another person as an object of sexual stimulation through sight. The second, developed through narcissism and the constitution of the ego, comes from identification with the image seen. Thus, in film terms, one implies a separation of the erotic identity of the subject from the object on the screen (active scopophilia), the other demands identification of the ego with the object on the screen through the spectator's fascination with and recognition of his like. The first is a function of the sexual instincts, the second of ego libido. This dichotomy was crucial for Freud. Although he saw the two as interacting and overlaying each other, the tension between instinctual drives and self-preservation polarises in terms of pleasure. But both are formative structures, mechanisms without intrinsic meaning. In themselves they have no signification, unless attached to an idealisation. Both pursue aims in indifference to perceptual reality, and motivate eroticised phantasmagoria that affect the subject's perception of the world to make a mockery of empirical objectivity.

During its history, the cinema seems to have evolved a particular illusion of reality in which this contradiction between libido and ego has found a beautifully complementary fantasy world. In *reality* the fantasy world of the screen is subject to the law which produces it. Sexual instincts and identification processes have a meaning within the symbolic order which articulates desire. Desire, born with language, allows the possibility of transcending the instinctual and the imaginary, but its point of reference continually returns to the traumatic moment of its birth: the castration complex. Hence the look, pleasurable in form, can be threatening in content, and it is woman as representation/image that crystallises this paradox.

III WOMAN AS IMAGE, MAN AS BEARER OF THE LOOK

A In a world ordered by sexual imbalance, pleasure in looking has been split between active/male and passive/female. The determining male gaze projects its fantasy onto the female figure, which is styled accordingly. In their traditional exhibitionist role women are simultaneously looked at and displayed, with their appearance coded for strong visual and erotic impact so that they can be said to connote *to-be-looked-at-ness*. Woman displayed as sexual object is the *leitmotif* of erotic spectacle: from pin-ups to strip-tease, from Ziegfeld to Busby Berkeley, she holds the look, and plays to and signifies male desire. Mainstream film neatly combines spectacle and narrative. (Note, however, how in the musical song-and-dance numbers interrupt the flow of the diegesis.) The presence of woman is an indispensable element of spectacle in normal narrative film, yet her visual presence tends to work against the development of a story-line, to freeze the flow of action in moments of erotic contemplation. This alien presence then has to be integrated into cohesion with the narrative. As Budd Boetticher has put it:

> What counts is what the heroine provokes, or rather what she represents. She is the one, or rather the love or fear she inspires in the hero, or else the concern he feels for her, who makes him act the way he does. In herself the woman has not the slightest importance.

(A recent tendency in narrative film has been to dispense with this problem altogether; hence the development of what Molly Haskell has called the "buddy movie," in which the active homosexual eroticism of the central male figures can carry the story without distraction.) Traditionally, the woman displayed has functioned on two levels: as erotic object for the characters within the screen story, and as erotic object for the spectator within the auditorium, with a shifting tension between the looks on either side of the screen. For instance, the device of the show-girl allows the two looks to be unified technically without any apparent break in the diegesis. A woman performs within the narrative; the gaze of the spectator and that of the male characters in the film are neatly combined without breaking narrative verisimilitude. For a moment the sexual impact of the performing woman takes the film into a no man's land outside its own time and space. Thus Marilyn Monroe's first appearance in *The River of No Return* and Lauren Bacall's songs in *To Have and Have Not*. Similarly, conventional close-ups of legs (Dietrich, for instance) or a face (Garbo) integrate into the narrative a different mode of eroticism. One part of a fragmented body destroys the Renaissance space, the illusion of depth demanded by the narrative; it gives flatness, the quality of a cut-out or icon, rather than verisimilitude, to the screen.

B An active/passive heterosexual division of labour has similarly controlled narrative structure. According to the principles of the ruling ideology and the psychical structures that back it up, the male figure cannot bear the burden of sexual objectification. Man is reluctant to gaze at his exhibitionist like. Hence the split between spectacle and narrative supports the man's role as the active one of advancing the story, making things happen. The man controls the film fantasy and also emerges as the representative of power in a further sense: as the bearer of the look of the spectator, transferring it behind the screen to neutralise the extra-diegetic tendencies represented by woman as spectacle. This is made possible through the processes set in motion by structuring the film around a main controlling figure with whom the spectator can identify. As the spectator identifies with the main male protagonist, he projects his look onto that of his like, his screen surrogate, so that the power of the male protagonist as he controls events coincides with the active power of the erotic look, both giving a satisfying sense of omnipotence. A male movie star's glamorous characteristics are thus not those of the erotic object of the gaze, but those of the more perfect, more complete, more powerful ideal ego conceived in the original moment of recognition in front of the mirror. The character in the story can make things happen and control events better than the subject/spectator, just as the image in the mirror was more in control of motor co-ordination.

In contrast to woman as icon, the active male figure (the ego ideal of the identification process) demands a three-dimensional space corresponding to that of the mirror recognition, in which the alienated subject internalised his own representation of his imaginary existence. He is a figure in a landscape. Here the function of film is to reproduce as accurately as possible the so-called natural conditions of human perception. Camera technology (as exemplified by deep focus in particular) and camera movements (determined by the action of the protagonist), combined with invisible editing (demanded by realism), all tend to blur the limits of screen space. The male protagonist is free to command the stage, a stage of spatial illusion in which he articulates the look and creates the action. (There are films with a woman as main protagonist, of course. To analyse this phenomenon seriously here would take me too far afield. Pam Cook and Claire Johnston's study of *The Revolt of Mamie Stover* in Phil Hardy (ed.), *Raoul Walsh* (Edinburgh, 1974), shows in a striking case how the strength of this female protagonist is more apparent than real.)

C1   Sections III A and B have set out a tension between a mode of representation of woman in film and conventions surrounding the diegesis. Each is associated with a look: that of the spectator in direct scopophilic contact with the female form displayed for his enjoyment (connoting male fantasy) and that of the spectator fascinated with the image of his like set in an illusion of natural space, and through him gaining control and possession of the woman within the diegesis. (This tension and the shift from one pole to the other can structure a single text. Thus both in *Only Angels Have Wings* and in *To Have and Have Not*, the film opens with the woman as object of the combined gaze of spectator and all the male protagonists in the film. She is isolated, glamorous, on display, sexualised. But as the narrative progresses she falls in love with the main male protagonist and becomes his property, losing her outward glamorous characteristics, her generalised sexuality, her show-girl connotations; her eroticism is subjected to the male star alone. By means of identification with him, through participation in his power, the spectator can indirectly possess her too.)

But in psychoanalytic terms, the female figure poses a deeper problem. She also connotes something that the look continually circles around but disavows: her lack of a penis, implying a threat of castration and hence unpleasure. Ultimately, the meaning of woman is sexual difference, the visually ascertainable absence of the penis, the material evidence on which is based the castration complex essential for the organisation of entrance to the symbolic order and the law of the father. Thus the woman as icon, displayed for the gaze and enjoyment of men, the active controllers of the look, always threatens to evoke the anxiety it originally signified. The male unconscious has two avenues of escape from this castration anxiety: preoccupation with the re-enactment of the original-trauma (investigating the woman, demystifying her mystery), counterbalanced by the devaluation, punishment or saving of the guilty object (an avenue typified by the concerns of the *film noir*); or else complete disavowal of castration by the substitution of a fetish object or turning the represented figure itself into a fetish so that it becomes reassuring rather than dangerous (hence overvaluation, the cult of the female star).

This second avenue, fetishistic scopophilia, builds up the physical beauty of the object, transforming it into something satisfying in itself. The first avenue, voyeurism, on the contrary, has associations with sadism: pleasure lies in ascertaining guilt (immediately associated with castration), asserting control and subjugating the guilty person through punishment or forgiveness. This sadistic side fits in well with narrative. Sadism demands a story, depends on making something happen, forcing a change in another person, a battle of will and strength, victory/defeat, all occurring in a linear time with a beginning and an end. Fetishistic scopophilia, on the other hand, can exist outside linear time as the erotic instinct is focused on the look alone. These contradictions and ambiguities can be illustrated more simply by using works by Hitchcock and Sternberg, both of whom take the look almost as the content or subject matter of many of their films. Hitchcock is the more complex, as he uses both mechanisms. Sternberg's work, on the other hand, provides many pure examples of fetishistic scopophilia.

C2   Sternberg once said he would welcome his films being projected upside-down so that story and character involvement would not interfere with the spectator's undiluted appreciation of the screen image. This statement is revealing but ingenuous: ingenuous in that his films do demand that the figure of the woman (Dietrich, in the cycle of films with her, as the ultimate example) should be identifiable; but revealing in that it emphasises the fact that for him the pictorial space enclosed by the frame is paramount, rather than narrative or identification processes. While Hitchcock goes into the investigative side of voyeurism, Sternberg produces the ultimate fetish, taking it to the point where the powerful look of the male protagonist (characteristic of traditional narrative film) is broken in favour of the image in direct erotic rapport with the spectator. The beauty of the woman as object and the screen space coalesce; she is no longer the bearer of guilt but a perfect product, whose body, stylised and fragmented by close-ups, is the content of the film and the direct recipient of the spectator's look.

Sternberg plays down the illusion of screen depth; his screen tends to be one-dimensional, as light and shade, lace, steam, foliage, net, streamers and so on reduce the visual field. There is little or no mediation of the look through the eyes of the main male protagonist. On the contrary, shadowy presences like La Bessière in *Morocco* act as surrogates for the director, detached as they are from audience identification. Despite Sternberg's insistence that his stories are irrelevant, it is significant that they are concerned with situation, not suspense, and cyclical rather than linear time, while plot complications revolve around misunderstanding rather than conflict. The most important absence is that of the controlling male gaze within the screen scene. The high point of emotional drama in the most typical Dietrich films, her supreme moments of erotic meaning, take place in the absence of the man she loves in the fiction. There are other witnesses, other spectators watching her on the screen, their gaze is one with, not standing in for, that of the audience. At the end of *Morocco*, Tom Brown has already disappeared into the desert when Amy Jolly kicks off her gold sandals and walks after him. At the end of *Dishonoured*, Kranau is indifferent to the fate of Magda. In both cases, the erotic impact, sanctified by death, is displayed as a spectacle for the audience. The male hero misunderstands and, above all, does not see.

In Hitchcock by contrast, the male hero does see precisely what the audience sees. However, although fascination with an image through scopophilic eroticism can be the subject of the film, it is the role of the hero to portray the contradictions and tensions experienced by the spectator. In *Vertigo* in particular, but also in *Marnie* and *Rear Window*, the look is central to the plot, oscillating between voyeurism and fetishistic fascination. Hitchcock has never concealed his interest in voyeurism, cinematic and non-cinematic. His heroes are exemplary of the symbolic order and the law—a policeman (*Vertigo*), a dominant male possessing money and power (*Marnie*)—but their erotic drives lead them into compromised situations. The power to subject another person to the will sadistically or to the gaze voyeuristically is turned onto the woman as the object of both. Power is backed by a certainty of legal right and the established guilt of the woman (evoking castration, psychoanalytically speaking). True perversion is barely concealed under a shallow mask of ideological correctness—the man is on the right side of the law, the woman on the wrong. Hitchcock's skilful use of identification processes and liberal use of subjective camera from the point of view of the male protagonist draw the spectators deeply into his position, making them share his uneasy gaze. The spectator is absorbed into a voyeuristic situation within the screen scene and diegesis, which parodies his own in the cinema.

In an analysis of *Rear Window*, Douchet takes the film as a metaphor for the cinema. Jeffries is the audience, the events in the apartment block opposite correspond to the screen. As he watches, an erotic dimension is added to his look, a central image to the drama. His girlfriend Lisa had been of little sexual interest to him, more or less a drag, so long as she remained on the spectator side. When she crosses the barrier between his room and the block opposite, their relationship is reborn erotically. He does not merely watch her through his lens, as a distant meaningful image, he also sees her as a guilty intruder exposed by a dangerous man threatening her with punishment, and thus finally giving him the opportunity to save her. Lisa's exhibitionism has already been established by her obsessive interest in dress and style, in being a passive image of visual perfection; Jeffries's voyeurism and activity have also been established through his work as a photo-journalist, a maker of stories and captor of images. However, his enforced inactivity, binding him to his seat as a spectator, puts him squarely in the fantasy position of the cinema audience.

In *Vertigo*, subjective camera predominates. Apart from one flashback from Judy's point of view, the narrative is woven around what Scottie sees or fails to see. The audience follows the growth of his erotic obsession and subsequent despair precisely from his point of view. Scottie's voyeurism is blatant: he falls in love with a woman he follows and spies on without speaking to. Its sadistic side is equally blatant: he has chosen (and freely chosen, for he had been a successful lawyer) to be a policeman, with all the attendant possibilities of pursuit and investigation. As a result, he follows, watches and falls in love with a perfect image of female beauty and mystery. Once he actually confronts her, his erotic drive is to break her down and force her *to tell* by persistent cross-questioning.

In the second part of the film, he re-enacts his obsessive involvement with the image he loved to watch secretly. He reconstructs Judy as Madeleine, forces her to conform in every detail to the actual physical appearance of his fetish. Her exhibitionism, her masochism, make her an ideal passive counterpart to Scottie's active sadistic voyeurism. She knows her part is to perform, and only by playing it through and then replaying it can she keep Scottie's erotic interest. But in the repetition he does break her down and succeeds in exposing her guilt. His curiosity wins through; she is punished.

Thus, in *Vertigo*, erotic involvement with the look boomerangs: the spectator's own fascination is revealed as illicit voyeurism as the narrative content enacts the processes and pleasures that he is himself exercising and enjoying. The Hitchcock hero here is firmly placed within the symbolic order, in narrative terms. He has all the attributes of the patriarchal superego. Hence the spectator, lulled into a false sense of security by the apparent legality of his surrogate, sees through his look and finds himself exposed as complicit, caught in the moral ambiguity of looking. Far from being simply an aside on the perversion of the police, *Vertigo* focuses on the implications of the active/looking, passive/looked-at split in terms of sexual difference and the power of the male symbolic encapsulated in the hero. Marnie, too, performs for Mark Rutland's gaze and masquerades as the perfect to-be-looked-at image. He, too, is on the side of the law until, drawn in by obsession with her guilt, her secret, he longs to see her in the act of committing a crime, make her confess and thus save her. So he, too, becomes complicit as he acts out the implications of his power. He controls money and words; he can have his cake and eat it.

IV SUMMARY

The psychoanalytic background that has been discussed in this article is relevant to the pleasure and unpleasure offered by traditional narrative film. The scopophilic instinct (pleasure in looking at another person as an erotic object) and, in contradistinction, ego libido (forming identification processes) act as formations, mechanisms, which mould this cinema's formal attributes. The actual image of woman as (passive) raw material for the (active) gaze of man takes the argument a step further into the content and structure of representation, adding a further layer of ideological significance demanded by the patriarchal order in its favourite cinematic form—illusionistic narrative film. The argument must return again to the psychoanalytic background: women in representation can signify castration, and activate voyeuristic or fetishistic mechanisms to circumvent this threat. Although none of these interacting layers is intrinsic to film, it is only in the film form that they can reach a perfect

New Woman will be, as an arrow quits the bow with a movement that gathers and separates the vibrations musically, in order to be more than her self.

I say that we must, for, with a few rare exceptions, there has not yet been any writing that inscribes femininity; exceptions so rare, in fact, that, after plowing through literature across languages, cultures, and ages,[2] one can only be startled at this vain scouting mission. It is well known that the number of women writers (while having increased very slightly from the nineteenth century on) has always been ridiculously small. This is a useless and deceptive fact unless from their species of female writers we do not first deduct the immense majority whose workmanship is in no way different from male writing, and which either obscures women or reproduces the classic representations of women (as sensitive—intuitive—dreamy, etc.)[3]

Let me insert here a parenthetical remark. I mean it when I speak of male writing. I maintain unequivocally that there is such a thing as *marked* writing; that, until now, far more extensively and repressively than is ever suspected or admitted, writing has been run by a libidinal and cultural—hence political, typically masculine—economy; that this is a locus where the repression of women has been perpetuated, over and over, more or less consciously, and in a manner that's frightening since it's often hidden or adorned with the mystifying charms of fiction; that this locus has grossly exaggerated all the signs of sexual opposition (and not sexual difference), where woman has never *her* turn to speak—this being all the more serious and unpardonable in that writing is precisely *the very possibility of change,* the space that can serve as a springboard for subversive thought, the precursory movement of a transformation of social and cultural structures.

Nearly the entire history of writing is confounded with the history of reason, of which it is at once the effect, the support, and one of the privileged alibis. It has been one with the phallocentric tradition. It is indeed that same self-admiring, self-stimulating, self-congratulatory phallocentrism.

With some exceptions, for there have been failures—and if it weren't for them, I wouldn't be writing (I-woman, escapee)—in that enormous machine that has been operating and turning out its "truth" for centuries. There have been poets who would go to any lengths to slip something by at odds with tradition—men capable of loving love and hence capable of loving others and of wanting them, of imagining the woman who would hold out against oppression and constitute herself as a superb, equal, hence "impossible" subject, untenable in a real social framework. Such a woman the poet could desire only by breaking the codes that negate her. Her appearance would necessarily bring on, if not revolution—for the bastion was supposed to be immutable—at least harrowing explosions. At times it is in the fissure caused by an earthquake, through that radical mutation of things brought on by a material upheaval when every structure is for a moment thrown off balance and an ephemeral wildness sweeps order away, that the poet slips something by, for a brief span, of woman. Thus did Kleist expend himself in his yearning for the existence of sister-lovers, maternal daughters, mother-sisters, who never hung their heads in shame. Once the palace of magistrates is restored, it's time to pay: immediate bloody death to the uncontrollable elements.

But only the poets—not the novelists, allies of representationalism. Because poetry involves gaining strength through the unconscious and because the unconscious, that other limitless country, is the place where the repressed manage to survive: women, or as Hoffmann would say, fairies.

She must write her self, because this is the invention of a *new insurgent* writing which, when the moment of her liberation has come, will allow her to carry out the indispensable ruptures and transformations in her history, first at two levels that cannot be separated.

a) Individually. By writing her self, woman will return to the body which has been more than confiscated from her, which has been turned into the uncanny stranger on display—the ailing or dead figure, which so often turns out to be the nasty companion, the cause and location of inhibitions. Censor the body and you censor breath and speech at the same time.

Write your self. Your body must be heard. Only then will the immense resources of the unconscious spring forth. Our naphtha will spread, throughout the world, without dollars—black or gold —nonassessed values that will change the rules of the old game.

To write. An act which will not only "realize" the decensored relation of woman to her sexuality, to her womanly being, giving her access to her native strength; it will give her back her goods, her pleasures, her organs, her immense bodily territories which have been kept under seal; it will tear her away from the superegoized structure in which she has always occupied the place reserved for the guilty (guilty of everything, guilty at every turn: for having desires, for not having any; for being frigid, for being "too hot"; for not being both at once; for being too motherly and not enough; for having children and for not having any; for nursing and for not nursing…)—tear her away by means of this research, this job of analysis and illumination, this emancipation of the marvelous text of her self that she must urgently learn to speak. A woman without a body, dumb, blind, can't possibly be a good fighter. She is reduced to being the servant of the militant male, his shadow. We must kill the false woman who is preventing the live one from breathing. Inscribe the breath of the whole woman.

b) An act that will also be marked by woman's seizing the occasion to *speak*, hence her shattering entry into history, which has always been based *on her suppression*. To write and thus to forge for herself the antilogos weapon. To become *at will* the taker and initiator, for her own right, in every symbolic system, in every political process.

It is time for women to start scoring their feats in written and oral language.

Every woman has known the torment of getting up to speak. Her heart racing, at times entirely lost for words, ground and language slipping away—that's how daring a feat, how great a transgression it is for a woman to speak—even just open her mouth—in public. A double distress, for even if she transgresses, her words fall almost always upon the deaf male ear, which hears in language only that which speaks in the masculine.

It is by writing, from and toward women, and by taking up the challenge of speech which has been governed by the phallus, that women will confirm women in a place other than that which is reserved in and by the symbolic, that is, in a place other than silence. Women should break out of the snare of silence. They shouldn't be conned into accepting a domain which is the margin or the harem.

Listen to a woman speak at a public gathering (if she hasn't painfully lost her wind). She doesn't "speak," she throws her trembling body forward; she lets go of herself, she flies; all of her passes into her voice, and it's with her body that she vitally supports the "logic" of her speech. Her flesh speaks true. She lays herself bare. In fact, she physically materializes what she's thinking; she signifies it with her body. In a certain way she *inscribes* what she's saying, because she doesn't deny her drives the intractable and impassioned part they have in speaking. Her speech, even when "theoretical" or political, is never simple or linear or "objectified," generalized: she draws her story into history.

There is not that scission, that division made by the common man between the logic of oral speech and the logic of the text, bound as he is by his antiquated relation—servile, calculating—to mastery. From which proceeds the niggardly lip service which engages only the tiniest part of the body, plus the mask.

In women's speech, as in their writing, that element which never stops resonating, which, once we've been permeated by it, profoundly and imperceptibly touched by it, retains the power of moving us—that element is the song: first music from the first voice of love which is alive in every woman. Why this privileged relationship with the voice? Because no woman stockpiles as many defenses for countering the drives as does a man. You don't build walls around yourself, you don't forego pleasure as "wisely" as he. Even if phallic mystification has generally contaminated good relationships, a woman is never far from "mother" (I mean outside her role functions: the "mother" as nonname and as source of goods). There is always within her at least a little of that good mother's milk. She writes in white ink.

Woman for women.—There always remains in woman that force which produces/is produced by the other—in particular, the other woman. *In* her, matrix, cradler; herself giver as her mother and child; she is her own sister-daughter. You might object, "What about she who is the hysterical offspring of a bad mother?" Everything will be changed once woman gives woman to the other woman. There is hidden and always ready in woman the source; the locus for the other. The mother, too, is a metaphor. It is necessary and sufficient that the best of herself be given to woman by another woman for her to be able to love herself and return in love the body that was "born" to her. Touch me, caress me, you the living no-name, give me my self as myself. The relation to the "mother," in terms of intense pleasure and violence, is curtailed no more than the relation to childhood (the child that she was, that she is, that she makes, remakes, undoes, there at the point where, the same, she others herself). Text: my body—shot through with streams of song; I don't mean the overbearing, clutchy "mother" but, rather, what touches you, the equivoice that affects you, fills your breast with an urge to come to language and launches your force; the rhythm that laughs you; the intimate recipient who makes all metaphors possible and desirable; body (body? bodies?), no more describable than god, the soul, or the Other; that part of you that leaves a space between yourself and urges you to inscribe in language your woman's style. In women there is always more or less of the mother who makes everything all right, who nourishes, and who stands up against separation; a force that will not be cut off but will knock the wind out of the codes. We will rethink womankind beginning with every form and every period of her body. The Americans remind us, "We are all Lesbians"; that is, don't denigrate woman, don't make of her what men have made of you.

Because the "economy" of her drives is prodigious, she cannot fail, in seizing the occasion to speak, to transform directly and indirectly *all* systems of exchange based on masculine thrift. Her libido will produce far more radical effects of political and social change than some might like to think.

Because she arrives, vibrant, over and again, we are at the beginning of a new history, or rather of a process of becoming in which several histories intersect with one another. As subject for history, woman always occurs simultaneously in several places. Woman un-thinks[4] the unifying, regulating history that homogenizes and channels forces, herding contradictions into a single battlefield. In woman, personal history blends together with the history of all women, as well as national and world history. As a militant, she is an integral part of all liberations. She must be farsighted, not limited to a blow-by-blow interaction. She foresees that her liberation will do more than modify power relations or toss the ball over to the other camp; she will bring about a mutation in human relations, in thought, in all praxis: hers is not simply a class struggle, which she carries forward into a much vaster movement. Not that in order to be a woman-in-struggle(s) you have to leave the class struggle or repudiate it; but you have to split it open, spread it out, push it forward, fill it with the fundamental struggle so as to prevent the class struggle, or any other struggle for the liberation of a class or people, from operating as a form of repression, pretext for postponing the inevitable, the staggering alteration in power relations and in the production of individualities. This alteration is already upon us—in the United States, for example, where millions of night crawlers are in the process of undermining the family and disintegrating the whole of American sociality.

The new history is coming; it's not a dream, though it does extend beyond men's imagination, and for good reason. It's going to deprive them of their conceptual orthopedics, beginning with the destruction of their enticement machine.

It is impossible to *define* a feminine practice of writing, and this is an impossibility that will remain, for this practice can never be theorized, enclosed, coded—which doesn't mean that it doesn't exist. But it will always surpass the discourse that regulates the phallocentric system; it does and will take place in areas other than those subordinated to philosophico-theoretical domination. It will be conceived of only by subjects who are breakers of automatisms, by peripheral figures that no authority can ever subjugate.

Hence the necessity to affirm the flourishes of this writing, to give form to its movement, its near and distant byways. Bear in mind to begin with (1) that sexual opposition, which has always worked for man's profit to the point of reducing writing, too, to his laws, is only a historico-cultural limit. There is, there will be more and more rapidly pervasive now, a fiction that produces irreducible effects of femininity. (2) That it is through ignorance that most readers, critics, and writers of both sexes hesitate to admit or deny outright the possibility or the pertinence of a distinction between feminine and masculine writing. It will usually be said, thus disposing of sexual difference: either that all writing, to the extent that it materializes, is feminine; or, inversely—but it comes to the same thing—that the act of writing is equivalent to masculine masturbation (and so the woman who writes cuts herself out a paper penis); or that writing is bisexual, hence neuter, which again does away with differentiation. To admit that writing is precisely working (in) the in-between, inspecting the process of the same and of the other without which nothing can live, undoing the work of death—to admit this is first to want the two, as well as both, the ensemble of the one and the other, not fixed in sequences of struggle and expulsion or some other form of death but infinitely dynamized by an incessant process of exchange from one subject to another. A process of different subjects knowing one another and beginning one another anew only from the living boundaries of the other: a multiple and inexhaustible course with millions of encounters and transformations of the same into the other and into the in-between, from which woman takes her forms (and man, in his turn; but that's his other history).

In saying "bisexual, hence neuter," I am referring to the classic conception of bisexuality, which, squashed under the emblem of castration fear and along with the fantasy of a "total" being (though composed of two halves), would do away with the difference experienced as an operation incurring loss, as the mark of dreaded sectility.

To this self-effacing, merger-type bisexuality, which would conjure away castration (the writer who puts up his sign: "bisexual written here, come and see," when the odds are good that it's neither one nor the other), I oppose the *other bisexuality* on which every subject not enclosed in the false theater of phallocentric representationalism has founded his/her erotic universe. Bisexuality: that is, each one's location in self (*répéperage en soi*) of the presence—variously manifest and insistent according to each person, male or female—of both sexes, nonexclusion either of the difference or of one sex, and, from this "self-permission," multiplication of the effects of the inscription of desire, over all parts of my body and the other body.

Now it happens that at present, for historico-cultural reasons, it is women who are opening up to and benefiting from this vatic bisexuality which doesn't annul differences but stirs them up, pursues them, increases their number. In a certain way, "woman is bisexual"; man—it's a secret to no one—being poised to keep glorious phallic monosexuality in view. By virtue of affirming the primacy of the phallus and of bringing it into play, phallocratic ideology has claimed more than one victim. As a woman, I've been clouded over by the great shadow of the scepter and been told: idolize it, that which you cannot brandish. But at the same time, man has been handed that grotesque and scarcely enviable destiny (just imagine) of being reduced to a single idol with clay balls. And consumed, as Freud and his followers note, by a fear of being a woman! For, if psychoanalysis was constituted from woman, to repress femininity (and not so successful a repression at that—men have made it clear), its account of masculine sexuality is now hardly refutable; as with all the "human" sciences, it reproduces the masculine view, of which it is one of the effects.

Here we encounter the inevitable man-with-rock, standing erect in his old Freudian realm, in the way that, to take the figure back to the point where linguistics is conceptualizing it "anew," Lacan preserves it in the sanctuary of the phallos (ϕ) "sheltered" from *castration's lack*! Their "symbolic" exists, it holds power—we, the sowers of disorder, know it only too well. But we are in no way obliged to deposit our lives in their banks of lack, to consider the constitution of the subject in terms of a drama manglingly restaged, to reinstate again and again the religion of the father. Because we don't want that. We don't fawn around the supreme hole. We have no womanly reason to pledge allegiance to the negative. The feminine (as the poets suspected) affirms: "... And yes," says Molly, carrying *Ulysses* off beyond any book and toward the new writing; "I said yes, I will Yes."

The Dark Continent is neither dark nor unexplorable.—It is still unexplored only because we've been made to believe that it was too dark to be explorable. And because they want to make us believe that what interests us is the white continent, with its monuments to Lack.

And we believed. They riveted us between two horrifying myths: between the Medusa and the abyss. That would be enough to set half the world laughing, except that it's still going on. For the phallologocentric sublation[5] is with us, and it's militant, regenerating the old patterns, anchored in the dogma of castration. They haven't changed a thing: they've theorized their desire for reality! Let the priests tremble, we're going to show them our sexts!

Too bad for them if they fall apart upon discovering that women aren't men, or that the mother doesn't have one. But isn't this fear convenient for them? Wouldn't the worst be, isn't the worst, in truth, that women aren't castrated, that they have only to stop listening to the Sirens (for the Sirens were men) for history to change its meaning? You only have to look at the Medusa straight on to see her. And she's not deadly. She's beautiful and she's laughing.

Men say that there are two unrepresentable things: death and the feminine sex. That's because they need femininity to be associated with death; it's the jitters that gives them a hard-on! for themselves! They need to be afraid of us. Look at the trembling Perseuses moving backward toward us, clad in apotropes. What lovely backs! Not another minute to lose. Let's get out of here.

Let's hurry: the continent is not impenetrably dark. I've been there often. I was overjoyed one day to run into Jean Genêt. It was in *Pompes funèbres*.[6] He had come there led by his Jean. There are some men (all too few) who aren't afraid of femininity.

Almost everything is yet to be written by women about femininity: about their sexuality, that is, its infinite and mobile complexity, about their eroticization, sudden turn-ons of a certain miniscule-immense area of their bodies; not about destiny, but about the adventure of such and such a drive, about trips, crossings, trudges, abrupt and gradual awakenings, discoveries of a zone at one time timorous and soon to be forthright. A woman's body, with its thousand and one thresholds of ardor—once, by smashing yokes and censors, she lets it articulate the profusion of meanings that run through it in every direction—will make the old single-grooved mother tongue reverberate with more than one language.

We've been turned away from our bodies, shamefully taught to ignore them, to strike them with that stupid sexual modesty; we've been made victims of the old fool's game: each one will love the other sex. I'll give you your body and you'll give me mine. But who are the men who give women the body that women blindly yield to them? Why so few texts? Because so few women have as yet won back their body. Women must write through their bodies, they must invent the impregnable language that will wreck partitions, classes, and rhetorics, regulations and codes, they must submerge, cut through, get beyond the ultimate reserve-discourse, including the one that laughs at the very idea of pronouncing the word "silence," the one that, aiming for the impossible, stops short before the word "impossible" and writes it as "the end."

Such is the strength of women that, sweeping away syntax, breaking that famous thread (just a tiny little thread, they say) which acts for men as a surrogate umbilical cord, assuring them—otherwise they couldn't come—that the old lady is always right behind them, watching them make phallus, women will go right up to the impossible.

When the "repressed" of their culture and their society returns, it's an explosive, *utterly* destructive, staggering return, with a force never yet unleashed and equal to the most forbidding of suppressions. For when the Phallic period comes to an end, women will have been either annihilated or borne up to the highest and most violent incandescence. Muffled throughout their history, they have lived in dreams, in bodies (though muted), in silences, in aphonic revolts.

And with such force in their fragility; a fragility, a vulnerability, equal to their incomparable intensity. Fortunately, they haven't sublimated; they've saved their skin, their energy. They haven't worked at liquidating the impasse of lives without futures. They have furiously inhabited these sumptuous bodies: admirable hysterics who made Freud succumb to many voluptuous moments impossible to confess, bombarding his Mosaic statue with their carnal and passionate body words, haunting him with their inaudible and thundering denunciations, dazzling, more than naked underneath the seven veils of modesty. Those who, with a single word of the body, have inscribed the vertiginous immensity of a history which is sprung like an arrow from the whole history of men and from biblico-capitalist society, are the women, the supplicants of yesterday, who come as forebears of the new women, after whom no intersubjective relation will ever be the same. You, Dora, you the indomitable, the poetic body, you are the true "mistress" of the Signifier. Before long your efficacity will be seen at work when your speech is no longer suppressed, its point turned in against your breast, but written out over against the other.

In body.—More so than men who are coaxed toward social success, toward sublimation, women are body. More body, hence more writing. For a long time it has been in body that women have responded to persecution, to the familial-conjugal enterprise of domestication, to the repeated attempts at castrating them. Those who have turned their tongues 10,000 times seven times before not speaking are either dead from it or more familiar with their tongues and their mouths than anyone else. Now, I-woman am going to blow up the Law: an explosion henceforth possible and ineluctable; let it be done, right now, *in* language.

Let us not be trapped by an analysis still encumbered with the old automatisms. It's not to be feared that language conceals an invincible adversary because it's the language of men and their grammar. We mustn't leave them a single place that's any more theirs alone than we are.

If woman has always functioned "within" the discourse of man, a signifier that has always referred back to the opposite signifier which annihilates its specific energy and diminishes or stifles its very different sounds, it is time for her to dislocate this "within," to explode it, turn it around and seize it; to make it hers, containing it, taking it in her own mouth, biting that tongue with her very own teeth to invent for herself a language to get inside of. And you'll see with what ease she will spring forth from that "within"—the "within" where once she so drowsily crouched—to overflow at the lips she will cover the foam.

Nor is the point to appropriate their instruments, their concepts, their places, or to begrudge them their position of mastery. Just because there's a risk of identification doesn't mean that we'll succumb. Let's leave it to the worriers, to masculine anxiety and its obsession with how to dominate the way things work—knowing "how it works" in order to "make it work." For us the point is not to take possession in order to internalize or manipulate, but rather to dash through and to "fly."[7]

Flying is woman's gesture—flying in language and making it fly. We have all learned the art of flying and its numerous techniques; for centuries we've been able to possess anything only by flying; we've lived in flight, stealing away, finding, when desired, narrow passageways, hidden crossovers. It's no accident that *voler* has a double meaning, that it plays on each of them and thus throws off the agents of sense. It's no accident: women take after birds and robbers just as robbers take after women and birds. They (*illes*)[8] go by, fly the coop, take pleasure in jumbling the order of space, in disorienting it, in changing around the furniture, dislocating things and values, breaking them all up, emptying structures, and turning propriety upside down.

What woman hasn't flown/stolen? Who hasn't felt, dreamt, performed the gesture that jams sociality? Who hasn't crumbled, held up to ridicule the bar of separation? Who hasn't inscribed with her body the differential, punctured the system of couples and opposition? Who, by some act of transgression, hasn't overthrown successiveness, connection, the wall of circumfusion?

A feminine text cannot fail to be more than subversive. It is volcanic; as it is written it brings about an upheaval of the old property crust, carrier of masculine investments; there's no other way. There's no room for her if she's not a he. If she's a her-she, it's in order to smash everything, to shatter the framework of institutions, to blow up the law, to break up the "truth" with laughter.

For once she blazes *her* trail in the symbolic, she cannot fail to make of it the chaosmos of the "personal"—in her pronouns, her nouns, and her clique of referents. And for good reason. There will have been the long history of gynocide. This is known by the colonized peoples of yesterday, the workers, the nations, the species off whose backs the history of men has made its gold; those who have known the ignominy of persecution derive from it an obstinate future desire for grandeur; those who are locked up know better than their jailers the taste of free air. Thanks to their history, women today know (how to do and want) what men will be able to conceive of only much later. I say woman overturns the "personal," for if, by means of laws, lies, blackmail, and marriage, her right to herself has been extorted at the same time as her name, she has been able, through the very movement of mortal alienation, to see more closely the inanity of "propriety," the reductive stinginess of the masculine-conjugal subjective economy, which she doubly resists. On the one hand she has constituted herself necessarily as that "person" capable of losing a part of herself without losing her integrity. But secretly, silently, deep down inside, she grows and multiplies, for, on the other hand, she knows far more about living and about the relation between the economy of the drives and the management of the ego than any man. Unlike man, who holds so dearly to his title and his titles, his pouches of value, his cap, crown, and everything connected with his head, woman couldn't care less about the fear of decapitation (or castration), adventuring, without the masculine temerity, into anonymity, which she can merge with without annihilating herself: because she's a giver.

I shall have a great deal to say about the whole deceptive problematic of the gift. Woman is obviously not that woman Nietzsche dreamed of who gives only in order to.[9] Who could ever think of the gift as a gift-that-takes? Who else but man, precisely the one who would like to take everything?

If there is a "propriety of woman," it is paradoxically her capacity to depropriate unselfishly: body without end, without appendage, without principal "parts." If she is a whole, it's a whole composed of parts that are wholes, not simple partial objects but a moving, limitlessly changing ensemble, a cosmos tirelessly traversed by Eros, an immense astral space not organized around any one sun that's any more of a star than the others.

This doesn't mean that she's an undifferentiated magma, but that she doesn't lord it over her body or her desire. Though masculine sexuality gravitates around the penis, engendering that centralized body (in political anatomy) under the dictatorship of its parts, woman does not bring about the same regionalization which serves the couple head/genitals and which is inscribed only within boundaries. Her libido is cosmic, just as her unconscious is worldwide. Her writing can only keep going, without ever inscribing or discerning contours, daring to make these vertiginous crossings of the other(s) ephemeral and passionate sojourns in him, her, them, whom she inhabits long enough to look at from the point closest to their unconscious from the moment they awaken, to love them at the point closest to their drives; and then further, impregnated through and through with these brief, identificatory embraces, she goes and passes into infinity. She alone dares and wishes to know from within, where she, the outcast, has never ceased to hear the resonance of fore-language. She lets the other language speak—the language of 1,000 tongues which knows neither enclosure nor death. To life she refuses nothing. Her language does not contain, it carries; it does not hold back, it makes possible. When id is ambiguously uttered—the wonder of being several—she doesn't defend herself against these unknown women whom she's surprised at becoming, but derives pleasure from this gift of alterability. I am spacious, singing flesh, on which is grafted no one knows which I, more or less human, but alive because of transformation.

Write! and your self-seeking text will know itself better than flesh and blood, rising, insurrectionary dough kneading itself, with sonorous, perfumed ingredients, a lively combination of flying colors, leaves, and rivers plunging into the sea we feed. "Ah, there's her sea," he will say as he holds out to me a basin full of water from the little phallic mother from whom he's inseparable. But look, our seas are what we make of them, full of fish or not, opaque or transparent, red or black, high or smooth, narrow or bankless; and we are ourselves sea, sand, coral, seaweed, beaches, tides, swimmers, children, waves.... More or less wavily sea, earth, sky—what matter would rebuff us? We know how to speak them all.

Heterogeneous, yes. For her joyous benefit she is erogenous; she is the erotogeneity of the heterogeneous: airborne swimmer, in flight, she does not cling to herself; she is dispersible, prodigious, stunning, desirous and capable of others, of the other woman that she will be, of the other woman she isn't, of him, of you.

Woman be unafraid of any other place, of any same, or any other. My eyes, my tongue, my ears, my nose, my skin, my mouth, my body-for-(the)-other—not that I long for it in order to fill up a hole, to provide against some defect of mine, or because, as fate would have it, I'm spurred on by feminine "jealousy"; not because I've been dragged into the whole chain of substitutions that brings that which is substituted back to its ultimate object. That sort of thing you would expect to come straight out of "Tom Thumb," out of the *Penisneid* whispered to us by old grandmother ogresses, servants to their father-sons. If they believe, in order to muster up some self-importance, if they really need to believe that we're dying of desire, that we are this hole fringed with desire for their penis—that's their immemorial business. Undeniably (we verify it at our own expense—but also to our amusement), it's their business to let us know they're getting a hard-on, so that we'll assure them (we the maternal mistresses of their little pocket signifier) that they still can, that it's still there—that men structure themselves only by being fitted with a feather. In the child it's not the penis that the woman desires, it's not that famous bit of skin around which every man gravitates. Pregnancy cannot be traced back, except within the historical limits of the ancients, to some form of fate, to those mechanical substitutions brought about by the unconscious of some eternal "jealous woman"; not to penis envies; and not to narcissism or to some sort of homosexuality linked to the ever-present mother! Begetting a child doesn't mean that the woman or the man must fall ineluctably into patterns or must recharge the circuit of reproduction. If there's a risk there's not an inevitable trap: may women be spared the pressure, under the guise of consciousness-raising, of a supplement of interdictions. Either you want a kid or you don't—*that's your business.* Let nobody threaten you; in satisfying your desire, let not the fear of becoming the accomplice to a sociality succeed the old-time fear of being "taken." And man, are you still going to bank on everyone's blindness and passivity, afraid lest the child make a father and, consequently, that in having a kid the woman land herself more than one bad deal by engendering all at once child—mother—father—family? No; it's up to you to break the old circuits. It will be up to man and woman to render obsolete the former relationship and all its consequences, to consider the launching of a brand-new subject, alive, with defamilialization. Let us demater-paternalize rather than deny woman, in an effort to avoid the co-optation of procreation, a thrilling era of the body. Let us defetishize. Let's get away from the dialectic which has it that the only good father is a dead one, or that the child is the death of his parents. The child is the other, but the other without violence, bypassing loss, struggle. We're fed up with the reuniting of bonds forever to be sev-ered, with the litany of castration that's handed down and genealogized. We won't advance backward anymore; we're not going to repress something so simple as the desire for life. Oral drive, anal drive, vocal drive—all these drives are our strengths, and among them is the gesta-tion drive—just like the desire to write: a desire to live self from within, a desire for the swol-len belly, for language, for blood. We are not going to refuse, if it should happen to strike our fancy, the unsurpassed pleasures of pregnancy which have actually been always exaggerated or conjured away—or cursed—in the classic texts. For if there's one thing that's been repressed here's just the place to find it: in the taboo of the pregnant woman. This says a lot about the power she seems invested with at the time, because it has always been suspected, that, when pregnant, the woman not only doubles her market value, but—what's more important—takes on intrinsic value as a woman in her own eyes and, undeniably, acquires body and sex.

There are thousands of ways of living one's pregnancy; to have or not to have with that still invisible other a relationship of another intensity. And if you don't have that particular yearn-ing, it doesn't mean that you're in any way lacking. Each body distributes in its own special way, without model or norm, the nonfinite and changing totality of its desires. Decide for yourself on your position in the arena of contradictions, where pleasure and reality embrace. Bring the other to life. Women know how to live detachment; giving birth is neither losing nor increas-ing. It's adding to life an other. Am I dreaming? Am I mis-recognizing? You, the defenders of "theory," the sacrosanct yes-men of Concept, enthroners of the phallus (but not of the penis):

Once more you'll say that all this smacks of "idealism," or what's worse, you'll splutter that I'm a "mystic."

And what about the libido? Haven't I read the "Signification of the Phallus"? And what about separation, what about that bit of self for which, to be born, you undergo an abla-tion—an ablation, so they say, to be forever commemorated by your desire?

Besides, isn't it evident that the penis gets around in my texts, that I give it a place and appeal? Of course I do. I want all. I want all of me with all of him. Why should I deprive myself of a part of us? I want all of us. Woman of course has a desire for a "loving desire" and not a jealous one. But not because she is gelded; not because she's deprived and needs to be filled out, like some wounded person who wants to console herself or seek vengeance; I don't want a penis to decorate my body with. But I do desire the other for the other, whole and entire, male or female; because living means wanting everything that is, everything that lives, and wanting it alive. Castration? Let others toy with it. What's a desire originating from a lack? A pretty meager desire.

The woman who still allows herself to be threatened by the big dick, who's still impressed by the commotion of the phallic stance, who still leads a loyal master to the beat of the drum: that's the woman of yesterday. They still exist, easy and numerous victims of the oldest of farces: either they're cast in the original silent version in which, as titanesses lying under the mountains they make with their quivering, they never see erected that theoretic monument to the golden phallus looming, in the old manner, over their bodies. Or, coming today out of their *infans* period and into the second, "enlightened" version of their virtuous debasement, they see themselves suddenly assaulted by the builders of the analytic empire and, as soon as they've begun to formulate the new desire, naked, nameless, so happy at making an appearance, they're taken in their bath by the new old men, and then, whoops! Luring them with flashy signifiers, the demon of interpretation—oblique, decked out in modernity—sells them the same old handcuffs, baubles, and chains. Which castration do you prefer? Whose degrading do you like better, the father's or the mother's? Oh, what pwetty eyes, you pwetty little girl. Here, buy my glasses and you'll see the Truth-Me-Myself tell you everything you should know. Put them on your nose and take a fetishist's look (you are me, the other analyst—that's what I'm telling you) at your body and the body of the other. You see? No? Wait, you'll have everything explained to you, and you'll know at last which sort of neurosis you're related to. Hold still, we're going to do your portrait, so that you can begin looking like it right away.

Yes, the naives to the first and second degree are still legion. If the New Women, arriving now, dare to create outside the theoretical, they're called in by the cops of the signifier, fingerprinted, remonstrated, and brought into the line of order that they are supposed to know; assigned by force of trickery to a precise place in the chain that's always formed for the benefit of a privileged signifier. We are pieced back to the string which leads back, if not to the Name-of-the-Father, then, for a new twist, to the place of the phallic-mother.

Beware, my friend, of the signifier that would take you back to the authority of a signified! Beware of diagnoses that would reduce your generative powers. "Common" nouns are also proper nouns that disparage your singularity by classifying it into species. Break out of the circles; don't remain within the psychoanalytic closure. Take a look around, then cut through!

And if we are legion, it's because the war of liberation has only made as yet a tiny breakthrough. But women are thronging to it. I've seen them, those who will be neither dupe nor domestic, those who will not fear the risk of being a woman; will not fear any risk, any desire, any space still unexplored in themselves, among themselves and others or anywhere else. They do not fetishize, they do not deny, they do not hate. They observe, they approach, they try to see the other woman, the child, the lover—not to strengthen their own narcissism or verify the solidity or weakness of the master, but to make love better, to invent.

Other love—In the beginning are our differences. The new love dares for the other, wants the other, makes dizzying, precipitous flights between knowledge and invention. The woman arriving over and over again does not stand still; she's everywhere, she exchanges, she is the desire-that-gives. (Not enclosed in the paradox of the gift that takes nor under the illusion of unitary fusion. We're past that.) She comes in, comes-in-between herself me and you, between the other me where one is always infinitely more than one and more than me, without the fear of ever reaching a limit; she thrills in our becoming. And we'll keep on becoming! She cuts through defensive loves, motherages, and devourations: beyond selfish narcissism, in the moving, open, transitional space, she runs her risks. Beyond the struggle-to-the-death that's been removed to the bed, beyond the love-battle that claims to represent exchange, she scorns at an Eros dynamic that would be fed by hatred. Hatred: a heritage, again, a remainder, a duping subservience to the phallus. To love, to watch-think-seek the other in the other, to despecularize, to unhoard. Does this seem difficult? It's not impossible, and this is what nourishes life—a love that has no commerce with the apprehensive desire that provides against the lack and stultifies the strange; a love that rejoices in the exchange that multiplies. Wherever history still unfolds as the history of death, she does not tread. Opposition, hierarchizing exchange, the struggle for mastery which can end only in at least one death (one master—one slave, or two nonmasters ≠ two dead)—all that comes from a period in time governed by phallocentric values. The fact that this period extends into the present doesn't prevent woman from starting the history of life somewhere else. Elsewhere, she gives. She doesn't "know" what she's giving, she doesn't measure it; she gives, though, neither a counterfeit impression nor something she hasn't got. She gives more, with no assurance that she'll get back even some unexpected profit from what she puts out. She gives that there may be life, thought, transformation. This is an "economy" that can no longer be put in economic terms. Wherever she loves, all the old concepts of management are left behind. At the end of a more or less conscious computation, she finds not her sum but her differences. I am for you what you want me to be at the moment you look at me in a way you've never seen me before: at every instant. When I write, it's everything that we don't know we can be that is written out of me, without exclusions, without stipulation, and everything we will be calls us to the unflagging, intoxicating, unappeasable search for love. In one another we will never be lacking.

NOTES

1. Men still have everything to say about their sexuality, and everything to write. For what they have said so far, for the most part, stems from the opposition activity/passivity, from the power relation between a fantasized obligatory virility meant to invade, to colonize, and the consequential phantasm of woman as a "dark continent" to penetrate and to "pacify." (We know what "pacify" means in terms of scotomizing the other and misrecognizing the self.) Conquering her, they've made haste to depart from her borders, to get out of sight, out of body. The way man has of getting out of himself and into her whom he takes not for the other but for his own, deprives him, he knows, of his own bodily territory. One can understand how man, confusing himself with his penis and rushing in for the attack, might feel resentment and fear of being "taken" by the woman, of being lost in her, absorbed, or alone.
2. I am speaking here only of the place "reserved" for women by the Western world.

3. Which works, then, might be called feminine? I'll just point out some examples: one would have to give them full readings to bring out what is pervasively feminine in their significance. Which I shall do elsewhere. In France (have you noted our infinite poverty in this field?—the Anglo-Saxon countries have shown resources of distinctly greater consequence), leafing through what's come out of the twentieth century—and it's not much—the only inscriptions of femininity that I have seen were by Colette, Marguerite Duras, ... and Jean Genét.

4. *"Dé-pense,"* a neologism formed on the verb *penser,* hence "unthinks," but also "spends" (from *dépenser*) (translator's note).

5. Standard English term for the Hegelian *Aufhebung,* the French *la relève.*

6. Jean Genêt, *Pompes funèbres* (Paris, 1948), p. 185.

7. Also, "to steal." Both meanings of the verb *voler* are played on, as the text itself explains the following paragraph (translator's note).

8. *Illes* is a fusion of the masculine pronoun *ils,* which refers back to birds and robbers, with the feminine pronoun *elles,* which refers to women (translator's note).

9. Reread Derrida's text, "Le Style de la femme," in *Nietzsche aujourd'hui* (Paris: Union Générale d'Editions, Coll. 10/18), where the philosopher can be seen operating an *Aufhebung* of all philosophy in its systematic reducing of woman to the place of seduction: she appears as the one who is taken for; the bait in person, all veils unfurled, the one who doesn't give but who gives only in order to (take).

THIS SEX WHICH IS NOT ONE (1977)

LUCE IRIGARAY

Translated from the French by Catherine Porter

Irigaray begins by rejecting the Freudian model of female sexuality, which sees women as failed men who "lack" a penis. She then proposes an alternative model of female sexuality that opposes what she sees as the singularity of male sexuality with what she sees as the doubleness or multiplicity of female sexuality. She sees male singularity and female doubleness or multiplicity as based in the anatomy of women's and men's sexual organs. Not all readers have agreed with her interpretations of women's or men's anatomy or with her reading of bodily forms as shaping sexual identities and even, in some of her other works, shaping the style of women's writing. While some feminists have celebrated the connection that Irigaray sees between women's bodies and minds, some have seen the connection as a needless restraint on women's minds. For a similar approach and a similar response, see the essay by Hélène Cixous in this volume. In proposing a "female imaginary," Irigaray draws on Jacques Lacan's idea of the imaginary (see the headnote to Lacan). She also draws on Marx's notions of use-value, exchange-value, and commodities to see women as often reduced to commodities exchanged between men. On the exchange of women between men, see also the selection in this volume by Eve Kosofsky Sedgwick.

Female sexuality has always been conceptualized on the basis of masculine parameters. Thus the opposition between "masculine" clitoral activity and "feminine" vaginal passivity, an opposition which Freud—and many others—saw as stages, or alternatives, in the development of a sexually "normal" woman, seems rather too clearly required by the practice of male sexuality. For the clitoris is conceived as a little penis pleasant to masturbate so long as castration anxiety does not exist (for the boy child), and the vagina is valued for the "lodging" it offers the male organ when the forbidden hand has to find a replacement for pleasure-giving.

In these terms, woman's erogenous zones never amount to anything but a clitoris-sex that is not comparable to the noble phallic organ, or a hole-envelope that serves to sheathe and massage the penis in intercourse: a non-sex, or a masculine organ turned back upon itself, self-embracing.

About woman and her pleasure, this view of the sexual relation has nothing to say. Her lot is that of "lack," "atrophy" (of the sexual organ), and "penis envy," the penis being the only sexual organ of recognized value. Thus she attempts by every means available to appropriate that organ for herself: through her somewhat servile love of the father-husband capable of giving her one, through her desire for a child-penis, preferably a boy, through access to the cultural values still reserved by right to males alone and therefore always masculine, and so on. Woman lives her own desire only as the expectation that she may at last come to possess an equivalent of the male organ.

Yet all this appears quite foreign to her own pleasure, unless it remains within the dominant phallic economy. Thus, for example, woman's autoeroticism is very different from man's. In order to touch himself, man needs an instrument: his hand, a woman's body, language... And this self-caressing requires at least a minimum of activity. As for woman, she touches herself in and of herself without any need for mediation, and before there is any way to distinguish activity from passivity. Woman "touches herself" all the time, and moreover no one can forbid her to do so, for her genitals are formed of two lips in continuous contact. Thus, within herself, she is already two— but not divisible into one(s)—that caress each other.

This autoeroticism is disrupted by a violent break-in: the brutal separation of the two lips by a violating penis, an intrusion that distracts and deflects the woman from this "self-caressing" she needs if she is not to incur the disappearance of her own pleasure in sexual relations. If the vagina is to serve *also,* but *not only,* to take over for the little boy's hand in order to assure an articulation between autoeroticism and heteroeroticism in intercourse (the encounter with the totally other always signifying death), how, in the classic representation of sexuality, can the perpetuation of autoeroticism for woman be managed? Will woman not be left with the impossible alternative between a defensive virginity, fiercely turned in upon itself, and a body open to penetration that no longer knows, in this "hole" that constitutes its sex, the pleasure of its own touch? The more or less exclusive—and highly anxious—attention paid to erection in Western sexuality proves to what extent the imaginary that governs it is foreign to the feminine. For the most part, this sexuality offers nothing but imperatives dictated by male rivalry: the "strongest" being the one who has the best "hard-on," the longest, the biggest, the stiffest penis, or even the one who "pees the farthest" (as in little boys' contests). Or else one finds imperatives dictated by the enactment of sadomasochistic fantasies, these in turn governed by man's relation to his mother: the desire to force entry, to penetrate, to appropriate for himself the mystery of this womb where he has been conceived, the secret of his begetting, of his "origin." Desire/need, also to make blood flow again in order to revive a very old relationship—intrauterine, to be sure, but also prehistoric—to the maternal.

Woman, in this sexual imaginary, is only a more or less obliging prop for the enactment of man's fantasies. That she may find pleasure there in that role, by proxy, is possible, even certain. But such pleasure is above all a masochistic prostitution of her body to a desire that is not her own, and it leaves her in a familiar state of dependency upon man. Not knowing what she wants, ready for anything, even asking for more, so long as he will "take" her as his "object" when he seeks his own pleasure. Thus she will not say what she herself wants; moreover, she does not know, or no longer knows, what she wants. As Freud admits, the beginnings of the sexual life of a girl child are so "obscure," so "faded with time," that one would have to dig down very deep indeed to discover beneath the traces of this civilization, of this history, the vestiges of a more archaic civilization that might give some clue to woman's sexuality. That extremely ancient civilization would undoubtedly have a different alphabet, a different language … Woman's desire would not be expected to speak the same language as man's; woman's desire has doubtless been submerged by the logic that has dominated the West since the time of the Greeks.

Within this logic, the predominance of the visual, and of the discrimination and individualization of form, is particularly foreign to female eroticism. Woman takes pleasure more from touching than from looking, and her entry into a dominant scopic economy signifies, again, her consignment to passivity: she is to be the beautiful object of contemplation. While her body finds itself thus eroticized, and called to a double movement of exhibition and of chaste retreat in order to stimulate the drives of the "subject," her sexual organ represents *the horror of nothing to see*. A defect in this systematics of representation and desire. A "hole" in its scoptophilic lens. It is already evident in Greek statuary that this nothing-to-see has to be excluded, rejected, from such a scene of representation. Woman's genitals are simply absent, masked, sewn back up inside their "crack."

This organ which has nothing to show for itself also lacks a form of its own. And if woman takes pleasure precisely from this incompleteness of form which allows her organ to touch itself over and over again, indefinitely, by itself, that pleasure is denied by a civilization that privileges phallomorphism. The value granted to the only definable form excludes the one that is in play in female autoeroticism. The *one* of form, of the individual, of the (male) sexual organ, of the proper name, of the proper meaning … supplants, while separating and dividing, that contact of *at least two* (lips) which keeps woman in touch with herself, but without any possibility of distinguishing what is touching from what is touched.

Whence the mystery that woman represents in a culture claiming to count everything, to number everything by units, to inventory everything as individualities. *She is neither one nor two*. Rigorously speaking, she cannot be identified either as one person, or as two. She resists all adequate definition. Further, she has no "proper" name. And her sexual organ, which is not *one* organ, is counted as *none*. The negative, the underside, the reverse of the only visible and morphologically designatable organ (even if the passage from erection to detumescence does pose some problems): the penis.

But the "thickness" of that "form," the layering of its volume, its expansions and contractions and even the spacing of the moments in which it produces itself as form—all this the feminine keeps secret. Without knowing it. And if woman is asked to sustain, to revive, man's desire, the request neglects to spell out what it implies as to the value of her own desire. A desire of which she is not aware, moreover, at least not explicitly. But one whose force and continuity are capable of nurturing repeatedly and at length all the masquerades of "femininity" that are expected of her.

It is true that she still has the child, in relation to whom her appetite for touch, for contact, has free rein, unless it is already lost, alienated by the taboo against touching of a highly obsessive civilization. Otherwise her pleasure will find, in the child, compensations for and diversions from the frustrations that she too often encounters in sexual relations per se. Thus maternity fills the gaps in a repressed female sexuality. Perhaps man and woman no longer caress each other except through that mediation between them that the child—preferably a boy—represents? Man, identified with his son, rediscovers the pleasure of maternal fondling; woman touches herself again by caressing that part of her body: her baby-penis-clitoris.

What this entails for the amorous trio is well known. But the Oedipal interdiction seems to be a somewhat categorical and factitious law—although it does provide the means for perpetuating the authoritarian discourse of fathers—when it is promulgated in a culture in which sexual relations are impracticable because man's desire and woman's are strangers to each other. And in which the two desires have to try to meet through indirect means, whether the archaic one of a sense-relation to the mother's body, or the present one of active or passive extension of the law of the father. These are regressive emotional behaviors, exchanges of words too detached from the sexual arena not to constitute an exile with respect to it: "mother" and "father" dominate the interactions of the couple, but as social roles. The division of labor prevents them from making love. They produce or reproduce. Without quite knowing how to use their leisure. Such little as they have, such little indeed as they wish to have. For what are they to do with leisure? What substitute for amorous resource are they to invent? Still…

Perhaps it is time to return to that repressed entity, the female imaginary. So woman does not have a sex organ? She has at least two of them, but they are not identifiable as ones. Indeed, she has many more. Her sexuality, always at least double, goes even further: it is *plural*. Is this the way culture is seeking to characterize itself now? Is this the way texts write themselves/are written now? Without quite knowing what censorship they are evading? Indeed, woman's pleasure does not have to choose between clitoral activity and vaginal passivity, for example. The pleasure of the vaginal caress does not have to be substituted for that of the clitoral caress. They each contribute, irreplaceably, to woman's pleasure. Among other caresses … Fondling the breasts, touching the vulva, spreading the lips, stroking the posterior wall of the vagina, brushing against the mouth of the uterus, and so on. To evoke only a few of the most specifically female pleasures. Pleasures which are somewhat misunderstood in sexual difference as it is imagined—or not imagined, the other sex being only the indispensable complement to the only sex.

But *woman has sex organs more or less everywhere*. She finds pleasure almost anywhere. Even if we refrain from invoking the hystericization of her entire body, the geography of her pleasure is far more diversified, more multiple in its differences, more complex, more subtle, than is commonly imagined—in an imaginary rather too narrowly focused on sameness.

"She" is indefinitely other in herself. This is doubtless why she is said to be whimsical, incomprehensible, agitated, capricious ... not to mention her language, in which "she" sets off in all directions leaving "him" unable to discern the coherence of any meaning. Hers are contradictory words, somewhat mad from the standpoint of reason, inaudible for whoever listens to them with ready-made grids, with a fully elaborated code in hand. For in what she says, too, at least when she dares, woman is constantly touching herself. She steps ever so slightly aside from herself with a murmur, an exclamation, a whisper, a sentence left unfinished ... When she returns, it is to set off again from elsewhere. From another point of pleasure, or of pain. One would have to listen with another ear, as if hearing an *"other meaning" always in the process of weaving itself, of embracing itself with words, but also of getting rid of words in order not to become fixed, congealed in them.* For if "she" says something, it is not, it is already no longer, identical with what she means. What she says is never identical with anything, moreover; rather, it is contiguous. *It touches* (*upon*). And when it strays too far from that proximity, she breaks off and starts over at "zero": her body-sex.

It is useless, then, to trap women in the exact definition of what they mean, to make them repeat (themselves) so that it will be clear; they are already elsewhere in that discursive machinery where you expected to surprise them. They have returned within themselves. Which must not be understood in the same way as within yourself. They do not have the interiority that you have, the one you perhaps suppose they have. Within themselves means *within the intimacy of that silent, multiple, diffuse touch.* And if you ask them insistently what they are thinking about, they can only reply: Nothing. Everything.

Thus what they desire is precisely nothing, and at the same time everything. Always something more and something else besides that *one*—sexual organ, for example—that you give them, attribute to them. Their desire is often interpreted, and feared, as a sort of insatiable hunger, a voracity that will swallow you whole. Whereas it really involves a different economy more than anything else, one that upsets the linearity of a project, undermines the goal-object of a desire, diffuses the polarization toward a single pleasure, disconcerts fidelity to a single discourse ...

Must this multiplicity of female desire and female language be understood as shards, scattered remnants of a violated sexuality? A sexuality denied? The question has no simple answer. The rejection, the exclusion of a female imaginary certainly puts woman in the position of experiencing herself only fragmentarily, in the little-structured margins of a dominant ideology, as waste, or excess, what is left of a mirror invested by the (masculine) "subject" to reflect himself, to copy himself. Moreover, the role of "femininity" is prescribed by this masculine specula(riza)tion and corresponds scarcely at all to woman's desire, which may be recovered only in secret, in hiding, with anxiety and guilt.

But if the female imaginary were to deploy itself, if it could bring itself into play otherwise than as scraps, uncollected debris, would it represent itself, even so, in the form of *one* universe? Would it even be volume instead of surface? No. Not unless it were understood, yet again, as a privileging of the maternal over the feminine. Of a phallic maternal, at that. Closed in upon the jealous possession of its valued product. Rivaling man in his esteem for productive excess. In such a race for power, woman loses the uniqueness of her pleasure. By closing herself off as volume, she renounces the pleasure that she gets from the *nonsuture of her lips:* she is undoubtedly a mother, but a virgin mother; the role was assigned to her by mythologies long ago. Granting her a certain social power to the extent that she is reduced, with her own complicity, to sexual impotence.

(Re-)discovering herself, for a woman, thus could only signify the possibility of sacrificing no one of her pleasures to another, of identifying herself with none of them in particular, *of never being simply one.* A sort of expanding universe to which no limits could be fixed and which would not be incoherence nonetheless—nor that polymorphous perversion of the child in which the erogenous zones would lie waiting to be regrouped under the primacy of the phallus.

Woman always remains several, but she is kept from dispersion because the other is already within her and is autoerotically familiar to her. Which is not to say that she appropriates the other for herself, that she reduces it to her own property. Ownership and property are doubtless quite foreign to the feminine. At least sexually. But not *nearness.* Nearness so pronounced that it makes all discrimination of identity, and thus all forms of property, impossible. Woman derives pleasure from what is *so near that she cannot have it, nor have herself.* She herself enters into a ceaseless exchange of herself with the other without any possibility of identifying either. This puts into question all prevailing economies: their calculations are irremediably stymied by woman's pleasure, as it increases indefinitely from its passage in and through the other.

However, in order for woman to reach the place where she takes pleasure as woman, a long detour by way of the analysis of the various systems of oppression brought to bear upon her is assuredly necessary. And claiming to fall back on the single solution of pleasure risks making her miss the process of going back through a social practice that *her* enjoyment requires.

For woman is traditionally a use-value for man, an exchange value among men; in other words, a commodity. As such, she remains the guardian of material substance, whose price will be established, in terms of the standard of their work and of their need/desire, by "subjects": workers, merchants, consumers. Women are marked phallicly by their fathers, husbands, procurers. And this branding determines their value in sexual commerce. Woman is never anything but the locus of a more or less competitive exchange between two men, including the competition for the possession of mother earth.

How can this object of transaction claim a right to pleasure without removing her/itself from established commerce? With respect to other merchandise in the marketplace, how could this commodity maintain a relationship other than one of aggressive jealousy? How could material substance enjoy her/itself without provoking the consumer's anxiety over the disappearance of his nurturing ground? How could that exchange—which can in no way be defined in terms "proper" to woman's desire—appear as anything but a pure mirage, mere foolishness, all too readily obscured by a more sensible discourse and by a system of apparently more tangible values?

A woman's development, however radical it may seek to be, would thus not suffice to liberate woman's desire. And to date no political theory or political practice has resolved, or sufficiently taken into consideration, this historical problem, even though Marxism has proclaimed its importance. But women do not constitute, strictly speaking, a class, and their dispersion among several classes makes their political struggle complex, their demands sometimes contradictory.

There remains, however, the condition of underdevelopment arising from women's submission by and to a culture that oppresses them, uses them, makes of them a medium of exchange, with very little profit to them. Except in the quasi monopolies of masochistic pleasure, the domestic labor force, and reproduction. The powers of slaves? Which are not negligible powers, moreover. For where pleasure is concerned, the master is not necessarily well served. Thus to reverse the relation, especially in the economy of sexuality, does not seem a desirable objective.

But if women are to preserve and expand their autoeroticism, their homo-sexuality, might not the renunciation of heterosexual pleasure correspond once again to that disconnection from power that is traditionally theirs? Would it not involve a new prison, a new cloister, built of their own accord? For women to undertake tactical strikes, to keep themselves apart from men long enough to learn to defend their desire, especially through speech, to discover the love of other women while sheltered from men's imperious choices that put them in the position of rival commodities, to forge for themselves a social status that compels recognition, to earn their living in order to escape from the condition of prostitute … these are certainly indispensable stages in the escape from their proletarization on the exchange market. But if their aim were simply to reverse the order of things, even supposing this to be possible, history would repeat itself in the long run, would revert to sameness: to phallocratism. It would leave room neither for women's sexuality, nor for women's imaginary, nor for women's language to take (their) place.

"IMAGES OF WOMEN" CRITICISM (1985)

TORIL MOI

In this chapter from her Sexual/Textual Politics: Feminist Literary Theory, *Moi picks out a dominant trend in early feminist literary criticism, a trend that continues today in the expectations that the general public brings to feminist criticism and in many classroom discussions. Images of women criticism tends to judge literary works by whether they represent female characters the way that critics would like to see actual women outside literature. Images criticism objects to writing that offers a derogatory view of women or does not provide "strong female characters" who can act as realistic and "positive role models." Such approaches risk assuming that the critic's own sense of the real matches the real of other readers. They also risk sliding into "prescriptive criticism," criticism that focuses too much on telling writers how to write as opposed to interpreting what they do write. Few critics would want to give up prescriptive criticism entirely, since most critics want to express preferences for some literature over other literature. But Moi calls our attention to the problem in dwelling too much on prescribing how writers should write. Images of women criticism risks overlooking the many things we look to literature for besides role models, such as literary language and form, humor, and irony. Given the long history of derogatory writing about women and of patriarchal interpretations of literature that early feminist critics set out to undermine, Moi looks with sympathy on images of women criticism, even as she sets out to encourage later feminists to move beyond it.*

Just as early feminist literary criticism focused on opposing derogatory images and role models and tended to give less attention to literary form, and just as that pattern continues today in the literary interpretation we often see in popular culture and in many classrooms, so the same can be said for the early and sometimes continuing criticism of literature that represents less powerful racial, ethnic, and sexual groups and colonized or formerly colonized peoples across the world. Critics interested in the representation of such groups often began by opposing derogatory images and calling for more affirming images, and then later critics, while not rejecting such approaches, sometimes saw the focus on images as too limiting. They sometimes began to give more attention to literary form. Now many approaches flourish, sometimes as allies and sometimes in opposition to each other. Moi's review of images of women criticism thus helps pose questions that continue to resonate both in and beyond feminist criticism.

For a related critique of liberal Western feminism, see the essay by Gayatri C. Spivak in this volume.

The "Images of Women" approach to literature has proved to be an extremely fertile branch of feminist criticism, at least in terms of the actual number of works it has generated: specialist bibliographies list hundreds if not thousands of items under this heading. In order to limit the amount of bibliographical references in the following account of its aims and methods, I will refer mainly to the articles printed in one central collection of essays, suitably enough entitled *Images of Women in Fiction: Feminist Perspectives*. In American colleges in the early 1970s, the great majority of courses on women in literature centered on the study of female stereotypes in male writing (Register, 28). *Images of Women in Fiction* was published in 1972 as the first hardback textbook aimed at this rapidly expanding academic market. The book obviously corresponded to a deeply felt need among teachers and students, since it was reprinted several times in rapid succession.[1] What kind of perspectives, then, does this book present as "feminist"? In her preface, the editor, Susan Koppelman Cornillon, states that the idea for the book came from her own experience in teaching women's studies:

> In all courses I felt the desperate need for books that would study literature as being writings about *people*. This volume is an effort to supply that need ... These essays lead us into fiction

and then back out again into reality, into ourselves and our own lives … This book will be a useful tool for raising consciousness not only in classrooms, but for those not involved in the academic world who are committed to personal growth.

The new field of feminist literary studies is here presented as one essentially concerned with nurturing personal growth and raising the individual consciousness by linking literature to life, particularly to the lived experience of the reader. This fundamental outlook is reflected in the essays of all the 21 contributors (19 women, 2 men). Both male and female authors, mostly from the nineteenth and twentieth centuries, are studied in these essays, and both sexes come in for harsh criticism for their creation of "unreal" female characters. Indeed, the editor, in her essay "The fiction of fiction," accuses women writers of being *worse* than male writers in this respect, since they, unlike the men, are betraying their own sex.

In "Images of Women" criticism the act of reading is seen as a communication between the life ("experience") of the author and the life of the reader. When the reader becomes a critic, her duty is to present an account of her own life that will enable *her* readers to become aware of the position from which she speaks. In one of the essays in *Images of Women in Fiction*, Florence Howe succinctly presents this demand for autobiography in criticism:

> I begin with autobiography because it is there, in our consciousness about our own lives, that the connection between feminism and literature begins. That we learn from lives is, of course, a fundamental assumption of literature and of its teacher-critics.

Such an emphasis upon the reader's right to learn about the writer's experience strongly supports the basic feminist contention that no criticism is "value-free," that we all speak from a specific position shaped by cultural, social, political and personal factors. It is authoritarian and manipulative to present this limited perspective as "universal," feminists claim, and the only democratic procedure is to supply the reader with all necessary information about the limitations of one's own perspective at the outset. The importance of this principle cannot be overestimated: it remains one of the fundamental assumptions of any feminist critic to date.

Problems do however arise if we are too sanguine about the actual possibility of making one's own position clear. Hermeneutical theory, for instance, has pointed out that we cannot fully grasp our own "horizon of understanding": there will always be unstated blindspots, fundamental presuppositions and "pre-understandings" of which we are unaware. Psychoanalysis furthermore informs us that the most powerful motivations of our psyche often turn out to be those we have most deeply repressed. It is therefore difficult to believe that we can ever fully be aware of our own perspective. The prejudices one is *able* to formulate consciously are precisely for that reason likely to be the least important ones. These theoretical difficulties are not just abstract problems for the philosophers among us: they return to manifest themselves quite evidently in the texts of the feminist critic who tries to practise the autobiographical ideal in her work. In trying to state her own personal experience as a necessary background for the understanding of her research interests, she may for instance discover, to her cost, that there is no obvious end to the amount of "relevant" detail that might be taken into account in such a context. She then runs the risk of reading like a more or less unwilling exhibitionist rather than a partisan of egalitarian criticism. One such extreme case can be found in a feminist study of Simone de Beauvoir, where, in the middle of the book, the critic suddenly decides to spend sixteen pages on an autobiographical account of her own life and her feelings about Beauvoir.[2] This kind of narcissistic delving into one's own self can only caricature the valuable point of principle made by feminist critics: that no criticism is neutral, and that we therefore have a responsibility to make our position reasonably apparent to our readers. Whether this is necessarily always best done through autobiographical statements about the critic's emotional and personal life is a more debatable point.

As one reads on in *Images of Women in Fiction*, one quickly becomes aware of the fact that to study "images of women" in fiction is equivalent to studying *false* images of women in fiction written by both sexes. The "image" of women in literature is invariably defined in opposition to the "real person" whom literature somehow never quite manages to convey to the reader. In Cornillon's volume, "reality" and "experience" are presented as the highest goals of literature, the essential truths that must be rendered by all forms of fiction. This viewpoint occasionally leads to an almost absurd "ultra-realist" position, as when, for instance, Cornillon points out that a significant part of the modern American woman's life is spent shaving her legs and removing hairs from various other parts of her body. She rightly emphasizes the degrading and oppressive nature of the male demand for well-shaved women, but then goes on to make her main literary point: "And yet, with all that attaches itself to female leg-shaving slavery, I have never seen any fictional character either shave or pluck a hair" (117).

I would not be surprised if Cornillon turned out to be right—toe-nail clipping and the disposal of sanitary towels also seem neglected as fictional themes—but her complaint rests on the highly questionable notion that art can and should reflect life accurately and inclusively in every detail. The extreme reflectionism (or "naturalism" in Lukács's sense of the word) advocated in *Images of Women in Fiction* has the advantage of emphasizing the way in which writers constantly *select* the elements they wish to use in their texts; but instead of acknowledging this as one of the basic facts of textual creativity, reflectionism posits that the artist's selective creation should be measured against "real life," thus assuming that the only constraint on the artist's work is his or her perception of the "real world." Such a view resolutely refuses to consider textual production as a highly complex, "over-determined" process with many different and conflicting literary and non-literary determinants (historical, political, social, ideological, institutional, generic, psychological and so on). Instead, writing is seen as a more or less faithful *reproduction* of an external reality to which we all have equal and unbiased access, and which therefore enables us to criticize the author on the grounds that he or she has created an *incorrect* model of the reality we somehow all know. Resolutely empiricist in its approach, this view fails to consider the proposition that the real is not only something we construct, but a controversial construct at that.

Literary works can and should of course be criticized for having selected and shaped their fictional universe according to oppressive and objectionable ideological assumptions, but that should not be confused with failing to be "true to life" or with not presenting "an authentic expression of real experience." Such an insistent demand for authenticity not only reduces all literature to rather simplistic forms of autobiography, it also finds itself ruling the greater part of world literature out of bounds. What these critics fail to perceive is the fact that though Shakespeare probably never in his life found himself mad and naked on a heath, *King Lear* nevertheless reads "authentically" enough for most people. It is significant that all the contributors to Cornillon's volume (with the notable exception of Josephine Donovan) adhere to a rather simple form of content analysis when confronted with the literary text. Extreme reflectionism simply cannot accommodate notions of formal and generic constraints on textual production, since to acknowledge such constraints is equivalent to accepting the inherent impossibility of ever achieving a total reproduction of reality in fiction.

The wider question at issue here is clearly the problem of realism as opposed to modernism. Predictably enough, several essays in the volume lash out against modernism, and its somewhat vaguely termed "formalist" fellow-traveller. The modernist is accused of neglecting the "exclusions based on class, race and sex" in order to "take refuge in his formalist concerns, secure in his conviction that other matters are irrelevant" (286). But this is not all:

> Modernism, by contrast, seeks to intensify isolation. It forces the work of art, the artist, the critic, and the audience outside of history. Modernism denies us the possibility of understanding ourselves as *agents* in the material world, for all has been removed to an abstract world of ideas, where interactions can be minimized or emptied of meaning and real consequences. Less than ever are we able to interpret the world—much less change it. (300–1)[3]

In another essay, feminist criticism is succinctly defined as "a materialist approach to literature which attempts to do away with the formalist illusion that literature is somehow divorced from reality" (326).[4] The "formalist" critics referred to in this passage seem to be identifiable as the American New Critics, concerned as they were with with the formal aspects of the literary work at the expense of historical and sociological factors. At this point, however, it is worth noting that though American feminist critics from Kate Millett onwards have consistently argued against the New Critics's ahistoricism, this has not prevented them from uncritically adopting the *aesthetic* ideals of the very same New Critics.

In *Images of Women in Fiction*, the double rejection of "modernist" literature and "formalist" criticism highlights the deep realist bias of Anglo-American feminist criticism. An insistence on authenticity and truthful reproduction of the "real world" as the highest literary values inevitably makes the feminist critic hostile to non-realist forms of writing. There is nevertheless no automatic connection between demands for a full reproduction of the totality of the real and what is known as a "realist" fiction. At least two famous literary attempts at capturing reality in its totality, *Tristram Shandy* and *Ulysses*, end up by mischievously transgressing traditional realism in the most radical fashion precisely *because of* their doomed attempt to be all-inclusive. And some feminist critics have for instance objected to Joyce's portrayal of Molly Bloom's chamberpot and menstrual cycle (there is no reference to leg-shaving) on the grounds that, in spite of their undeniable realism, these factors contribute precisely to presenting her as a biologically determined, earthbound creature that no woman reader can really *admire*.

In this case the demand for realism clashes with another demand: that for the representation of female role-models in literature. The feminist reader of this period not only wants to see her own experiences mirrored in fiction, but strives to identify with strong, impressive female characters. Cheri Register, in an essay published in 1975, succinctly sums up this demand: "A literary work should provide *role-models,* instill a positive sense of feminine identity by portraying women who are self-actualizing, whose identities are not dependent on men" (20).[5] This might however clash with the demand for authenticity (quite a few women are "authentically" weak and unimpressive); on this point Register is unambiguous: "It is important to note here that although female readers need literary models to emulate, characters should not be idealized beyond plausibility. The demand for authenticity supercedes all other requirement"(21).

Register's choice of words here ("should," "demand," "requirements") reflects the strong normative (or prescriptive, as she prefers to call it) aspect of much of this early feminist criticism. The "Images of Women" critics downgrade literature they find lacking in "authenticity" and "real experience" according to their own standards of what counts as "real." In case of doubt about the degree of authenticity in a work, Register recommends several tests: "One obvious check the reader might make on authenticity would be to compare the character's life with the author's" (12), she suggests. One may also use sociological data in order to check up on the social aspects of the author's work, though inner emotions must be subjected to a different form of control:

> While it is useful to compile statistical data on a collection of works from a limited time period to see how accurately they mirror female employment, educational attainment, marital status, birthrate, and the like, it is impossible to measure the authenticity of a single female protagonist's inner turmoil. The final test must be the subjective response of the female reader, who is herself familiar with "female reality." Does she recognize aspects of her own experience? (13)

Though Register hastens to warn us against too simplistic conclusions, since "female reality is not monolithic, but has many nuances and variations" (13) such a governess mentality (the "Big-Sister-is-watching-you" syndrome) must be considered one of the perhaps inevitable excesses of a new and rapidly expanding branch of research. In the 1970s, this approach led to a great number of published and unpublished papers dealing with literature from a kind of inverted sociological perspective: fiction was read in order to compare the empirical sociological facts in the literary work (as for instance the number of women working outside the home or doing the dishes) to the corresponding empirical data in the "real" world during the author's lifetime.

It is easy today to be reproving of this kind of criticism: to take it to task for not recognizing the "literariness" of literature, for tending towards a dangerous anti-intellectualism, for being excessively naive about the relationship between literature and reality and between author and text, and for being unduly censorious of the works of women writers who often wrote under ideological conditions that made it impossible for them to fulfil the demands of the feminist critics of early 1970s. Though it is impossible not to deplore the wholesale lack of theoretical (or even literary) awareness of these early feminist critics, their enthusiasm and commitment to the feminist cause are exemplary. For a generation educated within the ahistorical, aestheticizing discourse of New Criticism, the feminists' insistence on the *political* nature of any critical discourse, and their will to take historical and sociological factors into account must have seemed both fresh and exciting; to a large extent those are precisely the qualities present-day feminist critics still strive to preserve.

NOTES

1. I was unable to consult the 1972 original edition. My comments are therefore based on the 1973 reprint.
2. See Ascher, 107–22.
3. Robinson and Vogel's contribution.
4. Katz-Stoker's essay.
5. Register is here quoting Martin.

REFERENCES

Ascher, Carol. (1981) *Simone de Beauvoir: A Life of Freedom.* Brighton: Harvester.

Cornillon, Susan Koppelman (ed). (1972) *Images of Women in Fiction: Feminist Perspectives.* Bowling Green, Ohio: Bowling Green University Popular Press.

Donovan, Josephine. (1972) "Feminist style criticism," in Cornillon, Susan Koppelman (ed.), *Images of Women in Fiction: Feminist Perspectives.* Bowling Green University Popular Press, 341–54.

Millett, Kate. (1969) *Sexual Politics.* London: Virago, 1977.

Register, Cheri. (1975) "American feminist literary criticism: a bibliographical imroduction" in Donovan, Josephine (ed.), *Feminist Literary Criticism. Explorations in Theory.* Lexington: The University Press of Kentucky, 1–28.

Robinson, Lillian S., and Vogel, Lise. (1972) "Modernism and history," in Cornillon, Susan Koppelman (ed.), *Images of Women in Fiction: Feminist Perspectives.* Bowling Green, Ohio: Bowling Green University Popular Press, 278–307.

THE OPPOSITIONAL GAZE: BLACK FEMALE SPECTATORS (1992)

BELL HOOKS

Responding to Laura Mulvey's "Visual Pleasure and Narrative Cinema" (included in this volume), hooks rejects what she sees as Mulvey's sense that spectators all respond to film in the same way and all respond passively. Mulvey supposes that spectators typically accept, rather than criticize the cultural assumptions and patterns of looking in the films they watch. For hooks, by contrast, spectators vary according to their cultural position. Thus she proposes a culturally specific model of black spectators, especially black women spectators.

She also believes that spectators have often already reached the position of critical, nonpassive looking that Mulvey calls for but sees as the exception. The racially generic but implicitly white spectators that Mulvey describes get swept up in the ideological assumptions of the film. The black spectators that hooks describes sometimes get swept up in a similar way, as in the example from Toni Morrison's The Bluest Eye *or in hooks's remark that "many black women" are too "profoundly colonized, shaped by dominant ways of knowing," to respond critically. But often the spectators that hooks describes have more agency than Mulvey anticipates. They can laugh at a film and criticize it while it plays. Compared to the spectators that Mulvey describes, the spectators in hooks's essay take an oppositional, critical perspective.*

When thinking about black female spectators, I remember being punished as a child for staring, for those hard intense direct looks children would give grown-ups, looks that were seen as confrontational, as gestures of resistance, challenges to authority. The "gaze" has always been political in my life. Imagine the terror felt by the child who has come to understand through repeated punishments that one's gaze can be dangerous. The child who has learned so well to look the other way when necessary. Yet, when punished, the child is told by parents, "Look at me when I talk to you." Only, the child is afraid to look. Afraid to look, but fascinated by the gaze. There is power in looking.

Amazed the first time I read in history classes that white slave-owners (men, women, and children) punished enslaved black people for looking, I wondered how this traumatic relationship to the gaze had informed black parenting and black spectatorship. The politics of slavery, of racialized power relations, were such that the slaves were denied their right to gaze. Connecting this strategy of domination to that used by grown folks in southern black rural communities where I grew up, I was pained to think that there was no absolute difference between whites who had oppressed black people and ourselves. Years later, reading Michel Foucault, I thought again about these connections, about the ways power as domination reproduces itself in different locations employing similar apparatuses, strategies, and mechanisms of control. Since I knew as a child that the dominating power adults exercised over me and over my gaze was never so absolute that I did not dare to look, to sneak a peep, to stare dangerously, I knew that the slaves had looked. That all attempts to repress our/black peoples' right to gaze had produced in us an overwhelming longing to look, a rebellious desire, an oppositional gaze. By courageously looking, we defiantly declared: "Not only will I stare. I want my look to change reality." Even in the worst circumstances of domination, the ability to manipulate one's gaze in the face of structures of domination that would contain it, opens up the possibility of agency. In much of his work, Michel Foucault insists on describing domination in terms of "relations of power" as part of an effort to challenge the assumption that "power is a system of domination which controls everything and which leaves no room for freedom." Emphatically stating that in all relations of power "there is necessarily the possibility of resistance," he invites the critical thinker to search those margins, gaps, and locations on and through the body where agency can be found.

Stuart Hall calls for recognition of our agency as black spectators in his essay "Cultural Identity and Cinematic Representation." Speaking against the construction of white representations of blackness as totalizing, Hall says of white presence: "The error is not to conceptualize this 'presence' in terms of power, but to locate that power as wholly external to us as extrinsic force, whose influence can be thrown off like the serpent sheds its skin." What Frantz Fanon reminds us, in *Black Skin, White Masks*, is how power is inside as well as outside:

> ...the movements, the attitudes, the glances of the Other fixed me there, in the sense in which a chemical solution is fixed by a dye. I was indignant; I demanded an explanation. Nothing happened. I burst apart. Now the fragments have been put together again by another self. This "look," from—so to speak—the place of the Other, fixes us, not only in its violence, hostility and aggression, but in the ambivalence of its desire.

Spaces of agency exist for black people, wherein we can both interrogate the gaze of the Other but also look back, and at one another, naming what we see. The "gaze" has been and is a site of resistance for colonized black people globally. Subordinates in relations of power learn experientially that there is a critical gaze, one that "looks" to document, one that is oppositional. In resistance struggle, the power of the dominated to assert agency by claiming and cultivating "awareness" politicizes "looking" relations—one learns to look a certain way in order to resist.

When most black people in the United States first had the opportunity to look at film and television, they did so fully aware that mass media was a system of knowledge and power reproducing and maintaining white supremacy. To stare at the television, or mainstream movies, to engage its images, was to engage its negation of black representation. It was the oppositional black gaze that responded to these looking relations by developing independent black cinema. Black viewers of mainstream cinema and television could chart the progress of political movements for racial equality *via* the construction of images, and did so. Within my family's southern black working-class home, located in a racially segregated neighborhood, watching television was one way to develop critical spectatorship. Unless you went to work in the white world, across the tracks, you learned to look at white people by staring at them on the screen. Black looks, as they were constituted in the context of social movements for racial uplift, were interrogating gazes. We laughed at television shows like *Our Gang* and *Amos 'n' Andy*, at these white representations of blackness, but we also looked at them critically. Before racial integration, black viewers of movies and television experienced visual pleasure in a context where looking was also about contestation and confrontation.

Writing about black looking relations in "Black British Cinema: Spectatorship and Identity Formation in Territories," Manthia Diawara identifies the power of the spectator: "Every narration places the spectator in a position of agency; and race, class and sexual relations influence the way in which this subjecthood is filled by the spectator." Of particular concern for him are moments of "rupture" when the spectator resists "complete identification with the film's discourse." These ruptures define the relation between black spectators and dominant cinema prior to racial integration. Then, one's enjoyment of a film wherein representations of blackness were stereotypically degrading and dehumanizing co-existed with a critical practice that restored presence where it was negated. Critical discussion of the film while it was in progress or at its conclusion maintained the distance between spectator and the image. Black films were also subject to critical interrogation. Since they came into being in part as a response to the failure of white-dominated cinema to represent blackness in a manner that did not reinforce white supremacy, they too were critiqued to see if images were seen as complicit with dominant cinematic practices.

Critical, interrogating black looks were mainly concerned with issues of race and racism, the way racial domination of blacks by whites overdetermined representation. They were rarely concerned with gender. As spectators, black men could repudiate the reproduction of racism in cinema and television, the negation of black presence, even as they could feel as though they were rebelling against white supremacy by daring to look, by engaging phallocentric politics of spectatorship. Given the real life public circumstances wherein black men were murdered/lynched for looking at white womanhood, where the black male gaze was always subject to control and/or punishment by the powerful white Other, the private realm of television screens or dark theaters could unleash the repressed gaze. There they could "look" at white womanhood without a structure of domination overseeing the gaze, interpreting, and punishing. That white supremacist structure that had murdered Emmet Till after interpreting his look as violation, as "rape" of white womanhood, could not control black male responses to screen images. In their role as spectators, black men could enter an imaginative space of phallocentric power that mediated racial negation. This gendered relation to looking made the experience of the black male spectator radically different from that of the black female spectator. Major early black male independent filmmakers represented black women in their films as objects of male gaze. Whether looking through the camera or as spectators watching films, whether mainstream cinema or "race" movies such as those made by Oscar Micheaux, the black male gaze had a different scope from that of the black female.

Black women have written little about black female spectatorship, about our moviegoing practices. A growing body of film theory and criticism by black women has only begun to emerge. The prolonged silence of black women as spectators and critics was a response to absence, to cinematic negation. In "The Technology of Gender," Teresa de Lauretis, drawing on the work of Monique Wittig, calls attention to "the power of discourses to 'do violence' to people, a violence which is material and physical, although produced by abstract and scientific discourses as well as the discourses of the mass media." With the possible exception of early race movies, black female spectators have had to develop looking relations within a cinematic context that constructs our presence as absence, that denies the "body" of the black female so as to perpetuate white supremacy and with it a phallocentric spectatorship where the woman to be looked at and desired is "white." (Recent movies do not conform to this paradigm but I am turning to the past with the intent to chart the development of black female spectatorship.)

Talking with black women of all ages and classes, in different areas of the United States, about their filmic looking relations, I hear again and again ambivalent responses to cinema. Only a few of the black women I talked with remembered the pleasure of race movies, and even those who did, felt that pleasure interrupted and usurped by Hollywood. Most of the black women I talked with were adamant that they never went to movies expecting to see compelling representations of black femaleness. They were all acutely aware of cinematic racism—its violent erasure of black womanhood. In Anne Friedberg's essay "A Denial of Difference: Theories of Cinematic Identification" she stresses that "identification can only be made through recognition, and all recognition is itself an implicit confirmation of the ideology of the status quo." Even when representations of black women were present in film, our bodies and being were there to serve—to enhance and maintain white womanhood as object of the phallocentric gaze.

Commenting on Hollywood's characterization of black women in *Girls on Film*, Julie Burchill describes this absent presence:

> Black women have been mothers without children (Mammies—who can ever forget the sickening spectacle of Hattie MacDaniels waiting on the simpering Vivien Leigh hand and foot and enquiring like a ninny, "What's ma lamb gonna wear?")…Lena Horne, the first black performer signed to a long term contract with a major (MGM), looked gutless but was actually quite spirited. She seethed when Tallulah Bankhead complimented her on the paleness of her skin and the non-Negroidness of her features.

When black women actresses like Lena Horne appeared in mainstream cinema most white viewers were not aware that they were looking at black females unless the film was specifically coded as being about blacks. Burchill is one of the few white women film critics who has dared to examine the intersection of race and gender in relation to the construction of the category "woman" in film as object of the phallocentric gaze. With characteristic wit she asserts: "What does it say about racial purity that the best blondes have all been brunettes (Harlow, Monroe, Bardot)? I think it says that we are not as white as we think." Burchill could easily have said "we are not as white as we want to be," for clearly the obsession to have white women film stars be ultra-white was a cinematic practice that sought to maintain a distance, a separation between that image and the black female Other; it was a way to perpetuate white supremacy. Politics of race and gender were inscribed into mainstream cinematic narrative from *Birth of A Nation* on. As a seminal work, this film identified what the place and function of white womanhood would be in cinema. There was clearly no place for black women.

Remembering my past in relation to screen images of black womanhood, I wrote a short essay, "Do you remember Sapphire?" which explored both the negation of black female representation in cinema and television and our rejection of these images. Identifying the character of "Sapphire" from *Amos 'n' Andy* as that screen representation of black femaleness I first saw in childhood, I wrote:

> She was even then backdrop, foil. She was bitch—nag. She was there to soften images of black men, to make them seem vulnerable, easygoing, funny, and unthreatening to a white audience. She was there as man in drag, as castrating bitch, as someone to be lied to, someone to be tricked, someone the white and black audience could hate. Scapegoated on all sides. *She was not us.* We laughed with the black men, with the white people. We laughed at this black woman who was not us. And we did not even long to be there on the screen. How

could we long to be there when our image, visually constructed, was so ugly. We did not long to be there. We did not long for her. We did not want our construction to be this hated black female thing—foil, backdrop. Her black female image was not the body of desire. There was nothing to see. She was not us.

Grown black women had a different response to Sapphire; they identified with her frustrations and her woes. They resented the way she was mocked. They resented the way these screen images could assault black womanhood, could name us bitches, nags. And in opposition they claimed Sapphire as their own, as the symbol of that angry part of themselves white folks and black men could not even begin to understand.

Conventional representations of black women have done violence to the image. Responding to this assault, many black women spectators shut out the image, looked the other way, accorded cinema no importance in their lives. Then there were those spectators whose gaze was that of desire and complicity. Assuming a posture of subordination, they submitted to cinema's capacity to seduce and betray. They were cinematically "gaslighted." Every black woman I spoke with who was/is an ardent moviegoer, a lover of the Hollywood film, testified that to experience fully the pleasure of that cinema they had to close down critique, analysis; they had to forget racism. And mostly they did not think about sexism. What was the nature then of this adoring black female gaze—this look, that could bring pleasure in the midst of negation? In her first novel, *The Bluest Eye*, Toni Morrison constructs a portrait of the black female spectator; her gaze is the masochistic look of victimization. Describing her looking relations, Miss Pauline Breedlove, a poor working woman, maid in the house of a prosperous white family, asserts:

> The onliest time I be happy seem like was when I was in the picture show. Every time I got, I went, I'd go early, before the show started. They's cut off the lights, and everything be black. Then the screen would light up, and I's move right on in them picture. White men taking such good care of they women, and they all dressed up in big clean houses with the bath tubs right in the same room with the toilet. Them pictures gave me a lot of pleasure.

To experience pleasure, Miss Pauline sitting in the dark must imagine herself transformed, turned into the white woman portrayed on the screen. After watching movies, feeling the pleasure, she says, "But it made coming home hard."

We come home to ourselves. Not all black women spectators submitted to that spectacle of regression through identification. Most of the women I talked with felt that they consciously resisted identification with films—that this tension made moviegoing less than pleasurable; at times it caused pain. As one black woman put, "I could always get pleasure from movies as long as I did not look too deep." For black female spectators who have "looked too deep" the encounter with the screen hurt. That some of us chose to stop looking was a gesture of resistance, turning away was one way to protest, to reject negation. My pleasure in the screen ended abruptly when I and my sisters first watched *Imitation of Life*. Writing about this experience in the "Sapphire" piece, I addressed the movie directly, confessing:

I had until now forgotten you, that screen image seen in adolescence, those images that made me stop looking. It was there in *Imitation of Life,* that comfortable mammy image. There was something familiar about this hard-working black woman who loved her daughter so much, loved her in a way that hurt. Indeed, as young southern black girls watching this film, Peola's mother reminded us of the hardworking, churchgoing, Big Mamas we knew and loved. Consequently, it was not this image that captured our gaze; we were fascinated by Peola.

Addressing her, I wrote:

You were different. There was something scary in this image of young sexual sensual black beauty betrayed—that daughter who did not want to be confined by blackness, that "tragic mulatto" who did not want to be negated. "Just let me escape this image forever," she could have said. I will always remember that image. I remembered how we cried for her, for our unrealized desiring selves. She was tragic because there was no place in the cinema for her, no loving pictures. She too was absent image. It was better then, that we were absent, for when we were there it was humiliating, strange, sad. We cried all night for you, for the cinema that had no place for you. And like you, we stopped thinking it would one day be different.

When I returned to films as a young woman, after a long period of silence, I had developed an oppositional gaze. Not only would I not be hurt by the absence of black female presence, or the insertion of violating representation, I interrogated the work, cultivated a way to look past race and gender for aspects of content, form, language. Foreign films and U.S. independent cinema were the primary locations of my filmic looking relations, even though I also watched Hollywood films.

From "jump," black female spectators have gone to films with awareness of the way in which race and racism determined the visual construction of gender. Whether it was *Birth of A Nation* or Shirley Temple shows, we knew that white womanhood was the racialized sexual difference occupying the place of stardom in mainstream narrative film. We assumed white women knew it too. Reading Laura Mulvey's provocative essay, "Visual Pleasure and Narrative Cinema," from a standpoint that acknowledges race, one sees clearly why black women spectators not duped by mainstream cinema would develop an oppositional gaze. Placing ourselves outside that pleasure in looking, Mulvey argues, was determined by a "split between active/male and passive/female." Black female spectators actively chose not to identify with the film's imaginary subject because such identification was disenabling.

Looking at films with an oppositional gaze, black women were able to critically assess the cinema's construction of white womanhood as object of phallocentric gaze and choose not to identify with either the victim or the perpetrator. Black female spectators, who refused to identify with white womanhood, who would not take on the phallocentric gaze of desire and possession, created a critical space where the binary opposition Mulvey posits of "woman as image, man as bearer of the look" was continually deconstructed. As critical spectators, black women looked from a location that disrupted, one akin to that described by Annette Kuhn in *The Power of The Image:*

...the acts of analysis, of deconstruction and of reading "against the grain" offer an additional pleasure—the pleasure of resistance, of saying "no": not to "unsophisticated" enjoyment, by ourselves and others, of culturally dominant images, but to the structures of power which ask us to consume them uncritically and in highly circumscribed ways.

Mainstream feminist film criticism in no way acknowledges black female spectatorship. It does not even consider the possibility that women can construct an oppositional gaze via an understanding and awareness of the politics of race and racism. Feminist film theory rooted in an ahistorical psychoanalytic framework that privileges sexual difference actively suppresses recognition of race, reenacting and mirroring the erasure of black womanhood that occurs in films, silencing any discussion of racial difference—of racialized sexual difference. Despite feminist critical interventions aimed at deconstructing the category "woman" which highlight the significance of race, many feminist film critics continue to structure their discourse as though it speaks about "women" when in actuality it speaks only about white women. It seems ironic that the cover of the recent anthology *Feminism and Film Theory* edited by Constance Penley has a graphic that is a reproduction of the photo of white actresses Rosalind Russell and Dorothy Arzner on the 1936 set of the film *Craig's Wife* yet there is no acknowledgement in any essay in this collection that the woman "subject" under discussion is always white. Even though there are photos of black women from films reproduced in the text, there is no acknowledgment of racial difference.

It would be too simplistic to interpret this failure of insight solely as a gesture of racism. Importantly, it also speaks to the problem of structuring feminist film theory around a totalizing narrative of woman as object whose image functions solely to reaffirm and reinscribe patriarchy. Mary Ann Doane addresses this issue in the essay "Remembering Women: Psychical and Historical Construction in Film Theory":

> This attachment to the figure of a degeneralizible Woman as the product of the apparatus indicates why, for many, feminist film theory seems to have reached an impasse, a certain blockage in its theorization.... In focusing upon the task of delineating in great details the attributes of woman as effect of the apparatus, feminist film theory participates in the abstraction of women.

The concept "Woman" effaces the difference between women in specific socio-historical contexts, between women defined precisely as historical subjects rather than as *a* psychic subject (or non-subject). Though Doane does not focus on race, her comments speak directly to the problem of its erasure. For it is only as one imagines "woman" in the abstract, when woman becomes fiction or fantasy, can race not be seen as significant. Are we really to imagine that feminist theorists writing only about images of white women, who subsume this specific historical subject under the totalizing category "woman," do not "see" the whiteness of the image? It may very well be that they engage in a process of denial that eliminates the necessity of revisioning conventional ways of thinking about psychoanalysis as a paradigm of analysis and the need to rethink a body of feminist film theory that is firmly rooted in a denial of the reality that sex/sexuality may not be the primary and/or exclusive signifier of difference. Doane's essay appears in a very recent anthology, *Psychoanalysis and Cinema* edited by E. Ann Kaplan, where, once again, none of the theory presented acknowledges or discusses racial difference, with the exception of one essay, "Not Speaking with Language, Speaking with No Language," which problematizes notions of orientalism in its examination of Leslie Thornton's film *Adynata*. Yet in most of the essays, the theories espoused are rendered problematic if one includes race as a category of analysis.

Constructing feminist film theory along these lines enables the production of a discursive practice that need never theorize any aspect of black female representation or spectatorship. Yet the existence of black women within white supremacist culture problematizes, and makes complex, the overall issue of female identity, representation, and spectatorship. If, as Friedberg suggests, "identification is a process which commands the subject to be displaced by an other; it is a procedure which breeches the separation between self and other, and, in this way, replicates the very structure of patriarchy." If identification "demands sameness, necessitates similarity, disallows difference"— must we then surmise that many feminist film critics who are "over-identified" with the mainstream cinematic apparatus produce theories that replicate its totalizing agenda? Why is it that feminist film criticism, which has most claimed the terrain of woman's identity, representation, and subjectivity as its field of analysis, remains aggressively silent on the subject of blackness and specifically representations of black womanhood? Just as mainstream cinema has historically forced aware black female spectators not to look, much feminist film criticism disallows the possibility of a theoretical dialogue that might include black women's voices. It is difficult to talk when you feel no one is listening, when you feel as though a special jargon or narrative has been created that only the chosen can understand. No wonder then that black women have for the most part confined our critical commentary on film to conversations. And it must be reiterated that this gesture is a strategy that protects us from the violence perpetuated and advocated by discourses of mass media. A new focus on issues of race and representation in the field of film theory could critically intervene on the historical repression reproduced in some arenas of contemporary critical practice, making a discursive space for discussion of black female spectatorship possible.

When I asked a black woman in her twenties, an obsessive moviegoer, why she thought we had not written about black female spectatorship, she commented: "We are afraid to talk about ourselves as spectators because we have been so abused by 'the gaze'." An aspect of that abuse was the imposition of the assumption that black female looking relations were not important enough to theorize. Film theory as a critical "turf" in the United States has been and continues to be influenced by and reflective of white racial domination. Since feminist film criticism was initially rooted in a women's liberation movement informed by racist practices, it did not open up the discursive terrain and make it more inclusive. Recently, even those white film theorists who include an analysis of race show no interest in black female spectatorship. In her introduction to the collection of essays *Visual and Other Pleasures,* Laura Mulvey describes her initial romantic absorption in Hollywood cinema, stating:

> Although this great, previously unquestioned and unanalyzed love was put in crisis by the
> impact of feminism on my thought in the early 1970s, it also had an enormous influence

on the development of my critical work and ideas and the debate within film culture with which I became preoccupied over the next fifteen years or so. Watched through eyes that were affected by the changing climate of consciousness, the movies lost their magic.

Watching movies from a feminist perspective, Mulvey arrived at that location of disaffection that is the starting point for many black women approaching cinema within the lived harsh reality of racism. Yet her account of being a part of a film culture whose roots rest on a founding relationship of adoration and love indicates how difficult it would have been to enter that world from "jump" as a critical spectator whose gaze had been formed in opposition.

Given the context of class exploitation, and racist and sexist domination, it has only been through resistance, struggle, reading, and looking "against the grain," that black women have been able to value our process of looking enough to publicly name it. Centrally, those black female spectators who attest to the oppositionality of their gaze deconstruct theories of female spectatorship that have relied heavily on the assumption that, as Doane suggests in her essay, "Woman's Stake: Filming the Female Body," "woman can only mimic man's relation to language, that is assume a position defined by the penis-phallus as the supreme arbiter of lack." Identifying with neither the phallocentric gaze nor the construction of white womanhood as lack, critical black female spectators construct a theory of looking relations where cinematic visual delight is the pleasure of interrogation. Every black woman spectator I talked to, with rare exception, spoke of being "on guard" at the movies. Talking about the way being a critical spectator of Hollywood films influenced her, black woman filmmaker Julie Dash exclaims, "I make films because I was such a spectator!" Looking at Hollywood cinema from a distance, from that critical politicized standpoint that did not want to be seduced by narratives reproducing her negation, Dash watched mainstream movies over and over again for the pleasure of deconstructing them. And of course there is that added delight if one happens, in the process of interrogation, to come across a narrative that invites the black female spectator to engage the text with no threat of violation.

Significantly, I began to write film criticism in response to the first Spike Lee movie, *She's Gotta Have It*, contesting Lee's replication of mainstream patriarchal cinematic practices that explicitly represents woman (in this instance black woman) as the object of a phallocentric gaze. Lee's investment in patriarchal filmic practices that mirror dominant patterns makes him the perfect black candidate for entrance to the Hollywood canon. His work mimics the cinematic construction of white womanhood as object, replacing her body as text on which to write male desire with the black female body. It is transference without transformation. Entering the discourse of film criticism from the politicized location of resistance, of not wanting, as a working-class black woman I interviewed stated, "to see black women in the position white women have occupied in film forever," I began to think critically about black female spectatorship.

For years I went to independent and/or foreign films where I was the only black female present in the theater. I often imagined that in every theater in the United States there was another black woman watching the same film wondering why she was the only visible black female spectator. I remember trying to share with one of my five sisters the cinema I liked so much. She was "enraged" that I brought her to a theater where she would have to read subtitles. To her it was a violation of Hollywood notions of spectatorship, of coming to the movies to be entertained. When I interviewed her to ask what had changed her mind over the years, led her to embrace this cinema, she connected it to coming to critical consciousness, saying, "I learned that there was more to looking than I had been exposed to in ordinary (Hollywood) movies." I shared that though most of the films I loved were all white, I could engage them because they did not have in their deep structure a subtext reproducing the narrative of white supremacy. Her response was to say that these films demystified "whiteness," since the lives they depicted seemed less rooted in fantasies of escape. They were, she suggested, more like "what we knew life to be, the deeper side of life as well." Always more seduced and enchanted with Hollywood cinema than me, she stressed that unaware black female spectators must "break out," no longer be imprisoned by images that enact a drama of our negation. Though she still sees Hollywood films, because "they are a major influence in the culture"—she no longer feels duped or victimized.

Talking with black female spectators, looking at written discussions either in fiction or academic essays about black women, I noted the connection made between the realm of representation in mass media and the capacity of black women to construct ourselves as subjects in daily life. The extent to which black women feel devalued, objectified, dehumanized in this society determines the scope and texture of their looking relations. Those black women whose identities were constructed in resistance, by practices that oppose the dominant order, were most inclined to develop an oppositional gaze. Now that there is a growing interest in films produced by black women and those films have become more accessible to viewers, it is possible to talk about black female spectatorship in relation to that work. So far, most discussions of black spectatorship that I have come across focus on men. In "Black Spectatorship: Problems of Identification and Resistance" Manthia Diawara suggests that "the components of 'difference'" among elements of sex, gender, and sexuality give rise to different readings of the same material, adding that these conditions produce a "resisting" spectator. He focuses his critical discussion on black masculinity.

The recent publication of the anthology *The Female Gaze: Women as Viewers of Popular Culture* excited me, especially as it included an essay, "Black Looks," by Jacqui Roach and Petal Felix that attempts to address black female spectatorship. The essay posed provocative questions that were not answered: Is there a black female gaze? How do black women relate to the gender politics of representation? Concluding, the authors assert that black females have "our own reality, our own history, our own gaze—one which the sees the world rather differently from 'anyone else.'" Yet, they do not name/describe this experience of seeing "rather differently." The absence of definition and explanation suggests they are assuming an essentialist stance wherein it is presumed that black women, as victims of race and gender oppression, have an inherently different field of vision. Many black women do not "see differently" precisely because their perceptions of reality are so profoundly colonized, shaped by dominant ways of knowing. As Trinh T. Minh-ha points out in "Outside In, Inside Out": "Subjectivity does not merely consist of talking about oneself ... be this talking indulgent or critical."

Critical black female spectatorship emerges as a site of resistance only when individual black women actively resist the imposition of dominant ways of knowing and looking.

While every black woman I talked to was aware of racism, that awareness did not automatically correspond with politicization, the development of an oppositional gaze. When it did, individual black women consciously named the process. Manthia Diawara's "resisting spectatorship" is a term that does not adequately describe the terrain of black female spectatorship. We do more than resist. We create alternative texts that are not solely reactions. As critical spectators, black women participate in a broad range of looking relations, contest, resist, revision, interrogate, and invent on multiple levels. Certainly when I watch the work of black women filmmakers Camille Billops, Kathleen Collins, Julie Dash, Ayoka Chenzira, Zeinabu Davis, I do not need to "resist" the images even as I still choose to watch their work with a critical eye.

Black female critical thinkers concerned with creating space for the construction of radical black female subjectivity, and the way cultural production informs this possibility, fully acknowledge the importance of mass media, film in particular, as a powerful site for critical intervention. Certainly Julie Dash's film *Illusions* identifies the terrain of Hollywood cinema as a space of knowledge production that has enormous power. Yet, she also creates a filmic narrative wherein the black female protagonist subversively claims that space. Inverting the "real-life" power structure, she offers the black female spectator representations that challenge stereotypical notions that place us outside the realm of filmic discursive practices. Within the film she uses the strategy of Hollywood suspense films to undermine those cinematic practices that deny black women a place in this structure. Problematizing the question of "racial" identity by depicting passing, suddenly it is the white male's capacity to gaze, define, and know that is called into question.

When Mary Ann Doane describes in "Woman's Stake: Filming the Female Body" the way in which feminist filmmaking practice can elaborate "a special syntax for a different articulation of the female body," she names a critical process that "undoes the structure of the classical narrative through an insistence upon its repressions." An eloquent description, this precisely names Dash's strategy in *Illusions,* even though the film is not unproblematic and works within certain conventions that are not successfully challenged. For example, the film does not indicate whether the character Mignon will make Hollywood films that subvert and transform the genre or whether she will simply assimilate and perpetuate the norm. Still, subversively, *Illusions* problematizes the issue of race and spectatorship. White people in the film are unable to "see" that race informs their looking relations. Though she is passing to gain access to the machinery of cultural production represented by film, Mignon continually asserts her ties to black community. The bond between her and the young black woman singer Esther Jeeter is affirmed by caring gestures of affirmation, often expressed by eye-to-eye contact, the direct unmediated gaze of recognition. Ironically, it is the desiring objectifying sexualized white male gaze that threatens to penetrate her "secrets" and disrupt her process. Metaphorically, Dash suggests the power of black women to make films will be threatened and undermined by that white male gaze that seeks to reinscribe the black female body in a narrative of voyeuristic pleasure where the only relevant opposition is male/female, and the only location for the female is as a victim. These tensions are not resolved by the narrative. It is not at all evident that Mignon will triumph over the white supremacist capitalist imperialist dominating "gaze."

Throughout *Illusions,* Mignon's power is affirmed by her contact with the younger black woman whom she nurtures and protects. It is this process of mirrored recognition that enables both black women to define their reality, apart from the reality imposed upon them by structures of domination. The shared gaze of the two women reinforces their solidarity. As the younger subject, Esther represents a potential audience for films that Mignon might produce, films wherein black females will be the narrative focus. Julie Dash's recent feature-length film *Daughters of the Dust* dares to place black females at the center of its narrative. This focus caused critics (especially white males) to critique the film negatively or to express many reservations. Clearly, the impact of racism and sexism so over-determine spectatorship—not only what we look at but who we identify with—that viewers who are not black females find it hard to empathize with the central characters in the movie. They are adrift without a white presence in the film.

Another representation of black females nurturing one another *via* recognition of their common struggle for subjectivity is depicted in Sankofa's collective work *Passion of Remembrance.* In the film, two black women friends, Louise and Maggie, are from the onset of the narrative struggling with the issue of subjectivity, of their place in progressive black liberation movements that have been sexist. They challenge old norms and want to replace them with new understandings of the complexity of black identity, and the need for liberation struggles that address that complexity. Dressing to go to a party, Louise and Maggie claim the "gaze." Looking at one another, staring in mirrors, they appear completely focused on their encounter with black femaleness. How they see themselves is most important, not how they will be stared at by others. Dancing to the tune "Let's get Loose," they display their bodies not for a voyeuristic colonizing gaze but for that look of recognition that affirms their subjectivity—that constitutes them as spectators. Mutually empowered they eagerly leave the privatized domain to confront the public. Disrupting conventional racist and sexist stereotypical representations of black female bodies, these scenes invite the audience to look differently. They act to critically intervene and transform conventional filmic practices, changing notions of spectatorship. *Illusions, Daughters of the Dust,* and *A Passion of Remembrance* employ a deconstructive filmic practice to undermine existing grand cinematic narratives even as they retheorize subjectivity in the realm of the visual. Without providing "realistic" positive representations that emerge only as a response to the totalizing nature of existing narratives, they offer points of radical departure. Opening up a space for the assertion of a critical black female spectatorship, they do not simply offer diverse representations, they imagine new transgressive possibilities for the formulation of identity.

In this sense they make explicit a critical practice that provides us with different ways to think about black female subjectivity and black female spectatorship. Cinematically, they provide new points of recognition, embodying Stuart Hall's vision of a critical practice that acknowledges that identity is constituted "not outside but within representation," and invites us to see film "not as a second-order mirror held up to reflect what already exists, but as that form of representation which is able to constitute us as new

kinds of subjects, and thereby enable us to discover who we are." It is this critical practice that enables production of feminist film theory that theorizes black female spectatorship. Looking and looking back, black women involve ourselves in a process whereby
we see our history as counter-memory, using it as a way to know the present and invent
the future.

QUEER STUDIES

COMPULSORY HETEROSEXUALITY AND LESBIAN EXISTENCE (1980)

ADRIENNE RICH

Rich calls attention to the concept of compulsory heterosexuality, *the assumption, explicit or implicit, that people should be heterosexual or else something is wrong with them. Each year, for example, men and patriarchal economics pressure or force millions of women around the globe into marriage, rape, or concubinage. Even in its implicit form, when people say or do things that take for granted that everyone is or should be heterosexual, compulsory heterosexuality, Rich argues, costs many people with same-sex desires great and needless suffering.*

Focusing on women, Rich goes on to propose a lesbian continuum, *"a range—through each woman's life and throughout history—of woman-identified experience" regardless of whether "a woman has had or consciously desired genital sexual experience with another woman." The notion of a lesbian continuum has attracted both appreciation and criticism. Some feminist and lesbian critics find it oversimplifying. They fear that it desexualizes lesbianism or mutes its specificity and that the concept of a continuum can reestablish its opposite poles, leaving only a subtler form of the old, too simple binary opposition between straight women and lesbian women. It can also invite others to propose a heterosexual continuum, the same continuum as it appears from the other side of the binary. Nevertheless, by seeing lesbianism as ordinary and pervasive, Rich turns the tables on compulsory heterosexuality, recentering existence outside heterosexuality and inside queerness.*

For an essay that draws from Rich's argument, see Robert McRuer's "Compulsory Able-Bodiedness and Queer/Disabled Existence" in this volume.

FOREWORD

I want to say a little about the way "Compulsory Heterosexuality" was originally conceived and the context in which we are now living. It was written in part to challenge the erasure of lesbian existence from so much of scholarly feminist literature, an erasure which I felt (and feel) to be not just anti-lesbian, but anti-feminist in its consequences, and to distort the experience of heterosexual women as well. It was not written to widen divisions but to encourage heterosexual feminists to examine heterosexuality as a political institution which disempowers women—and to change it. I also hoped that other lesbians would feel the depth and breadth of woman identification and woman bonding that has run like a continuous though stifled theme through the heterosexual experience, and that this would become increasingly a politically activating impulse, not simply a validation of personal lives. I wanted the essay to suggest new kinds of criticism, to incite new questions in classrooms and academic journals, and to sketch, at least, some bridge over the gap between *lesbian* and *feminist*. I wanted, at the very least, for feminists to find it less possible to read, write, or teach from a perspective of unexamined heterocentricity.

Within the three years since I wrote "Compulsory Heterosexuality"—with this energy of hope and desire—the pressure to conform in a society increasingly conservative in mood have become more intense. The New Right's messages to women have been, precisely, that we are the emotional and sexual property of men, and that the autonomy and equality of women threaten family, religion, and state.

The institutions by which women have traditionally been controlled—patriarchal motherhood, economic exploitation, the nuclear family, compulsory heterosexuality—are being strengthened by legislation, religious fiat, media imagery, and efforts at censorship. In a worsening economy, the single mother trying to support her children confronts the feminization of poverty which Joyce Miller of the National Coalition of Labor Union Women has named one of the major issues of the 1980s. The lesbian, unless in disguise, faces discrimination in hiring and harassment and violence in the street. Even within feminist-inspired institutions such as battered-women's shelters and Women's Studies programs, open lesbians are fired and others warned to stay in the closet. The retreat into sameness—assimilation for those who can manage it—is the most passive and debilitating of responses to political repression, economic insecurity, and a renewed open season on difference.

I want to note that documentation of male violence against women—within the home especially—has been accumulating rapidly in this period (see note 9). At the same time, in the realm of literature which depicts woman bonding and woman identification as essential for female survival, a steady stream of writing and criticism has been coming from women of color in general and lesbians of color in particular—the latter group being even more profoundly erased in academic feminist scholarship by the double bias of racism and homophobia.[1]

There has recently been an intensified debate on female sexuality among feminists and lesbians, with lines often furiously and bitterly drawn, with *sadomasochism* and *pornography* as key words which are variously defined according to who is talking. The depth of women's rage and fear regarding sexuality and its relation to power and pain is real, even when the dialogue sounds simplistic, self-righteous, or like parallel monologues.

Because of all these developments, there are parts of this essay that I would word differently, qualify, or expand if I were writing it today. But I continue to think that heterosexual feminists will draw political strength for change from taking a critical stance toward the ideology which *demands* heterosexuality, and that lesbians cannot assume that we are untouched by that ideology and the institutions founded upon it. There is nothing about such a critique that requires us to think of ourselves as victims, as having been brainwashed or totally powerless. Coercion and compulsion are among the conditions in which women have learned to recognize our strength. Resistance is a major theme in this essay and in the study of women's lives, if we know what we are looking for.

I

> Biologically men have only one innate orientation—a sexual one that draws them to women,—while women have two innate orientations, sexual toward men and reproductive toward their young.[2]

> I was a woman terribly vulnerable, critical, using femaleness as a sort of standard or yard-stick to measure and discard men. Yes—something like that. I was an Anna who invited defeat from men without ever being conscious of it. (But I am conscious of it. And being conscious of it means I shall leave it all behind me and become—but what?) I was stuck fast in an emotion common to women of our time, that can turn them bitter, or Lesbian, or solitary. Yes, that Anna during that time was...

[Another blank line across the page:][3]

The bias of compulsory heterosexuality, through which lesbian experience is perceived on a scale ranging from deviant to abhorrent or simply rendered invisible, could be illustrated from many texts other than the two just preceding. The assumption made by Rossi, that women are "innately" sexually oriented only toward men, and that made by Lessing, that the lesbian is simply acting out of her bitterness toward men, are by no means theirs alone; these assumptions are widely current in literature and in the social sciences.

I am concerned here with two other matters as well: first, how and why women's choice of women as passionate comrades, life partners, co-workers, lovers, community has been crushed, invalidated, forced into hiding and disguise; and second, the virtual or total neglect of lesbian existence in a wide range of writings, including feminist scholarship. Obviously there is a connection here. I believe that much feminist theory and criticism is stranded on this shoal.

My organizing impulse is the belief that it is not enough for feminist thought that specifically lesbian texts exist. Any theory or cultural/political creation that treats lesbian existence as a marginal or less "natural" phenomenon, as mere "sexual preference," or as the minor image of either heterosexual or male homosexual relations is profoundly weakened thereby, whatever its other contributions. Feminist theory can no longer afford merely to voice a toleration of "lesbianism" as an "alternative life style" or make token allusion to lesbians. A feminist critique of compulsory heterosexual orientation for women is long overdue. In this exploratory paper, I shall try to show why.

I will begin by way of examples, briefly discussing four books that have appeared in the last few years, written from different viewpoints and political orientations, but all presenting themselves, and favorably reviewed, as feminist.[4] All take as a basic assumption that the social relations of the sexes are disordered and extremely problematic, if not disabling, for women; all seek paths toward change. I have learned more from some of these books than from others, but on this I am clear: each one might have been more accurate, more powerful, more truly a force for change had the author dealt with lesbian existence as a reality and as a source of knowledge and power available to women, or with the institution of heterosexuality itself as a beachhead of male domi-nance.[5] In none of them is the question ever raised as to whether, in a different context or other things being equal, women would *choose* heterosexual coupling and marriage; heterosexuality is presumed the "sexual preference" of "most women," either implicitly or explicitly. In none of these books, which concern themselves with mothering, sex roles, relationships, and societal pre-scriptions for women, is compulsory heterosexuality ever examined as an institution powerfully affecting all these, or the idea of "preference" or "innate orientation" even indirectly questioned.

In *For Her Own Good: 150 Years of the Experts' Advice to Women* by Barbara Ehrenreich and Deirdre English, the authors' superb pamphlets *Witches, Midwives and Nurses: A History of Women Healers* and *Complaints and Disorders: The Sexual Politics of Sickness* are developed into a provocative and complex study. Their thesis in this book is that the advice given to American women by male health professionals, particularly in the areas of marital sex, mater-nity, and child care, has echoed the dictates of the economic marketplace and the role capital-ism has needed women to play in production and/or reproduction. Women have become the consumer victims of various cures, therapies, and normative judgments in different periods (including the prescription to middle-class women to embody and preserve the sacredness of the home—the "scientific" romanticization of the home itself). None of the "experts'" advice has been either particularly scientific or women-oriented; it has reflected male needs, male fantasies about women, and male interest in controlling women—particularly in the realms of sexuality and motherhood—fused with the requirements of industrial capitalism. So much of this book is so devastatingly informative and is written with such lucid feminist wit, that I kept waiting as I read for the basic proscription against lesbianism to be examined. It never was.

This can hardly be for lack of information. Jonathan Katz's *Gay American History*[6] tells us that as early as 1656 the New Haven Colony prescribed the death penalty for lesbians. Katz provides many suggestive and informative documents on the "treatment" (or torture) of lesbians by the medical profession in the nineteenth and twentieth centuries. Recent work by the historian Nancy Sahli documents the crackdown on intense female friendships among college women at the turn of the present century.[7] The ironic title *For Her Own Good* might have referred first and foremost to the economic imperative to heterosexuality and marriage and to the sanctions imposed against single women and widows—both of whom have been and still are viewed as deviant. Yet, in this often enlightening Marxist-feminist overview of male prescriptions for female sanity and health, the economics of prescriptive heterosexuality go unexamined.[8]

Of the three psychoanalytically based books, one, Jean Baker Miller's *Toward a New Psychology of Women,* is written as if lesbians simply do not exist, even as marginal beings. Given Miller's title, I find this astonishing. However, the favorable reviews the book has received in feminist journals, including *Signs* and *Spokeswoman,* suggest that Miller's hetero-centric assumptions are widely shared. In *The Mermaid and the Minotaur: Sexual Arrangements and the Human Malaise,* Dorothy Dinnerstein makes an impassioned argument for the shar-ing of parenting between women and men and for an end to what she perceives as the male/female symbiosis of "gender arrangements," which she feels are leading the species further and further into violence and self-extinction. Apart from other problems that I have with this book (including her silence on the institutional and random terrorism men have practiced on women—and children—throughout history,[9] and her obsession with psychology to the neglect of economic and other material realities that help to create psychological reality), I find Dinnerstein's view of the relations between women and men as "a collaboration to keep history mad" utterly ahistorical. She means by this a collaboration to perpetuate social relations which are hostile, exploitative, and destructive to life itself. She sees women and men as equal partners in the making of "sexual arrangements," seemingly unaware of the repeated struggles of women to resist oppression (their own and that of others) and to change their condition. She ignores, specifically, the history of women who—as witches, *femmes seules*, marriage resisters, spinsters, autonomous widows, and/or lesbians—have managed on varying levels *not* to collaborate. It is this history, precisely, from which feminists have so much to learn and on which there is overall such blanketing silence. Dinnerstein acknowledges at the end of her book that "female separatism," though "on a large scale and in the long run wildly impractical," has something to teach us: "Separate, women could in principle set out to learn from scratch—undeflected by the opportunities to evade this task that men's presence has so far offered—what intact self-creative humanness is."[10] Phrases like "intact self-creative humanness" obscure the question of what the many forms of female separatism have actually been addressing. The fact is that women in every culture and throughout history *have* undertaken the task of independent, non heterosexual, woman-connected existence, to the extent made possible by their context, often in the belief that they were the "only ones" ever to have done so. They have undertaken it even though few women have been in an economic position to resist marriage altogether, and even though attacks against unmarried women have ranged from aspersion and mockery to deliberate gynocide, including the burning and torturing of millions of widows and spinsters during the witch persecutions of the fifteenth, sixteenth, and seventeenth centuries in Europe.

Nancy Chodorow does come close to the edge of an acknowledgment of lesbian existence. Like Dinnerstein, Chodorow believes that the fact that women, and women only, are responsible for child care in the sexual division of labor has led to an entire social organization of gender inequality, and that men as well as women must become primary carers for children if that inequality is to change. In the process of examining, from a psychoanalytic perspective, how mothering by women affects the psychological development of girl and boy children, she offers documentation that men are "emotionally secondary" in women's lives, that "women have a richer, ongoing inner world to fall back on ... men do not become as emotionally important to women as women do to men."[11] This would carry into the late twentieth century Smith-Rosenberg's findings about eighteenth- and nineteenth-century women's emotional focus on women. "Emotionally important" can, of course, refer to anger as well as to love, or to that intense mixture of the two often found in women's relationships with women—one aspect of what I have come to call the "double life of women." Chodorow concludes that because women have women as mothers, "the mother remains a primary internal object [*sic*] to the girl, so that heterosexual relationships are on the model of a nonexclusive, second relationship for her, whereas for the boy they re-create an exclusive, primary relationship." According to Chodorow, women "have learned to deny the limitations of masculine lovers for both psychological and practical reasons."[12]

But the practical reasons (like witch burnings, male control of law, theology, and science, or economic nonviability within the sexual division of labor) are glossed over. Chodorow's account barely glances at the constraints and sanctions which historically have enforced or ensured the coupling of women with men and obstructed or penalized women's coupling or allying in independent groups with other women. She dismisses lesbian existence with the comment that "lesbian relationships do tend to re-create mother-daughter emotions and connections, but most women are heterosexual" (implied: more mature, having developed beyond the mother-daughter connection?). She then adds: "This heterosexual preference and taboos on homosexuality, in addition to objective economic dependence on men, make the option of primary sexual bonds with other women unlikely—though more prevalent in recent years."[13] The significance of that qualification seems irresistible, but Chodorow does not explore it further. Is she saying that lesbian existence has become more *visible* in recent years (in certain groups), that economic and other pressures have changed (under capitalism, socialism, or both), and that consequently more women are rejecting the heterosexual "choice"? She argues that women want children because their heterosexual relationships lack richness and intensity, that in having a child a woman seeks to re-create her own intense relationship with her mother. It seems to me that on the basis of her own findings, Chodorow leads us implicitly to conclude that heterosexuality is not a "preference" for women, that, for one thing, it fragments the erotic from the emotional in a way that women find impoverishing and painful. Yet her book participates in mandating it. Neglecting the covert socializations and the overt forces which have channeled women into marriage and heterosexual romance, pressures ranging from the selling of daughters to the silences of literature to the images of the television screen, she, like Dinnerstein, is stuck with trying to reform a man-made institution—compulsory heterosexuality—as if, despite profound emotional impulses and complementarities drawing women toward women, there is a mystical/biological heterosexual inclination, a "preference" or "choice" which draws women toward men.

Moreover, it is understood that this "preference" does not need to be explained unless through the tortuous theory of the female Oedipus complex or the necessity for species reproduction. It is lesbian sexuality which (usually, and incorrectly, "included" under male homosexuality) is seen as requiring explanation. This assumption of female heterosexuality seems to me in itself remarkable: it is an enormous assumption to have glided so silently into the foundations of our thought.

The extension of this assumption is the frequently heard assertion that in a world of genuine equality, where men are nonoppressive and nurturing, everyone would be bisexual. Such a notion blurs and sentimentalizes the actualities within which women have experienced sexuality; it is a liberal leap across the tasks and struggles of here and now, the continuing process of sexual definition which will generate its own possibilities and choices. (It also assumes that women who have chosen women have done so simply because men are oppressive and emotionally unavailable, which still fails to account for women who continue to pursue relationships with oppressive and or emotionally unsatisfying men.) I am suggesting that heterosexuality, like motherhood, needs to be recognized and studied as a *political institution*—even, or especially, by those individuals who feel they are, in their personal experience, the precursors of a new social relation between the sexes.

II

If women are the earliest sources of emotional caring and physical nurture for both female and male children, it would seem logical, from a feminist perspective at least, to pose the following questions: whether the search for love and tenderness in both sexes does not originally lead toward women; why in fact women would ever redirect that search; why species survival, the means of impregnation, and emotional/erotic relationships should ever have become so rigidly identified with each other; and why such violent strictures should be found necessary to enforce women's total emotional, erotic loyalty and subservience to men. I doubt that enough feminist scholars and theorists have taken the pains to acknowledge the societal forces which wrench women's emotional and erotic energies away from themselves and other women and from woman-identified values. These forces, as I shall try to show, range from literal physical enslavement to the disguising and distorting of possible options.

I do not assume that mothering by women is a "sufficient cause" of lesbian existence. But the issue of mothering by women has been much in the air of late, usually accompanied by the view that increased parenting by men would minimize antagonism between the sexes and equalize the sexual imbalance of power of males over females. These discussions are carried on without reference to compulsory heterosexuality as a phenomenon, let alone as an ideology. I do not wish to psychologize here, but rather to identify sources of male power. I believe large numbers of men could, in fact, undertake child care on a large scale without radically altering the balance of male power in a male-identified society.

In her essay "The Origin of the Family," Kathleen Gough lists eight characteristics of male power in archaic and contemporary societies which I would like to use as a framework: "men's ability to deny women sexuality or to force it upon them; to command or exploit their labor to control their produce; to control or rob them of their children; to confine them physically and prevent their movement; to use them as objects in male transactions; to cramp their creativeness; or to withhold from them large areas of the society's knowledge and cultural attainments."[14] (Gough does not perceive these power characteristics as specifically enforcing heterosexuality, only as producing sexual inequality.) Gough's words appear in italics; the elaboration of each of her categories, in brackets, is my own.

Characteristics of male power include *the power of men*

1. *to deny women* [their own] *sexuality*—[by means of clitoridectomy and infibulation; chastity belts; punishment, including death, for female adultery; punishment, including death, for lesbian sexuality; psychoanalytic denial of the clitoris; strictures against masturbation; denial of maternal and postmenopausal sensuality; unnecessary hysterectomy; pseudolesbian images in the media and literature; closing of archives and destruction of documents relating to lesbian existence]

2. *or to force it* [male sexuality] *upon them*—[by means of rape (including marital rape) and wife beating; father-daughter, brother-sister incest; the socialization of women to feel that male sexual "drive" amounts to a right;[15] idealization of heterosexual romance in art, literature, the media, advertising, etc.; child marriage; arranged marriage; prostitution; the harem; psychoanalytic doctrines of frigidity and vaginal orgasm; pornographic

depictions of women responding pleasurably to sexual violence and humiliation (a sub-liminal message being that sadistic heterosexuality is more "normal" than sensuality between women)]

3. *to command or exploit their labor to control their produce*—[by means of the institutions of marriage and motherhood as unpaid production; the horizontal segregation of women in paid employment; the decoy of the upwardly mobile token woman; male control of abortion, contraception, sterilization, and childbirth; pimping; female infanticide, which robs mothers of daughters and contributes to generalized devaluation of women]

4. *to control or rob them of their children*—[by means of father right and "legal kidnaping";[16] enforced sterilization; systematized infanticide; seizure of children from lesbian moth-ers by the courts; the malpractice of male obstetrics; use of the mother as "token torturer"[17] in genital mutilation or in binding the daughter's feet (or mind) to fit her for marriage]

5. *to confine them physically and prevent their movement*—[by means of rape as terrorism, keeping women off the streets; purdah; foot binding; atrophying of women's athletic capabilities; high heels and "feminine" dress codes in fashion; the veil; sexual harass-ment on the streets; horizontal segregation of women in employment; prescriptions for "full-time" mothering at home; enforced economic dependence of wives]

6. *to use them as objects in male transactions*—[use of women as "gifts"; bride price; pimping; arranged marriage; use of women as entertainers to facilitate male deals—e.g., wife-host-ess, cocktail waitress required to dress for male sexual titillation, call girls, "bunnies," geisha, *kisaeng* prostitutes, secretaries]

7. *to cramp their creativeness*—[witch persecutions as campaigns against midwives and fe-male healers, and as pogrom against independent, "unassimilated" women;[18] definition of male pursuits as more valuable than female within any culture, so that cultural values become the embodiment of male subjectivity; restriction of female self-fulfillment to marriage and motherhood; sexual exploitation of women by male artists and teachers; the social and economic disruption of women's creative aspirations;[19] erasure of female tradition][20]

8. *to withhold from them large areas of the society's knowledge and cultural attainments*—[by means of noneducation of females; the "Great Silence" regarding women and particular-ly lesbian existence in history and culture;[21] sex-role tracking which deflects women from science, technology, and other "masculine" pursuits; male social/professional bonding which excludes women; discrimination against women in the professions]

These are some of the methods by which male power is manifested and maintained. Looking at the schema, what surely impresses itself is the tact that we are confronting not a simple maintenance of inequality and property possession, but a pervasive cluster of forces, ranging from physical brutality to control of consciousness, which suggests that an enor-mous potential counterforce is having to be restrained.

Some of the forms by which male power manifests itself are more easily recognizable as enforcing heterosexuality on women than are others. Yet each one I have listed adds to the cluster of forces within which women have been convinced that marriage and sexual orientation toward men are inevitable—even if unsatisfying or oppressive—components of their lives. The chastity belt; child marriage; erasure of lesbian existence (except as exotic and perverse) in art, literature, film; idealization of heterosexual romance and marriage—these are some fairly obvious forms of compulsion, the first two exemplifying physical force, the second two control of consciousness. While clitoridectomy has been assailed by feminists as a form of woman torture,[22] Kathleen Barry first pointed out that it is not simply a way of turning the young girl into a "marriageable" woman through brutal surgery. It intends that women in the intimate proximity of polygynous marriage will not form sexual relationships with each other, that—from a male, genital-fetishist perspective—female erotic connections, even in a sex-segregated situation, will be literally excised.[23]

The function of pornography as an influence on consciousness is a major public issue of our time, when a multibillion-dollar industry has the power to disseminate increasingly sadistic, women-degrading visual images. But even so-called soft-core pornography and advertising depict women as objects of sexual appetite devoid of emotional context, without individual meaning or personality—essentially as a sexual commodity to be consumed by males. (So-called lesbian pornography, created for the male voyeuristic eye, is equally devoid of emotional context or individual personality.) The most pernicious message relayed by pornography is that women are natural sexual prey to men and love it, that sexuality and violence are congruent, and that for women sex is essentially masochistic, humiliation pleasurable, physical abuse erotic. But along with this message comes another, not always recognized: that enforced submission and the use of cruelty, if played out in heterosexual pairing, is sexually "normal," while sensuality between women, including erotic mutuality and respect, is "queer," "sick," and either pornographic in itself or not very exciting compared with the sexuality of whips and bondage.[24] Pornography does not simply create a climate in which sex and violence are interchangeable; *it widens the range of behavior considered acceptable from men in heterosexual intercourse*—behavior which reiteratively strips women of their autonomy, dignity, and sexual potential, including the potential of loving and being loved by women in mutuality and integrity.

In her brilliant study *Sexual Harassment of Working Women: A Case of Sex Discrimination*, Catharine A. MacKinnon delineates the intersection of compulsory heterosexuality and economics. Under capitalism, women are horizontally segregated by gender and occupy a structurally inferior position in the workplace. This is hardly news, but MacKinnon raises the question why, even if capitalism "requires some collection of individuals to occupy low-status, low-paying positions... such persons must be biologically female," and goes on to point out that "the fact that male employers often do not hire qualified women, *even when they could pay them less than men* suggests that more than the profit motive is implicated" [emphasis added].[25] She cites a wealth of material documenting the fact that women are not only segregated in low-paying service jobs (as secretaries, domestics, nurses, typists, telephone operators, child-care workers, waitresses), but that "sexualization of the woman" is part of the job. Central and intrinsic to the economic realities of women's lives is the requirement that women will "market sexual attractiveness to men, who tend to hold the economic power and position to enforce their predilections." And MacKinnon documents that "sexual harassment perpetuates the interlocked structure by which women have been kept sexually in thrall to men at the bottom of the labor market. Two forces of American society converge: men's control over women's sexuality and capital's control over employees' work lives."[26] Thus, women in the workplace are at the mercy of sex as power in a vicious circle. Economically disadvantaged, women—whether waitresses or professors—endure sexual harassment to keep their jobs and learn to behave in a complaisantly and ingratiatingly heterosexual manner because they discover this is their true qualification for employment, whatever the job description. And, MacKinnon notes, the woman who too decisively resists sexual overtures in the workplace is accused of being "dried up" and sexless, or lesbian. This raises a specific difference between the experiences of lesbians and homosexual men. A lesbian, closeted on her job because of heterosexist prejudice, is not simply forced into denying the truth of her outside relationships or private life. Her job depends on her pretending to be not merely heterosexual, but a heterosexual *woman* in terms of dressing and playing the feminine, deferential role required of "real" women.

MacKinnon raises radical questions as to the qualitative differences between sexual harassment, rape, and ordinary heterosexual intercourse. ("As one accused rapist put it, he hadn't used 'any more force than is usual for males during the preliminaries.'") She criticizes Susan Brownmiller[27] for separating rape from the mainstream of daily life and for her unexamined premise that "rape is violence, intercourse is sexuality," removing rape from the sexual sphere altogether. Most crucially she argues that "taking rape from the realm of 'the sexual,' placing it in the realm of 'the violent' allows one to be against it without raising any questions about the extent to which the institution of heterosexuality has defined force as a normal part of 'the preliminaries.'"[28] "Never is it asked whether, under conditions of male supremacy, the notion of 'consent' has any meaning."[29]

The fact is that the workplace, among other social institutions, is a place where women have learned to accept male violation of their psychic and physical boundaries as the price of survival; where women have been educated—no less than by romantic literature or by pornography—to perceive themselves as sexual prey. A woman seeking to escape such casual violations along with economic disadvantage may well turn to marriage as a form of hoped-for protection, while bringing into marriage neither social nor economic power, thus entering that institution also from a disadvantaged position. MacKinnon finally asks:

> What if inequality is built into the social conceptions of male and female sexuality, of masculinity and femininity, of sexiness and heterosexual attractiveness? Incidents of sexual harassment suggest that male sexual desire itself may be aroused by female vulnerability.... Men feel they can take advantage, so they want to, so they do. Examination of sexual harassment, precisely because the episodes appear commonplace, forces one to confront the fact that sexual intercourse normally occurs between economic (as well as physical) unequals... the apparent legal requirement that violations of women's sexuality appear out of the ordinary before they will be punished helps prevent women from defining the ordinary conditions of their own consent.[30]

Given the nature and extent of heterosexual pressures—the daily "eroticization of women's subordination," as MacKinnon phrases it[31]—I question the more or less psychoanalytic perspective (suggested by such writers as Karen Horney, H. R. Hayes, Wolfgang Lederer, and, most recently, Dorothy Dinnerstein) that the male need to control women sexually results from some primal male "fear of women" and of women's sexual insatiability. It seems more probable that men really fear not that they will have women's sexual appetites forced on them or that women want to smother and devour them, but that women could be indifferent to them altogether, that men could be allowed sexual and emotional—therefore economic—access to women *only* on women's terms, otherwise being left on the periphery of the matrix.

The means of assuring male sexual access to women have recently received searching investigation by Kathleen Barry.[32] She documents extensive and appalling evidence for the existence, on a very large scale, of international female slavery, the institution once known as "white slavery" but which in fact has involved, and at this very moment involves, women of every race and class. In the theoretical analysis derived from her research, Barry makes the connection between all enforced conditions under which women live subject to men: prostitution, marital rape, father-daughter and brother-sister incest, wife beating, pornography, bride price, the selling of daughters, purdah, and genital mutilation. She sees the rape paradigm—where the victim of sexual assault is held responsible for her own victimization—as leading to the rationalization and acceptance of other forms of enslavement where the woman is presumed to have "chosen" her fate, to embrace it passively, or to have courted it perversely through rash or unchaste behavior. On the contrary, Barry maintains, "female sexual slavery is present in ALL situations where women or girls cannot change the conditions of their existence; where regardless of how they got into those conditions, e.g., social pressure, economic hardship, misplaced trust or the longing for affection, they cannot get out; and where they are subject to sexual violence and exploitation."[33] She provides a spectrum of concrete examples, not only as to the existence of a widespread international traffic in women, but also as to how this operates—whether in the form of a "Minnesota pipeline" funneling blonde, blue-eyed midwestern runaways to Times Square, or the purchasing of young women out of rural poverty in Latin America or Southeast Asia, or the providing of *maisons d'abattage* for migrant workers in the eighteenth arrondissement of Paris. Instead of "blaming the victim" or trying to diagnose her presumed pathology, Barry turns her floodlight on the pathology of sex colonization itself, the ideology of "cultural sadism" represented by the pornography industry and by the overall identification of women primarily as "sexual beings whose responsibility is the sexual service of men."[34]

Barry delineates what she names a "sexual domination perspective" through whose lens sexual abuse and terrorism of women by men has been rendered almost invisible by treating it as natural and inevitable. From its point of view, women are expendable as long as the sexual and emotional needs of the male can be satisfied. To replace this perspective of domination with a universal standard of basic freedom for women from gender-specific violence, from constraints on movement, and from male right of sexual and emotional access is the political purpose of her book. Like Mary Daly in *Gyn/Ecology*, Barry rejects structuralist and other cultural-relativist rationalizations for sexual torture and anti-woman violence. In her opening chapter, she asks of her readers that they refuse all handy escapes into ignorance and denial. "The only way we can come out of hiding, break through our paralyzing defenses, is to know it all—the full extent of sexual violence and domination of women.... In *knowing,* in facing directly, we can learn to chart our course out of this oppression, by envisioning and creating a world which will preclude sexual slavery."[35]

"Until we name the practice, give conceptual definition and form to it, illustrate its life over time and in space, those who are its most obvious victims will also not be able to name it or define their experience."

But women are all, in different ways and to different degrees, its victims; and part of the problem with naming and conceptualizing female sexual slavery is, as Barry clearly sees, compulsory heterosexuality.[36] Compulsory heterosexuality simplifies the task of the procurer and pimp in world-wide prostitution rings and "eros centers," while, in the privacy of the home, it leads the daughter to "accept" incest/rape by her father, the mother to deny that it is happening, the battered wife to stay on with an abusive husband. "Befriending or love" is a major tactic of the procurer, whose job it is to turn the runaway or the confused young girl over to the pimp for seasoning. The ideology of heterosexual romance, beamed at her from childhood out of fairy tales, television, films, advertising, popular songs, wedding pageantry, is a tool ready to the procurer's hand and one which he does not hesitate to use, as Barry documents. Early female indoctrination in "love" as an emotion may be largely a Western concept; but a more universal ideology concerns the primacy and uncontrollability of the male sexual drive. This is one of many insights offered by Barry's work:

> As sexual power is learned by adolescent boys through the social experience of their sex drive, so do girls learn that the locus of sexual power is male. Given the importance placed on the male sex drive in the socialization of girls as well as boys, early adolescence is probably the first significant phase of male identification in a girl's life and development.... As a young girl becomes aware of her own increasing sexual feelings... she turns away from her heretofore primary relationships with girlfriends. As they become secondary to her, recede in importance in her life, her own identity also assumes a secondary role and she grows into male identification.[37]

We still need to ask why some women never, even temporarily, turn away from "heretofore primary relationships" with other females. And why does male identification—the casting of one's social, political, and intellectual allegiances with men—exist among lifelong sexual lesbians? Barry's hypothesis throws us among new questions, but it clarifies the diversity of forms in which compulsory heterosexuality presents itself. In the mystique of the overpowering, all-conquering male sex drive, the penis-with-a-life-of-its-own, is rooted the law of male sex right to women, which justifies prostitution as a universal cultural assumption on the one hand, while defending sexual slavery within the family on the basis of "family privacy and cultural uniqueness" on the other.[38] The adolescent male sex drive, which, as both young women and men are taught, once triggered cannot take responsibility for itself or take no for an answer, becomes, according to Barry, the norm and rationale for adult male sexual behavior: a condition of *arrested sexual development*. Women learn to accept as natural the inevitability of this "drive" because they receive it as dogma. Hence, marital rape; hence, the Japanese wife resignedly packing her husband's suitcase for a weekend in the *kisaeng* brothels of Taiwan; hence, the psychological as well as economic imbalance of power between husband and wife, male employer and female worker, father and daughter, male professor and female student.

The effect of male identification means

> internalizing the values of the colonizer and actively participating in carrying out the colonization of one's self and one's sex.... Male identification is the act whereby women place men above women, including themselves, in credibility, status, and importance in most situations, regardless of the comparative quality the women may bring to the situation.... Interaction with women is seen as a lesser form of relating on every level.[39]

What deserves further exploration is the doublethink many women engage in and from which no woman is permanently and utterly free: However woman-to-woman relationships, female support networks, a female and feminist value system are relied on and cherished, indoctrination in male credibility and status can still create synapses in thought, denials of feeling, wishful thinking, a profound sexual and intellectual confusion.[40] I quote here from a letter I received the day I was writing this passage: "I have had very bad relationships with men—I am now in the midst of a very painful separation. I am trying to find my strength through women—without my friends, I could not survive." How many times a day do women speak words like these or think them or write them, and how often does the synapse reassert itself?

Barry summarizes her findings:

> Considering the arrested sexual development that is understood to be normal in the male population, and considering the numbers of men who are pimps, procurers, members of slavery gangs, corrupt officials participating in this traffic, owners, operators, employees of brothels and lodging and entertainment facilities, pornography purveyors, associated with prostitution, wife beaters, child molesters, incest perpetrators, johns (tricks) and rapists, one cannot but be momentarily stunned by the enormous male population engaging in female sexual slavery. The huge number of men engaged in these practices should be cause for declaration of an international emergency, a crisis in sexual violence. But what should be cause for alarm is instead accepted as normal sexual intercourse.[41]

Susan Cavin, in a rich and provocative, if highly speculative, dissertation, suggests that patriarchy becomes possible when the original female band, which includes children but ejects adolescent males, becomes invaded and outnumbered by males; that not patriarchal marriage, but the rape of the mother by the son, becomes the first act of male domination. The entering wedge, or leverage, which allows this to happen is not just a simple change in sex ratios; it is also the mother-child bond, manipulated by adolescent males in order to remain within the matrix past the age of exclusion. Maternal affection is used to establish male right of sexual access, which, however, must ever after be held by force (or through control of consciousness) since the original deep adult bonding is that of woman for woman.[42] I find this hypothesis extremely suggestive, since one form of false consciousness which serves compulsory heterosexuality is the maintenance of a mother-son relationship between women and men, including the demand that women provide maternal solace, nonjudgmental nurturing, and compassion for their harassers, rapists, and batterers (as well as for men who passively vampirize them).

But whatever its origins, when we look hard and clearly at the extent and elaboration of measures designed to keep women within a male sexual purlieu, it becomes an inescapable question whether the issue feminists have to address is not simple "gender inequality" nor the domination of culture by males nor mere "taboos against homosexuality," but the enforcement of heterosexuality for women as a means of assuring male right of physical, economic, and emotional access.[43] One of many means of enforcement is, of course, the rendering invisible of the lesbian possibility, an engulfed continent which rises fragmentedly into view from time to time only to become submerged again. Feminist research and theory that contribute to lesbian invisibility or marginality are actually working against the liberation and empowerment of women as a group.[44]

The assumption that "most women are innately heterosexual" stands as a theoretical and political stumbling block for feminism. It remains a tenable assumption partly because lesbian existence has been written out of history or catalogued under disease, partly because it has been treated as exceptional rather than intrinsic, partly because to acknowledge that for women heterosexuality may not be a "preference" at all but something that has had to be imposed, managed, organized, propagandized, and maintained by force is an immense step to take if you consider yourself freely and "innately" heterosexual. Yet the failure to examine heterosexuality as an institution is like failing to admit that the economic system called capitalism or the caste system of racism is maintained by a variety of forces, including both physical violence and false consciousness. To take the step of questioning heterosexuality as a "preference" or "choice" for women—and to do the intellectual and emotional work that follows—will call for a special quality of courage in heterosexually identified feminists, but I think the rewards will be great: a freeing-up of thinking, the exploring of new paths, the shattering of another great silence, new clarity in personal relationships.

III

I have chosen to use the terms *lesbian existence* and *lesbian continuum* because the word *lesbianism* has a clinical and limiting ring. *Lesbian existence* suggests both the fact of the historical presence of lesbians and our continuing creation of the meaning of that existence. I mean the term *lesbian continuum* to include a range—through each woman's life and throughout history—of woman-identified experience, not simply the fact that a woman has had or consciously desired genital sexual experience with another woman. If we expand it to embrace many more forms of primary intensity between and among women, including the sharing of a rich inner life, the bonding against male tyranny, the giving and receiving of practical and political support, if we can also hear it in such associations as *marriage resistance* and the "haggard" behavior identified by Mary Daly (obsolete meanings: "intractable," "willful," "wanton," and "unchaste," "a woman reluctant to yield to wooing"),[45] we begin to grasp breadths of female history and psychology which have lain out of reach as a consequence of limited, mostly clinical, definitions of *lesbianism*.

Lesbian existence comprises both the breaking of a taboo and the rejection of a compulsory way of life. It is also a direct or indirect attack on male right of access to women. But it is more than these, although we may first begin to perceive it as a form of naysaying to patriarchy, an act of resistance. It has, of course, included isolation, self-hatred, breakdown, alcoholism, suicide, and intrawoman violence; we romanticize at our peril what it means to love and act against the grain, and under heavy penalties; and lesbian existence has been lived (unlike, say, Jewish or Catholic existence) without access to any knowledge of a tradition, a continuity, a social underpinning. The destruction of records and memorabilia and letters documenting the realities of lesbian existence must be taken very seriously as a means of keeping heterosexuality compulsory for women, since what has been kept from our knowledge is joy, sensuality, courage, and community, as well as guilt, self-betrayal, and pain.[46]

Lesbians have historically been deprived of a political existence through "inclusion" as female versions of male homosexuality. To equate lesbian existence with male homosexuality because each is stigmatized is to erase female reality once again. Part of the history of lesbian existence is, obviously, to be found where lesbians, lacking a coherent female community, have shared a kind of social life and common cause with homosexual men. But there are differences: women's lack of economic and cultural privilege relative to men; qualitative differences in female and male relationships—for example, the patterns of anonymous sex among male homosexuals, and the pronounced ageism in male homosexual standards of sexual attractiveness. I perceive the lesbian experience as being, like motherhood, a profoundly *female* experience, with particular oppressions, meanings, and potentialities we cannot comprehend as long as we simply bracket it with other sexually stigmatized existences. Just as the term *parenting* serves to conceal the particular and significant reality of being a parent who is actually a mother, the term *gay* may serve the purpose of blurring the very outlines we need to discern, which are of crucial value for feminism and for the freedom of women as a group.[47]

As the term *lesbian* has been held to limiting, clinical associations in its patriarchal definition, female friendship and comradeship have been set apart from the erotic, thus limiting the erotic itself. But as we deepen and broaden the range of what we define as lesbian existence, as we delineate a lesbian continuum, we begin to discover the erotic in female terms: as that which is unconfined to any single part of the body or solely to the body itself; as an energy not only diffuse but, as Audre Lorde has described it, omnipresent in "the sharing of joy, whether physical, emotional, psychic," and in the sharing of work; as the empowering joy which "makes us less willing to accept powerlessness, or those other supplied states of being which are not native to me, such as resignation, despair, self-effacement, depression, self-denial."[48] In another context, writing of women and work, I quoted the autobiographical passage in which the poet H.D. described how her friend Bryher supported her in persisting with the visionary experience which was to shape her mature work:

> I knew that this experience, this writing-on-the-wall before me, could not be shared with anyone except the girl who stood so bravely there beside me. This girl said without hesitation, "Go on." It was she really who had the detachment and integrity of the Pythoness of Delphi. But it was I, battered and dissociated... who was seeing the pictures, and who was

reading the writing or granted the inner vision. Or perhaps, in some sense, we were "seeing" it together, for without her, admittedly, I could not have gone on.[49]

If we consider the possibility that all women—from the infant suckling at her mother's breast, to the grown woman experiencing orgasmic sensations while suckling her own child, perhaps recalling her mother's milk smell in her own, to two women, like Virginia Woolf's Chloe and Olivia, who share a laboratory,[50] to the woman dying at ninety, touched and handled by women—exist on a lesbian continuum, we can see ourselves as moving in and out of this continuum, whether we identify ourselves as lesbian or not.

We can then connect aspects of woman identification as diverse as the impudent, intimate girl friendships of eight or nine year olds and the banding together of those women of the twelfth and fifteenth centuries known as Beguines who "shared houses, rented to one another, bequeathed houses to their room-mates... in cheap subdivided houses in the artisans' area of town," who "practiced Christian virtue on their own, dressing and living simply and not associating with men," who earned their livings as spinsters, bakers, nurses, or ran schools for young girls, and who managed—until the Church forced them to disperse—to live independent both of marriage and of conventual restrictions.[51] It allows us to connect these women with the more celebrated "Lesbians" of the women's school around Sappho of the seventh century B.C., with the secret sororities and economic networks reported among African women, and with the Chinese marriage-resistance sisterhoods—communities of women who refused marriage or who, if married, often refused to consummate their marriages and soon left their husbands, the only women in China who were not footbound and who, Agnes Smedley tells us, welcomed the births of daughters and organized successful women's strikes in the silk mills.[52] It allows us to connect and compare disparate individual instances of marriage resistance: for example, the strategies available to Emily Dickinson, a nineteenth-century white woman genius, with the strategies available to Zora Neale Hurston, a twentieth-century Black woman genius. Dickinson never married, had tenuous intellectual friendships with men, lived self-convented in her genteel father's house in Amherst, and wrote a lifetime of passionate letters to her sister-in-law Sue Gilbert and a smaller group of such letters to her friend Kate Scott Anthon. Hurston married twice but soon left each husband, scrambled her way from Florida to Harlem to Columbia University to Haiti and finally back to Florida, moved in and out of white patronage and poverty, professional success, and failure; her survival relationships were all with women, beginning with her mother. Both of these women in their vastly different circumstances were marriage resisters, committed to their own work and selfhood, and were later characterized as "apolitical." Both were drawn to men of intellectual quality; for both of them women provided the ongoing fascination and sustenance of life.

If we think of heterosexuality as *the* natural emotional and sensual inclination for women, lives such as these are seen as deviant, as pathological, or as emotionally and sensually deprived. Or, in more recent and permissive jargon, they are banalized as "life styles." And the work of such women, whether merely the daily work of individual or collective survival and resistance or the work of the writer, the activist, the reformer, the anthropologist, or the artist—the work of self-creation—is undervalued, or seen as the bitter fruit of "penis envy" or the sublimation of repressed eroticism or the meaningless rant of a "man-hater." But when we turn the lens of vision and consider the degree to which and the methods whereby heterosexual "preference" has actually been imposed on women, not only can we understand differently the meaning of individual lives and work, but we can begin to recognize a central fact of women's history: that women have always resisted male tyranny. A feminism of action, often though not always without a theory, has constantly re-emerged in every culture and in every period. We can then begin to study women's struggle against powerlessness, women's radical rebellion, not just in male-defined "concrete revolutionary situations"[53] but in all the situations male ideologies have not perceived as revolutionary— for example, the refusal of some women to produce children, aided at great risk by other women;[54] the refusal to produce a higher standard of living and leisure for men (Leghorn and Parker show how both are part of women's unacknowledged, unpaid, and ununionized economic contribution). We can no longer have patience with Dinnerstein's view that women have simply collaborated with men in the "sexual arrangements" of history. We begin to observe behavior, both in history and in individual biography, that has hitherto been invisible or misnamed, behavior which often constitutes, given the limits of the counterforce exerted in a given time and place, radical rebellion. And we can connect these rebellions and the necessity for them with the physical passion of woman for woman which is central to lesbian existence: the erotic sensuality which has been, precisely, the most violently erased fact of female experience.

Heterosexuality has been both forcibly and subliminally imposed on women. Yet everywhere women have resisted it, often at the cost of physical torture, imprisonment, psychosurgery, social ostracism, and extreme poverty. "Compulsory heterosexuality" was named as one of the "crimes against women" by the Brussels International Tribunal on Crimes against Women in 1976. Two pieces of testimony from two very different cultures reflect the degree to which persecution of lesbians is a global practice here and now. A report from Norway relates:

> A lesbian in Oslo was in a heterosexual marriage that didn't work, so she started taking tranquillizers and ended up at the health sanatorium for treatment and rehabilitation.... The moment she said in family group therapy that she believed she was a lesbian, the doctor told her she was not. He knew from "looking into her eyes," he said. She had the eyes of a woman who wanted sexual intercourse with her husband. So she was subjected to so-called "couch therapy." She was put into a comfortably heated room, naked, on a bed, and for an hour her husband was to...try to excite her sexually....The idea was that the touching was always to end with sexual intercourse. She felt stronger and stronger aversion. She threw up and sometimes ran out of the room to avoid this "treatment." The more strongly she asserted that she was a lesbian, the more violent the forced heterosexual intercourse became. This treatment went on for about six months. She escaped from the hospital, but she was brought back. Again she escaped. She has not been there since. In the end she realized that she had been subjected to forcible rape for six months.

and from Mozambique:

> I am condemned to a life of exile because I will not deny that I am a lesbian, that my primary commitments are, and will always be to other women. In the new Mozambique, lesbianism is considered a left-over from colonialism and decadent Western civilization. Lesbians are sent to rehabilitation camps to learn through self-criticism the correct line about themselves....If I am forced to denounce my own love for women, if I therefore denounce myself, I could go back to Mozambique and join forces in the exciting and hard struggle of rebuilding a nation, including the struggle for the emancipation of Mozambiquan women. As it is, I either risk the rehabilitation camps, or remain in exile.[55]

Nor can it be assumed that women like those in Carroll Smith-Rosenberg's study, who married, stayed married, yet dwelt in a profoundly female emotional and passional world, "preferred" or "chose" heterosexuality. Women have married because it was necessary, in order to survive economically, in order to have children who would not suffer economic deprivation or social ostracism, in order to remain respectable, in order to do what was expected of women, because coming out of "abnormal" childhoods they wanted to feel "normal" and because heterosexual romance has been represented as the great female adventure, duty, and fulfillment. We may faithfully or ambivalently have obeyed the institution, but our feelings—and our sensuality—have not been tamed or contained within it. There is no statistical documentation of the numbers of lesbians who have remained in heterosexual marriages for most of their lives. But in a letter to the early lesbian publication *The Ladder*, the playwright Lorraine Hansberry had this to say:

> I suspect that the problem of the married woman who would prefer emotional-physical relationships with other women is proportionally much higher than a similar statistic for men. (A statistic surely no one will ever really have.) This because the estate of woman being what it is, how could we ever begin to guess the numbers of women who are not prepared to risk a life alien to what they have been taught all their lives to believe was their "natural" destiny—AND—their only expectation for ECONOMIC security. It seems to be that this is why the question has an immensity that it does not have for male homosexuals.... A woman of strength and honesty may, if she chooses, sever her marriage and marry a new male mate and society will be upset that the divorce rate is rising so—but there are few places in the United States, in any event, where she will be anything remotely akin to an "outcast." Obviously this is not true for a woman who would end her marriage to take up life with another woman.[56]

This *double life*—this apparent acquiescence to an institution founded on male interest and prerogative—has been characteristic of female experience: in motherhood and in many kinds of heterosexual behavior, including the rituals of courtship; the pretense of asexuality by the nineteenth-century wife; the simulation of orgasm by the prostitute, the courtesan, the twentieth-century "sexually liberated" woman.

Meridel LeSueur's documentary novel of the depression, *The Girl*, is arresting as a study of female double life. The protagonist, a waitress in a St. Paul working-class speakeasy, feels herself passionately attracted to the young man Butch, but her survival relationships are with Clara, an older waitress and prostitute, with Belle, whose husband owns the bar, and with Amelia, a union activist. For Clara and Belle and the unnamed protagonist, sex with men is in one sense an escape from the bedrock misery of daily life, a flare of intensity in the gray, relentless, often brutal web of day-to-day existence:

> It was like he was a magnet pulling me. It was exciting and powerful and frightening. He was after me too and when he found me I would run, or be petrified, just standing in front of him like a zany. And he told me not to be wandering with Clara to the Marigold where we danced with strangers. He said he would knock the shit out of me. Which made me shake and tremble, but it was better than being a husk full of suffering and not knowing why.[57]

Throughout the novel the theme of double life emerges; Belle reminisces about her marriage to the bootlegger Hoinck:

> You know, when I had that black eye and said I hit it on the cupboard, well he did it the bastard, and then he says don't tell anybody.... He's nuts, that's what he is, nuts, and I don't see why I live with him, why I put up with him a minute on this earth. But listen kid, she said, I'm telling you something. She looked at me and her face was wonderful. She said, Jesus Christ, Goddam him I love him that's why I'm hooked like this all my life, Goddam him I love him.[58]

After the protagonist has her first sex with Butch, her women friends care for her bleeding, give her whiskey, and compare notes.

> My luck, the first time and I got into trouble. He gave me a little money and I come to St. Paul where for ten bucks they'd stick a huge vet's needle into you and you start it and then you were on your own.... I never had no child. I've just had Hoinck to mother, and a hell of a child he is.[59]

> Later they made me go back to Clara's room to lie down....Clara lay down beside me and put her arms around me and wanted me to tell her about it but she wanted to tell about herself. She said she started it when she was twelve with a bunch of boys in an old shed. She said nobody had paid any attention to her before and she became very popular.... They like it so much, she said, why shouldn't you give it to them and get presents and attention? I never cared anything for it and neither did my mama. But it's the only thing you got that's valuable.[60]

Sex is thus equated with attention from the male, who is charismatic though brutal, infantile, or unreliable. Yet it is the women who make life endurable for each other, give physical affection without causing pain, share, advise, and stick by each other. *(I am trying to find my strength through women—without my friends, I could not survive.)* LeSueur's *The Girl* parallels Toni Morrison's remarkable *Sula*, another revelation of female double life:

> Nel was the one person who had wanted nothing from her, who had accepted all aspects of her.... Nel was one of the reasons Sula had drifted back to Medallion.... The men...had merged into one large personality: the same language of love, the same entertainments of love, the same cooling of love. Whenever she introduced her private thoughts into their rubbings and goings, they hooded their eyes. They taught her nothing but love tricks, shared nothing but worry, gave nothing but money. She had been looking all along for a friend, and it took her a while to discover that a lover was not a comrade and could never be—for a woman.

But Sula's last thought at the second of her death is "Wait'll I tell Nel." And after Sula's death, Nel looks back on her own life:

> "All that time, all that time, I thought I was missing Jude." And the loss pressed down on her chest and came up into her throat. "We was girls together," she said as though explaining something. "O Lord, Sula," she cried, "Girl, girl, girlgirlgirl!" It was a fine cry—loud and long—but it had no bottom and it had no top, just circles and circles of sorrow.[61]

The Girl and *Sula* are both novels which examine what I am calling the lesbian continuum, in contrast to the shallow or sensational "lesbian scenes" in recent commercial fiction.[62] Each shows us woman identification untarnished (till the end of LeSueur's novel) by romanticism; each depicts the competition of heterosexual compulsion for women's attention, the diffusion and frustration of female bonding that might, in a more conscious form, reintegrate love and power.

IV

Woman identification is a source of energy, a potential springhead of female power, curtailed and contained under the institution of heterosexuality. The denial of reality and visibility to women's passion for women, women's choice of women as allies, life companions, and community, the forcing of such relationships into dissimulation and their disintegration under intense pressure have meant an incalculable loss to the power of all women *to change the social relations of the sexes, to liberate ourselves and each other*. The lie of compulsory female heterosexuality today afflicts not just feminist scholarship, but every profession, every reference work, every curriculum, every organizing attempt, every relationship or conversation over which it hovers. It creates, specifically, a profound falseness, hypocrisy, and hysteria in the heterosexual dialogue, for every heterosexual relationship is lived in the queasy strobe light of that lie. However we choose to identify ourselves, however we find ourselves labeled, it flickers across and distorts our lives.[63]

The lie keeps numberless women psychologically trapped, trying to fit mind, spirit, and sexuality into a prescribed script because they cannot look beyond the parameters of the acceptable. It pulls on the energy of such women even as it drains the energy of "closeted" lesbians—the energy exhausted in the double life. The lesbian trapped in the "closet," the woman imprisoned in prescriptive ideas of the "normal" share the pain of blocked options, broken connections, lost access to self-definition freely and powerfully assumed.

The lie is many-layered. In Western tradition, one layer—the romantic—asserts that women are inevitably, even if rashly and tragically, drawn to men; that even when that attraction is suicidal (e.g., *Tristan and Isolde*, Kate Chopin's *The Awakening*), it is still an organic imperative. In the tradition of the social sciences it asserts that primary love between the sexes is "normal"; that women *need* men as social and economic protectors, for adult sexuality, and for psychological completion; that the heterosexually constituted family is the basic social unit; that women who do not attach their primary intensity to men must be, in functional terms, condemned to an even more devastating outsiderhood than their outsiderhood as women. Small wonder that lesbians are reported to be a more hidden population than male homosexuals. The Black lesbian-feminist critic Lorraine Bethel, writing on Zora Neale Hurston, remarks that for a Black woman—already twice an outsider—to choose to assume still another "hated identity" is problematic indeed. Yet the lesbian continuum has been a life line for Black women both in Africa and the United States.

> Black women have a long tradition of bonding together...in a Black/women's community that has been a source of vital survival information, psychic and emotional support for us. We have a distinct Black woman-identified folk culture based on our experiences as Black women in this society; symbols, language and modes of expression that are specific to the realities of our lives.... Because Black women were rarely among those Blacks and females who gained access to literary and other acknowledged forms of artistic expression, this Black female bonding and Black woman-identification has often been hidden and unrecorded except in the individual lives of Black women through our own memories of our particular Black female tradition.[64]

Another layer of the lie is the frequently encountered implication that women turn to women out of hatred for men. Profound skepticism, caution, and righteous paranoia about men may indeed be part of any healthy woman's response to the misogyny of male-dominated culture, to the forms assumed by "normal" male sexuality, and to *the failure even of "sensitive" or "political" men to perceive or find these troubling.* Lesbian existence is also represented as mere refuge from male abuses, rather than as an electric and empowering charge between women. One of the most frequently quoted literary passages on lesbian relationship is that in which Colette's Renée, in *The Vagabond*, describes "the melancholy and touching image of two weak creatures who have perhaps found shelter in each other's arms, there to sleep and weep, safe from man who is often cruel, and there to taste *better than any pleasure, the bitter happiness of feeling themselves akin, frail and forgotten* [emphasis added]."[65] Colette is often considered a lesbian writer. Her popular reputation has, I think, much to do with the fact that she writes about lesbian existence as if for a male audience; her earliest "lesbian" novels, the Claudine series, were written under compulsion for her husband and published under both their names. At all events, except for her writings on her mother, Colette is a less reliable source on the lesbian continuum than, I would think, Charlotte Brontë, who understood that while women may, indeed must, be one another's allies, mentors, and comforters in the female struggle for survival, there is quite extraneous delight in each other's company and attraction to each others' minds and character, which attend a recognition of each others's strengths.

By the same token, we can say that there is a *nascent* feminist political content in the act of choosing a woman lover or life partner in the face of institutionalized heterosexuality.[66] But for lesbian existence to realize this political content in an ultimately liberating form, the erotic choice must deepen and expand into conscious woman identification—into lesbian feminism.

The work that lies ahead, of unearthing and describing what i call here "lesbian existence," is potentially liberating for all women. It is work that must assuredly move beyond the limits of white and middle-class Western Women's Studies to examine women's lives, work, and groupings within every racial, ethnic, and political structure. There are differences, moreover, between "lesbian existence" and the "lesbian continuum," differences we can discern even in the movement of our own lives. The lesbian continuum, I suggest, needs delineation in light of the "double life" of women, not only women self-described as heterosexual but also of self-described lesbians. We need a far more exhaustive account of the forms the double life has assumed. Historians need to ask at every point how heterosexuality as institution has been organized and maintained through the female wage scale, the enforcement of middle-class women's "leisure," the glamorization of so-called sexual liberation, the withholding of education from women, the imagery of "high art" and popular culture, the mystification of the "personal" sphere, and much else. We need an economics which comprehends the institution of heterosexuality, with its doubled workload for women and its sexual divisions of labor, as the most idealized of economic relations.

The question inevitably will arise: Are we then to condemn all heterosexual relationships, including those which are least oppressive? I believe this question, though often heartfelt, is the wrong question here. We have been stalled in a maze of false dichotomies which prevents our apprehending the institution as a whole: "good" versus "bad" marriages; "marriage for love" versus arranged marriage; "liberated" sex versus prostitution; heterosexual intercourse versus rape; *Liebeschmerz* versus humiliation and dependency. Within the institution exist, of course, qualitative differences of experience; but the absence of choice remains the great unacknowledged reality, and in the absence of choice, women will remain dependent upon the chance or luck of particular relationships and will have no collective power to determine the meaning and place of sexuality in their lives. As we address the institution itself, moreover, we begin to perceive a history of female resistance which has never fully understood itself because it has been so fragmented, miscalled, erased. It will require a courageous grasp of the politics and economics, as well as the cultural propaganda, of heterosexuality to carry us beyond individual cases or diversified group situations into the complex kind of overview needed to undo the power men everywhere wield over women, power which has become a model for every other form of exploitation and illegitimate control.

AFTERWORD

In 1980, Ann Snitow, Christine Stansell, and Sharon Thompson, three Marxist-feminist activists and scholars, sent out a call for papers for an anthology on the politics of sexuality. Having just finished writing "Compulsory Heterosexuality" for *Signs*, I sent them that manuscript and asked them to consider it. Their anthology, *Powers of Desire*, was published by the Monthly Review Press New Feminist Library in 1983 and included my paper. During the intervening period, the four of us were in correspondence, but I was able to take only limited advantage of this dialogue due to ill health and resulting surgery. With their permission, I reprint here excerpts from that correspondence as a way of indicating that my essay should be read as one contribution to a long exploration in progress, not as my own "last word" on sexual politics. I also refer interested readers to *Powers of Desire* itself.

Dear Adrienne,

…In one of our first letters, we told you that we were finding parameters of left-wing/feminist sexual discourse to be far broader than we imagined. Since then, we have perceived what we believe to be a crisis in the feminist movement about sex, an intensifying debate (although not always an explicit one), and a questioning of assumptions once taken for granted. While we fear the link between sex and violence, as do Women Against Pornography, we wish we better understood its sources in ourselves as well as in men. In the Reagan era, we can hardly afford to romanticize any old norm of a virtuous and moral sexuality.

In your piece, you are asking the question, what would women choose in a world where patriarchy and capitalism did *not* rule? We agree with you that heterosexuality is an institution created between these grind stones, but we don't conclude, therefore, that it is entirely a male creation. You only allow for female historical agency insofar as women exist on the lesbian continuum while we would argue that women's history, like men's history, is created out of a dialectic of necessity and choice.

All three of us (hence one lesbian, two heterosexual women) had questions about your use of the term "false consciousness" for women's heterosexuality. In general, we think the false-consciousness model can blind us to the necessities and desires that comprise the lives of the oppressed. It can also lead to the too easy denial of others' experience when that experience is different from our own. We posit, rather, a complex social model in which all erotic life is a continuum, one which therefore includes relations with men.

Which brings us to this metaphor of the continuum. We know you are a poet, not an historian, and we look forward to reading your metaphors all our lives—and standing straighter as feminists, as women, for having read them. But the metaphor of the lesbian continuum is open to all kinds of misunderstandings, and these sometimes have odd political effects. For example, Sharon reports that at a recent meeting around the abortion-rights struggle, the notions of continuum arose in the discussion several times and underwent divisive transformation. Overall, the notion that two ways of being existed on the same continuum was interpreted to mean that those two ways were the *same*. The sense of range and gradation that your description evokes disappeared. Lesbianism and female friendship became exactly the same thing. Similarly, heterosexuality and rape became the same. In one of several versions of the continuum that evolved, a slope was added, like so:

This sloped continuum brought its proponents to the following conclusion: An appropriate, workable abortion-rights strategy is to inform all women that heterosexual penetration is rape, whatever their subjective experience to the contrary. All women will immediately recognize the truth of this and opt for the alternative of nonpenetration. The abortion-rights struggle will thus be simplified into a struggle against coercive sex and its consequences (since no enlightened woman would voluntarily undergo penetration unless her object was procreation—a peculiarly Catholic-sounding view).

The proponents of this strategy were young women who have worked hard in the abortion-rights movement for the past two or more years. They are inexperienced but they are dedicated. For this reason, we take their reading of your work seriously. We don't think, however, that it comes solely, or even at all, from the work itself. As likely a source is the tendency to dichotomize that has plagued the women's movement. The source of that tendency is harder to trace.

In that regard, the hints in "Compulsory" about the double life of women intrigue us. You define the double life as "the apparent acquiescence to an institution founded on male interest and prerogative." But that definition doesn't really explain your other references—to, for instance, the "intense mixture" of love and anger in lesbian relationships and to the peril of romanticizing what it means "to love and act against the grain." We think these comments raise extremely important issues for feminists right now; the problem of division and anger among us needs airing and analysis. Is this, by any chance, the theme of a piece you have in the works?

…We would still love it if we could have a meeting with you in the next few months. Any chance?… Greetings and support from us—in all your undertakings.

We send love,
Sharon, Chris, and Ann

New York City
April 19, 1981

Dear Ann, Chris, and Sharon,

…It's good to be back in touch with you, you who have been so unfailingly patient, generous, and persistent. Above all, it's important to me that you know that ill health, not a withdrawal because of political differences, delayed my writing back to you….

"False consciousness" can, I agree, be used as a term of dismissal for any thinking we don't like or adhere to. But, as I tried to illustrate in some detail, there is a real, identifiable system of heterosexual propaganda, of defining women as existing for the sexual use of men, which goes beyond "sex role" or "gender" stereotyping or "sexist imagery" to include a vast number of verbal and nonverbal messages. And this I call "control of consciousness." The possibility of a woman who does not exist sexually for men—the lesbian possibility—is buried, erased, occluded, distorted, misnamed, and driven underground. The feminist books—Chodorow, Dinnerstein, Ehrenreich and English, and others—which I discuss at the beginning of my essay contribute to this invalidation and erasure, and as such are part of the problem.

My essay is founded on the belief that we all think from within the limits of certain solipsisms—usually linked with privilege, racial, cultural, and economic as well as sexual—which present themselves as "the universal," "the way things are," "all women," etc., etc. I wrote it equally out of the belief that in becoming conscious of our solipsisms we have certain kinds of choices, that we can and must re-educate ourselves. I never have maintained that heterosexual feminists are walking about in a state of "brainwashed" false consciousness.

Nor have such phrases as "sleeping with the enemy" seemed to me either profound or useful. *Homophobia* is too diffuse a term and does not go very far in helping us identify and talk about the sexual solipsism of heterosexual feminism. In this paper I was trying to ask heterosexual feminists to examine their experience of heterosexuality critically and antagonistically, to critique the institution of which they are a part, to struggle with the norm and its implications for women's freedom, to become more open to the considerable resources offered by the lesbian-feminist perspective, to refuse to settle for the personal privilege and solution of the individual "good relationship" within the institution of heterosexuality.

As regards "female historical agency," I wanted, precisely, to suggest that the victim model is insufficient; that there *is* a history of female agency and choice which has actually challenged aspects of male supremacy; that, like male supremacy, these can be found in many different cultures.... It's not that I think all female agency has been solely and avowedly lesbian. But by erasing lesbian existence from female history, from theory, from literary criticism ... from feminist approaches to economic structure, ideas about "the family," etc., an enormous amount of female agency is kept unavailable, hence unusable. I wanted to demonstrate that that kind of obliteration continues to be acceptable in seriously regarded feminist texts. What surprised me in the responses to my essay, including your notes, is how almost every aspect of it has been considered, except this—to me—central one. I was taking a position which was neither lesbian/separatist in the sense of dismissing heterosexual women nor a "gay civil rights" plea for...openness to lesbianism as an "option" or an "alternate life style." I was urging that lesbian *existence* has been an unrecognized and unaffirmed claiming by women of their sexuality, thus a pattern of resistance, thus also a kind of borderline position from which to analyze and challenge the relationship of heterosexuality to male supremacy. And that lesbian existence, when recognized, demands a conscious restructuring of feminist analysis and criticism, not just a token reference or two.

I certainly agree with you that the term *lesbian continuum* can be misused. It was, in the example you report of the abortion-rights meeting, though I would think anyone who had read my work from *Of Woman Born* onward would know that my position on abortion and sterilization abuse is more complicated than that. My own problem with the phrase is that it can be, is, used by women who have not yet begun to examine the privileges and solipsisms of heterosexuality, as a safe way to describe their felt connections with women, without having to share in the risks and threats of lesbian existence. What I had thought to delineate rather complexly as a continuum has begun to sound more like "life-style shopping." *Lesbian continuum*—the phrase—came from a desire to allow for the greatest possible variation of female-identified experience, while paying a different kind of respect to *lesbian existence*—the traces and knowledge of women who have made their primary erotic and emotional choices for women. If I were writing the paper today, I would still want to make this distinction, but would put more caveats around *lesbian continuum*. I fully agree with you that Smith-Rosenberg's "female world" is not a social ideal, enclosed as it is within prescriptive middle-class heterosexuality and marriage.

My own essay could have been stronger had it drawn on more of the literature by Black women toward which Toni Morrison's *Sula* inevitably pointed me. In reading a great deal more of Black women's fiction I began to perceive a different set of valences from those found in white women's fiction for the most part: a different quest for the woman hero, a different relationship both to sexuality with men and to female loyalty and bonding....

You comment briefly on your reactions to some of the radical-feminist works I cited in my first footnote.[67] I am myself critical of some of them even as I found them vitally useful. What most of them share is a taking seriously of misogyny—of organized, institutionalized, normalized hostility and violence against women. I feel no "hierarchy of oppressions" is needed in order for us to take misogyny as seriously as we take racism, anti-Semitism, imperialism. To take misogyny seriously needn't mean that we perceive women merely as victims, without responsibilities or choices; it does mean recognizing the "necessity" in that "dialectic of necessity and choice"—identifying, describing, refusing to turn aside our eyes. I think that some of the apparent reductiveness, or even obsessiveness, of some white radical-feminist theory derives from racial and/or class solipsism, but also from the immense effort of trying to render woman hating visible amid so much denial....

Finally, as to poetry and history: I want both in my life; I need to see through both. If metaphor can be misconstrued, history can also lead to misconstrual when it obliterates acts of resistance or rebellion, wipes out transformational models, or sentimentalizes power relationships. I know you know this. I believe we are all trying to think and write out of our best consciences, our most open consciousness. I expect that quality in this book which you are editing, and look forward with anticipation to the thinking—and the actions—toward which it may take us.

In sisterhood,
Adrienne

Montague, Massachusetts,
November 1981

NOTES

1. See, for example, Paula Gunn Allen, *The Sacred Hoop: Recovering the Feminine in American Indian Traditions* (Boston: Beacon, 1986); Beth Brant, ed., *A Gathering of Spirit: Writing and Art by North American Indian Women* (Montpelier, Vt: Sinister Wisdom Books, 1984); Gloria Anzaldúa and Cherríe Moraga, eds., *This Bridge Called My Back: Writings by Radical Women of Color* (Watertown, Mass.: Persephone, 1981; distributed by Kitchen Table/Women of Color Press, Albany, N.Y.); J. R. Roberts, *Black Lesbians: An Annotated Bibliography* (Tallahassee, Fla.: Naiad, 1981); Barbara Smith, ed. *Home Girls: A Black Feminist Anthology* (Albany, N.Y.: Kitchen Table/Women of Color Press, 1984). As Lorraine Bethel and Barbara Smith pointed out in *Conditions 5: The Black Women's Issue* (1980), a great deal of fiction by Black women depicts primary relationships between women. I would like to cite here the work of Ama Ata Aidoo, Toni Cade Bambara, Buchi Emecheta, Bessie Head, Zora Neale Hurston, Alice Walker. Donna Allegra, Red Jordan Arobateau, Audre Lorde, Ann Allen Shockley, among others, write directly as Black lesbians. For fiction by other lesbians of color, see Elly Bulkin, ed., *Lesbian Fiction: An Anthology* (Watertown, Mass.: Persephone, 1981).

   See also, for accounts of contemporary Jewish-lesbian existence, Evelyn Torton Beck, ed., *Nice Jewish Girls: A Lesbian Anthology* (Watertown, Mass.: Persephone, 1982; distributed by Crossing Press, Trumansburg, N.Y 14886); Alice Bloch, *Lifetime Guarantee* (Watertown, Mass.: Persephone, 1982); and Melanie Kaye-Kantrowitz and Irena Klepfisz, eds., *The Tribe of Dina: A Jewish Women's Anthology* (Montpelier, Vt.: Sinister Wisdom Books, 1986).

The earliest formulation that I know of heterosexuality as an institution was in the lesbian-feminist paper *The Furies,* founded in 1971. For a collection of articles from that paper, see Nancy Myron and Charlotte Bunch, eds., *Lesbianism and the Women's Movement* (Oakland, Calif.: Diana Press, 1975; distributed by Crossing Press, Trumansburg, N.Y. 14886).

2. Alice Rossi, "Children and Work in the Lives of Women," paper delivered at the University of Arizona, Tuscon, February 1976.

3. Doris Lessing, *The Golden Notebook,* 1962 (New York: Bantam, 1977), p. 480.

4. Nancy Chodorow, *The Reproduction of Mothering* (Berkeley: University of California Press, 1978); Dorothy Dinnerstein, *The Mermaid and the Minotaur: Sexual Arrangements and the Human Malaise* (New York: Harper & Row, 1976); Barbara Ehrenreich and Deirdre English, *For Her Own Good: 150 Years of the Experts' Advice to Women* (Garden City, N.Y.: Doubleday, Anchor, 1978); Jean Baker Miller, *Toward a New Psychology of Women* (Boston: Beacon, 1976).

5. I could have chosen many other serious and influential recent books, including anthologies, which would illustrate the same point: e.g., *Our Bodies, Ourselves,* the Boston Women's Health Book Collective's best seller (New York: Simon and Schuster, 1976), which devotes a separate (and inadequate) chapter to lesbians, but whose message is that heterosexuality is most women's life preference; Berenice Carroll, ed., *Liberating Women's History: Theoretical and Critical Essays* (Urbana: University of Illinois Press, 1976), which does not include even a token essay on the lesbian presence in history, though an essay by Linda Gordon, Persis Hunt, *et al.* notes the use by male historians of "sexual deviance" as a category to discredit and dismiss Anna Howard Shaw, Jane Addams, and other feminists ("Historical Phallacies: Sexism in American Historical Writing"); and Renate Bridenthal and Claudia Koonz, eds., *Becoming Visible: Women in European History* (Boston: Houghton Mifflin, 1977), which contains three mentions of male homosexuality but no materials that I have been able to locate on lesbians. Gerda Lerner, ed., *The Female Experience: An American Documentary* (Indianapolis: Bobbs-Merril, 1977), contains an abridgment of two lesbian-feminist position papers from the contemporary movement but no other documentation of lesbian existence. Lerner does note in her preface, however, how the charge of deviance has been used to fragment women and discourage women's resistance. Linda Gordon, in *Woman's Body, Woman's Right: A Social History of Birth Control in America* (New York: Viking, Grossman, 1976), notes accurately that "it is not that feminism has produced more lesbians. There have always been many lesbians, despite the high levels of repression; and most lesbians experience their sexual preference as innate" (p. 410).

[A.R., 1986: I am glad to update the first annotation in this footnote. *"The New" Our Bodies, Ourselves* (New York: Simon and Schuster, 1984) contains an expanded chapter on "Loving Women: Lesbian Life and Relationships" and furthermore emphasizes *choices* for women throughout—in terms of sexuality, health care, family, politics, etc.]

6. Jonathan Katz, ed., *Gay American History: Lesbians and Gay Men in the U.S.A.* (New York: Thomas Y. Crowell, 1976).

7. Nancy Sahli, "Smashing Women's Relationships before the Fall," *Chrysalis: A Magazine of Women's Culture* 8 (1979): 17–27.

8. This is a book which I have publicly endorsed. I would still do so, though with the above caveat. It is only since beginning to write this article that I fully appreciated how enormous is the unasked question in Ehrenreich and English's book.

9. See, for example, Kathleen Barry, *Female Sexual Slavery* (Englewood Cliffs, N.J.: Prentice-Hall, 1979); Mary Daly, *Gyn/Ecology: The Metaethics of Radical Feminism* (Boston: Beacon, 1978); Susan Griffin, *Woman and Nature: The Roaring inside Her* (New York: Harper & Row, 1978); Diana Russell and Nicole van de Ven, eds., *Proceedings of the International Tribunal of Crimes against Women* (Millbrae, Calif.: Les Femmes, 1976); and Susan Brownmiller, *Against Our Will: Men, Women and Rape* (New York: Simon and Schuster, 1975); *Aegis: Magazine on Ending Violence against Women* (Feminist Alliance against Rape, P.O. Box 21033, Washington, D.C. 20009).

   [A.R., 1986: Work on both incest and on woman battering has appeared in the 1980s which I did not cite in the essay. See Florence Rush, *The Best-kept Secret* (New York: McGraw-Hill, 1980); Louise Armstrong, *Kiss Daddy Goodnight: A Speakout on Incest* (New York: Pocket Books, 1979); Sandra Butler, *Conspiracy of Silence: The Trauma of Incest* (San Francisco: New Glide, 1978); F. Delacoste and F. Newman, eds., *Fight Back!: Feminist Resistance to Male Violence* (Minneapolis: Cleis Press, 1981); Judy Freespirit, *Daddy's Girl: An Incest Survivor's Story* (Langlois, Ore.: Diaspora Distribution, 1982); Judith Herman, *Father-Daughter Incest* (Cambridge, Mass.: Harvard University Press, 1981); Toni McNaron and Yarrow Morgan, eds., *Voices in the Night: Women Speaking about Incest* (Minneapolis: Cleis Press, 1982); and Betsy Warrior's richly informative, multipurpose compilation of essays, statistics, listings, and facts, the *Battered Women's Directory* (formerly entitled *Working on Wife Abuse*), 8th ed. (Cambridge, Mass.: 1982).]

10. Dinnerstein, p. 272.

11. Chodorow, pp. 197–198.

12. Ibid, pp. 198–199.

13. Ibid, p. 200.

14. Kathleen Gough, "The Origin of the Family," in *Toward an Anthropology of women*, ed. Rayna [Rapp] Reiter (New York: Monthly Review Press, 1975), pp 69–70.

15. Barry, pp. 216–219.

16. Anna Demeter, *Legal Kidnapping* (Boston: Beacon, 1977), pp. xx, 126–128.

17. Daly, pp. 139–141, 163–165.

18. Barbara Ehrenreich and Deirdre English, *Witches, Midwives and Nurses: A History of Women Healers* (Old Westbury, N.Y.: Feminist Press, 1973); Andrea Dworkin, *Woman Hating* (New York: Dutton, 1974), pp. 118–154; Daly, pp. 178–222.

19. See Virginia Woolf, *A Room of One's Own* (London: Hogarth, 1929), and *id.*, *Three Guineas* (New York: Harcourt Brace, [1938] 1966); Tillie Olsen, *Silences* (Boston: Delacorte, 1978); Michelle Cliff, The Resonance of Interruption," *Chrysalis: A Magazine of Women's Culture* 8 (1979): 29–37.

20. Mary Daly, *Beyond God the Father* (Boston: Beacon, 1973), pp. 347–351; Olsen, pp. 22–46.

21. Daly, *Beyond God the Father*, p. 93.

22. Fran P. Hosken, "The Violence of Power: Genital Mutilation of Females," *Heresies: A Feminist Journal of Art and Politics* 6 (1979): 28–35; Russell and van de Ven, pp. 194–195.

   [A.R., 1986: See especially "Circumcision of Girls," in Nawal El Saadawi, *The Hidden Face of Eve: Women in the Arab World* (Boston: Beacon, 1982), pp. 33–43.]

23. Barry, pp. 163–164.

24. The issue of "lesbian sadomasochism" needs to be examined in terms of dominant cultures' teachings about the relation of sex and violence. I believe this to be another example of the "double life" of women.

25. Catharine A. MacKinnon, *Sexual Harassment of Working Women: A Case of Sex Discrimination* (New Haven, Conn.: Yale University Press, 1979), pp. 15–16.

26. Ibid, p.174.

27. Brownmiller, op. cit.

28. MacKinnon, p. 219. Susan Schecter writes: "The push for heterosexual union at whatever cost is so intense that... it has become a cultural force of its own that creates battering. The ideology of romantic love and its jealous possession of the partner as property provide the masquerade for what can become severe abuse" *(Aegis: Magazine on Ending Violence against Women* [July–August 1979]: 50–51).

29. MacKinnon, p. 298.

30. Ibid, p. 220.

31. Ibid, p. 221.

32. Barry, op. cit.
    [A.R., 1986: See also Kathleen Barry, Charlotte Bunch, and Shirley Castley, eds., *International Feminism: Networking against Female Sexual Slavery* (New York: International Women's Tribune Center, 1984)]

33. Barry, p. 33.

34. Ibid, p. 103.

35. Ibid, p. 5

36. Ibid, p. 100.
    [A.R., 1986: This statement has been taken as claiming that "all women are victims" purely and simply, or that "all heterosexuality equals sexual slavery." I would say, rather, that all women are affected, though differently, by dehumanizing attitudes and practices directed at women as a group.]

37. Ibid, p. 218.

38. Ibid, p. 140.

39. Ibid, p. 172.

40. Elsewhere I have suggested that male identification has been a powerful source of white women's racism and that it has often been women already seen as "disloyal" to male codes and systems who have actively battled against it (Adrienne Rich, "Disloyal to Civilization: Feminism, Racism, Gynephobia," in *On Lies, Secrets and Silence: Selected Prose, 1996–1978* [New York: W.W. Norton, 1979]).

41. Barry, p. 220.

42. Susan Cavin, "Lesbian Origins" (Ph.D. diss., Rutgers University, 1978), unpublished. ch. 6.
    [A.R. 1986: This dissertation was recently published as *Lesbian Origins* (San Francisco: Ism Press, 1986).]

43. For my perception of heterosexuality as an economic institution I am indebted to Lisa Leghorn and Katherine Parker, who allowed me to read the unpublished manuscript of their book *Woman's Worth: Sexual Economics and the World of Women* (London and Boston: Routledge & Kegan Paul, 1981).

44. I would suggest that lesbian existence has been most recognized and tolerated where it has resembled a "deviant" version of heterosexuality—e.g., where lesbians have, like Stein and Toklas, played heterosexual roles (or seemed to in public) and have been chiefly identified with male culture. See also Claude E. Schaeffer, "The Kuterai Female Berdache: Courier, Guide, Prophetess and Warrior," *Ethnohistory* 12, no. 3 (Summer 1965): 193–236. (Berdache: "an individual of a

definite physiological sex [m. or f.] who assumes the role and status of the opposite sex and who is viewed by the community as being of one sex physiologically but as having assumed the role and status of the opposite sex" [Schaeffer, p. 231].) Lesbian existence has also been relegated to an upper-class phenomenon, an elite decadence (as in the fascination with Paris salon lesbians such as Renée Vivien and Natalie Clifford Barney), to the obscuring of such "common women" as Judy Grahn depicts in her *The Work of a Common Woman* (Oakland, Calif.: Diana Press, 1978) and *True to Life Adventure Stories* (Oakland, Calif.: Diana Press, 1978).

45. Daly, *Gyn/Ecology*, p. 15.

46. "In a hostile world in which women are not supposed to survive except in relation with and in service to men, entire communities of women were simply erased. History trends to bury what it seeks to reject" (Blanche W. Cook, "'Women Alone Stir My Imagination': Lesbianism and the Cultural Tradition," *Signs: Journal of Women in Culture and Society* 4, no. 4 [Summer 1979]: 719–720). The Lesbian Herstory Archives in New York City is one attempt to preserve contemporary documents on lesbian existence—a project of enormous value and meaning, working against the continuing censorship and obliteration of relationships, networks, communities in other archives and elsewhere in the culture.

47. [A.R., 1986: The shared historical and spiritual "crossover" functions of lesbians and gay men in cultures past and present are traced by Judy Grahn in *Another Mother Tongue: Gay Words, Gay Worlds* (Boston: Beacon, 1984). I now think we have much to learn both from the uniquely female aspects of lesbian existence and from the complex "gay" identity we share with gay men.]

48. Audre Lorde, "Uses of the Erotic: The Erotic as Power," in *Sister Outsider* (Trumansburg, N.Y.: Crossing Press, 1984).

49. Adrienne Rich, "Conditions for Work: The Common World of Women," in *On Lies, Secrets, and Silence*, p. 209; H.D., *Tribute to Freud* (Oxford: Carcanet, 1971), pp. 50–54.

50. Woolf, *A Room of One's Own*, p. 126.

51. Gracia Clark, "The Beguines: A Mediaeval Women's Community," *Quest: A Feminist Quarterly* 1, no. 4 (1975): 73–80.

52. See Denise Paulmé, ed., *Women of Tropical Africa* (Berkeley: University of California Press, 1963), pp. 7, 266–267. Some of these sororities are described as "a kind of defensive syndicate against the male element," their aims being "to offer concerted resistance to an oppressive patriarchate," "independence in relation to one's husband and with regard to motherhood, mutual aid, satisfaction of personal revenge." See also Audre Lorde, "Scratching the Surface: Some Notes on Barriers to Women and Loving," in *Sister Outsider*, pp, 45–52; Marjorie Topley, "Marriage Resistance in Rural Kwangtung," in *Women in Chinese Society*, ed. M. Wolf and R. Witke (Stanford, Calif: Stanford University Press, 1978), pp. 67–89; Agnes Smedley, *Portraits of Chinese Women in Revolution*, ed. J. MacKinnon and S. MacKinnon (Old Westbury, NY.: Feminist Press, 1976), pp. 103–110.

53. See Rosalind Petchesky, "Dissolving the Hyphen: A Report on Marxist-Feminist Groups 1–5," in *Capitalist Patriarchy and the Case for Socialist Feminism*, ed. Zillah Eisenstein (New York: Monthly Review Press, 1979), p. 387.

54. [A.R., 1986: See Angelo Davis, *Women, Race and Class* (New York: Random House, 1981), p. 102; Orlando Patterson, *Slavery and Social Death: A Comparative Study* (Cambridge: Harvard University Press, 1982), p. 133.]

55. Russel and van de Ven, pp. 42–43, 56–57.

56. I am indebted to Jonathan Kate's *Gay American History* (*op. cit*) for bringing to my attention Hansberry's letters to *The Ladder* and to Barbara Grier for supplying me with copies of relevant pages from *The Ladder*, quoted here by permission of Barbara Grier. See also the reprinted series of *The Ladder*, ed. Jonathan Katz *et al.* (New York: Arno, 1975), and Deirdre Carmody, "Letters by Eleanor Roosevelt Detail Friendship with Lorena Hickok," *New York Times* (October 21, 1979).

57. Meridel LeSueur, *The Girl* (Cambridge, Mass.: West End Press, 1978), pp. 10–11. LeSueur describes, in an afterword, how this book was drawn from the writings and oral narrations of women in the Workers Alliance who met as a writers' group during the depression.

58. Ibid, p. 20.

59. Ibid, pp. 53–54.

60. Ibid, p. 55.

61. Toni Morrison, *Sula* (New York: Bantam, 1973), pp. 103–104, 149. I am indebted to Lorraine Bethel's essay "'This Infinity of Conscious Pain': Zora Neale Hurston and the Black Female Literary Tradition," in *All the Women Are White, All the Black An Men, but Some of Us Are Brave: Black Women's Studies*, ed. Gloria T. Hull, Patricia Bell Scott, and Barbara Smith (Old Westbury, N.Y.: Feminist Press, 1982).

62. See Maureen Brady and Judith McDaniel, "Lesbians in the Mainstream: The Image of Lesbians in Recent Commercial Fiction," *Conditions* 6 (1979): 82–105.

63. See Russell and van de Ven, p. 40: "Few heterosexual women realize their lack of free choice about their sexuality, and few realize how and why compulsory heterosexuality is also a crime against them."

64. Bethel, "'This Infinity of Conscious Pain,'" op. cit.

65. Dinnerstein, the most recent writer to quote this passage, adds ominously: "But what has to be added to her account is that these 'women enlaced' are sheltering each other not just from what men want to do to them, but also from what they want to do to each other" (Dinnerstein, p. 103). The fact is, however, that woman-to-woman violence is a minute grain in the universe of male-against-female violence perpetuated and rationalized in every social institution.

66. Conversation with Blanche W. Cook, New York City, March 1979.

67. See note 9.

THE STRAIGHT MIND (1980)

MONIQUE WITTIG

Wittig endorses the structuralist and poststructuralist belief that language shapes culture, but she looks sceptically on the heritage of structuralism and psychoanlysis that she sees in the writings of Claude Lévi-Strauss, Roland Barthes, and Jacques Lacan (each represented in this volume). She singles out Lévi-Strauss's idea that men shape culture by exchanging women, an argument rewritten by feminist and queer studies scholars, such as Gayle Rubin and Eve Kosofsky Sedgwick. (See the selection from Sedgwick in this volume.) Wittig also criticizes the way that Lacan takes heterosexuality as a given. Wittig astonished her first readers with her conclusion that "lesbians are not women." For Wittig, the very idea of gender, including the very idea of women and men, depends on taking heterosexual norms for granted. In other essays, she rejects second-wave feminist claims for a specifically women's culture, seeing such claims as depending on the sexist divisions between genders that feminists set out to oppose. Lesbians have no place, she believes, in the heterosexual way of thinking that naturalizes heterosexuality and centers on the experience of men. Therefore, she argues, the very presence of lesbians exposes a fraud in heterosexual assumptions, so that we should abolish altogether the distinction between women and men.

In recent years in Paris, language as a phenomenon has dominated modern theoretical systems and the social sciences and has entered the political discussions of the lesbian and women's liberation movements. This is because it relates to an important political field where what is at play is power, or more than that, a network of powers, since there is a multiplicity of languages that constantly act upon the social reality. The importance of language as such as a political stake has only recently been perceived.[2] But the gigantic development of linguistics, the multiplication of schools of linguistics, the advent of the sciences of communication, and the technicality of the metalanguages that these sciences utilize, represent the symptoms of the importance of what is politically at stake. The science of language has invaded other sciences, such as anthropology through Lévi-Strauss, psychoanalysis through Lacan, and all the disciplines which have developed from the basis of structuralism.

The early semiology of Roland Barthes nearly escaped from linguistic domination to become a political analysis of the different systems of signs, to establish a relationship between this or that system of signs—for example, the myths of the petit bourgeois class—and the class struggle within capitalism that this system tends to conceal. We were almost saved, for political semiology is a weapon (a method) that we need to analyze what is called ideology. But the miracle did not last. Rather than introducing into semiology concepts which are foreign to it—in this case Marxist concepts—Barthes quickly stated that semiology was only a branch of linguistics and that language was its only object.

Thus, the entire world is only a great register where the most diverse languages come to have themselves recorded, such as the language of the Unconscious,[3] the language of fashion, the language of the exchange of women where human beings are literally the signs which are used to communicate. These languages, or rather these discourses, fit into one another, interpenetrate one another, support one another, reinforce one another, auto-engender, and engender one another. Linguistics engenders semiology and structural linguistics, structural linguistics engenders structuralism, which engenders the Structural Unconscious. The ensemble of these discourses produces a confusing static for the oppressed, which makes them lose sight of the material cause of their oppression and plunges them into a kind of ahistoric vacuum.

For they produce a scientific reading of the social reality in which human beings are given as invariants, untouched by history and unworked by class conflicts, with identical psyches because genetically programmed. This psyche, equally untouched by history and unworked by class conflicts, provides the specialists, from the beginning of the twentieth century, with a whole arsenal of invariants: the symbolic language which very advantageously functions with very few elements, since, like digits (0–9), the symbols "unconsciously" produced by the psyche are not very numerous. Therefore, these symbols are very easy to impose, through therapy and theorization, upon the collective and individual unconscious. We are taught that the Unconscious, with perfectly good taste, structures itself upon metaphors, for example, the name-of-the-father, the Oedipus complex, castration, the murder-or-death-of-the-father, the exchange of women, etc. If the Unconscious, however, is easy to control, it is not just by anybody. Similar to mystical revelations, the apparition of symbols in the psyche demands multiple interpretations. Only specialists can accomplish the deciphering of the Unconscious. Only they, the psychoanalysts, are allowed (authorized?) to organize and interpret psychic manifestations which will show the symbol in its full meaning. And while the symbolic language is extremely poor and essentially lacunary, the languages or metalanguages which interpret it are developing, each one of them, with a richness, a display, that only theological exegeses of the Bible have equalled.

Who gave the psychoanalysts their knowledge? For example, for Lacan, what he calls the "psychoanalytic discourse," or the "analytical experience," both "teach" him what he already knows. And each one teaches him what the other one taught him. But can we deny that Lacan scientifically discovered, through the "analytical experience" (somehow an experiment), the structures of the Unconscious? Will we be irresponsible enough to disregard the discourses of the psychoanalyzed people lying on their couches? In my opinion, there is no doubt that Lacan found in the Unconscious the structures he said he found there, since he had previously put them there. People who did not fall into the power of the psychoanalytical institution may experience an immeasurable feeling of sadness at the degree of oppression (of manipulation) that the psychoanalyzed discourses show. In the analytical experience there is an oppressed person, the psychoanalyzed, whose need for communication is exploited and who (in the same way as the witches could, under torture, only repeat the language that the inquisitors wanted to hear) has no other choice, (if s/he does not want to destroy the implicit contract which allows her/him to communicate and which s/he needs), than to attempt to say what s/he is supposed to say. They say that this can last for a lifetime—cruel contract which constrains a human being to display her/his misery to an oppressor who is directly responsible for it, who exploits her/him economically, politically, ideologically and whose interpretation reduces this misery to a few figures of speech.

But can the need to communicate what this contract implies only be satisfied in the psychoanalytical situation, in being cured or "experimented" with? If we believe recent testimonies[4] by lesbians, feminists, and gay men, this is not the case. All their testimonies emphasize the political significance of the impossibility that lesbians, feminists, and gay men face in the attempt to communicate in heterosexual society, other than with a psychoanalyst. When the general state of things is understood (one is not sick or to be cured, one has an enemy) the result is that the oppressed person breaks the psychoanalytical contract. This is what appears in the testimonies, along with the teaching that the psychoanalytical contract was not a contract of consent but a forced one.

The discourses which particularly oppress all of us, lesbians, women, and homosexual men, are those which take for granted that what founds society, any society, is heterosexuality.[5] These discourses speak about us and claim to say the truth in an apolitical field, as if anything of that which signifies could escape the political in this moment of history, and as if, in what concerns us, politically insignificant signs could exist. These discourses of heterosexuality oppress us in the sense that they prevent us from speaking unless we speak in their terms. Everything which puts them into question is at once disregarded as elementary. Our refusal of the totalizing interpretation of psychoanalysis makes the theoreticians say that we neglect the symbolic dimension. These discourses deny us every possibility of creating our own categories. But their most ferocious action is the unrelenting tyranny that they exert upon our physical and mental selves.

When we use the overgeneralizing term "ideology" to designate all the discourses of the dominating group, we relegate these discourses to the domain of Irreal Ideas; we forget the material (physical) violence that they directly do to the oppressed people, a violence produced by the abstract and "scientific" discourses as well as by the discourses of the mass media. I would like to insist on the material oppression of individuals by discourses, and I would like to underline its immediate effects through the example of pornography.

Pornographic images, films, magazine photos, publicity posters on the walls of the cities, constitute a discourse, and this discourse covers our world with its signs, and this discourse has a meaning: it signifies that women are dominated. Semioticians can interpret the system of this discourse, describe its disposition. What they read in that discourse are signs whose function is not to signify and which have no raison d'être except to be elements of a certain system or disposition. But for us this discourse is not divorced from the real as it is for semioticians. Not only does it maintain very close relations with the social reality which is our oppression (economically and politically), but also it is in itself real since it is one of the aspects of oppression, since it exerts a precise power over us. The pornographic discourse is one of the strategies of violence which are exercised upon us: it humiliates, it degrades, it is a crime against our "humanity." As a harassing tactic it has another function, that of a warning. It orders us to stay in line, and it keeps those who would tend to forget who they are in step; it calls upon fear. These same experts in semiotics, referred to earlier, reproach us for confusing, when we demonstrate against pornography, the discourses with the reality. They do not see that this discourse *is* reality for us, one of the facets of the reality of our oppression. They believe that we are mistaken in our level of analysis.

I have chosen pornography as an example because its discourse is the most symptomatic and the most demonstrative of the violence which is done to us through discourses, as well as in the society at large. There is nothing abstract about the power that sciences and theories have to act materially and actually upon our bodies and our minds, even if the discourse that produces it is abstract. It is one of the forms of domination, its very expression. I would say, rather, one of its exercises. All of the oppressed know this power and have had to deal with it. It is the one which says: you do not have the right to speech because your discourse is not scientific and not theoretical, you are on the wrong level of analysis, you are confusing discourse and reality, your discourse is naive, you misunderstand this or that science.

If the discourse of modern theoretical systems and social science exert a power upon us, it is because it works with concepts which closely touch us. In spite of the historic advent of the lesbian, feminist, and gay liberation movements, whose proceedings have already upset the philosophical and political categories of the discourses of the social sciences, their categories (thus brutally put into question) are nevertheless utilized without examination by contemporary science. They function like primitive concepts in a conglomerate of all kinds of disciplines, theories, and current ideas that I will call the straight mind. (See *The Savage Mind* by Claude Lévi-Strauss.) They concern "woman," "man," "sex," "difference," and all of the series of concepts which bear this mark, including such concepts as "history," "culture," and the "real." And although it has been accepted in recent years that there is no such thing as nature, that everything is culture, there remains within that culture a core of nature which resists examination, a relationship excluded from the social in the analysis—a relationship whose characteristic is ineluctability in culture, as well as in nature, and which is the heterosexual relationship. I will call it the obligatory social relationship between "man" and "woman." (Here I refer to Ti-Grace Atkinson and her analysis of sexual intercourse as an institution.[6]) With its ineluctability as knowledge, as an obvious principle, as a given prior to any science, the straight mind develops a totalizing interpretation of history, social reality, culture, language, and all the subjective phenomena at the same time. I can only underline the oppressive character that the straight mind is clothed in in its tendency to immediately universalize its production of concepts into general laws which claim to hold true for all societies, all epochs, all individuals. Thus one speaks of *the* exchange of women, *the* difference between the sexes, *the* symbolic order, *the* Unconscious, Desire, *Jouissance,* Culture, History, giving an absolute meaning to these concepts when they are only categories founded upon heterosexuality, or thought which produces the difference between the sexes as a political and philosophical dogma.

The consequence of this tendency toward universality is that the straight mind cannot conceive of a culture, a society where heterosexuality would not order not only all human relationships but also its very production of concepts and all the processes which escape consciousness, as well. Additionally, these unconscious processes are historically more and more imperative in what they teach us about ourselves through the instrumentality of specialists. The rhetoric which expresses them (and whose seduction I do not underestimate) envelops itself in myths, resorts to enigma, proceeds by accumulating metaphors, and its function is to poeticize the obligatory character of the "you-will-be-straight-or-you-will-not-be."

In this thought, to reject the obligation of coitus and the institutions that this obligation has produced as necessary for the constitution of a society, is simply an impossibility, since to do this would mean to reject the possibility of the constitution of the other and to reject the "symbolic order," to make the constitution of meaning impossible, without which no one can maintain an internal coherence. Thus lesbianism, homosexuality, and the societies that we form cannot be thought of or spoken of, even though they have always existed. Thus, the straight mind continues to affirm that incest, and not homosexuality, represents its major interdiction. Thus, when thought by the straight mind, homosexuality is nothing but heterosexuality.

Yes, straight society is based on the necessity of the different/other at every level. It cannot work economically, symbolically, linguistically, or politically without this concept. This necessity of the different/other is an ontological one for the whole conglomerate of sciences and disciplines that I call the straight mind. But what is the different/other if not the dominated? For heterosexual society is the society which not only oppresses lesbians and gay men, it oppresses many different/others, it oppresses all women and many categories of men, all those who are in the position of the dominated. To constitute a difference and to control it is an "act of power, since it is essentially a normative act. Everybody tries to show the other as different. But not everybody succeeds in doing so. One has to be socially dominant to succeed in it."[7]

For example, the concept of difference between the sexes ontologically constitutes women into different/others. Men are not different, whites are not different, nor are the masters. But the blacks, as well as the slaves, are. This ontological characteristic of the difference between the sexes affects all the concepts which are part of the same conglomerate. But for us there is no such thing as being-woman or being-man. "Man" and "woman" are political concepts of opposition, and the copula which dialectically unites them is, at the same time, the one which abolishes them.[8] It is the class struggle between women and men which will abolish men and women.[9] The concept of difference has nothing ontological about it. It is only the way that the masters interpret a historical situation of domination. The function of difference is to mask at every level the conflicts of interest, including ideological ones.

In other words, for us, this means there cannot any longer be women and men, and that as classes and categories of thought or language they have to disappear, politically, economically, ideologically. If we, as lesbians and gay men, continue to speak of ourselves and to conceive of ourselves as women and as men, we are instrumental in maintaining heterosexuality. I am sure that an economic and political transformation will not dedramatize these categories of language. Can we redeem *slave*? Can we redeem *nigger, negress*? How is *woman* different? Will we continue to write *white, master, man*? The transformation of economic relationships will not suffice. We must produce a political transformation of the key concepts, that is of the concepts which are strategic for us. For there is another order of materiality, that of language, and language is worked upon from within by these strategic concepts. It is at the same time tightly connected to the political field, where everything that concerns language, science and thought refers to the person as subjectivity and to her/his relationship to society. And we cannot leave this within the power of the straight mind or the thought of domination.

If among all the productions of the straight mind I especially challenge the models of the Structural Unconscious, it is because: at the moment in history when the domination of social groups can no longer appear as a logical necessity to the dominated, because they revolt, because they question the differences, Lévi-Strauss, Lacan, and their epigones call upon necessities which escape the control of consciousness and therefore the responsibility of individuals.

They call upon unconscious processes, for example, which require the exchange of women as a necessary condition for every society. According to them, that is what the unconscious tells us with authority, and the symbolic order, without which there is no meaning, no language, no society, depends on it. But what does women being exchanged mean if not that they are dominated? No wonder then that there is only one Unconscious, and that it is heterosexual. It is an Unconscious which looks too consciously after the interests of the masters[10] in whom it lives for them to be dispossessed of their concepts so easily. Besides, domination is denied; there is no slavery of women, there is difference. To which I will answer with this statement made by a Rumanian peasant at a public meeting in 1848: "Why do the gentlemen say it was not slavery, for we know it to have been slavery, this sorrow that we have sorrowed." Yes, we know it, and this science of oppression cannot be taken away from us.

It is from this science that we must track down the "what-goes-without-saying" heterosexual, and (I paraphrase the early Roland Barthes) we must not bear "seeing Nature and History confused at every turn."[11] We must make it brutally apparent that psychoanalysis after Freud and particularly Lacan have rigidly turned their concepts into myths—Difference, Desire, the Name-of-the-father, etc. They have even "over-mythified" the myths, an operation that was necessary for them in order to systematically heterosexualize that personal dimension which suddenly emerged through the dominated individuals into the historical field, particularly through women, who started their struggle almost two centuries ago. And it has been done systematically, in a concert of interdisciplinarity, never more harmonious than since the heterosexual myths started to circulate with ease from one formal system to another, like sure values that can be invested in anthropology as well as in psychoanalysis and in all the social sciences.

This ensemble of heterosexual myths is a system of signs which uses figures of speech, and thus it can be politically studied from within the science of our oppression; "for-we-know-it-to-have-been-slavery" is the dynamic which introduces the diachronism of history into the fixed discourse of eternal essences. This undertaking should somehow be a political semiology, although with "this sorrow that we have sorrowed" we work also at the level of language/manifesto, of language/action, that which transforms, that which makes history.

In the meantime, in the systems that seemed so eternal and universal that laws could be extracted from them, laws that could be stuffed into computers, and in any case for the moment stuffed into the unconscious machinery, in these systems, thanks to our action and our language, shifts are happening. Such a model, as for example, the exchange of women, reengulfs history in so violent and brutal a way that the whole system, which was believed to be formal, topples over into another dimension of knowledge. This dimension of history belongs to us, since somehow we have been designated, and since, as Lévi-Strauss said, we talk, let us say that we break off the heterosexual contract.

So, this is what lesbians say everywhere in this country and in some others, if not with theories at least through their social practice, whose repercussions upon straight culture and society are still unenvisionable. An anthropologist might say that we have to wait for fifty years. Yes, if one wants to universalize the functioning of these societies and make their invariants appear. Meanwhile the straight concepts are undermined. What is woman? Panic, general alarm for an active defense. Frankly, it is a problem that the lesbians do not have because of a change of perspective, and it would be incorrect to say that lesbians associate, make love, live with women, for "woman" has meaning only in heterosexual systems of thought and heterosexual economic systems. Lesbians are not women.

NOTES

1. This text was first read in New York at the Modern Language Association Convention in 1978 and dedicated to American lesbians.
2. However, the classical Greeks knew that there was no political power without mastery of the art of rhetoric, especially in a democracy.
3. Throughout this paper, when Lacan's use of the term "the Unconscious" is referred to it is capitalized, following his style.
4. For example see Karla Jay and Allen Young, eds., *Out of the Closets* (New York: Links Books, 1972).
5. Heterosexuality: a word which first appears in the French language in 1911.
6. Ti-Grace Atkinson, *Amazon Odyssey* (New York: Links Books, 1974), pp. 13–23.
7. Claude Faugeron and Philippe Robert, *La Justice et son public et les représentations sociales du système pénal* (Paris: Masson, 1978).
8. See, for her definition of "social sex," Nicole-Claude Mathieu, "Notes pour une définition sociologique des catégories de sexe," *Epistémologie Sociologique* 11 (1971). Translated as *Ignored by Some, Denied by Others: The Social Sex Category in Sociology* (pamphlet), Explorations in Feminism 2 (London: Women's Research and Resources Centre Publications, 1977), pp. 16–37.
9. In the same way that in every other class struggle the categories of opposition are "reconciled" by the struggle whose goal is to make them disappear.
10. Are the millions of dollars a year made by the psychoanalysts symbolic?
11. Roland Barthes, *Mythologies* (New York: Hill and Wang, 1972), p. 11.

GENDER ASYMMETRY AND EROTIC TRIANGLES (1985)

EVE KOSOFSKY SEDGWICK

Through such influential volumes as Between Men: English Literature and Male Homoscial Desire, The Epistemology of the Closet, *and* Tendencies, *Sedgwick took a leading and provocative role in the development of queer studies in general and of literary queer studies in particular. In this early chapter from* Between Men, *Sedgwick introduces her argument that men tend to structure their relations to each other through their relations to women, so that even heterosexual relations in literature and culture often take their structure not only through the relation between women and men but also, and especially, through men's relations to each other. Thus the men in literary works, as Sedgwick goes on to argue in later chapters, often see women not so much in themselves as they see them as a means (as something to use) for men to shape their relation to other men. The desired woman, Sedgwick argues, gives the desiring man status with other men, a trophy, a sense of victory and power not only over women but also over observing, envious, or rival men.*

The graphic schema on which I am going to be drawing most heavily in the readings that follow is the triangle. The triangle is useful as a figure by which the "commonsense" of our intellectual tradition schematizes erotic relations, and because it allows us to condense into a juxtaposition with that folk-perception several somewhat different streams of recent thought.

René Girard's early book, *Deceit, Desire, and the Novel,* was itself something of a schematization of the folk-wisdom of erotic triangles. Through readings of major European fictions, Girard traced a calculus of power that was structured by the relation of rivalry between the two active members of an erotic triangle. What is most interesting for our purposes in his study is its insistence that, in any erotic rivalry, the bond that links the two rivals is as intense and potent as the bond that links either of the rivals to the beloved: that the bonds of "rivalry" and "love," differently as they are experienced, are equally powerful and in many senses equivalent. For instance, Girard finds many examples in which the choice of the beloved is determined in the first place, not by the qualities of the beloved, but by the beloved's already being the choice of the person who has been chosen as a rival. In fact, Girard seems to see the bond between rivals in an erotic triangle as being even stronger, more heavily determinant of actions and choices, than anything in the bond between either of the lovers and the beloved. And within the male-centered novelistic tradition of European high culture, the triangles Girard traces are most often those in which two males are rivals for a female; it is the bond between males that he most assiduously uncovers.

The index to Girard's book gives only two citations for "homosexuality" per se, and it is one of the strengths of his formulation not to depend on how homosexuality as an entity was perceived or experienced—indeed, on what was or was not considered sexual—at any given historical moment. As a matter of fact, the symmetry of his formulation always depends on *suppressing* the subjective, historically determined account of which feelings are or are not part of the body of "sexuality." The transhistorical clarity gained by this organizing move naturally has a cost, however. Psychoanalysis, the recent work of Foucault, and feminist historical scholarship all suggest that the place of drawing the boundary between the sexual and the not-sexual, like the place of drawing the boundary between the realms of the two genders, *is* variable, but is *not* arbitrary. That is (as the example of *Gone with the Wind* suggests), the placement of the boundaries in a particular society affects not merely the definitions of those terms themselves—sexual/nonsexual, masculine/feminine—but also the apportionment of forms of power that are not obviously sexual. These include control over the means of production and reproduction of goods, persons, and meanings. So that Girard's account, which thinks it is describing a dialectic of power abstracted from either the male/female or the sexual/nonsexual dichotomies, is leaving out of consideration categories that in fact preside over the distribution of power in every known society. And because the distribution of power according to these dichotomies is not and possibly cannot be symmetrical, the hidden symmetries that Girard's triangle helps us discover will always in turn discover hidden obliquities. At the same time, even to hear in mind the lurking possibility of the Girardian symmetry is to be possessed of a graphic tool for historical measure. It will make it easier for us to perceive and discuss the mutual inscription in these texts of male homosocial and heterosocial desire, and the resistances to them.

Girard's argument is of course heavily dependent, not only on a brilliant intuition for taking seriously the received wisdom of sexual folklore, but also on a schematization from Freud: the Oedipal triangle, the situation of the young child that is attempting to situate itself with respect to a powerful father and a beloved mother. Freud's discussions of the etiology of "homosexuality" (which current research seems to be rendering questionable as a set of generalizations about personal histories of "homosexuals")[1] suggest homo- and heterosexual outcomes in adults to be the result of a complicated play of desire for and identification with the parent of each gender: the child routes its desire/identification through the mother to arrive at a role like the father's, or vice versa. Richard Klein summarizes this argument as follows:

> In the normal development of the little boy's progress towards heterosexuality, he must pass, as Freud says with increasing insistence in late essays like "Terminable and Interminable Analysis," through the stage of the "positive" Oedipus, a homoerotic identification with his father, a position of effeminized subordination to the father, as a condition of finding a model for his own heterosexual role. Conversely, in this theory, the development of the male homosexual requires the postulation of the father's absence or distance and an abnormally strong identification by the child with the mother, in which the child takes the place of the father. There results from this scheme a surprising neutralization of polarities: heterosexuality in the male... presupposes a homosexual phase as the condition of its normal possibility: homosexuality, obversely, requires that the child experience a powerful heterosexual identification.[2]

I have mentioned that Girard's reading presents itself as one whose symmetry is undisturbed by such differences as gender; although the triangles that most shape his view tend, in the European tradition, to involve bonds of "rivalry" between males "over" a woman, in his view *any* relation of rivalry is structured by the same play of emulation and identification, whether the entities occupying the corners of the triangle be heroes, heroines, gods, books, or whatever. In describing the Oedipal drama, Freud notoriously tended to place a male in the generic position of "child" and treat the case of the female as being more or less the same, "mutatis mutandis"; at any rate, as Freud is interpreted by conventional American psychoanalysis, the enormous difference in the degree and kind of female and male power enters psychoanalytic view, when at all, as a result rather than as an active determinant of familial and intrapsychic structures of development. Thus, both Girard and Freud (or at least the Freud of this interpretive tradition) treat the erotic triangle as symmetrical—in the sense that its structure would be relatively unaffected by the power difference that would be introduced by a change in the gender of one of the participants.

In addition, the asymmetry I spoke of in section i of the Introduction—the radically disrupted continuum, in our society, between sexual and nonsexual male bonds, as against the relatively smooth and palpable continuum of female homosocial desire—might be expected to alter the structure of erotic triangles in ways that depended on gender, and for which neither Freud nor Girard would offer an account. Both Freud and Girard, in other words, treat erotic triangles under the Platonic light that perceives no discontinuity in the homosocial continuum—none, at any rate, that makes much difference—even in modern Western society. There is a kind of bravery about the proceeding of each in this respect, but a historical blindness, as well.

Recent rereadings and reinterpretations of Freud have gone much farther in taking into account the asymmetries of gender. In France, recent psychoanalytic discourse impelled by Jacques Lacan identifies power, language, and the Law itself with the phallus and the "name of the father." It goes without saying that such a discourse has the potential for setting in motion both feminist and virulently misogynistic analyses; it does, at any rate, offer tools, though not (so far) historically sensitive ones, for describing the mechanisms of patriarchal power in terms that are at once intrapsychic (Oedipal conflict) and public (language and the Law). Moreover, by distinguishing (however incompletely) the phallus, the locus of power, from the actual anatomical penis,[3] Lacan's account creates a space in which anatomic sex and cultural gender may be distinguished from one another and in which the different paths of *men's* relations to male power might be explored (e.g. in terms of class). In addition, it suggests ways of talking about the relation between the individual male and the cultural institutions of masculine domination that fall usefully under the rubric of representation.

A further contribution of Lacanian psychoanalysis that will be important for our investigation is the subtlety with which it articulates the slippery relation—already adumbrated in Freud—between desire and identification. The schematic elegance with which Richard Klein, in the passage I have quoted, is able to summarize the feminizing potential of desire for a woman and the masculinizing potential of subordination to a man, owes at least something to a Lacanian grinding of the lenses through which Freud is being viewed. In Lacan and those who have learned from him, an elaborate meditation on introjection and incorporation forms the link between the apparently dissimilar processes of desire and identification.

Recent American feminist work by Dorothy Dinnerstein and Nancy Chodorow also revises Freud in the direction of greater attention to gender/power difference. Coppélia Kahn summarizes the common theme of their argument (which she applies to Shakespeare) as follows:

> Most children, male or female, in Shakespeare's time, Freud's, or ours, are not only borne but raised by women. And thus arises a crucial difference between the girl's developing sense of identity and the boy's. For though she follows the same sequence of symbiotic union, separation and individuation, identification, and object love as the boy, her femininity arises in relation to a person of the *same* sex, while his masculinity arises in relation to a person of the *opposite* sex. Her femininity is reinforced by her original symbiotic union with her mother and by the identification with her that must precede identity, while his masculinity is threatened by the same union and the same identification. While the boy's sense of *self* begins in union with the feminine, his sense of *masculinity* arises against it.[4]

It should be clear, then, from what has gone before, on the one hand that there are many and thorough asymmetries between the sexual continuums of women and men, between female and male sexuality and homosociality, and most pointedly between homosocial and heterosocial object choices for males; and on the other hand that the status of women, and the whole question of arrangements between genders, is deeply and inescapably inscribed in the structure even of relationships that seem to exclude women—even in male homosocial/homosexual relationships. Heidi Hartmann's definition of patriarchy in terms of "relationships between men" (see Introduction i), in making the power relationships between men and women appear to be dependent on the power relationships between men and men, suggests that large-scale social structures are congruent with the male-male-female erotic triangles described most forcefully by Girard and articulated most thoughtfully by others. We can go further than that, to say that in any male-dominated society, there is a special relationship between male homosocial (*including* homosexual) desire and the structures for maintaining and transmitting patriarchal power: a relationship founded on an inherent and potentially active structural congruence. For historical reasons, this special relationship may take the form of ideological homophobia, ideological homosexuality, or some highly conflicted but intensively structured combination of the two. (Lesbianism also must always be in a special relation to patriarchy, but on different [sometimes opposite] grounds and working through different mechanisms.)

Perhaps the most powerful recent argument through (and against) a traditional discipline that bears on these issues has occurred within anthropology. Based on readings and critiques of Lévi-Strauss and Engels, in addition to Freud and Lacan, Gayle Rubin has argued in an influential essay that patriarchal heterosexuality can best be discussed in terms of one or another form of the traffic in women: it is the use of women as exchangeable, perhaps symbolic, property for the primary purpose of cementing the bonds of men with men. For example, Lévi-Strauss writes, "The total relationship of exchange which constitutes marriage is not established between a man and a woman, but between two groups or men, and the woman figures only as one of the objects in the exchange, not as one of the partners."[5] Thus, like Freud's "heterosexual" in Richard Klein's account, Lévi-Strauss's man uses a woman as a "conduit of a relationship" in which the true *partner* is a man.[6] Rejecting Lévi-Strauss's celebratory treatment of this relegation of women, Rubin offers, instead, an array of tools for specifying and analyzing it.

Luce Irigaray has used the Lévi-Straussian description of the traffic in women to make a resounding though expensive leap of register in her discussion of the relation of heterosexual to male homosocial bonds. In the reflections translated into English as "When the Goods Get Together," she concludes: "[Male] homosexuality is the law that regulates the sociocultural order. Heterosexuality amounts to the assignment of roles in the economy."[7] To begin to describe this relation as having the asymmetry of (to put it roughly) *parole* to *langue* is wonderfully pregnant; if her use of it here is not a historically responsive one, still it has potential for increasing our ability to register historical difference.

The expensiveness of Irigaray's vision of male homosexuality is, oddly, in a sacrifice of sex itself: the male "homosexuality" discussed here turns out to represent anything but actual sex between men, which—although it is also, importantly, called "homosexuality"— has something, like the same invariable, tabooed status for her larger, "real" "homosexuality" that incest has in principle for Lévi-Straussian kinship in general. Even Irigaray's supple machinery of meaning has the effect of transfixing, then sublimating, the quicksilver of sex itself.

The loss of the diachronic in a formulation like Irigaray's is, again, most significant, as well. Recent anthropology, as well as historical work by Foucault, Sheila Rowbotham, Jeffrey Weeks, Alan Bray, K. J. Dover, John Boswell, David Fernbach, and others, suggests that among the things that have changed radically in Western culture over the centuries, and vary across cultures, about men's genital activity with men are its frequency, its exclusivity, its class associations, its relation to the dominant culture, its ethical status, the degree to which it is seen as defining nongenital aspects of the lives of those who practice it, and, perhaps most radically, its association with femininity or masculinity in societies where gender is a profound determinant of power. The virility of the homosexual orientation of male desire seemed as self-evident to the ancient Spartans, and perhaps to Whitman, as its effeminacy seems in contemporary popular culture. The importance of women (not merely of "the feminine," but of actual women, as well) in the etiology and the continuing experience of male homosexuality seems to be historically volatile (across time, across class) to a similar degree. Its changes are inextricable from the changing shapes of the institutions by which gender and class inequality are structured.

Thus, Lacan, Chodorow and Dinnerstein, Rubin, Irigaray, and others, making critiques from within their multiple traditions, offer analytical tools for treating the erotic triangle not as an ahistorical, Platonic form, a deadly symmetry from which the historical accidents of gender, language, class, and power detract, but as a sensitive register precisely for delineating relationships of power and meaning, and for making graphically intelligible the play of desire and identification by which individuals negotiate with their societies for empowerment.

NOTES

1. On this, see Bell et al., *Sexual Preferences.*
2. Review of *Homosexualities,* p. 1077.
3. On this see Gallop, *Daughter's Seduction,* pp. 15–32.
4. Kahn, *Man's Estate,* pp. 9–10.
5. *The Elementary Structures of Kinship* (Boston: Beacon, 1969), p. 115; quoted in Rubin, "Traffic," p. 174.
6. Rubin, *ibid.*
7. Irigaray, "Goods," pp. 107–10.

BIBLIOGRAPHY

Bell, Alan P., Martin S. Weinberg, and Sue Kiefer Hammersmith. *Sexual Preference: Its Development in Men and Women.* Bloomington: Indiana University Press, 1981.

Boswell, John. *Christianity, Social Tolerance and Homosexuality: Gay People in Western Europe from the Beginning of the Christian Era to the Fourteenth Century.* Chicago: University of Chicago Press, 1980.

Bray, Alan. *Homosexuality in Renaissance England.* London: Gay Men's Press, 1982.

Chodorow, Nancy. *The Reproduction of Mothering: Psychoanalysis and the Sociology of Gender.* Berkeley: University of California Press, 1978.

Dover, K. J. *Greek Homosexuality.* New York: Random House–Vintage, 1980.

Fernbach, David. *The Spiral Path: A Gay Contribution to Human Survival.* Alyson Press, 1981

Foucault, Michel. *The History of Sexuality: Volume I. An Introduction.* Tr. Robert Hurley. New York: Pantheon, 1978.

Gallop, Jane. *The Daughter's Seduction: Feminism and Psychoanalysis.* Ithaca: Cornell University Press, 1982.

Girard, René. *Deceit, Desire, and the Novel: Self and Other in Literary Structure.* Tr. Yvonne Freccero. Baltimore: Johns Hopkins University Press, 1972.

Irigaray, Luce. "When the Goods Get Together." In *New French Feminisms,* ed. Elaine Marks and Isabelle de Courtivron. New York: Schocken, 1981, pp. 107–11

Kahn, Coppélia. *Man's Estate: Masculine Identity in Shakespeare.* Berkeley: University of California Press, 1981.

Klein, Richard. Review *of Homosexualities in French Literature. MLN* 95, no. 4 (May 1980), pp. 1070–80.

Lévi-Strauss, Claude. *The Elementary Structures of Kinship.* Boston: Beacon Press, 1969.

Rowbotham, Sheila, and Jeffrey Weeks. *Socialism and the New Life: The Personal and Sexual Politics of Edward Carpenter and Harelock Ellis.* London: Pluto Press, 1977.

Rubin, Gayle. "The Traffic in Women: Notes Toward a Political Economy of Sex." In *Toward an Authropology of Women.* Ed. Rayna Reiter. New York: Monthly Review Press, 1975, pp. 157—210,

Weeks, Jeffrey. *Coming Out: Homosexual Politics in Britain from the Nineteenth Century to the Present.* London: Quartet Books, 1977.

———. *Sex. Politics, and Society: The Regulation of Sexuality Since 1800.* London: Longman, 1981.

GENDER TROUBLE: FEMINISM AND THE SUBVERSION OF IDENTITY (1990)

JUDITH BUTLER

A philosopher, Butler draws on Foucault's Discipline and Punish *and the concept of compulsory heterosexuality as well as on feminism, psychoanalysis, and the work of Monique Wittig (Foucault, Rich, and Wittig are all represented in this volume). Butler describes identity as constructed by performance rather than as a static essence. She rejects what she calls the expressive model, the idea that a given anatomical sex (female or male) necessarily expresses a given gender (feminine or masculine). In the same vein of deconstructive argument, she rejects the idea that there is a prediscursive essence, a material factuality that comes before discourse, that is, that comes before the language we use to describe it. Instead, she argues, we perform gender by imitating other performances of gender. For Butler, performance suggests variation and continuous process, rather than an interior core of essential selfhood. Performing gender, and watching it performed in more or less the same way over and over, produces a taken-for-granted idea that certain ways are natural and right. Yet, repetitions are never perfect. We never do the same thing exactly the same way twice. And some repetitions vary from the model more than others. Thus, even as repetition irons in the model of an essentialized notion of gender, Butler argues that it also undermines that model, proliferating what it repeats into a series of variations. While we can see patterns in the ways that people perform gender, then, we can also see repetitions that change the patterns and even, with a sense of humor, repetitions that parody the patterns. Thus gender and subjectivity, to Butler, are not an essential core inside us but are instead something we constantly produce through what we do.*

This selection comes from the final pages of Gender Trouble. *For a controversial response to Butler's already controversial argument, see the essay in this volume by Martha C. Nussbaum.*

FROM INTERIORITY TO GENDER PERFORMATIVES

In *Discipline and Punish* Foucault challenges the language of internalization as it operates in the service of the disciplinary regime of the subjection and subjectivation of criminals.[1] Although Foucault objected to what he understood to be the psychoanalytic belief in the "inner" truth of sex in *The History of Sexuality,* he turns to a criticism of the doctrine of internalization for separate purposes in the context of his history of criminology. In a sense, *Discipline and Punish* can be read as Foucault's effort to rewrite Nietzsche's doctrine of internalization in *On the Genealogy of Morals* on the model of *inscription.* In the context of prisoners, Foucault writes, the strategy has been not to enforce a repression of their desires, but to compel their bodies to signify the prohibitive law as their very essence, style, and necessity. That law is not literally internalized, but incorporated, with the consequence that bodies are produced which signify that law on and through the body; there the law is manifest as the essence of their selves, the meaning of their soul, their conscience, the law of their desire. In effect, the law is at once fully manifest and fully latent, for it never appears as external to the bodies it subjects and subjectivates. Foucault writes:

> It would be wrong to say that the soul is an illusion, or an ideological effect. On the contrary, it exists, it has a reality, it is produced permanently *around, on, within,* the body by the functioning of a power that is exercised on those that are punished (my emphasis).[2]

The figure of the interior soul understood as "within" the body is signified through its inscription *on* the body, even though its primary mode of signification is through its very absence, its potent invisibility. The effect of a structuring inner space is produced through the signification of a body as a vital and sacred enclosure. The soul is precisely what the body lacks; hence, the body presents itself as a signifying lack. That lack which *is* the body signifies the soul as that which cannot show. In this sense, then, the soul is a surface signification that contests and displaces the inner/outer distinction itself, a figure of interior psychic space inscribed *on* the body as a social signification that perpetually renounces itself as such. In Foucault's terms, the soul is not imprisoned by or within the body, as some Christian imagery would suggest, but "the soul is the prison of the body."[3]

The redescription of intrapsychic processes in terms of the surface politics of the body implies a corollary redescription of gender as the disciplinary production of the figures of fantasy through the play of presence and absence on the body's surface, the construction of the gendered body through a series of exclusions and denials, signifying absences. But what determines the manifest and latent text of the body politic? What is the prohibitive law that generates the corporeal stylization of gender, the fantasied and fantastic figuration of the body? We have already considered the incest taboo and the prior taboo against homosexuality as the generative moments of gender identity, the prohibitions that produce identity along the culturally intelligible grids of an idealized and compulsory heterosexuality. That disciplinary production of gender effects a false stabilization of gender in the interests of the heterosexual construction and regulation of sexuality within the reproductive domain. The construction of coherence conceals the gender discontinuities that run rampant within heterosexual, bisexual, and gay and lesbian contexts in which gender does not necessarily follow from sex, and desire, or sexuality generally, does not seem to follow from gender— indeed, where none of these dimensions of significant corporeality express or reflect one another. When the disorganization and disaggregation of the field of bodies disrupt the regulatory fiction of heterosexual coherence, it seems that the expressive model loses its descriptive force. That regulatory ideal is then exposed as a norm and a fiction that disguises itself as a developmental law regulating the sexual field that it purports to describe.

According to the understanding of identification as an enacted fantasy or incorporation, however, it is clear that coherence is desired, wished for, idealized, and that this idealization is an effect of a corporeal signification. In other words, acts, gestures, and desire produce the effect of an internal core or substance, but produce this *on the surface* of the body, through the play of signifying absences that suggest, but never reveal, the organizing principle of identity as a cause. Such acts, gestures, enactments, generally construed, are *performative* in the sense that the essence or identity that they otherwise purport to express are *fabrications* manufactured and sustained through corporeal signs and other discursive means. That the gendered body is performative suggests that it has no ontological status apart from the various acts which constitute its reality. This also suggests that if that reality is fabricated as an interior essence, that very interiority is an effect and function of a decidedly public and social discourse, the public regulation of fantasy through the surface politics of the body, the gender border control that differentiates inner from outer, and so institutes the "integrity" of the subject. In other words, acts and gestures, articulated and enacted desires create the illusion of an interior and organizing gender core, an illusion discursively maintained for the purposes of the regulation of sexuality within the obligatory frame of reproductive heterosexuality. If the "cause" of desire, gesture, and act can be localized within the "self" of the actor, then the political regulations and disciplinary practices which produce that ostensibly coherent gender are effectively displaced from view. The displacement of a political and discursive origin of gender identity onto a psychological "core" precludes an analysis of the political constitution of the gendered subject and its fabricated notions about the ineffable interiority of its sex or of its true identity.

If the inner truth of gender is a fabrication and if a true gender is a fantasy instituted and inscribed on the surface of bodies, then it seems that genders can be neither true nor false, but are only produced as the truth effects of a discourse of primary and stable identity. In *Mother Camp: Female Impersonators in America*, anthropologist Esther Newton suggests that the structure of impersonation reveals one of the key fabricating mechanisms through which the social construction of gender takes place.[4] I would suggest as well that drag fully subverts the distinction between inner and outer psychic space and effectively mocks both the expressive model of gender and the notion of a true gender identity. Newton writes:

> At its most complex, [drag] is a double inversion that says, "appearance is an illusion." Drag says [Newton's curious personification] "my 'outside' appearance is feminine, but my essence 'inside' [the body] is masculine." At the same time it symbolizes the opposite inversion; "my appearance 'outside' [my body, my gender] is masculine but my essence 'inside' [myself] is feminine."[5]

Both claims to truth contradict one another and so displace the entire enactment of gender significations from the discourse of truth and falsity.

The notion of an original or primary gender identity is often parodied within the cultural practices of drag, cross-dressing, and the sexual stylization of butch/femme identities. Within feminist theory, such parodic identities have been understood to be either degrading to women, in the case of drag and cross-dressing, or an uncritical appropriation of sex-role stereotyping from within the practice of heterosexuality, especially in the case of butch/femme lesbian identities. But the relation between the "imitation" and the "original" is, I think, more complicated than that critique generally allows. Moreover, it gives us a clue to the way in which the relationship between primary identification—that is, the original meanings accorded to gender—and subsequent gender experience might be reframed. The performance of drag plays upon the distinction between the anatomy of the performer and the gender that is being performed. But we are actually in the presence of three contingent dimensions of significant corporeality: anatomical sex, gender identity, and gender performance. If the anatomy of the performer is already distinct from the gender of the performer, and both of those are distinct from the gender of the performance, then the performance suggests a dissonance not only between sex and performance, but sex and gender, and gender and performance. As much as drag creates a unified picture of "woman" (what its critics often oppose), it also reveals the distinctness of those aspects of gendered experience which are falsely naturalized as a unity through the regulatory fiction of heterosexual coherence. *In imitating gender, drag implicitly reveals the imitative structure of gender itself—as well as its contingency.* Indeed, part of the pleasure, the giddiness of the performance is in the recognition of a radical contingency in the relation between sex and gender in the face *of* cultural configurations of causal unities that are regularly assumed to be natural and necessary. In the place of the law of heterosexual coherence, we see sex and gender denaturalized by means of a performance which avows their distinctness and dramatizes the cultural mechanism of their fabricated unity.

The notion of gender parody defended here does not assume that there is an original which such parodic identities imitate. Indeed, the parody is *of* the very notion of an original; just as the psychoanalytic notion of gender identification is constituted by a fantasy of a fantasy, the transfiguration of an Other who is always already a "figure" in that double sense, so gender parody reveals that the original identity after which gender fashions itself is an imitation without an origin. To be more precise, it is a production which, in effect—that is, in its effect—postures as an imitation. This perpetual displacement constitutes a fluidity of identities that suggests an openness to resignification and recontextualization; parodic proliferation deprives hegemonic culture and its critics of the claim to naturalized or essentialist gender identities. Although the gender meanings taken up in these parodic styles are clearly part of hegemonic, misogynist culture, they are nevertheless denaturalized and mobilized through their parodic recontextualization. As imitations which effectively displace the meaning of the original. they imitate the myth of originality itself. In the place of an original identification which serves as a determining cause, gender identity might be reconceived as a personal/cultural history of received meanings subject to a set of imitative practices which refer laterally to other imitations and which, jointly, construct the illusion of a primary and interior gendered self or parody the mechanism of that construction

According to Fredric Jameson's "Postmodernism and Consumer Society," the imitation that mocks the notion of an original is characteristic of pastiche rather than parody:

> Pastiche is, like parody, the imitation of a peculiar or unique style, the wearing of a stylistic mask, speech in a dead language: but it is a neutral practice of mimicry, without parody's ulterior motive, without the satirical impulse, without laughter, without that still latent feeling that there exists something *normal* compared to which what is being imitated is rather comic. Pastiche is blank parody, parody that has lost it humor.[6]

The loss of the sense of "the normal," however, can be its own occasion for laughter, especially when "the normal," "the original" is revealed to be a copy, and an inevitably failed one, an ideal that no one *can* embody. In this sense, laughter emerges in the realization that all along the original was derived.

Parody by itself is not subversive, and there must be a way to understand what makes certain kinds of parodic repetitions effectively disruptive, truly troubling, and which repetitions become domesticated and recirculated as instruments of cultural hegemony. A typology of actions would clearly not suffice, for parodic displacement, indeed, parodic laughter, depends on a context and reception in which subversive confusions can be fostered. What performance where will invert the inner/outer distinction and compel a radical rethinking of the psychological presuppositions of gender identity and sexuality? What performance where will compel a reconsideration of the *place* and stability of the masculine and the feminine? And what kind of gender performance will enact and reveal the performativity of gender itself in a way that destabilizes the naturalized categories of identity and desire?

If the body is not a "being," but a variable boundary, a surface whose permeability is politically regulated, a signifying practice within a cultural field of gender hierarchy and compulsory heterosexuality, then what language is left for understanding this corporeal enactment, gender, that constitutes its "interior" signification on its surface? Sartre would perhaps have called this act "a style of being," Foucault, "a stylistics of existence." And in my earlier reading of Beauvoir, I suggest that gendered bodies are so many "styles of the flesh." These styles are never self-styled, for styles have a history, and those histories condition and limit the possibilities. Consider gender, for instance, as *a corporeal style,* an "act," as it were, which is both intentional and performative, where *"performative"* suggests a dramatic contingent construction of meaning.

Wittig understands gender as the workings of "sex," where "sex" is an obligatory injunction for the body to become a cultural sign, to materialize itself in obedience to a historically delimited possibility, and to do this, not once or twice, but as a sustained and repeated corporeal project. The notion of a "project," however, suggests the originating force of a radical will, and because gender is a project which has cultural survival as its end, the term *strategy* better suggests the situation of duress under which gender performance always and variously occurs. Hence, as a strategy of survival within compulsory systems, gender is a performance with clearly punitive consequences. Discrete genders are part of what "humanizes" individuals within contemporary culture; indeed, we regularly punish those who fail to do their gender right. Because there is neither an "essence" that gender expresses or externalizes nor an objective ideal to which gender aspires, and because gender is not a fact, the various acts of gender create the idea of gender, and without those acts, there would be no gender at all. Gender is, thus, a construction that regularly conceals its genesis; the tacit collective agreement to perform, produce, and sustain discrete and polar genders as cultural fictions is obscured by the credibility of those productions—and the punishments that attend not agreeing to believe in them; the construction "compels" our belief in its necessity and naturalness. The historical possibilities materialized through various corporeal styles are nothing other than those punitively regulated cultural fictions alternately embodied and deflected under duress.

Consider that a sedimentation of gender norms produces the peculiar phenomenon of a "natural sex" or a "real woman" or any number of prevalent and compelling social fictions, and that this is a sedimentation that over time has produced a set of corporeal styles which, in reified form, appear as the natural configuration of bodies into sexes existing in a binary relation to one another. If these styles are enacted, and if they produce the coherent gendered subjects who pose as their originators, what kind of performance might reveal this ostensible "cause" to be an "effect"?

In what senses, then, is gender an act? As in other ritual social dramas, the action of gender requires a performance that is *repeated.* This repetition is at once a reenactment and reexperiencing of a set of meanings already socially established; and it is the mundane and ritualized form of their legitimation.[7] Although there are individual bodies that enact these significations by becoming stylized into gendered modes, this "action" is a public action. There are temporal and collective dimensions to these actions, and their public character is not inconsequential; indeed, the performance is effected with the strategic aim of maintaining gender within its binary frame—an aim that cannot be attributed to a subject, but, rather, must be understood to found and consolidate the subject.

Gender ought not to be construed as a stable identity or locus of agency from which various acts follow; rather, gender is an identity tenuously constituted in time, instituted in an exterior space through *stylized repetition of acts*. The effect of gender is produced through the stylization of the body and, hence, must be understood as the mundane way in which bodily gestures, movements, and styles of various kinds constitute the illusion of an abiding gendered self. This formulation moves the conception of gender off the ground of a substantial model of identity to one that requires a conception of gender as a constituted *social temporality*. Significantly, if gender is instituted through acts which are internally discontinuous, then the *appearance of substance* is precisely that, a constructed identity, a performative accomplishment which the mundane social audience, including the actors themselves, come to believe and to perform in the mode of belief. Gender is also a norm that can never be fully internalized; "the internal" is a surface signification, and gender norms are finally phantasmatic, impossible to embody. If the ground of gender identity is the stylized repetition of acts through time and not a seemingly seamless identity, then the spatial metaphor of a "ground" will be displaced and revealed as a stylized configuration, indeed, a gendered corporealization of time. The abiding gendered self will then be shown to be structured by repeated acts that seek to approximate the ideal of a substantial ground of identity, but which, in their occasional *dis*continuity, reveal the temporal and contingent groundlessness of this "ground." The possibilities of gender transformation are to be found precisely in the arbitrary relation between such acts, in the possibility of a failure to repeat, a de-formity, or a parodic repetition that exposes the phantasmatic effect of abiding identity as a politically tenuous construction.

If gender attributes, however, are not expressive but performative, then these attributes effectively constitute the identity they are said to express or reveal. The distinction between expression and performativeness is crucial. If gender attributes and acts, the various ways in which a body shows or produces its cultural signification, are performative, then there is no preexisting identity by which an act or attribute might be measured; there would be no true or false, real or distorted acts of gender, and the postulation of a true gender identity would be revealed as a regulatory fiction. That gender reality is created through sustained social performances means that the very notions of an essential sex and a true or abiding masculinity or femininity are also constituted as part of the strategy that conceals gender's performative character and the performative possibilities for proliferating gender configurations outside the restricting frames of masculinist domination and compulsory heterosexuality.

Genders can be neither true nor false, neither real nor apparent, neither original nor derived. As credible bearers of those attributes, however, genders can also be rendered thoroughly and radically *incredible*.

CONCLUSION: FROM PARODY TO POLITICS

I began with the speculative question of whether feminist politics could do without a "subject" in the category of women. At stake is not whether it still makes sense, strategically or transitionally, to refer to women in order to make representational claims in their behalf. The feminist "we" is always and only a phantasmatic construction, one that has its purposes, but which denies the internal complexity and indeterminacy of the term and constitutes itself only through the exclusion of some part of the constituency that it simultaneously seeks to represent. The tenuous or phantasmatic status of the "we," however, is not cause for despair or, at least, it is not *only* cause for despair. The radical instability of the category sets into question the *foundational* restrictions on feminist political theorizing and opens up other configurations, not only of genders and bodies, but of politics itself.

The foundationalist reasoning of identity politics tends to assume that an identity must first be in place in order for political interests to be elaborated and, subsequently, political action to be taken. My argument is that there need not be a "doer behind the deed," but that the "doer" is variably constructed in and through the deed. This is not a return to an existential theory of the self as constituted through its acts, for the existential theory maintains a prediscursive structure for both the self and its acts. It is precisely the discursively variable construction of each in and through the other that has interested me here.

The question of locating "agency" is usually associated with the viability of the "subject," where the "subject" is understood to have some stable existence prior to the cultural field that it negotiates. Or, if the subject is culturally constructed, it is nevertheless vested with an agency, usually figured as the capacity for reflexive mediation, that remains intact regardless of its cultural embeddedness. On such a model, "culture" and "discourse" *mire* the subject, but do not constitute that subject. This move to qualify and enmire the preexisting subject has appeared necessary to establish a point of agency that is not fully *determined* by that culture and discourse. And yet, this kind of reasoning falsely presumes (a) agency can only be established through recourse to a prediscursive "I," even if that "I" is found in the midst of a discursive convergence, and (b) that to be *constituted* by discourse is to be *determined* by discourse, where determination forecloses the possibility of agency.

Even within the theories that maintain a highly qualified or situated subject, the subject still encounters its discursively constituted environment in an oppositional epistemological frame. The culturally enmired subject negotiates its constructions, even when those constructions are the very predicates of its own identity. In Beauvoir, for example, there is an "I" that does its gender, that becomes its gender, but that "I," invariably associated with its gender, is nevertheless a point of agency never fully identifiable with its gender. That *cogito* is never fully *of* the cultural world that it negotiates, no matter the narrowness of the ontological distance that separates that subject from its cultural predicates. The theories of feminist identity that elaborate predicates of color, sexuality, ethnicity, class, and ablebodiedness invariably close with an embarrassed "etc." at the end of the list. Through this horizontal trajectory of adjectives, these positions strive to encompass a situated subject, but invariably fail to be complete. This failure, however, is instructive: what political impetus is to be derived from the exasperated "etc." that so often occurs at the end of such lines? This is a sign of exhaustion as well as of the illimitable process of signification itself. It is the *supplément*, the excess that necessarily accompanies any effort to posit identity once and for all. This illimitable *et cetera*, however, offers itself as a new departure for feminist political theorizing.

If identity is asserted through a process of signification, if identity is always already signi-fied, and yet continues to signify as it circulates within various interlocking discourses, then the question of agency is not to be answered through recourse to an "I" that preexists signi-fication. In other words, the enabling conditions for an assertion of "I" are provided by the structure of signification, the rules that regulate the legitimate and illegitimate invocation of that pronoun, the practices that establish the terms of intelligibility by which that pronoun can circulate. Language is not an *exterior medium or instrument* into which I pour a self and from which I glean a reflection of that self. The Hegelian model of self-recognition that has been appropriated by Marx, Lukacs, and a variety of contemporary liberatory discourses presupposes a potential adequation between the "I" that confronts its world, including its language, as an object, and the "I" that finds itself as an object in that world. But the subject/object dichotomy, which here belongs to the tradition of Western epistemology, conditions the very problematic of identity that it seeks to solve.

What discursive tradition establishes the "I" and its "Other" in an epistemological con-frontation that subsequently decides where and how questions of knowability and agency are to be determined? What kinds of agency are foreclosed through the positing of an epis-temological subject precisely because the rules and practices that govern the invocation of that subject and regulate its agency in advance are ruled out as sites of analysis and critical intervention? That the epistemological point of departure is in no sense inevitable is naively and pervasively confirmed by the mundane operations of ordinary language—widely docu-mented within anthropology—that regard the subject/object dichotomy as a strange and contingent, if not violent, philosophical imposition. The language of appropriation, instru-mentality, and distanciation germane to the epistemological mode also belong to a strategy of domination that pits the "I" against an "Other" and, once that separation is effected, cre-ates an artificial set of questions about the knowability and recoverability of that Other.

As part of the epistemological inheritance of contemporary political discourses of iden-tity, this binary opposition is a strategic move within a given set of signifying practices, one that establishes the "I" in and through this opposition and which reifies that opposition as a necessity, concealing the discursive apparatus by which the binary itself is constituted. The shift from an *epistemological* account of identity to one which locates the problematic within practices of *signification* permits an analysis that takes the epistemological mode itself as one possible and contingent signifying practice. Further, the question of *agency* is refor-mulated as a question of how signification and resignification work. In other words, what is signified as an identity is not signified at a given point in time after which it is simply there as an inert piece of entitative language. Clearly, identities *can* appear as so many inert substantives; indeed, epistemological models tend to take this appearance as their point of theoretical departure. However, the substantive "I" only appears as such through a signify-ing practice that seeks to conceal its own workings and to naturalize its effects. Further, to qualify as a substantive identity is an arduous task, for such appearances are rule-generated identities, ones which rely on the consistent and repeated invocation of rules that condition and restrict culturally intelligible practices of identity. Indeed, to understand identity as a *practice*, and as a signifying practice, is to understand culturally intelligible subjects as the resulting effects of a rule-bound discourse that inserts itself in the pervasive and mundane signifying acts of linguistic life. Abstractly considered, language refers to an open system of signs by which intelligibility is insistently created and contested. As historically specific organizations of language, discourses present themselves in the plural, coexisting within temporal frames, and instituting unpredictable and inadvertent convergences from which specific modalities of discursive possibilities are engendered.

As a process, signification harbors within itself what the epistemological discourse refers to as "agency." The rules that govern intelligible identity, i.e., that enable and restrict the intelligible assertion of an "I," rules that are partially structured along matrices of gender hierarchy and compulsory heterosexuality, operate through *repetition*. Indeed, when the subject is said to be constituted, that means simply that the subject is a consequence of certain rule-governed discourses that govern the intelligible invocation of identity. The subject is not *determined* by the rules through which it is generated because signification is *not a founding act, but rather a regulated process of repetition* that both conceals itself and enforces its rules precisely through the production of substantializing effects. In a sense, all signification takes place within the orbit of the compulsion to repeat; "agency," then, is to be located within the possibility of a variation on that repetition. If the rules governing signification not only restrict, but enable the assertion of alternative domains of cultural intelligibility, i.e., new possibilities for gender that contest the rigid codes of hierarchical binarisms, then it is only *within* the practices of repetitive signifying that a subversion of identity becomes possible. The injunction *to be* a given gender produces necessary failures, a variety of incoherent configurations that in their multiplicity exceed and defy the injunction by which they are generated. Further, the very injunction to be a given gender takes place through discursive routes: to be a good mother, to be a heterosexually desirable object, to be a fit worker, in sum, to signify a multiplicity of guarantees in response to a variety of different demands all at once. The coexistence or convergence of such discursive injunctions produces the possibility of a complex reconfiguration and redeployment; it is not a transcendental subject who enables action in the midst of such a convergence. There is no self that is prior to the convergence or who maintains "integrity" prior to its entrance into this conflicted cultural field. There is only a taking up of the tools where they lie, where the very "taking up" is enabled by the tool lying there.

What constitutes a subversive repetition within signifying practices of gender? I have argued ("I" deploy the grammar that governs the genre of the philosophical conclusion, but note that it is the grammar itself that deploys and enables this "I," even as the "I" that insists itself here repeats, redeploys, and—as the critics will determine—contests the philosophical grammar by which it is both enabled and restricted) that, for instance, within the sex/gender distinction, sex poses as "the real" and the "factic," the material or corporeal ground upon which gender operates as an act of cultural *inscription*. And yet gender is not written on the body as the torturing instrument of writing in Kafka's "In the Penal Colony" inscribes itself unintelligibly on the flesh of the accused. The question is not: what meaning does that inscription carry within it, but what cultural apparatus arranges this meeting between instrument and body, what interventions into this ritualistic repetition are possible? The "real" and the "sexually factic" are phantasmatic constructions—illusions of substance—that bodies are compelled to approximate, but never can. What, then, enables the exposure of the rift between the phantasmatic and the real whereby the real admits itself as phantasmatic? Does this offer the possibility for a repetition that is not fully constrained by the injunction to reconsolidate naturalized identities? Just as bodily surfaces are enacted *as* the natural, so these surfaces can become the site of a dissonant and denaturalized performance that reveals the performative status of the natural itself.

Practices of parody can serve to reengage and reconsolidate the very distinction between a privileged and naturalized gender configuration and one that appears as derived, phantasmatic, and mimetic—a failed copy, as it were. And surely parody has been used to further a politics of despair, one which affirms a seemingly inevitable exclusion of marginal genders from the territory of the natural and the real. And yet this failure to become "real" and to embody "the natural" is, I would argue, a constitutive failure of all gender enactments for the very reason that these ontological locales are fundamentally uninhabitable. Hence, there is a subversive laughter in the pastiche-effect of parodic practices in which the original, the authentic, and the real are themselves constituted as effects. The loss of gender norms would have the effect of proliferating gender configurations, destabilizing substantive identity, and depriving the naturalizing narratives of compulsory heterosexuality of their central protagonists: "man" and "woman." The parodic repetition of gender exposes as well the illusion of gender identity as an intractable depth and inner substance. As the effects of a subtle and politically enforced performativity, gender is an "act," as it were, that is open to splittings, self-parody, self-criticism, and those hyperbolic exhibitions of "the natural" that, in their very exaggeration, reveal its fundamentally phantasmatic status.

I have tried to suggest that the identity categories often presumed to be foundational to feminist politics, that is, deemed necessary in order to mobilize feminism as an identity politics, simultaneously work to limit and constrain in advance the very cultural possibilities that feminism is supposed to open up. The tacit constraints that produce culturally intelligible "sex" ought to be understood as generative political structures rather than naturalized foundations. Paradoxically, the reconceptualization of identity as an *effect*, that is, as *produced* or *generated*, opens up possibilities of "agency" that are insidiously foreclosed by positions that take identity categories as foundational and fixed. For an identity to be an effect means that it is neither fatally determined nor fully artificial and arbitrary. That the *constituted* status of identity is misconstrued along these two conflicting lines suggests the ways in which the feminist discourse on cultural construction remains trapped within the unnecessary binarism of free will and determinism. Construction is not opposed to agency; it is the necessary scene of agency, the very terms in which agency is articulated and becomes culturally intelligible. The critical task for feminism is not to establish a point of view outside of constructed identities; that conceit is the construction of an epistemological model that would disavow its own cultural location and, hence, promote itself as a global subject, a position that deploys precisely the imperialist strategies that feminism ought to criticize. The critical task is, rather, to locate strategies of subversive repetition enabled by those constructions, to affirm the local possibilities of intervention through participating in precisely those practices of repetition that constitute identity and, therefore, present the immanent possibility of contesting them.

This theoretical inquiry has attempted to locate the political in the very signifying practices that establish, regulate, and deregulate identity. This effort, however, can only be accomplished through the introduction of a set of questions that extend the very notion of the political. How to disrupt the foundations that cover over alternative cultural configurations of gender? How to destabilize and render in their phantasmatic dimension the "premises" of identity politics?

This task has required a critical genealogy of the naturalization of sex and of bodies in general. It has also demanded a reconsideration of the figure of the body as mute, prior to culture, awaiting signification, a figure that cross-checks with the figure of the feminine, awaiting the inscription-as-incision of the masculine signifier for entrance into language and culture. From a political analysis of compulsory heterosexuality, it has been necessary to question the construction of sex as binary, as a hierarchical binary. From the point of view of gender as enacted, questions have emerged over the fixity of gender identity as an interior depth that is said to be externalized in various forms of "expression." The implicit construction of the primary heterosexual construction of desire is shown to persist even as it appears in the mode of primary bisexuality. Strategies of exclusion and hierarchy are also shown to persist in the formulation of the sex/gender distinction and its recourse to "sex" as the prediscursive as well as the priority of sexuality to culture and, in particular, the cultural construction of sexuality as the prediscursive. Finally, the epistemological paradigm that presumes the priority of the doer to the deed establishes a global and globalizing subject who disavows its own locality as well as the conditions for local intervention.

If taken as the grounds of feminist theory or politics, these "effects" of gender hierarchy and compulsory heterosexuality are not only misdescribed as foundations, but the signifying practices that enable this metaleptic misdescription remain outside the purview of a feminist critique of gender relations. To enter into the repetitive practices of this terrain of signification is not a choice, for the "I" that might enter is always already inside: there is no possibility of agency or reality outside of the discursive practices that give those terms the intelligibility that they have. The task is not whether to repeat, but how to repeat or, indeed, to repeat and, through a radical proliferation of gender, *to displace* the very gender norms that enable the repetition itself. There is no ontology of gender on which we might construct a politics, for gender ontologies always operate within established political contexts as normative injunctions, determining what qualifies as intelligible sex, invoking and consolidating the reproductive constraints on sexuality, setting the prescriptive requirements whereby sexed or gendered bodies come into cultural intelligibility. Ontology is, thus, not a foundation, but a normative injunction that operates insidiously by installing itself into political discourse as its necessary ground.

The deconstruction of identity is not the deconstruction of politics; rather, it establishes as political the very terms through which identity is articulated. This kind of critique brings into question the foundationalist frame in which feminism as an identity politics has been articulated. The internal paradox of this foundationalism is that it presumes, fixes, and constrains the very "subjects" that it hopes to represent and liberate. The task here is not to celebrate each and every new possibility *qua* possibility, but to redescribe those possibilities that *already* exist, but which exist within cultural domains designated as culturally unintelligible and impossible. If identities were no longer fixed as the premises of a political syllogism, and politics no longer understood as a set of practices derived from the alleged interests that belong to a set of ready-made subjects, a new configuration of politics would surely emerge from the ruins of the old. Cultural configurations of sex and gender might then proliferate or, rather, their present proliferation might then become articulable within the discourses that establish intelligible cultural life, confounding the very binarism of sex, and exposing its fundamental unnaturalness. What other local strategies for engaging the "unnatural" might lead to the denaturalization of gender as such?

NOTES

1. Parts of the following discussion were published in two different contexts, in my "Gender Trouble, Feminist Theory, and Psychoanalytic Discourse," in *Feminism/Postmodernism*, ed. Linda J. Nicholson (New York: Routledge, 1989) and "Performative Acts and Gender Constitution: An Essay in Phenomenology and Feminist Theory," *Theatre Journal*, Vol. 20, No. 3, Winter 1988.

2. Michel Foucault, *Discipline and Punish: the Birth of the Prison*, trans. Alan Sheridan (New York: Vintage, 1979), p. 29.

3. Ibid., p. 30.

4. See the chapter "Role Models" in Esther Newton, *Mother Camp: Female Impersonators in America* (Chicago: University of Chicago Press, 1972).

5. Ibid., p. 103.

6. Fredric Jameson, "Postmodernism and Consumer Society," in *The Anti-Aesthetic: Essays on Postmodern Culture*, ed. Hal Foster (Port Townsend, WA.: Bay Press, 1983), p. 114.

7. See Victor Turner, *Dramas, Fields and Metaphors* (Ithaca: Cornell University Press, 1974). See also Clifford Geertz, "Blurred Genres: The Refiguration of Thought," in *Local Knowledge, Further Essays in Interpretive Anthropology* (New York: Basic Books, 1983).

THE PROFESSOR OF PARODY: THE HIP DEFEATISM OF JUDITH BUTLER (1999)

MARTHA C. NUSSBAUM

Like Judith Butler, Nussbaum is a feminist philosopher, but their intellectual and verbal styles differ greatly. Nussbaum's critique of Butler has provoked some readers to outrage at Nussbaum and others to welcome her summary and criticism of Butler's ideas and style. Still other readers may prefer Butler's approach in some ways and Nussbaum's in other ways. Readers may wish to continue the dialogue, indirectly, by reading more of Butler's and Nussbaum's writing.

I

For a long time, academic feminism in America has been closely allied to the practical struggle to achieve justice and equality for women. Feminist theory has been understood by theorists as not just fancy words on paper; theory is connected to proposals for social change. Thus feminist scholars have engaged in many concrete projects: the reform of rape law; winning attention and legal redress for the problems of domestic violence and sexual harassment; improving women's economic opportunities, working conditions, and education; winning pregnancy benefits for female workers; campaigning against the trafficking of women and girls in prostitution; working for the social and political equality of lesbians and gay men.

Indeed, some theorists have left the academy altogether, feeling more comfortable in the world of practical politics, where they can address these urgent problems directly. Those who remain in the academy have frequently made it a point of honor to be academics of a committed practical sort, eyes always on the material conditions of real women, writing always in a way that acknowledges those real bodies and those real struggles. One cannot read a page of Catharine MacKinnon, for example, without being engaged with a real issue of legal and institutional change. If one disagrees with her proposals—and many feminists disagree with them—the challenge posed by her writing is to find some other way of solving the problem that has been vividly delineated.

Feminists have differed in some cases about what is bad, and about what is needed to make things better; but all have agreed that the circumstances of women are often unjust and that law and political action can make them more nearly just. MacKinnon, who portrays hierarchy and subordination as endemic to our entire culture, is also committed to, and cautiously optimistic about, change through law—the domestic law of rape and sexual harassment and international human rights law. Even Nancy Chodorow, who, in *The Reproduction of Mothering*, offered a depressing account of the replication of oppressive gender categories in child-rearing, argued that this situation could change. Men and women could decide, understanding the unhappy consequences of these habits, that they will henceforth do things differently; and changes in laws and institutions can assist in such decisions.

Feminist theory still looks like this in many parts of the world. In India, for example, academic feminists have thrown themselves into practical struggles, and feminist theorizing is closely tethered to practical commitments such as female literacy, the reform of unequal land laws, changes in rape law (which, in India today, has most of the flaws that the first generation of American feminists targeted), the effort to get social recognition for problems of sexual harassment and domestic violence. These feminists know that they live in the middle of a fiercely unjust reality; they cannot live with themselves without addressing it more or less daily, in their theoretical writing and in their activities outside the seminar room.

In the United States, however, things have been changing. One observes a new, disquieting trend. It is not only that feminist theory pays relatively little attention to the struggles of women outside the United States. (This was always a dispiriting feature even of much of the best work of the earlier period.) Something more insidious than provincialism has come to prominence in the American academy. It is the virtually complete turning from the material side of life, toward a type of verbal and symbolic politics that makes only the flimsiest of connections with the real situation of real women.

Feminist thinkers of the new symbolic type would appear to believe that the way to do feminist politics is to use words in a subversive way, in academic publications of lofty obscurity and disdainful abstractness. These symbolic gestures, it is believed, are themselves a form of political resistance; and so one need not engage with messy things such as legislatures and movements in order to act daringly. The new feminism, moreover, instructs its members that there is little room for large-scale social change, and maybe no room at all. We are all, more or less, prisoners of the structures of power that have defined our identity as women; we can never change those structures in a large-scale way, and we can never escape from them. All that we can hope to do is to find spaces within the structures of power in which to parody them, to poke fun at them, to transgress them in speech. And so symbolic verbal politics, in addition to being offered as a type of real politics, is held to be the only politics that is really possible.

These developments owe much to the recent prominence of French postmodernist thought. Many young feminists, whatever their concrete affiliations with this or that French thinker, have been influenced by the extremely French idea that the intellectual does politics by speaking seditiously, and that this is a significant type of political action. Many have also derived from the writings of Michel Foucault (rightly or wrongly) the fatalistic idea that we are prisoners of an all-enveloping structure of power, and that real-life reform movements usually end up serving power in new and insidious ways. Such feminists therefore find comfort in the idea that the subversive use of words is still available to feminist intellectuals. Deprived of the hope of larger or more lasting changes, we can still perform our resistance by the reworking of verbal categories, and thus, at the margins, of the selves who are constituted by them.

One American feminist has shaped these developments more than any other. Judith Butler seems to many young scholars to define what feminism is now. Trained as a philosopher, she is frequently seen (more by people in literature than by philosophers) as a major thinker about gender, power, and the body. As we wonder what has become of old-style feminist politics and the material realities to which it was committed, it seems necessary to reckon with Butler's work and influence, and to scrutinize the arguments that have led so many to adopt a stance that looks very much like quietism and retreat.

II

It is difficult to come to grips with Butler's ideas, because it is difficult to figure out what they are. Butler is a very smart person. In public discussions, she proves that she can speak clearly and has a quick grasp of what is said to her. Her written style, however, is ponderous and obscure. It is dense with allusions to other theorists, drawn from a wide range of different theoretical traditions. In addition to Foucault, and to a more recent focus on Freud, Butler's work relies heavily on the thought of Louis Althusser, the French lesbian theorist Monique Wittig, the American anthropologist Gayle Rubin, Jacques Lacan, J. L. Austin, and the American philosopher of language Saul Kripke. These figures do not all agree with one another, to say the least; so an initial problem in reading Butler is that one is bewildered to find her arguments buttressed by appeal to so many contradictory concepts and doctrines, usually without any account of how the apparent contradictions will be resolved.

A further problem lies in Butler's casual mode of allusion. The ideas of these thinkers are never described in enough detail to include the uninitiated (if you are not familiar with the Althusserian concept of "interpellation," you are lost for chapters) or to explain to the initiated how, precisely, the difficult ideas are being understood. Of course, much academic writing is allusive in some way: it presupposes prior knowledge of certain doctrines and positions. But in both the continental and the Anglo-American philosophical traditions, academic writers for a specialist audience standardly acknowledge that the figures they mention are complicated, and the object of many different interpretations. They therefore typically assume the responsibility of advancing a definite interpretation among the contested ones, and of showing by argument why they have interpreted the figure as they have, and why their own interpretation is better than others.

We find none of this in Butler. Divergent interpretations are simply not considered—even where, as in the cases of Foucault and Freud, she is advancing highly contestable interpretations that would not be accepted by many scholars. Thus one is led to the conclusion that the allusiveness of the writing cannot be explained in the usual way, by positing an audience of specialists eager to debate the details of an esoteric academic position. The writing is simply too thin to satisfy any such audience. It is also obvious that Butler's work is not directed at a non-academic audience eager to grapple with actual injustices. Such an audience would simply be baffled by the thick soup of Butler's prose, by its air of in-group knowingness, by its extremely high ratio of names to explanations.

To whom, then, is Butler speaking? It would seem that she is addressing a group of young feminist theorists in the academy who are neither students of philosophy, caring about what Althusser and Freud and Kripke really said, nor outsiders, needing to be informed about the nature of their projects and persuaded of their worth. This implied audience is imagined as remarkably docile. Subservient to the oracular voice of Butler's text, and dazzled by its patina of high-concept abstractness, the imagined reader poses few questions, requests no arguments and no clear definitions of terms.

Still more strangely, the implied reader is expected not to care greatly about Butler's own final view on many matters. For a large proportion of the sentences in any book by Butler—especially sentences near the end of chapters—are questions. Sometimes the answer that the question expects is evident. But often things are much more indeterminate. Among the non-interrogative sentences, many begin with "Consider..." or "One could suggest... "—in such a way that Butler never quite tells the reader whether she approves of the view described. Mystification as well as hierarchy are the tools of her practice, a mystification that eludes criticism because it makes few definite claims.

Take two representative examples:

What does, it mean for the agency of a subject to *presuppose* its own subordination? Is the act of *presupposing* the same as the act of *reinstating,* or is there a discontinuity between the power presupposed and the power reinstated? Consider that in the very act by which the subject reproduces the conditions of its own subordination, the subject exemplifies a temporally based vulnerability that belongs to those conditions, specifically, to the exigencies of their renewal.

And:

Such questions cannot be answered here, but they indicate a direction for thinking that is perhaps prior to the question of conscience, namely, the question that preoccupied Spinoza, Nietzsche, and most recently, Giorgio Agamben: How are we to understand the desire to be as a constitutive desire? Resituating conscience and interpellation within such an account, we might then add to this question another: How is such a desire exploited not only by a law in the singular, but by laws of various kinds such that we yield to subordination in order to maintain some sense of social "being"?

Why does Butler prefer to write in this teasing, exasperating way? The style is certainly not unprecedented. Some precincts of the continental philosophical tradition, though surely not all of them, have an unfortunate tendency to regard the philosopher as a star who fascinates, and frequently by obscurity, rather than as an arguer among equals. When ideas are stated clearly, after all, they may be detached from their author: one can take them away and pursue them on one's own. When they remain mysterious (indeed, when they are not quite asserted), one remains dependent on the originating authority. The thinker is heeded only for his or her turgid charisma. One hangs in suspense, eager for the next move. When Butler does follow that "direction for thinking," what will she say? What does it mean, tell us please, for the agency of a subject to presuppose its own subordination? (No clear answer to this question, so far as I can see, is forthcoming.) One is given the impression of a mind so profoundly cogitative that it will not pronounce on anything lightly: so one waits, in awe of its depth, for it finally to do so.

In this way obscurity creates an aura of importance. It also serves another related purpose. It bullies the reader into granting that, since one cannot figure out what is going on, there must be something significant going on, some complexity of thought, where in reality there are often familiar or even shopworn notions, addressed too simply and too casually to add any new dimension of understanding. When the bullied readers of Butler's books muster the daring to think thus, they will see that the ideas in these books are thin. When Butler's notions are stated clearly and succinctly, one sees that, without a lot more distinctions and arguments, they don't go far, and they are not especially new. Thus obscurity fills the void left by an absence of a real complexity of thought and argument.

Last year Butler won the first prize in the annual Bad Writing Contest sponsored by the journal *Philosophy and Literature,* for the following sentence:

The move from a structuralist account in which capital is understood to structure social relations in relatively homologous ways to a view of hegemony in which power relations are subject to repetition, convergence, and rearticulation brought the question of temporality into the thinking of structure, and marked a shift from a form of Althusserian theory that takes structural totalities as theoretical objects to one in which the insights into the contingent possibility of structure inaugurate a renewed conception of hegemony as bound up with the contingent sites and strategies of the rearticulation of power.

Now, Butler might have written: "Marxist accounts, focusing on capital as the central force structuring social relations, depicted the operations of that force as everywhere uniform. By contrast, Althusserian accounts, focusing on power, see the operations of that force as variegated and as shifting over time." Instead, she prefers a verbosity that causes the reader to expend so much effort in deciphering her prose that little energy is left for assessing the truth of the claims. Announcing the award, the journal's editor remarked that "it's possibly the anxiety-inducing obscurity of such writing that has led Professor Warren Hedges of Southern Oregon University to praise Judith Butler as 'probably one of the ten smartest people on the planet.'"(Such bad writing, incidentally, is by no means ubiquitous in the "queer theory" group of theorists with which Butler is associated. David Halperin, for example, writes about the relationship between Foucault and Kant, and about Greek homosexuality, with philosophical clarity and historical precision.)

Butler gains prestige in the literary world by being a philosopher; many admirers associate her manner of writing with philosophical profundity. But one should ask whether it belongs to the philosophical tradition at all, rather than to the closely related but adversarial traditions of sophistry and rhetoric. Ever since Socrates distinguished philosophy from what the sophists and the rhetoricians were doing, it has been a discourse of equals who trade arguments and counter-arguments without any obscurantist sleight-of-hand. In that way, he claimed, philosophy showed respect for the soul, while the others' manipulative methods showed only disrespect. One afternoon, fatigued by Butler on a long plane trip, I turned to a draft of a student's dissertation on Hume's views of personal identity. I quickly felt my spirits reviving. Doesn't she write clearly, I thought with pleasure, and a tiny bit of pride. And Hume, what a fine, what a gracious spirit: how kindly he respects the reader's intelligence, even at the cost of exposing his own uncertainty.

III

Butler's main idea, first introduced in *Gender Trouble* in 1989 and repeated throughout her books, is that gender is a social artifice. Our ideas of what women and men are reflect nothing that exists eternally in nature. Instead they derive from customs that embed social relations of power.

This notion, of course, is nothing new. The denaturalizing of gender was present already in Plato, and it received a great boost from John Stuart Mill, who claimed in *The Subjection of Women* that "what is now called the nature of women is an eminently artificial thing." Mill saw that claims about "women's nature" derive from, and shore up, hierarchies of power: womanliness is made to be whatever would serve the cause of keeping women in subjection, or, as he put it, "enslav[ing] their minds." With the family as with feudalism, the rhetoric of nature itself serves the cause of slavery. "The subjection of women to men being a universal custom, any departure from it quite naturally appears unnatural.... But was there ever any domination which did not appear natural to those who possessed it?"

Mill was hardly the first social-constructionist. Similar ideas about anger, greed, envy, and other prominent features of our lives had been commonplace in the history of philosophy since ancient Greece. And Mill's application of familiar notions of social-construction to gender needed, and still needs, much fuller development; his suggestive remarks did not yet amount to a theory of gender. Long before Butler came on the scene, many feminists contributed to the articulation of such an account.

In work published in the 1970s and 1980s, Catharine MacKinnon and Andrea Dworkin argued that the conventional understanding of gender roles is a way of ensuring continued male domination in sexual relations, as well as in the public sphere. They took the core of Mill's insight into a sphere of life concerning which the Victorian philosopher had said little. (Not nothing, though: in 1869 Mill already understood that the failure to criminalize rape within marriage defined woman as a tool for male use and negated her human dignity.) Before Butler, MacKinnon and Dworkin addressed the feminist fantasy of an idyllic natural sexuality of women that only needed to be "liberated"; and argued that social forces go so deep that we should not suppose we have access to such a notion of "nature." Before Butler, they stressed the ways in which male-dominated power structures marginalize and subordinate not only women, but also people who would like to choose a same-sex relationship. They understood that discrimination against gays and lesbians is a way of enforcing the familiar hierarchically ordered gender roles; and so they saw discrimination against gays and lesbians as a form of sex discrimination.

Before Butler, the psychologist Nancy Chodorow gave a detailed and compelling account of how gender differences replicate themselves across the generations: she argued that the ubiquity of these mechanisms of replication enables us to understand how what is artificial can nonetheless be nearly ubiquitous. Before Butler, the biologist Anne Fausto Sterling, through her painstaking criticism of experimental work allegedly supporting the naturalness of conventional gender distinctions, showed how deeply social power-relations had compromised the objectivity of scientists: *Myths of Gender* (1985) was an apt title for what she found in the biology of the time. (Other biologists and primatologists also contributed to this enterprise.) Before Butler, the political theorist Susan Moller Okin explored the role of law and political thought in constructing a gendered destiny for women in the family; and this project, too, was pursued further by a number of feminists in law and political philosophy. Before Butler, Gayle Rubin's important anthropological account of subordination, *The Traffic in Women* (1975), provided a valuable analysis of the relationship between the social organization of gender and the asymmetries of power.

So what does Butler's work add to this copious body of writing? *Gender Trouble* and *Bodies that Matter* contain no detailed argument against biological claims of "natural" difference, no account of mechanisms of gender replication, and no account of the legal shaping of the family; nor do they contain any detailed focus on possibilities for legal change. What, then, does Butler offer that we might not find more fully done in earlier feminist writings? One relatively original claim is that when we recognize the artificiality of gender distinctions, and refrain from thinking of them as expressing an independent natural reality, we will also understand that there is no compelling reason why the gender types should have been two (correlated with the two biological sexes), rather than three or five or indefinitely many. "When the constructed status of gender is theorized as radically independent of sex, gender itself becomes a free-floating artifice," she writes.

From this claim it does not follow, for Butler, that we can freely reinvent the genders as we like: she holds, indeed, that there are severe limits to our freedom. She insists that we should not naïvely imagine that there is a pristine self that stands behind society, ready to emerge all pure and liberated: "There is no self that is prior to the convergence or who maintains 'integrity' prior to its entrance into this conflicted cultural field. There is only a taking up of the tools where they lie, where the very 'taking up' is enabled by the tool lying there." Butler does claim, though, that we can create categories that are in some sense new ones, by means of the artful parody of the old ones. Thus her best known idea, her conception of politics as a parodic performance, is born out of the sense of a (strictly limited) freedom that comes from the recognition that one's ideas of gender have been shaped by forces that are social rather than biological. We are doomed to repetition of the power structures into which we are born, but we can at least make fun of them; and some ways of making fun are subversive assaults on the original norms.

The idea of gender as performance is Butler's most famous idea, and so it is worth pausing to scrutinize it more closely. She introduced the notion intuitively, in *Gender Trouble*, without invoking theoretical precedent. Later she denied that she was referring to quasi-theatrical performance, and associated her notion instead with Austin's account of speech acts in *How to Do Things with Words*. Austin's linguistic category of "performatives" is a category of linguistic utterances that function, in and of themselves, as actions rather than as assertions. When (in appropriate social circumstances) I say "I bet ten dollars," or "I'm sorry," or "I do" (in a marriage ceremony), or "I name this ship...," I am not reporting on a bet or an apology or a marriage or a naming ceremony, I am conducting one.

Butler's analogous claim about gender is not obvious, since the "performances" in question involve gesture, dress, movement, and action, as well as language. Austin's thesis, which is restricted to a rather technical analysis of a certain class of sentences, is in fact not especially helpful to Butler in developing her ideas. Indeed, though she vehemently repudiates readings of her work that associate her view with theater, thinking about the Living Theater's subversive work with gender seems to illuminate her ideas far more than thinking about Austin.

Nor is Butler's treatment of Austin very plausible. She makes the bizarre claim that the fact that the marriage ceremony is one of dozens of examples of performatives in Austin's text suggests "that the heterosexualization of the social bond is the paradigmatic form for those speech acts which bring about what they name." Hardly. Marriage is no more paradigmatic for Austin than betting or ship-naming or promising or apologizing. He is interested in a formal feature of certain utterances, and we are given no reason to suppose that their content has any significance for his argument. It is usually a mistake to read earth-shaking significance into a philosopher's pedestrian choice of examples. Should we say that Aristotle's use of a low-fat diet to illustrate the practical syllogism suggests that chicken is at the heart of Aristotelian virtue? Or that Rawls's use of travel plans to illustrate practical reasoning shows that *A Theory of Justice* aims at giving us all a vacation?

Leaving these oddities to one side, Butler's point is presumably this: when we act and speak in a gendered way, we are not simply reporting on something that is already fixed in the world, we are actively constituting it, replicating it, and reinforcing it. By behaving as if there were male and female "natures," we co-create the social fiction that these natures exist. They are never there apart from our deeds; we are always making them be there. At the same time, by carrying out these performances in a slightly different manner, a parodic manner, we can perhaps unmake them just a little.

Thus the one place for agency in a world constrained by hierarchy is in the small opportunities we have to oppose gender roles every time they take shape. When I find myself doing femaleness, I can turn it around, poke fun at it, do it a little bit differently. Such reactive and parodic performances, in Butler's view, never destabilize the larger system. She doesn't envisage mass movements of resistance or campaigns for political reform; only personal acts carried out by a small number of knowing actors. Just as actors with a bad script can subvert it by delivering the bad lines oddly, so too with gender: the script remains bad, but the actors have a tiny bit of freedom. Thus we have the basis for what, in *Excitable Speech*, Butler calls "an ironic hopefulness."

Up to this point, Butler's contentions, though relatively familiar, are plausible and even interesting, though one is already unsettled by her narrow vision of the possibilities for change. Yet Butler adds to these plausible claims about gender two other claims that are stronger and more contentious. The first is that there is no agent behind or prior to the social forces that produce the self. If this means only that babies are born into a gendered world that begins to replicate males and females almost immediately, the claim is plausible, but not surprising: experiments have for some time demonstrated that the way babies are held and talked to, the way their emotions are described, are profoundly shaped by the sex the adults in question believe the child to have. (The same baby will be bounced if the adults think it is a boy, cuddled if they think it is a girl; its crying will be labeled as fear if the adults think it is a girl, as anger if they think it is a boy.) Butler shows no interest in these empirical facts, but they do support her contention.

If she means, however, that babies enter the world completely inert, with no tendencies and no abilities that are in some sense prior to their experience in a gendered society, this is far less plausible, and difficult to support empirically. Butler offers no such support, preferring to remain on the high plane of metaphysical abstraction. (Indeed, her recent Freudian work may even repudiate this idea: it suggests, with Freud, that there are at least some presocial impulses and tendencies, although, typically, this line is not clearly developed.) Moreover, such an exaggerated denial of pre-cultural agency takes away some of the resources that Chodorow and others use when they try to account for cultural change in the direction of the better.

Butler does in the end want to say that we have a kind of agency, an ability to undertake change and resistance. But where does this ability come from, if there is no structure in the personality that is not thoroughly power's creation? It is not impossible for Butler to answer this question, but she certainly has not answered it yet, in a way that would convince those who believe that human beings have at least some pre-cultural desires—for food, for comfort, for cognitive mastery, for survival—and that this structure in the personality is crucial in the explanation of our development as moral and political agents. One would like to see her engage with the strongest forms of such a view, and to say, clearly and without jargon, exactly why and where she rejects them. One would also like to hear her speak about real infants, who do appear to manifest a structure of striving that influences from the start their reception of cultural forms.

Butler's second strong claim is that the body itself, and especially the distinction between the two sexes, is also a social construction. She means not only that the body is shaped in many ways by social norms of how men and women should be; she means also that the fact that a binary division of sexes is taken as fundamental, as a key to arranging society, is itself a social idea that is not given in bodily reality. What exactly does this claim mean, and how plausible is it?

Butler's brief exploration of Foucault on hermaphrodites does show us society's anxious insistence to classify every human being in one box or another, whether or not the individual fits a box; but of course it does not show that there are many such indeterminate cases. She is right to insist that we might have made many different classifications of body types, not necessarily focusing on the binary division as the most salient; and she is also right to insist that, to a large extent, claims of bodily sex difference allegedly based upon scientific research have been projections of cultural prejudice—though Butler offers nothing here that is nearly as compelling as Fausto Sterling's painstaking biological analysis.

And yet it is much too simple to say that power is all that the body is. We might have had the bodies of birds or dinosaurs or lions, but we do not; and this reality shapes our choices. Culture can shape and reshape some aspects of our bodily existence, but it does not shape all the aspects of it. "In the man burdened by hunger and thirst," as Sextus Empiricus observed long ago, "it is impossible to produce by argument the conviction that he is not so burdened." This is an important fact also for feminism, since women's nutritional needs (and their special needs when pregnant or lactating) are an important feminist topic. Even where sex difference is concerned, it is surely too simple to write it all off as culture; nor should feminists be eager to make such a sweeping gesture. Women who run or play basketball, for example, were right to welcome the demolition of myths about women's athletic performance that were the product of male-dominated assumptions; but they were also right to demand the specialized research on women's bodies that has fostered a better understanding of women's training needs and women's injuries. In short: what feminism needs, and sometimes gets, is a subtle study of the interplay of bodily difference and cultural construction. And Butler's abstract pronouncements, floating high above all matter, give us none of what we need.

IV

Suppose we grant Butler her most interesting claims up to this point: that the social structure of gender is ubiquitous, but we can resist it by subversive and parodic acts. Two significant questions remain. What should be resisted, and on what basis? What would the acts of resistance be like, and what would we expect them to accomplish?

Butler uses several words for what she takes to be bad and therefore worthy of resistance: the "repressive," the "subordinating," the "oppressive." But she provides no empirical discussion of resistance of the sort that we find, say, in Barry Adam's fascinating sociological study *The Survival of Domination* (1978), which studies the subordination of blacks, Jews, women, and gays and lesbians, and their ways of wrestling with the forms of social power that have oppressed them. Nor does Butler provide any account of the concepts of resistance and oppression that would help us, were we really in doubt about what we ought to be resisting.

Butler departs in this regard from earlier social-constructionist feminists, all of whom used ideas such as non-hierarchy, equality, dignity, autonomy, and treating as an end rather than a means, to indicate a direction for actual politics. Still less is she willing to elaborate any positive normative notion. Indeed, it is clear that Butler, like Foucault, is adamantly opposed to normative notions such as human dignity, or treating humanity as an end, on the grounds that they are inherently dictatorial. In her view, we ought to wait to see what the political struggle itself throws up, rather than prescribe in advance to its participants. Universal normative notions, she says, "colonize under the sign of the same."

This idea of waiting to see what we get—in a word, this moral passivity—seems plausible in Butler because she tacitly assumes an audience of like-minded readers who agree (sort of) about what the bad things are—discrimination against gays and lesbians, the unequal and hierarchical treatment of women—and who even agree (sort of) about why they are bad (they subordinate some people to others, they deny people freedoms that they ought to have). But take that assumption away, and the absence of a normative dimension becomes a severe problem.

Try teaching Foucault at a contemporary law school, as I have, and you will quickly find that subversion takes many forms, not all of them congenial to Butler and her allies. As a perceptive libertarian student said to me, Why can't I use these ideas to resist the tax structure, or the antidiscrimination laws, or perhaps even to join the militias? Others, less fond of liberty, might engage in the subversive performances of making fun of feminist remarks in class, or ripping down the posters of the lesbian and gay law students' association. These things happen. They are parodic and subversive. Why, then, aren't they daring and good?

Well, there are good answers to those questions, but you won't find them in Foucault, or in Butler. Answering them requires discussing which liberties and opportunities human beings ought to have, and what it is for social institutions to treat human beings as ends rather than as means—in short, a normative theory of social justice and human dignity. It is one thing to say that we should be humble about our universal norms, and willing to learn from the experience of oppressed people. It is quite another thing to say that we don't need any norms at all. Foucault, unlike Butler, at least showed signs in his late work of grappling with this problem; and all his writing is animated by a fierce sense of the texture of social oppression and the harm that it does.

Come to think of it, justice, understood as a personal virtue, has exactly the structure of gender in the Butlerian analysis: it is not innate or "natural," it is produced by repeated performances (or as Aristotle said, we learn it by doing it), it shapes our inclinations and forces the repression of some of them. These ritual performances, and their associated repressions, are enforced by arrangements of social power, as children who won't share on the playground quickly discover. Moreover, the parodic subversion of justice is ubiquitous in politics, as in personal life. But there is an important difference. Generally we dislike these subversive performances, and we think that young people should be strongly discouraged from seeing norms of justice in such a cynical light. Butler cannot explain in any purely structural or procedural way why the subversion of gender norms is a social good while the subversion of justice norms is a social bad. Foucault, we should remember, cheered for the Ayatollah, and why not? That, too, was resistance, and there was indeed nothing in the text to tell us that that struggle was less worthy than a struggle for civil rights and civil liberties.

There is a void, then, at the heart of Butler's notion of politics. This void can look liberating, because the reader fills it implicitly with a normative theory of human equality or dignity. But let there be no mistake: for Butler, as for Foucault, subversion is subversion, and it can in principle go in any direction. Indeed, Butler's naïvely empty politics is especially dangerous for the very causes she holds dear. For every friend of Butler, eager to engage in subversive performances that proclaim the repressiveness of heterosexual gender norms, there are dozens who would like to engage in subversive performances that flout the norms of tax compliance, of non-discrimination, of decent treatment of one's fellow students. To such people we should say, you cannot simply resist as you please, for there are norms of fairness, decency, and dignity that entail that this is bad behavior. But then we have to articulate those norms—and this Butler refuses to do.

V

What precisely does Butler offer when she counsels subversion? She tells us to engage in parodic performances, but she warns us that the dream of escaping altogether from the oppressive structures is just a dream: it is within the oppressive structures that we must find little spaces for resistance, and this resistance cannot hope to change the overall situation. And here lies a dangerous quietism.

If Butler means only to warn us against the dangers of fantasizing an idyllic world in which sex raises no serious problems, she is wise to do so. Yet frequently she goes much further. She suggests that the institutional structures that ensure the marginalization of lesbians and gay men in our society, and the continued inequality of women, will never be changed in a deep way; and so our best hope is to thumb our noses at them, and to find pockets of personal freedom within them. "Called by an injurious name, I come into social being, and because I have a certain inevitable attachment to my existence, because a certain narcissism takes hold of any term that confers existence, I am led to embrace the terms that injure me because they constitute me socially." In other words: I cannot escape the humiliating structures without ceasing to be, so the best I can do is mock, and use the language of subordination stingingly. In Butler, resistance is always imagined as personal, more or less private, involving no unironic, organized public action for legal or institutional change.

Isn't this like saying to a slave that the institution of slavery will never change, but you can find ways of mocking it and subverting it, finding your personal freedom within those acts of carefully limited defiance? Yet it is a fact that the institution of slavery can be changed, and was changed—but not by people who took a Butler-like view of the possibilities. It was changed because people did not rest content with parodic performance: they demanded, and to some extent they got, social upheaval. It is also a fact that the institutional structures that shape women's lives have changed. The law of rape, still defective, has at least improved; the law of sexual harassment exists, where it did not exist before; marriage is no longer regarded as giving men monarchical control over women's bodies. These things were changed by feminists who would not take parodic performance as their answer, who thought that power, where bad, should, and would, yield before justice.

Butler not only eschews such a hope, she takes pleasure in its impossibility. She finds it exciting to contemplate the alleged immovability of power, and to envisage the ritual subversions of the slave who is convinced that she must remain such. She tells us—this is the central thesis of *The Psychic Life of Power*—that we all eroticize the power structures that oppress us, and can thus find sexual pleasure only within their confines. It seems to be for that reason that she prefers the sexy acts of parodic subversion to any lasting material or institutional change. Real change would so uproot our psyches that it would make sexual satisfaction impossible. Our libidos are the creation of the bad enslaving forces, and thus necessarily sadomasochistic in structure.

Well, parodic performance is not so bad when you are a powerful tenured academic in a liberal university. But here is where Butler's focus on the symbolic, her proud neglect of the material side of life, becomes a fatal blindness. For women who are hungry, illiterate, disenfranchised, beaten, raped, it is not sexy or liberating to reenact, however parodically, the conditions of hunger, illiteracy, disenfranchisement, beating, and rape. Such women prefer food, schools, votes, and the integrity of their bodies. I see no reason to believe that they long sadomasochistically for a return to the bad state. If some individuals cannot live without the sexiness of domination, that seems sad, but it is not really our business. But when a major theorist tells women in desperate conditions that life offers them only bondage, she purveys a cruel lie, and a lie that flatters evil by giving it much more power than it actually has.

Excitable Speech, Butler's most recent book, which provides her analysis of legal controversies involving pornography and hate speech, shows us exactly how far her quietism extends. For she is now willing to say that even where legal change is possible, even where it has already happened, we should wish it away, so as to preserve the space within which the oppressed may enact their sadomasochistic rituals of parody.

As a work on the law of free speech, *Excitable Speech* is an unconscionably bad book. Butler shows no awareness of the major theoretical accounts of the First Amendment, and no awareness of the wide range of cases such a theory will need to take into consideration. She makes absurd legal claims: for example, she says that the only type of speech that has been held to be unprotected is speech that has been previously defined as conduct rather than speech. (In fact, there are many types of speech, from false or misleading advertising to libelous statements to obscenity as currently defined, which have never been claimed to be action rather than speech, and which are nonetheless denied First Amendment protection.) Butler even claims, mistakenly, that obscenity has been judged to be the equivalent of "fighting words." It is not that Butler has an argument to back up her novel readings of the wide range of cases of unprotected speech that an account of the First Amendment would need to cover. She just has not noticed that there is this wide range of cases, or that her view is not a widely accepted legal view. Nobody interested in law can take her argument seriously.

But let us extract from Butler's thin discussion of hate speech and pornography the core of her position. It is this: legal prohibitions of hate speech and pornography are problematic (though in the end she does not clearly oppose them) because they close the space within which the parties injured by that speech can perform their resistance. By this Butler appears to mean that if the offense is dealt with through the legal system, there will be fewer occasions for informal protest; and also, perhaps, that if the offense becomes rarer because of its illegality we will have fewer opportunities to protest its presence.

Well, yes. Law does close those spaces. Hate speech and pornography are extremely complicated subjects on which feminists may reasonably differ. (Still, one should state the contending views precisely: Butler's account of MacKinnon is less than careful, stating that MacKinnon supports "ordinances against pornography" and suggesting that, despite MacKinnon's explicit denial, they involve a form of censorship. Nowhere does Butler mention that what MacKinnon actually supports is a civil damage action in which particular women harmed through pornography can sue its makers and its distributors.)

But Butler's argument has implications well beyond the cases of hate speech and pornography. It would appear to support not just quietism in these areas, but a much more general legal quietism—or, indeed, a radical libertarianism. It goes like this: let us do away with everything from building codes to non-discrimination laws to rape laws, because they close the space within which the injured tenants, the victims of discrimination, the raped women, can perform their resistance. Now, this is not the same argument radical libertarians use to oppose building codes and anti-discrimination laws; even they draw the line at rape. But the conclusions converge.

If Butler should reply that her argument pertains only to speech (and there is no reason given in the text for such a limitation, given the assimilation of harmful speech to conduct), then we can reply in the domain of speech. Let us get rid of laws against false advertising and unlicensed medical advice, for they close the space within which poisoned consumers and mutilated patients can perform their resistance! Again, if Butler does not approve of these extensions, she needs to make an argument that divides her cases from these cases, and it is not clear that her position permits her to make such a distinction.

For Butler, the act of subversion is so riveting, so sexy, that it is a bad dream to think that the world will actually get better. What a bore equality is! No bondage, no delight. In this way, her pessimistic erotic anthropology offers support to an amoral anarchist politics.

VI

When we consider the quietism inherent in Butler's writing, we have some keys to understanding Butler's influential fascination with drag and cross-dressing as paradigms of feminist resistance. Butler's followers understand her account of drag to imply that such performances are ways for women to be daring and subversive. I am unaware of any attempt by Butler to repudiate such readings.

But what is going on here? The woman dressed mannishly is hardly a new figure. Indeed, even when she was relatively new, in the nineteenth century, she was in another way quite old, for she simply replicated in the lesbian world the existing stereotypes and hierarchies of male-female society. What, we may well ask, is parodic subversion in this area, and what a kind of prosperous middle-class acceptance? Isn't hierarchy in drag still hierarchy? And is it really true (as *The Psychic Life of Power* would seem to conclude) that domination and subordination are the roles that women must play in every sphere, and if not subordination, then mannish domination?

In short, cross-dressing for women is a tired old script—as Butler herself informs us. Yet she would have us see the script as subverted, made new, by the cross-dresser's knowing symbolic sartorial gestures; but again we must wonder about the newness, and even the subversiveness. Consider Andrea Dworkin's parody (in her novel *Mercy*) of a Butlerish parodic feminist, who announces from her posture of secure academic comfort:

> The notion that bad things happen is both propagandistic and inadequate.... To understand a woman's life requires that we affirm the hidden or obscure dimensions of pleasure, often in pain, and choice, often under duress. One must develop an eye for secret signs—the clothes that are more than clothes or decoration in the contemporary dialogue, for instance, or the rebellion hidden behind apparent conformity. There is no victim. There is perhaps an insufficiency of signs, an obdurate appearance of conformity that simply masks the deeper level on which choice occurs.

In prose quite unlike Butler's, this passage captures the ambivalence of the implied author of some of Butler's writings, who delights in her violative practice while turning her theoretical eye resolutely away from the material suffering of women who are hungry, illiterate, violated, beaten. There is no victim. There is only an insufficiency of signs.

Butler suggests to her readers that this sly send-up of the status quo is the only script for resistance that life offers. Well, no. Besides offering many other ways to be human in one's personal life, beyond traditional norms of domination and subservience, life also offers many scripts for resistance that do not focus narcissistically on personal self-presentation. Such scripts involve feminists (and others, of course) in building laws and institutions, without much concern for how a woman displays her own body and its gendered nature: in short, they involve working for others who are suffering.

The great tragedy in the new feminist theory in America is the loss of a sense of public commitment. In this sense, Butler's self-involved feminism is extremely American, and it is not surprising that it has caught on here, where successful middle-class people prefer to focus on cultivating the self rather than thinking in a way that helps the material condition of others. Even in America, however, it is possible for theorists to be dedicated to the public good and to achieve something through that effort.

Many feminists in America are still theorizing in a way that supports material change and responds to the situation of the most oppressed. Increasingly, however, the academic and cultural trend is toward the pessimistic flirtatiousness represented by the theorizing of Butler and her followers. Butlerian feminism is in many ways easier than the old feminism. It tells scores of talented young women that they need not work on changing the law, or feeding the hungry, or assailing power through theory harnessed to material politics. They can do politics in safety of their campuses, remaining on the symbolic level, making subversive gestures at power through speech and gesture. This, the theory says, is pretty much all that is available to us anyway, by way of political action, and isn't it exciting and sexy?

In its small way, of course, this is a hopeful politics. It instructs people that they can, right now, without compromising their security, do something bold. But the boldness is entirely gestural, and insofar as Butler's ideal suggests that these symbolic gestures really are political change, it offers only a false hope. Hungry women are not fed by this, battered women are not sheltered by it, raped women do not find justice in it, gays and lesbians do not achieve legal protections through it.

Finally there is despair at the heart of the cheerful Butlerian enterprise. The big hope, the hope for a world of real justice, where laws and institutions protect the equality and the dignity of all citizens, has been banished, even perhaps mocked as sexually tedious. Judith Butler's hip quietism is a comprehensible response to the difficulty of realizing justice in America. But it is a bad response. It collaborates with evil. Feminism demands more and women deserve better.

COMPULSORY ABLE-BODIEDNESS AND QUEER/ DISABLED EXISTENCE (2002)

ROBERT McRUER

Drawing on Adrienne Rich's essay about compulsory heterosexuality and Judith Butler's concept of gender trouble (both in this volume), McRuer merges queer studies and disability studies to propose concepts of compulsory able-bodiedness and ability trouble. McRuer builds on this essay in his later Crip Theory: Cultural Signs of Queerness and Disability (2006).

CONTEXTUALIZING DISABILITY

In her famous critique of compulsory heterosexuality Adrienne Rich opens with the suggestion that lesbian existence has often been "simply rendered invisible" (178), but the bulk of her analysis belies that rendering. In fact, throughout "Compulsory Heterosexuality and Lesbian Existence," one of Rich's points seems to be that compulsory heterosexuality depends as much on the ways in which lesbian identities are made visible (or, we might say, comprehensible) as on the ways in which they are made invisible or incomprehensible. She writes:

Any theory of cultural/political creation that treats lesbian existence as a marginal or less "natural" phenomenon, as mere "sexual preference," or as the mirror image of either heterosexual or male homosexual relations is profoundly weakened thereby, whatever its other contributions. Feminist theory can no longer afford merely to voice a toleration of "lesbianism" as an "alternative lifestyle," or make token allusion to lesbians. A feminist critique of compulsory heterosexual orientation for women is long overdue. (178)

The critique that Rich calls for proceeds not through a simple recognition or even valuation of "lesbian existence" but rather through an interrogation of how the system of compulsory heterosexuality utilizes that existence. Indeed, I would extract from her suspicion of mere "toleration" confirmation for the idea that one of the ways in which heterosexuality is currently constituted or founded, established as the foundational sexual identity for women, is precisely through the deployment of lesbian existence as always and everywhere supplementary—the margin to heterosexuality's center, the mere reflection of (straight and gay) patriarchal realities. Compulsory heterosexuality's casting of some identities as alternatives ironically buttresses the ideological notion that dominant identities are not really alternatives but rather the natural order of things.[1]

More than twenty years after it was initially published, Rich's critique of compulsory heterosexuality is indispensable, the criticisms of her ahistorical notion of a "lesbian continuum" notwithstanding.[2] Despite its continued relevance, however, the realm of compulsory heterosexuality might seem to be an unlikely place to begin contextualizing disability.[3] I want to challenge that by considering what might be gained by understanding "compulsory heterosexuality" as a key concept in disability studies. Through a reading of compulsory heterosexuality, I want to put forward a theory of what I call compulsory able-bodiedness. The Latin root for *contextualize* denotes the act of weaving together, interweaving, joining together, or composing. This essay thus contextualizes disability in the root sense of the word, because I argue that the system of compulsory able-bodiedness that produces disability is thoroughly interwoven with the system of compulsory heterosexuality that produces queerness; that—in fact—compulsory heterosexuality is contingent on compulsory able-bodiedness and vice versa. And, although I reiterate it in my conclusion, I want to make it clear at the outset that this particular contextualizing of disability is offered as part of a much larger and collective project of unraveling and decomposing both systems.[4]

The idea of imbricated systems is of course not new—Rich's own analysis repeatedly stresses the imbrication of compulsory heterosexuality and patriarchy. I would argue, however, as others have, that feminist and queer theories (and cultural theories generally) are not yet accustomed to figuring ability/disability into the equation, and thus this theory of compulsory able-bodiedness is offered as a preliminary contribution to that much-needed conversation.[5]

ABLE-BODIED HETEROSEXUALITY

In his introduction to *Keywords: A Vocabulary of Culture and Society,* Raymond Williams describes his project as

> the record of an inquiry into a vocabulary: a shared body of words and meanings in our
> most general discussions, in English, of the practices and institutions which we group as
> culture and society. Every word which I have included has at some time, in the course of
> some argument, virtually forced itself on my attention because the problems of its meaning
> seemed to me inextricably bound up with the problems it was being used to discuss. (15)

Although Williams is not particularly concerned in *Keywords* with feminism or gay and lesbian liberation, the processes he describes should be recognizable to feminists and queer
theorists, as well as to scholars and activists in other contemporary movements, such as
African American studies or critical race theory. As these movements have developed, increasing numbers of words have indeed forced themselves on our attention, so that an inquiry
into not just the marginalized identity but also the dominant identity has become necessary.
The problem of the meaning of masculinity (or even maleness), of whiteness, of heterosexuality has increasingly been understood as inextricably bound up with the problems the
term is being used to discuss.

One need go no further than the *Oxford English Dictionary* to locate problems with
the meaning of heterosexuality. In 1971 the *OED Supplement* defined *heterosexual* as "pertaining to or characterized by the normal relations of the sexes; opp. to homosexual." At
this point, of course, a few decades of critical work by feminists and queer theorists have
made it possible to acknowledge quite readily that heterosexual and homosexual are in
fact not equal and opposite identities. Rather, the ongoing subordination of homosexuality (and bisexuality) to heterosexuality allows heterosexuality to be institutionalized
as "the normal relations of the sexes," while the institutionalization of heterosexuality
as the "normal relations of the sexes" allows homosexuality (and bisexuality) to be
subordinated. And, as queer theory continues to demonstrate, it is precisely the introduction of normalcy into the system that introduces compulsion. "Nearly everyone,"
Michael Warner writes in *The Trouble with Normal: Sex, Politics, and the Ethics of Queer
Life,* "wants to be normal. And who can blame them, if the alternative is being abnormal, or deviant, or not being one of the rest of us? Put in those terms, there doesn't seem
to be a choice at all. Especially in America where [being] normal probably outranks all
other social aspirations" (53). Compulsion is here produced and covered over, with the
appearance of choice (sexual preference) mystifying a system in which there actually is
no choice.

A critique of normalcy has similarly been central to the disability rights movement and
to disability studies, with—for example—Lennard Davis's overview and critique of the historical emergence of normalcy *(Enforcing* 23–49) or Rosemarie Garland-Thomson's introduction of the concept of the "normate" *(Extraordinary Bodies* 8–9). Such scholarly and
activist work positions us to locate the problems of able-bodied identity, to see the problem of the meaning of able-bodiedness as bound up with the problems it is being used
to discuss. Arguably, able-bodied identity is at this juncture even more naturalized than
heterosexual identity. At the very least, many people not sympathetic to queer theory will
concede that ways of being heterosexual are culturally produced and culturally variable,
even if and even as they understand heterosexual identity itself to be entirely natural. The

same cannot be said, on the whole, for able-bodied identity. An extreme example that none-theless encapsulates currently hegemonic thought on ability and disability is a notorious *Salon* article attacking disability studies that appeared online in the summer of 1999. Nora Vincent writes, "It's hard to deny that something called normalcy exists. The human body is a machine, after all—one that has evolved functional parts: lungs for breathing, legs for walking, eyes for seeing, ears for hearing, a tongue for speaking and most crucially for all the academics concerned, a brain for thinking. This is science, not culture" ("Enabling").[6] In a nutshell, you either have an able body or you don't.

Yet the desire for definitional clarity might unleash more problems than it contains; if it's hard to deny that something called normalcy exists, it's even harder to pinpoint what that something is. The *OED* defines *able-bodied* redundantly and negatively as "having an able body, i.e. one free from physical disability, and capable of the physical exertions required of it; in bodily health; robust." Able-bodiedness, in turn, is defined vaguely as "soundness of bodily health; ability to work; robustness." The parallel structure of the definitions of ability and sexuality is quite striking: first, to be able-bodied is to be "free from physical disability," just as to be heterosexual is to be "the opposite of homosexual." Second, even though the language of "the normal relations" expected of human beings is not present in the definition of able-bodied, the sense of normal relations is, especially with the emphasis on work: being able-bodied means being capable of the normal physical exertions required in a particular system of labor. It is here, in fact, that both able-bodied identity and the *Oxford English Dictionary* betray their origins in the nineteenth century and the rise of indus-trial capitalism. It is here as well that we can begin to understand the compulsory nature of able-bodiedness: in the emergent industrial capitalist system, free to sell one's labor but not free to do anything else effectively meant free to have an able body but not particularly free to have anything else.

Like compulsory heterosexuality, then, compulsory able-bodiedness functions by cov-ering over, with the appearance of choice, a system in which there actually is no choice. I would not locate this compulsion, moreover, solely in the past, with the rise of industrial capitalism. Just as the origins of heterosexual/homosexual identity are now obscured for most people so that compulsory heterosexuality functions as a disciplinary formation seem-ingly emanating from everywhere and nowhere, so too are the origins of able-bodied/dis-abled identity obscured, allowing what Susan Wendell calls "the disciplines of normality" (87) to cohere in a system of compulsory able-bodiedness that similarly emanates from everywhere and nowhere. Able-bodied dilutions and misunderstandings of the minority thesis put forward in the disability rights movement and disability studies have even, in some ways, strengthened the system: the dutiful (or docile) able-bodied subject now recog-nizes that some groups of people have chosen to adjust to or even take pride in their "condi-tion," but that recognition, and the tolerance that undergirds it, covers over the compulsory nature of the able-bodied subject's own identity.[7]

Michael Bérubé's memoir about his son Jamie, who has Down syndrome, helps exem-plify some of the ideological demands currently sustaining compulsory able-bodiedness. Bérubé writes of how he "sometimes feel[s] cornered by talking about Jamie's intelligence, as if the burden of proof is on me, official spokesman on his behalf." The subtext of these encounters always seems to be the same: "In the end, aren't you disappointed to have a retarded child? [...] Do we really have to give this person our full attention?" (180). Bérubé 's excavation of this subtext pinpoints an important common experience that links all people with disabilities under a system of compulsory able-bodiedness—the experience of the able-bodied need for an agreed-on common ground. I can imagine that answers might be incredibly varied to similar questions—"In the end, wouldn't you rather be hearing?" and "In the end, wouldn't you rather not be HIV positive?" would seem, after all, to be very different questions, the first (with its thinly veiled desire for Deafness not to exist) more obviously genocidal than the second. But they are not really different questions, in that their constant repetition (or their presence as ongoing subtexts) reveals more about the able-bodied culture doing the asking than about the bodies being interrogated. The culture asking such questions assumes in advance that we all agree: able-bodied identities, able-bodied perspectives are preferable and what we all, collectively, are aiming for. A system of compulsory able-bodiedness repeatedly demands that people with disabilities embody for others an affirmative answer to the unspoken question, Yes, but in the end, wouldn't you rather be more like me?

It is with this repetition that we can begin to locate both the ways in which compulsory able-bodiedness and compulsory heterosexuality are interwoven and the ways in which they might be contested. In queer theory, Judith Butler is most famous for identifying the repetition required to maintain heterosexual hegemony:

> The "reality" of heterosexual identities is performatively constituted through an imitation that sets itself up as the origin and the ground of all imitations. In other words, heterosexuality is always in the process of imitating and approximating its own phantasmatic idealization of itself—and failing. Precisely because it is bound to fail, and yet endeavors to succeed, the project of heterosexual identity is propelled into an endless repetition of itself. ("Imitation" 21)

If anything, the emphasis on identities that are constituted through repetitive performances is even more central to compulsory able-bodiedness—think, after all, of how many institutions in our culture are showcases for able-bodied performance. Moreover, as with heterosexuality, this repetition is bound to fail, as the ideal able-bodied identity can never, once and for all, be achieved. Able-bodied identity and heterosexual identity are linked in their mutual impossibility and in their mutual incomprehensibility—they are incomprehensible in that each is an identity that is simultaneously the ground on which all identities supposedly rest and an impressive achievement that is always deferred and thus never really guaranteed. Hence Butler's queer theories of gender performativity could be easily extended to disability studies, as this slightly paraphrased excerpt from *Gender Trouble* suggests (I substitute, by bracketing, terms having to do literally with embodiment for Butler's terms of gender and sexuality):

> [Able-bodiedness] offers normative [...] positions that are intrinsically impossible to embody, and the persistent failure to identify fully and without incoherence with these positions reveals [able-bodiedness] itself not only as a compulsory law, but as an inevitable comedy. Indeed, I would offer this insight into [able-bodied identity] as both a

compulsory system and an intrinsic comedy, a constant parody of itself, as an alternative [disabled] perspective. (122)

In short, Butler's theory of gender trouble might be resignified in the context of queer/disability studies as what we could call "ability trouble"—meaning not the so-called problem of disability but the inevitable impossibility, even as it is made compulsory, of an able-bodied identity.

QUEER/DISABLED EXISTENCE

The cultural management of the endemic crisis surrounding the performance of both heterosexual and able-bodied identity effects a panicked consolidation of hegemonic identities. The most successful heterosexual subject is the one whose sexuality is not compromised by disability (metaphorized as queerness); the most successful able-bodied subject is the one whose ability is not compromised by queerness (metaphorized as disability). This consolidation occurs through complex processes of conflation and stereotype: people with disabilities are often understood as somehow queer (as paradoxical stereotypes of the asexual or oversexual person with disabilities would suggest), while queers are often understood as somehow disabled (as an ongoing medicalization of identity, similar to what people with disabilities more generally encounter, would suggest). Once these conflations are available in the popular imagination, queer/disabled figures can be tolerated and, in fact, utilized in order to maintain the fiction that able-bodied heterosexuality is not in crisis. As lesbian existence is deployed, in Rich's analysis, to reflect back heterosexual and patriarchal "realities," queer/disabled existence can be deployed to buttress compulsory able-bodiedness. Since queerness and disability both have the potential to disrupt the performance of able-bodied heterosexuality, both must be safely contained—embodied—in such figures.

In the 1997 film *As Good As It Gets*, for example, although Melvin Udall (Jack Nicholson), who is diagnosed in the film as obsessive-compulsive, is represented visually in many ways that initially position him in what Martin F. Norden calls "the cinema of isolation" (i.e., Melvin is represented in ways that link him to other representations of people with disabilities), the trajectory of the film is toward able-bodied heterosexuality. To effect the consolidation of heterosexual and able-bodied norms, disability and queerness in the film are visibly located elsewhere, in the gay character Simon Bishop (Greg Kinnear). Over the course of the film, Melvin progressively sheds his sense of inhabiting an anomalous body, and disability is firmly located in the nonheterosexual character, who is initially represented as able-bodied but ends up, after he is attacked and beaten by a group of burglars, using a wheelchair and cane for most of the film. More important, the disabled/queer figure, as in many other contemporary cultural representations, facilitates the heterosexual romance: Melvin first learns to accept the differences Simon comes to embody, and Simon then encourages Melvin to reconcile with his girlfriend, Carol Connelly (Helen Hunt). Having served their purpose, Simon, disability, and queerness are all hustled offstage together. The film concludes with a fairly traditional romantic reunion between the (able-bodied) male and female leads.[8]

CRITICALLY QUEER, SEVERELY DISABLED

The crisis surrounding heterosexual identity and able-bodied identity does not automatically lead to their undoing. Indeed, as this brief consideration of *As Good As It Gets* should suggest, this crisis and the anxieties that accompany it can be invoked in a wide range of cultural texts precisely to be (temporarily) resolved or alleviated. Neither gender trouble nor ability trouble is sufficient in and of itself to unravel compulsory heterosexuality or compulsory able-bodiedness. Butler acknowledges this problem: "This failure to approximate the norm [...] is not the same as the subversion of the norm. There is no promise that subversion will follow from the reiteration of constitutive norms; there is no guarantee that exposing the naturalized status of heterosexuality will lead to its subversion" ("Critically Queer" 22; qtd. in Warner, "Normal and Normaller" 168–69n87). For Warner, this acknowledgment in Butler locates a potential gap in her theory, "let us say, between virtually queer and critically queer" (Warner 168–69n87). In contrast to a virtually queer identity, which would be experienced by anyone who failed to perform heterosexuality without contradiction and incoherence (i.e., everyone), a critically queer perspective could presumably mobilize the inevitable failure to approximate the norm, collectively "working the weakness in the norm," to use Butler's phrase ("Critically Queer" 26).[9]

A similar gap can be located if we appropriate Butler's theories for disability studies. Everyone is virtually disabled, both in the sense that able-bodied norms are "intrinsically impossible to embody" fully and in the sense that able-bodied status is always temporary, disability being the one identity category that all people will embody if they live long enough. What we might call a critically disabled position, however, would differ from such a virtually disabled position; it would call attention to the ways in which the disability rights movement and disability studies have resisted the demands of compulsory able-bodiedness and have demanded access to a newly imagined and newly configured public sphere where full participation is not contingent on an able body.

We might, in fact, extend the concept and see such a perspective not as critically disabled but rather as severely disabled, with *severe* performing work similar to the critically queer work performed by *fabulous*. Tony Kushner writes:

> *Fabulous* became a popular word in the queer community—well, it was never unpopular, but for a while it became a battle cry of a new queer politics, carnival and camp, aggressively fruity, celebratory and tough like a streetwise drag queen: *"FAAAAABULOUS!"* [...] *Fabulous* is one of those words that provide a measure of the degree to which a person or event manifests a particular, usually oppressed, subculture's most distinctive, invigorating features. (vii)

Severe, though less common than *fabulous*, has a similar queer history: a severe critique is a fierce critique, a defiant critique, one that thoroughly and carefully reads a situation—and I mean reading in the street sense of loudly calling out the inadequacies of a given situation, person, text, or ideology. "Severely disabled," according to such a queer conception, would reverse the able-bodied understanding of severely disabled bodies as the most marginalized, the most excluded from a privileged and always elusive normalcy, and would instead suggest that it is precisely those bodies that are best positioned to refuse "mere toleration" and to call out the inadequacies of compulsory able-bodiedness. Whether it is the "army of one-breasted women" Audre Lorde imagines descending on the Capitol; the Rolling Quads, whose resistance sparked the independent living movement in Berkeley, California; Deaf students shutting down Gallaudet University in the Deaf President Now action; or ACT UP storming the National Institutes of Health or the Food and Drug Administration, severely disabled/critically queer bodies have already generated ability trouble that remaps the public sphere and reimagines and reshapes the limited forms of embodiment and desire proffered by the systems that would contain us all.[10]

Compulsory heterosexuality is intertwined with compulsory able-bodiedness; both systems work to (re)produce the able body and heterosexuality. But precisely because they depend on a queer/disabled existence that can never quite be contained, able-bodied heterosexuality's hegemony is always in danger of being disrupted. I draw attention to critically queer, severely disabled possibilities to further an incorporation of the two fields, queer theory and disability studies, in the hope that such a collaboration (which in some cases is already occurring, even when it is not acknowledged or explicitly named as such) will exacerbate, in more productive ways, the crisis of authority that currently besets heterosexual/able-bodied norms. Instead of invoking the crisis in order to resolve it (as in a film like *As Good As It Gets*), I would argue that a queer/disability studies (in productive conversations with disabled/queer movements outside the academy) can continuously invoke, in order to further the crisis, the inadequate resolutions that compulsory heterosexuality and compulsory able-bodiedness offer us. And in contrast to an able-bodied culture that holds out the promise of a substantive (but paradoxically always elusive) ideal, a queer/disabled perspective would resist delimiting the kinds of bodies and abilities that are acceptable or that will bring about change. Ideally, a queer/disability studies—like the term *queer* itself—might function "oppositionally and relationally but not necessarily substantively, not as a positivity but as a positionality, not as a thing, but as a resistance to the norm" (Halperin 66). Of course, in calling for a queer/disability studies without a necessary substance, I hope it is clear that I do not mean to deny the materiality of queer/disabled bodies, as it is precisely those material bodies that have populated the movements and brought about the changes detailed above. Rather, I mean to argue that critical queerness and severe disability are about collectively transforming (in ways that cannot necessarily be predicted in advance) the substantive uses to which queer/disabled existence has been put by a system of compulsory able-bodiedness, about insisting that such a system is never as good as it gets, and about imagining bodies and desires otherwise.

NOTES

1. In 1976, the Brussels Tribunal on Crimes against Women identified "compulsory heterosexuality" as one such crime (Katz, "Invention" 26). A year earlier, in her important article "The Traffic in Women: Notes on the 'Political Economy' of Sex," Gayle Rubin examined the ways in which "obligatory heterosexuality" and "compulsory heterosexuality" function in what she theorized as a larger sex/gender system (179, 198; qtd. in Katz, *Invention* 132). Rich's 1980 article, which has been widely cited and reproduced since its initial publication, was one of the most extensive analyses of compulsory heterosexuality in feminism. I agree with Jonathan Ned Katz's insistence that the concept is redundant because "any society split between heterosexual and homosexual is compulsory" (*Invention* 164), but I also acknowledge the historical and critical usefulness of the phrase. It is easier to understand the ways in which a society split between heterosexual and homosexual is compulsory precisely because of feminist deployments of the redundancy of compulsory heterosexuality. I would also suggest that popular queer theorizing outside the academy (from drag performances to activist street theater) has often employed redundancy performatively to make a critical point.

2. In an effort to forge a political connection among all women, Rich uses the terms "lesbian" and "lesbian continuum" to describe a vast array of sexual and affectional connections throughout history, many of which emerge from historical and cultural conditions quite different from those that have made possible the identity of lesbian ("Compulsory Heterosexuality" 192–99). Moreover, by using "lesbian continuum" to affirm the connection between lesbian and heterosexual women, Rich effaces the cultural and sexual specificity of contemporary lesbian existence.

3. The incorporation of queer theory and disability studies that I argue for here is still in its infancy. It is in cultural activism and cultural theory about AIDS (such as John Nguyet Erni's *Unstable Frontiers* or Cindy Patton's *Fatal Advice*) that a collaboration between queer theory and disability studies is already proceeding and has been for some time, even though it is not yet acknowledged or explicitly named as such. Michael Davidson's "Strange Blood: Hemophobia and the Unexplored Boundaries of Queer Nation" is one of the finest analyses to date of the connections between disability studies and queer theory.

4. The collective projects that I refer to are, of course, the projects of gay liberation and queer studies in the academy and the disability rights movement and disability studies in the academy. This chapter is part of my own contribution to these projects and is part of my longer work in progress, titled "De-composing Bodies: Cultural Signs of Queerness and Disability."

5. David Mitchell and Sharon Snyder are in line with many scholars working in disability studies when they point out the "ominous silence in the humanities" on the subject of disability (*Body* 1). See, for other examples, Simi Linton's discussion of the "divided curriculum" (71–116) and assertions by Rosemarie Garland-Thomson and by Lennard Davis about the necessity of examining disability alongside other categories of difference such as race, class, gender, and sexuality (Garland-Thomson, *Extraordinary Bodies* 5; Davis, *Enforcing Normalcy* xi).

6. Disability studies is not the only field Vincent has attacked in the mainstream media; see her article "The Future of Queer: Wedded to Orthodoxy," which mocks academic queer theory. Neither being disabled nor being gay or lesbian in and of itself guarantees the critical consciousness generated in the disability rights or queer movements or in queer theory or disability studies: Vincent is a lesbian journalist, but her writing clearly supports both able-bodied and hetero-

sexual norms. Instead of showing a stigmaphilic response to queer/disabled existence, finding "a commonality with those who suffer from stigma, and in this alternative realm [learning] to value the very things the rest of the world despises" (Warner, *Trouble* 43), Vincent reproduces the dominant culture's stigmaphobic response. See Warner's discussion of Erving Goffman's concepts of stigmaphobe and stigmaphile (41–45).

7. Michel Foucault's discussion of "docile bodies" and his theories of disciplinary practices are in the background of much of my analysis here (*Discipline* 135–69).

8. The consolidation of able-bodied and heterosexuality identity is probably most common in mainstream films and television movies about AIDS, even—or perhaps especially—when those films are marketed as new and daring. The 1997 Christopher Reeve–directed HBO film *In the Gloaming* is an example. In the film, the disabled/queer character (yet again, in a tradition that reaches back to *An Early Frost* [1985]) is eliminated at the end but not before effecting a healing of the heteronormative family. As Simon Watney writes about *An Early Frost*, "The closing shot [...] shows a 'family album' picture. [...] A traumatic episode is over. The family closes ranks, with the problem son conveniently dispatched, and life getting back to normal" (114). I am focusing on a non-AIDS-related film about disability and homosexuality, because I think the processes I theorize here have a much wider currency and can be found in many cultural texts that attempt to represent queerness or disability. There is not space here to analyze *As Good As It Gets* fully; for a more comprehensive close reading of how heterosexual/able-bodied consolidation works in the film and other cultural texts, see my forthcoming article "As Good As It Gets: Queer Theory and Critical Disability." I do not, incidentally, think that these processes are unique to fictional texts: the MLA's annual *Job Information List,* for instance, provides evidence of other locations where heterosexual and able-bodied norms support each other while ostensibly allowing for tolerance of queerness and disability. The recent high visibility of queer studies and disability studies on university press lists, conference proceedings, and even syllabi has not translated into more jobs for disabled/queer scholars.

9. See my discussion of Butler, Gloria Anzaldúa, and critical queerness in *Queer Renaissance* 149–53.

10. On the history of the AIDS Coalition to Unleash Power (ACT UP), see Douglas Crimp and Adam Rolston's *AIDS DemoGraphics.* Lorde recounts her experiences with breast cancer and imagines a movement of one-breasted women in *The Cancer Journals.* Joseph P. Shapiro recounts both the history of the Rolling Quads and the Independent Living Movement and the Deaf President Now action in *No Pity: People with Disabilities Forging a New Civil Rights Movement* (41–58, 74–85). Deaf activists have insisted for some time that deafness should not be understood as a disability and that people living with deafness, instead, should be seen as having a distinct language and culture. As the disability rights movement has matured, however, some Deaf activists and scholars in Deaf studies have rethought this position and have claimed disability (that is, disability revalued by a disability rights movement and disability studies) in an attempt to affirm a coalition with other people with disabilities. It is precisely such a reclaiming of disability that I want to stress here with my emphasis on severe disability.

REFERENCES

As Good As It Gets. Dir. James L. Brooks. Perf. Jack Nicholson, Helen Hunt, and Greg Kinnear. TriStar, 1997.

Bérubé, Michael. *Life As We Know It: A Father, a Family, and an Exceptional Child.* 1996. New York: Vintage, 1998

Crimp, Douglas, and Adam Rolston. *AIDS DemoGraphics.* Seattle: Bay, 1990.

Davidson, Michael. "Strange Blood: Hemophobia and the Unexplored Boundaries of Queer Nation." *Beyond the Binary: Reconstructing Cultural Identity in a Multicultural Context.* Ed. Timothy Powell. New Brunswick: Rutgers UP, 1999. 39–60.

Davis, Lennard J. *Enforcing Normalcy: Disability, Deafness, and the Body.* New York: Verso, 1995.

Erni, John Nguyet. *Unstable Frontiers: Technomedicine and the Cultural Politics of "Curing" AIDS.* Minneapolis: U of Minnesota P, 1994.

Foucault, Michel. *Discipline and Punish: The Birth of the Prison.* Trans. Alan Sheridan. New York: Vintage-Random 1977.

Garland-Thomson, Rosemarle. *Extraordinary Bodies: Figuring Physical Disability in American Culture and Literature.* New York: Columbia UP, 1997.

Halperin, David M. *Saint Foucault: Towards a Gay Hagiography.* New York: Oxford UP, 1995.

In the Gloaming. Dir. Christopher Reeve. Perf. Glenn Close, Robert Sean Leonard, and David Strathairn. HBO, 1997.

Katz, Jonathan Ned. *The Invention of Heterosexuality.* New York: Dutton, 1995.

Kushner, Tony. "Foreword: Notes toward a Theater of the Fabulous." *Staging Lives: An Anthology of Contemporary Gay Theater.* Ed. John M. Clum. Boulder: Westview, 1996. vii-ix.

Lorde, Audre. *The Cancer Journals.* San Francisco: Aunt Lute, 1980.

Mitchell, David T., and Sharon L. Snyder, eds. *The Body and Physical Difference: Discourses of Disability in the Humanities.* The Body, in Theory: Histories of Cultural Materialism. Ann Arbor: U of Michigan P, 1997.

Norden, Martin F. *The Cinema Of Isolation: A History of Physical Disability in the Movies.* New Brunswick: Rutgers UP, 1994

Patton, Cindy. *Fatal Advice: How Safe-Sex Education Went Wrong.* Durham: Duke UP, 1997.

Rich, Adrienne. "Compulsory Heterosexuality and Lesbian Existence." *Powers of Desire: The Politics of Sexuality.* Ed. Ann Snitow, Christine Stansell, and Sharon Thompson. New York: Monthly Rev., 1983. 177–205.

Shapiro, Joseph P. *No Pity: People with Disabilities Forging a New Civil Rights Movement.* New York: Times, 1993.

Vincent, Nora. "Enabling Disabled Scholarship." *Salon.* 18 Aug. 1999 <http://www.salon.com/books/it/1999/08/18/disability >.

Warner, Michael. "Normal and Normaller: Beyond Gay Marriage." *GLQ: A Journal of Lesbian and Gay Studies* 5.2 (1999): 119–71.

———. *The Trouble with Normal: Sex, Politics, and the Ethics of Queer Life.* New York Free, 1999.

Watney, Simon. *Policing Desire: Pornography, AIDS, and the Media.* 2nd ed. Minneapolis: U of Minnesota P, 1989.

Wendell, Susan. *The Rejected Body: Feminist Philosophical Reflections on Disability.* London: Routledge, 1996.

Williams, Raymond. *Keywords: A Vocabulary of Culture and Society.* Rev. ed. New York: Oxford UP, 1983.

QUEER TEMPORALITIES AND POSTMODERN GEOGRAPHIES (2005)

JUDITH HALBERSTAM

Halberstam's essay joins with that realm of queer studies that seeks, as she puts it, to "detach queerness from sexual identity" and "to disconnect queerness from an essential definition of homosexual embodiment." She asks questions about contemporary and queer contemporary time and space and their relation to postmodernist notions of time and Marxist interpretations of postmodernism. (This essay introduces Halberstam's book, In a Queer Time and Place: Transgender Bodies, Subcultural Lives. *She kindly rewrote the conclusion for this reprinting, replacing a discussion that introduces the remaining chapters of this book.)*

> How can a relational system be reached through sexual practices? Is it possible to create a homosexual mode of life?…To be "gay," I think, is not to identify with the psychological traits and the visible masks of the homosexual, but to try to define and develop a way of life.
>
> —*Michel Foucault, "Friendship as a Way of Life"*

> There is never one geography of authority and there is never one geography of resistance. Further, the map of resistance is not simply the underside of the map of domination—if only because each is a lie to the other, and each gives lie to the other.
>
> —*Steve Pile, "Opposition, Political Identities, and Spaces of Resistance"*

This book makes the perhaps overly ambitious claim that there is such a thing as "queer time" and "queer space." Queer uses of time and space develop, at least in part, in opposition to the institutions of family, heterosexuality, and reproduction. They also develop according to other logics of location, movement, and identification. If we try to think about queerness as an outcome of strange temporalities, imaginative life schedules, and eccentric economic practices, we detach queerness from sexual identity and come closer to understanding Foucault's comment in "Friendship as a Way of Life" that "homosexuality threatens people as a 'way of life' rather than as a way of having sex" (310). In Foucault's radical formulation, queer friendships, queer networks, and the existence of these relations in space and in relation to the use of time mark out the particularity and indeed the perceived menace of homosexual life. In this book, the queer "way of life" will encompass subcultural practices, alternative methods of alliance, forms of transgender embodiment, and those forms of representation dedicated to capturing these willfully eccentric modes of being. Obviously not all gay, lesbian, and transgender people live their lives in radically different ways from their heterosexual counterparts, but part of what has made queerness compelling as a form of self-description in the past decade or so has to do with the way it has the potential to open up new life narratives and alternative relations to time and space.

Queer time perhaps emerges most spectacularly, at the end of the twentieth century, from within those gay communities whose horizons of possibility have been severely diminished by the AIDS epidemic. In his memoir of his lover's death from AIDS, poet Mark Doty writes: "All my life I've lived with a future which constantly diminishes but never vanishes" (Doty 1996, 4). The constantly diminishing future creates a new emphasis on the here, the present, the now, and while the threat of no future hovers overhead like a storm cloud, the urgency of being also expands the potential of the moment and, as Doty explores, squeezes new possibilities out of the time at hand. In his poem "In Time of Plague," Thorn Gunn explores the erotics of compressed time and impending mortality: "My thoughts are crowded with death/and it draws so oddly on the sexual/that I am confused/confused to be attracted/by, in effect, my own annihilation" (Gunn 1993, 59). Queer time, as it flashes into view in the heart of a crisis, exploits the potential of what Charles-Pierre Baudelaire called in relation to modernism "The transient, the fleeting, the contingent." Some gay men have responded to the threat of AIDS, for example, by rethinking the conventional emphasis on longevity and futurity, and by making community in relation to risk, disease, infection, and death (Bersani 1996; Edelman 1998). And yet queer time, even as it emerges from the AIDS crisis, is not only about compression and annihilation; it is also about the potentiality of a life unscripted by the conventions of family, inheritance, and child rearing. In the sections on subcultures in this book, I will examine the queer temporalities that are proper to subcultural activities, and will propose that we rethink the adult/youth binary in relation to an "epistemology of youth" that disrupts conventional accounts of youth culture, adulthood, and maturity. Queer subcultures produce alternative temporalities by allowing their participants to believe that their futures can be imagined according to logics that lie outside of those paradigmatic markers of life experience—namely, birth, marriage, reproduction, and death.

These new temporal logics, again, have emerged most obviously in the literatures produced in relation to the AIDS epidemic. For example, in *The Hours*, Michael Cunningham's beautiful rewriting of Virginia Woolf's *Mrs. Dalloway*, Cunningham takes the temporal frame of Woolf's novel (life in a day) and emphasizes its new, but also queer rendering of time and space. Indeed, Cunningham rationalizes Woolf's authorial decision to have the young Clarissa Dalloway "love another girl" in terms of queer temporality. He explains: "Clarissa Dalloway in her first youth, will love another girl, Virginia thinks; Clarissa will believe that a rich, riotous future is opening before her, but eventually (how, exactly, will the change be accomplished?) she will come to her senses, as young women do and marry a suitable man" (Cunningham 1998, 81–82). The "riotous future," which emerges in Woolf's novel from a lesbian kiss in Clarissa's youth, becomes, in Cunningham's skillful rewrite, a queer time that is both realized and ultimately disappointing in its own narrative arc. Cunningham tracks Woolf's autobiographical story of a descent into madness and suicide alongside a contemporary narrative of Clarissa Vaughn, who has refused to "come to her senses" and lives with a woman named Sally while caring for her best friend, Richard, a writer dying of AIDS. Cunningham's elegant formulation of queer temporality opens up the possibility of a "rich, riotous future" and closes it down in the same aesthetic gesture. While Woolf, following Sigmund Freud, knows that Clarissa must come to her senses (and like Freud, Woolf cannot imagine "how the change [will] be accomplished"), Cunningham turns Clarissa away from the seemingly inexorable march of narrative time toward marriage (death) and uses not consummation but the kiss as the gateway to alternative outcomes. For Woolf, the kiss constituted one of those "moments of being" that her writing struggled to encounter and inhabit; for Cunningham, the kiss is a place where, as Carolyn Dinshaw terms it in *Getting Medieval*, different histories "touch" or brush up against each other, creating temporal havoc in the key of desire (Dinshaw 1999).

While there is now a wealth of excellent work focused on the temporality of lives lived in direct relation to the HIV virus (Edelman 1998), we find far less work on the other part of Cunningham's equation: those lives lived in "the shadow of an epidemic," the lives of women, transgenders, and queers who partake of this temporal shift in less obvious ways. Furthermore, the experience of HIV for heterosexual and queer people of color does not necessarily offer the same kind of hopeful reinvention of conventional understandings of time. As Cathy Cohen's work in *The Boundaries of Blackness: AIDS and the Breakdown of Black Politics* shows, some bodies are simply considered "expendable," both in mainstream and marginal communities, and the abbreviated life spans of black queers or poor drug users, say, does not inspire the same kind of metaphysical speculation on curtailed futures, intensified presents, or reformulated histories; rather, the premature deaths of poor people and people of color in a nation that pumps drugs into impoverished urban communities and withholds basic health care privileges, is simply business as usual (Cohen 1999). Samuel Delany articulates beautifully the difficulty in connecting radical political practice to exploited populations when he claims, "We must remember that it is only those workers—usually urban artists (a realization Marx did come to)—whose money comes from several different social class sources, up and down the social ladder, who can afford to entertain a truly radical political practice" (Reid-Pharr 2001, xii). And yet, as Robert Reid-Pharr argues in *Black Gay Man*, the book that Delany's essay introduces, the relation between the universal and the particular that allows for the elevation of white male experience (gay or straight) to the level of generality and the reduction of, say, black gay experience to the status of the individual, can only come undone through a consideration of the counterlogics that emerge from "the humdrum perversities of our existence" (12). *In a Queer Time and Place* seeks to unravel precisely those claims made on the universal from and on behalf of white male subjects theorizing postmodern temporality and geography.

Queer time and space are useful frameworks for assessing political and cultural change in the late twentieth and early twenty-first centuries (both what has changed and what must change). The critical languages that we have developed to try to assess the obstacles to social change have a way of both stymieing our political agendas and alienating nonacademic constituencies. I try here to make queer time and queer space into useful terms for academic and nonacademic considerations of life, location, and transformation. To give an example of the way in which critical languages can sometimes weigh us down, consider the fact that we have become adept within postmodernism at talking about "normativity," but far less adept at describing in rich detail the practices and structures that both oppose and sustain conventional forms of association, belonging, and identification. I try to use the concept of queer time to make clear how respectability, and notions of the normal on which it depends, may be upheld by a middle-class logic of reproductive temporality. And so, in Western cultures, we chart the emergence of the adult from the dangerous and unruly period of adolescence as a desired process of maturation; and we create longevity as the most desirable future, applaud the pursuit of long life (under any circumstances), and pathologize modes of living that show little or no concern for longevity. Within the life cycle of the Western human subject, long periods of stability are considered to be desirable, and people who live in rapid bursts (drug addicts, for example) are characterized as immature and even dangerous. But the ludic temporality created by drugs (captured by Salvador Dalí as a melting clock and by William Burroughs as "junk time") reveals the artificiality of our privileged constructions of time and activity. In the works of queer postmodern writers like Lynn Breedlove (*Godspeed*), Eileen Myles (*Chelsea Girls*), and others, speed itself (the drug as well as the motion) becomes the motor of an alternative history as their queer heroes rewrite completely narratives of female rebellion (Myles 1994; Breedlove 2002).

The time of reproduction is ruled by a biological clock for women and by strict bourgeois rules of respectability and scheduling for married couples. Obviously, not all people who have children keep or even are able to keep reproductive time, but many and possibly most people believe that the scheduling of repro-time is natural and desirable. Family time refers to the normative scheduling of daily life (early to bed, early to rise) that accompanies the practice of child rearing. This timetable is governed by an imagined set of children's needs, and it relates to beliefs about children's health and healthful environments for child rearing. The time of inheritance refers to an overview of generational time within which values, wealth, goods, and morals are passed through family ties from one generation to the next. It also connects the family to the historical past of the nation, and glances ahead to connect the family to the future of both familial and national stability. In this category we can include the kinds of hypothetical temporality—the time of "what if"—that demands protection in the way of insurance policies, health care, and wills.

In queer renderings of postmodern geography, the notion of a body-centered identity gives way to a model that locates sexual subjectivities within and between embodiment, place, and practice. But queer work on sexuality and space, like queer work on sexuality and time, has had to respond to canonical work on "postmodern geography" by Edward Soja, Fredric Jameson, David Harvey, and others that has actively excluded sexuality as a category for analysis precisely because desire has been cast by neo-Marxists as part of a ludic body politics that obstructs the "real" work of activism (Soja 1989; Harvey 1990; Jameson 1997). This foundational exclusion, which assigned sexuality to body/local/personal and took class/global/political as its proper frame of reference, has made it difficult to introduce questions of sexuality and space into the more general conversations about globalization and transnational capitalism. Both Anna Tsing and Steve Pile refer this problem as the issue of "scale." Pile, for example, rejects the notion that certain political arenas of struggle (say, class) are more important than others (say, sexuality), and instead he offers that we rethink these seemingly competing struggles in terms of scale by recognizing that while we tend to view local struggles as less significant than global ones, ultimately "the local and the global are not natural scales, but formed precisely out of the struggles that seemingly they only contain" (Pile 1997, 13).

A "queer" adjustment in the way in which we think about time, in fact, requires and produces new conceptions of space. And in fact, much of the contemporary theory seeking to disconnect queerness from an essential definition of homosexual embodiment has focused on queer space and queer practices. By articulating and elaborating a concept of queer time, I suggest new ways of understanding the nonnormative behaviors that have clear but not essential relations to gay and lesbian subjects. For the purpose of this book, "queer" refers to nonnormative logics and organizations of community, sexual identity, embodiment, and activity in space and time. "Queer time" is a term for those specific models of temporality that emerge within postmodernism once one leaves the temporal frames of bourgeois reproduction and family, longevity, risk/safety, and inheritance. "Queer space" refers to the place-making practices within postmodernism in which queer people engage and it also describes the new understandings of space enabled by the production of queer counterpublics. Meanwhile, "postmodernism" in this project takes on meaning in relation to new forms of cultural production that emerge both in sync with and running counter to what Jameson has called the "logic" of late capitalism in his book *Postmodernism* (1997). I see postmodernism as simultaneously a crisis and an opportunity—a crisis in the stability of form and meaning, and an opportunity to rethink the practice of cultural production, its hierarchies and power dynamics, its tendency to resist or capitulate. In his work on postmodern geography, Pile also locates postmodernism in terms of the changing relationship between opposition and authority; he reminds us, crucially, that "the map of resistance is not simply the underside of the map of domination" (6).

In *The Condition of Postmodernity,* Harvey demonstrates that our conceptions of space and time are social constructions forged out of vibrant and volatile social relations (Harvey 1990). Harvey's analysis of postmodern time and space is worth examining in detail both because he energetically deconstructs the naturalization of modes of temporality and because he does so with no awareness of having instituted and presumed a normative framework for his alternative understanding of time. Furthermore, Harvey's concept of "time/space compression" and his accounts of the role of culture in late capitalism have become hegemonic in academic contexts. Harvey asserts that because we experience time as some form of natural progression, we fail to realize or notice its construction. Accordingly, we have concepts like "industrial" time and "family" time, time of "progress," "austerity" versus "instant" gratification, "postponement" versus "immediacy." And to all of these different kinds of temporality, we assign value and meaning. Time, Harvey explains, is organized according to the logic of capital accumulation, but those who benefit from capitalism in particular experience this logic as inevitable, and they are therefore able to ignore, repress, or erase the demands made on them and others by an unjust system. We like to imagine, Harvey implies, both that our time is our own and, as the cliché goes, "there is a time and a place for everything." These formulaic responses to time and temporal logics produce emotional and even physical responses to different kinds of time: thus people feel guilty about leisure, frustrated by waiting, satisfied by punctuality, and so on. These emotional responses add to our sense of time as "natural."

Samuel Beckett's famous play *Waiting for Godot* can be read, for example, as a defamiliarization of time spent: a treatise on the feeling of time wasted, of inertia or time outside of capitalist propulsion. Waiting, in this play, seems to be a form of postponement until it becomes clear that nothing has been postponed and nothing will be resumed. In Beckett's play, the future does not simply become diminished, it actually begins to weigh on the present as a burden. If poetry, according to W. H. Auden, "makes nothing happen," the absurdist drama makes the audience wait for nothing to happen, and the experience of duration makes visible the formlessness of time. Since Beckett's clowns go nowhere while waiting, we also see the usually invisible fault lines between time and space as temporal stasis is figured as immobility.

The different forms of time management that Harvey mentions and highlights are all adjusted to the schedule of normativity without ever being discussed as such. In fact, we could say that normativity, as it has been defined and theorized within queer studies, is the big word missing from almost all the discussions of postmodern geography within a Marxist tradition. Since most of these discussions are dependent on the work of Foucault and since normativity was Foucault's primary understanding of the function of modern power, this is a huge oversight, and one with consequences for the discussion of sexuality in relation to time and space. Harvey's concept of time/space compressions, for instance, explains that all of the time cycles that we have naturalized and internalized (leisure, inertia, recreation, work/industrial, family/domesticity) are also spatial practices, but again, Harvey misses the opportunity to deconstruct the meaning of naturalization with regard to specific normalized ways of being. The meaning of space, Harvey asserts, undergoes the double process of naturalization: first it is naturalized in relation to use values (we presume that our use of space is the only and inevitable use of space—private property, for example); but second, we naturalize space by subordinating it to time. The construction of spatial practices, in other words, is obscured by the naturalization of both time and space. Harvey argues for multiple conceptions of time and space, but he does not adequately describe how time/space becomes naturalized, on the one hand, and how hegemonic constructions of time and space are uniquely gendered and sexualized on the other. His is an avowedly materialist analysis of time/space dedicated understandably to uncovering the processes of capitalism, but it lacks a simultaneous desire to uncover the processes of heteronormativity, racism, and sexism.

We need, for example, a much more rigorous understanding of the gendering of domestic space. Harvey could have pointed to the work within feminist history on the creation of separate spheres, for one, to show where and how the time/space continuum breaks down under the weight of critical scrutiny (Cott 1977; Smith-Rosenberg 1985). Feminist historians have claimed for some thirty years that in the eighteenth and nineteenth centuries, as the European bourgeoisie assumed class dominance over the aristocracy and proletariat, a separation of spheres graphically represented the gendered logic of the public/private binary and annexed middle-class women to the home, leaving the realm of politics and commerce to white men (McHugh 1999; Duggan 2000). Furthermore, as work by Paul Gilroy and Joseph Roach has shown, histories of racialization cannot avoid spatial conceptions of time, conflict, or political economy (Gilroy 1993; Roach 1996). Indeed, the histories of racialized peoples have been histories of immigration, diaspora, and forced migration. Only a single-minded focus on the history of the white working class and an abstract concept of capital can give rise to the kind of neat scheme that Harvey establishes whereby time dominates critical consciousness and suppresses an understanding of spatiality.

Lindon Barrett's *Blackness and Value: Seeing Double* provides one good antidote to Harvey's clean rendering of Enlightenment divisions of space and time (Barrett 1999). According to the account that Barrett gives in his book, Western philosophy can be historically located as a discourse that accompanies capitalism, and works to justify and rationalize a patently brutal and unjust system as inevitably scientific and organic. So seamlessly has capitalism been rationalized over the last two hundred years, in fact, that we no longer see the fault lines that divide black from white, work from play, subject from object. In true deconstructive form and with painstaking care, Barrett restores the original foundations of Western thought that were used to designate black as inhuman and white as human, black in association with idleness, perverse sexuality, and lack of self-consciousness, and white in association with diligence, legibility, the normal, the domestic, restraint, and self-awareness. By tracing this philosophical history, Barrett is able to explain the meaning of blackness in different historical periods in opposition to the seemingly inevitable, transparent, and neutral rhetorics of time and space that govern those periods.

Tsing also criticizes Harvey for making the breaks between space and time, modern and postmodern, economics and culture so clean and so distinct. She theorizes global capitalism much more precisely in relation to new eras of speed and connection, travel, movement, and communication; she lays out the contradictory results of global capitalism in terms of what it enables as well as what forms of oppression it enacts: Tsing reminds us that globalization makes a transnational politics (environmentalism, human rights, feminism) possible even as it consolidates U.S. hegemony. Harvey can only describe the condition of postmodernism in terms of new forms of domination and, like Jameson, can only think about cultural production as a channel for U.S. hegemony. Tsing, an anthropologist, is in many ways an unlikely defender of the nonsymmetrical relationship of cultural production to economic production, but her most important critique of Harvey concerns his characterization of postmodern culture as "a mirror of economic realities"(Tsing 2002, 466). Harvey's analysis, according to Tsing, suffers first from a simplistic mode of taking cultural shifts and then mapping them onto economic shifts; second, she claims that Harvey makes all of his assumptions about globalization without using an ethnographic research base. Finally, he overgeneralizes the "postmodern condition" on the basis of a flawed understanding of the role of culture, and then allows culture to stand in for all kinds of other evidence of the effect of globalization.

In relation to gender, race, and alternative or subcultural production, therefore, Harvey's grand theory of "the experience, of space and time" in postmodernity leaves the power structures of biased differentiation intact, and presumes that, in Pile's formulation, opposition can only be an "echo of domination" (Pile 1997, 13). But while Harvey, like Soja and Jameson, can be counted on at least to nod to the racialization and gendering of postmodern space, also like Soja and Jameson, he has nothing to say about sexuality and space. Both Soja and Harvey claim that it was Foucault's interviews on space and published lecture notes on "heterotopia" that, as Soja puts it, created the conditions for a postmodern geography. The Foucault who inspires the postmodern Marxist geographers is clearly the Foucault of *Discipline and Punish*, but not that of *The History of Sexuality*. Indeed, Harvey misses several obvious opportunities to discuss the naturalization of time and space in relation to sexuality. Reproductive time and family time are, above all, heteronormative time/space constructs. But while Harvey hints at the gender politics of these forms of time/space, he does not mention the possibility that all kinds of people, especially in postmodernity, will and do opt to live outside of reproductive and familial time as well as on the edges of logics of labor and production. By doing so, they also often live outside the logic of capital accumulation: here we could consider ravers, club kids, HIV-Positive barebackers, rent boys, sex workers, homeless people, drug dealers, and the unemployed. Perhaps such people could productively be called "queer subjects" in terms of the ways they live (deliberately, accidentally, or of necessity) during the hours when others sleep and in the spaces (physical, metaphysical, and economic) that others have abandoned, and in terms of the ways they might work in the domains that other people assign to privacy and family. Finally, as I will trace in this book, for some queer subjects, time and space are limned by risks they are willing to take: the transgender person who risks his life by passing in a small town, the subcultural musicians who risk their livelihoods by immersing themselves in normative practices, the queer performers who destabilize the normative values that make everyone else feel safe and secure; but also those people who live without financial safety nets, without homes, without steady jobs, outside the organizations of time and space that have been established for the purposes of protecting the rich few from everyone else.

Using the Foucault of *The History of Sexuality*, we can return to the concepts of time that Harvey takes for granted and expose their hidden but implicit logics (Foucault 1986). Stephen M. Barber and David L. Clark, in their introduction to a book of essays on Eve Kosofsky Sedgwick, present perhaps the most compelling reading to date of a queer temporality that emerges from Foucault's formulation of modernity as "an attitude rather than as a period of history" (Barber 2002, 304). Barber and Clark locate Foucault's comments on modernity alongside Sedgwick's comments on queerness in order to define queerness as a temporality—"a 'moment,' it is also then a force; or rather it is a crossing of temporality with force" (8). In Sedgwick, Barber and Clark identify an elaboration of the relation between temporality and writing; in Foucault, they find a model for the relation between temporality and ways of being. They summarize these currents in terms of a "moment," a "persistent present," or "a queer temporality that is at once indefinite and virtual but also forceful, resilient, and undeniable" (2). It is this model of time, the model that emerges between Foucault and Sedgwick, that is lost to and overlooked by Marxist geographers for whom the past represents the logic for the present, and the future represents the fruition of this logic.

Postmodern geography, indeed, has built on Foucault's speculative but powerful essay on heterotopia and on Foucault's claim in this essay that "the present epoch will be above all an epoch of space" (Foucault 1986, 22). Based on this insight, Soja and Harvey argue that critical theory has privileged time/history over space/geography with many different implications. But for both Harvey in *The Condition of Postmodernity* and Jameson in "The Cultural Logic of Postmodernism," postmodernism is a strange and even bewildering confusion of time and space where history has lost its (materialist) meaning, time has become a perpetual, present, and space has flattened out in the face of creeping globalization. Both theorists evince a palpable nostalgia for modernism with its apparent oppositional logics and its clear articulations of both alienation and revolution; and both theorists oppose the politics of the local within "an epoch of space" to the politics of the global—a global capitalism opposed by some kind of utopian global socialism, and no politics outside this framework registers as meaningful. Predictably, then, the "local" for postmodern geographers becomes the debased term in the binary, and their focus on the global, the abstract, and even the universal is opposed to the local with its associations with the concrete, the specific, the narrow, the empirical, and even the bodily. As Tsing puts it, the local becomes just a "stopping place for the global" in Marxist accounts, and all too often the local represents place, while the global represents circulation, travel, and migration. By refusing to set local/global up in a dialectical relation, Tsing allows for a logic of diversity: diverse locals, globals, capitalisms, temporalities (Tsing 2002).

Stuart Hall also reminds us in his essay on "The Global and the Local" that "the more we understand about the development of Capital itself, the more we understand that it is only part of the story" (Hall 1997). And as Doreen Massey says of Harvey's exclusive focus on capital, "In Harvey's account, capital always wins, and it seems capital can only win" (Massey 1994, 140). Massey suggests that alternatives are rarely suggested by those theorists of the dominant; we are always already trapped, and the more we find evidence of alternatives in local contexts, the more the local becomes mistrusted as "place bound," reactionary, and even fascist. Work on sexuality and space offers a far more complicated picture of globalization and the relationships between the global and the local than Harvey or Soja allow. Indeed, queer studies of sexuality and space present the opportunity for a developed understanding of the local, the nonmetropolitan (not the same thing, I know), and the situated. And while work on globalization will inevitably skim the surface of local variation and perhaps even reproduce the homogenizing effects of globalization in the process of attempting to offer a critique, queer studies of space, sexuality, and embodiment explore the postmodern politics of place in all of its contradiction, and in the process, they expose the contours of what I call in chapter 2 "metronormativity."

One theorist who has accounted for the possibility of "the end of capitalism" is J. K. Gibson-Graham, the collaborative moniker for the joint theories of Julie Graham and Katherine Gibson. In the original and inspirational call for an anticapitalist imaginary, Gibson-Graham argues that "it is the way capitalism has been 'thought' that has made it so difficult for people to imagine its supersession (Gibson-Graham 1991, 5). Drawing on feminist studies and queer theory, Gibson-Graham contends that capitalism has been unnecessarily stabilized within Marxist representations as a totalizing force and a unitary entity. If we destabilize the meaning of capitalism using poststructuralist critiques of identity and signification, then we can begin to see the multiplicity of noncapitalist forms that constitute, supplement, and abridge global capitalism, but we can also begin to imagine, by beginning to see, the alternatives to capitalism that already exist and are presently under construction. Gibson-Graham calls for the "querying" of globalization through a wide-ranging recognition of its incomplete status, its discontinuities, instabilities, and vulnerabilities. Gibson-Graham proposes "the severing of globalization from a fixed capitalist identity, a breaking apart of the monolithic significations of capitalism (market/commodity/capital) and a liberation of different economic beings and practices" (146).

The literature on sexuality and space is growing rapidly, but it tends to focus on gay men, and it is often comparative only to the extent that it takes white gay male sexual communities as a highly evolved model that other sexual cultures try to imitate and reproduce. One of the best studies of sexual space that does still focus on gay men, but recognizes the fault lines of class, race, and gender in the construction of sexual communities is Samuel R. Delany's *Times Square Red, Times Square Blue.* Delany's book breaks the mold in the genre of gay male accounts of space that often take the form of travelogues and then compare the author's sexual experiences with gay men in a variety of global locations, only to argue for a kind of universal homosexuality within which fluidity and flexibility are the order of the day (Browning 1996). In Delany's book, the geo-specific sexual practices he describes belong to the interactions between men of different classes and races in New York's porn shops and triple-X theaters. These practices develop and are assigned meaning only in the context of the porn theater, and their meanings shift and change when the men leave the darkened theater and reemerge into the city. Delany's study illustrates a few of the claims I have been making here about queer time and space: first, that oppositional cultures, or in Pile's terms, "geographies of resistance," are not symmetrical to the authority they oppose; second, that the relations between sexuality and time and space provide immense insight into the flows of power and subversion within postmodernism; and finally, that queers use space and time in ways that challenge conventional logics of development, maturity, adulthood, and responsibility (Delany 1999).

Delany's groundbreaking analysis of the destruction of sexual subcultures during the corporate development of New York City's Times Square allows him to take issue with the notion that increasing public safety was the main motivation behind the area's face-lift. While developers claimed that the sex industries in Times Square rendered the area wholly unsafe for women and families especially, Delany argues that there is no particular relationship between street safety and the presence or absence of sex workers. He states unequivocally: "What I see lurking behind the positive foregrounding of 'family values' (along with, in the name of such values, the violent suppression of urban social structures, economic, social and sexual) is a wholly provincial and absolutely small-town terror of cross-class contact" (153). While I want to return to this notion of the small-town terror of contact with otherness in my chapters on Brandon Teena, here I am interested in Delany's insights about urban sex cultures and their understandings of space and time.

Delany divides his book into two sections, as the title suggests, and while the first half provides an ethnographic account of the denizens of porn theaters, dotted with anecdotes of Delany's encounters with various men, the second half articulates a theory of space, intimacy, and bodily contact in postmodernism. In this latter section, Delany makes some big claims. First, he proposes that "given the mode of capitalism under which we live, life is at its most rewarding, productive, and pleasant when large numbers of people understand, appreciate and seek out interclass contact and communication conducted in a mode of good will" (111). The encounters between men in the sex cinemas of midtown Manhattan are one of the few remaining zones of pleasurable interclass contact, according to Delany, and by razing this area, the urban planners of the new Times Square are deploying a logic of "safety" to justify the destruction of an intricate subcultural system. In its place, the corporate developers will construct a street mall guaranteed to make the tourists who visit Times Square feel safe enough to spend their money there. The second proposal made by Delany redefines class struggle for a postmodern politics. He argues that class war works silently against the social practices through which interclass contact can take place. In other words, what we understand in this day and age as "class war" is not simply owners exploiting labor or labor rebelling against managers but a struggle between those who value interclass contact and work hard to maintain those arenas in which it can occur, and those who fear it and work to create sterile spaces free of class mixing.

In order to create and maintain new spaces for interclass contact, Delany asserts that we need to be able, first, to imagine such spaces; we have to find out where they are, and how they can be sustained and supported. Second, we need to theorize the new spaces. It is not enough simply to point to new sites for interclass contact but as Delany has done here, we have to create a complex discourse around them through narrative and the meticulous work of archiving. Third, we have to avoid nostalgia for what was and what has disappeared while creating a new formulation for future spaces and architectures. Finally, Delany urges us to narrate an account of the invisible institutions that prop up counterpublics, but also to tell the story of the new technologies that want to eradicate them through a moral campaign about cleaning up the city. Delany repeatedly claims in *Times Square Red* that small towns in the United States are (if measured in terms of the number of crimes per capita) far more violent than big cities and that the structure of violence, particularly violence against queers, say, in each location is quite different. In a small town, the violence tends to be predictable, he claims, since locals often initiate violence against strangers or outsiders; but in the city, violence is random and unpredictable. Delany suggests that we break away from the cozy fantasies of small-town safety and big-city danger, and reconsider the actual risks of different locations in terms of the different populations that inhabit them. Specifically, he recommends that we not design urban areas to suit suburban visitors, and that we start to consider the problem of small-town violence in terms of the lack of cross-class, cross-race, or cross-sexual contact in small towns and rural areas.

Women are tellingly absent from Delany's smart, engaging, and even revolutionary account of sexual subcultures, and one is led to conclude by the end of the book that as of now, there is no role for women in this subterranean world of public sex. While it is not my project here to discuss the possibilities for women to develop venues for public sex, I do want to address the absence of gender as a category of analysis in much of the work on sexuality and space by shifting the terms of discussion from the global to the local in relation to postmodern geographies; and by shifting the focus from urban to rural in relation to queer geographies. I will also argue for a new conception of space and sexuality—what I call a "technotopic" understanding of space in chapter 5—that opens up in queer art making.

The division between urban and rural or urban and small town has had a major impact on the ways in which queer community has been formed and perceived in the United States. Until recently, small towns were considered hostile to queers and urban areas were cast as the queer's natural environment. In contemporary debates about urban life, affluent gay populations are often described as part of a "creative class" that enhances the city's cultural life and cultural capital, and this class of gays are then cast in opposition to the small-town family life and values of midwestern Americans (Florida 2002). While there is plenty of truth to this division between urban and small-town life, between hetero-familial cultures and queer creative and sexual cultures, the division also occludes the lives of nonurban queers. *In a Queer Time and Place* both confirms that queer subcultures thrive in urban areas *and* contests the essential characterizations of queer life as urban. In an extended consideration of the life and death of Brandon Teena, a young transgender man who was murdered in small-town Nebraska, I look at how the transgender body functions in relation to time and space as a rich site for fantasies of futurity and anachronism, and I ask here why transgenderism holds so much significance in postmodernism....

Throughout this book, I return to the transgender body as a contradictory site in postmodernism. The gender ambiguous individual today represents a very different set of assumptions about gender than the gender inverted subject of the early twentieth century, and, as a model of gender inversion recedes into anachronism, the transgender body has emerged as futurity itself, a kind of heroic fulfillment of postmodern promises of gender flexibility. Why has gender flexibility become a site of both fascination and promise in the late twentieth century, and what did this new flexibility have to do with other economies of flexibility within postmodernism? As Emily Martin's book *Flexible Bodies* shows in relation to historically variable conceptions of the immune system, flexibility has become "one of our new taken-for-granted virtues for persons and their bodies" (Martin 1995). Martin continues: "Flexibility has also become a powerful commodity, something scarce and highly valued, that can be used to discriminate against some people" (xvii). While we have become used to thinking in terms of "flexible citizenship" and "flexible accumulation" as some of the sinister sides of this new "virtue," the contemporary interest in flexible genders, from talk shows to blockbuster movies, may also be a part of the conceptualization of a new global elite (Ong 1999).

Because bodily flexibility has become both a commodity (in the case of cosmetic surgeries for example) and a form of commodification, it is not enough in this "age of flexibility" to celebrate gender flexibility as simply another sign of progress and liberation. Promoting flexibility at the level of identity and personal choices may sound like a postmodern or even a queer program for social change. But it as easily describes the advertising strategies of huge corporations like the Gap, that sell their products by casting their consumers as simultaneously all the same and all different. Indeed, the new popularity of "stretch" fabrics accommodates precisely this model of bodily fluidity by creating apparel that can stretch to meet the demands of the unique and individual body that fills it. Advertising by other companies, like Dr Pepper, whose ads exhort the consumer to "be you!" and who sell transgression *as* individualism, also play with what could be called a "bad" reading of postmodern gender. Postmodern gender theory has largely been (wrongly) interpreted as both a description of and a call for greater degrees of flexibility and fluidity. Many young gays and lesbians think of themselves as part of a "postgender" world, and for them, the idea of "labeling" becomes a sign of an oppression they have happily cast off in order to move into a pluralistic world of infinite diversity. In other words, it has become commonplace and even clichéd for young urban (white) gays and lesbians to claim that they do not like "labels" and do not want to be "pigeonholed" by identity categories, even as those same identity categories represent the activist labors of previous generations that brought us to the brink of "liberation" in the first place. Many urban gays and lesbians of different age groups also express a humanistic sense that their uniqueness cannot be captured by the application of a blanket term. The emergence of this liberal, indeed neo-liberal, notion of "uniqueness as radical style" in hip queer urban settings must be considered alongside the transmutations of capitalism in late postmodernity. As Lisa Duggan claims: "new neo-liberal sexual politics ... might be termed the new homonormativity—it is a politics that does not contest dominant heteronorrnative assumptions and institutions, but upholds and sustains them, while promising the possibility of a semobilized gay constituency and a privatized, depoliticized gay culture anchored in domesticity and consumption" (Duggan 2003).

Harvey has characterized late capitalism in terms of "flexibility with respect to labour processes, labour markets, products and patterns of consumption" (Harvey 1990, 147). Increased flexibility, as we now know, leads to increased opportunities for the exploitation by transnational corporations of cheap labor markets in Third World nations and in immigrant communities in the First World. The local and intersubjective forms of flexibility may be said to contribute to what Anna Tsing calls the "charisma of globalization" by incorporating a seemingly radical ethic of flexibility into understandings of selfhood. In queer communities, what I will define as "transgressive exceptionalism" can be seen as a by-product of local translations of neo-liberalism.

This book tries to keep transgenderism alive as a meaningful designator of unpredictable gender identities and practices, and it locates the transgender figure as a central player in numerous postmodern debates about space and sexuality, subcultural production, rural gender roles, art and gender ambiguity, the politics of biography, historical conceptions of manhood, gender and genre, the local and the global. Queer lives offer incredible insights into possibilities for social change, but in order for such possibilities to be enacted, queer intellectual labor needs first to be recognized by those who would dismiss the logic of "body politics" altogether, and second it needs to speak to people for whom academic theory often reads like a foreign language. By championing dyke subcultural lives and performances in a shamelessly utopian way, I give in to the seduction of believing in some meaningful relationship between alternative cultural production and new ways of inhabiting time and space.

BIBLIOGRAPHY

Barber, S. M., and D. L. Clark. "Queer Moments: The Performative Temporalities of Eve Kosofsky Sedgwick." In *Regarding Sedgwick: Essays on Queer Culture and Critical Theory*, edited by S. M. Barber and D. L. Clark. New York: Routledge, 2002.

Barrett, L. *Blackness and Value: Seeing Double.* Cambridge: Cambridge University Press, 1999.

Baudelaire, Charles Pierre. *Painter of Modern Life and Other Essays.* New York: Da Capo Press, 1990.

Bersani, L. *Homos.* Cambridge, MA: Harvard University Press, 1996.

Breedlove, L. *Godspeed.* New York: St. Martin's Press, 2002.

Cohen, C. J. *The Boundaries of Blackness: AIDS and the Breakdown of Black Politics.* Chicago: University of Chicago Press, 1999.

Cott, N. *The Bonds of Womanhood: "Woman's Sphere" in New England, 1780–1835.* New Haven, CT: Yale University Press, 1977.

Cunningham, M. *The Hours.* New York: Picador, 1998.

Delany, S. *Times Square Red, Times Square Blue.* New York: New York University Press, 1999.

Dinshaw, C. *Getting Medieval: Sexualities and Communities, Pre- and Postmodern.* Durham, NC: Duke University Press, 1999.

Doty, M. *Heaven's Coast.* New York: Harper, 1996.

Duggan, L. *The Twilight of Equality: Neo-Liberalism, Cultural Politics and the Attack on Democracy.* Boston: Beacon Press, 2003.

Edelman, L. "The Future Is Kid Stuff: Queer Theory, Disidentification, and the Death Drive." *Narrative* 6 (1998): 18–30.

Florida, R. *The Rise of the Creative Class and How It's Transforming Work, Leisure, Community, and Everyday Life.* New York: Basic Books, 2002.

Foucault, M. "Friendship as a Way of Life." In *Foucault Live: Collected Interviews, 1961–1984,* edited by S. Lotringer, 204–12. New York: Semiotext(e), 1996.

———. "Of Other Spaces." Translated by Jay Miskowiec. *Diacritics* 16, no. 1 (1986): 22–27.

Gibson-Graham, J. K. *The End of Capitalism (as We Knew It).* Malden, MA: Blackwell, 1996.

Gilroy, P. *The Black Atlantic: Modernity and Double Consciousness.* Cambridge, MA: Harvard University Press, 1993.

Gunn, T. *The Man with Night Sweats.* Boston: Faber and Faber, 1993.

Hall, S. "The Global and the Local: Globalization and Ethnicity." In *Dangerous Liaisons: Gender, Nation, and Postcolonial Perspectives,* edited by Ann McClintock et al., 173–87. Minneapolis: University of Minnesota Press, 1997.

Harvey, D. *The Condition of Postmodernnity.* Oxford: Blackwell, 1990.

Jameson, F. *Postmodernism, or the Cultural Logic of Late Capitalism.* Durham, NC: Duke University Press, 1997.

Martin, E. *Flexible Bodies.* Boston: Beacon Press, 1995.

Massey, D. "The Political Place of Locality Studies." In *Space, Place, and Gender,* 125–45. Minneapolis: University of Minnesota Press, 1994.

McHugh, K. *American Domesticity: From How-To Manual to Hollywood Drama.* New York: Oxford University Press, 1999.

Myles, E. *Chelsea Girls.* Santa Rosa, CA: Black Sparrow Press, 1994.

Ong, A. *Flexible Citizenship: The Cultural Logics of Transnationality.* Durham, NC: Duke University Press, 1999.

Pile, S. "Introduction: Opposition, Political Identities, and Spaces of Resistance." In *Geographies of Resistance,* edited by M. Keith, 1–32, London: Routledge, 1997.

Reid-Pharr, R. *Black Gay Man: Essays.* Foreword by Samuel R. Delany. New York: New York University Press, 2001.

Roach, J. *Cities of the Dead: Circum-Atlantic Performance.* New York: Columbia University Press, 1996.

Smith-Rosenberg, C. *Disorderly Conduct: Visions of Gender in Victorian America.* New York: Knopf, 1985.

Soja, E. *Postmodern Geographies: The Reassertion of Space in Critical Social Theory.* New York: Verso, 1989.

Tsing, A. "Conclusion: The Global Situation." In *The Anthropology of Globalization: A Reader,* edited by J. X. Inda, 453–86. Oxford: Blackwell, 2002.

MARXISM

PREFACE TO *A CONTRIBUTION TO THE CRITIQUE OF POLITICAL ECONOMY* (1859)
THE FETISHISM OF COMMODITIES AND THE SECRET THEREOF (1867)
THE WORKING DAY (1867)

KARL MARX

While Marx's ideas and influence cannot be represented by a concise selection of his writings, a concise selection can still hold considerable interest and help readers follow how later writers and theorists draw on Marx's ideas. The brief excerpt from Marx's Preface to A Contribution to the Critique of Political Economy *provides a classic summary of his materialist understanding of history, economics, and human consciousness, including the relation between the base (economics) and the superstructure (the rest of culture, including law, politics, religion, aesthetics, and philosophy). The first section from* Capital *describes Marx's argument that capitalism leads people to fetishize commodities, that is, to suppose that commodities have mystical value. Such fetishizing, Marx argues, leads people to overlook how the value of commodities is socially produced rather than mystically inherent in the commodities themselves. Marx describes a series of epochs in the human understanding of commodities (epochs that he also mentions in the excerpt from the Preface to* A Contribution to the Critique of Political Economy*), ranging from the hypothetical isolated individual's relation to potential commodities (he takes the fictional Robinson Crusoe as an example) to what he describes as the movement from primitive economies to feudal and capitalist economies. Each of these epochs opposes Marx's ideal of a socialist economy that provides for people in proportion to their labor. (Marx's quotation from Dogberry refers to a comical character in Shakespeare's* Much Ado about Nothing.*) The second section focuses on how capital exploits workers. It shows the rhetorical power in some of Marx's writings, as when he complains about capital's "were-wolf hunger for surplus labour." (Marx refers to the Factory Acts, a series of laws in nineteenth-century Britain that put modest limits on abusive working conditions, including the number of hours that employers could hire children—ten or sometimes twelve hours per day, varying with the act, the industry, and the age of the children. He also refers to a law passed in Massachusetts in 1842 that limited employers from hiring children under twelve for more than ten hours per day. Marx's notes to* Capital *are not included.)*

PREFACE TO *A CONTRIBUTION TO THE CRITIQUE OF POLITICAL ECONOMY* (1859)

KARL MARX

Translated from the German by N. I. Stone

In the social production which men carry on they enter into definite relations that are indispensable and independent of their will; these relations of production correspond to a definite stage of development of their material powers of production. The sum total of these relations of production constitutes the economic structure of society—the real foundation, on which rise legal and political superstructures and to which correspond definite forms of social consciousness. The mode of production in material life determines the general character of the social, political and spiritual processes of life. It is not the consciousness of men that determines their existence, but, on the contrary, their social existence determines their consciousness. At a certain stage of their development, the material forces of production in society come in conflict with the existing relations of production, or—what is but a legal expression for the same thing—with the property relations within which they had been at work before. From forms of development of the forces of production these relations turn into their fetters. Then comes the period of social revolution. With the change of the economic foundation the entire immense superstructure is more or less rapidly transformed. In considering such transformations the distinction should always be made between the material transformation of the economic conditions of production which can be determined with the precision of natural science, and the legal, political, religious, aesthetic or philosophic—in short ideological forms in which men become conscious of this conflict and fight it out. Just as our opinion of an individual is not based on what he thinks of himself, so can we not judge of such a period of transformation by its own consciousness; on the contrary, this consciousness must rather be explained from the contradictions of material life, from the existing conflict between the social forces of production and the relations of production. No social order ever disappears before all the productive forces, for which there is room in it, have been developed; and new higher relations of production never appear before the material conditions of their existence have matured in the womb of the old society. Therefore, mankind always takes up only such problems as it can solve; since, looking at the matter more closely, we will always find that the problem itself arises only when the material conditions necessary for its solution already exist or are at least in the process of formation. In broad outlines we can designate the Asiatic, the ancient, the feudal, and the modern bourgeois methods of production as so many epochs in the progress of the economic formation of society. The bourgeois relations of production are the last antagonistic form of the social process of production—antagonistic not in the sense of individual antagonism, but of one arising from conditions surrounding the life of individuals in society; at the same time the productive forces developing in the womb of bourgeois society create the material conditions for the solution of that antagonism. This social formation constitutes, therefore, the closing chapter of the prehistoric stage of human society.

THE FETISHISM OF COMMODITIES AND THE SECRET THEREOF (1867)

KARL MARX

Translated from the German by Samuel Moore and Edward Aveling

A commodity appears, at first sight, a very trivial thing, and easily understood. Its analysis shows that it is, in reality, a very queer thing, abounding in metaphysical subtleties and theological niceties. So far as it is a value in use, there is nothing mysterious about it, whether we consider it from the point of view that by its properties it is capable of satisfying human wants, or from the point that those properties are the product of human labour. It is as clear as noon-day, that man, by his industry, changes the forms of the materials furnished by nature, in such a way as to make them useful to him. The form of wood, for instance, is altered, by making a table out of it. Yet, for all that, the table continues to be that common, every-day thing, wood. But, so soon as it steps forth as a commodity, it is changed into something transcendent. It not only stands with its feet on the ground, but, in relation to all other commodities, it stands on its head, and evolves out of its wooden brain grotesque ideas, far more wonderful than "table-turning" ever was.

The mystical character of commodities does not originate, therefore, in their use-value. Just as little does it proceed from the nature of the determining factors of value. For, in the first place, however varied the useful kinds of labour, or productive activities, may be, it is a physiological fact, that they are functions of the human organism, and that each such function, whatever may be its nature or form, is essentially the expenditure of human brain, nerves, muscles, &c. Secondly, with regard to that which forms the ground-work for the quantitative determination of value, namely, the duration of that expenditure, or the quantity of labour, it is quite clear that there is a palpable difference between its quantity and quality. In all states of society, the labour-time that it costs to produce the means of subsistence, must necessarily be an object of interest to mankind, though not of equal interest in different stages of development. And lastly, from the moment that men in any way work for one another, their labour assumes a social form.

Whence, then, arises the enigmatical character of the product of labour, so soon as it assumes the form of commodities? Clearly from this form itself. The equality of all sorts of human labour is expressed objectively by their products all being equally values; the measure of the expenditure of labour-power by the duration of that expenditure, takes the form of the quantity of value of the products of labour; and finally, the mutual relations of the producers, within which the social character of their labour affirms itself, take the form of a social relation between the products.

A commodity is therefore a mysterious thing, simply because in it the social character of men's labour appears to them as an objective character stamped upon the product of that labour; because the relation of the producers to the sum total of their own labour is presented to them as a social relation, existing not between themselves, but between the products of their labour. This is the reason why the products of labour become commodities, social things whose qualities are at the same time perceptible and imperceptible by the senses. In the same way the light from an object is perceived by us not as the subjective excitation of our optic nerve, but as the objective form of something outside the eye itself. But, in the act of seeing, there is at all events, an actual passage of light from one thing to another, from the external object to the eye. There is a physical relation between physical things. But it is different with commodities. There, the existence of the things *quâ* commodities, and the value relation between the products of labour which stamps them as commodities, have absolutely no connection with their physical properties and with the material relations arising therefrom. There it is a definite social relation between men, that assumes, in their eyes, the fantastic form of a relation between things. In order, therefore, to find an analogy, we must have recourse to the mist-enveloped regions of the religious world. In that world the productions of the human brain appear as independent beings endowed with life, and entering into relation both with one another and the human race. So it is in the world of commodities with the products of men's hands. This I call the Fetishism which attaches itself to the products of labour, so soon as they are produced as commodities, and which is therefore inseparable from the production of commodities.

This Fetishism of commodities has its origin, as the foregoing analysis has already shown, in the peculiar social character of the labour that produces them.

As a general rule, articles of utility become commodities, only because they are products of the labour of private individuals or groups of individuals who carry on their work independently of each other. The sum total of the labour of all these private individuals forms the aggregate labour of society. Since the producers do not come into social contact with each other until they exchange their products, the specific social character of each producer's labour does not show itself except in the act of exchange. In other words, the labour of the individual asserts itself as a part of the labour of society, only by means of the relations which the act of exchange establishes directly between the products, and indirectly, through them, between the producers. To the latter, therefore, the relations connecting the labour of one individual with that of the rest appear, not as direct social relations between individuals at work, but as what they really are, material relations between persons and social relations between things. It is only by being exchanged that the products of labour acquire, as values, one uniform social status, distinct from their varied forms of existence as objects of utility. This division of a product into a useful thing and a value becomes practically important, only when exchange has acquired such an extension that useful articles are produced for the purpose of being exchanged, and their character as values has therefore to be taken into account, beforehand, during production. From this moment the labour of the individual producer acquires socially a two-fold character. On the one hand, it must, as a definite useful kind of labour, satisfy a definite social want, and thus hold its place as part and parcel of the collective labour of all, as a branch of a social division of labour that has sprung up spontaneously. On the other hand, it can satisfy the manifold wants of the individual producer himself, only in so far as the mutual exchangeability of all kinds of useful private labour is an established social fact, and therefore the private useful labour of each producer ranks on an equality with that of all others. The equalisation of the most different kinds of labour can be the result only of an abstraction from their inequalities, or of reducing them to their common denominator, viz., expenditure of human labour power or human labour in the abstract. The two-fold social character of the labour of the individual appears to him, when reflected in his brain, only under those forms which are impressed upon that labour in everyday practice by the exchange of products. In this way, the character that his own labour possesses of being socially useful takes the form of the condition, that the product must be not only useful, but useful for others, and the social character that his particular labour has of being the equal of all other particular kinds of labour, takes the form that all the physically different articles that are the products of labour, have one common quality, viz., that of having value.

Hence, when we bring the products of our labour into relation with each other as values, it is not because we see in these articles the material receptacles of homogeneous human labour. Quite the contrary: wherever, by an exchange, we equate as values our different products, by that very act, we also equate, as human labour, the different kinds of labour expended upon them. We are not aware of this, nevertheless we do it. Value, therefore, does not stalk about with a label describing what it is. It is value, rather, that converts every product into a social hieroglyphic. Later on, we try to decipher the hieroglyphic, to get behind the secret of our own social products; for to stamp an object of utility as a value, is just as much a social product as language. The recent scientific discovery, that the products of labour, so far as they are values, are but material expressions of the human labour spent in their production, marks, indeed, an epoch in the history of the development of the human race, but, by no means, dissipates the mist through which the social character of labour appears to us to be an objective character of the products themselves. The fact, that in the particular form of production with which we are dealing, viz., the production of commodities, the specific social character of private labour carried on independently, consists in the equality of every kind of that labour, by virtue of its being human labour, which character, therefore, assumes in the product the form of the value—this fact appears to the producers, notwithstanding the discovery above referred to, to be just as real and final, as the fact, that, after the discovery by science of the component gases of air, the atmosphere itself remained unaltered.

What, first of all, practically concerns producers when they make an exchange, is the question, how much of some other product they get for their own? in what proportions the products are exchangeable? When these proportions have, by custom, attained a certain stability, they appear to result from the nature of the products, so that, for instance, one ton of iron and two ounces of gold appear as naturally to be of equal value as a pound of gold and a pound of iron in spite of their different physical and chemical qualities appear to be of equal weight. The character of having value, when once impressed upon products, obtains fixity only by reason of their acting and re-acting upon each other as quantities of value. These quantities vary continually, independently of the will, foresight and action of the producers. To them, their own social action takes the form of the action of objects, which rule the producers instead of being ruled by them. It requires a fully developed production of commodities before, from accumulated experience alone, the scientific conviction springs up, that all the different kinds of private labour, which are carried on independently of each other, and yet as spontaneously developed branches of the social division of labour, are continually being reduced to the quantitative proportions in which society requires them. And why? Because, in the midst of all the accidental and ever fluctuating exchange-relations between the products, the labour-time socially necessary for their production forcibly asserts itself like an over-riding law of nature. The law of gravity thus asserts itself when a house falls about our ears. The determination of the magnitude of value by labour-time is therefore a secret, hidden under the apparent fluctuations in the relative values of commodities. Its discovery, while removing all appearance of mere accidentality from the determination of the magnitude of the values of products, yet in no way alters the mode in which that determination takes place.

Man's reflections on the forms of social life, and consequently, also, his scientific analysis of those forms, take a course directly opposite to that of their actual historical development. He begins, post festum, with the results of the process of development ready to hand before him. The characters that stamp products as commodities, and whose establishment is a necessary preliminary to the circulation of commodities, have already acquired the stability of natural, self-understood forms of social life, before man seeks to decipher, not their historical character, for in his eyes they are immutable, but their meaning. Consequently it was the analysis of the prices of commodities that alone led to the determination of the magnitude of value, and it was the common expression of all commodities in money that alone led to the establishment of their characters as values. It is, however, just this ultimate money form of the world of commodities that actually conceals, instead of disclosing, the social character of private labour, and the social relations between the individual producers. When I state that coats or boots stand in a relation to linen, because it is the universal incarnation of abstract human labour, the absurdity of the statement is self-evident. Nevertheless, when the producers of coats and boots compare those articles with linen, or, what is the same thing, with gold or silver, as the universal equivalent, they express the relation between their own private labour and the collective labour of society in the same absurd form.

The categories of bourgeois economy consist of such like forms. They are forms of thought expressing with social validity the conditions and relations of a definite, historically determined mode of production, viz., the production of commodities. The whole mystery of commodities, all the magic and necromancy that surrounds the products of labour as long as they take the form of commodities, vanishes therefore, so soon as we come to other forms of production.

Since Robinson Crusoe's experiences are a favourite theme with political economists, let us take a look at him on his island. Moderate though he be, yet some few wants he has to satisfy, and must therefore do a little useful work of various sorts, such as making tools and furniture, taming goats, fishing and hunting. Of his prayers and the like we take no account, since they are a source of pleasure to him, and he looks upon them as so much recreation. In spite of the variety of his work, he knows that his labour, whatever its form, is but the activity of one and the same Robinson, and consequently, that it consists of nothing but different modes of human labour. Necessity itself compels him to apportion his time accurately between his different kinds of work. Whether one kind occupies a greater space in his general activity than another, depends on the difficulties, greater or less as the case may be, to be overcome in attaining the useful effect aimed at. This our friend Robinson soon learns by experience, and having rescued a watch, ledger, and pen and ink from the wreck, commences, like a true-born Briton, to keep a set of books. His stock-book contains a list of the objects of utility that belong to him, of the operations necessary for their production, and lastly, of the labour time that definite quantities of those objects have, on an average, cost him. All the relations between Robinson and the objects that form this wealth of his own creation, are here so simple and clear as to be intelligible without exertion, even to Mr. Sedley Taylor. And yet those relations contain all that is essential to the determination of value.

Let use now transport ourselves from Robinson's island bathed in light to the European middle ages shrouded in darkness. Here, instead of the independent man, we find everyone dependent, serfs and lords, vassals and suzerains, laymen and clergy. Personal dependence here characterises the social relations of production just as much as it does the other spheres of life organized on the basis of that production. But for the very reason that personal dependence forms the groundwork of society, there is no necessity for labour and its products to assume a fantastic form different from their reality. They take the shape, in the transactions of society, of services in kind and payments in kind. Here the particular and natural form of labour, and not, as in a society based on production of commodities, its general abstract form is the immediate social form of labour. Compulsory labour is just as properly measured by time, as commodity-producing labour; but every serf knows that what he expends in the service of his lord, is a definite quantity of his own personal labour-power. The tithe to be rendered to the priest is more matter of fact than his blessing. No matter, then, what we may think of the parts played by the different classes of people themselves in this society, the social relations between individuals in the performance of their labour, appear at all events as their own mutual personal relations, and are not disguised under the shape of social relations between the products of labour.

For an example of labour in common or directly associated labour, we have no occasion to go back to that spontaneously developed form which we find on the threshold of the history of all civilized races. We have one close at hand in the patriarchal industries of a peasant family, that produces corn, cattle, yarn, linen, and clothing for home use. These different articles are, as regards the family, so many products of its labour, but as between themselves, they are not commodities. The different kinds of labour, such as tillage, cattle tending, spinning, weaving and making clothes, which result in the various products, are in themselves, and such as they are, direct social functions, because functions of the family, which, just as much as a society based on the production of commodities, possesses a spontaneously developed system of division of labour. The distribution of the work within the family, and the regulation of the labour-time of the several members, depend as well upon differences of age and sex as upon natural conditions varying with the seasons. The labour-power of each individual, by its very nature, operates in this case merely as a definite portion of the whole labour-power of the family, and therefore, the measure of the expenditure of individual labour-power by its duration, appears here by its very nature as a social character of their labour.

Let us now picture to ourselves, by way of change, a community of free individuals, carrying on their work with the means of production in common, in which the labour-power of all the different individuals is consciously applied as the combined labour-power of the community. All the characteristics of Robinson's labour are here repeated, but with this difference, that they are social, instead of individual. Everything produced by him was exclusively the result of his own personal labour, and therefore simply an object of use for himself. The total product of our community is a social product. One portion serves as fresh means of product and remains social. But another portion is consumed by the members as means of subsistence. A distribution of this portion amongst them is consequently necessary. The mode of this distribution will vary with the productive organization of the community, and the degree of historical development attained by the producers. We will assume, but merely for the sake of a parallel with the production of commodities, that the share of each individual producer in the means of subsistence is determined by his labour-time. Labour-time would, in that case, play a double part. Its apportionment in accordance with a definite social plan maintains the proper proportion between the different kinds of work to be done and the various wants of the community. On the other hand, it also serves as a measure of the portion of the common labour borne by each individual, and of his share in the part of the total product destined for individual consumption. The social relations of the individual producers, with regards both to their labour and to its products, are in this case perfectly simple and intelligible, and that with regard not only to production but also to distribution.

The religious world is but the reflex of the real world. And for a society based upon the production of commodities, in which the producers in general enter into social relations with one another by treating their products as commodities and values, whereby they reduce their individual private labour to the standards of homogeneous human labour—for such a society, Christianity with its *cultus* of abstract man, more especially in its bourgeois developments, Protestantism, Deism, &c., is the most fitting form of religion. In the ancient Asiatic and other ancient modes of production, we find that the conversion of products into commodities, and therefore the conversion of men into producers of commodities, holds a subordinate place, which, however, increases in importance as the primitive communities approach nearer and nearer to their dissolution. Trading nations, properly so called, exist in the ancient world only in its interstices, like the gods of Epicurus in the Intermundia, or like Jews in the pores of Polish society. Those ancient social organisms of production are, as compared with bourgeois society, extremely simple and transparent. But they are founded either on the immature development of man individually, who has not yet severed the umbilical cord that unites him with his fellow men in a primitive tribal community, or upon direct relations of subjection. They can arise and exist only when the development of the productive power of labour has not risen beyond a low stage, and when, therefore, the social relations within the sphere of material life, between man and man, and between man and Nature, are correspondingly narrow. This narrowness is reflected in the ancient worship of Nature, and in the other elements of the popular religions. The religious reflex of the real world can, in any case, only then finally vanish, when the practical relations of everyday life offer to man none but perfectly intelligible and reasonable relations with regard to his fellowmen and to nature.

The life-process of society, which is based on the process of material production, does not strip off its mystical veil until it is treated as production by freely associated men, and is consciously regulated by them in accordance with a settled plan. This, however, demands for society a certain material groundwork or set of conditions of existence which in their turn are the spontaneous product of a long and painful process of development.

Political economy has indeed analysed, however incompletely, value and its magnitude, and has discovered what lie beneath these forms. But it has never once asked the question why labour is represented by the value of its product and labour time by the magnitude of that value. These formulæ, which bear stamped upon them in unmistakeable letters, that they belong to a state of society, in which the process of production has the mastery over man, instead of being controlled by him, such formulæ appear to the bourgeois intellect to be as much a self-evident necessity imposed by nature as productive labour itself. Hence forms of social production that preceded the bourgeois form, are treated by the bourgeoisie in much the same way as the Fathers of the Church treated pre-Christian religions.

To what extent some economists are misled by the Fetishism inherent in commodities, or by the objective appearance of the social characteristics of labour, is shown, amongst other ways, by the dull and tedious quarrel over the part played by Nature in the formation of exchange value. Since exchange value is a definite social manner of expressing the amount of labour bestowed upon an object, Nature has no more to do with it, than it has in fixing the course or exchange.

The mode of production in which the product takes the form of a commodity, or is produced directly for exchange, is the most general and most embryonic form of bourgeois production. It therefore makes its appearance at an early date in history, though not in the same predominating and characteristic manner as now-a-days. Hence its Fetish character is comparatively easy to be seen through. But when we come to more concrete forms, even this appearance of simplicity vanishes. Whence arose the illusions of the monetary system? To it gold and silver, when serving as money, did not represent a social relation between producers, but were natural objects with strange social properties. And modern economy, which looks down with such disdain on the monetary system, does not its superstition come out as clear as noon-day, whenever it treats of capital? How long is it since economy discarded the physiocratic illusion, that rents grow out of the soil and not out of society?

But not to anticipate, we will content ourselves with yet another example relating to the commodity form. Could commodities themselves speak, they would say: Our use-value may be a thing that interests men. It is no part of us as objects. What, however, does belong to us as objects, is our value. Our natural intercourse as commodities proves it. In the eyes of each other we are nothing but exchange values. Now listen how those commodities speak through the mouth of the economist. "Value"—(i.e., exchange value) "is a property of things, riches"—(i.e., use-value) "of man. Value, in this sense, necessarily implies exchanges, riches do not." "Riches"(use-value) "are the attribute of men, value is the attribute of commodities. A man or a community is rich, a pearl or a diamond is valuable...A pearl or a diamond is valuable" as a pearl or diamond. So far no chemist has ever discovered exchange value either in a pearl or a diamond. The economical discoverers of this chemical element, who by-the-bye lay special claim to critical acumen, find however that the use-value of objects belongs to them independently of their material properties, while their value, on the other hand, forms a part of them as objects. What confirms them in this view, is the peculiar circumstance that the use-value of objects is realised without exchange, by means of a direct relation between the objects and man, while, on the other hand, their value is realised only by exchange, that is, by means of a social process. Who fails here to call to mind our good friend, Dogberry, who informs neighbour Seacoal, that, "To be a well-favoured man is the gift of fortune; but reading and writing comes by nature."

THE WORKING DAY (1867)

KARL MARX

"What is a working day? What is the length of time during which capital may consume the labour-power whose daily value it buys? How far may the working day be extended beyond the working time necessary for the reproduction of labour-power itself?" It has been seen that to these questions capital replies: the working day contains the full 24 hours, with the deduction of the few hours of repose without which labour-power absolutely refuses its services again. Hence it is self-evident that the labourer is nothing else, his whole life through, than labour-power, that therefore all his disposable time is by nature and law labour-time, to be devoted to the self-expansion of capital. Time for education, for intellectual development, for the fulfilling of social functions and for social intercourse, for the free-play of his bodily and mental activity, even the rest time of Sunday (and that in a country of Sabbatarians!)—moonshine! But in its blind unrestrainable passion, its were-wolf hunger for surplus-labour, capital oversteps not only the moral, but even the merely physical maximum bounds of the working day. It usurps the time for growth, development, and healthy maintenance of the body. It steals the time required for the consumption of fresh air and sunlight. It higgles over a meal-time, incorporating it where possible with the process of production itself, so that food is given to the labourer as to a mere means of production, as coal is supplied to the boiler, grease and oil to the machinery. It reduces the sound sleep needed for the restoration, reparation, refreshment of the bodily powers to just so many hours of torpor as the revival of an organism, absolutely exhausted, renders essential. It is not the normal maintenance of the labour-power which is to determine the limits of the working day; it is the greatest possible daily expenditure of labour-power, no matter how diseased, compulsory, and painful it may be, which is to determine the limits of the labourers' period of repose. Capital cares nothing for the length of life of labour-power. All that concerns it is simply and solely the maximum of labour-power, that can be rendered fluent in a working day. It attains this end by shortening the extent of the labourer's life, as a greedy farmer snatches increased produce from the soil by robbing it of its fertility.

The capitalistic mode of production (essentially the production of surplus-value, the absorption of surplus-labour), produces thus, with the extension of the working day, not only the deterioration of human labour-power by robbing it of its normal, moral and physical, conditions of development and function. It produces also the premature exhaustion and death of this labour-power itself. It extends the labourer's time of production during a given period by shortening his actual lifetime.

But the value of the labour-power includes the value of the commodities necessary for the reproduction of the worker, or for the keeping up of the working class. If then the unnatural extension of the working day, that capital necessarily strives after in its unmeasured passion for self-expansion, shortens the length of life of the individual labourer, and therefore the duration of his labour-power, the forces used up have to be replaced at a more rapid rate and the sum of the expenses for the reproduction of labour-power will be greater; just as in a machine the part of its value to be reproduced every day is greater the more rapidly the machine is worn out. It would seem therefore that the interest of capital itself points in the direction of a normal working day.

The slave-owner buys his labourer as he buys his horse. If he loses his slave, he loses capital that can only be restored by new outlay in the slave-mart. But "the rice-grounds of Georgia, or the swamps of the Mississippi may be fatally injurious to the human constitution; but the waste of human life which the cultivation of these districts necessitates, is not so great that it cannot be repaired from the teeming preserves of Virginia and Kentucky. Considerations of economy, moreover, which, under a natural system, afford some security for humane treatment by identifying the master's interest with the slave's preservation, when once trading in slaves is practised, become reasons for racking to the uttermost the toil of the slave; for, when his place can at once be supplied from foreign preserves, the duration of his life becomes a matter of less moment than its productiveness while it lasts. It is accordingly a maxim of slave management, in slave-importing countries, that the most effective economy is that which takes out of the human chattel in the shortest space of time the utmost amount of exertion it is capable of putting forth. It is in tropical culture, where annual profits often equal the whole capital of plantations, that negro life is most recklessly sacrificed. It is the agriculture of the West Indies, which has been for centuries prolific of fabulous wealth, that has engulfed millions of the African race. It is in Cuba, at this day, whose revenues are reckoned by millions, and whose planters are princes, that we see in the servile class, the coarsest fare, the most exhausting and unremitting toil, and even the absolute destruction of a portion of its numbers every year."[1]

Mutato nomine de te fabula narratur. For slave-trade read labour-market, for Kentucky and Virginia, Ireland and the agricultural districts of England, Scotland, and Wales, for Africa, Germany. We heard how over-work thinned the ranks of the bakers in London. Nevertheless, the London labour-market is always over-stocked with German and other candidates for death in the bakeries. Pottery, as we saw, is one of the shortest-lived industries. Is there any want therefore of potters? Josiah Wedgwood, the inventor of modern pottery, himself originally a common workman, said in 1785 before the House of Commons that the whole trade employed from 15,000 to 20,000 people.[2] In the year 1861 the population alone of the town centres of this industry in Great Britain numbered 101,302. "The cotton trade has existed for ninety years. . . . It has existed for three generations of the English race, and I believe I may safely say that during that period it has destroyed nine generations of factory operatives."[3]

No doubt in certain epochs of feverish activity the labour-market shows significant gaps. In 1834, *e.g.* But then the manufacturers proposed to the Poor Law Commissioners that they should send the "surplus-population" of the agricultural districts to the north, with the explanation "that the manufacturers would absorb and use it up."[4] Agents were appointed with the consent of the Poor Law Commissioners. . . . An office was set up in Manchester, to which lists were sent of those workpeople in the agricultural districts wanting employment, and their names were registered in books. The manufacturers attended at these offices, and selected such persons as they chose; when they had selected such persons as their "wants required," they gave instructions to have them forwarded to Manchester, and they were sent, ticketed like bales of goods, by canals, or with carriers, others tramping on the road, and many of them were found on the way lost and half-starved. This system had grown up into a regular trade. This House will hardly believe it, but I tell them, that this traffic in human flesh was as well kept up, they were in effect as regularly sold to these [Manchester] manufacturers as slaves are sold to the cotton-grower in the United States. . . . In 1860, "the cotton trade was at its zenith." . . . The manufacturers again found that they were short of hands. . . . They applied to the "flesh agents," as they are called. Those agents sent to the southern downs of England, to the pastures of Dorsetshire, to the glades of Devonshire, to the people tending kine in Wiltshire, but they sought in vain. The surplus-population was "absorbed." The "Bury Guardian" said, on the completion of the French treaty, that "10,000 additional hands could be absorbed by Lancashire, and that 30,000 or 40,000 will be needed." After the "flesh agents and sub-agents" had in vain sought through the agricultural districts, "a deputation came up to London, and waited on the right hon. gentleman [Mr. Villiers, President of the Poor Law Board] with a view of obtaining poor children from certain union houses for the mills of Lancashire."[5]

What experience shows to the capitalist generally is a constant excess of population, *i.e.*, an excess in relation to the momentary requirements of surplus-labour-absorbing capital, although this excess is made up of generations of human beings stunted, short-lived, swiftly replacing each other, plucked, so to say, before maturity. And, indeed, experience shows to the intelligent observer with what swiftness and grip the capitalist mode of production, dating, historically speaking, only from yesterday, has seized the vital power of the people by the very root—shows how the degeneration of the industrial population is only retarded by the constant absorption of primitive and physically uncorrupted elements from the country—shows how even the country labourers, in spite of fresh air and the principle of natural selection, that works so powerfully amongst them, and only permits the survival of the strongest, are already beginning to die off. Capital that has such good reasons for denying the sufferings of the legions of workers that surround it, is in practice moved as much and as little by the sight of the coming degradation and final depopulation of the human race, as by the probable fall of the earth into the sun. In every stock-jobbing swindle every one knows that some time or other the crash must come, but every one hopes that it may fall on the head of his neighbour, after he himself has caught the shower of gold and placed it in safety. *Après moi le déluge!* is the watchword of every capitalist and of every capitalist nation. Hence Capital is reckless of the health or length of life of the labourer, unless under compulsion from society. To the outcry as to the physical and mental degradation, the premature death, the torture of overwork, it answers: Ought these to trouble us since they increase our profits? But looking at things as a whole, all this does not, indeed, depend on the good or ill will of the individual capitalist. Free competition brings out the inherent laws of capitalist production, in the shape of external coercive laws having power over every individual capitalist.

The establishment of a normal working day is the result of centuries of struggle between capitalist and labourer. The history of this struggle shows two opposed tendencies. Compare, *e.g.*, the English factory legislation of our time with the English Labour Statutes from the 14th century to well into the middle of the 18th. Whilst the modern Factory Acts compulsorily shortened the working-day, the earlier statutes tried to lengthen it by compulsion. Of course the pretensions of capital in embryo—when, beginning to grow, it secures the right of absorbing a *quantum sufficit* of surplus-labour, not merely by the force of economic relations, but by the help of the State—appear very modest when put face to face with the concessions that, growling and struggling, it has to make in its adult condition. It takes centuries ere the "free" labourer, thanks to the development of capitalistic production, agrees, *i.e.*, is compelled by social conditions, to sell the whole of his active life, his very capacity for work, for the price of the necessaries of life, his birthright for a mess of pottage. Hence it is natural that the lengthening of the working day, which capital, from the middle of the 14th to the end of the 17th century, tries to impose by State-measures on adult labourers, approximately coincides with the shortening of the working day which, in the second half of the 19th century, has here and there been effected by the State to prevent the coining of children's blood into capital. That which to-day, *e.g.*, in the State of Massachusetts, until recently the freest State of the North-American Republic, has been proclaimed as the statutory limit of the labour of children under 12, was in England, even in the middle of the 17th century, the normal working-day of able-bodied artizans, robust labourers, athletic blacksmiths.

The first "Statute of Labourers" (23 Edward III., 1349) found its immediate pretext (not its cause, for legislation of this kind lasts centuries after the pretext for it has disappeared) in the great plague that decimated the people, so that, as a Tory writer says, "The difficulty of getting men to work on reasonable terms (*i.e.*, at a price that left their employers a reasonable quantity of surplus-labour) grew to such a height as to be quite intolerable."[6] Reasonable wages were, therefore, fixed by law as well as the limits of the working day. The latter point, the only one that here interests us, is repeated in the Statute of 1496 (Henry VIII.). The working day for all artificers and field labourers from March to September ought, according to this statute (which, however, could not be enforced), to last from 5 in the morning to between 7 and 8 in the evening. But the meal times consist of 1 hour for breakfast, 1 1/2 hours for dinner, and 1/2 an hour for "noon-meate," *i.e.*, exactly twice as much as under the factory acts now in force. In winter, work was to last from 5 in the morning until dark, with the same intervals. A statute of Elizabeth of 1562 leaves the length of the working day for all labourers "hired for daily or weekly wage" untouched, but aims at limiting the intervals to 2 1/2 hours in the summer, or to 2 in the winter. Dinner is only to last 1 hour, and the "afternoon-sleep of half an hour" is only allowed between the middle of May and the middle of August. For every hour of absence 1d. is to be subtracted from the wage. In practice, however, the conditions were much more favourable to the labourers than in the statute-book. William Petty, the father of political economy, and to some extent the founder of Statistics, says in a work that he published in the last third of the 17th century: "Labouring-men (then meaning field-labourers) work 10 hours per diem, and make 20 meals per week, viz., 3 a day for working days, and 2 on Sundays; whereby it is plain, that if they could fast on Fryday nights, and dine in one hour and an half, whereas they take two, from eleven to one; thereby this working 1/20 more, and spending 1/20 less, the above-mentioned (tax) might be raised."[7] Was not Dr. Andrew Ure right in crying down the 12 hours' bill of 1833 as a retrogression to the times of the dark ages? It is true, these regulations contained in the statute mentioned by Petty, apply also to apprentices. But the condition of child-labour, even at the end of the 17th century, is seen from the following complaint: Tis not their practice (in Germany) as with us in this kingdom, to bind an apprentice for seven years; three or four is their common standard: and the reason is, because they are educated from their cradle to something of employment, which renders them the more apt and docile, and consequently the more capable of attaining to a ripeness and quicker proficiency in business. Whereas our youth, here in England, being bred to nothing before they come to be apprentices, make a very slow progress and require much longer time wherein to reach the perfection of accomplished artists.[8]

Still, during the greater part of the 18th century, up to the epoch of Modern Industry and machinism, capital in England had not succeeded in seizing for itself, by the payment of the weekly value of labour-power, the whole week of the labourer, with the exception, however, of the agricultural labourers. The fact that they could live for a whole week on the wage of four days, did not appear to the labourers a sufficient reason that they should work the other two days for the capitalist. One party of English economists, in the interest of capital, denounces this obstinacy in the most violent manner, another party defends the labourers. Let us listen, *e.g.*, to the contest between Postlethwayt whose Dictionary of Trade then had the same reputation as the kindred works of M'Culloch and M'Gregor to-day, and the author (already quoted) of the "Essay on Trade and Commerce."

Postlethwayt says among other things: "We cannot put an end to those few observations, without noticing that trite remark in the mouth of too many; that if the industrious poor can obtain enough to maintain themselves in five days, they will not work the whole six. Whence they infer the necessity of even the necessaries of life being made dear by taxes, or any other means, to compel the working artizan and manufacturer to labour the whole six days in the week, without ceasing. I must beg leave to differ in sentiment from those great politicians, who contend for the perpetual slavery of the working people of this kingdom; they forget the vulgar adage, all work and no play. Have not the English boasted of the ingenuity and dexterity of her working artists and manufacturers which have heretofore given credit and reputation to British wares in general? What has this been owing to? To nothing more probably than the relaxation of the working people in their own way. Were they obliged to toil the year round, the whole six days in the week, in a repetition of the same work, might it not blunt their ingenuity, and render them stupid instead of alert and dexterous; and might not our workmen lose their reputation instead of maintaining it by such eternal slavery? .... And what sort of workmanship could we expect from such hard-driven animals? .... Many of them will execute as much work in four days as a Frenchman will in five or six. But if Englishmen are to be eternal drudges, 'tis to be feared they will degenerate below the Frenchmen. As our people are famed for bravery in war, do we not say that it is owing to good English roast beef and pudding in their bellies, as well as their constitutional spirit of liberty? And why may not the superior ingenuity and dexterity of our artists and manufactures, be owing to that freedom and liberty to direct themselves in their own way, and I hope we shall never have them deprived of such privileges and that good living from whence their ingenuity no less than their courage may proceed."[9] Thereupon the author of the "Essay on Trade and Commerce" replies: "If the making of every seventh day an holiday is supposed to be of divine institution, as it implies the appropriating the other six days to labour (he means capital as we shall soon see) surely it will not be thought cruel to enforce it ..... That mankind in general, are naturally inclined to ease and indolence, we fatally experience to be true, from the conduct of our manufacturing populace, who do not labour, upon an average, above four days in a week, unless provisions happen to be very dear. ... Put all the necessaries of the poor under one denomination; for instance, call them all wheat, or suppose that ... the bushel of wheat shall cost five shillings and that he (a manufacturer) earns a shilling by his labour, he then would be obliged to work five days only in a week. If the bushel of wheat should cost but four shillings, he would be obliged to work but four days; but as wages in this kingdom are much higher in proportion to the price of necessaries .... the manufacturer, who labours four days, has a surplus of money to live idle with the rest of the week .... I hope I have said enough to make it appear that the moderate labour of six days in a week is no slavery. Our labouring people do this, and to all appearance are the happiest of all our labouring poor, but the Dutch do this in manufactures, and appear to be a very happy people. The French do so, when holidays do not intervene. But our populace have adopted a notion, that as Englishmen they enjoy a birthright privilege of being more free and independent than in any country in Europe. Now this idea, as far as it may affect the bravery of our troops, may be of some use; but the less the manufacturing poor have of it, certainly the better for themselves and for the State. The labouring people should never think themselves independent of their superiors. ..... It is extremely dangerous to encourage mobs in a commercial state like ours, where, perhaps, seven parts out of eight of the whole, are people with little or no property. The cure will not be perfect, till our manufacturing poor are contented to labour six days for the same sum which they now earn in four days."[10] To this end, and for "extirpating idleness, debauchery and excess," promoting a spirit of industry, "lowering the price of labour in our manufactories, and easing the lands of the heavy burden of poor's rates," our "faithful Eckart" of capital proposes this approved device: to shut up such labourers as become dependent on public support, in a word, paupers, in "an *ideal workhouse*." Such ideal workhouse must be made a "House of Terror," and not an asylum for the poor, "where they are to be plentifully fed, warmly and decently clothed, and where they do but little work."[11] In this "House of Terror," this "ideal workhouse, the poor shall work 14 hours in a day, allowing proper time for meals, in such manner that there shall remain 12 hours of neat-labour."[12]

Twelve working hours daily in the Ideal Workhouse, in the "House of Terror" of 1770! 63 years later, in 1833, when the English Parliament reduced the working day for children of 13 to 18, in four branches of industry to 12 full hours, the judgment day of English Industry had dawned! In 1852, when Louis Bonaparte sought to secure his position with the bourgeoisie by tampering with the legal working day, the French people cried out with one voice "the law that limits the working day to 12 hours is the one good that has remained to us of the legislation of the Republic!"[13]At Zürich the work of children over 10, is limited to 12 hours; in Aargau in 1862, the work of children between 13 and 16, was reduced from 12 1/2 to 12 hours; in Austria in 1860, for children between 14 and 16, the same reduction was made. "What a progress," since 1770! Macaulay would shout with exultation!

The "House of Terror" for paupers of which the capitalistic soul of 1770 only dreamed, was realized a few years later in the shape of a gigantic "Workhouse" for the industrial worker himself. It is called the Factory. And the ideal this time fades before the reality.

NOTES

1. Cairnes, "The Slave Power," p. 110, 111.
2. John Ward, "History of the Borough of Stoke-upon-Trent," London, 1843, p. 42.
3. Ferrand's Speech in the House of Commons, 27th April, 1863.
4. l. c.
5. l. c.
6. "Sophisms of Free Trade." 7th Ed. London, 1850, p. 205.
7. W. Petty, "Political Anatomy of Ireland, Verbatim Sapienti," 1672, Ed. 1691, p. 10.
8. "A Discourse on the necessity of encouraging Mechanick Industry," London, 1689, p. 13.
9. Postlethwayt, l. c., "First Preliminary Discourse," p. 14.
10. "An essay on trade and commerce, containing observations on Taxation, &c., London, 1770," p. 15, 41, 96, 97, 55, 57, 69.
11. l. c. p. 242.
12. l. c. p. 260.
13. "Rep. of Insp. of Fact.," 31st October, 1856, p. 80.

THE WORK OF ART IN THE AGE OF ITS MECHANICAL REPRODUCIBILITY (1936–1939)

WALTER BENJAMIN

Translated from the German by Harry Zohn and Edmund Jephcott

With the growth of mass culture and technological change, many people see technology as a threat to the arts. Writing during the Great Depression amid the growth of fascism (including Nazism) and anticipating World War II, Benjamin feels strongly the dangerous connections between mass culture and the fascist, dictatorial abuse of aesthetics. When Benjamin describes film, he is thinking both of silent film and of the new sound films that began within the decade prior to his writing. When he describes the fascist aestheticization of politics, he is thinking of the mass organization and mass rallies characteristic of fascism, as visible, for example, in Leni Riefenstahl's notorious Nazi propaganda film Triumph of the Will *(1935). Technological change and mass culture, Benjamin argues, undermine the traditional* aura *of art. Art can no longer seem autonomous, separate from the masses. But Benjamin also sees new technologies as transforming the arts in exciting ways and potentially as encouraging critical thinking, depending on how we use them. Unlike Horkheimer and Adorno, who see corporate, consumer culture as producing conformist consumers (see their essay in this volume), Benjamin believes that consumer culture can also produce critical consumers. Benjamin's sense of technology's threat to the arts and of its possibilities for the arts may resonate even more now that the age of technological reproducibility has evolved from the mechanical reproduction that Benjamin describes to the current age of electronic reproduction.*

The context clarifies most of Benjamin's many allusions. The French expression l'art pour l'art *refers to what is usually rendered in English as "art for art's sake." Benjamin also refers to Freud's* The Psychopathology of Everyday Life *(1901), which includes the famous argument that puns—now often called Freudian slips—are not mere accidents but instead reveal something repressed in the psyche. The closing Latin expression* Fiat ars— pereat mundus *can be translated as "Let art flourish—though the world perish."*

(This is the third of several versions of Benjamin's essay, which an earlier translation made famous under the less accurately translated title "The Work of Art in the Age of Mechanical Reproduction." In this reprinting, Benjamin's notes are moderately abridged. The translator's and editor's notes are not included.)

Our fine arts were developed, their types and uses were established, in times very different from the present, by men whose power of action upon things was insignificant in comparison with ours. But the amazing growth of our techniques, the adaptability and precision they have attained, the ideas and habits they are creating, make it a certainty that profound changes are impending in the ancient craft of the Beautiful. In all the arts, there is a physical component which can no longer be considered or treated as it used to be, which cannot remain unaffected by our modern knowledge and power. For the last twenty years, neither matter nor space nor time has been what it was from time immemorial. We must expect great innovations to transform the entire technique of the arts, thereby affecting artistic invention itself and perhaps even bringing about an amazing change in our very notion of art.

—PAUL VALÉRY, *Pièces sur l'art* ("La Conquête de l'ubiquité")

INTRODUCTION

When Marx undertook his analysis of the capitalist mode of production, this mode was in its infancy. Marx adopted an approach which gave his investigations prognostic value. Going back to the basic conditions of capitalist production, he presented them in a way which showed what could be expected of capitalism in the future. What could be expected, it emerged, was not only an increasingly harsh exploitation of the proletariat but, ultimately, the creation of conditions which would make it possible for capitalism to abolish itself.

Since the transformation of the superstructure proceeds far more slowly than that of the base, it has taken more than half a century for the change in the conditions of production to be manifested in all areas of culture. How this process has affected culture can only now be assessed, and these assessments must meet certain prognostic requirements. They do not, however, call for theses on the art of the proletariat after its seizure of power, and still less for any on the art of the classless society. They call for theses defining the tendencies of the development of art under the present conditions of production. The dialectic of these conditions of production is evident in the superstructure, no less than in the economy. Theses defining the developmental tendencies of art can therefore contribute to the political struggle in ways that it would be a mistake to underestimate. They neutralise a number of traditional concepts— such as creativity and genius, eternal value and mystery—which, used in an uncontrolled way (and controlling them is difficult today), allow factual material to be manipulated in the interests of fascism. *In what follows, the concepts which are introduced into the theory of art differ from those now current in that they are completely useless for the purposes of fascism. On the other hand, they are useful for the formulation of revolutionary demands in the politics of art [Kunstpolitik].*

I

In principle, the work of art has always been reproducible. Objects made by humans could always be copied by humans. Replicas were made by pupils in practicing for their craft, by masters in disseminating their works, and, finally, by third parties in pursuit of profit. But the technological reproduction of artworks is something new. Having appeared intermittently in history, at widely spaced intervals, it is now being adopted with ever-increasing intensity. The Greeks had only two ways of technologically reproducing works of art: casting and stamping. Bronzes, terracottas, and coins were the only artworks they could produce in large numbers. All others were unique and could not be technologically reproduced. Graphic art was first made technologically reproducible by the woodcut, long before written language became reproducible by movable type. The enormous changes brought about in literature by movable type, the technological reproducibility of writing, are well known. But they are only a special case, though an important one, of the phenomenon considered here from the perspective of world history. In the course of the Middle Ages the woodcut was supplemented by engraving and etching, and at the beginning of the nineteenth century by lithography.

Lithography marked a fundamentally new stage in the technology of reproduction. This much more direct process—distinguished by the fact that the drawing is traced on a stone, rather than incised on a block of wood or etched on a copper plate—first made it possible for graphic art to market its products not only in large numbers, as previously, but in daily changing variations. Lithography enabled graphic art to provide an illustrated accompaniment to everyday life. It began to keep pace with movable-type printing. But only a few decades after the invention of lithography, graphic art was surpassed by photography. For the first time, photography freed the hand from the most important artistic tasks in the process of pictorial reproduction—tasks that now devolved solely upon the eye looking into a lens. And since the eye perceives more swiftly than the hand can draw, the process of pictorial reproduction was enormously accelerated, so that it could now keep pace with speech. A cinematographer shooting a scene in the studio captures the images at the speed of an actor's speech. Just as the illustrated newspaper virtually lay hidden within lithography, so the sound film was latent in photography. The technological reproduction of sound was tackled at the end of the last century. These convergent endeavors made it possible to conceive of the situation that Paul Valéry describes in this sentence: "Just as water, gas, and electricity are brought into our houses from far off to satisfy our needs with minimal effort, so we shall be supplied with visual or auditory images, which will appear and disappear at a simple movement of the hand, hardly more than a sign."[1] *Around 1900, technological reproduction not only had reached a standard that permitted it to reproduce all known works of art, profoundly modifying their effect, but it also had captured a place of its own among the artistic processes.* In gauging this standard, we would do well to study the impact which its two different manifestations—the reproduction of artworks and the art of film—are having on art in its traditional form.

II

In even the most perfect reproduction, *one* thing is lacking: the here and now of the work of art—its unique existence in a particular place. It is this unique existence—and nothing else—that bears the mark of the history to which the work has been subject. This history includes changes to the physical structure of the work over time, together with any changes in ownership.[2] Traces of the former can be detected only by chemical or physical analyses (which cannot be performed on a reproduction), while changes of ownership are part of a tradition which can be traced only from the standpoint of the original in its present location.

The here and now of the original underlies the concept of its authenticity. Chemical analyses of the patina of a bronze can help to establish its authenticity, just as the proof that a given manuscript of the Middle Ages came from an archive of the fifteenth century helps to establish its authenticity. *The whole sphere of authenticity eludes technological—and, of course, not only technological—reproducibility.*[3] But whereas the authentic work retains its full authority in the face of a reproduction made by hand, which it generally brands a forgery, this is not the case with technological reproduction. The reason is twofold. First, technological reproduction is more independent of the original than is manual reproduction. For example, in photography it can bring out aspects of the original that are accessible only to the lens (which is adjustable and can easily change viewpoint) but not to the human eye; or it can use certain processes, such as enlargement or slow motion, to record images which escape natural optics altogether. This is the first reason. Second, technological reproduction can place the copy of the original in situations which the original itself cannot attain. Above all, it enables the original to meet the recipient halfway, whether in the form of a photograph or in that of a gramophone record. The cathedral leaves its site to be received in the studio of an art lover; the choral work performed in an auditorium or in the open air is enjoyed in a private room.

The situations into which the product of technological reproduction can be brought may leave the artwork's other properties untouched, but they certainly devalue the here and now of the artwork. And although this can apply not only to art but (say) to a landscape moving past the spectator in a film, in the work of art this process touches on a highly sensitive core, more vulnerable than that of any natural object. That core is its authenticity. The authenticity of a thing is the quintessence of all that is transmissible in it from its origin on, ranging from its physical duration to the historical testimony relating to it. Since the historical testimony is founded on the physical duration, the former, too, is jeopardized by reproduction, in which the physical duration plays no part. And what is really jeopardized when the historical testimony is affected is the authority of the object.

One might encompass the eliminated element within the concept of the aura, and go on to say: what withers in the age of the technological reproducibility of the work of art is the latter's aura. The process is symptomatic; its significance extends far beyond the realm of art. *It might be stated as a general formula that the technology of reproduction detaches the reproduced object from the sphere of tradition. By replicating the work many times over, it substitutes a mass existence for a unique existence. And in permitting the reproduction to reach the recipient in his or her own situation, it actualizes that which is reproduced.* These two processes lead to a massive upheaval in the domain of objects handed down from the past—a shattering of tradition which is the reverse side of the present crisis and renewal of humanity. Both processes are intimately related to the mass movements of our day. Their most powerful agent is film. The social significance of film, even—and especially—in its most positive form, is inconceivable without its destructive, cathartic side: the liquidation of the value of tradition in the cultural heritage. This phenomenon is most apparent in the great historical films. It is assimilating ever more advanced positions in its spread. When Abel Gance fervently proclaimed in 1927, "Shakespeare, Rembrandt, Beethoven will make films....All legends, all mythologies, and all myths, all the founders of religions, indeed, all religions,...await their celluloid resurrection, and the heroes are pressing at the gates," he was inviting the reader, no doubt unawares, to witness a comprehensive liquidation.[4]

III

Just as the entire mode of existence of human collectives changes over long historical periods, so too does their mode of perception. The way in which human perception is organized—the medium in which it occurs—is conditioned not only by nature but by history. The era of the migration of peoples, an era which saw the rise of the late-Roman art industry and the Vienna Genesis, developed not only an art different from that of antiquity but also a different perception. The scholars of the Viennese school Riegl and Wickhoff, resisting the weight of the classical tradition beneath which this art had been buried, were the first to think of using such art to draw conclusions about the organization of perception at the time the art was produced. However far-reaching their insight, it was limited by the fact that these scholars were content to highlight the formal signature which characterized perception in late-Roman times. They did not attempt to show the social upheavals manifested in these changes of perception—and perhaps could not have hoped to do so at that time. Today, the conditions for an analogous insight are more favorable. And if changes in the medium of present-day perception can be understood as a decay of the aura, it is possible to demonstrate the social determinants of that decay.

The concept of the aura which was proposed above with reference to historical objects can be usefully illustrated with reference to an aura of natural objects. We define the aura of the latter as the unique apparition of a distance, however near it may be. To follow with the eye—while resting on a summer afternoon—a mountain range on the horizon or a branch that casts its shadow on the beholder is to breathe the aura of those mountains, of that branch. In the light of this description, we can readily grasp the social basis of the aura's present decay. It rests on two circumstances, both linked to the increasing significance of the masses in contemporary life. Namely: *the desire of the present-day masses to "get closer" to things spatially and humanly, and their equally passionate concern for overcoming each thing's uniqueness [Überwindung des Einmaligen jeder Gegebenheit] by assimilating it as a reproduction.*[5] Every day the urge grows stronger to get hold of an object at close range in an image [*Bild*], or better, in a facsimile [*Abbild*], a reproduction. And the reproduction [*Reproduktion*], as offered by illustrated magazines and newsreels, differs unmistakably from the image. Uniqueness and permanence are as closely entwined in the latter as are transitoriness and repeatability in the former. The stripping of the veil from the object, the destruction of the aura, is the signature of a perception whose "sense for sameness in the world" has so increased that, by means of reproduction, it extracts sameness even from what is unique. Thus is manifested in the field of perception what in the theoretical sphere is noticeable in the increasing significance of statistics. The alignment of reality with the masses and of the masses with reality is a process of immeasurable importance for both thinking and perception.

IV

The uniqueness of the work of art is identical to its embeddedness in the context of tradition. Of course, this tradition itself is thoroughly alive and extremely changeable. An ancient statue of Venus, for instance, existed in a traditional context for the Greeks (who made it an object of worship) that was different from the context in which it existed for medieval clerics (who viewed it as a sinister idol). But what was equally evident to both was its uniqueness—that is, its aura. Originally, the embeddedness of an artwork in the context of tradition found expression in a cult. As we know, the earliest artworks originated in the service of rituals—first magical, then religious. And it is highly significant that the artwork's auratic mode of existence is never entirely severed from its ritual function. In other words: *the unique value of the "authentic" work of art has its basis in ritual, the source of its original use value.* This ritualistic basis, however mediated it may be, is still recognizable as secularized ritual in even the most profane forms of the cult of beauty.[6] The secular worship of beauty, which developed during the Renaissance and prevailed for three centuries, clearly displayed that ritualistic basis in its subsequent decline and in the first severe crisis which befell it. For when, with the advent of the first truly revolutionary means of reproduction (namely, photography, which emerged at the same time as socialism), art felt the approach of that crisis which a century later has become unmistakable, it reacted with the doctrine of *l'art pour l'art*—that is, with a theology of art. This in turn gave rise to a negative theology, in the form of an idea of "pure" art, which rejects not only any social function but any definition in terms of a representational content. (In poetry, Mallarmé was the first to adopt this standpoint.)

No investigation of the work of art in the age of its technological reproducibility can overlook these connections. They lead to a crucial insight: for the first time in world history, technological reproducibility emancipates the work of art from its parasitic subservience to ritual. To an ever-increasing degree, the work reproduced becomes the reproduction of a work designed for reproducibility.[7] From a photographic plate, for example, one can make any number of prints; to ask for the "authentic" print makes no sense. *But as soon as the criterion of authenticity ceases to be applied to artistic production, the whole social function of art is revolutionized. Instead of being founded on ritual, it is based on a different practice: politics.*

V

The reception of works of art varies in character, but in general two polar types stand out: one accentuates the artwork's cult value; the other, its exhibition value. Artistic production begins with figures in the service of a cult. One may assume that it was more important for these figures to be present than to be seen. The elk depicted by Stone Age man on the walls of his cave is an instrument of magic. He exhibits it to his fellow men, to be sure, but in the main it is meant for the spirits. Cult value as such tends today, it would seem, to keep the artwork out of sight: certain statues of gods are accessible only to the priest in the cella; certain images of the Madonna remain covered nearly all year round; certain sculptures on medieval cathedrals are not visible to the viewer at ground level. *With the emancipation of specific artistic practices from the service of ritual,·the opportunities for exhibiting their products increase.* It is easier to exhibit a portrait bust that can be sent here and there than to exhibit the statue of a divinity that has a fixed place in the interior of a temple. A panel painting can be exhibited more easily than the mosaic or fresco which preceded it. And although a Mass may have been no less suited to public presentation than a symphony, the symphony came into being at a time when the possibility of such presentation promised to be greater.

The scope for exhibiting the work of art has increased so enormously with the various methods of technologically reproducing it that, as happened in prehistoric times, a quantitative shift between the two poles of the artwork has led to a qualitative transformation in its nature. Just as the work of art in prehistoric times, through the absolute emphasis placed on its cult value, became first and foremost an instrument of magic which only later came to be recognized as a work of art, so today, through the absolute emphasis placed on its exhibition value, the work of art becomes a construct [*Gebilde*] with quite new functions. Among these, the one we are conscious of—the artistic function—may subsequently be seen as incidental.[8] This much is certain: today, photography and film are the most serviceable vehicles of this new understanding.

VI

In photography, exhibition value begins to drive back cult value on all fronts. But cult value does not give way without resistance. It falls back to a last entrenchment: the human countenance. It is no accident that the portrait is central to early photography. In the cult of remembrance of dead or absent loved ones, the cult value of the image finds its last refuge. In the fleeting expression of a human face, the aura beckons from early photographs for the last time. This is what gives them their melancholy and incomparable beauty. But as the human being withdraws from the photographic image, exhibition value for the first time shows its superiority to cult value. To have given this development its local habitation constitutes the unique significance of Atget, who, around 1900, took photographs of deserted Paris streets. It has justly been said that he photographed them like scenes of crimes. A crime scene, too, is deserted; it is photographed for the purpose of establishing evidence. With Atget, photographic records begin to be evidence in the historical trial [*Prozess*]. This constitutes their hidden political significance. They demand a specific kind of reception. Free-floating contemplation is no longer appropriate to them. They unsettle the viewer; he feels challenged to find a particular way to approach them. At the same time, illustrated magazines begin to put up signposts for him—whether these are right or wrong is irrelevant. For the first time, captions become obligatory. And it is clear that they have a character altogether different from the titles of paintings. The directives given by captions to those looking at images in illustrated magazines soon become even more precise and commanding in films, where the way each single image is understood appears prescribed by the sequence of all the preceding images.

VII

The nineteenth-century dispute over the relative artistic merit of painting and photography seems misguided and confused today. But this does not diminish its importance, and may even underscore it. The dispute was in fact an expression of a world-historical upheaval whose true nature was concealed from both parties. Insofar as the age of technological reproducibility separated art from its basis in cult, all semblance of art's autonomy disappeared forever. But the resulting change in the function of art lay beyond the horizon of the nineteenth century. And even the twentieth, which saw the development of film, was slow to perceive it.

Though commentators had earlier expended much fruitless ingenuity on the question of whether photography was an art—without asking the more fundamental question of whether the invention of photography had not transformed the entire character of art—film theorists quickly adopted the same ill-considered standpoint. But the difficulties which photography caused for traditional aesthetics were child's play compared to those presented by film. Hence the obtuse and hyperbolic character of early film theory. Abel Gance, for instance, compares film to hieroglyphs: "By a remarkable regression, we are transported back to the expressive level of the Egyptians.... Pictorial language has not matured, because our eyes are not yet adapted to it. There is not yet enough respect, not enough *cult,* for what it expresses."[9] Or, in the words of Séverin-Mars: "What other art has been granted a dream...at once more poetic and more real? Seen in this light, film might represent an incomparable means of expression, and only the noblest minds should move within its atmosphere, in the most perfect and mysterious moments of their lives."[10] Alexandre Arnoux, for his part, concludes a fantasy about the silent film with the question: "Do not all the bold descriptions we have given amount to a definition of prayer?"[11] It is instructive to see how the desire to annex film to "art" impels these theoreticians to attribute elements of cult to film—with a striking lack of discretion. Yet when these speculations were published, works like *A Woman of Paris* and *The Gold Rush* had already appeared. This did not deter Abel Gance from making the comparison with hieroglyphs, while Séverin-Mars speaks of film as one might speak of paintings by Fra Angelico. It is revealing that even today especially reactionary authors look in the same direction for the significance of film—finding, if not actually a sacred significance, then at least a supernatural one. In connection with Max Reinhardt's film version of *A Midsummer Night's Dream*, Werfel comments that it was undoubtedly the sterile copying of the external world—with its streets, interiors, railroad stations, restaurants, automobiles, and beaches—that had prevented film up to now from ascending to the realm of art. "Film has not yet realized its true purpose, its real possibilities.... These consist in its unique ability to use natural means to give incomparably convincing expression to the fairy-like, the marvelous, the supernatural."[12]

VIII

The artistic performance of a stage actor is directly presented to the public by the actor in person; that of a screen actor, however, is presented through a camera, with two consequences. The recording apparatus that brings the film actor's performance to the public need not respect the performance as an integral whole. Guided by the cameraman, the camera continually changes its position with respect to the performance. The sequence of positional views which the editor composes from the material supplied him constitutes the completed film. It comprises a certain number of movements, of various kinds and duration, which must be apprehended as such through the camera, not to mention special camera angles, close-ups, and so on. Hence, the performance of the actor is subjected to a series of optical tests. This is the first consequence of the fact that the actor's performance is presented by means of a camera. The second consequence is that the film actor lacks the opportunity of the stage actor to adjust to the audience during his performance, since he does not present his performance to the audience in person. This permits the audience to take the position of a critic, without experiencing any personal contact with the actor. *The audience's empathy with the actor is really an empathy with the camera. Consequently, the audience takes the position of the camera; its approach is that of testing.*[13] This is not an approach compatible with cult value.

IX

In the case of film, the fact that the actor represents someone else before the audience matters much less than the fact that he represents himself before the apparatus. One of the first to sense this transformation of the actor by the test performance was Pirandello. That his remarks on the subject in his novel *Si gira* [Shoot!] are confined to the negative aspects of this change, and to silent film only, does little to diminish their relevance. For in this respect, the sound film changed nothing essential. What matters is that the actor is performing for a piece of equipment—or, in the case of sound film, for two pieces of equipment. "The film actor," Pirandello writes, "feels as if exiled. Exiled not only from the stage but from his own person. With a vague unease, he senses an inexplicable void, stemming from the fact that his body has lost its substance, that he has been volatilized, stripped of his reality, his life, his voice, the noises he makes when moving about, and has been turned into a mute image that flickers for a moment on the screen, then vanishes into silence.... The little apparatus will play with his shadow before the audience, and he himself must be content to play before the apparatus."[14] The situation can also be characterized as follows: for the first time—and this is the effect of film—the human being is placed in a position, where he must operate with his whole living person, while forgoing its aura. For the aura is bound to his presence in the here and now. There is no facsimile of the aura. The aura surrounding Macbeth on the stage cannot be divorced from the aura which, for the living spectators, surrounds the actor who plays him. What distinguishes the shot in the film studio, however, is that the camera is substituted for the audience. As a result, the aura surrounding the actor is dispelled—and, with it, the aura of the figure he portrays.

It is not surprising that it should be a dramatist such as Pirandello who, in reflecting on the special character of film acting, inadvertently touches on the crisis now affecting the theater. Indeed, nothing contrasts more starkly with a work of art completely subject to (or, like film, founded in) technological reproduction than a stage play. Any thorough consideration will confirm this. Expert observers have long recognized that, in film, "the best effects are almost always achieved by 'acting' as little a possible.... The development," according to Rudolf Arnheim, writing in 1932, has been toward "using the actor as one of the 'props,' chosen for his typicalness and... introduced in the proper context."[15] Closely bound up with this development is something else. *The stage actor identifies himself with a role. The film actor very often is denied this opportunity.* His performance is by no means a unified whole, but is assembled from many individual performances. Apart from incidental concerns about studio rental, availability of other actors, scenery, and so on, there are elementary necessities of the machinery that split the actor's performance into a series of episodes capable of being assembled. In particular, lighting and its installation require the representation of an action—which on the screen appears as a swift, unified sequence—to be filmed in a series of separate takes, which may be spread over hours in the studio. Not to mention the more obvious effects of montage. A leap from a window, for example, can be shot in the studio as a leap from a scaffold, while the ensuing fall may be filmed weeks later at an outdoor location. And far more paradoxical cases can easily be imagined. Let us assume that an actor is supposed to be startled by a knock at the door. If his reaction is not satisfactory, the director can resort to an expedient: he could have a shot fired without warning behind the actor's back on some other occasion when he happens to be in the studio. The actor's frightened reaction at that moment could be recorded and then edited into the film. Nothing shows more graphically that art has escaped the realm of "beautiful semblance," which for so long was regarded as the only sphere in which it could thrive.

X

The film actor's feeling of estrangement in the face of the apparatus, as Pirandello describes this experience, is basically of the same kind as the estrangement felt before one's appearance [*Erscheinung*] in a mirror. But now the mirror image [*Bild*] has become detachable from the person mirrored, and is transportable. And where is it transported? To a site in front of the public.[16] The screen actor never for a moment ceases to be aware of this. *While he stands before the apparatus, the screen actor knows that in the end he is confronting the public, the consumers who constitute the market.* This market, where he offers not only his labor but his entire self, his heart and soul, is beyond his reach. During the shooting, he has as little contact with it as would any article being made in a factory. This may contribute to that oppression, that new anxiety which, according to Pirandello, grips the actor before the camera. Film responds to the shriveling of the aura by artificially building up the "personality" outside the studio. The cult of the movie star, fostered by the money of the film industry, preserves that magic of the personality which has long been no more than the putrid magic of its own commodity character. So long as moviemakers' capital sets the fashion, as a rule the only revolutionary merit that can be ascribed to today's cinema is the promotion of a revolutionary criticism of traditional concepts of art. We do not deny that in some cases today's films can also foster revolutionary criticism of social conditions, even of property relations. But the present study is no more specifically concerned with this than is western European film production.

It is inherent in the technology of film, as of sports, that everyone who witnesses these performances does so as a quasi-expert. This is obvious to anyone who has listened to a group of newspaper boys leaning on their bicycles and discussing the outcome of a bicycle race. It is no accident that newspaper publishers arrange races for their delivery boys. These arouse great interest among the participants, for the winner has a chance to rise from delivery boy to professional racer. Similarly, the newsreel offers everyone the chance to rise from passer-by to movie extra. In this way, a person might even see himself becoming part of work of art, think of Vertov's *Three Songs of Lenin* or Ivens' *Borinage. Any person today can lay claim to being filmed.* This claim can best be clarified by considering the historical situation of literature today.

For centuries it was in the nature of literature that a small number of writers confronted many thousands of readers. This began to change toward the end of the past century. With the growth and extension of the press, which constantly made new political, religious, scientific, professional, and local journals available to readers, an increasing number of readers—in isolated cases, at first—turned into writers. It began with the space set aside for "letters to the editor" in the daily press, and has now reached a point where there is hardly a European engaged in the work process who could not, in principle, find an opportunity to publish somewhere or other an account of a work experience, a complaint, a report, or something of the kind. Thus, the distinction between author and public is about to lose its axiomatic character. The difference becomes functional; it may vary from case to case. At any moment, the reader is ready to become a writer. As an expert—which he has had to become in any case in a highly specialized work process, even if only in some minor capacity—the reader gains access to authorship. In the Soviet Union, work itself is given a voice. And the ability to describe a job in words now forms part of the expertise needed to carry it out. Literary competence is no longer founded on specialized higher education but on polytechnic training, and thus is common property.[17]

All this can readily be applied to film, where shifts that in literature took place over centuries have occurred in a decade. In cinematic practice—above all, in Russia—this shift has already been partly realized. Some of the actors taking part in Russian films are not actors in our sense but people who portray *themselves*—and primarily in their own work process. In western Europe today, the capitalist exploitation of film obstructs the human being's legitimate claim to being reproduced. Under these circumstances, the film industry has an overriding interest in stimulating the involvement of the masses through illusionary displays and ambiguous speculations.

XI

The shooting of a film, especially a sound film, offers a hitherto unimaginable spectacle. It presents a process in which it is impossible to assign to the spectator a single viewpoint which would exclude from his or her field of vision the equipment not directly involved in the action being filmed—the camera, the lighting units, the technical crew, and so forth (unless the alignment of the spectator's pupil coincided with that of the camera). This circumstance, more than any other, makes any resemblance between a scene in a film studio and one onstage superficial and irrelevant. In principle, the theater includes a position from which the action on the stage cannot easily be detected as an illusion. There is no such position where a film is being shot. The illusory nature of film is of the second degree; it is the result of editing. That is to say: *In the film studio the apparatus has penetrated so deeply into reality that a pure view of that reality, free of the foreign body of equipment, is the result of a special procedure, namely, the shooting by the specially adjusted photographic device and the assembly of that shot with others of the same kind.* The equipment-free aspect of reality has here become the height of artifice, and the vision of immediate reality the Blue Flower in the land of technology.

This state of affairs, which contrasts so sharply with that which obtains in the theater, can be compared even more instructively to the situation in painting. Here we have to pose the question: How does the camera operator compare with the painter? In answer to this, it will be helpful to consider the concept of the operator as it is familiar to us from surgery. The surgeon represents the polar opposite of the magician. The attitude of the magician, who heals a sick person by a laying-on of hands differs from that of the surgeon, who makes an intervention in the patient. The magician maintains the natural distance between himself and the person treated; more precisely, he reduces it slightly by laying on his hands, but increases it greatly by his authority. The surgeon does exactly the reverse; he greatly diminishes the distance from the patient by penetrating the patient's body, and increases it only slightly by the caution with which his hand moves among the organs. In short: unlike the magician (traces of whom are still found in the medical practitioner), the surgeon abstains at the decisive moment from confronting his patient person to person; instead, he penetrates the patient by operating.— Magician is to surgeon as painter is to cinematographer. The painter maintains in his work a natural distance from reality, whereas the cinematographer penetrates deeply into its tissue. The images obtained by each differ enormously. The painter's is a total image, whereas that of the cinematographer is piecemeal, its manifold parts being assembled according to a new law. *Hence, the presentation of reality in film is incomparably the more significant for people of today, since it provides the equipment-free aspect of reality they are entitled to demand from a work of art and does so precisely on the basis of the most intensive interpenetration of reality with equipment.*

XII

The technological reproducibility of the artwork changes the relation of the masses to art. The extremely backward attitude toward a Picasso painting changes into a highly progressive reaction to a Chaplin film. The progressive reaction is characterized by an immediate, intimate fusion of pleasure—pleasure in seeing and experiencing—with an attitude of expert appraisal. Such a fusion is an important social index. As is clearly seen in the case of painting, the more reduced the social impact of an art form, the more widely criticism and enjoyment of it diverge in the public. The conventional is uncritically enjoyed, while the truly new is criticized with aversion. With regard to the cinema, the critical and uncritical attitudes of the public coincide. The decisive reason for this is that nowhere more than in the cinema are the reactions of individuals, which together make up the massive reaction of the audience, determined by the imminent concentration of reactions into a mass. No sooner are these reactions manifest than they regulate one another. Again, the comparison with painting is fruitful. A painting has always exerted a claim to be viewed primarily by a single person or by a few. The simultaneous viewing of paintings by a large audience, as happens in the nineteenth century, is an early symptom of the crisis in painting, a crisis triggered not only by photography but, in a relatively independent way, by the artwork's claim to the attention of the masses.

Painting, by its nature, cannot provide an object of simultaneous collective reception, as architecture has always been able to do, as the epic poem could do at one time, and as film is able to do today. And although direct conclusions about the social role of painting cannot be drawn from this fact alone, it does have a strongly adverse effect whenever painting is led by special circumstances, as if against its nature, to confront the masses directly. In the churches and monasteries of the Middle Ages, and at the princely courts up to about the end of the eighteenth century, the collective reception of paintings took place not simultaneously but in a manifold graduated and hierarchically mediated way. If that has changed, the change testifies to the special conflict in which painting has become enmeshed by the technological reproducibility of the image. And while efforts have been made to present paintings to the masses in galleries and salons, this mode of reception gives the masses no means of organizing and regulating their response.[18] Thus, the same public which reacts progressively to a slapstick comedy inevitably displays a backward attitude toward Surrealism.

XIII

Film can be characterized not only in terms of man's presentation of himself to the camera but also in terms of his representation of his environment by means of this apparatus. A glance at occupational psychology illustrates the testing capacity of the equipment. Psychoanalysis illustrates it in a different perspective. In fact, film has enriched our field of perception with methods that can be illustrated by those of Freudian theory. Fifty years ago, a slip of the tongue passed more or less unnoticed. Only exceptionally may such a slip have opened a perspective on depths in a conversation which had seemed to be proceeding on a superficial plane. Since the publication of *Zur Psychopathologie des Alltagslebens* (On the Psychopathology of Everyday Life), things have changed. This book isolated and made analyzable things which had previously floated unnoticed on the broad stream of perception. A similar deepening of apperception throughout the entire spectrum of optical—and now also auditory—impressions has been accomplished by film. One is merely stating the obverse of this fact when one says that actions shown in a movie can be analyzed much more precisely and from more points of view than those presented in a painting or on the stage. In contrast to what obtains in painting, filmed action lends itself more readily to analysis because it delineates situations far more precisely. In contrast to what obtains on the stage, filmed action lends itself more readily to analysis because it can be isolated more easily. This circumstance derives its prime importance from the fact that it tends to foster the interpenetration of art and science. Actually, if we think of a filmed action as neatly delineated within a particular situation—like a flexed muscle in a body—it is difficult to say which is more fascinating, its artistic value or its value for science. *Demonstrating that the artistic uses of photography are identical to its scientific uses—these two dimensions having usually been separated until now—will be one of the revolutionary functions of film.*

On the one hand, film furthers insight into the necessities governing our lives by its use of close-ups, by its accentuation of hidden details in familiar objects, and by its exploration of commonplace milieux through the ingenious guidance of the camera; on the other hand, it manages to assure us of a vast and unsuspected field of action [*Spielraum*]. Our bars and city streets, our offices and furnished rooms, our railroad stations and our factories seemed to close relentlessly around us. Then came film and exploded this prison-world with the dynamite of the split second, so that now we can set off calmly on journeys of adventure among its far-flung debris. With the close-up, space expands; with slow motion, movement is extended. And just as enlargement not merely clarifies what we see indistinctly "in any case," but brings to light entirely new structures of matter, slow motion not only reveals familiar aspects of movements, but discloses quite unknown aspects within them—aspects "which do not appear as the retarding of natural movements but have a curious gliding, floating character of their own."[19] Clearly, it is another nature which speaks to the camera as compared to the eye. "Other" above all in the sense that a space informed by human consciousness gives way to a space informed by the unconscious. Whereas it is a commonplace that, for example, we have some idea what is involved in the act of walking (if only in general terms), we have no idea at all what happens during the split second when a person actually takes a step. We are familiar with the movement of picking up a cigarette lighter or a spoon, but know almost nothing of what really goes on between hand and metal, and still less how this varies with different moods. This is where the camera comes into play, with all its resources for swooping and rising, disrupting and isolating, stretching or compressing a sequence, enlarging or reducing an object. It is through the camera that we first discover the optical unconscious, just as we discover the instinctual unconscious through psychoanalysis.

XIV

It has always been one of the primary tasks of art to create a demand whose hour of full satisfaction has not yet come. The history of every art form has critical periods in which the particular form strains after effects which can be easily achieved only with a changed technical standard—that is to say, in a new art form. The excesses and crudities of art which thus result, particularly in periods of so-called decadence, actually emerge from the core of its richest historical energies. In recent years, Dadaism has abounded in such barbarisms. Only now is its impulse recognizable: *Dadaism attempted to produce with the means of painting (or literature) the effects which the public today seeks in film.*

Every fundamentally new, pioneering creation of demand will overshoot its target. Dadaism did so to the extent that it sacrificed the market values so characteristic of film in favor of more significant aspirations—of which, to be sure, it was unaware in the form described here. The Dadaists attached much less importance to the commercial usefulness of their artworks than to the uselessness of those works as objects of contemplative immersion. They sought to achieve this uselessness not least by thorough degradation of their material. Their poems are "word-salad" containing obscene expressions and every imaginable kind of linguistic refuse. It is not otherwise with their paintings, on which they mounted buttons or train tickets. What they achieved by such means was a ruthless annihilation of the aura in every object they produced, which they branded as a reproduction through the very means of production. Before a painting by Arp or a poem by August Stramm, it is impossible to take time for concentration and evaluation, as one can before a painting by Derain or a poem by Rilke. Contemplative immersion—which, as the bourgeoisie degenerated, became a breeding ground for asocial behavior—is here opposed by distraction [*Ablenkung*] as a variant of social behavior.[20] Dadaist manifestations actually guaranteed a quite vehement distraction by making artworks the center of scandal. One requirement was paramount: to outrage the public.

From an alluring visual composition or an enchanting fabric of sound, the Dadaists turned the artwork into a missile. It jolted the viewer, taking on a tactile [*taktisch*] quality. It thereby fostered the demand for film, since the distracting element in film is also primarily tactile, being based on successive changes of scene and focus which have a percussive effect on the spectator. Let us compare the screen [*Leinwand*] on which a film unfolds with the canvas [*Leinwand*] of a painting. The painting invites the viewer to contemplation; before it, he can give himself up to his train of associations. Before a film image, he cannot do so. No sooner has he seen it than it has already changed. It cannot be fixed on. Duhamel, who detests the cinema and knows nothing of its significance, though he does know something about its structure, describes the situation as follows: "I can no longer think what I want to think. My thoughts have been replaced by moving images."[21] Indeed, the train of associations in the person contemplating these images is immediately interrupted by new images. This constitutes the shock effect of film, which, like all shock effects, seeks to induce heightened attention.[22] *By means of its technological structure, film has freed the physical shock effect—which Dadaism had kept wrapped, as it were, inside the moral shock effect—from this wrapping.*[23]

XV

The masses are a matrix from which all customary behavior toward works of art is today emerging newborn. Quantity has been transformed into quality: *the greatly increased mass of participants has produced a different kind of participation.* The fact that the new mode of participation first appeared in a disreputable form should not mislead the observer. Yet some people have launched spirited attacks against precisely this superficial aspect of the matter. Among these critics, Duhamel has expressed himself most radically. What he objects to most is the kind of participation which the movie elicits from the masses. Duhamel calls the movie "a pastime for helots, a diversion for uneducated, wretched, worn-out creatures who are consumed by their worries..., a spectacle which requires no concentration and presupposes no intelligence..., which kindles no light in the heart and awakens no hope other than the ridiculous one of someday becoming a 'star' in Los Angeles."[24] Clearly, this is in essence the ancient lament that the masses seek distraction, whereas art demands concentration from the spectator. That is a commonplace. The question remains whether it provides a basis for the analysis of film. This calls for closer examination. Distraction and concentration [*Zerstreuung und Sammlung*] form an antithesis, which may be formulated as follows. A person who concentrates before a work of art is absorbed by it; he enters into the work, just as, according to legend, a Chinese painter entered his completed painting while beholding it. By contrast, the distracted masses absorb the work of art into themselves. This is most obvious with regard to buildings. Architecture has always offered the prototype of an artwork that is received in a state of diffraction and through the collective. The laws of architecture's reception are highly instructive.

Buildings have accompanied human existence since primeval times. Many art forms have come into being and passed away. Tragedy begins with the Greeks, is extinguished along with them, and is revived centuries later, though only according to its "rules." The epic, which originates in the early days of peoples, dies out in Europe at the end of the Renaissance. Panel painting is a creation of the Middle Ages, and nothing guarantees its uninterrupted existence. But the human need for shelter is permanent. Architecture has never had fallow periods. Its history is longer than that of any other art, and its effect ought to be recognized in any attempt to account for the relationship of the masses to the work of art. Buildings are received in a twofold manner: by use and by perception. Or, better: tactilely and optically. Such reception cannot be understood in terms of the concentrated attention of a traveler before a famous building. On the tactile side, there is no counterpart to what contemplation is on the optical side. Tactile reception comes about not so much by way of attention as by way of habit. The latter largely determines even the optical reception of architecture, which spontaneously takes the form of casual noticing, rather than attentive observation. Under certain circumstances, this form of reception shaped by architecture acquires canonical value. *For the tasks which face the human apparatus of perception at historical turning points cannot be performed solely by optical means—that is, by way of contemplation. They are mastered gradually—taking their cue from tactile reception—through habit.*

Even the distracted person can form habits. What is more, the ability to master certain tasks in a state of distraction proves that their performance has become habitual. The sort of distraction that is provided by art represents a covert measure of the extent to which it has become possible to perform new tasks of apperception. Since, moreover, individuals are tempted to evade such tasks, art will tackle the most difficult and most important tasks wherever it is able to mobilize the masses. It does so currently in film. *Reception in distraction—the sort of reception which is increasingly noticeable in all areas of art and is a symptom of profound changes in apperception—finds in film its true training ground.* Film, by virtue of its shock effects, is predisposed to this form of reception. It makes cult value recede into the background, not only because it encourages an evaluating attitude in the audience but also because, at the movies, the evaluating attitude requires no attention. The audience is an examiner, but a distracted one.

EPILOGUE

The increasing proletarianization of modern man and the increasing formation of masses are two sides of the same process. Fascism attempts to organize the newly proletarianized masses while leaving intact the property relations which they strive to abolish. It sees its salvation in granting expression to the masses—but on no account granting them rights.[25] The masses have a right to changed property relations; fascism seeks to give them *expression* in keeping these relations unchanged. *The logical outcome of fascism is an aestheticizing of political life.* The violation of the masses, whom fascism, with its *Führer* cult, forces to their knees, has its counterpart in the violation of an apparatus which is pressed into serving the production of ritual values.

All efforts to aestheticize politics culminate in one point. That one point is war. War, and only war, makes it possible to set a goal for mass movements on the grandest scale while preserving traditional property relations. That is how the situation presents itself in political terms. In technological terms it can be formulated as follows: only war makes it possible to mobilize all of today's technological resources while maintaining property relations. It goes without saying that the fascist glorification of war does not make use of *these* arguments. Nevertheless, a glance at such glorification is instructive. In Marinetti's manifesto for the colonial war in Ethiopia, we read:

> For twenty-seven years we Futurists have rebelled against the idea that war is anti-aesthetic....We therefore state:...War is beautiful because—thanks to its gas masks, its terrifying megaphones, its flame throwers, and light tanks—it establishes man's dominion over the subjugated machine. War is beautiful because it inaugurates the dreamed-of metallization of the human body. War is beautiful because it enriches a flowering meadow with the fiery orchids of machine-guns. War is beautiful because it combines gunfire, barrages, cease-fires, scents, and the fragrance of putrefaction into a symphony. War is beautiful because it creates new architectures, like those of armored tanks, geometric squadrons of aircraft, spirals of smoke from burning villages, and much more....Poets and artists of Futurism,...remember these principles of an aesthetic of war, that they may illuminate...your struggles for a new poetry and a new sculpture![26]

This manifesto has the merit of clarity. The question it poses deserves to be taken up by the dialectician. To him, the aesthetic of modern warfare appears as follows: if the natural use of productive forces is impeded by the property system, then the increase in technological means, in speed, in sources of energy will press toward an unnatural use. This is found in war, and the destruction caused by war furnishes proof that society was not mature enough to make technology its organ, that technology was not sufficiently developed to master the elemental forces of society. The most horrifying features of imperialist war are determined by the discrepancy between the enormous means of production and their inadequate use in the process of production (in other words, by unemployment and the lack of markets). *Imperialist war is an uprising on the part of technology, which demands repayment in "human material" for the natural material society has denied it.* Instead of draining rivers, society directs a human stream into a bed of trenches; instead of dropping seeds from airplanes, it drops incendiary bombs over cities; and in gas warfare it has found a new means of abolishing the aura.

"Fiat ars—pereat mundus," says fascism, expecting from war, as Marinetti admits, the artistic gratification of a sense perception altered by technology. This is evidently the consummation of *l'art pour l'art*. Humankind, which once, in Homer, was an object of contemplation for the Olympian gods, has now become one for itself. Its self-alienation has reached the point where it can experience its own annihilation as a supreme aesthetic pleasure. *Such is the aestheticizing of politics, as practiced by fascism. Communism replies by politicizing art.*

NOTES

1. Paul Valéry, *Pièces sur l'art* (Paris), p. 105 ("La Conquête de l'ubiquité").
2. Of course, the history of a work of art encompasses more than this. The history of the *Mona Lisa*, for instance, encompasses the kinds and number of copies made of it in the seventeenth, eighteenth, and nineteenth centuries.
3. Precisely because authenticity is not reproducible, the intensive penetration of certain (technological) processes of reproduction was instrumental in differentiating and gradating authenticity. To develop such differentiations was an important function of the trade in works of art. Such trade had a manifest interest in distinguishing among various prints of a woodblock engraving (those before and those after inscription), of a copperplate engraving, and so on. The invention of the woodcut may be said to have struck at the root of the quality of authenticity even before its late flowering. To be sure, a medieval picture of the Madonna at the time it was created could not yet be said to be "authentic." It became "authentic" only during the succeeding centuries, and perhaps most strikingly so during the nineteenth.
4. Abel Gance, "Le Temps de l'image est venue!" (It Is Time for the Image!), in Léon Pierre-Quint, Germaine Dulac, Lionel Landry, and Abel Gance, *L'Art cinématographique*, vol. 2 (Paris, 1927), pp. 94–96.
5. Getting closer (in terms of human interest) to the masses may involve having one's social function removed from the field of vision. Nothing guarantees that a portraitist of today, when painting a famous surgeon at the breakfast table with his family, depicts his social function more precisely than a painter of the seventeenth century who showed the viewer doctors representing their profession, as Rembrandt did in his *Anatomy Lesson*.
6. To the extent that the cult value of a painting is secularized, the impressions of its fundamental uniqueness become less distinct. In the viewer's imagination, the uniqueness of the phenomena holding sway in the cult image is more and more displaced by the empirical uniqueness of the artist or of his creative achievement. To be sure, never completely so—the concept of authenticity always transcends that of proper attribution. (This is particularly apparent in the collector, who always displays some traits of the fetishist and who, through his possession of the artwork, shares in its cultic power.) Nevertheless, the concept of authenticity still functions as a determining factor in the evaluation of art; as art becomes secularized, authenticity displaces the cult value of the work.
7. In film, the technological reproducibility of the product is not an externally imposed condition of its mass dissemination, as it is, say, in literature or painting. *The technological reproducibility of films is based directly on the technology of their production. This not only makes possible the mass dissemination of films in the most direct way, but actually enforces it.* It does so because the process of producing a film is so costly that an individual who could afford to buy a painting, for example, could not afford to buy a [master print of a] film. It was calculated in 1927 that, in order to make a profit, a major film needed to reach an audience of nine million. Of course, the

advent of sound film [in that year] initially caused a movement in the opposite direction: its audience was restricted by language boundaries. And that coincided with the emphasis placed on national interests by fascism. But it is less important to note this setback (which in any case was mitigated by dubbing) than to observe its connection with fascism. The simultaneity of the two phenomena results from the economic crisis. The same disorders which led, in the world at large, to an attempt to maintain existing property relations by brute force induced film capital, under the threat of crisis, to speed up the development of sound film. Its introduction brought temporary relief, not only because sound film attracted the masses back into the cinema but because it consolidated new capital from the electricity industry with that of film. Thus, considered from the outside, sound film promoted national interests; but seen from the inside, it helped internationalize film production even more than before.

8. Bertolt Brecht, on a different level, engaged in analogous reflections: "If the concept of 'work of art' can no longer be applied to the thing that emerges once the work is transformed into a commodity, we have to eliminate this concept with due caution but without fear, lest we liquidate the function of the very thing as well. For it has to go through this phase unswervingly; there is no viable detour from the straight path. Rather, what happens here with the work of art will change it fundamentally, will erase its past to such an extent that—should the old concept be taken up again (and it will be; why not?)—it will no longer evoke any memory of the thing it once designated." Brecht, *Versuche* (Experiments), 8–10, no. 3 (Berlin, 1931), pp. 301–302 ("Der Dreigroschen-prozess" [The Threepenny Trial]).

9. Abel Gance, "Le Temps de l'image est venu," in *L' Art cinématograqhic*, vol. 2, p. 101.

10. Séverin-Mars, cited ibid., p. 100.

11. Alexandre Arnoux, *Cinéma* (Paris, 1929), p, 28.

12. Franz Werfel, "Ein Sommernachstraum: Ein Film von Shakespeare and Reinhardt," *Neues Wiener Journal*, cited in *Lu*, November 15, 1935.

13. "Film . . . provides—or could provide—useful insight into the details of human actions. . . . Character is never used as a source of motivation; the inner life of the persons represented never supplies the principal cause of the plot and seldom is its main result" (Bertolt Brecht, "Der Dreigroschenprozess," *Versuche*, p. 268). The expansion of the field of the testable which the filming apparatus brings about for the actor corresponds to the extraordinary expansion of the field of the testable brought about for the individual through economic conditions. Thus, vocational aptitude tests become constantly more important. What matters in these tests are segmental performances of the individual. The final cut of a film and the vocational aptitude test are both taken before a panel of experts. The director in the studio occupies a position identical to that of the examiner during aptitude tests.

14. Luigi Pirandello, *Si Gira*, cited in Léon Pierre-Quint, "Signification du cinéma," *L'Art cinématographique*, vol. 2, pp. 14–15.

15. Rudolf Arnheim, *Film als Kunst* (Berlin, 1932), pp. 176–177. In this context, certain apparently incidental details of film directing which diverge from practices on the stage take on added interest. For example, the attempt to let the actor perform without makeup, as in Dreyer's *Jeanne d'Arc*. Dreyer spent months seeking the forty actors who constitute the Inquisitors' tribunal. Searching for these actors was like hunting for rare props. Dreyer made every effort to avoid resemblances of age, build, and physiognomy in the actors. (See Maurice Schultz, "Le Maquillage" [Makeup], in *L'Art cinématographique*, vol. 6 [Paris, 1929], pp. 65–66.) If the actor thus becomes a prop, the prop, in its turn, not infrequently functions as actor. At any rate, it is not unusual for films to allocate a role to a prop. Rather than selecting examples at random from the infinite number

available, let us take just one especially revealing case. A clock that is running will always be a disturbance on the stage, where it cannot be permitted its role of measuring time. Even in a naturalistic play, real-life time would conflict with theatrical time. In view of this, it is very revealing that film—where appropriate—can readily make use of time as measured by a clock. This feature, more than many others, makes it clear that—circumstances permitting—each and every prop in a film may perform decisive functions. From here it is but a step to Pudovkin's principle, which states that "to connect the performance of an actor with an object, and to build that performance around the object, ... is always one of the most powerful methods of cinematic construction" (V. I. Pudovkin, *Film Regie und Filmmanuskript* [Film Direction and the Film Script] (Berlin, 1928), p. 126). Film is thus the first artistic medium which is able to show how matter plays havoc with human beings [*wie die Materie dem Menschen mitspielt*]. It follows that films can be an excellent means of materialist exposition.

16. The change noted here in the mode of exhibition—a change brought about by reproduction technology—is also noticeable in politics. The present crisis of the bourgeois democracies involves a crisis in the conditions governing the public presentation of leaders. Democracies exhibit the leader directly, in person, before elected representatives. The parliament is his public. But innovations in recording equipment now enable the speaker to be heard by an unlimited number of people while he is speaking, and to be seen by an unlimited number shortly afterward. This means that priority is given to presenting the politician before the recording equipment. Parliaments are becoming depopulated at the same time as theaters. Radio and film are changing not only the function of the professional actor but, equally, the function of those who, like the leaders, present themselves before these media. The direction of this change is the same for the film actor and for the leader, regardless of their different tasks. It tends toward the exhibition of controllable, transferable skills under certain social conditions. This results in a new form of selection—selection before an apparatus—from which the star and the dictator emerge as victors.

17. The privileged character of the respective techniques is lost. Aldous Huxley writes: "Advances in technology have led ... to vulgarity.... Process reproduction and the rotary press have made possible the indefinite multiplication of writing and pictures. Universal education and relatively high wages have created an enormous public who know how to read and can afford to buy reading and pictorial matter. A great industry has been called into existence in order to supply these commodities. Now, artistic talent is a very rare phenomenon; whence it follows ... that, at every epoch and in all countries, most art has been bad. But the proportion of trash in the total artistic output is greater now than at any other period. That it must be so is a matter of simple arithmetic. The population of Western Europe has a little more than doubled during the last century. But the amount of reading—and seeing—matter has increased, I should imagine, at least twenty and possibly fifty or even a hundred times. If there were n men of talent in a population of x millions, there will presumably be $2n$ men of talent among $2x$ millions. The situation may be summed up thus. For every page of print and pictures published a century ago, twenty or perhaps even a hundred pages are published today. But for every man of talent then living, there are now only two men of talent. It may be of course that, thanks to universal education, many potential talents which in the past would have been stillborn are now enabled to realize themselves. Let us assume, then, that there are now three or even four men of talent to every one of earlier times. It still remains true to say that the consumption of reading—and seeing—matter has far outstripped the natural production of gifted writers and draftsmen. It is the same with hearing-matter. Prosperity, the gramophone and the radio have created an audience of hearers who consume an amount of hearing-matter that has increased out of all proportion to

the increase of population and the consequent natural increase of talented musicians. It follows from all this that in all the arts the output of trash is both absolutely and relatively greater than it was in the past; and that it must remain greater for just so long as the world continues to consume the present inordinate quantities of reading-matter, seeing-matter, and hearing-matter." (Aldous Huxley, *Beyond the Mexique Bay: A Traveller's Journal* [1934; rpt. London, 1949], pp. 274ff.) This mode of observation is obviously not progressive.

18. This mode of observation may seem crude [*plump*]; but as the great theoretician Leonardo has shown, crude modes of observation may at times prove useful. Leonardo compares painting and music as follows: "Painting is superior to music because, unlike unfortunate music, it does not have to die as soon as it is born....Music, which is consumed in the very act of its birth, is inferior to painting, which the use of varnish has rendered eternal." Leonardo da Vinci, *Frammenti letterari e filosofici* (Literary and Philosophical Fragments), cited in Fernand Baldensperger, "Le Raffermissement des techniques dans la littérature occidentale de 1840" [The Strengthening of Techniques in Western Literature around 1840], *Revue de Littérature Comparée*, 15–16 (Paris, 1935): 79, note 1.

19. Rudolf Arnheim, *Film als Kunst*, p. 138.

20. The theological archetype of this contemplation is the awareness of being alone with one's God. Such awareness, in the heyday of the bourgeoisie, fostered a readiness to shake off clerical tutelage. During the decline of the bourgeoisie, this same awareness had to take into account the hidden tendency to remove from public affairs those forces which the individual puts to work in his communion with God.

21. Georges Duhamel, *Scènes de la vie future*, 2nd ed. (Paris, 1930), p. 52.

22. Film is the art form corresponding to the increased threat to life that faces people today. Humanity's need to expose itself to shock effects represents an adaptation to the dangers threatening it. Film corresponds to profound changes in the apparatus of apperception—changes that are experienced on the scale of private existence by each passerby in big-city traffic, and on a historical scale by every present-day citizen.

23. Film proves useful in illuminating Cubism and Futurism, as well as Dadaism. Both appear as deficient attempts on the part of art to take into account the pervasive interpenetration of reality by the apparatus [*Durchdringung der Wirklichkeit mit der Apparatur*]. Unlike film, these schools did not try to use the apparatus as such for the artistic representation of reality, but aimed at a sort of alloy of represented reality and represented apparatus. In Cubism, a premonition of the structure of this apparatus, which is based on optics, plays a dominant part; in Futurism, it is the premonition of the effects of the apparatus—effects which are brought out by the rapid coursing of the band of film.

24. Duhamel, *Scènes de la vie future*, p. 58.

25. A technological factor is important here, especially with regard to the newsreel, whose significance for propaganda purposes can hardly be overstated. *Mass reproduction is especially favored by the reproduction of the masses.* In great ceremonial processions, giant rallies, and mass sporting events, and in war, all of which are now fed into the camera, the masses come face to face with themselves. This process, whose significance need not be emphasized, is closely bound up with the development of reproduction and recording technologies. In general, mass movements are more clearly apprehended by the camera than by the eye. A bird's-eye view best captures assemblies of hundreds of thousands. And even when this perspective is no less accessible to the human eye than to the camera, the image formed by the eye cannot be enlarged in the same way as a photograph. This is to say that mass movements, including war, are a form of human behavior especially suited to the camera.

26. Cited in *La Stampa Torino*.

THE CULTURE INDUSTRY: ENLIGHTENMENT AS MASS DECEPTION (1944, 1947)

MAX HORKHEIMER AND THEODOR W. ADORNO

Translated from the German by Edmund Jephcott

"Culture today is infecting everything with sameness," argue Horkheimer and Adorno. Thus when they protest what they call "identity," they do not mean identity in the usual contemporary sense, as when people ask who and what we are. They mean identity as in sameness, the identicalness of seemingly different things. By the culture industry, Horkheimer and Adorno mean the entertainment industry. Large as it was when they wrote their essay in the 1940s, it has since grown enormously in size and influence and in the proportion it takes up of the overall economy, especially in industrialized countries that increasingly center on the service economy. Leaders of the so-called Frankfurt School in Germany, which focused on what is called "critical theory" (a narrower use of the expression than the more typical sense of critical theory that this book uses), Horkheimer and Adorno wanted to understand why the masses did not revolt against the system that Marxists find oppressive. After fleeing Nazi Germany, they wrote "The Culture Industry" while living in the United States, and readers can see their horrified yet fascinated response to American popular culture, including music, movies, and radio. They saw the culture industry as luring consumers of entertainment into a complacency that keeps consumers from looking critically at the inequities of the larger capitalist economy. The vast and beguiling menu of consumer choices, to Horkheimer and Adorno, disguises an underlying sameness, and the disguise charms consumers into overlooking how little the menu actually allows in the way of critical thinking and genuine choice. To Horkheimer and Adorno, such freedom as the culture industry offers its consumers finally "proves to be freedom to be the same." They see the consumption of industrially produced leisure as draining away the energies that could go into critical thinking and as accustoming consumers to the mechanized routine that industry expects from its workers. The consumption of culture shapes desire, so that desire only desires to consume culture, not to criticize it in any larger and meaningful way. Thus entertainment draws consumers' horizon around entertainment itself, until such resistance as they can muster comes only in the form of more entertainment. For a moderately more hopeful view of the culture industry, readers may compare Walter Benjamin's essay in this volume.

Horkheimer and Adorno wrote with an eye on how Hitler (whom they refer to as "the Führer"), Mussolini, and other fascist leaders expanded their power by exploiting mass culture. They also wrote when television had barely begun and before video, the Internet, and digital recordings of music or film. Readers may ask whether the explosive growth of the culture industry since Horkheimer and Adorno wrote their argument makes genuine change possible at last or ends up imposing conformity and reducing the chance for change all the more.

(Horkheimer and Adorno's essay appears here nearly in its entirety; one brief section has been excised. The current edition includes notes by Gunzelin Schmid Noerr, which often track variations between different versions of the essay. Only a few of Noerr's explanatory notes are retained here.)

The sociological view that the loss of support from objective religion and the disintegration of the last precapitalist residues, in conjunction with technical and social differentiation and specialization, have given rise to cultural chaos is refuted by daily experience. Culture today is infecting everything with sameness. Film, radio, and magazines form a system. Each branch of culture is unanimous within itself and all are unanimous together. Even the aesthetic manifestations of political opposites proclaim the same inflexible rhythm. The decorative administrative and exhibition buildings of industry differ little between authoritarian and other countries. The bright monumental structures shooting up on all sides show off the systematic ingenuity of the state-spanning combines, toward which the unfettered entrepreneurial system, whose monuments are the dismal residential and commercial blocks in the surrounding areas of desolate cities, was already swiftly advancing. The older buildings around the concrete centers already look like slums, and the new bungalows on the outskirts, like the flimsy structures at international trade fairs, sing the praises of technical progress while inviting their users to throw them away after short use like tin cans. But the town-planning projects, which are supposed to perpetuate individuals as autonomous units in hygienic small apartments, subjugate them only more completely to their adversary, the total power of capital. Just as the occupants of city centers are uniformly summoned there for purposes of work and leisure, as producers and consumers, so the living cells crystallize into homogenous, well-organized complexes. The conspicuous unity of macrocosm and microcosm confronts human beings with a model of their culture: the false identity of universal and particular. All mass culture under monopoly is identical, and the contours of its skeleton, the conceptual armature fabricated by monopoly, are beginning to stand out. Those in charge no longer take much trouble to conceal the structure, the power of which increases the more bluntly its existence is admitted. Films and radio no longer need to present themselves as art. The truth that they are nothing but business is used as an ideology to legitimize the trash they intentionally produce. They call themselves industries, and the published figures for their directors' incomes quell any doubts about the social necessity of their finished products.

Interested parties like to explain the culture industry in technological terms. Its millions of participants, they argue, demand reproduction processes which inevitably lead to the use of standard products to meet the same needs at countless locations. The technical antithesis between few production centers and widely dispersed reception necessitates organization and planning by those in control. The standardized forms, it is claimed, were originally derived from the needs of the consumers: that is why they are accepted with so little resistance. In reality, a cycle of manipulation and retroactive need is unifying the system ever more tightly. What is not mentioned is that the basis on which technology is gaining power over society is the power of those whose economic position in society is strongest. Technical rationality today is the rationality of domination. It is the compulsive character of a society alienated from itself. Automobiles, bombs, and films hold the totality together until their leveling element demonstrates its power against the very system of injustice it served. For the present the technology of the culture industry confines itself to standardization and mass production and sacrifices what once distinguished the logic of the work from that of society. These adverse effects, however, should not be attributed to the internal laws of technology itself but to its function within the economy today. Any need which might escape the central control is repressed by that of individual consciousness. The step from telephone to radio has clearly distinguished the roles. The former liberally permitted the participant to play the role of subject. The latter democratically makes everyone equally into listeners, in order to expose them in authoritarian fashion to the same programs put out by different stations. No mechanism of reply has been developed, and private transmissions are condemned to unfreedom. They confine themselves to the apocryphal sphere of "amateurs," who, in any case, are organized from above. Any trace of spontaneity in the audience of the official radio is steered and absorbed into a selection of specializations by talent-spotters, performance competitions, and sponsored events of every kind. The talents belong to the operation long before they are put on show; otherwise they would not conform so eagerly. The mentality of the public, which allegedly and actually favors the system of the culture industry, is a part of the system, not an excuse for it. If a branch of art follows the same recipe as one far removed from it in terms of its medium and subject matter; if the dramatic denouement in radio "soap operas" is used as an instructive example of how to solve technical difficulties—which are mastered no less in "jam sessions" than at the highest levels of jazz—or if a movement from Beethoven is loosely "adapted" in the same way as a Tolstoy novel is adapted for film, the pretext of meeting the public's spontaneous wishes is mere hot air. An explanation in terms of the specific interests of the technical apparatus and its personnel would be closer to the truth, provided that apparatus were understood in all its details as a part of the economic mechanism of selection. Added to this is the agreement, or at least the common determination, of the executive powers to produce or let pass nothing which does not conform to their tables, to their concept of the consumer, or, above all, to themselves.

If the objective social tendency of this age is incarnated in the obscure subjective intentions of board chairmen, this is primarily the case in the most powerful sectors of industry: steel, petroleum, electricity, chemicals. Compared to them the culture monopolies are weak and dependent. They have to keep in with the true wielders of power, to ensure that their sphere of mass society, the specific product of which still has too much of cozy liberalism and Jewish intellectualism about it, is not subjected to a series of purges. The dependence of the most powerful broadcasting company on the electrical industry, or of film on the banks, characterizes the whole sphere, the individual sectors of which are themselves economically, intertwined. Everything is so tightly clustered that the concentration of intellect reaches a level where it overflows the demarcations between company names and technical sectors. The relentless unity of the culture industry bears witness to the emergent unity of politics. Sharp distinctions like those between A and B films, or between short stories published in magazines in different price segments, do not so much reflect real differences as assist in the classification, organization, and identification of consumers. Something is provided for everyone so that no one can escape; differences are hammered home and propagated. The hierarchy of serial qualities purveyed to the public serves only to quantify it more completely. Everyone is supposed to behave spontaneously according to a "level" determined by indices and to select the category of mass product manufactured for their type. On the charts of research organizations, indistinguishable from those of political propaganda, consumers are divided up as statistical material into red, green, and blue areas according to income group.

The schematic nature of this procedure is evident from the fact that the mechanically differentiated products are ultimately all the same. That the difference between the models of Chrysler and General Motors is fundamentally illusory is known by any child, who is fascinated by that very difference. The advantages and disadvantages debated by enthusiasts serve only to perpetuate the appearance of competition and choice. It is no different with the offerings of Warner Brothers and Metro Goldwyn Mayer. But the differences, even between the more expensive and cheaper products from the same firm, are shrinking—in cars to the different number of cylinders, engine capacity, and details of the gadgets, and in films to the different number of stars, the expense lavished on technology, labor and costumes, or the use of the latest psychological formulae. The unified standard of value consists in the level of conspicuous production, the amount of investment put on show. The budgeted differences of value in the culture industry have nothing to do with actual differences, with the meaning of the product itself. The technical media, too, are being engulfed by an insatiable uniformity. Television aims at a synthesis of radio and film, delayed only for as long as the interested parties cannot agree. Such a synthesis, with its unlimited possibilities, promises to intensify the impoverishment of the aesthetic material so radically that the identity of all industrial cultural products, still scantily disguised today, will triumph openly tomorrow in a mocking fulfillment of Wagner's dream of the total art work. The accord between word, image, and music is achieved so much more perfectly than in *Tristan* because the sensuous elements, which compliantly document only the surface of social reality, are produced in principle within the same technical work process, the unity of which they express as their true content. This work process integrates all the elements of production, from the original concept of the novel, shaped by its sidelong glance at film, to the last sound effect. It is the triumph of invested capital. To impress the omnipotence of capital on the hearts of expropriated job candidates as the power of their true master is the purpose of all films, regardless of the plot selected by the production directors.

Even during their leisure time, consumers must orient themselves according to the unity of production. The active contribution which Kantian schematism still expected of subjects—that they should, from the first, relate sensuous multiplicity to fundamental concepts—is denied to the subject by industry. It purveys schematism as its first service to the customer. According to Kantian schematism, a secret mechanism within the psyche preformed immediate data to fit them into the system of pure reason. That secret has now been unraveled. Although the operations of the mechanism appear to be planned by those who supply the data, the culture industry, the planning is in fact imposed on the industry by the inertia of a society irrational despite all its rationalization, and this calamitous tendency, in passing through the agencies of business, takes on the shrewd intentionality peculiar to them. For the consumer there is nothing left to classify, since the classification has already been preempted by the schematism of production. This dreamless art for the people fulfils the dreamy idealism which went too far for idealism in its critical form. Everything comes from consciousness—from that of God for Malebranche and Berkeley, and from earthly production management for mass art. Not only do hit songs, stars, and soap operas conform to types recurring cyclically as rigid invariants, but the specific content of productions, the seemingly variable element, is itself derived from those types. The details become interchangeable. The brief interval sequence which has proved catchy in a hit song, the hero's temporary disgrace which he accepts as a "good sport," the wholesome slaps the heroine receives from the strong hand of the male star, his plain-speaking abruptness toward the pampered heiress, are, like all the details, ready-made clichés, to be used here and there as desired and always completely defined by the purpose they serve within the schema. To confirm the schema by acting as its constituents is their sole raison d'être. In a film, the outcome can invariably be predicted at the start—who will be rewarded, punished, forgotten—and in light music the prepared ear can always guess the continuation after the first bars of a hit song and is gratified when it actually occurs. The average choice of words in a short story must not be tampered with. The gags and effects are no less calculated than their framework. They are managed by special experts, and their slim variety is specifically tailored to the office pigeonhole. The culture industry has developed in conjunction with the predominance of the effect, the tangible performance, the technical detail, over the work, which once carried the idea and was liquidated with it. By emancipating itself, the detail had become refractory; from Romanticism to Expressionism it had rebelled as unbridled expression, as the agent of opposition, against organization. In music, the individual harmonic effect had obliterated awareness of the form as a whole; in painting the particular detail had obscured the overall composition; in the novel psychological penetration had blurred the architecture. Through totality, the culture industry is putting an end to all that. Although operating only with effects, it subdues their unruliness and subordinates them to the formula which supplants the work. It crushes equally the whole and the parts. The whole confronts the details in implacable detachment, somewhat like the career of a successful man, in which everything serves to illustrate and demonstrate a success which, in fact, it is no more than the sum of those idiotic events. The so-called leading idea is a filing compartment which creates order, not connections. Lacking both contrast and relatedness, the whole and the detail look alike. Their harmony, guaranteed in advance, mocks the painfully achieved harmony of the great bourgeois works of art. In Germany even the most carefree films of democracy were overhung already by the graveyard stillness of dictatorship.

The whole world is passed through the filter of the culture industry. The familiar experience of the moviegoer, who perceives the street outside as a continuation of the film he has just left, because the film seeks strictly to reproduce the world of everyday perception, has become the guideline of production. The more densely and completely its techniques duplicate empirical objects, the more easily it creates the illusion that the world outside is a seamless extension of the one which has been revealed in the cinema. Since the abrupt introduction of the sound film, mechanical duplication has become entirely subservient to this objective. According to this tendency, life is to be made indistinguishable from the sound film. Far more strongly than the theatre of illusion, film denies its audience any dimension in which they might roam freely in imagination—contained by the film's framework but unsupervised by its precise actualities—without losing the thread; thus it trains those exposed to it to identify film directly with reality. The withering of imagination and spontaneity in the consumer of culture today need not be traced back to psychological mechanisms. The products themselves, especially the most characteristic, the sound film, cripple those faculties through their objective makeup. They are so constructed that their adequate comprehension requires a quick, observant, knowledgeable cast of mind but positively debars the spectator from thinking, if he is not to miss the fleeting facts. This kind of alertness is so ingrained that it does not even need to be activated in particular cases, while still repressing the powers of imagination. Anyone who is so absorbed by the world of the film, by gesture, image, and word, that he or she is unable to supply that which would have made it a world in the first place, does not need to be entirely transfixed by the special operations of the machinery at the moment of the performance. The required qualities of attention have become so familiar from other films and other culture products already known to him or her that they appear automatically. The power of industrial society is imprinted on people once and for all. The products of the culture industry are such that they can be alertly consumed even in a state of distraction. But each one is a model of the gigantic economic machinery, which, from the first, keeps everyone on their toes, both at work and in the leisure time which resembles it. In any sound film or any radio broadcast something is discernible which cannot be attributed as a social effect to any one of them, but to all together. Each single manifestation of the culture industry inescapably reproduces human beings as what the whole has made them. And all its agents, from the producer to the women's organizations, are on the alert to ensure that the simple reproduction of mind does not lead on to the expansion of mind.

The complaints of art historians and cultural attorneys over the exhaustion of the energy which created artistic style in the West are frighteningly unfounded. The routine translation of everything, even of what has not yet been thought, into the schema of mechanical reproducibility goes beyond the rigor and scope of any true style—the concept with which culture lovers idealize the precapitalist past as an organic era. No Palestrina could have eliminated the unprepared or unresolved dissonance more puristically than the jazz arranger excludes any phrase which does not exactly fit the jargon. If he jazzes up Mozart, he changes the music not only where it is too difficult or serious but also where the melody is merely harmonized differently, indeed, more simply, than is usual today. No medieval patron of architecture can have scrutinized the subjects of church windows and sculptures more suspiciously than the studio hierarchies examine a plot by Balzac or Victor Hugo before it receives the imprimatur of feasibility. No cathedral chapter could have assigned the grimaces and torments of the damned to their proper places in the order of divine love more scrupulously than production managers decide the position of the torture of the hero or the raised hem of the leading lady's dress within the litany of the big film. The explicit and implicit, exoteric and esoteric catalog of what is forbidden and what is tolerated is so extensive that it not only defines the area left free but wholly controls it. Even the most minor details are modeled according to this lexicon. Like its adversary, avant-garde art, the culture industry defines its own language positively, by means of prohibitions applied to its syntax and vocabulary. The permanent compulsion to produce new effects which yet remain bound to the old schema, becoming additional rules, merely increases the power of the tradition which the individual effect seeks to escape. Every phenomenon is by now so thoroughly imprinted by the schema that nothing can occur that does not bear in advance the trace of the jargon, that is not seen at first glance to be approved. But the true masters, as both producers and reproducers, are those who speak the jargon with the same free-and-easy relish as if it were the language it has long since silenced. Such is the industry's ideal of naturalness. It asserts itself more imperiously the more the perfected technology reduces the tension between the culture product and everyday existence. The paradox of routine travestied as nature is detectable in every utterance of the culture industry, and in many is quite blatant. A jazz musician who has to play a piece of serious music, Beethoven's simplest minuet, involuntarily syncopates, and condescends to start on the beat only with a superior smile. Such "naturalness," complicated by the ever more pervasive and exorbitant claims of the specific medium, constitutes the new style, "a system of nonculture to which one might even concede a certain 'unity of style' if it made any sense to speak of a stylized barbarism."[1]

The general influence of this stylization may already be more binding than the official rules and prohibitions; a hit song is treated more leniently today if it does not respect the thirty-two bars or the compass of the ninth than if it includes even the most elusive melodic or harmonic detail which falls outside the idiom. Orson Welles is forgiven all his offences against the usages of the craft because, as calculated rudeness, they confirm the validity of the system all the more zealously. The compulsion of the technically conditioned idiom which the stars and directors must produce as second nature, so that the nation may make it theirs, relates to nuances so fine as to be almost as subtle as the devices used in a work of the avant-garde, where, unlike those of the hit song, they serve truth. The rare ability to conform punctiliously to the obligations of the idiom of naturalness in all branches of the culture industry becomes the measure of expertise. As in logical positivism, what is said and how it is said must be verifiable against everyday speech. The producers are experts. The idiom demands the most prodigious productive powers, which it absorbs and squanders. Satanically, it has rendered cultural conservatism's distinction between genuine and artificial style obsolete. A style might possibly be called artificial if it had been imposed from outside against the resistance of the intrinsic tendencies of form. But in the culture industry the subject matter itself, down to its smallest elements, springs from the same apparatus as the jargon into which it is absorbed. The deals struck between the art specialists and the sponsor and censor over some all-too-unbelievable lie tell us less about internal, aesthetic tensions than about a divergence of interests. The reputation of the specialist, in which a last residue of actual autonomy still occasionally finds refuge, collides with the business policy of the church or the industrial combine producing the culture commodity. By its own nature, however, the matter has already been reified as negotiable even before the various agencies come into conflict. Even before Zanuck acquired her, Saint Bernadette gleamed in the eye of her writer as an advert aimed at all the relevant consortia. To this the impulses of form have been reduced. As a result, the style of the culture industry, which has no resistant material to overcome, is at the same time the negation of style. The reconciliation of general and particular, of rules and the specific demands of the subject, through which alone style takes on substance, is nullified by the absence of tension between the poles: "the extremes which touch" have become a murky identity in which the general can replace the particular and vice versa.

Nevertheless, this caricature of style reveals something about the genuine style of the past. The concept of a genuine style becomes transparent in the culture industry as the aesthetic equivalent of power. The notion of style as a merely aesthetic regularity is a retrospective fantasy of Romanticism. The unity of style not only of the Christian Middle Ages but of the Renaissance expresses the different structures of social coercion in those periods, not the obscure experience of the subjects, in which the universal was locked away. The great artists were never those whose works embodied style in its least fractured, most perfect form but those who adopted style as a rigor to set against the chaotic expression of suffering, as a negative truth. In the style of these works expression took on the strength without which existence is dissipated unheard. Even works which are called classical, like the music of Mozart, contain objective tendencies which resist the style they incarnate. Up to Schönberg and Picasso, great artists have been mistrustful of style, which at decisive points has guided them less than the logic of the subject matter. What the Expressionists and Dadaists attacked in their polemics, the untruth of style as such, triumphs today in the vocal jargon of the crooner, in the adept grace of the film star, and even in the mastery of the photographic shot of a farm laborer's hovel. In every work of art, style is a promise. In being absorbed through style into the dominant form of universality, into the current musical, pictorial, or verbal idiom, what is expressed seeks to be reconciled with the idea of the true universal. This promise of the work of art to create truth by impressing its unique contours on the socially transmitted forms is as necessary as it is hypocritical. By claiming to anticipate fulfillment through their aesthetic derivatives, it posits the real forms of the existing order as absolute. To this extent the claims of art are always also ideology. Yet it is only in its struggle with tradition, a struggle precipitated in style, that art can find expression for suffering. The moment in the work of art by which it transcends reality cannot, indeed, be severed from style; that moment, however, does not consist in achieved harmony, in the questionable unity of form and content, inner and outer, individual and society, but in those traits in which the discrepancy emerges, in the necessary failure of the passionate striving for identity. Instead of exposing itself to this failure, in which the style of the great work of art has always negated itself, the inferior work has relied on its similarity to others, the surrogate of identity. The culture industry has finally posited this imitation as absolute. Being nothing other than style, it divulges style's secret: obedience to the social hierarchy. Aesthetic barbarism today is accomplishing what has threatened intellectual formations since they were brought together as culture and neutralized. To speak about culture always went against the grain of culture. The general designation "culture" already contains, virtually, the process of identifying, cataloging, and classifying which imports culture into the realm of administration. Only what has been industrialized, rigorously subsumed, is fully adequate to this concept of culture. Only by subordinating all branches of intellectual production equally to the single purpose of imposing on the senses of human beings, from the time they leave the factory in the evening to the time they clock on in the morning, the imprint of the work routine which they must sustain throughout the day, does this culture mockingly fulfill the notion of a unified culture which the philosophers of the individual personality held out against mass culture.

The culture industry, the most inflexible style of all, thus proves to be the goal of the very liberalism which is criticized for its lack of style. Not only did its categories and contents originate in the liberal sphere, in domesticated naturalism no less than in the operetta and the revue, but the modern culture combines are the economic area in which a piece of the circulation sphere otherwise in the process of disintegration, together with the corresponding entrepreneurial types, still tenuously survives. In that area people can still make their way, provided they do not look too closely at their true purpose and are willing to be compliant. Anyone who resists can survive only by being incorporated. Once registered as diverging from the culture industry, they belong to it as the land reformer does to capitalism. Realistic indignation is the trademark of those with a new idea to sell. Public authority in the present society allows only those complaints to be heard in which the attentive ear can discern the prominent figure under whose protection the rebel is suing for peace. The more immeasurable the gulf between chorus and leaders, the more certainly is there a place among the latter for anyone who demonstrates superiority by well-organized dissidence. In this way liberalism's tendency to give free rein to its ablest members survives in the culture industry. To open that industry to clever people is the function of the otherwise largely regulated market, in which, even in its heyday, freedom was the freedom of the stupid to starve, in art as elsewhere. Not for nothing did the system of the culture industry originate in the liberal industrial countries, just as all its characteristic media, especially cinema, radio, jazz, and magazines, also triumph there. Its progress, however, stems from the general laws of capital. Gaumont and Pathé,[2] Ullstein and Hugenberg did not follow the international trend to their own disadvantage; Europe's economic dependence on the USA after the war and the inflation also made its contribution. The belief that the barbarism of the culture industry is a result of "cultural lag," of the backwardness of American consciousness in relation to the state of technology, is quite illusory. Prefascist Europe was backward in relation to the monopoly of culture. But it was precisely to such backwardness that intellectual activity owed a remnant of autonomy, its last exponents their livelihood, however meager. In Germany the incomplete permeation of life by democratic control had a paradoxical effect. Many areas were still exempt from the market mechanism which had been unleashed in Western countries. The German educational system, including the universities, the artistically influential theatres, the great orchestras, and the museums were under patronage. The political powers, the state and the local authorities who inherited such institutions from absolutism, had left them a degree of independence from the power of the market as the princes and feudal lords had done up to the nineteenth century. This stiffened the backbone of art in its late phase against the verdict of supply and demand, heightening its resistance far beyond its actual degree of protection. In the market itself the homage paid to not yet marketable artistic quality was converted into purchasing power, so that reputable literary and musical publishers could support authors who brought in little more than the respect of connoisseurs. Only the dire and incessant threat of incorporation into commercial life as aesthetic experts finally brought the artists to heel. In former times they signed their letters, like Kant and Hume, "Your most obedient servant," while undermining the foundations of throne and altar. Today they call heads of government by their first names and are subject, in every artistic impulse, to the judgment of their illiterate principals. The analysis offered by de Tocqueville a hundred years ago has been fully borne out in the meantime. Under the private monopoly of culture tyranny does indeed "leave the body free and sets to work directly on the soul. The ruler no longer says: 'Either you think as I do or you die.' He says: 'You are free not to think as I do; your life, your property—all that you shall keep. But from this day on you will be a stranger among us.'"[3] Anyone who does not conform is condemned to an economic impotence which is prolonged in the intellectual powerlessness of the eccentric loner. Disconnected from the mainstream, he is easily convicted of inadequacy. Whereas the mechanism of supply and demand is today disintegrating in material production, in the superstructure it acts as a control on behalf of the rulers. The consumers are the workers and salaried employees, the farmers and petty bourgeois. Capitalist production hems them in so tightly, in body and soul, that they unresistingly succumb to whatever is proffered to them. However, just as the ruled have always taken the morality dispensed to them by the rulers more seriously than the rulers themselves, the defrauded masses today cling to the myth of success still more ardently than the successful. They, too, have their aspirations. They insist unwaveringly on the ideology by which they are enslaved. The pernicious love of the common people for the harm done to them outstrips even the cunning of the authorities. It surpasses the rigor of the Hays Office,[4] just as, in great epochs, it has inspired renewed zeal in greater agencies directed against it, the terror of the tribunals. It calls for Mickey Rooney rather than the tragic Garbo, Donald Duck rather than Betty Boop. The industry bows to the vote it has itself rigged. The incidental costs to the firm which cannot turn a profit from its contract with a declining star are legitimate costs for the system as a whole. By artfully sanctioning the demand for trash, the system inaugurates total harmony. Connoisseurship and expertise are proscribed as the arrogance of those who think themselves superior, whereas culture distributes its privileges democratically to all. Under the ideological truce between them, the conformism of the consumers, like the shamelessness of the producers they sustain, can have a good conscience. Both content themselves with the reproduction of sameness.

Unending sameness also governs the relationship to the past. What is new in the phase of mass culture compared to that of late liberalism is the exclusion of the new. The machine is rotating on the spot. While it already determines consumption, it rejects anything untried as a risk. In film, any manuscript which is not reassuringly based on a best-seller is viewed with mistrust. That is why there is incessant talk of ideas, novelty and surprises, of what is both totally familiar and has never existed before. Tempo and dynamism are paramount. Nothing is allowed to stay as it was, everything must be endlessly in motion. For only the universal victory of the rhythm of mechanical production and reproduction promises that nothing will change, that nothing unsuitable will emerge. To add anything to the proven cultural inventory would be too speculative. The frozen genres—sketch, short story, problem film, hit song—represent the average of late liberal taste threateningly imposed as a norm. The most powerful of the culture agencies, who work harmoniously with others of their kind as only managers do, whether they come from the ready-to-wear trade or college, have long since reorganized and rationalized the objective mind. It is as if some omnipresent agency had reviewed the material and issued an authoritative catalog tersely listing the products available. The ideal forms are inscribed in the cultural heavens where they were already numbered by Plato—indeed, were only numbers, incapable of increase or change.

Amusement and all the other elements of the culture industry existed long before the industry itself. Now they have been taken over from above and brought fully up to date. The culture industry can boast of having energetically accomplished and elevated to a principle the often inept transposition of art to the consumption sphere, of having stripped amusement of its obtrusive naiveties and improved the quality of its commodities. The more all-embracing the culture industry has become, the more pitilessly it has forced the outsider into either bankruptcy or a syndicate; at the same time it has become more refined and elevated, becoming finally a synthesis of Beethoven and the Casino de Paris.[5] Its victory is twofold: what is destroyed as truth outside its sphere can be reproduced indefinitely within it as lies. "Light" art as such, entertainment, is not a form of decadence. Those who deplore it as a betrayal of the ideal of pure expression harbor illusions about society. The purity of bourgeois art, hypostatized as a realm of freedom contrasting to material praxis, was bought from the outset with the exclusion of the lower class; and art keeps faith with the cause of that class, the true universal, precisely by freeing itself from the purposes of the false. Serious art has denied itself to those for whom the hardship and oppression of life make a mockery of seriousness and who must be glad to use the time not spent at the production line in being simply carried along. Light art has accompanied autonomous art as its shadow. It is the social bad conscience of serious art. The truth which the latter could not apprehend because of its social premises gives the former an appearance of objective justification. The split between them is itself the truth: it expresses at least the negativity of the culture which is the sum of both spheres. The antithesis can be reconciled least of all by absorbing light art into serious or vice versa. That, however, is what the culture industry attempts. The eccentricity of the circus, the peep show, or the brothel in relation to society is as embarrassing to it as that of Schönberg and Karl Kraus. The leading jazz musician Benny Goodman therefore has to appear with the Budapest String Quartet, more pedantic rhythmically than any amateur clarinetist, while the quartet play with the saccharine monotony of Guy Lombardo.[6] What is significant is not crude ignorance, stupidity or lack of polish. The culture industry has abolished the rubbish of former times by imposing its own perfection, by prohibiting and domesticating dilettantism, while itself incessantly committing the blunders without which the elevated style cannot be conceived. What is new, however, is that the irreconcilable elements of culture, art, and amusement have been subjected equally to the concept of purpose and thus brought under a single false denominator: the totality of the culture industry. Its element is repetition. The fact that its characteristic innovations are in all cases mere improvements to mass production is not extraneous to the system. With good reason the interest of countless consumers is focused on the technology, not on the rigidly repeated, threadbare and half-abandoned content. The social power revered by the spectators manifests itself more effectively in the technically enforced ubiquity of stereotypes than in the stale ideologies which the ephemeral contents have to endorse.

Nevertheless, the culture industry remains the entertainment business. Its control of consumers is mediated by entertainment, and its hold will not be broken by outright dictate but by the hostility inherent in the principle of entertainment to anything which is more than itself. Since the tendencies of the culture industry are turned into the flesh and blood of the public by the social process as a whole, those tendencies are reinforced by the survival of the market in the industry. Demand has not yet been replaced by simple obedience. The major reorganization of the film industry shortly before the First World War, the material precondition for its expansion, was a deliberate adaptation to needs of the public registered at the ticket office, which were hardly thought worthy of consideration in the pioneering days of the screen. That view is still held by the captains of the film industry, who accept only more or less phenomenal box-office success as evidence and prudently ignore the counterevidence, truth. Their ideology is business. In this they are right to the extent that the power of the culture industry lies in its unity with fabricated need and not in simple antithesis to it—or even in the antithesis between omnipotence and powerlessness. Entertainment is the prolongation of work under late capitalism. It is sought by those who want to escape the mechanized labor process so that they can cope with it again. At the same time, however, mechanization has such power over leisure and its happiness, determines so thoroughly the fabrication of entertainment commodities, that the off-duty worker can experience nothing but after-images of the work process itself. The ostensible content is merely a faded foreground; what is imprinted is the automated sequence of standardized tasks. The only escape from the work process in factory and office is through adaptation to it in leisure time. This is the incurable sickness of all entertainment. Amusement congeals into boredom, since, to be amusement, it must cost no effort and therefore moves strictly along the well-worn grooves of association. The spectator must need no thoughts of his own: the product prescribes each reaction, not through any actual coherence—which collapses once exposed to thought—but through signals. Any logical connection presupposing mental capacity is scrupulously avoided. Developments are to emerge from the directly preceding situation, not from the idea of the whole. There is no plot which could withstand the screenwriters' eagerness to extract the maximum effect from the individual scene. Finally, even the schematic formula seems dangerous, since it provides some coherence of meaning, however meager, when only meaninglessness is acceptable. Often the plot is willfully denied the development called for by characters and theme under the old schema. Instead, the next step is determined by what the writers take to be their most effective idea. Obtusely ingenious surprises disrupt the plot. The product's tendency to fall back perniciously on the pure nonsense which, as buffoonery and clowning, was a legitimate part of popular art up to Chaplin and the Marx brothers, emerges most strikingly in the less sophisticated genres. Whereas the films of Greer Garson and Bette Davis can still derive some claim to a coherent plot from the unity of the socio-psychological case represented, the tendency to subvert meaning has taken over completely in the text of novelty songs,[7] suspense films, and cartoons. The idea itself, like objects in comic and horror films, is massacred and mutilated. Novelty songs have always lived on contempt for meaning, which, as both ancestors and descendants of psychoanalysis, they reduce to the monotony of sexual symbolism. In crime and adventure films the spectators are begrudged even the opportunity to witness the resolution. Even in nonironic examples of the genre they must make do with the mere horror of situations connected in only the most perfunctory way.

Cartoon and stunt films were once exponents of fantasy against rationalism. They allowed justice to be done to the animals and things electrified by their technology, by granting the mutilated beings a second life. Today they merely confirm the victory of technological reason over truth. A few years ago they had solid plots which were resolved only in the whirl of pursuit of the final minutes. In this their procedure resembled that of slapstick comedy. But now the temporal relations have shifted. The opening sequences state a plot motif so that destruction can work on it throughout the action: with the audience in gleeful pursuit the protagonist is tossed about like a scrap of litter. The quantity of organized amusement is converted into the quality of organized cruelty. The self-elected censors of the film industry, its accomplices, monitor the duration of the atrocity prolonged into a hunt. The jollity dispels the joy supposedly conferred by the sight of an embrace and postpones satisfaction until the day of the pogrom. To the extent that cartoons do more than accustom the senses to the new tempo, they hammer into every brain the old lesson that continuous attrition, the breaking of all individual resistance, is the condition of life in this society. Donald Duck in the cartoons and the unfortunate victim in real life receive their beatings so that the spectators can accustom themselves to theirs.

The enjoyment of the violence done to the film character turns into violence against the spectator; distraction becomes exertion. No stimulant concocted by the experts may escape the weary eye; in face of the slick presentation no one may appear stupid even for a moment; everyone has to keep up, emulating the smartness displayed and propagated by the production. This makes it doubtful whether the culture industry even still fulfils its self-proclaimed function of distraction. If the majority of radio stations and cinemas were shut down, consumers probably would not feel too much deprived. In stepping from the street into the cinema, they no longer enter the world of dream in any case, and once the use of these institutions was no longer made obligatory by their mere existence, the urge to use them might not be so overwhelming. Shutting them down in this way would not be reactionary machine-wrecking. Those who suffered would not be the film enthusiasts but those who always pay the penalty in any case, the ones who had lagged behind. For the housewife, despite the films which are supposed to integrate her still further, the dark of the cinema grants a refuge in which she can spend a few unsupervised hours, just as once, when there were still dwellings and evening repose, she could sit gazing out of the window. The unemployed of the great centers find freshness in summer and warmth in winter in these places of regulated temperature. Apart from that, and even by the measure of the existing order, the bloated entertainment apparatus does not make life more worthy of human beings. The idea of "exploiting" the given technical possibilities, of fully utilizing the capacities for aesthetic mass consumption, is part of an economic system which refuses to utilize capacities when it is a question of abolishing hunger.

The culture industry endlessly cheats its consumers out of what it endlessly promises. The promissory note of pleasure issued by plot and packaging is indefinitely prolonged: the promise, which actually comprises the entire show, disdainfully intimates that there is nothing more to come, that the diner must be satisfied with reading the menu. The desire inflamed by the glossy names and images is served up finally with a celebration of the daily round it sought to escape. Of course, genuine works of art were not sexual exhibitions either. But by presenting denial as negative, they reversed, as it were, the debasement of the drive and rescued by mediation what had been denied. That is the secret of aesthetic sublimation: to present fulfillment in its brokenness. The culture industry does not sublimate: it suppresses. By constantly exhibiting the object of desire, the breasts beneath the sweater, the naked torso of the sporting hero, it merely goads the unsublimated anticipation of pleasure, which through the habit of denial has long since been mutilated as masochism. There is no erotic situation in which innuendo and incitement are not accompanied by the clear notification that things will never go so far. The Hays Office merely confirms the ritual which the culture industry has staged in any case: that of Tantalus. Works of art are ascetic and shameless; the culture industry is pornographic and prudish. It reduces love to romance. And, once reduced, much is permitted, even libertinage as a marketable specialty, purveyed by quota with the trade description "daring." The mass production of sexuality automatically brings about its repression. Because of his ubiquity, the film star with whom one is supposed to fall in love is, from the start, a copy of himself. Every tenor now sounds like a Caruso record, and the natural faces of Texas girls already resemble those of the established models by which they would be typecast in Hollywood. The mechanical reproduction of beauty—which, admittedly, is made only more inescapable by the reactionary culture zealots with their methodical idolization of individuality—no longer leaves any room for the unconscious idolatry with which the experience of beauty has always been linked. The triumph over beauty is completed by humor, the malicious pleasure elicited by any successful deprivation. There is laughter because there is nothing to laugh about. Laughter, whether reconciled or terrible, always accompanies the moment when a fear is ended. It indicates a release, whether from physical danger or from the grip of logic. Reconciled laughter resounds with the echo of escape from power; wrong laughter copes with fear by defecting to the agencies which inspire it. It echoes the inescapability of power. Fun is a medicinal bath which the entertainment industry never ceases to prescribe. It makes laughter the instrument for cheating happiness. To moments of happiness laughter is foreign; only operettas, and now films, present sex amid peals of merriment. But Baudelaire is as humorless as Hölderlin. In wrong society laughter is a sickness infecting happiness and drawing it into society's worthless totality. Laughter about something is always laughter at it, and the vital force which, according to Bergson, bursts through rigidity in laughter is, in truth, the irruption of barbarity, the self-assertion which, in convivial settings, dares to celebrate its liberation from scruple. The collective of those who laugh parodies humanity. They are monads, each abandoning himself to the pleasure—at the expense of all others and with the majority in support—of being ready to shrink from nothing. Their harmony presents a caricature of solidarity. What is infernal about wrong laughter is that it compellingly parodies what is best, reconciliation. Joy, however, is austere: *res severa verum gaudium.* The ideology of monasteries, that it is not asceticism but the sexual act which marks the renunciation of attainable bliss, is negatively confirmed by the gravity of the lover who presciently pins his whole life to the fleeting moment. The culture industry replaces pain, which is present in ecstasy no less than in asceticism, with jovial denial. Its supreme law is that its consumers shall at no price be given what they desire; and in that very deprivation they must take their laughing satisfaction. In each performance of the culture industry the permanent denial imposed by civilization is once more inflicted on and unmistakably demonstrated to its victims. To offer them something and to withhold it is one and the same. That is what the erotic commotion achieves. Just because it can never take place, everything revolves around the coitus. In film, to allow an illicit relationship without due punishment of the culprits is even more strictly tabooed than it is for the future son-in-law of a millionaire to be active in the workers' movement.

Unlike that of the liberal era, industrial no less than nationalist culture can permit itself to inveigh against capitalism, but not to renounce the threat of castration. This threat constitutes its essence. It outlasts the organized relaxation of morals toward the wearers of uniforms, first in the jaunty films produced for them and then in reality. What is decisive today is no longer Puritanism, though it still asserts itself in the form of women's organizations, but the necessity, inherent in the system, of never releasing its grip on the consumer, of not for a moment allowing him or her to suspect that resistance is possible. This principle requires that while all needs should be presented to individuals as capable of fulfillment by the culture industry, they should be so set up in advance that individuals experience themselves through their needs only as eternal consumers, as the culture industry's object. Not only does it persuade them that its fraud is satisfaction; it also gives them to understand that they must make do with what is offered, whatever it may be. The flight from the everyday world, promised by the culture industry in all its branches, is much like the abduction of the daughter in the American cartoon: the father is holding the ladder in the dark. The culture industry presents that same everyday world as paradise. Escape, like elopement, is destined from the first to lead back to its starting point. Entertainment fosters the resignation which seeks to forget itself in entertainment.

Amusement, free of all restraint, would be not only the opposite of art but its complementary extreme. Absurdity in the manner of Mark Twain, with which the American culture industry flirts from time to time, could be a corrective to art. The more seriously art takes its opposition to existence, the more it resembles the seriousness of existence, its antithesis: the more it labors to develop strictly according to its own formal laws, the more labor it requires to be understood, whereas its goal had been precisely to negate the burden of labor. In some revue films, and especially in grotesque stories and "funnies," the possibility of this negation is momentarily glimpsed. Its realization, of course, cannot be allowed. Pure amusement indulged to the full, relaxed abandon to colorful associations and merry nonsense, is cut short by amusement in its marketable form: it is disrupted by the surrogate of a coherent meaning with which the culture industry insists on endowing its products while at the same time slyly misusing them as pretexts for bringing on the stars. Biographies and other fables stitch together the scraps of nonsense into a feeble-minded plot. It is not the bells on the fool's cap that jingle but the bunch of keys of capitalist reason, which even in its images harnesses joy to the purpose of getting ahead. Every kiss in the revue film must contribute to the career of the boxer or hit-song expert whose success is being glorified. The deception is not that the culture industry serves up amusement but that it spoils the fun by its business-minded attachment to the ideological clichés of the culture which is liquidating itself. Ethics and taste suppress unbridled amusement as "naïve"—naivety being rated no more highly than intellectualism—and even restrict its technical possibilities. The culture industry is corrupt, not as a sink of iniquity but as the cathedral of higher gratification. At all its levels, from Hemingway to Emil Ludwig, from Mrs. Miniver[8] to the Lone Ranger, from Toscanini to Guy Lombardo, intellectual products drawn ready-made from art and science are infected with untruth. Traces of something better persist in those features of the culture industry by which it resembles the circus—in the stubbornly purposeless expertise of riders, acrobats, and clowns, in the "defense and justification of physical as against intellectual art."[9] But the hiding places of mindless artistry, which represents what is human against the social mechanism, are being relentlessly ferreted out by organizational reason, which forces everything to justify itself in terms of meaning and effect. It is causing meaninglessness to disappear at the lowest level of art just as radically as meaning is disappearing at the highest.

The fusion of culture and entertainment is brought about today not only by the debasement of culture but equally by the compulsory intellectualization of amusement. This is already evident in the fact that amusement is now experienced only in facsimile, in the form of cinema photography or the radio recording. In the age of liberal expansion amusement was sustained by an unbroken belief in the future: things would stay the same yet get better. Today, that belief has itself been intellectualized, becoming so refined as to lose sight of all actual goals and to consist only in a golden shimmer projected beyond the real. It is composed of the extra touches of meaning—running exactly parallel to life itself—applied in the screen world to the good guy, the engineer, the decent girl, and also to the ruthlessness disguised as character, to the sporting interest, and finally to the cars and cigarettes, even where the entertainment does not directly serve the publicity needs of the manufacturer concerned but advertises the system as a whole. Amusement itself becomes an ideal, taking the place of the higher values it eradicates from the masses by repeating them in an even more stereotyped form than the advertising slogans paid for by private interests. Inwardness, the subjectively restricted form of truth, was always more beholden to the outward rulers than it imagined. The culture industry is perverting it into a barefaced lie. It appears now only as the high-minded prattle tolerated by consumers of religious bestsellers, psychological films, and women's serials[10] as an embarrassingly agreeable ingredient, so that they can more reliably control their own human emotions. In this sense entertainment is purging the affects in the manner once attributed by Aristotle to tragedy and now by Mortimer Adler to film. The culture industry reveals the truth not only about style but also about catharsis.

The more strongly the culture industry entrenches itself, the more it can do as it chooses with the needs of consumers—producing, controlling, disciplining them; even withdrawing amusement altogether: here, no limits are set to cultural progress. But the tendency is immanent in the principle of entertainment itself, as a principle of bourgeois enlightenment. If the need for entertainment was largely created by industry, which recommended the work to the masses through its subject matter, the oleograph through the delicate morsel it portrayed and, conversely, the pudding mix through the image of a pudding, entertainment has always borne the trace of commercial brashness, of sales talk, the voice of the fairground huckster. But the original affinity between business and entertainment reveals itself in the meaning of entertainment itself: as society's apologia. To be entertained means to be in agreement. Entertainment makes itself possible only by insulating itself from the totality of the social process, making itself stupid and perversely renouncing from the first the inescapable claim of any work, even the most trivial: in its restrictedness to reflect the whole. Amusement always means putting things out of mind, forgetting suffering, even when it is on display. At its root is powerlessness. It is indeed escape, but not, as it claims, escape from bad reality but from the last thought of resisting that reality. The liberation which amusement promises is from thinking as negation. The shamelessness of the rhetorical question "What do people want?" lies in the fact that it appeals to the very people as thinking subjects whose subjectivity it specifically seeks to annul. Even on those occasions when the public rebels against the pleasure industry it displays the feebleness systematically instilled in it by that industry. Nevertheless, it has become increasingly difficult to keep the public in submission. The advance of stupidity must not lag behind the simultaneous advance of intelligence. In the age of statistics the masses are too astute to identify with the millionaire on the screen and too obtuse to deviate even minutely from the law of large numbers. Ideology hides itself in probability calculations. Fortune will not smile on all—just on the one who draws the winning ticket or, rather, the one designated to do so by a higher power—usually the entertainment industry itself, which presents itself as ceaselessly in search of talent. Those discovered by the talent scouts and then built up by the studios are ideal types of the new, dependent middle classes. The female starlet is supposed to symbolize the secretary, though in a way which makes her seem predestined, unlike the real secretary, to wear the flowing evening gown. Thus she apprises the female spectator not only of the possibility that she, too, might appear on the screen but still more insistently of the distance between them. Only one can draw the winning lot, only one is prominent, and even though all have mathematically the same chance, it is so minimal for each individual that it is best to write it off at once and rejoice in the good fortune of someone else, who might just as well be oneself but never is. Where the culture industry still invites naïve identification, it immediately denies it. It is no longer possible to lose oneself in others. Once, film spectators saw their own wedding in that of others. Now the happy couple on the screen are specimens of the same species as everyone in the audience, but the sameness posits the insuperable separation of its human elements. The perfected similarity is the absolute difference. The identity of the species prohibits that of the individual cases. The culture industry has sardonically realized man's species being. Everyone amounts only to those qualities by which he or she can replace everyone else: all are fungible, mere specimens. As individuals they are absolutely replaceable, pure nothingness, and are made aware of this as soon as time deprives them of their sameness. This changes the inner composition of the religion of success, which they are sternly required to uphold. The path *per aspera ad astra*, which presupposes need and effort, is increasingly replaced by the prize. The element of blindness in the routine decision as to which song is to be a hit, which extra a heroine, is celebrated by ideology. Films emphasize chance. By imposing an essential sameness on their characters, with the exception of the villain, to the point of excluding any faces which do not conform—for example, those which, like Garbo's, do not look as if they would welcome the greeting "Hello, sister"—the ideology does, it is true, make life initially easier for the spectators. They are assured that they do not need to be in any way other than they are and that they can succeed just as well without having to perform tasks of which they know themselves incapable. But at the same time they are given the hint that effort would not help them in any case, because even bourgeois success no longer has any connection to the calculable effect of their own work. They take the hint. Fundamentally, everyone recognizes chance, by which someone is sometimes lucky, as the other side of planning. Just because society's energies have developed so far on the side of rationality that anyone might become an engineer or a manager, the choice of who is to receive from society the investment and confidence to be trained for such functions becomes entirely irrational. Chance and planning become identical since, given the sameness of people, the fortune or misfortune of the individual, right up to the top, loses all economic importance. Chance itself is planned; not in the sense that it will affect this or that particular individual but in that people believe in its control. For the planners it serves as an alibi, giving the impression that the web of transactions and measures into which life has been transformed still leaves room for spontaneous, immediate relationships between human beings. Such freedom is symbolized in the various media of the culture industry by the arbitrary selection of average cases. In the detailed reports on the modestly luxurious pleasure trip organized by the magazine for the lucky competition winner—preferably a shorthand typist who probably won through contacts with local powers-that-be—the powerlessness of everyone is reflected. So much are the masses mere material that those in control can raise one of them up to their heaven and cast him or her out again: let them go hang with their justice and their labor. Industry is interested in human beings only as its customers and employees and has in fact reduced humanity as a whole, like each of its elements, to this exhaustive formula. Depending on which aspect happens to be paramount at the time, ideology stresses plan or chance, technology or life, civilization or nature. As employees people are reminded of the rational organization and must fit into it as common sense requires. As customers they are regaled, whether on the screen or in the press, with human interest stories demonstrating freedom of choice and the charm of not belonging to the system. In both cases they remain objects.

The less the culture industry has to promise and the less it can offer a meaningful explanation of life, the emptier the ideology it disseminates necessarily becomes. Even the abstract ideals of the harmony and benevolence of society are too concrete in the age of the universal advertisement. Abstractions in particular are identified as publicity devices. Language which appeals to mere truth only arouses impatience to get down to the real business behind it. Words which are not a means seem meaningless, the others seem to be fiction, untruth. Value judgments are perceived either as advertisements or as mere chatter. The noncommittal vagueness of the resulting ideology does not make it more transparent, or weaker. Its very vagueness, the quasiscientific reluctance to be pinned down to anything which cannot be verified, functions as an instrument of control. Ideology becomes the emphatic and systematic proclamation of what is. Through its inherent tendency to adopt the tone of the factual report, the culture industry makes itself the irrefutable prophet of the existing order. With consummate skill it maneuvers between the crags of demonstrable misinformation and obvious truth by faithfully duplicating appearances, the density of which blocks insight. Thus the omnipresent and impenetrable world of appearances is set up as the ideal. Ideology is split between the photographing of brute existence and the blatant lie about its meaning, a lie which is not articulated directly but drummed in by suggestion. The mere cynical reiteration of the real is enough to demonstrate its divinity. Such photological proof may not be stringent, but it is overwhelming. Anyone who continues to doubt in face of the power of monotony is a fool. The culture industry sweeps aside objections to itself along with those to the world it neutrally duplicates. One has only the choice of conforming or being consigned to the backwoods: the provincials who oppose cinema and radio by falling back on eternal beauty and amateur theatricals have already reached the political stance toward which the members of mass culture are still being driven. This culture is hardened enough either to poke fun at the old wishful dreams, the paternal ideal no less than unconditional feeling, or to invoke them as ideology, as the occasion demands. The new ideology has the world as such as its subject. It exploits the cult of fact by describing bad existence with utmost exactitude in order to elevate it into the realm of facts. Through such elevation existence itself becomes a surrogate of meaning and justice. Beauty is whatever the camera reproduces. The disappointed hope that one might oneself be the employee who won the world trip is matched by the disappointing appearance of the exactly photographed regions through which the journey might have led. What is offered is not Italy but evidence that it exists. The film can permit itself to show the Paris in which the young American woman hopes to still her longing as a desolately barren place, in order to drive her all the more implacably into the arms of the smart American boy she might equally well have met at home. That life goes on at all, that the system, even in its most recent phase, reproduces the lives of those who constitute it instead of doing away with them straight away, is even credited to the system as its meaning and value. The ability to keep going at all becomes the justification for the blind continuation of the system, indeed, for its immutability. What is repeated is healthy—the cycle in nature as in industry. The same babies grin endlessly from magazines, and endlessly the jazz machine pounds. Despite all the progress in the techniques of representation, all the rules and specialties, all the gesticulating bustle, the bread on which the culture industry feeds humanity, remains the stone of stereotype. It lives on the cyclical, on the admittedly well-founded amazement that, in spite of everything, mothers still give birth to children, that the wheels have not yet come completely to a halt. All this consolidates the immutability of the existing circumstances. The swaying cornfields at the end of Chaplin's film on Hitler give the lie to the antifascist speech about freedom. They resemble the blond tresses of the German maidens whose outdoor life in the summer wind is photographed by Ufa. Nature, in being presented by society's control mechanism as the healing antithesis of society, is itself absorbed into that incurable society and sold off. The solemn pictorial affirmation that the trees are green, the sky is blue, and the clouds are sailing overhead already makes them cryptograms for factory chimneys and gasoline stations. Conversely, wheels and machine parts are made to gleam expressively, debased as receptacles of that leafy, cloudy soul. In this way both nature and technology are mobilized against the alleged stuffiness, the faked recollection of liberal society as a world in which people idled lasciviously in plush-lined rooms instead of taking wholesome open-air baths as they do today, or suffered breakdowns in antediluvian Benz models instead of traveling at rocket speed from where they are in any case to where it is no different. The triumph of the giant corporation over entrepreneurial initiative is celebrated by the culture industry as the perpetuity of entrepreneurial initiative. The fight is waged against an enemy who has already been defeated, the thinking subject. The resurrection of *Hans Sonnenstößer*, the enemy of bourgeois philistines, in Germany, and the smug coziness of *Life with Father* have one and the same meaning....

It is not only the standardized mode of production of the culture industry which makes the individual illusory in its products. Individuals are tolerated only as far as their wholehearted identity with the universal is beyond question. From the standardized improvisation in jazz to the original film personality who must have a lock of hair straying over her eyes so that she can be recognized as such, pseudoindividuality reigns. The individual trait is reduced to the ability of the universal so completely to mold the accidental that it can be recognized as accidental. The sulky taciturnity or the elegant walk of the individual who happens to be on show is serially produced like the Yale locks which differ by fractions of a millimeter. The peculiarity of the self is a socially conditioned monopoly commodity misrepresented as natural. It is reduced to the moustache, the French accent, the deep voice of the prostitute, the "Lubitsch touch"—like a fingerprint on the otherwise uniform identity cards to which the lives and faces of all individuals, from the film star to the convict, have been reduced by the power of the universal. Pseudoindividuality is a precondition for apprehending and detoxifying tragedy: only because individuals are none but mere intersections of universal tendencies is it possible to reabsorb them smoothly into the universal. Mass culture thereby reveals the fictitious quality which has characterized the individual throughout the bourgeois era and is wrong only in priding itself on this murky harmony between universal and particular. The principle of individuality was contradictory from the outset. First, no individuation was ever really achieved. The class-determined form of self-preservation maintained everyone at the level of mere species being. Every bourgeois character expressed the same thing, even and especially when deviating from it: the harshness of competitive society. The individual, on whom society was supported, itself bore society's taint; in the individual's apparent freedom he was the product of society's economic and social apparatus. Power has always invoked the existing power relationships when seeking the approval of those subjected to power. At the same time, the advance of bourgeois society has promoted the development of the individual. Against the will of those controlling it, technology has changed human beings from children into persons. But all such progress of individuation has been at the expense of the individuality in whose name it took place, leaving behind nothing except individuals' determination to pursue their own purposes alone. The citizens whose lives are split between business and private life, their private life between ostentation and intimacy, their intimacy between the sullen community of marriage and the bitter solace of being entirely alone, at odds with themselves and with everyone, are virtually already Nazis, who are at once enthusiastic and fed up, or the city dwellers of today, who can imagine friendship only as "social contact" between the inwardly unconnected. The culture industry can only manipulate individuality so successfully because the fractured nature of society has always been reproduced within it. In the ready-made faces of film heroes and private persons fabricated according to magazine-cover stereotypes, a semblance of individuality—in which no one believes in any case—is fading, and the love for such hero-models is nourished by the secret satisfaction that the effort of individuation is at last being replaced by the admittedly more breathless one of imitation. The hope that the contradictory, disintegrating person could not survive for generations, that the psychological fracture within it must split the system itself, and that human beings might refuse to tolerate the mendacious substitution of the stereotype for the individual—that hope is vain. The unity of the personality has been recognized as illusory since Shakespeare's Hamlet. In the synthetically manufactured physiognomies of today the fact that the concept of human life ever existed is already forgotten. For centuries society has prepared for Victor Mature and Mickey Rooney.[11] They come to fulfill the very individuality they destroy.

The heroizing of the average forms part of the cult of cheapness. The highest-paid stars resemble advertisements for unnamed merchandise. Not for nothing are they often chosen from the ranks of commercial models. The dominant taste derives its ideal from the advertisement, from commodified beauty. Socrates' dictum that beauty is the useful has at last been ironically fulfilled. The cinema publicizes the cultural conglomerate as a totality, while the radio advertises individually the products for whose sake the cultural system exists. For a few coins you can see the film which cost millions, for even less you can buy the chewing gum behind which stand the entire riches of the world, and the sales of which increase those riches still further. Through universal suffrage the vast funding of armies is generally known and approved, if in absentia, while prostitution behind the lines is not permitted. The best orchestras in the world, which are none, are delivered free of charge to the home. All this mockingly resembles the land of milk and honey as the national community apes the human one. Something is served up for everyone. A provincial visitor's comment on the old Berlin Metropoltheater that "it is remarkable what can be done for the money" has long since been adopted by the culture industry and elevated to the substance of production itself. Not only is a production always accompanied by triumphant celebration that it has been possible at all, but to a large extent it is that triumph itself. To put on a show means to show everyone what one has and can do. The show is still a fairground, but one incurably infected by culture. Just as people lured by the fairground crier overcame their disappointment inside the booths with a brave smile, since they expected it in any case, the moviegoer remains tolerantly loyal to the institution. But the cheapness of mass-produced luxury articles, and its complement, universal fraud, are changing the commodity character of art itself. That character is not new: it is the fact that art now dutifully admits to being a commodity, abjures its autonomy and proudly takes its place among consumer goods, that has the charm of novelty. Art was only ever able to exist as a separate sphere in its bourgeois form. Even its freedom, as negation of the social utility which is establishing itself through the market, is essentially conditioned by the commodity economy. Pure works of art, which negated the commodity character of society by simply following their own inherent laws, were at the same time always commodities. To the extent that, up to the eighteenth century, artists were protected from the market by patronage, they were subject to the patrons and their purposes instead. The purposelessness of the great modern work of art is sustained by the anonymity of the market. The latter's demands are so diversely mediated that the artist is exempted from any particular claim, although only to a certain degree, since his autonomy, being merely tolerated, has been attended throughout bourgeois history by a moment of untruth, which has culminated now in the social liquidation of art. The mortally sick Beethoven, who flung away a novel by Walter Scott with the cry: "The fellow writes for money," while himself proving an extremely experienced and tenacious businessman in commercializing the last quartets—works representing the most extreme repudiation of the market—offers the most grandiose example of the unity of the opposites of market and autonomy in bourgeois art. The artists who succumb to ideology are precisely those who conceal this contradiction instead of assimilating it into the consciousness of their own production, as Beethoven did: he improvised on "Rage over a Lost Penny" and derived the metaphysical injunction "It must be," which seeks aesthetically to annul the world's compulsion by taking that burden onto itself, from his housekeeper's demand for her monthly wages. The principle of idealist aesthetics, purposiveness without purpose, reverses the schema socially adopted by bourgeois art: purposelessness for purposes dictated by the market. In the demand for entertainment and relaxation, purpose has finally consumed the realm of the purposeless. But as the demand for the marketability of art becomes total, a shift in the inner economic composition of cultural commodities is becoming apparent. For the use which is made of the work of art in antagonistic society is largely that of confirming the very existence of the useless, which art's total subsumption under usefulness has abolished. In adapting itself entirely to need, the work of art defrauds human beings in advance of the liberation from the principle of utility which it is supposed to bring about. What might be called use value in the reception of cultural assets is being replaced by exchange value; enjoyment is giving way to being there and being in the know, connoisseurship by enhanced prestige. The consumer becomes the ideology of the amusement industry, whose institutions he or she cannot escape. One has to have seen Mrs. Miniver, just as one must subscribe to *Life* and *Time*. Everything is perceived only from the point of view that it can serve as something else, however vaguely that other thing might be envisaged. Everything has value only in so far as it can be exchanged, not in so far as it is something in itself. For consumers the use value of art, its essence, is a fetish, and the fetish—the social valuation which they mistake for the merit of works of art—becomes its only use value, the only quality they enjoy. In this way the commodity character of art disintegrates just as it is fully realized. Art becomes a species of commodity, worked up and adapted to industrial production, saleable and exchangeable; but art as the species of commodity which exists in order to be sold yet not for sale becomes something hypocritically unsaleable as soon as the business transaction is no longer merely its intention but its sole principle. The Toscanini performance on the radio is, in a sense, unsaleable. One listens to it for nothing, and each note of the symphony is accompanied, as it were, by the sublime advertisement that the symphony is not being interrupted by advertisements—"This concert is brought to you as a public service." The deception takes place indirectly *via* the profit of all the united automobile and soap manufacturers, on whose payments the stations survive, and, of course, *via* the increased sales of the electrical industry as the producer of the receiver sets. Radio, the progressive latecomer to mass culture, is drawing conclusions which film's pseudomarket at present denies that industry. The technical structure of the commercial radio system makes it immune to liberal deviations of the kind the film industry can still permit itself in its own preserve. Film is a private enterprise which already represents the sovereign whole, in which respect it has some advantages over the other individual combines. Chesterfield is merely the nation's cigarette, but the radio is its mouthpiece. In the total assimilation of culture products into the commodity sphere radio makes no attempt to purvey its products as commodities. In America it levies no duty from the public. It thereby takes on the deceptive form of a disinterested, impartial authority, which fits fascism like a glove. In fascism radio becomes the universal mouthpiece of the *Führer;* in the loudspeakers on the street his voice merges with the howl of sirens proclaiming panic, from which modern propaganda is hard to distinguish in any case. The National Socialists knew that broadcasting gave their cause stature as the printing press did to the Reformation. The *Führer's* metaphysical charisma, invented by the sociology of religion, turned out finally to be merely the omnipresence of his radio addresses, which demonically parodies that of the divine spirit. The gigantic fact that the speech penetrates everywhere replaces its content, as the benevolent act of the Toscanini broadcast supplants its content, the symphony. No listener can apprehend the symphony's true coherence, while the *Führer*'s address is in any case a lie. To posit the human word as absolute, the false commandment, is the immanent tendency of radio. Recommendation becomes command. The promotion of identical commodities under different brand names, the scientifically endorsed praise of the laxative in the slick voice of the announcer between the overtures of *La Traviata* and *Rienzi,* has become untenable if only for its silliness. One day the *Diktat* of production, the specific advertisement, veiled by the semblance of choice, can finally become the *Führer*'s overt command. In a society of large-scale fascistic rackets which agree among themselves on how much of the national product is to be allocated to providing for the needs of the people, to invite the people to use a particular soap powder would, in the end, seem anachronistic. In a more modern, less ceremonious style, the *Führer* directly orders both the holocaust and the supply of trash.

Today works of art, suitably packaged like political slogans, are pressed on a reluctant public at reduced prices by the culture industry; they are opened up for popular enjoyment like parks. However, the erosion of their genuine commodity character does not mean that they would be abolished in the life of a free society but that the last barrier to their debasement as cultural assets has now been removed. The abolition of educational privilege by disposing of culture at bargain prices does not admit the masses to the preserves from which they were formerly excluded but, under the existing social conditions, contributes to the decay of education and the progress of barbaric incoherence. Someone who in the nineteenth or early twentieth century spent money to attend a drama or a concert, paid the performance at least as much respect as the money spent. The citizen who wanted a return for his outlay might occasionally try to establish some connection to the work. The guidebooks to Wagner's music dramas or the commentaries on *Faust* bear witness to this. They form a transition to the biographical glaze applied to works of art and the other practices to which works of art are subjected today. Even when the art business was in the bloom of youth, use value was not dragged along as a mere appendage by exchange value but was developed as a precondition of the latter, to the social benefit of works of art. As long as it was expensive, art kept the citizen within some bounds. That is now over. Art's unbounded proximity to those exposed to it, no longer mediated by money, completes the alienation between work and consumer, which resemble each other in triumphant reification. In the culture industry respect is vanishing along with criticism: the latter gives way to mechanical expertise, the former to the forgetful cult of celebrities. For consumers, nothing is expensive any more. Nevertheless, they are dimly aware that the less something costs, the less it can be a gift to them. The twofold mistrust of traditional culture as ideology mingles with that of industrialized culture as fraud. Reduced to mere adjuncts, the degraded works of art are secretly rejected by their happy recipients along with the junk the medium has made them resemble. The public should rejoice that there is so much to see and hear. And indeed, everything is to be had. The "screenos"[12] and cinema vaudevilles, the competitions in recognizing musical extracts, the free magazines, rewards, and gift articles handed out to the listeners of certain radio programs are not mere accidents, but continue what is happening to the culture products themselves. The symphony is becoming the prize for listening to the radio at all, and if the technology had its way the film would already be delivered to the apartment on the model of the radio. It is moving towards the commercial system. Television points the way to a development which easily enough could push the Warner brothers into the doubtless unwelcome position of little theatre performers and cultural conservatives. However, the pursuit of prizes has already left its imprint on consumer behavior. Because culture presents itself as a bonus, with unquestioned private and social benefits, its reception has become a matter of taking one's chances. The public crowds forward for fear of missing something. What that might be is unclear, but, at any rate, only those who join in have any chance. Fascism, however, hopes to reorganize the gift-receivers trained by the culture industry into its enforced adherents.

Culture is a paradoxical commodity. It is so completely subject to the law of exchange that it is no longer exchanged; it is so blindly equated with use that it can no longer be used. For this reason it merges with the advertisement. The more meaningless the latter appears under monopoly, the more omnipotent culture becomes. Its motives are economic enough. That life could continue without the whole culture industry is too certain; the satiation and apathy it generates among consumers are too great. It can do little to combat this from its own resources. Advertising is its elixir of life. But because its product ceaselessly reduces the pleasure it promises as a commodity to that mere promise, it finally coincides with the advertisement it needs on account of its own inability to please. In the competitive society advertising performed a social service in orienting the buyer in the market, facilitating choice and helping the more efficient but unknown supplier to find customers. It did not merely cost labor time, but saved it. Today, when the free market is coming to an end, those in control of the system are entrenching themselves in advertising. It strengthens the bond which shackles consumers to the big combines. Only those who can keep paying the exorbitant fees charged by the advertising agencies, and most of all by radio itself, that is, those who are already part of the system or are co-opted into it by the decisions of banks and industrial capital, can enter the pseudomarket as sellers. The costs of advertising, which finally flow back into the pockets of the combines, spare them the troublesome task of subduing unwanted outsiders; they guarantee that the wielders of influence remain among their peers, not unlike the resolutions of economic councils which control the establishment and continuation of businesses in the totalitarian state. Advertising today is a negative principle, a blocking device: anything which does not bear its seal of approval is economically suspect. All-pervasive advertising is certainly not needed to acquaint people with the goods on offer, the varieties of which are limited in any case. It benefits the selling of goods only directly. The termination of a familiar advertising campaign by an individual firm represents a loss of prestige, and is indeed an offence against the discipline which the leading clique imposes on its members. In wartime, commodities which can no longer be supplied continue to be advertised merely as a display of industrial power. At such times the subsidizing of the ideological media is more important than the repetition of names. Through their ubiquitous use under the pressure of the system, advertising techniques have invaded the idiom, the "style" of the culture industry. So complete is their triumph that in key positions it is no longer even explicit: the imposing buildings of the big companies, floodlit advertisements in stone, are free of advertising, merely displaying the illuminated company initials on their pinnacles, with no further need of self-congratulation. By contrast, the buildings surviving from the nineteenth century, the architecture of which still shamefully reveals their utility as consumer goods, their function as accommodation, are covered from basement to above roof level with hoardings and banners: the landscape becomes a mere background for signboards and symbols. Advertising becomes simply the art with which Goebbels presciently equated it, *l'art pour l'art*, advertising for advertising's sake, the pure representation of social power. In the influential American magazines *Life* and *Fortune* the images and texts of advertisements are, at a cursory glance, hardly distinguishable from the editorial section. The enthusiastic and unpaid picture story about the living habits and personal grooming of celebrities, which wins them new fans, is editorial, while the advertising pages rely on photographs and data so factual and lifelike that they represent the ideal of information to which the editorial section only aspires. Every film is a preview of the next, which promises yet again to unite the same heroic couple under the same exotic sun: anyone arriving late cannot tell whether he is watching the trailer or the real thing. The montage character of the culture industry, the synthetic, controlled manner in which its products are assembled—factory-like not only in the film studio but also, virtually, in the compilation of the cheap biographies, journalistic novels, and hit songs—predisposes it to advertising: the individual moment, in being detachable, replaceable, estranged even technically from any coherence of meaning, lends itself to purposes outside the work. The special effect, the trick, the isolated and repeatable individual performance have always conspired with the exhibition of commodities for advertising purposes, and today every close-up of a film actress is an advert for her name, every hit song a plug for its tune. Advertising and the culture industry are merging technically no less than economically. In both, the same thing appears in countless places, and the mechanical repetition of the same culture product is already that of the same propaganda slogan. In both, under the dictate of effectiveness, technique is becoming psychotechnique, a procedure for manipulating human beings. In both, the norms of the striking yet familiar, the easy but catchy, the worldly wise but straightforward hold good; everything is directed at overpowering a customer conceived as distracted or resistant.

Through the language they speak, the customers make their own contribution to culture as advertising. For the more completely language coincides with communication, the more words change from substantial carriers of meaning to signs devoid of qualities; the more purely and transparently they communicate what they designate, the more impenetrable they become. The demythologizing of language, as an element of the total process of enlightenment, reverts to magic. In magic word and content were at once different from each other and indissolubly linked. Concepts like melancholy, history, indeed, life, were apprehended in the word which both set them apart and preserved them. Its particular form constituted and reflected them at the same time. The trenchant distinction which declares the word itself fortuitous and its allocation to its object arbitrary does away with the superstitious commingling of word and thing. Anything in a given sequence of letters which goes beyond the correlation to the event designated is banished as unclear and as verbal metaphysics. As a result, the word, which henceforth is allowed only to designate something and not to mean it, becomes so fixated on the object that it hardens to a formula. This affects language and subject matter equally. Instead of raising a matter to the level of experience, the purified word exhibits it as a case of an abstract moment, and everything else, severed from now defunct expression by the demand for pitiless clarity, therefore withers in reality also. The outside-left in football, the blackshirt,[13] the Hitler Youth member, and others of their kind are no more than what they are called. If, before its rationalization, the word had set free not only longing but lies, in its rationalized form it has become a straightjacket more for longing than for lies. The blindness and muteness of the data to which positivism reduces the world passes over into language itself, which is limited to registering those data. Thus relationships themselves become impenetrable, taking on an impact, a power of adhesion and repulsion which makes them resemble their extreme antithesis, spells. They act once more like the practices of a kind of sorcery, whether the name of a diva is concocted in the studio on the basis of statistical data, or welfare government is averted by the use of taboo-laden words such as "bureaucracy" and "intellectuals," or vileness exonerates itself by invoking the name of a homeland. The name, to which magic most readily attaches, is today undergoing a chemical change. It is being transformed into arbitrary, manipulable designations, the power of which, although calculable, is for that reason as willful as that of archaic names. First names, the archaic residues, have been brought up to date either by stylizing them into advertising brands—film stars' surnames have become first names—or by standardizing them collectively. By contrast, the bourgeois, family name which, instead of being a trademark, individualized its bearers by relating them to their own prehistory, sounds old-fashioned. In Americans it arouses a curious unease. To conceal the uncomfortable distance existing between particular people they call themselves Bob and Harry, like replaceable members of teams. Such forms of interaction reduce human beings to the brotherhood of the sporting public, which protects them from true fraternity. Signification, the only function of the word admitted by semantics, is consummated in the sign. Its character as sign is reinforced by the speed with which linguistic models are put into circulation from above. Whether folksongs are rightly or wrongly called upper-class culture which has come down in the world, their elements have at least taken on their popular form in a long, highly mediated process of experience. The dissemination of popular songs, by contrast, is practically instantaneous. The American term "fad" for fashions which catch on epidemically—inflamed by the action of highly concentrated economic powers—referred to this phenomenon long before totalitarian advertising bosses had laid down the general lines of culture in their countries. If the German fascists launch a word like "intolerable" [*Untragbar*] over the loudspeakers one day, the whole nation is saying "intolerable" the next. On the same pattern, the nations against which the German *Blitzkrieg* was directed have adopted it in their own jargon. The universal repetition of the term denoting such measures makes the measures, too, familiar, just as, at the time of the free market, the brand name on everyone's lips increased sales. The blind and rapidly spreading repetition of designated words links advertising to the totalitarian slogan. The layer of experience which made words human like those who spoke them has been stripped away, and in its prompt appropriation language takes on the coldness which hitherto was peculiar to billboards and the advertising sections of newspapers. Countless people use words and expressions which they either have ceased to understand at all or use only according to their behavioral functions, just as trademarks adhere all the more compulsively to their objects the less their linguistic meaning is apprehended. The Minister of Public Education speaks ignorantly of "dynamic forces," and the hit songs sing endlessly of "reverie" and "rhapsody," hitching their popularity to the magic of the incomprehensible as if to some deep intimation of a higher life. Other stereotypes, such as "memory," are still partly comprehended, but become detached from the experience which might fulfill them. They obtrude into the spoken language like enclaves. On the German radio of Flesch and Hitler they are discernible in the affected diction of the announcer, who pronounces phrases like "Goodnight, listeners," or "This is the Hitler Youth speaking," or even "the *Führer*" with an inflection which passes into the mother tongue of millions. In such turns of phrase the last bond between sedimented experience and language, which still exerted a reconciling influence in dialect in the nineteenth century, is severed. By contrast, in the hands of the editor whose supple opinions have promoted him to the status of *Schriftleiter*, German words become petrified and alien. In any word one can distinguish how far it has been disfigured by the fascist "folk" community. By now, of course, such language has become universal, totalitarian. The violence done to words is no longer audible in them. The radio announcer does not need to talk in an affected voice; indeed, he would be impossible if his tone differed from that of his designated listeners. This means, however, that the language and gestures of listeners and spectators are more deeply permeated by the patterns of the culture industry than ever before, in nuances still beyond the reach of experimental methods. Today the culture industry has taken over the civilizing inheritance of the frontier and entrepreneurial democracy, whose receptivity to intellectual deviations was never too highly developed. All are free to dance and amuse themselves, just as, since the historical neutralization of religion, they have been free to join any of the countless sects. But freedom to choose an ideology, which always reflects economic coercion, everywhere proves to be freedom to be the same. The way in which the young girl accepts and performs the obligatory date, the tone of voice used on the telephone and in the most intimate situations, the choice of words in conversation, indeed, the whole inner life compartmentalized according to the categories of vulgarized depth psychology, bears witness to the attempt to turn oneself into an apparatus meeting the requirements of success, an apparatus which, even in its unconscious impulses, conforms to the model presented by the culture industry. The most intimate reactions of human beings have become so entirely reified, even to themselves, that the idea of anything peculiar to them survives only in extreme abstraction: personality means hardly more than dazzling white teeth and freedom from body odor and emotions. That is the triumph of advertising in the culture industry: the compulsive imitation by consumers of cultural commodities which, at the same time, they recognize as false.

NOTES

1. Nietzsche, *Unzeitgemässe Betrachtungen. Werke*, Leipzig 1917, Vol. 1, p. 187.
2. "Pathé": French film magnates.
3. A. de Tocqueville, *De la Démocratie en Amérique*, Paris 1864, Vol. II, p. 151.
4. "Hays Office": Voluntary censorship agency, set up in 1934 in Hollywood.
5. "Casino de Paris": Music hall in Paris, famous for its luxurious furnishings.
6. "Lombardo": Orchestra leader especially known for his annual musical broadcast on New Year's Eve.
7. "novelty songs": Hit songs with comic elements.
8. "Mrs. Miniver": Leading role in radio family serial; also filmed.
9. Frank Wedekind, *Gesammelte Werke*, Munich 1921, Vol. IX, p. 426.
10. "women's serials": Light novels in women's magazines.
11. "Mature...Rooney": Well-known film actors, embodiments of the hero and the antihero.
12. "screenos": Bingo games played by the audience between pictures.
13. "blackshirt": A term for fascists, after the black shirts of their uniforms, especially in Italy but also in other countries.

SHORT DESCRIPTION OF A NEW TECHNIQUE OF ACTING WHICH PRODUCES AN ALIENATION EFFECT (1940)

BERTOLT BRECHT

Translated from the German by John Willett

A playwright, Brecht called for a new style of acting, which he dubbed the alienation effect. The alienation effect encourages audiences not to identify with the performers on the stage or the roles that the performers play. Contrary to the usual Stanislavskian or "method" acting that asks performers to absorb themselves into their roles and invites audiences to lose themselves in a trance of realism, Brecht asked for staging and acting that calls attention to itself as performance. Let the lights go on, he said (versus the classical Hollywood assumptions of a darkened theater, as Laura Mulvey notes in her essay in this volume). Let the lights stay visible, and let the performers act in ways that expose their role as actresses and actors, so that audiences can have a critical distance that allows them to question ideological assumptions instead of letting interpellation smother their skepticism. Readers can transfer Brecht's argument about staging into parallel arguments about poetry or fiction that calls attention to itself as performed, constructed writing instead of encouraging audiences to see the literary text as a passive window to or transcript of unquestionable truth and realism.

Readers may compare Brecht's notion of an alienation effect to the notion of defamiliarization in Victor Shklovsky's essay in this volume.

While most of Brecht's notes are not included here, some of them centrally continue the argument of his essay, and those central notes are included.

What follows represents an attempt to describe a technique of acting which was applied in certain theatres with a view to taking the incidents portrayed and alienating them from the spectator. The aim of this technique, known as the alienation effect, was to make the spectator adopt an attitude of inquiry and criticism in his approach to the incident. The means were artistic.

The first condition for the A-effect's application to this end is that stage and auditorium must be purged of everything "magical" and that no "hypnotic tensions" should be set up. This ruled out any attempt to make the stage convey the flavour of a particular place (a room at evening, a road in the autumn), or to create atmosphere by relaxing the tempo of the conversation. The audience was not "worked up" by a display of temperament or "swept away" by acting with tautened muscles; in short, no attempt was made to put it in a trance and give it the illusion of watching an ordinary unrehearsed event. As will be seen presently, the audience's tendency to plunge into such illusions has to be checked by specific artistic means.[1]

The first condition for the achievement of the A-effect is that the actor must invest what he has to show with a definite gest of showing. It is of course necessary to drop the assumption that there is a fourth wall cutting the audience off from the stage and the consequent illusion that the stage action is taking place in reality and without an audience. That being so, it is possible for the actor in principle to address the audience direct.

It is well known that contact between audience and stage is normally made on the basis of empathy. Conventional actors devote their efforts so exclusively to bringing about this psychological operation that they may be said to see it as the principal aim of their art.[2] Our introductory remarks will already have made it clear that the technique which produces an A-effect is the exact opposite of that which aims at empathy. The actor applying it is bound not to try to bring about the empathy operation.

Yet in his efforts to reproduce particular characters and show their behaviour he need not renounce the means of empathy entirely. He uses these means just as any normal person with no particular acting talent would use them if he wanted to portray someone else, i.e., show how he behaves. This showing of other people's behaviour happens time and again in ordinary life (witnesses of an accident demonstrating to newcomers how the victim behaved, a facetious person imitating a friend's walk, etc.), without those involved making the least effort to subject their spectators to an illusion. At the same time they do feel their way into their characters' skins with a view to acquiring their characteristics.

As has already been said, the actor too will make use of this psychological operation. But whereas the usual practice in acting is to execute it during the actual performance, in the hope of stimulating the spectator into a similar operation, he will achieve it only at an earlier stage, at some time during rehearsals.

To safeguard against an unduly "impulsive," frictionless and uncritical creation of characters and incidents, more reading rehearsals can be held than usual. The actor should refrain from living himself into the part prematurely in any way, and should go on functioning as long as possible as a reader (which does not mean a reader-aloud). An important step is memorizing one's first impressions.

When reading his part the actor's attitude should be one of a man who is astounded and contradicts. Not only the occurrence of the incidents, as he reads about them, but the conduct of the man he is playing, as he experiences it, must be weighed up by him and their peculiarities understood; none can be taken as given, as something that "was bound to turn out that way," that was "only to be expected from a character like that." Before memorizing the words he must memorize what he felt astounded at and where he felt impelled to contradict. For these are dynamic forces that he must preserve in creating his performance.

When he appears on the stage, besides what he actually is doing he will at all essential points discover, specify, imply what he is not doing; that is to say he will act in such a way that the alternative emerges as clearly as possible, that his acting allows the other possibilities to be inferred and only represents one out of the possible variants. He will say for instance "You'll pay for that," and not say "I forgive you." He detests his children; it is not the case that he loves them. He moves down stage left and not up stage right. Whatever he doesn't do must be contained and conserved in what he does. In this way every sentence and every gesture signifies a decision; the character remains under observation and is tested. The technical term for this procedure is "fixing the 'not . . . but.' "

The actor does not allow himself to become completely transformed on the stage into the character he is portraying. He is not Lear, Harpagon, Schweik; he shows them. He reproduces their remarks as authentically as he can; he puts forward their way of behaving to the best of his abilities and knowledge of men; but he never tries to persuade himself (and thereby others) that this amounts to a complete transformation. Actors will know what it means if I say that a typical kind of acting without this complete transformation takes place when a producer or colleague shows one how to play a particular passage. It is not his own part, so he is not completely transformed; he underlines the technical aspect and retains the attitude of someone just making suggestions.

Once the idea of total transformation is abandoned the actor speaks his part not as if he were improvising it himself but like a quotation. At the same time he obviously has to render all the quotation's overtones, the remark's full human and concrete shape; similarly the gesture he makes must have the full substance of a human gesture even though it now represents a copy.

Given this absence of total transformation in the acting there are three aids which may help to alienate the actions and remarks of the characters being portrayed:

1. Transposition into the third person.
2. Transposition into the past.
3. Speaking the stage directions out loud.

Using the third person and the past tense allows the actor to adopt the right attitude of detachment. In addition he will look for stage directions and remarks that comment on his lines, and speak them aloud at rehearsal ("He stood up and exclaimed angrily, not having eaten:..., " or "He had never been told so before, and didn't know if it was true or not, " or "He smiled, and said with forced nonchalance:..."). Speaking the stage directions out loud in the third person results in a clash between two tones of voice, alienating the second of them, the text proper. This style of acting is further alienated by taking place on the stage after having already been outlined and announced in words. Transposing it into the past gives the speaker a standpoint from which he can look back at his sentence. The sentence too is thereby alienated without the speaker adopting an unreal point of view; unlike the spectator, he has read the play right through and is better placed to judge the sentence in accordance with the ending, with its consequences, than the former, who knows less and is more of a stranger to the sentence.

This composite process leads to an alienation of the text in the rehearsals which generally persists in the performance too.[3] The directness of the relationship with the audience allows and indeed forces the actual speech delivery to be varied in accordance with the greater or smaller significance attaching to the sentences. Take the case of witnesses addressing a court. The underlinings, the characters' insistence on their remarks, must be developed as a piece of effective virtuosity. If the actor turns to the audience it must be a whole-hearted turn rather than the asides and soliloquizing technique of the old-fashioned theatre. To get the full A-effect from the poetic medium the actor should start at rehearsal by paraphrasing the verse's content in vulgar prose, possibly accompanying this by the gestures designed for the verse. A daring and beautiful handling of verbal media will alienate the text. (Prose can be alienated by translation into the actor's native dialect.)

Gesture will be dealt with later, but it can at once be said that everything to do with the emotions has to be externalized; that is to say, it must be developed into a gesture. The actor has to find a sensibly perceptible outward expression for his character's emotions, preferably some action that gives away what is going on inside him. The emotion in question must be brought out, must lose all its restrictions so that it can be treated on a big scale. Special elegance, power and grace of gesture bring about the A-effect.

A masterly use of gesture can be seen in Chinese acting. The Chinese actor achieves the A-effect by being seen to observe his own movements.

Whatever the actor offers in the way of gesture, verse structure, etc., must be finished and bear the hallmarks of something rehearsed and rounded-off. The impression to be given is one of ease, which is at the same time one of difficulties overcome. The actor must make it possible for the audience to take his own art, his mastery of technique, lightly too. He puts an incident before the spectator with perfection and as he thinks it really happened or might have happened. He does not conceal the fact that he has rehearsed it, any more than an acrobat conceals his training, and he emphasizes that it is his own (actor's) account, view, version of the incident.

Because he doesn't identify himself with him he can pick a definite attitude to adopt towards the character whom be portrays, can show what he thinks of him and invite the spectator, who is likewise not asked to identify himself, to criticize the character portrayed.

The attitude which he adopts is a socially critical one. In his exposition of the incidents and in his characterization of the person he tries to bring out those features which come within society's sphere. In this way his performance becomes a discussion (about social conditions) with the audience he is addressing. He prompts the spectator to justify or abolish these conditions according to what class he belongs to.[4]

The object of the A-effect is to alienate the social gest underlying every incident. By social gest is meant the mimetic and gestural expression of the social relationships prevailing between people of a given period.[5]

It helps to formulate the incident for society, and to put it across in such a way that society is given the key, if titles are thought up for the scenes. These titles must have a historical quality.

This brings us to a crucial technical device: historicization.

The actor must play the incidents as historical ones. Historical incidents are unique, transitory incidents associated with particular periods. The conduct of the persons involved in them is not fixed and "universally human"; it includes elements that have been or may be overtaken by the course of history, and is subject to criticism from the immediately following period's point of view. The conduct of those born before us is alienated* from us by an incessant evolution.

It is up to the actor to treat present-day events and modes of behaviour with the same detachment as the historian adopts with regard to those of the past. He must alienate these characters and incidents from us.

Characters and incidents from ordinary life, from our immediate surroundings, being familiar, strike us as more or less natural. Alienating them helps to make them seem remarkable to us. Science has carefully developed a technique of getting irritated with the everyday, "self-evident", universally accepted occurrence, and there is no reason why this infinitely useful attitude should not be taken over by art.[6] It is an attitude which arose in science as a result of the growth in human productive powers. In art the same motive applies.

As for the emotions, the experimental use of the A-effect in the epic theatre's German productions indicated that this way of acting too can stimulate them, though possibly a different class of emotion is involved from those of the orthodox theatre. A critical attitude on the audience's part is a thoroughly artistic one. Nor does the actual practice of the A-effect seem anything like so unnatural as its description. Of course it is a way of acting that has nothing to do with stylization as commonly practised. The main advantage of the epic theatre with its A-effect, intended purely to show the world in such a way that it becomes manageable, is precisely its quality of being natural and earthly, its humour and its renunciation of all the mystical elements that have stuck to the orthodox theatre from the old days.

NOTES

1. E.g., such mechanical means as very brilliant illumination of the stage (since a half-lit stage plus a completely darkened auditorium makes the spectator less level-headed by preventing him from observing his neighbour and in turn hiding him from his neighbour's eyes) and also *making visible the sources of light.*

MAKING VISIBLE THE SOURCES OF LIGHT

There is a point in showing the lighting apparatus openly, as it is one of the means of preventing an unwanted element of illusion; it scarcely disturbs the necessary concentration. If we light the actors and their performance in such a way that the lights themselves are within the spectator's field of vision we destroy part of his illusion of being present at a spontaneous, transitory, authentic, unrehearsed event. He sees that arrangements have been made to show

---

*   *Entfremdet.*

something; something is being repeated here under special conditions, for instance in a very brilliant light. Displaying the actual lights is meant to be a counter to the old-fashioned theatre's efforts to hide them. No one would expect the lighting to be hidden at a sporting event, a boxing match for instance. Whatever the points of difference between the modern theatre's presentations and those of a sporting promoter, they do not include the same concealment of the sources of light as the old theatre found necessary. *(Brecht: "Der Bühnenbau des epischen Theaters")*

2. Cf. these remarks by Poul Reumert, the best-known Danish actor:

...If I feel I am *dying*, and if I *really* feel it, then so does everybody else; if I act as though I had a dagger in my hand, and am entirely filled by the one idea of killing the child, then everybody shudders....The whole business is a matter of mental activity being communicated by emotions, or the other way round if you prefer it: a feeling so strong as to be an obsession, which is translated into thoughts. If it comes off it is the most infectious thing in the world: anything external is then a matter of complete indifference....

And Rapaport, "The Work of the Actor," *Theater Workshop*, October 1936:

...On the stage the actor is surrounded entirely by fictions....The actor must be able to regard all this as though it were true, as though he were convinced that all that surrounds him on the stage is a living reality and, along with himself, he must convince the audience as well. This is the central feature of our method of work on the part....Take any object, a cap for example; lay it on the table or on the floor and try to regard it as though it were a rat; make believe that it is a rat, and not a cap....Picture what sort of a rat it is; what size, colour?...We thus commit ourselves to believe quite naïvely that the object before us is something other than it is and, at the same time, learn to compel the audience to believe....

This might be thought to be a course of instruction for conjurers, but in fact it is a course of acting, supposedly according to Stanislavsky's method. One wonders if a technique that equips an actor to make the audience see rats where there aren't any can really be all that suitable for disseminating the truth. Given enough alcohol it doesn't take acting to persuade almost anybody that he is seeing rats: pink ones.

3. The theatre can create the corresponding A-effect in the performance in a number of ways. The Munich production of *Edward II* for the first time had titles preceding the scenes, announcing the contents. The Berlin production of *The Threepenny Opera* had the titles of the songs projected while they were sung. The Berlin production of *Mann ist Mann* had the actors' figures projected on big screens during the action.

4. Another thing that makes for freedom in the actor's relationship with his audience is that he does not treat it as an undifferentiated mass. He doesn't boil it down to a shapeless dumpling in the stockpot of the emotions. He does not address himself to everybody alike; he allows the existing divisions within the audience to continue, in fact he widens them. He has friends and enemies in the audience; he is friendly to the one group and hostile to the other. He takes sides, not necessarily with his character but if not with it then against it. (At least, that is his basic attitude, though it too must be variable and change according to what the character may say at different stages. There may, however, also be points at which everything is in the balance and the actor must withhold judgment, though this again must be expressly shown in his acting.)

5. If *King Lear* (in Act I, scene 1) tears up a map when he divides his kingdom between his daughters, then the act of division is alienated. Not only does it draw our attention to his kingdom,

but by treating the kingdom so plainly as his own private property he throws some light on the basis of the feudal idea of the family. In *Julius Caesar* the tyrant's murder by Brutus is alienated if during one of his monologues accusing Caesar of tyrannical motives he himself maltreats a slave waiting on him. Weigel as *Maria Stuart* suddenly took the crucifix hanging round her neck and used it coquettishly as a fan, to give herself air. (See too Brecht: "Übungsstücke für Schauspieler" in *Versuche 11*, p. 107.)

6. THE A-EFFECT AS A PROCEDURE IN EVERYDAY LIFE

The achievement of the A-effect constitutes something utterly ordinary, recurrent; it is just a widely-practised way of drawing one's own or someone else's attention to a thing, and it can be seen in education as also in business conferences of one sort or another. The A-effect consists in turning the object of which one is to be made aware, to which one's attention is to be drawn, from something ordinary, familiar, immediately accessible, into something peculiar, striking and unexpected. What is obvious is in a certain sense made incomprehensible, but this is only in order that it may then be made all the easier to comprehend. Before familiarity can turn into awareness the familiar must be stripped of its inconspicuousness; we must give up assuming that the object in question needs no explanation. However frequently recurrent, modest, vulgar it may be it will now be labelled as something unusual.

A common use of the A-effect is when someone says: "Have you ever really looked carefully at your watch?" The questioner knows that I've looked at it often enough, and now his question deprives me of the sight which I've grown used to and which accordingly has nothing more to say to me. I used to look at it to see the time, and now when he asks me in this importunate way I realize that I have given up seeing the watch itself with an astonished eye; and it is in many ways an astonishing piece of machinery. Similarly it is an alienation effect of the simplest sort if a business discussion starts off with the sentence: "Have you ever thought what happens to the waste from your factory which is pumped into the river twenty-four hours a day?" This waste wasn't just swept down the river unobserved; it was carefully channelled into the river; men and machines have worked on it; the river has changed colour, the waste has flowed away most conspicuously, but just as waste. It was superfluous to the process of manufacture, and now it is to become material for manufacture; our eye turns to it with interest. The asking of the question has alienated it, and intentionally so. The very simplest sentences that apply in the A-effect are those with "Not—But": (He didn't say "come in" but "keep moving." He was not pleased but amazed). They include an expectation which is justified by experience but, in the event, disappointed. One might have thought that...but one oughtn't to have thought it. There was not just one possibility but two; both are introduced, then the second one is alienated, then the first as well. To see one's mother as a man's wife one needs an A-effect; this is provided, for instance, when one acquires a stepfather. If one sees one's teacher hounded by the bailiffs an A-effect occurs: one is jerked out of a relationship in which the teacher seems big into one where he seems small. An alienation of the motor-car takes place if after driving a modern car for a long while we drive an old model T Ford. Suddenly we hear explosions once more; the motor works on the principle of explosion. We start feeling amazed that such a vehicle, indeed any vehicle not drawn by animal-power, can move; in short, we understand cars, by looking at them as something strange, new, as a triumph of engineering and to that extent something unnatural. Nature, which certainly embraces the motor-car, is suddenly imbued with an element of unnaturalness, and from now on this is an indelible part of the concept of nature.

The expression "in fact" can likewise certify or alienate. (He wasn't in fact at home; he said he would be, but we didn't believe him and had a look; or again, we didn't think it possible for him not to be at home, but it was a fact.) The term "actually" is just as conducive to alienation. ("I don't actually agree.") Similarly the Eskimo definition "A car is a wingless aircraft that crawls along the ground" is a way of alienating the car.

In a sense the alienation effect itself has been alienated by the above explanation; we have taken a common, recurrent, universally-practiced operation and tried to draw attention to it by illuminating its peculiarity. But we have achieved the effect only with those people who have truly ("in fact") grasped that it does "not" result from every representation "but" from certain ones: only "actually" is it familiar.

IDEOLOGY AND IDEOLOGICAL STATE APPARATUSES (NOTES TOWARDS AN INVESTIGATION) (1970)

LOUIS ALTHUSSER

Translated from the French by Ben Brewster

Althusser proposes that for the economy and state to continue producing they must reproduce themselves. And production, he argues, reproduces itself through ideology. Laborers continue to labor because they absorb the ideology that tells them to labor. Althusser then moves to three constellations of related concepts: ideological state apparatuses, ideology as the imaginary relationship to real conditions, and interpellation. Let us introduce those three concepts one by one.

The state depends on what Althusser calls the repressive state apparatus (RSA) and the ideological state apparatuses (ISAs). The RSA—the police, military, courts, and prisons—rules by violence or the potential for violence. The ISAs—schools, the family, religion, the legal system, the political system, political parties, unions, the media, the arts, sports—rule by ideology. What, then, is ideology? According to Althusser (and here is where the current selection from his essay begins, a little over halfway through), ideology is our imaginary relationship to real conditions. We misrecognize the world around us. We do not see its real conditions. Instead, we see the ideology that paints the world in imaginary ways, telling us that we are free subjects. The term subject *can mean agent, like the subject of a sentence. But in reality, Althusser argues, we are subjects in a different sense. We are subjects to ideology, in the same sense that someone may be subject to the law or the king. Ideology reproduces itself by masking reality in our imaginary relationships. It recruits us as subjects, making us believe that by going along with the system, we work for our own good, even though the system actually goes against our own interests. The RSA does not usually need to act because the ISAs, especially schools and families, teach us to believe in the dominant ideology without recognizing it. We do not recognize that we are in ideology. Even so, ideology calls out to us, enticing us to misrecognize it as reality; to believe in the naturalness, rightness, and inevitability of the capitalist economy and state; to believe that we are free subjects, although in reality our freedom is only imaginary.*

Althusser names that calling out interpellation *(which means calling) or* hailing *(which means calling out and saying hello). Interpellation is thus the process of being passively, unconsciously absorbed into the assumptions of the dominant culture, even against our best interests. Althusser thus invites us to ask how and when literary and cultural discourses implicitly call to us (interpellate or hail us), such as when, for example, they use words like "you," "us," or "we" (as in this headnote) or when a national anthem plays, or in yet subtler ways, drawing us into accepting the culture's assumptions without even realizing it. The ideology of the dominant culture comes to seem natural, obvious, inevitable, true, like common sense, and only by seeming natural, obvious, inevitable, true, and like common sense can it persuade us to go along with its assumptions, to overlook the real condition that the ruling ideology is not any of those things and that we would do better to oppose it.*

IDEOLOGY IS A "REPRESENTATION" OF THE IMAGINARY RELATIONSHIP OF INDIVIDUALS TO THEIR REAL CONDITIONS OF EXISTENCE

In order to approach my central thesis on the structure and functioning of ideology, I shall first present two theses, one negative, the other positive. The first concerns the object which is "represented" in the imaginary form of ideology, the second concerns the materiality of ideology.

THESIS I: Ideology represents the imaginary relationship of individuals to their real conditions of existence.

We commonly call religious ideology, ethical ideology, legal ideology, political ideology, etc., so many "world outlooks." Of course, assuming that we do not live one of these ideologies as the truth (e.g. "believe" in God, Duty, Justice, etc....), we admit that the ideology we are discussing from a critical point of view, examining it as the ethnologist examines the myths of a "primitive society," that these "world outlooks" are largely imaginary, i.e., do not "correspond to reality."

However, while admitting that they do not correspond to reality, i.e., that they constitute an illusion, we admit that they do make allusion to reality, and that they need only be "interpreted" to discover the reality of the world behind their imaginary representation of that world (ideology = *illusion/allusion*).

There are different types of interpretation, the most famous of which are the *mechanistic* type, current in the eighteenth century (God is the imaginary representation of the real King), and the "*hermeneutic*" interpretation, inaugurated by the earliest Church Fathers, and revived by Feuerbach and the theologico-philosophical school which descends from him, e.g., the theologian Barth (to Feuerbach, for example, God is the essence of real Man). The essential point is that on condition that we interpret the imaginary transposition (and inversion) of ideology we arrive at the conclusion that in ideology "men represent their real conditions of existence to themselves in an imaginary form."

Unfortunately, this interpretation leaves one small problem unsettled: why do men "need" this imaginary transposition of their real conditions of existence in order to "represent to themselves" their real conditions of existence?

The first answer (that of the eighteenth century) proposes a simple solution: Priests or Despots are responsible. They "forged" the Beautiful Lies so that, in the belief that they were obeying God, men would in fact obey the Priests and Despots, who are usually in alliance in their imposture, the Priests acting in the interests of the Despots or vice versa, according to the political positions of the "theoreticians" concerned. There is therefore a cause for the imaginary transposition of the real conditions of existence: that cause is the existence of a small number of cynical men who base their domination and exploitation of the "people" on a falsified representation of the world which they have imagined in order to enslave other minds by dominating their imaginations.

The second answer (that of Feuerbach, taken over word for word by Marx in his Early Works) is more "profound," i.e., just as false. It, too, seeks and finds a cause for the imaginary transposition and distortion of men's real conditions of existence, in short, for the alienation in the imaginary of the representation of men's conditions of existence. This cause is no longer Priests or Despots, nor their active imagination and the passive imagination of their victims. This cause is the material alienation which reigns in the conditions of existence of men themselves. This is how, in *The Jewish Question* and elsewhere, Marx defends the Feuerbachian idea that men make themselves an alienated (= imaginary) representation of their conditions of existence because these conditions of existence are themselves alienating (in the *1844 Manuscripts:* because these conditions are dominated by the essence of alienated society—"*alienated labour*").

All these interpretations thus take literally the thesis which they presuppose, and on which they depend, i.e., that what is reflected in the imaginary representation of the world found in an ideology is the conditions of existence of men, i.e., their real world.

Now I can return to a thesis which I have already advanced: it is not their real conditions of existence, their real world, that "men" "represent to themselves" in ideology, but above all it is their relation to those conditions of existence which is represented to them there. It is this relation which is at the centre of every ideological, i.e., imaginary, representation of the real world. It is this relation that contains the "cause" which has to explain the imaginary distortion of the ideological representation of the real world. Or rather, to leave aside the language of causality it is necessary to advance the thesis that it is the *imaginary nature of this relation* which underlies all the imaginary distortion that we can observe (if we do not live in its truth) in all ideology.

To speak in a Marxist language, if it is true that the representation of the real conditions of existence of the individuals occupying the posts of agents of production, exploitation, repression, ideologization and scientific practice, does in the last analysis arise from the relations of production, and from relations deriving from the relations of production, we can say the following: all ideology represents in its necessarily imaginary distortion not the existing relations of production (and the other relations that derive from them), but above all the (imaginary) relationship of individuals to the relations of production and the relations that derive from them. What is represented in ideology is therefore not the system of the real relations which govern the existence of individuals, but the imaginary relation of those individuals to the real relations in which they live.

If this is the case, the question of the "cause" of the imaginary distortion of the real relations in ideology disappears and must be replaced by a different question: why is the representation given to individuals of their (individual) relation to the social relations which govern their conditions of existence and their collective and individual life necessarily an imaginary relation? And what is the nature of this imaginariness? Posed in this way, the question explodes the solution by a "clique,"[1] by a group of individuals (Priests or Despots) who are the authors of the great ideological mystification, just as it explodes the solution by the alienated character of the real world. We shall see why later in my exposition. For the moment I shall go no further.

THESIS II: Ideology has a material existence.

I have already touched on this thesis by saying that the "ideas" or "representations," etc., which seem to make up ideology do not have an ideal (*idéale* or *idéelle*) or spiritual existence, but a material existence. I even suggested that the ideal (*idéale, idéelle*) and spiritual existence of "ideas" arises exclusively in an ideology of the "idea" and of ideology, and let me add, in an ideology of what seems to have "founded" this conception since the emergence of the sciences, i.e., what the practicians of the sciences represent to themselves in their spontaneous ideology as "ideas," true or false. Of course, presented in affirmative form, this thesis is unproven. I simply ask that the reader be favourably disposed towards it, say, in the name of materialism. A long series of arguments would be necessary to prove it.

This hypothetical thesis of the not spiritual but material existence of "ideas" or other "representations" is indeed necessary if we are to advance in our analysis of the nature of ideology. Or rather, it is merely useful to us in order the better to reveal what every at all serious analysis of any ideology will immediately and empirically show to every observer, however critical.

While discussing the ideological State apparatuses and their practices, I said that each of them was the realization of an ideology (the unity of these different regional ideologies—religious, ethical, legal, political, aesthetic, etc.—being assured by their subjection to the ruling ideology). I now return to this thesis: an ideology always exists in an apparatus, and its practice, or practices. This existence is material.

Of course, the material existence of the ideology in an apparatus and its practices does not have the same modality as the material existence of a paving-stone or a rifle. But, at the risk of being taken for a Neo-Aristotelian (NB Marx had a very high regard for Aristotle), I shall say that "matter is discussed in many senses," or rather that it exists in different modalities, all rooted in the last instance in "physical" matter.

Having said this, let me move straight on and see what happens to the "individuals" who live in ideology, i.e., in a determinate (religious, ethical, etc.) representation of the world whose imaginary distortion depends on their imaginary relation to their conditions of existence, in other words, in the last instance, to the relations of production and to class relations (ideology = an imaginary relation to real relations). I shall say that this imaginary relation is itself endowed with a material existence.

Now I observe the following.

An individual believes in God, or Duty, or Justice, etc. This belief derives (for everyone, i.e., for all those who live in an ideological representation of ideology, which reduces ideology to ideas endowed by definition with a spiritual existence) from the ideas of the individual concerned, i.e., from him as a subject with a consciousness which contains the ideas of his belief. In this way, i.e., by means of the absolutely ideological "conceptual" device (*dispositif*) thus set up (a subject endowed with a consciousness in which he freely forms or freely recognizes ideas in which he believes), the (material) attitude of the subject concerned naturally follows.

The individual in question behaves in such and such a way, adopts such and such a practical attitude, and, what is more, participates in certain regular practices which are those of the ideological apparatus on which "depend" the ideas which he has in all consciousness freely chosen as a subject. If he believes in God, he goes to Church to attend Mass, kneels, prays, confesses, does penance (once it was material in the ordinary sense of the term) and naturally repents and so on. If he believes in Duty, he will have the corresponding attitudes, inscribed in ritual practices "according to the correct principles." If he believes in Justice, he will submit unconditionally to the rules of the Law, and may even protest when they are violated, sign petitions, take part in a demonstration, etc.

Throughout this schema we observe that the ideological representation of ideology is itself forced to recognize that every "subject" endowed with a "consciousness" and believing in the "ideas" that his "consciousness" inspires in him and freely accepts, must *act* according to his ideas," must therefore inscribe his own ideas as a free subject in the actions of his material practice. If he does not do so, "that is wicked."

Indeed, if he does not do what he ought to do as a function of what he believes, it is because he does something else, which, still as a function of the same idealist scheme, implies that he has other ideas in his head as well as those he proclaims, and that he acts according to these other ideas, as a man who is either "inconsistent" ("no one is willingly evil") or cynical, or perverse.

In every case, the ideology of ideology thus recognizes, despite its imaginary distortion, that the "ideas" of a human subject exist in his actions, or ought to exist in his actions, and if that is not the case, it lends him other ideas corresponding to the actions (however perverse) that he does perform. This ideology talks of actions: I shall talk of actions inserted into *practices. And* I shall point out that these practices are governed by the *rituals* in which these practices are inscribed, within the *material existence of an ideological apparatus,* be it only a small part of that apparatus: a small mass in a small church, a funeral, a minor match at a sports' club, a school day, a political party meeting, etc.

Besides, we are indebted to Pascal's defensive "dialectic" for the wonderful formula which will enable us to invert the order of the notional schema of ideology. Pascal says more or less: "Kneel down, move your lips in prayer, and you will believe." He thus scandalously inverts the order of things, bringing, like Christ, not peace but strife, and in addition something hardly Christian (for woe to him who brings scandal into the world)—scandal itself. A fortunate scandal which makes him stick with Jansenist defiance to a language that directly names the reality.

I will be allowed to leave Pascal to the arguments of his ideological struggle with the religious ideological State apparatus of his day. And I shall be expected to use a more directly Marxist vocabulary, if that is possible, for we are advancing in still poorly explored domains.

I shall therefore say that, where only a single subject (such and such an individual) is concerned, the existence of the ideas of his belief is material in that *his ideas are his material actions inserted into material practices governed by material rituals which are themselves defined by the material ideological apparatus from which derive the ideas of that subject.* Naturally, the four inscriptions of the adjective "material" in my proposition must be affected by different modalities: the materialities of a displacement for going to mass, of kneeling down, of the gesture of the sign of the cross, or of the *mea culpa*, of a sentence, of a prayer, of an act of contrition, of a penitence, of a gaze, of a hand-shake, of an external verbal discourse or an "internal" verbal discourse (consciousness), are not one and the same materiality. I shall leave on one side the problem of a theory of the differences between the modalities of materiality.

It remains that in this inverted presentation of things, we are not dealing with an "inversion" at all, since it is clear that certain notions have purely and simply disappeared from our presentation, whereas others on the contrary survive, and new terms appear.

Disappeared: the term *ideas*.
Survive: the terms *subject, consciousness, belief, actions*.
Appear: the terms *practices, rituals, ideological apparatus*.

It is therefore not an inversion or overturning (except in the sense in which one might say a government or a glass is overturned), but a reshuffle (of a non-ministerial type), a rather strange reshuffle, since we obtain the following result.

Ideas have disappeared as such (insofar as they are endowed with an ideal or spiritual existence), to the precise extent that it has emerged that their existence is inscribed in the actions of practices governed by rituals defined in the last instance by an ideological apparatus. It therefore appears that the subject acts insofar as he is acted by the following system (set out in the order of its real determination): ideology existing in a material ideological apparatus, prescribing material practices governed by a material ritual, which practices exist in the material actions of a subject acting in all consciousness according to his belief.

But this very presentation reveals that we have retained the following notions: subject, consciousness, belief, actions. From this series I shall immediately extract the decisive central term on which everything else depends: the notion of the *subject*.

And I shall immediately set down two conjoint theses:
1. there is no practice except by and in an ideology;
2. there is no ideology except by the subject and for subjects.
I can now come to my central thesis.

IDEOLOGY INTERPELLATES INDIVIDUALS AS SUBJECTS

This thesis is simply a matter of making my last proposition explicit: there is no ideology except by the subject and for subjects. Meaning, there is no ideology except for concrete subjects, and this destination for ideology is only made possible by the subject: meaning, *by the category of the subject* and its functioning.

By this I mean that, even if it only appears under this name (the subject) with the rise of bourgeois ideology, above all with the rise of legal ideology,[2] the category of the subject (which may function under other names: e.g., as the soul in Plato, as God etc.) is the constitutive category of all ideology, whatever its determination (regional or class) and whatever its historical date—since ideology has no history.

I say: the category of the subject is constitutive of all ideology, but at the same time and immediately I add that *the category of the subject is only constitutive of all ideology insofar as all ideology has the function (which defines it) of "constituting" concrete individuals as subjects.* In the interaction of this double constitution exists the functioning of all ideology, ideology being nothing but its functioning in the material forms of existence of that functioning.

In order to grasp what follows, it is essential to realize that both he who is writing these lines and the reader who reads them are themselves subjects, and therefore ideological subjects (a tautological proposition), i.e., that the author and the reader of these lines both live "spontaneously" or "naturally" in ideology in the sense in which I have said that "man is an ideological animal by nature."

That the author, insofar as he writes the lines of a discourse which claims to be scientific, is completely absent as a "subject" from "his" scientific discourse (for all scientific discourse is by definition a subject-less discourse, there is no "Subject of science" except in an ideology of science) is a different question which I shall leave on one side for the moment.

As St. Paul admirably put it, it is in the "Logos," meaning in ideology, that we "live, move and have our being." It follows that, for you and for me, the category of the subject is a primary "obviousness" (obviousnesses are always primary): it is clear that you and I are subjects (free, ethical, etc. ...). Like all obviousnesses, including those that make a word "name a thing" or "have a meaning" (therefore including the obviousness of the "transparency" of language), the "obviousness" that you and I are subjects—and that does not cause any problems—is an ideological effect, the elementary ideological effect.[3] It is indeed a peculiarity of ideology that it imposes (without appearing to do so, since these are "obviousnesses") obviousnesses as obviousnesses, which we cannot *fail to recognize* and before which we have the inevitable and natural reaction of crying out (aloud or in the "still, small voice of conscience"): "That's obvious! That's right! That's true!"

At work in this reaction is the ideological *recognition* function which is one of the two functions of ideology as such (its inverse being the function of *misrecognition—méconnaissance*).

To take a highly "concrete" example, we all have friends who, when they knock on our door and we ask, through the door, the question "Who's there?" answer (since "it's obvious") "It's me." And we recognize that "it is him" or "her." We open the door, "and it's true, it really was she who was there." To take another example, when we recognize somebody of our (previous) acquaintance ((*re*)–*connaissance*) in the street, we show him that we have recognized him (and have recognized that he has recognized us) by saying to him "Hello, my friend," and shaking his hand (a material ritual practice of ideological recognition in everyday life—in France, at least; elsewhere, there are other rituals).

In this preliminary remark and these concrete illustrations, I only wish to point out that you and I are *always already* subjects, and as such constantly practice the rituals of ideological recognition, which guarantee for us that we are indeed concrete, individual, distinguishable and (naturally) irreplaceable subjects. The writing I am currently executing and the reading you are currently[4] performing are also in this respect rituals of ideological recognition, including the "obviousness" with which the "truth" or "error" of my reflections may impose itself on you.

But to recognize that we are subjects and that we function in the practical rituals of the most elementary everyday life (the hand-shake, the fact of calling you by your name, the fact of knowing, even if I do not know what it is, that you "have" a name of your own, which means that you are recognized as a unique subject, etc.)—this recognition only gives us the "consciousness" of our incessant (eternal) practice of ideological recognition—its consciousness, i.e., its *recognition*—but in no sense does it give us the (scientific) *knowledge* of the mechanism of this recognition. Now it is this knowledge that we have to reach, if you will, while speaking in ideology, and from within ideology we have to outline a discourse which tries to break with ideology, in order to dare to be the beginning of a scientific (i.e., subjectless) discourse on ideology.

Thus in order to represent why the category of the "subject" is constitutive of ideology, which only exists by constituting concrete subjects as subjects, I shall employ a special mode of exposition: "concrete" enough to be recognized, but abstract enough to be thinkable and thought, giving rise to a knowledge.

As a first formulation I shall say: *all ideology hails or interpellates concrete individuals as concrete subjects, by the functioning of the category of the subject.*

This is a proposition which entails that we distinguish for the moment between concrete individuals on the one hand and concrete subjects on the other, although at this level concrete subjects only exist insofar as they are supported by a concrete individual.

I shall then suggest that ideology "acts" or "functions" in such a way that it "recruits" subjects among the individuals (it recruits them all), or "transforms" the individuals into subjects (it transforms them all) by that very precise operation which I have called *interpellation* or hailing, and which can be imagined along the lines of the most commonplace everyday police (or other) hailing: "Hey, you there."[5]

Assuming that the theoretical scene I have imagined takes place in the street, the hailed individual will turn round. By this mere one-hundred-and-eighty-degree physical conversion, he becomes a *subject*. Why? Because he has recognized that the hail was "really" addressed to him, and that "it was *really him* who was hailed" (and not someone else). Experience shows that the practical telecommunication of hailing is such that they hardly ever miss their man: verbal call or whistle, the one hailed always recognizes that it is really him who is being hailed. And yet it is a strange phenomenon, and one which cannot be explained solely by "guilt feelings," despite the large numbers who "have something on their consciences."

Naturally for the convenience and clarity of my little theoretical theatre I have had to present things in the form of a sequence, with a before and an after, and thus in the form of a temporal succession. There are individuals walking along. Somewhere (usually behind them) the hail rings out: "Hey, you there!" One individual (nine times out of ten it is the right one) turns round, believing/suspecting/knowing that it is for him, i.e., recognizing that "it really is he" who is meant by the hailing. But in reality these things happen without any succession. The existence of ideology and the hailing or interpellation of individuals as subjects are one and the same thing.

I might add: what thus seems to take place outside ideology (to be precise, in the street), in reality takes place in ideology. What really takes place in ideology seems therefore to take place outside it. That is why those who are in ideology believe themselves by definition outside ideology: one of the effects of ideology is the practical *denegation* of the ideological character of ideology by ideology: ideology never says, "I am ideological." It is necessary to be outside ideology, i.e., in scientific knowledge, to be able to say: I am in ideology (a quite exceptional case) or (the general case): I was in ideology. As is well known, the accusation of being in ideology only applies to others, never to oneself (unless one is really a Spinozist or a Marxist, which, in this matter, is to be exactly the same thing). Which amounts to saying that ideology *has no outside* (for itself), but at the same time *that it is nothing but outside* (for science and reality).

Spinoza explained this completely two centuries before Marx, who practiced it but without explaining it in detail. But let us leave this point, although it is heavy with consequences, consequences which are not just theoretical, but also directly political, since, for example, the whole theory of criticism and self-criticism, the golden rule of the Marxist-Leninist practice of the class struggle, depends on it.

Thus ideology hails or interpellates individuals as subjects. As ideology is eternal, I must now suppress the temporal form in which I have presented the functioning of ideology, and say: ideology has always-already interpellated individuals as subjects, which amounts to making it clear that individuals are always-already interpellated by ideology as subjects, which necessarily leads us to one last proposition: *individuals are always-already subjects.* Hence individuals are "abstract" with respect to the subjects which they always already are. This proposition might seem paradoxical.

That an individual is always-already a subject, even before he is born, is nevertheless the plain reality, accessible to everyone and not a paradox at all. Freud shows that individuals are always "abstract" with respect to the subjects they always-already are, simply by noting the ideological ritual that surrounds the expectation of a "birth," that "happy event." Everyone knows how much and in what way an unborn child is expected. Which amounts to saying, very prosaically, if we agree to drop the "sentiments," i.e., the forms of family ideology (paternal/maternal/conjugal/fraternal) in which the unborn child is expected: it is certain in advance that it will bear its Father's Name, and will therefore have an identity and be irreplaceable. Before its birth, the child is therefore always-already a subject, appointed as a subject in and by the specific familial ideological configuration in which it is "expected" once it has been conceived. I hardly need add that this familial ideological configuration is, in its uniqueness, highly structured, and that it is in this implacable and more or less "pathological" (presupposing that any meaning can be assigned to that term) structure that the former subject-to-be will have to "find" "its" place, i.e., "become" the sexual subject (boy or girl) which it already is in advance. It is clear that this ideological constraint and pre-appointment, and all the rituals of rearing and then education in the family, have some relationship with what Freud studied in the forms of the pre-genital and genital "stages" of sexuality, i.e., the "grip" of what Freud registered by its effects as being the unconscious. But let us leave this point, too, on one side.

Let me go one step further. What I shall now turn my attention to is the way the "actors" in this *mise en scène* of interpellation, and their respective roles, are reflected in the very structure of all ideology.

AN EXAMPLE: THE CHRISTIAN RELIGIOUS IDEOLOGY

As the formal structure of all ideology is always the same, I shall restrict my analysis to a single example, one accessible to everyone, that of religious ideology, with the proviso that the same demonstration can be produced for ethical, legal, political, aesthetic ideology, etc.

Let us therefore consider the Christian religious ideology. I shall use a rhetorical figure and "make it speak," i.e., collect into a fictional discourse what it "says" not only in its two Testaments, its Theologians, Sermons, but also in its practices, its rituals, its ceremonies and its sacraments. The Christian religious ideology says something like this:

It says: I address myself to you, a human individual called Peter (every individual is called by his name, in the passive sense, it is never he who provides his own name), in order to tell you that God exists and that you are answerable to Him. It adds: God addresses himself to you through my voice (Scripture having collected the Word of God, Tradition having transmitted it, Papal Infallibility fixing it for ever on "nice" points). It says: this is who you are: you are Peter! This is your origin, you were created by God for all eternity, although you were born in the 1920th year of Our Lord! This is your place in the world! This is what you must do! By these means, if you observe the "law of love" you will be saved, you, Peter, and will become part of the Glorious Body of Christ! Etc....

Now this is quite a familiar and banal discourse, but at the same time quite a surprising one.

Surprising because if we consider that religious ideology is indeed addressed to individuals,[6] in order to "transform them into subjects" by interpellating the individual, Peter, in order to make him a subject, free to obey or disobey the appeal, i.e., God's commandments; if it calls these individuals by their names, thus recognizing that they are always-already interpellated as subjects with a personal identity (to the extent that Pascal's Christ says: "It is for you that I have shed this drop of my blood!"); if it interpellates them in such a way that the subject responds: *"Yes; it really is me!"* if it obtains from them the *recognition* that they really do occupy the place it designates for them as theirs in the world, a fixed residence: "It really is me, I am here, a worker, a boss or a soldier!" in this vale of tears: if it obtains from them the recognition of destination (eternal life or damnation) according to the respect or contempt they show to "God's Commandments," Law become Love;—if everything does happen in this way (in the practice of the well-known rituals of baptism, confirmation, communion, confession and extreme unction, etc....), we should note that all this "procedure" to set up Christian religious subjects is dominated by a strange phenomenon: the fact that there can only be such a multitude of possible religious subjects on the absolute condition that there is a Unique, Absolute, *Other Subject,* i.e., God.

It is convenient to designate this new and remarkable Subject by writing Subject with a capital S to distinguish it from ordinary subjects, with a small s.

It then emerges that the interpellation of individuals as subjects presupposes the "existence" of a Unique and central Other Subject, in whose Name the religious ideology interpellates all individuals as subjects. All this is clearly[7] written in what is rightly called the Scriptures. "And it came to pass at that time that God the Lord (Yahweh) spoke to Moses in the cloud. And the Lord cried to Moses, 'Moses!' And Moses replied 'It is (really) I! I am Moses thy servant, speak and I shall listen!' And the Lord spoke to Moses and said to him, *'I am that I am.' "*

God thus defines himself as the Subject *par excellence,* he who is through himself and for himself ("I am that I am"), and he who interpellates his subject, the individual subjected to him by his very interpellation, i.e., the individual named Moses. And Moses, interpellated-called by his Name, having recognized that it "really" was he who was called by God, recognizes that he is a subject, a subject *of* God, a subject subjected to God, *a subject through the Subject and subjected to the Subject.* The proof: he obeys him, and makes his people obey God's Commandments.

God is thus the Subject, and Moses and the innumerable subjects of God's people, the Subject's interlocutors-interpellates: his *mirrors,* his *reflections.* Were not men made *in the image* of God? As all theological reflection proves, whereas He "could" perfectly well have done without men, God needs them, the Subject needs the subjects, just as men need God, the subjects need the Subject. Better: God needs men, the great Subject needs subjects, even in the terrible inversion of his image in them (when the subjects wallow in debauchery, i.e., sin).

Better: God duplicates himself and sends his Son to the Earth, as a mere subject "forsaken" by him (the long complaint of the Garden of Olives which ends in the Crucifixion), subject but Subject, man but God, to do what prepares the way for the final Redemption, the Resurrection of Christ. God thus needs to "make himself" a man, the Subject needs to become a subject, as if to show empirically, visibly to the eye, tangibly to the hands (see St. Thomas) of the subjects, that, if they are subjects, subjected to the Subject, that is solely in order that finally, on Judgment Day, they will re-enter the Lord's Bosom, like Christ, i.e., re-enter the Subject.[8]

Let us decipher into theoretical language this wonderful necessity for the duplication of *the Subject into subjects* and of *the Subject itself into a subject-Subject.*

We observe that the structure of all ideology, interpellating individuals as subjects in the name of a Unique and Absolute Subject is *speculary,* i.e., a mirror-structure, and *doubly* speculary: this mirror duplication is constitutive of ideology and ensures its functioning. Which means that all ideology is *centred,* that the Absolute Subject occupies the unique place of the Centre, and interpellates around it the infinity of individuals into subjects in a double mirror-connexion such that it *subjects* the subjects to the Subject, while giving them in the Subject in which each subject can contemplate its own image (present and future) the *guarantee* that this really concerns them and Him, and that since everything takes place in the Family (the Holy Family: the Family is in essence Holy), "God will *recognize* his own in it," i.e., those who have recognized God, and have recognized themselves in Him, will be saved.

Let me summarize what we have discovered about ideology in general.

The duplicate mirror-structure of ideology ensures simultaneously:

1. the interpellation of "individuals" as subjects;
2. their subjection to the Subject;
3. the mutual recognition of subjects and Subject, the subjects' recognition of each other, and finally the subject's recognition of himself;[9]
4. the absolute guarantee that everything really is so, and that on condition that the subjects recognize what they are and behave accordingly, everything will be all right: Amen—"*So be it.*"

Result: caught in this quadruple system of interpellation as subjects, of subjection to the Subject, of universal recognition and of absolute guarantee, the subjects "work," they "work by themselves" in the vast majority of cases, with the exception of the "bad subjects" who on occasion provoke the intervention of one of the detachments of the (repressive) State apparatus. But the vast majority of (good) subjects work all right "all by themselves," i.e., by ideology (whose concrete forms are realized in the Ideological State Apparatuses). They are inserted into practices governed by the rituals of the ISAs. They "recognize" the existing state of affairs (*das Bestehende*), that "it really is true that it is so and not otherwise," and that they must be obedient to God, to their conscience, to the priest, to de Gaulle, to the boss, to the engineer, that thou shalt "love thy neighbor as thyself," etc. Their concrete, material behaviour is simply the inscription in life of the admirable words of the prayer: *"Amen—So be it."*

Yes, the subjects "work by themselves." The whole mystery of this effect lies in the first two moments of the quadruple system I have just discussed, or, if you prefer, in the ambiguity of the term *subject*. In the ordinary use of the term, subject in fact means: (1) a free subjectivity, a centre of initiatives, author of and responsible for its actions; (2) a subjected being, who submits to a higher authority, and is therefore stripped of all freedom except that of freely accepting his submission. This last note gives us the meaning of this ambiguity, which is merely a reflection of the effect which produces it: the individual *is interpellated as a (free) subject in order that he shall submit freely to the commandments of the Subject, i.e., in order that he shall (freely) accept his subjection,* i.e., in order that he shall make the gestures and actions of his subjection "all by himself." *There are no subjects except by and for their subjection.* That is why they "work all by themselves."

"So be it!…" This phrase which registers the effect to be obtained proves that it is not "naturally" so ("naturally": outside the prayer, i.e., outside the ideological intervention). This phrase proves that it *has* to be so if things are to be what they must be, and let us let the words slip: if the reproduction of the relations of production is to be assured, even in the processes of production and circulation, every day, in the "consciousness," i.e., in the attitudes of the individual-subjects occupying the posts which the socio-technical division of labour assigns to them in production, exploitation, repression, ideologization, scientific practice, etc. Indeed, what is really in question in this mechanism of the mirror recognition of the Subject and of the individuals interpellated as subjects, and of the guarantee given by the Subject to the subjects if they freely accept their subjection to the Subject's "commandments"? The reality in question in this mechanism, the reality which is necessarily *ignored* (*méconnue*) in the very forms of recognition (ideology = misrecognition/ignorance) is indeed, in the last resort, the reproduction of the relations of production and of the relations deriving from them.

NOTES

1. I use this very modern term deliberately. For even in Communist circles, unfortunately, it is a commonplace to "explain" some political deviation (left or right opportunism) by the action of a "clique."
2. Which borrowed the legal category of "subject in law" to make an ideological notion: man is by nature a subject.
3. Linguists and those who appeal to linguistics for various purposes often run up against difficulties which arise because they ignore the action of the ideological effect in all discourses—including even scientific discourses.
4. NB: this double "currently" is one more proof of the fact that ideology is "eternal," since these two "currently" are separated by an indefinite interval; I am writing these lines on 6 April 1969, you may read them at any subsequent time.
5. Hailing as an everyday practice subject to a precise ritual takes a quite "special" from in the policeman's practice of "hailing" which concerns the hailing of "suspects."
6. Although we know that the individual is always already a subject, we go on using this term, convenient because of the contrasting effect it produces.
7. I am quoting in a combined way, not to the letter but "in spirit and truth."
8. The dogma of the Trinity is precisely the theory of the duplication of the Subject (the Father) into a subject (the Son) and of their mirror-connexion (the Holy Spirit).
9. Hegel is (unknowingly) an admirable "theoretician" of ideology insofar as he is a "theoretician" of Universal Recognition who unfortunately ends up in the ideology of Absolute Knowledge. Feuerbach is an astonishing "theoretician" of the mirror connexion, who unfortunately ends up in the ideology of the Human Essence. To find the material with which to construct a theory of the guarantee, we most turn to Spinoza.

DOMINANT, RESIDUAL, AND EMERGENT (1977)

RAYMOND WILLIAMS

Williams was a prolific critic and a founding figure of what came to be called cultural materialism. Cultural materialism helped inspire cultural studies. To a degree, it eventually merged with cultural studies, although cultural materialists often write more about literary history and cultural studies scholars typically focus more on contemporary and popular culture.

Drawing on the concept of hegemony from Antonio Gramsci, meaning dominant cultural patterns that achieve and sustain their dominance by encouraging—but not forcing—people to believe in them, Williams's influential concepts of the dominant, residual, and emergent bring out a sense of process rather than an absolute and unchangeable control by ruling forces. The flexible model of dominant, residual, and emergent expands on the implications of process, power, and potential vulnerability in the notion of the hegemony, breaking the hegemony into multiple dimensions. Williams's focus on the multiple dimensions of the dominant appealed to critics who, influenced by deconstruction, wanted to see process and multiplicity in cultural formations of power and dominance. Williams called the dominant, residual, and emergent patterns of a given time or period its "structures of feeling."

The complexity of a culture is to be found not only in its variable processes and their social definitions—traditions, institutions, and formations—but also in the dynamic interrelations, at every point in the process, of historically varied and variable elements. In what I have called "epochal" analysis, a cultural process is seized as a cultural system, with determinate dominant features: feudal culture or bourgeois culture or a transition from one to the other. This emphasis on dominant and definitive lineaments and features is important and often, in practice, effective. But it then often happens that its methodology is preserved for the very different function of historical analysis, in which a sense of movement within what is ordinarily abstracted as a system is crucially necessary, especially if it is to connect with the future as well as with the past. In authentic historical analysis it is necessary at every point to recognize the complex interrelations between movements and tendencies both within and beyond a specific and effective dominance. It is necessary to examine how these relate to the whole cultural process rather than only to the selected and abstracted dominant system. Thus "bourgeois culture" is a significant generalizing description and hypothesis, expressed within epochal analysis by fundamental comparisons with "feudal culture" or "socialist culture." However, as a description of cultural process, over four or five centuries and in scores of different societies, it requires immediate historical and internally comparative differentiation. Moreover, even if this is acknowledged or practically carried out, the "epochal" definition can exert its pressure as a static type against which all real cultural process is measured, either to show "stages" or "variations" of the type (which is still historical analysis) or, at its worst, to select supporting and exclude "marginal" or "incidental" or "secondary" evidence.

Such errors are avoidable if, while retaining the epochal hypothesis, we can find terms which recognize not only "stages" and "variations," but the internal dynamic relations of any actual process. We have certainly still to speak of the "dominant" and the "effective," and in these senses of the hegemonic. But we find that we have also to speak, and indeed with further differentiation of each, of the "residual" and the "emergent," which in any real process, and at any moment in the process, are significant both in themselves and in what they reveal of the characteristics of the "dominant."

By "residual" I mean something different from the "archaic," though in practice these are often very difficult to distinguish. Any culture includes available elements of its past, but their place in the contemporary cultural process is profoundly variable. I would call the "archaic" that which is wholly recognized as an element of the past, to be observed, to be examined, or even on occasion to be consciously "revived," in a deliberately specializing way. What I mean by the "residual" is very different. The residual, by definition, has been effectively formed in the past, but it is still active in the cultural process, not only and often not at all as an element of the past, but as an effective element of the present. Thus certain experiences, meanings, and values which cannot be expressed or substantially verified in terms of the dominant culture, are nevertheless lived and practiced on the basis of the residue—cultural as well as social—of some previous social and cultural institution or formation. It is crucial to distinguish this aspect of the residual, which may have an alternative or even oppositional relation to the dominant culture, from that active manifestation of the residual (this being its distinction from the archaic) which has been wholly or largely incorporated into the dominant culture. In three characteristic cases in contemporary English culture this distinction can become a precise term of analysis. Thus organized religion is predominantly residual, but within this there is a significant difference between some practically alternative and oppositional meanings and values (absolute brotherhood, service to others without reward) and a larger body of incorporated meanings and values (official morality, or the social order of which the otherworldly is a separated neutralizing or ratifying component). Again, the idea of rural community is predominantly residual, but is in some limited respects alternative or oppositional to urban industrial capitalism, though for the most part it is incorporated, as idealization or fantasy, or as an exotic—residential or escape—leisure function of the dominant order itself. Again, in monarchy, there is virtually nothing that is actively residual (alternative or oppositional), but, with a heavy and deliberate additional use of the archaic, a residual function has been wholly incorporated as a specific political and cultural function—marking the limits as well as the methods—of a form of capitalist democracy.

A residual cultural element is usually at some distance from the effective dominant culture, but some part of it, some version of it—and especially if the residue is from some major area of the past—will in most cases have had to be incorporated if the effective dominant culture is to make sense in these areas. Moreover, at certain points the dominant culture cannot allow too much residual experience and practice outside itself, at least without risk. It is in the incorporation of the actively residual—by reinterpretation, dilution, projection, discriminating inclusion and exclusion—that the work of the selective tradition is especially evident. This is very notable in the case of versions of "the literary tradition," passing through selective versions of the character of literature to connecting and incorporated definitions of what literature now is and should be. This is one among several crucial areas, since it is in some alternative or even oppositional versions of what literature is (has been) and what literary experience (and in one common derivation, other significant experience) is and must be, that, against the pressures of incorporation, actively residual meanings and values are sustained.

By "emergent" I mean, first, that new meanings and values, new practices, new relationships and kinds of relationship are continually being created. But it is exceptionally difficult to distinguish between those which are really elements of some new phase of the dominant culture (and in this sense "species-specified") and those which are substantially alternative or oppositional to it: emergent in the strict sense, rather than merely novel. Since we are always considering relations within a cultural process, definitions of the emergent, as of the residual, can be made only in relation to a full sense of the dominant. Yet the social location of the residual is always easier to understand, since a large part of it (though not all) relates to earlier social formations and phases of the cultural process, in which certain real meanings and values were generated. In the subsequent default of a particular phase of a dominant culture there is then a reaching back to those meanings and values which were created in actual societies and actual situations in the past, and which still seem to have significance because they represent areas of human experience, aspiration, and achievement which the dominant culture neglects, undervalues, opposes, represses, or even cannot recognize.

The case of the emergent is radically different. It is true that in the structure of any actual society, and especially in its class structure, there is always a social basis for elements of the cultural process that are alternative or oppositional to the dominant elements. One kind of basis has been valuably described in the central body of Marxist theory: the formation of a new class, the coming to consciousness of a new class, and within this, in actual process, the (often uneven) emergence of elements of a new cultural formation. Thus the emergence of the working class as a class was immediately evident (for example, in nineteenth-century England) in the cultural process. But there was extreme unevenness of contribution in different parts of the process. The making of new social values and institutions far outpaced the making of strictly cultural institutions, while specific cultural contributions, though significant, were less vigorous and autonomous than either general or institutional innovation. A new class is always a source of emergent cultural practice, but while it is still, as a class, relatively subordinate, this is always likely to be uneven and is certain to be incomplete. For new practice is not, of course, an isolated process. To the degree that it emerges, and especially to the degree that it is oppositional rather than alternative, the process of attempted incorporation significantly begins. This can be seen, in the same period in England, in the emergence and then the effective incorporation of a radical popular press. It can be seen in the emergence and incorporation of working-class writing, where the fundamental problem of emergence is clearly revealed, since the basis of incorporation, in such cases, is the effective predominance of received literary forms—an incorporation, so to say, which already conditions and limits the emergence. But the development is always uneven. Straight incorporation is most directly attempted against the visibly alternative and oppositional class elements: trade unions, working-class political parties, working-class life styles (as incorporated into "popular" journalism, advertising, and commercial entertainment). The process of emergence, in such conditions, is then a constantly repeated, an always renewable, move beyond a phase of practical incorporation: usually made much more difficult by the fact that much incorporation looks like recognition, acknowledgement, and thus a form of *acceptance*. In this complex process there is indeed regular confusion between the locally residual (as a form of resistance to incorporation) and the generally emergent.

Cultural emergence in relation to the "emergence" and growing strength of a class is then always of major importance, and always complex. But we have also to see that it is not the only kind of emergence. This recognition is very difficult, theoretically, though the practical evidence is abundant. What has really to be said, as a way of defining important elements of both the residual and the emergent, and as a way of understanding the character of the dominant, is that *no mode of production and therefore no dominant social order and therefore no dominant culture ever in reality includes or exhausts all human practice, human energy, and human intention*. This is not merely a negative proposition, allowing us to account for significant things which happen outside or against the dominant mode. On the contrary it is a fact about the modes of domination, that they select from and consequently exclude the full range of human practice. What they exclude may often be seen as the personal or the private, or as the natural or even the metaphysical. Indeed it is usually in one or other of these terms that the excluded area is expressed, since what the dominant has effectively seized is indeed the ruling definition of the social.

It is this seizure that has especially to be resisted. For there is always, though in varying degrees, practical consciousness, in specific relationships, specific skills, specific perceptions, that is unquestionably social and that a specifically dominant social order neglects, excludes, represses, or simply fails to recognize. A distinctive and comparative feature of any dominant social order is how far it reaches into the whole range of practices and experiences in an attempt at incorporation. There can be areas of experience it is willing to ignore or dispense with: to assign as private or to specialize as aesthetic or to generalize as natural. Moreover, as a social order changes, in terms of its own developing needs, these relations are variable. Thus in advanced capitalism, because of changes in the social character of labour, in the social character of communications, and in the social character of decision-making, the dominant culture reaches much further than ever before in capitalist society into hitherto "reserved" or "resigned" areas of experience and practice and meaning. The area of effective penetration of the dominant order into the whole social and cultural process is thus now significantly greater. This in turn makes the problem of emergence especially acute, and narrows the gap between alternative and oppositional elements. The alternative, especially in areas that impinge on significant areas of the dominant, is often seen as oppositional and, by pressure, often converted into it. Yet even here there can be spheres of practice and meaning which, almost by definition from its own limited character, or in its profound deformation, the dominant culture is unable in any real terms to recognize. Elements of emergence may indeed be incorporated, but just as often the incorporated forms are merely facsimiles of the genuinely emergent cultural practice. Any significant emergence, beyond or against a dominant mode, is very difficult under these conditions; in itself and in its repeated confusion with the facsimiles and novelties of the incorporated phase. Yet, in our own period as in others, the fact of emergent cultural practice is still undeniable, and together with the fact of actively residual practice is a necessary complication of the would-be dominant culture.

This complex process can still in part be described in class terms. But there is always other social being and consciousness which is neglected and excluded: alternative perceptions of others, in immediate relationships; new perceptions and practices of the material world. In practice these are different in quality from the developing and articulated interests of a rising class. The relations between these two sources of the emergent—the class and the excluded social (human) area—are by no means necessarily contradictory. At times they can be very close and on the relations between them much in political practice depends. But culturally and as a matter of theory the areas can be seen as distinct.

What matters, finally, in understanding emergent culture, as distinct from both the dominant and the residual, is that it is never only a matter of immediate practice; indeed it depends crucially on finding new forms or adaptations of form. Again and again what we have to observe is in effect a pre-emergence, active and pressing but not yet fully articulated, rather than the evident emergence which could be more confidently named. It is to understand more closely this condition of pre-emergence, as well as the more evident forms of the emergent, the residual, and the dominant, that we need to explore the concept of structures of feeling.

COGNITIVE MAPPING (1988)

FREDRIC JAMESON

This essay, a talk given at a conference on "Marxism and the Interpretation of Culture," summarizes many of Jameson's most provocative and influential ideas. Jameson connects economic history to the history of literary form. He frames his talk partly as a response to the growth of what is sometimes called "post-Marxism," which tends to give less weight than earlier Marxism to economics as the determinant of culture and thus less weight to class.

While this essay reads more easily than much of Jameson's other work, a summary of its basic ideas may make them more accessible. Jameson traces three stages in the history of capital and the expansion of commodification. In the first stage, capital organizes space through the industrial organization of labor, the Enlightenment, secularization and desacralization, a shift (characteristic, Marx argued, of the growth of capitalism through commodities) from the use value of built objects to their exchange value. Such economic changes proceeded hand in hand, in Jameson's eyes, with the growth of realistic novels— such as Don Quixote or the novels of Balzac—that demystify novels of transcendence. The realistic novel, he argues, transformed natural desire into the desire for commodities and for "success."

Then, in the second stage, as the economic system changes from market capitalism to monopoly capitalism, including imperialism, people imagine their lives in a way that allows them to romanticize their own supposed individuality at the cost of failing to recognize the larger economic structures that shape their beliefs, behaviors, and understandings, even their understanding of themselves. Lived or felt experience no longer matches the actual structure of experience. Jameson's sense of a gap between felt experience and the actual structure draws on the concept of interpellation that Louis Althusser describes in his essay in this volume. Thus a novel about London thinks that it is indeed about London, and its readers think that the novel is about London, but actually the structure of life in London depends on what British monopoly capitalism and imperialism do in India, Jamaica, and Hong Kong. Londoners and readers of British novels thus misrecognize their own lives by not recognizing how bound up they are with Empire, with far away lands, and yet with far away lands that in another, disguised sense are not far away at all. Thus a truthful cognitive mapping no longer lines up with individual experience as people—or as subjects—imagine their experience. And therefore, Jameson argues, modernist art responds by inventing new and seemingly distorted forms that represent the gap between experience and the truths of economic and political life, the true totality of global class relations that experience masks. The individualist focus and characteristic irony of modernist writing may seem to zero in on middle-class individuality, but indirectly the individualism and irony are secondary. They are symptoms that express, that figure, the colonialism and monopoly capitalism that make the appearance of middle-class individuality possible in the nations that depend on colonizing other peoples and lands.

In the third stage, then, the stage of "late capitalism" when multinational, global, corporate capitalism eclipses the modernist cities and even the nation-states, the distorted figurations magnify, leading to a "postmodernist space" that relentlessly saturates "the postmodern body" with "a perceptual barrage of immediacy from which all sheltering layers and intervening mediations have been removed." The "decentering of global capital" in "the fragmented and schizophrenic decentering and dispersion" of postmodernism then also threaten the coordination required for socialist politics.

I am addressing a subject about which I know nothing whatsoever, except for the fact that it does not exist. The description of a new aesthetic, or the call for it, or its prediction—these things are generally done by practicing artists whose manifestos articulate the originality they hope for in their own work, or by critics who think they already have before their eyes the stirrings and emergences of the radically new. Unfortunately, I can claim neither of those positions, and since I am not even sure how to imagine the kind of art I want to propose here, let alone affirm its possibility, it may well be wondered what kind of an operation this will be, to produce the concept of something we cannot imagine.

Perhaps all this is a kind of blind, in that something else will really be at stake. I have found myself obliged, in arguing an aesthetic of cognitive mapping, to plot a substantial detour through the great themes and shibboleths of post-Marxism, so that to me it does seem possible that the aesthetic here may be little more than a pretext for debating those theoretical and political issues. So be it. In any case, during this Marxist conference I have frequently had the feeling that I am one of the few Marxists left. I take it I have a certain responsibility to restate what seem to me to be a few self-evident truths, but which you may see as quaint survivals of a religious, millenarian, salvational form of belief.

In any case, I want to forestall the misapprehension that the aesthetic I plan to outline is intended to displace and to supercede a whole range of other, already extant or possible and conceivable aesthetics of a different kind. Art has always done a great many different things, and had a great many distinct and incommensurable functions: let it continue to do all that—which it will, in any case, even in Utopia. But the very pluralism of the aesthetic suggests that there should be nothing particularly repressive in the attempt to remind ourselves and to revive experimentally one traditional function of the aesthetic that has in our time been peculiarly neglected and marginalized, if not interdicted altogether.

"To teach, to move, to delight": of these traditional formulations of the uses of the work of art, the first has virtually been eclipsed from contemporary criticism and theory. Yet the pedagogical function of a work of art seems in various forms to have been an inescapable parameter of any conceivable Marxist aesthetic, if of few others; and it is the great historical merit of the work of Darko Suvin to repeatedly insist on a more contemporary formulation of this aesthetic value, in the suggestive slogan of the *cognitive*, which I have made my own today. Behind Suvin's work, of course, there stands the immense, yet now partially institutionalized and reified, example of Brecht himself, to whom any cognitive aesthetic in our time must necessarily pay homage. And perhaps it is no longer the theater but the poetry of Brecht that is for us still the irrefutable demonstration that cognitive art need not raise any of the old fears about the contamination of the aesthetic by propaganda or the instrumentalization of cultural play and production by the message or the extra-aesthetic (basely practical) impulse. Brecht's is a poetry of thinking and reflection; yet no one who has been stunned by the sculptural density of Brecht's language, by the stark simplicity with which a contemplative distance from historical events is here powerfully condensed into the ancient forms of folk wisdom and the proverb, in sentences as compact as peasants' wooden spoons and bowls, will any longer question the proposition that in his poetry at least—so exceptionally in the whole history of contemporary culture—the cognitive becomes in and of itself the immediate source of profound aesthetic delight.

I mention Brecht to forestall yet another misunderstanding, that it will in any sense be a question here of the return to some older aesthetic, even that of Brecht. And this is perhaps the moment to warn you that I tend to use the charged word "representation" in a different way than it has consistently been used in poststructuralist or post-Marxist theory: namely, as the synonym of some bad ideological and organic realism or mirage of realistic unification. For me "representation" is, rather, the synonym of "figuration" itself, irrespective of the latter's historical and ideological form. I assume, therefore, in what follows, that all forms of aesthetic production consist in one way or another in the struggle with and for representation—and this whether they are perspectival or trompe l'oeil illusions or the most reflexive and diacritical, iconoclastic or form-breaking modernisms. So, at least in my language, the call for new kinds of representation is not meant to imply the return to Balzac or Brecht; nor is it intended as some valorization of content over form—yet another archaic distinction I still feel is indispensable and about which I will have more to say shortly.

In the project for a spatial analysis of culture that I have been engaged in sketching for the teaching institute that preceded this conference, I have tried to suggest that the three historical stages of capital have each generated a type of space unique to it, even though these three stages of capitalist space are obviously far more profoundly interrelated than are the spaces of other modes of production. The three types of space I have in mind are all the result of discontinuous expansions or quantum leaps in the enlargement of capital, in the latter's penetration and colonization of hitherto uncommodified areas. You will therefore note in passing that a certain unifying and totalizing force is presupposed here—although it is not the Hegelian Absolute Spirit, nor the party, nor Stalin, but simply capital itself; and it is on the strength of such a view that a radical Jesuit friend of mine once publicly accused me of monotheism. It is at least certain that the notion of capital stands or falls with the notion of some unified logic of this social system itself, that is to say, in the stigmatized language I will come back to later, that both are irrecoverably totalizing concepts.

I have tried to describe the first kind of space of classical or market capitalism in terms of a logic of the grid, a reorganization of some older sacred and heterogeneous space into geometrical and Cartesian homogeneity, a space of infinite equivalence and extension of which you can find a kind of dramatic or emblematic shorthand representation in Foucault's book on prisons. The example, however, requires the warning that a Marxian view of such space grounds it in Taylorization and the labor process rather than in that shadowy and mythical Foucault entity called "power." The emergence of this kind of space will probably not involve problems of figuration so acute as those we will confront in the later stages of capitalism, since here, for the moment, we witness that familiar process long generally associated with the Enlightenment, namely, the desacralization of the world, the decoding and secularization of the older forms of the sacred or the transcendent, the slow colonization of use value by exchange value, the "realistic" demystification of the older kinds of transcendent narratives in novels like *Don Quixote,* the standardization of both subject and object, the denaturalization of desire and its ultimate displacement by commodification or, in other words, "success," and so on.

The problems of figuration that concern us will only become visible in the next stage, the passage from market to monopoly capital, or what Lenin called the "stage of imperialism"; and they may be conveyed by way of a growing contradiction between lived experience and structure, or between a phenomenological description of the life of an individual and a more properly structural model of the conditions of existence of that experience. Too rapidly we can say that, while in older societies and perhaps even in the early stages of market capital, the immediate and limited experience of individuals is still able to encompass and coincide with the true economic and social form that governs that experience, in the next moment these two levels drift ever further apart and really begin to constitute themselves into that opposition the classical dialectic describes as *Wesen* and *Erscheinung,* essence and appearance, structure and lived experience.

At this point the phenomenological experience of the individual subject—traditionally, the supreme raw materials of the work of art—becomes limited to a tiny corner of the social world, a fixed-camera view of a certain section of London or the countryside or whatever. But the truth of that experience no longer coincides with the place in which it takes place. The truth of that limited daily experience of London lies, rather, in India or Jamaica or Hong Kong; it is bound up with the whole colonial system of the British Empire that determines the very quality of the individual's subjective life. Yet those structural coordinates are no longer accessible to immediate lived experience and are often not even conceptualizable for most people.

There comes into being, then, a situation in which we can say that if individual experience is authentic, then it cannot be true; and that if a scientific or cognitive model of the same content is true, then it escapes individual experience. It is evident that this new situation poses tremendous and crippling problems for a work of art; and I have argued that it is as an attempt to square this circle and to invent new and elaborate formal strategies for overcoming this dilemma that modernism or, perhaps better, the various moderisms as such emerge: in forms that inscribe a new sense of the absent global colonial system on the very syntax of poetic language itself, a new play of absence and presence that at its most simplified will be haunted by the erotic and be tattooed with foreign place names, and at its most intense will involve the invention of remarkable new languages and forms.

At this point I want to introduce another concept that is basic to my argument, that I call the "play of figuration." This is an essentially allegorical concept that supposes the obvious, namely, that these new and enormous global realities are inaccessible to any individual subject or consciousness—not even to Hegel, let alone Cecil Rhodes or Queen Victoria—which is to say that those fundamental realities are somehow ultimately unrepresentable or, to use the Althusserian phrase, are something like an absent cause, one that can never emerge into the presence of perception. Yet this absent cause can find figures through which to express itself in distorted and symbolic ways: indeed, one of our basic tasks as critics of literature is to track down and make conceptually available the ultimate realities and experiences designated by those figures, which the reading mind inevitably tends to reify and to read as primary contents in their own right.

Since we have evoked the modernist moment and its relationship to the great new global colonial network, I will give a fairly simple but specialized example of a kind of figure specific to this historical situation. Everyone knows how, toward the end of the nineteenth century, a wide range of writers began to invent forms to express what I will call "monadic relativism." In Gide and Conrad, in Fernando Pessoa, in Pirandello, in Ford, and to a lesser extent in Henry James, even very obliquely in Proust, what we begin to see is the sense that each consciousness is a closed world, so that a representation of the social totality now must take the (impossible) form of a coexistence of those sealed subjective worlds and their peculiar interaction, which is in reality a passage of ships in the night, a centrifugal movement of lines and planes that can never intersect. The literary value that emerges from this new formal practice is called "irony"; and its philosophical ideology often takes the form of a vulgar appropriation of Einstein's theory of relativity. In this context, what I want to suggest is that these forms, whose content is generally that of privatized middle-class life, nonetheless stand as symptoms and distorted expressions of the penetration even of middle-class lived experience by this strange new global relativity of the colonial network. The one is then the figure, however deformed and symbolically rewritten, of the latter; and I take it that this figural process will remain central in all later attempts to restructure the form of the work of art to accommodate content that must radically resist and escape artistic figuration.

If this is so for the age of imperialism, how much more must it hold for our own moment, the moment of the multinational network, or what Mandel calls "late capitalism," a moment in which not merely the older city but even the nation-state itself has ceased to play a central functional and formal role in a process that has in a new quantum leap of capital prodigiously expanded beyond them, leaving them behind as ruined and archaic remains of earlier stages in the development of this mode of production.

At this point I realize that the persuasiveness of my demonstration depends on your having some fairly vivid perceptual sense of what is unique and original in postmodernist space—something I have been trying to convey in my course, but for which it is more difficult here to substitute a shortcut. Briefly, I want to suggest that the new space involves the suppression of distance (in the sense of Benjamin's aura) and the relentless saturation of any remaining voids and empty places, to the point where the postmodern body—whether wandering through a postmodern hotel, locked into rock sound by means of headphones, or undergoing the multiple shocks and bombardments of the Vietnam War as Michael Herr conveys it to us—is now exposed to a perceptual barrage of immediacy from which all sheltering layers and intervening mediations have been removed. There are of course, many other features of this space one would ideally want to comment on—most notably, Lefebvre's concept of abstract space as what is simultaneously homogeneous and fragmented—but I think that the peculiar disorientation of the saturated space I have just mentioned will be the most useful guiding thread.

You should understand that I take such spatial peculiarities of postmodernism as symptoms and expressions of a new and historically original dilemma, one that involves our insertion as individual subjects into a multidimensional set of radically discontinuous realities, whose frames range from the still surviving spaces of bourgeois private life all the way to the unimaginable decentering of global capital itself. Not even Einsteinian relativity, or the multiple subjective worlds of the older modernists, is capable of giving any kind of adequate figuration to this process, which in lived experience makes itself felt by the so-called death of the subject, or, more exactly, the fragmented and schizophrenic decentering and dispersion of this last (which can no longer even serve the function of the Jamesian reverberator or "point of view"). And although you may not have realized it, I am talking about practical politics here: since the crisis of socialist internationalism, and the enormous strategic and tactical difficulties of coordinating local and grassroots or neighborhood political actions with national or international ones, such urgent political dilemmas are all immediately functions of the enormously complex new international space I have in mind.

Let me here insert an illustration, in the form of a brief account of a book that is, I think, not known to many of you but in my opinion of the greatest importance and suggestiveness for problems of space and politics. The book is nonfiction, a historical narrative of the single most significant political experience of the American 1960s: *Detroit: I Do Mind Dying,* by Marvin Surkin and Dan Georgakis. (I think we have now come to be sophisticated enough to understand that aesthetic, formal, and narrative analyses have implications that far transcend those objects marked as fiction or as literature.) *Detroit* is a study of the rise and fall of the League of Black Revolutionary Workers in that city in the late 1960s.[1] The political formation in question was able to conquer power in the workplace, particularly in the automobile factories; it drove a substantial wedge into the media and informational monopoly of the city by way of a student newspaper; it elected judges; and finally it came within a hair's breadth of electing the mayor and taking over the city power apparatus. This was, of course a remarkable political achievement, characterized by an exceedingly sophisticated sense of the need for a multilevel strategy for revolution that involved initiatives on the distinct social levels of the labor process, the media and culture, the juridical apparatus, and electoral politics.

Yet it is equally clear—and far clearer in virtual triumphs of this kind than in the earlier stages of neighborhood politics—that such strategy is bound and shackled to the city form itself. Indeed, one of the enormous strengths of the superstate and its federal constitution lies in the evident discontinuities between city, state, and federal power: if you cannot make socialism in one country, how much more derisory, then, are the prospects for socialism in one city in the United States today? Indeed, our foreign visitors may not be aware that there exist in this country four or five socialist communes, near one of which, in Santa Cruz, California, I lived until recently; no one would want to belittle these local successes, but it seems probable that few of us think of them as the first decisive step toward the transition to socialism.

If you cannot build socialism in one city, then suppose you conquer a whole series of large key urban centers in succession. This is what the League of Black Revolutionary Workers began to think about; that is to say, they began to feel that their movement was a political model and ought to be generalizable. The problem that arises is spatial: how to develop a *national* political movement on the basis of a *city* strategy and politics. At any rate, the leadership of the League began to spread the word in other cities and traveled to Italy and Sweden to study workers' strategies there and to explain their own model; reciprocally, out-of-town politicos came to Detroit to investigate the new strategies. At this point it ought to be clear that we are in the middle of the problem of representation, not the least of it being signaled by the appearance of that ominous American word "leadership." In a more general way, however, these trips were more than networking, making contacts, spreading information: they raised the problem of how to represent a unique local model and experience to people in other situations. So it was logical for the League to make a film of their experience, and a very fine and exciting film it is.

Spatial discontinuities, however, are more devious and dialectical, and they are not overcome in any of the most obvious ways. For example, they returned on the Detroit experience as some ultimate limit before which it collapsed. What happened was that the jet-setting militants of the League had become media stars; not only were they becoming alienated from their local constituencies, but, worse than that, nobody stayed home to mind the store. Having acceded to a larger spatial plane, the base vanished under them; and with this the most successful social revolutionary experiment of that rich political decade in the United States came to a sadly undramatic end. I do not want to say that it left no traces behind, since a number of local gains remain, and in any case every rich political experiment continues to feed the tradition in underground ways. Most ironic in our context, however, is the very success of their failure: the representation—the model of this complex spatial dialectic—triumphantly survives in the form of a film and a book, but in the process of becoming an image and a spectacle, the referent seems to have disappeared, as so many people from Debord to Baudrillard always warned us it would.

Yet this very example may serve to illustrate the proposition that successful spatial representation today need not be some uplifting socialist-realist drama of revolutionary triumph but may be equally inscribed in a narrative of defeat, which sometimes, even more effectively, causes the whole architectonic of postmodern global space to rise up in ghostly profile behind itself, as some ultimate dialectical barrier or invisible limit. This example also may have given a little more meaning to the slogan of cognitive mapping to which I now turn.

I am tempted to describe the way I understand this concept as something of a synthesis between Althusser and Kevin Lynch—a formulation that, to be sure, does not tell you much unless you know that Lynch is the author of a classic work, *The Image of the City*, which in its turn spawned the whole low-level subdiscipline that today takes the phrase "cognitive mapping" as its own designation.[2] Lynch's problematic remains locked within the limits of phenomenology, and his book can no doubt be subjected to many criticisms on its own terms (not the least of which is the absence of any conception of political agency or historical process). My use of the book will be emblematic, since the mental map of city space explored by Lynch can be extrapolated to that mental map of the social and global totality we all carry around in our heads in variously garbled forms. Drawing on the downtowns of Boston, Jersey City, and Los Angeles, and by means of interviews and questionnaires in which subjects were asked to draw their city context from memory, Lynch suggests that urban alienation is directly proportional to the mental unmapability of local cityscapes. A city like Boston, then, with its monumental perspectives, its markers and monuments, its combination of grand but simple spatial forms, including dramatic boundaries such as the Charles River, not only allows people to have, in their imaginations, a generally successful and continuous location to the rest of the city, but in addition gives them something of the freedom and aesthetic gratification of traditional city form.

I have always been struck by the way in which Lynch's conception of city experience—the dialectic between the here and now of immediate perception and the imaginative or imaginary sense of the city as an absent totality—presents something like a spatial analogue of Althusser's great formulation of ideology itself, as "the Imaginary representation of the subject's relationship to his or her Real conditions of existence." Whatever its defects and problems, this positive conception of ideology as a necessary function in any form of social life has the great merit of stressing the gap between the local positioning of the individual subject and the totality of class structures in which he or she is situated, a gap between phenomenological perception and a reality that transcends all individual thinking or experience; but this ideology, as such, attempts to span or coordinate, to map, by means of conscious and unconscious representations. The conception of cognitive mapping proposed here therefore involves an extrapolation of Lynch's spatial analysis to the realm of social structure, that is to say, in our historical moment, to the totality of class relations on a global (or should I say multinational) scale. The secondary premise is also maintained, namely, that the incapacity to map socially is as crippling to political experience as the analogous incapacity to map spatially is for urban experience. It follows that an aesthetic of cognitive mapping in this sense is an integral part of any socialist political project.

In what has preceded I have infringed so many of the taboos and shibboleths of a faddish post-Marxism that it becomes necessary to discuss them more openly and directly before proceeding. They include the proposition that class no longer exists (a proposition that might be clarified by the simple distinction between class as an element in small-scale models of society, class consciousness as a cultural event, and class analysis as a mental operation); the idea that this society is no longer motored by production but rather reproduction (including science and technology)—an idea that, in the midst of a virtually completely built environment, one is tempted to greet with laughter; and, finally, the repudiation of representation and the stigmatization of the concept of totality and of the project of totalizing thought. Practically, this last needs to be sorted into several different propositions—in particular, one having to do with capitalism and one having to do with socialism or communism. The French *nouveaux philosophes* said it most succinctly, without realizing that they were reproducing or reinventing the hoariest American ideological slogans of the cold war: totalizing thought is totalitarian thought; a direct line runs from Hegel's Absolute Spirit to Stalin's Gulag.

As a matter of self-indulgence, I will open a brief theoretical parenthesis here, particularly since Althusser has been mentioned. We have already experienced a dramatic and instructive melt-down of the Althusserian reactor in the work of Barry Hindess and Paul Hirst, who quite consequently observe the incompatibility of the Althusserian attempt to secure semi-autonomy for the various levels of social life, and the more desperate effort of the same philosopher to retain the old orthodox notion of an "ultimately determining instance" in the form of what he calls "structural totality." Quite logically and consequently, then, Hindess and Hirst simply remove the offending mechanism, whereupon the Althusserian edifice collapses into a rubble of autonomous instances without any necessary relationship to each other whatsoever—at which point it follows that one can no longer talk about or draw practical political consequences from any conception of social structure; that is to say, the very conceptions of something called capitalism and something called socialism or communism fall of their own weight into the ash can of History. (This last, of course, then vanishes in a puff of smoke, since by the same token nothing like History as a total process can any longer be conceptually entertained.) All I wanted to point out in this high theoretical context is that the baleful equation between a philosophical conception of totality and a political practice of totalitarianism is itself a particularly ripe example of what Althusser calls "expressive causality," namely, the collapsing of two semiautonomous (or, now, downright autonomous) levels into one another. Such an equation, then, is possible for unreconstructed Hegelians but is quite incompatible with the basic positions of any honest post-Althusserian post-Marxism.

To close the parenthesis, all of this can be said in more earthly terms. The conception of capital is admittedly a totalizing or systemic concept: no one has ever seen or met the thing itself; it is either the result of scientific reduction (and it should be obvious that scientific thinking always reduces the multiplicity of the real to a small-scale model) or the mark of an imaginary and ideological vision. But let us be serious: anyone who believes that the profit motive and the logic of capital accumulation are not the fundamental laws of this world, who believes that these do not set absolute barriers and limits to social changes and transformations undertaken in it—such a person is living in an alternative universe; or, to put it more politely, in this universe such a person—assuming he or she is progressive—is doomed to social democracy, with its now abundantly documented treadmill of failures and capitulations. Because if capital does not exist, then clearly socialism does not exist either. I am far from suggesting that no politics at all is possible in this new post-Marxian Nietzschean world of micropolitics—that is observably untrue. But I do want to argue that without a conception of the social totality (and the possibility of transforming a whole social system), no properly socialist politics is possible.

About socialism itself we must raise more troubling and unsolved dilemmas that involve the notion of community or the collective. Some of the dilemmas are very familiar, such as the contradiction between self-management on the local level and planning on the global scale; or the problems raised by the abolition of the market, not to mention the abolition of the commodity form itself. I have found even more stimulating and problematical the following propositions about the very nature of society itself: it has been affirmed that, with one signal exception (capitalism itself, which is organized around an economic mechanism), there has never existed a cohesive form of human society that was not based on some form of transcendence or religion. Without brute force, which is never but a momentary solution, people cannot in this vein be asked to live cooperatively and to renounce the omnivorous desires of the id without some appeal to religious belief or transcendent values, something absolutely incompatible with any conceivable socialist society. The result is that these last achieve their own momentary coherence only under seige circumstances, in the wartime enthusiasm and group effort provoked by the great blockades. In other words, without the nontranscendent economic mechanism of capital, all appeals to moral incentives (as in Che) or to the primacy of the political (as in Maoism) must fatally exhaust themselves in a brief time, leaving only the twin alternatives of a return to capitalism or the construction of this or that modern form of "oriental despotism." You are certainly welcome to believe this prognosis, provided you understand that in such a case any socialist politics is strictly a mirage and a waste of time, which one might better spend adjusting and reforming an eternal capitalist landscape as far as the eye can see.

In reality this dilemma is, to my mind, the most urgent task that confronts Marxism today. I have said before that the so-called crisis in Marxism is not a crisis in Marxist science, which has never been richer, but rather a crisis in Marxist ideology. If ideology—to give it a somewhat different definition—is a vision of the future that grips the masses, we have to admit that, save in a few ongoing collective experiments, such as those in Cuba and in Yugoslavia, no Marxist or Socialist party or movement anywhere has the slightest conception of what socialism or communism as a social system ought to be and can be expected to look like. That vision will not be purely economic, although the Marxist economists are as deficient as the rest of us in their failure to address this Utopian problem in any serious way. It is, as well, supremely social and cultural, involving the task of trying to imagine how a society without hierarchy, a society of free people, a society that has at once repudiated the economic mechanisms of the market, can possibly cohere. Historically, all forms of hierarchy have always been based ultimately on gender hierarchy and on the building block of the family unit, which makes it clear that this is the true juncture between a feminist problematic and a Marxist one—not an antagonistic juncture, but the moment at which the feminist project and the Marxist and socialist project meet and face the same dilemma: how to imagine Utopia.

Returning to the beginning of this lengthy excursus, it seems unlikely that anyone who repudiates the concept of totality can have anything useful to say to us on this matter, since for such persons it is clear that the totalizing vision of socialism will not compute and is a false problem within the random and undecidable world of microgroups. Or perhaps another possibility suggests itself, namely, that our dissatisfaction with the concept of totality is not a thought in its own right but rather a significant symptom, a function of the increasing difficulties in thinking of such a set of interrelationships in a complicated society. This would seem, at least, to be the implication of the remark of the Team X architect Aldo van Eyck, when, in 1966, he issued his version of the death of modernism thesis: "We know nothing of vast multiplicity—we cannot come to terms with it—not as architects or planners or anybody else." To which he added, and the sequel can easily be extrapolated from architecture to social change itself: "But if society has no form—how can architects build its counterform?"[3]

You will be relieved to know that at this point we can return both to my own conclusion and to the problem of aesthetic representation and cognitive mapping, which was the pretext of this essay. The project of cognitive mapping obviously stands or falls with the conception of some (unrepresentable, imaginary) global social totality that was to have been mapped. I have spoken of form and content, and this final distinction will allow me at least to say something about an aesthetic, of which I have observed that I am, myself, absolutely incapable of guessing or imagining its form. That postmodernism gives us hints and examples of such cognitive mapping on the level of content is, I believe, demonstrable.

I have spoken elsewhere of the turn toward a thematics of mechanical reproduction, of the way in which the autoreferentiality of much of postmodernist art takes the form of a play with reproductive technology—film, tapes, video, computers, and the like—which is, to my mind, a degraded figure of the great multinational space that remains to be cognitively mapped. Fully as striking on another level is the omnipresence of the theme of paranoia as it expresses itself in a seemingly inexhaustible production of conspiracy plots of the most elaborate kinds. Conspiracy, one is tempted to say, is the poor person's cognitive mapping in the postmodern age; it is a degraded figure of the total logic of late capital, a desperate attempt to represent the latter's system, whose failure is marked by its slippage into sheer theme and content.

Achieved cognitive mapping will be a matter of form, and I hope I have shown how it will be an integral part of a socialist politics, although its own possibility may well be dependent on some prior political opening, which its task would then be to enlarge culturally. Still, even if we cannot imagine the productions of such an aesthetic, there may, nonetheless, as with the very idea of Utopia itself, be something positive in the attempt to keep alive the possibility of imagining such a thing.

NOTES

1. Dan Georgakis and Marvin Surkin, *Detroit: I Do Mind Dying. A Study in Urban Revolution* (New York: St. Martin's Press, 1975).
2. Kevin Lynch, *The Image of the City* (Cambridge: MIT Press, 1960).
3. Quoted in Kenneth Frampton, *Modern Architecture: A Critical History* (New York: Oxford University Press, 1980), pp. 276–77.

HISTORICISM AND CULTURAL STUDIES

THE HISTORICAL TEXT AS LITERARY ARTIFACT
(1974, 1978)[1]

HAYDEN WHITE

Building on his book Metahistory *(1973), which studied the literary forms of nineteenth-century history writing, in this article White sees history as literary. For White, history is not the recording of the real so much as the telling of a story. We tend to think that the real determines the story, but White argues that the story determines the real. The best history, therefore, does not just present the facts. Instead, with "critical self-consciousness," it contemplates competing ways of figuring those facts into a story, what White calls an "emplotment." Drawing on structuralist notions from Claude Lévi-Strauss and Roman Jakobson, White anticipates the new historicist idea that facts do not lead to interpretation so much as interpretation shapes or produces what we recognize as facts. Working with Jakobson's "Linguistics and Poetics," White builds on the opposition between metaphor and metonymy and on the notion of encoding and decoding. Readers can compare White's ideas to Stuart Hall's elaboration of the same process in "Encoding and Decoding."*

One of the ways that a scholarly field takes stock of itself is by considering its history. Yet it is difficult to get an objective history of a scholarly discipline, because, if the historian is himself a practitioner of it, he is likely to be a devotee of one or another of its sects and hence biased; and if he is not a practitioner, he is unlikely to have the expertise necessary to distinguish between the significant and the insignificant events of his field's development. One might think that these difficulties would not arise in the field of history itself, but they do and not only for the reasons mentioned above. In order to write the history of any given scholarly discipline or even of a science, one must be prepared to ask questions *about* it of a sort that do not have to be asked in the practice *of* it. One must try to get behind or beneath the presuppositions which sustain a given type of inquiry and ask the questions that can be begged in its practice in the interest of determining why this type of inquiry has been designed to solve the problems it characteristically tries to solve. This is what metahistory seeks to do. It addresses itself to such questions as: What is the structure of a peculiarly *historical* consciousness? What is the epistemological status of historical *explanations*, as compared with other kinds of explanations that might be offered to account for the materials with which historians ordinarily deal? What are the possible *forms* of historical representation and what are their bases? What authority can historical accounts claim as contributions to a secured knowledge of reality in general and to the human sciences in particular?

Now, many of these questions have been dealt with quite competently over the last quarter-century by philosophers concerned to define history's relationships to other disciplines, especially the physical and social sciences, and by historians interested in assessing the success of their discipline in mapping the past and determining the relationship of that past to the present. But there is one problem that neither philosophers nor historians have looked at very seriously and to which literary theorists have given only passing attention. This question has to do with the status of the historical narrative, considered purely as a verbal artifact which purports to be a model of structures and processes that are long past and cannot therefore be subjected to either experimental or observational controls. This is not to say that historians and philosophers of history have failed to take notice of the essentially provisional and contingent nature of historical representations and of their susceptibility to infinite revision in the light of new evidence or more sophisticated conceptualization of problems. One of the marks of a good professional historian is the consistency with which he reminds his readers of the purely provisional nature of his characterizations of events, agents, and agencies found in the always incomplete historical record. Nor is it to say that literary theorists have *never* studied the structure of historical narratives. But in general there has been a reluctance to consider historical narratives as what they most manifestly are: that is to say verbal fictions, the contents of which are as much *invented* as *found* and the forms of which have more in common with their counterparts in literature than they have with those in the sciences.

Now, it is obvious that this conflation of mythic and historical consciousness will offend some historians and disturb those literary theorists whose conception of literature presupposes a radical opposition of history to fiction or of fact to fancy. As Northrop Frye has remarked, "In a sense the historical is the opposite of the mythical, and to tell the historian that what gives shape to his book is a myth would sound to him vaguely insulting." Yet Frye himself grants that "when a historian's scheme gets to a certain point of comprehensiveness it becomes mythical in shape, and so approaches the poetic in its structure." He even speaks of different kinds of historical myths: Romantic myths "based on a quest or pilgrimage to a City of God or classless society;" Comic "myths of progress through evolution or revolution;" Tragic myths of "decline and fall like the works of Gibbon and Spengler;" and Ironic "myths of recurrence or casual catastrophe." But Frye appears to believe that these myths are operative only in such victims of what might be called the "poetic fallacy" as Hegel, Marx, Nietzsche, Spengler, Toynbee, and Sartre—historians whose fascination with the "constructive" capacity of human thought has deadened their responsibility to the "found" data. "The historian works inductively," he says, "collecting his facts and trying to avoid any informing patterns except those he sees, or is honestly convinced he sees, in the facts themselves." He does not work "from" a "unifying form," as the poet does, but "toward" it; and it therefore follows that the historian, like any writer of discursive prose, is to be judged "by the truth of what he says, or by the adequacy of his verbal reproduction of his external model," whether that external model be the actions of past men or the historian's own thought about such actions.

What Frye says is true enough as a statement of the *ideal* that has inspired historical writing since the time of the Greeks, but that ideal presupposes an opposition between myth and history that is as problematical as it is venerable. It serves Frye's purposes very well, since it permits him to locate the specifically "fictive" in the space between the two concepts of the "mythic" and the "historical." As readers of Frye's *Anatomy of Criticism* will remember, Frye conceives fictions to consist in part of sublimates of archetypal myth-structures. These structures have been displaced to the interior of verbal artifacts in such a way as to serve as their latent meanings. The fundamental meanings of all fictions, their thematic content, consist, in Frye's view, of the "pre-generic plot-structures" or "mythoi" derived from the corpora of Classical and Judaeo-Christian religious literature. According to this theory, we understand *why* a particular story has "turned out" as it has when we have identified the archetypal myth, or pre-generic plot-structure, of which the story is an exemplification. And we see the "point" of a story when we have identified its theme (Frye's translation of *dianoia*), which makes of it a "parable or illustrative fable." "Every work of literature," Frye insists, "has both a fictional and a thematic aspect," but as we move from "fictional projection" toward the overt articulation of theme, the writing tends to take on the aspect of "direct address, or straight discursive writing and cease (s) to be literature." And in Frye's view, as we have seen, history (or at least "proper history") belongs to the category of "discursive writing," so that when the fictional element—or mythic plot-structure—is *obviously* present in it, ceases to be history altogether and becomes a bastard genre, product of an unholy, though not unnatural, union between history and poetry.

Yet—I would argue—histories gain part of their explanatory effect by their success in making stories out of *mere* chronicles; and stories in turn are made out of chronicles by an operation which I have elsewhere called "emplotment." And by emplotment I mean simply the encodation of the facts contained in the chronicle as components of specific *kinds* of plot-structures, in precisely the way that Frye has suggested is the case with "fictions" in general.

The late R. G. Collingwood insisted that the historian was above all a story-teller and suggested that historical sensibility was manifested in the capacity to make a plausible story out of a congeries of "facts" which, in their unprocessed form, made no sense at all. In their efforts to make sense of the historical record, which is fragmentary and always incomplete, historians have to make use of what Collingwood called "the constructive imagination" which told the historian—as it tells the competent detective—what "must have been the case" given the available evidence and the formal properties it displayed to the consciousness capable of putting the right question to it. This constructive imagination functions in much the same way that Kant supposed the a priori imagination functions when it tells us that, even though we cannot perceive both sides of a tabletop simultaneously, we can be certain it has *two* sides if it has one, because the very concept of *one side* entails at least *one other*. Collingwood suggested that historians come to their evidence endowed with a sense of the *possible* forms that different kinds of recognizably human situations *can* take. He called this sense the nose for the "story" contained in the evidence or for the "true" story that was buried in or hidden behind the "apparent" story. And he concluded that historians provide plausible explanations for bodies of historical evidence when they succeed in discovering the "story" or complex of "stories" inplicitly contained within them.

What Collingwood failed to see was that no given set of casually recorded historical events in themselves constitute a story; the most that they offer to the historian are story *elements*. The events are *made* into a story by the suppression or subordination of certain of them and the highlighting of others, by characterization, motific repetition, variation of tone and point of view, alternative descriptive strategies, and the like—in short, all of the techniques that we would normally expect to find in the emplotment of a novel or a play. For example, no historical event is *intrinsically tragic*; it can only be conceived as such from a particular point of view or from within the context of a structured set of events of which it is an element enjoying a privileged place. For in history what is tragic from one perspective is comic from another, just as in society what appears to be "tragic" from the standpoint of one class may be, as Marx purported to show of the 18th Brumaire of Louis Buonaparte, only a "farce" from that of another class. Considered as potential elements of a story, historical events are value-neutral. Whether they find their place finally in a story that is tragic, comic, romantic or ironic—to use Frye's categories—depends upon the historian's decision to configure them according to the imperatives of one plot-structure or mythos rather than another. The same set of events can serve as components of a story that is tragic *or* comic, as the case may be, depending on the historian's choice of the plot-structure that he considers most appropriate for ordering events of that kind so as to make them into a comprehensible story.

This suggests that what the historian brings to his consideration of the historical record is a notion of the *types* of configurations of events that can be recognized as stories by the audience for which he is writing. True, he can misfire. I do not suppose that anyone would accept the emplotment of the life of President Kennedy as comedy, but whether it ought to be emplotted romantically, tragically, or satirically is an open question. The important point is that most historical sequences can be emplotted in a number of different ways, so as to provide different interpretations of those events and to endow them with different meanings. Thus, for example, what Michelet in his great history of the French Revolution construed as a drama of Romantic transcendence, his contemporary Tocqueville emplotted as an ironic Tragedy. Neither can be said to have had more knowledge of the "facts" contained in the record; they simply had different notions of the kind of story that best fitted the facts they knew. Nor should it be thought that they told different stories of the Revolution because they had discovered different *kinds* of facts, political on the one hand, social on the other. They sought out different kinds of facts because they had different kinds of stories to tell. But why did these alternative, not to say mutually exclusive, representations of what was substantially the same set of events appear equally plausible to their respective audiences? Simply because the historians shared with their audiences certain preconceptions about how the Revolution might be emplotted, in response to imperatives that were generally extra-historical, ideological, aesthetic, or mythical, in nature.

Collingwood once remarked that you could never explicate a tragedy to anyone who was not already acquainted with the kinds of situations that are regarded as "tragic" in our culture. Anyone who has taught or taken one of those omnibus courses, usually entitled Western Civilization or Introduction to the Classics of Western Literature, will know what Collingwood had in mind. Unless you have some idea of the generic attributes of tragic, comic, romantic, or ironic situations, you will be unable to recognize them as such when you come upon them in a literary text. But historical situations do not have built into them intrinsic meanings in the way that literary texts do. Historical situations are not *inherently* tragic, comic, or romantic. They may all be inherently ironic but they need not be emplotted that way. All the historian needs to do to transform a tragic into a comic situation is to shift his point of view or change the scope of his perceptions. Anyway, we only think of situations as tragic or comic because these concepts are part of our generally cultural and specifically literary heritage. *How* a given historical situation is to be configured depends on the historian's subtlety in matching up a specific plot-structure with the set of historical events which he wishes to endow with a meaning of a particular kind. This is essentially a literary, that is to say fiction-making, operation. And to call it that in no way detracts from the status of historical narratives as providing a kind of knowledge. For not only are the pre-generic plot-structures by which sets of events can be constituted as stories of a particular kind limited in number, as Frye and other archetypal critics suggest; but the encodation of events in terms of such plot-structures is one of the ways that a culture has of making sense of both personal and public pasts.

We can make sense of sets of events in a number of different ways. One of the ways is to subsume the events under the causal laws which may have governed their concatenation in order to produce the particular configuration that the events appear to assume when considered as "effects of mechanical forces. This is the way of scientific explanation. Another way we make sense of a set of events which appears strange, enigmatic, or mysterious in its immediate manifestations is to encode the set in terms of culturally provided categories, such as metaphysical concepts, religious beliefs, or story-forms. The effect of such encodations is to familiarize the unfamiliar, and in general this is the way of historiography, whose "data" are always immediately strange, not to say exotic, simply by virtue of their distance from us in time and their origination in a way of life different from our own.

The historian shares with his audience *general notions* of the *forms* that significant human situations *must* take by virtue of his participation in the specific processes of sense-making which identify him as a member of one cultural endowment rather than another. In the process of studying a given complex of events, he begins to perceive the *possible* story-form that such events *may* figure. In his narrative account of how this set of events took on the shape which he perceives to inhere within it, he emplots his account as a story of a particular kind. The reader, in the process of following the historian's account of those events, gradually comes to realize that the story he is reading is of one kind rather than another: romance, tragedy, comedy, satire, epic, or what have you. And when he has perceived the class or type of stories to which the story that he is reading belongs, he experiences the effect of having the events in the story explained to him. He has at this point not only successfully *followed* the story, he has grasped the point of it, *understood* it, as well. The original strangeness, mystery, or exoticism of the events is dispelled and they take on a familiar aspect, not in their details, but in their functions as elements of a familiar kind of configuration. They are rendered comprehensible by being subsumed under the categories of the plot-structure in which they are encoded as a story of a particular kind. They are familiarized, not only because the reader now has more *information* about the events, but also because he has been shown how the data conform to an *icon* of a comprehensible finished process, a plot-structure with which he is familiar as a part of his cultural endowment.

This is not unlike what happens, or is supposed to happen, in psychotherapy. The set of events in the patient's past which are the presumed cause of his distress, manifested in the neurotic syndrome, have been defamiliarized, rendered strange, mysterious, and threatening and assumed a meaning that he can neither accept nor effectively reject. It is not that the patient does not *know* what those events were, does not know the facts; for if he did not in some sense know the facts, he would be unable to recognize them and repress them whenever they arise in his consciousness. On the contrary, he knows them all too well. He knows them so well, in fact, that he lives with them constantly and in such a way as to make it impossible for him to see any other facts except through the coloration that the set of events in question gives to his perception of the world. We might say that, according to the theory of psycho-analysis, the patient has over-emplotted these events, has charged them with a meaning so intense that, whether real or merely imagined, they continue to shape both his perceptions and his responses to the world long after they should have become "past history." The therapist's problem, then, is not to hold up before the patient the "real facts" of the matter, the "truth" as against the "fantasy" that obsesses him. Nor is it to give him a short course in psychoanalytical theory by which to enlighten him as to the true nature of his distress by cataloguing it as a manifestation of some "complex." This is what the analyst might do in relating the patient's case to a third party, and especially to another analyst. But psychoanalytic theory recognizes that the patient will resist both of these tactics in the same way that he resists the intrusion into consciousness of the traumatized memory traces in the *form* that he obsessively remembers them. The problem is to get the patient to "re-emplot" his whole life history in such a way as to change the *meaning* of those events for him and their *significance* for the economy of the whole set of events that make up his life. As thus envisaged, the therapeutic process is an exercise in the refamiliarization of events that have been defamiliarized, rendered alienated from the patient's life-history, by virtue of their over-determination as causal forces. And we might say that the events are detraumatized by being removed from the plot-structure in which they have a dominant place and inserted in another in which they have a subordinate or simply ordinary function as elements of a life shared with all other men.

Now, I am not interested in forcing the analogy between psychotherapy and historiography; I use the example merely to illustrate a point about the fictive component in historical narratives. Historians seek to refamiliarize us with events which have been forgotten through either accident, neglect, or repression. Moreover, the greatest historians have always dealt with those events in the histories of their cultures which are "traumatic" in nature and the meaning of which is either problematical or overdetermined in the significance that they still have for current life, events such as revolutions, civil wars, large scale processes such as industrialization and urbanization, or institutions which have lost their original function in a society but continue to play an important role on the current social scene. In looking at the ways in which such structures took shape or evolved, historians *re*familiarize them, not only by providing more information about them, but also by showing how their developments conformed to one or another of the story types that we conventionally invoke to make sense of our own life-histories.

Now, if any of this is plausible as a characterization of the explanatory effect of historical narrative, it tells us something important about the *mimetic* aspect of historical narratives. It is generally maintained—as Frye said—that a history is a verbal model of a set of events external to the mind of the historian. But it is wrong to think of a history as a model similar to a scale model of an airplane or ship, a map, or a photograph. For with this latter kind of model, we can check its adequacy by going and looking at the original and, by applying the necessary rules of translation, seeing in what respect the model has actually succeeded in reproducing aspects of the original. But historical structures and processes are not like these originals; we cannot go and look at them in order to see if the historian has adequately reproduced them in his narrative. Nor should we want to, even if we could; for after all it was the very strangeness of the original as it appeared in the documents that inspired the historian's efforts to make a model of it in the first place. If the historian only did that for us we should be in the same situation as the patient whose analyst merely told him, on the basis of interviews with his parents, siblings and childhood friends, what the "true facts" of the patient's early life were. We would have no reason to think that anything at all had been *explained* to us.

This is what leads me to think that historical narratives are not only models of past events and processes but also metaphorical statements which suggest a relation of similitude between such events and processes and the story-types that we conventionally use to endow the events of our lives with culturally sanctioned meanings. Viewed in a purely formal way, a historical narrative is not only a *reproduction* of the events reported in it, it is also a *complex of symbols* which gives us directions for finding an *icon* of the structure of those events in our literary tradition.

I am here of course invoking the distinctions between sign, symbol, and icon which C. S. Peirce developed in his philosophy of language. I think that these distinctions will help us to understand what is fictive in all putatively realistic representations of the world and what is realistic in all manifestly fictive ones. They help us, in short, to answer the question: what are historical representations *representations of*? It seems to me that we must say of histories what Frye seems to think is true only of poetry or philosophies of history, namely that, considered as a system of signs, the historical narrative points in two directions simultaneously: *toward* the events described in the narrative and *toward* the story-type or mythos which the historian has chosen to serve as the icon of the structure of the events. The narrative itself is not the icon; what it does is *describe* events in the historical record in such a way as to inform the reader *what to take as an icon* of the events so as to render them "familiar" to him. The historical narrative thus mediates between the events reported in it on the one side and pre-generic plot-structures conventionally used in our culture to endow unfamiliar events and situation with meanings.

The evasion of the implications of the fictive nature of historical narrative is in part a consequence of the utility of the concept "history" for the definition of other types of discourse. "History" can be set over against "science" by virtue of its want of conceptual rigor and failure to produce the kinds of universal laws that the sciences characteristically seek to produce. Similarly, "history" can be set over against "literature" by virtue of its interest in the "actual" rather than the "possible," which is supposedly the object of representation of "literary" works. Thus, within a long and distinguished critical tradition that has sought to determine what is "real" and what is "imagined" in the novel, "history" has served as a kind of archetype of the "realistic" pole of representation. I am thinking of Frye, Auerbach, Booth, Scholes and Kellogg, and others. Nor is it unusual for literary theorists, when they are speaking about the "context" of a literary work, to suppose that this "context," the "historical milieu," has a concreteness and an accessibility that the work itself can never have: as if it were easier to perceive the reality of a past world put together from a thousand historical documents than it is to probe the depths of a single literary work that is present to the critic studying it. But the presumed concreteness and accessibility of historical milieux, these "contexts" of the "texts" that literary scholars study, are themselves products of the fictive capability of the historians who have studied those contexts. The historical documents are not less opaque than the texts studied by the literary critic. Nor is the world those documents figure more accessible. The one is no more "given" than the other. In fact, the opaqueness of the world figured in historical documents is, if anything, increased by the production of historical narratives. Each new historical work only adds to the number of possible texts that have to be interpreted if a full and accurate picture of a given historical milieu is to be faithfully drawn. The relationship between the past to be analyzed and historical works produced by analysis of the documents is paradoxical; the *more* we know about the past, the more difficult it is to generalize about it.

But if the increase in our knowledge of the past makes it more difficult to generalize about it, it should make it easier for us to generalize about the forms in which that knowledge is transmitted to us. Our knowledge of the past may increase incrementally, but our understanding of it does not. Nor does our understanding of the past progress by the kind of revolutionary breakthroughs that we associate with the development of the physical sciences. Like literature, history progresses by the production of classics, the nature of which is such that they cannot be disconfirmed or negated, in the way that the principal conceptual schemata of the sciences are. And it is their nondisconfirmability that testifies to the essentially *literary* nature of historical classics. There is something in a historical masterpiece that cannot be negated, and this non-negatable element is its form, the form which is its fiction.

It is frequently forgotten or, when remembered, denied, that no given set of events attested by the historical record comprises a *story* manifestly finished and complete. This is as true of the events that comprise the life of an individual as it is of an institution, a nation, or a whole people. We do not *live* stories, even if we give our lives meaning by retrospectively casting them in the form of stories. And so too with nations or whole cultures. In an essay on the "mythical" nature of historiography, Lévi-Strauss remarks on the astonishment that a visitor from another planet would feel if confronted by the thousands of histories actually written about the French Revolution. For in those works, the "authors do not always make use of the same incidents; when they do, the incidents are revealed in different lights. And yet these are variations which have to do with the same country, the same period, and the same events—events whose reality is scattered across every level of a multilayered structure." He goes on to suggest that the criterion of validity by which historical accounts might be assessed cannot depend on their "elements," that is to say their putative "factual" content. On the contrary, he notes, "Pursued in isolation, each element shows itself to be beyond grasp. But certain of them derive consistency from the fact that they can be integrated into a system whose terms are more or less credible when set against the overall coherence of the series." But this "coherence of the series" cannot be the coherence of the *chronological* series, that sequence of "facts" organized into the temporal order of their original occurrence. For the "chronicle" of events, out of which the historian fashions his story of "what really happened," already comes pre-encoded. There are "hot" and "cold" chronologies, chronologies in which more or less numbers of dates appear to demand inclusion in a full "chronicle" of "what happened." Moreover, the "dates" themselves come to us already grouped into "classes of dates," classes which are constitutive of putative "domains" of the historical field, domains which appear as problems for the historian to solve if he is to give a full and culturally responsible account of the past.

All this suggests to Lévi-Strauss that, when it is a matter of working up a comprehensive account of the various "domains" of the historical record in the form of a story, the "alleged historical continuities" that the historian purports to find in the record are "secured only by dint of fraudulent outlines" imposed by the historian on record. These "fraudulent outlines" are, in his view, a product of "abstraction" and a means of escape from the "threat of an infinite regress" that always lurks at the interior of every complex of historical "facts." We can construct a comprehensible story of the past, Lévi-Strauss insists, only by a decision to "give up" one or more of the domains of facts offering themselves for inclusion in our accounts. Our *explanations* of historical structures and processes are thus determined more by what we leave out of our representations than by what we put in. For it is in this brutal capacity to exclude certain facts in the interest of constituting others as components of comprehensible stories that the historian displays his tact as well as his understanding. The "overall coherence" of any given "series" of historical facts is the coherence of story, but this coherence is achieved only by a tailoring of the "facts" to the requirements of the story-form. And thus Lévi-Strauss concludes: "In spite of worthy and indispensible efforts to bring another moment in history alive and to possess it, a clairvoyant history should admit that it never completely escapes from the nature of myth."

It is this mediative function that permits us to speak of a historical narrative as an extended metaphor. As a symbolic structure, the historical narrative does not *reproduce* the events it describes; it tells us in what direction to think about the events and charges our thought about the events with different emotional valences. The historical narrative does not *image* the things it indicates, it *calls to mind* images of the things it indicates in the same way that a metaphor does. When a given concourse of events is emplotted as a "tragedy," this simply means that the historian has so described the events as to *remind us* of that form of fiction which we associate with the concept "tragic." Properly understood, histories ought never to be read as unambiguous signs of the events they report, but rather as symbolic structures, extended metaphors, that "liken" the events reported in them to some form with which we have already become familiar in our literary culture.

Perhaps I should indicate briefly what is meant by the *symbolic* and *iconic* aspects of a metaphor. The hackneyed phrase, "My love, a rose," is not, obviously, intended to be understood as suggesting that the loved one is *actually* a rose. It is not even meant to suggest that the loved one has the specific attributes of a rose, that is to say, that the loved one is red, yellow, orange or black, is a plant, has thorns, needs sunlight, should be sprayed regularly with insecticides, and so on. It is meant to be understood as indicating that the beloved shares the *qualities* which the rose has come to *symbolize* in the customary linguistic usages of Western culture. That is to say, considered as a message, the metaphor gives directions for finding an entity that will evoke the images associated *with loved ones and roses alike* in our culture. The metaphor does not *image* the thing it seeks to characterize, *it gives directions* for finding the set of images that are intended to be associated with that thing. It functions as a symbol, rather than as a sign: which is to say that it does not give us either a *description* or an *icon* of the thing it represents, but *tells us* what images to look for in our culturally encoded experience in order to determine how we *should feel* about the thing represented.

So too for historical narratives. They succeed in endowing sets of past events with meanings, over and above whatever comprehension they provide by appeal to putative causal laws, by exploiting the metaphorical similarities between sets of real events and the conventional structures of our fictions. By the very constitution of a set of events in such a way as to make a comprehensible story out of them, the historian changes those events with the sympolic significance of a comprehensible plot-structure. Historians may not like to think of their works as translations of "fact" into "fictions"; but this is one of the effects of their works. By suggesting alternative emplotments of a given sequence of historical events, historians provide historical events with all of the possible meanings with which the literary art of their culture is capable of endowing them. The real dispute between the "proper historian" and the "philosopher of history" has to do with the latter's insistence that events can be emplotted in one and only one story-form. History writing thrives on the discovery of all the possible plot-structures that might be invoked to endow sets of events with different meanings. And our understanding of the past increases precisely in the degree to which we succeed in determining how far that past conforms to the strategies of sense-making that are contained in their purest forms in literary art.

Conceiving historical narratives in this way may give us some insight into the crisis in historical thinking which has been under way since the beginning of our century. Let's imagine that the problem of the historian is to make sense of a hypothetical *set* of events by arranging them in a *series* that is at once chronological *and* syntactically structured, in the way that any discourse from a sentence all the way up to a novel is structured. We can see immediately that the imperatives of chronological arrangement of the events constituting the set must exist in tension with the imperatives of the syntactical strategies alluded to whether the latter are conceived as those of logic (the syllogism) or those of narrative (the plot structure).

Thus, we have a set of events :

1. a, b, c, d, e,.........n,

ordered chronologically but requiring description and characterization as elements of plot or argument by which to give them meaning. Now, the series can be emplotted in a number of different ways and thereby endowed with different meanings without violating the imperatives of the chronological arrangement at all. We may briefly characterize some of these emplotments in the following way:

2. A, b, c, d, e,.........n
3. a, B, c, d, e,.........n
4. a, b, C, d, e,.........n
5. a, b, c, D, e,.........n

And so on.

The capitalized letters indicate the privileged status given to certain events or sets of events in the series by which they are endowed with explanatory force, either as causes explaining the structure of the whole series or as symbols of the plot-structure of the series considered as a story of a specific kind. We might say that any history which endows any putatively "original" event (a) with the status of a decisive factor (A) in the structuration of the whole series of events following after it is "deterministic." The emplotments of the history of "society" by Rousseau in his *Second Discourse*, Marx in the *Manifesto*, and Freud in *Totem and Taboo* would fall into this category. So too any history which endows the last event in the series (e), whether real or only speculatively projected, with the force of full explanatory power (E) is of the type of all eschatological or apocalyptical histories. St. Augustine's *City of God* and the various versions of the Joachite notion of the advent of a millenium, Hegel's *Philosophy of History*, and in general all Idealist histories are of this sort. In between we would have the various forms of historiography which appeal to plot-structures of a distinctively "fictional" sort (Romance, Comedy, Tragedy, and Satire) by which to endow the series with a perceivable form and a conceivable "meaning."

If the series were simply recorded in the order in which the events originally occurred, under the assumption that the ordering of the events in their temporal sequence itself provided a kind of explanation of why they occurred when and where they did, we would have the pure form of the *chronicle*. This would be a "naive" form of chronicle however, inasmuch as the categories of time and space alone served as the informing interpretative principles. Over against the "naive" form of chronicle we could postulate as a logical possibility its "sentimental" counterpart, the ironic denial that historical series have any kind of larger significance or describe any imaginable plot structure or indeed can even be construed as a story with a discernible beginning, middle, and end. We could conceive such accounts of history as intending to serve as antidotes to their false or over-emplotted counterparts (Nos. 2, 3, 4 and 5) and could represent them as an ironic return to mere chronicle as constituting the only sense which any cognitively responsible history could take. We could characterize such histories thus:

6. "a, b, c, d, e,.........n"

with the quotation marks indicating the conscious interpretation of the events as having nothing other than seriality as their meaning.

This schema is of course highly abstract and does not do justice to the possible mixtures of and variations within the types that it is meant to distinguish. But it helps us, I think, to conceive how events might be emplotted in different ways without violating the imperatives of the chronological order of the events (however they are construed) so as to yield alternative, mutually exclusive, and yet, equally plausible interpretations of the set. I have tried to show in *Metahistory* how such mixtures and variations occur in the writings of the master historians of the 19th century; and I have suggested in that book that classic historical accounts always represent attempts both to emplot the historical series adequately and implicitly to come to terms with other plausible emplotments. It is this dialectical tension between two or more possible emplotments that signals the element of critical self-consciousness present in any historian of recognizably classical stature.

Histories, then, are not only about events but also about the possible sets of relationships that those events can be demonstrated to figure. These sets of relationships are not, however, immanent in the events themselves; they exist only in the mind of the historian reflecting on them. Here they are present as the modes of relationships conceptualized in the myth, fable, and folklore, scientific knowledge, religion, and literary art of the historian's own culture. But more importantly, they are—I suggest—immanent in the very language which the historian must use to *describe* events prior to a scientific analysis of them or a fictional emplotment of them. For if the historian's aim is to familarize us with the unfamiliar, he must use figurative, rather than technical, language. Technical languages are familiarizing only *to* those who have been indoctrinated in their uses and only *of* those sets of events which the practitioners of a discipline have agreed to describe in a uniform terminology. History possesses no such generally accepted technical terminology and in fact no agreement on what kind of events make up its specific subject-matter. The historian's characteristic instrument of encodation, communication, and exchange is ordinary educated speech. This implies that the only instruments that he has for endowing his data with meaning, of rendering the strange familiar, and of rendering the mysterious past comprehensible, are the techniques of *figurative* language. All historical narratives presuppose figurative characterizations of the events they purport to represent and explain. And this means that historical narratives, considered purely as verbal artifacts, can be characterized by the mode of figurative discourse in which they are cast.

If this is case, then it may well be that the kind of emplotment that the historian decides to use to give meaning to a set of historical events is dictated by the dominant figurative mode of the language he has used to *describe* the elements of his account *prior* to his composition of a narrative. Geoffrey Hartman once remarked in my hearing, at a conference on literary history, that he was not sure that he knew what historians of literature might want to do, but he did know that to write a history meant to place an event within a context, by relating it as a part to some conceivable whole. He went on to suggest that as far as he knew, there were only two ways of relating parts to wholes, by metonymy and by synecdoche. Having been engaged for some time in the study of the thought of Giambattista Vico, I was much taken with this thought, because it conformed to Vico's notion that the "logic" of all "poetic wisdom" was contained in the relationships which language itself provided in the four principal modes of figurative representation: metaphor, metonymy, synecdoche, and irony. My own hunch—and it is a hunch which I find confirmed in Hegel's reflections on the nature of non-scientific discourse—is that in any field of study which, like history, has not yet become disciplinized to the point of constructing a formal terminological system for describing its objects, in the way that physics and chemistry have, it is the types of figurative discourse that dictate the fundamental forms of the data to be studied. This means that the *shape* of the *relationships* which will appear to be inherent in the objects inhabiting the field will in reality have been imposed on the field by the investigator in the very *act of identifying and describing* the objects that he finds there. The implication is that historians *constitute* their subjects as possible objects of narrative representation by the very language they use to *describe* them. And if this is the case, it means that the different kinds of historical interpretations that we have of the same set of events, such as the French Revolution as interpreted by Michelet, Tocqueville, Taine, and others, are little more than projections of the linguistic protocols that these historians used to *pre*-figure that set of events prior to writing their narratives of it. It is only a hypothesis, but it seems possible that the conviction of the historian that he has "found" the form of his narrative in the events themselves, rather than imposed it upon them, in the way the poet does, is a result of a certain lack of linguistic self-consciousness which obscures the extent to which descriptions of events *already* constitute interpretations of their nature. As thus envisaged, the difference between Michelet's and Tocqueville's accounts of the Revolution does not reside only in the fact that the former emplotted his story in the modality of a Romance and the latter his in the modality of Tragedy; it resides as well in the tropological mode—metaphorical and metonymic respectively—which each brought to his apprehension of the facts as they appeared in the documents.

I do not have the space to try to demonstrate the plausibility of this hypothesis, which is the informing principle of my book *Metahistory*. But I hope that this essay may serve to suggest an approach to the study of such discursive prose forms as historiography, an approach that is as old as the study of rhetoric and as new as modern linguistics. Such a study would proceed along the lines laid out by Roman Jakobson in a paper on "Linguistics and Poetics," in which he characterized the difference between Romantic poetry and the various forms of 19th century Realistic prose as residing in the essentially Metaphorical nature of the former and the essentially Metonymical nature of the latter. I think that this characterization of the difference between poetry and prose is too narrow, because it presupposes that complex macrostructural narratives such as the novel are little more than projections of the "selective" (i.e., phonemic) axis of all speech acts. Poetry, and especially Romantic poetry, is then characterized by Jakobson as a projection of the "combinatory" (i.e., morphemic) axis of language. Such a binary theory pushes the analyst toward a dualistic opposition between poetry and prose which appears to rule out the possibility of a Metonymical poetry and a Metaphorical prose. But the fruitfulness of Jakobson's theory lies in its suggestion that the various forms of both poetry and prose, all of which have their counterparts in narrative in general and therefore in historiography too, can be characterized in terms of the dominant trope which serves as the paradigm, provided by language itself, of all significant relationships conceived to exist in the world by anyone wishing to represent those relationships in language.

Narrative, or the syntagmatic dispersion of events across a temporal series presented as a prose discourse, in such a way as to display their progressive elaboration as a comprehensible form, would represent the "inward turn" that discourse takes when it tries to *show* the reader the true form of things existing behind a merely apparent formlessness. Narrative *style* in history as well as in the novel would then be construed as the modality of the movement from a representation of some original state of affairs to some subsequent state. The primary *meaning* of a narrative would then consist of the de-structuration of a set of events (real or imagined) originally encoded in one tropological mode and the progressive re-structuration of the set in another tropological mode. As thus envisaged, narrative would be a process of de-codation and re-codation in which an original perception is clarified by being cast in a figurative mode different from that in which it has come encoded by convention, authority, or custom. And the explanatory force of the narrative would then depend on the contrast between the original encodation and the later one.

For example, let us suppose that a set of experiences comes to us as a grotesque, i.e., as unclassified and unclassifiable. Our problem is to identify the modality of the relationships that bind the discernible elements of the formless totality together in such a way as to make of it a whole of some sort. If we stress the similarities among the elements, we are working in the mode of Metaphor; if we stress the differences among them, we are working in the mode of Metonymy. Of course, in order to make sense of any set of experiences, we must obviously identify both the parts of a thing that appear to make it up and the nature of the shared aspects of the parts that make them identifiable as a totality. This implies that all original characterizations of anything must utilize *both* Metaphor and Metonymy in order to "fix" it as something about which we can meaningfully discourse.

In the case of historiography, the attempts of commentators to make sense of the French Revolution are instructive in this regard. Burke decodes the events of the Revolution which his contemporaries experience as a grotesque by re-coding it in the mode of Irony; Michelet recodes these events in the mode of Synecdoche; Tocqueville recodes them in the mode of Metonymy. In each case, however, the movement from code to recode is narratively described, i.e., laid out on a time-line in such a way as to make the interpretation of the events that made up the "Revolution" a kind of drama that we can recognize as Satirical, Romantic, and Tragic respectively. This drama can be followed by the reader of the narrative in such a way as to be experienced as a progressive revelation of what the *true* nature of the events consists of. The revelation is not experienced, however, as a restructuring of perception so much as an illumination of a field of occurrence. But actually what has happened is that a set of events originally encoded in one way is simply being decoded by being recoded in another. The events themselves are not substantially changed from one account to another. That is to say, the data that are to be analyzed are not significantly different in the different accounts. What is different are the modalities of their relationships. These modalities, in turn, although they *may* appear to the reader to be based on different theories of the nature of society, politics, and history, ultimately have their origin in the figurative characterizations of the whole set of events as representing wholes of fundamentally different sorts. It is for this reason that, when it is a matter of setting different interpretations of the same set of historical phenomena over against one another in an attempt to decide which is the best or most convincing, we are often driven to confusion or ambiguity. This is not to say that we cannot distinguish between good and bad historiography, since we can always fall back on such criteria as responsibility to the rules of evidence, the relative fullness of narrative detail, logical consistency, and the like to determine this issue. But it is to say that the effort to distinguish between good and bad interpretations of a historical event such as the Revolution is not as easy as it might at first appear when it is a matter of dealing with alternative interpretations produced by historians of relatively equal learning and conceptual sophistication. After all, a great historical classic cannot be disconfirmed or nullified either by the discovery of some new datum that might call a specific explanation of some element of the whole account into question or by the generation of new methods of analysis which permit us to deal with questions that earlier historians might not have taken under consideration. And it is precisely because great historical classics, such as works by Gibbon, Michelet, Thucydides, Mommsen, Ranke, Burckhardt, Bancroft, and so on, cannot be definitely disconfirmed that we must look to the specifically literary aspects of their work as crucial, and not merely subsidiary, elements in their historiographical technique.

What all this points to is the necessity of revising the distinction conventionally drawn between poetic and prose discourse in discussion of such narrative forms as historiography and recognizing that the distinction, as old as Aristotle, between history and poetry obscures as much as it illuminates about both. If there is an element of the historical in all poetry, there is an element of poetry in every historical account of the world. And this because in our account of the historical world we are dependent, in ways perhaps that we are not in the natural sciences, on the techniques of *figurative language* both for our *characterization* of the objects of our narrative representations and for the *strategies* by which to constitute narrative accounts of the transformations of those objects in time. And this because history has no stipulatable subject matter uniquely its own; it is always written as part of a contest between contending poetic figurations of what the past *might* consist of.

The older distinction between fiction and history, in which fiction is conceived as the representation of the imaginable and history as the representation of the actual, must give place to the recognition that we can only know the *actual* by contrasting it with or likening it to the *imaginable*. As thus conceived, historical narratives are complex structures in which a world of experience is imagined to exist under at least two modes, one of which is encoded as "real," the other of which is "revealed" to have been illusory in the course of the narrative. Of course, it is a fiction of the historian that the various states of affairs which he constitutes as the beginning, the middle, and the end of a course of development are all "actual" or "real" and that he is merely recording "what happened" in the transition from the inaugural to the terminal phase. But both the beginning state of affairs and the ending one are inevitably poetic constructions, and as such dependent upon the modality of the figurative language used to give them the appearance of coherence. This implies that all narrative is not simply a recording of "what happened" in the transition from one state of affairs to another, but a progressive *redescription* of sets of events in such a way as to dismantle a structure encoded in one verbal mode in the beginning so as to justify a recoding of it in another mode at the end. This is what the "middle" of all narratives consists of.

All of this is highly schematic, and I know that this insistence on the fictive element in all historical narratives is certain to arouse the ire of historians who believe that they are doing something fundamentally different from the novelist, by virtue of the fact that they deal with "real," while the novelist deals with "imagined," events. But neither the form nor the explanatory power of narrative derives from the different contents it is presumed to be able to accommodate. In point of fact, history—the real world as it evolves in time—is made sense of in the same way that the poet or novelist tries to make sense of it, i.e., by endowing what originally appears as problematical and mysterious with the aspect of a recognizable, because it is a familiar, form. It does not matter whether the world is conceived to be real or only imagined, the manner of making sense of it is the same.

So too, to say that we make sense of the real world by imposing upon it the formal coherency that we customarily associate with the products of writers of fiction in no way detracts from the status as knowledge which we ascribe to historiography. It would only detract from it if we were to believe that literature did not teach us anything about reality, but was a product of an imagination which was not of this world but of some other, inhuman, one. In my view, we experience the "fictionalization" of history as an "explanation" for the same reason that we experience great fiction as an illumination of a world that we inhabit along with the author. In both we re-cognize the forms by which consciousness both constitutes and colonizes the world it seeks to inhabit comfortably.

Finally, it may be observed that if historians were to recognize the fictive element in their narratives, this would not mean the degradation of historiography to the status of ideology or propaganda. In fact, this recognition would serve as a potent antidote to the tendency of historians to become captive of ideological preconceptions which they do not recognize as such but honor as the "correct" perception of "the way things *really* are." By drawing historiography nearer to its origins in literary sensibility, we should be able to identify the ideological, because it is the fictive, element in our own discourse. We are always able to see the "fictive" element in those historians with whose interpretations of a given set of events we disagree; we seldom perceive that element in our own prose. So, too, if we recognized the literary or fictive element in every historical account, we would be able to move the teaching of historiography onto a higher level of self-consciousness than it currently occupies.

What teacher has not lamented his inability to give instruction to apprentices in the *writing* of history? What graduate student of history has not despaired at trying to comprehend and imitate the model which his instructors *appear* to honor but the principles of which remain uncharted? If we recognize that there is a fictive element in all historical narrative, we would find in the theory of language and narrative itself the basis for a more subtle presentation of what historiography consists of than that which simply tells the student to go and "find out the facts" and write them up in such a way as to tell "what really happened."

In my view, history as a discipline is in bad shape today because it has lost sight of its origins in the literary imagination. In the interest of *appearing* scientific and objective, it has repressed and denied to itself its own greatest source of strength and renewal. By drawing historiography back once more to an intimate connection with its literary basis, we should not only be putting ourselves on guard against *merely* ideological distortions, we should be by way of arriving at that "theory" of history without which it cannot pass for a "discipline" at all.

NOTES

1. This essay is a revised version of a lecture given before the Comparative Literature Colloquium of Yale University on January 24, 1974. In it I have tried to elaborate some of the themes that I originally discussed in an article, "The Structure of Historical Narrative," *CLIO*, I (1972), 5–20. I have also drawn upon the materials of my book *Metahistory: The Historical Imagination in Nineteenth Century Europe* (Baltimore, 1973), especially the introduction entitled "The Poetics of History." The essay profited from conversations with Michael Holquist and Geoffrey Hartman, both of Yale University and both experts in the theory of narrative. The quotations from Claude Lévi-Strauss are taken from his *The Savage Mind* (London, 1966) and "Overture to Le Cru et le cuit," in *Structuralism*, ed. Jacques Ehrmann (New York, 1970). The remarks on the iconic nature of metaphor draw upon Paul Henle, *Language, Thought and Culture* (Ann Arbor, 1966). Jakobson's notions of the tropological nature of style are in "Linguistics and Poetics," in *Style and Language*, ed. Thomas A. Sebeok (New York and London, 1960). In addition to Northrop Frye's *Anatomy of Criticism* (Princeton, 1957), see also his essay on philosophy of history, "New Directions from Old," in *Fables of Identity* (New York, 1963). On story and plot in historical narrative in R. G. Collingwood's thought, see of course *The Idea of History* (Oxford, 1956).

PANOPTICISM (1975)

MICHEL FOUCAULT

Translated from the French by Alan Sheridan

In this section from Discipline and Punish: The Birth of the Prison *(slightly abridged here), Foucault proposes that the Panopticon, a prison designed (and never built) by the English philosopher Jeremy Bentham, offers a model of modern culture. Bentham designed the Panopticon with prison cells circling around a guard tower so that a guard can watch each prisoner, yet the prisoners cannot tell when a guard watches them. Because prisoners would know that a guard might be watching them at any time, Bentham reasoned, they would internalize the rules and police their own behavior, whether or not a guard was actually watching. To Foucault, modern society works like the Panopticon. In an earlier era, the rulers ruled—enforced* discipline—*by punishment, Now, those in authority rule by sur-*veillance, *by watching, by a pervasive cultural observation that leads us to internalize the surveiling discipline and* regulate, police, *ourselves. Instead of punishment, the panoptic, internalized surveillance works, for example, through sympathy with the criminal, which leads us to ask what about ourselves may go wrong and worry about how we can regulate and police ourselves. Directly or figuratively, therapy replaces punishment at the means of regulation. As part of our watching, we "measure, assess, diagnose, cure, transform" each other—and ourselves. We live in a world of video cameras, to the point that we become our own video cameras watching ourselves. Self-policing, Foucault contends, has reached* *the point where it is more pervasive and powerful than the old policing and regulating that stayed outside ourselves.*

The following, according to an order published at the end of the seventeenth century, were the measures to be taken when the plague appeared in a town.[1]

First, a strict spatial partitioning: the closing of the town and its outlying districts, a prohibition to leave the town on pain of death, the killing of all stray animals; the division of the town into distinct quarters, each governed by an intendant. Each street is placed under the authority of a syndic, who keeps it under surveillance; if he leaves the street, he will be condemned to death. On the appointed day, everyone is ordered to stay indoors: it is forbidden to leave on pain of death. The syndic himself comes to lock the door of each house from the outside; he takes the key with him and hands it over to the intendant of the quarter; the intendant keeps it until the end of the quarantine. Each family will have made its own provisions; but, for bread and wine, small wooden canals are set up between the street and the interior of the houses, thus allowing each person to receive his ration without communicating with the suppliers and other residents; meat, fish and herbs will be hoisted up into the houses with pulleys and baskets. If it is absolutely necessary to leave the house, it will be done in turn, avoiding any meeting. Only the intendants, syndics and guards will move about the streets and also, between the infected houses, from one corpse to another, the "crows" who can be left to die: these are "people of little substance who carry the sick, bury the dead, clean and do many vile and abject offices." It is a segmented, immobile, frozen space. Each individual is fixed in his place. And, if he moves, he does so at the risk of his life, contagion or punishment.

Inspection functions ceaselessly. The gaze is alert everywhere: "A considerable body of militiary commanded by good officers and men of substance" guards at the gates, at the town hall and in every quarter to ensure the prompt obedience of the people and the most absolute authority of the magistrates, "as also to observe all disorder, theft and extortion." At each of the town gates there will be an observation post; at the end of each street sentinels. Every day, the intendant visits the quarter in his charge, inquires whether the syndics have carried out their tasks, whether the inhabitants have anything to complain of; they "observe their actions." Every day, too, the syndic goes into the street for which he is responsible; stops before each house: gets all the inhabitants to appear at the windows (those who live overlooking the courtyard will be allocated a window looking onto the street at which no one but they may show themselves); he calls each of them by name; informs himself as to the state of each and every one of them—"in which respect the inhabitants will be compelled to speak the truth under pain of death"; if someone does not appear at the window, the syndic must ask why: "In this way he will find out easily enough whether dead or sick are being concealed." Everyone locked up in his cage, everyone at his window, answering to his name and showing himself when asked—it is the great review of the living and the dead.

This surveillance is based on a system of permanent registration: reports from the syndics to the intendants, from the intendants to the magistrates or mayor. At the beginning of the "lock up," the role of each of the inhabitants present in the town is laid down, one by one; this document bears "the name, age, sex of everyone, notwithstanding his condition": a copy is sent to the intendant of the quarter, another to the office of the town hall, another to enable the syndic to make his daily roll call. Everything that may be observed during the course of the visits—deaths, illnesses, complaints, irregularities—is noted down and transmitted to the intendants and magistrates. The magistrates have complete control over medical treatment; they have appointed a physician in charge; no other practitioner may treat, no apothecary prepare medicine, no confessor visit a sick person without having received from him a written note "to prevent anyone from concealing and dealing with those sick of the contagion, unknown to the magistrates." The registration of the pathological must be constantly centralized. The relation of each individual to his disease and to his death passes through the representatives of power, the registration they make of it, the decisions they take on it.

Five or six days after the beginning of the quarantine, the process of purifying the houses one by one is begun. All the inhabitants are made to leave; in each room "the furniture and goods" are raised from the ground or suspended from the air; perfume is poured around the room; after carefully sealing the windows, doors and even the keyholes with wax, the perfume is set alight. Finally, the entire house is closed while the perfume is consumed; those who have carried out the work are searched, as they were on entry, "in the presence of the residents of the house, to see that they did not have something on their persons as they left that they did not have on entering." Four hours later, the residents are allowed to re-enter their homes.

This enclosed, segmented space, observed at every point, in which the individuals are inserted in a fixed place, in which the slightest movements are supervised, in which all events are recorded, in which an uninterrupted work of writing links the centre and periphery, in which power is exercised without division, according to a continuous hierarchical figure, in which each individual is constantly located, examined and distributed among the living beings, the sick and the dead—all this constitutes a compact model of the disciplinary mechanism. The plague is met by order; its function is to sort out every possible confusion: that of the disease, which is transmitted when bodies are mixed together; that of the evil, which is increased when fear and death overcome prohibitions. It lays down for each individual his place, his body, his disease and his death, his well-being, by means of an omnipresent and omniscient power that subdivides itself in a regular, uninterrupted way even to the ultimate determination of the individual, of what characterizes him, of what belongs to him, of what happens to him. Against the plague, which is a mixture, discipline brings into play its power, which is one of analysis. A whole literary fiction of the festival grew up around the plague: suspended laws, lifted prohibitions, the frenzy of passing time, bodies mingling together without respect, individuals unmasked, abandoning their statutory identity and the figure under which they had been recognized, allowing a quite different truth to appear. But there was also a political dream of the plague, which was exactly its reverse: not the collective festival, but strict divisions; not laws transgressed, but the penetration of regulation into even the smallest details of everyday life through the mediation of the complete hierarchy that assured the capillary functioning of power; not masks that were put on and taken off, but the assignment to each individual of his "true" name, his "true" place, his "true" body, his "true" disease. The plague as a form, at once real and imaginary, of disorder had as its medical and political correlative discipline. Behind the disciplinary mechanisms can be read the haunting memory of "contagions" of the plague, of rebellions, crimes, vagabondage, desertions, people who appear and disappear, live and die in disorder.

If it is true that the leper gave rise to rituals of exclusion, which to a certain extent pro-vided the model for and general form of the great Confinement, then the plague gave rise to disciplinary projects. Rather than the massive, binary division between one set of people and another, it called for multiple separations, individualizing distributions, an organiza-tion in depth of surveillance and control, an intensification and a ramification of power. The leper was caught up in a practice of rejection, of exile-enclosure; he was left to his doom in a mass among which it was useless to differentiate; those sick of the plague were caught up in a meticulous tactical partitioning in which individual differentiations were the constricting effects of a power that multiplied, articulated and subdivided itself; the great confinement on the one hand; the correct training on the other. The leper and his separation; the plague and its segmentations. The first is marked; the second analysed and distributed. The exile of the leper and the arrest of the plague do not bring with them the same political dream. The first is that of a pure community, the second that of a disciplined society. Two ways of exercising power over men, of controlling their relations, of separating out their dangerous mixtures. The plague-stricken town, traversed throughout with hierarchy, surveillance, obser-vation, writing; the town immobilized by the functioning of an extensive power that bears in a distinct way over all individual bodies—this is the utopia of the perfectly governed city. The plague (envisaged as a possibility at least) is the trial in the course of which one may define ideally the exercise of disciplinary power. In order to make rights and laws function accord-ing to pure theory, the jurists place themselves in imagination in the state of nature; in order to see perfect disciplines functioning, rulers dreamt of the state of plague. Underlying disci-plinary projects the image of the plague stands for all forms of confusion and disorder; just as the image of the leper, cut off from all human contact, underlies projects of exclusion.

They are different projects, then, but not incompatible ones. We see them coming slowly together, and it is the peculiarity of the nineteenth century that it applied to the space of exclusion of which the leper was the symbolic inhabitant (beggars, vagabonds, madmen and the disorderly formed the real population) the technique of power proper to disci-plinary partitioning. Treat "lepers" as "plague victims," project the subtle segmentations of discipline onto the confused space of internment, combine it with the methods of ana-lytical distribution proper to power, individualize the excluded, but use procedures of indi-vidualization to mark exclusion—this is what was operated regularly by disciplinary power from the beginning of the nineteenth century in the psychiatric asylum, the penitentiary, the reformatory, the approved school and, to some extent, the hospital. Generally speaking, all the authorities exercising individual control function according to a double mode; that of binary division and branding (mad/sane; dangerous/harmless; normal/abnormal); and that of coercive assignment, of differential distribution (who he is; where he must be; how he is to be characterized; how he is to be recognized; how a constant surveillance is to be exer-cised over him in an individual way, etc.). On the one hand, the lepers are treated as plague victims; the tactics of individualizing disciplines are imposed on the excluded; and, on the other hand, the universality of disciplinary controls makes it possible to brand the "leper" and to bring into play against him the dualistic mechanisms of exclusion. The constant divi-sion between the normal and the abnormal, to which every individual is subjected, brings us back to our own time, by applying the binary branding and exile of the leper to quite different objects; the existence of a whole set of techniques and institutions for measuring, supervising and correcting the abnormal brings into play the disciplinary mechanisms to which the fear of the plague gave rise. All the mechanisms of power which, even today, are disposed around the abnormal individual, to brand him and to alter him, are composed of those two forms from which they distantly derive.

Bentham's *Panopticon* is the architectural figure of this composition. We know the principle on which it was based; at the periphery, an annular building; at the centre, a tower; this tower is pierced with wide windows that open onto the inner side of the ring; the peripheric building is divided into cells, each of which extends the whole width of the building; they have two windows, one on the inside, corresponding to the windows of the tower; the other, on the outside, allows the light to cross the cell from one end to the other. All that is needed, then, is to place a supervisor in a central tower and to shut up in each cell a madman, a patient, a condemned man, a worker or a schoolboy. By the effect of backlighting, one can observe from the tower, standing out precisely against the light, the small captive shadows in the cells of the periphery. They are like so many cages, so many small theatres, in which each actor is alone, perfectly individualized and constantly visible. The panoptic mechanism arranges spatial unities that make it possible to see constantly and to recognize immediately. In short, it reverses the principle of the dungeon; or rather of its three functions—to enclose, to deprive of light and to hide—it preserves only the first and eliminates the other two. Full lighting and the eye of a supervisor capture better than darkness, which ultimately protected. Visibility is a trap.

To begin with, this made it possible—as a negative effect—to avoid those compact, swarming, howling masses that were to be found in places of confinement, those painted by Goya or described by Howard. Each individual, in his place, is securely confined to a cell from which he is seen from the front by the supervisor; but the side walls prevent him from coming into contact with his companions. He is seen, but he does not see; he is the object of information, never a subject in communication. The arrangement of his room, opposite the central tower, imposes on him an axial visibility; but the divisions of the ring, those separated cells, imply a lateral invisibility. And this invisibility is a guarantee of order. If the inmates are convicts, there is no danger of a plot, an attempt at collective escape, the planning of new crime for the future, bad reciprocal influences; if they are patients, there is no danger of contagion; if they are madmen there is no risk of their committing violence upon one another; if they are schoolchildren, there is no copying, no noise, no chatter, no waste of time; if they are workers, there are no disorders, no theft, no coalitions, none of those distractions that slow down the rate of work, make it less perfect or cause accidents. The crowd, a compact mass, a locus of multiple exchanges, individualities merging together, a collective effect, is abolished and replaced by a collection of separated individualities. From the point of view of the guardian, it is replaced by a multiplicity that can be numbered and supervised; from the point of view of the inmates, by a sequestered and observed solitude (Bentham, 60–64).

Hence the major effect of the Panopticon: to induce in the inmate a state of conscious and permanent visibility that assures the automatic functioning of power. So to arrange things that the surveillance is permanent in its effects, even if it is discontinuous in its action; that the perfection of power should tend to render its actual exercise unnecessary; that this architectural apparatus should be a machine for creating and sustaining a power relation independent of the person who exercises it; in short, that the inmates should be caught up in a power situation of which they are themselves the bearers. To achieve this, it is at once too much and too little that the prisoner should be constantly observed by an inspector: too little, for what matters is that he knows himself to be observed; too much, because he has no need in fact of being so. In view of this, Bentham laid down the principle that power should be visible and unverifiable. Visible: the inmate will constantly have before his eyes the tall outline of the central tower from which he is spied upon. Unverifiable: the inmate must never know whether he is being looked at at any one moment; but he must be sure that he may always be so. In order to make the presence or absence of the inspector unverifiable, so that the prisoners, in their cells, cannot even see a shadow, Bentham envisaged not only Venetian blinds on the windows of the central observation hall, but, on the inside, partitions that intersected the hall at right angles and, in order to pass from one quarter to the other, not doors but zig-zag openings; for the slightest noise, a gleam of light, a brightness in a half-opened door would betray the presence of the guardian.[2] The Panopticon is a machine for dissociating the see/being seen dyad: in the peripheric ring, one is totally seen, without ever seeing; in the central tower, one sees everything without ever being seen.[3]

It is an important mechanism, for it automatizes and disindividualizes power. Power has its principle not so much in a person as in a certain concerted distribution of bodies, surfaces, lights, gazes; in an arrangement whose internal mechanisms produce the relation in which individuals are caught up. The ceremonies, the rituals, the marks by which the sovereign's surplus power was manifested are useless. There is a machinery that assures dissymmetry, disequilibrium, difference. Consequently, it does not matter who exercises power. Any individual, taken almost at random, can operate the machine: in the absence of the director, his family, his friends, his visitors, even his servants (Bentham, 45). Similarly, it does not matter what motive animates him: the curiosity of the indiscreet, the malice of a child, the thirst for knowledge of a philosopher who wishes to visit this museum of human nature, or the perversity of those who take pleasure in spying and punishing. The more numerous those anonymous and temporary servers are, the greater the risk for the inmate of being surprised and the greater his anxious awareness of being observed. The Panopticon is a marvellous machine which, whatever use one may wish to put it to, produces homogeneous effects of power.

A real subjection is born mechanically from a fictitious relation. So it is not necessary to use force to constrain the convict to good behaviour, the madman to calm, the worker to work, the schoolboy to application, the patient to the observation of the regulations. Bentham was surprised that panoptic institutions could be so light: there were no more bars, no more chains, no more heavy locks; all that was needed was that the separations should be clear and the openings well arranged. The heaviness of the old "houses of security," with their fortress-like architecture, could be replaced by the simple, economic geometry of a "house of certainty." The efficiency of power, its constraining force have, in a sense, passed over to the other side—to the side of its surface of application. He who is subjected to a field of visibility, and who knows it, assumes responsibility for the constraints of power; he makes them play spontaneously upon himself; he inscribes in himself the power relation in which he simultaneously plays both roles; he becomes the principle of his own subjection. By this very fact, the external power may throw off its physical weight; it tends to the non-corporal; and, the more it approaches this limit, the more constant, profound and permanent are its effects: it is a perpetual victory that avoids any physical confrontation and which is always decided in advance.

Bentham does not say whether he was inspired, in his project, by Le Vaux's menagerie at Versailles: the first menagerie in which the different elements are not, as they traditionally were, distributed in a park (Loisel, 104–7). At the centre was an octagonal pavilion which, on the first floor, consisted of only a single room, the king's *salon;* on every side large windows looked out onto seven cages (the eighth side was reserved for the entrance), containing different species of animals. By Bentham's time, this menagerie had disappeared. But one finds in the programme of the Panopticon a similar concern with individualizing observation, with characterization and classification, with the analytical arrangement of space. The Panopticon is a royal menagerie; the animal is replaced by man, individual distribution by specific grouping and the king by the machinery of a furtive power. With this exception, the Panopticon also does the work of a naturalist. It makes it possible to draw up differences: among patients, to observe the symptoms of each individual, without the proximity of beds, the circulation of miasmas, the effects of contagion confusing the clinical tables; among schoolchildren, it makes it possible to observe performances (without there being any imitation or copying), to map aptitudes, to assess characters, to draw up rigorous classifications and, in relation to normal development, to distinguish "laziness and stubbornness" from "incurable imbecility"; among workers, it makes it possible to note the aptitudes of each worker, compare the time he takes to perform a task, and if they are paid by the day, to calculate their wages (Bentham, 60–64).

So much for the question of observation. But the Panopticon was also a laboratory; it could be used as a machine to carry out experiments, to alter behaviour, to train or correct individuals. To experiment with medicines and monitor their effects. To try out different punishments on prisoners, according to their crimes and character, and to seek the most effective ones. To teach different techniques simultaneously to the workers, to decide which is the best. To try out pedagogical experiments—and in particular to take up once again the well-debated problem of secluded education, by using orphans. One would see what would happen when, in their sixteenth or eighteenth year, they were presented with other boys or girls; one could verify whether, as Helvetius thought, anyone could learn anything; one would follow "the genealogy of every observable idea"; one could bring up different children according to different systems of thought, making certain children believe that two and two do not make four or that the moon is a cheese, then put them together when they are twenty or twenty-five years old; one would then have discussions that would be worth a great deal more than the sermons or lectures on which so much money is spent; one would have at least an opportunity of making discoveries in the domain of metaphysics. The Panopticon is a privileged place for experiments on men, and for analysing with complete certainty the transformations that may be obtained from them. The Panopticon may even provide an apparatus for supervising its own mechanisms. In this central tower, the director may spy on all the employees that he has under his orders: nurses, doctors, foremen, teachers, warders; he will be able to judge them continuously, alter their behaviour, impose upon them the methods he thinks best; and it will even be possible to observe the director himself. An inspector arriving unexpectedly at the centre of the Panopticon will be able to judge at a glance, without anything being concealed from him, how the entire establishment is functioning. And in any case, enclosed as he is in the middle of this architectural mechanism, is not the director's own fate entirely bound up with it? The incompetent physician who has allowed contagion to spread, the incompetent prison governor or workshop manager will be the first victims of an epidemic or a revolt. "By every tie I could devise," said the master of the Panopticon, "my own fate had been bound up by me with theirs" (Bentham, 177). The Panopticon functions as a kind of laboratory of power. Thanks to its mechanism of observation, it gains in efficiency and in the ability to penetrate into men's behaviour; knowledge follows the advances of power, discovering new objects of knowledge over all the surfaces on which power is exercised.

The plague-stricken town, the panoptic establishment—the differences are important. They mark, at a distance of a century and a half, the transformations of the disciplinary programme. In the first case, there is an exceptional situation: against an extraordinary evil, power is mobilized; it makes itself everywhere present and visible; it invents new mechanisms; it separates, it immobilizes, it partitions; it constructs for a time what is both a counter-city and the perfect society; it imposes an ideal functioning, but one that is reduced, in the final analysis, like the evil that it combats, to a simple dualism of life and death: that which moves brings death, and one kills that which moves. The Panopticon, on the other hand, must be understood as a generalizable model of functioning; a way of defining power relations in terms of the everyday life of men. No doubt Bentham presents it as a particular institution, closed in upon itself. Utopias, perfectly closed in upon themselves, are common enough. As opposed to the ruined prisons, littered with mechanisms of torture, to be seen in Piranese's engravings, the Panopticon presents a cruel, ingenious cage. The fact that it should have given rise, even in our own time, to so many variations, projected or realized, is evidence of the imaginary intensity that it has possessed for almost two hundred years. But the Panopticon must not be understood as a dream building: it is the diagram of a mechanism of power reduced to its ideal form; its functioning, abstracted from any obstacle, resistance or friction, must be represented as a pure architectural and optical system: it is in fact a figure of political technology that may and must be detached from any specific use.

It is polyvalent in its applications; it serves to reform prisoners, but also to treat patients, to instruct schoolchildren, to confine the insane, to supervise workers, to put beggars and idlers to work. It is a type of location of bodies in space, of distribution of individuals in relation to one another, of hierarchical organization, of disposition of centers and channels of power, of definition of the instruments and modes of intervention of power, which can be implemented in hospitals, workshops, schools, prisons. Whenever one is dealing with a multiplicity of individuals on whom a task or a particular form of behaviour must be imposed, the panoptic schema may be used. It is—necessary modifications apart—applicable "to all establishments whatsoever, in which, within a space not too large to be covered or commanded by buildings a number of persons are meant to be kept under inspection" (Bentham 40; although Bentham takes the penitentiary house as his prime example, it is because it has many different functions to fulfil—safe custody, confinement, solitude, forced labour and instruction).

In each of its applications, it makes it possible to perfect the exercise of power. It does this in several ways: because it can reduce the number of those who exercise it, while increasing the number of those on whom it is exercised. Because it is possible to intervene at any moment and because the constant pressure acts even before the offences, mistakes or crimes have been committed. Because, in these conditions, its strength is that it never intervenes, it is exercised spontaneously and without noise, it constitutes a mechanism whose effects follow from one another. Because, without any physical instrument other than architecture and geometry, it acts directly on individuals; it gives "power of mind over mind." The panoptic schema makes any apparatus of power more intense: it assures its economy (in material, in personnel, in time); it assures its efficacity by its preventative character, its continuous functioning and its automatic mechanisms. It is a way of obtaining from power "in hitherto unexampled quantity" "a great and new instrument of government...; its great excellence consists in the great strength it is capable of giving to *any* institution it may be thought proper to apply it to" (Bentham, 66).

It's a case of "its easy once you've thought of it" in the political sphere. It can in fact be integrated into any function (education, medical treatment, production, punishment); it can increase the effect of this function, by being linked closely with it; it can constitute a mixed mechanism in which relations of power (and of knowledge) may be precisely adjusted, in the smallest detail, to the processes that are to be supervised; it can establish a direct proportion between "surplus power" and "surplus production." In short, it arranges things in such a way that the exercise of power is not added on from the outside, like a rigid, heavy constraint, to the functions it invests, but is so subtly present in them as to increase their efficiency by itself increasing its own points of contact. The panoptic mechanism is not simply a hinge, a point of exchange between a mechanism of power and a function; it is a way of making power relations function in a function, and of making a function function through these power relations. Bentham's Preface to *Panopticon* opens with a list of the benefits to be obtained from his "inspection-house": "*Morals reformed—health preserved—industry invigorated—instruction diffused—public burthens lightened*—Economy seated, as it were, upon a rock—the gordian knot of the Poor-Laws not cut, but united—all by a simple idea in architecture" (Bentham, 39).

Furthermore, the arrangement of this machine is such that its enclosed nature does not preclude a permanent presence from the outside: we have seen that anyone may come and exercise in the central tower the functions of surveillance, and that, this being the case, he can gain a clear idea of the way in which the surveillance is practiced. In fact, any panoptic institution, even if it is as rigorously closed as a penitentiary, may without difficulty be subjected to such irregular and constant inspections: and not only by the appointed inspectors, but also by the public; any member of society will have the right to come and see with his own eyes how the schools, hospitals, factories, prisons function. There is no risk, therefore, that the increase of power created by the panoptic machine may degenerate into tyranny; the disciplinary mechanism will be democratically controlled, since it will be constantly accessible "to the great tribunal committee of the world."[4] This Panopticon, subtly arranged so that an observer may observe, at a glance, so many different individuals, also enables everyone to come and observe any of the observers. The seeing machine was once a sort of dark room into which individuals spied; it has become a transparent building in which the exercise of power may be supervised by society as a whole.

The panoptic schema, without disappearing as such or losing any of its properties, was destined to spread throughout the social body; its vocation was to become a generalized function. The plague-stricken town provided an exceptional disciplinary model: perfect, but absolutely violent; to the disease that brought death, power opposed its perpetual threat of death; life inside it was reduced to its simplest expression; it was, against the power of death, the meticulous exercise of the right of the sword. The Panopticon, on the other hand, has a role of amplification; although it arranges power, although it is intended to make it more economic and more effective, it does so not for power itself, nor for the immediate salvation of a threatened society: its aim is to strengthen the social forces—to increase production, to develop the economy, spread education, raise the level of public morality; to increase and multiply.

How is power to be strengthened in such a way that, far from impeding progress, far from weighing upon it with its rules and regulations, it actually facilitates such progress? What intensificator of power will be able at the same time to be multiplicator of production? How will power, by increasing its forces, be able to increase those of society instead of confiscating them or impeding them? The Panopticon's solution to this problem is that the productive increase of power can be assured only if, on the one hand, it can be exercised continuously in the very foundations of society, in the subtlest possible way, and if, on the other hand, it functions outside these sudden, violent, discontinuous forms that are bound up with the exercise of sovereignty. The body of the king, with its strange material and physical presence, with the force that he himself deploys or transmits to some few others, is at the opposite extreme of this new physics of power represented by panopticism; the domain of panopticism is, on the contrary, that whole lower region, that region of irregular bodies, with their details, their multiple movements, their heterogeneous forces, their spatial relations; what are required are mechanisms that analyse distributions, gaps, series, combinations, and which use instruments that render visible, record, differentiate and compare: a physics of a relational and multiple power, which has its maximum intensity not in the person of the king, but in the bodies that can be individualized by these relations. At the theoretical level, Bentham defines another way of analysing the social body and the power relations that traverse it; in terms of practice, he defines a procedure of subordination of bodies and forces that must increase the utility of power while practising the economy of the prince. Panopticism is the general principle of a new "political anatomy" whose object and end are not the relations of sovereignty but the relations of discipline.

The celebrated, transparent, circular cage with its high tower, powerful and knowing, may have been for Bentham a project of a perfect disciplinary institution; but he also set out to show how one may "unlock" the disciplines and get them to function in a diffused, multiple, polyvalent way throughout the whole social body. These disciplines, which the classical age had elaborated in specific, relatively enclosed places—barracks, schools, workshops—and whose total implementation had been imagined only at the limited and temporary scale of a plague-stricken town, Bentham dreamt of transforming into a network of mechanisms that would be everywhere and always alert, running through society without interruption in space or in time. The panoptic arrangement provides the formula for this generalization. It programmes, at the level of an elementary and easily transferable mechanism, the basic functioning of a society penetrated through and through with disciplinary mechanisms.

There are two images, then, of discipline. At one extreme, the discipline-blockade, the enclosed institution, established on the edges of society, turned inwards towards negative functions: arresting evil, breaking communications, suspending time. At the other extreme, with panopticism, is the discipline-mechanism: a functional mechanism that must improve the exercise of power by making it lighter, more rapid, more effective, a design of subtle coercion for a society to come. The movement from one project to the other, from a schema of exceptional discipline to one of a generalized surveillance, rests on a historical transformation: the gradual extension of the mechanisms of discipline throughout the seventeenth and eighteenth centuries, their spread throughout the whole social body, the formation of what might be called in general the disciplinary society....

The organization of the police apparatus in the eighteenth century sanctioned a generalization of the disciplines that became co-extensive with the state itself. Although it was linked in the most explicit way with everything in the royal power that exceeded the exercise of regular justice, it is understandable why the police offered such slight resistance to the rearrangement of the judicial power; and why it has not ceased to impose its prerogatives upon it, with ever-increasing weight, right up to the present day; this is no doubt because it is the secular arm of the judiciary; but it is also because, to a far greater degree than the judicial institution, it is identified, by reason of its extent and mechanisms, with a society of the disciplinary type. Yet it would be wrong to believe that the disciplinary functions were confiscated and absorbed once and for all by a state apparatus.

"Discipline" may be identified neither with an institution nor with an apparatus; it is a type of power, a modality for its exercise, comprising a whole set of instruments, techniques, procedures, levels of application, targets; it is a "physics" or an "anatomy" of power, a technology. And it may be taken over either by "specialized" institutions (the penitentiaries or "houses of correction" of the nineteenth century), or by institutions that use it as an essential instrument for a particular end (schools, hospitals), or by pre-existing authorities that find in it a means of reinforcing or reorganizing their internal mechanisms of power (one day we should show how intra-familial relations, essentially in the parents–children cell, have become "disciplined," absorbing since the classical age external schemata, first educational and military, then medical, psychiatric, psychological, which have made the family the privileged locus of emergence for the disciplinary question of the normal and the abnormal); or by apparatuses that have made discipline their principle of internal functioning (the disciplinarization of the administrative apparatus from the Napoleonic period), or finally by state apparatuses whose major, if not exclusive, function is to assure that discipline reigns over society as a whole (the police).

On the whole, therefore, one can speak of the formation of a disciplinary society in this movement that stretches from the enclosed disciplines, a sort of social "quarantine" to an indefinitely generalizable mechanism of "panopticism." Not because the disciplinary modality of power has replaced all the others; but because it has infiltrated the others, sometimes undermining them, but serving as an intermediary between them, linking them together, extending them and above all making it possible to bring the effects of power to the most minute and distant elements. It assures an infinitesimal distribution of the power relations.

A few years after Bentham, Julius gave this society its birth certificate (Julius, 384–6). Speaking of the panoptic principle, he said that there was much more there than architectural ingenuity: it was an event in the "history of the human mind." In appearance, it is merely the solution of a technical problem; but, through it, a whole type of society emerges. Antiquity had been a civilization of spectacle. "To render accessible to a multitude of men the inspection of a small number of objects": this was the problem to which the architecture of temples, theatres and circuses responded. With spectacle, there was a predominance of public life, the intensity of festivals, sensual proximity. In these rituals in which blood flowed, society found new vigor and formed for a moment a single great body. The modern age poses the opposite problem: "To procure for a small number, or even for a single individual, the instantaneous view of a great multitude." In a society in which the principal elements are no longer the community and public life, but, on the one hand, private individuals and, on the other, the state, relations can be regulated only in a form that is the exact reverse of the spectacle: "It was to the modern age, to the ever-growing influence of the state, to its ever more profound intervention in all the details and all the relations of social life, that was reserved the task of increasing and perfecting its guarantees, by using and directing towards that great aim the building and distribution of buildings intended to observe a great multitude of men at the same time."

Julius saw as a fulfilled historical process that which Bentham had described as a technical programme. Our society is one not of spectacle, but of surveillance; under the surface of images, one invests bodies in depth; behind the great abstraction of exchange, there continues the meticulous, concrete training of useful forces; the circuits of communication are the supports of an accumulation and a centralization of knowledge; the play of signs defines the anchorages of power; it is not that the beautiful totality of the individual is amputated, repressed, altered by our social order, it is rather that the individual is carefully fabricated in it, according to a whole technique of forces and bodies. We are much less Greeks than we believe. We are neither in the amphitheatre, nor on the stage, but in the panoptic machine, invested by its effects of power, which we bring to ourselves since we are part of its mechanism. The importance, in historical mythology, of the Napoleonic character probably derives from the fact that it is at the point of junction of the monarchical, ritual exercise of sovereignty and the hierarchical, permanent exercise of indefinite discipline. He is the individual who looms over everything with a single gaze which no detail, however minute, can escape: "You may consider that no part of the Empire is without surveillance, no crime, no offence, no contravention that remains unpunished, and that the eye of the genius who can enlighten all embraces the whole of this vast machine, without, however, the slightest detail escaping his attention" (Treilhard, 14). At the moment of its full blossoming, the disciplinary society still assumes with the Emperor the old aspect of the power of spectacle. As a monarch who is at one and the same time a usurper of the ancient throne and the organizer of the new state, he combined into a single symbolic, ultimate figure the whole of the long process by which the pomp of sovereignty, the necessarily spectacular manifestations of power, were extinguished one by one in the daily exercise of surveillance, in a panopticism in which the vigilance of intersecting gazes was soon to render useless both the eagle and the sun....

To return to the problem of legal punishments, the prison with all the corrective technology at its disposal is to be resituated at the point where the codified power to punish turns into a disciplinary power to observe; at the point where the universal punishments of the law are applied selectively to certain individuals and always the same ones; at the point where the redefinition of the juridical subject by the penalty becomes a useful training of the criminal; at the point where the law is inverted and passes outside itself, and where the counter-law becomes the effective and institutionalized content of the juridical forms. What generalizes that power to punish, then, is not the universal consciousness of the law in each juridical subject; it is the regular extension, the infinite minute web of panoptic techniques.

Taken one by one, most of these techniques have a long history behind them. But what was new, in the eighteenth century, was that, by being combined and generalized, they attained a level at which the formation of knowledge and the increase of power regularly reinforce one another in a circular process. At this point, the disciplines crossed the "technological" threshold. First the hospital, then the school, then, later, the workshop were not simply "reordered" by the disciplines; they became, thanks to them, apparatuses such that any mechanism of objectification could be used in them as an instrument of subjection, and any growth of power could give rise in them to possible branches of knowledge; it was this link, proper to the technological systems, that made possible within the disciplinary element the formation of clinical medicine, psychiatry, child psychology, educational psychology, the rationalization of labour. It is a double process, then: an epistemological "thaw" through refinement of power relations; a multiplication of the effects of power through the formation and accumulation of new forms of knowledge.

The extension of the disciplinary methods is inscribed in a broad historical process: the development at about the same time of many other technologies—agronomical, industrial, economic. But it must be recognized that, compared with the mining industries, the emerging chemical industries or methods of national accountancy, compared with the blast furnaces or the steam engine, panopticism has received little attention. It is regarded as not much more than a bizarre little Utopia, a perverse dream—rather as though Bentham had been the Fourier of a police society, and the Phalanstery had taken on the form of the Panopticon. And yet this represented the abstract formula of a very real technology, that of individuals. There were many reasons why it received little praise; the most obvious is that the discourses to which it gave rise rarely acquired, except in the academic classifications, the status of sciences; but the real reason is no doubt that the power that it operates and which it augments is a direct, physical power that men exercise upon one another. An inglorious culmination had an origin that could be only grudgingly acknowledged. But it would be unjust to compare the disciplinary techniques with such inventions as the steam engine or Amici's microscope. They are much less; and yet, in a way, they are much more. If a historical equivalent or at least a point of comparison had to be found for them, it would be rather in the "inquisitorial" technique.

The eighteenth century invented the techniques of discipline and the examination, rather as the Middle Ages invented the judicial investigation. But it did so by quite different means. The investigation procedure, an old fiscal and administrative technique, had developed above all with the reorganization of the Church and the increase of the princely states in the twelfth and thirteenth centuries. At this time it permeated to a very large degree the jurisprudence first of the ecclesiastical courts, then of the lay courts. The investigation as an authoritarian search for a truth observed or attested was thus opposed to the old procedures of the oath, the ordeal, the judicial duel, the judgment of God or even of the transaction between private individuals. The investigation was the sovereign power arrogating to itself the right to establish the truth by a number of regulated techniques. Now, although the investigation has since then been an integral part of western justice (even up to our own day), one must not forget either its political origin, its link with the birth of the states and of monarchical sovereignty, or its later extension and its role in the formation of knowledge. In fact, the investigation has been the no doubt crude, but fundamental element in the constitution of the empirical sciences; it has been the juridical-political matrix of this experimental knowledge, which, as we know, was very rapidly released at the end of the Middle Ages. It is perhaps true to say that, in Greece, mathematics were born from techniques of measurement; the sciences of nature, in any case, were born, to some extent, at the end of the Middle Ages, from the practices of investigation. The great empirical knowledge that covered the things of the world and transcribed them into the ordering of an indefinite discourse that observes, describes and establishes the "facts" (at a time when the western world was beginning the economic and political conquest of this same world) had its operating model no doubt in the Inquisition—that immense invention that our recent mildness has placed in the dark recesses of our memory. But what this politico-juridical, administrative and criminal, religious and lay, investigation was to the sciences of nature, disciplinary analysis has been to the sciences of man. These sciences, which have so delighted our "humanity" for over a century, have their technical matrix in the petty, malicious minutiae of the disciplines and their investigations. These investigations are perhaps to psychology, psychiatry, pedagogy, criminology, and so many other strange sciences, what the terrible power of investigation was to the calm knowledge of the animals, the plants or the earth. Another power, another knowledge. On that threshold of the classical age, Bacon, lawyer and statesman, tried to develop a methodology of investigation for the empirical sciences. What Great Observer will produce the methodology of examination for the human sciences? Unless, of course, such a thing is not possible. For, although it is true that, in becoming a technique for the empirical sciences, the investigation has detached itself from the inquisitorial procedure, in which it was historically rooted, the examination has remained extremely close to the disciplinary power that shaped it. It has always been and still is an intrinsic element of the disciplines. Of course it seems to have undergone a speculative purification by integrating itself with such sciences as psychology and psychiatry. And, in effect, its appearance in the form of tests, interviews, interrogations and consultations is apparently in order to rectify the mechanisms of discipline: educational psychology is supposed to correct the rigors of the school, just as the medical or psychiatric interview is supposed to rectify the effects of the discipline of work. But we must not be misled; these techniques merely refer individuals from one disciplinary authority to another, and they reproduce, in a concentrated or formalized form, the schema of power-knowledge proper to each discipline (on this subject, cf. Tort). The great investigation that gave rise to the sciences of nature has become detached from its politico-juridical model; the examination, on the other hand, is still caught up in disciplinary technology.

In the Middle Ages, the procedure of investigation gradually superseded the old accusatory justice, by a process initiated from above; the disciplinary technique, on the other hand, insidiously and as if from below, has invaded a penal justice that is still, in principle, inquisitorial. All the great movements of extension that characterize modern penalty—the problematization of the criminal behind his crime, the concern with a punishment that is a correction, a therapy, a normalization, the division of the act of judgement between various authorities that are supposed to measure, assess, diagnose, cure, transform individuals—all this betrays the penetration of the disciplinary examination into the judicial inquisition.

What is now imposed on penal justice as its point of application, its "useful" object, will no longer be the body of the guilty man set up against the body of the king; nor will it be the juridical subject of an ideal contract; it will be the disciplinary individual. The extreme point of penal justice under the Ancien Régime was the infinite segmentation of the body of the regicide: a manifestation of the strongest power over the body of the greatest criminal, whose total destruction made the crime explode into its truth. The ideal point of penality today would be an indefinite discipline: an interrogation without end, an investigation that would be extended without limit to a meticulous and ever more analytical observation, a judgement that would at the same time be the constitution of a file that was never closed, the calculated leniency of a penalty that would be interlaced with the ruthless curiosity of an examination, a procedure that would be at the same time the permanent measure of a gap in relation to an inaccessible norm and the asymptotic movement that strives to meet in infinity. The public execution was the logical culmination of a procedure governed by the Inquisition. The practice of placing individuals under "observation" is a natural extension of a justice imbued with disciplinary methods and examination procedures. Is it surprising that the cellular prison, with its regular chronologies, forced labour, its authorities of surveillance and registration, its experts in normality, who continue and multiply the functions of the judge, should have become the modern instrument of penality? Is it surprising that prisons resemble factories, schools, barracks, hospitals, which all resemble prisons?

NOTES

1. Archives militaries de Vincennes, A 1, 516–91 sc. Pièce. This regulation is broadly similar to a whole series of others that date from the same period and earlier.
2. In the *Postscript to the Panopticon,* 1791, Bentham adds dark inspection galleries painted in black around the inspector's lodge, each making it possible to observe two storeys of cells.
3. In his first version of the *Panopticon,* Bentham had also imagined an acoustic surveillance, operated by means of pipes leading from the cells to the central tower. In the *Postscript* he abandoned the idea, perhaps because he could not introduce into it the principle of dissymmetry and prevent the prisoners from hearing the inspector as well as the inspector hearing them. Julius tried to develop a system of dissymmetrical listening (Julius, 18).
4. Imagining this continuous flow of visitors entering the central tower by an underground passage and then observing the circular landscape of the Panopticon, was Bentham aware of the Panoramas that Barker was constructing at exactly the same period (the first seems to have dated from 1787) and in which the visitors, occupying the central place, saw unfolding around them a landscape, a city or a battle. The visitors occupied exactly the place of the sovereign gaze.

BIBLIOGRAPHY

Archieves militaries de Vincennes, A 1 516–91 sc.
Bentham, J., *Works,* ed. Bowring, IV, 1843.
Julius, N. H, *Leçons sur les prisons,* I, 1831 (Fr. trans.).

Loisel, G., *Histoire des ménageries*, II, 1912.

Tort, Michel, *Q.I.*, 1974.

Treilhard, J. B., *Motifs du code d'instruction criminelle*, 1808.

SUBCULTURE: THE MEANING OF STYLE (1979)

DICK HEBDIGE

As a cultural studies scholar, Hebdige brings the study of popular culture, youth culture, and subculture together with the theoretical movements emerging from structuralism (as in the structuralism of Claude Lévi-Strauss and Roland Barthes) and contemporary Marxism (as in the work of Louis Althusser). He lets cultural studies and new methods of critical theory influence each other. Like many cultural studies scholars, he asks how youth subcultures do and do not have agency, the ability to shape and change the culture around them. That is to say, he asks how the protests by youth subcultures genuinely change things, and how they offer sensationalist yet superficial changes that end up reinforcing what they set out to change.

Since Hebdige's classic study, scholars who study subcultures, arguably even those who call themselves post-subcultures scholars, also study how subcultures regulate themselves and how they separate themselves from the larger commercial culture or buy into it, increasingly through online communication as well as through the club and live-music scenes. Like Hebdige, they debate how and how much subcultures resist or submit to the larger culture and how much they produce their own alternative communities. They continue to ask, for example, whether youth styles genuinely express political opposition or instead siphon off potentially rebellious energy, buying into a cultural system that absorbs youth expressiveness into the larger machine of commodity culture.

Subculture: The Unnatural Break

I felt unclean for about 48 hours

> (*G. L. C. councillor after seeing a concert by the Sex Pistols [reported* New Musical Express, *18 July 1977]*)

[Language is] of all social institutions, the least amenable to initiative. It blends with the life of society, and the latter, inert by nature, is a prime conservative force.

Saussure, 1974

Subcultures represent "noise" (as opposed to sound): interference in the orderly sequence which leads from real events and phenomena to their representation in the media. We should therefore not underestimate the signifying power of the spectacular subculture not only as a metaphor for potential anarchy "out there" but as an actual mechanism of semantic disorder: a kind of temporary blockage in the system of representation. As John Mepham (1972) has written:

> Distinctions and identities may be so deeply embedded in our discourse and thought about the world whether this be because of their role in our practical lives, or because they are cognitively powerful and are an important aspect of the way in which we appear to make sense of our experience, that the theoretical challenge to them can be quite startling.

Any elision, truncation or convergence of prevailing linguistic and ideological categories can have profoundly disorienting effects. These deviations briefly expose the arbitrary nature of the codes which underlie and shape all forms of discourse. As Stuart Hall (1974) has written (here in the context of explicitly political deviance):

> New…developments which are both dramatic and "meaningless" within the consensually validated norms, pose a challenge to the normative world. They render problematic not only how the…world is defined, but how it ought to be. They "breach our expectancies."…

Notions concerning the sanctity of language are intimately bound up with ideas of social order. The limits of acceptable linguistic expression are prescribed by a number of apparently universal taboos. These taboos guarantee the continuing "transparency" (the taken-for-grantedness) of meaning.

Predictably then, violations of the authorized codes through which the social world is organized and experienced have considerable power to provoke and disturb. They are generally condemned, in Mary Douglas' words (1967), as "contrary to holiness" and Levi-Strauss has noted how, in certain primitive myths, the mispronunciation of words and the misuse of language are classified along with incest as horrendous aberrations capable of "unleashing storm and tempest" (Levi-Strauss, 1969). Similarly, spectacular subcultures express forbidden contents (consciousness of class, consciousness of difference) in forbidden forms (transgressions of sartorial and behavioural codes, law breaking, etc.). They are profane articulations, and they are often and significantly defined as "unnatural." The terms used in the tabloid press to describe those youngsters who, in their conduct or clothing, proclaim subcultural membership ("freaks," "animals…who find courage, like rats, in hunting in packs"[1]) would seem to suggest that the most primitive anxieties concerning the sacred distinction between nature and culture can be summoned up by the emergence of such a group. No doubt, the breaking of rules is confused with the "absence of rules" which according to Levi-Strauss (1969), seems to provide the surest criteria for distinguishing a natural from a cultural process. Certainly, the official reaction to the punk subculture, particularly to the Sex Pistols' use of "foul language" on television[2] and record,[3] and to the vomiting and spitting incidents at Heathrow Airport[4] would seem to indicate that these basic taboos are no less deeply sedimented in contemporary British society.

TWO FORMS OF INCORPORATION

> Has not this society, glutted with aestheticism, already integrated former romanticisms, surrealism, existentialism and even Marxism to a point? It has, indeed, through trade, in the form of commodities. That which yesterday was reviled today

> becomes cultural consumer-goods, consumption thus engulfs what was intended to
> give meaning and direction.
>
> *Lefebvre, 1971*

We have seen how subcultures "breach our expectancies," how they represent symbolic challenges to a symbolic order. But can subcultures always be effectively incorporated and if so, how? The emergence of a spectacular subculture is invariably accompanied by a wave of hysteria in the press. This hysteria is typically ambivalent: it fluctuates between dread and fascination, outrage and amusement. Shock and horror headlines dominate the front page (e.g. "Rotten Razored," *Daily Mirror*, 28 June 1977) while, inside, the editorials positively bristle with "serious" commentary[5] and the centrespreads or supplements contain delirious accounts of the latest fads and rituals (see, for example, *Observer* colour supplements 30 January, 10 July 1977, 12 February 1978). Style in particular provokes a double response: it is alternately celebrated (in the fashion page) and ridiculed or reviled (in those articles which define subcultures as social problems).

In most cases, it is the subculture's stylistic innovations which first attract the media's attention. Subsequently deviant or "anti-social" acts—vandalism, swearing, fighting, "animal behaviour"—are "discovered" by the police, the judiciary, the press; and these acts are used to "explain" the subculture's original transgression of sartorial codes. In fact, either deviant behaviour or the identification of a distinctive uniform (or more typically a combination of the two) can provide the catalyst for a moral panic. In the case of the punks, the media's sighting of punk style virtually coincided with the discovery or invention of punk deviance. The *Daily Mirror* ran its first series of alarmist centrespreads on the subculture, concentrating on the bizarre clothing and jewellery during the week (29 Nov–3 Dec 1977) in which the Sex Pistols exploded into the public eye on the Thames *Today* programme. On the other hand, the mods, perhaps because of the muted character of their style, were not identified as a group until the Bank Holiday clashes of 1964, although the subculture was, by then, fully developed, at least in London. Whichever item opens the amplifying sequence, it invariably ends with the simultaneous diffusion and defusion of the subcultural style.

As the subculture begins to strike its own eminently marketable pose, as its vocabulary (both visual and verbal) becomes more and more familiar, so the referential context to which it can be most conveniently assigned is made increasingly apparent. Eventually, the mods, the punks, the glitter rockers can be incorporated, brought back into line, located on the preferred "map of problematic social reality" (Geertz, 1964) at the point where boys in lipstick are "just kids dressing up," where girls in rubber dresses are "daughters just like yours" (see pp. 98–9; 158–9, n. 8). The media, as Stuart Hall (1977) has argued, not only record resistance, they "situate it within the dominant framework of meanings" and those young people who choose to inhabit a spectacular youth culture are simultaneously *returned*, as they are represented on T.V. and in the newspapers, to the place where common sense would have them fit (as "animals" certainly, but also "in the family," "out of work," "up to date," etc.). It is through this continual process of recuperation that the fractured order is repaired and the subculture incorporated as a diverting spectacle within the dominant mythology from which it in part emanates: as "folk devil," as Other, as Enemy. The process of recuperation takes two characteristic forms:

1. the conversion of subcultural signs (dress, music, etc.) into mass-produced objects (i.e., the commodity form);

2. the "labelling" and re-definition of deviant behaviour by dominant groups—the police, the media, the judiciary (i.e. the ideological form).

THE COMMODITY FORM

The first has been comprehensively handled by both journalists and academics. The relationship between the spectacular subculture and the various industries which service and exploit it is notoriously ambiguous. After all, such a subculture is concerned first and foremost with consumption. It operates exclusively in the leisure sphere ("I wouldn't wear my punk outfit for work—there's a time and a place for everything"). It communicates through commodities even if the meanings attached to those commodities are purposefully distorted or overthrown. It is therefore difficult in this case to maintain any absolute distinction between commercial exploitation on the one hand and creativity/originality on the other, even though these categories are emphatically opposed in the value systems of most subcultures. Indeed, the creation and diffusion of new styles is inextricably bound up with the process of production, publicity and packaging which must inevitably lead to the defusion of the subculture's subversive power—both mod and punk innovations fed back directly into high fashion and mainstream fashion. Each new subculture establishes new trends, generates new looks and sounds which feed back into the appropriate industries. As John Clarke (1976) has observed:

> The diffusion of youth styles from the subcultures to the fashion market is not simply a "cultural process" but a real network or infrastructure of new kinds of commercial and economic institutions. The small-scale record shops, recording companies—the boutiques and one- or two-woman manufacturing companies—these versions of artisan capitalism, rather than more generalized and unspecific phenomena, situate the dialectic of commercial "manipulation."

However, it would be mistaken to insist on the absolute autonomy of "cultural" and commercial processes. As Lefebvre (1971) puts it: "Trade is…both a social and an intellectual phenomenon," and commodities arrive at the market-place already laden with significance. They are, in Marx's words (1970), "social hieroglyphs" and their meanings are inflected by conventional usage.

Thus, as soon as the original innovations which signify "subcultures" are translated into commodities and made generally available, they become "frozen." Once removed from their private contexts by the small entrepreneurs and big fashion interests who produce them on a mass scale, they become codified, made comprehensible, rendered at once public property and profitable merchandise. In this way, the two forms of incorporation (the semantic/ideological and the "real"/commercial) can be said to converge on the commodity form. Youth cultural styles may begin by issuing symbolic challenges, but they must inevitably end by establishing new sets of conventions; by creating new commoditics, new industries or rejuvenating old ones (think of the boost punk must have given haberdashery!). This occurs irrespective of the subculture's political orientation: the macrobiotic restaurants, craft shops and "antique markets" of the hippie era were easily converted into punk boutiques and record shops. It also happens irrespective of the startling content of the style: punk clothing and insignia could be bought mail-order by the summer of 1977, and in September of that year *Cosmopolitan* ran a review of Zandra Rhodes' latest collection of couture follies which consisted entirely of variations on the punk theme. Models smoldered beneath mountains of safety pins and plastic (the pins were jeweled, the "plastic" wet-look satin) and the accompanying article ended with an aphorism—"To shock is chic"—which presaged the subculture's imminent demise.

THE IDEOLOGICAL FORM

The second form of incorporation—the ideological—has been most adequately treated by those sociologists who operate a transactional model of deviant behaviour. For example, Stan Cohen has described in detail how one particular moral panic (surrounding the mod-rocker conflict of the mid-60s) was launched and sustained.[6] Although this type of analysis can often provide an extremely sophisticated explanation of why spectacular subcultures consistently provoke such hysterical outbursts, it tends to overlook the subtler mechanisms through which potentially threatening phenomena are handled and contained. As the use of the term "folk devil" suggests, rather too much weight tends to be given to the sensational excesses of the tabloid press at the expense of the ambiguous reactions which are, after all, more typical. As we have seen, the way in which subcultures are represented in the media makes them both more *and less* exotic than they actually are. They are seen to contain both dangerous aliens and boisterous kids, wild animals and wayward pets. Roland Barthes furnishes a key to this paradox in his description of "identification"—one of the seven rhetorical figures which, according to Barthes, distinguish the meta-language of bourgeois mythology. He characterizes the petit-bourgeois as a person"…unable to imagine the Other…the Other is a scandal which threatens his existence"(Barthes, 1972).

Two basic strategies have been evolved for dealing with this threat. First, the Other can be trivialized, naturalized, domesticated. Here, the difference is simply denied ("Otherness is reduced to sameness"). Alternatively, the Other can be transformed into meaningless exotica, a "pure object, a spectacle, a clown" (Barthes, 1972). In this case, the difference is consigned to a place beyond analysis. Spectacular subcultures are continually being defined in precisely these terms. Soccer hooligans, for example, are typically placed beyond "the bounds of common decency" and are classified as "animals" ("These people aren't human beings," football club manager quoted on the *News at Ten*, Sunday, 12 March 1977.) (See Stuart Hall's treatment of the press coverage of football hooligans in *Football Hooliganism* (edited by Roger Ingham, 1978).) On the other hand, the punks tended to be resituated by the press in the family, perhaps because members of the subculture deliberately obscured their origins, refused the family and willingly played the part of folk devil, presenting themselves as pure objects, as villainous clowns. Certainly, like every other youth culture, punk was perceived as a threat to the family. Occasionally this threat was represented in literal terms. For example, the *Daily Mirror* (1 August 1977) carried a photograph of a child lying in the road after a punk–ted confrontation under the headline "VICTIM OF THE PUNK ROCK PUNCH-UP: THE BOY WHO FELL FOUL OF THE MOB." In this case, punk's threat to the family was made "real" (that could be my child!) through the ideological framing of photographic evidence which is popularly regarded as unproblematic.

None the less, on other occasions, the opposite line was taken. For whatever reason, the inevitable glut of articles gleefully denouncing the latest punk outrage was counterbalanced by an equal number of items devoted to the small details of punk family life. For instance, the 15 October 1977 issue of *Woman's Own* carried an article entitled "Punks and Mothers" which stressed the classless, fancy dress aspects of punk. Photographs depicting punks with smiling mothers, reclining next to the family pool, playing with the family dog, were placed above a text which dwelt on the ordinariness of individual punks: "It's not as rocky horror as it appears." … "punk can be a family affair" … "punks as it happens are non-political," and, most insidiously, albeit accurately, "Johnny Rotten is as big a household name as Hughie Green." Throughout the summer of 1977, the *People* and the *News of the World* ran items on punk babies, punk brothers, and punk–ted weddings. All these articles served to minimize the Otherness so stridently proclaimed in punk style, and defined the subculture in precisely those terms which it sought most vehemently to resist and deny.

Once again, we should avoid making any absolute distinction between the ideological and commercial "manipulations" of subculture. The symbolic restoration of daughters to the family, of deviants to the fold, was undertaken at a time when the widespread "capitulation" of punk musicians to market forces was being used throughout the media to illustrate the fact that punks were "only human after all." The music papers were filled with the familiar success stories describing the route from rags to rags and riches—of punk musicians flying to America, of bank clerks become magazine editors or record producers, of harassed seamstresses turned overnight into successful business women. Of course, these success stories had ambiguous implications. As with every other "youth revolution" (e.g., the beat boom, the mod explosion and the Swinging Sixties) the relative success of a few individuals created an impression of energy, expansion and limitless upward mobility. This ultimately reinforced the image of the open society which the very presence of the punk subculture—with its rhetorical emphasis on unemployment, high-rise living and narrow options—had originally contradicted. As Barthes (1972) has written: "myth can always, as a last resort, signify the resistance which is brought to bear against it" and it does so typically by imposing its own ideological terms, by substituting in this case "the fairy tale of the artist's creativity" for an art form "within the compass of every consciousness," a "music" to be judged, dismissed or marketed for "noise"—a logically consistent, self-constituted chaos. It does so finally by replacing a subculture engendered by history, a product of real historical contradictions, with a handful of brilliant nonconformists, satanic geniuses who, to use the words of Sir John Read, Chairman of E.M.I. "become in the fullness of time, wholly acceptable and can contribute greatly to the development of modern music."[7]

STYLE AS INTENTIONAL COMMUNICATION

> I speak through my clothes.
>
> *Eco, 1973*

The cycle leading from opposition to defusion, from resistance to incorporation encloses each successive subculture. We have seen how the media and the market fit into this cycle. We must now turn to the subculture itself to consider exactly how and what subcultural style communicates. Two questions must be asked which together present us with something of a paradox: how does a subculture make sense to its members? How is it made to signify disorder? To answer these questions we must define the meaning of style more precisely.

In "The Rhetoric of the Image," Roland Barthes contrasts the "intentional" advertising image with the apparently "innocent" news photograph. Both are complex articulations of specific codes and practices, but the news photo appears more "natural" and transparent than the advertisement. He writes—"the signification of the image is certainly intentional...the advertising image is clear, or at least emphatic." Barthes' distinction can be used analogously to point up the difference between subcultural and "normal" styles. The subcultural stylistic ensembles—those emphatic combinations of dress, dance, argot, music, etc.—bear approximately the same relation to the more conventional formulae ("normal" suits and ties, casual wear, twin-sets, etc.) that the advertising image bears to the less consciously constructed news photograph.

Of course, signification need not be intentional, as semioticians have repeatedly pointed out. Umberto Eco writes "not only the expressly intended communicative object...but every object may be viewed ... as a sign" (Eco, 1973). For instance, the conventional outfits worn by the average man and woman in the street are chosen within the constraints of finance, "taste," preference, etc. and these choices are undoubtedly significant. Each ensemble has its place in an internal system of differences—the conventional modes of sartorial discourse—which fit a corresponding set of socially prescribed roles and options. These choices contain a whole range of messages which are transmitted through the finely graded distinctions of a number of interlocking sets—class and status, self-image and attractiveness, etc. Ultimately, if nothing else, they are expressive of "normality" as opposed to "deviance" (i.e., they are distinguished by their relative invisibility, their appropriateness, their "naturalness"). However, the intentional communication is of a different order. It stands apart—a visible construction, a loaded choice. It directs attention to itself; it gives itself to be read.

This is what distinguishes the visual ensembles of spectacular subcultures from those favoured in the surrounding culture(s). They are *obviously* fabricated (even the mods, precariously placed between the worlds of the straight and the deviant, finally declared themselves different when they gathered in groups outside dance halls and on sea fronts). They *display* their own codes (e.g., the punk's ripped T-shirt) or at least demonstrate that codes are there to be used and abused (e.g., they have been thought about rather than thrown together). In this they go against the grain of a mainstream culture whose principal defining characteristic, according to Barthes, is a tendency to masquerade as nature, to substitute "normalized" for historical forms, to translate the reality of the world into an image of the world which in turn presents itself as if composed according to "the evident laws of the natural order" (Barthes, 1972).

As we have seen, it is in this sense that subcultures can be said to transgress the law of "man's second nature."[8] By repositioning and recontextualizing commodities, by subverting their conventional uses and inventing new ones, the subcultural stylist gives the lie to what Althusser has called the "false obviousness of everyday practice" (Althusser and Balibar, 1968), and opens up the world of objects to new and covertly oppositional readings. The communication of significant *difference*, then (and the parallel communication of a group *identity*), is the "point" behind the style of all spectacular subcultures. It is the superordinate term under which all the other significations are marshalled, the message through which all the other messages speak. Once we have granted this initial difference a primary determination over the whole sequence of stylistic generation and diffusion, we can go back to examine the internal structure of individual subcultures. To return to our earlier analogy: if the "spectacular" subculture is an intentional communication, if it is, to borrow a term from linguistics, "motivated," what precisely is being communicated and advertised?

STYLE AS *BRICOLAGE*

> It is conventional to call "monster" any blending of dissonant elements....I call "monster" every original, inexhaustible beauty.
>
> *Alfred Jarry*

The subcultures with which we have been dealing share a common feature apart from the fact that they are all predominantly working class. They are, as we have seen, cultures of conspicuous consumption—even when, as with the skinheads and the punks, certain types of consumption are conspicuously refused—and it is through the distinctive rituals of consumption, through style, that the subculture at once reveals its "secret" identity and communicates its forbidden meanings. It is basically the way in which commodities are *used* in subculture which mark the subculture off from more orthodox cultural formations.

Discoveries made in the field of anthropology are helpful here. In particular, the concept of *bricolage* can be used to explain how subcultural styles are constructed. In *The Savage Mind* Levi-Strauss shows how the magical modes utilized by primitive peoples (superstition, sorcery, myth) can be seen as implicitly coherent, though explicitly bewildering, systems of connection between things which perfectly equip their users to "think" their own world. These magical systems of connection have a common feature: they are capable of infinite extension because basic elements can be used in a variety of improvised combinations to generate new meanings within them. *Bricolage* has thus been described as a "science of the concrete" in a recent definition which clarifies the original anthropological meaning of the term:

> [Bricolage] refers to the means by which the non-literate, non-technical mind of so-called "primitive" man responds the world around him. The process involves a "science of the concrete" (as opposed to our "civilised" science of the "abstract") which far from lacking logic, in fact carefully and precisely orders, classifies and arranges into structures the *minutiae* of the physical world in all their profusion by means of a "logic" which is not our own. The structures "improvised" or made up (these are rough translations of the process of *bricoler*) as *ad hoc* responses to an environment, then serve to establish homologies and analogies between the ordering of nature and that of society, and so satisfactorily "explain" the world and make it able to be lived in. (Hawkes, 1977)

The implications of the structured improvisations of *bricolage* for a theory of spectacular subculture as a system of communication have already been explored. For instance, John Clarke has stressed the way in which prominent forms of discourse (particularly fashion) are radically adapted, subverted and extended by the subcultural *bricoleur*:

> Together, object and meaning constitute a sign, and, within any one culture, such signs are assembled, repeatedly, into characteristic forms of discourse. However, when the bricoleur re-locates the significant object in a different position within that discourse, using the same overall repertoire of signs, or when that object is placed within a different total ensemble, a new discourse is constituted, a different message conveyed. (Clarke, 1976)

In this way the teddy boy's theft and transformation of the Edwardian style revived in the early 1950s by Savile Row for wealthy young men about town can be construed as an act of *bricolage*. Similarly, the mods could be said to be functioning as *bricoleurs* when they appropriated another range of commodities by placing them in a symbolic ensemble which served to erase or subvert their original straight meanings. Thus pills medically prescribed for the treatment of neuroses were used as ends-in-themselves, and the motor scooter, originally an ultra-respectable means of transport, was turned into a menacing symbol of group solidarity. In the same improvisatory manner, metal combs, honed to a razor-like sharpness, turned narcissism into an offensive weapon. Union jacks were emblazoned on the backs of grubby parka anoraks or cut up and converted into smartly tailored jackets. More subtly, the conventional insignia of the business world—the suit, collar and tie, short hair, etc.—were stripped of their original connotations—efficiency, ambition, compliance with authority—and transformed into "empty" fetishes, objects to be desired, fondled and valued in their own right.

At the risk of sounding melodramatic, we could use Umberto Eco's phrase "semiotic guerilla walfare" (Eco, 1972) to describes these subversive practises. The war may be conducted at a level beneath the consciousness of the individual members of a spectacular subculture (though the subculture is still, at another level, an intentional communication (see pp. 513–15) but with the emergence of such a group, "war—and it is Surrealism's war—is declared on a world of surfaces" (Annette Michelson, quoted Lippard, 1970).

The radical aesthetic practices of Dada and Surrealism—dream work, collage, "readymades," etc.—are certainly relevant here. They are the classic modes of "anarchic" discourse. Breton's manifestos (1924 and 1929) established the basic premise of surrealism: that a new "surreality" would emerge through the subversion of common sense, the collapse of prevalent logical categories and oppositions (e.g., dream/reality, work/play) and the celebration of the abnormal and the forbidden. This was to be achieved principally through "juxtaposition of two more or less distant realities" (Reverdy, 1918) exemplified for Breton in Lautreamont's bizarre phrase: "Beautiful like the chance meeting of an umbrella and a sewing machine on a dissecting table" Lautréamont, 1970). In *The Crisis of the Object*, Breton further theorized this "collage aesthetic," arguing rather optimistically that an assault on the syntax of everyday life which dictates the ways in which the most mundane objects are used, would instigate

> ... a *total revolution of the object:* acting to divert the object from its ends by coupling it to a new name and signing it.... Perturbation and deformation are in demand here for their own sakes.... Objects thus reassembled have in common the fact that they derive from and yet succeed in differing from the objects which surround us, by simple *change of role.* (Breton, 1936)

Max Ernst (1948) puts the same point more cryptically: "He who says collage says the irrational."

Obviously, these practices have their corollary in *bricolage*. The subcultural *bricoleur*, like the "author" of a surrealist collage, typically "juxtaposes" two apparently incompatible realities (i.e., 'flag': 'jacket'; 'hole': 'teeshirt'; 'comb': 'weapon') on an apparently unsuitable scale... and... it is there that the explosive junction occurs" (Ernst, 1948). Punk exemplifies most clearly the subcultural uses of these anarchic modes. It too attempted through "perturbation and deformation" to disrupt and reorganize meaning. It too, sought the "explosive junction." But what, if anything, were these subversive practices being used to signify? How do we "read" them? By singling out punk for special attention, we can look more closely at some of the problems raised in a reading of style.

STYLE IN REVOLT: REVOLTING STYLE

> Nothing was holy to us. Our movement was neither mystical, communistic nor anarchistic. All of these movements had some sort of programme, but ours was completely nihilistic. We spat on everything, including ourselves. Our symbol was nothingness, a vacuum, a void.
>
> *George Grosz on Dada*

> We're so pretty, oh so pretty... vac-unt.
>
> *The Sex Pistols*

Although it was often directly offensive (T-shirts covered in swear words) and threatening (terrorist/guerilla outfits) punk style was defined principally through the violence of its "cut ups." Like Duchamp's "ready mades"—manufactured objects which qualified as art because he chose to call them such, the most unremarkable and inappropriate items—a pin, a plastic clothes peg, a television component, a razor blade, a tampon—could be brought within the province of punk (un)fashion. Anything within or without reason could be turned into part of what Vivien Westwood called "confrontation dressing" so long as the rupture between "natural" and constructed context was clearly visible (i.e., the rule would seem to be: if the cap doesn't fit, wear it).

Objects borrowed from the most sordid of contexts found a place in the punks' ensembles: lavatory chains were draped in graceful arcs across chests encased in plastic bin-liners. Safety pins were taken out of their domestic "utility" context and worn as gruesome ornaments through the cheek, ear or lip. "Cheap" trashy fabrics (PVC, plastic, lurex, etc.) in vulgar designs (e.g. mock leopard skin) and "nasty" colours, long discarded by the quality end of the fashion industry as obsolete kitsch, were salvaged by the punks and turned into garments (fly boy drainpipes, "common" miniskirts) which offered self-conscious commentaries on the notions of modernity and taste. Conventional ideas of prettiness were jettisoned along with the traditional feminine lore of cosmetics. Contrary to the advice of every woman's magazine, make-up for both boys and girls was worn to be seen. Faces became abstract portraits: sharply observed and meticulously executed studies in alienation. Hair was obviously dyed (hay yellow, jet black, or bright orange with tufts of green or bleached in question marks), and T-shirts and trousers told the story of their own construction with multiple zips and outside seams clearly displayed. Similarly, fragments of school uniform (white brinylon shirts, school ties) were symbolically defiled (the shirts covered in graffiti, or fake blood; the ties left undone) and juxtaposed against leather drains or shocking pink mohair tops. The perverse and the abnormal were valued intrinsically. In particular, the illicit iconography of sexual fetishism was used to predictable effect. Rapist masks and rubber wear, leather bodices and fishnet stockings, implausibly pointed stiletto heeled shoes, the whole paraphernalia of bondage—the belts, straps and chains—were exhumed from the boudoir, closet and the pornographic film and placed on the street where they retained their forbidden connotations. Some young punks even donned the dirty raincoat—that most prosaic symbol of sexual "kinkiness"—and hence expressed their deviance in suitably proletarian terms.

Of course, punk did more than upset the wardrobe. It undermined every relevant discourse. Thus dancing, usually an involving and expressive medium in British rock and mainstream pop cultures, was turned into a dumbshow of blank robotics. Punk dances bore absolutely no relation to the desultory frugs and clinches which Geoff Mungham describes as intrinsic to the respectable working-class ritual of Saturday night at the Top Rank or Mecca. Indeed, overt displays of heterosexual interest were generally regarded with contempt and suspicion (who let the BOF/wimp[9] in?) and conventional courtship patterns found no place on the floor in dances like the pogo, the pose and the robot. Though the pose did allow for a minimum sociability (i.e., it could involve two people) the "couple" were generally of the same sex and physical contact was ruled out of court as the relationship depicted in the dance was a "professional" one. One participant would strike a suitable cliché fashion pose while the other would fall into a classic "Bailey" crouch to snap an imaginary picture. The pogo forebade even this much interaction, though admittedly there was always a good deal of masculine jostling in front of the stage. In fact the pogo was a caricature—a *reductio ad absurdum* of all the dance styles associated with rock music. It resembled the "anti-dancing" of the "Leapniks" which Melly describes in connection with the trad boom (Melly, 1972). The same abbreviated gestures—leaping into the air, hands clenched to the sides, to head an imaginary ball—were repeated without variation in time to the strict mechanical rhythms of the music. In contrast to the hippies' languid, free-form dancing, and the "idiot dancing" of the heavy metal rockers...the pogo made improvisation redundant: the only variations were imposed by changes in the tempo of the music—fast numbers being "interpreted" with manic abandon in the form of frantic on-the-spots, while the slower ones were pogoed with a detachment bordering on the catatonic.

The robot, a refinement witnessed only at the most exclusive punk gatherings, was both more "expressive" and less "spontaneous" within the very narrow range such terms acquired in punk usage. It consisted of barely perceptible twitches of the head and hands or more extravagant lurches (Frankenstein's first steps?) which were abruptly halted at random points. The resulting pose was held for several moments, even minutes, and the whole sequence was as suddenly, as unaccountably, resumed and re-enacted. Some zealous punks carried things one step further and choreographed whole evenings, turning themselves for a matter of hours, like Gilbert and George,[10] into automata, living sculptures.

The music was similarly distinguished from mainstream rock and pop. It was uniformly basic and direct in its appeal, whether through intention or lack of expertise. If the latter, then the punks certainly made a virtue of necessity ("We want to be amateurs"—Johnny Rotten). Typically, a barrage of guitars with the volume and treble turned to maximum accompanied by the occasional saxophone would pursue relentless (un)melodic lines against a turbulent background of cacophonous drumming and screamed vocals. Johnny Rotten succinctly defined punk's position on harmonics: "We're into chaos not music."

The names of the groups (the Unwanted, the Rejects, the Sex Pistols, the Clash, the Worst, etc.) and the titles of the songs: "Belsen was a Gas," "If You Don't Want to Fuck me, Fuck Off," "I Wanna be Sick on You," reflected the tendency towards wilful desecration and the voluntary assumption of outcast status which characterized the whole punk movement. Such tactics were, to adapt Levi-Strauss's famous phrase, "things to whiten mother's hair with." In the early days at least, these "garage bands" could dispense with musical pretensions and substitute, in the traditional romantic terminology, "passion" for "technique," the language of the common man for the arcane posturings of the existing elite, the now familiar armoury of frontal attacks for the bourgeois notion of entertainment or the classical concept of "high art."

It was in the performance arena that punk groups posed the clearest threat to law and order. Certainly, they succeeded in subverting the conventions of concert and nightclub entertainment. Most significantly, they attempted both physically and in terms of lyrics and life-style to move closer to their audiences. This in itself is by no means unique: the boundary between artist and audience has often stood as a metaphor in revolutionary aesthetics (Brecht, the surrealists, Dada, Marcuse, etc.) for that larger and more intransigent barrier which separates art and the dream from reality and life under capitalism.[11] The stages of those venues secure enough to host "new wave" acts were regularly invaded by hordes of punks, and if the management refused to tolerate such blatant disregard for ballroom etiquette, then the groups and their followers could be drawn closer together in a communion of spittle and mutual abuse. At the Rainbow Theatre in May 1977 as the Clash played "White Riot," chairs were ripped out and thrown at the stage. Meanwhile, every performance, however apocalyptic, offered palpable evidence that things could change, indeed were changing: that performance itself was a possibility no authentic punk should discount. Examples abounded in the music press of "ordinary fans" (Siouxsie of Siouxsie and the Banshees, Sid Vicious of the Sex Pistols, Mark P *of Sniffin Glue,* Jordan of the Ants) who had made the symbolic crossing from the dance floor to the stage. Even the humbler positions in the rock hierarchy could provide an attractive alternative to the drudgery of manual labour, office work or a youth on the dole. The Finchley Boys, for instance, were reputedly taken off the football terraces by the Stranglers and employed as roadies.

If these "success stories" were, as we have seen, subject to a certain amount of "skewed" interpretation in the press, then there were innovations in other areas which made opposition to dominant definitions possible. Most notably, there was an attempt, the first by a predominantly working-class youth culture, to provide an alternative critical space within the subculture itself to counteract the hostile or at least ideologically inflected coverage which punk was receiving in the media. The existence of an alternative punk press demonstrated that it was not only clothes or music that could be immediately and cheaply produced from the limited resources at hand. The fanzines *(Sniffin Glue, Ripped and Torn, etc.)* were journals edited by an individual or a group, consisting of reviews, editorials and interviews with prominent punks, produced on a small scale as cheaply as possible, stapled together and distributed through a small number of sympathetic retail outlets.

The language in which the various manifestoes were framed was determinedly "working class" (i.e., it was liberally peppered with swear words) and typing errors and grammatical mistakes, misspellings and jumbled pagination were left uncorrected in the final proof. Those corrections and crossings out that were made before publication were left to be deciphered by the reader. The overwhelming impression was one of urgency and immediacy, of a paper produced in indecent haste, of memos from the front line.

This inevitably made for a strident buttonholing type of prose which, like the music it described, was difficult to "take in" in any quantity. Occasionally a wittier, more abstract item—what Harvey Garfinkel (the American ethnomethodologist) might call an "aid to sluggish imaginations"—might creep in. For instance, *Sniffin Glue*, the first fanzine and the one which achieved the highest circulation, contained perhaps the single most inspired item of propaganda produced by the subculture—the definitive statement of punk's do-it-yourself philosophy—a diagram showing three finger positions on the neck of a guitar over the caption: "Here's one chord, here's two more, now form your own band."

Even the graphics and typography used on record covers and fanzines were homologous with punk's subterranean and anarchic style. The two typographic models were graffiti which was translated into a flowing "spray can" script, and the ransom note in which individual letters cut up from a variety of sources (newspapers, etc.) in different type faces were pasted together to form an anonymous message. The Sex Pistols' "God Save the Queen" sleeve (later turned into T-shirts, posters, etc.) for instance incorporated both styles: the roughly assembled legend was pasted across the Queen's eyes and mouth which were further disfigured by those black bars used in pulp detective magazines to conceal identity (i.e., they connote crime or scandal). Finally, the process of ironic self-abasement which characterized the subculture was extended to the name "punk" itself which, with its derisory connotations of "mean and petty villainy," "rotten," "worthless," etc. was generally preferred by hardcore members of the subculture to the more neutral "new wave."

NOTES

1. This was part of a speech made by Dr George Simpson, a Margate magistrate, after the mod-rocker clashes of Whitsun 1964. For sociologists of deviance, this speech has become *the* classic example of rhetorical overkill and deserves quoting in full: "These long-haired, mentally unstable, petty little hoodlums, these sawdust Caesars who can only find courage like rats, in hunting in packs" (quoted in Cohen, 1972).
2. On 1 December 1976 the Sex Pistols appeared on the Thames twilight programme *Today.* During the course of the interview with Bill Grundy they used the words "sod," "bastard" and "fuck." The papers carried stories of jammed switchboards, shocked parents, etc. and there were some unusual refinements. The *Daily Mirror* (2 December) contained a story about a lorry driver who had been so

incensed by the Sex Pistols' performance that he had kicked in the screen of his colour television: "I can swear as well as anyone, but I don't want this sort of muck coming into my home at teatime."

3. The police brought an unsuccessful action for obscenity against the Sex Pistols after their first L.P. "Never Mind the Bollocks" was released in 1977.

4. On 4 January, 1977 the Sex Pistols caused an incident at Heathrow Airport by spitting and vomiting in front of airline staff. The *Evening News* quoted a check-in desk girl as saying: "The group are the most revolting people I have ever seen in my life. They were disgusting, sick and obscene." Two days after this incident was reported in the newspapers, E.M.I. terminated the group's contract.

5. The 1 August 1977 edition of the *Daily Mirror* contained just such an example of dubious editorial concern. Giving "serious" consideration to the problem of ted–punk violence along the King's Road, the writer makes the obvious comparison with the seaside disturbances of the previous decade: "[The clashes] must not be allowed to grow into the pitched battles like the mods and rockers confrontations at several seaside towns a few years back." Moral panics can be recycled; even the same events can be recalled in the same prophetic tones to mobilise the same sense of outrage.

6. The definitive study of a moral panic is Cohen's *Folk Devils and Moral Panics.* The mods and rockers were just two of the "folk devils"—"the gallery of types that society erects to show its members which roles should be avoided"—which periodically become the centre of a "moral panic."

Societies appear to be subject, every now and then, to periods of moral panic. A condition, episode, person or group of persons emerges to become defined as a threat to societal values and interests; its nature is presented in a stylised and stereotypical fashion by the mass media; the moral barricades are manned by editors, bishops, politicians and other right-thinking people; socially accredited experts pronounce their diagnoses and solutions; ways of coping are evolved or (more often) resorted to; the condition then disappears, submerges or deteriorates and becomes more visible. (Cohen, 1972)

Official reactions to the punk subculture betrayed all the classic symptoms of a moral panic. Concerts were cancelled; clergymen, politicians and pundits unanimously denounced the degeneracy of youth. Among the choicer reactions, Marcus Lipton, the late M.P. for Lambeth North, declared: "If pop music is going to be used to destroy our established institutions, then it ought to be destroyed first." Bernard Brook-Partridge, M.P. for Havering-Romford, stormed, "I think the Sex Pistols are absolutely bloody revolting. I think their whole attitude is calculated to incite people to misbehaviour....It is a deliberate incitement to anti-social behaviour and conduct" (quoted in *New Musical Express,* 15 July 1977).

7. On 7 December one month before E.M.I. terminated its contract with the Sex Pistols, Sir John Read, the record company's Chairman, made the following statement at the annual general meeting:

Thoughout its history as a recording company, E.M.I. has always sought to behave within contemporary limits of decency and good taste—taking into account not only the traditional rigid conventions of one section of society, but also the increasingly liberal attitudes of other (perhaps larger) sections...at any given time...What is decent or in good taste compared to the attitudes of, say, 20 or even 10 years ago?

It is against this present-day social background that E.M.I. has to make value judgements about the content of records...Sex Pistols is a pop group devoted to a new form of music known as "punk rock." It was contracted for recording purposes by E.M.I. . . . in October, 1976 . . . In this context, it must be remembered that the recording industry has signed many pop groups, initially controversial, who have in the fullness of time become wholly acceptable and contributed greatly to the development of modern music . . . E.M.I should not set itself up as public censor, but it does seek to encourage restraint, (quoted in Vermore, 1978)

Despite the eventual loss of face (and some £40,000 paid out to the Pistols when the contract was terminated) E.M.I, and the other record companies tended to shrug off the apparent contradictions involved in signing up groups who openly admitted to a lack of professionalism, musicianship, and commitment to the profit motive. During the Clash's famous performance of "White Riot" at the Rainbow in 1977 when seats were ripped out and thrown at the stage, the last two rows of the theatre (left, of course, intact) were occupied almost exclusively by record executives and talent scouts: C.B.S. paid for the damage without complaint. There could be no clearer demonstration of the fact that symbolic assaults leave real institutions intact. Nonetheless, the record companies did not have everything their own way. The Sex Pistols received five-figure sums in compensation from both A & M and E.M.I. and when their L.P. (recorded at last by Virgin) finally did reach the shops, it contained a scathing attack on E.M.I.

8. Hall (1977) states: " . . . culture is the accumulated growth of man's power over nature, materialised in the instruments and practice of labour and in the medium of signs, thought, knowledge and language through which it is passed on from generation to generation as man's "second nature."

9. BOF = Boring old Fart
    Wimp= "wet".

10. Gilbert and George mounted their first exhibition in 1970 when, clad in identical conservative suit, with metallized hands and faces, a glove, a stick and a tape recorder, they won critical acclaim by performing a series of carefully controlled and endlessly repeated movements on a dais while miming to Flanagan and Allen's "Underneath the Arches". Other pieces with titles like "Lost Day" and "Normal Boredom" have since been performed at a variety of major art galleries throughout the world.

11. Of course, rock music had always threatened to dissolve these categories, and rock performances were popularly associated with all forms of riot and disorder—from the slashing of cinema seats by teddy boys through Beatlemania to the hippy happenings and festivals where freedom was expressed less aggressively in nudity, drug taking and general "spontaneity" However punk represented a new departure.

BIBLIOGRAPHY

Barthes, R. (1971), "The Rhetoric of the Image," *W.P.C.S.* I, University of Birmingham, retranslated in S. Heath (ed.), *Image, Music, Text*, Fontana, 1977.

———. (1972), *Mythologies*, Paladin.

Breton, A. (1924), "The First Surrealist Manifesto," in R. Seaver and H. Lane (eds), *Manifestoes of Surrealism*, University of Michigan Press, 1972.

———. (1929), "The Second Surrealist Manifesto," in R. Seaver and H. Lane (eds), *Manifestoes of Surrealism*, University of Michigan Press, 1972.

———. (1936), "Crisis of the Object", in L. Lippard (ed.), *Surrealists on Art*, Spectrum, 1970.

Clarke, J. (1976), "Style," in S. Hall *et al.* (eds), *Resistance Through Rituals*, Hutchinson.

Cohen, S. (1972), *Folk Devils and Moral Panics*, MacGibbon & Kee.

Douglas, M. (1967), *Purity and Danger*, Penguin.

Eco, U. (1972), "Towards a Semiotic Enquiry into the Television Message," *W.P.C.S.* 3, University of Birmingham.

———. (1973), "Social Life as a Sign System," in D. Robey (ed.), *Structuralism: The Wolfson College Lectures 1972*, Cape.

Ernst, M. (1948), *Beyond Painting and Other Writing by the Artist and His Friends*, ed. B. Karpel, Sculz.

Geertz, C. (1964), "Ideology as a Cultural System," in D.E. Apter (ed.), *Ideololgy and Discontent*, Free Press.

Hall, S. (1974), "Deviancy, Politics and the Media," in P. Rock and M. McIntosh (eds.), *Deviance and Social Control*, Tavistock.

———. (1977), "Culture, the Media and the 'Ideologial Effect,'" in J. Curran *et al.* (eds.), *Mass Communication and Society*, Arnold.

Hawkes, T. (1977), *Structuralism and Semiotics*, Methuen.

Ingham, R. (ed.) (1977), *Football Hooliganism*, Inter-action Imprint.

Lautréamont, Comte de (1970), *Chants du Maldoror*, Alison & Busby.

Lefebvre, H. (1971), *Everyday Life in the Modern World*, Allen Lane.

Levi–Strauss, C. (1969), *The Elementary Structures of Kinship*, Eyre & Spottiswood.

Lippard, L. (ed.) (1970), *Surrealists on Art*, Spectrum.

Marx, K. and Engels, F. (1970), *The German Ideology*, Lawrence & Wishart.

Melly, G. (1972), *Revolt into Style*, Penguin.

Mepham, J. (1972), "The Structuralist Sciences and Philosophy," in D. Robey (ed.), *Structuralism: The Wolfson College Lectures 1972*, Cape, 1973.

Reverdy, P. (1918), *Nord-Sud*.

Vermorel, F. and Vermorel, J. (1978), *The Sex Pistols*, Tandem.

JACKIE MAGAZINE: ROMANTIC INDIVIDUALISM AND THE TEENAGE GIRL (1977, 1991)

ANGELA McROBBIE

Angela McRobbie works in part from a concern that even the best studies of youth subcultures by cultural studies scholars, including Dick Hebdige's Subcultures, *give too little attention to gender. She argues that cultural studies scholars, without seeming to realize it, tend to represent youth in general by focusing on boys and young men, with girls only as props in the background. McRobbie developed her own research through fieldwork among British girls and through this classic structuralist and feminist study of* Jackie, *a popular magazine for British girls. (Here there is space for only the first half of McRobbie's essay. The second half continues with a discussion of codes of personal life, fashion and beauty, and pop music.)*

Another useful expression, though, is the pathetic appealing look, which brings out
a boy's protective instinct and has him desperate to get you another drink/help you

on with your coat/give you a lift home. It's best done by opening your eyes wide and dropping the mouth open a little, looking (hanging your head slightly) directly into the eyes of the boy you're talking to. Practice this.

Jackie, 15 February 1975

One of the main reasons for choosing *Jackie* for analysis is its great success as a weekly magazine. Since it first appeared in 1964 its sales have risen from an initial average of 350,000 (with a drop in 1965 to 250,000) to 451,000 in 1968 and 605,947 in 1976. This means that it has been Britain's biggest-selling teen magazine for over ten years. *Boyfriend,* first published in 1959, started off with sales figures averaging around 418,000 but had fallen to 199,000 in 1965 when publication ceased. *Mirabelle,* launched in 1956, sold over 540,000 copies each week, a reflection of the "teenage boom" of the mid-1950s, but by 1968 its sales had declined to 175,000.[1]

The object of this study, however, is not to grapple with those factors upon which this success appears to be based. Instead it will be to mount a systematic critique of *Jackie* as a system of messages, a signifying system and a bearer of a certain ideology, an ideology which deals with the construction of teenage femininity.

Jackie is one of a large range of magazines, newspapers and comics published by D. C. Thomson of Dundee (five newspapers in Scotland, 32 titles in all). With a history of vigorous anti-unionism, D. C. Thomson is not unlike other mass communication groups.[2] Like Walt Disney, for example, it produces for a young market and operates a strict code of censorship on content. But its conservatism is most evident in its newspapers. The *Sunday Post* with a reputed readership of around 3 million (i.e., 79 per cent of the entire population of Scotland over the age of 15) is comforting, reassuring, and parochial in tone. Consisting, in the main, of anecdotal incidents drawn to the attention of the reader in "couthie" language, it serves as a Sunday entertainer, reminding its readers of the pleasure of belonging to a particular national culture.

One visible result of this success has been enviably high profit margins of 20 per cent or more, at a time of inflation and crisis in the publishing world.[3] D. C. Thomson has also expanded into other associated fields with investments, for example, in the Clyde Paper Company and Southern TV3. Without adhering to a "conspiracy plot" thesis, it would nonetheless be naive to imagine that the interests of such a company lie purely in the realisation of profit. In *Jackie,* D. C. Thomson is not merely "giving girls what they want." Each magazine, newspaper or comic has its own conventions and its own style. But within these conventions, and through them, a concerted effort is nevertheless made to win and shape the consent of the readers to a particular set of values.

The work of this branch of the media involves framing the world for its readers, and through a variety of techniques endowing with importance those topics chosen for inclusion. The reader is invited to share this world with *Jackie.* It is no coincidence that the title is also a girl's name. This is a sign that the magazine is concerned with the "category of the subject,"[4] in particular the individual girl and the feminine persona. *Jackie* is both the magazine and the ideal girl. The short snappy name carries a string of connotations—British, fashionable (particularly in the 1960s), modern and cute. With the "pet-form" abbreviated ending, it sums up all those desired qualities which the reader is supposedly seeking.

This ideological work is also grounded on certain natural, even biological, categories. *Jackie* expresses the natural features of adolescence in much the same way as Disney comics capture the natural essence of childhood. As Dorfman and Mattelart writing on Disney point out, each has a "virtually biologically captive predetermined authence."[5] *Jackie* introduces the girl to adolescence, outlining its landmarks and characteristics in detail and stressing the problematic features as well as the fun. Of course *Jackie* is not solely responsible for nurturing this ideology of femininity. Nor would such an ideology cease to exist if *Jackie* disappeared.

Unlike other fields of mass culture, the magazines of teenage girls have not yet been subject to rigorous critical analysis, yet from the most cursory of readings it is clear that they too, like those other forms more immediately associated with the sociology of the press, TV, film, radio—are powerful ideological forces. In fact, women's and girls' weeklies occupy a privileged position. Addressing themselves solely to a female market, their concern is with promoting a feminine culture for their readers. They define and shape the woman's world, spanning every stage from early childhood to old age. From *Mandy, Bunty, Judy* and *Jackie* to *House and Home,* the exact nature of the woman's role is spelt out in detail, according to her age and status. She progresses from adolescent romance where there are no explicitly sexual encounters, to the more sexual world of *19, Honey,* or *Over 21,* which in turn give way to marriage, childbirth, home-making, child-care and *Woman's Own.* There are no male equivalents to these products. Male magazines tend to be based on particular leisure pursuits or hobbies, motorcycling, fishing, cars or even pornography. There is no consistent attempt to link interests with age, nor is there a sense of natural or inevitable progression from one to another complementary to the life-cycle. Instead there are a variety of leisure options available, many of which involve participation outside the home.

It will be argued that the way *Jackie* addresses girls as grouping—as do all the other magazines—serves to obscure differences of, for example, class or race, between women. *Jackie* asserts a class-less, race-less sameness, a kind of false unity which assumes a common experience of womanhood or girlhood. By isolating a particular phase or age as the focus of interest, one which coincides roughly with that of its readers, the magazine is ascribing to age, certain ideological meanings. Adolescence comes to be synonymous with *Jackie*'s definition of it. The consensual totality of feminine adolescence means that all girls want to know how to catch a boy, lose weight, look their best and be able to cook. This allows few opportunities for other feminine modes, other kinds of adolescence. Dissatisfaction with the present is responded to in terms of looking forward to the next stage. In this respect girls are being invited to join a closed sorority of shared feminine values which actively excludes other possible values. Within the world of *Jackie* what we find is a cloyingly claustrophobic environment where the dominant emotions are fear, insecurity, competitiveness and even panic.

There are several ways in which we can approach *Jackie* magazine as part of the media and of mass culture in general. The first of these is the traditionalist thesis. In this, magazines are seen as belonging to popular or mass culture, something which is inherently inferior to high culture, or the arts. Cheap, superficial, exploitative and debasing, mass culture reduces its audience to a mass of mindless morons:

> the open sagging mouths and glazed eyes, the hands mindlessly drumming in time to the music, the broken stiletto heels, the shoddy, stereotyped "with it" clothes: here apparently, is a collective portrait of a generation enslaved by a commercial machine.[6]

Alderson, writing explicitly on girls' weeklies takes a similar position. Claiming, correcly, that what they offer their readers is a narrow and restricted view of life, she proposed as an alternative, better literature, citing *Jane Eyre* as an example.[7]

The problems with such an approach are manifest. "High" culture becomes a cure for all ills. It is, to quote Willis, "a repository of quintessential human values,"[8] playing a humanising role by elevating the emotions and purifying the spirit. What this argument omits to mention are the material requirements necessary to purchase such culture. And underpinning it is an image of the deprived, working-class youngster (what Alderson calls the "Newsom girl") somehow lacking in those qualities which contact with the arts engenders. Mass culture is seen as a manipulative, vulgar, profit-seeking industry offering cheap and inferior versions of the arts to the more impressionable and vulnerable sectors of the population. This concept of culture is inadequate because it is ahistorical, and is based on unquestioned qualitative judgements. It offers no explanations as to how these forms develop and are distributed. Nor does it explain why one form has a particular resonance for one class in society rather than another.

The second interpretation has much in common with this approach, although it is generally associated with more radical critics. This is the conspiracy thesis and it, too, sees mass culture as fodder for the masses; the result of a ruling-class plot whose objective it is to keep the working classes docile and subordinate and to divert them into entertainments. Writing on TV, Hall, Connell and Curti describe this approach, "from this position the broadcaster is conceived of as nothing more than the ideological agent of his political masters."[9]

Orwell, writing on boys' magazines in the 1930s, can be seen to take such a position, "Naturally, the politics of the *Gem* and *Magnet* are Conservative...All fiction from the novels in the mushroom libraries downwards is censored in the interests of the ruling class."[10] By this logic, *Jackie* is merely a mouthpiece for ruling-class ideology, focused on young adolescent girls. Again, mass culture is seen as worthless and manipulative. Not only is this argument also ahistorical, but it fails to locate the operations of different apparatuses in the social formation (politics, the media, the law, education, the family) each of which is relatively autonomous, has its own level and its own specific material practices. While private sectors of the economy do ultimately work together with the State, there is a necessary separation, between them. Each apparatus has its own uneven development and one cannot be collapsed with another.

The third argument reverses both the first two arguments, to the extent that it points to pop music and pop culture as meaningful activities: "for most young people today...pop music and pop culture is their only expressive outlet."[11] Such a position does have some relevance to our study of *Jackie*. It hinges on the assumption that this culture expresses and offers, albeit in consumerist terms, those values and ideas held both by working-class youth and by sections of middle-class youth. Youth, that is, is defined in terms of values held, which are often in opposition to those held by the establishment, by their parents, the school, in work, and so on. Such a definition does not consider youth's relation to production, but to consumption, and it is this approach which has characterised that huge body of work, the sociology of culture and of youth subcultural theory, and delinquency theory.

To summarise a familiar argument which finds expression in most of these fields: working-class youth, denied access to other "higher" forms of culture, and associating these in any case with "authority" and with the middle classes, turns to those forms available on the market. Here they can at least exert some power in their choice of commodities. These commodities often come to be a hallmark of the subcultural group in question but not exactly in their original forms. The group subverts the original meaning by bestowing additional implied connotations to the object thereby extending the range of its signifying power. These new meanings undermine and can even negate the previous or established meanings so that the objects come to represent an oppositional ideology linked to the subculture or youth grouping, in question. It then summarises for the outside observer, the group's disaffection from the wider society. This process of re-appropriation can be seen in, for example, the "style" of the skinheads, the "mod" suit, the "rocker" motor-bike, or even the "punk" safety-pin.[12]

But this approach, which hinges on explaining the choice of cultural artefacts—clothes, records or motor-bikes—is of limited usefulness when applied to teenage girls and their magazines. They play little, if any, role in shaping their own pop culture and their choice in consumption is materially extremely narrow. Indeed the forms made available to them make re-appropriation difficult. *Jackie* offers its readers no active "presence" in which girls are invited to participate. The uses are, in short, prescribed by the "map." Yet this does not mean that *Jackie* cannot be used in subversive ways. Clearly girls do use it as a means of signalling their boredom and disaffection, in the school, for example. The point here is that despite these possible uses, the magazine itself has a powerful ideological presence as a form, and as such demands analysis carried out apart from these uses or "readings."

The fourth and final interpretation is the one most often put forward by media practitioners themselves. Writing on the coverage of political affairs on TV, Stuart Hall et al. label this the *laissez-faire* thesis:

> Programming is conceived, simply, as a "window" on the campaign; it reflects, and therefore, does not shape, or mould, the political debate. In short, the objectives of television are to provide objective information... so that they—the public—may make up their own minds in a "rational" manner.[13]

By this logic, *Jackie,* instead of colouring the way girls think and act merely reflects and accurately portrays their pre-existing interests, giving them "what they want" and offering useful advice on the way.

While the argument made here will include strands from the positions outlined above, its central thrust will represent a substantial shift away from them. What I want to suggest is that *Jackie* occupies the sphere of the personal or private, what Gramsci calls "Civil Society" ("the ensemble of organisms that are commonly called Private").[14] Hegemony is sought uncoercively on this terrain, which is relatively free of direct State interference. Consequently it is seen as an arena of "freedom," of "free choice" and of "free time." This sphere includes, "not only associations and organisations like political parties and the press, but also the family, which combines ideological and economic functions"[15] and as Hall, Lumley and McLennan observe, this distinctness from the State has "pertinent effects—for example, in the manner in which different aspects of the class struggle are ideologically inflected."[16] *Jackie* exists within a large, powerful, privately-owned publishing apparatus which produces a vast range of newspapers, magazines and comics. It is on this level of the magazine that teenage girls are subjected to an explicit attempt to win consent to the dominant order—in terms of femininity, leisure and consumption, i.e., at the level of culture.

The "teen" magazine is a highly previlaged "site." Here the girls' consent is sought uncoercively and in their leisure time. As Frith observes, "The ideology of leisure in a capitalist society...is that people work in order to be able to enjoy leisure. Leisure is their 'free' time and so the values and choices, expressed in leisure and independent of work—they are the result of ideological conditions."[17] While there is a strongly coercive element to those other terrains which teenage girls inhabit—the school and the family—in her leisure time the girl is officially free to do as she pleases. It is on the open market that girls are least constrained by the display of social control. The only qualification here is the ability to buy a ticket, magazine or Bay City Roller T-shirt. Here they remain relativity free from interference by authority. Frith notes that there are three main purposes for capitalist society with regard to leisure:[18] (1) the reproduction of labour physically (food, rest, relaxation); (2) the reproduction of labour ideologically (so that the work-force will willingly return to work each day); (3) the provision of a market for the consumption of goods, thus the realisation of surplus value.

While *Jackie* readers are not yet involved in production, they are already being pushed in this direction ideologically, at school, in the home and in the youth club. *Jackie* as a commodity designed for leisure covers all three points noted above. It encourages good health and "beauty sleep," and it is both a consumer object which encourages further consumption and a powerful ideological force.

So, using *Jackie* as an example, we can see that leisure and its exploitation in the commercial and private sector also provides capital with space to carry out ideological work. Further, it can be argued that the very way in which leisure is set up and defined is itself ideological. Work is a necessary evil, possibly dull and unrewarding. But its rationale is to allow the worker to look forward to his or her leisure as an escape. That is, leisure is equated with free choice and free time and exists in opposition to work, which is associated with necessity, coercion and authority. In this sphere of individual self-expression and relaxation, the State remains more or less hidden revealing itself only when it is deemed politically necessary (for example at football matches and rock concerts; through the laws relating to obscene publications and through licensing and loitering laws, etc.)

Commercial leisure enterprises with their illusion of freedom have, then, an attraction for youth. And this freedom is pursued, metaphorically, inside the covers of *Jackie*. With an average readership age of 10 to 14, *Jackie* prefigures girls' entry into the labour market as young workers, and its pages are crammed full of the "goodies" which this later freedom promises. (*Jackie* girls are never at school, they are enjoying the fruits of their labour on the open market. They live in large cities, frequently in flats shared with other young wage-earners like themselves.)

This image of freedom has a particular resonance for girls when it is located within and intersects with the longer and again ideologically constructed "phase" they inhabit in the present. Leisure has a special importance in this period of "brief flowering,"[19] that is, in those years prior to marriage and settling down, after which they become dual labourers in the home and in production. Leisure in their "single" years is especially important because it is here that their future is secured. It is in *this* sphere that they go about finding a husband and thereby sealing their fate.

In pursuit of this image of freedom and of free choice it is in the interests of capital that leisure be to some extent removed from direct contact with the State, despite the latter's welfare and leisure provisions for youth. Thus a whole range of consumer goods, pop music, pubs, discos and in this case teen magazines occupy a space which promise greater personal freedom for the consumer. *Jackie* exists in this private sphere. The product of a privately owned industry and the prime exponent of the world of the private or personal emotions. Frith makes the point that

> The overall result for capital is that control of leisure has been exercised indirectly, leisure choices can't be determined but they do have to be limited—the problem is to ensure that workers' leisure activities don't affect their discipline, skill or willingness to work.[20]

That is, capital needs to provide this personal space for leisure, but it also needs to control it. This is clearly best done through consumption. Hence ultimately State and private spheres do function "beneath the ruling ideology" but they also have different "modes of insertion" on a day-to-day basis, which, as pointed out earlier, in turn produce *"pertinent effects."* There is an *unspoken* consensus existing between those ideologies carried in State organised leisure, and those included in *Jackie*. The former is typically blunt in its concern with moral training, discipline, team spirit, patriotism, allowing the latter to dedicate itself to fun and romance!

What then are the key features which characterise *Jackie?* First there is a lightness of tone, a non-urgency, which holds true right through the magazine particularly in the use of colour, graphics and advertisements. It asks to be read at a leisurely pace indicating that its subject matter is not wholly serious, and is certainly not "news." Since entertainment and leisure goods are designed to arouse feelings of pleasure as well as interest, the appearance of the magazine is inviting, its front cover shows a pretty girl smiling happily. The dominance of the visual level, which is maintained throughout the magazine reinforces this notion of leisure. It is to be glanced through, looked at and only finally read. Published at weekly intervals, the reader has time to peruse each item at her own speed. She also has time to pass it round her friends or swap it for another magazine.

Rigid adherence to a certain style of lay-out and patterning of features ensures a familiarity with its structure(s). The reader can rely on *Jackie* to cheer her up, entertain her, or solve her problems each week. The style of the magazine once established, facilitates and encourages partial and uneven reading, in much the same way as newspapers also do. The girl can quickly turn to the centre page for pin-up, glance at the fashion page and leave the problems and picture stories which are the main substance of the magazine, till she has more time.

Articles and features are carefully arranged to avoid one "heavy" feature following another. The black-and-white-picture stories taking up between 2 1/2 and 3 full pages are always broken up by a coloured advertisement or beauty feature, and the magazine opens and closes by inviting the reader to participate directly through the letters or the problem pages.

This sense of solidness and resistance to change (*Jackie*'s style has not been substantially altered since it began publication) is reflected and paralleled in its thematic content. Each feature consists of workings and reworkings of a relatively small repertoire of specific themes or concerns which sum up the girls' world. These topics saturate the magazine. Entering the world of *Jackie* means suspending interest in the real world of school, family or work, and participating in a sphere which is devoid of history and resistant to change.

Jackie deals primarily with the terrain of the personal and it marks a turning inwards to the sphere of the "soul," the "heart" or the emotions. On the one hand, of course, certain features do change—fashion is itself predicated upon change and upon being "up to date." But the degree of change even here is qualified—certain features remain the same, e.g., the model's looks, poses, the style of drawing and its positioning within the magazine and so on.

Above all, *Jackie*, like the girl it symbolises, is intended to be looked at. This overriding concern with visuals affects every feature. But its visual appearance and style also reflects the spending power of its readers. There is little of the extravagant or exotic in *Jackie*. The paper on which it is printed is thin and not glossy. The fashion and beauty pages show clothes priced within the girls' range and the advertisements are similarly focused on a low-budget market, featuring principally personal toiletries, tampons, shampoos and lipsticks, rather than larger consumer goods.

This is how the reader looks at *Jackie*, but how is it best analysed? How does the sociologist look at the magazine? Instead of drawing on the well-charted techniques of content analysis, I will be using approaches associated with *semiology*, the science of signs. However, this approach offers no fool proof methodology. As a science it is still in its infancy, yet it has more to offer than traditional content analysis,[21] because it is not solely concerned with the numerative *appearance* of the content, but with the messages which such contents signify. Magazines are specific signifying systems where particular messages are produced and articulated. Quantification is therefore rejected and replaced with understanding media messages as *structured wholes* and combinations of structures, polarities and oppositions are endowed with greater significance than their mere numerative existence.

Semiological analysis proceeds by isolating sets of codes around which the message is constructed. These conventions operate at several levels, visual and narrative, and also include sets of subcodes, such as those of fashion, beauty, romance, personal/domestic life and pop music. These codes constitute the "rules" by which different meanings are produced and it is the identification and consideration of these in detail that provides the basis to the analysis. In short, semiology is concerned with the internal structuring of a text or signifying system, with what Barthes calls "immanent analysis":

> The relevance shown by semiological research centres by definition round the signification of the objects analysed: they are examined only in relation to the meaning which is theirs without bringing on—at least prematurely, that is, before the system is reconstituted as far as possible—the other determining factors of these objects (whether psychological, socio-logical or physical). These other factors must of course not be denied. . . . The principle of relevance evidently has a consequence for the analyst, a situation of immanence; one ob-serves a given system from the inside.[22]

How then do we apply such an analysis to *Jackie?* Given the absence of any definitive rules of procedure—an absence which stems from the polysemic qualities of the image ("It is precisely this polysemy which invites interpretation and therefore makes the imposition of one dominant reading among the variants ... possible"),[23] my approach is necessarily exploratory, First then, I will attempt to locate the more general structural qualities of *Jackie.* Having described the nature and organisation of the codes which hold it together, I will then go on to consider these separately in some detail although in practice they rarely appear in such as "pure" form.

One of the most immediate and outstanding features of *Jackie* as it is displayed on book-stalls, newspaper stands and counters, up and down the country, is its ability to look "natu-ral." It takes its place easily within that whole range of women's magazines which rarely change their format and which (despite new arrivals which quickly achieve this solidness if they are to succeed) always seem to have been there. Its existence is taken for granted. Yet this front obscures the "artificiality" of the magazine, its "product-ness" and its existence as a commodity.

Jackie is the result of a certain kind of labour which involves the implementation and arrangement of a series of visual and narrative signs. Its meanings derive from the practice of encoding "raw material" (or re-encoding already-coded material) which results in the creation of new meanings. These new meanings depend upon the specific organisation of different codes all of which in turn involve different kinds of labour—photography, mount-ing, framing, drawing, headlining, and so on.

There is nonetheless, a real problem as to what constitutes raw material. It can be argued that any such material by virtue of its existence within a set social relation is already encoded. But does "raw material" refer merely to the material existence of 13–15-year-old girls? Or does it recognise that they have already been in constant contact with various ideologies since early childhood? That is, does it assume an already existing culture of femininity? I would argue that it is the latter which is the case. For raw material we can read that preexis-tent level of femininity which both working-class and middle-class girls can hardly avoid. As part of the dominant ideology it has saturated their lives, colouring the way they dress, the way they act and the way they talk to each other. This ideology is predicated upon their future roles as wives and mothers. Each of the codes combines within it, two separate levels: the denotative—the literal—and the connotative. It is this latter which is of the greater interest to the semiologist, "connotative codes are the configurations of meaning which permit a sign to signify in addition to its denotative reference, other additional, implied meanings."[24] Connotation then, "refers subjects to social relations, social structures, to our routinised knowledge of the social formation."[25] And as Barthes comments, "As for the signified of connotation, its character is at once general, global and diffuse; it is, if you like, a fragment of ideology."[26] Codes of connotation depend on prior social knowledge on the part of the reader, observer, or audience, they are "cultural, conventionalised and historical."[27]

A large range of codes operate in *Jackie* (see Figure 1), but for present purposes I have identified four subcodes, and organised the study around them.[28] These are: (1) the code of romance; (2) the code of personal/domestic life; (3) the code of fashion and beauty; and (4) the code of pop music

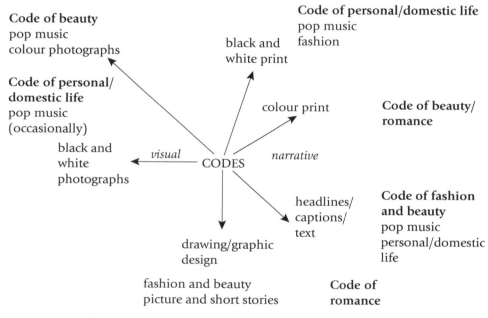

Figure 1 The codes operating in *Jackie*

THE CODE OF ROMANCE: THE MOMENT OF BLISS

> The hero of romance knows how to treat women. Flowers, little gifts, love-letters, maybe poems to her eyes and hair, candlelit meals on moonlit terraces and muted strings. Nothing hasty, physical. Some heavy breathing... Mystery, magic, champagne, ceremony... women never have enough of it.[29]

Jackie picture stories are similar in form to those comic strips, and tales of adventure, time-travel, rivalry and intrigue which regularly fill the pages of children's weeklies. Yet there is something distinctive about these stories which indicates immediately their concern with romance. First, the titles clearly announce a concern with "you, me, love and happiness." Romantic connotations are conveyed through the relationship between titles and the names of "pop" songs and ballads. (*Jackie* however, does not use the older *Boyfriend* technique of using a well-known pop song and its singer both to inspire the story and to give it moral weight!)

The titles anchor the stories they introduce. In our sample these include:

> "The Happiest Xmas Ever"
> "Meet Me On The Corner"
> "As Long As I've Got You"
> "Come Fly With Me"
> "Where Have All The Flowers Gone?"

This concern with romance pervades every story and is built into them through the continued use of certain formal techniques and styles. For a start, the way the characters look indicates clearly that this is serious. They are all older and physically more mature than the intended reader. Each character conforms to a well-established and recognisable standard of beauty or handsomeness and they are all smart, fairly sophisticated young adults, rather than adolescents or teenagers.

The most characteristic feature of "romance" in *Jackie* is the concern with the narrow and restricted world of the emotions. No attempt is made to fill out social events or backgrounds. The picture story is the realm, par excellence, of the individual. Each story revolves round one figure and the tiny web of social relationships surrounding him or, usually, her. Rarely are there more than two or three characters in each plot and where they do exist it is merely as part of the background or scenery—in the cafe, at the disco or in the street.

Unlike comic strips, where the subject is fun, excitement or adventure, these stories purport to deal with the more serious side of life—hence the semi-naturalistic style of the drawings and the use of black and white. This, along with the boldness of the drawings, the starkness of stroke and angularity of the figures, conspires to create an impression of realism and seriousness. The form of the stories alone tells us that romance is important, serious and relevant. Yet simultaneously in the content, we are told that it is fun; the essence and meaning of life; the key to happiness, and so on. It is this blend which gives the *Jackie* romance its characteristic flavour. In general terms this is nothing new, these stories owe a great deal to popular cinema romances, and to novelettes. The characters closely resemble the anonymous but distinctive type of the film-star—dewy-eyed women and granite-jawed heroes. Their poses are equally soaked in the language of film—the clinch; the rejected lover alone by herself as the sun sets—the moon comes up—to name but a few. But this cinematic resemblance is based on more than just association. The very form of the comic strip has close links with the film. Strung together, in a series of clips, set out across and down the page—the stories rise to a climax and resolution, graphically illustrated in larger images erupting across the page.

From these clips we can see clearly that the emotional life is defined and lived in terms of *romance* which in turn is equated with great moments rather than long-term processes. Hence the centrality and visual impact of the clinch, the proposal, the wedding-day. Together these moments constitute a kind of orchestration of time: through them the feminine career is constructed. The picture stories consist of a set of visual images composed and set within a series of frames laid out across the page to be "read" like a text. But these frames communicate visually, resemble film-clips and tell the story by "freezing" the action into sets of "stills." Unlike other comics (*Bunty* or *Judy*), *Jackie* stories do not conform to the convention of neatly mounted images set uniformly across the page. Instead, a whole range of loose frames indicating different kinds of situations or emotions are used. These produce a greater continuity between "form" and "content," so that as the pace of the story accelerates, the visuals erupt with the breathless emotional feelings, spilling out over the page.

Each separate image which makes up the story is "anchored" with sets of verbal messages illuminating the action and eliminating ambiguity. This is necessary since "all images are polysemic; they imply, underlying their signifiers, a 'floating chain' of signifieds, among which the reader can choose a few and ignore the rest."[30] But anchorage refers to only one part of the written message accompanying the image in the comic strip, that is the caption, title and statement of fact ("the next day," "later that evening," etc.). The second function of the linguistic message here is "relay." Again quoting Barthes:

> words (most often a snippet of dialogue) and image stand in complementary relationship; the words like the images, are thus fragments of a more general syntagma, and the unity of the message occurs at a superior level, the level of the story, anecdote, narrative.... The two functions of the linguistic message can co-exist in an iconic group but the dominance of one or the other is not a matter of indifference for the general economy of the work.... In some strips which are meant to be read quickly, the narrative is entrusted above all to the word, and the image gathers up the attributive, paradigmatic information (the stereotyped status of persons).[31]

Thus the moments of reading and looking are collapsed into one, and the reader is spared the boredom of having to read more lengthy descriptions; she merely "takes it in" and hurries on to the next image. The techniques through which this relay operates are well-known—dialogue is indicated by the use of balloons issuing from the mouths of the speakers and filled with words, and thoughts are conveyed through a series of small bubbles which drift upwards away from the character's mouth—thinking being associated with a "higher" level of discourse, an "intellectual" pursuit.

The central and most dramatic incident in each story is specified by the spilling-out of one visual image over the page. This image sums up graphically the fraught nature of the moment; the moment when the timid shy heroine catches sight of her handsome boyfriend fascinated by her irresistible best-friend at a party to which she stupidly invited her: or when the girl, let down by her boy rushes out of the coffee bar across the street to be hit by a passing car... and so on.

Each frame represents a selection from the development of the plot, and is credited with an importance which those intervening moments are not. Thus the train, supermarket, and office have meaning, to the extent that they represent potential meeting-places where the girl could well bump into the prospective boyfriend, who lurks round every corner. It is this which determines their inclusion in the plot; the possibility that everyday life could be transformed into social life.

Within the frames themselves the way the figures look, act, and pose also contributes to the ideology of romance. For a start there is very little variation in types of physical appearance. This homogeneity hinges on a blend of modernity and conservatism which typifies the *Jackie* look. The girls are "mod" but neat and conventional, rarely are they "way-out." Boys may look acceptably scruffy and disheveled by displaying a kind of managed untidiness.

The appearance is matched by language. Deriving seemingly from the days of the teenage commercial boom it has a particularly 1950s ring about it.[32] Bereft of accent, dialect, slang or vulgarity it remains the invention of the media—the language of pop, and of Radio 1 disc jockeys. Distantly modern it is also quite unthreatening, peppered with phrases like "rave"; "yacked"; "zacked"; "scrummy hunk"; "dishy"; "fare"; "come-on, let's blow this place"; "I'm the best mover in town"—all of which convey an image of youth "on the move," of "a whole scene going," and of "wowee, dig the slick chick in the corner"; "a nice piece or talent," teenagers "doing their own thing." But these teenagers are a strangely anonymous and unrecognisable grouping, similar only, perhaps, to the "Young Generation" seen on TV variety shows or the young people in Coca-Cola or Levi Jeans advertisements. It is a language of action, of "good time," of enjoyment and of consumerism. The characters in *Jackie* stories and in Coca-Cola TV advertisements at least seem to be getting things done. They are constantly seen "raving it up" at discos, going for trips in boyfriends' cars, or else going on holiday. And yet, as we shall see, the female and male characters in *Jackie* are simultaneously doing nothing but pursuing each other, and far from being a pleasure-seeking *group*, these stories in fact consist of isolated individuals, distrusting even their best-friends and in search of fulfillment only through a partner. The anonymity of the language, then, parallels the strangely amorphous *Jackie* girls. Marked by a rootlessness, lack of ties or sense of region, the reader is unable to "locate" them in any social context: They are devoid of history. Bound together by an invisible "generational consciousness" they inhabit a world where no disruptive values exist. At the "heart" of this world is the individual girl looking for romance. But romance is not itself an unproblematic category and what I will be arguing here is that its central contradiction is glaringly clear and unavoidable even to the girl herself who is so devoted to its cause. This contradiction is based round the fact that the *romantic moment,* its central tenet, cannot be reconciled with its promise *of eternity.* The code of romance realises, but cannot accept, that the man can adore, love, "cherish" and be sexually attracted to his girlfriend and simultaneously be "aroused" by other girls. It is the recognition of this fact that sets all girls against each other, and forms the central theme in the picture stories. Hence the girl constantly worries, as she is passionately embraced; "can it last?" or "how can I be sure his love is for ever?"

Earlier we asserted that *Jackie* was concerned with "the category of the subject,"[33] with the constitution of the feminine personality. Indeed "personality" itself forms an important organising category in the magazine. Each week there is some concern with "your" personality, how to know it, change it or understand those of your friends, boyfriends, families.[34] In the picture stories "personality" takes on an important role alongside looks. The characters depend for their meaning on well-known stereotypes. That is, to "read" correctly the reader must possess previous cultural knowledge of the types of subjects which inhabit his or her social world.

Jackie boys fall into four categories. First, there is the fun-loving, grinning, flirtatious boy who is irresistible to all girls; second, the tousled, scatterbrained "zany" youth who inspires maternal feelings in girls; third, the emotional, shy, sensitive and even arty type; and fourth, the juvenile delinquent usually portrayed on his motor-bike looking wild and aggressive but sexy, and whom the girl must tame.

In every case the male figure is idealised and romanticised so that there is a real discrepancy between *Jackie* boys and those boys who are discussed on the Cathy and Claire page. The central point here, is that *Jackie*'s boys are as interested in romance as the girls, "Mm! I wish Santa would bring me that for Christmas... so how do we get together?" and this, as countess sociological studies, novels and studies of sexual behaviour indicate, simply does not ring true. Boys in contemporary capitalist society are socialised to be interested in sex although this does not mean they do not want to find the "ideal" girl or wife.

Female characters, significantly, show even less variation in personality. In fact they can be summarised as three contrasting types. The blonde, quiet, timid, loving and trusting girl who either gets her boy in the end or is tragically abandoned; and the wild, fun-loving "brunette" (often the blonde's best-friend) who will resort to plotting and conniving to get the man she wants. This "bitch" character is charming and irresistible to men although all women can immediately "see through" her. Finally there is the non-character, the friendly, open, fun-loving "ordinary" girl (who may perhaps be slightly scatty or absent-minded). She is remarkable in being normal and things tend to happen to her rather than at her instigation. Frequently she figures in stories focusing on the supernatural.

Most of these characters have changed little since the magazine first appeared in 1964. Their style is still rooted in the "Swinging London" of the mid-1960s. The girls have large, heavily made-up eyes, pale lips and tousled hair, turned-up noses and tiny mouths. They wear clothes at least partly reminiscent of the 1960s, hipster skirts with large belts, polo-neck sweaters and, occasionally, flared trousers. Despite the fact that several of these girls introduce themselves as plain, their claims are contradicted by the accompanying image indicating that they are, without exception, beautiful. Likewise the men (or boys) are ruggedly handsome, young versions of James Bond (to the extent that some even wear 1950s-style short raincoats with "turned-up" collars). They have thick eyebrows, smiling eyes, and granite jaws.

While some of the stories seem to be set in London, the majority give no indication of locale. The characters speak without an accent and are usually without family or community ties. They have all left school, but work hovers invisibly in the background as a necessary time-filler between one evening and the next, or may sometimes be a pathway to a glamour, fame or romance. Recognisable social backgrounds are rare. The small town—equated with boredom—is signified through the use of strangely anachronistic symbols—the coffee bar, the motor-bike and the narrow street. The country-side on the other hand, is where the girl escapes *to*, after a broken romance or an unhappy love affair. But when her problems are resolved, she invariably returns to the city where things really happen. But the city that these teenagers inhabit is strangely lacking in population. There are no foreigners, black teenagers, old people or children, no married couples and rarely any families or siblings. It is a world occupied almost solely by young adults on the brink of pairing-up as couples.

The messages which these images and stories together produce are limited and unambiguous, and are repeated endlessly over the years. These are:

1. the girl has to fight to *get* and *keep* her man;
2. she can *never* trust another woman unless she is old and "hideous" in which case she does not appear in these stories anyway;
3. despite this, romance, and being a girl, are fun.

No story ever ends with *two* girls alone together and enjoying each other's company. Occasionally the flat-mate or best-friend appears in a role as "confidante" but these appearances are rare and by implication unimportant. A happy ending means a happy couple; a sad one—a single girl. Having eliminated the possibility of strong supportive relationships between girls themselves, and between people of different ages, *Jackie* stories must elevate to dizzy heights the supremacy of the heterosexual romantic partnership.

This is, it may be argued, unsurprising and predictable. But these stories do more than this. They cancel out completely the possibility of any relationship other than the romantic one between girl and boy. They make it impossible for any girl to talk to, or think about, a boy in terms other than those of romance. (A favourite story in both picture-form and as a short story, is the platonic relationship which the girl enjoys. She likes him as a friend—but when she is made jealous by his showing an interest in another girl, she realises that it is *really* love that she feels for him and their romance blossoms.)

Boys and men, then, are not sex objects but romantic objects. The code of romance neatly displaces that of sexuality which hovers somewhere in the background appearing fleetingly in the guise of passion, or the "clinch." Romance is about the public and *social* effects and implications of "love" relationships. That is, it is concerned with impressing one's friends with a new handsome boyfriend, with being flattered by the attention and compliments lavished by admirers. It is about playing games which skirt about sexuality, and which include sexual innuendo, but which are somehow nicer, cleaner and less sordid. Romance is the girls' reply to male sexuality. It stands in opposition to their "just being after the one thing," and consequently it makes sex seem dirty, sordid, and unattractive. The girl's sexuality is understood and experienced not in terms of a physical need or her own body, but in terms of the romantic attachment. In depicting romantic partnerships, *Jackie* is therefore also constructing male and female roles ensuring that they are separate and as distinct as possible. They are as different as they look different and any interchange between the sexes invariably exudes *romantic* possibilities. What *Jackie* does is to map out all those *differences* which exist between the sexes but to assert that what they do *share* is a common interest—indeed devotion to—romance.

So far, I have outlined in some detail the organising principles around which this discourse (the picture-story) is structured. While I would not hold the separation of form and content as being either possible, or necessary, for analysis, there are a number of recurring themes which can be identified through a process of extrapolation from both the image and the accompanying text. Thus, temporarily holding constant the formal features of the picture-story; the "balloon" form of dialogue; the action through "relay"; and the style of illustration—we can go on to deal with the patterns, combinations and permutations of those stock situations which give *Jackie* its characteristic thematic unity.

The stories themselves can be categorised as follows:

1. the traditional "love" story;
2. the romantic adventure serial;
3. the "pop" special (where the story revolves around a famous pop star);
4. the "zany" tale;
5. the historical romance.

But these story-types are worked through and expounded by the use of certain conventions or devices and it is through these that the thematic structure can be seen most clearly.

THE CONVENTION OF "TIME" OR OF THE TEMPORAL

FLASHBACK   Here the opening clips signify aloneness conveyed through images of isolation; a single figure against a rugged, beautiful, threatening, landscape. Along this same chain of signifieds and following "aloneness" comes the explanation—that is—"alone-and rejected-by-a-loved-one" or "separated-from-a-loved-one." Next comes the elucidation— what has caused such a state of unhappiness or misery, and this is classified and expounded upon through the use of the flashback—"I remember only a year ago and it was all so…" "But Dave was different from the others even then." The reader is transported into the narrator's past and confronted with scenes of love, tenderness, excitement, etc. The difference between the past and present state is emphasised by changes of season, and particularly by changes of expression. Warm weather, for example, goes with smiling, happy faces gazing in mutual pleasure at one another.

From this point onwards different conventions intervene to carry the story along, and it is nearly concluded with a return to the present, and a magical or intentionally un-magical resolution. (The boy reappears, or does not reappear, or a new one takes his place. Through this device the reader is invited to interpret her life, past and present, in terms of romantic attachment—her life has meaning through him.)

THE DIARY   Again this allows the reader access to the innermost secrets of its writer, sometimes mediated through a guilty best-friend reading her friend's outpourings.

HISTORY   This is the most popular device. By locating the characters in a specific period the scriptwriter and artist are provided immediately with a whole string of easy, and ideologically constructed, concepts with which they can fill out the plot. History means particular styles of clothing, quaint language, strange customs and rituals. Thus we have the Victorian heroine connoted through her dress and background dissatisfied with her life and bored by her persistent suitor. When she is transported—magically—into the present, she is, however, so horrified by liberated women (policewomen and girls in bikinis) that she is glad to return to her safe and secure environment. Thus, culturally-defined notions of the Victorian period, are used to glamorise the past and criticise the present which is, by implication, bereft of romance. At the same time, this story is incorporating popularised notions of present phenomena which might conceivably be seen as threatening the established moral order, and in doing so it is thereby diluting and ridiculing them. (This technique has been well-documented elsewhere and is also described by Dorfman and Mattelart discussing similar processes in Disney comics.)[35] Likewise the Edwardian period—again recognisable through costume and this time carrying connotations of more active women—is used to relate a simple love story, jealousy and reconciliation, with its participants (literally) carrying out their romances on bicycle saddles.

But history is not just novelty, it is also used to demonstrate the intransigence of much-hallowed social values, and "natural resistance" to change. When a patrician (in the setting of Ancient Rome) falls for a slave girl he can only die for her thereby allowing her to escape with her slave boyfriend: he cannot escape or be paired off with her. Similarly when a flower-girl is attracted by a gentleman her thoughts only become romantic when she discovers that he is not really a gentleman but a rather Bohemian artist. A nineteenth-century woman and her child arrive at the doorstep on Christmas but are turned away. Two guests help them and it emerges that the woman is the disinherited daughter of a wealthy man...the messages are clear: love conquers poverty and simultaneously renders it unimportant. At any rate poverty only "exists" in the past (and is thus contained and manageable). People marry into their own class and their own race. (When a nurse falls for a wounded German prisoner in war-time Britain she knows her love cannot be fulfilled...and the prisoner returns to Germany.) Similarly, social class—too controversial an issue to appear in stories set in the present—can be acknowledged as *having* existed in the past.

History then provides *Jackie* with a whole set of issues which are more safely dealt with in the past; social problems, social class, foreigners and war. But history also means unchanging eras characterised primarily by splendid costumes (the code of fashion), exoticism (language and customs) and adventure. And yet, despite this, the reader can derive reassurance which lingers on in a recognition of the sameness which links past and present. Underpinning all the adventures and historical tableaux is romance, the young girl in pursuit of it, or being pursued by it. Love, it is claimed, transcends time and is all-important, and history is, again, denied.

THE SEASONS The importance of weather in reflecting moods and creating atmosphere is a feature throughout the stories. "Love" takes different forms at different times of the year, and holiday romances give way to autumnal "blues."

CONVENTION OF THE EXIGENCIES OF PLOT

THE ZANY TALE Here romance is blended with comedy. Here the drawings are less dramatic and are characterised by softer lines. The plots revolve around unusual, unlikely events and coincidences resulting in romantic meetings. At their centre is the zany boy whose bizarre hobbies lead him through a number of disasters until eventually he finds a steady girl who tames him. ("Now they're crazy about each other.") Zany girls of this type are rare. Girls are not really interested in anything outside the confines of femininity, and anyway no girl would willingly make a public comic spectacle of herself in this way.

Animals, always the subject of sentiment, often figure strongly in these stories. A camel escapes from the zoo, is caught by a young girl in the city centre who has to await the arrival of the handsome, young, zookeeper. Another favourite centres on the ritual of walking the dog and taking an evening stroll in the local park where numerous handsome young men are doing the same thing or are willing to be pestered by *her* dog—and so on: "Hmm, funny names you call your cats."

Again the message is clear—a "zany" absent-minded boyfriend is a good bet. He is unlikely to spend his time chasing other girls and is indeed incapable of doing so, he is the lovable "twit" who needs mothering as well as loving. He is a character most often found in television situation comedies like "Some Mothers Do 'Ave 'Em'" or "It Ain't 'Arf Hot, Mum."

THE PLOT WHICH DEPENDS ON A RECOGNISABLE SOCIAL LOCALE   The hospital appears frequently and carries rich connotations of romance and drama. A girl, for example, is recovering from a throat operation and discovers her boyfriend is going out with someone else, but she overcomes her disappointment by meeting someone new in the hospital. In another story a dashing young man catches sight of a pretty girl and follows her to her place of work, a blood-bank. Terrified to sign up to give blood he thinks of ways of getting to know her...

Hospitals are not the only places where romance can happen—at the bus stop, on the bus, in the park, in the flat downstairs—depending on luck, coincidence or "stars." "He must be on day release... he's on the train Mondays and Wednesdays but not the rest of the week." And there is a moral here, if love strikes, or simply happens "out of the blue," then all the girl needs to do is look out for it, be alert without actively seeking it. In fact this allows her, once again, to remain passive, she certainly cannot approach somebody, only a coincidence may bring them together (though she may work on bringing about such a coincidence).

THE CONVENTION OF EXTENDING LUCK OR COINCIDENCE BY THE INTRODUCTION OF SUPERNATURAL DEVICES

This way the reader is invited to share a fantasy, or a dream come true. These devices may include leprechauns, magic lamps and straightforward dreams. The dream or fantasy occupies a central place in the girls' life anyway—to an extent all the picture stories are fantasies, and escapist. Likewise real-life boys are frequently described as "dreamy." Daydreaming is an expected "normal" activity on the part of girls, an adolescent phase. But dreaming of this sort is synonymous with passivity—and as we have already seen, romance is the language of passivity. The romantic girl, in contrast to the sexual man, is taken in a kiss, or embrace. Writing on the development of female sexuality in little girls, Mitchell describes their retreat into the Oedipus complex where the desire to be loved can be fulfilled in the comforting and secure environment of the family.[36] Likewise in *Jackie* stories the girl is chosen. "Hmm, this mightn't be so bad after all—if I can get chatting to that little lady later": *is taken* in an embrace, "Hmm, I could enjoy teaching you, love... very, very much," and is herself *waiting to be loved.* "I must be a nut! But I'm really crazy about Jay. If only I could make him care."

THE CONVENTION OF PERSONAL OR DOMESTIC LIFE

Here the girl is at odds with her family and siblings (who rarely appear in person) and eventually is saved by the appearance of a boyfriend. Thus we have a twin, madly jealous of her pretty sister, who tries to steal the sister's boyfriend when the sister has to stay in bed with flu. "Story of my life! Just Patsy's twin. He doesn't even know my name, I bet. Just knows me as the other one. The quiet one."

Another common theme (echoed in the problem page) is the girl with the clever family. In one case a handsome young man sees a girl reading Shakespeare in the park. When he begins to take her out she insists on going to art galleries and museums, but gives herself away when his clever friend shows that she does not know what she is talking about. Breaking down she admits to reading cheap romances inside the covers of highbrow drama! Through this humiliation and admission of inferiority she wins the love of the boy. All the girl needs is a good personality, looks and confidence. Besides, boys do not like feeling threatened by a "brainy" girl.

Jackie asserts the absolute and natural separation of sex roles. Girls can take humiliation and be all the more attractive for it, as long as they are pretty and unassertive. Boys can *be* footballers, pop stars, even juvenile delinquents, but girls can only be feminine. The girl's life is defined through emotions—jealousy, possessiveness and devotion. Pervading the stories is a fundamental fear, fear of losing your boy, or of never getting one. Romance as a code or a way of life, precipitates individual neurosis and prohibits collective action as a means of dealing with it.

By displacing all vestiges or traces of adolescent sexuality and replacing it with concepts of love, passion and eternity, romance gets trapped within its own contradictions, and hence we have the "problem page."

Once declared and reciprocated this love is meant to be lasting, and is based on fidelity and premarital monogamy. But the girl knows that while she, in most cases, will submit to those, there is always the possibility that her boy's passion may be roused by almost any attractive girl at the bus-stop, outside the home, etc. The way this paradox is handled is the introduction of terms which express resignation, despair, fatalism—it's "all in the game." Love is a roulette and it has its losers, but for the girl who has lost there is always the chance that it will happen again, this time with a more reliable boy. Girls do not fight back. Female flirts almost always come to a bad end. They are abandoned by their admirers who soon turn their attention back to the quiet, trusting girls who have always been content to sit in the background.

NOTES

1. Figures taken from C. L. White, *Women's Magazines 1963–1968*, London, Michael Joseph, 1970; Appendix IV, and from *British Rate and Data* (June 1977).
2. G. Rosei, "The Private Life of Lord Snooty," in the *Sunday Times* magazine, 29 July 1973, pp. 8–16.
3. Ibid., see also *Willing's Press Guide*, 1977, and McCarthy Information Ltd (June 1977) where it is noted that "Among the enviably high profit-margin firms are Shopfitters (Lancs); Birmingham

satchel maker Ralph Martindale, and 'Dandy' and 'Beano' published by D.C. Thomson—all with profit margins of 20% or more." See also Extel Card March 1977 for D. C. Thomson.

Year	Turnover	Profit after tax
1974	£18 556 000	£2 651 000
1975	£23 024 000	£2 089 000
1976	£28 172 000	£2 092 000

4. L. Althusser, "Ideology and the State," in *Lenin and Philosophy and Other Essays,* London, New Left Books, 1971, p. 163.

5. A. Dorfman and A. Mattelart, *How to Read Donald Duck,* 1971, p. 30.

6. Paul Johnson in the *New Statesman,* 28 February 1964.

7. C. Alderson, *The Magazines Teenagers Read,* London, 1968, p. 3.

8. P. Willis, "Symbolism and Practice: A Theory for the Social Meaning of Pop Music," CCCS, Birmingham University, stencilled paper, p. 2.

9. S. Hall, I. Connell and L. Curti "The Unity of Current Affairs Television," in Working Paper in *Cultural Studies,* CCCS, University of Birmingham, no. 9, 1976, p. 51.

10. George Orwell, "Boys' Weeklies" in his book *Inside the Whale and Other Essays,* Harmondsworth, Penguin, 1969, pp. 185–203, first published in 1939.

11. Willis, "Symbolism and Practice," op cit. p. 1.

12. J. Clarke, S. Hall, T. Jefferson and B. Roberts, "Subcultures, Cultures and Classes," in S. Hall (ed.), *Resistance Through Rituals,* London, Hutchinson, 1976, p. 55.

13. S. Hall, I. Connell and L. Curti, "The Unity of Current Affairs Television," in Working Papers in *Cultural Studies,* CCCS, University of Birmingham, no 9, 1978, p. 53.

14. Antonio Gramsci, *Selections from the Prison Notebooks,* quoted in S. Hall, B. Lumley and G. McLennan, "Politics and Ideology: Gramsci in 'On Ideology,'" *Cultural Studies,* no. 10, 1977, p. 51.

15. Ibid., p. 51.

16. Ibid., p. 67.

17. Simon Frith, *Sound Effects,* New York, Pantheon, 1981.

18. Ibid.

19. Richard Hoggart, *The Uses of Literacy,* Harmondsworth, Penguin, 1957, p. 51.

20. Frith, *Sound Effects,* op.cit

21. B. Berelson defines C.A. as "a research technique for the objective, systematic and quantitative description of the manifest content of communication," in B. Berelson, *Content Analysis in Communication Research,* London, 1952, p. 18.

22. R. Barthes, *Elements of Semiology,* London, Jonathan Cape, 1967, pp. 95, 96.

23. S. Hall, "The Determination of News Photographs," in *Cultural Studies,* CCCS, University of Birmingham no. 3, 1972, p. 69.

24. Ibid., p. 64.

25. Ibid., p. 65.

26. Quoting R. Barthes, *Elements of Semiology,* London, Jonathan Cape, 1967, p. 91.

27. Ibid., p. 66.

28. My analysis based on these codes is by no means exhaustive, nor does it cover every different kind of feature. Absent are advertisements, personality quiz games, on-the-spot interviews and short stories. However, each of these does fit into the coded outlines, some into more than one. Personality games and on-the-spot interviews obviously would be examined under the code of personal domestic life, short stories under romance.

29. G. Greer, *The Female Eunuch*, London, MacGibbon & Kee, 1970, p. 173.

30. R. Barthes, "The Rhetoric of the Image," in Working Paper in *Cultural Studies*, CCCS, University of Birmingham, no. 1, 1971, p. 43.

31. Ibid., p. 44.

32. The language is remarkably reminiscent of the "hip" language of commentaries of the "teen-age scene" in the 1950s, e.g., "Hey, gang—some square's giving Jules trouble," and "Hey, what you at man? Like, I don't mind sharing my thoughts with all mankind but I draw a line at the furniture, dig?"

33. L. Althusser, "Ideology and the State," in *Lenin and Philosophy and Other Essays*, London, New Left Books, 1971, p. 163.

34. These take the form of quizzes, articles and features on birth signs, all of which are designed to help *"you"* know *"yourself,"* e.g., the reader is asked to pick, from a selection of possible responses, what she would do, in a number of given situations. Her answers are then tallied up numerically and there is a particular personality profile which allegedly corresponds to her "total."

35. Dorfman and Mattelart, *How to Read Donald Duck*, op.cit., p. 56:

    The second strategy is called recuperation; the utilisation of a potentially dangerous phenomenon of the social body in such a way that it serves to justify the continued need of the social system and its values, and very often justifies the violence and repression which are part of that system.

36. J. Mitchell, *Psychoanalysis and Feminism*, Harmondsworth, Penguin, 1974, p. 117.

CULTURAL IDENTITY AND CINEMATIC REPRESENTATION (1989)

STUART HALL

Drawing on Frantz Fanon's ideas about national culture (including his critique of Négritude), Ferdinand de Saussure's concept of the sign, and Jacques Derrida's deconstructive critique of Saussure's ideas (all included in this volume), Hall asks how we can think about cultural identity amid the deconstructive uncertainly exposed by Derrida. To critics who misconstrue Derrida's argument, cultural identity seems too unstable to carry meaning. To Hall, by contrast, deconstruction expands rather than erases our understanding of cultural identity.

Born and raised in Jamaica, Hall considers Jamaican identity for his example, though readers can use Hall's model to find similar ways to think about other cultural identities, sexual, national, racial, class-based, religious, regional, and so on. Hall notes that some people have described Jamaican identity as African, others as European, and others as American. Rather than allow any one of these influences to characterize Jamaican identity by itself, Hall chooses all three, so that he reads each history in multiple ways. He triangulates the three histories to describe Jamaican identity not as an essence but as a process.

In this view, identity is not a stable signified that a single signifier passively represents. Instead, identity is a continuous process of multiple signifiers and signifieds circulating through each other, producing identities, not merely labeling identities that are already statically there. In addition to applying Hall's model to Jamaican identity, we could choose a similar structure, with different but still particular multiple components, to describe any cultural identity. Indeed, Hall's interpretation of a particular example of cultural identity that resonates broadly both for that and for other examples bears comparison to Susan Koshy's essay on the fiction of Asian American literature elsewhere in this volume.

Both the new "Caribbean cinema," which has now joined the company of the other "Third Cinemas" and the emerging cinemas of Afro-Caribbean blacks in the "diasporas" of the West, put the issue of cultural identity in question. Who is this emergent, new subject of the cinema? From where does it speak? The practices of representation always implicate the positions from which we speak or write—the positions of *enunciation*. What recent theories of enunciation suggest is that, though we speak, so to say "in our own name," of ourselves and from our own experience, nevertheless who speaks, and the subject who is spoken of, are never exactly in the same place. Identity is not as transparent or unproblematic as we think. Perhaps, instead of thinking of identity as an already accomplished historical fact, which the new cinematic discourses then represent, we should think, instead, of identity as a "production" which is never complete, always in process, and always constituted within, not outside, representation. But this view problematizes the very authority and authenticity to which the term, "cultural identity," lays claim.

In this paper, then, I seek to open a dialogue, an investigation, on the subject of cultural identity and cinematic representation. The "I" who writes here must also be thought of as, itself, "enunciated." We all write and speak from a particular place and time, from a history and a culture which is specific. What we say is always "in context," *positioned*. I was born into and spent my childhood and adolescence in a lower-middle class family in Jamaica. I have lived all my adult life in England, in the shadow of the black diaspora—"in the belly of the beast." I write against the background of a lifetime's work in cultural studies. If the paper seems preoccupied with the diaspora experience and its narratives of displacement, it is worth remembering that all discourse is "placed," and the heart has its reasons.

There are at least two different ways of thinking about "cultural identity." The first position defines "cultural identity" in terms of the idea of one, shared culture, a sort of collective "one true self," hiding inside the many other, more superficial or artificially imposed "selves," which people with a shared history and ancestry hold in common. Within the terms of this definition, our cultural identities reflect the common historical experiences and shared cultural codes which provide us, as "one people," with stable, unchanging and continuous frames of reference and meaning, beneath the shifting divisions and vicissitudes of our actual history. This "oneness," underlying all the other, more superficial differences, is the truth, the essence, of "Caribbeaness." It is this identity which a Caribbean cinema must discover, excavate, bring to light and express through cinematic representation.

Such a conception of cultural or national identity played a critical role in all the post-colonial struggles which have so profoundly reshaped our world. It lay at the centre of the vision of the poets of "Negritude" like Aimee Cesaire and Leopold Senghor, and of the Pan-African political project, earlier in the century. It continues to be a very powerful and creative force in emergent forms of representation amongst hitherto marginalised peoples. In post-colonial societies, the rediscovery of this identity is often the object of what Frantz Fanon once called a "passionate research . . . directed by the secret hope of discovering beyond the misery of today, beyond self-contempt, resignation and abjuration, some very beautiful and splendid era whose existence rehabilitates us both in regard to ourselves and in regard to others." New forms of cultural practice in these societies address themselves to this project for the very good reason that, as Fanon puts it, in the recent past, "Colonisation is not satisfied merely with holding a people in its grip and emptying the native's brain of all form and content. By a kind of perverted logic, it turns to the past of the oppressed people, and distorts, disfigures and destroys it" (Fanon, Wretched of the Earth, "On National Culture," p. 170, 1963).

The question which Fanon's observation poses is, what is the nature of this "profound research" which drives the new forms of visual and cinematic representtation? Is it only a matter of unearthing that which the colonial experience buried and overlaid, bringing to light the hidden continuities it suppressed? Or is a quite different practice entailed—not the rediscovery but the *production* of identity? Not an identity grounded in the archaeology, but in the *re-telling* of the past?

We cannot and should not, for a moment, underestimate or neglect the importance of the act of imaginative re-discovery. "Hidden histories" have played a critical role in the emergence of some of the most important social movements of our time. The photographic work of a visual artist like Armet Francis, a Jamaican-born photographer who has lived in Britain since the age of eight, is a testimony to the continuing creative power of this conception of identity within the practices of representation. His photographs of the peoples of The Black Triangle, taken in Africa, the Caribbean, the US and the UK, attempt to reconstruct in visual terms "the underlying unity of the black people whom, colonisation and slavery distributed across the African diaspora." His text is an act of imaginary re-unification.

Crucially, his images find a way of imposing an imaginary coherence on the experience of dispersal and fragmentation, which is the history of all enforced diasporas. He does this by representing or "figuring" Africa as the mother of these different civilisations. His Triangle is, after all, "centred" in Africa. Africa is the name of the missing term, the great aporia, which lies at the centre of our cultural identity and gives it a meaning which, until recently, it lacked. No one who looks at these textual images now, in the light of the history of transportation, slavery and migration, can fail to understand how the rift of separation, the "loss of identity" which has been integral to the Caribbean experience only begins to be healed when these forgotten connections are once more set in place. Such texts restore an imaginary fullness or plenitude, to set against the broken rubric of our past. They are resources of resistance and identity, with which to confront the fragmented and pathological ways in which that experience has been re-constructed within the dominant regimes of cinematic and visual representation of the West.

There is, however, a related but different view of cultural identity, which qualifies, even if it does not replace, the first. This second position recognises that, as well as the many points of similarity, there are also critical points of deep and significant *difference* which constitute "what we really are": or rather—since history has intervened—"what we have become." We cannot speak for very long, with any exactness, about "one experience, one identity," without acknowledging its other sides—the differences and discontinuities which constitute, precisely, the Caribbean's "uniqueness." Cultural identity, in this second sense, is a matter of "becoming" as well as of "being." It belongs to the future as much as to the past. It is not something which already exists, transcending place, time, history and culture. Cultural identities come from somewhere, have histories. But, like everything which is historical, they undergo constant transformation. Far from being eternally fixed in some essentialised past, they are subject to the continuous "play" of history, culture and power. Far from being grounded in a mere "recovery" of the past, which is waiting to be found, and which, when found, will secure our sense of ourselves into eternity, identities are the names we give to the different ways we are positioned by, and position ourselves within, the narratives of the past.

It is only from this second position that we can properly understand the truly traumatic character of "the colonial experience." The ways we have been positioned and subjected in the dominant regimes of representation were a critical exercise of cultural power and normalisation, precisely because they were not superficial. They had the power to make us see and experience ourselves as "Other." Every regime of representation is a regime of power formed, as Foucault reminds us, by the fatal couplet, "power/knowledge." And this kind of knowledge is internal, not external. It is one thing to place some person or set of peoples as the Other of a dominant discourse. It is quite another thing to subject them to that "knowledge," not only as a matter of imposed will and domination, by the power of inner compulsion and subjective con-formation to the norm. That is the lesson—the sombre majesty—of Fanon's insight into the colonising experience in BLACK SKIN, WHITE MASKS.

This expropriation of cultural identity cripples and deforms. If its silences are not resisted, they produce, in Fanon's vivid phrase, "individuals without an anchor, without horizon, colourless, stateless, rootless—a race of angels" (Fanon, WRETCHED OF THE EARTH, p. 176). Nevertheless, it also changes our conception of what "cultural identity" is. In this perspective, cultural identity is not a fixed essence at all, lying unchanged outside history and culture. It is not some universal and transcendental spirit inside us on which history has made no fundamental mark. It is not once-and-for-all. It is not a fixed origin to which we can make some final and absolute Return. Of course, it is not a mere phantasm, either. It is *something*—not a mere trick of the imagination. It has its histories—and histories have their real, material and symbolic effects. The past continues to speak to us. But this is no longer a simple, factual "past," since our relation to it is, like the child's relation to the mother, always-already "after the break." It is always constructed through memory, fantasy, narrative and myth. Cultural identities are the points of identification, the unstable points of identification or suture, which are made, within the discourses of history and culture. Not an essence but a *positioning*. Hence, there is always a politics of position, which has no absolute guarantee in an unproblematic, transcendental "law of history."

This second view of cultural history is much less familiar, and unsettling. But it is worth spending a few moments tracing its formations. We might think of Caribbean identities as "framed" by two axes or vectors, simultaneously operative: the vector of similarity and continuity; and the vector of difference and rupture. Caribbean identities always have to be thought of in terms of the dialogic relationship between these two axes. The one gives us some grounding in, some continuity with, the past. The second reminds us that what we share is precisely the experience of a profound discontinuity. The peoples dragged into slavery by the triangular Atlantic trade came predominantly from Africa—though when that supply ended, it was temporarily refreshed by indentured labour from the Asian sub-continent. This neglected fact explains why, when you visit Guyana or Trinidad, you suddenly see, symbolically inscribed in the faces of their peoples, the paradoxical "truth" of Christopher Columbus's mistake: you *can* find "Asia" by sailing west, if you know where to look! The great majority of slaves were from Africa—already figured, in the European imaginary, as "the Dark Continent." But they were also from different countries, tribal communities, villages, languages and gods. African religion, which has been so profoundly formative in Caribbean spiritual life, is precisely *different* from Christian monotheism in having, not one, but a proliferation of gods. These gods live on, in an underground existence, in the pantheon of black Saints which people the hybridised religious universe of Latin American Catholicism. The paradox is that it was the uprooting of slavery and transportation and the insertion into the plantation economy (as well as the symbolic economy) of the Western world that "unified" these peoples across their differences, in the same moment as it cut them off from direct access to that past.

Difference, therefore, persists—in and alongside continuity. And this is so, not only for the past but in the present. To return to the Caribbean after any long absence is to experience again the shock of the "doubleness" of similarity and difference. As a Jamaican returning for the First Caribbean Film Festival, I "recognized" Martinique instantly, though I was seeing it for the first time. I also saw at once how different Martinique is from, say, Jamaica: and this is no mere difference of topography or climate. It is also a profound difference of culture and history. And the difference *matters*. It positions Martiniquains and Jamaicans as *both* the same *and* different. Moreover, the boundaries of difference are continually repositioned in relation to different points of reference. Vis-à-vis the developed West, we are very much "the same." We belong to the marginal, the under-developed, the periphery "the other." We are at the outer edge, the "rim" of the metropolitan world—always "South" to someone else's *El Norte*.

At the same time, we do not stand in the same relation of "otherness" to the metropolitan centres. Each has negotiated its economic, political and cultural dependency differently. And this "difference," whether we like it or not, is already inscribed in our cultural identities. In turn, it is this negotiation of identity which makes us, vis-à-vis other Latin American people, with a very similar history, different. Caribbeans—*les Antilliennes*: "islanders" to their mainland. And yet, vis-à-vis one another, Jamaican, Haitian, Cuban, Guadeloupean, Barbadian, etc.

How, then, to describe this play of "difference" within identity? The common history—transportation, slavery, colonisation—has been profoundly formative. It was also, metaphorically as well as literally, a trans-lation. The inscription of difference is also specific and critical. I use the word "play" because the double meaning of the metaphor is important. It suggests, on the one hand, the instability, the permanent unsettlement, the lack of any final resolution. On the other hand, it reminds us that the place where this "doubleness" is most powerfully to be heard is "playing" within the varieties of Caribbean musics. This cultural "play" could not be represented, cinematically, as a simple, binary opposition—"past/present" "them/us." Its complexity exceeds this binary structure of representation. At different places, times, in relation to different questions, the boundaries are re-sited. They become, not only what they have, at times, certainly been—mutually excluding categories: but also, what they sometimes are—differential points along a sliding scale.

One trivial example is the way Martinique both *is* and *is not* "French." Superficially, Fort de France is a much richer, more "fashionable" place than Kingston—which is not only visibly poorer, but itself at a point of transition between being "in fashion" in an Anglo-African and Afro-American way—for those who can afford to be in any sort of fashion at all. Yet, what is distinctively "Martiniquais" can only be described in terms of that special and peculiar supplement which the black and mulatto skin adds to the "refinement" and sophistication of a Parisian-derived haute couture: that is, a sophistication which, because it is black, is always transgressive.

To capture this sense of difference which is not pure "otherness," we need to deploy the play on words of a theorist like Jacques Derrida. Derrida uses the anomalous a in his way of writing "difference"—*differance*—as a marker which sets up a disturbance in our settled understanding or translation of the concept. It sets the word in motion to new meanings without obscuring the trace of its other meanings. His sense of *differance,* as Christopher Norris puts it, thus "remains suspended between the two French verbs 'to differ' and 'to defer' (postpone), both of which contribute to its textual force but neither of which can fully capture its meaning. Language depends on difference, as Saussure showed.... the structure of distinctive propositions which make up its basic economy. Where Derrida breaks new ground .... is in the extent to which differ shades into 'defer' ... the idea that meaning is always deferred, perhaps to the point of an endless supplementarity, by the play of signification" (Norris, 1982, p. 32). This second sense of difference challenges the fixed binaries which stabilise meaning and representation and show how meaning is never finished or completed in this way, but keeps on moving to encompass other, additional or supplementary meanings, which, as Norris puts it elsewhere (Norris, 1987, p. l5) "disturb the classical economy of language and representation." Without relations of difference, no representation could occur. But what is then constituted within representation is always open to being deferred, staggered, serialized,

Where, then, does identity come in to this infinite postponement of meaning? Derrida does not help us as much as he might here—and this is precisely where, in my view, he has permitted his profound theoretical insights to be re-appropriated into a celebration of formal "playfulness," which evacuates it of its political meaning. For if signification depends upon the endless re-positioning of its differential terms, meaning, in any specific instance, depends on the contingent and arbitrary stop—the necessary and temporary "break" in the infinite semiosis of language. This does not detract from the original insight. It only threatens to do so if we mistake this "cut" of identity—this *positioning,* which makes meaning possible—as a natural and permanent, rather than an arbitrary and contingent "ending." Whereas, I understand every such position as "strategic." And arbitrary, in the sense that there is no permanent equivalence between the particular sentence we close, and its true meaning, as such. Meaning continues to unfold, so to speak, beyond the arbitrary closure which makes it, at any moment, possible. It is always either over—or underdetermined—either an excess or a supplement. There is always something "left over."

It is possible, with this conception of "difference," to rethink the positionings and re-positionings of Caribbean cultural identities in relation to at least three "presences," to borrow Aimee Cesaire's and Leopold Senghor's metaphor: Presence Africaine, Presence Europeanne, and the third, most ambiguous, presence of all—the sliding term "Presence American." I mean America, here, not in its "first world" sense—the big cousin to the North whose "rim" we occupy, but in the second, broader sense: America, the New Found Land, the "New World," *Terra Incognita*.

"Presence Africaine" is the site of the repressed. Apparently silenced beyond memory by the power of the new cultures of slavery, it was, in fact present everywhere: in the everyday life and customs of the slave quarters, in the languages and patois of the plantations, in names and words, often disconnected from their taxonomies, in the secret syntactical structures through which other languages were spoken, in the stories and tales told to children, in religious practices and beliefs, in the spiritual life, the arts, crafts, musics and rhythms of slave and post-emancipation society. Africa, the signified which could not be represented, remained the unspoken, unspeakable "presence" in Caribbean culture. It is "hiding" behind every verbal inflection, every narrative twist of Caribbean cultural life. It is the secret code with which every Western text was "re-read." *This* was—is—the "Africa" that "is alive and well in the diaspora" (Hall, 1976).

When I was growing up as a child in Kingston, I was surrounded by the signs, music, and rhythms of this Africa of the diaspora, which only existed as a result of a long and discontinuous series of transformations. But, although almost everyone around me was some shade of brown or black (Africa "speaks"!), I never once heard a single person refer to themselves or to others as, in some way, or as having been at some time in the past, "African." It was only in the 1970s that this Afro-Caribbean identity became historically available to the great majority of Jamaican people, at home and abroad. In this historic moment, the great majority of Jamaicans discovered themselves to be "black"—just as they discovered themselves to be the sons and daughters of "slavery."

This profound cultural discovery, however, was not, and could not be, made directly, without "mediation." It could only be made through the impact on popular life of the postcolonial revolution, the civil rights struggles, the culture of Rastafarianism and the music of reggae—the metaphors, the figures or signifiers, of a new construction of "Jamaican-ness." This is a "new" Africa, grounded in an "old" Africa, now, as part of a spiritual journey of discovery that led, in the Caribbean, to an indigenous cultural revolution. "Africa," as we might say, necessarily "deferred"—as a spiritual, cultural and political metaphor.

It is the presence/absence of the "otherness" of Africa, in this form, which made it also the privileged signifier of new conceptions of Caribbean identity. Everyone in the Caribbean, of whatever ethnic background, must sooner or later come to terms with this African Presense.

Black, brown, mulatto, white—all must look "Presense Africaine" in the face, speak its name. But whether it is, in this sense, an *origin* of our identities, unchanged by four hundred years of displacement, dismemberment, transportation, to which we could in any final or literal sense, return, is more open to doubt. The original "Africa" is no longer there. It too has been transformed. History is, in that sense, irreversible. We must not collude with the West which, precisely "normalizes" and appropriates Africa by freezing it into some timeless zone of the "primitive, unchanging past." Africa must at last be reckoned with, by Caribbean people. But it cannot in any simple sense be merely recovered. It belongs irrevocably, for us, to what Edward Said once called an "imaginative geography and history," which helps "the mind to intensify its own sense of itself by dramatising the difference between what is close to it and what is far away" (Said, Orientalism, p. 55). It "has acquired an imaginative or figurative value we can name and feel" *(*Said, ibid.*)*. Our belongingness to it constitutes what Benedict Anderson calls "an imagined community." To *this* "Africa," which is a necessary part of the Caribbean imaginary, we can't literally go home again.

The character of this displaced "homeward" journey—its length and complexity—comes across vividly, not yet in the Caribbean cinemas, but in other texts. Tony Sewell's text and documentary archival photographs, Garvey's Children: The Legacy Of Marcus Garvey, tells the story of a "return" to an African identity for Caribbean people which went, necessarily, by the long route through London and the United States. It "ends," not in Ethiopia but with Garvey's statue in front of the St. Ann Parish Library in Jamaica, with the music of Burning Spear and Bob Marley's Redemption Song. This is our "long journey" home. Derek Bishton's remarkably courageous visual and written text, Black Heart Man—the story of the journey of a *white* photographer "on the trail of the promised land," starts in England, and goes, through Sashamene, the place in Ethiopia to which many Jamaican people have found their way on their search for the Promised Land, and the story of slavery; but it ends in Pinnacle, Jamaica, where the first Rastafarian settlement was established, and "beyond"—among the dispossessed of twentieth century Kingston and the streets of Handsworth, where Bishton's voyage of discovery first began. This symbolic journey is necessary for us all—and necessarily circular.

This is the Africa we must return to but "by another route": what Africa has *become* in the New World, what we have made of "Africa." "Africa"—as we re-tell it through politics, memory and desire.

What of the second, troubling, term in the identity equation—the European Presense? For many of us, this is a matter, not of too little but of too much. Where Africa was a case of the unspoken, Europe was a case of that which is endlessly speaking—and endlessly speaking *us*. The European presense thus interrupts the innocence of the whole discourse of "difference" in the Caribbean by introducing the question of power. "Europe" belongs irrevocably to the question of power, to the lines of force and consent, to the pole of the *dominant* in Caribbean culture. In terms of colonialism, underdevelopment, poverty and the racism of colour, the European Presense is that which, in visual representation has positioned us within its dominant regimes of representation: the colonial discourse, the literatures of adventure and exploration, the romance of the exotic, the ethnographic and travelling eye, the tropical languages of tourism, travel brochure and Hollywood and the violent, pornographic languages *of ganja* and urban violence.

The error is not to conceptualise this "presence" in terms of power, but to locate that power as wholly external to us—an extrinsic force, whose influence can be thrown off like the serpent sheds its skin. What Frantz Fanon reminds us, in *Black Skin, White Masks*, is how its power is inside as well as outside: "the movements, the attitudes, the glances of the other fixed me there, in the sense in which a chemical solution is fixed by a dye. I was indignant; I demanded an explanation. Nothing happened. I burst apart. Now the fragments have been put together again by another self." (BSWM p. 109) This "look" from—so to speak—the place of the Other, fixes us, not only in its violence, hostility and aggression, but in the ambivalence of its desire. This brings us face to face, not simply with the dominating European presense as the site or "scene" of integration where those other presences which it had actively disaggregated were recomposed—re-framed, put together in a new way; but as the site of a profound splitting and doubling: what Homi Bhabba has called "the ambivalent identifications of the racist world" ... the "'otherness' of the self inscribed in the perverse palimpsest of colonial identity" (Intro to Fanon, p. xv).

The dialogue of power and resistance, of refusal and recognition, with and against "Presence Europeenne" is almost as complex as the so-called "dialogue" with Africa. In terms of popular cultural life, it is nowhere to be found in its pure, pristine state. It is always already fused, syncretised, with other cultural elements. It is always-already creolised. Not "lost" beyond the Middle Passage, but ever-present, the harmonics in our musics to the ground-bass of Africa, traversing and intersecting our lives at every point. How can we stage this dialogue so that, finally, we can place it, without terror, rather than being forever placed by it? Can we ever recognise its irreversible influence, whilst resisting its imperialising eye? The enigma is impossible, so far, to resolve. It requires the most complex of cultural strategies. Think, for example, of the dialogue of every Caribbean film maker, one way or another, with the dominant cinemas of the "West"—of European and American film making. Who could describe this tense and tortured dialogue as a "one way trip"?

I think of the third "New World" Presence, not so much in terms of power, as of ground, place, territory. It is the juncture-point where the other cultural tributaries met, the "empty" land (the European colonisers emptied it) where strangers from every other part of the globe met. None of the people who now occupy the islands—black, brown, white, African, European, American, Spanish, French, East Indian, Chinese, Portugese, Jew, Dutch—originally "belonged" there. It is the space where the creolisations and assimilations and syncretisms were negotiated. The New World is the third term—the primal scene where the fateful/fatal encounter was staged between Africa and the West. It has to be understood as the place of displacements: of the original pre-Columbian inhabitants, the Arawaks, permanently displaced from their homelands; of peoples displaced in different ways from Africa, Asia and Europe; the displacements of slavery, colonisation and conquest. It stands for the endless ways in which Caribbean people have been destined to "migrate"; it is the signifier of migration itself—of travelling, voyaging, and return as fate, as destiny; of the Antillean as the prototype of the modern or post-modern New World nomad, continually moving between centre and periphery. This preoccupation with movement and migration Caribbean cinema shares with many other "Third Cinemas," but it is one of our defining themes, and is destined to cross the narrative of every film script or cinematic image.

Presence Americaine also has its silences, its suppressions. Peter Hulme, in his essay on "Islands of Enchantment" (NEW FORMATIONS, no. 3, Winter, 1987) reminds us that the word "Jamaica" is the Hispanic form of the indigenous Arawak name of the island—"land of wood and water"—which Columbus' re-naming ("Santiago") never replaced. The Arawak "presence" remains a ghostly one, visible in the islands mainly in their museums and archeological sites, part of the barely knowable or usable "past." It is not represented in the emblem of the Jamaican National Heritage Trust, for example, which chose, instead, the figure of Diego Pimtenta, "an African who fought for his Spanish masters against the English invasion of the island in 1655"—a deferred, metonuymic, sly and sliding representation of Jamaican identity if ever there was one! Peter Hulme recounts the story of how Prime Minister Edward Seaga tried to alter the Jamaican coat-of-arms, which consists of two Arawak figures holding a shield with five pineapples, surmounted by an alligator. "Can the crushed and extinct Arawaks represent the dauntless character of Jamaicans? Does the low-slung, near extinct crocodile, a cold-blooded reptile, symbolise the warm, soaring spirit of Jamaicans?" Prime Minister Seaga asked, rhetorically (JAMAICA HANSARD, vol. 9, p. 363: 1983 –4. Quoted in Hulme op.cit). There can be few political statements which so eloquently testify to the complexities entailed in the process of trying to represent a diverse people with a diverse history through a single, hegemonic "identity." Fortunately, Mr. Seaga's invitation to the Jamaican people, who are overwhelmingly of African descent, to start their "remembering" by first "forgetting" something else, got the comeuppance it so richly deserved.

Thus I think of the New World Presences—America, Terra Incognita—as itself the beginning of diaspora, of diversity, of difference: as what makes Afro-Caribbean people already the people of a diaspora. I use this term here metaphorically, not literally. I do not mean those scattered tribes whose identity can only be secured in relation to some sacred homeland to which they must at all costs return, even if it means pushing other people into the sea. This is the old, the imperialising, the hegemonising, form of "ethnicity." We have seen the fate of the people of Palestine at the hands of this backward-looking conception of diaspora—and the complicity of the West with it. The diaspora experience as I intend it here is defined, not by essence or purity, but by the recognition of a necessary heterogeneity, diversity; by a conception of "identity" which lives with and through, not despite, difference; by *hybridity*. Diaspora identities are those which are constantly producing and reproducing themselves anew, through transformation and difference. One can only think here of what is uniquely—"essentially"—Caribbean: precisely the mixes of colour, pigmentation, physiogromic type; the "blends" of tastes that is Caribbean cuisine; the aesthetics of the "cross-overs" of "cut-and-mix," to borrow Dick Hebdige's telling phrase, which is the heart and soul of black music.

Young black cultural practitioners and critics in Britain are increasingly coming to acknowledge and explore in their work this "diaspora aesthetic": "Across a whole range of cultural forms there is a 'syncretic' dynamic which critically appropriates elements from the master-codes of the dominant culture and 'creolises' them, disarticulating given signs and re-articulating their symbolic meaning. The subversive force of this hybridising tendency is most apparent at the level of language itself where creoles, patois and black English decentre, destabilise and carnivalise the linguistic domination of 'English'—the nation-language of master discourse—through strategic inflections, accentuations and other performative moves in semantic, syntactic and lexical codes" (Kobena Mercer, BLACK FRAMES, p. 57).

It is because this "New World" is constituted for us as place, a narrative of displacement, that it gives rise so profoundly to a certain imaginary plenitude, recreating the endless desire to return to "lost origins," to be one again with the mother, to go back to the beginning. Who can ever forget, when once seen rising up out of that blue-green Caribbean, those islands of enchantment. And yet, this "return to the beginning" is like the Imaginary in Lacan—it can neither be fulfilled nor requited, and hence is the beginning of the symbolic, of representation, the infinitely renewable source of desire, memory, myth, search, discovery—in short, the reservoir of our cinematic narratives.

I have been trying, in a series of metaphors, to put in play a different sense of our relationship to the past, and thus a different way of thinking about cultural identity, which might begin to constitute new points of recognition in the discourses of the emerging Caribbean cinema. I have been trying to speak of identity as constituted, not outside but within representation; and hence of cinema, not as a second-order mirror held up to reflect what already exists, but as that form of representation which is able to constitute us as new kinds of subjects, and thereby enable us to discover who we are. Communities, Benedict Anderson argues in *Imagined Communities* are to be distinguished, not by their falsity/genuineness, but by the style in which they are imagined. (p. 15) This is the vocation of a modern Caribbean cinema: by allowing us to see and recognise the different parts and histories of ourselves, to construct those points of identification, those positionalities we call "a cultural identity."

"We must not therefore be content," Fanon warns us, "with delving into the past of a people in order to find coherent elements which will counteract colonialism's attempts to falsify and harm.... "A national culture is not a folk-lore, nor an abstract populism that believes it can discover a people's true nature. A national culture is the whole body of efforts made by a people in the sphere of thought to describe, justify and praise the action through which that people has created itself and keeps itself in existence"(TWOTE, p. 188).

THE CIRCULATION OF SOCIAL ENERGY (1988)

STEPHEN GREENBLATT

In this introductory chapter to his Shakespearean Negotiations, *Greenblatt describes his concept of cultural poetics, a term he prefers to new historism, though he is the leading historicist literary critic. Drawing implicitly on deconstructionist skepticism about organic unity, Greenblatt relishes the marginal, the fragmentary, rather than the new critical "whole reading." He does not see his call for historicist reading as asking us to explain how literature reflects its culture and history. For new historicists, to concentrate on how literature reflects history is to see literature as merely passive. Instead, they see literature as actively engaging with and speaking to history. Greenblatt takes an interest in the way that literature and history exchange and circulate cultural energy. Idiosyncratically, he lists a series of "abjurations," practices he invites critics to renounce. The point of each abjuration is to say that everything is sociohistorical, that nothing is an essence unto itself, for everything is connected to other things. Cultural productions are collective, not individual. As Greenblatt puts it, "there is no escape from contingency," from the way that everything depends on other things. He sees art as always having an origin, not in the sense of an ultimate essence, the sense that Derrida rejects, but in the sense of motive, something social, historical, and cultural that, as Greenblatt says, it comes "from." Readers seeking to work with Greenblatt's way of interpreting can ask what specific social energies circulate in a movie, poem, novel, play, song, or other cultural object and then interpret those energies by drawing on Greenblatt's model of the modes of circulation: appropriation, purchase, and symbolic acquisition. Greenblatt invites us to ask how works of literature take, buy, or represent specific energies, forces, and ideas from the the culture around them and then change those energies by recasting them as literature.*

(This reprinting leaves out the next-to-last paragraph, where Greenblatt summarizes the later chapters of Shakespearean Negotiations.*)*

I began with the desire to speak with the dead.

This desire is a familiar, if unvoiced, motive in literary studies, a motive organized, professionalized, buried beneath thick layers of bureaucratic decorum: literature professors are salaried, middle-class shamans. If I never believed that the dead could hear me, and if I knew that the dead could not speak, I was nonetheless certain that I could re-create a conversation with them. Even when I came to understand that in my most intense moments of straining to listen all I could hear was my own voice, even then I did not abandon my desire. It was true that I could hear only my own voice, but my own voice was the voice of the dead, for the dead had contrived to leave textual traces of themselves, and those traces make themselves heard in the voices of the living. Many of the traces have little resonance, though every one, even the most trivial or tedious, contains some fragment of lost life; others seem uncannily full of the will to be heard. It is paradoxical, of course, to seek the living will of the dead in fictions, in places, where there was no live bodily being to begin with. But those who love literature tend to find more intensity in simulations—in the formal, self-conscious miming of life—than in any of the other textual traces left by the dead, for simulations are undertaken in full awareness of the absence of the life they contrive to represent, and hence they may skillfully anticipate and compensate for the vanishing of the actual life that has empowered them. Conventional in my tastes, I found the most satisfying intensity of all in Shakespeare.

I wanted to know how Shakespeare managed to achieve such intensity, for I thought that the more I understood this achievement, the more I could hear and understand the speech of the dead.

The question then was how did so much life get into the textual traces? Shakespeare's plays, it seemed, had precipitated out of a sublime confrontation between a total artist and a totalizing society. By a total artist I mean one who, through training, resourcefulness, and talent, is at the moment of creation complete unto himself; by a totalizing society I mean one that posits an occult network linking all human, natural, and cosmic powers and that claims on behalf of its ruling elite a privileged place in this network. Such a society generates vivid dreams of access to the linked powers and vests control of this access in a religious and state bureaucracy at whose pinnacle is the symbolic figure of the monarch. The result of this confrontation between total artist and totalizing society was a set of unique, inexhaustible, and supremely powerful works of art.

In the book I have written something of this initial conception survives, but it has been complicated by several turns in my thinking that I had not foreseen. I can summarize those turns by remarking that I came to have doubts about two things: "total artist" and "totalizing society."

I did not, to be sure, doubt that the plays attributed to Shakespeare were in large part written by the supremely gifted alumnus of the Stratford grammar school. Nor did I cease to believe that Renaissance society was totalizing in intention. But I grew increasingly uneasy with the monolithic entities that my work had posited. No individual, not even the most brilliant, seemed complete unto himself—my own study of Renaissance self-fashioning had already persuaded me of this—and Elizabethan and Jacobean visions of hidden unity seemed like anxious rhetorical attempts to conceal cracks, conflict, and disarray. I had tried to organize the mixed motives of Tudor and Stuart culture under the rubric *power,* but that term implied a structural unity and stability of command belied by much of what I actually knew about the exercise of authority and force in the period.

If it was important to speak of power in relation to Renaissance literature—not only as the object but as the enabling condition of representation itself—it was equally important to resist the integration of all images and expressions into a single master discourse. For if Renaissance writers themselves often echoed the desire of princes and prelates for just such a discourse, brilliant critical and theoretical work in recent years by a large and diverse group of scholars had demonstrated that this desire was itself constructed out of conflicting and ill-sorted motives. Even those literary texts that sought most ardently to speak for a monolithic power could be shown to be the sites of institutional and ideological contestation.

But what does it mean to pull back from a notion of artistic completeness, on the one hand, and totalizing power, on the other? It can mean a return to the text itself as the central object of our attention. To speak of such a return has a salutary ring—there are days when I long to recover the close-grained formalism of my own literary training—but the referent of the phrase "the text itself" is by no means clear. Indeed in the case of Shakespeare (and of the drama more generally), there has probably never been a time since the early eighteenth century when there was less confidence in the "text." Not only has a new generation of textual historians undermined the notion that a skilled editorial weaving of folio and quarto readings will give us an authentic record of Shakespeare's original intentions, but theater historians have challenged the whole notion of the text as the central, stable locus of theatrical meaning. There are textual traces—a bewildering mass of them— but it is impossible to take the "text itself" as the perfect, unsubstitutable, freestanding container of all of its meanings.

The textual analyses I was trained to do had as their goal the identification and celebration of a numinous literary authority, whether that authority was ultimately located in the mysterious genius of an artist or in the mysterious perfection of a text whose intuitions and concepts can never be expressed in other terms.[1] The great attraction of this authority is that it appears to bind and fix the energies we prize, to identify a stable and permanent source of literary power, to offer an escape from shared contingency.

This project, endlessly repeated, repeatedly fails for one reason: there is no escape from contingency.

All the same, we do experience unmistakable pleasure and interest in the literary traces of the dead, and I return to the question how it is possible for those traces to convey lost life. Over the past several generations this question has been addressed principally by close reading of the textual traces, and I believe that sustained, scrupulous attention to formal and linguistic design will remain at the center of literary teaching and study. But in the essays that follow I propose something different: to look less at the presumed center of the literary domain than at its borders, to try to track what can only be glimpsed, as it were, at the margins of the text. The cost of this shift in attention will be the satisfying illusion of a "whole reading," the impression conveyed by powerful critics that had they but world enough and time, they could illuminate every corner of the text and knit together into a unified interpretive vision all of their discrete perceptions. My vision is necessarily more fragmentary, but I hope to offer a compensatory satisfaction: insight into the half-hidden cultural transactions through which great works of art are empowered.

I propose that we begin by taking seriously the collective production of literary pleasure and interest. We know that this production is collective since language itself, which is at the heart of literary power, is the supreme instance of a collective creation. But this knowledge has for the most part remained inert, either cordoned off in prefatory acknowledgments or diffused in textual analyses that convey almost nothing of the social dimension of literature's power. Instead the work seems to stand only for the skill and effort of the individual artist, as if whole cultures possessed their shared emotions, stories, and dreams only because a professional caste invented them and parceled them out. In literary criticism Renaissance artists function like Renaissance monarchs: at some level we know perfectly well that the power of the prince is largely a collective invention, the symbolic embodiment of the desire, pleasure, and violence of thousands of subjects, the instrumental expression of complex networks of dependency and fear, the agent rather than the maker of the social will. Yet we can scarcely write of prince or poet without accepting the fiction that power directly emanates from him and that society draws upon this power.[2]

The attempt to locate the power of art in a permanently novel, untranslatable formal perfection will always end in a blind alley, but the frustration is particularly intense in the study of the Shakespearean theater for two reasons. First, the theater is manifestly the product of collective intentions. There may be a moment in which a solitary individual puts words on a page, but it is by no means clear that this moment is the heart of the mystery and that everything else is to be stripped away and discarded. Moreover, the moment of inscription, on closer analysis, is itself a social moment. This is particularly clear with Shakespeare, who does not conceal his indebtedness to literary sources, but it is also true for less obviously collaborative authors, all of whom depend upon collective genres, narrative patterns, and linguistic conventions.[3] Second, the theater manifestly addresses its audience as a collectivity.

The model is not, as with the nineteenth-century novel, the individual reader who withdraws from the public world of affairs to the privacy of the hearth but the crowd that gathers together in a public play space.[4] The Shakespearean theater depends upon a felt community: there is no dimming of lights, no attempt to isolate and awaken the sensibilities of each individual member of the audience, no sense of the disappearance of the crowd.

If the textual traces in which we take interest and pleasure are not sources of numinous authority, if they are the signs of contingent social practices, then the questions we ask of them cannot profitably center on a search for their untranslatable essence. Instead we can ask how collective beliefs and experiences were shaped, moved from one medium to another, concentrated in manageable aesthetic form, offered for consumption. We can examine how the boundaries were marked between cultural practices understood to be art forms and other, contiguous, forms of expression. We can attempt to determine how these specially demarcated zones were invested with the power to confer pleasure or excite interest or generate anxiety. The idea is not to strip away and discard the enchanted impression of aesthetic autonomy but to inquire into the objective conditions of this enchantment, to discover how the traces of social circulation are effaced.

I have termed this general enterprise—study of the collective making of distinct cultural practices and inquiry into the relations among these practices—a poetics of culture. For me the inquiry is bound up with a specific interest in Renaissance modes of aesthetic empowerment: I want to know how cultural objects, expressions, and practices—here, principally, plays by Shakespeare and the stage on which they first appeared—acquired compelling force. English literary theorists in the period needed a new word for that force, a word to describe the ability of language, in Puttenham's phrase, to cause "a stir to the mind"; drawing on the Greek rhetorical tradition, they called it *energia*.[5] This is the origin in our language of the term "energy," a term I propose we use, provided we understand that its origins lie in rhetoric rather than physics and that its significance is social and historical. We experience that energy within ourselves, but its contemporary existence depends upon an irregular chain of historical transactions that leads back to the late sixteenth and early seventeenth centuries.[6] Does this mean that the aesthetic power of a play like *King Lear* is a direct transmission from Shakespeare's time to our own? Certainly not. That play and the circumstances in which it was originally embedded have been continuously, often radically, refigured. But these refigurations do not cancel history, locking us into a perpetual present; on the contrary, they are signs of the inescapability of a historical process, a structured negotiation and exchange, already evident in the initial moments of empowerment. That there is no direct, unmediated link between ourselves and Shakespeare's plays does not mean that there is no link at all. The "life" that literary works seem to possess long after both the death of the author and the death of the culture for which the author wrote is the historical consequence, however transformed and refashioned, of the social energy initially encoded in those works.

But what is "social energy"? The term implies something measurable, yet I cannot provide a convenient and reliable formula for isolating a single, stable quantum for examination. We identify *energia* only indirectly, by its effects: it is manifested in the capacity of certain verbal, aural, and visual traces to produce, shape, and organize collective physical and mental experiences. Hence it is associated with repeatable forms of pleasure and interest, with the capacity to arouse disquiet, pain, fear, the beating of the heart, pity, laughter, tension, relief, wonder. In its aesthetic modes, social energy must have a minimal predictability—enough to make simple repetitions possible—and a minimal range: enough to reach out beyond a single creator or consumer to some community, however constricted. Occasionally, and we are generally interested in these occasions, the predictability and range will be far greater: large numbers of men and women of different social classes and divergent beliefs will be induced to explode with laughter or weep or experience a complex blend of anxiety and exaltation. Moreover, the aesthetic forms of social energy are usually characterized by a minimal adaptability—enough to enable them to survive at least some of the constant changes in social circumstance and cultural value that make ordinary utterances evanescent. Whereas most collective expressions moved from their original setting to a new place or time are dead on arrival, the social energy encoded in certain works of art continues to generate the illusion of life for centuries. I want to understand the negotiations through which works of art obtain and amplify such powerful energy.

If one longs, as I do, to reconstruct these negotiations, one dreams of finding an originary moment, a moment in which the master hand shapes the concentrated social energy into the sublime aesthetic object. But the quest is fruitless, for there is no originary moment, no pure act of untrammeled creation. In place of a blazing genesis, one begins to glimpse something that seems at first far less spectacular: a subtle, elusive set of exchanges, a network of trades and trade-offs, a jostling of competing representations, a negotiation between joint-stock companies. Gradually, these complex, ceaseless borrowings and lendings have come to seem to me more important, more poignant even, than the epiphany for which I had hoped.

The textual traces that have survived from the Renaissance and that are at the center of our literary interest in Shakespeare are the products of extended borrowings, collective exchanges, and mutual enchantments. They were made by moving certain things— principally ordinary language but also metaphors, ceremonies, dances, emblems, items of clothing, well-worn stories, and so forth—from one culturally demarcated zone to another. We need to understand not only the construction of these zones but also the process of movement across the shifting boundaries between them. Who decides which materials can be moved and which must remain in place? How are cultural materials prepared for exchange? What happens to them when they are moved?

But why are we obliged to speak of movement at all? Except in the most material instances—items of clothing, stage properties, the bodies of actors—nothing is literally moved onto the stage. Rather, the theater achieves its representations by gesture and language, that is, by signifiers that seem to leave the signifieds completely untouched. Renaissance writers would seem to have endorsed this intangibility by returning again and again to the image of the mirror; the purpose of playing, in Hamlet's conventional words, is "to hold as 'twere the mirror up to nature: to show virtue her feature, scorn her own image, and the very age and body of the time his form and pressure" (3.2.21–24). The mirror is the emblem of instantaneous and accurate reproduction; it takes nothing from what it reflects and adds nothing except self-knowledge.

Perhaps this is what the players actually thought they were doing, but it is worth considering how convenient and self-protective the image of the mirror must have seemed. Artists in a time of censorship and repression had ample reason to claim that they had taken nothing from the world they represented, that they had never dreamed of violating the distance demanded by their superiors, that their representations only reflected faithfully the world's own form. Yet even in Hamlet's familiar account, the word *pressure*—that is, impression, as with a seal or signet ring—should signal to us that for the Renaissance more is at stake in mirrors than an abstract and bodiless reflection. Both optics and mirror lore in the period suggested that something was actively passing back and forth in the production of mirror images, that accurate representation depended upon material emanation and exchange.[7] Only if we reinvest the mirror image with a sense of pressure as well as form can it convey something of its original strangeness and magic. And only with the recovery of this strangeness can we glimpse a whole spectrum of representational exchanges where we had once seen simple reflection alone. In some exchanges the object or practice mimed onstage seems relatively untouched by the representation; in others, the object or practice is intensified, diminished, or even completely evacuated by its encounter with the theater; in still others, it is marked as a prize—something "up for grabs"—in an unresolved struggle between competing representational discourses. The mistake is to imagine that there is a single, fixed, mode of exchange; in reality, there are many modes, their character is determined historically, and they are continually renegotiated.

The range of these modes is treated in detail in the chapters that follow, but it might be useful to note some of the more common types:

1. Appropriation.   There seems to be little or no payment or reciprocal understanding or quid pro quo. Objects appear to be in the public domain, hence in the category of "things indifferent" (adiaphora): there for the taking. Or, alternatively, objects appear to be vulnerable and defenseless, hence graspable without punishment or retaliation.

The prime example of adiaphora is ordinary language: for literary art this is the single greatest cultural creation that may be appropriated without payment. One of the simplest and most sublime instances is Lear's anguished "Never, never, never, never, never." But once we pass beyond the most conventional and familiar expressions, we come upon instances of language use that are charged with potential dangers, powerful social charms that cannot be simply appropriated. And under certain circumstances even ordinary language may be surprisingly contested.

The prime example of the vulnerable is the lower classes, who may at most times be represented almost without restraint.

2. Purchase. Here something, most often money, is paid by the theater company for an object (or practice or story) that is staged. The clearest instances are properties and costumes. The inventories that have survived suggest that theater companies were prepared to pay a high price for objects with a high symbolic valence: "Item, 1 popes miter"; "Item, 3 Imperial crowns; 1 plain crown"; "Bought a doublet of white satin laid thick with gold lace, and pair of round paned hose of cloth of silver, the panes laid with gold lace. . . £7.00."[8] Some of the costumes were made directly for the players; others came via transactions that reveal the circuitous channels through which social energy could be circulated: suits were given by gentlemen to their servants in lieu of cash payment (or in addition to such payment); the servants sold the clothes to the players; the players appeared onstage in clothes that might actually have belonged to members of the audience.

The companies did not pay for "rights" to stories, so far as I know—at least not in the modern sense—but the playwright or company did pay for the books used as sources (for example, Holinshed or Marguerite of Navarre or Giraldi Cinthio), and the playwright himself was paid.

3. Symbolic Acquisition. Here a social practice or other mode of social energy is transferred to the stage by means of representation. No cash payment is made, but the object acquired is not in the realm of things indifferent, and something is implicitly or explicitly given in return for it. The transferring agency has its purposes, which may be more or less overt; the theater picks up what it can get and gives in return what it must (for example, public celebration or humiliation). In chapter 4 I discuss the way the charismatic religious practice of exorcism, under attack by the official church, is brought on to the stage, where its power is at once exploited and marked out as a fraud: "Five fiends have been in poor Tom at once: of lust, as Obidicut; Hobbididence, prince of dumbness; Mahu, of stealing; Modo, of murder; Flibbertigibbet, of mopping and mowing, who since possesses chambermaids and waiting-women."

We can further distinguish three types of symbolic acquistion:

A. Acquisition Through Simulation. The actor simulates what is already understood to be a theatrical representation. The most extreme instance is the theater's own self-representations—that is, simulations of actors performing plays, as in The Spanish Tragedy, Hamlet, The Knight of the Burning Pestle, or The Roman Actor—but many of the most resonant instances involve more complex simulations of the histrionic elements in public ceremonials and rituals. For example, as I shall show in chapter 5, the spectacular royal pardons that were understood by observers to be the theatrical occasions in plays such as Measure for Measure.

B. Metaphorical Acquisition. Here a practice (or a set of social energies) is acquired indirectly. For example, after 1606 players were forbidden to take the name of the Lord in vain—that is, every use of the words "God" or "Christ Jesus" or the "Holy Ghost" or the "Trinity" onstage, even in wholly pious contexts, would be subject to a £10 fine.[9] The regulation threatened to remove from the performances not simply a set of names but a whole range of powerful energies, rituals, and experiences. The players' simple and effective response, sanctioned by a long tradition, was to substitute for the interdicted words names like Jove and Jupiter, each a miniature metaphor for the Christian God. To take a slightly more complex example, when the fairies in *A Midsummer Night's Dream* "consecrate" the marriage beds with field-dew, they are, in a mode at once natural and magical, enacting (and appropriating to the stage) the Catholic practice of anointing the marriage bed with holy water.[10]

Metaphorical acquisition works by teasing out latent homologies, similitudes, systems of likeness, but it depends equally upon a deliberate distancing or distortion that precedes the disclosure of likeness. Hence a play will insist upon the difference between its representation and the "real," only to draw out the analogy or proportion linking them. The chorus in *Henry V* urgently calls attention to the difference between the theater's power to command the imagination of the audience and the prince's power to command his subjects, but as the play unfolds, those powers become revealingly confounded (see chapter 2). Or again, the strategies of the theater and the family, seemingly far removed, are revealed by *King Lear* to be mirrors of each other.[11]

C. Acquisition Through Synecdoche or Metonymy.   Here the theater acquires cultural energy by isolating and performing one part or attribute of a practice, which then stands for the whole (often a whole that cannot be represented). For example, as I argue in chapter 3, verbal chafing becomes in Shakespeare's comedies not only a sign but a vital instance of an encompassing erotic heat otherwise impossible to stage in the public theater.

Inquiries into the relation between Renaissance theater and society have been situated most often at the level of reflection: images of the monarchy, the lower classes, the legal profession, the church, and so forth. Such studies are essential, but they rarely engage questions of dynamic exchange. They tend instead to posit two separate, autonomous systems and then try to gauge how accurately or effectively the one represents the other. But crucial questions typically remain outside the range of this critical practice: How is it determined what may be staged? To what extent is the object of theatrical representation itself already a representation? What governs the degree of displacement or distortion in theatrical representation? Whose interests are served by the staging? What is the effect of representation on the object or practice represented? Above all, how is the social energy inherent in a cultural practice negotiated and exchanged?

If we are to attempt an answer to these questions, it would be well to begin with certain abjurations:

1. There can be no appeals to genius as the sole origin of the energies of great art.
2. There can be no motiveless creation.
3. There can be no transcendent or timeless or unchanging representation.
4. There can be no autonomous artifacts.
5. There can be no expression without an origin and an object, a *from* and a *for*.
6. There can be no art without social energy.
7. There can be no spontaneous generation of social energy.

Bound up with these negations are certain generative principles:

1. Mimesis is always accompanied by—indeed is always produced by—negotiation and exchange.
2. The exchanges to which art is a party may involve money, but they may involve other currencies as well. Money is only one kind of cultural capital.

3. The agents of exchange may appear to be individuals (most often, an isolated artist is imagined in relation to a faceless, amorphous entity designated society or culture), but individuals are themselves the products of collective exchange. In the Renaissance theater this collective nature is intensified by the artists' own participation in versions of joint-stock companies. In such companies individual ventures have their own sharply defined identities and interests (and their own initial capital), but to succeed they pool their resources, and they own essential properties in common.

If there is no expressive essence that can be located in an aesthetic object complete unto itself, uncontaminated by interpretation, beyond translation or substitution—if there is no mimesis without exchange—then we need to analyze the collective dynamic circulation of pleasures, anxieties, and interests.[12] This circulation depends upon a separation of artistic practices from other social practices, a separation produced by a sustained ideological labor, a consensual classification. That is, art does not simply exist in all cultures; it is made up along with other products, practices, discourses of a given culture. (In practice, "made up" means inherited, transmitted, altered, modified, reproduced far more than it means invented: as a rule, there is very little pure invention in culture.) Now the demarcation is rarely, if ever, absolute or complete, nor can we account for it by a single theoretical formulation. We can think up various metaphors to describe the process: the building of a set of walls or fences to separate one territory from adjacent territories; the erection of a gate through which some people and objects will be allowed to pass and others prohibited; the posting of a sign detailing the acceptable code of behavior within the walled territory; the development of a class of functionaries who specialize in the customs of the demarcated zone; the establishment, as in a children's game, of ritualized formulas that can be endlessly repeated. In the case of the public theater of the late sixteenth and early seventeenth centuries, these metaphors were literalized: there was the actual construction of a building, the charging of admission to cross the threshold, the set of regulations governing what could and could not be presented on the stage, a set of tacit understandings (for example, no one was actually to be killed or tortured, no one was to have sex onstage, no one was really cursing or praying or conjuring, and so forth), the writing of scripts that could be screened ahead of time by the censors, rehearsals, the relative nonparticipation of the audience, the existence of theater companies of professional actors.

This literalization and institutionalization of the place of art makes the Renaissance theater particularly useful for an analysis of the cultural circulation of social energy, and the stakes of the analysis are heightened by the direct integration of Shakespeare's plays— easily the most powerful, successful, and enduring artistic expressions in the English language— with this particular mode of artistic production and consumption. We are not, that is, dealing with texts written outside the institution and subsequently attached to it or with encysted productions staged in a long-established and ideologically dormant setting but with literary creations designed in intimate and living relation to an emergent commercial practice. For the most part these creations seem intended at once to enhance the power of the theater as an institution and to draw upon the power this institution has already accumulated. The desire to enhance the general practice of which any particular work is an instance is close to the center of all artistic production, but in the drama this desire is present in a direct, even coarse, sense because of the overwhelming importance and immediacy of material interests. Shakespeare the shareholder was presumably interested not simply in a good return on an individual play but in the health and success of his entire company as it related both to those who helped regulate it and to its audience. Each individual play may be said to make a small contribution to the general store of social energy possessed by the theater and hence to the sustained claim that the theater can make on its real and potential audience.

If each play is bound up with the theater's long-term institutional strategy, it is none-theless important to avoid the assumption that the relation between mode and individual performance is always harmonious. It is possible for a playwright to be in tension with his own medium, hostile to its presuppositions and conditions, eager to siphon off its powers and attack its pleasures. Ben Jonson's career makes this tension manifest, and one can even glimpse it at moments in Shakespeare's. We can say, perhaps, that an individual play medi-ates between the mode of the theater, understood in its historical specificity, and elements of the society out of which that theater has been differentiated. Through its representational means, each play carries charges of social energy onto the stage; the stage in its turn revises that energy and returns it to the audience.

Despite the wooden walls and the official regulations, the boundaries between the the-ater and the world were not fixed, nor did they constitute a logically coherent set; rather they were a sustained collective improvisation. At any given time, the distinction between the theater and the world might be reasonably clear and the boundaries might assume the qual-ity of self-evidence, so that the very cataloging of distinctions might seem absurd: for exam-ple, *of course* the theater audience could not intervene in the action on stage, *of course* the violence could only be mimed. But one can think of theaters that swept away every one of the supposedly self-evident distinctions, and more important for our purposes, Renaissance players and audiences could think of such counter-examples.

In consequence, the ratio between the theater and the world, even at its most stable and unchallenged moments, was never *perfectly* taken for granted, that is, experienced as something wholly natural and self-evident. Forces both within and without the theater were constantly calling attention to theatrical practices that violated the established conventions of the English playhouse. When Protestant polemicists characterized the Catholic Mass as theater, the attack conjured up a theater in which (1) the playhouse disguised itself as a holy place; (2) the audience did not think of itself as an audience but as a community of believers; (3) the theatrical performance—with its elaborate costumes and rituals—not only refused to concede that it was an illusion but claimed to be the highest truth; (4) the actors did not fully grasp that they were actors but actually believed in the roles they played and in the symbolic actions they mimed; and (5) the spectacle demanded of the audience not a few pennies and the pleasant wasting of several hours but a lifelong commitment to the institu-tion that staged the show. Similarly, the playwrights themselves frequently called attention in the midst of their plays to alternative theatrical practices. Thus, for example, the denoue-ment of Massinger's *Roman Actor* (like that of Kyd's *Spanish Tragedy*) turns upon the staging of a mode of theater in which princes and nobles take part in plays and in which the killing turns out to be real. It required no major act of imagination for a Renaissance audience to conceive of either of these alternatives to the conventions of the public playhouse: both were fully operative in the period itself, in the form of masques and courtly entertainments, on the one hand, and public maimings and executions, on the other.

Thus the conventional distinction between the theater and the world, however firmly grasped at a given moment, was not one that went without saying; on the contrary, it was constantly said. This "saying" did not necessarily subvert the distinction; often, in fact, it had the opposite effect, shoring up and insisting upon the boundaries within which the public theater existed. Nor did recognizing alternatives necessarily make these boundaries seem "merely" arbitrary; attacks on illegitimate forms of theater tended to moralize the existing practice. But the consciousness in the sixteenth century, as now, of other ways to construe the relation between the theater and the world heightened awareness of the theater as a contingent practice, with a set of institutional interests, motives, and constraints and with the concomitant possibility of inadvertently or deliberately violating these very interests. This possibility, even if never put into practice, affected the relation of the theater both to social and political authorities and to its own sense of itself: even the theater's moments of docile self-regulation, the instances of its willingness to remain well within conventional limits, were marked out as strategies, institutional decisions taken to secure the material well-being of the playing company.

The sustained cultural representation of alternative theatrical practices was probably sufficient by itself to call attention to the specific interests, vulnerabilities, and objective social conditions of the public stage. Even without transgression or persecution, the theater would have been denied the luxury at times granted to privileged cultural institutions, particularly those that perform public rites and preserve cultural memory: the luxury of forgetting that its representatives have a concrete, material interest in the rituals they perform and the boundaries they observe. But in fact the theater in the sixteenth and seventeenth centuries constantly violated its interests and transgressed its boundaries. Indeed these boundaries were defined in relation to transgressions that were fully understood as such only after the fact, and the interests of the theater could be clearly understood only when they had been violated. The Tudor and Stuart regulations governing the public stage were confused, inconsistent, and haphazard, the products neither of a traditional, collective understanding nor of a coherent, rational attempt to regularize and define a new cultural practice. They were instead a jumble of traditional rules and offices designed to govern older, very different theatrical practices and a set of ordinances drawn up hastily in response to particular and local pressures. As a result, even the relatively peaceful and prosperous moments in the troubled life of a theater company had an air of improvisation rather than of established and settled fact.[13]

This institutional improvisation frames the local improvisations of individual playwrights. Hence Shakespeare's representational equipment included not only the ideological constraints within which the theater functioned as an institution but also a set of received stories and generic expectations, including, as his career progressed, those established by his own earlier plays. And though in many of his materials he worked within fairly well-defined boundaries—he could not, for example, have Prince Hal lose the battle of Agincourt— Shakespeare actually had at every point a surprising range of movement. The choices he made were not purely subjective or individual or disinterested, but they were choices: there are dozens of tellings of the Lear story—it is part of the ideology of the family in the late Middle Ages and Renaissance—yet in none of them, so far as I know, does Cordelia die in Lear's arms.

But if we grant the Elizabethan theater this provisional character, should we not say that its air of improvisatory freedom is countered by a still greater insistence on the contained and scripted nature of the represented actions? After all, theatrical performance is distinct from most other social practices precisely insofar as its character is predetermined and enclosed, as it forces its audience to grant that retrospective necessity was prospective: the formal necessity disclosed when one looks back on events that have already occurred was in fact the necessity disclosed in the existence, before the performance itself, of the script.[14] Life outside the theater is full of confusion, schemes imperfectly realized, arbitrary interference, unexpected and unpredictable resistances from the body. On the stage this confusion is at once mimed and revealed to be only scripted. Of course, we may say that even onstage there is no certainty: the actors may forget their lines or blurt them out before their cue or altogether refuse to perform, the clown may decide to improvise, individuals in the audience may abandon the voluntary submission expected of them and intervene in the performance, the scaffolding may collapse and force the cancellation of the show. But this absurd, almost entirely theoretical contingency only gives the touch of freedom that seasons that disclosure of necessity.

We could argue further that one of the ideological functions of the theater was precisely to create in its audience the sense that what seemed spontaneous or accidental was in fact fully plotted ahead of time by a playwright carefully calculating his effects, that behind experienced uncertainty there was design, whether the design of the human patriarchs—the fathers and rulers who unceasingly watched over the errant courses of their subjects—or the overarching design of the divine patriarch. The theater then would confirm the structure of human experience as proclaimed by those on top and would urge us to reconfirm this structure in our pleasure.

But if the improvisational provisionality of the theater is not necessarily subversive ideologically, neither is the hidden order of scripted performance necessarily orthodox. Not only can the audience withhold its confirmation of that order and refuse to applaud, but the order itself is marked out as theatrical and to that extent unreal. In applauding, the audience need only be confirming its own practical interests in the playhouse.

Can we speak, however, of "practical interests" in this context? Should we not say that the theater escapes from the network of practices that governs the circulation of social energy? The public theater would seem to be of no *use* to the audience at all in providing material or symbolic strategic advantage: the events depicted on the stage do not impinge directly on the practical arrangements of the members of the audience, and via the script an abstractness, an atemporality, is concealed behind the powerful illusion of unfolding life.

These special conditions, though important, do not constitute the theater as a place radically detached from the realm of social practice. In the first place, the theater does have obvious use-value for several classes of people: those who act, write for it, regulate it, provide costumes, build and maintain the playhouses, ferry customers across the river, pick pockets or pick up tricks during the performance, provide refreshment, sweep up after the crowd, and so forth. Only one group—the audience—appears to be excluded from practical activity, and an activity cannot become nonpractical because it excludes a social group, for then virtually all activities would become nonpractical. Second, the audience's pleasure is in some important senses useful. The Renaissance had theories, as we do, arguing on both physiological and psychological grounds for the practical necessity of recreation, and these were supplemented by explicitly political theories. An audience watching a play, Nashe suggested, would not be hatching a rebellion. Third, the practical usefulness of the theater depends largely on the illusion of its distance from ordinary social practice. The triumphant cunning of the theater is to make its spectators forget that they are participating in a practical activity, to invent a sphere that seems far removed from the manipulations of the everyday. Shakespeare's theater is powerful and effective precisely to the extent that the audience believes it to be nonuseful and hence nonpractical.[15] And this belief gives the theater an unusually broad license to conduct its negotiations and exchanges with surrounding institutions, authorities, discourses, and practices.

These negotiations were defined by the unequivocal *exclusion* of relatively little from the privileged space of the playhouse, even though virtually everything represented on the stage was at least potentially dangerous and hence could be scrutinized and censored. The Elizabethan theater could, within limits, represent the sacred as well as the profane, contemporary as well as ancient times, stories set in England as well as as those set in distant lands. Allusions to the reigning monarch, and even to highly controversial issues in the reign, were not necessarily forbidden (though the company had to tread cautiously); the outlawed practices and agents of the Catholic faith could be represented with considerable sympathy, along with Turks, Jews, witches, demons, fairies, wild men, ghosts. Above all—and the enabling agent of this range of representational resources—the language of the theater was astonishingly open: the most solemn formulas of the church and state could find their way onto the stage and mingle with the language of the marketplace, just as elevated verse could alternate in the same play with the homeliest of prose. The theater is marked off from the "outside world" and licensed to operate as a distinct domain, but its boundaries are remarkably permeable.

For the circulation of social energy by and through the stage was not part of a single coherent, totalizing system. Rather it was partial, fragmentary, conflictual; elements were crossed, torn apart, recombined, set against each other; particular social practices were magnified by the stage, others diminished, exalted, evacuated. What then is the social energy that is being circulated? Power, charisma, sexual excitement, collective dreams, wonder, desire, anxiety, religious awe, free-floating intensities of experience: in a sense the question is absurd, for everything produced by the society can circulate unless it is deliberately excluded from circulation. Under such circumstances, there can be no single method, no overall picture, no exhaustive and definitive cultural poetics. . . .

I had dreamed of speaking with the dead, and even now I do not abandon this dream. But the mistake was to imagine that I would hear a single voice, the voice of the other. If I wanted to hear one, I had to hear the many voices of the dead. And if I wanted to hear the voice of the other, I had to hear my own voice. The speech of the dead, like my own speech, is not private property.

NOTES

1. The classic formulation is by W. K. Wimsatt, Jr.: "In each poem there is something (an individual intuition—or a concept) which can never be expressed in other terms" ("The Structure of the 'Concrete Universal' in Literature," in *Criticism: The Foundations of Modern Literary Judgment*, ed. Mark Schorer, Josephine Miles, and Gordon McKenzie, rev. ed. [New York: Harcourt, Brace, and World, 1958], p. 403).
2. To be sure, a wide range of literary studies have implicity, and on occasion explicitly, addressed the collective experience of theater: E. K. Chambers's encyclopedic studies of the theatrical institutions in the Middle Ages and the Renaissance, Glynne Wickham's volumes on early English stages, Robert Weimann's analysis of Shakespeare and the popular tradition, C.L. Barber's discussion of Shakespeare and folk rituals, a large number of books and articles on the rhetorical materials with which Shakespeare worked, and so forth. The present study is an attempt to supplement these volumes by exploring the poetics of Renaissance culture.
3. We may posit (and feel) the presence of a powerful and highly individuated creative intelligence, but that creativity does not lead us back to a moment of pure sublime invention, nor does it secure a formal textual autonomy.
4. Novels may have been read aloud to members of the household, but the differentiation of the domestic group is alien to the organization of the theatrical audience.
5. George Puttenham, *The Arte of English Poesie*, in *Elizabethan Critical Essays*, ed. G. Gregory Smith, 2 vols. (London: Oxford University Press, 1904) 2:148. See, likewise, Sir Philip Sidney, *An Apologie for Poetrie*, in Smith, 1:201. The term derives ultimately from Aristotle's *Rhetoric* (33.2.2), as interpreted especially by Quintilian (*Institutio* 8.3.89) and Scaliger (*Poetices* 3.27).
6. And back before the late sixteenth and early seventeenth centuries as well, since the transactions that enable the creation of Shakespeare's plays are possible only because of prior transactions. Theoretically, at least, the chain has no end, though any inquiry has practical limits and, moreover, certain moments seem more important than others.
7. Jurgis Baltrusaitis, *Le Miroir: Essai sur une légende scientifique; Révélations, science fiction, et fallacies* (Paris: Elmayan, 1978).
8. These items are from the inventory of the Lord Admiral's Men in *Henslowe's Diary*, ed. R. A. Foakes and R. T. Rickert (Cambridge: Cambridge University Press, 1961), app. 2, pp. 320–25.
9. For the terms of "An Acte to Restraine Abuses of Players," see E. K. Chambers, *The Elizabethan Stage*, 4 vols. (Oxford: Clarendon, 1923), 4:338–9. It is not clear how strictly this regulation was enforced.
10. These maneuvers were not always successful. In 1639 it is reported that "Thursday last the players of the Fortune were fined 1000£ for setting up an altar, a bason, and two candlesticks, and bowing down before it upon the stage, and although they allege that it was an old play revived, and an altar to the heathen gods, yet it was apparent that this play was revived on purpose in contempt of the ceremonies of the Church" (quoted in Gerald Eades Bentley, *The Jacobean and*

Caroline Stage, 7 vols. [Oxford: Clarendon, 1941–68], 1:277). Bentley expresses some reservations about the accuracy of this account.

11. Stephen Greenblatt, "The Cultivation of Anxiety: King Lear and His Heirs," *Raritan* 2 (1982): 92–124. I should add that the members of joint-stock companies in the early modern period customarily referred to each other in familial terms.

12. "Dynamic circulation" is Michel Foucault's phrase *(L'Usage des plaisirs,* vol. 2 of *Histoire de la sexualité* [Paris: Gallimard, 1984], pp. 52–53).

13. Glynne Wickham, who has argued that the Elizabethan regulations were somewhat more methodical than I have allowed, emphasizes the players' creative flexibility in response: "It is this freedom from rigidly doctrinaire approaches to play writing and play production, coupled with the will to adapt and improvise creatively within the limits of existing opportunities, which ultimately explains the triumph of Elizabethan drama over the censorship and the triumph of Jacobean and Caroline actors in bringing this drama successfully to birth despite the determined efforts of the clergy, town-councillors and Chambers of Commerce to suppress it" (*Early English Stages, 1300–1660*, vol. 2, part 2: 1576–1660 [London: Routledge and Kegan Paul, 1972], p. 208). But we might add—as Wickham himself recognizes—that some of the most severe regulations, such as those suppressing the great mystery cycles and prohibiting unlicensed playing troupes, very much helped the major Elizabethan and Jacobean companies.

14. For reflections on this distinction between retrospective and prospective necessity, see Pierre Bourdieu, *Outline of a Theory of Practice,* trans. Richard Nice (Cambridge: Cambridge University Press, 1977). I have found Bourdieu's book extremely suggestive.

15. In this regard, we may invoke what Bourdieu calls "a restricted definition of economic interest" that is the historical product of capitalism:

> The constitution of relatively autonomous areas of practice is accompanied by a process through which symbolic interests (often described as "spiritual" or "cultural") come to be set up in opposition to strictly economic interests as defined in the field of economic transactions by the fundamental tautology "business is business"; strictly "cultural" or "aesthetic" interest, disinterested interest, is the paradoxical product of the ideological labour in which writers and artists, those most directly interested, have played an important part and in the course of which symbolic interests become autonomous by being opposed to material interests, i.e., by being symbolically nullified as interests, (p. 177)

THE POLITICS OF CONTAINMENT (1991)

JONATHAN DOLLIMORE

Dollimore has written extensively about queer and bisexual history and theory, about early modern (Renaissance) drama, and about cultural materialism, the Marxist-

oriented tradition of cultural criticism in the tradition of Raymond Williams. In "The Politics of Containment", a section from his Sexual Dissidence: Augustine to Wilde, Freud to Foucault, *Dollimore addresses "containment theory," which some critics have associated with cultural materialism and its cousin or analogue in literary criticism, new historicism. Containment theorists suppose that those in power (the dominant or hegemonic forces) can contain the resistance to their power. They mean "contain" not in the sense of include but in the sense of confine and limit. Containment theorists have been accused of excess pessimism, of underestimating how resistance can overcome abusive power. Dollimore tries to strike a balance between resistance to abusive power and the ability of abusive power to contain resistance. He takes containment seriously but also argues that resistance cannot be completely contained. At the same time, he declines what he sees as an easy optimism about resistance, for such resistance as he finds possible he also believes will make its way only with great difficulty and at a great price. Dollimore strikes a balance between readings of containment and resistance that he sees as too optimistic or too pessimistic. He tries to specify the mechanisms and structures of resistance that ends up as co-opted by, absorbed into the dominant, and resistance that manages, either more or less, to escape co-optation and emerge as genuine subversion. To Dollimore, cultural conflicts do not typically end up at either extreme of resistance or containment, an insight that parallels the deconstructive sense of internal contradiction and multiplicity, though Dollimore, working from more Marxist traditions, does not pursue that parallel.*

In his next chapter, Dollimore provides three brief examples, one from the Nazi persecution of homosexuals; one from Oscar Wilde's De Profundis, *written in prison; and one from George Jackson's* Soledad Brother, *also written in prison. The selection here includes only the most extended of those examples, the discussion of Wilde. Dollimore's discussion of Wilde draws on Foucault's* Discipline and Punish *(see the selection from Foucault's book in this volume), which argues that the dominant ways of thinking have come to influence people to go along with them not so much by direct enforcement as by training people to internalize the discourses that shape their behavior, and thus by training people to believe that they* choose *to act in the ways that the dominant discourses pressure them to act. While Foucault had a number of differences with Marxist theory, for Dollimore's purposes here Foucault's notion of internalized "discipline" carries many similarities to Dollimore's Marxist sense of how people internalize abusive ideology, abusive patterns of social assumption. (Some of Dollimore's passing references to other parts of his book are not included in this selection. His reference to Hall in 1928 is to Radclyffe Hall's* The Well of Loneliness, *a famous lesbian novel from 1928.)*

Humanist transgression in the name of an essential self has proved wanting, and its adherents have lost their faith. This is part of a wider crisis: with the post/modern repudiation of the very existence of the essential self, there are those who have become sceptical about the possibilities of effective transgression, and pessimistic about the possibilities of radical change. Most worryingly perhaps, the belief in an autonomous self, that experiential focus apparently necessary for successful opposition to a repressive social order, seems to be unfounded; in those haunting words of Michel Foucault, "there is no single locus of great Refusal, no soul of revolt, source of all rebellions, or pure law of the revolutionary" *(History, 95–6)*.

For the radical humanist especially, the post/modern repudiation of the unified subject seems to disempower the marginal, robbing it of that independence and autonomy which was the assumed precondition of its possessing any subversive agency of its own, or at least any independent cultural identity. The disappearance of the independent experiential *locus* for opposition further suggests that repression infiltrates and constructs consciousness itself: where we once thought there was an essential self, a liberating, uncontaminated otherness/ difference constituting the soul of revolt, we find instead only the power which it promised to liberate us from. Even worse, it seems as if the existing social order might actively forestall resistance because somehow preceding and informing it: subversion and transgression are not merely defeated by law, but actually produced by law in a complex process of (re)legitimation.

From such anxious perceptions there emerges the so-called subversion/containment problematic wherein repressive laws are seen not only to defeat us coercively—that much was always obvious—but to inhabit us in ways which ensure our defeat prior to, in ways other than, direct force. Resistance from the margins seems doomed to replicate internally the strategies, structures, and even the values of the dominant.

Unless, that is, resistance is otherwise, and derives in part from the inevitable incompleteness and surplus of control itself? If so perhaps we should think of resistance not in terms of an originating identity, but a reactive agency? Such thoughts lead us to the practice of transgressive reinscription. But consideration of that practice must wait upon a fuller account of the containment argument....

VERSIONS OF CONTAINMENT

The arguments for containment come in diverse forms. One of its most important developments has been in relation to the early modern period; another is in recent analysis of colonialist discourse.[1] Some of these precede or have developed adjacently to the post/modern critique of the subject (and usefully enlarge its scope), since containment theories have always recognized that identity is an effect of the social domains which subversion and transgression would contest.

First there is the anthropological version which sees allegedly transgressive practices like carnival as not at all disturbing of dominant values but rather their guarantor—a licensed release of social tension, a kind of safety-valve effect which, far from undermining the existing order, actually contributes to its survival.

Second are the psychological versions to the effect that (1) true faith paradoxically lies in honest doubt; (2) it is the sacrilegious who, most knowing the true value of the sacred, are thereby most beholden unto it, *even as* they seek to destroy it; (3) there is nothing so bourgeois as the desire to scandalize the bourgeoisie. A further version of this argument is Richard Sennett's theory of "disobedient dependence." Transgression, says Sennett, is perhaps the most forceful element in disobedient dependence, since it involves a defiance based on dependence, a rebellion not against authority but within it: "the transgressor disobeys but authority relates the terms." As such this rebellion "has very little to do with genuine independence or autonomy"; moreover, "the world into which a person has entered through the desire to transgress is seldom … a real world of its own, a true alternative which blots out that past" (*Authority*, 33–4).[2]

Third is the theoretical version . . . which says that to invert a binary opposition (e.g., masculine/feminine) is to remain within rather than overthrow its oppressive structure. This might be the critique, in theoretical guise, of the "mannish lesbian."

A fourth category of containment is developed most persuasively by Michel Foucault in relation to sexuality, but can be formulated more generally to include the other three. I outline it in relation to Foucault in Chapter 14, but will briefly rehearse it here. We have become used to thinking of sexuality as an anarchic and hence potentially subversive energy which conservatives want to control, radicals want to liberate. However, Foucault sees it in terms of socially created identities and desires which enable rather than hinder the operations of power within the realm of the psychosexual. In short, sexuality, far from being an energy which "power" is afraid of, is actually a discursive construct which power works through.

Containment theory is sometimes seen as having little to do with materialist critique, and is sometimes conveniently disavowed, often by gestural materialists, as a kind of bourgeois intellectual bad faith. But Raymond Williams for one knew otherwise; in 1977, before most current debates were underway, he gave this astute summary of the crucial issue:

> The major theoretical problem … is to distinguish between alternative and oppositional initiatives and contributions which are made within or against a specific hegemony (which then sets certain limits to them or which can succeed in neutralizing, changing or actually incorporating them) and other kinds of initiative and contribution which are irreducible to the terms of the original…hegemony, and are in that sense independent. It can be persuasively argued that all or nearly all initiatives and contributions, even when they take on manifestly alternative or oppositional forms, are in practice tied to the hegemonic: that the dominant culture, so to say, at once produces and limits its own forms of counter-culture. *There is more evidence for this view…than we usually admit.* (*Marxism and Literature*, 114, my emphasis.)

Williams rightly insists, nevertheless, that significant breaks with the dominant *have* occurred, and will of course continue to do so. But such breaks can neither be adequately recognized nor developed if the realities and complexity of containment are disavowed. To that end his account is indebted to but also departs from a European Marxist tradition of cultural critique,[3] one which has recognized the complexity and indirect effectiveness of domination, and is acutely aware of the fact that human potentialities have not only been savagely repressed, but also abandoned and repudiated by their former adherents and those with most to gain from them. Some of the most effective Marxist cultural critique this century has attended to the reasons for the failure of potential to be realized in circumstances which should have enabled it. An obvious instance concerns the way that, after the First World War, when conditions seemed right for the development of socialism, fascism won out instead.

Moreover, far from opting for the facile optimism dictated by party dogma, writers as diverse as Walter Benjamin, Antonio Gramsci, Theodor Adorno, Herbert Marcuse, and Louis Althusser have felt it necessary to describe the complexity, the flexible resilience of power structures, and their psychic internalization. These writers have been without illusion—even pessimistic—about the short- or medium-term possibilities of progressive change, and it is not surprising that today there are those living in the societies of advanced capitalism who find a continuing relevance in their work. Specifically, some of the current debates around subversion and containment, and the reactionary or repressive dimensions of high culture, are benefiting from renewed attention to that work. It is in such a spirit that I approach it here: though on balance more critical than accepting of containment theory, I believe it is too often caricatured and disavowed by those unwilling to face its challenge.

OBJECTIONS

For example, there are those who construe containment theory as saying that resistance is *only ever* an effect of power. This simplistic version of the theory, deriving more from its critics than its advocates, represents power as "seamless and all pervasive" and resistance, where it exists at all, as "ultimately self-deceived" (Belsey, "Towards Cultural History," 164). Resistance is supposed to be self-deceived because it was only ever the ruse of the power which created it—a manufactured threat whose "suppression" is a strategy of control by the power which produced it. Actually, even this version of containment theory might offer more space for resistance than its advocates sometimes, and its critics usually, allow, since the very activity of producing the threat requires giving it a visibility and identity, both of which, even though initially a charade, may then or subsequently be occupied or appropriated by oppositional forces. Always, though, at a certain cost, and the more so to those implicated in the earlier stages of this process.

Further, when containment theorists are reproached for representing the prevailing structures and mechanisms of power as so unified and omnipotent that resistance appears impossible, the implication is that resistance is never impossible. Perhaps not, but the fact of possibility says little about the likelihood of success. Just as containment theorists should not judge a priori that all subversion is contained, so its opponents cannot decide a priori that all power structures are subvertible; each instance, if it can be decided at all, can only be done so historically.

My own objections to containment theory are as follows:

1. Sometimes it involves a conceptual confusion: subversion, and even more transgression, necessarily *presuppose* the law, but they do not thereby necessarily *ratify* the law. A logical presupposition is elided with a contingent one. It is tempting to imagine that the converse is also true—that containment necessarily presupposes subversion. But this does not in fact follow; we should say rather that containment is always susceptible (in principle, not a priori) to subversion by the selfsame challenge it has either incorporated, imagined, or actually produced (via containment).

2. Containment theory often presupposes an agency of change too subjective and a criterion of success too total. Thus subversion or transgression are implicitly judged by impossible criteria: complete transformation of the social (i.e. revolution), or total personal liberation within, or escape from it (i.e. redemption). Their impossibility is partly guaranteed by the fact that the agency involved in both subversion and transgression is usually assumed to be a local or limited one, and often explicitly subjective or voluntarist. Recall that Sennett tells us that in disobedient dependence the transgressor fails to achieve "genuine independence or autonomy," a "real world" of his or her own or a "true alternative" to that being resisted. But what could such a utopian—not to say idealist—vision of freedom be, in actual political practice, remembering that the transgressor typically emerges from a position of marginality, subordination, and repression—i.e., *relative powerlessness?* What for example, to recall our earlier discussion, could it have been for Hall and other lesbians in 1928?

So although containment theory is not obviously essentialist, and in some respects is just the opposite in that it partly emerges from a perceived failure of essentialist radicalism, and the associated realization that the essential unified self is an illusion, it remains a theory nevertheless generated by, and in the space of, an essential absence of the subject. Hence the unwillingness of some of its advocates to concede that any particular episode of containment may be a stage in a larger process of change in which an apparent "personal" failure becomes a stage in a longer term success. In idealist culture individual failure or loss is always a kind of absolute failure or loss. But, by the same token, to accuse containment theory of being fatalistic, negative, and even cynical[4] may be to miss the point, since, some at least of those persuaded by it subscribe to a residual (philosophical) idealism that has lost its faith but not its criteria.

3. This brings me to a third objection, one which relates to each of the others, but is independently identified here because most important for my purposes: the containment theorist, like the radical humanist, overlooks the part played by contradiction and dislocation in the mutually reactive process of transgression and its control. The best way to elucidate contradiction and dislocation is through an account of what they both presuppose, and are in turn presupposed by, namely ideology.

IDEOLOGY, DISLOCATION, CONTRADICTION

> It seems we have no other test of truth and reason than the example and pattern of the opinions and customs of the country we live in. *There* is always the perfect religion, the perfect government, the perfect and accomplished manner in all things.
>
> Montaigne, *"Of Cannibals,"* Essays, *ed. Frame, 152*

Ideology typically fixes meaning, naturalizing or eternalizing its prevailing forms by putting them beyond question, and thereby also effacing the contradictions and conflicts of the social domain.[5] Materialist cultural critique aims to contest ideology in this sense, and via several strategies. First, by restoring meanings to their histories, it tries to show how meaning is powerfully controlled; Marx's formulation of how ruling classes also rule ideas remains a valid point of departure. At the same time this critique shows the historical contingency of meaning but in a way which does not then imply the arbitrariness of meaning, if by that is meant that it can be simply, subjectively, or unilaterally altered. On the contrary, to recognize that meanings are historically grounded and partly or largely (but never entirely) controlled by powerful interests is also, usually, to show them incapable of easy alterations. Even so, there is rarely a ruling bloc which controls meaning uncontested. As well as being contested by other classes or groups, it will typically also be contested from within: conflict between ruling fractions is an important factor in change, and in the destabilization of ideology.

So the critique of ideology identifies the contingency of the social (it could always be otherwise), and its potential instability (ruling groups doubly contested from without and within), but does not underestimate the difficulty of change (existing social arrangements are powerfully invested and are not easily made otherwise). The apparent need for propaganda bears out the first and second propositions, the brute force which both supplements propaganda and takes over when it fails, often successfully, bears out the third.

In highlighting the contingency of the social, the critique of ideology may also intensify its internal instabilities, doing so in part by disarticulating or disaligning existing ideological configurations. To borrow a now obsolete seventeenth-century word, the dislocation which the critique aims for is not so much an incoherence as a *dis*coherence—an incongruity verging on a meaningful contradiction.[6] In the process of being made to discohere, meanings are returned to circulation, thereby becoming the more vulnerable to appropriation, transformation, and reincorporation in new configurations. Such in part are the processes whereby the social is unmade and remade, disarticulated and rearticulated.

The critique whose objective is discoherence further seeks to reveal and maybe reactivate the contradictions which are effaced by ideology as an aspect of the control of meaning. I am using the term contradiction in its materialist sense to denote the way a social process develops according to an inner logic which simultaneously, or subsequently, helps effect its negation. Mass communication provides a commonplace example in the censorship which becomes, via the controversy it provokes, the publicist for what it seeks to repress.

Contradictions are manifested in and through representation, infecting its most elementary categories. An instance of this is the way binarism, that most static of structures, produces internal instabilities in and through the very categories it deploys *in order* to clarify, divide, and stabilize the world. Thus the opposition us/them produces the anomaly of the internal dissident. As we have seen with Wilde, and will do again in the discussion of Renaissance cross-dressing (Chapter 19), binarism affords the opportunity for transgression *in and of its own terms;* transgression is in part enabled by the very logic which would prevent it.

At a much wider level I draw on three classic paradigms of contradiction deriving from Hegel, Marx, and Freud; each paradigm has changed human history in the course of analysing it: Hegel's theory of the master/slave dialectic, Marx's theory of the fundamental contradiction between the forces and relations of production, and the Freudian proposition that the repressed returns via the mode of its repression. Each paradigm is different from the other two and, arguably, incompatible with them. However, with regard to subversion and transgression they have something in common.

In a revolutionary conjuncture contradictions may contribute to the disintegration of an existing order though only (usually) through terrible suffering, victimization, and struggle. That has to be said. In a non-revolutionary conjuncture contradictions render social process the site of contest, struggle, and change. And, again, suffering, victimization, and struggle. The contradictions which surface in times of crisis are especially revealing: they tell us that no matter how successful authority may be in its repressive strategies, there remains something potentially uncontrollable not only in authority's objects but in its enterprise, its rationale, and even its origin. In short: change, contest, and struggle are in part made possible by contradiction. But also suffering, victimization, and struggle.

TRANSGRESSIVE KNOWLEDGE

The surfacing of contradictions is enabled by and contributes to transgressive or dissident knowledge. I propose this as a category additional to those of resistance and subversion and one which might modify the way we use them. The suspicious thing about the concepts of subversion and resistance, at least as they are sometimes used in critical theory, is that they tend always to turn up where we want to find them, and never where we do not—i.e., in relation to ourselves.[7] Also, the very search for subversion sometimes presupposes a view of history as in perpetual crisis, so inherently unstable that the least resistance has instant revolutionary potential. In fact, we should never expect transgression or subversion miraculously to change the social order. If transgression subverts, it is less in terms of immediate undermining or immediate gains, than in terms of the dangerous knowledge it brings with it, or produces, or which is produced *in and by* its containment in the cultural sphere. This is the transgression that this study explores: the kind which seizes upon and exploits contradictions and which, as a political act, inspires recognition first, that the injustices of the existing social order are not inevitable—that they are, in other words, contingent and not eternal; second, that injustice is only overcome by a radical transformation of the conditions that produce and sustain it; third, that all such transformations are the cost of destructive struggle.

Thus in the case of Elizabethan and Jacobean drama (one of the principal areas to which containment theory has been applied), my own view is that it contributes not a vision of political freedom, but a searching knowledge of political domination. That knowledge is often incomplete, sometimes confused yet always dangerous. But one simply cannot slide from the dangerous knowledge to political vision, or instantly produce the second from the first. This knowledge *was* challenging: working culturally, it subverted, interrogated, and disarticulated dominant ideologies, helping to precipitate them into discoherence and crisis. But history tells us time and again that from such crisis there may emerge not freedom but brutal repression. And such repression emerges not because the subversive was only ever contained—a ruse of power to consolidate itself—but because the challenge really *was* subversive.

The dangerous knowledge produced by and in relation to transgression must include awareness of that always present, always potentially tragic dialectic between authority and resistance whereby instability becomes a force of repression much more than a force of liberation; dominant social formations can and do reconstitute themselves around the self-same contradictions that destabilize them, and change can also thereby become an impetus for reaction.

Theories of containment become somewhat more persuasive when we recognize that, like resistance, it too may work dialectically—through, for instance, the displacement of social crisis, generated within and by the dominant, onto the subordinate. Displacement often involves the demonizing of relatively powerless minorities, although it may be misleading to isolate this process from others. In abstraction there are at least three ways whereby the dominant identifies the subordinate (or the deviant) as threatening "other." The first is paranoid: the threat is imagined only; in actuality the subordinate is relatively powerless and unthreatening. The second is subversive: the threat is actually or potentially dangerous. The third involves the displacement of crisis and anxiety etc. onto the deviant. In practice some of these will typically coexist, e.g., the first with the third, or the second with the third.

The process of displacement/demonizing can never be assured of success, because it is usually a consequence of some kind of instability in the dominant (perhaps the consequence of another, effective, challenge—the second above), and because here too the demonized must be given a voice, one which can be subsequently inhabited or appropriated subversively (the second is thereby fashioned out of the third). But what stacks the odds in favour of displacement succeeding is the brute fact of the minority's relative powerlessness and probable disrepute. Also of course the struggle is usually in and for representation, especially of *how* instability is represented, and those who control the means of representation have more than a head start. The power of domination is also the power to fashion, apparently rationally but usually violently, the more "truthful" narrative.

None of this should surprise us; and to point it out is not fatalistic. Indeed it takes us back to the possibilities of resistance as already outlined: since power is dependent upon (though not reducible to) control of representation, to destabilize representation *is* potentially subversive, but this kind of resistance, like any other kind, rarely, if ever, instantly disempowers controlling interests; often it provokes them into reaction; and what then follows is by definition a contest between unequally matched contenders. Established power structures often prove resilient even, or specially, when destabilized. It is de rigueur for critics of containment theory to insist that there are always spaces and contradictions for resistance. So there are, but in saying so we would do well to remember the costs of subversion. It is too easy to appropriate the resistance of others for optimistic theoretical narratives of our own, while leaving behind the fuller histories that would complicate those narratives.

In summary then, we have to reckon not only with conflict and contradictions, but with the disavowals and displacements by which they may be reconstituted as, and in, new forces of repression. Tyranny endlessly provokes social disruption within those it subordinates, intentionally or not. That disruption is often marked by a potentially explosive combination of dangerous knowledge, political discontent, and legitimate claim. Equally certain however is that tyranny relegitimates itself in the eyes of some or many precisely by suppressing the discontent it provokes. It deploys its "superior" forces in the name of law and order; in other words it is a suppression working simultaneously in terms of brute force and intense ideological work at the level of representation. At the same time or separately, tyranny typically displaces crises generated within the dominant (for example between competing factions) onto the subordinate, whose control and extra-repression again serves to relegitimate and sometimes reintegrate the dominant. It is these aspects of the subversion/containment dialectic which seem to me to require analysis; the next chapter considers them in the context of some specific histories. The first two indicate the significance of the histories of sexual dissidence to the subversion/containment dialectic, while the third suggests a connection (via Genet) between this and other kinds of dissidence....

ART OF EXPIATION: WILDE IN PRISON

Experience of suffering in the present may turn us towards the past, maybe to discover something forgotten which contributed towards our suffering, or because every present defeat has a history of other past defeats. But it is exactly then, when the past is potentially most informative in relation to a present vulnerability, that our relation to it runs the risk of becoming most conservative: we find in the past an explanation of the present which is also a comforting deception. Often it comes in the form of "tradition," wherein we rediscover the eternal verities, and fatalistically accept the recurrence of the past as the only kind of future, possibly the best kind of future.

Tradition thereby becomes a rationalization of a painfully inadequate present, and maybe even of defeat in the present. The repressions inherent in the very notion of tradition must be recognized and confronted.

Oscar Wilde's *De Profundis*, written in prison, involves a conscious renunciation of his transgressive aesthetic and a reaffirmation of tradition as focused in the depth model of identity. This is a work which registers many things, not least Wilde's courage and his despair during imprisonment. It also shows how he responded to the unendurable by investing suffering with meaning, and this within a confessional narrative whose aim is a deepened self-awareness: "I could not bear [my sufferings] to be without meaning. Now I find hidden somewhere away in my nature something that tells me that nothing in the whole world is meaningless...that something ... is Humility." Such knowledge and such humility are achieved through deep renunciation; in effect Wilde repositions himself as the authentic, sincere subject which hitherto he had subverted: "the supreme vice is shallowness" he says in this work, and he says it more than once. And later: "The moment of repentance is the moment of initiation" (Wilde, *Letters*, 467, 425, 487).

This may be seen as that suffering into truth, that redemptive knowledge pointing to the transcendent realization of self beyond the social, so cherished within idealist culture. Those who see *De Profundis* as Wilde's most mature work, and equate maturity with renunciation and expiation, often interpret it thus. It can be regarded differently, as a containment, a tragic defeat of the kind which only ideological coercion, reinforced by overt brutality, can effect. Atonement, expiation, and renunciation—along with their "natural" medium, confession—are experienced as voluntary and self-confirming but they are in truth massively coerced through incarceration and suffering. They involve a response to suffering which has profoundly religious antecedents: Wilde survives by rescuing an imaginary spiritual autonomy from a situation which affords no actual autonomy. What Wilde says here of the law is true also of his new relationship to the culture he had hitherto transgressed: "I found myself . . . constrained to appeal to the very things against which I had always protested" *(Letters, 492–3)*.

I mentioned earlier Wilde's remark in 1898 that "something is killed in me"; prison had, he said, destroyed him body and soul. Commenting on *De Profundis*, Gide remarked that "Society knows quite well how to go about it when it wants to dispose of a man, and knows means subtler than death . . . For two years Wilde had suffered too much and too passively. His will had been broken . . . Nothing remained in his shattered life but the mournful musty odour of what he had once been" (*Oscar Wilde*, 42).

Ellmann believed that Gide never acknowledged the full extent of his debt to Wilde, and remarked also Gide's tendency to belittle Wilde as a writer.[8] It has also been suggested that Gide exaggerated the extent of Wilde's deterioration as a result of his prison experience (Gide, *Oscar Wilde*, 45). Harsh as it is, and for whatever motives, Gide's critique of *De Profundis* is to the point. He sees it as "the sobbing of a wounded man" and Wilde's affirmation of humility as a rationalization of the only retreat left to him. And it is a retreat covered over "with all the sophistries he can muster." In short, "*humility was only a pompous name that he gave to his impotence*" (*Oscar Wilde*, 50–3). But there is more to Wilde's prison experience than Gide allowed. For one thing Wilde's new-found humility was, as he told Gide later, inseparable from a pity for others which also kept him from killing himself. Both the humility and the pity were a continuation of Wilde's long-standing attraction towards the figure of Christ, most obviously in his view of Christ as the supreme artist.

But in prison the conception had changed. Some of Wilde's earlier remarks about Christ suggested what might just have been the most daring of all transgressive reinscriptions—an oppositional Christ for our own time who would blast the pieties of the conservatively religious into kingdom come and rescue Christ from his adherents.[9] Wilde used to tell several wonderfully heretical parables; Gide and W. B. Yeats, among others, recorded them. Yeats recollects Wilde telling him one day that he had been inventing a Christian heresy:

he told a detailed story, in the style of some early Father, of how Christ recovered after the Crucifixion, and escaping from the tomb, lived on for many years, the one man upon earth who knew the falsehood of Christianity. Once Saint Paul visited his town and he alone in the carpenters' quarter did not go to hear him preach. Henceforth the other carpenters noticed that, for some unknown reason, he kept his hands covered. (*Autobiographies*, 136–7)

What *De Profundis* offers is no such transgressive appropriation but a tame accommodation of self to Christian humility or, as Gide described it, an enforced retreat into it. Gide also said that it was the only retreat left to Wilde. This raises a profound question about the nature of tradition.

In *Discipline and Punish*, a book which he describes as a "correlative history of the modern soul," Foucault speaks of a crucial change taking place in Western culture towards punishment:

> The expiation that once rained down upon the body must be replaced by a punishment that acts in depth on the heart, the thoughts, the will, the inclinations. Mably formulated the principle once and for all: "Punishment, if I may put it, should strike the soul rather than the body" … A new character came on the scene, masked. It was the end of a certain kind of tragedy: comedy began, with shadow play, faceless voices, impalpable entities. (pp. 23, 16–17)

The distinction between physical coercion and "punishment which acts in depth upon the heart" is an important one, and might seem especially applicable to Wilde as I am interpreting his imprisonment: an incarceration which coerces the subject into expiation. But in Wilde's case it is not so much that incarceration is supplemented with some more insidious targeting of his soul by penal authority—clearly, and amusingly, access to the prison chaplain and the Bible did not count as such; rather, Wilde brings with him the cultural history which will facilitate his spiritual expiation, and he calls it Art. There is no actual penal targeting of *his* soul; it, or rather *the* soul, has already been massively targeted in the aesthetic and cultural traditions in which Wilde is steeped.

Foucault distinguishes between the soul of Christian theology, "born in sin and subject to punishment," and the modern soul, "born rather out of methods of punishment, supervision and constraint," creating a subject who is

> *already in himself the effect of a subjection much more profound than himself.* A "soul" inhabits him and brings him to existence, which is itself a factor in the mastery that power exercises over the body. The soul is the effect and instrument of a political anatomy; the soul is the prison of the body. (pp. 29–30, my emphasis).

I have suggested elsewhere how Foucault's "modern soul" is already anticipated in the early modern period, and in relation to Christianity. The case of Wilde further suggests how art, especially in so far as it derives from that history, is also a constitutive element in the production of a soul that is the prison of the body, producing its adherent as, in Foucault's terms, an "effect of a subjection much more profound than himself."

My account of Wilde's renunciation of his transgressive aesthetic is not reproachful, and not only because I cannot even conceive of a reproach which, given Wilde's prison experience, would not be crass. I am concerned rather with the ways that art itself, like religion, is source of both liberation and containment, of both Wilde's transgressive aesthetic and its renunciation. Wilde's imprisonment painfully exemplifies the proposition of Frankfurt School theorists like Theodor Adorno, as paraphrased by Martin Jay in an allusion to Marx which rightly connects religion and art: Jay refers to "the inherently ambiguous nature of high-culture," at once "a false consolation for real suffering and an embattled refuge of the utopian hopes for overcoming that very misery" ("Hierarchy and the Humanities," 133). It leads me to speculate that, had Wilde escaped incarceration and turned his transgressive aesthetic on Christianity, and created his oppositional Christ, it might just have been not the supreme instance of containment, not a fatal "essentialist" complicity, but his most radical work.

NOTES

1. See Greenblatt, *Renaissance Self-Fashioning,* esp. ch. 5; id., "Invisible Bullets"; Mullaney, *The Place of the Stage;* Dollimore, *Political Shakespeare,* ch. 1, and the introduction to *Radical Tragedy* (2nd edn.); Sinfield, "Power and Ideology: An Outline Theory and Sidney's *Arcadia.*" On recent work on colonial discourse, see Benita Parry's "Problems in Current Theories of Colonial Discourse," which addresses the writing of Frantz Fanon, Gayatri Spivak, Homi Bhabha, Abdul JanMohamed, and others. The subversion/containment debate is an additionally significant instance of the development described in Ch. 2 whereby theory reads history and vice versa: a theoretical framework enables a historical enquiry which eventually shows the need to modify the theoretical framework.
2. Cf. Freud, who in a discussion of transference remarks that "defiance signifies dependence as much as obedience does, though with a 'minus' instead of a 'plus' sign before it" (Freud, *Introductory Lectures on Psychoanalysis,* i. 495).
3. It is described in Anderson's *Considerations on Western Marxism.*
4. Ryan, *Shakespeare,* 8, and Lentricchia, *Ariel and the Police,* 99.
5. To use ideology in this specific and limited sense does not assume the non-ideological to be a value-free scientific discourse. On the contrary, I adhere to this limited sense of the concept in order to indicate that a materialist criticism is always finally *also* an ethical perspective. So my usage precisely differs from that which would describe as ideological *any* system of values. Thus Sumner in *Reading Ideologies* defines ideology as "the basic or simple elements (the ideas, images, impressions, notions etc) of any form of social consciousness" (20). To designate thus any affirmation of value to be as ideological as (e.g.) a position which seeks to naturalize or universalize its own authority is to rob the concept of ideology of its capacity to distinguish between these crucially different positions. Thus the view that homosexuals are naturally inferior to heterosexuals is (in my sense) ideological; the view that homosexuals are equal with heterosexuals, and deserving of equal rights in law is not, resting rather on an openly admitted ethical commitment to equality (from which the practice of a materialist/political criticism arises). For a philosophical defence of the limited notion of ideology adopted here see Bhaskar, *Scientific Realism and Human Emancipation,* ch. 2. Bhaskar sees as mistaken the development in Marxism which uses the concept of ideology "positively" to express "the values or world view of a

particular social class (group or sometimes milieu)." Bhaskar also rejects the extension of the concept "to embrace the entire cultural sphere, understood as more or less mystificatory" (p. 242).

6. The *OED* cites Hooker from 1600: "An opinion of discoherence … between the justice of God and the state of men in this world."

7. In Greenblatt's famous adaptation of Kafka, "There is subversion, no end of subversion, only not for us" ("Invisible Bullets," 46).

8. Ellmann, *Oscar Wilde: Critical Essays,* 4; see also Ellmann's "Corydon and Ménalque," 84–5, 90, and *passim,* and his 1987 biography, *Oscar Wilde,* 336–41.

9. Interestingly Gide, shortly after his encounter with Wilde in Algiers, contemplated something similar—a book called *Christianisme contre le Christ.*

10. Wilde's encounters with prison chaplains make dismal, farcical reading. One chaplain suggested that Wilde ended up in prison because he had omitted to conduct morning prayers in his household; another, suspecting Wilde of masturbation, wrote to the authorities that "perverse sexual practices are again getting the mastery over him"; to a third Wilde complained that he could not see the sky from his cell window. The chaplain replied that his mind should not "dwell on the clouds, but on Him who is above the clouds." Wilde called him a damned fool and threw him out of the cell (Ellmann, *Oscar Wilde,* 454, 464, 466–7).

BIBLIOGRAPHY

Anderson, Perry, *Considerations on Western Marxism* (London: NLB, 1976).

Belsey, Catherine, "Towards Cultural History" *Textual Practice,* 3 (1989), 159–72.

Bhaskar, Roy, *Scientific Realism and Human Emancipation* (London: Verso, 1986).

Dollimore, Jonathan and Sinfield, Alan (eds.), *Political Shakespeare: New Essays in Cultural Materialism* (Manchester: Manchestes University Press, 1985).

Ellman, R., "Corydon and Ménalque," in *Golden Codgers: Biographical Speculations* (London: Oxford University Press, 1973), 81–100.

———. *Oscar Wilde* (London: Hamish Hamilton, 1987).

Foucault, Michel, *Discipline and Punish: The Birth of the Prison,* trans. Alan Sheridan (New York: Pantheon, 1977).

———. *The History of Sexuality,* i: *An Introduction* (New York: Vintage Books [1978], 1980).

Freud, Sigmund, *The Pelican Freud Library,* 15 vols., general ed. Angela Richards (Harmondsworth: Penguin, 1974–86): i: *Introductory Lectures on Psychoanalysis.*

Gide, André, *Oscar Wilde,* trans. Bernard Frechtman (London: William Kimber, 1951).

Greenblatt, Stephen, *Renaissance Self-Fashioning from More to Shakespeare* (Chicago: University of Chicago Press, 1980).

———. "Invisible Bullets: Renaissance Authority and its Subversion," in J. Dollimore and A. Sinfield (eds.), *Political Shakespeare* (Manchester: Manchester University Press, 1985).

Jay, Martin, "Hierarchy and the Humanities: The Radical Implications of a Conservative Idea," *Telos,* 62 (Winter 1984–5), 131–44.

Lientricchia, Frank, *Ariel and the Police: Michel Foucault, William James, Wallace Stevens* (Brighton: Harvester Press, 1988).

Montaigne, Michel, *Essays,* ed. D. M. Frame (Stanford, Calif.: Stanford University Press, 1958).

Mullaney, Steven, *The Place of the Stage: Licence, Play and Power in Renaissance England* (Chicago: University of Chicago Press, 1988).

Parry, Benita, "Problems in Current Theories of Colonial Discourse", *Oxford Literary Review,* 9 (1987), 27–58.

Ryan, Kiernan, *Shakespeare* (Harvester New Readings) (Hemel Hempstead: Harvester Wheatsheaf, 1989).

Sennett, Richard, *Authority* (London: Secker, 1980).

Sinfield, Alan, "Power and Ideology: An Outline Theory and Sidney's *Arcadia,*" *ELH* 52. (1985), 259–77.

Sumner, Colin, *Reading Ideologies: An Investigation into the Marxist Theory of Ideology and Law* (New York: Academic Press, 1979).

Wilde, Oscar, *The Letters of Oscar Wilde,* ed. Rupert Hart-Davis (New York: Harcourt Brace & World, 1962).

———, *De Profundis* [1897], in *The Letters of Oscar Wilde,* ed. Rupert Hart-Davis (New York: Harcourt Brace & World, 1962).

Williams, Raymond, *Marxism and Literature* (Oxford: Oxford University Press, 1977).

Yeats, W.B., *Autobiographies* (London: Macmillan, 1955).

THE CONTRADICTORY POLITICS OF POPULAR CULTURE: RESISTING, SELLING OUT, AND "HOT SEX" (1993)

TRICIA ROSE

In her book The Hip Hop Wars: What We Talk about When We Talk about Hip Hop, *cultural studies scholar Rose asks questions about agency that are central to cultural studies and Marxist studies and that are similar to the questions that Gayatri C. Spivak asks in "Can the Subaltern Speak?" As a scholar and admirer of hip hop, Rose believes that most popular hip hop has degraded over the years, centering more and more on what she calls the tragic trinity of "gangstas, pimps, and hoes," degrading the people, particularly African American people, that it supposedly celebrates. She tries to understand who makes the decisions, who is the agent, when someone decides to listen to gangsta, pimp, and ho hip hop. In the process of asking about agency, Rose considers the cultural setting of hip hop, including the economic setting, and not just the setting of its listeners but also the setting of its producers and, not the least, its distributors (the music industry, the radio stations). She sees the site of agency as dispersed across more agents than the individual listeners who think and to some extent are made to think that they make their own decisions when they choose from a menu that in many ways others provide for them. Thus the supposedly direct expression of hip hop is mediated by many cultural agents and is not just the individual, personal choice of musicians or listeners. Similarly, in this shorter essay (a response to questions at a symposium) Rose explores the contradictory politics of resistance and complicity in popular culture. Sometimes, she argues, popular culture that seems to resist one kind of cultural problem, such as racism, encourages another kind, such as consumerism or sexism. We can appreciate the resistance to racism while abhorring the sexism, and we may wonder if the sexism undermines the resistance to racism. The desire to see popular culture and art as all at one extreme or the other, as heroically resistant to oppression or as quick to cave into it, can therefore, Rose argues, oversimplify its contradictory politics.*

(Rose's essay is untitled; the present title was supplied by the editor.)

Since my work often deals with contemporary popular culture, rap music and hip hop culture in particular, I am often asked what I think of the latest hip hop controversy. I am called on to comment on the most recent popular trend or conflict anywhere—at parties, at conferences, by the coffee machine. This, of course, has kept me quite busy over the past few years. For example, the cryptic and anti-Semitic lyrics of Chuck D's "Welcome to the Terrordome" followed me around like the plague. "So what do you think of PE's anti-Semitism?" people would ask, as if they had caught me in a trap. The 2 Live Crew and Luke Skywalker's public defense of their (t)horny work nearly drove me out of academia and back into public housing management. "Tricia," friends and colleagues would ask, "you can't possibly defend 2 Live Crew's disgusting and violent lyrics as parody, *too*? Could you?" A few years ago, a group of feminist undergraduate activists inquired pointedly: "How could you think of Salt-n-Pepa as feminists? They wear makeup, high heels, and lipstick!" Imagine that—lipstick. More recently, I have ducked comments about Ice-T and "Cop Killer." "By pulling the controversial 'Cop Killer' off his heavy metal band's debut album, Ice-T is bowing to corporate and law enforcement pressure, isn't he? … I thought he was committed to cultural resistance." And then they add casually, "What do you think?" And so it goes.

Buried in these paraphrased exchanges are standards for politically progressive and consistent popular culture expression. Also concealed are utopian notions of the popular culture terrain as a site of absolute resistance to dominant institutions and discourses, as if cultural workers' identities, status, and popularity were derived from a total immunity to political and social contradictions. If a popular culture figure's work exhibits sexism, anti-Semitism, or bows to institutional pressure in any way, then, for many left critics, his/her name is withdrawn from the venerable log of "known politically resistant cultural workers" with a disappointed sigh.

It is my hope to persuade you that this "zero sum method of culture analysis" (by this I mean notions of popular cultural resistance as an all-or-nothing proposition) is a no-win scenario. Cultural expressions are rarely, if ever, consistently and totally oppositional. One would have to have rather deeply rose-tinted lenses to miss the abundant and persistent existence of "nonprogressive elements" throughout the history of cultural expressions—popular, state-sponsored or avant garde, black or otherwise. For the most part, popular expressions are contradictory and partial forms of cultural resistance. And so, Chuck D's critical interventions against racial oppression coupled with his anti Semitic comments; Luke Skywalker's challenge to community standards and free speech rhetoric coupled with his misogynist visions; Ice-T's frontal assault on censorship followed by his subsequent retreat; and NWA's antipolice stance along with its violent misogynist fantasies are not exceptions but, instead, represent the messy and contradictory nature of all cultural expression.

A quest for a seamless web of resistant or oppositional popular practice is a misguided journey fraught with romantic and problematic notions of resistance and opposition. Such a quest not only imagines absolute resistance, but also avoids grappling with the reality of resistance and the muddy waters which often surround it. Rather than embark on these expeditions we must explore and critique the contradictions in popular expression. I am not saying that we should simply acknowledge them ("Hey, Dr. Dre fights police repression and is a sexist pig, what do you want from me?"), but that we should confront them— incorporate them into an analysis which explores how and why they retain currency—not simply dismiss them because they do not measure up to an imaginary standard of politically consistent expression.

In what follows I would like to explore two examples of hip hop-related cultural expressions/symbols which are generally resistive but have important contradictory and regressive effects. They are, first, the resurgence of Malcolm X as a black cultural symbol and, second, the winter 1992–93 hip hop guerrilla fashion accessory—the face mask.

X MARKS THE CAP

Malcolm X's currency in the mass media is both a moment of intense commodification and a very clear act of collective historical counter-memory and oppositional identity formation for black youth in the U.S. The revival of his role, image, and presence in American culture is clearly counter to dominant representations of Malcolm over the last twenty-five years, which were infrequent and frighteningly manipulated. For the most part the process of naming Martin "the king" resulted in the erasure of Malcolm and his intellectual legacy from the popular/political history of the 1960s.

Through rap lyrics and video imagery, Public Enemy, KRS-One, Intelligent Hoodlum, Paris, and other rappers brought Malcolm X into the spotlight for black teenagers in the latter half of the 1980s. These rappers sampled and looped various sections of his speeches, and some rapped them as part of their own lyrics. It would be an understatement to say that prior to and during these late eighties' interventions, Malcolm X was rarely/barely conjured in media black history sound bytes. During the eighties I heard a number of teachers' horror stories about black teenagers' inquiries regarding this political character named "Malcolm Ten." Among other things, this speaks to the severity of Malcolm's erasure from American history and from the popular imagination of sixties black resistance movements. It was decided that Martin Luther King and integrationist dreams were to be the remembered facets of "our" memories of the sixties. And so, Malcolm X disappeared; a magic trick that took a lot of work—particularly given his substantial currency among black Americans and left activists in general. Clearly, his absence was achieved not via benign neglect, but through malignant and aggressive dominant institutional attempts (e.g., in public school textbooks) to erase him and his legacy. Black teens picked up on this, sensed that his absence was strategic, "knew" that a collective memory of him would be critical to their attempts at resistance. By forcing his presence back into high school curricula and raising questions about his ideas, this generation of black urban youth forced Malcolm and his forthright and aggressively black politics into the public spotlight.

This glowing interpretation of how Malcolm reemerged into national consciousness sounds nothing short of heroic. But (there is always a but) there is another, less glamorous side to this: the *way* Malcolm has entered the public arena. (And here I am not even referring to the selective resurrection of his ideas or the way Malcolm's political transformation has been transformed.) Malcolm's entrance into the public arena has been propelled by consumption and commodification of his iconic power. Not surprising, this is a serious problem for more traditional left scholars/activists. Lately "Malcolm X" is everywhere: he's on air fresheners, potato chip bags, on T-shirts, sneakers, and baseball caps. He's being "worn" by whites in rich suburban enclaves. Could there be a worse "resurrection" of Malcolm than as a fashion statement for the white middle class? Isn't this a sign of his demise, a sign of his (re)erasure?

I think his current status in popular culture and politics is a crystallization of the kinds of contradictions with which we must come to terms. We cannot say that Malcolm X is "just" a commercially orchestrated object when his (re)presence has been fueled by a culturally resistant context that uses commodities to oppositional ends (albeit not unfettered). Nor can we rightfully say that this is an erasure of him when he was virtually invisible (an invisibility that was facilitated by publishing industries, educational institutions, and popular mass media at all levels) prior to this "commercial" intervention. How do we deal with this sort of contradiction? How do we interpret the resistive and incorporated facets of Malcolm X's contemporary presence without falling into old and blinding binary oppositions between resistance and cooptation? This, it seems to me, is the central question for people who want to study popular culture and processes of resistive and progressive collective memory formation. (By the way, some of my lefty friends said they were living with this tension in Malcolm's contemporary identity *until* the ubiquitous X was on a bag of barbecue chips—that's where they drew the line.)

Inside this commodification, wearers/sharers of his image, from a variety of subject positions, use his symbolism to mean a number of different things—myself included. When I was in Cuba two years ago, I gave exiled Black Liberation Army leader Assata Shakuur my "By Any Means Necessary" T-shirt which featured a long strong black arm pulling up the fragile hand of another black body from the invisible space beneath the fabric. I was thrilled to be able to give her something of emotional and political value and she seemed very pleased to accept it. She had asked me where I "had it made" a few days before I gave it to her and seemed genuinely excited about what it might suggest. The exchange between us was complex and powerful for me. And yet, at the same time, I was aware of the contradictory politics of our interaction. Shakuur is exiled, while I can move freely; I give her a T-shirt most likely not manufactured and distributed by blacks (as Malcolm might have liked), and yet perhaps she can use this visualization/interpretation of his most famous slogan to organize Afro-Cubans, to let them know that they are part of a larger process of black liberation. I was fraught with knowledge of the ways in which such counterhegemonic exchanges are continually remade, recast, and manipulated by dominant forces.

HOT SEX

My second example concerns a recent fashion trend in hip hop style: the insulated stretch face mask. This mask, which looks like a skier's cousin to a hockey goalie mask or an s/m leather face mask, has really taken hold among urban b-boys this past winter. The mask is usually worn halfway up the face— it is very confining and too hot to wear full face in New York City—but you know what it is when you see it hanging around the chin. There is also a half-face version which attaches around the face below the eyes. Seeing this mask produces a succession of complicated and contradictory responses. On the one hand, it makes me think of hockey, but only for a second or so. The next thing that comes to mind is the urban guerrilla, the postindustrial urban warrior who wears an "all weather" mask for "all weather" occasions. It has a very rugged, outback sort of thing. It is a super-masculine accessory that signifies the confidence, physical prowess, and power associated with the hunter. Add other hip hop winter gear: a hoody, snooty, parka, and Tims, and you've got a serious arctic urban guerrilla on your hands.[1]

Then, I begin to think about why this mask is popular among black teenagers.[2] I think about the overall gear and its role as protection against the psychological and physical elements, rather than as a climatic shield. This mask masks one's identity, perhaps also masking young black males' disturbing lack of public confidence which results from relentless physical and psychological surveillance. This generation of black males and females knows that its rights to public space and services are in a permanent state of suspension. The males especially (to borrow a phrase from Cornel West) know what "blacks cannot not know": that they are—categorically—understood as a dangerous element, as outsiders in their own territory, with no place else to go. This mask provides a physical buffer zone which mediates against public interpolation, shields them from others' hostility (police rifle sites, car doors being suddenly locked, white men clutching their "women" [sic], white women clutching their purses). It temporarily protects them from the perennial rather than seasonal elements.

But this mask also masks vulnerability, hides the fear that knowing who you are to them produces, a fear that produces more anger and hostility. Behind this mask, you can prevent yourself from being seen easily and clearly; in your anonymity you exercise power—momentary but significant. This is particularly valuable when you know you are always/already in the rifle's sight; when you are usually the hunted.

At a more general level, this mask is also part of recent horror film imagery. You don't have to be a horror film freak to know that this sort of face mask has a great deal of popular culture currency from films like *Friday the 13th*, the cult classic *Texas Chainsaw Massacre*, and *Silence of the Lambs*. In horror film language this mask says: "I am a psychotic murderer. Not only will I probably torture and kill you, but I will do this for pleasure rather than for money." The specter of this character has clear gender implications. Horror films usually involve extreme and often sexual violence against women at the hands of men. Now this mask conjures my distinctly female fear of the disguised, physically powerful, and "psychotic" male figure who can rape me and then escape without identification. (At this point, I hear a small voice in my head: "Officer, maybe this description will help: he was wearing Timberland boots, a Triple Fat brand goose down overcoat, a snooty, and ... ummm, a *face mask*.")

Part of this mask's b-boy popularity stems from Q-Tip's appearance in the music video for "Hot Sex," a song from the soundtrack to the Eddie Murphy film *Boomerang*. A bald-headed Q-Tip wore this mask full face throughout the entire video, which was staged in a grand yet empty theater decorated in blood red velvet curtains, red seats, and red carpeting. Much of the footage captured Q-Tip rapping from the stage and in the aisles while scenes from *Boomerang* were projected onto the screen behind him, sometimes behind a sheer curtain. Accompanied by dissonant and dark beats, "Hot Sex" tells the tale of a Tribe Called Quest's prowess mostly by describing how they can get "hot sex on a platter" from the girl-friends of other men who think they have their women "locked up," or "in the pocket" (sic). In one passage, Q-Tip says he's "the undercover brother—dump your ho' in the trunk."[3]

I must confess that when I first began to see this mask on kids in New York City, rape and fear of physical domination were the *very first* things that came to mind, and this was long before I saw the video. As a black woman who is committed to exploring black cultural resistance, I responded by pushing this intense and focused fear to the back of my mind and trying to assure myself that terrorizing black women was not the primary motivation for this fashion statement's popularity. But still, I felt that this mask was somehow taking things a bit too far. In conversations with a black male friend, cultural critic and artist Arthur Jafa, I found myself unwilling to explore anything else but my initial reaction: this mask, in this context, was a hostile symbolic act toward black women. This is not to say that I was *unaware* of the range of contradictory symbolic meanings embedded in the mask as a hip hop sign. It is to say that as a form of self-protection I was refusing to entertain these other interpretations. In an attempt to demonstrate my awareness of these other crucial interpretive contexts, I gave A. J. a multifaceted analysis of the other ways the mask might be interpreted, not unlike what has transpired here. In the process, I began to realize that my desire to reject these more politically resistive and/or sympathetic readings was completely connected to my initial interpretation of this mask as a sexually violent symbol. My frustration centered on the point at which these two lines of analysis intersected.

I was angry and frustrated because I felt that to explore the anger and pain associated with young black masculine identity seemed to involve giving permission to or excusing the female-directed anger and violence embedded in this symbol. Why should I explore, re-center, male pain at my expense, at the expense of black women in general? How can I manage and explore these tensions, remain focused on the point of intersection, and refuse the magnetic pull toward either of the binary oppositional alternatives that hover in the distance?

These sorts of contradictions are at work at the same time and they are in constant motion. Even in this relatively small symbol, we need to deal with the regressive elements at the same time that we attempt to figure out *what range of forces they serve*. I'm not suggesting that we just accept these regressive forces as "reality" and offer black male experiences as justification. Along these lines, I have little or no patience for the "I'm reflecting reality, not producing realities" argument sometimes offered by rappers who spin tales of ghetto "cultural pathology" to the delight of the Right. On the other hand, sewing up Q-Tip's, Ice-T's, Ice Cube's, or Bushwick Bill's mouth will not bind the ruptures in the social fabric which have been orchestrated by the state; such censorship instead hinders a collective way of thinking about such realities which, in turn, hinders a collective way of organizing against such realities.

In the terms offered in the symposium questions, I think it is crucial that we acknowledge the fact that all cultural forms of resistance, *popular or otherwise,* carry "contradictory forces" as a starting point for talking about the complexity of their relationships with audiences and communities. (I'm erasing the phrase "political impurity" from question 2 and replacing it here with "contradictory forces," because purity and impurity have troubling political and ideological legacies. Also, deploying the term "impurity" implies that we can take "purity" seriously.) We need to explore the ways in which various subjectivities can produce blind spots and/or useful reappropriations of dominant ideas that may not fit into contemporary theoretical paradigms for cultural resistance. However, we must also face—head on—those political and cultural expressions and ideas which we find regressive, problematic, and unacceptable— interrogate these articulations, interrogate our expectations and our relationships to them.

NOTES

1. A hoody is a hooded sweatshirt or jacket; a snooty is a skullcap-style hat; and Tims is short for Timberland boots.
2. These masks are also worn by Latino b-boys who are also under severe police surveillance, but given my focus I am not exploring that here.
3. A Tribe Called Quest, "Hot Sex," *Boomerang* soundtrack (LaFace Records, 1992).

THE EMERGENCE OF ENVIRONMENTAL CRITICISM (2005)

LAWRENCE BUELL

Buell surveys the history of environmental literary studies. He divides environmental criticism roughly into a first and a second wave, following a loose analogy to earlier and later feminism and the not-exactly-linear movement of racial and ethnic studies from first-wave celebrations to more skeptically second-wave complications. As he hints early in this essay, Buell's work, like other ecocriticism, can fit loosely within a broad definition of cultural studies.Still,here and elsewhere Buell distances his work from new historicism and from cultural studies, and perhaps ecocriticism does not fit neatly under any of the rubrics that organize this volume.

Until the end of the twentieth century, such a book as this could not have been written. The environmental turn in literary and cultural studies emerged as a self-conscious movement little more than a dozen years ago. Since then it has burgeoned, however. A tell-tale index is the growth within the last decade of the Association for the Study of Literature and Environment (ASLE) from a localized North American ferment into a thousand-member organization with chapters worldwide from the UK to Japan and Korea to Australia–New Zealand. The "Who's listening?" question which nagged me when I first entered the arena of environmental criticism has given way to "How can I keep pace with all this new work?"

To burgeon is not necessarily to mature or to prevail. "Ecocriticism," the commonest omnibus term for an increasingly heterogeneous movement, has not yet achieved the standing accorded (say) to gender or postcolonial or critical race studies. Eventually I believe it will; but it is still finding its path, a path bestrewn by obstacles both external and self-imposed.

At first sight, the belatedness and liminality of the recent environmental turn in literary-critical studies seems strange. For creative art and critical reflection have always taken a keen interest in how the material world is engaged, absorbed, and reshaped by theory, imagination, and *techne*. Humankind's earliest stories are of earth's creation, of its transformation by gods or by human ingenuity's "second nature," as Cicero first called it—tales that frame environmental ethics in varied ways. In at least one case they may have significantly influenced the course of world history. The opening chapters of Genesis, the first book in Hebrew and Christian scripture, have been blamed as the root cause of western technodomination-ism: God's mandate to man to take "dominion" over the creatures of the sea and earth and "subdue" them. Others retort that this thesis misreads both history and the biblical text: that "cultivate" is the more crucial term, implying pious stewardship rather than transforma-tion.[1] My point in mentioning this debate is not to arbitrate it but merely to call attention to the antiquity and durability of environmental discourse—and its variety both within indi-vidual thought traditions and worldwide. By contrast to either reading of Judaeo-Christian thought, for example, Mayan mythography represents the gods as fashioning human beings after several false starts from corn gathered with the help of already-created animals, thereby symbolizing "the collective survival that must exist between humans, plants, and animals," whereas in Mäori cosmology, creation is an ongoing process: "humanity and all things of the natural world are always emerging, always unfolding."[2]

All this goes to show that if environmental criticism today is still an emergent discourse it is one with very ancient roots. In one form or another the "idea of nature" has been a dominant or at least residual concern for literary scholars and intellectual historians ever since these fields came into being.[3] That legacy calls into question just how marked a break from previous practice the contemporary movement is. What can be really new and differ-ent, much less "radical," about an area of inquiry that for more than a century has been an eminently safe and reputable pursuit? For one who knows the history of the permutations of critical thought about Romantic poetry, on the face of it early ecocriticism's insistence—in the face of then-fashionable poststructuralist and new historicist approaches—that Wordsworth was a poet of nature after all has a suspiciously retro, neo-Victorian ring, even when the argument is recast to emphasize not just love of nature but proto-ecological knowledge and environmentalist commitment. This is a specter that has bedeviled ecocriticism from its birth: the suspicion that it might not boil down to much more than old-fashioned enthusi-asms dressed up in new clothes.

Yet the marked increase and sophistication of environmentality as an issue within liter-ary and cultural studies since the 1980s is a countervailing fact, despite the wrangling over what it means and what should be done about it that will surely continue for some time to come. It testifies to the need to correct somehow against the marginalization of environmental issues in most versions of critical theory that dominated literary and cultural studies through the 1980s—even as "the environment" was becoming an increasingly salient public concern and a major topic of research in science, economics, law, and public policy—and certain humanities fields as well, notably history and ethics. In the book on Wordsworth that inaugurated British ecocriticism, Jonathan Bate framed the problem with the pardonable zeal of the insurgent: Geoffrey "Hartman threw out nature to bring us the transcendent imagination; [Jerome] McGann throws out the transcendent imagination to bring us history and society," after which Alan Liu categorically denies that there is such a thing as nature in Wordsworth except as "'constituted by acts of political definition'" (Bate 1991: 8, 18). Those prior imbalances, notwithstanding the brilliance with which they were argued, invited correction. Since then, indeed, British Romanticism has proven to be as fertile and varied ground for ecocritical revisionism as it was for previous critical revolutions from phenomenology through new historicism (e.g., Kroeber 1994; McKusick 2000; Morton 1994, 2000; Oerlemans 2002; Fletcher 2004; Hess 2004).

The imbalance to which Bate objected actually predated the late twentieth-century revolution in critical theory that began with Hartman's generation. My own literary education bears witness to this. As a schoolchild in the northeastern United States, I imbibed a commonly taught, watered-down version of Aristotelian poetic theory that defined "setting" as one of literature's four basic building blocks other than language itself—"plot," "character," and "theme" being the others. But the term was vaguely defined and required nothing more in practice than a few perfunctory sentences about the locale of the work in question. In such rare cases as Thomas Hardy's *The Return of the Native*, we were given to understand that a nonhuman entity like Egdon Heath might be a book's main "character" or agential force. Otherwise, "setting" was mere backdrop for the human drama that really counted, even in texts like Wordsworth's "Tintern Abbey" or Thoreau's *Walden*. Although I first read them at roughly the same time as the controversy provoked by the serialization of Rachel Carson's *Silent Spring* in *The New Yorker*, and although my late father was fighting Carson-like battles as a member of our local planning commission, I doubt that any of this would have much affected my early *literary* training even if my instructors had taken notice of it. One of them assigned us a section of her previous bestseller *The Sea Around Us* (1950) as an example of mastery of the art of descriptive language. A description of trying on a suit of new clothes or of beholding oneself in a mirror would have served equally well.

Symptomatic of the mentality I assimilated was US writer Eudora Welty's demure apology at the start of her luminous essay on "Place in Fiction" for place as "one of the lesser angels that watch over the racing hand of fiction" relative to "character, plot, symbolic meaning," and especially "feeling, who in my eyes carries the crown, soars highest of them all and rightly relegates place into the shade" (Welty 1970: 125).

Why do the discourses of environment seem more crucial today than they did to Welty in the 1940s? The most obvious answer is that during the last third of the twentieth century "the environment" became front-page news. As the prospect of a sooner-or-later apocalypse by unintended environmental disaster came to seem likelier than apocalypse by deliberate nuclear *machismo*, public concern about the state and fate of "the environment" took increasing hold, initially in the West but now worldwide. The award of the 2004 Nobel Peace Prize to Kenyan environmental activist Wangari Maathai is, at this moment of writing, the latest sign of an advancing level of concern, which the "war against terror" since September 11, 2001 has upstaged but by no means suppressed. Underlying the advance has been a growing malaise about modern industrial society's inability to manage its unintended environmental consequences that Ulrich Beck, the Rachel Carson of contemporary social theory, calls "reflexive modernization," meaning in particular the fear that even the privileged classes of the world inhabit a global "risk society" whose hazards cannot be anticipated, calculated, and controlled, much less escaped (Beck, Giddens, and Lash 1994: 6; cf. Beck 1986; Willms 2004).

Environmental issues, in turn, have become an increasing provocation both for artists and for academics, giving rise within colleges and universities to cross-disciplinary environmental studies programs often galvanized by student demand as much as by faculty research agendas. Though natural and social scientists have so far been the major players in such programs, considerable numbers of humanists have also been drawn in, many of them bringing preexisting commitments of a citizenly kind to bear in environmentally directed teaching and scholarship. Indeed, many nonhumanists would agree—often more readily than doubt-prone humanists do—that issues of vision, value, culture, and imagination are keys to today's environmental crises at least as fundamental as scientific research, technological know-how, and legislative regulation. If we feel tokenized as players in environmental dialogue, both within the university and without, that may be more because of our own internal disputes and uncertainties about role, method, and voice than because of any stigma attached to the "impracticality" of the humanities either within academe or the wider world.

FIN-DE-SIÉCLE FERMENT: A SNAPSHOT

Literature scholars who took the environmental turn in the 1980s and 1990s found themselves entering a mind-expanding though also vertiginous array of cross-disciplinary conversations—with life scientists, climatologists, public policy specialists, geographers, cultural anthropologists, landscape architects, environmental lawyers, even applied mathematicians and environmental engineers—conversations that tended to produce or reinforce disenchantment with the protocols of their home discipline. Two opposite reactions arising from this state of ferment that look more antipodal than they may actually have been were resistance to prevalent models of critical theory and the quest for theory.

A number of early ecocritics looked to the movement chiefly as a way of "rescuing" literature from the distantiations of reader from text and text from world that had been ushered in by the structuralist revolution in critical theory. These ecocritical dissenters sought to reconnect the work of (environmental) writing and criticism with environmental experience—meaning in particular the *natural* world.[4] I recall an intense exchange at the first international conference of the still-new ASLE in Fort Collins, Colorado, over the question of whether nature writing could be properly taught without some sort of outdoor *practicum* component, preferably *in situ*. Environmental literacy was seen as indispensable to such a pedagogy.[5] No less striking was the alliance at that gathering—an alliance that continues—between critics, writer-practitioners, and environmental activists. (These can be overlapping categories, of course.) The ecocritical movement's primary publications, the American *ISLE* (International Studies in Literature and Environment) and its younger British counterpart *Green Letters,* are remarkable among scholarly association journals for their mixture of scholarly, pedagogical, creative, and environmentalist contributions.

The conception of ecocriticism as an alliance of academic critics, artists, environmental educators, and green activists reinforced the penchant within the movement for decrying "the metropolitan tendency in literary studies towards high theory and abstraction," as one Australian ecocritic put it.[6] This undertone of complaint, in turn, fed mainstream academic critics' suspicions that ecocriticism was more an amateur enthusiasm than a legitimate new "field." Another ground of skepticism might have been the movement's provenance as an offshoot of an association of second-level prestige whose principal support base lay mostly outside the most prominent American university literature departments. For the Western American Literature Association to presume to instigate a revolution in literary studies seemed to some observers the equivalent of a new school of criticism in China being fomented from some outpost in that country's own "far west," Sinjiang.

But cross-disciplinary and extra-academic alliances also have had the positive and permanent advantages of stretching the new movement's horizons beyond the academy and of provoking a self examination of premises that has intensified as the movement has evolved beyond an initial concentration on nature-oriented literature and on traditional forms of environmental education to take into account urban as well as rural loci and environmental justice concerns as well as nature preservation. From the start, calls "to reconnect the study of literature with the living earth" have focused participants' attention on the connection between academic work and public citizenship and advocacy.[7] The symbiosis between artistic accomplishment and environmentalist commitment in such writers as the American poets Gary Snyder and A. R. Ammons—to name but two among the scores of writers worldwide of whom the same might be said—has enriched the movement conceptually as well as aesthetically.[8]

Up to a point early ecocriticism's appeal to the authority of experiential immersion and the efficacy of practice over against the authority of "theory" reprised first-wave race, feminism, and sexuality studies ("Speaking as a woman/an African American/a gay white male, I…"). But an obvious difference between ecocriticism and emergent discourses on behalf of silenced or disempowered social groups was in the kind of identitarian claims that could plausibly be made in that context. One can speak as an environmentalist, one can "speak a word for Nature, for absolute freedom and wildness," as Thoreau did,[9] but self-evidently no human can speak *as* the environment, *as* nature, *as* a nonhuman animal. How do we know what it is like to be a bat, philosopher Thomas Nagel asks rhetorically, in a celebrated article.[10] Well, we don't. At most we can attempt to speak from the standpoint of understanding humans to be part of what Aldo Leopold called "the biotic community"—attempt, that is, to speak in cognizance of human being as ecologically or environmentally embedded. Although there is something potentially noble about human attempts to speak ecocentrically against human dominationism, unless one proceeds very cautiously there soon becomes something quixotic and presumptuous about it too. All too often, arguments about curbing species self-interest boil down to setting limits you mostly want to see other people observe.

This is where the distanced abstractions of the kind of theory ecocriticism initially reacted against can show to advantage. Take, for example, Michel Foucault's conception of "biopolitics"—the endeavor "to rationalize the problems presented to governmental practice by the phenomena characteristic of a group of living human beings constituted as a population: health, sanitation, birthrate, longevity, race" (Foucault 1994: 73). Early ecocriticism would have been likely to bristle at this lumping together of such heterogeneous categories under the sign of political practice; but one also needs an inner voice like Foucault's as reminder that the "who" that engages in ecocritical work is neither as individuated nor as extricated from social institutions as one might wish to think. One of the main differences between what I shall be calling first-wave and second-wave environmental criticism is that the revisionists have absorbed this sociocentric perspective to a greater degree.[11]

Given that it is self-evidently more problematic for an ecocritic to presume to speak for "nature" than for (say) a black critic to speak for black experience, one might suppose that early ecocriticism would have been driven quickly to pass through the appeal-to-experience stage into a discourse of theoretical reflection. Yet if your ultimate interest is the remediation of humankind's alienation from the natural world, you may well decide on principle to resist the abstractifications of theoretical analysis, indeed to resist standard modes of formal argument altogether in favor of a discourse where critical reflection is embedded within narratives of encounter with nature. A number of ecocritics have preferred this alternative path of "narrative scholarship," as Scott Slovic (1994) has called it.[12] A prominent example is pioneer ecocritic and recent ASLE president John Elder. Elder's first book (1985) was a largely analytical study of nature poetry and the conception of nature–culture relations more generally in the light of Whiteheadian process philosophy. But he cast his next in the form of a series of semi-autobiographical narratives of place, which are put in conversation with Robert Frost's "Directive," a poem of imagined return to a decayed farmstead in the same upper New England region (Elder 1998). We find a similar approach to the enlistment of environmental psychology in former ASLE president Ian Marshall's (2003) stirring book of mountaineering narratives and the conceptualization of islanded solitude in ecophilosopher Kathleen Dean Moore's (2004) narrative of an Alaskan summer.

Of course, there is nothing inherently untheoretical about rejecting standard modes of critical argument—Nietzsche and Derrida did that too—or in narrative scholarship as such. It can yield a higher degree of critical self-consciousness than otherwise, as the narrative-reflexive turn in cultural anthropology demonstrates. Anna Lowenhaupt Tsing's *In the Realm of the Diamond Queen* (1993), for instance, offers an account of the endangered Meratus peoples of Kalimantan (Indonesia) in which the author's portrayal of her halting acquisition of native environmental literacy plays a crucial part, as she skillfully weaves back and forth between her outsider's position in relation to her informants and the marginality of the Meratus themselves contending with the dominant cultures of their island, their nation, and transnational capitalism. The best ecocritical work of this kind is as insightful as Tsing's environmental ethnography. Besides, it would be a great mistake to interpret resistance to dominant strains of theory as proof of resistance to theory *tout court*.

On the contrary, literature-and-environment studies have striven almost from the start to define their position on the critical map analytically as well as through narrative practice. One strategy has been to build selectively on poststructuralist theory while resisting the totalizing implications of its linguistic turn and its aftermaths, such that the word-world gets decoupled from the material world to the point of making it impossible to conceive of literary discourse as other than tropology or linguistic play or ideological formation. From this standpoint, "theory and ecology" might be seen as a fruitful, energizing collaboration to the end of calling into "question the concepts on which the old hierarchies are built" (meaning for this writer androcentrism specifically and anthropocentrism more generally), even as one resists an exclusive focus on "textuality, as networks of signifying systems of all kinds" that would privilege "networks of language and culture" to the eclipse of culture's imbrication in "the networks of the land" (Campbell 1989: 128, 133, 136). In a similar spirit, Verena Conley plumbs the archive of French critical theory over the past half-century, hoping to confirm the hypothesis "that the driving force of poststructural thought is indissolubly linked to ecology" (Conley 1997: 7), and succeeding in a number of instances (most notably Felix Guattari, Michel Serres, and Luce Irigiray), though she admits to not being able to do much with Derrida or Baudrillard. British ecocritic Dominic Head suggests a ground for dialogue between "the broader Green movement" and postmodern theory with respect to a comparable "deprivileging of the human subject" (Head 1998a: 28). Dana Phillips commends anthropologist of science Bruno Latour's canny reflections on the inextricable hybridization of nature and culture as a corrective against ecocriticism's incautious attempts to distinguish cleanly between the two (Phillips 2003: esp. 30–4).

Altogether, the story of literary ecotheory's relation to critical models has been unfolding less as a story of dogged recalcitrance—though there has been some of that—than as a quest *for* adequate models of inquiry from the plethora of possible alternatives that offer themselves from whatever disciplinary quarter. Cybernetics, evolutionary biology, landscape ecology, risk theory, phenomenology, environmental ethics, feminist theory, ecotheology, anthropology, psychology, science studies, critical race studies, postcolonial theory, environmental history—all these and more, each fraught with its own internal wranglings—have presented themselves as correctives or enhancements to literary theory's preexisting toolkit. The menu of approaches continues to expand, and the combinatorics have become ever more proliferate and complex.

The environmental turn in literary studies is best understood, then, less as a monolith than as a concourse of discrepant practices. In her introduction to the first significant critical collection, Cheryll Glotfelty was being candid rather than evasive in defining ecocriticism in extremely sweeping terms, as "the study of the relationship between literature and the physical environment," in whatever way these terms be defined (Glotfelty and Fromm 1996: xviii). It is not a revolution in the name of a dominant methodology in the sense that Russian and new critical formalism, phenomenology, deconstruction, and new historicism have been. It lacks the kind of paradigm-defining statement that, for example, Edward Said's *Orientalism* (1978) supplied for colonial discourse studies.[13] More like (say) feminism in this respect, ecocriticism gathers itself around a commitment to environmentality from whatever critical vantage point. A map of feminism must recognize fault lines dividing historical from poststructuralist feminisms, western traditions of women's studies from "womanist" approaches to the study of disprivileged women of color; and must recognize how these differences interact with other critical genealogies, such as postcolonial theory in the case of womanist revisionism. Broadly speaking, this is the kind of direction in which literary ecotheory has been evolving, toward increasing acknowledgment of ecocultural complexity after an initial concentration now increasingly (though by no means universally) thought to have been too narrowly focused. One of the catalysts, indeed, has been ecofeminism, itself an evolving congeries, on which more below.

That the environmental turn in literary studies has been more issue-driven than method or paradigm-driven is one reason why the catchy but totalizing rubric of "ecocriticism" is less indicative than "environmental criticism" or "literary-environmental studies." Being less cumbersome and (so far) much more widely used, "ecocriticism" may well be here to stay. I have found it a convenient shorthand I cannot do without. But the term implies a nonexistent methodological holism. It overstates the degree to which the environmental turn in literary studies was ever a coordinated project.[14] The stigma of critical amateurism attached by skeptics at the start of the ecocritical insurgency, for which the media is as responsible as the movement,[15] has itself created internal disaffection with the rubric, a bit like the way a number of the so-called American Transcendentalists tended to shy away from that lumping label, which had been slapped on the movement by conservative detractors as a synonym for "German nonsense." Today, a number of younger scholars, in whose hands the future of environmental criticism lies, often seem to prefer not to self-identify as "ecocritics." On the other hand, the same was true in the 1980s for many putative new historicists who are now looked back upon as exemplars of that movement.[16]

A more substantive reason for belaboring the terminological issue is the implicit narrowness of the "eco," insofar as it connotes the "natural" *rather than* the "built" environment and, still more specifically, the field of ecology. "Ecocriticism is a name that implies more ecological literacy than its advocates now possess," pithily observes one who hopes to see more (Howarth 1996: 69). Although attempted reformation of literary studies via *rapprochement* with life sciences has been *one* of the movements distinctive projects, it is only one such project—and a minority endeavor at that. From the start, and increasingly, the "eco" of practicing so-called ecocritics has been more aesthetic, ethical, and sociopolitical than scientist. The looser rubric of ASLE's flagship journal *ISLE* (Interdisciplinary Studies in Literature and Environment) better fits the actual mix, and all the more so now that environmental criticism's working conception of "environment" has broadened in recent years from "natural" to include also the urban, the interweave of "built" and "natural" dimensions in every locale, and the interpenetration of the local by the global.

On the other hand, "ecocriticism" suffices if—like poet-critic Gary Snyder—one is careful to use the term in mindfulness of its etymology and of its metaphorical stretch. "Ecology" derives etymologically from the Greek *oikos*, household, and in modern usage refers both to "the study of biological interrelationships and the flow of energy through organisms and inorganic matter." Metaphorically, furthermore, "ecology" can be stretched to cover "energy-exchange and interconnection" in "other realms" too: from technology-based communication systems to the "ecology" of thinking or composition (Snyder 2004: 5, 9). Indeed, "the ecology movement," particularly outside the United States, sometimes serves as a synonym for environmentalism. Looked at this way, a perfectly plausible case can be made for speaking of environmentally valenced work in literature studies as "ecocriticism."

FROM "NATURE" IN LITERATURE X TO THE BEGINNINGS OF ECOCRITICISM

The term "ecocriticism" was coined in the late 1970s (Rueckert 1996), but its antecedents stretch back much further. The quest for an inception point can trap one in an infinite regress. For US settler-culture literature, one would need to go back at least as far as the 1920s—the decade when it first established itself as a professional specialization—and Norman Foerster's *Nature in American Literature* (1923), sometimes said to have "inaugurated the new academic field" of American literature (Mazel 2001: 6).[17] Some Americanists might argue that the origin should be set much earlier, at least as far back as Ralph Waldo Emerson's *Nature* (1836), the first canonical work of US literature to unfold a theory of nature with special reference to poetics.[18] But for present purposes it should suffice to begin with the two precontemporary books of literary and cultural studies of greatest influence for later Anglo-American environmental criticism: in American Studies, Leo Marx's *The Machine and the Garden: Technology and the Pastoral Ideal in American Culture* (1964), the earliest book listed among the "top fifteen" recommended in *The Ecocriticism Reader*'s bibliography (Glotfelty and Fromm 1996: 395–6), and in British Studies, Raymond Williams' *The Country and the City* (1973), which has been praised as "a masterpiece of ecocriticism *avant la lettre*" (Head 2002: 24).

Marx and Williams both focused on the cultural history and literary instantiation of the intertwined history of attitudes toward nature vs. (for Williams) urbanism and (for Marx) industrial technology. Both dwelt upon the salience and durability of their respective national penchants to identify national essence symbolically with "country" (Williams) or a bucolic "middle landscape" between settlement and frontier or wilderness (Marx). Both also stressed the seductiveness and the mendacity of nostalgia for rurality: how it characteristically expressed itself in the form of wishful prettifying palliatives that disguised the irreversible transformation of landscape wrought by economic power and/or class interest. Both accounts were given further torque and bite by a shared cultural Marxist commitment to conceiving the modernization process as an ironic grand narrative of industrial capitalism's inevitable triumph over the counter-cultures of pastoral opposition (Marx) and traditional local life (Williams).

The importance of these two books and the essays that succeeded them for the subsequent turn in environmental studies lay especially in their identification of the dynamics of the history of what we would now call national imaginaries in terms of a symbiotic opposition between contrasting prototypical landscapes.

Marx and Williams defined the stakes quite differently. Williams concerned himself much more with the actualities of environmental history and landscape transformation than did Marx, who was a leading exemplar of the "myth-symbol" school of American Studies, according to which the key to the dynamics of national history lay in its cultural symbolics. Williams' heroes were endangered country folk and the culture of rural working-class life, and such writers as peasant poet John Clare and regional novelist Thomas Hardy, whose works rendered these most faithfully, despite the threat of cooptation by the stereotypical "green language" of romanticism and the false consciousness implanted by deference to patrons or marketplace. Marx's heroes, on the other hand, were a small group of high canonical literati, from Henry Thoreau to William Faulkner, who practiced a "complex pastoral" that resisted prettified, anodyne mainstream "simple pastoral" by using green tropes to critique advancing machine culture. For Marx, such visions of a lost or possible future golden age had "nothing to do with the environment" per se (Marx 1964: 264). The payoff was entirely political and aesthetic.

Williams more closely anticipated later literature-and-environment studies in his keen interest in the facts of environmental history, in literature's (mis)representation of them, and (in his later essays) the possibilities of the greening of socialism into a "socialist ecology" that might stand as a latter-day equivalent of Victorian poet and culture critic William Morris (Williams 1989: 210–26). Marx, by contrast, was a technodeterminist who declared the demise of anti-establishment pastoral in the first half of the twentieth century and the need for "new symbols of possibility"—although he has since revised that judgment (Marx 1964: 365; 1988: 291–314). But Marx's partiality for complex or critical pastoral, together with the pronounced right-wing tendency of British country writing during the interwar period, helps explain why contemporary American ecocritics have been less quick to share British critics' "cynicism toward the pastoral" as the classist closed circuit that Williams saw it as being. Marx's work has helped energize British ecocritic Terry Gifford's account of an intellectually and politically robust "post-pastoral" mode in contemporary British poetry that calls into question Williams' dismissal of the mode (Gifford 2002: 51–3), and my own argument that "pastoral outrage" at landscape degradation has been key to the "toxic discourse" of recent environmental justice advocacy (Buell 2001: 35–58).[19] It helps also to explain why Scott Hess's critique of "postmodern pastoral," an update of Marx's "simple" or mainstream tradition whereby the machine becomes "no longer a potential interruption but the central site of the pastoral order" (as in virtual imaging technology), nonetheless works round to envisaging the possibility of a "sustainable pastoral" that would not cater to consumerist passivity, but promote more self-conscious "action and participation" through its cognizance of humanity's ongoing interaction with "the non-human forces in which our lives are embedded" (Hess 2004: 77, 95).

Neither Marx nor Williams seems to have been influenced by the other, or by other countries' nature-based nationalisms. (Williams took no interest in American literature, whereas Marx's training and literary research were squarely in American Studies.)[20] More recent environmental criticism within literary studies has likewise generally concentrated on individual nations' literary histories and is only now starting to think intensively in comparatist terms.[21] Of course, Marx and Williams bear no special responsibility for the practice of reading environmental imagination as a barometer of *national* imagination. In this they followed the bias of literary professionalism toward nation-based specialties that marked the work of their own mentors and that still runs strong.[22] Nor is nation-based specialization altogether unjustified in this case. Nations *do* generate distinctive forms of pastoral or outback nationalism (e.g., the myth of the Bush for Australia; the mystique of the far North for Canada; the iconicity of the Black Forest for German culture; the myth of the jungle for Creole cultures of Brazil, Venezuela, and other Latin American nations).[23] Whatever the limits of their analytical horizons, Marx and Williams provided usable models for critical thinking about such national imaginaries, as well as about specific texts and genres.

Their work was not so much directly catalytic for the environmental turn in literary studies, however, as it was retrospectively enlisted once the movement got underway. The work today considered the starting point for American ecocriticism proper, Joseph Meeker's *The Comedy of Survival* (1972, revd. 1997), gives Marx no more than passing mention in the process of denigrating pastoral's anthropocentrism. Jonathan Bate's *Romantic Ecology* (1991) appears to gather a certain amount of energy from Williams, but is mainly concerned to rehabilitate the green language to which Williams himself gave short shrift over against the tendency of new historicism—which reckons Williams as a significant precursor[24]—to dismiss Wordsworth's devotion to "nature" as conservative politics. For Meeker and Bate were committed, as Williams and Marx were not, to the proposition that "an ecological *ethic* must be reaffirmed in our contemporary structure of values" (Bate 1991: 11). Ecocriticism had begun to arrive. But it arrived not as a program so much as a bevy of disparate, semi-intercommunicating practitioners ranging from professional outliers like Meeker to central figures within academe like Bate, who went on to become the general editor of the monumental new *Oxford History of English Literature*.

THE ENVIRONMENTAL TURN ANATOMIZED

No definitive map of environmental criticism in literary studies can therefore be drawn. Still, one can identify several trend-lines marking an evolution from a "first wave" of ecocriticism to a "second" or newer revisionist wave or waves increasingly evident today. This first–second distinction should not, however, be taken as implying a tidy, distinct succession. Most currents set in motion by early ecocriticism continue to run strong, and most forms of second-wave revisionism involve building on as well as quarreling with precursors. In this sense, "palimpsest" would be a better metaphor than "wave." As has been said of the irregular advance of the idea of sustainable development (or "ecological modernization" as some prefer to call it), the history of literary-environmental studies might be thought of as a loose-hanging "discourse coalition" comprised of semi-fortuitously braided story-lines, each of which encapsulates "complex disciplinary debates" (Hajer 1995: 65).

The initiative that first visibly distinguished ecocriticism from the work of Williams and Marx was the push in some quarters, though by no means all, for closer alliance with environmental sciences, especially the life sciences. This is the standpoint from which the "eco" of "ecocriticism" makes most coherent sense. Meeker reconceives literature under the sign of biology, especially the ethological studies of Konrad Lorenz. He offers an ingeniously offbeat brief for comedy as a mode that values traits humans share with nonhumans—species survival, adaptation to circumstance, community, veniality, and play—as against what he sees as tragedy's anthropocentric haughtiness toward the natural order (Meeker 1997). Since then, others have also taken up the argument that ecocriticism's progress hinges significantly if not crucially on its becoming more science-literate. Specific prescriptions vary greatly, however. Joseph Carroll (1995) and Glen A. Love (2003) look to evolutionary biology for critical models; William Howarth seems rather to favor bringing humanities and science together in the context of studying specific landscapes and regions (Howarth 1996), to which end geology is at least as important as the life sciences (Howarth 1999). Ursula Heise, on the other hand, has recently turned to a branch of applied mathematics, risk theory, as a window onto literature's exploration of the kind of contemporary anxieties underscored by Ulrich Beck (Heise 2002), while for N. Katherine Hayles the prosthetics of environment information technology, artificial intelligence, and virtual reality become crucial in measuring the transit from human to "posthuman" modes of being in the world, and fiction's imagination of these (Hayles 1999).[25]

The story-line encapsulated here is not only one of increasing variety but also of assumed certitudes placed under question. First-wave ecocritical calls for greater scientistic literacy tend to presuppose a bedrock "human" condition, to commend the scientific method's ability to describe natural laws, and to look to science as a corrective to critical subjectivism and cultural relativism. Love is particularly emphatic: the promise of ecocriticism lies in building upon the sociobiology-based "consilience" of disciplines as envisioned by Edward O. Wilson, for whom aesthetic and social theory must ultimately be obedient to evolutionary genetics, whereas "a cultural constructionist position … plays into the hands of the destroyers" (Love 2003: 21). From this standpoint, cultural theory's anthropocentric arrogance and ignorant disdain for science cost it the "science wars" that roiled the American academy during the 1990s. From the standpoint of second-wave science-oriented environmental critics like Heise and Hayles, by contrast, the borderline between science and culture is less clearcut. Both would argue for "a scientifically informed foregrounding of green issues in literature" as Heise (1997: 6) states, but they envisage science's relationship to human culture as a feedback loop in which science is viewed both as objectified discipline and humanly directed enterprise, and the terms of scientistic discourse have significant implications for environmental criticism of literature but do not serve as an authoritative model. The discourses of science and literature must be read both with and against each other.

For a number of other ecocritics, the arrogance of scientism has loomed up as greater hazard than the insouciance of cultural theory in reducing science to cultural construct or the slickness of underinformed literary criticism in its loose "metaphoric transfer" (Heise's phrase) of the lexicon of "eco"-terms. (Of course, the text-as-organism metaphor has a much longer history in critical theory, dating back through new critical formalism to Romanticism, which in turn has much older roots in the mystical idea of the world as text, the *liber mundi.*) Ecofeminist work presents an instructive example of such skepticism. Ecofeminism is itself a multiverse, but inquiry starts from the premise of a correlation between the history of institutionalized patriarchy and human domination of the non-human. As an initiative within literary studies, it has taken shape as an intertwinement of revisionist history of science, with Carolyn Merchant and Donna Haraway the most visibly influential figures; of resistance to androcentric traditions of literary interpretation exemplified by such critics as Annette Kolodny and Louise Westling; of feminist ecotheology inaugurated by Mary Daly and Rosemary Radford Ruether; and of the environmental philosophy of Val Plumwood, Karen Warren, and others.[26] An ecofeminist might claim that the analogy between "woman" and "nature" is inherent, or (increasingly) that it is historically contingent. One might assert, or might disclaim, that environmental ethics properly hinges on an "ethics of care," which women are culturally if not also biologically constructed to undertake more readily than men. One might stake a position within science studies, or one might self-position remotely afield from it, for example as a theologian arguing for the recuperation of maternal images of deity, or as a neopagan advocate for revival of the prehistoric "Goddess" overthrown by the agro-pastoral and monotheistic revolutions. By no means all ecofeminists would position themselves as "anti-science," even many whose particular interests led them away from science as a topic of inquiry. But most would likely sympathize with (if not accept without qualification) the claim that "natural disorder is man-induced"[27]—as well as with the claim that traditions of differential conditioning of the sexes in western history helps explain the instrumental rationalism that made possible modern science and technology and the broader linkage between the history of male dominance and confidence (not confined to scientists) in the knowledge/power of instrumental rationalism to control the nonhuman environment.

Neither ecofeminists nor any other group of environmental critics hold a monopoly on pondering the question of the objectivity vs. the constructedness of science's methods and findings. If anything, that is the special province of science studies. None has written about it with more brilliance and panache than Bruno Latour. An ethnographer of scientific practices, he gleefully exposes the myth of the "Great Divide" between Nature and Society as an artifact of what he mock-grandiosely calls the modern "Constitution," which he cleverly schematizes as paradoxically ordaining both the absolute separation and absolute authority of both science and politics—thereby ensuring the very opposite: their hybridization (Latour 1993: 13–48).[28] Latour doesn't want to undermine science's authority so much as to redefine it contextually in such a way as to deny both science's exemption from human agency and its reduction only to that. Science's "facts" are "neither real nor fabricated"; the microbial revolution hinged on a certain kind of orchestrated laboratory performance, without which science history would have taken a different path, but the discovery/invention was not fictitious, either. Latour ingeniously proposes the neologism "factish" (a collage of "fact" and "fetish") to describe this understanding of the "facts" of science: "types of action that do not fall into the comminatory choice between fact and belief" (Latour 1999: 295, 306).[29]

Several second-wave ecocritics have commended Latour as a wholesome antidote to simplistic endorsement either of science's authority over against the claims and frames of literary and cultural theory or of "theory's" purported demolition of science as nothing more than discursive or cultural construction.[30] Not that Latour, who shows scant interest in literature and the arts, will likely become the all-purpose theorist of literary studies' environmental turn. Ecocritical interest in his work betokens, rather, a more reflexive approach to science on the part of those who look to it to energize literary studies (ASLE can here be seen as playing catchup to the Society for the Study of Literature and Science), by provoking a more sophisticated rethinking of the nature and place of "nature" itself. This brings us to the next of our story-lines.

For first-wave ecocriticism, "environment" effectively meant "natural environment." In practice if not in principle, the realms of the "natural" and the "human" looked more disjunct than they have come to seem for more recent environmental critics—one of the reasons for preferring "environmental criticism" to "ecocriticism" as more indicative of present practice. Ecocriticism was initially understood to be synchronous with the aims of earthcare. Its goal was to contribute to "the struggle to preserve the 'biotic community'" (Coupe 2000: 4). The paradigmatic first-wave ecocritic appraised "the effects of culture upon nature, with a view toward celebrating nature, berating its despoilers, and reversing their harm through political action" (Howarth 1996: 69). In the process, the ecocritic might seek to redefine the concept of culture itself in organicist terms with a view to envisioning a "philosophy of organism" that would break down "the hierarchical separations between human beings and other elements of the natural world" (Elder 1985: 172).

Second-wave ecocriticism has tended to question organicist models of conceiving both environment and environmentalism. Natural and built environments, revisionists point out, are long since all mixed up; the landscape of the American "West" is increasingly the landscape of metropolitan sprawl rather than the outback of Rocky Mountain "wilderness"; the two spheres are as intertwined, now and historically, as surely as Los Angeles and Las Vegas have siphoned water from the Colorado basin from the hinterlands for the past century (Comer 1999). Literature-and-environment studies must develop a "social ecocriticism" that takes urban and degraded landscapes just as seriously as "natural" landscapes (Bennett 2001: 32). Its traditional commitment to the nature protection ethic must be revised to accommodate the claims of environmental justice (Adamson, Evans, and Stein 2002)—or (more broadly) "the environmentalism of the poor," as one ecological economist has called it (Martinez-Alier 2002).

This shift has divided but enriched the movement. Certainly it has influenced my own work. It was the most important impetus behind the change of focus from my *Environmental Imagination* to *Writing for an Endangered World.* The earlier book centered on the question of the extent to which (certain kinds of) literature can be thought to model ecocentric values, as exemplified in particular by the directional movement of Henry David Thoreau's career and by American nature writing more generally. In these respects, *The Environmental Imagination* was a representative work of first-wave ecocriticism. Although I believed then and continue to believe that the literatures of nature *do* bear important witness against "the arrogance of humanism" (Ehrenfeld 1978), I found myself agreeing with those who thought the concentration on "environment" as "nature" and on nature writing as the most representative environmental genre were too restrictive, and that a mature environmental aesthetics—or ethics, or politics—must take into account the interpenetration of metropolis and outback, of anthropocentric as well as biocentric concerns.

It remains to be seen just how far the discourses of urbanism and environmental justice can be coordinated with the discourses of nature and the protectionist agendas they tend to imply. Some significant divisions separate first-wave projects to reconnect humans with the natural world from second-wave skepticism "that more can be learned from the 'black hole' of a weasel's eyes than from, say, the just-closed eyes of a child of the ghetto killed by lead-poisoning from ingesting the peeling paint in his/her immediate environment."[31] According to the former way of thinking, the prototypical human figure is a solitary human and the experience in question activates a primordial link between human and nonhuman. According to the latter, the prototypical human figure is defined by social category and the "environment" is artificially constructed. Is there any common ground here to indicate that environmental criticism might grow rather than fall apart from this kind of schism?

I think so. First and foremost because in both instances the understanding of personhood is defined for better or for worse by environmental entanglement. Whether individual or social, being doesn't stop at the border of the skin. If the weasel epiphany sounds too rarefied, set beside the image of the poisoned child this declaration by a Native American writer quoted by an ecocritic/nature writer of more traditional persuasion. "You could cut off my hand, and I would still live…You could take out my eyes, and I would still live…Take away the sun, and I die. Take away the plants and animals, and I die. So why should I think my body is more a part of me than the sun and the earth?" (K. D. Moore 2004: 58–9). This too has the marks of the first-wave mentality (environment = nature, nature = nurture, the exemplar and the idiom = more or less what one would expect from the paradigmatic "ecological Indian," the model minority sage of green wisdom) (Krech 1999). But the underlying view of the environment-constructed body, of environmentality as crucial to health or disease, life or death, is quite similar.

The image of the poisoned child is also in its own way as much an idealization as the image of the eco-sensitive indigene. Its underlying valorization of "the natural" tends not to be so different from the first wave's as one might suppose. Second-wave ecocriticism has so far concentrated strongly, for example, on locating vestiges of nature within cities and/or exposing crimes of eco-injustice against society's marginal groups. In this there should be enough shared ground for ongoing conversation if not *rapprochement*. Skittishness at modernization's aggressive, accelerating, inequitable transformations of "natural" into "constructed" space is a common denominator crucial to giving ecocriticism, both waves of it, its edge of critique. This is ecocriticism's equivalent as it were to queer studies, with which some environmental writers and critics have in fact begun to affiliate (see Sandilands 1999): to unsettle normative thinking about environmental status quos. Not that there is anything anti-normative about environmental concern as such. On the contrary, environmental concern is more mainstream than homophobia. But not as a high-priority issue. The mainstream view, in the United States at least, is that "the environment" will be society's top problem "tomorrow"—a quarter century from now, say—but not today (Guber 2003: 44, 54). Environmental concern is normal. But *vehement* concern still looks queer.

That is a consensus environmental criticism of whatever stripe is out to disrupt. To adapt the terms of Niklas Luhmann's model of systems analysis, the insistence on environmentality—whether it be the ecological Indian or the poisoned child—interjects the disruptive "anxiety" element that "cannot be regulated away by any of the function systems" that comprise modernized society (the institution of economics, law, etc.) (Luhmann 1989: 127).[33]

Second-wave ecocriticism's revision of first-wave horizons was partially anticipated in several ways. To begin with, the movement's latitudinarian definitions of "environment" increased from the get-go the likelihood that a de facto equation of environment = nature would be disputed sooner rather than later. And all the more so because of a certain degree of anticipatory eclecticism within early ecocriticism itself,[34] an eclecticism foreshadowed in some degree by first-wave ecocriticism's pantheon of significant late twentieth century environmental writers. A preeminent example was Rachel Carson's swerve from her first book *Under the Sea Wind* (1941), a quite traditional performance in the nature writing vein, to *Silent Spring* two decades later, even while carrying over many of the resources and implicit values of the former. That swerve has since been taken further in the self-conscious hybridization of traditional rural-focused nature writing and epidemiological analysis in such post-Carson feminist writers as Terry Tempest Williams and Sandra Steingraber, whose autobiographical narratives of environmental cancer-clusters self-consciously interlace metropolitan and exurban genres and locales. This work brings us to the heart of second-wave ecocriticism's defining concerns. More on that in chapter 4.

The revised and expanded sense of environmentality just noted has altered ecocriticism's working sense of its proper canon more sweepingly than I have so far indicated. Once I thought it helpful to try to specify a subspecies of "environmental text," the first stipulation of which was that the nonhuman environment must be envisaged not merely as a framing device but as an active presence, suggesting human history's implication in natural history. Now, it seems to me more productive to think inclusively of environmentality as a property of any text—to maintain that all human artifacts bear such traces, and at several stages: in the composition, the embodiment, and the reception (Buell 1995: 7–8 vs. Buell 2001: 2–3). These second thoughts seem broadly to typify the directional momentum of environmental criticism. Some of the earlier significant ecocritical interventions already show cognizance of this. I think especially of Robert Pogue Harrison's *Forests: The Shadows of Civilization*, which traces permutations of forest imagination in Western thought and literature, and Louise Westling's *The Green Breast of the New World*, a study of patriarchal misprisions of landscape (together with certain resistances thereto). Both sweep from the ancient Sumerian epic of *Gilgamesh* to the near-present.

Between these two books, significantly, the overlap in the primary texts discussed turns out to be rather slight. Forest phenomenology in the Western high canon and ecofeminism in (chiefly) US literary discourse lead the two authors down quite different paths. Heterogeneity and with it the possibilities for both intense contestation and for ships passing by each other unnoticed are bound to increase exponentially as the consensual understanding of what might count as environmental literature expands. For example, one second-wave appraisal plausibly contends that "eco-criticism becomes most interesting and useful...when it aims to recover the environmental character or orientation of works whose conscious or foregrounded interests lie elsewhere" (Kern 2000: 11). What this critic has in mind is landscape semiotics in Jane Austen's fiction, particularly the impact on Elizabeth Bennet of her visit in *Pride and Prejudice* to Darcy's estate at Pemberley, the direct experience of which begins to dispel her dislike of him. Jonathan Bate enlists *Emma, Sense and Sensibility,* and *Mansfield Park* with fuller reference to nineteenth-century environmental history in a paired study of Austen and Hardy (Bate 2000: 1–23). But depending on what one means by "environmental character or orientation," one might wish to privilege a completely different set of texts, as with environmental justice criticism's emphasis on contemporary works by nonwhite writers that confront the issue of environmental racism, only a relative few of which were on the radar screens of first-wave ecocritics (Adamson, Evans, and Stein). Here a case for including Austen's fiction in the picture might still be made; but it would require one to foreground rather than mention in passing Edward Said's reading of *Mansfield Park*, which centers on the dependence of the Bertrams' elegant lifestyle on the family estate in Antigua, sustained by slave labor (Said 1993: 84–97).

ASLE's journal, *ISLE*, has reflected these tendencies. It still prints articles on nature writing, Wordsworthian poetry, and pastoral theory. But the last and only number to feature a special section on Henry David Thoreau was in fact the very first (spring 1993); and the past few years have seen essays on British and American film, Australian place-making, Latin American environmental justice poetry, immigrant autobiography, and a revisionist interpretation of animal encounters in medieval lives of St. Francis as a strategy of Franciscan apologetics.

As this last example suggests, no less striking than the expansion of the range of ecocritical texts and topics has been the reframing of the first-wave's preferred canon. As Lance Newman writes in a provocative essay on "Marxism and Ecocriticism," "nature writing is not a stable form of reaction to a stable problem (the ideologically-driven human domination of nature). It is a dynamic tradition of response to the rise and development of the capitalist ecosocial order…how nature writers see and understand nature has everything to do with how they see and understand the society whose relations with it they hope to change" (Newman 2002: 18–19). Newman is *not* making the same claim here about a text like *Walden* that Leo Marx made, namely that Thoreau's interest in the natural world is significant as symbolic theater for political critique and ceases to become of interest to us as the text's interest in natural history becomes more literal. Newman's argument is the obverse: that understanding "ecocentric consciousness" requires a "historical consciousness" attentive to the "coevolution of material social and natural systems that has produced the present crisis" of environmental endangerment against which nature writing implicitly if not explicitly positions itself (Newman 2002: 21). Taking its cue, as here, from critical theory on the one hand and from the increasing politicization of post-Carson nature writing on the other, the newer environmental criticism is likely to continue to press for more cosmopolitan ways of understanding the work of ecodiscourse in the canon of original concentration, even as it takes in a wider range of literary history so as ultimately to include, in principle, any text whatsoever.

Might this process of cosmopolitanization wind up amounting to a forfeiture of the original mission? To a taming down of first-wave ecocriticism's original schismatic disaffection with business-as-usual literary studies? To the consolidation of environmental criticism as just another niche within the culture of academic professionalism, now that it is on the way to becoming more "critically sophisticated," increasingly more engaged with the other critical games in town? My own response to such concerns, which will take the rest of this book to unfold, is "Probably so, to some extent." But the promise is well worth the risk, both on the intrinsics and the pragmatics—especially if the alternatives are a too narrow conception of enviromentalism and environmentality, and the (re)production of the unemployable.

Right now, as I see it, environmental criticism is in the tense but enviable position of being a wide-open movement still sorting out its premises and its powers. Its reach is increasingly worldwide and from bottom to top within academe: from graduate studies in (some) major university literature departments to courses in entry-level composition. It is wide open to alliances with environmental writers, environmental activists, and extra-academic environmental educators. Not the least of its attractions is the prospect of encompassing all these roles. Increasing critical sophistication may make environmental criticism more professionally cautious and more internally stratified. But its intellectual zest and its activist edge are likely to gain more from its future evolution than they sacrifice.

NOTES

1. These generalizations encapsulate almost four decades of controversy touched off by Lynn White's "The Historical Roots of Our Ecologic Crisis" (White 1967), which pinned responsibility for technodominationism on Judaeo-Christianity. White's thesis has been disputed by biblical scholars, theologians, and environmental ethicists, who have convincingly exposed its tendentiousness without having permanently laid the charge to rest. Many of the responses have been collected by Timothy Weiskel, "The Environmental Crisis and Western Civilization: The Lynn White Controversy" (http://ecoethics.net/bib/1997/enca-001.htm). Adjudication is complicated by sharp variance between the different creation accounts in Genesis 1–2 by the scribes known respectively as "Priestly" and "Jahwist," the former being much more dominationist than the latter. Here I especially follow the analysis of Theodore Hiebert, "The Human Vocation: Origins and Transformations in Christian Traditions," *Christianity and Ecology: Seeking the Well-Being of Earth and Humans*, ed. Dieter T. Hessel and Rosemary Radford Ruether (Cambridge, MA: Harvard University Press, 2000), 135–54, a concise follow-up to Hiebert's *The Yahwist's Landscape: Nature and Religion in Early Israel* (New York: Oxford University Press, 1996).
2. Victor D. Montejo, "The Road to Heaven: Jakaltek Maya Beliefs, Religion, and the Ecology," in *Indigenous Traditions and Ecology: The Interbeing of Cosmology and Community*, ed. John A. Grim (Cambridge, MA: Harvard University Press, 2001), 177; Manuka Henare, "*Tapu, Mana, Mauri, Hau, Waima*: A Maori-Philosophy of Vitalism and Cosmos," in the same volume, 198. Montejo's Mayan source is the *Popul Vuh*, Book III, Chapter 1—a post-conquest transcription.
3. Here I adapt Raymond Williams' useful distinction between residual, dominant, and emergent cultures (Williams 1977: 121—7)—useful in part because Williams does not minimize the difficulty of distinguishing "emergent" from "dominant" or from copycat "facsimiles of the genuinely emergent cultural practice": 126. As we shall see, especially in chapter 4, it is no small matter to distinguish what is and is not genuinely radical in environmental criticism.
4. See, for example, the 1994 forum, "Defining Ecocritical Theory and Practice," posted on the ASLE website (www.asle.umn.edu/archive). Only one of the sixteen contributors made a point of strongly emphasizing the potential significance of urban writing and landscapes. Overwhelmingly, "environmental" literary study is here seen to be a matter of "the ways that the relationship between humans and nature are reflected in literary texts" (Stephanie Sarver, "What Is Ecocriticism," 1994 forum).

5. For presentations of this philosophy of teaching in action by two participants in that discussion, see Elder (1999) and Tallmadge (2000).

6. This from Australian ecocritic Bruce Bennett's recollection of a conversation with environmental writer Barry Lopez as "we walked along a line of cork oaks by the Swan River at Matilda Bay." See Bennett, "Some Dynamics of Literary Placemaking," *ISLE,* 10 (summer 2003): 99.

7. Quotation from Elder (1999: 649). The essay as a whole describes one such pedagogical experiment. The ASLE website, *ISLE,* and *Green Letters* make clear the movement's intelligent commitment to environmental education in the broadest sense. See, for example, Terry Gifford's notes from a 2000 Taiwan conference session led by him and two American ecocritics, Scott Slovic and Patrick Murphy: "Introducing Ecocriticism into the University Curriculum," *Green Letters,* 4 (spring 2003): 40–1.

8. The bibliography of *The Ecocriticism Reader* lists Snyder's bioregional manifesto, *The Practice of the Wild* (1990), as one of its "top fifteen choices" (Glotfelty and Fromm 1996: 397). Phillips' otherwise caustic assessment of what he takes to be early ecocriticism's high-minded simplisms ends by commending Ammons' book-length poem *Garbage* for its wily, sardonic, self-reflexive perceptiveness (Phillips 2003: 240–7).

9. Henry David Thoreau, "Walking," *The Norton Anthology of American Literature,* 6th edn., ed. Nina Baym et al. (New York: Norton, 2003), B: 1993.

10. Thomas Nagel, "What Is It Like to Be a Bat?" *Philosophical Review,* 83 (October 1974): 435–50.

11. Timothy Morton's (2000) study of Romantic-era consumerism in the case of the spice trade is a good example of such internalization, even though it makes only passing reference to Foucault.

12. For further insights into ecocritical understanding of the relation of narrative and critical practices, see the introductions, notes, and selected interviews in Satterfield and Slovic (2004).

13. See Buell (1999: 700–4) and Reed (2002: 148–9) for (non-identical) taxonomies of discrepant practices.

14. This is in no sense meant to denigrate the efforts and impact of such particular individuals as Scott Slovic (University of Nevada–Reno), *ISLE*'s editor during the period of its emergence into a journal of real significance, and a catalytic influence on the creation of ASLE chapters in Japan and Australia.

15. See Jay Parini, "The Greening of the Humanities," *New York Times* (Sunday magazine), October 29, 1995, pp. 52–3—an article that was significantly cut and altered by editorial fiat from the author's original version. Its provocative, editorially bestowed subtitle is "Deconstruction is compost"; and some of the interlocutors are reduced to misleadingly simplistic sound bites like "Literary theory wasn't real. Nature is tangible."

16. The Texas A & M University faculty group hosting the 1980s visiting lecture series on new historicism, that led to Jeffrey N. Cox and Larry Reynolds (eds.), *New Historical Literary Study: Essays on Reproducing Texts, Representing History* (Princeton, NJ: Princeton University Press, 1997), expressed bemusement and frustration at the reluctance of their guests, among whom I was privileged to be one, to confess to being new historicists. "It seems there are more discussions than actual examples of it," the editors remark (p. 6).

17. *American Literature,* the original flagship journal in the field, annually offers a prize in Foerster's name for the year's best essay in *AL.*

18. The first item in Mazel's (2001) anthology of "early ecocriticism" dates from 1864.

19. This is not to imply agreement on all points, of course. For the most recently published of a series of exchanges, see Marx (2003) and L. Buell (2003).

20. Marx does devote a limited amount of attention to the pastoral formation as a transplanted Eurocentric desire, particularly in his discussion of "Shakespeare's American Fable," *The Tempest* (March 1964: 34–72), and Williams' final chapter ("Cities and Countries") sketchily anticipates postcolonial studies by imagining Britain and its colonies as a symbolic opposition of metropolitan and outback (pp. 289–306). See also Marx's thoughtful review of *The Country and the City* (Marx 1973: 422–4).

21. An auspicious exception is *The Green Studies Reader: From Romanticism to Ecocriticism* (Coupe 2000), a British counterpart to Glotfelty and Fromm (1996), which includes a range of British and American ecocritical work together with relevant continental theory. Of course, these items are juxtaposed rather than critically compared at any length.

22. For Williams, the most significant precursor in the present context was F. R. Leavis, and the key book was Leavis and Denys Thompson, *Culture and Environment: The Training of Critical Awareness* (1933). For Marx, it was Perry Miller, and the key works were certain essays collected in Miller's *Errand into the Wilderness* (1956) and (posthumously) *Nature's Nation* (1967).

23. *As* to US literary studies, Mazel (2001: 5–6) overstates, but not by much, in remarking with Norman Foerster in mind (and quoting the subtitle of Devall and Sessions 1985), that "it was only by reading literature *as if nature mattered*—by practicing an early ecocriticism—that American literary criticism came to be professionalized."

24. Catherine Gallagher and Stephen Greenblatt, *Practicing New Historicism* (Chicago: University of Chicago Press, 2000), 60–6.

25. Some ecocritics might consider Heise or at least Hayles to be scholars of "literature and science" rather than ecocritics, but both have published in ecocritical venues and Heise in particular has taken a significant part in ASLE forums and conferences.

26. Strictly speaking, "ecofeminism" is a French invention, the term having been coined by Françoise d'Eaubonne (in *Le Féminisme ou la mort*, 1974). But the movement is of Anglophone origins (Merchant 1992: 184).

27. Conley (1997: 132), paraphrasing Luce Irigiray.

28. Latour dedicates *We Have Never Been Modern* to Donna Haraway, whose briefs on behalf of hybrids ("monsters," "cyborgs") respectfully cite Latour (Haraway 1991: 149–81, 295–337).

29. For Latour on the microbial revolution, see *The Pasteurization of France* (Cambridge, MA: Harvard University Press, 1988).

30. Clarke (2001: 152–4) states this case "affirmatively" (Latour attempting to move "beyond the culture of denunciation"); Phillips (2003: esp. 30–4) states it negatively (Latour as exposing the stupid extremisms of scientistic arrogance and postmodernist denial).

31. Bennett (1998: 53). He refers here to a passage from Annie Dillard's *Pilgrim at Tinker Creek,* not so much to chide the book itself (which he teaches to urban students) but to rebut environmental critic Neil Evernden's claim, citing the same passage, that one's place in the natural world can be found only through direct contact with the "ultrahuman" (Evernden 1992: 118–23).

32. William Schneider, "Everybody's an Environmentalist Now," *National Journal*, 22 (April 28, 1990): 1062.

33. The mordant Luhmann views ecological anxiety mainly as a "self-inductive" form of "self-certainty" in its own right, rather than as a reliable mechanism for ameliorating "the relation of society to its environment"; but he grants it the power to disrupt business-as-usual norms by creating a climate of critical self-reflexive moralism (Luhmann 1989: 129–31).

34. For example, Glotfelty and Fromm's *The Ecocriticism Reader* (1996) includes Cynthia Deitering's 1992 essay "The Postnatural Novel: Toxic Consciousness in Fiction of the 1980s"—right after Scott Russell Sanders' first-wave "Speaking a Word for Nature." The treatment of Don DeLillo's *White Noise* in both these essays, in turn, has been seized upon by one ecojustice revisionist as an indicator of how much further ecocriticism needs to go in the direction of pinpointing "the invasive, pervasive effects of corporate capitalism" and the workings of "the racial–class dynamic" (Reed 2002: 151), according to which Sanders' essay is judged clueless and Deitering's commendable but underconceptualized.

BIBLIOGRAPHY

Adamson, Joni, Mei Mei Evans, and Rachel Stein (eds.) 2002. *The Environmental Justice Reader: Politics, Poetics, and Pedagogy.* Tucson: University of Arizona Press.

Bate, Jonathan 1991. *Romantic Ecology: Wordsworth and the Environmental Tradition.* London: Routledge.

——. 2000. *The Song of the Earth.* Cambridge, MA: Harvard University Press.

Beck, Ulrich, Anthony Giddens, and Scott Lash 1994. *Reflexive Modernization: Politics, Tradition and Aesthetics in the Modern Social Order.* Stanford, CA: Stanford University Press.

Bennett, Michael 1998. "Urban Nature: Teaching Tinker Creek by the East River," *ISLE,* 5 (winter): 49–59.

Buell, Lawrence 2001. *Writing for an Endangered World: Literature, Culture, and Environment in the United States and Beyond.* Cambridge, MA: Harvard University Press.

Carroll, Joseph 1995. *Evolution and Literary Theory.* Columbia: University of Missouri Press.

Clarke, Bruce 2001. "Science, Theory, and Systems: A Response to Glen A. Love and Jonathan Levin," *ISLE,* 8 (winter): 149–65.

Comer, Krista 1999. *Landscapes of the New West: Gender and Geography in Contemporary Women's Writing.* Chapel Hill: University of North Carolina Press.

Conley, Verena 1997. *Ecopolitics: The Environment in Poststructuralist Thought.* London: Routledge.

Coupe, Laurence (ed.) 2000. *The Green Studies Reader: From Romantiasm to Ecocriticism.* London: Routledge.

Devall, Bill and George Sessions 1985. *Deep Ecology: Living as if Nature Mattered.* Salt Lake City, UT: Gibbs Smith.

Ehrenfeld, David W. 1978. *The Arrogance of Humanism.* Oxford: Oxford University Press.

Elder, John 1985. *Imagining the Earth: Poetry and the Vision of Nature.* Urbana: University of Illinois Press.

——. 1998. *Reading the Mountains of Home.* Cambridge, MA: Harvard University Press.

——. 1999. "The Poetry of Experience," *New Literary History,* 30 (summer): 649–59.

Fletcher, Angus 2004. *A New Theory for American Poetry: Democracy, the Environment, and the Future of Imagination.* Cambridge, MA: Harvard University Press.

Foucatt, Michel 1994. "The Birth of Biopolitics." In *Ethics: Subjectivity and Truth.* Trans. Robert Hurley et al. Ed. Paul Rabinow. New York: New Press, 73–9.

Gifford, Terry 2002 "Towards a Post-Pastoral View of British Poetry." In *The Environmental Tradition in English Literature.* Ed. John Parham. Aldershot: Ashgate, 35–58.

Glotfelty, Cheryll and Harold Fromm (eds.) 1996. *The Ecocriticism Reader: Landmarks in Literary Ecology.* Athens: University of Georgia Press.

Guber, Deborah Lynn 2003. *The Grassroots of a Green Revolution: Polling America on the Environment.* Cambridge, MA: MIT Press.

Hajer, Maarten A. 1995. *The Politics of Environmental Discourse: Ecological Modernization and the Policy Process.* Oxford: Clarendon Press.

Haraway, Donna 1991. *Simians, Cyborgs, and Women: The Reinvention of Nature.* New York: Routedge.

Harrison, Robert Pogue 1992. *Forests: The Shadow of Civilization.* Chicago: University of Chicago Press.

Hayles, N. Katherine 1999. *How We Became Posthuman: Virtual Bodies in Cybernetics, Literature, and Informatics.* Chicago: University of Chicago Press.

Head, Dominic 1998. "The (Im)possibility of Ecocriticism." In *Writing the Environment: Eccrititism and Literature.* Ed. Richard Kerridge and Neil Sammells. London: Zed Books, 27–39.

——. 2002, "Beyond 2000: Raymond Williams and the Ecocritic's Task." In *The Environmental Tradition in English Literature.* Ed. John Parham. Aldershot: Ashgate, 24–36.

Heise, Ursula 2002. "Toxins, Drugs, and Global Systems: Risk and Narrative in the Contemporary Novel." *American Literature,* 74 (December): 747–78.

Hess, Scott 2004. "Postmodern Pastoral, Advertising, and the Masque of Technology," *ISLE,* 11 (winter): 71–100.

Howarth, William 1996. "Some Principles of Ecocriticism." In *The Ecocriticism Reader: Landmarks in Literary Ecology.* Ed. Cheryll Glotfelty and Harold Fromm. Athens: University of Georgia Press.

Kern, Robert 2000. "Ecocriticism—What Is It Good For?" *ISLE,* 7 (winter): 9–32.

Krech, Shepard, III 1999. *The Ecological Indian: Myth and History.* New York: Norton.

Kroeber, Karl 1994. *Ecological Literary Criticism: Romantic Imagining and the Biology of Mind.* New York: Columbia University Press.

Latour, Bruno 1993. *We Have Never Been Modern.* Trans. Catherine Porter. Cambridge, MA: Harvard University Press.

——. 1999. *Pandora's Hope: Essays on the Reality of Science Studies.* Cambridge, MA: Harvard University Press.

Love, Glen A. 2003. *Practical Ecocriticism: Literature, Biology, and the Environment.* Charlottesville: University Press of Virginia.

Luhmann, Niklas 1989. *Ecological Communication.* Trans. John Bednarz, Jr. Chicago: University of Chicago Press.

McKusick, James C. 2000. *Green Writing: Romanticism and Ecology.* New York: St. Martin's Press.

Marshall, Ian 2003. *Peak Experiences: Walking Meditations on Literature, Nature, and Need.* Charlottesville: University Press of Virginia.

Mártinez-Alier, Joan 2002. *The Environmentalism of the Poor: A Study of Ecological Conflicts and Valuation.* Cheltenham: Elgar.

Marx, Leo 1964. *The Machine in the Garden: Technology and the Pastoral Ideal in America.* New York: Oxford University Press.

——. 1973. "Between Two Landscapes." *RIBA Journal,* 8 (August): 422–4.

——. 2003. "The Pandering Landscape: On American Nature as Illusion." In *"Natures Nation" Revisited: American Concepts of Nature from Wonder to Ecological Crisis* Ed. Hans Bak and Walter W. Hölbling. Amsterdam: VU University Press, 30–42.

Mazel, David (ed.) 2001. *A Century of Early Ecocriticism.* Athens: University of Georgia Press.

Meeker, Joseph W. 1997. *The Comedy of Survival: Literary Ecology and a Play Ethic*, 3rd edn. Tucson: University of Arizona Press. Orig. edn. 1972.

Merchant, Carolyn 1992. *Radical Ecology: The Search for a Livable World*. New York: Routledge.

Moore, Kathleen Dean 2004. *The Pine Island Paradox*. Minneapolis, MN: Milkweed.

Morton, Timothy 1994. *Shelley and the Revolution in Taste: The Body and the National World*. Cambridge: Cambridge University Press.

———. 2000. *The Poetics of Spice: Romantic Consumerism and the Exotic*. Cambridge: Cambridge University Press.

Newman, Lance 2002. "Marxism and Ecocriticism," *ISLE*, 9 (summer): 1–25.

Oerlemans, Onno 2002. *Romanticism and the Materiality of Nature*. Toronto: University of Toronto Press.

Phillips, Dana 2003. *The Truth of Ecology: Nature, Culture, and Literature in America*. New York: Oxford University Press.

Reed, T. V. 2002. "Toward an Environmental Justice Ecocriticism." In *The Environmental Justice Reader: Politics, Poetics, and Pedagogy*. Ed. Joni Adamson, Mei Mei Evans, and Rachel Stein. Tucson: University of Arizona Press, 145–62.

Rueckert, William 1996. "Literature and Ecology: An Experiment in Ecocriticism." Rpt. from 1978. In *The Erocriticism Reader. Landmarks in Literary Ecology*. Ed. Cheryll Glotfelty and Harold Fromm. Athens: University of Georgia Press, 105–23.

Said, Edward 1978. *Orientalism*. New York: Random House.

———. 1993. *Cultural and Imperialism*. New York: Knopf.

Sandilands, Catriona 1999. *The Good-Natured Feminist: Ecofeminism and the Quest for Democracy*. Minneapolis: University of Minnesota Press.

Satterfield, Terre and Scott Slovic (ed.) 2004. *What's Nature Worth? Narrative Expressions of Environmental Values*. Salt Like City: University of Utah Press.

Snyder, Gary 2004. "Ecology, Literature, and the New World Disorder," *ISLE*, 11 (winter): 1–13.

Tallmadge, John 2000. "Toward a Natural History of Reading," *ISLE*, 7 (winter): 33–45.

Tsing, Anna Lowenhaupt 1993. *In the Realm of the Diamond Queen: Marginality in an Out-of-the-Way Place*. Princeton, NJ: Princeton University Press.

Welty, Eudora 1970. "Place in Fiction." In *The Eye of the Story*. New York: Random House.

Westling, Louise H. 1996. *The Green Breast of the New World: Landscape, Gender, and American Fiction*. Athens: University of Georgia Press.

White, Lynn, Jr. 1967. "The Historical Roots of Our Ecologic Crisis," *Science*, 155 (March 10): 1203–7.

Williams, Raymond 1973. *The Country and the City*. New York: Oxtord University Press.

———. 1977. *Marxism and Literature*. New York: Oxford University Press

———. 1989. "Socialism and Ecology." In *Resources of Hope: Culture, Democracy, Socialism*. Ed. Robin Gable. London: Verso, 210–26.

Willms, Johannes 2004. *Conversations with Ulrich Beck*. Trans. Michael Pollak. Cambridge: Polity Press.

HOW FORMALISM BECAME A DIRTY WORD, AND WHY WE CAN'T DO WITHOUT IT (2002)

RICHARD STRIER

In recent years, some critics have called for a "new formalism." Such critics sometimes fear that criticism committed to political goals and drawing on such movements as Marxism, feminism, cultural studies, historicism, queer studies, disability studies, or ecocriticism has lost track of its literary interest and turned into a version of sociology, history, or political science that happens to include examples from literature. Joining the dialogue about new formalism, Strier offers a deeply historicist call to keep literary criticism and interpretation formalist as well as historicist. Steeped in the history of twentieth-century criticism, including Cleanth Brooks and Paul de Man (both included in this volume), Strier reminds us that even so representative a formalist as the new critic Brooks called for literary criticism to draw on and speak to history. Noting that new historicists like to see how a literary text speaks back to history, Strier asks us to read literary form not just for patterns that connect one part of a text to another but also as an index of the culture that helps produce form and that form both reflects and speaks back to. Strier believes that "The level of style and syntax is the true level of 'lived' experience." That belief can keep us from reducing literary form to its role as a window we look through to an exterior life that provides the text's value. Instead, the textual window is itself always already part of what we look at while we also look through it.

To Strier, new historicist writing takes a valuable but nonliterary approach to literature. Others may object that while some new historicist writing takes a nonliterary approach, some takes a partly literary approach, or that the line between the literary and the nonliterary is not so firm as Strier assumes when he draws on René Wellek's distinction between monuments (literary) and documents (nonliterary). Part of our response to Strier's stance may depend on how firmly we believe that we can distinguish the literary from the nonliterary, or, if we can distinguish them, how avidly we choose to pursue the distinction. Strier himself invites us to bring the questions of formalist literary interpretation to the interpretation of documents as well as of monuments. If we do so, will that diminish the distinction between monuments and documents, or would we export the method without exporting the literariness that we associate with it? However we answer such questions, the distinction between the literary and the nonliterary or less literary remains central to the discussion of formalist interpretations of literature.

(For another call for a return to the study of literary form, see the essay in this volume by Susan J. Wolfson.)

I'm afraid that in my rather eighteenth-century title, "Wherein the author, etc.," I certainly promise more than I am going to deliver. In particular, I am not going to give a proper historical account but only the merest sketch of a history. I am also not truly going to show why—in absolute terms—we can't do without formalism. Much of my effort will go into distinguishing between two different kinds of "formalism" and considering the implications and underlying premises of each of them. I will argue that we give up a lot if we do, in fact, want to do without "formalism" in either of these senses. And I will argue this in relation to both literary and historical studies.

My modest and inadequate historical sketch is as follows. Formalism got to be a dirty word partly through essays like de Man's "The Dead-End of Formalist Criticism," written (in French) in the fifties but widely disseminated (in English) in the seventies (and echoed in Hartman's *Beyond Formalism* in 1970); partly through the resurgence of a certain kind of Marxist criticism; and partly through a very widespread misunderstanding of the phrase, "new historicism." To begin where I have begun, de Man's essay, when one actually looks at it and reads more than the title, turns out (like so many things) to be rather peculiar and complex. The "Dead-End" (or, properly, "Impasse") essay is deeply involved with Hegelian and Heideggerian notions like "the deep division of Being itself."[1] The central premise of the essay is the necessity of "the unhappy consciousness" which literature, especially poetry, is said to dramatize or reveal. Formalist criticism in its *echt* or naive state is held to be criticism expressing the false or "happy consciousness," which believes in a perfect adequation of language and the world, and of intention and meaning. I. A. Richards in the Anglo-Saxon world and Roland Barthes in France are associated with this position. De Man's major point about the "impasse" of formalism is that it must necessarily, by following out the logic of its own premises and techniques, produce deconstruction. In "Form and Intent in American New Criticism," he states the point clearly. New Criticism, he there argues, starts with the assumption of wholeness, unity, and reconciliation, but ends by revealing ironies, ambiguities and discontinuities.[2] Empson is the hero of the "Impasse" essay because Empson recognized this.

Yet despite de Man's stated desire to open criticism to "the sorrowful time of patience, i.e., history" ("Impasse," 245), deconstruction was too easily seen not as a negation but as a version of formalism—as one that privileged the aesthetic by giving up the category, and remained focused on textual matters. New historicism has been widely taken as announcing the arrival of "historicism" on the literary-critical scene—and this despite the deterministic premises of nineteenth-century "historicism," and despite the historical fact that the point of the phrase "new historicism" was the contrast with an older kind of historicism, not with formalism.[3] The point was *new* historicism, not new *historicism*—though "the profession" has steadfastly refused to see this. There is a great desire to see historicism—in some loose sense—as in itself the new thing, and therefore to demonize "formalism" as its (falsely) presumed opposite. We are "new" in that we are historicists, not formalists. This claim is particularly odd in fields like Renaissance and Romantic studies, where historical work continued to thrive through the heyday of the New Criticism. But the myth—like all successful myths—retains its power in the face of facts. The bad consequences of this include not only the demonization of literary formalism—even while a formalism is established elsewhere—but also the production in current graduate students of a remarkable and complacent ignorance of earlier (pre-1980) works of historical scholarship as well as of "formalist" criticism.[4] It seems to me that as few of my graduate students have read Rosemond Tuve or D. C. Allen as have read Cleanth Brooks or, for that matter, William Empson. But that's an initiative for another occasion—the defense of "old" historicism.[5]

With regard to formalism, I want to distinguish formalism as an ideology from formalism as a practice, and then to make some distinctions within the realm—not, of course, entirely nonideological—of practice. By formalism as an ideology, I mean the view that literature, like all other arts, is best studied by the detailed observation of what is taken to constitute the formal structure of individual works. As the mention of other arts suggests, literary formalism in this sense is part of general aesthetics. The critic's aim is to reveal the significant patterns within the work, and the assumption is that the revelation and "explication" of these patterns will serve to demonstrate (or, more rarely, establish) the aesthetic value of the work in question. This kind of criticism is necessarily committed to the question of value (and, somewhat against its will, to that of disvalue).[6] Explication, as W. K. Wimsatt explained, becomes criticism insofar as it reveals value.[7] This kind of criticism is also committed to an interest in what makes works of art special—in the case of literature to some conception of "literariness." This quality can be conceived in different ways, just as quite different formal features can be held to be crucial (imagery versus plot, for instance), but the question of literary value is built into the approach.[8] In giving up formalist ideology, we tend, therefore, to give up both the question of value and the conception of "the literary." Perhaps we (collectively) do want to give up these things, but surely we need (collectively) to think much more about this than we have.

One of the ways that the ideology of formalism expresses itself is in the importance it attaches to phrases like "in itself" and "as such"—the work "itself" or "in itself" or "as such." We should all remember (and some of us do) books with titles like "the poem itself." The idea was, first, that the work of (literary) art was different from other things (other kinds of writing); and second, that such a work was, if valuable, a worthy object of study on its own, without "external" materials. This is a position that is easily parodied. As René Wellek (who popularized the "internal-external" distinction) says, "A straw man is set up: the New Critic who supposedly denies that a work of art can be illuminated by historical knowledge at all."[9] But in practice the critic can indeed focus on formal patterns—imagery, plot, or whatever— that are intelligibly regarded as internal to the work. If one is interested in individual works (or texts) at all, one cannot avoid attempting analysis something like this. But perhaps we are not interested in individual works. I will return to this.

The "internalist" critic runs into trouble when the work "itself" is filled with allusions or, especially, references.[10] Allusions can keep us within a formal system of works, but references are trickier. In a once-famous essay attempting to sort out the relations between "criticism" and "history," Cleanth Brooks rather bravely took Marvell's "Horatian Ode" to Cromwell as his test case. Although Brooks disingenuously claimed that he did not choose the "Ode" as a hard case but as a normal one, Brooks acknowledged the debt of the figure he called "the critic" to the lexicographer for access to the meanings of words in the text, and he noted that since, in this particular (but supposedly non-special) case, "many of the words of this poem are [historical] proper nouns," the critic owes a debt to the historian as well.[11] Brooks nonetheless argued that despite these unavoidable debts, the critic, meaning the formalist, "has a significant function even in relation to this text." Despite some false steps, I think that Brooks does, in fact, prove this. Most of the false steps in Brooks' analysis derive from implicit historical and political assumptions that have nothing to do with his general procedures. For reasons that have to do more with his own politics than with his critical method, Brooks has trouble believing that any intelligent person could *praise* Cromwell. So Brooks devotes himself to finding implied criticisms and undercuttings in Marvell's poem, and these are often forced, over-ingenious, and conventionally moralizing. Yet some of Brooks' formal observations are simply true. In the early part of the poem, Cromwell *is* treated as a force rather than as a person; "the thunderbolt simile of the first part of the poem" *does* give way "to the falcon simile" in the second; and this latter figure surely "revises and qualifies the former" (116–17). I take it that such observations are data about the poem "as such." I also take it that such observations are data about Andrew Marvell's attitude toward Oliver Cromwell in 1650. Brooks backs away from the latter—"I have tried to read the poem," he says, "not Andrew Marvell's mind." But this retreat is not a very happy, stable, or successful one. Brooks goes on to concede that the poem "may tell us a great deal about Marvell's attitude toward Cromwell." He even goes so far as to say that "it probably does" so before he begins (partially) backing away again (125). But he needn't have backed away at all. Despite some confusion on the matter, formalist ideology is only committed to rejecting a crude form of intentionalism.[12]

When Brooks asserts that what the poem "says" is a question "for the critic rather than for the historian to answer" (127), he means that what the poem "says" can be ascertained only by detailed analysis that takes imagery and development into account and does not rely on quotations out of context or on gross generalizations. Brooks makes the (I think) extremely important point—though not one that he was in fact very interested in—that the critic, who is reading with "literary" sensitivity, "may on occasion be able to make a return on his debt to the historian" (127). The results of a formalist analysis, in other words, may themselves be *data* for historical understanding. The "literary" nuances of the poem "itself" may help us understand its historical moment, just as, in turn, detailed knowledge of the historical moment may—in a richer way than Brooks suggests—help us understand the nuances of a poem.

Moreover, and here I move from the ideology to the practice of formalism, the literary scholar trained in, let's call it, internalist reading can "make a return on his debt to the historian" in another way as well. Once we discard, at least for most purposes, Wellek's distinction between "monuments" and "documents"—between works and texts—and recognize that, insofar as the historian's sources are written, the analyst has as direct access to them as to literary works, then "internalist" reading of (so-called) documents becomes a possible practice.[13] And, I would argue, a highly desirable and informative one. Very few historical documents—meaning nonliterary and practically significant texts—have been subjected to "close reading" in the formalist sense. They have been very closely read for factual references and implications (names, places, dates, and datable references) and, occasionally, for keywords and key concepts (as in Hexter, Pocock, and Skinner), but they have not been *read* in the formalist sense at all.[14] Their patterns of imagery and rhetorical development have overwhelmingly not been noticed. I can testify from my own experience that surprising insights emerge when such patterns in "documents" are perceived. I tried the experiment of attempting an "old-fashioned close-reading" of two famous "documents" from early in the English Revolution. The results were startling. I discovered that the first of these documents, now always known as the "Root and Branch" Petition, should not properly be referred in this way, since the title phrase never, in fact, appears in the text in the grammatically singular form. Moreover, it turns out that the plural form—"roots and branches"—is crucial to the vision of widespread corruption that the text is presenting. A close reading of the "Grand Remonstrance" was equally productive, showing this text to be much more optimistic and consciously revolutionary than it is normally taken to be.[15]

But let me return to formalist practices in relation to literary texts. When one takes as model formalists figures like Leo Spitzer or Eric Auerbach, rather than Cleanth Brooks, one moves into a different world of formalist ideology and practice. The essential premise of critics like Spitzer or Auerbach is not the importance of detecting formal patterns within texts but the premise, as de Man puts it, of a "continuity between depth and surface"— the belief, that is, that formal features of a text, matters of style, can be indices to large intellectual and cultural matters.[16] I would call this practice and ideology "indexical" rather than aesthetic formalism. In his most famous book, Auerbach took on the task of studying "the representation of reality in Western literature" by considering minute details of style in selected passages from selected texts. In the famous opening chapter, on Homer and the Hebrew bible, Auerbach moves from kinds of syntax to kinds of narrative to matters of social, psychological, and religious world-view.[17] It does not matter, for my general point, whether Auerbach's conception of Homer is adequate (I think that it is suggestive but oversimplified); what matters is the premise that questions of style, minutely conceived, can be indices to large issues. This premise can be used by thoroughly historical critics. It is meant, in fact, to be a historical tool. In English Renaissance studies, for instance, we can think of the extraordinarily rich work of Morris Croll on the implications of baroque or Attic or Senecan style.[18] Even closer to Auerbach, we can point to how richly an Auerbachian insistence on "mixed" style and diction in Shakespeare has borne fruit in the work of Robert Weimann.[19] This kind of formalist believes, with Empson—who was himself a formalist *of this kind*—that "a profound enough criticism could extract an entire cultural history from a simple lyric."[20]

Let me give a brief and spectacular but by no means unusual example of this sort of "extraction," an example not tied to a particular conception of style. The procedure at issue is that of noting and giving full cultural weight to tiny anomalies and discontinuities. The point of such an analysis is not to deconstruct the text but to understand it. In Herbert's "Longing," this stanza (addressed to God) occurs:

Indeed the world's thy book,
   Where all things have their leafe assign'd:
Yet a meek look
Hath interlin'd.
   Thy board is full, yet humble guests
Finde nests. (49–54)[21]

What struck me, on reading this stanza "closely"—that is, with attention and with the assumption that details matter—was the concessive and insistently adversative structure of it. "*Indeed* the world's thy book ... *Yet* a meek look...Thy board is full, *yet*..." I wanted to know why the speaker was not, like Dante at the ecstatic end of the *Paradiso*, happy that the cosmos was God's "book,/Where all things have their leafe assigned." Why did he have to introduce the messy intrusion of "interlining"? Similarly, I wanted to know why the vision of "fullness"—Pleroma—was not ecstatic.[22] To get an answer required recognizing in the image of the book and the mention of "fullness" the cosmology of the Great Chain of Being, which, as Lovejoy has taught us, places great weight on inclusiveness, position, and plenitude.[23] And one then had to recognize that the stanza dramatized the difference between what Tertullian called "the God of the Philosophers," whose glory is cosmological, and the God of devotion, whose glory is dynamism and immediate responsiveness.[24] All this out of an "indeed" and two "yet"'s.

But why would one *want* to do "cultural history" in this way, from a (not so) simple lyric? Why begin at the micro-level? If there is a "continuity between depth and surface," why not skip the surface? Why not go to the grand issues directly? The answer to these questions has to do with a belief that one has to know the texture as well as the content of ideas to do intellectual or cultural history with true sensitivity, and with a corollary belief that this texture is most fully experienced at the level of verbal and stylistic detail, where tensions are manifested in texts in very subtle and unpredictable ways. The level of style and syntax is the true level of "lived" experience.[25]

Finally, let us consider what it would mean truly to give up all formalist premises. It would mean that we would give up on taking matters of style and textual disruptions as loci of significance. It would mean giving up on the individual literary work as a significant object of study. New historicism comes close, at times, to doing these things. It tends, first of all, to proceed from passages rather than from works as a whole. It will rightly be noted that a formalist like Auerbach does this as well, but the relevant difference is that new historicists tend to treat their passages almost entirely in terms of content. The relation between formalism of any sort and new historicism in literary studies might be captured by the "use-mention" distinction familiar in the work of Quine and other analytic philosophers.[26] Formalists are concerned with the uses to which details in literary (and other) texts are put. Their premise is that *the work provides the initial context* for understanding the significance of any particular item in a text. The question is "How is feature X used in this text?" New historicism, like very old historicism, is concerned with mentions. The fact that some item that is taken to be culturally or politically significant is mentioned in a text—in passing, in a metaphor, it doesn't matter how—is sufficient to get the machinery of "archeology" and archive-churning going.[27] Much that is rich and strange is turned up in this way, but the object of this kind of study is not literature, or any text, but some aspect of a culture in general. Ultimately, I think, the question of formalism is tied up with the question of whether a *literary* approach is valuable and worthwhile—both "in itself" and in relation to the whole world of texts, including "documents."

NOTES

1. Paul de Man, "The Dead-End of Formalist Criticism," in *Blindness and Insight: Essays in the Rhetoric of Contemporary Criticism,* 2nd ed. (Minneapolis: University of Minnesota Press, 1983), 229–245.

2. Paul de Man, "Form and Intent in American New Criticism," in *Blindness and Insight*, 20–35, esp. 28.

3. For Stephen Greenblatt's struggle with the term "historicism," see his "Resonance and Wonder" in *Learning to Curse: Essays in Early Modern Culture* (New York: Routledge, 1990), 161–183, esp. 164–5.

4. On the formalism of Clifford Geertz's anthropologic work—the model for much new historicism—see, *inter alia,* my remarks in "Historicism Old and New: Excerpts from a Panel Discussion," in *"The Muses Common-weale": Poetry and Politics in the Seventeenth Century*, ed. Claude J. Summers and Ted-Larry Pebworth (Columbia: University of Missouri Press, 1988), 214; and Vincent P. Pecora, "The Limits of Local Knowledge," in *The New Historicism*, ed. H. Aram Veeser (New York: Routledge, 1989), 243–276.

5. For an attempt at a balanced assessment of the need for and accomplishments of both "new" and "old," see Richard Strier, *Resistant Structures: Particularity, Radicalism, and Renaissance Texts* (Berkeley: University of California Press, 1995), ch. 4.

6. See the wonderful chapter "Badness in Poetry" in I. A. Richards, *Principles of Literary Criticism* (New York: Harcourt, 1925), 199–206.

7. See Wimsatt's title essay in *Explication as Criticism: Selected Papers from the English Institute, 1941–1952* (New York: Columbia University Press, 1963), 1–26; also W. K. Wimsatt, *The Verbal Icon: Studies in the Meaning of Poetry* (Lexington: University of Kentucky Press, 1954), 234–265.

8. The sometimes bitter conflict between the "Chicago school" and the Yale and other New Critics was entirely a matter of which formal features were held to have priority. See the essays by R. S. Crane and W. R. Keast on New Criticism in *Critics and Criticism, Ancient and Modern*, ed. R. S. Crane (Chicago: University of Chicago Press, 1952). I took my stand with the "Chicago school" in "The Poetics of Surrender: An Exposition and Critique of New Critical Poetics," *Critical Inquiry* 2 (1975): 171–189.

9. René Wellek, "Literary Theory, Criticism, and History," in René Wellek, *Concepts of Criticism*, ed. Stephen G. Nichols (New Haven: Yale University Press, 1963), 6.

10. Quentin Skinner's distinction between "relatively autonomous" and "relatively heteronomous" works is of use here. See Skinner, "Hermeneutics and the Role of History," *New Literary History* 7 (1975): 209–232, esp. 222–3.

11. Cleanth Brooks, "Literary Criticism: Marvell's Horatian Ode" (1946), in Wimsatt, ed., *Explication as Criticism*, 106. Further page references will appear in the text.

12. For Empson's puzzlement at the anti-intentionalism of Brooks and Wimsatt, see his review of Brooks' *The Well Wrought Urn*, "Thy Darling in an Urn" (1947), reprinted in William Empson, *Argufying: Essays on Literature and Culture*, ed. John Haffenden (Iowa City: University of Iowa Press, 1988), 282–88; and Empson's comments upon Wimsatt's *The Verbal Icon*, "Still the Strange Necessity" (1955), reprinted in *Argufying*, 120–128.

13. For the distinction between "monuments" and "documents," see Wellek, "Literary Theory, Criticism, and History," 15.

14. See the textual analyses in J. H. Hexter, *The Vision of Politics on the Eve of the Reformation: More, Machiavelli, and Seysell* (New York: Basic, 1973); in J. G. A. Pocock, *The Machiavellian Moment: Florentine Political Thought and the Atlantic Republican Tradition* (Princeton: Princeton University Press, 1975); and in Quentin Skinner, *The Foundations of Modern Political Thought*, 2 vols. (Cambridge: Cambridge University Press, 1978). For calls for what Hexter calls "macroanalysis" of historical "documents," see J. H. Hexter, "The Rhetoric of History," in *Doing History* (Bloomington: University of Indiana Press, 1971), 48–50, and Dominick LaCapra, "Rethinking Intellectual

History and Reading Texts," in *Rethinking Intellectual History: Texts, Contexts, Language* (Ithaca: Cornell University Press, 1983), 32–35.

15. See Richard Strier, "From Diagnosis to Operation: The 'Root and Branch' Petition and the Grand Remonstrance," in *The Theatrical City: Culture, Theatre, and Politics in London, 1576–1649,* ed. David L. Smith, Richard Strier, and David Bevington (Cambridge: Cambridge University Press, 1995), 224–244.

16. De Man, "Form and Intent in American New Criticism," 23.

17. Eric Auerbach, *Mimesis: The Representation of Reality in Western Literature,* trans. Willard R. Trask (Princeton: Princeron University Press, 1953), ch. 1. For Spitzer, see Leo Spitzer, *Essays on English and American Literature,* ed. Anna Hatcher (Princeton: Princeton University Press, 1962).

18. See Morris Croll, *Style, Rhetoric, and Rhythm: Essays by Morris W. Croll,* ed. J. Max Patrick and Robert O. Evans, with John M. Wallace and R. J. Schoeck (Princeton: Princeton University Press, 1966).

19. 19. See, for instance, Robert Weimann, "'Appropriation' and Modern History in Renaissance Prose Narrative," *New Literary History* 14 (1983): 459–95; and Weimann, "History and the Issue of Authority in Representation: The Elizabethan Theater and the Reformation," *New Literary History* 17 (1986): 449–76.

20. William Empson, "The Verbal Analysis" (1950), in Empson, *Argufying,* 107. On the historicism of Empson, see Strier, *Resistant Structures,* ch. 1.

21. From *The Works of George Herbert,* ed. F. E. Hutchinson (Oxford: Clarendon, 1941).

22. For the "Pleroma," see Hans Jonas, *The Gnostic Religion: The Message of the Alien God and the Beginnings of Christianity,* 2nd ed. (Boston: Beacon, 1963), esp. ch. 8.

23. See Arthur O. Lovejoy, *The Great Chain of Being: A Study of the History of an Idea* (Cambridge: Harvard University Press, 1936), ch. 1.

24. For a fuller version of this reading, see Strier, *Love Known: Theology and Experience in George Herbert's Poetry* (Chicago: University of Chicago Press, 1983), 166–173.

25. For defense and exemplification of this claim, see the "close reading" of Donne's third satire in Strier, *Resistant Structures,* ch. 6.

26. W. V. Quine, *Methods of Logic,* 4th ed. (Cambridge: Harvard University Press, 1982) 50, l46n., 268.

27. This model of "archeology" derives, of course, from Foucault. See Michel Foucault, *The Archeology of Knowledge* [1969], trans. A. M. Sheridan Smith (New York: Pantheon, 1972), and *The Order of Things: An Archeology of the Human. Sciences* [1966], trans. A. M. Sheridan Smith [?] (New York: Pantheon, 1970).

READING FOR FORM (2000,2006)

SUSAN J. WOLFSON

Charting the history of ideas about literary form in Anglo-American literary criticism of the twentieth century, Wolfson reacts against a movement, from about the 1980s on, away from the study of literary form. In this selection from her introduction to an anthology of essays called Reading for Form, *she responds to the history of criticism tracked across much of this volume. The new critics intensified the study of literary form. Later, and partly in response, Marxist and new historicist critics turned to sociocultural readings of literature. Wolfson sees sociocultural criticism as allowing its objection to new criticism to lead critics away from studying form, even from studying it in sociocultural and historicist ways. Thus while recent critics who think of themselves as new formalists sometimes seem to yearn for the social and political conservatism or indifference of new criticism, Wolfson invites critics to merge the study of form with the study of history revived by new historicism. Some critics might question whether recent criticism buries literary form as much as Wolfson contends, but she is certainly right that many current critics ignore or even sneer at the study of literary form.*

(For another call for a return to the study of literary form, see the essay in this volume by Richard Strier.)

Have you observ'd a sitting hare,
    Listening, and fearful of the storm
Of horns and hounds, clap back her ear,
    Afraid to keep, or leave her form?

So wrote Matthew Prior in *The Dove*, back in the eighteenth century. It could have been a satiric squib on the plight of formalist criticism at the end of the twentieth. Though some of us had never stopped reading for form, the practice in general, as a disciplinary love, devotion, and commitment, had gone underground or out to the margins. It was an aggrieved, counter-hegemonic, coterie remnant of an earlier critical heyday, at odds with sociocultural critique, or, if added into its mix, usually put there to expose complicity with dominant oppressions and false consciousness. Or at least that's the way it felt at the fin de siècle, with no little elegy for the loss of attention to the most complex, stimulating work (and play) of literary agency. Thus it was no news in 2003 to see W. J. T. Mitchell beginning an invitational essay with a wry sigh about this addiction: "Everyone knows that the concept of form has outlived its usefulness in discussions of literature, the arts, and media."[1]

Reading for Form was tracking alongside Mitchell's obituary headline, pressing against that world in which "everyone knows" the score—often, we thought, without knowing how to read for form in the first place. In exception to the "everyone" that Mitchell performatively overstated, formalist criticism was not only still alive in the 1990s but was exercising new muscle, first in informal discussions, then in a gathering at MLA 1997, then in a landmark issue of *Modern Language Quarterly* that branded the title of this expanded anthology. If those reading for form might seem to a generation of cultural critics like so many form-addicted hares not knowing how to survive the storms of history, in our point of view, a care for form was irreducibly, inextricably the force of literature in history. Let's return, just for a moment, to Prior's invitation to observe. The very fun of this local satire of form-addiction depends on the lively attention of the "you" whom he addresses, a *you* that is assumed to be, if not an addict, then at the very least dedicated to the audible and visible communications of form. Prior's verse converses with readers able to register the press of *storm* across *horn* to reach its rhyme in *form*—that safety to which storm lays a claim and against which it gets its own visibility. Prior's letter-press no less than his figure of hare-sense plays a game of keep and leave: the a-rhyme cued by *hare* hits the atonal, splayed lettering of *her ear*. Not a rhyme but a disarray of sight and sound. The natural form of the hare—as if starting out of embodied form into the derangements of poetic form— works conspicuously, proactively, in excess of the definition Dr. Johnson gave *form* in his dictionary (citing these very lines as his instance): "the seat or bed of a hare."

Keeping with form without being embedded in fearful addictions, we decided to begin in earnest our conversations about the creative and critical work of written forms. We weren't compacting with that 1980s-Reagan-era school of American poetry called "New Formalism," a throwback to the New Formalism of the 1950s, and, like it, invested in a reactionary poetics and politics. Nor were we calling for a new New Criticism, let alone its disciplinary constraints and enforcements. The most instructive New Criticism was always more open and dialectical, anyway. The ventures of deconstructive criticism and the expansion of inquiry into the agency of history and institution gave the best formalisms and the best historicisms new energy. We were unabashed readers for form, against the grain of those rigors that seemed more intent on information, and inattentive to its involvements with form. Even so, the *MLQ* event was no counter-manifesto for a new formalism, though some thought this was the only mode of impact. Thus one reviewer of the *MLQ* issue complained, "it does not hold together as a coherent statement about formalist criticism and its aims; ... is not a manifesto of 'a new formalism.' ... It's hard to see a new program for formalist literary studies emerging from this volume" (anonymous report). We thought of putting this on the dust jacket as a positive advertisement. Certainly, as the essays within demonstrate, again and again, the vitality of reading for form is freedom from program and manifesto, from any uniform discipline.

A uniform discipline becomes most interesting in its unraveling. In 1998, as the winter of the Starr impeachment inquiry daily dissolved the Clinton presidency into scandals of Gap dress and power tie, the *New York Times* gave us a brief relief with a foray into teen culture. "Cracking the Dress Code: How a School Uniform Becomes a Fashion Statement" reported a bracing bit of cultural formation.[2] "It's how you *want* to look," said one student, unflapped by the prescription at the School of the Incarnation for white blouse, navy skirt, or slacks for girls, white shirt and navy slacks for boys. With the dressers performing as both critics and artists, the basic material proved negotiable, the dress code itself an inspiring resource. Subtle accessorizing (just cautious enough to evade a bust) was one route, a use of artful supplement, perhaps so artful that only the wearer knew for sure. The school uniform itself became multiform, its deformation producing the syntax of fashion-statement: the arrangement of collars and cuffs, the interpretation of *white,* the use or nonuse of sweater buttons, the number of rolls to take in a skirt waistband, formfitting to baggy-slouching pants, knotting the tie, indulging the frisson of unseen underwear—all opportunities to perform with and within the uniform.

One student's gloss on this material culture casually and cannily fell into the form of an irregular couplet (I render the lines):

> They know you're not going to totally conform
> because half the time you don't want to be in perfect uniform.

My nonce couplet form, appropriately, can only almost conform to traditional formal prescription. What an exuberant playing out, by the teens, of art historian T. J. Clark's argument that "the work of art may have an ideology (in other words, those ideas, images, and values which are generally accepted, dominant) as its material, but it *works* that material; it gives it a new form and at certain times that new form is in itself a subversion of ideology."[3]

A reading of activist formalism was one of the things lost in "the radical transformation of literary study that has taken place over the last decade" (i.e., into the early 1990s), described by George Levine in his introduction to *Aesthetics and Ideology*. Levine noted two related negative effects on formalist criticism: first, a regard of literature as "indistinguishable from other forms of language" (refuting the key tenet of "New Criticism"), and second, a more pointed hostility, "a virtually total rejection of, even contempt for, 'formalism.'" Levine himself, though meaning to be hospitable to a formalist criticism refreshed for the 1990s, slipped into negative descriptions and defensiveness.[4] And no wonder. The most influential stories in criticism typically proffered the narrowest versions of literary form to serve accounts of its covert work.

Assaults on formalist criticism came from many quarters, some with critiques of social isolationism; others, of intellectual constraints. It was not attention to form per se that was discredited; it was the impulse to regard it as the product of any historically disinterested, internally coherent aesthetics. Critics as various as Harold Bloom and Terry Eagleton found common ground. Bloom indicted the "impasse of Formalist criticism."[5] Eagleton's influential essay "Ideology and Literary Form" read literary form as shaped and limited by the social forms of its historical situation and typically in the business, consciously or not, of recasting "historical contradictions into ideologically resolvable form." A formalist criticism was useful only insofar as it teased out the "ideological struggles" that literary form was said to displace through "naturalising, moralising, and mythifying devices." These struggles, "marginalised yet … querulously present," took possession of literary form in two chief modes that the astute formalist critic could expose: in forms that seemed to get away with it and proffer resolution, the critical work was to compel "organic closures [to] betray their *constructing* functions"; in works riddled with "self-contradictory forms," "fissures and hiatuses—formal displacements," "formal discontinuities," or "formal dissonances," the critic could argue these events as necessarily part of the work's "historical meaning."[6]

Form in these exposures was virtually equivalent to structure, whether constructing, or prone to deconstruction. Exposing the fragile facticity of form and its incomplete cover-ups was the most powerful form-attentive criticism in the post- (and anti-) New Critical climate. To read for form was to read against formalism: no longer New Critical explication, the project was now New Historicist critique. Thus Jerome J. McGann's influential but restrictive description of the business in the so-called "Romantic Ideology" that invests poetic form: "Unlike non-aesthetic utterance," poetic form offers social evaluations "to the reader *under the sign of completion.*" While formalists take this sign "as their object of study," historicists will measure both the "experience of finality and completion" and the "trans-historical" claim as the product of a specific discourse of "historical totality." "Integral form is the sign of this seeming knowledge—and it persuades its reader that such a totality is not just a poetic illusion, but a truth." Aesthetic form, in this regard, is totalized into "ideological formation." The "specialized" analysis of the "formal" will matter only insofar as it can (rather, "must") find its "raison d'être in the socio-historical ground."[7] The project, as Catherine Gallagher describes it, was to undo the "false resolution" of aesthetic form, and to read out "the original contradiction and the formal signs of its irresolvability."[8] Even with different theoretical stakes, the other powerful post-New Critical critique of formalism, deconstruction, shared this interest in contradictions. Paul de Man challenged the New Critical "theory of signifying form" (language as containing, reflecting, or referring to experience) not only with a critique of organic closure and verbal iconicity, but also with a theory of "constituting form," with which, inasmuch as it pointed toward a formalism tuned for social and ideological analyses, even Marxists could make peace.[9]

These are ironic developments for an American formalist criticism that itself emerged in revolt against another moribund critical institution, old historicism. The radical claim of the "new" formalists of the mid-twentieth century was that the writing and reading of literature not only could not avoid, but in fact compelled, a recognition of its formal arrangements—of form, in Jan Mukařovský's words, as "an indirect semantic factor."[10] In *Theory of Literature,* a once influential advocacy for "intrinsic study," René Wellek and Austin Warren called for a reading of the "work of art" as "a whole system of signs, or structure of signs, serving a specific aesthetic purpose." This approach answered their dissatisfaction with "the old dichotomy" between "form as the factor aesthetically active and a content aesthetically indifferent"; they wanted an account of the means by which words become "aesthetically effective."[11] Against a then dominant emphasis on content (manifest or repressed), R. S. Crane similarly argued, with a tighter focus on poetry, that nothing "is matter or content merely, in relation to which something else is form.... Everything is formed, and hence rendered poetic."[12] It is revealing that Geoffrey H. Hartman, who by the late 1960s felt ready to move "beyond formalism," diagnosed his own addiction to it in 1975 as an inability to discover a "method to distinguish clearly what is formal and what is not."[13] This unfolding discussion, claiming a wider and wider field for form, was more than an intervention: it was a radical reorganization of the subject and the method of reading. No small part of this work was a primary, foundational claim for the agency of language in the world.

Designating aesthetic agency—the deepest rationale of mid-twentieth-century formalist criticism—had a double force. Form was read as significant; yet warding off the old contextual claims meant courting a kind of isolationism, if not in the best practitioners, then in the general atmosphere. Hartman dedicated *Beyond Formalism* to the arch anti-formalist Bloom. Seeking a critical mode for a Bloomlike "engaged reflection of personal myths and communal dreams," he wanted "to go beyond formalism and to define art's role in the life of the artist, his culture, and the human community" (ix). Hartman sharpened this goal against two institutions: first, the socialist view of formalism as the aesthetic opponent of social progress (ix), and second, the high New Critical "Yale formalism" (René Wellek, Cleanth Brooks, W. K. Wimsatt), which seemed to isolate aesthetic form from human content. The *Beyond* that was Hartman's titular preposition (and proposition) was already cast ironically, however, for the book's eponymous essay wound up (or always planned on) saying that "to go beyond formalism" may be to go "against the nature of understanding"; the crucial question was whether it is possible to get "beyond formalism without going through the study of forms" (42). One seemed to find oneself thinking in forms even about the possibility of thinking otherwise. "There are many ways to transcend formalism," Hartman was sure, but "the worst," he was just as sure, "is not to study forms" (56).

No sooner had he advertised a move beyond formalism than Hartman found himself "more rather than less impressed ... by how hard it is to advance 'beyond formalism' in the understanding of literature" *(Fate,* vii). Hartman's addiction was not his alone. Tony Bennett, noting Louis Althusser's argument that "the real difference between art and science lies in the *specific form*" of presentation, remarked that the question "of specifying the features which uniquely distinguish works of literature from other ideological and cultural forms" is as much the "matter of prime importance" for Marxist analysis as it was for Russian formalism (their version of New Critical aesthetics).[14] So even as he observed Althusser and Pierre Macherey defining "literature" by its unique "capacity to reveal or rupture from within the terms of seeing proposed by the categories of dominant ideologies," Bennett also saw their task tied to "understanding the formal processes through which literary texts work upon and transform dominant ideological forms" (Bennett, 8). Meanwhile, Eagleton was modifying his earlier polemics on the mystificatory work of literary form. By 1986, as the new wave of anti-formalist critique was laying claim to ever wider grounds of analysis, Eagleton was not at the vanguard, where we might have expected to find him, but rethinking the principles into an unpredictable play of constraint and lively interrogation: "a literary text is in one sense constrained by the formal principles of *langue,* but at any moment it can also put these principles into question." And poetry, the former perpetrator of nefarious formalist business, was now the new hero of this interrogative potential. This "dynamic" putting-into-question, Eagleton proposed (unembarrassed by the sort of sentence we might expect to find in Wimsatt's *The Verbal Icon* or Brooks's *The Well Wrought Urn),* may be "most evident in a poem, which deploys words usually to be found in the lexicon, but by combining and condensing them generates an irreducible specificity of force and meaning."[15]

Eagleton was doing no more, or less, than recovering old but still fertile ground. Resisting the isolationist formalism of early-century modernism, Georg Lukács had already declared that "the truly social element in literature is the form."[16] The social register of form was never really in doubt in European theory. Even that grand master of formal play, Roland Barthes, had insisted on the necessary relation of (old) historicism to form. Writing in France in the 1950s, when it was not New Critical formalism but structuralism that was challenging historicism, Barthes sought to reconcile the terms that this polemic, however heuristically, had put asunder: on the one hand, the "literary," defined by a display of form; and on the other, "history," the language of fact and idea. Historicizing formalist questions in terms that briefly interested even de Man, Barthes insisted that any "total criticism" had to pursue a "dialectical co-ordination" between "ideology," the historically produced content, and "semiology," the "science of forms [that] studies significations apart from their content." His famous aphorism was that "a little formalism turns one away from History, but… a lot brings one back to it." One might also add the reciprocal in the wake of new historicism: if a little history (say, the anecdote) turns one away from formalism, a lot of history brings one back to it. There is really no necessary standoff: not only is formalism a "necessary principle" of analysis, but "the more a system is specifically defined in its forms, the more amenable it is to historical criticism."[17] The specificities of historical contingency become intelligible in their forms of articulation. Actions or form are enmeshed in, and even exercise agency within, networks of social and historical conditions. So if an investigation of cultural formations will improve our sense of the production of literary forms, reading for form will also improve our sense of how cultural forms are produced.

The essays in *Reading for Form* are nuanced by the work of historical criticism, but none tries to justify or rehabilitate formalist criticism at the outset of the twenty-first century by smuggling in formalist criticism under the cover of historicist criticism, as if that were the only legitimacy.

Amid what James E. B. Breslin has termed "an historically informed formalist criticism," our essays exercise readings for form with a sophisticated yet unembarrassed sense of literary value—and pleasure.[18] To suggest that *Reading for Form* is an intervention, however, is to imply that its force is oppositional, disruptive, previously unaccommodated and now urgently needed to break an impasse or turn the lights on. Our care is rather to heighten attention to the analytical force of forms for our reading, even as we reread the traditions of aesthetic theory. In 1990 Garrett Stewart proposed that a "formalist...return to textual theory" is necessary for "registering the *forms* of cultural dissemination in both the literary instance and its alternative discursive modes"; in the same year, Peter J. Manning, sensitive to New Criticism's strictures as well as to its general antipathy to Romanticism, and wanting to stay formalist and Romantic, thought there was an advantage in joining formalism to wider concerns, reading Romantic poetry in connection with "the motives from which it springs and the social relations within which it exists." Two years earlier, Stephen Greenblatt had conceded, in the thick of new historicism celebrity, both a yearning "to recover the closegrained formalism of my own literary training" and a recognition that "sustained, scrupulous attention to formal and linguistic design will remain at the center of literary teaching and study."[19]

Greenblatt's tone is complexly layered, and perhaps pressed by uncomfortable evasions and addictions. Is he sadly resigned, or somewhat relieved? A dozen years on (originally in 2000, and reprinted in this volume), Heather Dubrow wryly observed that "in the current critical climate, many scholars are far more comfortable detailing their sexual histories in print than confessing to an interest in literary form." The essays convened in *Reading for Form* make one thing clear: while everyone is unhappy with the turn against form, everyone is unhappy in a different way. When Marshall Brown and I first began assembling the conversation of these pages, we were struck by how various the cases for "form," "formalism," and "formalist criticism" seemed in different hands.[20] We had no interest in massaging a message out of the mess, let alone anything as dreary as a manifesto. Yet within this unpredictable variety of interests and approaches, one thing was becoming clear. If the equation of "literary" criticism with "formalist" criticism (narrowly conceived) was no longer satisfactory, another lively equation was emerging: of attention to form, however defined, with "reading"—the activity featured in Hartman's, Garrett Stewart's, and Manning's titles, and powerfully if ambivalently acknowledged by Greenblatt. What Marshall Brown has said of style—"Through their style, cultural expressions become literary by resisting the idealizing universals into which our ideologies otherwise slide"—is sharpened in the stylistic performance of the literary that we mean to call "form."[21]

The readings for form that follow—"for" as attention to and as advocacy for such attention—show, if no consensus about what form signifies, then a conviction of why it still has to matter. All share a sense that the reductive critique of formalism, in publication and pedagogy, has had unfortunate results, not the least a dulling of critical instruments and a loss of sensitivity to the complexity of literary form: its various and surprising work, its complex relation to traditions, and its interaction with extra-literary culture. "Reading for form" implies the activity as well as the object. Many of our contributors focus on the meta-form of form: poetry. D. Vance Smith, Susan Stewart, Marjorie Perloff, J. Paul Hunter, Heather Dubrow, Robert Kaufman, and Ronald Levao sharpen our sense of how events of poetic form (as Derek Attridge writes) resist incorporation "into the kind of interpretation we habitually give to linguistic utterances"; they are not transparent but invite "apprehension as a formal entity, quite apart from its semantic import."[22] Yet their essays go further, suggesting how formal events in poetry also work semantically, especially when questions of form— literary and social—are at stake.

NOTES

1. W. J. T. Mitchell, "The Commitment to Form; or, Still Crazy after All These Years," *PMLA* 118.2 (2003): 321.
2. William L. Hamilton, "Cracking the Dress Code: How a Fashion School Uniform becomes Statement," *New York Times,* 19 February 1998, BI, B8.
3. Clark, *Image of the People: Gustave Courbet and the Second French Republic, 1848–1851* (Greenwich, Conn.: New York Graphic Society, 1973), 13.
4. Levine, "Introduction: Reclaiming the Aesthetic," in *Aesthetics and Ideology,* ed. George Levine (New Brunswick, N.J.: Rutgers University Press, 1994), 1–2. On Levine's ambivalence about the work of formalism in this reclamation, see Heather Dubrow's essay here, and my remarks in *Formal Charges: The Shaping of Poetry in British Romanticism* (Stanford, Calif.: Stanford University Press, 1997), 227–28.
5. Bloom, *The Anxiety of Influence: A Theory of Poetry* (New York: Oxford University Press, 1973), 12
6. Eagleton, *Criticism and Ideology: A Study in Marxist Literary Theory* (1976; London: Verso, 1978), 114, 124–25, 128–29. Theodor W. Adomo gives the rubric: "The unsolved antagonisms of reality return in artworks as immanent problems of form" (*Aesthetic Theory,* ed. Gretel Adorno and Rolf Tiedemann, trans. Robert Hullot-Kentor [Minneapolis: University of Minnesota Press, 1997], 6).
7. McGann, "Keats and the Historical Method in Literacy Criticism" (1979), in *The Beauty of Inflections: Literary Investigations in Historical Method and Theory* (Oxford: Clarendon, 1985), 21–22; McGann, *The Romantic Ideology: A Critical Investigation* (Chicago: University of Chicago Press, 1983), 3. Similarly, Fredric Jameson reads aesthetic form as a business of ideologically produced acts "with the function of inventing imaginary or formal 'solutions' to unresolvable social contradictions," indeed, "a purely formal resolution in the aesthetic realm" (*The Political Unconscious: Narrative as a Socially Symbolic Act* [Ithaca, N.Y.: Cornell University Press, 1981], 79).
8. Gallagher, "Marxism and the New Historicism," in *The New Historicism,* ed. H. Aram Veeser (New York: Routledge, 1989), 39.
9. De Man, "The Dead-End of Formalist Criticism" (1971), in *Blindness and Insight: Essays in the Rhetoric of Contemporary Criticism,* 2d ed. (Minneapolis: University of Minnesota Press, 1983), 232. For the political critique of aesthetic formalization in de Man's late essays see Christopher Norris, *Paul de Man: Deconstruction and the Critique of Aesthetic Ideology* (New York: Routledge, 1988), 62–63, 116–24.
10. "Poetic Designation and the Aesthetic Function of Language" (1938), in *The Word and Verbal Art: Selected Essays by Jan Mukařovský,* ed. and trans. John Burbank and Peter Steiner (New Haven, Conn.: Yale University Press, 1977), 68. For my fuller discussion of this history see *Formal Charges,* 1–30.
11. Wellek and Warren, *Theory of Literature,* 3d ed. (1942; New York: Harcourt, Brace and World, 1956), 140–41.
12. Crane, *The Languages of Criticism and the Structure of Poetry* (Toronto: University of Toronto Press, 1953), 153.
13. Hartman, *The Fate of Reading and Other Essays* (Chicago: University of Chicago Press, 1975), vii. The essay "Beyond Formalism," originally published in 1966, is reprinted in *Beyond Formalism: Literary Essays, 1958–1970* (New Haven, Conn.: Yale University Press, 1970), 42–57.

14. Althusser, "A Letter on Art" (1966), in *Lenin and Philosophy, and Other Essays*, trans. Ben Brewster (London: New Left Books, 1971), 205; Bennett, *Formalism and Marxism* (London: Methuen, 1979), 122, 41–42. It is a matter of debate just how isolationist Russian formalism was; see Bennett, 108–9; my discussion in *Formal Charges*, 18–19; and Virgil Nemoianu's essay in this volume.

15. Eagleton, *William Shakespeare* (Oxford: Blackwell, 1986), 35–36.

16. Lukács, *The Evolution of Modern Drama*, quoted in Eagleton, *Marxism and Literary Criticism* (Berkeley: University of California Press, 1977), 20. Remarking that this "is not the kind of comment which has come to be expected of Marxist criticism," which "has traditionally opposed all kinds of literary formalism" as a reduction of literature "to an aesthetic game" (20), Eagleton cites Lukács as an instance of a counter-tradition with which he is sympathetic: a Marxist criticism that can stay interested in the complex shaping of forms by a relatively autonomous literary history, by "certain dominant ideological structures" in specific historical moments, and, within these, by "a specific set of relations between author and audience" (26; see 20–34).

17. Barthes, "Myth Today" (1957), trans. Annette Lavers, in *Mythologies* (New York: Hill and Wang, 1972), 111–12. De Man describes a politics of form in Barthes that, like Russian formalism, treats its conspicuousness as significant. In epochs when social and political freedoms are "curtailed," an artist's "choice of form becomes problematic": form ceases to be "transparent" and becomes "an object of reflection"—a transformation that amounts to a potentially "revolutionary action" (de Man, 234).

18. Breslin, *From Modern to Contemporary: American Poetry: 1945–1965* (Chicago: University of Chicago Press, 1984), xiv.

19. Stewart, *Reading Voices: Literature and the Phonotext* (Berkeley: University of California Press, 1990), 16; Manning, *Reading Romantics: Texts and Contexts* (New York: Oxford University Press, 1990), 3; Greenblatt, *Shakespearean Negotiations: The Circulation of Social Energy in Renaissance England* (Berkeley: University of California Press, 1988), 3–4)

20. Our "reading for form" does not imply formalism, in the traditional political, literary, and critical sense of an ideologically toned discipline that prioritizes form over other possible locations of value. Although we have learned from the techniques of mid twentieth-century criticism, our orientations and purposes are otherwise. In reading for form in the twenty-first century, the contributors to this volume share a concern both with how poetic form is articulated and valued, in James Breslin's phrasing, "with the changing theories and practices of poetic form" (xiv).

21. Brown, " 'Le Style Est l'Homme Même': The Action of Literature," *College English* 59, no. 7 (1997): 56; see also Brown, "Why Style Matters: The Lessons of Taine's *History of English Literature*," in *Turning Points: Essays in the History of Cultural Expressions* (Stanford, Calif.: Stanford University Press, 1997), 33–87.

22. Attridge, *The Rhythms of English Poetry* (London: Longman, 1982), 311, 307.

POSTCOLONIAL AND RACE STUDIES

ON NATIONAL CULTURE (1963)

FRANTZ FANON

Translated from the French by Richard Philcox

A Martiniquan psychiatrist, Fanon fought with the Free French against the Nazis in World War II and then with the Algerian independence movement against the French in the 1950s. He draws many of his ideas from the anticolonialist struggle for the independence of African nations. Fanon took inspiration from the poets and philosophers of Négritude, although he also looked on their ideas critically. The Négritude writers called for pride in blackness. They believed that black people, whether from Africa or (like Fanon) the African diaspora, share a collective personality that differs radically from the personality of the European colonizers. To Fanon, the Négritude writers exaggerated the common culture of African and black peoples. He thought that the Négritude movement reinvigorated the same stereotypes that the colonizers believed in, celebrating a supposed sensuality and communalism that colonizers saw as depraved and uncivilized. In this essay, Fanon recognizes why, in reaction against colonialism, colonized peoples often sought to romanticize their precolonial history and civilization and their racial commonality. After all, the colonizers taught them that they were inferior and had no history or civilization. But he also believes that the precolonial past can never be recovered because colonized cultures—like all cultures—change continuously. Thus, while Fanon respects the impulse of artists and intellectuals to identify with a glorious precolonial past, he calls for contemporary anticolonial art and writing to concentrate on the immediate needs of anticolonial politics. For Fanon, a merging of national consciousness and artistic consciousness can make possible an anticolonialist future.

(Fanon's essay appears here nearly in its entirety; one long example from a poem has been excised.)

It is not enough to write a revolutionary hymn to be a part of the African revolution, one has to join with the people to make this revolution. Make it with the people and the hymns will automatically follow. For an act to be authentic, one has to be a vital part of Africa and its thinking, part of all that popular energy mobilized for the liberation, progress and happiness of Africa. Outside this single struggle there is no place for either the artist or the intellectual who is not

committed and totally mobilized with the people in the great fight waged by
Africa and suffering humanity.

SÉKOU TOURÉ[1]

Each generation must discover its mission, fulfill it or betray it, in relative opacity. In the
underdeveloped countries preceding generations have simultaneously resisted the insidious
agenda of colonialism and paved the way for the emergence of the current struggles. Now that
we are in the heat of combat, we must shed the habit of decrying the efforts of our forefathers or
feigning incomprehension at their silence or passiveness. They fought as best they could with the
weapons they possessed at the time, and if their struggle did not reverberate throughout the international arena, the reason should be attributed not so much to a lack of heroism but to a fundamentally different international situation. More than one colonized subject had to say, "We've
had enough," more than one tribe had to rebel, more than one peasant revolt had to be quelled,
more than one demonstration to be repressed, for us today to stand firm, certain of our victory.

For us who are determined to break the back of colonialism, our historic mission is to
authorize every revolt, every desperate act, and every attack aborted or drowned in blood.

In this chapter we shall analyze the fundamental issue of the legitimate claim to a nation.
The political party that mobilizes the people, however, is little concerned with this issue of
legitimacy. Political parties are concerned solely with daily reality, and it is in the name of
this reality, in the name of this immediacy, which influences the present and future of men
and women, that they make their call to action. The political party may very well speak of the
nation in emotional terms, but it is primarily interested in getting the people who are listening to understand that they must join in the struggle if they want quite simply to exist.

We now know that in the first phase of the national struggle colonialism attempts to defuse
nationalist demands by manipulating economic doctrine. At the first signs of a dispute, colonialism feigns comprehension by acknowledging with ostentatious humility that the territory is
suffering from serious underdevelopment that requires major social and economic reforms.

And it is true that certain spectacular measures such as the opening of work sites for the
unemployed here and there delay the formation of a national consciousness by a few years. But
sooner or later colonialism realizes it is incapable of achieving a program of socio-economic
reforms that would satisfy the aspirations of the colonized masses. Even when it comes to filling
their bellies, colonialism proves to be inherently powerless. The colonialist state very quickly
discovers that any attempt to disarm the national parties at a purely economic level would be
tantamount to practicing in the colonies what it did not want to do on its own territory. And it
is no coincidence that today the doctrine of Cartierism is on the rise just about everywhere.

Cartier's bitter disillusionment with France's stubborn determination to retain ties with
people it will have to feed, whereas so many French citizens are in dire straits, reflects colonialism's inability to transform itself into a nonpartisan aid program. Hence once again no

need to waste time repeating "Better to go hungry with dignity than to eat one's fill in slavery." On the contrary we must persuade ourselves that colonialism is incapable of procuring for colonized peoples the material conditions likely to make them forget their quest for dignity. Once colonialism has understood where its social reform tactics would lead it, back come the old reflexes of adding police reinforcements, dispatching troops, and establishing a regime of terror better suited to its interests and its psychology.

Within the political parties, or rather parallel to them, we find the cultured class of colonized intellectuals. The recognition of a national culture and its right to exist represent their favorite stamping ground. Whereas the politicians integrate their action in the present, the intellectua6ls place themselves in the context of history. Faced with the colonized intellectual's debunking of the colonialist theory of a precolonial barbarism, colonialism's response is mute. It is especially mute since the ideas put forward by the young colonized intelligentsia are widely accepted by metropolitan specialists. It is in fact now commonly recognized that for several decades numerous European researchers have widely rehabilitated African, Mexican, and Peruvian civilizations. Some have been surprised by the passion invested by the colonized intellectuals in their defense of a national culture. But those who consider this passion exaggerated are strangely apt to forget that their psyche and their ego are conveniently safeguarded by a French or German culture whose worth has been proven and which has gone unchallenged.

I concede the fact that the actual existence of an Aztec civilization has done little to change the diet of today's Mexican peasant. I concede that whatever proof there is of a once mighty Songhai civilization does not change the fact that the Songhais today are undernourished, illiterate, abandoned to the skies and water, with a blank mind and glazed eyes. But, as we have said on several occasions, this passionate quest for a national culture prior to the colonial era can be justified by the colonized intellectuals' shared interest in stepping back and taking a hard look at the Western culture in which they risk becoming ensnared. Fully aware they are in the process of losing themselves, and consequently of being lost to their people, these men work away with raging heart and furious mind to renew contact with their people's oldest, inner essence, the farthest removed from colonial times.

Let us delve deeper; perhaps this passion and this rage are nurtured or at least guided by the secret hope of discovering beyond the present wretchedness, beyond this self-hatred, this abdication and denial, some magnificent and shining era that redeems us in our own eyes and those of others. I say that I have decided to delve deeper. Since perhaps in their unconscious the colonized intellectuals have been unable to come to loving terms with the present history of their oppressed people, since there is little to marvel at in its current state of barbarity, they have decided to go further, to delve deeper, and they must have been overjoyed to discover that the past was not branded with shame, but dignity, glory, and sobriety. Reclaiming the past does not only rehabilitate or justify the promise of a national culture. It triggers a change of fundamental importance in the colonized's psycho-affective equilibrium. Perhaps it has not been sufficiently demonstrated that colonialism is not content merely to impose its law on the colonized country's present and future. Colonialism is not satisfied with snaring the people in its net or of draining the colonized brain of any form or substance. With a kind of perverted logic, it turns its attention to the past of the colonized people and distorts it, disfigures it, and destroys it. This effort to demean history prior to colonization today takes on a dialectical significance.

When we consider the resources deployed to achieve the cultural alienation so typical of the colonial period, we realize that nothing was left to chance and that the final aim of colonization was to convince the indigenous population it would save them from darkness. The result was to hammer into the heads of the indigenous population that if the colonist were to leave they would regress into barbarism, degradation, and bestiality. At the level of the unconscious, therefore, colonialism was not seeking to be perceived by the indigenous population as a sweet, kind-hearted mother who protects her child from a hostile environment, but rather a mother who constantly prevents her basically perverse child from committing suicide or giving free rein to its malevolent instincts. The colonial mother is protecting the child from itself, from its ego, its physiology, its biology, and its ontological misfortune.

In this context there is nothing extravagant about the demands of the colonized intellectual, simply a demand for a coherent program. The colonized intellectual who wants to put his struggle on a legitimate footing, who is intent on providing proof and accepts to bare himself in order to better display the history of his body, is fated to journey deep into the very bowels of his people.

This journey into the depths is not specifically national. The colonized intellectual who decides to combat these colonialist lies does so on a continental scale. The past is revered. The culture which has been retrieved from the past to be displayed in all its splendor is not his national culture. Colonialism, little troubled by nuances, has always claimed that the "nigger" was a savage, not an Angolan or a Nigerian, but a "nigger." For colonialism, this vast continent was a den of savages, infested with superstitions and fanaticism, destined to be despised, cursed by God, a land of cannibals, a land of "niggers." Colonialism's condemnation is continental in scale. Colonialism's claim that the precolonial period was akin to a darkness of the human soul refers to the entire continent of Africa. The colonized's endeavors to rehabilitate himself and escape the sting of colonialism obey the same rules of logic. The colonized intellectual, steeped in Western culture and set on proving the existence of his own culture, never does so in the name of Angola or Dahomey. The culture proclaimed is African culture. When the black man, who has never felt as much a "Negro" as he has under white domination, decides to prove his culture and act as a cultivated person, he realizes that history imposes on him a terrain already mapped out, that history sets him along a very precise path and that he is expected to demonstrate the existence of a "Negro" culture.

And it is all too true that the major responsibility for this racialization of thought, or at least the way it is applied, lies with the Europeans who have never stopped placing white culture in opposition to the other noncultures. Colonialism did not think it worth its while denying one national culture after the other. Consequently the colonized's response was immediately continental in scope. In Africa, colonized literature over the last twenty years has not been a national literature but a "Negro" literature. The concept of negritude for example was the affective if not logical antithesis of that insult which the white man had leveled at the rest of humanity. This negritude, hurled against the contempt of the white man, has alone proved capable in some sectors of lifting taboos and maledictions. Because the Kenyan and Guinean intellectuals were above all confronted with a generalized ostracism and the syncretic contempt of the colonizer, their reaction was one of self-regard and celebration. Following the unconditional affirmation of European culture came the unconditional affirmation of African culture. Generally speaking the bards of negritude would contrast old Europe versus young Africa, dull reason versus poetry, and stifling logic versus exuberant Nature; on the one side there stood rigidity, ceremony, protocol, and skepticism, and on the other, naïveté, petulance, freedom, and, indeed, luxuriance. But also irresponsibility.

The bards of negritude did not hesitate to reach beyond the borders of the continent. Black voices from America took up the refrain on a larger scale. The "black world" came into being, and Busia from Ghana, Birago Diop from Senegal, Hampaté Ba from Mali and Saint-Clair Drake from Chicago were quick to claim common ties and identical lines of thought. This might be an appropriate time to look at the example of the Arab world. We know that most of the Arab territories came under colonial domination. Colonialism used the same tactics in these regions to inculcate the notion that the precolonial history of the indigenous population had been steeped in barbarity. The struggle for national liberation was linked to a cultural phenomenon commonly known as the awakening of Islam. The passion displayed by contemporary Arab authors in reminding their people of the great chapters of Arab history is in response to the lies of the occupier. The great names of Arabic literature have been recorded and the past of the Arab civilization has been brandished with the same zeal and ardor as that of the African civilizations. The Arab leaders have tried to revive that famous Dar el Islam, which exerted such a shining influence in the twelfth, thirteenth and fourteenth centuries.

Today, at a political level, the Arab League is a concrete example of this determination to revive the legacy of the past and carry it to a conclusion. Today Arab physicians and poets hail each other across borders in their endeavor to launch a new Arab culture, a new Arab civilization. They join forces in the name of Arabism, which is the guiding light for their thoughts. In the Arab world, however, even under colonial domination, nationalist feeling has been kept alive at an intensity unknown in Africa. As a result the Arab League shows no signs of that spontaneous solidarity between members of the group. On the contrary, para-doxically, each member endeavors to praise the achievements of his nation. Although the cultural element has been freed from that lack of differentiation that is characteristic of the African world, the Arabs do not always manage to forget their common identity when faced with an objective. Their actual cultural experience is not national but Arab. The issue at stake is not yet to secure a national culture, not yet to plunge into the groundswell of nations, but rather to pit an Arab or African culture against the universal condemnation of the colonizer. From both the Arab and African perspectives, the claims of the colonized intellectual are syncretic, continental in scope and, in the case of the Arabs, global.

This historical obligation to racialize their claims, to emphasize an African culture rather than a national culture leads the African intellectuals into a dead end. Let us take as an example the African Society for Culture. This Society was created by African intellectuals for a mutual exchange of ideas, experiences, and research. The aim of the Society was therefore to establish the existence of an African culture, to detail it nation by nation and reveal the inner dynamism of each of the national cultures. But at the same time this Society was responding to another demand: the need to take its place within the ranks of the European Society for Culture that threatened to turn into the Universal Society for Culture. At the root of this decision there was therefore the preoccupation with taking its place on an equal footing in the universal arena, armed with a culture sprung from the very bowels of the African continent. Very quickly, however, this Society proved incapable of handling these assignments and members' behavior was reduced to window-dressing operations such as proving to the Europeans that an African culture did exist and pitting themselves against the narcissism and ostentation of the Europeans. We have demonstrated that such an attitude was normal and drew its legitimacy from the lie propagated by the European intellectuals. But the aims of this Society were to deteriorate seriously once the concept of negritude had been elaborated. The African Society for Culture was to become the Cultural Society for the Black World and was forced to include the black diaspora, i.e., the dozens of millions of blacks throughout the Americas.

The blacks who lived in the United States, Central, and Latin America in fact needed a cultural matrix to cling to. The problem they were faced with was not basically any different from that of the Africans. The whites in America had not behaved any differently to them than the white colonizers had to the Africans. We have seen how the whites were used to putting all "Negroes" in the same basket. During the First Congress of the African Society for Culture in Paris in 1956 the black Americans spontaneously considered their problems from the same standpoint as their fellow Africans. By integrating the former slaves into African civilization the African intellectuals accorded them an acceptable civil status. But gradually the black Americans realized that their existential problems differed from those faced by the Africans. The only common denominator between the blacks from Chicago and the Nigerians or Tanganyikans[2] was that they all defined themselves in relation to the whites. But once the initial comparisons had been made and subjective feelings had settled down, the black Americans realized that the objective problems were fundamentally different. The principle and purpose of the freedom rides whereby black and white Americans endeavor to combat racial discrimination have little in common with the heroic struggle of the Angolan people against the iniquity of Portuguese colonialism. Consequently, during the Second Congress of the African Society for Culture the black Americans decided to create the American Society for African Culture.

Negritude thus came up against its first limitation, namely, those phenomena that take into account the historicizing of men. "Negro" or "Negro-African" culture broke up because the men who set out to embody it realized that every culture is first and foremost national, and that the problems for which Richard Wright or Langston Hughes had to be on the alert were fundamentally different from those faced by Léopold Senghor or Jomo Kenyatta. Likewise certain Arab states, who had struck up the glorious hymn to an Arab renaissance, were forced to realize that their geographical position and their region's economic interdependence were more important than the revival of their past. Consequently the Arab states today are organically linked to Mediterranean societies and cultures. The reason being that these states are subject to modern pressures and new commercial channels, whereas the great trade routes of the days of Arab expansion have now disappeared. But above all there is the fact that the political regimes of certain Arab states are so heterogenous and alien to each other that any encounter, even cultural, between these states proves meaningless.

It is clear therefore that the way the cultural problem is posed in certain colonized countries can lead to serious ambiguities. Colonialism's insistence that "niggers" have no culture, and Arabs are by nature barbaric, inevitably leads to a glorification of cultural phenomena that become continental instead of national, and singularly racialized. In Africa, the reasoning of the intellectual is Black-African or Arab-Islamic. It is not specifically national. Culture is increasingly cut off from reality. It finds safe haven in a refuge of smoldering emotions and has difficulty cutting a straightforward path that would, nevertheless, be the only one likely to endow it with productiveness, homogeneity, and substance.

Though historically limited the fact remains that the actions of the colonized intellectual do much to support and justify the action of the politicians. And it is true the attitude of the colonized intellectual sometimes takes on the aspect of a cult or religion. But under closer analysis it clearly reflects he is only too aware that he is running the risk of severing the last remaining ties with his people. This stated belief in the existence of a national culture is in feet a burning, desperate return to anything. In order to secure his salvation, in order to escape the supremacy of white culture the colonized intellectual feels the need to return to his unknown roots and lose himself, come what may, among his barbaric people. Because he feels he is becoming alienated, in other words the living focus of contradictions which risk becoming insurmountable, the colonized intellectual wrenches himself from the quagmire which threatens to suck him down, and determined to believe what he finds, he accepts and ratifies it with heart and soul. He finds himself bound to answer for everything and for everyone. He not only becomes an advocate, he accepts being included with the others, and henceforth he can afford to laugh at his past cowardice.

This painful and harrowing wrench is, however, a necessity. Otherwise we will be faced with extremely serious psycho-affective mutilations: individuals without an anchorage, without borders, colorless, stateless, rootless, a body of angels. And it will come as no surprise to hear some colonized intellectuals state: "Speaking as a Senegalese and a Frenchman.... Speaking as an Algerian and a Frenchman." Stumbling over the need to assume two nationalities, two determinations, the intellectual who is Arab and French, or Nigerian and English, if he wants to be sincere with himself, chooses the negation of one of these two determinations. Usually, unwilling or unable to choose, these intellectuals collect all the historical determinations which have conditioned them and place themselves in a thoroughly "universal perspective."

The reason being that the colonized intellectual has thrown himself headlong into Western culture. Like adopted children who only stop investigating their new family environment once their psyche has formed a minimum core of reassurance, the colonized intellectual will endeavor to make European culture his own. Not content with knowing Rabelais or Diderot, Shakespeare or Edgar Allan Poe, he will stretch his mind until he identifies with them completely.

La dame n'était pas seule
Elle avait un mari
Un mari très comme il faut
Qui citait Racine et Corneille
Et Voltaire et Rousseau
Et le Père Hugo et le jeune Musset
Et Gide et Valéry
Et tant d'autres encore.[3]

In some cases, however, at the very moment when the nationalist parties mobilize the people in the name of national independence, the colonized intellectual rejects his accomplishments, suddenly feeling them to be alienating. But this is easier said than done. The intellectual who has slipped into Western civilization through a cultural back door, who has managed to embody, or rather change bodies with, European civilization, will realize that the cultural model he would like to integrate for authenticity's sake offers little in the way of figureheads capable of standing up to comparison with the many illustrious names in the civilization of the occupier. History, of course, written by and for Westerners, may periodically enhance the image of certain episodes of the African past. But faced with his country's present-day status, lucidly and "objectively" observing the reality of the continent he would like to claim as his own, the intellectual is terrified by the void, the mindlessness, and the savagery. Yet he feels he must escape this white culture. He must look elsewhere, anywhere; for lack of a cultural stimulus comparable to the glorious panorama flaunted by the colonizer, the colonized intellectual frequently lapses into heated arguments and develops a psychology dominated by an exaggerated sensibility, sensitivity, and susceptibility. This movement of withdrawal, which first of all comes from a petitio principi in his psychological mechanism and physiognomy, above all calls to mind a muscular reflex, a muscular contraction.

The foregoing is sufficient to explain the style of the colonized intellectuals who make up their mind to assert this phase of liberating consciousness. A jagged style, full of imagery, for the image is the drawbridge that lets out the unconscious forces into the surrounding meadows. An energetic style, alive with rhythms bursting with life. A colorful style too, bronzed, bathed in sunlight and harsh. This style, which Westerners once found jarring, is not, as some would have it, a racial feature, but above all reflects a single-handed combat and reveals how necessary it is for the intellectual to inflict injury on himself, to actually bleed red blood and free himself from that part of his being already contaminated by the germs of decay. A swift, painful combat where inevitably the muscle had to replace the concept.

Although this approach may take him to unusual heights in the sphere of poetry, at an existential level it has often proved a dead end. When he decides to return to the routine of daily life, after having been roused to fever pitch by rubbing shoulders with his people, whoever they were and whoever they may be, all he brings back from his adventures are terribly sterile clichés. He places emphasis on customs, traditions, and costumes, and his painful, forced search seems but a banal quest for the exotic. This is the period when the intellectuals extol every last particular of the indigenous landscape. The flowing dress of the *boubou* is regarded as sacred and shoes from Paris or Italy are shunned for Muslim slippers, *babouches*. The language of the colonizer suddenly scorches his lips. Rediscovering one's people sometimes means in this phase wanting to be a "nigger," not an exceptional "nigger," but a real "nigger," a "dirty nigger," the sort defined by the white man. Rediscovering one's people means becoming a "filthy Arab," or going as native as possible, becoming unrecognizable; it means clipping those wings which had been left to grow.

The colonized intellectual decides to draw up a list of the bad old ways characteristic of the colonial world, and hastens to recall the goodness of the people, this people who have been made guardians of truth. The scandal this approach triggers among the colonists strengthens the determination of the colonized. Once the colonists, who had relished their victory over these assimilated intellectuals, realize that these men they thought saved have begun to merge with the "nigger scum," the entire system loses its bearings. Every colonized intellectual won over, every colonized intellectual who confesses, once he decides to revert to his old ways, not only represents a setback for the colonial enterprise, but also symbolizes the pointlessness and superficiality of the work accomplished. Every colonized intellectual who crosses back over the line is a radical condemnation of the method and the regime, and the uproar it causes justifies his abdication and encourages him to persevere.

If we decide to trace these various phases of development in the works of colonized writers, three stages emerge. First, the colonized intellectual proves he has assimilated the colonizer's culture. His works correspond point by point with those of his metropolitan counterparts. The inspiration is European and his works can be easily linked to a well-defined trend in metropolitan literature. This is the phase of full assimilation where we find Parnassians, Symbolists, and Surrealists among the colonized writers.

In a second stage, the colonized writer has his convictions shaken and decides to cast his mind back. This period corresponds approximately to the immersion we have just described. But since the colonized writer is not integrated with his people, since he maintains an outsider's relationship to them, he is content to remember. Old childhood memories will surface, old legends be reinterpreted on the basis of a borrowed aesthetic, and a concept of the world discovered under other skies. Sometimes this precombat literature is steeped in humor and allegory, at other times in anguish, malaise, death, and even nausea. Yet underneath the self-loathing, the sound of laughter can be heard.

Finally, a third stage, a combat stage where the colonized writer, after having tried to lose himself among the people, with the people, will rouse the people. Instead of letting the people's lethargy prevail, he turns into a galvanizer of the people. Combat literature, revolutionary literature, national literature emerges. During this phase a great many men and women who previously would never have thought of writing, now that they find themselves in exceptional circumstances, in prison, in the resistance or on the eve of their execution, feel the need to proclaim their nation, to portray their people and become the spokesperson of a new reality in action.

Sooner or later, however, the colonized intellectual realizes that the existence of a nation is not proved by culture, but in the people's struggle against the forces of occupation. No colonialism draws its justification from the fact that the territories it occupies are culturally nonexistent. Colonialism will never be put to shame by exhibiting unknown cultural treasures under its nose. The colonized intellectual, at the very moment when he undertakes a work of art, fails to realize he is using techniques and a language borrowed from the occupier. He is content to cloak these instruments in a style that is meant to be national but which is strangely reminiscent of exoticism. The colonized intellectual who returns to his people through works of art behaves in fact like a foreigner. Sometimes he will not hesitate to use the local dialects to demonstrate his desire to be as close to the people as possible, but the ideas he expresses, the preoccupations that haunt him are in no way related to the daily lot of the men and women of his country. The culture with which the intellectual is preoccupied is very often nothing but an inventory of particularisms. Seeking to cling close to the people, he clings merely to a visible veneer. This veneer, however, is merely a reflection of a dense, subterranean life in perpetual renewal. This reification, which seems all too obvious and characteristic of the people, is in fact but the inert, already invalidated outcome of the many, and not always coherent, adaptations of a more fundamental substance beset with radical changes. Instead of seeking out this substance, the intellectual lets himself be mesmerized by these mummified fragments which, now consolidated, signify, on the contrary, negation, obsolescence, and fabrication. Culture never has the translucency of custom. Culture eminently eludes any form of simplification. In its essence it is the very opposite of custom, which is always a deterioration of culture. Seeking to stick to tradition or reviving neglected traditions is not only going against history, but against one's people. When a people support an armed or even political struggle against a merciless colonialism, tradition changes meaning. What was a technique of passive resistance may, in this phase, be radically doomed. Traditions in an underdeveloped country undergoing armed struggle are fundamentally unstable and crisscrossed by centrifugal forces. This is why the intellectual often risks being out of step. The peoples who have waged the struggle are increasingly impermeable to demagoguery, and by seeking to follow them too closely, the intellectual turns out to be nothing better than a vulgar opportunist, even behind the times.

In the field of visual arts, for example, the colonized creator who at all costs wants to create a work of art of national significance confines himself to stereotyping details. These artists, despite having been immersed in modern techniques and influenced by the major contemporary trends in painting and architecture, turn their backs on foreign culture, challenge it, and, setting out in search of the true national culture, they give preference to what they think to be the abiding features of national art. But these creators forget that modes of thought, diet, modern techniques of communication, language, and dress have dialectically reorganized the mind of the people and that the abiding features that acted as safeguards during the colonial period are in the process of undergoing enormous radical transformations.

This creator, who decides to portray national truth, turns, paradoxically enough, to the past, and so looks at what is irrelevant to the present. What he aims for in his inner intentionality is the detritus of social thought, external appearances, relics, and knowledge frozen in time. The colonized intellectual, however, who strives for cultural authenticity, must recognize that national truth is first and foremost the national reality. He must press on until he reaches that place of bubbling trepidation from which knowledge will emerge.

Before independence the colonized painter was insensitive to the national landscape. He favored therefore the nonrepresentational or, more often, specialized in still life. After independence his desire to reunite with the people confines him to a point by point representation of national reality which is flat, untroubled, motionless, reminiscent of death rather than life. The educated circles go ecstatic over such careful renditions of truth, but we have every right to ask ourselves whether this truth is real, whether in fact it is not outmoded, irrelevant, or called into question by the heroic saga of the people hacking their way into history.

Much the same could be said about poetry. After the assimilation period of rhyming verse, the beat of the poetic drum bursts onto the scene. Poetry of revolt, but which is also analytical and descriptive. The poet must, however, understand that nothing can replace the rational and irreversible commitment on the side of the people in arms. Let us quote Depestre once again:

La dame n'était pas seule
Elle avait un mari
Un mari qui savait tout
Mais à parler franc qui ne savait rien
Parce que la culture ne va pas sans concessions
Une concession de sa chair et de son sang
Une concession de soi-même aux autres
Une concession qui vaut le
Classicisme et le romantisme
Et tout ce dont on abreuve notre esprit.[4]

The colonized poet who is concerned with creating a work of national significance, who insists on describing his people, misses his mark, because before setting pen to paper he is in no fit state to make that fundamental concession which Depestre mentions. The French poet René Char fully understood this when he reminds us that "the poem emerges from a subjective imposition and an objective choice. The poem is a moving assembly of decisive original values, in topical relation with someone whom such an undertaking brings to the foreground."[5]

Yes, the first duty of the colonized poet is to clearly define the people, the subject of his creation. We cannot go resolutely forward unless we first realize our alienation. We have taken everything from the other side. Yet the other side has given us nothing except to sway us in its direction through a thousand twists, except lure us, seduce us, and imprison us by ten thousand devices, by a hundred thousand tricks. To take also means on several levels being taken. It is not enough to try and disengage ourselves by accumulating proclamations and denials. It is not enough to reunite with the people in a past where they no longer exist. We must rather reunite with them in their recent counter move which will suddenly call everything into question; we must focus on that zone of hidden fluctuation where the people can be found, for let there be no mistake, it is here that their souls are crystallized and their perception and respiration transfigured. . . .

When the colonized intellectual writing for his people uses the past he must do so with the intention of opening up the future, of spurring them into action and fostering hope. But in order to secure hope, in order to give it substance, he must take part in the action and commit himself body and soul to the national struggle. You can talk about anything you like, but when it comes to talking about that one thing in a man's life that involves opening up new horizons, enlightening your country and standing tall alongside your own people, then muscle power is required.

The colonized intellectual is responsible not to his national culture, but to the nation as a whole, whose culture is, after all, but one aspect. The colonized intellectual should not be concerned with choosing how or where he decides to wage the national struggle. To fight for national culture first of all means fighting for the liberation of the nation, the tangible matrix from which culture can grow. One cannot divorce the combat for culture from the people's struggle for liberation. For example, all the men and women fighting French colonialism in Algeria with their bare hands are no strangers to the national culture of Algeria. The Algerian national culture takes form and shape during the fight, in prison, facing the guillotine, and in the capture and destruction of the French military positions.

We should not therefore be content to delve into the people's past to find concrete examples to counter colonialism's endeavors to distort and depreciate. We must work and struggle in step with the people so as to shape the future and prepare the ground where vigorous shoots are already sprouting. National culture is no folklore where an abstract populism is convinced it has uncovered the popular truth. It is not some congealed mass of noble gestures, in other words less and less connected with the reality of the people. National culture is the collective thought process of a people to describe, justify, and extol the actions whereby they have joined forces and remained strong. National culture in the underdeveloped countries, therefore, must lie at the very heart of the liberation struggle these countries are waging. The African intellectuals who are still fighting in the name of "Negro-African" culture and who continue to organize conferences dedicated to the unity of that culture should realize that they can do little more than compare coins and sarcophagi.

There is no common destiny between the national cultures of Guinea and Senegal, but there is a common destiny between the nations of Guinea and Senegal dominated by the same French colonialism. If we want the national culture of Senegal to resemble the national culture of Guinea it is not enough for the leaders of the two countries to address the problems of independence, labor unions, and the economy from a similar perspective. Even then they would not be absolutely identical since the people and the leaders operate at a different pace.

There can be no such thing as rigorously identical cultures. To believe one can create a black culture is to forget oddly enough that "Negroes" are in the process of disappearing, since those who created them are witnessing the demise of their economic and cultural supremacy.[6] There will be no such thing as black culture because no politician imagines he has the vocation to create a black republic. The problem is knowing what role these men have in store for their people, the type of social relations they will establish and their idea of the future of humanity. That is what matters. All else is hot air and mystification.

In 1959 the African intellectuals meeting in Rome constantly spoke of unity. But one of the leading bards of this cultural unity is Jacques Rabemananjara, today a minister in the government of Madagascar, who toed his government's line to vote against the Algerian people at the United Nations General Assembly. Rabe, if he had been sincere with himself, should have resigned from the government and denounced those men who claim to represent the will of the Malagasy people. The ninety thousand dead of Madagascar did not authorize Rabe to oppose the aspirations of the Algerian people at the UN General Assembly.

"Negro-African" culture grows deeper through the people's struggle, and not through songs, poems, or folklore. Senghor, who is also a member of the African Society for Culture and who has worked with us on this issue of African culture, had no scruples either about instructing his delegation to back the French line on Algeria. Support for "Negro-African" culture and the cultural unity of Africa is first contingent on an unconditional support for the people's liberation struggle. One cannot expect African culture to advance unless one contributes realistically to the creation of the conditions necessary for this culture, i.e., the liberation of the continent.

Once again, no speech, no declaration on culture will detract us from our fundamental tasks which are to liberate the national territory; constantly combat the new forms of colonialism; and, as leaders, stubbornly refuse to indulge in self-satisfaction at the top.

MUTUAL FOUNDATIONS FOR NATIONAL CULTURE AND LIBERATION STRUGGLES

The sweeping, leveling nature of colonial domination was quick to dislocate in spectacular fashion the cultural life of a conquered people. The denial of a national reality, the new legal system imposed by the occupying power, the marginalization of the indigenous population and their customs by colonial society, expropriation, and the systematic enslavement of men and women, all contributed to this cultural obliteration.

Three years ago at our first congress I demonstrated that in a colonial situation any dynamism is fairly rapidly replaced by a reification of attitudes. The cultural sphere is marked out by safety railings and signposts, every single one of them defense mechanisms of the most elementary type, comparable in more ways than one to the simple instinct of self-preservation. This period is interesting because the oppressor is no longer content with the objective nonexistence of the conquered nation and culture. Every effort is made to make the colonized confess the inferiority of their culture, now reduced to a set of instinctive responses, to acknowledge the unreality of their nation and, in the last extreme, to admit the disorganized, half-finished nature of their own biological makeup.

The reactions of the colonized to this situation vary. Whereas the masses maintain intact traditions totally incongruous with the colonial situation, whereas the style of artisanship ossifies into an increasingly stereotyped formalism, the intellectual hurls himself frantically into the frenzied acquisition of the occupier's culture, making sure he denigrates his national culture, or else confines himself to making a detailed, methodical, zealous, and rapidly sterile inventory of it.

What both reactions have in common is that they both result in unacceptable contradictions. Renegade or substantialist, the colonized subject is ineffectual precisely because the colonial situation has not been rigorously analyzed. The colonial situation brings national culture virtually to a halt. There is no such thing as national culture, national cultural events, innovations, or reforms within the context of colonial domination, and there never will be. There are scattered instances of a bold attempt to revive a cultural dynamism, and reshape themes, forms, and tones. The immediate, tangible, and visible effects of these minor convulsions is nil. But if we follow the consequences to their very limit there are signs that the veil is being lifted from the national consciousness, oppression is being challenged and there is hope for the liberation struggle.

National culture under colonial domination is a culture under interrogation whose destruction is sought systematically. Very quickly it becomes a culture condemned to clandestinity. This notion of clandestinity can immediately be perceived in the reactions of the occupier who interprets this complacent attachment to traditions as a sign of loyalty to the national spirit and a refusal to submit. This persistence of cultural expression condemned by colonial society is already a demonstration of nationhood. But such a demonstration refers us back to the laws of inertia. No offensive has been launched, no relations redefined. There is merely a desperate clinging to a nucleus that is increasingly shriveled, increasingly inert, and increasingly hollow.

After one or two centuries of exploitation the national cultural landscape has radically shriveled. It has become an inventory of behavioral patterns, traditional costumes, and miscellaneous customs. Little movement can be seen. There is no real creativity, no ebullience. Poverty, national oppression, and cultural repression are one and the same. After a century of colonial domination culture becomes rigid in the extreme, congealed, and petrified. The atrophy of national reality and the death throes of national culture feed on one another. This is why it becomes vital to monitor the development of this relationship during the liberation struggle. Cultural denial, the contempt for any national demonstration of emotion or dynamism and the banning of any type of organization help spur aggressive behavior in the colonized. But this pattern of behavior is a defensive reaction, nonspecific, anarchic, and ineffective. Colonial exploitation, poverty, and endemic famine increasingly force the colonized into open, organized rebellion. Gradually, imperceptibly, the need for a decisive confrontation imposes itself and is eventually felt by the great majority of the people. Tensions emerge where previously there were none. International events, the collapse of whole sections of colonial empires and the inherent contradictions of the colonial system stimulate and strengthen combativity, motivating and invigorating the national consciousness.

These new tensions, which are present at every level of the colonial system, have repercussions on the cultural front. In literature, for example, there is relative overproduction. Once a pale imitation of the colonizer's literature, indigenous production now shows greater diversity and a will to particularize. Mainly consumer during the period of oppression, the intelligentsia turns productive. This literature is at first confined to the genre of poetry and tragedy. Then novels, short stories, and essays are tackled. There seems to be a kind of internal organization, a law of expression, according to which poetic creativity fades as the objectives and methods of the liberation struggle become clearer. There is a fundamental change of theme. In fact, less and less do we find those bitter, desperate recriminations, those loud, violent outbursts that, after all, reassure the occupier. In the previous period, the colonialists encouraged such endeavors and facilitated their publication. The occupier, in fact, likened these scathing denunciations, outpourings of misery, and heated words to an act of catharsis. Encouraging these acts would, in a certain way, avoid dramatization and clear the atmosphere.

But such a situation cannot last. In fact the advances made by national consciousness among the people modify and clarify the literary creation of the colonized intellectual. The people's staying power stimulates the intellectual to transcend the lament. Complaints followed by indictments give way to appeals. Then comes the call for revolt. The crystallization of the national consciousness will not only radically change the literary genres and themes but also create a completely new audience. Whereas the colonized intellectual started out by producing work exclusively with the oppressor in mind—either in order to charm him or to denounce him by using ethnic or subjectivist categories—he gradually switches over to addressing himself to his people.

It is only from this point onward that one can speak of a national literature. Literary creation addresses and clarifies typically nationalist themes. This is combat literature in the true sense of the word, in the sense that it calls upon a whole people to join in the struggle for the existence of the nation. Combat literature, because it informs the national consciousness, gives it shape and contours, and opens up new, unlimited horizons. Combat literature, because it takes charge, because it is resolve situated in historical time.

At another level, oral literature, tales, epics, and popular songs, previously classified and frozen in time, begin to change. The storytellers who recited inert episodes revive them and introduce increasingly fundamental changes. There are attempts to update battles and modernize the types of struggle, the heroes' names, and the weapons used. The method of allusion is increasingly used. Instead of "a long time ago," they substitute the more ambiguous expression "What I am going to tell you happened somewhere else, but it could happen here today or perhaps tomorrow." In this respect the case of Algeria is significant. From 1952–53 on, its storytellers, grown stale and dull, radically changed both their methods of narration and the content of their stories. Once scarce, the public returned in droves. The epic, with its standardized forms, reemerged. It has become an authentic form of entertainment that once again has taken on a cultural value. Colonialism knew full well what it was doing when it began systematically arresting these storytellers after 1955.

The people's encounter with this new song of heroic deeds brings an urgent breath of excitement, arouses forgotten muscular tensions and develops the imagination. Every time the storyteller narrates a new episode, the public is treated to a real invocation. The existence of a new type of man is revealed to the public. The present is no longer turned inward but channeled in every direction. The storyteller once again gives free rein to his imagination, innovates, and turns creator. It even happens that unlikely characters for such a transformation, social misfits such as outlaws or drifters, are rediscovered and rehabilitated. Close attention should be paid to the emergence of the imagination and the inventiveness of songs and folk tales in a colonized country. The storyteller responds to the expectations of the people by trial and error and searches for new models, national models, apparently on his own, but in fact with the support of his audience. Comedy and farce disappear or else lose their appeal. As for drama, it is no longer the domain of the intellectual's tormented conscience. No longer characterized by despair and revolt, it has become the people's daily lot, it has become part of an action in the making or already in progress.

In artisanship, the congealed, petrified forms loosen up. Wood carving, for example, which turned out set faces and poses by the thousands, starts to diversify. The expressionless or tormented mask comes to life, and the arms are raised upwards in a gesture of action. Compositions with two, three, or five figures emerge. An avalanche of amateurs and dissidents encourages the traditional schools to innovate. This new stimulus in this particular cultural sector very often goes unnoticed. Yet its contribution to the national struggle is vital. By bringing faces and bodies to life, by taking the group set on a single socle as creative subject, the artist inspires concerted action.

The awakening national consciousness has had a somewhat similar effect in the sphere of ceramics and pottery. Formalism is abandoned. Jugs, jars, and trays are reshaped, at first only slightly and then quite radically. Colors, once restricted in number, governed by laws of traditional harmony, flood back, reflecting the effects of the revolutionary upsurge. Certain ochers, certain blues that were apparently banned for eternity in a given cultural context, emerge unscathed. Likewise, the taboo of representing the human face, typical of certain clearly defined regions according to sociologists, is suddenly lifted. The metropolitan anthropologists and experts are quick to note these changes and denounce them all, referring rather to a codified artistic style and culture developing in tune with the colonial situation. The colonialist experts do not recognize these new forms and rush to the rescue of indigenous traditions. It is the colonialists who become the defenders of indigenous style. A memorable example, and one that takes on particular significance because it does not quite involve a colonial reality, was the reaction of white jazz fans when after the Second World War new styles such as bebop established themselves. For them jazz could only be the broken, desperate yearning of an old "Negro," five whiskeys under his belt, bemoaning his own misfortune and the racism of the whites. As soon as he understands himself and apprehends the world differently, as soon as he elicits a glimmer of hope and forces the racist world to retreat, it is obvious he will blow his horn to his heart's content and his husky voice will ring out loud and clear. The new jazz styles are not only born out of economic competition. They are one of the definite consequences of the inevitable, though gradual, defeat of the Southern universe in the USA. And it is not unrealistic to think that in fifty years or so the type of jazz lament hiccuped by a poor, miserable "Negro" will be defended by only those whites believing in a frozen image of a certain type of relationship and a certain form of negritude.

We would also uncover the same transformations, the same progress and the same eagerness if we enquired into the fields of dance, song, rituals, and traditional ceremonies. Well before the political or armed struggle, a careful observer could sense and feel in these arts the pulse of a fresh stimulus and the coming combat. Unusual forms of expression, original themes no longer invested with the power of invocation but the power to rally and mobilize with the approaching conflict in mind. Everything conspires to stimulate the colonized's sensibility, and to rule out and reject attitudes of inertia or defeat. By imparting new meaning and dynamism to artisanship, dance, music, literature, and the oral epic, the colonized subject restructures his own perception. The world no longer seems doomed. Conditions are ripe for the inevitable confrontation.

We have witnessed the emergence of a new energy in the cultural sphere. We have seen that this energy, these new forms, are linked to the maturing of the national consciousness, and now become increasingly objectivized and institutionalized. Hence the need for nationhood at all costs.

A common mistake, hardly defensible, moreover, is to attempt cultural innovations and reassert the value of indigenous culture within the context of colonial domination. Hence we arrive at a seemingly paradoxical proposition: In a colonized country, nationalism in its most basic, most rudimentary and undifferentiated form is the most forceful and effective way of defending national culture. A culture is first and foremost the expression of a nation, its preferences, its taboos, and its models. Other taboos, other values, other models are formed at every level of the entire society. National culture is the sum of all these considerations, the outcome of tensions internal and external to society as a whole and its multiple layers. In the colonial context, culture, when deprived of the twin supports of the nation and the state, perishes and dies. National liberation and the resurrection of the state are the preconditions for the very existence of a culture.

The nation is not only a precondition for culture, its ebullition, its perpetual renewal and maturation. It is a necessity. First of all it is the struggle for nationhood that unlocks culture and opens the doors of creation. Later on it is the nation that will provide culture with the conditions and framework for expression. The nation satisfies all those indispensable requirements for culture which alone can give it credibility, validity, dynamism, and creativity. It is also the national character that makes culture permeable to other cultures and enables it to influence and penetrate them. That which does not exist can hardly have an effect on reality or even influence it. The restoration of the nation must therefore give life in the most biological sense of the term to national culture.

We have thus traced the increasingly essential fissuring of the old cultural strata, and on the eve of the decisive struggle for national liberation, grasped the new forms of expression and the flight of the imagination.

There now remains one fundamental question. What is the relationship between the struggle, the political or armed conflict, and culture? During the conflict is culture put on hold? Is the national struggle a cultural manifestation? Must we conclude that the liberation struggle, though beneficial for culture a posteriori, is in itself a negation of culture? In other words, is the liberation struggle a cultural phenomenon?

We believe the conscious, organized struggle undertaken by a colonized people in order to restore national sovereignty constitutes the greatest cultural manifestation that exists. It is not solely the success of the struggle that consequently validates and energizes culture; culture does not go into hibernation during the conflict. The development and internal progression of the actual struggle expand the number of directions in which culture can go and hint at new possibilities. The liberation struggle does not restore to national culture its former values and configurations. This struggle, which aims at a fundamental redistribution of relations between men, cannot leave intact either the form or substance of the people's culture. After the struggle is over, there is not only the demise of colonialism, but also the demise of the colonized.

This new humanity, for itself and for others, inevitably defines a new humanism. This new humanism is written into the objectives and methods of the struggle. A struggle, which mobilizes every level of society, which expresses the intentions and expectations of the people, and which is not afraid to rely on their support almost entirely, will invariably triumph. The merit of this type of struggle is that it achieves the optimal conditions for cultural development and innovation. Once national liberation has been accomplished under these conditions, there is none of that tiresome cultural indecisiveness we find in certain newly independent countries, because the way a nation is born and functions exerts a fundamental influence on culture. A nation born of the concerted action of the people, which embodies the actual aspirations of the people and transforms the state, depends on exceptionally inventive cultural manifestations for its very existence.

The colonized who are concerned for their country's culture and wish to give it a universal dimension should not place their trust in a single principle—that independence is inevitable and automatically inscribed in the people's consciousness—in order to achieve this aim. National liberation as objective is one thing, the methods and popular components of the struggle are another. We believe that the future of culture and the richness of a national culture are also based on the values that inspired the struggle for freedom.

And now the moment has come to denounce certain pharisees. Humanity, some say, has got past the stage of nationalist claims. The time has come to build larger political unions, and consequently the old-fashioned nationalists should correct their mistakes. We believe on the contrary that the mistake, heavy with consequences, would be to miss out on the national stage. If culture is the expression of the national consciousness, I shall have no hesitation in saying, in the case in point, that national consciousness is the highest form of culture.

Self-awareness does not mean closing the door on communication. Philosophy teaches us on the contrary that it is its guarantee. National consciousness, which is not nationalism, is alone capable of giving us an international dimension. This question of national consciousness and national culture takes on a special dimension in Africa. The birth of national consciousness in Africa strictly correlates with an African consciousness. The responsibility of the African toward his national culture is also a responsibility toward "Negro-African" culture. This joint responsibility does not rest upon a metaphysical principle but mindfulness of a simple rule which stipulates that any independent nation in an Africa where colonialism still lingers is a nation surrounded, vulnerable, and in permanent danger.

If man is judged by his acts, then I would say that the most urgent thing today for the African intellectual is the building of his nation. If this act is true, i.e., if it expresses the manifest will of the people, if it reflects the restlessness of the African peoples, then it will necessarily lead to the discovery and advancement of universalizing values. Far then from distancing it from other nations, it is the national liberation that puts the nation on the stage of history. It is at the heart of national consciousness that international consciousness establishes itself and thrives. And this dual emergence, in fact, is the unique focus of all culture.

NOTES

1. "The Political Leader as Representative of a Culture." Paper presented at the Second Congress of Black Writers and Artists, Rome, 1959.
2. Translator's Note: Present-day Tanzanians.
3. "The lady was not alone/She had a husband/A fine, upstanding husband/Who recited Racine and Corneille/And Voltaire and Rousseau/And old Hugo and the young Musset/And Gide and Valéry/And so many others as well." René Depestre, *"Face à la nuit."*

4. "The lady was not alone/She had a husband/A husband who knew everything/But to tell the truth knew nothing/Because culture does not come without making concessions/Without conceding your flesh and blood/Without conceding yourself to others/A concession worth just as much as/Classicism or Romanticism/And all that nurtures our soul." René Depestre, *"Face à la nuit."*

5. René Char, *"Partage Formel."*

6. At the last school prize-giving ceremony in Dakar, the president of the Republic of Senegal, Léopold Senghor, announced that negritude should be included in the school curriculum. If this decision is an exercise in cultural history, it can only be approved. But if it is a matter of shaping black consciousness it is simply turning one's back on history which has already noted the fact that most "Negroes" have ceased to exist.

THE LANGUAGE OF AFRICAN LITERATURE (1986)

NGUGI WA THIONG'O

Introducing Decolonising the Mind: The Politics of Language in African Literature, *his collection of essays that includes "The Language of African Literature," Ngugi says "This book,* Decolonising the Mind, *is my farewell to English as a vehicle for any of my writings. From now on it is Gikuyu and Kiswahili all the way." After publishing novels and essays in English, Ngugi shifted to writing in Gikuyu (while still publishing his works in English translations). "African literature can only be written in African languages," he argues in this controversial essay. African writers who disagree with Ngugi argue that because Africans use the languages of the colonizers—such as English, French, and Portuguese—and use them in distinctly African ways, they have made them into African languages as well as European languages. For Ngugi, however, the languages of the colonizers, even when Africans use them, remain the languages of the colonizers.*

I

The language of African literature cannot be discussed meaningfully outside the context of those social forces which have made it both an issue demanding our attention and a problem calling for a resolution.

On the one hand is imperialism in its colonial and neo-colonial phases continuously press-ganging the African hand to the plough to turn the soil over, and putting blinkers on him to make him view the path ahead only as determined for him by the master armed with the bible and the sword. In other words, imperialism continues to control the economy, politics, and cultures of Africa. But on the other, and pitted against it, are the ceaseless struggles of African people to liberate their economy, politics and culture from that Euro-American-based stranglehold to usher a new era of true communal self-regulation and self-determination. It is an ever-continuing struggle to seize back their creative initiative in history through a real control of all the means of communal self-definition in time and space. The choice of language and the use to which language is put is central to a people's definition of themselves in relation to their natural and social environment, indeed in relation to the entire universe. Hence language has always been at the heart of the two contending social forces in the Africa of the twentieth century.

The contention started a hundred years ago when in 1884 the capitalist powers of Europe sat in Berlin and carved an entire continent with a multiplicity of peoples, cultures, and languages into different colonies. It seems it is the fate of Africa to have her destiny always decided around conference tables in the metropolises of the western world: her submergence from self-governing communities into colonies was decided in Berlin; her more recent transition into neo-colonies along the same boundaries was negotiated around the same tables in London, Paris, Brussels and Lisbon. The Berlin-drawn division under which Africa is still living was obviously economic and political, despite the claims of bible-wielding diplomats, but it was also cultural. Berlin in 1884 saw the division of Africa into the different languages of the European powers. African countries, as colonies and even today as neo-colonies, came to be defined and to define themselves in terms of the languages of Europe: English-speaking, French-speaking or Portuguese-speaking African countries.[1]

Unfortunately writers who should have been mapping paths out of that linguistic encirclement of their continent also came to be defined and to define themselves in terms of the languages of imperialist imposition. Even at their most radical and pro-African position in their sentiments and articulation of problems they still took it as axiomatic that the renaissance of African cultures lay in the languages of Europe.

I should know!

II

In 1962 I was invited to that historic meeting of African writers at Makerere University College, Kampala, Uganda. The list of participants contained most of the names which have now become the subject of scholarly dissertations in universities all over the world. The title? "A Conference of *African Writers of English Expression*."[2]

I was then a student of *English* at Makerere, an overseas college of the University of London. The main attraction for me was the certain possibility of meeting Chinua Achebe. I had with me a rough typescript of a novel in progress, *Weep Not, Child*, and I wanted him to read it. In the previous year, 1961, I had completed *The River Between*, my first-ever attempt at a novel, and entered it for a writing competition organised by the East African Literature Bureau. I was keeping in step with the tradition of Peter Abrahams with his output of novels and autobiographies from *Path of Thunder* to *Tell Freedom* and followed by Chinua Achebe with his publication of *Things Fall Apart* in 1959. Or there were their counterparts in French colonies, the generation of Sédar Senghor and David Diop included in the 1947/48 Paris edition of *Anthologie de la nouvelle poésie nègre et malgache de langue française*. They all wrote in European languages as was the case with all the participants in that momentous encounter on Makerere hill in Kampala in 1962.

The title "A Conference of African Writers of English Expression," automatically excluded those who wrote in African languages. Now on looking back from the self-questioning heights of 1986, I can see this contained absurd anomalies. I, a student, could qualify for the meeting on the basis of only two published short stories, "The Fig Tree (Mūgumo)" in a student journal, *Penpoint*, and "The Return" in a new journal, *Transition*. But neither Shabaan Robert, then the greatest living East African poet with several works of poetry and prose to his credit in Kiswahili, nor Chief Fagunwa, the great Nigerian writer with several published titles in Yoruba, could possibly qualify.

The discussions on the novel, the short story, poetry, and drama were based on extracts from works in English and hence they excluded the main body of work in Swahili, Zulu, Yoruba, Arabic, Amharic and other African languages. Yet, despite this exclusion of writers and literature in African languages, no sooner were the introductory preliminaries over than this Conference of "African Writers of English Expression" sat down to the first item on the agenda: "What is African Literature?"

The debate which followed was animated: Was it literature about Africa or about the African experience? Was it literature written by Africans? What about a non-African who wrote about Africa: did his work qualify as African literature? What if an African set his work in Greenland: did that qualify as African literature? Or were African languages the criteria? OK: what about Arabic, was it not foreign to Africa? What about French and English, which had become African languages? What if an European wrote about Europe in an African language? If...if...if...this or that, except the issue: the domination of our languages and cultures by those of imperialist Europe: in any case there was no Fagunwa or Shabaan Robert or any writer in African languages to bring the conference down from the realms of evasive abstractions. The question was never seriously asked: did what we wrote qualify as African literature? The whole area of literature and audience, and hence of language as a determinant of both the national and class audience, did not really figure: the debate was more about the subject matter and the racial origins and geographical habitation of the writer.

English, like French and Portuguese, was assumed to be the natural language of literary and even political mediation between African people in the same nation and between nations in Africa and other continents. In some instances these European languages were seen as having a capacity to unite African peoples against divisive tendencies inherent in the multiplicity of African languages within the same geographic state. Thus Ezekiel Mphahlele later could write, in a letter to *Transition* number 11, that English and French have become the common language with which to present a nationalist front against white oppressors, and even "where the whiteman has already retreated, as in the independent states, these two languages are still a unifying force."[3] In the literary sphere they were often seen as coming to save African languages against themselves. Writing a foreword to Birago Diop's book *Contes d'Amadou Koumba* Sédar Senghor commends him for using French to rescue the spirit and style of old African fables and tales. "However while rendering them into French he renews them with an art which, while it respects the genius of the French language, that language of gentleness and honesty, preserves at the same time all the virtues of the negro-african languages."[4] English, French and Portuguese had come to our rescue and we accepted the unsolicited gift with gratitude. Thus in 1964, Chinua Achebe, in a speech entitled "The African Writer and the English Language," said:

> Is it right that a man should abandon his mother tongue for someone else's? It looks like a dreadful betrayal and produces a guilty feeling. But for me there is no other choice. I have been given the language and I intend to use it.[5]

See the paradox: the possibility of using mother-tongues provokes a tone of levity in phrases like "a dreadful betrayal" and "a guilty feeling"; but that of foreign languages produces a categorical positive embrace, what Achebe himself, ten years later, was to describe as this "fatalistic logic of the unassailable position of English in our literature."[6]

The fact is that all of us who opted for European languages—the conference participants and the generation that followed them—accepted that fatalistic logic to a greater or lesser degree. We were guided by it and the only question which preoccupied us was how best to make the borrowed tongues carry the weight of our African experience by, for instance, making them "prey" on African proverbs and other peculiarities of African speech and folklore. For this task, Achebe (*Things Fall Apart; Arrow of God*), Amos Tutuola (*The Palm-wine Drinkard; My Life in the Bush of Ghosts*), and Gabriel Okara (*The Voice*) were often held as providing the three alternative models. The lengths to which we were prepared to go in our mission of enriching foreign languages by injecting Senghorian "black blood" into their rusty joints, is best exemplified by Gabriel Okara in an article reprinted in *Transition*:

> As a writer who believes in the utilization of African ideas, African philosophy and African folklore and imagery to the fullest extent possible, I am of the opinion the only way to use them effectively is to translate them almost literally from the African language native to the writer into whatever European language he is using as medium of expression. I have endeavoured in my words to keep as close as possible to the vernacular expressions. For, from a word, a group of words, a sentence and even a name in any African language, one can glean the social norms, attitudes and values of a people.

> In order to capture the vivid images of African speech, I had to eschew the habit of expressing my thoughts first in English. It was difficult at first, but I had to learn. I had to study each Ijaw expression I used and to discover the probable situation in which it was used in order to bring out the nearest meaning in English. I found it a fascinating exercise.[7]

Why, we may ask, should an African writer, or any writer, become so obsessed by taking from his mother-tongue to enrich other tongues? Why should he see it as his particular mission? We never asked ourselves: how can we enrich our languages? How can we "prey" on the rich humanist and democratic heritage in the struggles of other peoples in other times and other places to enrich our own? Why not have Balzac, Tolstoy, Sholokov, Brecht, Lu Hsun, Pablo Neruda, H. C. Anderson, Kim Chi Ha, Marx, Lenin, Albert Einstein, Galileo, Aeschylus, Aristotle and Plato in African languages? And why not create literary monuments in our own languages? Why in other words should Okara not sweat it out to create in Ijaw, which he acknowledges to have depths of philosophy and a wide range of ideas and experiences? What was our responsibility to the struggles of African peoples? No, these questions were not asked. What seemed to worry us more was this: after all the literary gymnastics of preying on our languages to add life and vigour to English and other foreign languages, would the result be accepted as good English or good French? Will the owner of the language criticise our usage? Here we were more assertive of our rights! Chinua Achebe wrote:

I feel that the English language will be able to carry the weight of my African experience. But it will have to be a new English, still in full communion with its ancestral home but altered to suit new African surroundings.[8]

Gabriel Okara's position on this was representative of our generation:

Some may regard this way of writing English as a desecration of the language. This is of course not true. Living languages grow like living things, and English is far from a dead language. There are American, West Indian, Australian, Canadian and New Zealand versions of English. All of them add life and vigour to the language while reflecting their own respective cultures. Why shouldn't there be a Nigerian or West African English which we can use to express our own ideas, thinking and philosophy in our own way?[9]

How did we arrive at this acceptance of "the fatalistic logic of the unassailable position of English in our literature," in our culture and in our politics? What was the route from the Berlin of 1884 via the Makerere of 1962 to what is still the prevailing and dominant logic a hundred years later? How did we, as African writers, come to be so feeble towards the claims of our languages on us and so aggressive in our claims on other languages, particularly the languages of our colonization?

Berlin of 1884 was effected through the sword and the bullet. But the night of the sword and the bullet was followed by the morning of the chalk and the blackboard. The physical violence of the battlefield was followed by the psychological violence of the classroom. But where the former was visibly brutal, the latter was visibly gentle, a process best described in Cheikh Hamidou Kane's novel *Ambiguous Adventure* where he talks of the methods of the colonial phase of imperialism as consisting of knowing how to kill with efficiency and to heal with the same art.

On the Black Continent, one began to understand that their real power resided not at all in the cannons of the first morning but in what followed the cannons. Therefore behind the cannons was the new school. The new school had the nature of both the cannon and the magnet. From the cannon it took the efficiency of a fighting weapon. But better than the cannon it made the conquest permanent. The cannon forces the body and the school fascinates the soul.[10]

In my view language was the most important vehicle through which that power fascinated and held the soul prisoner. The bullet was the means of the physical subjugation. Language was the means of the spiritual subjugation. Let me illustrate this by drawing upon experiences in my own education, particularly in language and literature.

III

I was born into a large peasant family: father, four wives and about twenty-eight children. I also belonged, as we all did in those days, to a wider extended family and to the community as a whole.

We spoke Gĩkũyũ as we worked in the fields. We spoke Gĩkũyũ in and outside the home. I can vividly recall those evenings of storytelling around the fireside. It was mostly the grown-ups telling the children but everybody was interested and involved. We children would re-tell the stories the following day to other children who worked in the fields picking the pyrethrum flowers, tea-leaves or coffee beans of our European and African landlords.

The stories, with mostly animals as the main characters, were all told in Gĩkũyũ. Hare, being small, weak but full of innovative wit and cunning, was our hero. We identified with him as he struggled against the brutes of prey like lion, leopard, hyena. His victories were our victories and we learnt that the apparently weak can outwit the strong. We followed the animals in their struggle against hostile nature—drought, rain, sun, wind—a confrontation often forcing them to search for forms of co-operation. But we were also interested in their struggles amongst themselves, and particularly between the beasts and the victims of prey. These twin struggles, against nature and other animals, reflected real-life struggles in the human world.

Not that we neglected stories with human beings as the main characters. There were two types of characters in such human-centred narratives: the species of truly human beings with qualities of courage, kindness, mercy, hatred of evil, concern for others; and a man-eat-man two-mouthed species with qualities of greed, selfishness, individualism and hatred of what was good for the larger co-operative community. Co-operation as the ultimate good in a community was a constant theme. It could unite human beings with animals against ogres and beasts of prey, as in the story of how dove, after being fed with castor-oil seeds, was sent to fetch a smith working far away from home and whose pregnant wife was being threatened by these man-eating two-mouthed ogres.

There were good and bad story-tellers. A good one could tell the same story over and over again, and it would always be fresh to us, the listeners. He or she could tell a story told by someone else and make it more alive and dramatic. The differences really were in the use of words and images and the inflexion of voices to effect different tones.

We therefore learnt to value words for their meaning and nuances. Language was not a mere string of words. It had a suggestive power well beyond the immediate and lexical meaning. Our appreciation of the suggestive magical power of language was reinforced by the games we played with words through riddles, proverbs, transpositions of syllables, or through nonsensical but musically arranged words.[11] So we learnt the music of our language on top of the content. The language, through images and symbols, gave us a view of the world, but it had a beauty of its own. The home and the field were then our pre-primary school but what is important, for this discussion, is that the language of our evening teach-ins, and the language of our immediate and wider community, and the language of our work in the fields were one.

And then I went to school, a colonial school, and this harmony was broken. The language of my education was no longer the language of my culture. I first went to Kamaandura, missionary run, and then to another called Maanguũ run by nationalists grouped around the Gĩkũyũ Independent and Karinga Schools Association. Our language of education was still Gĩkũyũ. The very first time I was ever given an ovation for my writing was over a composition in Gĩkũyũ. So for my first four years there was still harmony between the language of my formal education and that of the Limuru peasant community.

It was after the declaration of a state of emergency over Kenya in 1952 that all the schools run by patriotic nationalists were taken over by the colonial regime and were placed under District Education Boards chaired by Englishmen. English became the language of my formal education. In Kenya, English became more than a language: it was *the* language, and all the others had to bow before it in deference.

Thus one of the most humiliating experiences was to be caught speaking Gĩkũyũ in the vicinity of the school. The culprit was given corporal punishment—three to five strokes of the cane on bare buttocks—or was made to carry a metal plate around the neck with inscriptions such as I AM STUPID or I AM A DONKEY. Sometimes the culprits were fined money they could hardly afford. And how did the teachers catch the culprits? A button was initially given to one pupil who was supposed to hand it over to whoever was caught speaking his mother tongue. Whoever had the button at the end of the day would sing who had given it to him and the ensuing process would bring out all the culprits of the day. Thus children were turned into witch-hunters and in the process were being taught the lucrative value of being a traitor to one's immediate community.

The attitude to English was the exact opposite: any achievement in spoken or written English was highly rewarded; prizes, prestige, applause; the ticket to higher realms. English became the measure of intelligence and ability in the arts, the sciences, and all the other branches of learning. English became *the* main determinant of a child's progress up the ladder of formal education.

As you may know, the colonial system of education in addition to its apartheid racial demarcation had the structure of a pyramid: a broad primary base, a narrowing secondary middle, and an even narrower university apex. Selections from primary into secondary were through an examination, in my time called Kenya African Preliminary Examination, in which one had to pass six subjects ranging from Maths to Nature Study and Kiswahili. All the papers were written in English. Nobody could pass the exam who failed the English language paper no matter how brilliantly he had done in the other subjects. I remember one boy in my class of 1954 who had distinctions in all subjects except English, which he had failed. He was made to fail the entire exam. He went on to become a turn boy in a bus company. I who had only passes but a credit in English got a place at the Alliance High School, one of the most elitist institutions for Africans in colonial Kenya. The requirements for a place at the University, Makerere University College, were broadly the same: nobody could go on to wear the undergraduate red gown, no matter how brilliantly they had performed in all the other subjects unless they had a credit—not even a simple pass!—in English. Thus the most coveted place in the pyramid and in the system was only available to the holder of an English language credit card. English was the official vehicle and the magic formula to colonial elitedom.

 Literary education was now determined by the dominant language while also reinforcing that dominance. Orature (oral literature) in Kenyan languages stopped. In primary school I now read simplified Dickens and Stevenson alongside Rider Haggard. Jim Hawkins, Oliver Twist, Tom Brown—not Hare, Leopard and Lion—were now my daily companions in the world of imagination. In secondary school, Scott and G. B. Shaw vied with more Rider Haggard, John Buchan, Alan Paton, Captain W. E. Johns. At Makerere I read English: from Chaucer to T. S. Eliot with a touch of Graham Greene.

Thus language and literature were taking us further and further from ourselves to other selves, from our world to other worlds.

What was the colonial system doing to us Kenyan children? What were the consequences of, on the one hand, this systematic suppression of our languages and the literature they carried, and on the other the elevation of English and the literature it carried? To answer those questions, let me first examine the relationship of language to human experience, human culture, and the human perception of reality.

IV

Language, any language, has a dual character: it is both a means of communication and a carrier of culture. Take English. It is spoken in Britain and in Sweden and Denmark. But for Swedish and Danish people English is only a means of communication with non-Scandinavians. It is not a carrier of their culture. For the British, and particularly the English, it is additionally, and inseparably from its use as a tool of communication, a carrier of their culture and history. Or take Swahili in East and Central Africa. It is widely used as a means of communication across many nationalities. But it is not the carrier of a culture and history of many of those nationalities. However in parts of Kenya and Tanzania, and particularly in Zanzibar, Swahili is inseparably both a means of communication and a carrier of the culture of those people to whom it is a mother-tongue.

Language as communication has three aspects or elements. There is first what Karl Marx once called the language of real life,[12] the element basic to the whole notion of language, its origins and development: that is, the relations people enter into with one another in the labour process, the links they necessarily establish among themselves in the act of a people, a community of human beings, producing wealth or means of life like food, clothing, houses. A human community really starts its historical being as a community of co-operation in production through the division of labour; the simplest is between man, woman and child within a household; the more complex divisions are between branches of production such as those who are sole hunters, sole gatherers of fruits or sole workers in metal. Then there are the most complex divisions such as those in modern factories where a single product, say a shirt or a shoe, is the result of many hands and minds. Production is co-operation, is communication, is language, is expression of a relation between human beings and it is specifically human.

The second aspect of language as communication is speech and it imitates the language of real life, that is communication in production. The verbal signposts both reflect and aid communication or the relations established between human beings in the production of their means of life. Language as a system of verbal signposts makes that production possible. The spoken word is to relations between human beings what the hand is to the relations between human beings and nature. The hand through tools mediates between human beings and nature and forms the language of real life: spoken words mediate between human beings and form the language of speech.

The third aspect is the written signs. The written word imitates the spoken. Where the first two aspects of language as communication through the hand and the spoken word historically evolved more or less simultaneously, the written aspect is a much later historical development. Writing is representation of sounds with visual symbols, from the simplest knot among shepherds to tell the number in a herd or the hieroglyphics among the Agĩkũyũ gicaandi singers and poets of Kenya, to the most complicated and different letter and picture writing systems of the world today.

In most societies the written and the spoken languages are the same, in that they represent each other: what is on paper can be read to another person and be received as that language which the recipient has grown up speaking. In such a society there is broad harmony for a child between the three aspects of language as communication. His interaction with nature and with other men is expressed in written and spoken symbols or signs which are both a result of that double interaction and a reflection of it. The association of the child's sensibility is with the language of his experience of life.

But there is more to it: communication between human beings is also the basis and process of evolving culture. In doing similar kinds of things and actions over and over again under similar circumstances, similar even in their mutability, certain patterns, moves, rhythms, habits, attitudes, experiences and knowledge emerge. Those experiences are handed over to the next generation and become the inherited basis for their further actions on nature and on themselves. There is a gradual accumulation of values which in time become almost self-evident truths governing their conception of what is right and wrong, good and bad, beautiful and ugly, courageous and cowardly, generous and mean in their internal and external relations. Over a time this becomes a way of life distinguishable from other ways of life. They develop a distinctive culture and history. Culture embodies those moral, ethical and aesthetic values, the set of spiritual eyeglasses, through which they come to view themselves and their place in the universe. Values are the basis of a people's identity, their sense of particularity as members of the human race. All this is carried by language. Language as culture is the collective memory bank of a people's experience in history. Culture is almost indistinguishable from the language that makes possible its genesis, growth, banking, articulation and indeed its transmission from one generation to the next.

Language as culture also has three important aspects. Culture is a product of the history which it in turn reflects. Culture in other words is a product and a reflection of human beings communicating with one another in the very struggle to create wealth and to control it. But culture does not merely reflect that history, or rather it does so by actually forming images or pictures of the world of nature and nurture. Thus the second aspect of language as culture is as an image-forming agent in the mind of a child. Our whole conception of ourselves as a people, individually and collectively, is based on those pictures and images which may or may not correctly correspond to the actual reality of the struggles with nature and nurture which produced them in the first place. But our capacity to confront the world creatively is dependent on how those images correspond or not to that reality, how they distort or clarify the reality of our struggles. Language as culture is thus mediating between me and my own self; between my own self and other selves; between me and nature. Language is mediating in my very being. And this brings us to the third aspect of language as culture. Culture transmits or imparts those images of the world and reality through the spoken and the written language, that is through a specific language. In other words, the capacity to speak, the capacity to order sounds in a manner that makes for mutual comprehension between human beings is universal. This is the universality of language, a quality specific to human beings. It corresponds to the universality of the struggle against nature and that between human beings. But the particularity of the sounds, the words, the word order into phrases and sentences, and the specific manner, or laws, of their ordering is what distinguishes one language from another. Thus a specific culture is not transmitted through language in its universality but in its particularity as the language of a specific community with a specific history. Written literature and orature are the main means by which a particular language transmits the images of the world contained in the culture it carries.

Language as communication and as culture are then products of each other. Communication creates culture: culture is a means of communication. Language carries culture, and culture carries, particularly through orature and literature, the entire body of values by which we come to perceive ourselves and our place in the world. How people perceive themselves affects how they look at their culture, at their politics and at the social production of wealth, at their entire relationship to nature and to other beings. Language is thus inseparable from ourselves as a community of human beings with a specific form and character, a specific history, a specific relationship to the world.

V

So what was the colonialist imposition of a foreign language doing to us children?

The real aim of colonialism was to control the people's wealth: what they produced, how they produced it, and how it was distributed; to control, in other words, the entire realm of the language of real life. Colonialism imposed its control of the social production of wealth through military conquest and subsequent political dictatorship. But its most important area of domination was the mental universe of the colonised, the control, through culture, of how people perceived themselves and their relationship to the world. Economic and political control can never be complete or effective without mental control. To control a people's culture is to control their tools of self-definition in relationship to others.

For colonialism this involved two aspects of the same process: the destruction or the deliberate undervaluing of a people's culture, their art, dances, religions, history, geography, education, orature and literature, and the conscious elevation of the language of the colo-niser. The domination of a people's language by the languages of the colonising nations was crucial to the domination of the mental universe of the colonised.

Take language as communication. Imposing a foreign language, and suppressing the native languages as spoken and written, were already breaking the harmony previously exist-ing between the African child and the three aspects of language. Since the new language as a means of communication was a product of and was reflecting the "real language of life" else-where, it could never as spoken or written properly reflect or imitate the real life of that com-munity. This may in part explain why technology always appears to us as slightly external, *their* product and not *ours*. The word "missile" used to hold an alien far-away sound until I recently learnt its equivalent in Gĩkũyũ, *ngurukuhĩ*, and it made me apprehend it differently. Learning, for a colonial child, became a cerebral activity and not an emotionally felt experience.

But since the new, imposed languages could never completely break the native languages as spoken, their most effective area of domination was the third aspect of language as communication, the written. The language of an African child's formal education was foreign. The language of the books he read was foreign. The language of his conceptualisation was foreign. Thought, in him, took the visible form of a foreign language. So the written language of a child's upbringing in the school (even his spoken language within the school compound) became divorced from his spoken language at home. There was often not the slightest relationship between the child's written world, which was also the language of his schooling, and the world of his immediate environment in the family and the community. For a colonial child, the harmony existing between the three aspects of language as communication was irrevocably broken. This resulted in the disassociation of the sensibility of that child from his natural and social environment, what we might call colonial alienation. The alienation became reinforced in the teaching of history, geography, music, where bourgeois Europe was always the centre of the universe.

This disassociation, divorce, or alienation from the immediate environment becomes clearer when you look at colonial language as a carrier of culture.

Since culture is a product of the history of a people which it in turn reflects, the child was now being exposed exclusively to a culture that was a product of a world external to himself. He was being made to stand outside himself to look at himself. *Catching Them Young* is the title of a book on racism, class, sex, and politics in children's literature by Bob Dixon. "Catching them young" as an aim was even more true of a colonial child. The images of this world and his place in it implanted in a child take years to eradicate, if they ever can be.

Since culture does not just reflect the world in images but actually, through those very images, conditions a child to see that world in a certain way, the colonial child was made to see the world and where he stands in it as seen and defined by or reflected in the culture of the language of imposition.

And since those images are mostly passed on through orature and literature it meant the child would now only see the world as seen in the literature of his language of adoption. From the point of view of alienation, that is of seeing oneself from outside oneself as if one was another self, it does not matter that the imported literature carried the great humanist tradition of the best in Shakespeare, Goethe, Balzac, Tolstoy, Gorky, Brecht, Sholokhov, Dickens. The location of this great mirror of imagination was necessarily Europe and its history and culture and the rest of the universe was seen from that centre.

But obviously it was worse when the colonial child was exposed to images of his world as mirrored in the written languages of his coloniser. Where his own native languages were associated in his impressionable mind with low status, humiliation, corporal punishment, slow-footed intelligence and ability or downright stupidity, non-intelligibility and barbarism, this was reinforced by the world he met in the works of such geniuses of racism as a Rider Haggard or a Nicholas Monsarrat; not to mention the pronouncement of some of the giants of western intellectual and political establishment, such as Hume ("...the negro is naturally inferior to the whites..."),[13] Thomas Jefferson ("...the blacks...are inferior to the whites on the endowments of both body and mind..."),[14] or Hegel with his Africa comparable to a land of childhood still enveloped in the dark mantle of the night as far as the development of self-conscious history was concerned. Hegel's statement that there was nothing harmonious with humanity to be found in the African character is representative of the racist images of Africans and Africa such a colonial child was bound to encounter in the literature of the colonial languages.[15] The results could be disastrous.

In her paper read to the conference on the teaching of African literature in schools held in Nairobi in 1973, entitled "Written Literature and Black Images,"[16] the Kenyan writer and scholar Professor Mĩcere Mũgo related how a reading of the description of Gagool as an old African woman in Rider Haggard's *King Solomon's Mines* had for a long time made her feel mortal terror whenever she encountered old African women. In his autobiography *This Life* Sydney Poitier describes how, as a result of the literature he had read, he had come to associate Africa with snakes. So on arrival in Africa and being put up in a modern hotel in a modern city, he could not sleep because he kept on looking for snakes everywhere, even under the bed. These two have been able to pinpoint the origins of their fears. But for most others the negative image becomes internalised and it affects their cultural and even political choices in ordinary living.

Thus Léopold Sédar Senghor has said very clearly that although the colonial language had been forced upon him, if he had been given the choice he would still have opted for French. He becomes lyrical in his subservience to French:

> We express ourselves in French since French has a universal vocation and since our message is also addressed to French people and others. In our languages [i.e., African languages] the halo that surrounds the words is by nature merely that of sap and blood; French words send out thousands of rays like diamonds.[17]

Senghor has now been rewarded by being anointed to an honoured place in the French Academy—that institution for safe-guarding the purity of the French language.

In Malawi, Banda has erected his own monument by way of an institution, The Kamuzu Academy, designed to aid the brightest pupils of Malawi in their mastery of English.

> It is a grammar school designed to produce boys and girls who will be sent to universities like Harvard, Chicago, Oxford, Cambridge and Edinburgh and be able to compete on equal terms with others elsewhere.

> The President has instructed that Latin should occupy a central place in the curriculum. All teachers must have had at least some Latin in their academic background. Dr. Banda has often said that no one can fully master English without knowledge of languages such as Latin and French...[18]

For good measure no Malawian is allowed to teach at the academy—none is good enough—and all the teaching staff has been recruited from Britain. A Malawian might lower the standards, or rather, the purity of the English language. Can you get a more telling example of hatred of what is national, and a servile worship of what is foreign even though dead?

In history books and popular commentaries on Africa, too much has been made of the supposed differences in the policies of the various colonial powers, the British indirect rule (or the pragmatism of the British in their lack of a cultural programme!) and the French and Portuguese conscious programme of cultural assimilation. These are a matter of detail and emphasis. The final effect was the same: Senghor's embrace of French as this language with a universal vocation is not so different from Chinua Achebe's gratitude in 1964 to English— "those of us who have inherited the English language may not be in a position to appreciate the value of the inheritance."[19] The assumptions behind the practice of those of us who have abandoned our mother-tongues and adopted European ones as the creative vehicles of our imagination, are not different either.

Thus the 1962 conference of "African Writers of English Expression" was only recognising, with approval and pride of course, what through all the years of selective education and rigorous tutelage, we had already been led to accept: the "fatalistic logic of the unassailable position of English in our literature." The logic was embodied deep in imperialism; and it was imperialism and its effects that we did not examine at Makerere. It is the final triumph of a system of domination when the dominated start singing its virtues.

VI

The twenty years that followed the Makerere conference gave the world a unique literature— novels, stories, poems, plays written by Africans in European languages—which soon consolidated itself into a tradition with companion studies and a scholarly industry.

Right from its conception it was the literature of the petty-bourgeoisie born of the colonial schools and universities. It could not be otherwise, given the linguistic medium of its message. Its rise and development reflected the gradual accession of this class to political and even economic dominance. But the petty-bourgeoisie in Africa was a large class with different strands in it. It ranged from that section which looked forward to a permanent alliance with imperialism in which it played the role of an intermediary between the bourgeoisie of the western metropolis and the people of the colonies—the section which in my book *Detained: A Writer's Prison Diary* I have described as the comprador bourgeoisie—to that section which saw the future in terms of a vigorous independent national economy in African capitalism or in some kind of socialism, what I shall here call the nationalistic or patriotic bourgeoisie. This literature by Africans in European languages was specifically that of the nationalistic bourgeoisie in its creators, its thematic concerns and its consumption.[20]

Internationally the literature helped this class, which in politics, business, and education, was assuming leadership of the countries newly emergent from colonialism, or of those struggling to so emerge, to explain Africa to the world: Africa had a past and a culture of dignity and human complexity.

Internally the literature gave this class a cohesive tradition and a common literary frame of references, which it otherwise lacked with its uneasy roots in the culture of the peasantry and in the culture of the metropolitan bourgeoisie. The literature added confidence to the class: the petty-bourgeoisie now had a past, a culture and a literature with which to confront the racist bigotry of Europe. This confidence—manifested in the tone of the writing, its sharp critique of European bourgeois civilisation, its implications, particularly in its negritude mould, that Africa had something new to give to the world—reflects the political ascendancy of the patriotic nationalistic section of the petty-bourgeoisie before and imme-diately after independence.

So initially this literature—in the post-war world of national democratic revolutionary and anti-colonial liberation in China and India, armed uprisings in Kenya and Algeria, the independence of Ghana and Nigeria with others impending—was part of that great anti-colonial and anti-imperialist upheaval in Asia, Africa, Latin America and Caribbean islands. It was inspired by the general political awakening; it drew its stamina and even form from the peasantry: their proverbs, fables, stories, riddles, and wise sayings. It was shot through and through with optimism. But later, when the comprador section assumed political ascen-dancy and strengthened rather than weakened the economic links with imperialism in what was clearly a neo-colonial arrangement, this literature became more and more critical, cyni-cal, disillusioned, bitter and denunciatory in tone. It was almost unanimous in its portrayal, with varying degrees of detail, emphasis, and clarity of vision, of the post-independence betrayal of hope. But to whom was it directing its list of mistakes made, crimes and wrongs committed, complaints unheeded, or its call for a change of moral direction? The imperial-ist bourgeoisie? The petty-bourgeoisie in power? The military, itself part and parcel of that class? It sought another audience, principally the peasantry and the working class or what was generally conceived as the people. The search for new audience and new directions was reflected in the quest for simpler forms, in the adoption of a more direct tone, and often in a direct call for action. It was also reflected in the content. Instead of seeing Africa as one undifferentiated mass of historically wronged blackness, it now attempted some sort of class analysis and evaluation of neo-colonial societies. But this search was still within the con-fines of the languages of Europe whose use it now defended with less vigour and confidence. So its quest was hampered by the very language choice, and in its movement toward the people, it could only go up to that section of the petty-bourgeoisie—the students, teachers, secretaries for instance—still in closest touch with the people. It settled there, marking time, caged within the linguistic fence of its colonial inheritance.

Its greatest weakness still lay where it has always been, in the audience—the petty-bourgeoisie readership automatically assumed by the very choice of language. Because of its indeterminate economic position between the many contending classes, the petty-bourgeoi-sie develops a vacillating psychological make-up. Like a chameleon it takes on the colour of the main class with which it is in the closest touch and sympathy. It can be swept to activity by the masses at a time of revolutionary tide; or be driven to silence, fear, cynicism, with-drawal into self-contemplation, existential anguish, or to collaboration with the powers-that-be at times of reactionary tides. In Africa this class has always oscillated between the imperialist bourgeoisie and its comprador neo-colonial ruling elements on the one hand, and the peasantry and the working class (the masses) on the other. This very lack of iden-tity in its social and psychological make-up as a class, was reflected in the very literature it produced: the crisis of identity was assumed in that very preoccupation with definition at the Makerere conference. In literature as in politics it spoke as if its identity or the crisis of its own identity was that of society as a whole. The literature it produced in European languages was given the identity of African literature as if there had never been literature in African languages. Yet by avoiding a real confrontation with the language issue, it was clearly wearing false robes of identity: it was a pretender to the throne of the mainstream of African literature. The practitioner of what Janheinz Jahn called neo-African literature tried to get out of the dilemma by over-insisting that European languages were really African languages or by trying to Africanise English or French usage while making sure it was still recognisable as English or French or Portuguese.

In the process this literature created, falsely and even absurdly, an English-speaking (or French or Portuguese) African peasantry and working class, a clear negation or falsification of the historical process and reality. This European-language-speaking peasantry and working class, existing only in novels and dramas, was at times invested with the vacillating mentality, the evasive self-contemplation, the existential anguished human condition, or the man-torn-between-two-worlds-facedness of the petty-bourgeoisie.

In fact, if it had been left entirely to this class, African languages would have ceased to exist—with independence!

VII

But African languages refused to die. They would not simply go the way of Latin to become the fossils for linguistic archaeology to dig up, classify, and argue about the international conferences.

These languages, these national heritages of Africa, were kept alive by the peasantry. The peasantry saw no contradiction between speaking their own mother-tongues and belonging to a larger national or continental geography. They saw no necessary antagonistic contradiction between belonging to their immediate nationality, to their multinational state along the Berlin-drawn boundaries, and to Africa as a whole. These people happily spoke Wolof, Hausa, Yoruba, Ibo, Arabic, Amharic, Kiswahili, Gĩkũyũ, Luo, Luhya, Shona, Ndebele, Kimbundu, Zulu or Lingala without this fact tearing the multinational states apart. During the anti-colonial struggle they showed an unlimited capacity to unite around whatever leader or party best and most consistently articulated an anti-imperialist position. If anything it was the petty-bourgeoisie, particularly the compradors, with their French and English and Portuguese, with their petty rivalries, their ethnic chauvinism, which encouraged these vertical divisions to the point of war at times. No, the peasantry had no complexes about their languages and the cultures they carried!

In fact when the peasantry and the working class were compelled by necessity or history to adopt the language of the master, they Africanised it without any of the respect for its ancestry shown by Senghor and Achebe, so totally as to have created new African languages, like Krio in Sierra Leone or Pidgin in Nigeria, that owed their identities to the syntax and rhythms of African languages. All these languages were kept alive in the daily speech, in the ceremonies, in political struggles, above all in the rich store of orature—proverbs, stories, poems, and riddles.

The peasantry and the urban working class threw up singers. These sang the old songs or composed new ones incorporating the new experiences in industries and urban life and in working-class struggle and organisations. These singers pushed the languages to new limits, renewing and reinvigorating them by coining new words and new expressions, and in generally expanding their capacity to incorporate new happenings in Africa and the world.

The peasantry and the working class threw up their own writers, or attracted to their ranks and concern intellectuals from among the petty-bourgeoisie, who all wrote in African languages. It is these writers like Heruy Wäldä Sellassie, Germacäw Takla Hawaryat, Shabaan Robert, Abdullatif Abdalla, Ebrahim Hussein, Euphrase Kezilahabi, B. H. Vilakazi, Okot p'Bitek, A. C. Jordan, P. Mboya, D. O. Fagunwa, Mazisi Kunene and many others rightly celebrated in Albert Gérard's pioneering survey of literature in African language from the tenth century to the present, called *African Language Literatures* (1981), who have given our languages a written literature. Thus the immortality of our languages in print has been ensured despite the internal and external pressures for their extinction. In Kenya I would like to single out Gakaara wa Wanjaū, who was jailed by the British for the ten years between 1952 and 1962 because of his writing in Gĩkũyũ. His book, *Mwandĩki wa Mau Mau Ithaamirĩoinĩ*, a diary he secretly kept while in political detention, was published by Heinemann Kenya and won the 1984 Noma Award. It is a powerful work, extending the range of the Gĩkũyũ language prose, and it is a crowning achievement to the work he started in 1946. He has worked in poverty, in the hardships of prison, in post-independence isolation when the English language held sway in Kenya's schools from nursery to University and in every walk of the national printed world, but he never broke his faith in the possibilities of Kenya's national languages. His inspiration came from the mass anti-colonial movement of Kenyan people, particularly the militant wing grouped around Mau Mau or the Kenya Land and Freedom Army, which in 1952 ushered in the era of modern guerrilla warfare in Africa. He is the clearest example of those writers thrown up by the mass political movements of an awakened peasantry and working class.

And finally from among the European-language-speaking African petty-bourgeoisie, there emerged a few who refused to join the chorus of those who had accepted the "fatalistic logic" of the position of European languages in our literary being. It was one of these, Obi Wali, who pulled the carpet from under the literary feet of those who gathered at Makerere in 1962 by declaring in an article published in *Transition* (10, September 1963), "that the whole uncritical acceptance of English and French as the inevitable medium for educated African writing is misdirected, and has no chance of advancing African literature and culture," and that until African writers accepted that any true African literature must be written in African languages, they would merely be pursuing a dead end.

> What we would like future conferences on African literature to devote time to, is the all-important problem of African writing in African languages, and all its implications for the development of a truly African sensibility.

Obi Wali had his predecessors. Indeed people like David Diop of Senegal had put the case against this use of colonial languages even more strongly.

> The African creator, deprived of the use of his language and cut off from his people, might turn out to be only the representative of a literary trend (and that not necessarily the least gratuitous) of the conquering nation. His works, having become a perfect illustration of the assimilationist policy through imagination and style, will doubtless rouse the warm applause of a certain group of critics. In fact, these praises will go mostly to colonialism

which, when it can no longer keep its subjects in slavery, transforms them into docile intellectuals patterned after Western literary fashions which besides, is another more subtle form of bastardization.[21]

David Diop quite correctly saw that the use of English and French was a matter of temporary historical necessity.

> Surely in an Africa freed from oppression it will not occur to any writer to express, otherwise than in his rediscovered language, his feelings and the feelings of his people.[22]

The importance of Obi Wali's intervention was in tone and timing: it was published soon after the 1962 Makerere conference of African writers of English expression; it was polemical and aggressive, poured ridicule and scorn on the choice of English and French, while being unapologetic in its call for the use of African languages. Not surprisingly it was met with hostility and then silence. But twenty years of uninterrupted dominance of literature in European languages, the reactionary turn that political and economic events in Africa have taken, and the search for a revolutionary break with the neo-colonial status quo, all compel soul-searching among writers, raising once again the entire question of the language of African literature.

VIII

The question is this: we as African writers have always complained about the neo-colonial economic and political relationship to Euro-America. Right. But by our continuing to write in foreign languages, paying homage to them, are we not on the cultural level continuing that neo-colonial slavish and cringing spirit? What is the difference between a politician who says Africa cannot do without imperialism and the writer who says Africa cannot do without European languages?

While we were busy haranguing the ruling circles in a language which automatically excluded the participation of the peasantry and the working class in the debate, imperialist culture and African reactionary forces had a field day: the Christian bible is available in unlimited quantities in even the tiniest African language. The comprador ruling cliques are also quite happy to have the peasantry and the working class all to themselves: distortions, dictatorial directives, decrees, museum-type fossils paraded as African culture, feudalistic ideologies, superstitions, lies, all these backward elements and more are communicated to the African masses in their own languages without any challenges from those with alternative visions of tomorrow who have deliberately cocooned themselves in English, French, and Portuguese. It is ironic that the most reactionary African politician, the one who believes in selling Africa to Europe, is often a master of African languages; that the most zealous of European missionaries who believed in rescuing Africa from itself, even from the paganism of its languages, were nevertheless masters of African languages, which they often reduced to writing. The European missionary believed too much in his mission of conquest not to communicate it in the languages most readily available to the people: the African writer believes too much in "African literature" to write it in those ethnic, divisive and underdeveloped languages of the peasantry!

The added irony is that what they have produced, despite any claims to the contrary, is not African literature. The editors of the Pelican Guides to Engish literature in their latest volume were right to include a discussion of this literature as part of twentieth-century English literature, just as the French Academy was right to honour Senghor for his genuine and talented contribution to French literature and language. What we have created is another hybrid tradition, a tradition in transition, a minority tradition that can only be termed as Afro-European literature; that is, the literature written by Africans in European languages.[23] It has produced many writers and works of genuine talent: Chinua Achebe, Wole Soyinka, Ayi Kwei Armah, Sembene Ousmane, Agostino Neto, Sédar Senghor and many others. Who can deny their talent? The light in the products of their fertile imaginations has certainly illuminated important aspects of the African being in its continuous struggle against the political and economic consequences of Berlin and after. However we cannot have our cake and eat it! Their work belongs to an Afro-European literary tradition which is likely to last for as long as Africa is under this rule of European capital in a neo-colonial set-up. So Afro-European literature can be defined as literature written by Africans in European languages in the era of imperialism.

But some are coming round to the inescapable conclusion articulated by Obi Wali with such polemical vigour twenty years ago: African literature can only be written in African languages, that is, the languages of the African peasantry and working class, the major alliance of classes in each of our nationalities and the agency for the coming inevitable revolutionary break with neo-colonialism.

I X

I started writing in Gĩkũyũ language in 1977 after seventeen years of involvement in Afro-European literature, in my case Afro-English literature. It was then that I collaborated with Ngũgĩ wa Mĩriĩ in the drafting of the playscript, *Ngaahika Ndeenda* (the English translation was *I Will Marry When I Want*). I have since published a novel in Gĩkũyũ, *Caitaani Mũtharabainĩ* (English translation: *Devil on the Cross*) and completed a musical drama, *Maitũ Njugĩra*, (English translation: *Mother Sing for Me*); three books for children, *Njamba Nene na Mbaathi i Mathagu*, *Bathitoora ya Njamba Nene*, *Njamba Nene na Cibũ Kĩng'ang'i*, as well as another novel manuscript: *Matigari Ma Njirũũngi*. Wherever I have gone, particularly in Europe, I have been confronted with the question: why are you now writing in Gĩkũyũ? Why do you now write in an African language? In some academic quarters I have been confronted with the rebuke, "Why have you abandoned us?" It was almost as if, in choosing to write in Gĩkũyũ, I was doing something abnormal. But Gĩkũyũ is my mother tongue! The very fact that what common sense dictates in the literary practice of other cultures is being questioned in an African writer is a measure of how far imperialism has distorted the view of African realities. It has turned reality upside down: the abnormal is viewed as normal and the normal is viewed as abnormal. Africa actually enriches Europe: but Africa is made to believe that it needs Europe to rescue it from poverty. Africa's natural and human resources continue to develop Europe and America: but Africa is made to feel grateful for aid from the same quarters that still sit on the back of the continent.

Africa even produces intellectuals who now rationalize this upside-down way of looking at Africa.

I believe that my writing in Gĩkũyũ language, a Kenyan language, an African language, is part and parcel of the anti-imperialist struggles of Kenyan and African peoples. In schools and universities our Kenyan languages—that is the languages of the many nationalities which make up Kenya—were associated with negative qualities of backwardness, underdevelopment, humiliation and punishment. We who went through that school system were meant to graduate with a hatred of the people and the culture and the values of the language of our daily humiliation and punishment. I do not want to see Kenyan children growing up in that imperialist-imposed tradition of contempt for the tools of communication developed by their communities and their history. I want them to transcend colonial alienation.

Colonial alienation takes two interlinked forms: an active (or passive) distancing of oneself from the reality around; and an active (or passive) identification with that which is most external to one's environment. It starts with a deliberate disassociation of the language of conceptualisation, of thinking, of formal education, of mental development, from the language of daily interaction in the home and in the community. It is like separating the mind from the body so that they are occupying two unrelated linguistic spheres in the same person. On a larger social scale it is like producing a society of bodiless heads and headless bodies.

So I would like to contribute towards the restoration of the harmony between all the aspects and divisions of language so as to restore the Kenyan child to his environment, understand it fully so as to be in a position to change it for his collective good. I would like to see Kenya peoples' mother-tongues (our national languages!) carry a literature reflecting not only the rhythms of a child's spoken expression, but also his struggle with nature and his social nature. With that harmony between himself, his language and his environment as his starting point, he can learn other languages and even enjoy the positive humanistic, democratic and revolutionary elements in other people's literatures and cultures without any complexes about his own language, his own self, his environment. The all-Kenya national language (i.e., Kiswahili); the other national languages (i.e., the languages of the nationalities like Luo, Gĩkũyũ, Maasai, Lunya, Kallenjin, Kamba, Mijikenda, Somali, Galla, Turkana, Arabic-speaking people, etc.); other African languages like Hausa, Wolof, Yoruba, Ibo, Zulu, Nyanja, Lingala, Kimbundu; and foreign languages—that is foreign to Africa—like English, French, German, Russian, Chinese, Japanese, Portuguese, Spanish will fall into their proper perspective in the lives of Kenyan children.

Chinua Achebe once decried the tendency of African intellectuals to escape into abstract universalism in the words that apply even more to the issue of the language of African literature:

> Africa has had such a fate in the world that the very adjective *African* can call up hideous fears of rejection. Better then to cut all the links with this homeland, this liability, and become in one giant leap the universal man. Indeed I understand this anxiety. *But running away from oneself seems to me a very inadequate way of dealing with an anxiety* [italics mine]. And if writers should opt for such escapism, who is to meet the challenge?[24]

Who indeed?

We African writers are bound by our calling to do for our languages what Spencer, Milton and Shakespeare did for English; what Pushkin and Tolstoy did for Russian; indeed what all writers in world history have done for their languages by meeting the challenge of creating a literature in them, which process later opens the languages for philosophy, science, technology and all the other areas of human creative endeavours.

But writing in our languages per se—although a necessary first step in the correct direction—will not itself bring about the renaissance in African cultures if that literature does not carry the content of our people's anti-imperialist struggles to liberate their productive forces from foreign control; the content of the need for unity among the workers and peasants of all the nationalities in their struggle to control the wealth they produce and to free it from internal and external parasites.

In other words writers in African languages should reconnect themselves to the revolutionary traditions of an organised peasantry and working class in Africa in their struggle to defeat imperialism and create a higher system of democracy and socialism in alliance with all the other peoples of the world. Unity in that struggle would ensure unity in our multilingual diversity. It would also reveal the real links that bind the people of Africa to the peoples of Asia, South America, Europe, Australia and New Zealand, Canada and the U.S.A.

But it is precisely when writers open out African languages to the real links in the struggles of peasants and workers that they will meet their biggest challenge. For to the comprador-ruling regimes, their real enemy is an awakened peasantry and working class. A writer who tries to communicate the message of revolutionary unity and hope in the languages of the people becomes a subversive character. It is then that writing in African languages becomes a subversive or treasonable offence with such a writer facing possibilities of prison, exile or even death. For him there are no "national" accolades, no new year honours, only abuse and slander and innumerable lies from the mouths of the armed power of a ruling minority—ruling, that is, on behalf of U.S.-led imperialism—and who see in democracy a real threat. A democratic participation of the people in the shaping of their own lives or in discussing their own lives in languages that allow for mutual comprehension is seen as being dangerous to the good government of a country and its institutions. African languages addressing themselves to the lives of the people become the enemy of a neo-colonial state.

NOTES

1. "European languages became so important to the Africans that they defined their own identities partly by reference to those languages. Africans began to describe each other in terms of being either Francophone or English-speaking Africans. The continent itself was thought of in terms of French-speaking states, English-speaking states and Arabic-speaking states."
   Ali A. Mazrui, *Africa's International Relations,* London: 1977, p. 92.

   Arabic does not quite fall into that category. Instead of Arabic-speaking states as an example, Mazrui should have put Portuguese-speaking states. Arabic is now an African language unless we want to write off all the indigenous populations of North Africa, Egypt, Sudan as not being Africans.

And as usual with Mazrui his often apt and insightful descriptions, observations, and comparisons of the contemporary African realities as affected by Europe are, unfortunately, often tinged with approval or a sense of irreversible inevitability.

2. The conference was organized by the anti-Communist Paris-based but American-inspired and financed Society for Cultural Freedom which was later discovered actually to have been financed by CIA. It shows how certain directions in our cultural, political, and economic choices can be masterminded from the metropolitan centres of imperialism.

3. This is an argument often espoused by colonial spokesmen. Compare Mphahlele's comment with that of Geoffrey Moorhouse in *Manchester Guardian Weekly,* 15 July 1964, as quoted by Ali A. Mazrui and Michael Tidy in their work *Nationalism and New States in Africa,* London: 1984.

   "On both sides of Africa, moreover, in Ghana and Nigeria, in Uganda and in Kenya, the spread of education has led to an increased demand for English at primary level. *The remarkable thing is that English has not been rejected as a symbol of Colonialism; it has rather been adopted as a politically neutral language beyond the reproaches of tribalism.* It is also a more attractive proposition in Africa than in either India or Malaysia because comparatively few Africans are completely literate in the vernacular tongues and even in the languages of regional communication, Hausa and Swahili, which are spoken by millions, and only read and written by thousands." (My italics)

   Is Moorehouse telling us that the English language is politically neutral vis-à-vis Africa's confrontation with neo-colonialism? Is he telling us that by 1964 there were more Africans literate in European languages than in African languages? That Africans could not, even if that was the case, be literate in their own national languages or in the regional languages? Really is Mr Moorehouse tongue-tying the African?

4. The English title is *Tales of Amadou Koumba,* published by Oxford University Press. The translation of this particular passage from the *Présence Africaine,* Paris edition of the book was done for me by Dr Bachir Diagne in Bayreuth.

5. The paper is now in Achebe's collection of essays *Morning Yet on Creation Day,* London: 1975.

6. In the introduction to *Morning Yet on Creation Day* Achebe obviously takes a slightly more critical stance from his 1964 position. The phrase is apt for a whole generation of us African writers.

7. *Transition* No. 10, September 1963, reprinted from *Dialogue,* Paris.

8. Chinua Achebe "The African Writer and the English Language," in *Morning Yet on Creation Day.*

9. Gabriel Okara, *Transition* No. 10, September 1963.

10. Cheikh Hamidou Kane *L'aventure Ambiguë.* (English translation: *Ambiguous Adventure*). This passage was translated for me by Bachir Diagne.

11. Example from a tongue twister: "Kaana ka Nikoora koona koora koora: na ko koora koona kaana ka Nikoora koora koora." I'm indebted to Wangui wa Goro for this example. "Nichola's child saw a baby frog and ran away: and when the baby frog saw Nichola's child it also ran away." A Gĩkũyũ speaking child has to get the correct tone and length of vowel and pauses to get it right. Otherwise it becomes a jumble of *k*'s and *r*'s and *na*'s.

12. "The production of ideas, of conceptions, of consciousness, is at first directly interwoven with the material activity and the material intercourse of men, the language of real life.

Conceiving, thinking, the mental intercourse of men, appear at this stage as the direct efflux of their material behaviour. The same applies to mental production as expressed in the language of politics, laws, morality, religion, metaphysics, etc., of a people. Men are the producers of their conceptions, ideas etc.—real, active men, as they are conditioned by a definite development of their productive forces and of the intercourse corresponding to these, up to its furthest form." Marx and Engels, German Ideology, the first part published under the title, *Feuerbach: Opposition of the Materialist and Idealist Outlooks,* London: 1973, p. 8.

13. Quoted in Eric Williams *A History of the People of Trinidad and Tobago,* London 1964, p. 32.

14. Eric Williams, ibid., p. 31.

15. In references to Africa in the introduction to his lectures in *The Philosophy of History,* Hegel gives historical, philosophical, rational expression and legitimacy to every conceivable European racist myth about Africa. Africa is even denied her own geography where it does not correspond to the myth. Thus Egypt is not part of Africa; and North Africa is part of Europe. Africa proper is the especial home of ravenous beasts, snakes of all kinds. The African is not part of humanity. Only slavery to Europe can raise him, possibly, to the lower ranks of humanity. Slavery is good for the African. "Slavery is in and for itself *injustice,* for the essence of humanity is *freedom;* but for this man must be matured. The gradual abolition of slavery is therefore wiser and more equitable than its sudden removal.' (Hegel *The Philosophy of History,* Dover edition), New York: 1956, pp. 91–9.) Hegel clearly reveals himself as the nineteenth-century Hitler of the intellect.

16. The paper is now in Akivaga and Gachukiah's *The Teaching of African Literature in Schools,* published by Kenya Literature Bureau.

17. Senghor, Introduction to his poems, "Éthiopiques, le 24 Septembre 1954," in answering the question: "Pourquoi, dès lors, écrivez-vous en français?" Here is the whole passage in French. See how lyrical Senghor becomes as he talks of his encounter with French language and French literature.

Mais on me posera la question: "Pourquoi, dès lors, écrivez-vous en français?" parce que nous sommes des métis culturels, parce que, si nous sentons en nègres, nous nous exprimons en français, parce que le français est une langue à vocation universelle, que notre message s'adresse *aussi* aux Français de France et aux autres hommes, parce que le français est une langue "de gentillesse et d'honnêteté." Qui a dit que c'était une langue grise et atone d'ingénieurs et de diplomates? Bien sûr, moi aussi, je l'ai dit un jour, pour les besoins de ma thèse. On me le pardonnera. Car je sais ses ressources pour l'avoir goûté, mâché, enseigné, et qu'il est la langue des dieux. Ecoutez donc Corneille, Lautréamont, Rimbaud, Péguy et Claudel. Écoutez le grand Hugo. Le français, ce sont les grandes orgues qui se prêtent à tous les timbres, à tous les effets, des douceurs les plus suaves aux fulgurances de l'orage. Il est, tour à tour ou en même temps, flûte, hautbois, trompette, tamtam et même canon. Et puis le français nous a fait don de ses mots abstraits—si rares dans nos langues maternelles—, où les larmes se font pierres précieuses. Chez nous, les mots sont naturellement nimbés d'un halo de sève et de sang; les mots du français rayonnent de mille feux, comme des diamants. Des fusées qui éclairent notre nuit.

See also Senghor's reply to a question on language in an interview by Armand Guiber and published in *Présence Africaine* 1962 under the title, Leópold Sédar Senghor:

Il est vrai que le français n'est pas ma langue maternelle. J'ai commencé de l'apprendre à sept ans, par des mots comme "confitures" et "chocolat." Aujourd' hui, je pense naturellement en Français, et je comprend le Français—faut-il en avoir honte? Mieux qu'aucune autre langue. C'est dire que le Français n'est plus pour moi un "véhicule étranger" mais la forme d'expression naturelle de ma pensée.

Ce qui m'est étrange dans le français, c'est peut-être son style:

Son architecture classique. Je suis naturellement porté à gonfler d'image son cadre étroit, sans la poussée de la chaleur émotionelle.

18. *Zimbabwe Herald* August 1981.
19. Chinua Achebe "The African Writer and the English Language" in *Morning Yet on Creation Day* p. 59.
20. Most of the writers were from Universities. The readership was mainly the product of schools and colleges. As for the underlying theme of much of that literature, Achebe's statement in his paper, "The Novelists as a Teacher," is instructive:

"If I were God I would regard as the very worst our acceptance—for whatever reason—of racial inferiority. It is too late in the day to get worked up about it or to blame others, much as they may deserve such blame and condemnation. What we need to do is to look back and try and find out where we went wrong, where the rain began to beat us.

"Here then is an adequate revolution for me to espouse—to help my society regain belief in itself and put away the complexes of the years of denigration and self-abasement." *Morning Yet on Creation Day,* p. 44.

Since the peasant and the worker had never really had any doubts about their Africanness, the reference could only have been the "educated" or the petty-bourgeois African. In fact if one substitutes the words "the petty-bourgeois" for the word "our" and "the petty-bourgeois class" for "my society" the statement is apt, accurate, and describes well the assumed audience. Of course, an ideological revolution in this class would affect the whole society.
21. David Diop "Contribution to the Debate on National Poetry," *Présence Africaine* 6, 1956.
22. David Diop, ibid.
23. The term "Afro-European Literature" may seem to put too much weight on the European-ness of the literature. Euro-African literature? Probably, the English, French, and Portuguese components would then be "Anglo-African literature," "Franco-African literature" or "Luso-African literature." What is important is that this minority literature forms a distinct tradition that needs a different term to distinguish it from *African Literature,* instead of usurping the title *African Literature* as is the current practice in literary scholarship. There have even been arrogant claims by some literary scholars who talk as if the literature written in European languages is necessarily closer to the Africanness of its inspiration than similar works in African languages, the languages of the majority. So thoroughly has the minority "Afro-European Literature"(Euro-African literature?) usurped the name "African literature" in the current scholarship that literature by Africans in African languages is the one that needs qualification. Albert Gérard's otherwise timely book is titled *African Language Literatures.*
24. Chinua Achebe "Africa and her Writers" in *Morning Yet on Creation Day,* p. 27.

ON MIMICRY AND MAN: THE AMBIVALENCE OF COLONIAL DISCOURSE (1983, 1994)

HOMI K. BHABHA

Bhabha describes cultural ambivalence as dramatized in what he calls mimicry. Inevitably, in a world of cultural mixing and differences of power, colonized people often end up mimicking their colonizers, adopting the colonizers' language, educational systems, governmental systems (parliament or congress, courts, constitution, laws), clothing, music, and so on. While some may see such mimicry as a form of internalized colonization or self-colonization, as in Ngugi wa Thiong'o's critique of African writing in European languages (see the selection by Ngugi in this volume), Bhabha calls attention to the way that the colonized's mimicry of the colonizers can express the colonized's ambivalence and, in turn, can provoke ambivalence and doubt in the colonizers. When the colonizers gaze in the mirror of the colonized's mimicry, the image they see looks, as Bhabha puts it, "almost the same, but not quite." The blend of repetition and difference can threaten the colonizers' sense of their own power and superiority. It can even threaten their sense of racial privilege when they begin to recognize that the mimicry is also, as Bhabha puts it, "Almost the same but not white." The signifiers slip far enough away from what they supposedly signify that they tilt the mimicry into mockery. The colonizers may suppose that their surveillance of the colonized, in Foucauldian terms, disciplines the colonized. But when the colonizers gaze at the colonized and see the mimicking colonized's displacement of the colonizers' gaze turned back on the colonizers, it alienates the colonizers from their confidence in their own essence, and, therefore, Bhabha argues, colonized people's mimicry of the colonizers destabilizes colonialism itself.

> Mimicry reveals something in so far as it is distinct from what might be called an itself that is behind. The effect of mimicry is camouflage.... It is not a question of harmonizing with the background, but against a mottled background, of becoming mottled—exactly like the technique of camouflage practised in human warfare.
>
> —JACQUES LACAN,
> "The Line and Light," *Of the Gaze*

It is out of season to question at this time of day, the original policy of conferring on every colony of the British Empire a mimic representation of the British Constitution. But if the creature so endowed has sometimes forgotten its real insignificance and under the fancied importance of speakers and maces, and all the paraphernalia and ceremonies of the imperial legislature, has dared to defy the mother country, she has to thank herself for the folly of conferring such privileges on a condition of society that has no earthly claim to so exalted a position. A fundamental principle appears to have been forgotten or overlooked in our system of colonial policy—that of colonial dependence. To give to a colony the forms of independence is a mockery; she would not be a colony for a single hour if she could maintain an independent station.

—Sir Edward Cust,
"Reflections on West African Affairs...addressed to the Colonial Office," Hatchard, London 1839

The discourse of post-Enlightenment English colonialism often speaks in a tongue that is forked, not false. If colonialism takes power in the name of history, it repeatedly exercises its authority through the figures of farce. For the epic intention of the civilizing mission, "human and not wholly human" in the famous words of Lord Rosebery, "writ by the finger of the Divine"[1] often produces a text rich in the traditions of *trompe l'oeil*, irony, mimicry, and repetition. In this comic turn from the high ideals of the colonial imagination to its low mimetic literary effects, mimicry emerges as one of the most elusive and effective strategies of colonial power and knowledge.

Within that conflictual economy of colonial discourse which Edward Said[2] describes as the tension between the synchronic panoptical vision of domination—the demand for identity, stasis—and the counter-pressure of the diachrony of history—change, difference—mimicry represents an *ironic* compromise. If I may adapt Samuel Weber's formulation of the marginalizing vision of castration,[3] then colonial mimicry is the desire for a reformed, recognizable Other, as *a subject of a difference that is almost the same, but not quite*. Which is to say, that the discourse of mimicry is constructed around an *ambivalence*; in order to be effective, mimicry must continually produce its slippage, its excess, its difference. The authority of that mode of colonial discourse that I have called mimicry is therefore stricken by an indeterminacy: mimicry emerges as the representation of a difference that is itself a process of disavowal. Mimicry is, thus, the sign of a double articulation; a complex strategy of reform, regulation, and discipline, which "appropriates" the Other as it visualizes power. Mimicry is also the sign of the inappropriate, however, a difference or recalcitrance which coheres the dominant strategic function of colonial power, intensifies surveillance, and poses an immanent threat to both "normalized" knowledges and disciplinary powers.

The effect of mimicry on the authority of colonial discourse is profound and disturbing. For in "normalizing" the colonial state or subject, the dream of post-Enlightenment civility alienates its own language of liberty and produces another knowledge of its norms. The ambivalence which thus informs this strategy is discernible, for example, in Locke's Second Treatise which *splits* to reveal the limitations of liberty in his double use of the word "slave": first simply, descriptively as the locus of a legitimate form of ownership, then as the trope for an intolerable, illegitimate exercise of power. What is articulated in that distance between the two uses is the absolute, imagined difference between the "Colonial" State of Carolina and the Original State of Nature.

It is from this area between mimicry and mockery, where the reforming, civilizing mission is threatened by the displacing gaze of its disciplinary double, that my instances of colonial imitation come. What they all share is a discursive process by which the excess or slippage produced by the *ambivalence* of mimicry (almost the same, *but not quite*) does not merely "rupture" the discourse, but becomes transformed into an uncertainty which fixes the colonial subject as a "partial" presence. By "partial" I mean both "incomplete" and "virtual." It is as if the very emergence of the "colonial" is dependent for its representation upon some strategic limitation or prohibition *within* the authoritative discourse itself. The success of colonial appropriation depends on a proliferation of inappropriate objects that ensure its strategic failure, so that mimicry is at once resemblance and menace.

A classic text of such partiality is Charles Grant's "Observations on the State of Society among the Asiatic Subjects of Great Britain" (1792)[4] which was only superseded by James Mills's *History of India* as the most influential early nineteenth-century account of Indian manners and morals. Grant's dream of an evangelical system of mission education conducted uncompromisingly in English was partly a belief in political reform along Christian lines and partly an awareness that the expansion of company rule in India required a system of "interpellation"—a reform of manners, as Grant put it, that would provide the colonial with "a sense of personal identity as we know it." Caught between the desire for religious reform and the fear that the Indians might become turbulent for liberty, Grant implies that it is, in fact the "partial" diffusion of Christianity, and the "partial" influence of moral improvements which will construct a particularly appropriate form of colonial subjectivity. What is suggested is a process of reform through which Christian doctrines might collude with divisive caste practices to prevent dangerous political alliances. Inadvertently, Grant produces a knowledge of Christianity as a form of social control which conflicts with the enunciatory assumptions which authorize his discourse. In suggesting, finally, that "partial reform" will produce an empty form of "the *imitation* of English manners which will induce them [the colonial subjects] to remain under our protection,"[5] Grant mocks his moral project and violates the Evidences of Christianity—a central missionary tenet—which forbade any tolerance of heathen faiths.

The absurd extravagance of Macaulay's *Infamous Minute* (1835)—deeply influenced by Charles Grant's *Observations*—makes a mockery of Oriental learning until faced with the challenge of conceiving of a "reformed" colonial subject. Then the great tradition of European humanism seems capable only of ironizing itself. At the intersection of European learning and colonial power, Macaulay can conceive of nothing other than "a class of interpreters between us and the millions whom we govern—a class of persons Indian in blood and colour, but English in tastes, in opinions, in morals and in intellect"[6]—in other words a mimic man raised "through our English School," as a missionary educationist wrote in 1819, "to form a corps of translators and be employed in different departments of Labour."[7] The line of descent of the mimic man can be traced through the works of Kipling, Forester, Orwell, Naipaul, and to his emergence, most recently, in Benedict Anderson's excellent essay on nationalism, as the anomalous Bipin Chandra Pal.[8] He is the effect of a flawed colonial mimesis, in which to be Anglicized, is *emphatically* not to be English.

The figure of mimicry is locatable within what Anderson describes as "the inner incompatibility of empire and nation."[9] It problematizes the signs of racial and cultural priority, so that the "national" is no longer naturalizable. What emerges between mimesis and mimicry is a *writing*, a mode of representation, that marginalizes the monumentality of history, quite simply mocks its power to be a model, that power which supposedly makes it imitable. Mimicry *repeats* rather than *re-presents* and in that diminishing perspective emerges Decoud's displaced European vision of Sulaco as the endlessness of civil strife where folly seemed even harder to bear than its ignominy... the lawlessness of a populace of all colours and races, barbarism, irremediable tyranny. ...America is ungovernable.[10]

Or Ralph Singh's apostasy in Naipaul's *The Mimic Men:*

> We pretended to be real, to be learning, to be preparing ourselves for life, we mimic men of the New World, one unknown corner of it, with all its reminders of the corruption that came so quickly to the new.[11]

Both Decoud and Singh, and in their different ways Grant and Macaulay, are the parodists of history. Despite their intentions and invocations they inscribe the colonial text erratically, eccentrically across a body politic that refuses to be representative, in a narrative that refuses to be representational. The desire to emerge as "authentic" through mimicry—through a process of writing and repetition—is the final irony of partial representation.

What I have called mimicry is not the familiar exercise of *dependent* colonial relations through narcissistic identification so that, as Fanon has observed,[12] the black man stops being an action person for only the white man can represent his self-esteem. Mimicry conceals no presence or identity behind its mask: it is not what Césaire describes as "colonization-thingification"[13] behind which there stands the essence of the *présence Africaine*. The *menace* of mimicry is its *double* vision which in disclosing the ambivalence of colonial discourse also disrupts its authority. And it is a double-vision that is a result of what I've described as the partial representation/recognition of the colonial object. Grant's colonial as partial imitator, Macaulay's translator, Naipaul's colonial politician as play-actor, Decoud as the scene setter of the *opéra bouffe* of the New World, these are the appropriate objects of a colonialist chain of command, authorized versions of otherness. But they are also, as I have shown, the figures of a doubling, the part-objects of a metonymy of colonial desire which alienates the modality and normality of those dominant discourses in which they emerge as "inappropriate" colonial subjects. A desire that, through the repetition of *partial presence,* which is the basis of mimicry, articulates those disturbances of cultural, racial, and historical difference that menace the narcissistic demand of colonial authority. It is a desire that reverses "in part" the colonial appropriation by now producing a partial vision of the colonizer's presence. A gaze of otherness, that shares the acuity of the genealogical gaze which, as Foucault describes it, liberates marginal elements and shatters the unity of man's being through which he extends his sovereignty.[14]

I want to turn to this process by which the look of surveillance returns as the displacing gaze of the disciplined, where the observer becomes the observed and "partial" representation rearticulates the whole notion of *identity* and alienates it from essence. But not before observing that even an exemplary history like Eric Stokes's *The English Utilitarians in India* acknowledges the anomalous gaze of otherness but finally disavows it in a contradictory utterance:

> Certainly India played *no* central part in fashioning the distinctive qualities of English civilisation. In many ways it acted as a disturbing force, a magnetic power placed at the periphery tending to distort the natural development of Britain's character....[15]

What is the nature of the hidden threat of the partial gaze? How does mimicry emerge as the subject of the scopic drive and the object of colonial surveillance? How is desire disciplined, authority displaced?

If we turn to a Freudian figure to address these issues of colonial textuality, that form of difference that is mimicry—*almost the same but not quite*—will become clear. Writing of the partial nature of fantasy, caught *inappropriately*, between the unconscious and the preconscious, making problematic, like mimicry, the very notion of "origins," Freud has this to say:

> Their mixed and split origin is what decides their fate. We may compare them with individuals of mixed race who taken, all round resemble white men but who betray their coloured descent by some striking feature or other and on that account are excluded from society and enjoy none of the privileges.[16]

Almost the same but not white: the visibility of mimicry is always produced at the site of interdiction. It is a form of colonial discourse that is uttered *inter dicta:* a discourse at the crossroads of what is known and permissible and that which though known must be kept concealed; a discourse uttered between the lines and as such both against the rules and within them. The question of the representation of difference is therefore always also a problem of authority. The "desire" of mimicry, which is Freud's *striking feature* that reveals so little but makes such a big difference, is not merely that impossibility of the Other which repeatedly resists signification. The desire of colonial mimicry—an interdictory desire—may not have an object, but it has strategic objectives which I shall call the *metonymy of presence*.

Those inappropriate signifiers of colonial discourse—the difference between being English and being Anglicized; the identity between stereotypes which, through repetition, also become different; the discriminatory identities constructed across traditional cultural norms and classifications, the Simian Black, the Lying Asiatic—all these are metonymies of presence. They are strategies of desire in discourse that make the anomalous representation of the colonized something other than a process of "the return of the repressed," what Fanon unsatisfactorily characterized as collective catharsis.[17] These instances of metonymy are the nonrepressive productions of contradictory and multiple belief. They cross the boundaries of the culture of enunciation through a strategic confusion of the metaphoric and metonymic axes of the cultural production of meaning. For each of these instances of "a difference that is almost the same but not quite" inadvertently creates a crisis for the cultural priority given to the *metaphoric* as the process of repression and substitution which negotiates the difference between paradigmatic systems and classifications. In mimicry, the representation of identity and meaning is rearticulated along the axis of metonymy. As Lacan reminds us, mimicry is like camouflage, not a harmonization or repression of difference, but a form of resemblance that differs/defends presence by displaying it in part, metonymically. Its threat, I would add, comes from the prodigious and strategic production of conflictual, fantastic, discriminatory "identity effects" in the play of a power that is elusive because it hides no essence, no "itself." And that form of *resemblance* is the most terrifying thing to behold, as Edward Long testifies in his *History of Jamaica* (1774). At the end of a tortured, negrophobic passage, that shifts anxiously between piety, prevarication, and perversion, the text finally confronts its fear; nothing other than the repetition of its resemblance "in part":

(Negroes) are represented by all authors as the vilest of human kind, to which they have little more pretension of resemblance *than what arises from their exterior forms* (my italics).[18]

From such a colonial encounter between the white presence and its black semblance, there emerges the question of the ambivalence of mimicry as a problematic of colonial subjection. For if Sade's scandalous theatricalization of language repeatedly reminds us that discourse can claim "no priority," then the work of Edward Said will not let us forget that the "ethnocentric and erratic will to power from which texts can spring"[19] is itself a theater of war. Mimicry, as the metonymy of presence is, indeed, such an erratic, eccentric strategy of authority in colonial discourse. Mimicry does not merely destroy narcissistic authority through the repetitious slippage of difference and desire. It is the process of the *fixation* of the colonial as a form of cross-classificatory, discriminatory knowledge in the defiles of an interdictory discourse, and therefore necessarily raises the question of the *authorization* of colonial representations. A question of authority that goes beyond the subject's lack of priority (castration) to a historical crisis in the conceptuality of colonial man as an *object* of regulatory power, as the subject of racial, cultural, national representation.

"This culture…fixed in its colonial status," Fanon suggests, "(is) both present and mummified, it testified against its members. It defines them in fact without appeal."[20] The ambivalence of mimicry—almost but not quite—suggests that the fetishized colonial culture is potentially and strategically an insurgent counter-appeal. What I have called its "identity-effects," are always crucially *split*. Under cover of camouflage, mimicry, like the fetish, is a part-object that radically revalues the normative knowledges of the priority of race, writing, history. For the fetish mimes the forms of authority at the point at which it deauthorizes them. Similarly, mimicry rearticulates presence in terms of its "otherness," that which it disavows. There is a crucial difference between this *colonial* articulation of man and his doubles and that which Foucault describes as "thinking the unthought"[21] which, for nineteenth-century Europe, is the ending of man's alienation by reconciling him with his essence. The colonial discourse that articulates an *interdictory* "otherness" is precisely the "other scene" of this nineteenth-century European desire for an authentic historical consciousness.

The "unthought" across which colonial man is articulated is that process of classificatory confusion that I have described as the metonymy of the substitutive chain of ethical and cultural discourse. This results in the *splitting* of colonial discourse so that two attitudes towards external reality persist; one takes reality into consideration while the other disavows it and replaces it by a product of desire that repeats, rearticulates "reality" as mimicry.

So Edward Long can say with authority, quoting variously, Hume, Eastwick, and Bishop Warburton in his support, that:

Ludicrous as the opinion may seem I do not think that an orangutang husband would be any dishonour to a Hottentot female.[22]

Such contradictory articulations of reality and desire—seen in racist stereotypes, statements, jokes, myths—are not caught in the doubtful circle of the return of the repressed. They are the effects of a disavowal that denies the differences of the other but produces in its stead forms of authority and multiple belief that alienate the assumptions of "civil" discourse. If, for a while, the ruse of desire is calculable for the uses of discipline soon the repetition of guilt, justification, pseudoscientific theories, superstition, spurious authorities, and classifications can be seen as the desperate effort to "normalize" *formally* the disturbance of a discourse of splitting that violates the rational, enlightened claims of its enunciatory modality. The ambivalence of colonial authority repeatedly turns from *mimicry*—a difference that is almost nothing but not quite—to *menace*—a difference that is almost total but not quite. And in that other scene of colonial power, where history turns to farce and presence to "a part," can be seen the twin figures of narcissism and paranoia that repeat furiously, uncontrollably.

In the ambivalent world of the "not quite/not white," on the margins of metropolitan desire, the *founding objects* of the Western world become the erratic, eccentric, accidental *objets trouvés* of the colonial discourse—the part-objects of presence. It is then that the body and the book loose their representational authority. Black skin splits under the racist gaze, displaced into signs of bestiality, genitalia, grotesquerie, which reveal the phobic myth of the undifferentiated whole white body. And the holiest of books—the Bible—bearing both the standard of the cross and the standard of empire finds itself strangely dismembered. In May 1817 a missionary wrote from Bengal:

> Still everyone would gladly receive a Bible. And why?—that he may lay it up as a curiosity for a few pice; or use it for waste paper. Such it is well known has been the common fate of these copies of the Bible....Some have been bartered in the markets, others have been thrown in snuff shops and used as wrapping paper.[23]

NOTES

1. Cited in Eric Stokes, *The Political Ideas of English Imperialism*, Oxford, Oxford University Press, 1960, pp. 17–18.
2. Edward Said, *Orientalism*, New York, Pantheon Books, 1978, p. 240.
3. Samuel Weber: "The Sideshow, Or: Remarks on a Canny Moment," *Modern Language Notes*, vol. 88, no. 6 (1973), p. 1112.
4. Charles Grant. "Observations on the State of Society among the Asiatic Subjects of Great Britain," *Sessional Papers 1812–13*, X (282), East India Company.
5. Ibid., chap. 4, p. 104.
6. T. B. Macaulay, "Minute on Education," in *Sources of Indian Tradition*, vol. II, ed. William Theodore de Bary, New York, Columbia University Press, 1958, p. 49.
7. Mr. Thomason's communication to the Church Missionary Society, September 5, 1819, in *The Missionary Register*, 1821, pp. 54–55.
8. Benedict Anderson, *Imagined Communities*, London, Verso, 1983, p. 88.
9. Ibid., pp. 88–89.
10. Joseph Conrad, *Nostromo*, London, Penguin, 1979, p. 161.
11. V. S. Naipaul, *The Mimic Men*, London, Penguin, 1967, p. 146.
12. Frantz Fanon, *Black Skin, White Masks*, London, Paladin, 1970, p. 109.
13. Aimé Césaire, *Discourse on Colonialism*, New York, Monthly Review Press, 1972, p. 21.
14. Michel Foucault, "Nietzsche, Genealogy, History," in *Language, Counter-Memory, Practice*, trans. Donald F. Bouchard and Sherry Simon, Ithaca, Cornell University Press, p. 153.

15. Eric Stokes, *The English Utilitarians and India*, Oxford University Press, 1959, p. xi.

16. Sigmund Freud, "The Unconscious" (1915), *SE*, XIV, pp. 190–191.

17. Fanon, p. 103.

18. Edward Long, *A History of Jamaica*, 1774, vol. II, p. 353.

19. Edward Said, "The Text, the World, the Critic," in *Textual Strategies*, ed. J. V. Harari, Ithaca, Cornell University Press, 1979, p. 184.

20. Frantz Fanon, "Racism, and Culture," in *Toward the African Revolution*, London, Pelican, 1967, p. 44.

21. Michel Foucault, *The Order of Things*, New York, Pantheon, 1970, part II, chap. 9.

22. Long, p. 364.

23. *The Missionary Register*, May 1817, p. 186.

CAN THE SUBALTERN SPEAK? SPECULATIONS ON WIDOW-SACRIFICE (1985)

GAYATRI C. SPIVAK

Weaving together feminism, deconstruction, Marxism, and postcolonial theory, in this and other essays Spivak challenges the way that Western feminists celebrate "strong women" (as in images of women criticism—see the selection by Toril Moi in this volume), including the literary celebration of individualist heroines discovering and expressing (speaking) their selfhood. She sees the privileged Western feminist self as surreptitiously built on the backs of subaltern, colonized peoples, not the least subaltern women. (A subaltern is someone with less power.) Spivak's dense, digressive, and allusive style can make explanation and summary helpful.

To follow Spivak's central example, readers need to know about the controversial Hindu practice of "sati," meaning widow burning. In India, British colonialists decided that widows could be burned only if they first agreed to be burned. The literal meaning of "sati" is "good wife." Thus to some Hindus, for a widow to be a good wife meant that she must want to be burned. That literal meaning made it harder to undermine the practice of sati, even though many Hindus opposed it.

When a widow says that she wants to be burned, who is speaking? Is she choosing for herself, Spivak asks, or is that impossible because she has been interpellated into a misogynist set of expectations? (On interpellation, see Louis Althusser's essay in this volume.) Is she speaking for herself, or has she been so absorbed into patriarchal culture that she speaks for the patriarchy, even if she believes that she speaks for herself? Can we even tell whether it is one or the other, and, if so, how can we tell? Can people who oppose or support sati speak for the sati better than she can speak for herself?

As a Derridean, Spivak is skeptical of what she sees as the romanticizing notion that anyone can voice an inner, true, and complete self, an essence. As a Marxist, she believes that we often exaggerate our individuality and do not realize how much we speak for larger, often oppressive ideologies—like sexism and patriarchy—that we have been interpellated into believing are our own. As a feminist, she suspects that widows who say they want to be burned to death are speaking for the patriarchy, not for themselves, even if they think they speak for themselves. And yet, as a feminist, she also wants to take seriously what women say and think. She fears that it is terribly presumptuous to tell a woman that what the woman says she thinks is not really what she thinks but is only what the patriarchy wants her to think. Putting all this together, Spivak finds the question of whether the subaltern can speak for herself or even for a larger subaltern group, such as women, colonized Indians, or Indian women, an aporia, an undecidable impasse, a question that, no matter how urgent, cannot be answered.

At the end of her article, Spivak says "The subaltern cannot speak." People who follow her argument always understood that she did not mean that sentence as a conclusion. It only names a tempting conclusion that she is not ready to accept. But other people seized on that one sentence and used it to represent the whole argument. They attacked Spivak for saying that subalterns cannot speak, wondering how she could say that, as a speaking subaltern herself. In the latest version of her article, Spivak regrets that she wrote that sentence, clarifying that she did not mean it as a conclusion. (Her article appears in several versions. The shortest version is reprinted here.)

Across criticism and popular culture, many people celebrate the voice and expression of the subaltern—of people who hold less power on such grounds as race, sexuality, colonization, disability, class, religion, region, or any combination of these or related reasons. Spivak proposes, by contrast, that such celebrations are a form of reverse ethnocentrism that finally serves those in power more than they serve subalterns. She believes that such celebrations oversimplify subalterns, as if all people in a group think the same thing, control all their thoughts, and understand their own motives. In the process, she argues, the celebration of subaltern voices romanticizes subaltern peoples, allowing those in power to praise themselves for their sympathy with people who have less power, once again judging the colonized and subaltern by their use-value for the privileged West instead of changing the politics that produce inequity.

In seeking to learn to speak to (rather than listen to or speak for) the historically muted subject of the non-elite ("subaltern") woman in the imperialist theater, the post-colonial intellectual *systematically* "unlearns" her privilege. This systematic unlearning involves her in learning to critique post-colonial discourse with the best tools that it can itself provide and not simply to substitute the lost figure of the colonized. Thus, to question the unquestioned "muting" of the subaltern woman even within the anti-imperialist project is not, as Jonathan Culler suggests, to "produce difference by differing," or to "appeal...to a sexual identity defined as essential and [to] privilege experiences associated with that identity."[1]

Culler's version of the feminist project is possible within what Elizabeth Fox-Genovese has called "the contribution of the bourgeois-democratic revolutions to the social and political individualism of women."[2] Many of us were still obliged to understand the feminist project as Culler now describes it when we were still agitating as U.S. academics.[3] It was certainly a necessary stage in my own education in "unlearning" and has consolidated the belief that the mainstream project of feminism in Western Europe and the United States may be described broadly as continuing and displacing the battle over the right to individualism between women and men in situations of upward class mobility. In this connection, one suspects, though one cannot demonstrate, that the opposite debate, between United States feminism and European "theory" (generally represented by women from the United States or Britain), occupies a not insignificant corner of that very terrain. I am generally sympathetic with the call to make United States feminism more "theoretical." It seems, however, that the problem of the muted subject of the subaltern woman, although not solved by an "essentialist" search for lost origins, cannot be served by the call for more "theory" in Anglo-America either.

That call is most often given in the name of a critique of "positivism." "Positivism" is here seen as identical with "essentialism." Yet the great work of Hegel, the modern inaugurator (in this broad compass one must assume the periodizing strategy of histories of European philosophy) of "the work of the negative," was not a stranger to the notion of essences. For Marx, whose own work is often fully identified with national "Marxisms" by these particular spokeswomen for "theory," the curious persistence of essentialism within the dialectic was a profound and productive problem.

Thus the stringent binary opposition between positivism/essentialism (read: U.S.) and "theory" (read: French, or Franco-German via Anglo-U.S.) may be in its own context spurious. Apart from repressing the ambiguous complicity between essentialism and critiques of positivism, it also makes the mistake of implying that positivism is not a theory. This move allows the emergence then of a proper name, a positive essence, Theory with a capital T. On both sides, the position of the investigator remains unquestioned. And, if this territorial debate (on Anglo-U.S. ground in the name of Europe) turns its glance upon the Third World, no particular change in the question of method is to be discerned. This debate cannot take into account that, in the case of the woman as subaltern, no ingredients for the constitution of the itinerary of the trace of a sexed subject can be gathered to locate the possibility of dissemination.

Yet I remain generally sympathetic in aligning feminism with the critique of positivism and the defetishization of the concrete. I am also far from averse to learning from the work of Western theorists, although I have also learned to insist upon marking their positionality as indeed the positionality of any investigating subject. Given these conditions, and as a literary critic, I confront the immense problem of the consciousness of the woman as subaltern tactically, in the following way: reinventing the problem in a sentence and transforming it into the object of a simple semiosis: What does this sentence mean? The anology here is between the ideological victimage of a Freud and the positionality of the post-colonial intellectual as investigating subject.

As Sarah Kofman has shown, the deep ambiguity of Freud's use of woman as scapegoat is a reaction-formation to an initial and continuing desire to give the hysteric a voice, to transform her at least into the *subject* of hysteria.[4] The masculist-imperialist ideological formation that operated that desire into "the daughter's seduction" is part of the "same" formation that constructs the monolithic "Third World Woman." As a post-colonial intellectual, I am operated by that formation as well. Part of our "unlearning" project is to articulate that ideological formation into our *object* of investigation. Thus, when confronted with the question: "Can the subaltern speak?, and, can the subaltern (as woman) speak?" I am aware that our efforts to give the subaltern a voice in history will be at least doubly open to the dangers run by Freud's discourse. It is as a product of these considerations that I have put together the following sentence:

White men are saving brown women from brown men in a spirit not unlike the one to be encountered in Freud's investigations of the sentence:

A child is being beaten.[5]

Freud is here invoked also as an example of the usefulness of First World male thinkers. It is of course understood that only the elite playing at self-marginalization can afford the impossible luxury of turning their backs on those resources.

The use of Freud here is not an isomorphic analogy between subject-formation and the behavior of social collectives. In other words, I am not suggesting that "white men are saving brown women from brown men" is a sentence indicating a *collective* fantasy that is symptomatic of a *collective* itinerary of sadomasochistic repression in the imperialist enterprise viewed as a *collective* project. There is a certain satisfying symmetry in such an allegory, but the methodology of this part of my essay would rather invite the reader to consider it a problem in "wild psychoanalysis" than a clinching solution.[6] Just as in Freud's insistence on making the woman the scapegoat in "A Child is Being Beaten" and elsewhere, his political interests are, however imperfectly, disclosed; so also, our insistence upon imperialist subject-production as the occasion for this sentence discloses our politics. The place of the investigator must not be rendered transparent.

Further, we are attempting to borrow the general methodological aura of Freud's strategy toward the sentence that he constructed *as a sentence* out of the many approximately similar substantive accounts given to him by his patients. This does not mean that the essay intends to offer, in these pages, a case of transference-in-analysis as an isomorphic model for the transaction between reader and text (here my sentence). The analogy between transference and literary criticism or historiography is at best no more than productive catachresis. To say that the subject is a text does not authorize the converse pronouncement: the verbal text is a subject.[7]

We are fascinated rather by how Freud predicates a *history* of repression that produces the final sentence. It is a history with a double origin, one hidden in the amnesia of the infant, the other lodged in the archaic past of humankind itself, assuming by implication a pre-originary space where man and animal were not yet differentiated.[8] We are driven to impose a homologue of this Freudian strategy upon the Marxian narrative of capitalist imperialism to explain the ideological dissimulation of imperialist political economy and outline a history of repression that produces a sentence like the one we have sketched. This history also has a double origin, one hidden in the maneuverings behind the abolition of widow sacrifice by the British in 1829; the other lodged in the classical and Vedic past of Hindu India, the *Rg-Veda* and the *Dharmaśāstra*. I cannot locate my assumption of an undifferentiated preoriginary space that supports this history, but no doubt there is one.

(If I do not cite here Lata Mani's "The Production of Colonial Discourse: Sati in Early Nineteenth Century Bengal," a work whose inception I shared, and which has opened up that problematic field to the very margin within which, but for a few deviations, I shall hold myself, it is neither by omission nor by presumption of independence. Rather, not to fragment the debt and to presuppose it every moment in its totality.[9])

The sentence I have constructed is one among many displacements describing the relationship between brown and white men (sometimes brown and white women worked in). It takes its place among some sentences of hyperbolical admiration or of pious guilt that today is the mark of a reverse ethnocentrism. The relationship between the imperialist subject and the subject of imperialism is at least ambiguous.

The Hindu widow ascends the pyre of the dead husband and immolates herself upon it. This is widow sacrifice. The conventional transcription of the Sanskrit name of the widow would be *sati*. The early colonial British transcribed it *suttee*.

The rite was not practiced universally and was not caste or class-fixed in any rigid way. The abolition of this rite by the British in 1829 has been generally understood as a case of "white men saving brown women from brown men." White women did not produce an alternative understanding, as one can see from perusing the nineteenth century British Missionary Registers down to Mary Daly.[10] Against this is the Indian nativist argument, a parody of the nostalgia for lost origins. "The women actually wanted to die."

The two sentences go a long way to legitimize each other.[11] One never encounters the testimony of the women's voice-consciousness. Such a testimony would not be ideology-transcendent or "fully" subjective, of course; but it would have constituted the ingredients for producing a counter-sentence. As one goes down the grotesquely mistranscribed names of these women, the sacrificed widows, in the police reports included in the records of the East India Company, one cannot put together a "voice." The most one can sense is the immense heterogeneity breaking through even such a skeletal and ignorant (castes are regularly described as tribes) account. Faced with the dialectically interlocking sentences that are constructible: "White men are saving brown women from brown men" and "the women wanted to die," the post-colonial woman intellectual asks the question of simple semiosis—"What does this mean?"—and begins to plot a history.

To mark the moment when not only a civil but a good society is born out of domestic confusion, singular events that break the letter of the law to install its spirit are often invoked. The protection of women by men often provides such an event.[12] If we remember that absolute equity toward and noninterference with native custom/law was at least the declared boast of the British, an invocation of this sanctioned transgression of the letter for the sake of the spirit may be read in the following remark by J.D.M. Derrett: "The very first legislation upon Hindu Law was carried through without the assent of a single Hindu." The legislation is not named here. The next sentence, where the measure is named, is equally interesting if one considers the implications of the survival of a colonially established "good" society after decolonization: "The recurrence of *sati* in independent India is probably an obscurantist revival which cannot long survive even in a very backward part of the country."[13]

Whether this observation is correct or not, what interests us is that the protection of woman (today the "Third World Woman") becomes a signifier for the establishment of a *good* society which must, at such inaugurative moments, transgress mere legality, or equity of legal policy. In this particular case, the process also allowed the re-definition as crime of what had been tolerated, known, or adulated as ritual. In other words, this one item in Hindu Law jumped the frontier between the private and the public domain.

Although Foucault's *historical narrative,* focusing solely on Western Europe, sees merely a tolerance for the criminal antedating the development of criminology in the late eighteenth century, his *theoretical description* of the *episteme* is most pertinent here: "The *episteme* is the 'apparatus' which makes possible the separation not of the true from the false, but of what may from what may not be characterized as scientific"—ritual as opposed to crime, the one fixed by superstition, the other by legal science.[14]

The leap of *suttee* from private to public has a clear and complex relationship with the changeover from a mercantile and commercial to a territorial and administrative British presence in India and can be followed especially in the exchange of correspondence among the police stations, the lower and the higher courts, the Court of Directors, the Prince Regent's Court, and the like. To anchor the leap within intellectual history, any extended treatment of the subject must refer to the correspondence of Lord William Bentinck, reigning governor-general at the time of the abolition.[15] My immediate concern with the semiosis of subject-constitution and object-formation here keeps me restricted to the other end of the spectrum of ideological production.

> It is interesting to note that, from the point of view of the native "colonial subject," also emergent from the feudalism-capitalism transition, *sati* is a signifier with the reverse social charge: "Groups rendered psychologically marginal by their exposure to Western impact...had come under pressure to demonstrate, to others as well as to themselves, their ritual purity and allegiance to traditional high culture. To many of them *sati* became an important proof of their conformity to older norms at a time when these norms had become shaky within."[16]

If this is the first historical "origin" of my "sentence," it is thus seen to be lost in the history of "man" as work, the story of capitalist expansion, the slow "freeing" of labor-power as commodity, what the narrative of the modes of production would mark as the transition from feudalism via mercantilism to capitalism. Yet the precarious normativity of this very narrative is sustained through the putatively changeless stopgap of the "Asiatic" mode of production which steps in to sustain it whenever it might become evident that the story of capital logic is the story of the West, that imperialism is a way to establish the universal normativity of the mode of production narrative, that to ignore the subaltern today is, willy nilly, to continue the imperialist project. This "origin" of my sentence is thus lost in the shuffle between other more powerful discourses. Is it still possible to wonder if, given that the abolition of *Sati* was in itself admirable, a perception of the "origin" of our sentence might contain interventionist possibilities?

The dissimulation of imperialism as the establisher of the good society is marked by the espousal of the woman as *object* of protection from her own kind. How should one examine the dissimulation of patriarchal strategy, which apparently grants the woman free choice as *subject*? In the other words, how does one make the move from "Britain" to "Hinduism"? Even the attempt shows that Imperialism is not identical with "chromatism" or mere prejudice against people of color. To approach this question, I will touch briefly upon the *Dharmaśāstra* (the sustaining scriptures) and the *Ṛg-Veda* (Praise-Knowledge). They represent the "archaic" origin in my homology of Freud. It is to belabor the obvious that my treatment is not exhaustive. My readings are rather an "interested" and inexpert examination, by a post-colonial woman, of the fabrication of a "repression," a constructed counter-narrative of woman's consciousness, thus woman's being, thus woman's being good, thus the good woman's desire, thus woman's desire. It is an attempt to tabulate a psychobiographical norm that is neither psychoanalytic nor proto- or counter-psychoanalytic.[17] Paradoxically, what we are witnessing at the same to time is the unfixed place of woman as a signifier in the inscription of the social individual.

The two moments in the *Dharmaśāstra* that I am interested in are the discourse on sanctioned suicides and the nature of the rites for the dead.[18] Framed in these two discourses, the self-immolation of widows seems to be caught within the structure of exceptions to the rule, in the following way:

The general scriptural doctrine about suicide is that it is reprehensible. Room is made, however, for certain forms of suicide which, by their formulaic performance, lose the phenomenal identity of being-suicide. The first broad category of sanctioned suicides arises out of *tattvajnāna*, or the knowledge of truth. Here presumably the knowing subject comprehends the insubstantiality or mere phenomenality (which may be "the same thing" as non-phenomenality) of its identity. At a certain point in time, *tat tva* was certainly interpreted as "that you," but even without that, *tattva* is thatness or quiddity. Thus, this enlightened self truly knows the "thatness" of its identity. Its demolition of that identity is not *ātmaghatā* (a killing of the self). The paradox of the knowledge of the limits of knowledge is thus that the strongest assertion of agency, to negate the possibility of agency, cannot be an example of itself. (Curiously enough, the self-*sacrifice* of gods is sanctioned rather by natural ecology, useful for the working of the economy of Nature and the Universe, than by self-knowledge. In this *logically* anterior stage, inhabited by gods rather than human beings, of this particular chain of displacements, suicide, and sacrifice (*ātmaghāta*; and *ātmadāna*) seem as little distinct as an "interior" (self-knowledge) and an "exterior" (ecology) sanction.)

This philosophical space, however, does not accommodate the self-immolating woman. For her, we must move another degree, where room is made to sanction suicides that cannot claim truth-knowledge as a state that is, at any rate, not easily verifiable, and belongs in the area of *Sruti* (what was heard or revealed) rather than *Smriti* (what is remembered or inscribed). This second degree of exception to the general rule about suicide annuls the phenomenal identity of self-immolation if performed in certain places, rather than in a certain state of enlightenment. As we thus move from an "interior" sanction (truth-knowledge) to an "exterior" one (place of pilgrimage), a topological guarantee of anamnesia is offered. It is possible for a woman to perform this type of (non)suicide.[19]

Yet even this is not the *proper* place for the woman to annul the proper name of suicide through the destruction of her proper self. For her alone is sanctioned self-immolation on a dead spouse's pyre. (The few male examples, cited in Hindu antiquity, of self-immolation on another's pyre, being proofs of enthusiasm and devotion to a master or superior, reveal the structure of domination within the rite.) This suicide which is not a suicide may be read as as simulacrum of both truth-knowledge and piety of place. If the former, it is as if the knowledge *in a subject* of its own insubstantiality and mere phenomenality is dramatized so that the dead husband becomes the exteriorized example and place of the extinguished subject and the widow the (non)agent who "acts it out." If the latter, it is as if the metonym for all sacred places is now that burning bed of wood, constructed by elaborate ritual, where the woman's subject, legally displaced from herself, is being consumed.[20] It is in terms of this profound ideology of the displaced place of the female subject that the paradox of free choice comes into play. In the case of the male subject, it is the felicity of the suicide, a felicity that will annul rather than establish its status as such, that is noted. In the case of the female "subject," a sanctioned self-immolation, even as it takes away the effect of "fall" (*pataka*) attached to an act of simple unsanctioned suicide, brings, on another register, praise for the act of choice. By the inexorable functioning of the ideological production of the sexed subject, such a death can be understood by the female subject as an *exceptional* signifier of her own desire, exceeding the general rule of a widow's conduct.

It is well known that, in certain periods and in certain areas, this exceptional rule became the general rule in a class-specific way. Ashis Nandy has related its marked prevalence in eighteenth and early nineteenth century Bengal to a spectrum of factors ranging from population control to communal misogyny.[21] It is certainly true that its prevalence there in the previous centuries was because in Bengal, unlike anywhere else in India, widows could inherit property. Thus, what the British see as poor victimized women going to the slaughter is in fact an ideological battleground. As P.V. Kane, the great historian of the *Dharmaśāstra*, has correctly observed: "In Bengal, [the fact that] the widow of a sonless member even in a joint Hindu family is entitled to practically the same rights over joint family property which her deceased husband would have had...must have frequently induced the surviving members to get rid of the widow by appealing at a most distressing hour to her devotion to and love for her husband" (HD II.2, 635).

It cannot however be ignored that benevolent and enlightened males were and are sympathetic with the "courage" of the woman's free choice in the matter. They thus accept the production of the sexed subaltern subject that we are discussing here: "Modern India does not justify the practice of *sati*, but it is a warped mentality that rebukes modern Indians for expressing admiration and reverence for the cool and unfaltering courage of Indian women in becoming *satis* or performing the *jauhar* for cherishing their ideals of womanly conduct" (HD II.2, 636).

What Jean-François Lyotard has termed the "*différend*," the inaccessibility of, or untranslatibility from, one mode of discourse in a dispute to another, is vividly illustrated here.[22] As the discourse of what the British perceive as heathen ritual is sublated (but not, Lyotard would argue, translated) into what the British perceive as crime, one diagnosis of female free will is substituted for another.

Let us remind ourselves that the self-immolation of widows was not *invariable* ritual prescription. *If, however, the widow does decide thus to exceed the letter of ritual,* to turn back is a transgression for which a particular type of penance is prescribed.[23] With the local British Police Officer supervising the immolation, to be dissuaded after a decision was, by contrast, a mark of real free choice, a choice of freedom. The ambiguity of the position of the indigenous colonial elite is disclosed in the nationalist romanticization of the purity, strength, and love of these self-sacrificing women. The two set-pieces are Rabindranath Tagore's paean to the "self-renouncing paternal grandmothers of Bengal" and Ananda Coomaraswamy's eulogy of "suttee" as "this last proof of the perfect unity of body and soul."[24]

It must be understood that I am not speaking for the killing of widows. I am suggesting that, within the two contending versions of freedom, the constitution of the female subject *in life* is the place of the *différend*. For in the case of widow self-immolation, ritual is not being re-defined as superstition, but being re-inscribed as *crime*. Edward Thompson's understanding of *sati* as "punishment" is thus far off the mark. The gravity of *sati* was that it was ideologically cathected as "reward," just as the gravity of imperialism was that it was ideologically cathected as "social mission." Here is Thompson's passage:

> It may seem unjust and illogical that the Moguls, who freely impaled and flayed alive, or nationals of Europe, whose countries had such ferocious penal codes and had known, scarcely a century before suttee began to shock the English conscience, orgies of witch-burning and religious persecution, should have felt as they did about suttee. But the difference seemed to them this—the victims of their cruelties were tortured by a law which considered them offenders, whereas the victims of suttee were punished for no offence but the physical weakness which had placed them at man's mercy. The rite seemed to prove a depravity and arrogance such as no other human offence had brought to light.[25]

All through the mid- and late eighteenth century, in the spirit of the codification of the Law, the British in India had consistently collaborated and consulted with learned Brahmins to inspect the "suttee" to verify if it was legal by their homogenized version of Hindu Law. The collaboration was often idiosyncratic, as in the case of the significance of being dissuaded. Sometimes, as in the case of the general Sāstric prohibition against the immolation of widows with small children, the British collaboration seems confused.[26]

In the beginning of the nineteenth century, the British authorities, and especially the British in England, repeatedly suggested that thus to collaborate made it appear as if the British condoned this practice. When the Law was finally written, the history of the fairly long period of initial collaboration was effaced, and the language celebrated the noble Hindu who was against the bad Hindu, the latter given to savage atrocities: "The practice of suttee…is revolting to the feelings of human nature…In many instances, acts of atrocity have been perpetrated, which have been shocking to the Hindoos themselves…Actuated by these considerations the Governor-General in Council, without intending to depart from one of the first and most important principles of the system of British Government in India that all classes of the people be secure in the observance of their religious usages, so long as that system can be adhered to without violation of the paramount dictates of justice and humanity, has deemed it right to establish the following rules…" (HD II.2, 624–625).[27]

That this was an alternative ideology of the graded sanctioning of suicide as exeeption, rather than its inscription as sin, was of course not understood. Perhaps *Sati* should have been read with martyrdom, with the defunct husband standing in for the transcendental One; or with war, with the husband standing in for sovereign or State, for whose sake an intoxicating ideology of self-sacrifice can be mobilized. In the event, it was categorized with murder, infanticide, and the lethal exposure of the very old. The dubious place of the free will of the constituted sexed subject as female was successfully effaced. There is no itinerary we can retrace here. Since the other sanctioned suicides did not involve the scene of this constitution, they entered neither the ideological battleground at the "archaic" origin—the tradition of the *Dharmaśāstra*— nor the scene of the re-inscription of ritual as crime—the British abolition. The only transmogrification was Mahatma Gandhi's re-inscription of the notion of *satyāgraha* or hunger strike as resistance. This is not the place to discuss the details of that sea-change. We would merely invite the reader to consider the auras of widow sacrifice and Gandhian resistance within the same determination. The root in the first part of *satyāgraha* and in *sati* are the same.

Since the beginning of the Puranic era (c. 400 A.D.), learned Brahmins debated the doctrinal appropriateness of *Sati* as of sanctioned suicides in sacred places in general. (This debate continues today in an academic way.) Sometimes the caste-provenance of the practice was in question. The *general* law for widows, that they should observe *brahmacarya*, was, however, hardly ever debated. It is not enough to translate *brahmacarya* as celibacy. It should he recognized that, of the four ages of man in Hindu (or Brahminical) *regulative* psychobiography, *brahmacarya* is the social practice anterior to the kinship inscription of marriage. The man—widower or husband—graduates through *vānaprastha* (forest-life) into the mature celibacy and renunciation of *samnyāsa* (laying aside).[28] The woman as *wife* is indispensable for *gārhasthya* or householdership, and may accompany her husband into forest life. She has no access (according to Brahminical sanction) to the final celibacy of asceticism or *samnyāsa*. The woman as *widow*, by the *general* law of sacred doctrine, must regress to an anteriority transformed into stasis. The *institutional* evils attendant upon this law are well known. We are considering its asymmetrical effect upon the *ideological* formation of the sexed subject. It is thus of much greater significance that there was no debate upon this non-exceptional fate of widows—either among Hindus or between Hindus and British—than that the *exceptional* prescription of self-immolation was actively contended.[29] Here the possibility of recovering a (sexually) subaltern subject is once again shown to be lost and overdetermined.

It is of course abundantly obvious that this legally programmed ad hoc asymmetry in the status of the subject, which effectively defines the woman as object of one husband, operates in the interest of the legally symmetrical subject-status of the male. The self-immolation of the widow, in such a reading, becomes the extreme case of the general law rather than an exception to it. It is not surprising then to read of the following heavenly reward for the *sati*, where the quality of being the object of a unique possessor is emphasized by way of rivalization with other females, those ecstatic heavenly dancers, paragons of female beauty and male pleasure who sing her praise: "In heaven she[,] being solely devoted to her husband

[,and] praised by groups of *apsarās* [heavenly dancers], sports with her husband as long as fourteen Indras rule" (HD II.2, 631).

The profound irony in locating the woman's free will in self-immolation is once again revealed in a verse accompanying the earlier passage: "As long as the woman [as wife: *stri*] does not burn herself in fire on the death of her husband[,] she is never released [*mucyate* from her female body [*strisarīr*— i.e., in the cycle of births]." Even as it operates the most subtle release from individual agency in general principle, the sanctioned suicide peculiar to woman draws its ideological strength by *identifying* individual agency with the supra-individual: kill yourself on your husband's pyre now, and you may kill your female body in the entire cycle of birth.

In a further twist of the paradox, this emphasis on free will establishes the peculiar misfortune of holding a female body. It is noticeable that the word for the self that is actually burned is the standard word for spirit in the noblest sense [*ātman*], while the verb "release," though the root for salvation in the noblest sense [*muc—moksha*], is in the passive [*mocy-ate*], and the word for that which is annulled in the cycle of birth is the everyday word for the body. The ideological message thus constituted writes itself in the benevolent twentieth century male historian's admiration: "The Jauhar [see below] practiced by the Rajput ladies of Chitor and other places for saving themselves from unspeakable atrocities at the hands of the victorious Moslems are too well known to need any lengthy notice" (HD II.2, 629).

Although, first, *jauhar*, the group self-immolation of aristocratic Rajput war-widows or imminent war-widows, is not, strictly speaking, an act of *Sati*, and, second, I should not wish to speak for the sanctioned sexual violence of conquering (male) armies, "Moslems" or otherwise, it cannot be denied that female self-immolation in the face of it is a legitimation of rape as "natural," and works, in the long run, in the interest of unique genital possession of the female. The group rape perpetrated by the conquerors is a metonymic celebration of territorial acquisition. Just as the "general" law for widows was unquestioned, so also this act of female "heroism" continues to be part of the patriotic tales told to children, thus operating on the crudest level of ideological reproduction. It has also played a tremendous role, precisely as an overdetermined signifier, in the acting out of Hindu communalism. Simultaneously, the broader question of the constitution of the sexed "subject" is dissimulated by the foregrounding of the *visible* violence of *Sati*. To repeat, then, the task of recovering a (sexually) subaltern subject is lost in an "institutional textuality" at the "archaic" origin.

Indeed, as I have mentioned above, when the status of the legal subject as property-holder could be temporarily bestowed upon the *female* relict, the practice of the self-immolation of widows was stringently enforced. Raghunandana, the late fifteenth/sixteenth century legalist whose interpretations are supposed to lend the greatest authority to such enforcement, takes as his text a curious passage from the *Rg-Veda*, the most ancient of the Hindu sacred texts, the first of the *Srutis*. In doing so, he is following a centuries-old tradition, commemorating a peculiar and transparent misreading at the very place of sanction. Here is the verse outlining certain steps within the rites for the dead. Even at a simple reading it is clear that it is "not addressed to widows at all, but to ladies of the deceased man's household whose husbands were living." Why then was it taken as authoritative? This, the unemphatic transposition of the dead for the living husband, is a different order of mystery at the archaic origin from the ones we have been discussing. "Let these women whose husbands are worthy and are living enter the house with clarified butter in their eyes. Let these wives first step into the house, tearless, healthy, and well adorned" (HD II.2, 634). But this crucial transposition is not the only "mistake" here. The authority is lodged in a disputed passage and an alternate reading. At the beginning of the second line, here translated "Let these wives first step into the house," the word for first is अग्रे (*agré*). Some have read it as अग्ने (*agné*, "O fire"). As Kane makes clear, however, "even without this change Aparārka and others rely for the practice of *Sati* on this verse" (HD IV.2, 199). Here is another screen around one origin of the history of the subaltern female subject. Is it a historical oneirocritique that one should perform on a statement such as: "Therefore it must be admitted that either the MSS are corrupt or Raghunandana committed an innocent slip"? (HD II.2, 634) For it should be mentioned, in addition, that the rest of the poem is about that general law of *brahmacarya*-in-stasis for widows to which *Sati* is an exception. Alternatively, the rest of the poem is about *niyoga*—"the appointing of a brother or any near kinsman to raise up issue to a deceased husband by marrying his widow."[30]

If P.V. Kane is the authority on the *history* of the *Dharmaśāstra*, Mulla's *Principles of Hindu Law* is the *practical* guide to Hindu Law. It is part of the historical text of what Freud calls "kettle logic" that we are unravelling here, that Mulla's textbook adduces, just as definitively, that the *Ṛg-Vedic* verse under consideration was proof that "remarriage of widows and divorce are recognised in some of the old texts."[31]

One cannot begin to wonder about the role of the word *yōni* here. In context, with the localizing adverb *agré* (in front), there can be no doubt that the word "means" "dwelling-place." But that does not efface the recognition of its primary sense of "genital" (not yet perhaps specifically *female* genital). What is it to take as the *authority* for the choice of a *widow's* self-*immolation* a passage celebrating the entry of adorned *wives* into a dwelling place invoked on this occasion by its *yōni*-name, so that the extra-contextual icon is almost one of entry into civic production or birth? Paradoxically, the imagic propinquity of vagina and fire seems to lend a kind of strength to the authority-claim.[32] This paradox is further strengthened by Raghunandana's modification of the verse so as to read "let them first ascend the *fluid* abode (or origin, with, of course, the *yōni*-name—*ā rohantu jalayōnimagné*), O fire (or of fire)." Why should one accept that this "probably mean[s] 'may fire be to them as cool as water'"? (HD II.2, 634) The fluid genital of fire, a "corrupt" phrasing, might figure forth a sexual indeterminacy that would provide a simulacrum for the intellectual indeterminacy of *tattva-jnāna* (truth-knowledge).

We have written above of a constructed counter-narrative of woman's consciousness, thus woman's being, thus woman's being-good, thus the good woman's desire, thus woman's desire. This slippage can be seen by way of the fracture inscribed in the very word *sati*.

It is the feminine gender of *sat*. *Sat* transcends any gender-specific notion of masculinity and moves up not only into human but spiritual universality. It is the present participle of the verb "to be" and as such means not only being but the True, the Good, the Right. In the sacred texts it is essence, universal spirit. Even as a prefix it indicates appropriate, felicitous, fit. It is noble enough to have entered the most privileged discourse of modern

Western philosophy, Heidegger's meditation on Being.[33] *Sati*, the feminine of this word, simply means "good wife."[34]

It is now time to disclose that *sati* or *suttee* as the proper name of the rite of widow self-immolation commemorates a grammatical error on the part of the British, quite as the nomenclature "American Indian" eommemorates a factual error on the part of Columbus. The word in the various Indian languages is "the burning of the *sati*" or of the good wife, who then does not enter the regressive stasis of the widow in *brahmacarya*. Here we have an example of the extent of the race-class-gender overdeterminations of the situation. It can perhaps be caught even when it is flattened out: white men, seeking to save brown women from brown men, impose upon those women a greater ideological constriction by absolutely identifying, *within discursive practice*, good-wifehood with self-immolation on the husband's pyre. On the other side of thus constituting the *object*, the abolition (or removal) of which will provide the occasion for the establishment of a good, as distinguished from a merely civil society, is the Hindu manipulation of female *subject*-constitution that I have tried to discuss in the last few pages.

I have already mentioned Edward Thompson's *Suttee*, published in 1928. I cannot do justice here to this perfect specimen of the justification of imperialism as a civilizing mission. Nowhere in this book, written by someone who avowedly "loves India," is there any questioning of the "beneficial ruthlessness" of the British in India as motivated by territorial expansionism or mismanagement of industrial capital.[35] The problem with this book is indeed a problem of "representation," the construction of a continuous and "homogeneous" "India" in terms of heads of state and British administrators, from the perspective of "a man of good sense" who would be transparent as the voice of reasonable humanity. "India" can then be "represented," in the other sense, by its imperial masters. The reason for referring to *Suttee* here is Thompson's finessing of the word *sati* as "faithful" in the very first sentence of his book, an inaccurate translation which is nonetheless an English permit for the insertion of the female subject into twentieth century discourse.[36]

Thompson praises General Charles Hervey's appreciation of the problem of *Sati* in the following way: "Hervey has a passage which brings out the pity of a system which looked only for prettiness and constancy in woman. He obtained the names of satis who had died on the pyres of Bikanir Rajas; they were such names as: 'Ray Queen, Sun-ray, Love's Delight, Garland, Virtue Found, Echo, Soft Eye, Comfort, Moonbeam, Love-lorn, Dear Heart, Eye-play, Arbour-born, Smile, Love-bud, Glad Omen, Mist-clad, or Cloud-sprung—the last a favourite name.'" Once again, imposing the upper-class Victorian's typical demands upon "his woman" (Thompson's preferred phrase), Thompson is appropriating the Hindu woman as his to save against the "system." Bikaner is in Rajasthan. As we have suggested, any discussion of widow-burnings of Rajasthan, especially within the ruling class, was intimately linked to the positive or negative construction of Hindu (or Aryan) communalism. A look at the pathetically mispelled names of the *satis* of the artisanal, peasant, village-priestly, moneylender, clerical and comparable social groups in Bengal, where *Satis* were most common, would not have yielded such a harvest. (Thompson's preferred adjective for Bengalis is "imbecilic.") Or perhaps it would. There is no more dangerous pastime than transposing proper names into common nouns, translating them, and using them as sociological evidence. I attempted to reconstruct the names on that list and began to feel Hervey-Thompson's arrogance. What, for instance, might "Comfort" have been? Was it "Shanti"? Readers are reminded of the last line of T.S. Eliot's *The Waste Land.* There the word hears the mark of one kind of stereotyping of India—the grandeur of the ecumenical Upanishads. Or was it "Swāsti?" Readers are reminded of the *swastikā*, the brahmanic ritual mark of domestic comfort (as in "God Bless Our Home"), stereotyped into a criminal parody of Aryan hegemony. Between these two appropriations, where is our pretty and constant burnt widow? The aura of the names owes more to writers like Edward Fitzgerald, the "translator" of the *Rubayyat of Omar Khayyam,* who helped to construct a certain picture of the oriental woman through the supposed "objectivity" of translation, than to sociological exactitude. (Edward Said's *Orientalism* remains the authoritative text here.[37] By this sort of reckoning the translated proper names of any random collection of contemporary French philosophers, or Boards of Directors of prestigious Southern U.S. corporation would give evidence of a ferocious investment in an archangelic and hagiocentric theocracy. These kinds of sleights-of-pen can be perpetrated upon "common nouns" as well, of course. There is that parody of the ethnographic construction of the other—the description of an English breakfast—where "egg" is translated "unfertilized ova of domestic fowl." But the proper name is most susceptible to the trick. And it is the British trick with the proper name *Sati* that we are discussing here.

After such a taming of the subject, Thompson can write, under the heading "The Psychology of the 'Satis'": "I had intended to try to examine this; but the truth is, it has ceased to seem a puzzle to me."[38]

Between patriarchy and imperialism, subject-constitution and object-formation, the figure of the woman disappears, not into a pristine nothingness, but into a violent shuttling which is the displaced figuration of the "Third World Woman" caught between tradition and modernization. These considerations would revise every detail of a judgment that seems valid when a history of sexuality "in the West" is broached: "Such would be the property of repression [*le propre de la repression*], that which distinguishes it from the prohibitions maintained by simple penal law: repression functions well [*fonctionne bien*] as a sentence to disappear, but also as an injunction to silence, affirmation of non-existence; and consequently states [*constat*] that of all this there is nothing to say, to see, to know.[39] The case of *suttee* as exemplum of the woman-in-imperialism would challenge and deconstruct this opposition between subject (law) and object-of-knowledge (repression), and mark the place of "disappearance" with something other than silence and non-existence, a violent aporia between subject- and object-status.

Sati as a woman's proper name is in fairly widespread use in India today. Naming a female infant "a good wife" has its own proleptic irony. The irony is all the greater because this sense of the common noun is not the primary operator in the proper name.[40] Behind the naming of the infant is the *Sati* of Hindu mythology, Durga in her manifestation as good wife.[41]

In the part of the story that is useful for us, *Sati*— she is already called that—arrives at her father's court uninvited, in the absence, even, of an invitation for her divine husband

Siva. Her father starts to abuse *Siva* and *Sati* dies in pain. *Siva* arrives in fury and dances over the universe with *Sati's* corpse on his shoulder. *Visnu* dismembers her body by arrow or wheel and the bits are strewn over the earth. Around each such relic bit is a great place of pilgrimage.

Figures like the goddess Athena—"father's daughters self-professedly uncontaminated by the womb"—are useful for establishing women's ideological self-debasement, which is to be distinguished from a deconstructive attitude toward the essentialist subject.[42] The figure of the mythic *Sati*, reversing every narrateme of the rite (the living husband avenges the wife's death, a transaction between great male gods fulfills the destruction of the female body and thus inscribes the earth as sacred geography), performs a similar function. To see this as proof of the feminism of classical Hinduism or of Indian culture as goddess-centered and therefore feminist, is as ideologically contaminated by nativism or reverse ethnocentrism as it was imperialist to erase the image of the luminous fighting Mother Durga and invest the proper noun *Sati* with no signification other than the ritual burning of the helpless widow as sacrificial offering who can then be saved. There is no space from where the subaltern (sexed) subject can speak.

Can the ideology of *Sati*, coming from the history of the periphery, be sublated into any model of interventionist practice?

Since this essay operates on the notion that all such clear-cut nostalgia for lost origins are suspect, especially as grounds for counter-hegemonic ideological production, we must proceed here by way of an example. But first a couple of cautions.

A position against nostalgia as a basis of counter-hegemonic ideological production does not endorse its negative use. Within the complexity of contemporary political economy, it would, for example, be highly questionable to urge that the current Indian working class crime of burning wives who bring insufficient dowries and of subsequently disguising the murder as suicide is either a *use* or *abuse* of the tradition of *Sati*-suicide. The most that can be claimed is that it is a displacement on a chain of semiosis with the female subject as signifier, which would lead us back into the narrative we have been unravelling. There is no doubt that one must work to stop the crime of bride-burning *in every way*. If, however, that work is accompanied by unexamined nostalgia or its opposite, it will assist actively in the substitution of race/ethnos or sheer genitalism as a signifier in the place of the female subject.

It should therefore be understood that the example I discuss below is in no way a plea for some violent Hindu sisterhood of self-destruction. The definition of the British Indian as Hindu in Hindu Law is one of the marks of the ideological war of the British against the Islamic Mughal rulers of India at the time of the former's entry: a significant skirmish in that as yet unfinished war was the division of the subcontinent, or the recent massacre of the Sikhs.[43] It should also be noted that, in my view, individual examples of this sort are tragic failures as *models* of interventionist practice, a view that would question the production of models as such. As objects of discourse analysis for the non-self-abdicating intellectual who is on tap, they can illuminate a section of the social text, in however haphazard a way.

A young woman of sixteen or seventeen, Bhuvaneswari Bhaduri by name, hanged herself in her father's modest apartment in North Calcutta in the year 1926. The suicide was a bit of a puzzle since, as Bhuvaneswari was menstruating at the time, it was clearly not a case of illicit pregnancy. Nearly a decade later, it was discovered that she had been a member of one of the many groups involved in the armed struggle for Indian independence. She had been finally entrusted with a political assassination. Unable to confront the task and yet aware of the practical need for trust, she had killed herself.

Bhuvaneswari had known that her death would be diagnosed as the outcome of illegitimate passion. She had therefore waited for the onset of menstruation. In that interim period of waiting, Bhuvaneswari, the *brahmacārini* who was no doubt looking forward to good wifehood, perhaps rewrote the social text of *Sati*-suicide in an interventionist way. (One tentative explanation of her inexplicable act had been a possible melancholia brought on by her brother-in-law's repeated taunts that she was too old to be not-yet-a-wife.) She generalized the sanctioned motive for female suicide by taking immense trouble to displace (not merely to deny), in the physiological inscription of her body, its imprisonment within legitimate possession by a single male. In the immediate context, her act became absurd, a case of delirium rather than sanity. It could not earn the status of the forgetfulness of the mother tongue in the correct use of a foreign language that is one metaphor for revolutionary practice in Marx's *The Eighteenth Brumaire*. The displacing gesture—waiting for menstruation—is at first a reversal of the interdict against a menstruating widow's right to immolate herself; the unclean widow too must wait, publicly, until the cleansing bath of the fourth day, when she is *no longer menstruating*, in order to claim her dubious privilege.

In this reading, Bhuvaneswari Bhaduri's suicide is an unemphatic, ad hoc, subaltern rewriting of the social text of *Sati*-suicide as much as the hegemonic account of the blazing, fighting, familial Durga. The emergent dissenting possibilities of that hegemonic account of the fighting mother are well documented and popularly well remembered through the discourse of the male leaders and participants in the Independence Movement. The subaltern as female cannot be heard or read. As follows:

I know of Bhuvaneswari's life and death through family connections. Preliminary to investigating them more thoroughly, I asked a Bengali woman, a philosopher and Sanskritist whose early intellectual production is almost identical with mine, to start the process. Two responses:

(a) Why, when her two sisters, Saileswari and Raseswari, led such full and wonderful lives, are you interested in the hapless Bhuvaneswari?

(b) I asked (my informant reported) her nieces. It appears that it was a case of illicit love.

The subaltern cannot speak. There is no virtue in global laundry lists with "women" as a pious item. Representation has not withered away: in spite of the heterogeneous information-retrieval about her, the monolithic subject assigned the proper name "Third World Woman"—consolidating a certain desire for the narcissistic Other—stands as evidence. The post-colonial intellectual—*as intellectual*—has a circumscribed task of recording this evidence, which she must not disown with a flourish.

NOTES

1. Jonathan Culler, *On Deconstruction: Theory and Criticism After Structuralism* (Ithaca: Cornell University Press, 1982), p. 48.

2. Elizabeth Fox-Genovese, "Placing Women's History in History," *New Left Review* 133 (May–June 1982), p. 21.

3. I have attempted to develop this idea in a somewhat autobiographical way in "Finding Feminist Readings: Dance-Years," in *American Criticism in the Poststructuralist* Age, ed. Ira Konigsberg (Ann Arbor: University of Michigan Press, 1981).

4. Sarah Kofman, *L'énigme de la femme: la femme dans les textes de Freud* (Paris: Galilée, 1980).

5. Sigmund Freud, "'A Child is Being Beaten': A Contribution to the Study of the Origin of Sexual Perversions," *The Standard Edition of the Complete Psychological Works of Sigmund Freud,* trans. James Strachey, et al. (London: Hogarth Press, 1955), vol. 17.

6. Freud, "'Wild' Psycho-Analysis, "*Standard Edition,* vol. 17.

7. I have tried to develop this critique in "The Letter as Cutting Edge," in *Literature and Psychoanalysis: Reading Otherwise,* ed. Shoshana Pelman (New Haven: Yale University Press, 1981).

8. Freud, "'A Child is Being Beaten,'" p. 188. This narrative of a double origin repeats a morphological clue given by Derrida in his early essay "Differance," in *Margins of Philosophy,* trans. Alan Bass (Chicago: University of Chicago Press, 1982). I attempt to pick up this clue—which I call "the double session of differance"—in "Twelve Varieties of Deconstructive Practice," lecture delivered at the School of Theory and Criticism, Northwestern University, June 1982.

9. Jacques Derrida, *Spurs,* trans. Barbara Harlow (Chicago: University of Chicago Press, 1970), p. 37. Mani's monograph is a masters thesis submitted to the History Board at the University of California at Santa Cruz.

10. Mary Daly, *Gyn-Ecology: The Metaethics of Radical Feminism* (Boston: Beacon Press, 1978), pp. 113–133. The existence of one or two Indian social reformers—Rammohun Roy is the only name that can be confidently cited—who were strongly opposed to widow-sacrifice, does not contradict the ideological generality of such an understanding. A more extended focus would discuss Roy under the heading of the "Production of the Colonial Subject."

11. Here I part company from Mani who, as a Foucauldian, seems to privilege the women's unrepresentable individual willing subjectivity.

12. I have been able to develop this point in my study of two texts as different from each other as Charlotte Bronte's *Jane Eyre,* and Mahasveta Devi's "Draupadi" in "Three Women's Texts and A Critique of Imperialism," forthcoming in *Critical Inquiry,* and "'Draupadi': by Mahasveta Devi," in *Writing and Sexual Difference,* ed. Elizabeth Abel (Chicago: University of Chicago Press, 1982).

13. J.D.M. Derrett, *Hindu Law Past and Present: Being An Account of the Controversy Which Preceded the Enactment of the Hindu Code, and Text of the Code as Enacted, And Some Comments Thereon* (Calcutta: A. Mukherjee & Co., 1957), p. 46.

14. Michel Foucault, *Power/Knowledge: Selected Interviews and Other Writings, 1972–1977,* trans. Colin Gordon, et al. (New York: Pantheon, 1980), p. 41.

15. C.H. Philips, ed. *The Correspondence of Lord William Cavendish Bentinck, Governor-General of India, 1828–1835,* 2 vols. (Oxford: Oxford University Press, 1977).

16. Ashis Nandy, "Sati: A Nineteenth Century Tale of Women, Violence and Protest," in *Rammohun Roy and the Process of Modernization in India,* ed. V.C. Joshi (Delhi: Vikas Publishing House, 1975), p. 68.

17. I have discussed this at greater length in an interview with Elizabeth Gross forthcoming in *Thesis Eleven*.

18. The following account leans heavily on Pandurang Vaman Kane, *History of Dharmaśāstra*, 5 vols. (Poona: Bhandarkar Oriental Research Institute, 1930–1962). Hereafter cited in texts as HD, with volume, part, and page numbers following.

19. Upendra Thakur, *The History of Suicide in India: An Introduction* (Delhi: Munshi Ram Manohar Lal, 1963), p. 9, has a useful list of Sanskrit primary sources on sacred places. This laboriously decent book betrays all the signs of the schizophrenia of the colonial subject, such as bourgeois nationalism, patriarchal communalism, and an "enlightened reasonableness."

20. An interesting typological parallel may be found in Freud's location of the function of the superego of the female *in the male* in the famous instance of penis-envy. See Catherine Millot, "Le surmoi féminin," *Ornicar?* 29 (April–June 1984), p. 124.

21. Nandy, "Sati," pp. 172–173.

22. Jean-François Lyotard, *Le différend* (Paris: Minuit, 1984).

23. HD II.2, p. 633. There are suggestions that this "prescribed penance" was far exceeded by social practice. In the passage below, published in 1938, notice the Hindu patristic assumptions about the freedom of female will at work in phrases like "courage" and "strength of character." The unexamined presuppositions of the passage might be that the complete objectification of the widow-concubine was just punishment for abdication of the right to courage, signifying subject status: "Some widows, however, had not the courage to go through this inhuman fiery ordeal; nor had they sufficient strength of mind and character to live up to the high ascetic ideal prescribed for them [*brahmacarya*]. It is sad to record that they were driven to lead the life of a concubine or *avaruddha stri* [incarcerated wife]." A.S. Altekar, *The Position of Women in Hindu Civilization: From Prehistoric Times to the Present Day* (Delhi: Motilal Banarsidass, 1938), p. 156; interpolations mine.

24. Quoted in Sena, *Brhat-Banga*, vol. 2, pp. 913–914.

25. Edward Thompson, *Suttee: A Historical and Philosophical Inquiry into the Hindu Rite of Widow-Burning* (London: Allen and Unwin, 1928), p. 32.

26. Here, as well as for the brahmin debates over *Sati*, see Mani, "Production," p. 71f.

27. I have written of the deployment of fantastic race-divisive, historical demographies *within* the ranks of the colonized in "Overdeterminations of Imperialism: David Ochterlony and the Ranee of Sirmoor," paper presented at the Sociology of Literature Conference, University of Essex, July 1984.

28. We are speaking here of the regulative norms of Brahminism, rather than "things as they were." See Robert Lingat, *The Classical Law of India*, trans. J.D.M. Derrett (Berkeley: University of Callifornia Press, 1973), p. 46.

29. Both the vestigial possibility of widow re-marriage in ancient India and the legal institution of widow re-marriage in 1856 are transactions among men. Widow re-marriage is very much an exception, perhaps because it left the program of subject-formation untouched. In all the "lore" of widow re-marriage, it is the father and the husband who are applauded for their reformist courage and selflessness.

30. Sir Monier Monier-Williams, *Sanskrit-English Dictionary* (Oxford: Clarendon Press, 1899), p. 552. Historians are often impatient if modernists seem to be attempting to import "feministic" judgments into ancient patriarchies. The real question is, of course, why structures of patriarchal domination should be unquestioningly recorded. Historical sanctions for collective action toward social justice can only be developed if people outside of the discipline question standards of "objectivity" preserved as such by the hegemonic tradition. It does not seem inap-

propriate to notice that so "objective" an instrument as a dictionary can use the deeply sexist-partisan explanatory expression: "raise up issue to a deceased husband!"

31. Sunderlal T. Desai, *Mulla: Principles of Hindu Law* (Bombay: N.M. Tripathi, 1982), p. 184.

32. I am grateful to Professor Alison Finley of Trinity College for discussing the passage with me. Professor Finley is an expert on the *Rg-Veda*. I hasten to add that she would find my reading as irresponsibly "literary-critical" as the ancient historian would find it "modernist" (see note 30).

33. Martin Heidegger, *An Introduction to Metaphysics*, trans. Ralph Manheim (New York: Doubleday Anchor, 1961), p. 58.

34. I was able to develop a similar point—about how "meaning" is demoted when the gender changes from masculine to feminine—with reference to a text so remote in time and place from my present concern as Henry James' *The Turn of the Screw* ("Finding Feminist Readings," pp. 43–44, note 2).

35. Thompson, *Suttee*, p. 37.

36. Ibid., p. 15. For the status of the proper name as "mark," see Derrida, "Taking Chances," in *Taking Chances: Derrida, Psychoanalysis, and Literature,* ed. Joseph H. Smith and William Kerrigan (Baltimore: John Hopkins University Press, 1984).

37. Edward Said, *Orientalism* (New York: Pantheon, 1978).

38. Thompson, *Suttee*, p. 137.

39. Foucault, *The History of Sexuality,* trans. Robert Hurley (New York: Vintage Books, 1980), vol. I, p, 4.

40. The fact that the word was also used as a form of address for well-born women ("lady") complicates matters.

41. It should be remembered that this account does not exhaust her many manifestations within the pantheon.

42. I have discussed this in "Displacements and the Discourse of Woman," *In Displacement: Derrida and After,* ed. Mark Krupnick (Bloomington: Indiana University Press, 1983), p. 174.

43. The complexity of the representation of Islamic India can become part of the historical pre-text of Said, *Covering Islam: How the Media and the Experts Determine How We See the Rest of the World* (New York: Pantheon, 1981).

UNDER WESTERN EYES: FEMINIST SCHOLARSHIP AND COLONIAL DISCOURSES (1988)

CHANDRA TALPADE MOHANTY

Mohanty argues that many Western feminists writing about women in the Third World have oversimplified Third World women by writing as if they were all alike. She sees Western feminists who oversimplify women from outside the West as upholding their own self-image as progressive Western feminists by opposing it to a distorted image of Third World women. Such distortions can reduce Third World women to victims of the patriarchal oppression that Western feminists see themselves as resisting. Mohanty's article contributed to the feminist desire to see the variety among women, as opposed to the tendency among some feminists to generalize too broadly about women and underestimate women's multiplicity. Mohanty thus helped Western feminists recognize the differences between women in different parts of the world and in different class positions, including the differences within any particular group of women.

It ought to be of some political significance at least that the term "colonization" has come to denote a variety of phenomena in recent feminist and left writings in general. From its analytic value as a category of exploitative economic exchange in both traditional and contemporary Marxisms (cf. particularly such contemporary scholars as Baran, Amin and Gunder-Frank) to its use by feminist women of colour in the US, to describe the appropriation of their experiences and struggles by hegemonic white women's movements,[1] the term "colonization" has been used to characterize everything from the most evident economic and political hierarchies to the production of a particular cultural discourse about what is called the "Third World."[2] However sophisticated or problematical its use as an explanatory construct, colonization almost invariably implies a relation of structural domination, and a discursive or political suppression of the heterogeneity of the subject(s) in question. What I wish to analyse here specifically is the production of "Third World Woman" as a singular monolithic subject in some recent (western) feminist texts. The definition of colonization I invoke is a predominantly *discursive* one, focusing on a certain mode of appropriation and codification of "scholarship" and "knowledge" about women in the third world by particular analytic categories employed in writings on the subject which take as their primary point of reference feminist interests as they have been articulated in the US and western Europe.

My concern about such writings derives from my own implication and investment in contemporary debates in feminist theory, and the urgent political necessity of forming strategic coalitions across class, race and national boundaries. Clearly, western feminist discourse and political practice is neither singular nor homogeneous in its goals, interests or analyses. However, it is possible to trace a coherence of *effects* resulting from the implicit assumption of "the west" (in all its complexities and contradictions) as the primary referent in theory and praxis. Thus, rather than claim simplistically that "western feminism" is a monolith, I would like to draw attention to the remarkably similar effects of various analytical categories and even strategies which codify their relationship to the Other in implicitly hierarchical terms. It is in this sense that I use the term "western feminist." Similar arguments pertaining to questions of methods of analysis can be made in terms of middle-class, urban African and Asian scholars producing scholarship on or about their rural or working-class sisters which assumes their own middle-class culture as the norm, and codifies peasant and working-class histories and cultures as Other. Thus, while this article focuses specifically on western feminist discourse on women in the third world, the critiques I offer also pertain to identical analytical principles employed by third-world scholars writing about their own cultures.

Moreover, the analytical principles discussed later serve to distort western feminist political practices, and limit the possibility of coalitions among (usually white) western feminists and working-class and feminist women of colour around the world. These limitations are evident in the construction of the (implicitly consensual) priority of issues around which apparently *all* women are expected to organize. The necessary and integral connection between feminist scholarship and feminist political practice and organizing determines the significance and status of western feminist writings on women in the third world, for feminist scholarship, like most other kinds of scholarship, does not comprise merely "objective" knowledge about a certain subject. It is also a directly political and discursive *practice* insofar as it is purposeful and ideological. It is best seen as a mode of intervention into particular hegemonic discourses (for example, traditional anthropology, sociology, literary criticism, etc.), and as a political praxis which counters and resists the totalizing imperative of age-old "legitimate" and "scientific" bodies of knowledge. Thus, feminist scholarly practices exist within relations of power—relations which they counter, redefine, or even implicitly support. There can, of course, be no apolitical scholarship.

The relationship between Woman—a cultural and ideological composite Other constructed through diverse representational discourse (scientific, literary, juridical, linguistic, cinematic, etc.)—and women—real, material subjects of their collective histories—is one of the central questions the practice of feminist scholarship seeks to address. This connection between women as historical subjects and the re-presentation of Woman produced by hegemonic discourses is not a relation of direct identity, or a relation of correspondence or simple implication.[3] It is an arbitrary relation set up in particular cultural and historical contexts. I would like to suggest that the feminist writings I analyse here discursively colonize the material and historical heterogeneities of the lives of women in the third world, thereby producing/representing a composite, singular "third-world woman"—an image which appears arbitrarily constructed but nevertheless carries with it the authorizing signature of western humanist discourse.[4] I argue that assumptions of privilege and ethnocentric universality on the one hand, and inadequate self-consciousness about the effect of western scholarship on the "third world" in the context of a world system dominated by the west on the other, characterize a sizable extent of western feminist work on women in the third world. An analysis of "sexual difference" in the form of a cross-culturally singular, monolithic notion of patriarchy or male dominance leads to the construction of a similarly reductive and homogeneous notion of what I shall call the "third-world difference"—that stable, ahistorical something that apparently oppresses most if not all the women in these countries. It is in the production of this "third-world difference" that western feminisms appropriate and colonize the constitutive complexities which characterize the lives of women in these countries. It is in this process of discursive homogenization and systematization of the oppression of women in the third world that power is exercised in much of recent western feminist writing, and this power needs to be defined and named.

In the context of the west's hegemonic position today, of what Anouar Abdel-Malek calls a struggle for "control over the orientation, regulation and decision of the process of world development on the basis of the advanced sector's monopoly of scientific knowledge and ideal creativity" (1981: especially 145), western feminist scholarship on the third world must be seen and examined precisely in terms of its inscription in these particular relations of power and struggle. There is, it should be evident, no universal patriarchal framework which this scholarship attempts to counter and resist—unless one posits an international male conspiracy or a monolithic, transhistorical power structure. There is, however, a particular world balance of power within which any analysis of culture, ideology, and socio-economic conditions has to be necessarily situated. Abdel-Malek is useful here, again, in reminding us about the inherence of politics in the discourses of "culture":

> Contemporary imperialism is, in a real sense, a hegemonic imperialism, exercising to a maximum degree a rationalized violence taken to a higher level than ever before—through fire and sword, but also through the attempt to control hearts and minds. For its content is defined by the combined action of the military-industrial complex and the hegemonic cultural centers of the West, all of them founded on the advanced levels of development attained by monopoly and finance capital, and supported by the benefits of both the scientific and technological revolution and the second industrial revolution itself. (1981: 145–6)

Western feminist scholarship cannot avoid the challenge of situating itself and examining its role in such a global economic and political framework. To do any less would be to ignore the complex interconnections between first- and third-world economies and the profound effect of this on the lives of women in *all* countries. I do not question the descriptive and informative value of most western feminist writings on women in the third world. I also do not question the existence of excellent work which does not fall into the analytic traps I am concerned with. In fact I deal with an example of such work later on. In the context of an overwhelming silence about the experiences of women in these countries, as well as the need to forge international links between women's political struggles, such work is both pathbreaking and absolutely essential. However, it is both to the *explanatory potential* of particular analytic strategies employed by such writing, and to their *political effect* in the context of the hegemony of western scholarship, that I want to draw attention here. While feminist writing in the US is still marginalized (except perhaps from the point of view of women of colour addressing privileged white women), western feminist writing on women in the third world must be considered in the context of the global hegemony of western scholarship—i.e., the production, publication, distribution and consumption of information and ideas. Marginal or not, this writing has political effects and implications beyond the immediate feminist or disciplinary audience. One such significant effect of the dominant "representations" of western feminism is its conflation with imperialism in the eyes of particular third-world women.[5] Hence the urgent need to examine the *political* implications of our *analytic* strategies and principles.

My critique is directed at three basic analytical presuppositions which are present in (western) feminist discourse on women in the third world. Since I focus primarily on the Zed Press "Women in the Third World" series, my comments on western feminist discourse are circumscribed by my analysis of the texts in this series.[6] This is a way of focusing my critique. However, even though I am dealing with feminists who identify themselves as culturally or geographically from the "west," as mentioned earlier, what I say about these presuppositions or implicit principles holds for anyone who uses these analytical strategies, whether third-world women in the west, or third-world women in the third world writing on these issues and publishing in the west. Thus, I am not making a culturalist argument about ethnocentrism; rather, I am trying to uncover how ethnocentric universalism is produced in certain analyses. As a matter of fact, my argument holds for any discourse that sets up its own authorial subjects as the implicit referent, i.e., the yardstick by which to encode and represent cultural Others. It is in this move that power is exercised in discourse.

The first analytical presupposition I focus on is involved in the strategic location or situation of the category "women" vis-à-vis the context of analysis. The assumption of women as an already constituted and coherent group with identical interests and desires, regardless of class, ethnic or racial location, implies a notion of gender or sexual difference or even patriarchy which can be applied universally and cross-culturally. (The context of analysis can be anything from kinship structures and the organization of labour to media representations.) The second analytical presupposition is evident on the methodological level, in the uncritical way "proof" of universality and cross-cultural validity are provided. The third is a more specifically political presupposition, underlying the methodologies and the analytic strategies, i.e., the model of power and struggle they imply and suggest. I argue that as a result of the two modes—or, rather, frames—of analysis described earlier, a homogeneous notion of the oppression of women as a group is assumed, which, in turn, produces the image of an "average third-world woman." This average third-world woman leads an essentially truncated life based on her feminine gender (read: sexually constrained) and being "third world" (read: ignorant, poor, uneducated, tradition-bound, religious, domesticated, family-oriented, victimized, etc.). This, I suggest, is in contrast to the (implicit) self-representation of western women as educated, modern, as having control over their own bodies and sexualities, and the "freedom" to make their own decisions. The distinction between western feminist re-presentation of women in the third world, and western feminist self-presentation is a distinction of the same order as that made by some Marxists between the "maintenance" function of the housewife and the real "productive" role of wage-labour, or the characterization by developmentalists of the third world as being engaged in the lesser production of "raw materials" in contrast to the "real" productive activity of the first world. These distinctions are made on the basis of the privileging of a particular group as the norm or referent. Men involved in wage-labour, first-world producers, and, I suggest, western feminists who sometimes cast third-world women in terms of "ourselves undressed" (Michelle Rosaldo's term; Rosaldo, 1980: 389–412, especially 392), all construct themselves as the normative referent in such a binary analytic.

"WOMEN" AS CATEGORY OF ANALYSIS, OR: WE ARE ALL SISTERS IN STRUGGLE

By women as a category of analysis, I am referring to the crucial presupposition that all of us of the same gender, across classes and cultures, are somehow socially constituted as a homogeneous group identifiable prior to the process of analysis. The homogeneity of women as a group is produced not on the basis of biological essentials, but rather on the basis of secondary sociological and anthropological universals. Thus, for instance, in any given piece of feminist analysis, women are characterized as a singular group on the basis of a shared oppression. What binds women together is a sociological notion of the "sameness" of their oppression It is at this point that an elision takes place between "women" as a discursively constructed group and "women" as material subjects of their own history.[7] Thus, the discursively consensual homogeneity of "women" as a group is mistaken for the historically specific material reality of groups of women. This results in an assumption of women as an always-already constituted group, one which has been labelled "powerless," "exploited," "sexually harassed," etc., by feminist scientific, economic, legal and sociological discourses. (Notice that this is quite similar to sexist discourse labelling women as weak, emotional, having math anxiety, etc.) The focus is not on uncovering the material and ideological specificities that constitute a group of women as "powerless" in a particular context. It is rather on finding a variety of cases of "powerless" groups of women to prove the general point that women as a group are powerless.[8]

In this section I focus on five specific ways in which "women" as a category of analysis is used in western feminist discourse on women in the third world to construct "third-world women" as a homogeneous "powerless" group often located as implicit *victims* of particular cultural and socio-economic systems. I have chosen to deal with a variety of writers—from Fran Hosken, who writes primarily about female genital mutilation, to writers from the Women in International Development school who write about the effect of development policies on third-world women for both western and third-world audiences. I do not intend to equate all the texts that I analyse, nor ignore their respective strengths and weaknesses. The authors I deal with write with varying degrees of care and complexity; however, the *effect* of the representation of third-world women in these texts is a coherent one. In these texts women are variously defined as victims of male violence (Fran Hosken); victims of the colonial process (M. Cutrufelli); victims of the Arab familial system (Juliette Minces); victims of the economic development process (B. Lindsay and the—liberal—WID school); and finally, victims of the economic basis of *the* Islamic code (P. Jeffery). This mode of defining women primarily in terms of their *object status* (the way in which they are affected or not affected by certain institutions and systems) is what characterizes this particular form of the use of "women" as a category of analysis. In the context of western women writing about and studying women in the third world, such objectification (however benevolently motivated) needs to be both named and challenged. As Valerie Amos and Pratibha Parmar argue quite eloquently, "Feminist theories which examine our cultural practices as 'feudal residues' or label us 'traditional' also portray us as politically immature women who need to be versed and schooled in the ethos of western feminism. They need to be continually challenged" (1984: 7).

WOMEN AS VICTIMS OF MALE VIOLENCE

Fran Hosken, in writing about the relationship between human rights and female genital mutilation in Africa and the Middle East, bases her whole discussion and condemnation of genital mutilation on one privileged premise: the goal of genital mutilation is "to mutilate the sexual pleasure and satisfaction of woman" (1981: 3–24, especially 11).[9] This, in turn, leads her to claim that woman's sexuality is controlled, as is her reproductive potential.

According to Hosken, "male sexual politics" in Africa and around the world "share the same political goal: to assure female dependence and subservience by any and all means." Physical violence against women (rape, sexual assault, excision, infibulation, etc.) is thus carried out "with an astonishing consensus among men in the world" (14). Here, women are defined systematically as the *victims* of male control—the "sexually oppressed." Although it is true that the potential of male violence against women circumscribes and elucidates their social position to a certain extent, defining women as archetypal victims freezes them into "objects-who-defend-themselves," men into "subjects-who-perpetrate-violence," and (every) society into a simple opposition between the powerless (read: women) and the powerful (read: men) groups of people. Male violence (if that indeed is the appropriate label) must be theorized and interpreted *within* specific societies, both in order to understand it better, as well as in order to effectively organize to change it.[10] Sisterhood cannot be assumed on the basis of gender; it must be forged in concrete historical and political praxis.

WOMEN AS UNIVERSAL DEPENDANTS

Beverley Lindsay's conclusion to the book, *Comparative Perspectives on Third World Women: The Impact of Race, Class and Sex* states: "Dependency relationships, based upon race, sex and class, are being perpetuated through social, educational, and economic institutions. These are the linkages among Third World Women" (1983: especially 298, 306). Here, as in other places, Lindsay implies that third-world women constitute an identifiable group purely on the basis of shared dependencies. If shared dependencies were all that was needed to bind us together as a group, third-world women would always be seen as an apolitical group with no subject status! Instead, if anything, it is the *common context* of political struggle against class, race, gender and imperialist hierarchies that may constitute third-world women as a strategic group at this historical juncture. Lindsay also states that linguistic and cultural differences exist between Vietnamese and Black American women, but "both groups are victims of race, sex and class." Again, Black and Vietnamese women are characterized and defined simply in terms of their victim status.

Similarly, examine statements like: "My analysis will start by stating that all African women are politically and economically dependent" (Cutrufelli, 1983: especially 13). Or: "Nevertheless, either overtly or covertly, prostitution is still the main if not the only source of work for African women" (Cutrufelli, 1983: 33). *All* African women are dependent. Prostitution is the only work option for African women as a *group*. Both statements are illustrative of generalizations sprinkled liberally through a recent Zed Press publication, *Women of Africa: Roots of Oppression*, by Maria Rosa Cutrufelli, who is described on the cover as an "Italian Writer, Sociologist, Marxist and Feminist." In the 1980s is it possible to imagine writing a book entitled "Women of Europe: Roots of Oppression"? I am not objecting to the use of universal groupings for descriptive purposes. Women from the continent of Africa can be descriptively characterized as "Women of Africa." It is when "women of Africa" becomes a homogeneous sociological grouping characterized by common dependencies or powerlessness (or even strengths) that problems arise—we say too little and too much at the same time.

This is because descriptive gender differences are transformed into the division between men and women. Women are constituted as a group via dependency relationships vis-à-vis men, who are implicitly held responsible for these relationships. When "women of Africa" (versus "men of Africa" as a group?) are seen as a group precisely because they are generally dependent and oppressed, the analysis of specific historical differences becomes impossible, because reality is always apparently structured by divisions between two mutually exclusive and jointly exhaustive groups, the victims and the oppressors. Here the sociological is substituted for the biological in order, however, to create the same—a unity of women. Thus, it is not the descriptive potential of gender difference but the privileged positioning and explanatory potential of gender difference as the *origin* of oppression that I question. In using "women of Africa" (as an already constituted group of oppressed peoples) as a category of analysis, Cutrufelli denies any historical specificity to the location of women as subordinate, powerful, marginal, central, or otherwise, vis-à-vis particular social and power networks. Women are taken as a unified "powerless" group prior to the historical and political analysis in question. Thus, it is then merely a matter of specifying the context *after the fact*. "Women" are now placed in the context of the family, or in the workplace, or within religious networks, almost as if these systems existed outside the relations of women with other women, and women with men.

The problem with this analytical strategy is, let me repeat, that it assumes men and women are already constituted as sexual–political subjects prior to their entry into the arena of social relations. Only if we subscribe to this assumption is it possible to undertake analysis which looks at the "effects" of kinship structures, colonialism, organization of labour, etc., on women, who are defined in advance as a group. The crucial point that is forgotten is that women are produced through these very relations as well as being implicated in forming these relations. As Michelle Rosaldo argues, "woman's place in human social life is not in any direct sense a product of the things she does (or even less, a function of what, biologically, she is) but the meaning her activities acquire through concrete social interactions" (1980: 400). That women mother in a variety of societies is not as significant as the value attached to mothering in these societies. The distinction between the act of mothering and the status attached to it is a very important one—one that needs to be stated and analysed contextually.

MARRIED WOMEN AS VICTIMS OF THE COLONIAL PROCESS

In Levi-Strauss's theory of kinship structures as a system of the exchange of women, what is significant is that exchange itself is not constitutive of the subordination of women; women are not subordinate because of the *fact* of exchange, but because of the *modes* of exchange instituted, and the values attached to these modes. However, in discussing the marriage ritual of the Bemba, a Zambian matrilocal, matrilineal people, Cutrufelli in *Women of Africa* focuses on the fact of the marital exchange of women before and after western colonization, rather than the value attached to this exchange in this particular context. This leads to her definition of Bemba women as a coherent group affected in a particular way by colonization. Here again, Bemba women are constituted rather unilaterally as the victims of western colonization. Cutrufelli cites the marriage ritual of the Bemba as a multi-stage event "whereby a young man becomes incorporated into his wife's family group as he takes up residence with them and gives his services in return for food and maintenance" (1983: 43). This ritual extends over many years, and the sexual relationship varies according to the degree of the girl's physical maturity. It is only after the girl undergoes an initiation ceremony at puberty that intercourse is sanctioned, and the man acquires legal rights over the woman. This initiation ceremony is the most important act of the consecration of women's reproductive power, so that the abduction of an uninitiated girl is of no consequence, while heavy penalty is levied for the seduction of an initiated girl. Cutrufelli asserts that the effect of European colonization has changed the whole marriage system. Now the young man is entitled to take his wife away from her people in return for money. The implication is that Bemba women have now lost the protection of tribal laws. However, while it is possible to see how the structure of the traditional marriage contract (as opposed to the post-colonial marriage contract) offered women a certain amount of control over their marital relations, only an analysis of the political significance of the actual practice which privileges an initiated girl over an uninitiated one, indicating a shift in female power relations as a result of this ceremony, can provide an accurate account of whether Bemba women were indeed protected by tribal laws *at all times.*

However, it is not possible to talk about Bemba women as a homogeneous group within the traditional marriage structure. Bemba women *before* the initiation are constituted within a different set of social relations compared to Bemba women *after* the initiation. To treat them as a unified group, characterized by the fact of their "exchange" between male kin, is to deny the specificities of their daily existence, and the differential *value* attached to their exchange before and after their initiation. It is to treat the initiation ceremony as a ritual with no political implications or effects. It is also to assume that in merely describing the *structure* of the marriage contract, the situation of women is exposed. Women as a group are positioned within a given structure, but there is no attempt made to trace the effect of the marriage practice in constituting women within an obviously changing network of power relations. Thus, women are assumed to be sexual-political subjects prior to entry into kinship structures.

WOMEN AND FAMILIAL SYSTEMS

Elizabeth Cowie, in another context (1978: 49–63), points out the implications of this sort of analysis when she emphasizes the specifically political nature of kinship structures which must be analysed as ideological practices which designate men and women as father, husband, wife, mother, sister, etc. Thus, Cowie suggests, women as women are not simply *located* within the family. Rather, it is in the family, as an effect of kinship structures, that women as women are *constructed*, defined within and by the group. Thus, for instance, when Juliette Minces (1980: especially 23) cites *the* patriarchal family as the basis for "an almost identical vision of women" that Arab and Muslim societies have, she falls into this very trap. Not only is it problematical to speak of a vision of women shared by Arab and Muslim societies, without addressing the particular historical and ideological power structures that construct such images, but to speak of the patriarchal family or the tribal kinship structure as the origin of the socio-economic status of women is again to assume that women are sexual-political subjects prior to their entry into the family. So while on the one hand women attain value or status within the family, the assumption of a singular patriarchal kinship system (common to all Arab and Muslim societies, i.e., over twenty different countries) is what apparently structures women as an oppressed group in these societies! This singular, coherent kinship system presumably influences another separate and given entity, "women." Thus all women, regardless of class and cultural differences, are seen as being similarly affected by this system. Not only are *all* Arab and Muslim women seen to constitute a homogeneous oppressed group, but there is no discussion of the specific *practices* within the family which constitute women as mothers, wives, sisters, etc. Arabs and Muslims, it appears, don't change at all. Their patriarchal family is carried over from the times of the Prophet Muhammad. They exist, as it were, outside history.

WOMEN AND RELIGIOUS IDEOLOGIES

A further example of the use of "women" as a category of analysis is found in cross-cultural analyses which subscribe to a certain economic reductionism in describing the relationship between the economy and factors such as politics and ideology. Here, in reducing the level of comparison to the economic relations between "developed" and "developing" countries, the question of women is denied any specificity. Mina Modares, in a careful analysis of women and Shi'ism in Iran, focuses on this very problem when she criticizes feminist writings which treat Islam as an ideology separate from and outside social relations and practices, rather than a discourse which includes rules for economic, social and power relations within society (Modares, 1981: 62–82). Patricia Jeffery's otherwise informative work on Pirzada women in purdah (1979) considers Islamic ideology as a partial explanation for the status of women in that it provides a justification for the purdah. Here, Islamic ideology is reduced to a set of ideas whose internalization by Pirzada women contributes to the stability of the system. The primary explanation for purdah is located in the control that Pirzada men have over economic resources, and the personal security purdah gives to Pirzada women. By taking a specific version of Islam as *the* Islam, Jeffery attributes a singularity and coherence to it. Modares notes, "'Islamic Theology' then becomes imposed on a separate and given entity called 'women.' A further unification is reached: Women (meaning *all women*), regardless of their differing positions within societies, come to be affected or not affected by Islam. These conceptions provide the right ingredients for an unproblematic possibility of a cross-cultural study of women" (1981: 63). Marnia Lazreg makes a similar argument when she addresses the reductionism inherent in scholarship on women in the Middle East and North Africa:

> A ritual is established whereby the writer appeals to religion as *the* cause of gender inequality just as it is made the source of underdevelopment in much of modernization theory. In an uncanny way, feminist discourse on women from the Middle East and North Africa mirrors that of theologians' own interpretation of women in Islam....

> The overall effect of this paradigm is to deprive women of self-presence, of being. Because women are subsumed under religion presented in fundamental terms, they are inevitably seen as evolving in nonhistorical time. They have virtually no history. Any analysis of change is therefore foreclosed. (Lazreg, 1988: 87)

While Jeffery's analysis does not quite succumb to this kind of unitary notion of religion (Islam), it does collapse all ideological specificities into economic relations, and universalizes on the basis of this comparison.

WOMEN AND THE DEVELOPMENT PROCESS

The best examples of universalization on the basis of economic reductionism can be found in the liberal "Women in Development" literature. Proponents of this school seek to examine the effect of development on third-world women, sometimes from self-designated feminist perspectives. At the very least, there is an evident interest in and commitment to improving the lives of women in "developing" countries. Scholars like Irene Tinker, Ester Boserup, and Perdita Huston[11] have all written about the effect of development policies on women in the third world. All three women assume that "development" is synonymous with "economic development" or "economic progress." As in the case of Minces' patriarchal family, Hosken's male sexual control, and Cutrufelli's western colonization, "development" here becomes the all-time equalizer. Women are seen as being affected positively or negatively by economic development policies, and this is the basis for cross-cultural comparison.

For instance, Perdita Huston states that the purpose of her study is to describe the effect of the development process on the "family unit and its individual members" in Egypt, Kenya, Sudan, Tunisia, Sri Lanka and Mexico. She states that the "problems" and "needs" expressed by rural and urban women in these countries all centre around education and training, work and wages, access to health and other services, political participation and legal rights. Huston relates all these "needs" to the lack of sensitive development policies which exclude women as a group. For her, the solution is simple: improved development policies which emphasize training for women field-workers, use women trainees and women rural development officers, encourage women's cooperatives, etc. Here, again women are assumed to be a coherent group or category prior to their entry into "the development process." Huston assumes that all third-world women have similar problems and needs. Thus, they must have similar interests and goals. However, the interests of urban, middle-class, educated Egyptian housewives, to take only one instance, could surely not be seen as being the same as those of their uneducated, poor maids. Development policies do not affect both groups of women in the same way. Practices which characterize women's status and roles vary according to class. Women are constituted as women through the complex interaction between class, culture, religion and other ideological institutions and frameworks. They are not "women"—a coherent group—solely on the basis of a particular economic system or policy. Such reductive cross-cultural comparisons result in the colonization of the specifics of daily existence and the complexities of political interests which women of different social classes and cultures represent and mobilize.

Thus it is revealing that for Perdita Huston women in the third-world countries she writes about have "needs" and "problems," but few if any have "choices" or the freedom to act. This is an interesting representation of women in the third world, one which is significant in suggesting a latent self-presentation of western women which bears looking at. She writes, "What surprised and moved me most as I listened to women in such very different cultural settings was the striking commonality—whether they were educated or illiterate, urban or rural—of their most basic values: the importance they assign to family, dignity, and service to others" (Huston, 1979: 115). Would Huston consider such values unusual for women in the west?

What is problematical, then, about this kind of use of "women" as a group, as a stable category of analysis, is that it assumes an ahistorical, universal unity among women based on a generalized notion of their subordination. Instead of analytically *demonstrating* the production of women as socio-economic political groups within particular local contexts, this analytical move—and the presuppositions it is based on—limits the definition of the female subject to gender identity, completely bypassing social class and ethnic identities. What characterizes women as a group is their gender (sociologically not necessarily biologically defined) over and above everything else, indicating a monolithic notion of sexual difference. Because women are thus constituted as a coherent group, sexual difference becomes coterminus with female subordination, and power is automatically defined in binary terms: people who have it (read: men), and people who do not (read: women). Men exploit, women are exploited. Such simplistic formulations are both historically reductive; they are also ineffectual in designing strategies to combat oppressions. All they do is reinforce binary divisions between men and women.

What would an analysis which did not do this look like? Maria Mies's work is one such example. It is an example which illustrates the strength of western feminist work on women in the third world and which does not fall into the traps just discussed. Maria Mies's study of the lace-makers of Narsapur, India (1982), attempts to analyse carefully a substantial household industry in which "housewives" produce lace doilies for consumption in the world market. Through a detailed analysis of the structure of the lace industry, production and reproduction relations, the sexual division of labour, profits and exploitation, and the overall consequences of defining women as "non-working housewives" and their work as "leisure-time activity," Mies demonstrates the levels of exploitation in this industry and the impact of this production system on the work and living conditions of the women involved in it. In addition, she is able to analyse the "ideology of the housewife," the notion of a woman sitting in the house, as providing the necessary subjective and socio-cultural element for the creation and maintenance of a production system that contributes to the increasing pauperization of women, and keeps them totally atomized and disorganized as workers. Mies's analyses show the effect of a certain historically and culturally specific mode of patriarchal organization, an organization constructed on the basis of the definition of the lace-makers as "non-working housewives" at familial, local, regional, statewide and international levels. The intricacies and the effects of particular power networks are not only emphasized; they also form the basis of Mies's analysis of how this particular group of women is situated at the centre of a hegemonic, exploitative world market.

This is a good example of what careful, politically focused, local analyses can accomplish. It illustrates how the category of woman is constructed in a variety of political contexts that often exist simultaneously and overlaid on top of one another. There is no easy generalization in the direction of "women" in India, or "women in the third world"; nor is there a reduction of the political construction of the exploitation of the lace-makers to cultural explanations about the passivity or obedience that might characterize these women and their situation. Finally, this mode of local political analysis which generates theoretical categories from within the situation and context being analysed, also suggests corresponding effective strategies for organizing against the exploitations faced by the lace-makers.

Here Narsapur women are not mere victims of the production process, because they resist, challenge, and subvert the process at various junctures. This is one instance of how Mies delineates the connections between the housewife ideology, the self-consciousness of the lace-makers and their inter-relationships as contributing to the latent resistances she perceives among the women:

> The persistence of the housewife ideology, the self-perception of the lace makers as petty commodity producers rather than as workers, is not only upheld by the structure of the industry as such but also by the deliberate propagation and reinforcement of reactionary patriarchal norms and institutions. Thus, most of the lace makers voiced the same opinion about the rules of *purdah* and seclusion in their communities which were also propagated by the lace exporters. In particular, the *Kapu* women said that they had never gone out of their houses, that women of their community could not do any other work than housework and lace work etc. but in spite of the fact that most of them still subscribed fully to the patriarchal norms of the *gosha* women, there were also contradictory elements in their consciousness. Thus, although they looked down with contempt upon women who were able to work outside the house—like the untouchable *Mala* and *Madiga* women or women of other lower castes, they could not ignore the fact that these women were earning more money precisely because they were *not* respectable housewives but workers. At one discussion, they even admitted that it would be better if they could also go out and do coolie work. And when they were asked whether they would be ready to come out of their houses and work in one place in some sort of a factory, they said they would do that. This shows that the *purdah* and housewife ideology, although still fully internalized, already had some cracks, because it has been confronted with several contradictory realities. (Mies, 1982: 157)

It is only by understanding the *contradictions* inherent in women's location within various structures that effective political action and challenges can be devised. Mies's study goes a long way towards offering such an analysis. While there are now an increasing number of western feminist writings in this tradition,[12] there is also unfortunately a large block of writing which succumbs to the cultural reductionism discussed earlier.

METHODOLOGICAL UNIVERSALISMS, OR: WOMEN'S OPPRESSION IS A GLOBAL PHENOMENON

Western feminist writings on women in the third world subscribe to a variety of methodologies to demonstrate the universal cross-cultural operation of male dominance and female exploitation. I summarize and critique three such methods below, moving from the most simple to the most complex methodologies.

First, proof of universalism is provided through the use of an arithmetic method. The argument goes like this: the more the number of women who wear the veil, the more universal is the sexual segregation and control of women (Deardon, 1975: 4–5). Similarly, a large number of different, fragmented examples from a variety of countries also apparently add up to a universal fact. For instance, Muslim women in Saudi Arabia, Iran, Pakistan, India and Egypt all wear some sort of a veil. Hence, this indicates that the sexual control of women is a universal fact in those countries in which the women are veiled (Deardon, 1975:

7, 10). Fran Hosken writes: "Rape, forced prostitution, polygamy, genital mutilation, pornography, the beating of girls and women, purdah (segregation of women) are all violations of basic human rights" (1981: 15). By equating purdah with rape, domestic violence, and forced prostitution, Hosken asserts its "sexual control" function as the primary explanation for purdah, whatever the context. Institutions of purdah are thus denied any cultural and historical specificity and contradictions and potentially subversive aspects are totally ruled out. In both these examples, the problem is not in asserting that the practice of wearing a veil is widespread. This assertion can be made on the basis of numbers. It is a descriptive generalization. However, it is the analytic leap from the practice of veiling to an assertion of its general significance in controlling women that must be questioned. While there may be a physical similarity in the veils worn by women in Saudi Arabia and Iran, the specific meaning attached to this practice varies according to the cultural and ideological context. In addition, the symbolic space occupied by the practice of purdah may be similar in certain contexts, but this does not automatically indicate that the practices themselves have identical significance in the social realm. For example, as is well known, Iranian middle-class women veiled themselves during the 1979 revolution to indicate solidarity with their veiled working-class sisters, while in contemporary Iran mandatory Islamic laws dictate that all Iranian women wear veils. While in both these instances similar reasons might be offered for the veil (opposition to the Shah and western cultural colonization in the first case, and the true Islamicization of Iran in the second), the concrete *meanings* attached to Iranian women wearing the veil are clearly different in the two historical contexts. In the first case, wearing the veil is both an oppositional and revolutionary gesture on the part of Iranian middle-class women; in the second case it is a coercive, institutional mandate.[13] It is on the basis of such context-specific differentiated analysis that effective political strategies can be generated. To assume that the mere practice of veiling women in a number of Muslim countries indicates the universal oppression of women through sexual segregation is not only analytically reductive, but also proves to be quite useless when it comes to the elaboration of oppositional political strategy.

Second, concepts like reproduction, the sexual division of labour, the family, marriage, household, patriarchy, etc., are often used without their specification in local cultural and historical contexts. These concepts are used by feminists in providing explanations for women's subordination, apparently assuming their universal applicability. For instance, how is it possible to refer to "the" sexual division of labour when the *content* of this division changes radically from one environment to the next, and from one historical juncture to another? At its most abstract level, it is the fact of the differential assignation of tasks according to sex that is significant; however, this is quite different from the *meaning* or *value* that the content of this sexual division of labour assumes in different contexts. In most cases the assigning of tasks on the basis of sex has an ideological origin. There is no question that a claim such as "women are concentrated in service-oriented occupations in a large number of countries around the world" is descriptively valid. Descriptively, then, perhaps the existence of a similar sexual division of labour (where women work in service occupations like nursing, social work, etc., and men in other kinds of occupations) in a number of different countries can be asserted. However, the concept of the "sexual division of labour" is more than just a descriptive category. It indicates the differential *value* placed on "men's work" versus "women's work."

Often the mere existence of a sexual division of labour is taken to be proof of the oppression of women in various societies. This results from a confusion between and collapsing together of the descriptive and explanatory potential of the concept of the sexual division of labour. Superficially similar situations may have radically different, historically specific explanations, and cannot be treated as identical. For instance, the rise of female-headed households in middle-class America might be construed as indicating women's independence and progress, whereby women are considered to have *chosen* to be single parents, there are increasing numbers of lesbian mothers, etc. However, the recent increase in female-headed households in Latin America,[14] where women might be seen to have more decision-making power, is concentrated among the poorest strata, where life choices are the most constrained economically. A similar argument can be made for the rise of female-headed families among Black and Chicana women in the US. The positive correlation between this and the level of poverty among women of colour and white working-class women in the US has now even acquired a name: the feminization of poverty. Thus, while it is possible to state that there is a rise in female-headed households in the US and in Latin America, this rise cannot be discussed as a universal indicator of women's independence, nor can it be discussed as a universal indicator of women's impoverishment. The *meaning* and *explanation* for the rise must obviously be specified according to the socio-historical context.

Similarly, the existence of a sexual division of labour in most contexts cannot be sufficient explanation for the universal subjugation of women in the workforce. That the sexual division of labour does indicate a devaluation of women's work must be shown through analysis of particular local contexts. In addition, devaluation of *women* must also be shown through careful analysis. In other words, the "sexual division of labour" and "women" are not commensurate analytical categories. Concepts like the sexual division of labour can be useful only if they are generated through local, contextual analyses.[15] If such concepts are assumed to be universally applicable, the resultant homogenization of class, race, religious, and daily material practices of women in the third world can create a false sense of the commonality of oppressions, interests and struggles between and amongst women globally. Beyond sisterhood there is still racism, colonialism and imperialism!

Finally, some writers confuse the use of gender as a superordinate category of organizing analysis with the universalistic proof and instantiation of this category. In other words, empirical studies of gender differences are confused with the analytical organization of cross-cultural work. Beverley Brown's review (1983) of the book *Nature, Culture and Gender* (1980) best illustrates this point. Brown suggests that nature:culture and female:male are superordinate categories which organize and locate lesser categories (like wild/domestic and biology/technology) within their logic. These categories are universal in the sense that they organize the universe of a system of representations. This relation is totally independent of the universal substantiation of any particular category. Her critique hinges on the fact that rather than clarify the generalizability of nature:culture::female:male as superordinate organizational categories, *Nature, Culture and Gender,* the book, construes the universality of this equation to lie at the level of empirical truth, which can be investigated through field-work. Thus, the usefulness of the nature:culture::female:male paradigm as a universal mode of the organization of representation within any particular socio-historical system is lost. Here, methodological universalism is assumed on the basis of the reduction of the nature:culture::female:male analytic categories to a demand for empirical proof of its existence in different cultures. Discourses of representation are confused with material realities, and the distinction between "Woman" and "women" is lost. Feminist work on women in the third world which blurs this distinction (a distinction which interestingly enough is often present in certain western feminists' self-representation) eventually ends up constructing monolithic images of "Third World Women" by ignoring the complex and mobile relationships between their historical materiality on the level of specific oppressions and political choices on the one hand and their general discursive representations on the other.

To summarize: I have discussed three methodological moves identifiable in feminist (and other academic) cross-cultural work which seeks to uncover a universality in women's subordinate position in society. The next and final section pulls together the previous sections attempting to outline the political effects of the analytical strategies in the context of western feminist writing on women in the third world. These arguments are not against generalization as much as they are for careful historically specific generalizations responsive to complex realities. Nor do these arguments deny the necessity of forming strategic political identities and affinities. Thus, while Indian women of different backgrounds might forge a political unity on the basis of organizing against police brutality towards women,[16] an *analysis* of police brutality must be contextual. Strategic coalitions which construct oppositional political identities for themselves are based on generalization and provisional unities, but the analysis of these group identities cannot be based on universalistic, ahistorical categories.

THE SUBJECT(S) OF POWER

This last section returns to an earlier point about the inherently political nature of feminist scholarship, and attempts to clarify my point about the possibility of detecting a colonialist move in the case of a structurally unequal first/third-world relation in scholarship. The nine texts in the Zed Press "Women in the Third World" series that I have discussed[17] focused on the following common areas in discussing women's "status" within various societies: religion, family/kinship structures, the legal system, the sexual division of labour, education and, finally, political resistance. A large number of western feminist writings on women in the third world focus on these themes. Of course, the Zed texts have varying emphases. For instance, two of the studies, *Women of Palestine* (1982) and *Indian Women in Struggle* (1980), focus explicitly on female militancy and political involvement, while *Women in Arab Society* (1980) deals with Arab women's legal, religious and familial status. In addition, each text evidences a variety of methodologies and degrees of care in making generalizations. Interestingly enough, however, almost all the texts assume "women" as a category of analysis in the manner designated earlier. Clearly this is an analytical strategy which is neither limited to these Zed Press publications, nor symptomatic of Zed Press publications in general. However, in the particular texts under question, each text assumes "women" have a coherent group identity within the different cultures discussed, prior to their entry into social relations. Thus, Omvedt can talk about "Indian Women" while referring to a particular group of women in the State of Maharashtra, Cutrufelli about "Women of Africa" and Minces about "Arab Women" as if these groups of women have some sort of obvious cultural coherence, distinct from men in these societies. The "status" or "position" of women is assumed to be self-evident because women as an already constituted group are *placed* within religious, economic, familial and legal structures. However, this focus on the position of women whereby women are seen as a coherent group across contexts, regardless of class or ethnicity, structures the world in ultimately binary, dichotomous terms, where women are always seen in opposition to men, patriarchy is always necessarily male dominance, and the religious, legal, economic and familial systems are implicitly assumed to be constructed by men. Thus, both men and women are always seen as preconstituted whole populations, and relations of dominace and exploitation are also posited in terms of whole peoples—wholes coming into exploitative relations. It is only when men and women are seen as different categories or groups possessing different *already constituted* categories of experience, cognition and interests as *groups* that such a simplistic dichotomy is possible.

What does this imply about the structure and functioning of power relations? The setting up of the commonality of third-world women's struggles across classes and cultures against a general notion of oppression (primarily the group in power—i,e., men) necessitates the assumption of something like what Michel Foucault calls the "juridico-discursive" model of power (1980: 134–45), the principal features of which are: "a negative relation" (limit and lack); an "insistence on the rule" (which forms a binary system); a "cycle of prohibition"; the "logic of censorship"; and a "uniformity" of the apparatus functioning at different levels. Feminist discourse on the third world which assumes a homogeneous category—or group—called "women" necessarily operates through such a setting up of *originary* power divisions. Power relations are structured in terms of a unilateral and undifferentiated source of power and a cumulative reaction to power. Opposition is a generalized phenomenon created as a response to power—which, in turn, is possessed by certain groups of people. The major problem with such a definition of power is that it locks all revolutionary struggles into binary structures—possessing power versus being powerless. Women are powerless, unified groups. If the struggle for a just society is seen in terms of the move from powerless to powerful for women as a *group*, and this is the implication in feminist discourse which structures sexual difference in terms of the division between the sexes, then the new society would be structurally identical to the existing organization of power relations, constituting itself as a simple *inversion* of what exists. If relations of domination and exploitation are defined in terms of binary divisions—groups which dominate and groups which are dominated—surely the implication is that the accession to power of women as a group is sufficient to dismantle the existing organization of relations? But women as a group are not in some sense essentially superior or infallible. The crux of the problem lies in that initial assumption of women as a homogeneous group or category ("the oppressed"), a familiar assumption in western radical and liberal feminisms.[18]

What happens when this assumption of "women as a oppressed group" is situated in the context of western feminist writing about third-world women? It is here that I locate the colonialist move. By contrasting the representation of women in the third world with what I referred to earlier as western feminisms' self-presentation in the same context, we see how western feminists alone become the true "subjects" of this counter-history. Third-world women, on the other hand, never rise above the debilitating generality of their "object" status.

While radical and liberal feminist assumptions of women as a sex class might elucidate (however inadequately) the autonomy of particular women's struggles in the west, the application of the notion of women as a homogeneous category to women in the third world colonizes and appropriates the pluralities of the simultaneous location of different groups of women in social class and ethnic frameworks; in doing so it ultimately robs them of their historical and political *agency*. Similarly, many Zed Press authors, who ground themselves in the basic analytic strategies of traditional Marxism, also implicitly create a "unity" of women by substituting "women's activity" for "labour" as the primary theoretical determinant of women's situation. Here again, women are constituted as a coherent group not on the basis of "natural" qualities or needs, but on the basis of the sociological "unity" of their role in domestic production and wage labour.[19] In other words, western feminist discourse, by assuming women as a coherent, already constituted group which is placed in kinship, legal and other structures, defines third-world women as subjects *outside* of social relations, instead of looking at the way women are constituted as women *through* these very structures. Legal, economic, religious and familial structures are treated as phenomena to be judged by western standards. It is here that ethnocentric universality comes into play. When these structures are defined as "underdeveloped" or "developing" and women are placed within these structures, an implicit image of the "average third-world woman" is produced. This is the transformation of the (implicitly western) "oppressed woman" into the "oppressed third-world woman." While the category of "oppressed woman" is generated through an exclusive focus on gender difference "the oppressed third-world woman" category has an additional attribute—the "third-world difference"! The "third-world difference" includes a paternalistic attitude towards women in the third world. Since discussions of the various themes I identified earlier (e.g., kinship, education, religion, etc.) are conducted in the context of the relative "underdevelopment" of the third world (which is nothing less than unjustifiably confusing development with the separate path taken by the west in its development, as well as ignoring the unidirectionality of the first/third-world power relationship), third-world women as a group or category are automatically and necessarily defined as: religious (read "not progressive"), family oriented (read "traditional"), legal minors (read "they-are-still-not-conscious-of-their-rights"), illiterate (read "ignorant"), domestic (read "backward") and sometimes revolutionary (read "their-country-is-in-a-state-of-war; they-must-fight!"). This is how the "third-world difference" is produced.

When the category of "sexually oppressed women" is located within particular systems in the third world which are defined on a scale which is normed through Eurocentric assumptions, not only are third-world women defined in a particular way prior to their entry into social relations, but since no connections are made between first- and third-world power shifts, it reinforces the assumption that people in the third world just have not evolved to the extent that the west has. This mode of feminist analysis, by homogenizing and systematizing the experiences of different groups of women, erases all marginal and resistant modes of experiences.[21] It is significant that none of the texts I reviewed in the Zed Press series focuses on lesbian politics or the politics of ethnic and religious marginal organizations in third-world women's groups. Resistance can thus only be defined as cumulatively reactive, not as something inherent in the operation of power. If power, as Michel Foucault has argued recently, can really be understood only in the context of resistance,[22] this misconceptualization of power is both analytically as well as strategically problematical. It limits theoretical analysis as well as reinforcing western cultural imperialism. For in the context of a first/third-world balance of power, feminist analyses which perpetuate and sustain the hegemony of the idea of the superiority of the west produce a corresponding set of universal images of the "third-world woman," images like the veiled woman, the powerful mother, the chaste virgin, the obedient wife, etc. These images exist in universal ahistorical splendour, setting in motion a colonialist discourse which exercises a very specific power in defining, coding and maintaining existing first/third-world connections.

To conclude, then, let me suggest some disconcerting similarities between the typically authorizing signature of such western feminist writings on women in the third world, and the authorizing signature of the project of humanism in general—humanism as a western ideological and political project which involves the necessary recuperation of the "East" and "Woman" as Others. Many contemporary thinkers like Foucault, Derrida, Kristeva, Deleuze, and Said have written at length about the underlying anthropomorphism and ethnocentrism which constitutes a hegemonic humanistic problematic that repeatedly confirms and legitimates (western) Man's centrality.[23] Feminist theorists like Luce Irigaray, Sarah Kofman, Hélène Cixous, and others have also written about the recuperation and absence of woman/women within western humanism.[24] The focus of the work of all these thinkers can be stated simply as an uncovering of the political *interests* that underlie the binary logic of humanistic discourse and ideology whereby, as a valuable recent essay puts it, "the first (majority) term (Identity, Universality, Culture, Disinterestedness, Truth, Sanity, Justice, etc.), which is, in fact, secondary and derivative (a construction), is privileged over and colonizes the second (minority) term (difference, temporality, anarchy, error, interestedness, insanity, deviance, etc.), which is in fact, primary and originative" (Spanos, 1984). In other words, it is only in so far as "Woman/Women" and "the East" are defined as *Others*, or as peripheral, that (western) Man/Humanism can represent him/itself as the centre. It is not the centre that determines the periphery, but the periphery that, in its boundedness, determines the centre.

Just as feminists like Kristeva, Cixous, Irigaray and others deconstruct the latent anthropomorphism in western discourse, I have suggested a parallel strategy in this article in uncovering a latent ethnocentrism in particular feminist writings on women in the third world.[25]

As discussed earlier, a comparison between western feminist self-presentation and western feminist re-presentation of women in the third world yields significant results. Universal images of "the third-world woman" (the veiled woman, chaste virgin, etc.), images constructed from adding the "third-world difference" to "sexual difference," are predicated on (and hence obviously bring into sharper focus) assumptions about western women as secular, liberated, and having control over their own lives. This is not to suggest that western women are secular and liberated and have control over their own lives. I am referring to a *discursive* self-presentation, not necessarily to material reality. If this were a material reality there would be no need for feminist political struggle in the west. Similarly, only from the vantage point of the west is it possible to define the "third world" as underdeveloped and economically dependent. Without the overdetermined discourse that creates the *third* world, there would be no (singular and privileged) first world. Without the "third-world woman," the particular self-presentation of western women mentioned above would be problematical. I am suggesting, in effect, that the one enables and sustains the other. This is not to say that the signature of western feminist writings on the third world has the same authority as the project of western humanism. However, in the context of the hegemony of the western scholarly establishment in the production and dissemination of texts, and in the context of the legitimating imperative of humanistic and scientific discourse, the definition of "the third-world woman" as a monolith might well tie into the larger economic and ideological praxis of "disinterested" scientific inquiry and pluralism which are the surface manifestations of a latent economic and cultural colonization of the "non-western" world. It is time to move beyond the ideological framework in which even Marx found it possible to say: They cannot represent themselves; they must be represented.

NOTES

1. See especially the essays in Moraga and Anzaldua (1983); Smith (1983); Joseph and Lewis (1981) and Moraga (1984).
2. Terms like "third" and "first" world are very problematical both in suggesting over-simplified similarities between and amongst countries labelled "third" or "first" world, as well as implicitly reinforcing existing economic, cultural, and ideological hierarchies. I use the term "third world" with full awareness of its problems, only because this is the terminology available to us at the moment. The use of quotation marks is meant to suggest a continuous questioning of the designation "third world." Even when I do not use quotation marks, I mean to use the term critically.
3. I am indebted to Teresa de Lauretis for this particular formulation of the project of feminist theorizing. See especially her introduction to de Lauretis (1984); see also Sylvia Wynter, "The Politics of Domination," unpublished manuscript.

4. This argument is similar to Homi Bhabha's (1983) definition of colonial discourse as strategically creating a space for a subject peoples through the production of knowledges and the exercise of power. The full quote reads: "[colonial discourse is] an apparatus of power...an apparatus that turns on the recognition and disavowal of racial/cultural/historical differences. Its predominant strategic function is the creation of a space for a 'subject peoples' through the production of knowledges in terms of which surveillance is exercised and a complex form of pleasure/unpleasure is incited. It [i.e., colonial discourse] seeks authorization for its strategies by the production of knowledges by colonizer and colonized which are stereotypical but antithetically evaluated."

5. A number of documents and reports on the UN International Conferences on Women, Mexico City 1975, and Copenhagen 1980, as well as the 1976 Wellesley Conference on Women and Development attest to this. Nawal el Saadawi, Fatima Mernissi and Mallica Vajarathon in "A Critical Look At The Wellesley Conference" (*Quest*, IV:2, Winter 1978, pp. 101–7), characterize this conference as "American-planned and organized," situating third world participants as passive audiences. They focus especially on the lack of self-consciousness of western women's implication in the effects of imperialism and racism in their assumption of an "international sisterhood." Amos and Parmar (1984) characterize Euro-American feminism which seeks to establish itself as the only legitimate feminism as "imperial."

6. The Zed Press "Women in the Third World" series is unique in its conception. I choose to focus on it because it is the only contemporary series of books I have found which assumes that "women in the Third World" is a legitimate and separate subject of study and research. Since 1985, when this essay was first written, numerous new titles have appeared in the Zed "Women in the Third World" series. Thus, I suspect that Zed has come to occupy a rather privileged position in the dissemination and construction of discourses by and about third-world women. A number of the books in this series are excellent, especially those which deal directly with women's resistance struggles. In addition, Zed Press consistently publishes progressive, feminist, anti-racist and anti-imperialist texts. However, a number of texts written by feminist sociologists, anthropologists, and journalists are symptomatic of the kind of western feminist work on women in the third world that concerns me. Thus, an analysis of a few of these particular texts in this series can serve as a representative point of entry into the discourse I am attempting to locate and define. My focus on these texts is therefore an attempt at an internal critique: I simply expect and demand more from this series. Needless to say, progressive publishing houses also carry their own authorizing signatures.

7. Elsewhere I have discussed this particular point in detail in a critique of Robin Morgan's construction of "women's herstory" in her introduction to *Sisterhood Is Global: The International Women's Movement Anthology* (1984) (see Mohanty) "Feminist Encounters" pp. 30–44, especially pp. 35–7.

8. My analysis in this section of the paper has been influenced by Felicity Eldhom, Olivia Harris and Kate Young's excellent discussions (Eldhom, Harris and Young, 1977). They examine the use of the concepts of "reproduction" and the "sexual division of labour" in anthropological work on women, suggesting the inevitable pull towards universals inherent in the use of these categories to determine "women's position."

9. Another example of this kind of analysis is Mary Daly's *Gyn/Ecology*. Daly's assumption in this text, that women as a group are sexually victimized, leads to her very problematic comparison between

the attitudes towards women witches and healers in the west, Chinese footbinding, and the genital mutilation of women in Africa. According to Daly, women in Europe, China, and Africa constitute a homogeneous group as victims of male power. Not only does this label (sexual victims) eradicate the specific historical realities which lead to and perpetuate practices like witch-hunting and genital mutilation, but it also obliterates the differences, complexities and heterogeneities of the lives of, for example, women of different classes, religions and nations in Africa. As Audre Lorde pointed out, women in Africa share a long tradition of healers and goddesses that perhaps binds them together more appropriately than their victim status. However, both Daly and Lorde fall prey to universalistic assumptions about "African women" (both negative and positive). What matters is the complex, historical range of power differences, commonalities and resistances that exist among women in Africa which construct African women as "subjects" of their own politics. See Daly (1978: 107–312) Lorde in Moraga and Anzaldua (1983).

10. See Eldhom, Harris and Young (1977) for a good discussion of the necessity to theorize male violence within specific societal frameworks, rather than to assume it as a universal fact.

11. These views can also be found in differing degrees in collections like: Wellesley Editorial Committee, ed., *Women and National Development: The Complexities of Change* Chicago: University of Chicago Press 1977, and *Signs*, Special Issue, "Development and the Sexual Division of Labor," 7.2, (Winter 1981). For an excellent introduction to WID issues see ISIS, *Women in Development: A Resource Guide for Organization and Action* Philadelphia: New Society Publishers, 1984. For a politically focused discussion of feminism and development and the stakes for poor third-world women, see Sen and Grown, (1987).

12. See essays by Vanessa Maher, Diane Elson and Ruth Pearson, and Maila Stevens in Young, Walkowitz and McCullagh (1981); and essays by Vivian Mota and Michelle Mattelart in Nash and Safa (1980). For examples of excellent self-conscious work by feminists writing about women in their own historical and geographical locations, see Lazreg (1988) on Algerian women; Gayatri Chakravorty Spivak's "A Literary Representation of the Subaltern: A Woman's Text from the Third World," in Spivak (1987), and Lata Mani's essay, "Contentious Traditions: The Debate on SATI in Colonial India," *Cultural Critique* No. 7, Fall 1987, pp. 119–56.

13. See Tabari (1980) for a detailed discussion of these instances.

14. Olivia Harris in Harris (1983: 4–7) Other MRG reports include Deardon (1975) and Jahan (1980).

15. See Eldhom, Harris and Young (1977) for an excellent discussion of this.

16. See Kishwar and Vanita (1984) for a discussion of this aspect of Indian women's struggles.

17. List of Zed Press Publications: Patricia Jeffery, *Frogs in a Well: Indian Women in Purdah*, 1979; Latin American and Caribbean Women's Collective, *Slaves of Slaves: The Challenge of Latin American Women*, 1980; Gale Omvedt, *We Shall Smash this Prison: Indian Women in Struggle*, 1980; Juliette Minces, *The House of Obedience: Women in Arab Society*, 1980; Bobby Siu, *Women of China: Imperialism and Women's Resistance 1900–1949*, 1981; Ingela Bendt and James Downing, *We Shall Return: Women of Palestine*, 1982; Maria Rosa Cutrufelli, *Women of Africa: Roots of Oppression*, 1983; Maria Mies, *The Lace Makers of Narsapur: Indian Housewives Produce for the World Market*, 1983; Miranda Davis, ed., *Third World/Second Sex: Women's Struggles and National Liberation*, 1983.

18. For succinct discussion of western radical and liberal feminisms, see Eisenstein (1983) and Eisenstein (1981).
19. See Haraway (1985: 65–108, especially 76).
20. Amos and Parmar (1984: 9) describe the cultural stereotypes present in Euro-American feminist thought: "The image is of the passive Asian woman subject to oppressive practices within the Asian family, with an emphasis on wanting to 'help' Asian women liberate themselves from their role. Or there is the strong, dominant Afro-Caribbean woman, who despite her "strength" is exploited by the "sexism" which is seen as being a strong feature in relationships between Afro-Caribbean men and women." These images illustrate the extent to which *paternalism* is an essential element of feminist thinking which incorporates the above stereotypes, a paternalism which can lead to the definition of priorities for women of colour by Euro-American feminists.
21. I discuss the question of theorizing experience in my "Feminist Encounters" (1987), and in an essay co-authored with Biddy Martin in de Lauretis (1986).
22. This is one of Foucault's central points in his reconceptualization of the strategies and workings of power networks. See Foucault (1978 and 1980).
23. Foucault (1978 and 1980); Derrida (1974); Kristeva (1980); Said (1978); and Deleuze and Guattari (1977).
24. Irigaray (1981); Cixous (1981). For a good discussion of Sarah Kofman's work, see Berg (1982: 11–20).
25. For an argument which demands a *new* conception of humanism in work on third-world women, see Lazreg (1988). While Lazreg's position might appear to be diametrically opposed to mine, I see it as a provocative and potentially positive extension of some of the implications that follow from my arguments. In criticizing the feminist rejection of humanism in the name of "essential Man," Lazreg points to what she calls an "essentialism of difference" within these very feminist projects. She asks: "To what extent can western feminism dispense with an ethics of responsibility when writing about 'different' women? The point is neither to subsume other women under one's own experience nor to uphold a separate truth for them. Rather, it is to allow them to *be* while recognizing that what they are is just as meaningful, valid, and comprehensible as what 'we' are. . . . Indeed, when feminists essentially deny other women the humanity they claim for themselves, they dispense with any ethical constraint. They engage in the act of splitting the social universe into 'us' and 'them,' 'subjects' and 'objects'" (99–100).

    This essay by Lazreg and an essay by S.P. Mohanty entitled "Us and Them: On the Philosophical Bases of Political Criticism," forthcoming in *The Yale Journal of Criticism* in March 1989 (Vol. 2, No. 2), suggest positive directions for self-conscious cross-cultural analyses, analyses which move beyond the deconstructive to a fundamentally productive mode in designating overlapping areas for cross-cultural comparison. The latter essay calls not for a "humanism" but for a reconsideration of the question of the "human" in a post-humanist context. It argues that (1) there is no necessary "incompatibility between the deconstruction of western humanism" and such "a positive elaboration" of the human; and moreover that (2) such an elaboration is essential if contemporary political-critical discourse is to avoid the incoherences and weaknesses of a relativist position.

REFERENCES

Abdel-Malek, Anouar (1981) *Social Dialectics: Nation and Revolution* Albany: State University of New York Press.

Amin, Samir (1977) *Imperialism and Unequal Development* New York: Monthly Review Press.

Amos, Valerie and Parmar, Pratibha (1984) "Challenging Imperial Feminism," *Feminist Review* No. 17.

Baran, Paul A. (1962) *The Political Economy of Growth* New York: Monthly Review Press.

Berg, Elizabeth (1982) "The Third Woman," *Diacritics,* Summer.

Bhabha, Homi (1983) "The Other Question—The Stereotype and Colonial Discourse" *Screen* 24:6, p. 23.

Boserup, Ester (1970) *Women's Role in Economic Development* New York: St Martin's Press; London: Allen & Unwin.

Brown, Beverly (1983) "Displacing the Difference—Review, Nature, Culture and Gender," *m/f* No. 8.

Cixous, Hélène (1981) "The Laugh of the Medusa" in Marks and Decourtivron (1981).

Cowie, Elizabeth (1978) "Woman as Sign," *m/f* No. 1.

Cutrufelli, Maria Rosa (1983) *Women of Africa: Roots of Oppression* London: Zed Press.

Daly, Mary (1978) *Gyn/Ecology: The Metaethics of Radical Feminism* Boston: Beacon Press.

De Lauretis, Teresa (1984) *Alice Doesn't: Feminism, Semiotics, Cinema* Bloomington: Indiana University Press.

De Lauretis, Teresa (1986) editor *Feminist Studies/Critical Studies* Bloomington: Indiana University Press.

Deardon, Ann (1975) editor *Arab Women* London: Minority Rights Group Report No. 27.

Deleuze, Giles and Guattari, Felix (1977) *Anti-Oedipus: Capitalism and Schizophrenia* New York: Viking.

Derrida, Jacques (1974) *Of Grammatology* Baltimore: Johns Hopkins University Press.

Eisenstein, Hester (1983) *Contemporary Feminist Thought* Boston: G. K. Hall & Co.

Eisenstein, Zillah (1981) *The Radical Future of Liberal Feminism* New York: Longman.

Eldhom, Felicity, Harris, Olivia and Young, Kate (1977) "Conceptualising Women," *"Critique of Anthoropology* "Women's Issue" No. 3.

Foucault, Michel (1978) *History of Sexuality Volume One* New York: Random House.

Foucault, Michel (1980) *Power/Knowledge* New York: Pantheon.

Gunder-Frank, Andre (1967) *Capitalism and Underdevelopment in Latin America* New York: Monthly Review Press.

Haraway, Donna (1985) "A Manifesto for Cyborgs: Science, Technology and Socialist Feminism in the 1980s," *Socialist Review* No. 80.

Harris, Olivia (1983a) "Latin American Women—An Overview" in Harris (1983).

Harris, Olivia (1983b) editor *Latin American Women* London: Minority Rights Group Report No. 57.

Hosken, Fran (1981) "Female Genital Multilation and Human Rights," *Feminist Issues* 1:3.

Huston, Perdita (1979) *Third World Women Speak Out* New York: Praeger.

Irigaray, Luce (1981) "This Sex Which Is Not One" and "When the Goods Get Together" in Marks and De Courtivron (1981).

Jahan, Rounaq (1980) editor *Women in Asia* London: Minority Rights Group Report No. 45.

Jeffery, Patricia (1979) *Frogs in a Well: Indian Women in Purdah* London: Zed Press.

Joseph, Gloria and Lewis, Jill (1981) *Common Differences: Conflicts in Black and White Feminist Perspectives* Boston: Beacon Press.

Kishwar, Madhu and Vanita, Ruth (1984) *In Search of Answers: Indian Women's Voices from Manushi* London: Zed Press.

Kristeva, Julia (1980) *Desire in Language* New York: Columbia University Press.

Lazreg, Marnia (1988) "Feminism and Difference: The Perils of Writing as a Woman on Women in Algeria," *Feminist Issues* 14:1.

Lindsay, Beverley (1983) editor *Comparative Perspectives of Third World Women: The Impact of Race, Sex and Class* New York: Praeger.

Lorde, Andre (1983) "An Open Letter to Mary Daly" in Moraga and Anzaldua (1983).

Marks, Elaine and De Courtivron, Isobel (1981) editors *New French Feminisms* New York: Schoken Books.

Mies, Maria (1982) *The Lace Makers of Narsapur: Indian Housewives Produce for the World Market* London: Zed Press.

Minces, Juliette (1980) *The House of Obedience: Women in Arab Society* London: Zed Press.

Modares, Mina (1981) "Women and Shi'ism in Iran" *m/f* Nos. 5 and 6.

Mohanty, Chandra and Martin, Biddy (1986) "Feminist Politics: What's Home Got to Do With It?" in De Lauretis (1986).

Mohanty, Chandra (1987) "Feminist Encounters: Locating the Politics of Experience," *Copyright* 1, "Fin de Siecle 2000."

Moraga, Cherrie and Anzaldua, Gloria (1983) editors *This Bridge Called My Back: Writings by Radical Women of Color* New York: Kitchen Table Press.

Moraga, Cherrie (1984) *Loving in the War Years* Boston: South End Press.

Morgan, Robin (1984) editor *Sisterhood is Global: The International Women's Movement Anthology* New York: Anchor Press/Doubleday; Harmondsworth: Penguin.

Nash, June and Safa, Helen I. (1980) editors *Sex and Class in Latin America: Women's Perspectives on Politics, Economics and the Family in the Third World* Massachusetts: Bergin & Garvey.

Rozaldo, M.Z. (1980) "The Use and Abuse of Anthropology: Reflections on Feminism and Cross-Cultural Understanding," *Signs* 5:3

Said, Edward (1978) *Orientalism* New York: Random House

Sen, Sita and Grown, Caren (1987) *Development Crises and Alternative Visions: Third World Women's Perspectives* New York: Monthly Review Press.

Smith, Barbara (1983) editor *Home Girls: A Black Feminist Anthology* New York: Kitchen Table Press.

Spanos, William V. (1984) "Boundary 2 and the Polity of Interest: Humanisim, the 'Center Elsewhere,' and Power," *Boundary 2*, Vol. XII, No. 3/Vol. XIII, No. 1, Spring/Fall.

Spivak, Gayatri Chakravorty (1987) *In Other Worlds: Essays in Cultural Politics* London and New York: Methuen.

Strathern, Marilyn and McCormack, Carol (1980) editors *Nature, Culture and Gender* Cambridge: Cambridge University Press.

Tabari, Azar (1980) "The Enigma of the Veiled Iranian Women," *Feminist Review* No. 5.

Tinker, Irene and Bramsen, Michelle Bo (1972) editors *Women and World Development* Washington DC: Overseas Development Council.

Young, Kate, Walkowitz, Carol and McCullagh, Roslyn (1981) editors *Of Marriage and the Market: Women's Subordination in International Perspective* London: CSE Books.

NARRATIVE AND SOCIAL SPACE (1993)

EDWARD W. SAID

Said is known for his postcolonial criticism and theory, including Orientalism *(1978), one of the founding works of modern postcolonial studies. He is also known for political commentary about the West's relations with Palestine and the Middle East. In this section from his book* Culture and Imperialism, *Said argues that imperialism plays a shaping role in Western culture and in the Western literary imagination, even when a work of literature's direct references to imperialism seem minor. Many readers think of imperialism as something that takes place far from the setting of European culture and novels, but Said shows how the central novels of English and French literary history draw on and contribute to a sense of social and narrative space that relies on imperial, colonialist privilege.*

Nearly everywhere in nineteenth- and early-twentieth-century British and French culture we find allusions to the facts of empire, but perhaps nowhere with more regularity and frequency than in the British novel. Taken together, these allusions constitute what I have called a structure of attitude and reference. In *Mansfield Park*, which within Jane Austen's work carefully defines the moral and social values informing her other novels, references to Sir Thomas Bertram's overseas possessions are threaded through; they give him his wealth, occasion his absences, fix his social status at home and abroad, and make possible his values, to which Fanny Price (and Austen herself) finally subscribes. If this is a novel about "ordination," as Austen says, the right to colonial possessions helps directly to establish social order and moral priorities at home. Or again, Bertha Mason, Rochester's deranged wife in *Jane Eyre*, is a West Indian, and also a threatening presence, confined to an attic room. Thackeray's Joseph Sedley in *Vanity Fair* is an Indian nabob whose rambunctious behavior and excessive (perhaps undeserved) wealth is counterpointed with Becky's finally unacceptable deviousness, which in turn is contrasted with Amelia's propriety, suitably rewarded in the end; Joseph Dobbin is seen at the end of the novel engaged serenely in writing a history of the Punjab. The good ship *Rose* in Charles Kingsley's *Westward Ho!* wanders through the Caribbean and South America. In Dickens's *Great Expectations*, Abel Magwitch is the convict transported to Australia whose wealth—conveniently removed from Pip's triumphs as a provincial lad flourishing in London in the guise of a gentleman—ironically makes possible the great expectations Pip entertains. In many other Dickens novels businessmen have connections with the empire, Dombey and Quilp being two noteworthy examples. For Disraeli's *Tancred* and Eliot's *Daniel Deronda*, the East is partly a habitat for native peoples (or immigrant European populations), but also partly incorporated under the sway of empire. Henry James's Ralph Touchett in *Portrait of a Lady* travels in Algeria and Egypt. And when we come to Kipling, Conrad, Arthur Conan Doyle, Rider Haggard, R. L. Stevenson, George Orwell, Joyce Cary, E. M. Forster, and T. E. Lawrence, the empire is everywhere a crucial setting.

The situation in France was different, insofar as the French imperial vocation during the early nineteenth century was different from England's, buttressed as it was by the continuity and stability of the English polity itself. The reverses of policy, losses of colonies, insecurity of possession, and shifts in philosophy that France suffered during the Revolution and the Napoleonic era meant that its empire had a less secure identity and presence in French culture. In Chateaubriand and Lamartine one hears the rhetoric of imperial grandeur; and in painting, in historical and philological writing, in music and theater one has an often vivid apprehension of France's outlying possessions. But in the culture at large—until after the middle of the century—there is rarely that weighty, almost philosophical sense of imperial mission that one finds in Britain.

There is also a dense body of American writing, contemporary with this British and French work, which shows a peculiarly acute imperial cast, even though paradoxically its ferocious anti-colonialism, directed at the Old World, is central to it. One thinks, for example, of the Puritan "errand into the wilderness" and, later, of that extraordinarily obsessive concern in Cooper, Twain, Melville, and others with United States expansion westward, along with the wholesale colonization and destruction of native American life (as memorably studied by Richard Slotkin, Patricia Limerick, and Michael Paul Rogin);[1] an imperial motif emerges to rival the European one. (In Chapter Four of this book I shall deal with other and more recent aspects of the United States in its late-twentieth-century imperial form.)

As a reference, as a point of definition, as an easily assumed place of travel, wealth, and service, the empire functions for much of the European nineteenth century as a codified, if only marginally visible, presence in fiction, very much like the servants in grand households and in novels, whose work is taken for granted but scarcely ever more than named, rarely studied (though Bruce Robbins has recently written on them),[2] or given density. To cite another intriguing analogue, imperial possessions are as usefully *there*, anonymous and collective, as the outcast populations (analyzed by Gareth Stedman Jones)[3] of transient workers, part-time employees, seasonal artisans; their existence always counts, though their names and identities do not, they are profitable without being fully there. This is a literary equivalent, in Eric Wolf's somewhat self-congratulatory words, of "people without History,"[4] people on whom the economy and polity sustained by empire depend, but whose reality has not historically or culturally required attention.

In all of these instances the facts of empire are associated with sustained possession, with far-flung and sometimes unknown spaces, with eccentric or unacceptable human beings, with fortune-enhancing or fantasized activities like emigration, money-making, and sexual adventure. Disgraced younger sons are sent off to the colonies, shabby older relatives go there to try to recoup lost fortunes (as in Balzac's *La Cousine Bette*), enterprising young travellers go there to sow wild oats and to collect exotica. The colonial territories are realms of possibility, and they have always been associated with the realistic novel. Robinson Crusoe is virtually unthinkable without the colonizing mission that permits him to create a new world of his own in the distant reaches of the African, Pacific, and Atlantic wilderness. But most of the great nineteenth-century realistic novelists are less assertive about colonial rule and possessions than either Defoe or late writers like Conrad and Kipling, during whose time great electoral reform and mass participation in politics meant that imperial competition became a more intrusive domestic topic. In the closing year of the nineteenth century, with the scramble for Africa, the consolidation of the French imperial Union, the American annexation of the Philippines, and British rule in the Indian subcontinent at its height, empire was a universal concern.

What I should like to note is that these colonial and imperial realities are overlooked in criticism that has otherwise been extraordinarily thorough and resourceful in finding themes to discuss. The relatively few writers and critics who discuss the relationship between culture and empire—among them Martin Green, Molly Mahood, John McClure, and, in particular, Patrick Brantlinger—have made excellent contributions, but their mode is essentially narrative and descriptive—pointing out the presence of themes, the importance of certain historical conjunctures, the influence or persistence of ideas about imperialism—and they cover huge amounts of material.[5] In almost all cases they write critically of imperialism, of that way of life that William Appleman Williams describes as being compatible with all sorts of other ideological persuasions, even antinomian ones, so that during the nineteenth century "imperial outreach made it necessary to develop an appropriate ideology" in alliance with military, economic, and political methods. These made it possible to "preserve and extend the empire without wasting its psychic or cultural or economic substance." There are hints in these scholars' work that, again to quote Williams, imperialism produces troubling self-images, for example, that of "a benevolent progressive policeman."[6]

But these critics are mainly descriptive and positivist writers strikingly different from the small handful of generally theoretical and ideological contributions—among them Jonah Raskin's *The Mythology of Imperialism*, Gordon K. Lewis's *Slavery, Imperialism, and Freedom*, and V. G. Kiernan's *Marxism and Imperialism* and his crucial work, *The Lords of Human Kind*.[7] All these books, which owe a great deal to Marxist analysis and premises, point out the centrality of imperialist thought in modern Western culture.

Yet none of them has been anywhere as influential as they should have been in changing our ways of looking at the canonical works of nineteenth- and twentieth-century European culture. The major critical practitioners simply ignore imperialism. In recently rereading Lionel Trilling's fine little book on E. M. Forster, for instance, I was struck that in his otherwise perceptive consideration of *Howards End* he does not once mention imperialism, which, in my reading of the book, is hard to miss, much less ignore. After all, Henry Wilcox and his family are colonial rubber growers: "They had the colonial spirit, and were always making for some spots where the white man might carry his burden unobserved."[8] And Forster frequently contrasts and associates that fact with the changes taking place in England, changes that affect Leonard and Jacky Bast, the Schlegels, and Howards End itself. Or there is the more surprising case of Raymond Williams, whose *Culture and Society* does not deal with the imperial experience at all. (When in an interview Williams was challenged about this massive absence, since imperialism "was not something which was secondary and external—it was absolutely constitutive of the whole nature of the English political and social order...*the* salient fact"[9]—he replied that his Welsh experience, which ought to have enabled him to think about the imperial experience, was "very much in abeyance" at the time he wrote *Culture and Society*.)[10] The few tantalizing pages in *The Country and the City* that touch on culture and imperialism are peripheral to the book's main idea.

Why did these lapses occur? And how was the centrality of the imperial vision registered and supported by the culture that produced it, then to some extent disguised it, and also was transformed by it? Naturally, if you yourself happen to have a colonial background, the imperial theme is a determining one in your formation, and it will draw you to it if you also happen to be a dedicated critic of European literature. An Indian or African scholar of English literature reads *Kim*, say, or *Heart of Darkness* with a critical urgency not felt in quite the same way by an American or British one. But in what way can we formulate the relationship between culture and imperialism beyond the asseverations of personal testimony? The emergence of formerly colonial subjects as interpreters of imperialism and its great cultural works has given imperialism a perceptible, not to say obtrusive identity as a subject for study and vigorous revision. But how can that particular kind of post-imperial testimony and study, usually left at the margins of critical discourse, be brought into active contact with current theoretical concerns?

To regard imperial concerns as constitutively significant to the culture of the modern West is, I have suggested, to consider that culture from the perspective provided by anti-imperialist resistance as well as pro-imperialist apology. What does this mean? It means remembering that Western writers until the middle of the twentieth century, whether Dickens and Austen, Flaubert or Camus, wrote with an exclusively Western audience in mind, even when they wrote of characters, places, or situations that referred to, made use of, overseas territories held by Europeans. But just because Austen referred to Antigua in *Mansfield Park* or to realms visited by the British navy in *Persuasion* without any thought of possible responses by the Caribbean or Indian natives resident there is no reason for us to do the same. We now know that these non-European peoples did not accept with indifference the authority projected over them, or the general silence on which their presence in variously attenuated forms is predicated. We must therefore read the great canonical texts, and perhaps also the entire archive of modern and pre-modern European and American culture, with an effort to draw out, extend, give emphasis and voice to what is silent or marginally present or ideologically represented (I have in mind Kipling's Indian characters) in such works.

In practical terms, "contrapuntal reading" as I have called it means reading a text with an understanding of what is involved when an author shows, for instance, that a colonial sugar plantation is seen as important to the process of maintaining a particular style of life in England. Moreover, like all literary texts, these are not bounded by their formal historic beginnings and endings. References to Australia in *David Copperfield* or India in *Jane Eyre* are made because they *can be*, because British power (and not just the novelist's fancy) made passing references to these massive appropriations possible; but the further lessons are no less true: that these colonies were subsequently liberated from direct and indirect rule, a process that began and unfolded while the British (or French, Portuguese, Germans, etc.) were still there, although as part of the effort at suppressing native nationalism only occasional note was taken of it. The point is that contrapuntal reading must take account of both processes, that of imperialism and that of resistance to it, which can be done by extending our reading of the texts to include what was once forcibly excluded—in *L'Etranger*, for example, the whole previous history of France's colonialism and its destruction of the Algerian state, and the later emergence of an independent Algeria (which Camus opposed).

Each text has its own particular genius, as does each geographical region of the world, with its own overlapping experiences and interdependent histories of conflict. As far as the cultural work is concerned, a distinction between particularity and sovereignty (or hermetic exclusiveness) can usefully be made. Obviously no reading should try to generalize so much as to efface the identity of a particular text, author, or movement. By the same token it should allow that what was, or appeared to be, certain for a given work or author may have become subject to disputation. Kipling's India, in *Kim*, has a quality of permanence and inevitability that belongs not just to that wonderful novel, but to British India, its history, administrators, and apologists and, no less important, to the India fought for by Indian nationalists as their country to be won back. By giving an account of this series of pressures and counter-pressures in Kipling's India, we understand the process of imperialism itself as the great work of art engages them, and of later anti-imperialist resistance. In reading a text, one must open it out both to what went into it and to what its author excluded. Each cultural work is a vision of a moment, and we must juxtapose that vision with the various revisions it later provoked—in this case, the nationalist experiences of post-independence India.

In addition, one must connect the structures of a narrative to the ideas, concepts, experiences from which it draws support. Conrad's Africans, for example, come from a huge library of *Africanism*, so to speak, as well as from Conrad's personal experiences. There is no such thing as a *direct* experience, or reflection, of the world in the language of a text. Conrad's impressions of Africa were inevitably influenced by lore and writing about Africa, which he alludes to in *A Personal Record*; what he supplies in *Heart of Darkness* is the result of his impressions of those texts interacting creatively, together with the requirements and conventions of narrative and his own special genius and history. To say of this extraordinarily rich mix that it "reflects" Africa, or even that it reflects an experience of Africa, is somewhat pusillanimous and surely misleading. What we have in *Heart of Darkness*—a work of immense influence, having provoked many readings and images—is a politicized, ideologically saturated Africa which to some intents and purposes was the imperialized place, with those many interests and ideas furiously at work in it, not just a photographic literary "reflection" of it.

This is, perhaps, to overstate the matter, but I want to make the point that far from *Heart of Darkness* and its image of Africa being "only" literature, the work is extraordinarily caught up in, is indeed an organic part of, the "scramble for Africa" that was contemporary with Conrad's composition. True, Conrad's audience was small, and, true also, he was very critical of Belgian colonialism. But to most Europeans, reading a rather rarefied text like *Heart of Darkness* was often as close as they came to Africa, and in that limited sense it was part of the European effort to hold on to, think about, plan for Africa. To represent Africa is to enter the battle over Africa, inevitably connected to later resistance, decolonization, and so forth.

Works of literature, particularly those whose manifest subject is empire, have an inherently untidy, even unwieldy aspect in so fraught, so densely charged a political setting. Yet despite their formidable complexity, literary works like *Heart of Darkness* are distillations, or simplifications, or a set of choices made by an author that are far less messy and mixed up than the reality. It would not be fair to think of them as abstractions, although fictions such as *Heart of Darkness* are so elaborately fashioned by authors and so worried over by readers as to suit the necessities of narrative which as a result, we must add, makes a highly specialized entry into the struggle over Africa.

So hybrid, impure, and complex a text requires especially vigilant attention as it is interpreted. Modern imperialism was so global and all-encompassing that virtually nothing escaped it; besides, as I have said, the nineteenth-century contest over empire is still continuing today. Whether or not to look at the connections between cultural texts and imperialism is therefore to take a position *in fact taken*—either to study the connection in order to criticize it and think of alternatives for it, or not to study it in order to let it stand, unexamined and, presumably, unchanged. One of my reasons for writing this book is to show how far the quest for, concern about, and consciousness of overseas dominion extended—not just in Conrad but in figures we practically never think of in that connection, like Thackeray and Austen—and how enriching and important for the critic is attention to this material, not only for the obvious political reasons, but also because, as I have been arguing, this particular kind of attention allows the reader to interpret canonical nineteenth- and twentieth-century works with a newly engaged interest.

Let us return to *Heart of Darkness*. In it Conrad offers an uncannily suggestive starting point for grappling at close quarters with these difficult matters. Recall that Marlow contrasts Roman colonizers with their modern counterparts in an oddly perceptive way, illuminating the special mix of power, ideological energy, and practical attitude characterizing European imperialism. The ancient Romans, he says, were "no colonists; their administration was merely a squeeze and nothing more." Such people conquered and did little else. By contrast, "what saves us is efficiency—the devotion to efficiency," unlike the Romans, who relied on brute force, which is scarcely more than "an accident arising from the weakness of others." Today, however,

> the conquest of the earth, which mostly means the taking it away from those who have a different complexion or slightly flatter noses than ourselves, is not a pretty thing when you look into it too much. What redeems it is the idea only. An idea at the back of it; not a sentimental pretence but an idea; and an unselfish belief in the idea—something you can set up, and bow down before, and offer a sacrifice to.... [11]

In his account of his great river journey, Marlow extends the point to mark a distinction between Belgian rapacity and (by implication) British rationality in the conduct of imperialism.[12]

Salvation in this context is an interesting notion. It sets "us" off from the damned, despised Romans and Belgians, whose greed radiates no benefits onto either their consciences or the lands and bodies of their subjects. "We" are saved because first of all we needn't look directly at the results of what we do; we are ringed by and ring ourselves with the practice of efficiency, by which land and people are put to use completely; the territory and its inhabitants are totally incorporated by our rule, which in turn totally incorporates us as we respond efficiently to its exigencies. Further, through Marlow, Conrad speaks of redemption, a step in a sense beyond salvation. If salvation saves us, saves time and money, and also saves us from the ruin of mere short-term conquest, then redemption extends salvation further still. Redemption is found in the self-justifying practice of an idea or mission over time, in a structure that completely encircles and is revered by you, even though you set up the structure in the first place, ironically enough, and no longer study it closely because you take it for granted.

Thus Conrad encapsulates two quite different but intimately related aspects of imperialism: the idea that is based on the power to take over territory, an idea utterly clear in its force and unmistakable consequences; and the practice that essentially disguises or obscures this by developing a justificatory regime of self-aggrandizing, self-originating authority interposed between the victim of imperialism and its perpetrator.

We would completely miss the tremendous power of this argument if we were merely to lift it out of *Heart of Darkness*, like a message out of a bottle. Conrad's argument is inscribed right in the very form of narrative as he inherited it and as he practiced it. Without empire, I would go so far as saying, there is no European novel as we know it, and indeed if we study the impulses giving rise to it, we shall see the far from accidental convergence between the patterns of narrative authority constitutive of the novel on the one hand, and, on the other, a complex ideological configuration underlying the tendency to imperialism.

Every novelist and every critic or theorist of the European novel notes its institutional character. The novel is fundamentally tied to bourgeois society; in Charles Morazé's phrase, it accompanies and indeed is a part of the conquest of Western society by what he calls *les bourgeois conquérants*. No less significantly, the novel is inaugurated in England by *Robinson Crusoe*, a work whose protagonist is the founder of a new world, which he rules and reclaims for Christianity and England. True, whereas Crusoe is explicitly enabled by an ideology of overseas expansion—directly connected in style and form to the narratives of sixteenth- and seventeenth-century exploration voyages that laid the foundations of the great colonial empires—the major novels that come after Defoe, and even Defoe's later works, seem not to be single-mindedly compelled by the exciting overseas prospects. *Captain Singleton* is the story of a widely travelled pirate in India and Africa, and *Moll Flanders* is shaped by the possibility in the New World of the heroine's climactic redemption from a life of crime, but Fielding, Richardson, Smollett, and Sterne do not connect their narratives so directly to the act of accumulating riches and territories abroad.

These novelists do, however, situate their work in and derive it from a carefully surveyed territorial greater Britain, and that *is* related to what Defoe so presciently began. Yet while distinguished studies of eighteenth-century English fiction—by Ian Watt, Lennard Davis, John Richetti, and Michael McKeon—have devoted considerable attention to the relationship between the novel and social space, the imperial perspective has been neglected.[13] This is not simply a matter of being uncertain whether, for example, Richardson's minute constructions of bourgeois seduction and rapacity actually relate to British military moves against the French in India occurring at the same time. Quite clearly they do not in a literal sense; but in both realms we find common values about contest, surmounting odds and obstacles, and patience in establishing authority through the art of connecting principle with profit over time. In other words, we need to have a critical sense of how the great spaces of *Clarissa* or *Tom Jones* are two things together: a domestic accompaniment to the imperial project for presence and control abroad, and a practical narrative about expanding and moving about in space that must be actively inhabited and enjoyed before its discipline or limits can be accepted.

I am not trying to say that the novel—or the culture in the broad sense—"caused" imperialism, but that the novel, as a cultural artefact of bourgeois society, and imperialism are unthinkable without each other. Of all the major literary forms, the novel is the most recent, its emergence the most datable, its occurrence the most Western, its normative pattern of social authority the most structured; imperialism and the novel fortified each other to such a degree that it is impossible, I would argue, to read one without in some way dealing with the other.

Nor is this all. The novel is an incorporative, quasi-encyclopedic cultural form. Packed into it are both a highly regulated plot mechanism and an entire system of social reference that depends on the existing institutions of bourgeois society, their authority and power. The novelistic hero and heroine exhibit the restlessness and energy characteristic of the enterprising bourgeoisie, and they are permitted adventures in which their experiences reveal to them the limits of what they can aspire to, where they can go, what they can become. Novels therefore end either with the death of a hero or heroine (Julien Sorel, Emma Bovary, Bazarov, Jude the Obscure) who by virtue of overflowing energy does not fit into the orderly scheme of things, or with the protagonists' accession to stability (usually in the form of marriage or confirmed identity, as is the case with novels of Austen, Dickens, Thackeray, and George Eliot).

But, one might ask, why give so much emphasis to novels, and to England? And how can we bridge the distance separating this solitary aesthetic form from large topics and undertakings like "culture" or "imperialism"? For one thing, by the time of World War One the British empire had become unquestionably dominant, the result of a process that had started in the late sixteenth century; so powerful was the process and so definitive its result that, as Seeley and Hobson argued toward the end of the nineteenth century, it was the central fact in British history, and one that included many disparate activities.[14] It is not entirely coincidental that Britain also produced and sustained a novelistic institution with no real European competitor or equivalent. France had more highly developed intellectual institutions—academies, universities, institutes, journals, and so on—for at least the first half of the nineteenth century, as a host of British intellectuals, including Arnold, Carlyle, Mill, and George Eliot, noted and lamented. But the extraordinary compensation for this discrepancy came in the steady rise and gradually undisputed dominance of the British novel. (Only as North Africa assumes a sort of metropolitan presence in French culture after 1870 do we see a comparable aesthetic and cultural formation begin to flow: this is the period when Loti, the early Gide, Daudet, Maupassant, Mille, Psichari, Malraux, the exoticists like Segalen, and of course Camus project a global concordance between the domestic and imperial situations.)

By the 1840s the English novel had achieved eminence as *the* aesthetic form and as a major intellectual voice, so to speak, in English society. Because the novel gained so important a place in "the condition of England" question, for example, we can see it also as participating in England's overseas empire. In projecting what Raymond Williams calls a "knowable community" of Englishmen and women, Jane Austen, George Eliot, and Mrs. Gaskell shaped the idea of England in such a way as to give it identity, presence, ways of reusable articulation.[15] And part of such an idea was the relationship between "home" and "abroad." Thus England was surveyed, evaluated, made known, whereas "abroad" was only referred to or shown briefly without the kind of presence or immediacy lavished on London, the countryside, or northern industrial centers such as Manchester or Birmingham.

This steady, almost reassuring work done by the novel is unique to England and has to be taken as an important cultural affiliation domestically speaking, as yet undocumented and unstudied, for what took place in India, Africa, Ireland, or the Caribbean. An analogy is the relationship between Britain's foreign policy and its finance and trade, a relationship which *has* been studied. We get a lively sense of how dense and complex it was from D.C.M. Platt's classic (but still debated) study of it, *Finance, Trade and Politics in British Foreign Policy, 1819–1914*, and how much the extraordinary twinning of British trade and imperial expansion depended on cultural and social factors such as education, journalism, intermarriage, and class. Platt speaks of "social and intellectual contact [friendship, hospitality, mutual aid, common social and educational background] which energized the actual pressure on British foreign policy," and he goes on to say that "concrete evidence [for the actual accomplishments of this set of contacts] has probably never existed." Nevertheless, if one looks at how the government's attitude to such issues as "foreign loans...the protection of bondholders, and the promotion of contracts and concessions overseas" developed, one can see what he calls a "departmental view," a sort of consensus about the empire held by a whole range of people responsible for it. This would "suggest how officials and politicians were likely to react."[16]

How best to characterize this view? There seems to be agreement among scholars that until about 1870 British policy was (according to the early Disraeli, for example) not to expand the empire but "to uphold and maintain it and to protect it from disintegration."[17] Central to this task was India, which acquired a status of astonishing durability in "departmental" thought. After 1870 (Schumpeter cites Disraeli's Crystal Palace speech in 1872 as the hallmark of aggressive imperialism, "the catch phrase of domestic policy")[18] protecting India (the parameters kept getting larger) and defending against other competing powers, e.g., Russia, necessitated British imperial expansion in Africa, and the Middle and Far East. Thereafter, in one area of the globe after another, "Britain was indeed preoccupied with holding what she already had," as Platt puts it, "and whatever she gained was demanded because it helped her to preserve the rest. She belonged to the party of *les satisfaits*, but she had to fight ever harder to stay with them, and she had by far the most to lose."[19] A "departmental view" of British policy was fundamentally careful; as Ronald Robinson and John Gallagher put it in their redefinition of Platt's thesis, "the British would expand by trade and influence if they could, but by imperial rule if they must."[20] We should not minimize or forget, they remind us, that the Indian army was used in China three times between 1829 and 1856, at least once in Persia (1856), Ethiopia and Singapore (1867), Hong Kong (1868), Afghanistan (1878), Egypt (1882), Burma (1885), Ngasse (1893), Sudan and Uganda (1896).

In addition to India, British policy obviously made the bulwark for imperial commerce mainland Britain itself (with Ireland a continuous colonial problem), as well as the so-called white colonies (Australia, New Zealand, Canada, South Africa, and even the former American possessions). Continuous investment and routine conservation of Britain's overseas and home territories were without significant parallel in other European or American powers, where lurches, sudden acquisitions or losses, and improvisations occurred far more frequently.

In short, British power was durable and continually reinforced. In the related and often adjacent cultural sphere, that power was elaborated and articulated in the novel, whose central continuous presence is not comparably to be found elsewhere. But we must be as fastidious as possible. A novel is neither a frigate nor a bank draft. A novel exists first as a novelist's effort and second as an object read by an audience. In time novels accumulate and become what Harry Levin has usefully called an institution of literature, but they do not ever lose either their status as events or their specific density as part of a continuous enterprise recognized and accepted as such by readers and other writers. But for all their social presence, novels are not reducible to a sociological current and cannot be done justice to aesthetically, culturally, and politically as subsidiary forms of class, ideology, or interest.

Equally, however, novels are not *simply* the product of lonely genius (as a school of modern interpreters like Helen Vendler try to suggest), to be regarded only as manifestations of unconditioned creativity. Some of the most exciting recent criticism—Fredric Jameson's *The Political Unconscious* and David Miller's *The Novel and the Police* are two celebrated examples[21]—shows the novel generally, and narrative in particular, to have a sort of regulatory social presence in West European societies. Yet missing from these otherwise valuable descriptions are adumbrations of the actual world in which the novels and narratives take place. Being an English writer meant something quite specific and different from, say, being a French or Portuguese writer. For the British writer, "abroad" was felt vaguely and ineptly to be out there, or exotic and strange, or in some way or other "ours" to control, trade in "freely," or suppress when the natives were energized into overt military or political resistance. The novel contributed significantly to these feelings, attitudes, and references and became a main element in the consolidated vision, or departmental cultural view, of the globe.

I should specify how the novelistic contribution was made and also, conversely, how the novel neither deterred nor inhibited the more aggressive and popular imperialist feelings manifest after 1880.[22] Novels are pictures of reality at the very early or the very late stage in the reader's experience of them: in fact they elaborate and maintain a reality they inherit from other novels, which they rearticulate and repopulate according to their creator's situation, gifts, predilections. Platt rightly stresses *conservation* in the "departmental view"; this is significant for the novelist, too: the nineteenth-century English novels stress the continuing existence (as opposed to revolutionary overturning) of England. Moreover, they *never* advocate giving up colonies, but take the long-range view that since they fall within the orbit of British dominance, *that* dominance is a sort of norm, and thus conserved along with the colonies.

What we have is a slowly built up picture with England—socially, politically, morally charted and differentiated in immensely fine detail—at the center and a series of overseas territories connected to it at the peripheries. The *continuity* of British imperial policy throughout the nineteenth century—in fact a narrative—is actively accompanied by this novelistic process, whose main purpose is not to raise more questions, not to disturb or otherwise preoccupy attention, but to keep the empire more or less in place. Hardly ever is the novelist interested in doing a great deal more than mentioning or referring to India, for example, in *Vanity Fair* and *Jane Eyre*, or Australia in *Great Expectations*. The idea is that (following the general principles of free trade) outlying territories are available for use, at will, at the novelist's discretion, usually for relatively simple purposes such as immigration, fortune, or exile. At the end of *Hard Times*, for example, Tom is shipped off to the colonies. Not until well after mid-century did the empire become a principal subject of attention in writers like Haggard, Kipling, Doyle, Conrad as well as in emerging discourses in ethnography, colonial administration, theory and economy, the historiography of non-European regions, and specialized subjects like Orientalism, exoticism, and mass psychology.

The actual interpretative consequences of this slow and steady structure of attitude and reference articulated by the novel are diverse. I shall specify four. The first is that, in literary history, an unusual organic continuity can be seen between the earlier narratives that are normally not considered to have much to do with empire and the later ones explicitly *about* it. Kipling and Conrad are prepared for by Austen and Thackeray, Defoe, Scott, and Dickens; they are also interestingly connected with their contemporaries like Hardy and James, regularly supposed to be only coincidentally associated with the overseas exhibits presented by their rather more peculiar novelistic counterparts. But both the formal characteristics and the contents of all these novelists' works belong to the same cultural formation, the differences being those of inflection, emphasis, stress.

Second, the structure of attitude and reference raises the whole question of power. Today's critic cannot and should not suddenly give a novel legislative or direct political authority: we must continue to remember that novels participate in, are part of, contribute to an extremely slow, infinitesimal politics that clarifies, reinforces, perhaps even occasionally advances perceptions and attitudes about England and the world. It is striking that never, in the novel, is that world beyond seen except as subordinate and dominated, the English presence viewed as regulative and normative. Part of the extraordinary novelty of Aziz's trial in *A Passage to India* is that Forster admits that "the flimsy framework of the court"[23] cannot be sustained because it is a "fantasy" that compromises British power (real) with impartial justice for Indians (unreal). Therefore he readily (even with a sort of frustrated impatience) dissolves the scene into India's "complexity," which twenty-four years before in Kipling's *Kim* was just as present. The main difference between the two is that the impinging disturbance of resisting natives had been thrust on Forster's awareness. Forster could not ignore something that Kipling easily incorporated (as when he rendered even the famous "Mutiny" of 1857 as mere waywardness, not as a serious Indian objection to British rule).

There can be no awareness that the novel underscores and accepts the disparity in power unless readers actually register the signs in individual works, and unless the history of the novel is seen to have the coherence of a continuous enterprise. Just as the sustained solidity and largely unwavering "departmental view" of Britain's outlying territories were maintained throughout the nineteenth century, so too, in an altogether literary way, was the aesthetic (hence cultural) grasp of overseas lands maintained as a part of the novel, sometimes incidental, sometimes very important. Its "consolidated vision" came in a whole series of overlapping affirmations by which a neat unanimity of view was sustained. That this was done within the terms of each medium or discourse (the novel, travel writing, ethnography) and not in terms imposed from outside, suggests conformity, collaboration, willingness but not necessarily an overtly or explicitly held political agenda, at least not until later in the century, when the imperial program was itself more explicit and more a matter of direct popular propaganda.

A third point can best be made by rapid illustration. All through *Vanity Fair* there are allusions to India, but none is anything more than incidental to the changes in Becky's fortunes, or in Dobbin's, Joseph's, and Amelia's positions. All along, though, we are made aware of the mounting contest between England and Napoleon, with its climax at Waterloo. This overseas dimension scarcely makes *Vanity Fair* a novel exploiting what Henry James was later to call "the international theme," any more than Thackeray belongs to the club of Gothic novelists like Walpole, Radcliffe, or Lewis who set their works rather fancifully abroad. Yet Thackeray and, I would argue, all the major English novelists of the mid-nineteenth century, accepted a globalized world-view and indeed could not (in most cases did not) ignore the vast overseas reach of British power. As we saw in the little example cited earlier from *Dombey and Son*, the domestic order was tied to, located in, even illuminated by a specifically *English* order abroad. Whether it is Sir Thomas Bertram's plantation in Antigua or, a hundred years later, the Wilcox Nigerian rubber estate, novelists aligned the holding of power and privilege abroad with comparable activities at home.

When we read the novels attentively, we get a far more discriminating and subtle view than the baldly "global" and imperial vision I have described thus far. This brings me to the fourth consequence of what I have been calling the structure of attitude and reference. In insisting on the integrity of an artistic work, as we must, and refusing to collapse the various contributions of individual authors into a general scheme, we must accept that the structure connecting novels to one another has no existence outside the novels themselves, which means that one gets the particular, concrete experience of "abroad" only in individual novels; conversely that only individual novels can animate, articulate, embody the relationship, for instance, between England and Africa. This obliges critics to read and analyze, rather than only to summarize and judge, works whose paraphrasable content they might regard as politically and morally objectionable. On the one hand, when in a celebrated essay Chinua Achebe criticizes Conrad's racism, he either says nothing about or overrides the limitations placed on Conrad by the novel as an aesthetic form. On the other hand, Achebe shows that he understands how the form works when, in some of his own novels, he rewrites—painstakingly and with originality—Conrad.[24]

All of this is especially true of English fiction because only England had an overseas empire that sustained and protected itself over such an area, for such a long time, with such envied eminence. It is true that France rivalled it, but, as I have said elsewhere, the French imperial consciousness is intermittent until the late nineteenth century, the actuality too impinged on by England, too lagging in system, profit, extent. In the main, though, the nineteenth-century European novel is a cultural form consolidating but also refining and articulating the authority of the status quo. However much Dickens, for example, stirs up his readers against the legal system, provincial schools, or the bureaucracy, his novels finally enact what one critic has called a "fiction of resolution."[25] The most frequent figure for this is the reunification of the family, which in Dickens's case always serves as a microcosm of society. In Austen, Balzac, George Eliot, and Flaubert—to take several prominent names together—the consolidation of authority includes, indeed is built into the very fabric of, both private property and marriage, institutions that are only rarely challenged.

The crucial aspect of what I have been calling the novel's consolidation of authority is not simply connected to the functioning of social power and governance, but made to appear both normative and sovereign, that is, self-validating in the course of the narrative. This is paradoxical only if one forgets that the constitution of a narrative subject, however abnormal or unusual, is still a social act par excellence, and as such has behind or inside it the authority of history and society. There is first the authority of the author—someone writing out the processes of society in an acceptable institutionalized manner, observing conventions, following patterns, and so forth. Then there is the authority of the narrator, whose discourse anchors the narrative in recognizable, and hence existentially referential, circumstances. Last, there is what might be called the authority of the community, whose representative most often is the family but also is the nation, the specific locality, and the concrete historical moment. Together these functioned most energetically, most noticeably, during the early nineteenth century as the novel opened up to history in an unprecedented way. Conrad's Marlow inherits all this directly.

Lukacs studied with remarkable skill the emergence of history in the European novel[26]—how Stendhal and particularly Scott place their narratives in and as part of a public history, making that history accessible to everyone and not, as before, only to kings and aristocrats. The novel is thus a concretely historical narrative shaped by the real history of real nations. Defoe locates Crusoe on an unnamed island somewhere in an outlying region, and Moll is sent to the vaguely apprehended Carolinas, but Thomas Bertram and Joseph Sedley derive specific wealth and specific benefits from historically annexed territories—the Caribbean and India, respectively—at specific historical moments. And, as Lukacs shows so persuasively, Scott constructs the British polity in the form of a historical society working its way out of foreign adventures[27] (the Crusades, for example) and internecine domestic conflict (the 1745 rebellion, the warring Highland tribes) to become the settled metropolis resisting local revolution and continental provocation with equal success. In France, history confirms the post-revolutionary reaction embodied by the Bourbon restoration, and Stendhal chronicles its—to him—lamentable achievements. Later Flaubert does much the same for 1848. But the novel is assisted also by the historical work of Michelet and Macaulay, whose narratives add density to the texture of national identity.

The appropriation of history, the historicization of the past, the narrativization of society, all of which give the novel its force, include the accumulation and differentiation of social space, space to be used for social purposes. This is much more apparent in late-nineteenth-century, openly colonial fiction: in Kipling's India, for example, where the natives and the Raj inhabit differently ordained spaces, and where with his extraordinary genius Kipling devised Kim, a marvelous character whose youth and energy allow him to explore both spaces, crossing from one to the other with daring grace as if to confound the authority of colonial barriers. The barriers within social space exist in Conrad too, and in Haggard, in Loti, in Doyle, in Gide, Psichari, Malraux, Camus, and Orwell.

Underlying social space are territories, lands, geographical domains, the actual geographical underpinnings of the imperial, and also the cultural contest. To think about distant places, to colonize them, to populate or depopulate them: all of this occurs on, about, or because of land. The actual geographical possession of land is what empire in the final analysis is all about. At the moment when a coincidence occurs between real control and power, the idea of what a given place was (could be, might become), and an actual place—at that moment the struggle for empire is launched. This coincidence is the logic both for Westerners taking possession of land and, during decolonization, for resisting natives reclaiming it. Imperialism and the culture associated with it affirm both the primacy of geography and an ideology about control of territory. The geographical sense makes projections—imaginative, cartographic, military, economic, historical, or in a general sense cultural. It also makes possible the construction of various kinds of knowledge, all of them in one way or another dependent upon the perceived character and destiny of a particular geography.

Three fairly restricted points should be made here. First, the spatial differentiations so apparent in late-nineteenth-century novels do not simply and suddenly appear there as a passive reflection of an aggressive "age of empire," but are derived in a continuum from earlier social discriminations already authorized in earlier historical and realistic novels.

Jane Austen sees the legitimacy of Sir Thomas Bertram's overseas properties as a natural extension of the calm, the order, the beauties of Mansfield Park, one central estate validating the economically supportive role of the peripheral other. And even where colonies are not insistently or even perceptibly in evidence, the narrative sanctions a spatial moral order, whether in the communal restoration of the town of Middlemarch centrally important during a period of national turbulence, or in the outlying spaces of deviation and uncertainty seen by Dickens in London's underworld, or in the Brontë stormy heights.

A second point. As the conclusions of the novel confirm and highlight an underlying hierarchy of family, property, nation, there is also a very strong spatial *hereness* imparted to the hierarchy. The astounding power of the scene in *Bleak House* where Lady Dedlock is seen sobbing at the grave of her long dead husband *grounds* what we have felt about her secret past—her cold and inhuman presence, her disturbingly unfertile authority—in the graveyard to which as a fugitive she has fled. This contrasts not only with the disorderly jumble of the Jellyby establishment (with its eccentric ties to Africa), but also with the favored house in which Esther and her guardian-husband live. The narrative explores, moves through, and finally endows these places with confirmatory positive and/or negative values.

This moral commensuration in the interplay between narrative and domestic space is extendable, indeed reproducible, in the world beyond metropolitan centers like Paris or London. In turn such French or English places have a kind of export value: whatever is good or bad about places at home is shipped out and assigned comparable virtue or vice abroad. When in his inaugural lecture in 1870 as Slade Professor at Oxford, Ruskin speaks of England's pure race, he can then go on to tell his audience to turn England into a "country again [that is] a royal throne of kings; a sceptred isle, for all the world a source of light, a centre of peace." The allusion to Shakespeare is meant to re-establish and relocate a preferential feeling for England. This time, however, Ruskin conceives of England as functioning *formally* on a world scale; the feelings of approbation for the island kingdom that Shakespeare had imagined principally but not exclusively confined at home are rather startlingly mobilized for imperial, indeed aggressively colonial service. Become colonists, found "colonies as fast and as far as [you are] able," he seems to be saying.[28]

My third point is that such domestic cultural enterprises as narrative fiction and history (once again I emphasize the narrative component) are premised on the recording, ordering, observing powers of the central authorizing subject, or ego. To say of this subject, in a quasi-tautological manner, that it writes because it *can* write is to refer not only to domestic society but to the outlying world. The capacity to represent, portray, characterize, and depict is not easily available to just any member of just any society; moreover, the "what" and "how" in the representation of "things," while allowing for considerable individual freedom, are circumscribed and socially regulated. We have become very aware in recent years of the constraints upon the cultural representation of women, and the pressures that go into the created representations of inferior classes and races. In all these areas—gender, class, and race—criticism has correctly focussed upon the institutional forces in modern Western societies that shape and set limits on the representation of what are considered essentially subordinate beings; thus representation itself has been characterized as keeping the subordinate subordinate, the inferior inferior.

NOTES

1. Richard Slotkin, *Regeneration Through Violence: The Mythology of the American Frontier, 1600–1860* (Middletown: Wesleyan University Press, 1973); Patricia Nelson Limerick, *The Legacy of Conquest: The Unbroken Past of the American West* (New York: Norton, 1988); Michael Paul Rogin, *Fathers and Children: Andrew Jackson and the Subjugation of the American Indian* (New York: Knopf, 1975).
2. Bruce Robbins, *The Servant's Hand: English Fiction from Below* (New York: Columbia University Press, 1986).
3. Gareth Stedman Jones, *Outcast London: A Study in the Relationship Between the Classes in Victorian Society* (1971; rprt. New York: Pantheon, 1984).
4. Eric Wolf, *Europe and the People Without History* (Berkeley: University of California Press, 1982).
5. Martin Green, *Dreams of Adventure, Deeds of Empire* (New York: Basic Books, 1979); Molly Mahood, *The Colonial Encounter: A Reading of Six Novels* (London: Rex Collings, 1977); John A. McClure, *Kipling and Conrad: The Colonial Fiction* (Cambridge, Mass.: Harvard University Press, 1981); Patrick Brantlinger, *The Rule of Darkness: British Literature and Imperialism 1830–1914* (Ithaca: Cornell University Press, 1988). See also John Barrell, *The Infection of Thomas de Quincey: A Psychopathology of Imperialism* (New Haven: Yale University Press, 1991).
6. William Appleman Williams, *Empire as a Way of Life* (New York and Oxford: Oxford University Press, 1980), pp. 112–13.
7. Jonah Raskin, *The Mythology of Imperialism* (New York: Random House, 1971); Gordon K. Lewis, *Slavery, Imperialism, and Freedom: Studies in English Radical Thought* (New York: Monthly Review, 1978); V. G. Kiernan, *The Lords of Human Kind: Black Man, Yellow Man, and White Man in an Age of Empire* (1969; rprt. New York: Columbia University Press, 1986), and *Marxism and Imperialism* (New York: St. Martin's Press, 1974). A more recent work is Eric Cheyfitz, *The Poetics of Imperialism: Translation and Colonization from* The Tempest *to* Tarzan (New York: Oxford University Press, 1991). Benita Parry, *Conrad and Imperialism* (London: Macmillan, 1983), cogently discusses these and other works in the context provided by Conrad's fiction.
8. E. M. Forster, *Howards End* (New York: Knopf, 1921), p. 204.

9. Raymond Williams, *Politics and Letters: Interviews with New Left Review* (London: New Left, 1979), p. 118.

10. Williams's *Culture and Society, 1780–1950*, was published in 1958 (London: Chatto & Windus).

11. Joseph Conrad, "Heart of Darkness," in *Youth and Two Other Stories* (Garden City: Doubleday, Page, 1925), pp. 50–51. For a demystifying account of the connection between modern culture and redemption, see Leo Bersani, *The Culture of Redemption* (Cambridge, Mass.: Harvard University Press, 1990).

12. Theories and justifications of imperial style—ancient versus modern, English versus French, and so on—were in plentiful supply after 1880. See as a celebrated example Evelyn Baring (Cromer), *Ancient and Modern Imperialism* (London: Murray, 1910). See also C. A. Bodelsen, *Studies in Mid-Victorian Imperialism* (New York: Howard Fertig, 1968), and Richard Faber, *The Vision and the Need: Late Victorian Imperialist Aims* (London: Faber & Faber, 1966). An earlier but still useful work is Klaus Knorr, *British Colonial Theories* (Toronto: University of Toronto Press, 1944).

13. Ian Watt, *The Rise of the Novel* (Berkeley: University of California Press, 1957); Lennard Davis, *Factual Fictions: The Origins of the English Novel* (New York: Columbia University Press, 1983); John Richetti, *Popular Fiction Before Richardson* (London: Oxford University Press, 1969); Michael McKeon, *The Origin of the English Novel, 1600–1740* (Baltimore: Johns Hopkins University Press, 1987).

14. J. R. Seeley, *The Expansion of England* (1884; rprt. Chicago: University of Chicago Press, 1971), p. 12; J. A. Hobson, *Imperialism: A Study* (1902; rprt. Ann Arbor: University of Michigan Press, 1972), p. 15. Although Hobson implicates other European powers in the perversions of imperialism, England stands out.

15. Raymond Williams, *The Country and the City* (New York: Oxford University Press, 1973), pp. 165–82 and *passim*.

16. D.C.M. Platt, *Finance, Trade and Politics in British Foreign Policy, 1815–1914* (Oxford: Clarendon Press, 1968), p. 536

17. Ibid., p. 357.

18. Joseph Schumpeter, *Imperialism and Social Classes*, trans. Heinz Norden (New York: Augustus M. Kelley, 1951), p. 12.

19. Platt, *Finance, Trade and Politics*, p. 359.

20. Ronald Robinson and John Gallagher, with Alice Denny, *Africa and the Victorians: The official Mind of Imperialism* (1961; new ed. London: Macmillan, 1981), p. 10. But for a vivid sense of what effects this thesis has had in scholarly discussion of empire, see William Roger Louis, ed., *Imperialism: The Robinson and Gallagher Controversy* (New York: Franklin Watts, 1976). An essential compilation for the whole field of study is Robin Winks, ed., *The Historiography of the British Empire-Commonwealth: Trends, Interpretations, and Resources* (Durham: Duke University Press, 1966). Two compilations mentioned by Winks (p. 6) are *Historians of India, Pakistan and Ceylon*, ed. Cyril H. Philips, and *Historians of South East Asia*, ed. D.G.E. Hall.

21. Fredric Jameson, *The Political Unconscious: Narrative as a Socially Symbolic Act* (Ithaca: Cornell University Press, 1981); David A. Miller, *The Novel and the Police* (Berkeley: University of California Press, 1988). See also Hugh Ridley, *Images of Imperial Rule* (London: Croom Helm, 1983).

22. In John MacKenzie, *Propaganda and Empire: The Manipulation of British Public Opinion, 1880–1960* (Manchester: Manchester University Press, 1984), there is an excellent account of how popular culture was effective in the official age of empire. See also MacKenzie, ed., *Imperialism and Popular Culture* (Manchester: Manchester University Press, 1986); for more subtle manipulations of the English national identity during the same period, see Robert Colls and Philip

Dodd, eds., *Englishness: Politics and Culture, 1880–1920* (London: Croom Helm, 1987). See also Raphael Samuel, ed., *Patriotism; The Making and Unmaking of British National Identity*, 3 vols. (London: Routledge, 1989).

23. E. M. Forster, *A Passage to India* (1924; rprt. New York: Harcourt, Brace & World, 1952), p. 231.

24. For the attack on Conrad, see Chinua Achebe, "An Image of Africa: Racism in Conrad's *Heart of Darkness,*" in *Hopes and Impediments: Selected Essays* (New York: Doubleday, Anchor, 1989), pp. 1–20. Some of the issues raised by Achebe are well discussed by Brantlinger, *Rule of Darkness*, pp. 269–74.

25. Deirdre David, *Fictions of Resolution in Three Victorian Novels* (New York: Columbia University Press, 1981).

26. Georg Lukacs, *The Historical Novels*, trans. Hannah and Stanley Mitchell (London: Merlin Press, 1962), pp. 19–88.

27. Ibid., pp. 30–63.

28. A few lines from Ruskin are quoted and commented on in R. Koebner and H. Schmidt, *Imperialism: The Story and Significance of a Political World, 1840–1866* (Cambridge: Cambridge University Press, 1964), p. 99.

BORDERLANDS / LA FRONTERA: THE NEW MESTIZA (1987, 1999)

GLORIA ANZALDÚA

Blending poetry and prose, English, Spanish, Spanglish, and Nahuatl and drawing on her vision of a feminist and queer blending of autobiography, history, theory, and advocacy, Anzaldúa insists on a mixing of national, racial, sexual, and gendered cultures and identities—Mexican, Chicana, Indian, mestiza (racially "mixed"), lesbian, working class, Tejana. She sees colonialist and patriarchal assumptions as denying the ordinariness of such mixtures and denying the porousness of the border that cultural mixtures evoke. For Anzaldúa, borders and cultural mixtures are metaphors of each other. She calls for crossing the borders of multiple identities instead of supposing that different identities can run along separate paths. Anzaldúa sees the political and cultural border between Mexico and the United States as a figure of the irrepressible yet contested mobility of Latina/Latino peoples and their cultures. Following Anzaldúa, some critics continue to expand the metaphor of the border and see it as a figure of the multiplicity of all history and of contemporary and postmodern global mixing, crossing, and mobility. This selection is the second chapter of Borderlands / La Frontera.

Movimentos de rebeldía y las culturas que traicionan

Esos movimientos de rebeldía que tenemos en la sangre nosotros los mexicanos surgen como ríos desbocanados en mis venas. Y como mi raza que cada en cuando deja caer esa esclavitud de obedecer; de callarse y aceptar, en mi está la rebeldía encimita de mi carne. Debajo de mi humillada mirada está una cara insolente lista para explotar. Me costó muy caro mi rebeldía—acalambrada con desvelos y dudas, sintiéndome inútil, estúpida, e impotente.

Me entra una rabia cuando alguien—sea mi mamá, la Iglesia, la cultura de los anglos—me dice haz esto, haz eso sin considerar mis deseos.

Repele. Hable pa' 'tras. Fui muy hocicona. Bra indiferente a muchos valores de mi culture. No me dejé de los hombres. No fui buena ni obediente.

Pero he crecido. Ya no sólo paso toda mi vida botando las costumbres y los valores de mi cultura que me traicionan. También recojo las costumbres que por el tiempo se han probado y las costumbres de respeto a las mujeres. But despite my growing tolerance, for this Chicana *la guerra de independencia* is a constant.

THE STRENGTH OF MY REBELLION

I have a vivid memory of an old photograph: I am six years old. I stand between my father and mother, head cocked to the right, the toes of my flat feet gripping the ground. I hold my mother's hand.

To this day I'm not sure where I found the strength to leave the source, the mother, disengage from my family, *mi tierra, mi gente,* and all that picture stood for. I had to leave home so I could find myself, find my own intrinsic nature buried under the personality that had been imposed on me.

I was the first in six generations to leave the Valley, the only one in my family to ever leave home. But I didn't leave all the parts of me: I kept the ground of my own being. On it I walked away, taking with me the land, the Valley, Texas. *Gané mi camino y me largué. Muy andariega mi hija.* Because I left of my own accord *me dicen, "¿Cómo te gusta la mala vida?"*

At a very early age I had a strong sense of who I was and what I was about and what was fair. I had a stubborn will. It tried constantly to mobilize my soul under my own regime, to live life on my own terms no matter how unsuitable to others they were. *Terca.* Even as a child I would not obey. I was "lazy." Instead of ironing my younger brothers' shirts or cleaning the cupboards, I would pass many hours studying, reading, painting, writing. Every bit of self-faith I'd painstakingly gathered took a beating daily. Nothing in my culture approved of me. *Había agarrado malos pasos.* Something was "wrong" with me. *Estaba más allá de la tradición.*

There is a rebel in me—the Shadow-Beast. It is a part of me that refuses to take orders from outside authorities. It refuses to take orders from my conscious will, it threatens the sovereignty of my rulership. It is that part of me that hates constraints of any kind, even those self-imposed. At the least hint of limitations on my time or space by others, it kicks out with both feet. Bolts.

CULTURAL TYRANNY

Culture forms our beliefs. We perceive the version of reality that it communicates. Dominant paradigms, predefined concepts that exist as unquestionable, unchallengeable, are transmitted to us through the culture. Culture is made by those in power—men. Males make the rules and laws; women transmit them. How many times have I heard mothers and mothers-in-law tell their sons to beat their wives for not obeying them, for being *hociconas* (big mouths), for being *callejeras* (going to visit and gossip with neighbors), for expecting their husbands to help with the rearing of children and the housework, for wanting to be something other than housewives?

The culture expects women to show greater acceptance of, and commitment to, the value system than men. The culture and the Church insist that women are subservient to males. If a woman rebels she is a *mujer mala*. If a woman doesn't renounce herself in favor of the male, she is selfish. If a woman remains a *virgen* until she marries, she is a good woman. For a woman of my culture there used to be only three directions she could turn: to the Church as a nun, to the streets as a prostitute, or to the home as a mother. Today some of us have a fourth choice: entering the world by way of education and career and becoming self-autonomous persons. A very few of us. As a working class people our chief activity is to put food in our mouths, a roof over our heads and clothes on our backs. Educating our children is out of reach for most of us. Educated or not, the onus is still on woman to be a wife/mother—only the nun can escape motherhood. Women are made to feel total failures if they don't marry and have children. "*¿Y cuándo te casas, Gloria? Se te va a pasar el tren.*" Y yo les digo, "*Pos si me caso, no va ser con un hombre.*" Se quedan calladitas. Sí, soy hija de la Chingada. I've always been her daughter. *No 'tés chingando.*

Humans fear the supernatural, both the undivine (the animal impulses such as sexuality, the unconscious, the unknown, the alien) and the divine (the superhuman, the god in us). Culture and religion seek to protect us from these two forces. The female, by virtue of creating entities of flesh and blood in her stomach (she bleeds every month but does not die), by virtue of being in tune with nature's cycles, is feared. Because, according to Christianity and most other major religions, woman is carnal, animal, and closer to the undivine, she must be protected. Protected from herself. Woman is the stranger, the other. She is man's recognized nightmarish pieces, his Shadow-Beast. The sight of her sends him into a frenzy of anger and fear.

La gorra, el rebozo, la mantilla are symbols of my culture's "protection" of women. Culture (read males) professes to protect women. Actually it keeps women in rigidly defined roles. It keeps the girlchild from other men—don't poach on my preserves, only I can touch my child's body. Our mothers taught us well, "*Los hombres nomás quieren una cosa*"; men aren't to be trusted, they are selfish and are like children. Mothers made sure we didn't walk into a room of brothers or fathers or uncles in nightgowns or shorts. We were never alone with men, not even those of our own family.

Through our mothers, the culture gave us mixed messages: *No voy a dejar que ningún pelado desgraciado maltrate a mis hijos.* And in the next breath it would say, *La mujer tiene que hacer lo que le diga el hombre.* Which was it to be—strong, or submissive, rebellious or conforming?

Tribal rights over those of the individual insured the survival of the tribe and were necessary then, and, as in the case of all indigenous peoples in the world who are still fighting off intentional, premeditated murder (genocide), they are still necessary.

Much of what the culture condemns focuses on kinship relationships. The welfare of the family, the community, and the tribe is more important than the welfare of the individual. The individual exists first as kin—as sister, as father, as *padrino*—and last as self.

In my culture, selfishness is condemned, especially in women; humility and selflessness, the absence of selfishness, is considered a virtue. In the past, acting humble with members outside the family ensured that you would make no one *envidioso* (envious); therefore he or she would not use witchcraft against you. If you get above yourself, you're an *envidiosa*. If you don't behave like everyone else, *la gente* will say that you think you're better than others, *que te crees grande*. With ambition (condemned in the Mexican culture and valued in the Anglo) comes envy. *Respeto* carries with it a set of rules so that social categories and hierarchies will be kept in order: respect is reserved for *la abuela, papá, el patrón*, those with power in the community. Women are at the bottom of the ladder one rung above the deviants. The Chicano, *mexicano*, and some Indian cultures have no tolerance for deviance. Deviance is whatever is condemned by the community. Most societies try to get rid of their deviants. Most cultures have burned and beaten their homosexuals and others who deviate from the sexual common.[1] The queer are the mirror reflecting the heterosexual tribe's fear: being different, being other and therefore lesser, therefore subhuman, in-human, non-human.

HALF AND HALF

There was a *muchacha* who lived near my house. *La gente del pueblo* talked about her being *una de las otras*, "of the Others." They said that for six months she was a woman who had a vagina that bled once a month, and that for the other six months she was a man, had a penis and she peed standing up. They called her half and half, *mita'y mita'*, neither one nor the other but a strange doubling, a deviation of nature that horrified, a work of nature inverted. But there is a magic aspect in abnormality and so-called deformity. Maimed, mad, and sexually different people were believed to possess supernatural powers by primal cultures' magico-religious thinking. For them, abnormality was the price a person had to pay for her or his inborn extraordinary gift.

There is something compelling about being both male and female, about having an entry into both worlds. Contrary to some psychiatric tenets, half and halfs are not suffering from a confusion of sexual identity, or even from a confusion of gender. What we are suffering from is an absolute despot duality that says we are able to be only one or the other. It claims that human nature is limited and cannot evolve into something better. But I, like other queer people, am two in one body, both male and female. I am the embodiment of the *hieros gamos:* the coming together of opposite qualities within.

FEAR OF GOING HOME: HOMOPHOBIA

For the lesbian of color, the ultimate rebellion she can make against her native culture is through her sexual behavior. She goes against two moral prohibitions: sexuality and homosexuality. Being lesbian and raised Catholic, indoctrinated as straight, I *made the choice to be queer* (for some it is genetically inherent). It's an interesting path, one that continually slips in and out of the white, the Catholic, the Mexican, the indigenous, the instincts. In and out of my head. It makes for *loquería*, the crazies. It is a path of knowledge—one of knowing (and of learning) the history of oppression of our *raza*. It is a way of balancing, of mitigating duality.

In a New England college where I taught, the presence of a few lesbians threw the more conservative heterosexual students and faculty into a panic. The two lesbian students and we two lesbian instructors met with them to discuss their fears. One of the students said, "I thought homophobia meant fear of going home after a residency."

And I thought, how apt. Fear of going home. And of not being taken in. We're afraid of being abandoned by the mother, the culture, *la Raza*, for being unacceptable, faulty, damaged. Most of us unconsciously believe that if we reveal this unacceptable aspect of the self our mother/culture/race will totally reject us. To avoid rejection, some of us conform to the values of the culture, push the unacceptable parts into the shadows. Which leaves only one fear—that we will be found out and that the Shadow-Beast will break out of its cage. Some of us take another route. We try to make ourselves conscious of the Shadow-Beast, stare at the sexual lust and lust for power and destruction we see on its face, discern among its features the undershadow that the reigning order of heterosexual males project on our Beast. Yet still others of us take it another step: we try to waken the Shadow-Beast inside us. Not many jump at the chance to confront the Shadow-Beast in the mirror without flinching at her lidless serpent eyes, her cold clammy moist hand dragging us underground, fangs bared and hissing. How does one put feathers on this particular serpent? But a few of us have been lucky—on the face of the Shadow-Beast we have seen not lust but tenderness; on its face we have uncovered the lie.

INTIMATE TERRORISM: LIFE IN THE BORDERLANDS

The world is not a safe place to live in. We shiver in separate cells in enclosed cities, shoulders hunched, barely keeping the panic below the surface of the skin, daily drinking shock along with our morning coffee, fearing the torches being set to our buildings, the attacks in the streets. Shutting down. Woman does not feel safe when her own culture, and white culture, are critical of her; when the males of all races hunt her as prey.

Alienated from her mother culture, "alien" in the dominant culture, the woman of color does not feel safe within the inner life of her Self. Petrified, she can't respond, her face caught between *los intersticios*, the spaces between the different worlds she inhabits.

The ability to respond is what is meant by responsibility, yet our cultures take away our ability to act—shackle us in the name of protection. Blocked, immobilized, we can't move forward, can't move backwards. That writhing serpent movement, the very movement of life, swifter than lightning, frozen.

We do not engage fully. We do not make full use of our faculties. We abnegate. And there in front of us is the crossroads and choice: to feel a victim where someone else is in control and therefore responsible and to blame (being a victim and transferring the blame on culture, mother, father, ex-lover, friend, absolves me of responsibility), or to feel strong, and, for the most part, in control.

My Chicana identity is grounded in the Indian woman's history of resistance. The Aztec female rites of mourning were rites of defiance protesting the cultural changes which disrupted the equality and balance between female and male, and protesting their demotion to a lesser status, their denigration. Like *la Llorona*, the Indian woman's only means of protest was wailing.

So *mamá, Raza,* how wonderful, *no tener que rendir cuentas a nadie.* I feel perfectly free to rebel and to rail against my culture. I fear no betrayal on my part because, unlike Chicanas and other women of color who grew up white or who have only recently returned to their native cultural roots, I was totally immersed in mine. It wasn't until I went to high school that I "saw" whites. Until I worked on my master's degree I had not gotten within an arm's distance of them. I was totally immersed *en lo mexicano,* a rural, peasant, isolated, *mexicanismo.* To separate from my culture (as from my family) I had to feel competent enough on the outside and secure enough inside to live life on my own. Yet in leaving home I did not lose touch with my origins because *lo mexicano* is in my system. I am a turtle, wherever I go I carry "home" on my back.

Not me sold out my people but they me. So yes, though "home" permeates every sinew and cartilage in my body, I too am afraid of going home. Though I'll defend my race and culture when they are attacked by non-*mexicanos, conozco el malestar de mi cultura.* I abhor some of my culture's ways, how it cripples its women, *como burras,* our strengths used against us, lowly *burras* bearing humility with dignity. The ability to serve, claim the males, is our highest virtue. I abhor how my culture makes *macho* caricatures of its men. No, I do not buy all the myths of the tribe into which I was born. I can understand why the more tinged with Anglo blood, the more adamantly my colored and colorless sisters glorify their colored culture's values—to offset the extreme devaluation of it by the white culture. It's a legitimate reaction. But I will not glorify those aspects of my culture which have injured me and which have injured me in the name of protecting me.

So, don't give me your tenets and your laws. Don't give me your lukewarm gods. What I want is an accounting with all three cultures—white, Mexican, Indian. I want the freedom to carve and chisel my own face, to staunch the bleeding with ashes, to fashion my own gods out of my entrails. And if going home is denied me then I will have to stand and claim my space, making a new culture—*una cultura mestiza*—with my own lumber, my own bricks and mortar and my own feminist architecture.

THE WOUNDING OF THE *INDIA*-MESTIZA

Estas carnes indias que despreciamos nosotros los mexicanos asi como despreciamos condenamos a nuestra madre, Malinali. Nos condenamos a nosotros mismos. Esta raza vencida, enemigo cuerpo.

Not me sold out my people but they me. *Malinali Tenepat,* or *Malintzín,* has become known as *la Chingada*—the fucked one. She has become the bad word that passes a dozen times a day from the lips of Chicanos. Whore, prostitute, the woman who sold out her people to the Spaniards are epithets Chicanos spit out with contempt.

The worst kind of betrayal lies in making us believe that the Indian woman in us is the betrayer. We, *indias y mestizas,* police the Indian in us, brutalize and condemn her. Male culture has done a good job on us. *Son las costumbres que traicionan. La india en mí es la sombra: La Chingada, Tlazolteotl, Coatlicue. Son ellas que oyemos lamentando a sus hijas perdidas.*

Not me sold out my people but they me. Because of the color of my skin they betrayed me. The dark-skinned woman has been silenced, gagged, caged, bound into servitude with marriage, bludgeoned for 300 years, sterilized and castrated in the twentieth century. For 300 years she has been a slave, a force of cheap labor, colonized by the Spaniard, the Anglo, by her own people (and in Mesoamerica her lot under the Indian patriarchs was not free of wounding). For 300 years she was invisible, she was not heard. Many times she wished to speak, to act, to protest, to challenge. The odds were heavily against her. She hid her feelings; she hid her truths; she concealed her fire; but she kept stoking the inner flame. She remained faceless and voiceless, but a light shone through her veil of silence. And though she was unable to spread her limbs and though for her right now the sun has sunk under the earth and there is no moon, she continues to tend the flame. The spirit of the fire spurs her to fight for her own skin and a piece of ground to stand on, a ground from which to view the world—a perspective, a homeground where she can plumb the rich ancestral roots into her own ample *mestiza* heart. She waits till the waters are not so turbulent and the mountains not so slippery with sleet. Battered and bruised she waits, her bruises throwing her back upon herself and the rhythmic pulse of the feminine. *Coatlalopeuh* waits with her.

> *Aquí en la soledad prospera su rebeldía.*
> *En la soledad Ella prospera.*

NOTE

1. Francisco Guerra, *The Pre-Columbian Mind: A study into the aberrant nature of sexual drives, drugs affecting behaviour, and the attitude towards life and death, with a survey of psychotherapy in pre-Columbian America* (New York, NY: Seminar Press, 1971).

TALKING BLACK: CRITICAL SIGNS OF THE TIMES (1988, 1992)

HENRY LOUIS GATES, JR.

Some readers who are not white resent and try to avoid critical theory because they suppose it is too white or too European. In this essay, first written for a panel called "Integrity and the Black Tradition," Gates offers his response to that resentment. Gates might have challenged the assumptions underlying the reluctance to engage with critical theory. After all, it is not possible to have no theory, for that, too, would be a theory. And not all whites or Europeans share the same ideas. They often disagree with each other, to say the least. Moreover, although a majority of the theorists who have most influenced Anglo-American and European critical thinking are white, many are not. Even Jacques Derrida, often described as French, was from Algeria in north Africa, although he moved to France at age nineteen. Instead of raising such questions, though, Gates focuses on the position of African Americans. He argues against segregating African American thinking from the rest of the world, even though the rest of the world has often thought in racist ways. (As an example he cites the Southern Agrarians, who were close intellectual colleagues of some of the key new critics.) Gates also argues that African American thinkers, in dialogue with the rest of the world, should develop their own theorizing, drawing on African American language, traditions, and "structures of thought and feeling." (Even in such an expression, Gates draws on the white British leftist critic Raymond Williams's concept of "structures of feeling.") In The Signifying Monkey: A Theory of African-American Literary Criticism, *Gates himself proposes a language for black theory by drawing on patterns from African American speech, including the tradition of "signi-fyin'" (playful language that signifies on or plays off earlier language, as in the language-game known as "the dozens"). Gates weaves black notions of signifyin' with Saussurean and Derridean (structuralist and deconstructionist) notions of signifying to propose a new African American theory of African American literature. This essay is a call for other critics and readers to remain engaged with the wide range of critical theory and to change it, as Gates himself changes it, by taking up the challenge of making an African American critical theory.*

For a language acts in diverse ways, upon the spirit of a people; even as the spirit of a people acts with a creative and spiritualizing force upon a language.

—Alexander Crummell, 1860

A new vision began gradually to replace the dream of political power—a powerful movement, the rise of another ideal to guide the unguided, another pillar of fire by night after a clouded day. It was the ideal of "book-learning"; the curiosity, born of compulsory ignorance, to know and test the power of the cabalistic letters of the white man, the longing to know. Here at last seemed to have been discovered the mountain path to Canaan; longer than the highway of Emancipation and law, steep and rugged, but straight, leading to heights high enough to overlook life.

—W.E.B. Du Bois, 1903

The knowledge which would teach the white world was Greek to his own flesh and blood. . . . and he could not articulate the message of another people.

—W.E.B. Du Bois, 1903

Alexander Crummell, a pioneering nineteenth-century Pan-Africanist, statesman, and missionary who spent the bulk of his creative years as an Anglican minister in Liberia, was also a pioneering intellectual and philosopher of language, founding the American Negro Academy in 1897 and serving as the intellectual godfather of W.E.B. Du Bois. For his first annual address as president of the academy, delivered on December 28, 1897, Crummell selected as his topic "The Attitude of the American Mind Toward the Negro Intellect." Given the occasion of the first annual meeting of the great intellectuals of the race, he could not have chosen a more timely or appropriate subject.

Crummell wished to attack, he said, "the denial of intellectuality in the Negro; the assertion that he was not a human being, that he did not belong to the human race." He argued
that the desire "to becloud and stamp out the intellect of the Negro" had led to the enactment of "laws and Statutes, closing the pages of every book printed to the eyes of Negroes;
barring the doors of every school-room against them!" This, he concluded, "was the systematized method of the intellect of the South, to stamp out the brains of the Negro!"—a
program that created an "almost Egyptian darkness [which] fell upon the mind of the race,
throughout the whole land."

Crummell next shared with his audience a conversation between two Boston lawyers
which he had overheard when he was "an errand boy in the Anti-slavery office in New York
City" in 1833 or 1834:

> While at the Capitol they happened to dine in the company of the great John C. Calhoun,
> then senator from South Carolina. It was a period of great ferment upon the question of
> Slavery, States' Rights, and Nullification; and consequently the Negro was the topic of con-
> versation at the table. One of the utterances of Mr. Calhoun was to this effect—"That if he
> could find a Negro who knew the Greek syntax, he would then believe that the Negro was a
> human being and should be treated as a man."

"Just think of the crude asininity," Crummell concluded rather generously, "of even a great
man!"

The salient sign of the black person's humanity—indeed, the only sign for Calhoun—
would be the mastering of the very essence of Western civilization, of the very foundation
of the complex fiction upon which white Western culture had been constructed. It is likely
that "Greek syntax," for John C. Calhoun, was merely a hyperbolic figure of speech, a trope
of virtual impossibility; he felt driven to the hyperbolic mode, perhaps, because of the long
racist tradition in Western letters of demanding that black people *prove* their full humanity.
We know this tradition all too well, dotted as it is with the names of the great intellectual
Western racialists, such as Francis Bacon, David Hume, Immanuel Kant, Thomas Jefferson,
and G. W. F. Hegel. Whereas each of these figures demanded that blacks write poetry to
prove their humanity, Calhoun—writing in a post-Phillis Wheatley era—took refuge in, yes,
Greek syntax.

In typical African-American fashion, a brilliant black intellectual accepted Calhoun's
challenge. The anecdote Crummell shared with his fellow black academicians turned out
to be his shaping scene of instruction. For Crummell himself jumped on a boat, sailed to
England, and matriculated at Queens' College, Cambridge, where he mastered the intricacies of Greek syntax. Calhoun, we suspect, was not impressed.

Crummell never stopped believing that mastering the master's tongue was the sole
path to civilization, intellectual freedom, and social equality for the black person. It was
Western "culture," he insisted, that the black person "must claim as his rightful heritage,
as a man—not stinted training, not a caste education, not," he concluded prophetically,
"a Negro curriculum." As he argued so passionately in his speech of 1860, "The English
Language in Liberia," the acquisition of the English language, along with Christianity, is the
wonderful sign of God's providence encoded in the nightmare of African enslavement in the

racist wilderness of the New World. English, for Crummell, was "the speech of Chaucer and Shakespeare, of Milton and Wordsworth, of Bacon and Burke, of Franklin and Webster," and its potential mastery was "this one item of compensation" that "the Almighty has bestowed upon us" in exchange for "the exile of our fathers from their African homes to America." In the English language are embodied "the noblest theories of liberty" and "the grandest ideas of humanity." If black people master the master's tongue, these great and grand ideas will become African ideas, because "ideas conserve men, and keep alive the vitality of nations."

In dark contrast to the splendors of the English language, Crummell set the African vernacular languages, which, he wrote, have "definite marks of inferiority connected with them all, which place them at the widest distances from civilized languages." Any effort to render the master's discourse in our own black tongue is an egregious error, for we cannot translate sublime utterances "in[to] broken English—a miserable caricature of their noble tongue." We must abandon forever both indigenous African vernacular languages and the neo-African vernacular languages that our people have produced in the New World:

> All low, inferior, and barbarous tongues are, doubtless, but the lees and dregs of noble languages, which have gradually, as the soul of a nation has died out, sunk down to degradation and ruin. We must not suffer this decay on these shores, in this nation. We have been made, providentially, the deposit of a noble trust; and we should be proud to show our appreciation of it. Having come to the heritage of this language we must cherish its spirit, as well as retain its letter. We must cultivate it among ourselves; we must strive to infuse its spirit among our reclaimed and aspiring natives.

I cite the examples of John C. Calhoun and Alexander Crummell as metaphors for the relation between the critic of black writing and the broader, larger institution of literature. Learning the master's tongue, for our generation of critics, has been an act of empowerment, whether that tongue be New Criticism, humanism, structuralism, Marxism, poststructuralism, feminism, new historicism, or any other "ism." Each of these critical discourses arises from a specific set of texts within the Western tradition. At least for the past decade, many of us have busied ourselves with the necessary task of learning about these movements in criticism, drawing upon their modes of reading to explicate the texts in our own tradition.

This is an exciting time for critics of Afro-American literature. More critical essays and books are being produced than ever before, and there have never been more jobs available teaching Afro-American literature in white colleges and universities. In a few years, we shall at last have our very own Norton anthology, a sure sign that the teaching of Afro-American literature is being institutionalized. Our pressing question now becomes this: In what languages shall we choose to speak, and write, our own criticisms? What are we now to do with the enabling masks of empowerment that we have donned as we have practiced one mode of formal criticism or another?

There is a long history of resistance to (white) theory in the (black) tradition. Unlike almost every other, the Afro-American literary tradition was generated as a response to allegations that its authors did not, and *could not* create literature, considered the signal measure of a race's innate "humanity." The African living in Europe or in the New World seems to have felt compelled to create a literature not only to demonstrate that blacks did indeed possess the intellectual ability to create a written art, but also to indict the several social and economic institutions that delimited the "humanity" of all black people in Western cultures.

So insistent did these racist allegations prove to be, at least from the eighteenth to the early twentieth century, that it is fair to describe the subtext of the history of black letters in terms of the urge to refute them. Even as late as 1911, when J. E. Casely-Hayford published *Ethiopia Unbound* (the "first" African novel), he felt it necessary to address this matter in the first two paragraphs of this text. "At the dawn of the twentieth century," the novel opens, "men of light and leading both in Europe and in America had not yet made up their minds as to what place to assign to the spiritual aspirations of the black man." Few literary traditions have begun with such a complex and curious relation to criticism: allegations of an absence led directly to a presence, a literature often inextricably bound in a dialogue with its harshest critics.

Black literature and its criticism, then, have been put to uses that were not primarily aesthetic; rather, they have formed part of a larger discourse on the nature of the black, and of his or her role in the order of things. The relation among theory, tradition, and integrity within black culture has not been, and perhaps cannot be, a straightforward matter.

Despite the fact that critics of black literature are often attacked for using theory and that some black readers respond to their work by remarking that it's all Greek to them, it is probably true that critics of Afro-American literature are more concerned with the complex relation between literature and theory than ever before. There are many reasons for this, not the least of which is our increasingly central role in "the profession" precisely when our colleagues are engulfed in their own extensive debates about the intellectual merit of so much theorizing. Theory, as a second-order reflection upon a primary gesture, has *always* been viewed with suspicion by scholars who find it presumptuous and even decadent when criticism claims the right to stand on its own: theoretical texts breed equally "decadent" theoretical responses in a creative process that can be very far removed from a poem or a novel.

For the critic of Afro-American literature, this process is even more perilous because most of the contemporary literary theory derives from critics of Western European languages and literatures. Is the use of theory to write about Afro-American literature merely another form of intellectual indenture, a mental servitude as pernicious in its intellectual implications as any other kind of enslavement? The key word implied in this panel discussion is *integrity*. To quote the *Oxford English Dictionary*'s definition of the word, does theorizing about a text or a literary tradition "mar," "violate," "impair," or "corrupt" the "soundness" of an "original perfect state" of a black text or of the black tradition? To argue that it does is to align oneself with the New Critics—who often seem not to have cared particularly for, or about, the writing of Afro-Americans—and with their view that texts are "organic wholes" in the first place. This is a critical error.

The sense of "integrity" as it seems to arise in the Afro-American tradition is more akin to the notion of "ringing true," or to Houston Baker's concept of "sounding." (One of the most frequently used critical judgments in the African-American tradition is "That just don't sound right," or, as Alice Walker puts it in *The Color Purple*, "Look like to me only a fool would want to talk in a way that feel peculiar to your mind.") That is the sense that black nationalists call on here, without understanding how problematic this can be. Doubleness, alienation, equivocality—since the turn of the century at least, these have been recurrent tropes for the black tradition.

To be sure, this matter of criticism and "integrity" has a long and rather tortured history in black letters. It was David Hume, after all, who called Francis Williams, the Jamaican poet of Latin verse, "a parrot who merely speaks a few words plainly." Phillis Wheatley, too, has long suffered from the spurious attacks of black and white critics alike for being the *rara avis* of a school of so-called mockingbird poets, whose use of European and American literary conventions has been considered a corruption of a "purer" black expression, found in forms such as the blues, signifying, spirituals, and Afro-American dance. Can we, as critics, escape a "mockingbird" relation to theory? And can we escape the racism of so many critical theorists, from Hume and Kant through the Southern Agrarians and the Frankfurt School?

Only recently have some scholars attempted to convince critics of black literature that we can. Perhaps predictably, a number of these attempts share a concern with that which has been most repressed in the received tradition of Afro-American criticism: close readings of the texts themselves. My advocacy of theory's value for such readings is meant as a prelude to the definition of critical principles peculiar to the black literary traditions, related to contemporary theory generally and yet, as Robert Farris Thompson puts it, "indelibly black." I have tried to work through contemporary theories of literature not to "apply" them to black texts, but to transform by translating them into a new rhetorical realm—to recreate, through revision, the critical theory at hand. As our familiarity with the black tradition and with literary theory expands, we shall invent our own black, text-specific theories, as some of us have begun to do. We must learn to read a black text within a black formal cultural matrix, as well as its "white" matrix.

This is necessary because the existence of a black canon is a historically contingent phenomenon; it is not inherent in the nature of "blackness," not vouchsafed by the metaphysics of some racial essence. The black tradition exists only insofar as black artists enact it. Only because black writers have read and responded to other black writers with a sense of recognition and acknowledgment can we speak of a black literary inheritance, with all the burdens and ironies that has entailed. Race is a text (an array of discursive practices), not an essence. It must be *read* with painstaking care and suspicion, not imbibed.

I have tried to employ contemporary theory to defamiliarize the texts of the black tradition: ironically, it is necessary to create distance between reader and texts in order to go beyond reflexive responses and achieve critical insight into and intimacy with their formal workings. I have done this to respect the "integrity" of these texts, by trying to avoid confusing my experience as an Afro-American with the act of language that defines a black text. This is the challenge of the critic of black literature in the 1980s: not to shy away from white power—that is, literary theory—but to translate it into the black idiom, *renaming* principles of criticism where appropriate, but especially *naming* indigenous black principles of criticism and applying them to our own texts. *Any* tool that enables the critic to explain the complex workings of the language of a text is appropriate here. For it is language, the black language of black texts, that expresses the distinctive quality of our literary tradition. Once it may have seemed that the only critical implements black critics needed were the pom-pom and the twirled baton; in fact, there is no deeper form of literary disrespect. We will not protect the "integrity" of our tradition by remaining afraid of, or naive about, literary theory; rather, we will inflict upon it the violation of reflexive, stereotypical readings—or nonreading. We are the keepers of the black literary tradition. No matter what theories we embrace, we have more in common with each other than we do with any other critic of any other literature. We write for each other, and for our own contemporary writers. This relation is a critical trust.

It is also a *political* trust. How can the demonstration that our texts sustain ever closer and more sophisticated readings *not* be political at a time when all sorts of so-called canonical critics mediate their racism through calls for "purity" of the "tradition," demands as implicitly racist as anything the Southern Agrarians said? How can the deconstruction of the forms of racism itself not be political? How can the use of literary analysis to explicate the racist social text in which we still find ourselves be anything *but* political? To be political, however, does not mean that I have to write at the level of a Marvel comic book. My task, as I see it, is to help guarantee that black and so-called Third World literature is taught to black and Third World and white students by black and Third World and white professors in heretofore white mainstream departments of literature, and to train students to think, to read, and to write clearly, to expose false uses of language, fraudulent claims, and muddled arguments, propaganda, and vicious lies—from all of which our people have suffered just as surely as we have from an economic order in which we were zeros and a metaphysical order in which we were absences. These are the "values" which should be transmitted through critical theory.

In the December 1986 issue of the *Voice Literary Supplement,* in an essay entitled "Cult-Nats Meet Freaky-Deke," Greg Tate argued cogently and compellingly that "black aestheticians need to develop a coherent criticism to communicate the complexities of our culture. There's no periodical on black cultural phenomena equivalent to *The Village Voice* or *Artforum,* no publication that provides journalism on black visual art, philosophy, politics, economics, media, literature, linguistics, psychology, sexuality, spirituality, and pop culture. Though there are certainly black editors, journalists, and academics capable of producing such a journal, the disentregration of the black cultural nationalist movement and the brain-drain of black intellectuals to white institutions have destroyed the vociferous public dialogue that used to exist between them." While I would argue that *Sage, Callaloo,* and *Black American Literature Forum (BALF)* are indeed fulfilling that function for academic critics, I am afraid that the truth of Tate's claim is irresistible.

But his most important contribution to the future of black criticism is to be found in his most damning allegation. "What's unfortunate," he writes, "is that while black artists have opened up the entire 'text of blackness' for fun and games, not many black critics have produced writing as fecund, eclectic, and freaky-deke as the art, let alone the culture, itself.... For those who prefer exegesis with a polemical bent, just imagine how critics as fluent in black and Western culture as the postliberated artists could strike terror into that bastion of white supremacist thinking, the Western art [and literary] world[s]." To which I can only say, echoing Shug in Alice Walker's *The Color Purple,* "Amen. Amen."

Tate's challenge is a serious one because neither ideology nor criticism nor blackness can exist as entities of themselves, outside the forms of their texts. This is the central theme of Ralph Ellison's *Invisible Man* and Ishmael Reed's *Mumbo Jumbo,* for example. But how can we write or read the text of "Black Theory"? What language(s) do black people use to represent their critical or ideological positions? In what forms of language do we speak or write? Can we derive a valid, integral "black" text or criticism or ideology from borrowed or appropriated forms? Can a black woman's text emerge "authentically" as borrowed, or "liberated," or revised, from the patriarchal forms of the slave narratives, on the one hand, or from the white matriarchal forms of the sentimental novel, on the other, as Harriet Jacobs and Harriet Wilson attempted to do in *Incidents in the Life of a Slave Girl* (1861) and *Our Nig* (1859)? Where lies the liberation in revision, the ideological integrity of defining freedom in the modes and forms of difference charted so cogently by so many poststructural critics of black literature?

For it is in these spaces of difference that black literature has dwelled. And while it is crucial to read these patterns of difference closely, we must understand as well that the quest was lost, in a major sense, before it had even begun, simply because the terms of our own self-representation have been provided by the master. It is not enough for us to show that refutation, negation, and revision exist, and to define them as satisfactory gestures of ideological independence. Our next concern must be to address the black political signified, that is, the cultural vision and the critical language that underpin the search through literature and art for a profound reordering and humanizing of everyday existence. We must urge our writers and critics to undertake the fullest and most ironic exploration of the manner and matter, the content and form, the structure and sensibility so familiar and poignant to us in our most sublime form of art, black music, where ideology and art are one, whether we listen to Bessie Smith or to postmodern and poststructural John Coltrane.

Just as we must urge our writers to meet this challenge, we as critics must turn to own peculiarly black structures of thought and feeling to develop our own languages of criticism. We must do so by drawing on the black vernacular, the language we use to speak to each other when no outsiders are around. Unless we look to the vernacular to ground our theories and modes of reading, we will surely sink in the mire of Nella Larsen's quicksand, remain alienated in the isolation of Harriet Jacob's garret, or masked in the received stereotype of the Black Other helping Huck to return to the raft, singing "China Gate" with Nat King Cole under the Da Nang moon, or reflecting our bald heads in the shining flash of Mr. T's signifying gold chains.

We must redefine theory itself from within our own black cultures, refusing to grant the racist premise that theory is something that white people do, so that we are doomed to imitate our white colleagues, like reverse black minstrel critics done up in whiteface. We are all heirs to critical theory, but critics are also heir to the black vernacular critical tradition as well. We must not succumb, as did Alexander Crummell, to the tragic lure of white power, the mistake of accepting the empowering language of white critical theory as "universal" or as our only language, the mistake of confusing the enabling mask of theory with our own black faces. Each of us has, in some literal or figurative manner, boarded a ship and sailed to a metaphorical Cambridge, seeking to master the master's tools. (I myself, being quite literal-minded, booked passage some fourteen years ago on the *QE2*.) Now we must at last don the empowering mask of blackness and talk *that* talk, the language of black difference. While it is true that we must, as Du Bois said so long ago, "know and test the power of the cabalistic letters of the white man," we must also know and test the dark secrets of a black discursive universe that awaits its disclosure through the black arts of interpretation. For the future of theory, in the remainder of this century, is black indeed.

IMPERIALIST NOSTALGIA (1989)

RENATO ROSALDO

In this opening section from a longer chapter of Culture and Truth: The Remaking of Social Analysis, *anthropologist Rosaldo observes how colonialist cultures often romanticize the people they colonize, thus trying to hide from themselves their own responsibility for the social change and devastation that colonialism causes. The remainder of Rosaldo's chapter, not included here, draws on examples from anthropologists' writing about the Ilongots, a people in the Philippines, including examples from Rosaldo's own writing.*

My anger at recent films that portray imperialism with nostalgia informs this chapter. Consider the enthusiastic reception of *Heat and Dust, A Passage to India, Out of Africa,* and *The Gods Must Be Crazy.* The white colonial societies portrayed in these films appear decorous and orderly, as if constructed in accord with the norms of classic ethnography. Hints of these societies' coming collapse only appear at the margins where they create not moral indignation but an elegiac mode of perception. Even politically progressive North American audiences have enjoyed the elegance of manners governing relations of dominance and subordination between the "races." Evidently, a mood of nostalgia makes racial domination appear innocent and pure.

Much as the previous chapter showed that the language of social analysis is not a neutral medium, this one argues that the observer is neither innocent nor omniscient. In my view, it is a mistake to urge social analysts to strive for a position of innocence designated by such adjectives as detached, neutral, or impartial. Under imperialism, metropolitan observers are no more likely to avoid a certain complicity with domination than they are to avoid having strong feelings toward the people they study. Such recognitions need not lead either to confessional breast-beating or to galloping bias. If social analysts realize that they cannot be perfectly "clean," they no more should become as "dirty" as possible than airline pilots, invoking the limitations of human fallibility, should blind their eyes. The usual notions of evidence, accuracy, and argumentation continue to apply for their studies.

Because researchers are necessarily both somewhat impartial and somewhat partisan, somewhat innocent and somewhat complicit, their readers should be as informed as possible about what the observer was in a position to know and not know. To return to this book's introduction, has the writer of an ethnography on death suffered a serious personal loss?

MOURNING FOR WHAT ONE HAS DESTROYED

Curiously enough, agents of colonialism—officials, constabulary officers, missionaries, and other figures from whom anthropologists ritually dissociate themselves—often display nostalgia for the colonized culture as it was "traditionally" (that is, when they first encountered it). The peculiarity of their yearning, of course, is that agents of colonialism long for the very forms of life they intentionally altered or destroyed. Therefore, my concern resides with a particular kind of nostalgia, often found under imperialism, where people mourn the passing of what they themselves have transformed.

Imperialist nostalgia revolves around a paradox: A person kills somebody, and then mourns the victim. In more attenuated form, someone deliberately alters a form of life, and then regrets that things have not remained as they were prior to the intervention. At one more remove, people destroy their environment, and then they worship nature. In any of its versions, imperialist nostalgia uses a pose of "innocent yearning" both to capture people's imaginations and to conceal its complicity with often brutal domination.

Imperialist nostalgia occurs alongside a peculiar sense of mission, "the white man's burden," where civilized nations stand duty-bound to uplift so-called savage ones. In this ideologically constructed world of ongoing progressive change, putatively static savage societies become a stable reference point for defining (the felicitous progress of) civilized identity. "We" (who believe in progress) valorize innovation, and then yearn for more stable worlds, whether these reside in our own past, in other cultures, or in the conflation of the two. Such forms of longing thus appear closely related to secular notions of progress. When the so-called civilizing process destabilizes forms of life, the agents of change experience transformations of other cultures as if they were personal losses.

Nostalgia is a particularly appropriate emotion to invoke in attempting to establish one's innocence and at the same time talk about what one has destroyed. Don't most people feel nostalgic about childhood memories? Aren't these memories genuinely innocent? Indeed, much of imperialist nostalgia's force resides in its association with (indeed, its disguise as) more genuinely innocent tender recollections of what is at once an earlier epoch and a previous phase of life. For my generation, one can, for example, evoke nostalgia by imitating radio voices saying "Call for Philip Morris," "The Shadow knows," or "Who was that masked man?" The relatively benign character of most nostalgia facilitates imperialist nostalgia's capacity to transform the responsible colonial agent into an innocent bystander. If most such recollections were not fairly harmless, the imperialist variety would not be nearly as effective as it is.

To "us," feelings of nostalgia seem almost as "natural" as motor reflexes. How can one help but feel nostalgic about childhood memories? Don't all people in all times and in all places feel nostalgia? Yet even the history of the concept in Western Europe reveals the historical and cultural specificity of our notion of nostalgia. Far from being eternal, the term *nostalgia* dates from the late seventeenth century, when, according to sociologist Fred Davis, a Swiss physician coined the term (from the Greek *nostos*, a return home, and *algos*, a painful condition) to refer to pathological conditions of homesickness among his nation's mercenaries who were fighting far from their homeland. (Even in its origins, the term appears to have been associated with processes of domination.) Davis explains that the symptoms of "nostalgia" among the Swiss mercenaries included "despondency, melancholia, lability of emotion, including profound bouts of weeping, anorexia, a generalized 'wasting away', and, not infrequently, attempts at suicide."[1] Evidently, nostalgia in the late seventeenth century was a weightier matter than the more innocent mood "we" at times experience in recalling our youths. In any case, the changing meanings of "nostalgia" in Western Europe (not to mention that many cultures have no such concept at all) indicate that "our" feelings of tender yearning are neither as natural nor as pan-human, and therefore not necessarily as innocent, as one might imagine.

Imperialist nostalgia has recently been analyzed by a number of scholars who regard the process of yearning for what one has destroyed as a form of mystification, although they do not use the term *imperialist nostalgia*. In a manuscript on the invention of Appalachia as a cultural category, anthropologist Allen Batteau, for example, studies the phenomenon in historical perspective.[2] He argues that during the last decade of the nineteenth century, as the frontier was closing, racism was codified and people began to deify nature and its Native American inhabitants. This attitude of reverence toward the natural developed at the same time that North Americans intensified the destruction of their human and natural environment. In showing how cultural notions about Appalachia were part of a larger dynamic, Batteau likens this process of idealization to forms of sacrifice where people draw a line between the profane (their civilization) and the sacred (nature), and then worship the very thing their civilizing process is destroying.

In a related analysis, North American historian Richard Slotkin suggests that frontier mythology in part revolves around a hunter hero who lives out his dreams in spiritual sympathy with the creatures of the wilderness who teach him their secret lore. "But his intention," Slotkin says, "is always to use the acquired skill against the teachers, to kill or assert his dominance over them. The consummation of his hunting quest in the killing of the quarry confirms him in his new and higher character and gives him full possession of the powers of the wilderness."[3] In this analysis, the disciple turns on his spiritual masters and achieves redemption by killing them. This frontier myth, which Slotkin calls regeneration through violence, shaped American experience from the westward expansion through the imperialist venture in the Philippines to the early official rhetoric of the Vietnam War.

Yet other scholars attempt to demystify imperialist nostalgia through a more frontal assault: They vigorously assert that the past was no better, and most probably worse, than the present. Rather than claim that nostalgia conceals guilt, they try to eliminate altogether the validity of elegiac postures toward small towns and rural communities. In a recent stimulating book on modernity, for example, social critic Marshall Berman attacks reverential postures toward traditional society by claiming that they are "idealized fantasies" designed to gloss over violence and brutality. The devastating portrait of such a society in Goethe's Gretchen tragedy in *Faust*, he says, "should etch in our minds forever the cruelty and brutality of so many of the forms of life that modernization has wiped out. So long as we remember Gretchen's fate, we will be immune to nostalgic yearning for the worlds we have lost."[4] Although Berman and I both aspire to "immunize" readers from such nostalgia, he apparently misses the paradox in his claim that modernization has "wiped out" brutal forms of life. His vigorous denial appears peculiar when one considers that the author, who condemns past "cruelty and brutality" (does he mean barbarism?), lives in a modern world noted for napalm, concentration camps, atomic bombs, torture, and systematic genocide. In my view, Berman combats overly romantic visions of bygone harmonious societies by simply standing them on their head. Instead of inflating the value of small-scale communities, he comes uncomfortably close to reproducing an ideology of progress that celebrates modernity at the expense of other forms of life.

1. Fred Davis, *Yearning for Yesterday: A Sociology of Nostalgia* (New York: Free Press, 1979), pp. 1–2. See also, David Lowenthal, *The Past Is a Foreign Country* (New York: Cambridge University Press, 1985).
2. Allen Batteau, "Romantic Appalachia: The Semantics of Social Creation and Control" (1986, book typescript).
3. Richard Slotkin, *Regeneration through Violence: The Mythology of the American Frontier, 1600–1860* (Middletown, Conn.: Wesleyan University Press, 1973), p. 551.
4. Marshall Berman, *All That Is Solid Melts into Air: The Experience of Modernity* (New York: Simon and Schuster, 1982), p. 60.

DISCOURSE AND DAT COURSE: POSTCOLONIALITY AND AFROCENTRICITY (1996)

ANN DUCILLE

Ann duCille's essay explains its contexts so lucidly that it needs little introduction. Leery of the abstract theorizing in much of postcolonial studies, she theorizes (in concrete terms) its relation to contemporary university politics and asks what African American studies, Afrocentrism, and postcolonial studies have in common, how they differ, and how they can learn from each other.

After the Egyptian and Indian, the Greek and Roman, the Teuton and Mongolian, the Negro is a sort of seventh son, born with a veil, and gifted with second-sight in this American world,—a world which yields him no true self-consciousness, but only lets him see himself through the revelation of the other world. It is a peculiar sensation, this double-consciousness, this sense of always looking at one's self through the eyes of others, of measuring one's soul by the tape of a world that looks on in amused contempt and pity.

—W. E. B. Du Bois, *The Souls of Black Folk* (1903)

For every action there is an equal and opposite reaction. For every doubly conscious racial or ethnic other constructed by institutions, there is a self attempting to assert its subjectivity. For many intellectuals, asserting a racial or national self has meant claiming as "familiar" everything African, Indian, or Caribbean and expelling as "foreign" all things British, French, Spanish, or even Anglo-American. Yet centuries of close encounters of the Columbian kind have produced a world out of joint, and often it is the would-be familiar that is foreign and the self that is alien. Black Americans, many of whom will never see Dakar or Lagos, choose African names from books (most likely published in the United States or Britain) in unknowing contradiction of the very cultural traditions they wish to celebrate.

In many traditional West African societies—the Yoruba of Nigeria, for instance—naming is an essential postnatal ritual, a communal event that generally takes place after birth, after a child has been presented to a waiting extended family, which only then christens the infant in ceremonial splendor and cultural specificity. For Africans whose names were so chosen, the would-be Afrocentric American tradition of christening a child *in utero*—with the aid of a book of African names—is close to sacrilege. Much the same is true for the Afrocentric practice whereby black adults rename themselves. Ghanaian names are especially popular among African Americans seeking to reclaim what slavery stripped them of; but for many Ghanaians the idea of an adult man born on a Monday naming himself Kofi (Friday) rather than Kojo (Monday) is at once laughable and lamentable.

This misnaming and other efforts to reclaim a homeland reinscribe our cultural dislocation. We sport Afros and don dreadlocks as visible signs of our essential Africanness, unaware that in most contemporary African societies, these "specifically diasporean" styles would identify us with the west, with the first world and not the third.[1]

Even the language in which we write at once underscores our alienation from "home" and our arrival within the academy; it is not in Hindi or Yoruba that we contemplate our postcoloniality and Afrocentricity, but in the fine and proper English of the colonizer. What we seek is a precolonial connection; what we theorize is a postcolonial condition; what we're stuck with is a perennial colonial contradiction. Illiterate in the languages of the homeland, we must use the master's tongue to talk our way out of his house—even when that house is on *our* land. As we labor to expel the alien within, our acts of intellectual and political exorcism, however culturally empowering, often produce blindspots that misshape our postcolonial conditions and our Afrocentric ideas.

ETHNIC NOTIONS

Afrocentric ideas are everywhere, it seems—from the "African Pride" hair straighteners sold in the "Ethnic Needs" aisle at Super Stop & Shop, to the fake kente placemats available though J.C. Penney's "Afrocentric" catalogue. In academic arenas, Afrocentrism has at times joined forces with multiculturalism in challenging the Eurocentric bent of public education and lobbying for curriculum changes at both the elementary and secondary school levels. In other instances, demands for Afrocentric curricula in urban areas such as Detroit and Milwaukee have led to the establishment of academies devoted exclusively to the education of young black men. When it comes to higher education, the epicenter of Afrocentricism is, indisputably, the African American Studies department at Temple University, home to Molefi Kete Asante—the nation's premier proponent of Afrocentricity (a term he coined)—and over two hundred graduate students.

Because the term has been used to include everything from food and fashion to racial fundamentalism, Afrocentrism has become a hot topic both within and outside the academy. Academic journals have fanned the flames of the increasingly heated debate between black intellectuals such as Henry Louis Gates—head of Afro-American Studies at Harvard—and cultural nationalists like Asante, who heads Temple's African American Studies department. What's at stake in this ideological campaign, most spectators agree, is the very future of black studies.

While academia waits eagerly to see if Gates and Harvard's black intelligentsia can indeed "kick Asante's ass,"[2] the media are busy tracking what they perceive to be the more radical (hence more newsworthy) antics of "loud-mouth extremists" and conspiracy theorists, such as Louis Farrakhan and Khalid Muhammad of the Nation of Islam and Leonard Jeffries of the City University of New York. Indeed, the popular press seems to take special delight in linking academic Afrocentrism of the Asante kind with what it calls the loony theories and antisemitic utterings of the likes of Jeffries, who—in the words of one set of reporters—"seems to believe in a conspiracy to oppress blacks that stretches from classrooms to the Mafia and Jewish movie producers."[3]

Tempting as these topics are, I would rather focus on the increasingly fraught (but less often discussed) relationship between postcoloniality and Afrocentricity as intellectual perspectives, as acclaimed and disclaimed discourses respectively. Occupied with each other, some Afrocentrists and multiculturalists have little noticed that the academy has opened its doors to another oppositional discourse: postcolonial studies. Others have not only noticed; they have begun to fear for their own intellectual lives.

As an African Americanist, I make no claim of neutrality, but I do want to say that I am neither a proponent of Afrocentricity nor an opponent of postcoloniality. My hope is, first, to discuss what these two disciplines have in common as therapeutic antidotes to imperialism and, second, to explore their different deployments within academia. What does it mean, for example, when Afrocentricity is dismissed as methodologically sloppy, anti-intellectual identity politics, while postcoloniality is affirmed as theoretically sophisticated oppositional discourse? The most critical factor in the reception of these two resistance narratives may have more to do with market than with methodology—with the academic merchandising of *different* difference.

If postcoloniality is discourse—an exotic, foreign field whose time has come within the U.S. academy—Afrocentricity is "dat course"—local color (homeboys and homegirls) whose time has come and gone, if indeed it ever was. Blacks are after all, in the words of Richard Wright, America's metaphor. Our otherness has become in some ways too familiar. In American feminist studies, the enslavement and breeding of African women is yesterday's news, like the Doberman biting the mailman. Widow burning, on the other hand, is not simply history; it is story.

POPULARIZING THE POSTCOLONIAL

In a special issue of *Social Text*, which, among other things, interrogates such phrases as "third world" and "postcolonial," Ella Shohat defines the latter term as "a new designation for critical discourses which thematize issues emerging from colonial relations and their aftermath."[4] Indira Karamcheti has also taken note of the increasing popularity of all things "postcolonial": postcolonial theory, postcolonial studies, and postcolonial literature. "The stars of postcolonial literary studies shine brightly in the dim skies of academe," Karamcheti writes, citing Edward Said, Gayatri Chakravorty Spivak, Kwame Anthony Appiah, Gauri Viswanathan, Sara Suleri, R. Radhakrishnan, Abdul JanMohamed, and Rey Chow.[5]

Like the presence of these luminary scholars, interest in postcoloniality is everywhere in the academy: in journal articles, including several special issues devoted entirely to postcolonial themes (in *Representations*, *PMLA*, *Callaloo*, and *Social Text*); at university presses that have started postcolonial series; in job announcements calling for specialists in postcolonial literary, theoretical, and cultural studies; in learned societies whose annual meetings for the past few years have sponsored panels devoted to postcolonial themes. For many of us who regularly read such publications and attend such conferences, these times have felt more and more like the dawning of a new age.

Although the designation "postcolonial" may be new, the study of power relations between colonizer and colonized is not. In the United States, black intellectuals such as W. E. B. Du Bois, Alexander Crummell, Pauline Hopkins, and Anna Julia Cooper discussed such themes in the late nineteenth and early twentieth centuries. More recently, but still decades before the rise of postcoloniality as an academic discipline, black activists and scholars, writers such as Marcus Garvey, Claude McKay, C. L. R. James, Frantz Fanon, and Aimé Césaire explored and exploded colonial and postcolonial power relations. In current academic theaters, Stuart Hall, Sylvia Wynter, Selwyn Cudjoe, Cedric Robinson, Alex Dupuy, Paget Henry, Paul Gilroy, Hazel Carby, bell hooks, Audre Lorde, Angela Davis, and Cheikh Anta Diop are among the many scholars of African descent who continue to probe the relationship between Prospero and Caliban, metropole and province.

The difference between my list of black scholars and the earlier inventory of Asian postcolonial theorists is a distinction that has inspired at least two kinds of charges from some Afrocentrists: that once again foreigners have taken over *our* field, and that it takes the interest of outsiders to legitimize a discourse of which the academy took little note when it was dominated by diasporic blacks. Although these charges have a certain history, they may not be pertinent to the rise of postcolonial studies. There is at least one other causal relation that Afrocentrism has all but ignored: spontaneous generation, in which postcoloniality (like Afrocentricity) developed as an equal and opposite reaction to the oppressions of imperialism. Postcoloniality is not so much the heir apparent to and beneficiary of other resistance narratives as it is their coincidence—an oppositional discourse with its own history of what Paget Henry calls "discursive insurrection," played out in the texts of native writers throughout the subaltern.[6]

Were I well versed in other "minority literatures," I could no doubt rattle off an impressive list of Indian, Middle Eastern, or Southeast Asian textual insurrectionists. The first-world academy in which so many of us are trained, however, has rarely fostered knowledge of either the non-European self or the foreign other. In attending so narrowly to its own racial and cultural self, Afrocentrism—more correctly, some brands of Afrocentrism—perpetuates the same divide-and-conquer ignorance on which imperialism has depended.

But if Afrocentricity errs in its cultural ethnocentrism, postcoloniality, precisely because it is taken more seriously by the academy, has an even more dangerously myopic relation to the company it keeps and the company that keeps it. Like Afrocentricity, it suffers from a limited perspective that sees its own colonized body in relation to a particular imperial force, even as it claims a global view. Moreover, the academy to which it has become attached has a vested interest in promoting the illusions of grandeur that the very term *postcolonial* suggests. From the ivory tower, conceptualizing a politically correct postcolonial globe makes it easier to get around the fact that much of the world's population lives in conditions that are hardly "postcolonial." This is particularly true of women who, as Anne McClintock notes, "do 2/3 of the world's work, earn 10% of the world's income, and own less than 1% of the world's property."[7] False universals, such as the postcolonial woman, the postcolonial other, the postcolonial condition, and even the postcolonial critic, camouflage the variety of neo-colonial circumstances in which masses of people live, work, and theorize. If Afrocentricity has an overdetermined (and some say grossly exaggerated) sense of its own glorious past, the false universals of postcoloniality often obscure both its lineage and its connection to other narratives of marginality.

Postcolonial discourse rises today in the U.S. academy as a more elegant incarnation of what used to be called world literature, third-world literature, Commonwealth studies, or area studies—all contemplations of the exotic, foreign other. As an academic discipline, postcoloniality takes its current preeminence not only from the traditional, often orientalist, and remarkably well-funded area studies it has somewhat eclipsed, but also from the very resistance narratives it seems to threaten: black studies and women's studies, for example. Unlike African American and other local narratives of marginality, postcoloniality is being figured as a universal master narrative containing all difference. "If it continues to be developed as a totalizing narrative cut off from a local place," Indira Karamcheti warns, "it can be used within academia to displace those minority groups whose social struggles for inclusion, empowerment, and representation cleared the space within which postcoloniality operates."[8] Put another way, its ties to poststructuralism and the dissolution of the essential features of many minority discourses make postcoloniality not simply a resistance narrative but a containment strategy.

Karamcheti is not alone in warning of the potential abuses of academic postcoloniality. Noting that some ethnic-studies scholars feel set adrift by the rising tide of postcolonial studies in English departments, Ella Shohat suggests that the term *postcolonial* has received ready institutional endorsement because it enables a "partial containment of the POCs (people of color)." In the North American context, she adds, "one has the impression that the 'postcolonial' is privileged precisely because it seems safely distant from 'the belly of the beast,' the United States."[9] Whereas the critique from African American studies and the alternative worldview from Afrocentricity cut uncomfortably close to home, postcoloniality seems to pose its opposition from a distance—as Gayatri Spivak might say, "in other worlds."

DISLOCATED DISCOURSES

But postcoloniality is a discourse still in the process of locating itself. It has been taken up by an academy that does not necessarily know what it is. Afrocentricity, by contrast, has been dismissed by the same academy that knows only too well what it is. Despite a current breath of life from Molefi Asante, the Afrocentric idea is hardly a new one. Speaking perhaps reductively, one could say that this effort to read diasporic experiences through reconstituted African ideals, belief systems, and cultural traditions has led other lives as Pan-Africanism, Garveyism, and back-to-African-ism in the 1920s, as negritude in the 1930s, and as the black-arts, black-power, and black-is-beautiful movements of the 1960s.

However empowering it may be for some black scholars, Afrocentricity has been spurned not only by much of the white European and Anglo-American academy but also by such leading black intellectuals as Clarence Walker, Cornel West, and Gates. West, for example, defines Afrocentrism as a contemporary brand of black nationalism that is gallant in its focus on "black doings and sufferings," but misguided in its fear of cultural hybridization, its inattention to issues of class, and its retrograde views on gender and sexuality.[10] Barbara Ransby, who sees Afrocentricity as a much misunderstood concept whose very definition is contested, reminds us that cultural nationalists like Asante do not have a monopoly on the term. (Patricia Hill Collins, for one, defines her decidedly black feminist perspective as Afrocentric, though her sociological work bears little resemblance to the male-centered theorizing of Asante.) Ransby rightly credits Asante for his role in forcing the academy to confront its Eurocentrism, but she also details some of the weaknesses in his brand of Afrocentrism, including sexism and homophobia. Analyzing the work of Haki Madhubuti and Na'im Akbar as well, Ransby argues that their brand of Afrocentrism denies the contributions of gay and lesbian activists and ignores the oppression of black women.[11]

Rejected even by what it would take to be "its own," Afrocentricity is a kind of bad-kid ideology within academia, a thankless-child anti-intellectualism that denies daddy, resists paternity, refuses to acknowledge Europe as its great white father. As its very name implies, postcoloniality, by contrast, seems to be a properly indebted, if rebellious, intellectual offspring. Its name announces its relation not to Mother Africa or India or China but to Father Europe, the colonizer without whom there would be neither colonial nor postcolonial. Where Afrocentricity is culturally exclusive and self-centered, postcoloniality is intellectually elastic and decentered. Where the former disdains theory, the latter thrives on it. Where the one is "unembarrassingly black," in the words of Joyce Joyce, the other is black only by default—de fault of being nonwhite.

The nonwhite, no-fault "blackness" of Indian, Bengali, Asian, Arab, Egyptian, and other "brown" postcolonial scholars has proven a boon for the North American academy. For one thing, affirmative action need no longer be an act of contrition. The displacement of cultural and geopolitical difference has enabled an easier diversity, a "black" presence without the historical and political particularities of Spivak's "black blacks." The academy, in effect, gets to eat its chocolate cake and have it too. Among the ingredients it leaves out, however, are racial identity, geopolitical ethnicity, and cultural specificity.

Both Afrocentricity and postcoloniality, it seems to me, have their origins in this hard-to-swallow difference—in an alterity that is at once institutionally promoted and intellectually denied. By this I mean that, on the one hand, the academy fosters a kind of skin trade that has made alterity the bestseller in the intellectual marketplace. On the other hand, it theorizes racial differences in solipsisms that obscure color, class, caste, culture, gender, sexuality, and place. Blackness becomes the metonymic expression of race, and the rainbow coalition is viewed on a dichromatic scale that only sees black and white. Put another way, though race may be a sign of irreducible difference, it also may be a sign of reducible *sameness*—of a homogenization that refuses specificity.[12] Let me clarify the point I'm trying to make by returning to the example of the Indian.

At one point in my research on Barbie dolls, I was in desperate pursuit of Indian Barbie. Dealers, collectors, and salesclerks understood readily enough what I meant when I asked for Eskimo Barbie or Spanish Barbie or Malaysian Barbie or Jamaican Barbie, but when I said I was looking for Indian Barbie, the response was either a question—"American or East Indian?"—or the assumption that I meant the doll Mattel markets as Native American Barbie.

In the continental United States, "Indians" have red skin and live on reservations, where they play bingo, build casinos, and plot to take over white people's land. Columbus discovered and named these people five hundred years ago. Marlon Brando rediscovered them in the 1960s, as did Kevin Costner in the 1990s. Even though it repeats Columbus's blunder, we continue to call these people Indians. Our current use of "Indian" as a synonym both for "native" and for "Native American" replicates the fifteenth- and sixteenth-century usage of the term as a generic designation for "nonwhite"—a misnomenclature that, through the centuries, has given the world Asian, African, Australian, Mexican, Caribbean, Hawaiian, and many varieties of North and South American "Indians." What does this mean for natives of the Indian subcontinent—for people of the Indus—whose own cultural, racial, and geopolitical specificity is denied by this generic use of the name they would call themselves?

For the postcolonial from the jewel in the crown of the British Raj, claiming self—claiming "Indianness"—in the United States begins not only with the assertion of India, the land Columbus did not discover, but with the unnaming of the "Indians," the people he supposedly did. Then, too, there are the multiracial, ethnically variegated inhabitants of the Caribbean, the "West Indians." What are we to make of them? Contemplating all these Indians (something we rarely do in the academy) brings back the silly song I learned in elementary school: "One little, two little, three little Indians." Even if some of them appear without warpaint and tomahawks, three little Indians are at least two too many for intellectual ease and theoretical comfort. First-world academia gets around this problem, it seems to me, by erasing "Indianness" from its lexicon, if not its cultural consciousness. It has largely ignored Columbus's misnamed Indian, except where the discourse of political correctness and romantic notions of native spirituality have necessitated a kind of lip-service to the "Native American."[13] It has translated the multivocality, racial diversity, and ethnic variety of what it calls the West Indian into a monochromatic scale of ubiquitous blackness, ignoring both Indians from India and the native Caribs and Arawaks. The "one little, two little, three little Indians" have been replaced by "the black" or, more recently, "the postcolonial"; that is to say, the same academy that rushed to validate postcoloniality has done away with Indianness. The alterity of the Indian as postcolonial is generic, categorical, locational, but, interestingly enough, not racial or at least not racially specific. Race, it seems, is the proper attribute of black or African people.

In Great Britain, Indians are considered "black," along with Africans, Afro-Caribbeans, and African Americans. In the United States, the racial status of Indians and several other minorities has varied with the political and social agenda of the historical moment. Anthropologically, Indians in India were classified as Caucasians, but when migration to the United States began in the early 1900s, that designation did not necessarily entitle them to the rights and privileges of other white immigrants, particularly naturalization, landownership, and citizenship. In 1922, the Supreme Court in *U.S. v. Thind* ruled that Bhagat Sigh Thind, a high-caste Punjabi, was not eligible for U.S. citizenship because he was not white in the sense intended by the framers of the Constitution. Academically, in this country, the racial status of Indians has been even more ambiguous. I know of more than one institution of higher learning that either by accident, ignorance, or design has augmented its statistics on the recruitment of black professors by counting Indian and other "brown" scholars among its black faculty.

On both sides of the Atlantic, a Eurocentric vision that sees only white and nonwhite translates the object of its intellectual gaze into white and black, where black is the metonym for all racial alterity. Within the U.S. academy, it is blackness, not Indianness, that has racial and cultural currency. Ironically, it is postcoloniality and not Afrocentricity that has intellectual cachet.

Returning to theories of action and reaction, I think the joke may be on the academy. I began by invoking Newton's law of motion to suggest that, for every constructed other, there is a self attempting to assert its subjectivity. Afrocentricity is, in some measure, such a reaction—an attempt to assert a distinctly African racial and cultural subjectivity, a truly black consciousness or an authentically black identity. Unfortunately, this particular effort denies cultural specificity and geopolitical ethnicity and reproduces racial hierarchies (who's blacker than whom) just as the academy does.

The vitriolic exchange in the pages of *New Literary History* (Winter 1987) between Joyce Joyce, on the one hand, and Henry Louis Gates and Houston Baker, on the other, is a glaring case in point. Arguing from an Afrocentric perspective, Joyce accuses Gates and Baker of not being black enough, even as they charge her with being too black. Similar blacker-than-thou politics are at work in Asante's response to Gates's threatened ass-kicking: "I am clear that the aping of whites is the road to neither intellectual respect nor ethical decency. Africans who exhibit confusion about their personal identities cannot hope to be clear about cultural identity."[14] Precisely the point that Gates and other multiculturalists insist on is that culture is not "clear," transhistorical, or one-dimensional—whether the assumed center is Europe or Africa.

Although the empowering premise of Afrocentric methodology offers a challenge to the universality of European paradigms, it does not sufficiently address the question of cultural mediation. Although it acknowledges blacks in the Americas as an African-derived people with their own cultural legacies, it does not adequately consider the degree to which Euro-American culture is intertwined with those around it. Nor does it consider the global implications of the imperialist agenda or what Spivak and others refer to as the colonial object.

"Cultures are not containable," the white deconstructionist Barbara Johnson tells us, and even the terms black and white are fallacious. They "imply a relation of mutual exclusion"—a binarism based on the notion of "pure, unified, and separate traditions"[15]—in the face of what are, I would add, interlocking cultural and linguistic phenomena. But in some Afrocentric circles, my acknowledgment of cultural symbiosis is a kind of heresy likely to place my blackness, like Gates's and Baker's, under suspicion. Many Afrocentrists, perhaps in reaction against notions of hybridity and the encroachments that come with them, have tried to purge themselves and African diasporic discourses of what Larry Neal called the "white thing" within. If my appropriation of Newton's ("white thing") theory holds, I wonder what the consequences will be when the postcolonial other "takes physic." Will the action of cultural erasure and racial transfiguration lead to intensified ethnic identification, sectarian struggle, and geopolitical contestation?

In part because of its engagement with theories of difference, postcoloniality as a discipline has the potential to present, in global proportions, the kind of finely honed critique of hegemonic systems that Afrocentricity as a perspective—as a therapeutic essentialism—has restricted to its own local politics. In the early 1990s I noted that the majority of scholars actively engaged in carving out the contours of postcolonial discourse were Indians. I predicted at the time that the more currency postcoloniality gained within the academy, the less this would be true. The inevitable turn away from the "authentic" Indian postcolonial to the intellectually produced postcolonialist was presaged, I argued, by a number of events around the university, including the arrival of a new generation of graduate students seeking training not in British, American, or even African American literature but in postcolonial studies.

Today there is considerable evidence that the intellectual tide has already turned, including the different first-world locations taken up in several recent publications that announce themselves as postcolonial texts. Several of these texts claim the United States, Canada, Australia, Ireland, and New Zealand as paradigmatic postcolonies, whose colonial subjects are not the native inhabitants of the land but the European settlers and their descendants. In these configurations, canonical white male authors such as Washington Irving, James Fenimore Cooper, and Herman Melville become the premier postcolonial writers. In other words, the oppositional "minority discourse" of postcoloniality is used to reaffirm the European or Anglo-American center. Such appropriations of postcolonial status may represent a form of intellectual imperialism that erases the line between colonizer and colonized. Will Indian scholars fight to hold that line, theorizing an "Indocentricity"?

As a reconstituted cultural-historical narrative, Afrocentricity serves a therapeutic function not unlike that served by other sacred texts, including the Bible and the Koran. Like the Old Testament, it is a kind of creation myth that gives a displaced people a home and a history, even as it denies the hybridity that is part of the history. My playful speculation about Indo-centricity notwithstanding, I would not wish the blind spots of Afrocentricity on another discourse. What I would wish for postcoloniality—as self-congratulating as it may seem—is not the therapeutic essentialism of Afrocentricity but the strategic essentialism of an interculturally oriented African American studies. I know the faults of my own discipline too well to hold it up as a perfect model. Instead I mean only to suggest that, as a politicized discourse, African American studies falls somewhere between the hyperlocalization and nativism of Asante's Afrocentricity and the global or universal delocalization of postcoloniality. Among other things, in its insistence on a local place, African American studies implicates the same United States that postcoloniality, for the most part, lets off the imperialist hook.

I began this chapter with Du Bois's famous ruminations on double-consciousness. I want to close my own ruminations by quoting Edward Said:

> No one today is purely *one* thing. Labels like Indian, or woman, or Muslim, or American are not more than starting-points, which if followed into actual experience for only a moment are quickly left behind. Imperialism consolidated the mixture of cultures and identities on a global scale. But its worst and most paradoxical gift was to allow people to believe that they were only, mainly, exclusively, white, or Black, or Western, or Oriental.[16]

Despite the decades and the racial and cultural differences that separate them, the visions of Du Bois and Said are remarkably similar. They both address how imperialism and colonization have turned the planet and its peoples upside down and inside out, so that no one is purely any one thing. But what do we do with this knowledge? To what use do we put this sense of our multiplicity, our interrelatedness, and our interdependence?

It is no accident, I suppose, that I am drawn to both Du Bois and Said—to African American discourse and to postcolonial theory. But what of Afrocentricity? Is it simply a straw man or false idol in the company of "legitimate" studies? If we could see beyond the tufts of straw and the feet of clay, I wonder what practitioners of these three discourses—African American studies, postcoloniality, and Afrocentricity—might learn from one another, and in particular what we might teach one another about the white academy that both claims and disclaims us. As we go about our intellectual business and launch our critiques, we would perhaps do well to be less suspicious of one another and more suspicious of the academy that promotes, demotes, and divides us. For if the world is out of joint, the university—traditionally a bastion of white male authority—is a perilous place to put it right.

NOTES

1. See Kobena Mercer, "Black Hair/Style Politics," in Russell Ferguson, Martha Gever, Trinh T. Minh-ha, and Cornel West, eds., *Out There: Marginalization and Contemporary Cultures* (New York and Cambridge: New Museum of Contemporary Art and MIT Press, 1992), pp. 247–264. Mercer writes that "however strongly these styles express a desire to 'return to the roots' among black peoples in the diaspora, in Africa *as it is* they would speak of a 'modern' orientation, a modelling of oneself according to metropolitan images of blackness" (p. 256).
2. See Greg Thomas, "The Black Studies War," *Village Voice*, January 17, 1995, pp. 23–29.

3. See Jerry Adler et al., "African Dreams," *Newsweek*, September 23, 1991, pp. 42–43.

4. Ella Shohat, "Notes on the 'Post-Colonial,' " *Social Text* 31–32 (1992), 101.

5. Indira Karamcheti, "Disciplining Postcoloniality: or, Taking Liberties with Countee Cullen," paper given at the Johns Hopkins University, Baltimore, April 30, 1993.

6. See Paget Henry and Paul Buhle, "Caliban as Deconstructionist: C.L.R. James and Post-Colonial Discourse," in Henry and Buhle, eds., *C.L.R. James's Caribbean* (Durham: Duke University Press, 1992), pp. 111–142; see also Edward Said, *Culture and Imperialism* (New York: Knopf, 1993). Said traces the history of textual or discursive insurrection—what he calls an "oppositional strain"—in the works of a variety of writers who, in one way or another and often in the "master's" own tongue, challenged the colonial order.

7. Anne McClintock, "The Angel of Progress: Pitfalls of the Term 'Post-Colonialism,' " *Social Text* 31–32 (1992), 91–92.

8. Karamcheti, "Disciplining Postcoloniality," pp. 2–3, 4–5.

9. Shohat, "Notes on the 'Post-Colonial,' " p. 108.

10. Cornel West, *Race Matters* (Boston: Beacon Press, 1993), p. 4.

11. See Barbara Ransby, "Afrocentrism, Cultural Nationalism, and the Problem with Essentialist Definitions of Race, Gender, and Sexuality," *Race and Reason* 1 (1994), 31–34.

12. Henry Louis Gates Jr., "Writing 'Race' and the Difference It Makes," in Gates, ed., *"Race," Writing, and Difference* (Chicago: University of Chicago Press, 1985), p. 5; Gayatri Chakravorty Spivak, "Interview with Sneja Gunew," in Sarah Harasym, ed., *The Post-Colonial Critic: Interview, Strategies, Dialogues* (New York: Routledge, 1990), p. 64.

13. There is of course much irony in this nomenclature, since the term "Native American" also invokes the colonizer, Amerigo Vespucci, for whom the Americas are named.

14. As quoted in Thomas, "The Black Studies War," p. 23.

15. Barbara Johnson, "Canon-Formation and the Afro-American Tradition," in Houston A. Baker Jr. and Patricia Redmond, eds., *Afro-American Literary Studies in the 1990s* (Chicago: University of Chicago Press, 1989), p. 42.

16. Said, *Culture and Imperialism*, p. 336.

THE FICTION OF ASIAN AMERICAN LITERATURE (1996)

SUSAN KOSHY

Koshy addresses the historically and culturally specific challenges of characterizing and interpreting a specific identity formation—or alliance of identity formations—and its literature, namely, Asian Americans and Asian American literature. She reviews the temptation to oversimplify identities and literary histories through essentialist categories. More provocatively, she reviews how even the resistance to oversimplifying essentialist categories can latch onto supposedly anti-essentialist versions of multiplicity that slide back into the easy answers they set out to resist. In place of such formulations, Koshy calls for a more nuanced and specific sense of how the shifting multiplicities of history and culture shape cultural and political alliances and identifications. Her interpretation of a particular example of cultural identity that resonates broadly both for that and for other examples bears comparison to Stuart Hall's essay on cultural identity elsewhere in this volume.

(Koshy's essay appears here nearly in its entirety; one brief section near the end has been excised.)

Epistemology is true as long as it accounts for the impossibility of its own beginning and lets itself be driven at every stage by its inadequacy to the things themselves. It is, however, untrue in the pretension that success is at hand and that states of affairs would ever simply correspond to its constructions and aporetic concepts.
—*Theodor W. Adorno*

ASIAN AMERICAN LITERATURE: INSTITUTIONAL LEGACIES

The boundaries of what constitutes Asian American literature have been periodically interrogated and revised, but its validity as an ordering rubric has survived these debates and repeatedly been salvaged by pointing to some existing or imminent stage of ethnogenesis, in which its representational logic would be manifest. Inherent in more recent definitions of the term has been the practice of a strategic deferral—an invocation of the work of culture-building that the debates themselves perform, and through which Asian American identity and its concomitant literature would come into being. Unlike African American, Native American or Chicano literature, Asian American literature inhabits the highly unstable temporality of the "about-to-be," its meanings continuously reinvented after the arrival of new groups of immigrants and the enactment of legislative changes.[1] However, the tactic of deferral in the interests of institutional consolidation has had its costs, and it is these costs that this essay will consider.

The affirmation of ethnic identity as a means of political and institutional space-claiming, and the very newness of the field which originated in the late sixties, have deferred questions about its founding premises. But it is precisely this question, "How are we to conceptualize Asian American literature taking into account the radical disjunctions in the emergence of the field?" that it has now become historically and politically most urgent to ask, because of pressures both inside and outside the community. The radical demographic shifts produced within the Asian American community by the 1965 immigration laws have transformed the nature and locus of literary production, creating a highly stratified, uneven and heterogeneous formation, that cannot easily be contained within the models of essentialized or pluralized ethnic identity suggested by the rubric Asian American literature, or its updated post-modern avatar Asian American literatures.[2] Moreover, we have entered a transnational era where ethnicity is increasingly produced at multiple local and global sites rather than, as before, within the parameters of the nation-state. This dispersal of ethnic identity has been intensified, in the case of Americans of Asian origin, by dramatic geopolitical realignments under way in the Pacific, that have reshaped the political imaginaries of "Asia" and "America" and the conjunctions between these two entities. Asian American literary production takes place within and participates in this transformed political and cultural landscape. Asian American Studies is, however, only just beginning to undertake a theoretical investigation of these changes, rendering itself peripheral to the developments inside its constituent group. Instead of an engagement with the new critical forces shaping its interdisciplinary project, much of the scholarship in the field has either continued to rely on paradigms of ethnicity produced in the inaugural moment of the field, or has sought to incorporate the changes through the fashionable but derivative vocabulary of post-modernism, post-colonialism or post-structuralism; formulaic invocations of "multiculturalism," "hybridity," "plural identities," or "border-crossing" are used promiscuously without any effort to link them to the material, cultural or historical specificities of the various Asian American experiences. Although substantial historical scholarship has been produced, the field has been weak in theoretical work, especially when compared to Chicano, Native American and African American Studies. The lack of significant theoretical work has affected its development and its capacity to address the stratifications and differences that constitute its distinctness within ethnic studies.

I will substantiate these arguments by reviewing the interpretive methods adopted thus far in delineating the boundaries of Asian American literature. I will do this by examining three paradigmatic attempts to discuss what constitutes Asian American literature, and analyzing the methodological problems and impasses revealed in these critical works: Frank Chin's Preface and Introduction to *Aiiieeeee! An Anthology of Asian-American Writers* (1974); Elaine Kim's full-length study *Asian American Literature: An Introduction to the Writings and Their Social Context* (1982), and her shorter essay on the subject, "Defining Asian American Realities Through Literature" (1987); and two essays by Shirley Geok-lin Lim, "Twelve Asian American Writers: In Search of Self-Definition" (1990), and "Assaying the Gold: Or, Contesting the Ground of Asian American Literature" (1993).[3] The methodological problems in these essays partake of larger historical/political and institutional legacies: the inadequacy of the pluralistic idiom of inclusion to confront the contradictions and heterogeneities within the field; the tensions between the formulation of a political identity and the critical task of situating the heterogeneity of ethnic literary production; the risks of archival recovery of ethnic texts without adequate theoretical and comparative work on the various literatures that constitute the field; and finally, the failure to come to terms with the scope and transformative impact of transnationalism on Asian American ethnicity. As an Asian American and a scholar in the field, I feel our most urgent task is to theoretically engage these problems and generate new conceptual frames that work in the interests of social change.

One of the major preoccupations in the field of Asian American literature has thus far been in documenting and compiling a rapidly expanding corpus, both through the recovery of older, neglected writers,[4] and the incorporation of new writers from the established and from the less-known immigrant groups from Korea, Southeast and South Asia. Since the official categorization of some of these groups under the designation "Asian American" is as recent as 1980 when, for instance, Asian Indians classified since 1950 as "other white" lobbied for and won reclassification in the census, the work of compilation is obviously one of urgency within the field. Moreover, the recognition ethnicity has recently accrued within an academy anxiously reconstituting its American canon has led to an increase in courses, job openings, and student interest in this emergent field. Hence, the proliferation of anthologies and bibliographies within the field bringing together the range of primary source material in order to meet this recent surge in demands.[5] But if the expansion of the field proceeds at this pace, without a more substantial theoretical investigation of the premises and assumptions underlying our constructions of commonalty and difference, we run the risk of unwittingly annexing the newer literary productions within older paradigms, overlooking radical disjunctions within more established formations like Chinese and Japanese American literature, and perpetuating hierarchies within the field.

The pluralism of inclusion, while appropriate for the task of building what Alastair Fowler has defined as the "potential canon" or "the entire written corpus, together with all surviving oral literature," can only fulfill a short-term, though crucial purpose.[6] I share with John Guillory a suspicion of a "liberal consensus whose name is 'pluralism' and whose pedagogic agenda has been exhausted in the gesture of 'opening the canon.'"[7] Pluralism offers us a means of expanding the potential canon, certainly, but as Werner Sollors has noted, this expansion is undertaken in the name of the very categories through which exclusion formerly operated; the pluralist method thus always carries the danger of reifying the categories that canonical change should work to transform.[8] Sollors offers some necessary cautions about the "mosaic procedure" that organizes many anthologies of ethnic literature: "The published results of this 'mosaic' procedure are the readers and compendiums made up of diverse essays on groups of ethnic writers who may have little in common except so-called ethnic roots while, at the same time, obvious and important literary and cultural connections are obfuscated." The latest Asian American anthologies (even more so than the earlier ones) cannot even assume the existence of common ethnic roots, since they work to include the writings of as many of their different constituent groups as possible. Moreover, since the category Asian American is itself so novel, and has undergone such radical changes of meaning in a very short while, its value as an organizing framework for literary production is much more problematic than even Sollors's generalized critique would suggest. If the theoretical challenge posed by the nomenclature is met with the assertion of an outmoded identity politics, or the more recent trend towards the postulation of a nebulous pan-Asian American consciousness, we risk repressing important connections between Asian and Asian American literature and misconceiving the dynamic, nomadic and dispersed nature of ethnogenesis in a transnational era, in the interests of recuperating a fictional notion of unity.

Although Shirley Lim has confidently asserted that "the pluralizing 's' which does not appear in discussions of Asian American literature is everywhere today assumed when critics discuss the emerging shape of Asian American literary studies" ("CGA," 162), I would argue, firstly, that such tacit acknowledgements do not relieve us of responsibility for theoretical articulations of the multiple, conflicted and emergent formations that constitute Asian American literature and, secondly, that critical work which proceeds in the absence of such theoretical delineations avoids what is one of the major challenges facing the field today, namely, to examine the impact of the recent demographic and geopolitical changes on the reconstitution of ethnicity among all the Asian American groups. The pluralism that Lim invokes merely offers an "additive approach," when what we need is a transformation of the paradigms ("CP," 276). Elaine Kim's *Asian American Literature: An Introduction to the Writings and Their Social Context*, which focuses on the writings of Chinese, Japanese, Filipino and Korean Americans, an invaluable contribution to the field in its time, offers now an obsolete mapping of the field. It remains, to date, the only book-length study that attempts to treat Asian American literature as a whole. Most other critical work offers thematic, sociohistorical, or rhetorical analyses of individual texts, authors or ethnic groups focusing on generational narratives, assimilation, motifs of resistance or feminist emergence, or the challenge to stereotypes or cliches.

SHIFTING BOUNDARIES OF ASIAN AMERICAN ETHNICITY

What makes the category "Asian American" so complex is that it has undergone reconfiguration more rapidly and to an extent that none of the other ethnic categories have. A brief summary will help elucidate this. The following account provides merely an overview: it is not intended to delineate exhaustively the many shifts, nuances and disjunctures in the historical constitution of Asian Americans. There are legitimate differences of interpretation over the content and significance of each pattern; however, such differences and debates are beyond the scope of my concerns here. Broadly speaking, then, one can chart five different historical patterns of ethnicity formation.

1) From the mid-nineteenth century to World War II, ethnicity was shaped by policies of containment and exclusion that the various Asian national groups encountered on their arrival in the U.S.[9] Economic competition and racist ideologies triggered the hostility of the white working class, particularly on the West Coast, leading to the passage of exclusionary immigration laws that were enacted first against the Chinese, then against the Japanese, Indians and Filipinos, barring their entry into the country.[10] Between the late nineteenth and early twentieth century, over 600 pieces of anti-Asian legislation were passed limiting or excluding Asians from access to housing, education, intermarriage, employment and land ownership.[11] Immigration laws limiting the entry of women, laws against miscegenation, and harsh, nomadic working conditions produced bachelor communities with such a skewed gender ratio among Chinese, Indians and Filipinos that communities were unable to reproduce themselves.[12]

The status of the various Asian national groups within the U.S. fluctuated historically, since it depended in part on the relations between the U.S. and their home governments. However, all the Asian groups posed the threat of economic competition domestically, and thus, as employers recruited new groups of Asians to fill the vacuum created by the exclusion of others, the hostility of nativist workers was redirected against the newcomers.

Legislative policies of exclusion and containment shaped the contours of the early Asian immigrant communities, as did the loyalties and allegiances of the various immigrant groups. Each of the groups identified itself by regional or national origin, and often occupied ethnic enclaves that reinforced these associations. Frequently, patterns of labor recruitment created narrow and cohesive sub-national identities: most of the earliest Chinese immigrants were from Guangdong province, the Japanese laborers were primarily from four prefectures in

Japan, and the Indian workers from three districts in Punjab. Although the earliest Korean immigrants were more heterogeneous in origin, religious affinities did exist among them: 40% were Christian. Among Filipinos, 90% were Catholic (*SFD*, 31–62). Language barriers and the existence of strong national rivalries in their home-countries often led the different Asian ethnic groups to actively dissociate from each other. Despite their sense of cultural distinctiveness, however, in the popular imagination, Asians were commonly identified as "Orientals" or "Asiatics" and were seen as sharing physical and psychological attributes.

2) The next historical shift in ethnic formation took place between World War II and the beginning of the protest movements of the sixties.[13] This period produced significant changes in the composition, status and boundaries of Asian American communities. The alignments of the War redefined the relationships of the various Asian national groups to each other and to the U.S. With World War II, Chinese and Filipino Americans found themselves viewed as favored allies; the enmity Korean Americans had long felt towards their colonizers, the Japanese, suddenly coincided with public sentiment; Asian Indians gained public consideration because of their country's strategic importance to Allied plans to block the Japanese advancement westward.[14] For Japanese Americans, however, Pearl Harbor was a wrenching, isolating and harrowing experience: they were classified as "enemy aliens," interned, and their communities on the West Coast destroyed.

The war against Nazism overseas and the need to combat Japanese propaganda calling for a pan-Asian alliance to fight Euro-American racism, made impossible the continuance of discriminatory practices and immigration laws. Consequently, the conditions of Asian Americans improved significantly. Restrictions on housing, employment, land ownership, naturalization, and miscegenation were gradually lifted. Furthermore, changes in immigration law allowed for the revitalization and augmentation of declining ethnic communities. Immigration from the Philippines, China and India was reopened, although severely restricted. However, loopholes in the law and the passage of the 1948 Displaced Persons Act and the 1953 Refugee Relief Act increased the number of immigrants. Most importantly, the War Brides Act, which allowed Asian wives and children of U.S. servicemen to enter on a non-quota basis, substantially increased the size of ethnic communities and created a more balanced gender ratio. Most immigrants entering at this time were women. The Chinese American community tripled in size between 1940 and 1960; for other groups the changes were less dramatic, but important. The Korean War also prompted a new wave of immigration from that country. Illegal immigration was prevalent among all groups, but most significant among Chinese Americans; in fact, the Border Patrol, now associated in the public consciousness with Mexican Americans, was established to combat illegal Chinese entries (*MRA*, 74).

While the 1940s focused public antagonism on Japanese Americans, the anti-Communist witch-hunts of the 1950s shifted attention to Chinese Americans. Raids, deportations, surveillance and the implementation of a Confession Program (involving information gathering and loyalty tests) fractured and terrorized the Chinese American community. In Ronald Takaki's succinct formulation: "The new peril was seen as yellow in race and red in ideology" (*SFD*, 415).

3) The identity-category "Asian American" was a product of the struggles of the 1960s but has been used to organize and interpret this set of immigrant experiences retrospectively

and prospectively. The struggles of the 1960s also led to the establishment of the academic discipline of Asian American Studies. The term "Asian American" emerged in the context of civil rights, Third World and anti-Vietnam war movements and was self-consciously adopted (in preference to "Oriental" or "Yellow") primarily on university campuses where the Asian American Movement enjoyed the broadest support.[15] The opening up of higher education and the demographic changes of the post-War years made possible, for the first time, the presence of Japanese, Filipino and Chinese American students in significant numbers on some university campuses. From these beginnings, the term "Asian American" has passed into academic and bureaucratic, and thence into popular usage.

The Asian American Movement was pivotal in creating a pan-Asian identity politics that represented their "unequal circumstances and histories as being related."[16] Asian American was a political subject position formulated to make visible a history of exclusion and discrimination against immigrants of Asian origin. This identity was then extended to represent the interests and circumstances of a very different group of Asian newcomers, who were entering the country with the change in immigration laws in 1965, and were destined to alter radically the demographic make-up of the constituency into which they were incorporated.

4) The next pattern of ethnic formation emerged with the change in immigration laws in 1965 and extended to the end of the next decade. During the Cold War, the U.S. claim to world leadership in the name of democracy and justice created pressure for changes in immigration policies that would place Asians on an equal footing with Europeans. Simultaneously, the Civil Rights Movement intensified domestic and international awareness of and opposition to racial discrimination. The passage of the 1965 immigration laws was a result of these combined internal and external pressures. The new laws allowed for an annual quota of 20,000 from each Asian country and the reunification of immediate family members on a non-quota basis. As a result, Asian Americans, who were under 1% of the U.S. population in 1965, increased to 2.8% in 1990, and are projected at 10.1% by 2050, making them the fastest growing minority group in the country. Japanese Americans, who comprised the largest group in 1960 representing 47% of the Asian American population, have declined rapidly to third position in the 1990 Census (11.7%), barely ahead of Asian Indians (11.2%) and Korean Americans (10.9%). Chinese Americans make up the largest group in the 1990 Census (23%), closely followed by Filipino Americans (19%).[17] The influx of newer groups has further diversified the identity of Asian Americans. After 1975, large numbers of Vietnamese, Lao, Hmong, Mien and Cambodians entered the United States as refugees. In the 1980 Census, immigrants from India lobbied for and won reclassification from the "other white" category to Asian Indian.

The arrival of new immigrants after 1965 has transformed the group from a predominantly American-born constituency to a group which is 65% foreign-born.[18] The new immigrants carry strong homeland identifications, speak many different languages, practice various religions and have a multiplicity of political affiliations. Some of the recent immigrants, especially Chinese and Indians, are part of "second phase migrations" arriving in the U.S. not from their countries of origin, but from Chinese diasporas in Singapore, Malaysia, and Cambodia or Indian diasporas in Uganda, Surinam, Fiji or Trinidad. Even when joining older groups, the newer immigrants add layers of class difference: whereas many of the earlier Chinese, Filipino and Indian immigrants were nonliterate laborers, the new arrivals from these groups include large numbers of middle-class professionals. The incorporation of such diverse groups within the notion of an Asian American identity has proved very difficult since their arrival has profoundly de-stabilized the formation. Highlighting the ironies of the new immigration, B.O. Hing, an Asian American leader, observes: "The success of one thing that we have fought for, namely, fair and equal immigration policies, has institutionalized a system which keeps us in constant flux" (Quoted in *AAP*, 95). Hing's comments overlook a further stratification in the constituency produced by the substantial number of Asians who are entering the country illegally, and are subsequently trapped within the most exploitative conditions of existence as workers in sweatshops, restaurants and brothels. This destabilization of the Asian American constituency has been engaged within the discipline primarily through the rhetoric of pluralism. Once we include the experiences of all the constituent groups, it is reasoned, the representational logic of the rubric will become apparent. Furthermore, the conventional wisdom goes, the dissemination of a pan-Asian consciousness will eventually unify the various Asian groups.

5) Finally, the fifth and latest historical pattern of ethnic identity formation has emerged in the last decade or so, and the scripts it has produced have further transformed the constituency we refer to as Asian America. This shift has been initiated by the reconfiguration of aspects of ethnicity within a transnational context. During this period, relations between the U.S. and Asia have undergone dramatic change and we have entered a transnational era that is remaking economic, political, and cultural relations in the Pacific. As a result, ethnicity can no longer be solely contextualized within the problematic of whether and how Asian Americans will be incorporated into the American body politic, but must also be read through the deterritorialization of ethnic identity. This transformation has begun to be engaged within the discipline, but is generally treated as a product or added feature of the fourth pattern, and addressed, if at all, through the overstrained and inadequate vocabulary of pluralism. The remaking of aspects of Asian American ethnicity during this period will be the subject of the last section of my essay. In historicizing these developments, I do not mean to imply that they are linear or progressive in their emergence; older formations often nest inside newer identity formations, or are unevenly developed across and within generations or ethnic groups. Certain patterns may be more significant in the experience of some groups than others. It is precisely because of the discontinuities and stratifications produced during these different periods that the concept of Asian American identity becomes such a complex one. The rhetoric and tropes that have been generated within the discipline to address or contain these differentiations, including the founding rubric of the discipline, are breaking under the strain of representing such heterogeneity. In the face of the staggering diversity of these emergent formations, interpellated by the transition from ethnicity to panethnicity, occupying differential positions in the vast imaginaries called "Asia," "America" and "Asian America," we face the theoretical challenge of constructing and examining our literatures and histories, without erasing our differences and conflicts.

DEFINING THE LITERATURE: THE ARITHMETIC OF INCLUSION

In this section I will examine three paradigmatic discussions of Asian American literature. Each of them attempts to map the field of Asian American literary production, and the boundaries they draw reveal the political temper of their historical moment, as well as the defining forces within the field of Asian American Studies. It is, therefore, critical to examine these attempts as definitive moments in the development of the field. Despite the progressively greater "inclusiveness" that marks the efforts of these different critics, the practice of an additive approach leaves unresolved, and even obscures, fundamental theoretical questions about the rubric as an enunciatory and interpretive category. For Chin and Kim, Chinese American and Japanese American literature forms the core of the field, the source of the tropes, themes and paradigms of ethnicity that constitute the literature. For all three critics, "other" Asian American literatures (Filipino, Korean, South Asian, Southeast Asian) are added on as auxiliary formations in deference to numerical ratios, the changing Census classifications, or the critic's own ethnic affiliation; or incorporated through the free-floating idioms of postmodernism (multiplicity, hybridity) that lack any historical specificity or cultural thickness. To use numbers as a gauge of our ability to integrate various literary traditions is fundamentally fallacious; it offers the palliative of inclusion without requiring any serious theoretical engagement with analyzing the grounds of our commonalty/differences. The certainty and precision of numbers assume the power within critical discourse of signifying integration and coverage: note the rhetorical echoes in Shirley Lim's title "Twelve Asian American Writers: In Search of Self-Definition," or Jessica Hagedorn's insistence in her recent anthology, *Charlie Chan Is Dead*, that her inclusion of forty-eight different writers is an index of her commitment to the meanings of contemporary Asian American fiction.

In choosing these particular critical texts for analysis, I am attempting to investigate the modalities of primary definition. As a result, the concern of the essay is not to provide a comprehensive survey of all the participants in these debates, but to examine some of the influential ones. Furthermore, I am not suggesting that all these efforts were part of either a self-conscious, individual or collaborative effort to shape and authorize an Asian American literary canon. Canon-formation does not take place through a single referendum but is rather the product, as Barbara Herrnstein Smith's deft summary indicates, "of a series of continuous interactions among a variably constituted object, emergent conditions, and the mechanisms of cultural selection and transmission."[19] Within a new field like Asian American literary studies, certain emergent conditions and mechanisms of cultural transmission have exercised a critical influence over the definition of Asian American literature. Firstly, the pace of production of critical and theoretical statements about the writings has lagged well behind the prolific production of anthologies of Asian American literature. This is, in part, because significant scholarly energy has been directed towards editing and introducing the works of individual or groups of Asian American authors. This practice of what Wendell Harris has called "fortunate sponsorship" has almost become a cottage industry in the field (112). Certainly, some degree of effort in sponsoring the work of newer or unfamiliar writers is constructive in an emergent field, but it cannot assume a disproportionate importance, nor can the task be discharged through biographical summary or thematic observations on the texts, the favored modes in many introductions. One of the consequences of this prioritization of scholarly activity has been a theoretical weakness within the field.[20] When this problem is compounded by other conditions like the status of Asian American literature as an emergent field, and the enormous demand among readers and teachers of American literature for guidance in interpreting this literature, it becomes clearer why the influence of the few critical texts to undertake an analysis of the entire field has been so great. Thus, often inadvertently, these evaluations have assumed a canon-forming power. Moreover, it has become commonplace in the discipline for even leading scholars to refer to Chinese and Japanese American texts as the "canonical" Asian American texts and to refer to other Asian American texts as "marginal," "peripheral," or "emergent" Asian American literatures. It is thus not so much a canon, but a phantom canon that the analysis of the following works will reveal.

The category "Asian American literature" gained recognition with the publication of several anthologies in the 1970s among which Frank Chin's offers the most polemical and influential elaboration of Asian American literature. Chin's anthology was published in the aftermath of the Asian American Movement of the 1960s and works from many of its ideological premises: that the separate circumstances of Asian ethnic groups are linked by a common history of exclusion and racism, that the myth of assimilation has been used to neutralize ethnic resistance and deny racial stratification, and that an assertive identity politics can be the basis of challenging Anglo hegemony. Chin's anthology works aggressively to enunciate and promote an Asian American identity that is independent of the determinations of white supremacy, and the search for autonomy leads him to formulate such authenticity in purist and separatist terms. He distinguishes between "real" Asian Americans who are "American born and raised, who got their China and Japan from the radio, off the silver screen, from television, out of comic books, from the pushers of white American culture" and "Americanized Asians," first-generation immigrants who maintain strong cultural ties to their countries of origin while fulfilling the subservient stereotype of the humble and passive Oriental (*AA*, vii). The authentic Asian American is here defined as a prototypical No-No Boy[21]: a political subject who says no to Asia, no to America and is decidedly male.[22] Paradoxically, in order to claim an Asian American identity in defiance of hegemonic codifications, Chin is led to disclaim connections with Asia. He focuses on the domestic context of ethnic identity formation and on generational distance from Asia. Clearly, Chin's rejection of the Asian part of his identity is an effort to repudiate the prevailing stereotype of Asians as perpetual foreigners in America, and to affirm the experiences of the many Asians in America *at this time,* who are several generations removed from the homeland experience. But this formulation is vitiated by its obsession with the white gaze.

Chin's Introduction also put in place the idea of an essential Asian American identity derived from the experiences and narratives of American-born Chinese and Japanese Americans which he names "the Asian American sensibility" (*AA*, ix). This notion has long survived Chin's anthology and often functions as a founding assumption in other discussions in Asian American Studies, often despite critics' heated disagreement with Chin's other views. Recent discussions of Asian American Literature (including Kim's and Lim's), have taken issue with Chin's anti-feminist and anti-immigrant postulations of Asian American literature; however, in their privileging of Chinese and Japanese American texts, and their inability to theorize the relationship between the newer and older formations, they inadvertently reproduce the framework employed by him. Even the current shift to the use of the plural *literatures* usually functions as a semantic cover for the continued reliance on essentialist paradigms through a token acknowledgement of the need for change. But the theorizing of this change is deferred—described as being beyond the scope of the current project, or reassuringly projected as being likely to be undertaken by others in the field. When such practices of deferral are accompanied by a tendency to group-specific research undertaken by "insiders" that eschews any comparative or theoretical work, the cumulative effect is a theoretical weakness in our conceptualization of the field as a whole.

Elaine Kim's discussion of Asian American literature increases the number of groups covered, by adding Korean American literature to Chin's list of Chinese, Japanese and Filipino American texts, but this expansion of the field seems arbitrarily based on the accident of ethnic affiliation rather than on any critical or literary criteria. As Kim admits in a later retrospective evaluation of her exclusion of South and Southeast Asian literatures from her study:

> I admitted at the time that this definition was arbitrary, prompted by my own inability to read Asian languages and my own lack of access to South and Southeast Asian communities. But for these shortcomings, I wrote, I would have included in my introductory study works written in Asian languages and works written by writers from Vietnamese American, Indian American, and other communities. Nonetheless, it is true that I wanted to delineate and draw boundaries around *whatever I thought of as* Asian American identity and literature [italics mine]. (*CC*, viii)

The *carte-blanche* Kim accorded her own decisions on defining Asian American literature is evidence of the degree of cultural authority that sometimes attaches to insiderism, and which, unchecked by vigilant scrutiny and challenge, can operate in powerfully exclusionary forms.[23]

The focus in Kim's analysis, as in Chin's, is on positing a literature that is expressive of the Asian American experience understood as sociologically distinct, separate from the mainstream, and shaped by settlement in the United States and the effects of American racism. But since Kim rejects Chin's central distinction between "real" and "fake" Asian American sensibilities—the crucial idea of authenticity that demarcates the boundaries of the Chin tradition—her definition of the literature incorporates the writings of first-generation immigrants and sojourners, which Chin had dismissed as the ventriloquist production of white racism. Instead of the notion of authenticity or "cultural integrity," Kim opts for an organizing framework that is chronological. Projecting the idea of a linear evolutionary pattern onto the emergence of Asian American identity allows her to claim a constitutive logic to the rubric "Asian American literature." Her projections of such a development are tentative but hopeful: "Distinctions among the various national groups sometimes do blur after a generation or two, when it is easier for us to see what we share as members of an American racial minority…" (*AIW*, xii). Focusing on chronological emergence allows her to shift the emphasis from the internal stratifications and differences within Asian American literature to a unity-in-the-making. Moreover, such a formulation not only fails to recognize the differential and uneven insertion of the various national groups into America by locating them in the same progressive march toward greater unity, it also fails to account for the fact that the increasing racial diversity of Asian Americans disallows any easy assumption of a unifying racial identity.

In her later essay, Kim also argues that a broad thematic concern "claiming America" characterizes the writing ("DA," 88). Methodologically, the study seems to be straining to construct a notion of commonalty. The purported commonalty is so broad as to be inclusive of other ethnic literatures, even though it is described as unique to Asian American literature. Another effect of the thematic criteria she introduces is to suture the quite disparate productions of Filipino and Korean Americans to Asian American literature by repressing the historical contexts of colonization, exile and post-colonial modernization that render their representation as local, American-based literatures much more problematic than in the case of earlier Chinese or Japanese American literature. The unique specificities of the colonial relationship between the U.S. and the Philippines, the topos of return that haunts Filipino American writing, and the continuities between Filipino and Filipino American writing create a distinctive literary formation that does not conform to prescriptions about Asian American writing derived from Japanese American and Chinese American literature.[24] Finally, much of the more recent writing, as I will show, is situated in a transnational context where America is not the exclusive locus of identification. While, on the one hand, Kim's delineation of Asian American literature is more inclusive than Chin's, her defining criteria work to reproduce the hegemony of the forms of Japanese and Chinese American literature by failing to reconfigure the field through the specificities of Korean and Filipino American writing.

Similarly, when Kim seeks to include Burmese American Wendy Law-Yone's *The Coffin Tree* within the same schema, she fails to distinguish between the refugee experience of forced dislocation, radical discontinuity and political uncertainty, and the voluntary experience of migration, except by treating the former as a more extreme expression of the drive to "claim America" common to both. Kim's methods of incorporation are symptomatic of a larger problem. With a new self-consciousness in the field about the hegemony of Japanese and Chinese American literatures, essayists and anthologists seeking to include underrepresented Asian American groups often use one particular group to stand in for the rest. References to Filipino and Vietnamese American literature, in particular, have come to operate in this fashion in the field. While the task of creating new conceptual models is avoided, such annexing of newer formations has acquired the persuasive force of comprehensiveness now. What it institutionalizes is a perception of the transposability of the newer literatures and the foundational status of the established ones. One generic outcome of such scholarly procedures is that the critical essay breaks down into lists of thematic similarities that invoke a "tradition" through sheer numerical force and the power of proxies. Another result of the rush to incorporate the newer groups is that with the quantity of available materials quite low in many cases, an industry is emerging to produce materials to fill this demand. While on the one hand, the effort to encourage writers from less-known groups is commendable, publishing numerous hastily-compiled, weakly-conceived anthologies is, finally, counter-productive. Availability of texts cannot be an end in itself. Furthermore, since the newer material is frequently being made available through collaborative autobiographies and student writing, where the extent of mediation is very high (especially where translation complicates the process of transmission), we need to interrogate the structures that determine literary production. In the case of collaborative autobiographies, where the reconstitution of the absent figure of the underrepresented is caught up in the epistemic violence of a disciplinary emphasis on concrete experience and sovereign subjectivity, and where the place of the collaborator is marked by a singular transparency, we cannot proceed without a historical critique of the collaborating/editorial subject. Autobiographical voicing is a fraught project in this context. An uncritical recourse to productivity in order to facilitate inclusion might only create a disciplinary formation where some of the groups stand in quasi-ethnographical relation to others.

In Lim's earlier essay "Twelve Asian American Writers: In Search of Self-Definition," the number stands in for breadth of coverage although all the writers discussed as "Asian American" are either Japanese or Chinese American. What is most troubling about this kind of slippage is its institutional reproduction over several decades in the field, as we have seen in the criticism of Chin and Kim. Lim notes that Asian American writing is part of the macrocosm of American writing but also reveals "certain inextricably Asian psychological and philosophical perspectives. A strong Confucian patriarchal orientation is a dominant element and with that the corollary of female inferiority..." (237). Not only is this statement incredibly reductive, but the collapsing of the distinctions between Asian and Confucian reveals what Gayatri Spivak has called a "sanctioned ignorance" about the cultural diversity of Asia that, interestingly enough, has its antecedents in American Orientalist writings, which have long centralized East Asian cultures because of a history of trade, military and missionary contacts between these areas and the U.S.[25]

This problem is compounded by the publication of Lim's essay in the MLA anthology *Redefining American Literary History* that undertakes as its project precisely what the essay most neglects to perform within the context of its own field. Moreover, the two other essays on Asian American literature included in the anthology focus on the work of Maxine Hong Kingston. The narrowness in the scope of what is covered as Asian American writing, and the complete absence of reference to this as an issue, suggest a kind of axiomatic force such an equivalence has gathered within the discipline, from which it is being disseminated amongst general readers of ethnic and American literature.

What is heartening are the significant critical shifts in the theoretical assumptions about Asian American literature between Lim's two essays. Shirley Lim's recent essay "Assaying the Gold" shows itself to be more aware of the dangers of an uncritical acceptance of the rubric Asian American literature, although the analytic methods and lexicon employed within the essay often finesse rather than confront the problems raised. Although she acknowledges, on the one hand, that "the rubric 'Asian American literature'... is both exceedingly contemporary, a newly invented epistemological tool, and already collapsing under the weight of its own contradictions," Lim avoids the implications of her own insight by settling for the nostalgic prediction that the increasing heterogeneity of the field will produce a greater pan-Asian consciousness among writers and readers. The evidence Lim summons to support this hope is rather slender and shifts between literary and sociological arenas. According to Lim, there are more signs of "biculturalism," "multiculturalism," and "borderland" negotiations in recent Asian American literary texts. By way of sociological support for her position, Lim argues that a greater solidarity has emerged among Asian Americans in response to mainstream American discrimination and as a result of coalition building among Asian Americans. And these factors, we are told, augur well for the emergence of a new phase in Asian American writing: "The stage is set for the transformation of Asian American literature into Pan-Asian American readings, from the old singular ethnic body into a multiethnic body...and we are already reading the scripts" (164–165).

The major problem with Lim's critical assertions is that they make predictions about the growth of a socio-historical, political, economic and cultural phenomenon like pan-Asian consciousness by using evidence drawn from a limited arena. In this respect, Lim repeats an error often made by cultural critics who read in the changes effected in the academy seismic socio-cultural transformations. Pan-Asian consciousness has enjoyed its greatest success on college campuses, as researchers of the Asian American movement have pointed out, but its political effectivity and acceptance in the Asian American constituency as a whole has been much more uneven. Contrary to Lim's neat predictions, sociological research on the future of Asian American panethnicity is more mixed in its findings, indicating simultaneously the growth of pan-Asian organizations and increased conflicts among them.[26] Yen Le Espiritu has identified the ethnic and class inequality within the pan-Asian structure, the influx of post-65 immigrants, and the reduction of public funding sources as causes of potential conflict among the various Asian ethnic groups (51). Moreover, contrary to the early hopes of activists, the institutionalization of Asian American Studies has had little effect on the various communities and, over time, the gulf between the community and the academy has only widened. I will also argue in greater detail later that changes in the political distribution system are likely to further interrupt the growth of pan-Asian consciousness. The projection of a pan-Asian framework as encompassing the future direction of the literature is premature, unsubstantiated and seeks to effect an emotional resolution to the problems of political identity raised by the very use of the term "Asian American." As in the work of Kim, the legitimacy of the rubric is finally salvaged as a signifier by pointing to a future in which it shall come to be. In the case of Kim and Lim, pluralism offers the avenue for that deferral: once everyone has been included, the representational truth of the rubric will be made manifest: "the next stage is for Asian Americans to become reflective of the multiple ethnicities that already compose their identity" ("CGA," 164).

Lim uses the terms "biculturalism," "multiculturalism," and "borderland" consciousness to represent some of the shifts discernible in the coding of ethnicity in contemporary Asian American literature, and then lists the work of writers who exemplify these new paradigms like Jessica Hagedorn, Bharati Mukherjee and David Henry Hwang. Multiculturalism is a term so capacious that recognition of it as a textual feature signals a critic's self-positioning as progressive and up-to-date, rather than illuminating in any specific way the dynamics of the text. If it is a reference to an official policy that shapes the terms of social interaction and literary production, then a term like "multiculturalism" would mean something very different in the case of a Mukherjee novel like *Jasmine* than, say, in the case of a Hagedorn novel like *Dogeaters*.[27] But Lim makes no effort to differentiate between the usages—consequently, the terminology functions as a loose and free-floating signifier of Asian Americanness that lacks any cultural density. *Jasmine* begins in a Punjab enmeshed in religious conflict between Sikhs and Hindus—the post-colonial sequel to the fostering of ethno-religious separatism, in the interests of political control, by the British colonial regime in India—an official multicultural policy that in colonialist and nationalist forms has had murderous consequences. Once she arrives in the U.S., Jasmine enters into a different version of a multicultural imaginary, where her cultural difference as an Indian female (which lacks referential density in the U.S.), is reinscribed as exotic sexual power. In Hagedorn's text, the legacy of Spanish and American colonialism have created a society obsessed with colonial genealogies and infatuated with Hollywood films, caught in a modernity marked by political corruption and poverty, where sexual desire becomes the site for the inscription of the incoherence, exploitation and violence that signify its experience of "multiculturalism." It could be argued that multiculturalism operates in so many different registers in these two texts that it differentiates them from each other rather than unifies them *as Asian American texts*. Finally, the use of multiculturalism as a unifying feature of contemporary Asian American texts leaves so many questions unanswered. Do Asian American texts operate the category of multiculturalism any differently from other ethnic texts? Do they share more in common with each other in this respect than they do with "mainstream" texts? Since multiculturalism in its broadest sense has become a feature of most modern societies and texts, surely we need some more finely honed criteria if we are to argue for its common existence in these two and other Asian American texts. Critics of Asian American literature need to be particularly vigilant that their institutional location as interpreters of "Asian American literature" does not predispose them to recycle and accommodate disparate cultural products into the existing categories of their discipline, or into the convenient catch-all terms generated by pluralism. Instead, the expansion of the literature must be accompanied by the generation of new criteria on the basis of which our selections are made. Cultural production is a much messier process than the available categories of ethnicity allow for. It is therefore imperative, as Werner Sollors points out, "that the categorization of writers—and literary critics—as 'members' of ethnic groups is understood to be a very partial, temporary and insufficient categorization at best" (256). In the case of Asian Americans, who are categorized within the most novel and artificial of ethnic formations, the mutability and fictionality of membership is a much more intense experience, one that needs to be foregrounded and not dispelled in our theorizations of Asian American literature.

Before I turn to the last part of my argument, I would like to briefly analyze a recent heated exchange between Jessica Hagedorn, the editor of one of the latest anthologies of Asian American fiction, *Charlie Chan Is Dead*, and Sven Birkerts, who reviewed the anthology for *The New York Times Book Review*.[28] The exchange serves as a critical parable for the arguments I have made thus far about the axiomatic status of Asian American literature within the discipline, the theoretical weakness within the field, and the recourse to the affirmation of ethnic identity to defer addressing the challenges of its heterogeneity. My comments on the following exchange also prepare the way for the last part of my essay in which I will discuss the effects of transnational forces on Asian American ethnicity, the failure of the discipline to take up this challenge in a significant way, and the incoherence that attaches to the term as a result of this failure.

The conflict between Hagedorn and Birkerts takes place over the ordering rubric for her collection—"Asian American fiction." For Birkerts, the problem with the anthology is its insufficiently formulated inclusiveness:

> To begin with, there are just too many different kinds of inclusions, everything from Indian-born Meena Alexander's aggressively hip "Manhattan Music" to "I Would Remember," a simple and powerful story by Carlos Bulosan, a Filipino born in 1913. "Asian American" has here become a term so hospitable that half the world's population can squeeze in under its banner. Generous and catholic, yes—but the mix is also jarring and too eclectic. The chaos is compounded—if chaos can be—by Ms. Hagedorn's reliance on an alphabetical ordering (effectively eliminating any impression of generational change) and by the unevenness of the contributions. First-rate work by authors like Joy Kogawa, David Wong Louie, Jose Garcia Villa, John Yau and Jocelyn Lieu must sit side by side with a number of less than distinguished stories from the post-modernist grab bag.

Hagedorn's acid retort to the reviewer directs his attention once again to the inclusiveness of the collection as its defining feature. But she neither explains the need for, or grounds of, such inclusiveness within the contemporary context of Asian American fiction:

> Rather than dealing with the literature presented in "Charlie Chan Is Dead: An Anthology of Contemporary Asian American Fiction" (Dec. 19), Sven Birkerts spends more than half of his review obsessing over the writers' bloodlines, and complaining that my inclusion of 48 writers as "Asian American" may have been too "hospitable." What exactly are his criteria for categorizing someone as Asian American? Since this is the first anthology of its kind, is this really the time to be narrow? . . .

> Is Mr. Birkerts an immigration official or a literary critic? Should we all send in our passports and green cards for verification? . . . What I hope from any reviewer of "Charlie Chan Is Dead" is that he or she treat seriously the form and substance of our literature.[29]

Birkerts's perplexity in confronting the staggering range of writings in the anthology is hardly surprising given the lack of an adequate theoretical or historical framework, a clear articulation of the criteria of selection, or in the absence of either, an explanation about the inability to provide such statements given the exceeding novelty of the field, the artificial conjunctions it effects, and the enormous transformations it has undergone within the last decades. Instead, both Elaine Kim, who has written a brief Preface, and Jessica Hagedorn, who provides an Introduction, invoke the celebration of differences, and the "international," as heady auguries of the new and liberating future that belongs to Asian American literature, and a sign of its break from the narrow cultural nationalism of its founding moment in the sixties. Hagedorn's page-length catalog that characterizes the "hipness" of her selections as "funky," "sassy," "sexy," substitutes affirmation for analysis. All too often the critical responsibilities that attend the task of introducing an inaugural volume ("the first anthology of Asian American fiction by a commercial publisher in this country") to a largely unfamiliar public are discharged by citing difference within a dizzying post-modern schema of montage and juxtaposition: "Some of these writers were originally poets, some still are. Others only write fiction. Some were born in the Philippines, some in Seattle. A few in Hawaii. Others in Toronto or London....Seoul. Greeley, Colorado. India. Penang. Moscow, Idaho" (xxix-xxx). This technique has the effect of positing the arbitrariness of the category at the level of haphazard global positionings that emerge as signifiers of the unpredictable and the provocative, rather than as the product of specific historical conditions. The only gloss Hagedorn provides on the relationship between her category and the global list of place names is the following summation: "Asian American literature? Too confining a term, maybe. World literature? Absolutely" (xxx). Why, then, has the editor retained the first label when a clearly better one is at hand? Or, to quote the Michael Jackson song, what does it mean for Asian Americans to say "We are the World"? Both the Introduction and the Preface list (but do not explain or theorize) the dizzying array of differences but then move on to achieve closure by sounding the note of "celebration." The overwhelming need seems to be to reconstitute wholeness at the level of mood, so that identity can emerge at the level of emotion, when it cannot be created through theoretical or critical interpretation.

For his part, the conflation of the ethnic with the local/domestic is the grounding assumption in Birkerts's understanding of ethnic literature. His primary difficulty in reading the anthology and locating its rationale derives from his understanding of how "difference" operates as a signifier in literary production—as a category or categories of intelligibility that narrow the focus, producing a kind of "special interest subjectivity."[30] Contrary to his expectations, the Chan anthology "turns the funnel upside down" on the trend among anthologists to "narrow the focus, screening down by race, sex, ethnicity, sexual orientation, geography, age or topical criteria." In this anthology, the locus of the ethnic shifts to the global. The term "minority" which is popularly taken to signify the fractional, peripheral, tangential seems to counter its own logic in assuming another aspect as overwhelming, or engulfing: "half the world's population can squeeze in under its banner." His consternation with the range of writings is imaged through the very geography that assumes the burden of imposing coherence on the notion of identity. The distance between the two perspectives that emerges in this encounter—between the Asian American writer-anthologist and the general reader—operating as it does as a site of charged accusations and defences, points to the necessary theoretical work that needs to be undertaken in elucidating the fictionality of the rubric.

We have now entered an era in which the dispersion and re-configuration of ethnic identity among Asian Americans will only accelerate, and it is to these new forces, which will recast aspects of ethnic formation, that I will now turn, in order to make some suggestions for the reorientation of theoretical investigations within the field.

RETHINKING AMERICAN LITERATURE AND THEORY

The emergence of pan-Asian ethnicity has been a vexed, conflicted and incomplete process, especially in the recent past, and is further complicated by the fact that no readily available symbols or grounds of cultural commonalty exist within such a heterogeneous formation. But Yen Le Espiritu argues that the problem of a lack of cultural commonalties, far from being unique to Asian Americans, is in fact typical, in various degrees, of the process of pan-ethnicization in the U.S.: "culture has followed panethnic boundaries rather than defined them" because "panethnic groups in the United States are products of political and social processes, rather than of cultural bonds" (13). While Espiritu's statement has certainly been true of the historical experiences of African Americans and Native Americans, for groups like Latin Americans and Asian Americans who have a shorter, more internally uneven history of being shaped by American location, and whose panethnic formation is being continuously de-stabilized and transformed by fresh waves of immigration, the presumption of a progressive development of panethnicity is much less predictable.

Two structural factors will significantly interrupt the formation of panethnicity in patterns that were conceivable in the past: a more conservative political climate that is increasingly hostile to structuring access along ethnic lines, and changes in the global economy that will significantly impact ethnic formation. I will analyze the transformative potential of both definitive shifts.

The 1994 elections have produced a transformed political landscape in which a more conservative agenda has defined discussions of welfare, affirmative action, and immigration. In addition, the recent recession, the temporization of the workforce, the numerous layoffs and decline in real wages, and the reduction in federal spending have created an embattled public that, mobilized by conservative rhetoric, has shown support for the curtailment of affirmative action and welfare programs and restrictions on immigration. The recent Supreme Court rulings that have mandated standards of "compelling federal interest" and "strict scrutiny" for affirmative action programs in education and federal contracts have reinforced this trend. "What we see as a result of these changes that are already under way (and only likely to intensify) is that a polity which structured access along ethnic lines since the civil rights era is slowly curtailing these policies. As social scientists have pointed out, the ascriptive force of the state is crucial to the production and consolidation of ethnicity. Joane Nagel notes that ethnic resurgences are strongest when the state uses the ethnic category as a unit in economic allocations and political representations (Quoted in *AAP*, 10). When these identifications are reinforced over a period of time through the coincidence of political and economic interests, the emergence of panethnicity is encouraged despite lack of common cultural bonds. In other words, "shifts in ethnic boundaries are often a direct response to changes in the political distribution system" (*AAP*, 11). The recent structural changes in the political distribution system would seem to suggest that the state's increasing unwillingness to legitimize ethnic labels as determinants of access may lead to a weakening of panethnicity, especially among predominantly foreign-born Asian American populations.

To suggest that the panethnic rubric may not be as effective in producing the more stable formations of the past is not to argue that the alternative narrative of assimilation will define the orientation and identifications of Asians in the U.S. Contrary to a long-standing tradition amongst critics that sets ethnicization in opposition to assimilation, I would argue that ethnicization will be influenced by a transnational context through polyethnic contacts across and within ethnic groups both inside and outside the country. It is here that I differ from Werner Sollors, who also challenges the ethnic identity versus assimilation opposition;

however, Sollors undoes the opposition only to recuperate the transethnic within a narrowly domestic conception of American national identity.[31] For this reason, Sollors's formulations about ethnic literature are more successful in the analysis of aspects of the African American tradition or second- and third-generation writers from other groups, but are inadequate to addressing the patterns found in more recent immigrant writing. Americanization/assimilation which was earlier associated with "Anglo conformity" will probably give way to a process of Americanization where most groups can, as Arjun Appadurai puts it, "renegotiate their links to their diasporic identities from their American vantage points."[32] It is precisely because the assimilationary process is losing its former power that presidential candidate Patrick Buchanan and conservative critic Peter Brimelow (author of *Alien Nation*) have issued alarmist calls for a "pause" in immigration similar to the one between 1924 and 1965; or, for a restriction to European-only immigration to reinvigorate the absorptive process.[33] At present, entry into the U.S. entails an adjustment to American codes and practices (what we have called assimilation), but it also enables investments/remittances that reestablish links to the home-country, return visits under a new status, and the entry of family members into the U.S. Within this context, becoming American does not necessarily involve a loss of the home culture, or a choice between ethnicity or mainstreaming as in earlier patterns of immigration to this country.

The globalization of capital, the transnationalization of production, the migrations of diverse peoples, the varying trajectories of arrival, departure and return (immigrants, exiles, refugees, temporary workers, intellectual exchange visitors), the creation of global information superhighways, and the electronic transfer of images and capital, have seen an exponential increase in the sites, frequency and variety of cross-cultural exchange. The shift from multinational corporations to transnational corporations with a global strategy has proliferated the points of exchange, transfer and contact. The world-wide move away from socialist policies following the collapse of the Soviet Union, accompanied by the lowering of trade barriers and the spread of consumer culture, has encouraged this shift. Whereas multinationals maintained autonomous subsidiaries with separate strategies in various countries, transnational companies support a global strategy that is conceived and implemented in a world-wide setting. As a result, they create circuits of capital, personnel and information that have multiple nodes, each more closely linked and dependent on the others, than within the older multinational system.

The rapid economic growth of parts of Asia (Japan, Singapore, Taiwan, Korea, Hong Kong, and now China, Vietnam, Malaysia, Philippines, Indonesia and India) over the last few decades has led to the proliferation of such transnational networks linking America and Asia, and as we move into what is being called the Pacific Century, these processes will only accelerate and proliferate. The emergence of the "borderless economy" has intensified linkages that defy containment within the nation state. Plans are under way to establish a free trade zone between the U.S. and Pacific Rim countries modelled on NAFTA; Chinese government officials are establishing a Special Economic Zone linking the Yunan region to Laos and Vietnam; trade links within ASEAN and SAARC countries have increased and strengthened.[34] The effect of these changes on Asian Americans will be substantial. Asian Americans, who have historically disavowed their connections to Asia in order to challenge racist stereotypes as perpetual foreigners, will be able to renegotiate their links to Asia; mainstream Americans will reencounter Asia within changed geopolitical alignments, which will not allow easy assumptions of patronage and wardship that stemmed from privileges of extraterritoriality and conquest in the nineteenth and early twentieth century.[35]

What we see appearing are global networks that do not conform to earlier models of departure from Asia and settlement in America that occurred within a vastly different geopolitical economy. For instance, China's impending takeover of Hong Kong has led to the dispersal of capital and family connections across a number of sites in Canada, Britain, Australia and the U.S., with the possibility of return or realignment pending an uncertain political future. Furthermore, patterns of reverse migration are beginning to emerge among Taiwanese Americans and Korean Americans due to strengthened economic conditions and the increase in living standards in their home-countries, and a decline in living standards in the U.S. Over the last four years, the number of people who received immigration visas from South Korea to the U.S. has fallen by more than half, from 25,500 in 1990 to 10,800 in 1994; simultaneously, in each of these four years between 5,000 and 6,500 people have returned to Korea, compared to 800 in 1980.[36] Such reverse migrations may also take place amongst the other Asian American groups if the economic and political situations in their home countries improve.

Nor is migration exclusively a sign of "cosmopolitan" class privilege. Poverty and gender do not impede migration but inflect the forms it takes. Garment sweatshops in some of the major US. cities draw on immigrant female workers, most of whom are Asian and Latin American.[37] Owners of ethnic grocery stores, restaurants, or the ubiquitous 7-11 convenience stores employ impoverished workers from their home countries for low wages, sometimes using the prospective green card as a lure. Tony Chan's film *Combination Platter* provides a sympathetic view of the predicament of the restaurant owner of The Szechuan Inn, Mr. Lee, and the undocumented workers whom he employs, both of whom are under siege by the INS, while they purvey to oblivious New Yorkers one of the staples of their ethnic experience—Chinese take-out at cheap rates. The film cuts between the hectic, hot and crowded male world of the kitchen workers and the leisurely, loquacious and self-absorbed world of the dining-room clientele, connected by commerce and separated from contact. Asian Americans inhabit both sides of the divide in this film, highlighting class differentiations within the group. The film follows Robert, who works as a waiter in the restaurant while he pursues, during his off-hours, his elusive quest for a green card, always under threat of exposure and deportation to Hong Kong.

Gender further defines the forms and trajectories of migration and the production of ethnicity in a transnational context. The international sex-trade has connected Thailand and the Philippines to America, Japan and Europe through package flesh tours, prostitution smuggling rings and mail-order bride catalogs (representations of these global networks appear in Jessica Hagedorn's *Dogeaters* and Wanwadee Larsen's *Confessions of a Mail Order Bride*).[38] The debt-crisis in countries like Sri Lanka and the Philippines has created an enormous outflow of female migrant workers to the Middle East, Japan, Hong Kong, Singapore, the U.S. and Europe, just as the entry of large numbers of middle-class women into the workforce in the West, and the increased prosperity of some Middle Eastern and Asian countries, has led to an enormous demand for such labor.[39] By March 1988, approximately 175,000 Filipinas were working overseas (about 81,000 as domestic workers) and sending home between $60–$100 million in foreign exchange (*BBB*, 187–188). The recent protests in the Philippines against governmental indifference to the plight of its foreign workers—following the execution by the Singapore government of Flor Contemplacion, an overseas Filipina maid—highlight the growing symbolic importance of the migrant worker in the Filipino national consciousness.[40] The short story "Jasmine" from Bharati Mukherjee's collection *The Middleman and Other Stories* explores the layered ironies in the relationship between Lara, a white feminist who is a performance artist, and Jasmine, the young Indian woman from Trinidad, whom she employs as a nanny or "day-mommy."[41] Lara's professionalism and feminism are enabled and subsidized by Jasmine's illegal status in the country, the underside to the successes of a liberal women's movement that argued from a platform of access, individual rights and emancipation from domesticity.

The sites for the production of heterogeneous Asian ethnicities, therefore, defy easy containment within national boundaries. Ethnicity metamorphoses at multiple sites of transit, return, and arrival in the movement between and within nations; it can no longer be solely defined through the negotiation between origin and destination. It is imperative that Asian American Studies move beyond comforting affirmations of pluralism and the celebration of differences as the terms of their engagement with these transformative processes taking place.

The disjunctions and multiple migrations that deterritorialize ethnicity are the subject of many of the newer stories produced by Asian Americans. When ethnic identity is produced through multiple locations, ethnic categories become de-stabilized and, consequently, open to misrecognition and reinscription. Once the narrator leaves Pakistan in Sara Suleri's *Meatless Days,* her family experience of the trauma of Partition and the genocidal divisiveness of the Bangladesh War render her loath to attach identity to place. The luminous and elliptical prose of the narrative refuses to name in the language of belonging the spaces through which she moves after her arrival in the U.S.[42] Her discourse discreetly skirts the available American categories of identity, "ethnic" "minority" or "Asian American," locating itself instead in the transmogrifications to which identity is subject in the spaces opened up by death and displacement in her stories. The potential for reinscription of ethnic codings is taken up in a comic mode in Mira Nair's *Mississippi Masala.* Her story revises prototypical narratives of ethnic formation, and the rubric "Asian American" strains to contain the displacements through which ethnicity travels. The film moves between Africa and America but the result is not a narrative of African America as we have come to think about it. Instead, the story is the unfamiliar one of displaced Indians moving across two continents. India as the space of "origin" never materializes as locale in the film; instead, India emerges in the Ugandan context as the boundary produced by British colonialism in the insertion of a middleman minority into an African colonial state, and then redrawn in post-Independence Idi Amin's Uganda, to reassert black nationhood through the expulsion of "foreign" elements. Within the racialized imagination of Mississippi, Ugandan "Indians" are an unfamiliar category misrecognized through older categories (Indian? American Indian—African? African American?). If the film unsettles our ideas about the category Asian American, it also ironizes the confidence with which we read the category African American by offering us an-other African American story set in Mississippi. The fictions of the putatively more stable Asian ethnic formations, like Chinese Americans and Japanese Americans, also show the effects of the diasporic renegotiation of identities as in Peter Wang's film *The Great Wall* or in David Mura's *Turning Japanese,* both stories of return to the country of origin.[43] The topos of return, which had appeared in earlier Asian American narratives as an imagined or actual end-point to the action allowing for resolution to the dilemmas of identification, appears as one more nodal point in an ongoing action that highlights the perplexities and paradoxes of belonging. Many of these stories deliberately avoid closure, ending with their characters beginning a new journey, in transit, or on the road.

However, travel possesses a different valence in each story because of important political and material differences. Suleri enters the U.S. as a student, a voluntary migration enabled by her class status, although her decision to leave seems to be precipitated by the political crises that follow the Bangladesh War. In *Mississippi Masala,* once again, political turmoil prompts the journey but this journey is a forced migration. Turned into political refugees, the Ugandan Indian extended family arrives in the U.S. with sufficient capital (that circulates through a diasporic ethnic network) to enter into a niche market at an opportune moment when the motel business was being abandoned by other Americans. The Chinese American family in *The Great Wall* is financially stable enough to afford an extended visit to China which, like Mura's, is a journey of cultural recovery. Mura himself is the beneficiary of a cultural exchange program that funds his one-year visit to Japan, and the cultural links that are sponsored by the two countries are underwritten by economic and political interests. The journeys undertaken from America are visits supported by a "strong" passport and a "hard" currency and involve an eventual return to a comfortable existence.

The earlier patterns of Asian immigrant experiences created more bounded immigrant communities where differentiations were experienced most keenly in separation from the dominant culture, from the home country, or across gender and generational divisions. The distance between Asia and America was more formidable at that time, the passages more dangerous, and the communications more tenuous, as the stories of Maxine Hong Kingston's *China Men* suggest.[44] The temporality of immigration as it emerges through the tropes of amnesia, exhaustion, and deferral mythifies the experience of Chinese laborers who made the journey to America fired by the ambition to make money and return, but were forced by harsh working conditions, poor salaries or new attachments to delay or abandon the idea of return. But some of the newer fictions of Asian American writers show the emergence of different "chronotopes" of immigration that represent the production of ethnicity in passage through a smaller world where national borders are more porous.[45] Arjun Appadurai delineates the challenges that the transnational poses for theorizations of American ethnicity:

> The formula of hyphenation (as in Italian-Americans, Asian-Americans, and African-Americans) is reaching the point of saturation, and the right-hand side of the hyphen can barely contain the unruliness of the left-hand side. . . . The politics of ethnic identity in the United States is inseparably linked to the global spread of originally local national identities. For every nation-state that has exported significant numbers of its populations

to the United States as refugees, tourists, or students, there is now a delocalized *transnation*, which retains a special ideological link to a putative place of origin but is otherwise a thoroughly diasporic collectivity. No existing conception of Americanness can contain this large variety of transnations. (424)...

It is clear from the foregoing analysis that the boundary marking of the field is caught up in a perception of competing needs: the tension between the need for political identity and the need to represent the conflicted and heterogeneous formation we call "Asian American." These needs are antagonistic to each other only if we work from the assumption that there is a "real" Asian American identity to which our vocabulary and procedures can be adequated. Hence, the pluralist computation that the sum of the parts will give us the whole. I would contend that "Asian American" offers us a rubric that we cannot not use. But our usage of the term should rehearse the catachrestic status of the formation. I use the term "catachresis" to indicate that there is no literal referent for the rubric "Asian American," and, as such, the name is marked by the limits of its signifying power. It then becomes our responsibility to articulate the inner contradictions of the term and to enunciate its representational inconsistencies and dilemmas. For, as Adorno notes, "criticizing epistemology also means...retaining it."[46] Asian American Studies is uniquely positioned to intervene in current theoretical discussions on ethnicity, representation and writing not despite, but because of, the contested and contestatory nature of its formation.

NOTES

1. The newest group of Asian immigrants are Tibetans who had been living in exile in India and Nepal after the Chinese takeover of Tibet in 1959. The Tibetan-U.S. Resettlement Project has succeeded in bringing 1,000 refugees to the U.S. since 1990. The Tibetan provisions in the U.S. Immigration Act of 1990 refer to them as "displaced persons" and admit them to the U.S. as "immigrants," not "refugees," a reflection of the unwillingness of the government to jeopardize U.S.-China relations at this point in time. See Karma Gyatsho Zurkhang, "Strangers in a Strange Land," *Utne Reader* Mar/Apr 1993: 94–97.
2. The first critical anthology that deals exclusively with Asian American literary studies was published under the title *Reading the Literatures of Asian America,* ed. Shirley Geok-lin Lim and Amy Ling (Philadelphia: Temple University Press, 1992).
3. *Aiiieeeee! An Anthology of Asian-American Writers,* ed. Chin et al. (Washington, D.C.: Howard University Press, 1974), hereafter abbreviated *AA*; Kim, *Asian American Literature: An Introduction to the Writings and Their Social Context* (Philadelphia: Temple University Press, 1982), hereafter abbreviated *AIW*; Kim, "Defining Asian American Realities Through Literature," *Cultural Critique* 6/7 (1987): 87–111, hereafter abbreviated "DA"; Lim, "Twelve Asian American Writers: In Search of Self-Definition," in *Redefining American Literary History,* ed. A. LaVonne Brown Ruoff and Jerry W. Ward Jr. (New York: Modern Language Association of America, 1990), 237–250; and Lim, "Assaying the Gold: Or, Contesting the Ground of Asian American Literature," *New Literary History* 24 (1993): 147–169, hereafter abbreviated "CGA."
4. See *Island: Poetry and History of Chinese Americans on Angel Island, 1910–1940,* ed. Him Mark Lai et al. (San Francisco, 1980); *Songs of Gold Mountain: Cantonese Rhymes from San Francisco's Chinatown,* ed. and trans. Marlon K. Horn (Berkeley: University of California Press, 1987); Amy Ling,

Between Worlds: Women Writers of Chinese Ancestry (New York: Pergamon Press, 1990); *Ayumi: A Japanese American Anthology,* ed. Janice Mirikitani (San Francisco, 1980). The University of Washington Press has played a very important role in reprinting the work of older writers like John Okada, Carlos Bulosan, Monica Sone and many others.

5. Some of the important anthologies and bibliographies include *Asian-American Authors,* ed. Kai-yu Hsu and Helen Palubinskas (Boston, 1972); *Asian American Heritage: An Anthology of Prose and Poetry,* ed. David Hsin-Fu Wand (New York, 1974); *Breaking Silence: An Anthology of Contemporary Asian American Poets,* ed. Joseph Bruchac (New York, 1983); *Asian American Literature: An Annotated Bibliography,* ed. King-Kok Cheung and Stan Yogi (New York: Modern Language Association of America, 1988); *The Forbidden Stitch: An Asian American Women's Anthology,* ed. Shirley Geok-lin Lim and Mayumi Tsutakawa (Corvallis, Or.: Calyx Books, 1989); *Making Waves,* ed. Asian Women United of California (Boston: Beacon Press, 1989); *Charlie Chan Is Dead: An Anthology of Contemporary Asian American Fiction,* ed. Jessica Hagedorn (New York: Penguin Books, 1993), hereafter abbreviated *CC.*

6. Quoted in Wendell V. Harris, "Canonicity," *PMLA* 106.1 (1991): 112.

7. John Guillory, "Canon, Syllabus, List: A Note on the Pedagogic Imaginary," *Transition* 52 1991): 39.

8. Werner Sollors, "A Critique of Pure Pluralism," in *Reconstructing American Literary History,* ed. Sacvan Bercovitch (Cambridge, Mass.: Harvard University Press, 1986), 255, hereafter abbreviated "CP."

9. For comprehensive accounts of Asian American history see Sucheng Chan, *Asian Americans: An Interpretive History* (Boston: Twayne, 1991), hereafter abbreviated *AAIH;* Ronald Takaki, *Strangers From a Different Shore* (Boston: Little, Brown, 1989), hereafter abbreviated *SFD;* and *Dictionary of Asian American History,* ed. Hyung-Chan Kim (New York: Greenwood Press, 1986).

10. See *Labor Immigration Under Capitalism: Asian Workers in the United States Before World War II,* ed. Lucie Cheng and Edna Bonacich (Berkeley: University of California Press, 1984); Joan M. Jensen, *Passage From India: Asian Indian Immigrants in North America* (New Haven: Yale University Press, 1988); H. Brett Melendy, *Asians in America: Filipinos, Koreans, and East Indians* (Boston: Twayne, 1977); Alexander Saxton, *The Indispensable Enemy: Labor and the Anti-Chinese Movement in California* (Berkeley: University of California Press, 1971); and Roger Daniels, *The Politics of Prejudice: The Anti-Japanese Movement in California and the Struggle for Japanese Exclusion* (New York: Atheneum, 1968).

11. Yen Le Espiritu, *Asian American Panethnicity: Bridging Institutions and Identities* (Philadelphia: Temple University Press, 1992), 135, hereafter abbreviated *AAP.*

12. The Japanese government encouraged the emigration of women to create more stable immigrant communities, and retained a loophole in the 1907 Gentlemen's Agreement that restricted the emigration of laborers, but allowed the parents, wives and children of laborers already in America to enter (*SFD,* 46–7). As a result, 46% of Japanese in Hawaii and 34.5% on the mainland by 1920 were women. Korean immigrant communities also had a higher ratio of women (21% by 1920). The women were drawn by the more attractive conditions for family life in Hawaii; and many entered the United States as picture brides with Japanese passports issued to them as Japanese colonial subjects under the Gentlemen's Agreement (56). Numbers of Indian and Filipino men married Mexican women.

13. See Bill Ong Hing, *Making and Remaking Asian America Through Immigration Policy, 1850–1990* (Stanford: Stanford University Press, 1993), especially 43–78, hereafter abbreviated as *MRA; SFD,* 357–420; *AAIH,* 121–144.

and anthropological theories, for instance—but it is arguably poststructuralism, with its tenacious attention to the materiality of human signification, that has generated some of the most far-reaching ramifications for the ways we approach questions of objectivity and questions of subjectivity alike.

The one indisputable accomplishment of poststructuralist theory in the past several decades has been its systematic unsettling of the stability of meaning, its interruption of referentiality. If such meaning had never been entirely stable even in pretheory days, what poststructuralist theory provides is a metalanguage in which it (meaning) can now be defined anew as a repetitive effect produced in the chain of signification in the form of an exact but illusory correspondence between signifier and signified. While referentiality as such may continue to exist, for the new metalanguage it is the movements in the realm of signification that matter, that command critical interest as the (shifting) basis for meaning. Henceforth, *meaning* is a term that occurs within scare quotes. With the emphasis on material signifiers comes the determining function of difference—to be further differentiated as both differing and deferring—which would from now on take the place of sameness and identity as the condition for signification. Ferdinand de Saussure's summary statements may be conveniently recalled here: "In language there are only differences. Even more important: a difference generally implies positive terms between which the difference is set up; but in language there are only differences *without positive terms.*" *"Language is a form and not a substance."*[1] The foregrounding of differencing means that it is no longer possible to speak casually about any anchorage for meaning. If intelligibility itself is now understood as the effect of a movement of differencing, a movement that always involves delays and deferrals, then no longer can the old-fashioned belief in epistemological groundedness hold. In its stead the conception of (linguistic) identity becomes structurally defined, with (linguistic) signifiers mutually dependent on one another for the generation of what makes sense. Rather than being that which follows identity, difference now precedes identity. It is difference that creates an object of study.

It is necessary, in any consideration of the vicissitudes of theory, to acknowledge the substantial impact made by poststructuralism's landmark demotion and refusal of referentiality. The exercise of bracketing referentiality is enormously useful because adherence to referentiality has often led to a conservative clinging to a "reality" that is presumed to exist, in some unchanging manner, independently of language and signification. This a priori real world is, moreover, often given the authority of what authenticates, of what bestows the value of transcendental truth on language and signification. The dismantling of such a metaphysics of presence is hence most effective in disciplines in which the presumption of a factographic form of knowing has traditionally gone uncontested (as in some practices of history, for instance), but it is groundbreaking also in areas in which the naturalness of an object of knowledge—such as literature, for instance—has seldom been put into question. By intensifying our awareness of (linguistic) signification as first and foremost *self-referential,* poststructuralist theory opens a way for the ingrained ideological presuppositions behind such practices of knowledge production to be rethought.

From these fundamental revelations of poststructuralism, many critics have gone on pragmatically to explore differencing and its liberating egalitarianism in various social and historical contexts. They do so, for instance, by translating the open-endedness of linguistic signification into the fluidity of the human subject. When transplanted into the tradition of individualism, significatory differencing quite logically means the multiplication of selves. Nowadays, what is commonly referred to as identity politics typically takes as its point of departure the problematizing and critiquing of essentialist notions that are attached to personhood, subjectivity, and identity formation.[2] Such branching off from high theory into democratic investigations of selfhood (through a thematization of differencing) is in many cases justifiable, but it has also left certain problems intact. In this regard I think it is important not simply to practice antiessentialist differencing ad infinitum but also to reconsider such a practice in conjunction with the rejection of referentiality that lies at the origins of poststructuralism. Exactly what is being thrown out when referentiality is theoretically rejected? I hope the significance of this point will become clear as I move through my arguments, for it bears on what I think is the conundrum in the critical study of marginalized groups and non-Western cultures today.

To begin, let me briefly revisit the question of how poststructuralist theory has methodologically radicalized the very production not only of the subject but also of the notion of an object of study. Albeit discussed much less frequently these days (simply because objectivity itself, it is assumed, can no longer be assumed), the issues that surround this topic remain instructive.

Consider the discipline of literature, for which one ongoing concern on which poststructuralist theory has helped to shed light is the problem of literariness, of what is specific to literature. At one level, this is of course precisely a question about referentiality. What is literature all about? To what does it refer? What reality does it represent? Old-fashioned though it may sound, such a preoccupation with literariness has surprising affinities with the contemporary cultural politics that clusters around identity. Let us retrace some of the well-known attempts at approaching this problem.

Marx's and Engels's discussion of literary writing and aesthetic representation provides a good instance of this because it is contextualized in their more general concern for social revolution and radical political practice. In their exchanges with authors seeking advice on writing fiction, Marx and Engels, we remember, made some rather startling statements.[3] Albeit theoretically forward looking, they were careful to warn these writers against turning literature into socialist propaganda in which fictional characters simply become mouthpieces for revolutionary doctrines. "The solution of the problem," writes Engels, "must become manifest from the situation and the action themselves without being expressly pointed out and . . . the author is not obliged to serve the reader on a platter the future historical resolution of the social conflicts which he describes."[4] Embedded in these brief remarks is an intuitive sense that theoretical and literary discourses are distinguished from each other by an essential articulatory difference, and that literary discourse, which specializes in indirection, can only become dull and mediocre should one turn it into a platform for direct proletarian pronouncements. Even where the subject matter cries out for justice to be done on some people's behalf, literary writing, they suggest, tends to accomplish its task more effectively when it does not explicitly solicit the reader's sympathy as such. In literature, the modus operandi is not to speak about something expressly even when one feels one must, in a manner quite opposite the clarity and forthrightness of theoretical argumentation. "The more the opinions of the author remain hidden, the better for the work of art";[5] in other words, a very different kind of power for producing change is in play. David Craig summarizes this point succinctly: "Surely, if literature affects action or changes someone's life, it is not by handing out a recipe for the applying but rather by disturbing us emotionally, mentally, because it *finds* us . . . , so that, after a series of such experiences and along with others that work with it, we feel an urge to 'do something' or at least to ask ourselves the question (the great question put by Chernyshevsky, Lenin, and Silone): 'What is to be done?' "[6]

What remains illuminating in these discussions is a perception of the work of indirection that seemed, to Marx and Engels at least, to be the unique characteristic of literary discourse; this is remarkable especially in light of their political belief in asserting the necessity to reform and revolutionize society, a belief that, in discursive terms, would be more in line with direct, straightforward, clear-cut expression—the very antithesis of their observations about literary writing. As political theorists, Marx and Engels nonetheless recognized that literary production could not be reduced to a mechanical mirroring of some reality out there, and that whatever literature is "about," such referentiality occurs, by definition, in a refracted manner rather than by straightforward declaration.[7]

In subsequent debates it was the critics who were overtly concerned with form (rather than with politics) who would continue the elaboration of this observation of literature-as-indirection, even though indirection was now theorized in different terms. For instance, the Russian Formalists' effort in defining the defamiliarizing capacity of art and literature—of art's capacity for presenting something familiar in such a manner as to call attention to its "artfulness," or its capacity for taking readers by surprise through the process of de-formation—can in retrospect be understood as an attempt to identify, perhaps to construct, a kind of rupture and distance from within a conventional discourse, so that the shock and alienating effect produced can be described as what is specific to art and literary expression. Such shock and alienation, again, are not a matter of direct expression but, rather, of a sensitively perceived differential—the more implicitly the differential is grasped, the greater the effect of artfulness and literariness—so much so that the art object itself takes on only secondary importance.

In the Anglo-American world the literary-theoretical avant-garde of the twentieth century was represented by New Criticism, which specializes in the discernment of a literary work's specificity through close reading. The contradiction between the aim and the practice of New Criticism has been well noted. Between the nostalgic desire to produce a complete, intrinsic reading that would exemplify the literary work as a self-sufficient world with rules that apply only to itself,[8] on the one hand, and the ambiguous open-endedness of meaning that results ironically from such desire-in-practice, on the other, lies the aporia that becomes, for a deconstructive critic such as Paul de Man, New Criticism's unwitting self-undoing. De Man demonstrates this by reintroducing the dimension of temporality—hence of postponements, deferrals, and belatedness—in the process of coming to terms with literary discourse: "The temporal factor, so persistently forgotten, should remind us that the form is never anything but a process on its way to completion."[9] Whereas New Criticism is still invested in a kind of time-less reading of the work of literature, a reading that circumvents temporality by the ideological projection of the work's organic wholeness, deconstruction would distinguish its comparable interest in literary specificity by underscoring the effects of time as manifested through the negative momentum of language. In de Man's hands, the previous attempts to get at literature's indirectness culminate in a sophisticated reformulation by way of the originary constitutive role of temporal difference, one that consistently undermines textual presence and plenitude. If literature is indirect, defamiliarizing, ambiguous, ironic, allegorical, and so forth—if, in other words, it is never straightforwardly referential—it is because human linguistic signification itself is always already mediated by the slow but indismissible labor of temporality.

But the perception of time alone does not necessarily account for the derailing of reference. One is reminded of the great humanist literary critic Erich Auerbach, for instance, for whom the noticeable temporal shifts in modernist literary representation, shifts he describes with animation and verve, nonetheless do not challenge the basic idea that there exists something common to all of our lives even in the midst of diversities.[10] From a poststructuralist, difference-oriented perspective, this statement from the end of Auerbach's *Mimesis* is quite astonishing, particularly in view of the sensitive close readings he has performed:

> The more it is exploited, the more the elementary things which our lives have in common come to light. The more numerous, varied, and simple the people are who appear as subjects of such random moments, the more effectively must what they have in common shine forth. In this unprejudiced and exploratory type of representation we cannot but see to what an extent—below the surface conflicts—the differences between men's ways of life and forms of thought have already lessened. The strata of societies and their different ways of life have become inextricably mingled. There are no longer even exotic peoples. A century ago (in Mérimée for example), Corsicans or Spaniards were still exotic; today the term would be quite unsuitable for Pearl Buck's Chinese peasants.[11]

In spite of his grasp of the changes in literary, representational time, referentiality itself is not a problem for Auerbach because he remains convinced of a universal something called human reality. Mimesis is simply a way of accessing it; accessibility itself is not an issue.

The contribution made by poststructuralist theory, then, lies not merely in its articulation of temporality but also in its insistence that time does not coincide with itself. This recurrent slippage and intrinsic irreconcilability—between speaking and writing, between sign and meaning, and between fiction and reality—allows deconstructionist critics to assert that deconstruction is a rigorously historical process. As Geoff Bennington writes, "Deconstruction, insofar as it insists on the necessary non-coincidence of the present with itself, is in fact in some senses the most historical of discourses imaginable."[12] For Marian Hobson, the point of deconstruction-as-history is precisely that identity is never possible and that such impossibility is itself plural: "It is trace, track, which makes identity impossible. But this impossibility is itself plural, not simple. It is not a straight negative—not simple, identical, non-identity. Trace, lack of self-coincidence, is on the contrary a plurality of impossibilities, a disjunction of negatives."[13] If conventional practices of history may be criticized on the basis of a premature projection of the referent, deconstruction's response is that history resides, rather, in the permanently self-undermining process of differentiation, a process that, by the sheer force of its logic, need not have an end in sight.

This potential alliance between the lack of (temporal and ontological) self-presence and differentiation-as-historicity is one major reason poststructuralism has left such indelible imprints on those areas of knowledge production that do not at first seem to have much to do with semiotics or, for that matter, with the revamping of metalanguages, but that are intimately linked to empirical issues such as culture and group identity. It is not difficult to see that the basic tenets of structuralist linguistics and semiotics—difference, identity, value, arbitrariness, convention, and systematicity—carry within them connotations that have res-onances well beyond the terrain of a narrow sense of language. With the bracketing of the object of knowledge and the foregrounding of the process of signification, as introduced by poststructuralism, it is inevitable that the certitude of the identities involved—epistemolog-ical, subjective, or collective—can no longer be safely taken for granted. It is not surprising, therefore, that one of the most prevalent uses of the poststructuralist metalanguage of differ-encing is to be found in areas in which existential identity is most at stake: multiculturalism, postcoloniality, and ethnicity.[14]

If this is the case, how is it that in these areas of study there is currently also a persistent refrain that non-Western subjects and subject matters are "oppositional" and "resistant" to Western theory? About fifteen to twenty years ago, even though the same ambivalent gesture toward the West might have been made, theory itself was not an issue. Nowadays, as can be surmised from journals, conferences, anthologies, and single-author publications, not only are more trendy topics such as transgender politics, Asian pop music, Third World urban geogra-phy, or cultural translation obligated to gesture toward one kind of Western theory or another; even the study of ancient ethnic poems and narratives must, in order to argue the case of their uniqueness, their beyond-comparison status, somehow demonstrate an awareness of the background of Western theoretical issues. If all this is testimony to the hegemony enjoyed by Western theory, why are claims of resistance and opposition at the same time so adamant?

If the exploration of literary difference was in order to ground literary specificity—that is, to define literature as an object with its essential attributes, attributes that make litera-ture definitively unlike anything else—then one of the consequences of such exploration is, ironically, the dissipation of this "object" altogether. From the nineteenth-century percep-tion of its essence (in Marx and Engels) as indirection to the late-twentieth-century asser-tion (by deconstructionist critics) of its noncoincidence with itself, the object of literariness seems to have become theoretically unsustainable exactly at the moment of its concrete definition: it "is" what it always is not. If the ongoing efforts to define literary difference have brought to light all that has been repressed, neglected, or ignored, such efforts have also shown how literature does not and cannot stop at the mere restoration or redemption of such difference. Inevitably, difference as such will continue to fragment and dismantle whatever specificity that may have been established through it, once again rendering the goal of stable objectification impossible.

Permanent differentiation and permanent impermanence: these are the key features of poststructuralist theoretical practice as we find it today. The example of literature has simply demonstrated the Pyrrhic victory of the scientific or social scientific attempt to produce an object of knowledge by way of differencing. If literariness is that which tends to disappear into something else at the moment of its being objectified, then literature is, ultimately, a historically mobile, changing relationship (of writing) rather than a concrete essence. Might this lesson about literariness be extended beyond the discipline of literature?

Consider now the study of X, those areas that, as I mentioned at the beginning, often attain visibility by gesturing toward and resisting Western theory at the same time. As in the case of literariness, we may set out to define X as an object with certain attributes. But we already know from the example of literariness that such an attempt at discovering the specificity of X will lead first to the process of differencing and eventually to the dissipation of X itself as a stable referent. Should we then say that, ultimately, X as such does not exist, that X, like literariness, is a permanently shifting, non-self-identical relationship? What might be the implications of proclaiming, let us say, that African American, Asian American, and gay and lesbian specificities do not exist? Such proclamations are, to be sure, intolerable to many, but it is perhaps less because these "people" really do exist than because the theoretical claim for their existence is inseparable from the hierarchical politics of race, class, gender, and ethnicity that structure Western and non-Western societies alike. In the face of the practical struggles that go on daily against different forms of social injustice, it is, for many, unacceptable to declare, in accordance with poststructuralist theoretical logic, that these versions of X do not exist. Yet the alternative—the insistence that they are real, that they are out there, that their empirical existence is absolutely incontestable, and that they are thus a core from which to stage resistance to the virtual claims of high theory—is equally untenable because it is theoretically naive.

The conundrum we face today in the wake of theory may thus be described as follows: In their attempts to argue the specificity of their objects of study, critics of marginalized historical areas often must rhetorically assert their resistance to or distrust of Western theory. But what exactly is the nature of that which they are resisting and distrusting? As these critics try to defend the viability of their proposed objects, they are compelled, against their own proclaimed beliefs, to set into motion precisely the poststructuralist operation of differencing, of making essentialist categories of identity disintegrate. Indeed, differencing is often the very weapon with which they mount their criticisms of Western theory. While they criticize Western theory, then, these critics are meanwhile implementing the bracketing of anchored, referential meanings that constitutes one of contemporary Western theory's most profound influences. Since there is nothing inherent in the methodological mechanism of structural differentiation that calls for resistance or differentiation at a level beyond the chain of signification, the objects to which these critics cling—in resistance—inevitably dissipate over time in a manner similar to that in which the object of literariness dissipates. To truly argue for resistance, they would in fact need to go against or abandon altogether the very theoretical premises (of poststructuralist differencing) on which they make their criticisms in the first place.[15]

Put in a different way, the attempt to argue the specificity of X as such, even as it discredits Western theory, tends to reproduce the very terms—and the very problems—that once surrounded the theoretical investigation of literariness. Like literature, X is often constructed (negatively) as what defamiliarizes, what departs from conventional expectations, what disrupts the norm, and so forth, terms that are invested in constructing specificity by way of differentiation. Like the attempt to define literariness also, the attempt to define *X* seems doomed to destroy its own object in the process of objectification. More disturbing still, if representation of *X* as such is recognizable in these similar theoretical terms, does it not mean that there is no essential difference between *X* and high theory—that the articulation of *X*, however historically specific it may be, is somehow already *within* the trajectory mapped out by high theory?

This is the juncture at which a rethinking of poststructuralist theory is in order, not once again by way of temporal differencing but, more significantly, by way of reexamining theory's interruption of referentiality. By bracketing referentiality, separating it from the signified, and making the signified part of the chain of signification and an effect produced by the play of signifiers, poststructuralism has devised an epistemological framework in which what lies "outside" can be recoded as what is inside. There is hence no outside to the text. At the same time, however, this also means that poststructuralism really does not offer a way of thinking about any outside except by reprogramming it into part of an ongoing interior (chain) condition. This is not exactly the same as saying that poststructuralism is a closed system of permutations; rather, it is simply that its mechanism of motility, which provides a set of terms that redefines referentiality effectively as the illusion produced by the play of temporal differences, also tends to preclude any other way of getting at the outside than by directing it inward. My point, then, is this: rather than systematicity per se (which was the problem characteristic of structuralism), the problem here is perhaps none other than temporality rendered as nonpresence.

Although it constitutes what is arguably poststructuralism's most radical intervention in European thought, the notion of time's noncoincidence with itself may nevertheless have a substantially contrary set of reverberations once we go beyond the parameters of Europe. Where otherness stands as an empirical and a cultural as well as a theoretical issue, the assertion of temporal disjunction as such (as an absolute force that structures all signification) may coincide, or become complicit, with the anthropological problematic that Johannes Fabian has called, in his well-known phrase, the denial of coevalness—"*a persistent and systematic tendency to place the referent(s) of anthropology in a Time other than the present of the producer of anthropological discourse.*"[16] In other words, whereas the insistence on the noncoincidence of the present with itself may indeed be a revolutionary charge within the philosophical and epistemological terrains from which poststructuralism stems, such an insistence, when seen in light of Europe's history with its colonized others, may turn out to be no more than another current of what Fabian calls allochronic discourse, in which other peoples who are our contemporaries are discursively confined each to their culture gardens/ethnic ghettos, in the name, precisely, of difference. Be it temporal, ontological, linguistic, or identitarian, noncoincidence can hardly be considered groundbreaking in the global circuits of colonialism and imperialism because the non-Western others are already, by definition, classified as noncoincident, discontinuous, and fundamentally different (from populations in the West, from the times and languages of Western ethnographers). To emphasize noncoincidence as such is thus merely to reify and raise to the level of metalanguage a rather conventional anthropological attitude toward the other's otherness—which is often unproblematically upheld as a fact—without actually confronting the conditions that enable such assumptions of noncoincidence to stand in the first place. Referring to the relevance of Fabian's work for the study of colonial America, for instance, Carlos Alonso comments on one such manifestation of the (principle of) noncoincidence inherent to the rhetoric of temporality—the expression of amazement: "Europe's rhetoric of amazement vis-à-vis America . . . necessitates the ceaseless deferral of total cognitive mastery. But rather than being deployed in order to maintain an irreducible alterity, the European figuration of the New World as new posited a continuity between itself and the new territories that made possible European appropriation of the recently discovered lands while simultaneously affirming their exoticism."[17]

Let me push my point one step further: the definition of time as noncoincidental with itself, I would like to suggest, means that poststructuralism ultimately does not offer any viable way of thinking about an *act of exclusion* except by recoding it as a (passive) *condition of exteriority*. Once recoded (in the form of an "always already"), this condition is channeled into an existing interior in such a manner as to become part of this interior's infinite series of differentiations over time, always open ended and incomplete, always ready for further differentiation to be sure, yet never again directed at the primary, originary moment involving the as yet unresolved outside. At the level of metalanguage, this outside, or what has been banished there, is none other than referentiality, which must henceforth live the life of the exiled, the exotic, and the exorcised—that which is barred once and for all from entering, from migrating into the interior of, the chain of signification.

It follows that when one is dealing with sexual, cultural, and ethnic others, it is always considered premature in poststructuralist theory to name and identify such references as such; instead, deconstruction's preferred benevolent gesture is to displace and postpone these others to a utopian, unrealizable realm, to a spectral dimension whose radicalness lies precisely in its spectrality, the fact that it cannot materialize *in the present*. Again, Alonso's observations about the discursive place occupied by America in the European imagination during the colonial epoch are pointedly on the mark. From being perceived as novel, he writes, America gradually shifted into the position of the future:

> Almost imperceptibly, the coevalness that the narrative of newness required was replaced by a narrative paradigm in which America occupied a position of *futurity* vis-à-vis the Old World. This transformation from novelty to futurity was significant because, among other things, it created the conditions for a permanent exoticization of the New World—the sort that cannot be undermined or dissolved by actual experience or objective analysis: safely ensconced in an always postponed future, America could become the object of a ceaselessly regenerating discourse of mystification and perpetual promise.[18]

This inability to deal with the other except by temporal displacement returns us to the scenario with which I began this essay. When scholars of marginalized groups and non-Western subjects rely on notions of resistance and opposition (to Western theory) in their attempts to argue the specificity of *X*, they are unwittingly reproducing the epistemological conundrum by which the specificity of an object of study is conceived of in terms of a differential—a differential, moreover, that has to be included in the chain of signification in order to be recognized. However, by virtue of its mechanism of postponement and displacement, this kind of logic implies the eventual dissolution of the object without being able to address *how* X presents not just a condition (exteriority) that has always already existed but more importantly an active politics of exclusion and discrimination. Within the bounds of this logic, the more resistive and oppositional (that is, on the outside) X is proclaimed to be, the more inevitably it is to lose its specificity (that is, become incorporated) in the larger framework of the systematic production of differences, while the circumstances that make this logic possible (that is, that enable it to unfold and progress as a self-regulating interior) remain unchallenged. This is one reason why so many new projects of articulating alternative identities, cultures, and group formations often seem so predictable in the end. Whether the topic under discussion is a particular ethnic work or the identity of an ethnic person, what has become predictable is precisely the invocation of "ambivalence," "multiplicity," "hybridity," "heterogeneity," "disruptiveness," "resistance," and the like, and no matter how new an object of study may appear to be, it is bound to lose its novelty once the play of temporal difference is set into motion. The moves permitted by the rules of the originary exclusion—the difference that makes the difference, as it were—have already been exhausted, and critics dealing with X can only repeatedly run up against the incommensurability between the experience of temporality as self-deconstruction (with its radical theoretical nuances) and the experience of temporality as allochronism (with its racialist anthropological ramifications).

In sum, contemporary uses of poststructuralist theory have tended to adopt poststructuralism's solution, differencing, without sufficiently reflecting on its flip side, its circumvention of exclusion. Yet contemporary issues of identity and cultural conflict almost invariably involve the politics of exclusion. Can these mutually incompatible states of affairs be reconciled with each other? How can they be reconciled? Can specificity be imagined in terms other than a naturalized differential, an automatized discontinuity? Are there perhaps forms of closure, limits, and references that should not be prematurely disavowed, because the act of disavowing them inevitably becomes a self-contradictory move, leading only to a theoretical impasse? (That is, the act of reprogramming everything as part of an interior inevitably becomes an act to exclude, with what is excluded being, first and foremost, the assertion of the violence of exclusion itself.)

The reference that is social injustice—itself a type of differential but a differential hierarchized with value—cannot be as easily postponed or displaced, because the mechanisms of postponement and displacement do not by themselves address the hierarchical or discriminatory nature of the differential involved. As a result, however permanently the issue may be deferred, the originary differential of inequality will not and cannot go away. The kind of theoretical mechanism that works by dissolving specificities into differences is therefore incapable of addressing the concerns implied here, because there is nothing inherent in such a mechanism that would necessitate the recognition of the inequality and injustice that may indeed, for lack of a better term, be "out there" yet that may not be immediately or entirely incorporable into the chain of signification. Referentiality, reformulated in this manner, may in the end require us to accept it precisely as the limit, the imperfect, irreducible difference that is not pure difference but difference thoroughly immersed in and corrupted by the errors and delusions of history.

For similar reasons, an awareness of historical asymmetries of power, aggression, social antagonism, inequality of representation, and their like cannot simply be accomplished through an adherence to the nebulous concept of resistance and opposition. That concept itself is often constituted with the logic of differentiation—of disruption and departure—within a theoretical framework whose success lies precisely in its perennial capacity for including and absorbing that which is on the outside. Resistance that imagines itself as purely premised on the outside is thus a futile exercise in the wake of poststructuralist theory. In its stead, it would be more productive to let referentiality interrupt, to reopen the poststructuralist closure on this issue, to acknowledge the inevitability of reference even in the most avantgarde of theoretical undertakings, and to demand a thorough reassessment of an originary act of repudiation/exclusion in terms that can begin to address the "scandal of domination and exploitation of one part of mankind by another."[19]

NOTES

1. Ferdinand de Saussure, *Course in General Linguistics,* intro. Jonathan Culler, ed. Charles Bally and Albert Sechehaye in collaboration with Albert Reidlinger, trans. Wade Baskin (Glasgow: Collins, 1974), 120, 122; emphases in the original.
2. The greatly influential work of Judith Butler is exemplary in this regard.
3. For useful discussions of the problematic of (aesthetic) reflection in Marxist theory, see, for instance, Pierre Macherey, *A Theory of Literary Production,* trans. Geoffrey Wall (London: Routledge, 1978), and Terry Eagleton, *Criticism and Ideology* (London: Verso, 1978). For related discussions, see Henri Arvon, *Marxist Esthetics,* trans. Helen R. Lane, intro. Fredric Jameson (Ithaca: Cornell University Press, 1973); *Marxism and Art: Essays Classic and Contemporary,* selected and with historical and critical commentary by Maynard Solomon (New York: Knopf, 1973); and Theodor Adorno, Walter Benjamin, Ernst Bloch, Bertolt Brecht, and Georg Lukács, *Aesthetics and Politics,* afterword by Fredric Jameson, trans. Ronald Taylor (London: Verso, 1980), as well as the essays in David Craig, ed., *Marxists on Literature: An Anthology* (New York: Penguin, 1975).
4. Friedrich Engels, "Letter to Minna Kautsky," in Craig, *Marxists on Literature,* 268. See also chaps. 8, 9 (Marx's and Engels's letters to Lasalle), and 13 (Engels's letter to Margaret Harkness), all reprinted from Karl Marx and Friedrich Engels, *Selected Correspondence* (Moscow: n.p., n.d.).
5. Engels, "Letter to Margaret Harkness," in Craig, *Marxists on Literature,* 270.
6. David Craig, introduction to Craig, *Marxists on Literature,* 22.
7. Pierre Macherey's discussion of Lenin's reading of Leo Tolstoy (and the question of reflection in Tolstoy's works) remains one of the most illuminating accounts in this regard. See Macherey, *Theory of Literary Production,* 105–35, 299–323.
8. See John Bender and David E. Wellbery, "Rhetoricality: On the Modernist Return of Rhetoric," in *The Ends of Rhetoric: History, Theory, Practice,* ed. John Bender and David E. Wellbery (Stanford, Calif.: Stanford University Press, 1990), 3–39. The authors see modernist rhetoricality, with its emphasis on the groundlessness of truth, as a legacy of Friedrich Nietzsche.
9. Paul de Man, "Form and Intent in the American New Criticism," "The Rhetoric of Temporality," and "The Dead-End of Formalist Criticism," in *Blindness and Insight: Essays in the Rhetoric of*

Contemporary Criticism, 2d ed., rev., intro. Wlad Godzich (Minneapolis: University of Minnesota Press, 1983), 20–35, 187–228, 229–45. The quotation is on p. 31.

10. Erich Auerbach, *Mimesis: The Representation of Reality in Western Literature,* trans. Willard R. Trask (Princeton, N.J.: Princeton University Press, 1953). See especially his perceptive discussion of Virginia Woolf, in whose work, as he notes, external events often have only the vaguest contours while the rich and sensitively registered internal time of the characters has led to the abdication of authorial objectivity and hegemony.

11. Ibid., 552.

12. Geoff Bennington, "Demanding History," in *Post-structuralism and the Question of History,* ed. Derek Attridge, Geoff Bennington, and Robert Young (New York: Cambridge University Press, 1987), 17.

13. Marian Hobson, "History Traces," in Attridge, Bennington, and Young, *Post-structuralism and the Question of History,* 102–3.

14. I discuss this in greater detail in "The Secrets of Ethnic Abjection," in *Traces* 2 (2001): 53–77. A few passages from that essay have been incorporated with modifications into the present one.

15. For a succinct critique of the contradictions that accompany poststructuralist theory and that have had a profound impact on the multiculturalist trends in the humanities, see Masao Miyoshi, "Ivory Tower in Escrow," *boundary 2* 27.1 (2000), in particular 39–50.

16. Johannes Fabian, *Time and the Other: How Anthropology Makes Its Object* (New York: Columbia University Press, 1983), 31; emphasis in the original.

17. Carlos J. Alonso, *The Burden of Modernity: The Rhetoric of Cultural Discourse in Spanish America* (New York: Oxford University Press, 1998), 7.

18. Ibid., 8; emphasis in the original.

19. Fabian, *Time and the Other,* x. In Miyoshi's terms, this would mean restoring the hitherto discredited function of so-called metanarratives: "The academics' work in this marketized world . . . is to learn and watch problems in as many sites as they can keep track of, not in any specific areas, nations, races, ages, genders, or cultures, but in all areas, nations, races, ages, genders, and cultures. In other words, far from abandoning the master narratives, the critics and scholars in the humanities must restore the public rigor of the metanarratives" ("Ivory Tower in Escrow," 49).

READER RESPONSE

ENCODING/DECODING (1973, 1980)

STUART HALL

Reconsidering Jakobson's model (see Jakobson's "Linguistics and Poetics" in this volume) of addresser (or sender), message, and addressee (or receiver), Hall observes that a communication system is not perfectly efficient. It is asymmetrical; what gets sent is not the same as what gets received. When a message is sent, it has to be encoded, and the encoding shapes the message because the message is mediated, influenced, by the encoders' discourses, ideologies, and technologies. When the message is received, it has to be decoded. In that sense, the structure may seem symmetrical. But the decoding, like the encoding, shapes the message because it, too, is mediated by another set of discourses, ideologies, and technologies. Therefore, the message is never the signified itself, stable and secure. Instead, it is always a discourse of signifiers in process. The decodings vary according to whether the decoders accept, question, or object to the encoders' cultural assumptions. Hall uses the example of a television news program, although he could just as well take examples from other kinds of messages, such as a song, a poem, a movie, or a novel.

Traditionally, mass-communications research has conceptualized the process of communication in terms of a circulation circuit or loop. This model has been criticized for its linearity—sender/message/receiver—for its concentration on the level of message exchange and for the absence of a structured conception of the different moments as a complex structure of relations. But it is also possible (and useful) to think of this process in terms of a structure produced and sustained through the articulation of linked but distinctive moments—production, circulation, distribution/consumption, reproduction. This would be to think of the process as a "complex structure in dominance," sustained through the articulation of connected practices, each of which, however, retains its distinctiveness and has its own specific modality, its own forms and conditions of existence. This second approach, homologous to that which forms the skeleton of commodity production offered in Marx's *Grundrisse* and in *Capital*, has the added advantage of bringing out more sharply how a continuous circuit—production-distribution-production—can be sustained through a "passage of forms."[1] It also highlights the specificity of the forms in which the product of the process "appears" in each moment, and thus what distinguishes discursive "production" from other types of production in our society and in modern media systems.

The "object" of these practices is meanings and messages in the form of sign-vehicles of a specific kind organized, like any form of communication or language, through the operation of codes within the syntagmatic chain of a discourse. The apparatuses, relations and practices of production thus issue, at a certain moment (the moment of "production/circulation") in the form of symbolic vehicles constituted within the rules of "language." It is in this discursive form that the circulation of the "product" takes place. The process thus requires, at the production end, its material instruments—its "means"—as well as its own sets of social (production) relations—the organization and combination of practices within media apparatuses. But it is in the *discursive* form that the circulation of the product takes place, as well as its distribution to different audiences. Once accomplished, the discourse must then be translated—transformed, again—into social practices if the circuit is to be both completed and effective. If no "meaning" is taken, there can be no "consumption." If the meaning is not articulated in practice, it has no effect. The value of this approach is that while each of the moments, in articulation, is necessary to the circuit as a whole, no one moment can fully guarantee the next moment with which it is articulated. Since each has its specific modality and conditions of existence, each can constitute its own break or interruption of the "passage of forms" on whose continuity the flow of effective production (that is, "reproduction") depends.

Thus while in no way wanting to limit research to "following only those leads which emerge from content analysis,"[2] we must recognize that the discursive form of the message has a privileged position in the communicative exchange (from the viewpoint of circulation), and that the moments of "encoding" and "decoding," though only "relatively autonomous" in relation to the communicative process as a whole, are *determinate* moments. A "raw" historical event cannot, *in that form*, be transmitted by, say, a television newscast. Events can only be signified within the aural-visual forms of the televisual discourse. In the moment when a historical event passes under the sign of discourse, it is subject to all the complex formal "rules" by which language signifies. To put it paradoxically, the event must become a "story" before it can become a *communicative event*. In that moment the formal sub-rules of discourse are "in dominance," without, of course, subordinating out of existence the historical event so signified, the social relations in which the rules are set to work or the social and political consequences of the event having been signified in this way. The "message form" is the necessary "form of appearance" of the event in its passage from source to receiver. Thus the transposition into and out of the "message form" (or the mode of symbolic exchange) is not a random "moment," which we can take up or ignore at our convenience. The "message form" is a determinate moment; though, at another level, it comprises the surface movements of the communications system only and requires, at another stage, to be integrated into the social relations of the communication process as a whole, of which it forms only a part.

From this general perspective, we may crudely characterize the television communicative process as follows. The institutional structures of broadcasting, with their practices and networks of production, their organized relations and technical infrastructures, are required to produce a programme. Using the analogy of *Capital,* this is the "labour process" in the discursive mode. Production, here, constructs the message. In one sense, then, the circuit begins here. Of course, the production processes is not without its "discursive" aspect: it, too, is framed throughout by meanings and ideas: knowledge-in-use concerning the routines of production, historically defined technical skills, professional ideologies, institutional knowledge, definitions and assumptions, assumptions about the audience and so on frame the constitution of the programme through this production structure. Further, though the production structures of television originate the television discourse, they do not constitute a closed system. They draw topics, treatments, agendas, events, personnel, images of the audience, "definitions of the situation" from other sources and other discursive formations within the wider socio-cultural and political structure of which they are a differentiated part. Philip Elliott has expressed this point succinctly, within a more traditional framework, in his discussion of the way in which the audience is both the "source" and the "receiver" of the television message. Thus—to borrow Marx's terms—circulation and reception are, indeed, "moments" of the production process in television and are reincorporated, via a number of skewed and structure "feedbacks," into the production process itself. The consumption or reception of the television message is thus also itself a "moment" of the production process in its larger sense, though the latter is "predominant" because it the "point of departure for the realization" of the message. Production and reception of the television message are not, therefore, identical, but they are related: they are differentiated moments within the totality formed by the social relations of the communicative process as a whole.

At a certain point, however, the broadcasting structures must yield encoded messages in the form of a meaningful discourse. The institution-societal relations of production must pass under the discursive rules of language for its product to be "realized." This initiates a further differentiated moment, in which the formal rules of discourse and language are in dominance. Before this message can have an "effect" (however defined), satisfy a "need" or be put to a "use," it must first be appropriated as a meaningful discourse and be meaningfully decoded. It is this set of decoded meanings which "have an effect," influence, entertain, instruct or persuade, with very complex perceptual, cognitive, emotional, ideological or behavioural consequences. In a "determinate" moment the structure employs a code and yields a "message": at another determinate moment the "message," via its decodings, issues into the structure of social practices. We are now fully aware that this re-entry into the practices of audience reception and "use" cannot be understood in simple behavioural terms. The typical processes identified in positivistic research on isolated elements—effects, uses, "gratifications"—are themselves framed by structures of understanding, as well as being produced by social and economic relations, which shape their "realization" at the reception end of the chain and which permit the meanings signified in the discourse to be transposed into practice or consciousness (to acquire social use value or political effectivity).

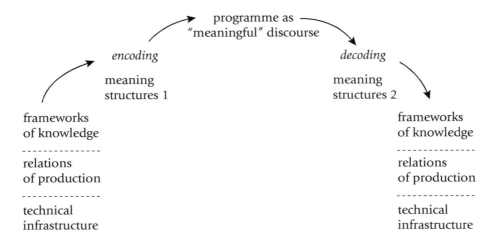

Clearly, what we have labeled in the diagram "meaning structures 1" and "meaning structures 2" may not be the same. They do not constitute an "immediate identity." The codes of encoding and decoding may not be perfectly symmetrical. The degrees of symmetry—that is, the degrees of "understanding" and "misunderstanding" in the communicative exchange—depend on the degrees of symmetry/asymmetry (relations of equivalence) established between the positions of the "personifications," encoder-producer and decoder-receiver. But this in turn depends on the degrees of identity/non-identity between the codes which perfectly or imperfectly transmit, interrupt or systematically distort what has been transmitted. The lack of fit between the codes has a great deal to do with the structural difference of relation and position between broadcasters and audiences, but it also has something to do with the asymmetry between the codes of "source" and "receiver" at the moment of transformation into and out of the discursive form. What are called "distortions" or "misunderstandings" arise precisely from the *lack of equivalence* between the two sides in the communicative exchange. Once again, this defines the "relative autonomy," but "determinateness," of the entry and exit of the message in its discursive moments.

The application of this rudimentary paradigm has already begun to transform our understanding of the older term, television "content." We are just beginning to see how it might also transform our understanding of audience reception, "reading" and response as well. Beginnings and endings have been announced in communications research before, so we must be cautious. But there seems some ground for thinking that a new and exciting phase in so-called audience research, of a quite new kind, may be opening up. At either end of the communicative chain the use of the semiotic paradigm promises to dispel the lingering behaviourism which has dogged mass-media research for so long, especially in its approach to content. Though we know the television programme is not a behavioural input, like a tap on the knee cap, it seems to have been almost impossible for traditional researchers to conceptualize the communicative process without lapsing into one or other variant of low-flying behaviourism. We know, as Gerbner has remarked, that representations of violence on the TV screen "are not violence but messages about violence"[3]: but we have continued to research the question of violence, for example, as if we were unable to comprehend this epistemological distinction.

The televisual sign is a complex one. It is itself constituted by the combination of two types of discourse, visual and aural. Moreover, it is an iconic sign, in Peirce's terminology, because "it possesses some of the properties of the thing represented."[4] This is a point which has led to a great deal of confusion and has provided the site of intense controversy in the study of visual language. Since the visual discourse translates a three-dimensional world into two-dimensional planes, it cannot, of course, *be* the referent or concept it signifies. The dog in the film can bark but it cannot bite! Reality exists outside language, but it is constantly mediated by and through language: and what we can know and say has to be produced in and through discourse. Discursive "knowledge" is the product not of the transparent representation of the "real" in language but of the articulation of language on real relations and conditions. Thus there is no intelligible discourse without the operation of a code. Iconic signs are therefore coded signs too—even if the codes here work differently from those of other signs. There is no degree zero in language. Naturalism and "realism"—the apparent fidelity of the representation to the thing or concept represented—is the result, the effect, of a certain specific articulation of language on the "real." It is the result of a discursive practice.

Certain codes may, of course, be so widely distributed in a specific language community or culture, and be learned at so early an age, that they appear not to be constructed—the effect of an articulation between sign and referent—but to be "naturally" given. Simple visual signs appear to have achieved a "near-universality" in this sense: though evidence remains that even apparently "natural" visual codes are culture-specific. However, this does not mean that no codes have intervened; rather, that the codes have been profoundly *naturalized*. The operation of naturalized codes reveals not the transparency and "naturalness" of language but the depth, the habituation and the near-universality of the codes in use. They produce apparently "natural" recognitions. This has the (ideological) effect of concealing the practices of coding which are present. But we must not be fooled by appearances. Actually, what naturalized codes demonstrate is the degree of habituation produced when there is a fundamental alignment and reciprocity—an achieved equivalence—between the encoding and decoding sides of an exchange of meanings. The functioning of the codes on the decoding side will frequently assume the status of naturalized perceptions. This leads us to think that the visual sign for "cow" actually *is* (rather than *represents*) the animal, cow. But if we think of the visual representation of a cow in a manual on animal husbandry—and, even more, of the linguistic sign "cow"—we can see that both, in different degrees, are *arbitrary* with respect to the concept of the animal they represent. The articulation of an arbitrary sign—whether visual or verbal—with the concept of a referent is the product not of nature but of convention, and the conventionalism of discourses requires the intervention, the support, of codes. Thus Eco has argued that iconic signs "look like objects in the real world because they reproduce the conditions (that is, the codes) of perception in the viewer."[5] These "conditions of perception" are, however, the result of a highly coded, even if virtually unconscious, set of operations—decodings. This is as true of the photographic or televisual image as it is of any other sign. Iconic signs are, however, particularly vulnerable to being "read" as natural because visual codes of perception are very widely distributed and because this type of sign is less arbitrary than a linguistic sign: the linguistic sign, "cow" possesses *none* of the properties of the thing represented, whereas the visual sign appears to possess *some* of those properties.

This may help us to clarify a confusion in current linguistic theory and to define precisely how some key terms are being used in this article. Linguistic theory frequently employs the distinction "denotation" and "connotation." The term "denotation" is widely equated with literal meaning of a sign: because this literal meaning is almost universally recognized, especially when visual discourse is being employed, "denotation" has often been confused with a literal transcription of "reality" in language—and thus with a "natural sign," one produced without the intervention of a code. "Connotation," on the other, hand, is employed simply to refer to less fixed and therefore more conventionalized and changeable, associative meanings, which clearly vary from instance to instance and therefore must depend on the intervention of codes.

We do *not* use the distinction—denotation/connotation—in this way. From our point of view, the distinction is an *analytic* one only. It is useful, in analysis, to be able to apply a rough rule of thumb which distinguishes those aspects of a sign which appear to be taken, in any language community at any point in time, as its "literal" meaning (denotation) from the more associative meanings for the sign which it is possible to generate (connotation). But analytic distinctions must not be confused with distinctions in the real world. There will be very few instances in which signs organized in a discourse signify *only* their "literal" (that is, near-universally consensualized) meaning. In actual discourse most signs will combine both the denotative and the connotative *aspects* (as redefined above). It may, then, be asked why we retain the distinction at all. It is largely a matter of analytic value. It is because signs appear to acquire their full ideological value—appear to be open to articulation with wider ideological discourses and meanings—at the level of their "associative" meanings (that is, at the connotative level)—for here "meanings" are *not* apparently fixed in natural perception (that is, they are not fully naturalized), and their fluidity of meaning and association can be more fully exploited and transformed.[6] So it is at the connotative *level* of the sign that situational ideologies alter and transform signification. At this level we can see more clearly the active intervention of ideologies in and on discourse: here, the sign is open to new accentuations and, in Vološinov's terms, enters fully into the struggle over meanings—the class struggle in language.[7] This does not mean that the denotative or "literal" meaning is outside ideology. Indeed, we could say that its ideological value is strongly *fixed*—because it has become so fully universal and "natural." The terms "denotation" and "connotation," then, are merely useful analytic tools for distinguishing, in particular contexts, between not the presence/absence of ideology in language but the different levels at which ideologies and discourses intersect.[8]

The level of connotation of the visual sign, of its contextual reference and positioning in different discursive fields of meaning and association, is the point where *already coded* signs intersect with the deep semantic codes of a culture and take on additional, more active ideological dimensions. We might take an example from advertising discourse. Here, too, there is no "purely denotative," and certainly no "natural," representation. Every visual sign in advertising connotes a quality, situation, value or inference, which is present as an implication or implied meaning, depending on the connotational positioning. In Barthes's example, the sweater always signifies a "warm garment" (denotation) and thus the activity/value of "keeping warm." But it is also possible, at its more connotative levels, to signify "the coming of winter" or "a cold day." And, in the specialized sub-codes of fashion, sweater may also connote a fashionable style of *haute couture* or, alternatively, an informal style of dress. But set against the right visual background and positioned by the romantic sub-code, it may connote "long autumn walk in the woods."[9] Codes of this order clearly contract relations for the sign with the wider universe of ideologies in a society. These codes are the means by which power and ideology are made to signify in particular discourses. They refer signs to the "maps of meaning" into which any culture is classified; and those "maps of social reality" have the whole range of social meanings, practices, and usages, power and interest "written in" to them. The connotative levels of signifiers, Barthes remarked, "have a close communication with culture, knowledge, history, and it is through them, so to speak, that the environmental world invades the linguistic and semantic system. They are, if you like, the fragments of ideology."[10]

The so-called denotative *level* of the televisual sign is fixed by certain, very complex (but limited or "closed") codes. But its connotative *level*, though also bounded, is more open, subject to more active *transformations*, which exploit its polysemic values. Any such already constituted sign is potentially transformable into more than one connotative configuration. Polysemy must not, however, be confused with pluralism. Connotative codes are *not* equal among themselves. Any society/culture tends, with varying degrees of closure, to impose its classifications of the social and cultural and political world. These constitute a *dominant cultural order*, though it is neither univocal nor uncontested. This question of the "structure of discourses in dominance" is a crucial point. The different areas of social life appear to be mapped out into discursive domains, hierarchically organized into *dominant or preferred meanings*. New, problematic or troubling events, which breach our expectancies and run counter to our "common-sense constructs," to our "taken-for granted" knowledge of social structures, must be assigned to their discursive domains before they can be said to "make sense." The most common way of "mapping" them is to assign the new to some domain or other of the existing "maps of problematic social reality." We say *dominant*, not "determined," because it is always possible to order, classify, assign and decode an event within more than one "mapping." But we say "dominant" because there exists a pattern of "preferred readings"; and these both have the institutional/political/ideological order imprinted in them and have themselves become institutionalized.[11] The domains of "preferred meanings" have the whole social order embedded in them as a set of meanings, practices and beliefs: the everyday knowledge of social structures, of "how things work for all practical purposes in this culture," the rank order of power and interest and the structure of legitimations, limits and sanctions. Thus to clarify a "misunderstanding" at the connotative level, we must refer, *through* the codes, to the orders of social life, of economic and political power and of ideology. Further, since these mappings are "structured in dominance" but not closed, the communicative process consists not in the unproblematic assignment of every visual item to its given position within a set of prearranged codes, but of *performative rules*—rules of competence and use, of logics-in-use—which seek actively to *enforce* or *prefer* one semantic domain over another and rule items into and out of their appropriate meaning-sets. Formal semiology has too often neglected this practice of *interpretative work*, though this constitutes, in fact, the real relations of broadcast practices in television.

In speaking of *dominant meanings*, then, we are not talking about a one-sided process which governs how all events will be signified. It consists of the "work" required to enforce, win plausibility for and command as legitimate a *decoding* of the event within the limit of dominant definitions in which it has been connotatively signified. Terni has remarked:

> By the word *reading* we mean not only the capacity to identify and decode a certain num-
> ber of signs, but also the subjective capacity to put them into a creative relation between
> themselves and with other signs: a capacity which is, by itself, the condition for a complete
> awareness of one's total environment.[12]

Our quarrel here is with the notion of "subjective capacity," as if the referent of a televisional discourse were an objective fact but the interpretative level were an individualized and private matter. Quite the opposite seems to be the case. The televisual practice takes "objective" (that is, systemic) responsibility precisely for the relations which disparate signs contract with one another in any discursive instance, and thus continually rearranges, delimits and prescribes into what "awareness of one's total environment" these items are arranged.

This brings us to the question of misunderstandings. Television producers who find their message "failing to get across" are frequently concerned to straighten out the kinks in the communication chain, thus facilitating the "effectiveness" of their communication. Much research which claims the objectivity of "policy-oriented analysis" reproduces this administrative goal by attempting to discover how much of a message the audience recalls and to improve the extent of understanding. No doubt misunderstandings of a literal kind do exist. The viewer does not know the terms employed, cannot follow the complex logic of argument or exposition, is unfamiliar with the language, finds the concepts too alien or difficult or is foxed by the expository narrative. But more often broadcasters are concerned that the audience has failed to take the meaning as they—the broadcasters—intended. What they really mean to say is that viewers are not operating within the "dominant" or "preferred" code. Their ideal is "perfectly transparent communication." Instead, what they have to confront is "systematically distorted communication."[13]

In recent years discrepancies of this kind have usually been explained by reference to "selective perception." This is the door via which a residual pluralism evades the compulsions of a highly structured, asymmetrical and non-equivalent process. Of course, there will always be private, individual, variant readings. But "selective perception" is almost never as selective, random or privatized as the concept suggests. The patterns exhibit, across individual variants, significant clusterings. Any new approach to audience studies will therefore have to begin with a critique of "selective perception" theory.

It was argued earlier that since there is no necessary correspondence between encoding and decoding, the former can attempt to "pre-fer" but cannot prescribe or guarantee the latter, which has its own conditions of existence. Unless they are wildly aberrant, encoding will have the effect of constructing some of the limits and parameters within which decodings will operate. If there were no limits, audiences could simply read whatever they liked into any message. No doubt some total misunderstandings of this kind do exist. But the vast range must contain *some* degree of reciprocity between encoding and decoding moments, otherwise we could not speak of an effective communicative exchange at all. Nevertheless, this "correspondence" is not given but constructed. It is not "natural" but the product of an articulation between two distinct moments. And the former cannot determine or guarantee, in a simple sense, which decoding codes will be employed. Otherwise communication would be a perfectly equivalent circuit, and every message would be an instance of "perfectly transparent communication." We must think, then, of the variant articulations in which encoding/decoding can be combined. To elaborate on this, we offer a hypothetical analysis of some possible decoding positions, in order to reinforce the point of "no necessary correspondence."[14]

We identify *three* hypothetical positions from which decodings of a televisual discourse may be constructed. These need to be empirically tested and refined. But the argument that decodings do not follow inevitably from encodings, that they are not identical, reinforces the argument of "no necessary correspondence." It also helps to deconstruct the commonsense meaning of "misunderstanding" in terms of a theory of "systematically distorted communication."

The first hypothetical position is that of the *dominant-hegemonic position*. When the viewer takes the connoted meaning from, say, a television newscast or current affairs programme full and straight, and decodes the message in terms of the reference code in which it has been encoded, we might say that the viewer *is operating inside dominant code*. This is the ideal-typical case of "perfectly transparent communication"—or as close as we are likely to come to it "for all practical purposes." Within this we can distinguish the positions produced by the *professional code*. This is the position (produced by what we perhaps ought to identify as the operation of a "metacode") which the professional broadcasters assume when encoding a message which has *already* been signified in a hegemonic manner. The professional code is "relatively independent" of the dominant code, in that it applies criteria and transformational operations of its own, especially those of a technico-practical nature. The professional code, however, operates *within* the "hegemony" of the dominant code. Indeed, it serves to reproduce the dominant definitions precisely by bracketing their hegemonic quality and operating instead with displaced professional codings which foreground such apparently neutral-technical questions as visual quality, news and presentational values, televisual quality, "professionalism" and so on. The hegemonic interpretations of, say, the politics of Northern Ireland, or the Chilean *coup* or the Industrial Relations Bill are principally generated by political and military elites: the particular choice of presentational occasions and formats, the selection of personnel, the choice of images, the staging of debates are selected and combined through the operation of the professional code. How the broadcasting professionals are able *both* to operate with "relatively autonomous" codes of their own *and* to act in such a way as to reproduce (not without contradiction) the hegemonic signification of events is a complex matter which cannot be further spelled out here. It must suffice to say that the professionals are linked with the defining elites not only by the institutional position of broadcasting itself as an "ideological apparatus,"[15] but also by the structure of *access* (that is, the systematic "lover-accessing" of selective elite personnel and their "definition of the situation" in television). It may even be said that the professional codes serve to reproduce hegemonic definitions specifically by *not overtly* biasing their operations in a dominant direction: ideological reproduction therefore takes place here inadvertently, unconsciously, "behind men's backs."[16] Of course, conflicts, contradictions and even misunderstandings regularly arise between the dominant and the professional significations and their signifying agencies.

The second position we would identify is that of the *negotiated code* or position. Majority audiences probably understand quite adequately what has been dominantly defined and professionally signified. The dominant definitions, however, are hegemonic precisely because they represent definitions of situations and events which are "in dominance" (*global*). Dominant definitions connect events, implicitly or explicitly, to grand totalizations, to the great syntagmatic views-of-the-world: they take "large views" of issues: they relate events to the "national interest" or to the level of geo-politics, even if they make these connections in truncated, inverted or mystified ways. The definition of a hegemonic viewpoint is (a) that it defines within its terms the mental horizon, the universe, of possible meanings, of a whole sector of relations in a society or culture; and (b) that it carries with it the stamp of legitimacy—it appears coterminous with what is "natural," "inevitable," "taken for granted" about the social order. Decoding within the *negotiated version* contains a mixture of adaptive and oppositional elements: it acknowledges the legitimacy of the hegemonic definitions to make the grand significations (abstract), while, at a more restricted, situational (situated) level, it makes its own ground rules—it operates with exceptions to the rule. It accords the privileged position to the dominant definitions of events while reserving the right to make a more negotiated application to "local conditions," to its own more *corporate* positions. This negotiated version of the dominant ideology is thus shot through with contradictions, though these are only on certain occasions brought to full visibility. Negotiated codes operate through what we might call particular or situated logics: and these logics are sustained by their differential and unequal relation to the discourses and logics of power. The simplest example of a negotiated code is that which governs the response of a worker to the notion of an Industrial Relations Bill limiting the right to strike or to arguments for a wages freeze. At the level of the "national interest" economic debate the decoder may adopt the hegemonic definition, agreeing that "we must all pay ourselves less in order to combat inflation." This, however, may have little or no relation to his/her willingness to go on strike for better pay and conditions or to oppose the Industrial Relations Bill at the level of shop-floor or union organization. We suspect that the great majority of so-called "misunderstandings" arise from the contradictions and disjunctures between hegemonic-dominant encodings and negotiated-corporate decodings. It is just these mismatches in the levels which most provoke defining elites and professionals to identify a "failure in communications."

Finally, it is possible for a viewer perfectly to understand both the literal and the connotative inflection given by a discourse but to decode the message in a *globally* contrary way. He/she detotalizes the message in the preferred code in order to retotalize the message within some alternative framework of reference. This is the case of the viewer who listens to a debate on the need to limit wages but "reads" every mention of the "national interest" as "class interest." He/she is operating with what we must call an *oppositional code*. One of the most significant political moments (they also coincide with crisis points within the broadcasting organizations themselves, for obvious reasons) is the point when events which are normally signified and decoded in a negotiated way begin to be given an oppositional reading. Here the "politics of signification"—the struggle in discourse—is joined.

NOTES

1. For an explication and commentary on the methodological implications of Marx's argument, see S. Hall, 'A reading of Marx's 1857 *Introduction to the Grundrisse*', in *WPCS 6* (1974).
2. J.D. Halloran, 'Understanding television', Paper for the Council of Europe Colloquy on 'Understanding Television' (University of Leicester 1973).
3. G. Gerbner *et al.*, *Violence in TV Drama: A Study of Trends and Symbolic Functions* (The Annenberg School, University of Pennsylvania 1970).
4. Charles Peirce, *Speculative Grammar*, in *Collected Papers* (Cambridge, Mass.: Harvard University Press 1931–58).
5. Umberto Eco, 'Articulations of the cinematic code', in *Cinemantics*, no. 1.
6. See the argument in S. Hall, 'Determinations of news photographs', in *WPCS* 3 (1972).
7. Vološinov, *Marxism And The Philosophy of Language* (The Seminar Press 1973).
8. For a similar clarification, see Marina Camargo Heck, 'Ideological dimensions of media messages', pages 122–7 above.
9. Roland Barthes, 'Rhetoric of the image', in *WPCS* 1 (1971).
10. Roland Barthes, *Elements of Semiology* (Cape 1967).
11. For an extended critique of 'preferred reading', see Alan O'Shea, 'Preferred reading' (unpublished paper, CCCS, University of Birmingham)
12. P. Terni, 'Memorandum', Council of Europe Colloquy on 'Understanding Television' (University of Leicester 1973).
13. The phrase is Habermas's, in 'Systematically distorted communications', in P. Dretzel (ed.), *Recent Sociology 2* (Collier-Macmillan 1970). It is used here, however, in a different way.
14. For a sociological formulation which is close, in some ways, to the positions outlined here but which does not parallel the argument about the theory of discourse, see Frank Parkin, *Class Inequality and Political Order* (Macgibbon and Kee 1971).
15. See Louis Althusser, 'Ideology and ideological state apparatuses', in *Lenin and Philosophy and Other Essays* (New Left Books 1971).
16. For an expansion of this argument, see Stuart Hall, 'The external/internal dialectic in broadcasting', *4th Symposium on Broadcasting* (University of Manchester 1972), and 'Broadcasting and the state: the independence/impartiality couplet', AMCR Symposium, University of Leicester 1976 (CCCS unpublished paper).

VALUE/EVALUATION (1990, 1995)

BARBARA HERRNSTEIN SMITH

What are the great films, poems, plays, or novels, and how do you know? What makes a work great—or not great? Who decides? Whose judgment do we value and why? In the past three or four decades, teachers, students, and critics have dramatically changed the ways they choose—and the ways that they think about how they choose—the literature and popular culture they read, teach, study, and write about. The literary canon—the works that a consensus of critics and teachers most value—has rapidly enlarged. In the study of English, for example, the canon continues to include the works written by British and American white men that once dominated the canon, but now it also includes many other works of literature, film, and popular culture, and it continues to grow and change rapidly. Smith reviews the history, principles, and practice of value and evaluation as they look from a perspective influenced by these relatively recent and still ongoing changes. She eventually ends up revaluing the specificity of perspective that she notes more traditional critics dismiss as bias. In her Contingencies of Value: Alternative Perspectives for Critical Theory, *Smith rejects the traditional belief that value is absolute and definite across variables of culture and identity. Instead, she sees value as contingent, as variable according to conditions exterior to the object evaluated. In this essay, for example, Smith eventually argues that gender can influence value and evaluation and also briefly acknowledges the role of age, class, and region. Readers may find it helpful to consider what other identity categories, perhaps in combination with gender, age, class, and region, can influence value and evaluation. At the same time, recognizing that people of one identity group do not all share the same tastes and judgments, we may ask how or whether we should, as Smith urges, consider identity in relation to our understanding and practices of value and evaluation. If value, taste, and evaluation are contingent, we may ask exactly how and on what they are contingent and how their contingency shapes our very concepts of value, taste, and evaluation.*

INTRODUCTION

Issues of value and evaluation tend to recur whenever literature, art, and other forms of cultural activity become a focus of discussion, whether in informal or institutional contexts. Some of those issues, moreover, though musty-sounding and unresolvable in their traditional formulations, retain considerable contemporary force: for example, the significance of such labels as "classic" and "masterpiece," the extent to which the value of literary works is "intrinsic" to them or a matter of "fashion," whether literary judgments can claim "objective validity" or are only "expressions of personal preference," whether there are underlying standards of taste based on universals of "human nature," and so forth. While such questions, formulated in one set of terms or another, have been central to Western critical theory for at least the past two hundred years, the past decade has witnessed the emergence of both significantly new perspectives on them and also dramatically transformed and expanded agendas for their exploration.

These new and changing interests and approaches arise from a number of sources, among them the increasing interaction between the theory of criticism and recent work in social, political and cultural studies. An important result of this interaction has been a recognition of the ways in which evaluation operates as a characteristic activity not only of individuals but of institutions and cultures, and also the extent to which value is itself a product of such activities. Reformulations of traditional questions in this general area also reflect important intellectual developments in philosophy and related fields: the growing dominance, for example, of various forms of skepticism, especially with respect to the ways in which beliefs and judgments, whether in science, political theory, ethics, or literary criticism, have traditionally been justified as "true" or "valid."

Within literary studies itself, these issues have been of particular concern to feminist and Marxist critics and to others who, from one perspective or another, have debated the structure—exclusions, inclusions, and priorities—of the standard academic canon and also its standard justifications. Also, the various concepts and methods developed by such contemporary critical approaches as reception-theory, psychoanalytic theory, and deconstruction have proved to be suggestive in relation to problems of value and evaluation as well as to those of meaning and interpretation.

VALUE

Like certain other terms, such as "meaning" "truth," and "reality," that have strong currency in everyday speech and also long histories as the focus of philosophical analysis, the term "value" seems to name an aspect of the world so fundamental to our thinking—so elementary and at the same time so general—as to be both irreducible and irreplaceable: it defies attempts to analyze it into simpler concepts, and efforts to explain, define or even paraphrase it seem obliged sooner or later to return to the term itself.

As can be seen from the following extracts, the *Oxford English Dictionary* solves the problem of recursive definition by defining "value" in terms of "worth" and vice versa:

VALUE

1. The equivalent (in material worth) of a specified sum or amount....
2. Worth or worthiness (of persons) in respect of rank or personal qualities. *Obs[olete]* b. Worth or efficacy in combat or warfare; manliness, valor.
3. The relative status of a thing, or the estimate in which it is held, according to its supposed worth, usefulness or importance....

WORTH

1. Pecuniary value; price; money. b. The equivalent of a specified sum or amount.
2. The relative value of a thing in respect of its qualities or of the estimation in which it is held (1961, 12: 29–30, 326).

It appears that the English wordform "value" has always maintained two related but more or less distinct senses. One is the material or monetary *equivalence-in-exchange* of something: for example, an object's price in some market or, as it is sometimes said, its "exchange value." In the other broad sense, "value" is not monetary, and not obviously or necessarily material, but a more abstract matter of relative quantity or measure. Examples of the value of something (or someone) in this second and rather more elusive sense include its relative effectiveness in performing some function or meeting some need, the relative degree of satisfaction it gives someone, its comparative handiness or suitability for advancing some purpose, and the object's (or person's) rank on some scale: for example, a scale of strength and courage in battle, as in the now obsolete sense of value as "valor"; or a scale of duration of sound, as in the "value" of tones in music; or a scale of sheer abstract numerosity, as when we speak of the "value" of some variable in a mathematical equation. These examples suggest that what "value" in this second sense means is something like *relative [amount of] positivity*. Since both senses of the term involve two key ideas, namely *comparison* and *amount*, that relate to an exceptionally broad range of practices and domains of human life, it is not surprising that "value" seems to name so fundamental an aspect of the world.

The history of the term also indicates that, while it has long had, as one of its central senses, the extent to which something is "held in esteem" (presumably by *people*), "value" is nevertheless often conceived as something residing or embodied in *objects themselves:* some essential quality or inherent property of a thing, in other words, that is independent not only of what amount of money (or anything else) it might fetch in some market but also independent of its performing any functions, or giving satisfaction to anyone, or being esteemed (or, in effect, "valued" or found valuable) in any of these or other ways by anyone. Though increasingly problematic, these latter conceptions remain common, and much usage of the term continues to suggest that value is an inherent property of things (something like *weight* in a conception of the latter that we would now regard as naive), or that it is itself a kind of ineffable *thing*. Contemporary discussions of the concept of value, especially in disciplines such as aesthetics and ethics, are complicated by the related fact that denials and inversions of the senses discussed above are also current, as where the ("absolute," "essential," "intrinsic," "pure," and so on) value of something, such as an artwork or person, is said to be precisely that about it which (rather like its *soul*) is unique, immeasurable, and independent of anyone's experience of it.

In literary theory, further complications are introduced by the notion that there is a special kind of value that characterizes certain texts after all specifiable values or sources of interest—e.g., market value, use value, historical interest, personal interest, and political or ideological interest—have been subtracted. This special value, often referred to as the text's "essential *literary* value," or its "value *as* a work of literature," is sometimes said to reside in the text's purely "formal" as opposed to "material" qualities, or in its "structure" as opposed to its "meaning," or in its "underlying meaning" as opposed to any obvious "theme," "subject," or ostensible "message." This special kind of value, the possession of which is sometimes said to mark off genuine works of literature from all other texts (e.g., those that are "nonliterary" or "subliterary"), is also commonly associated with a text's inherent capacity to produce some purely sensory/perceptual gratification, independent of any other kind of interest, or some purely passive and intellectual gratification, independent of any practical, active, or material response to the text. (Such notions are comparable to, and typically derived from, the conception of pure aesthetic value, or "beauty," developed by Immanuel Kant in his *Critique of Judgment* [1790].) Notions of this special kind of value are, however, increasingly subject to skeptical scrutiny, with questions focusing largely on (a) whether anything *is* left over when all those other forms of value and sources of interest are subtracted, (b) whether any of those critical distinctions can actually be drawn as clearly and firmly as is required, and (c) whether the various types of purity of response and experience posited by such notions are possible at all among human beings.

Although the term "value" is characteristically produced in singular and genitive constructions (that is, as "*the value of*" something), it does not seem possible to reduce the value of anything, including an artwork or work of literature, to a single, simple property or possession. It is sometimes useful, therefore, to think of "value" as a general name given to a variety of different positive *effects*. In relation to literature, "the-value-of" a particular text—say, Charlotte Brontë's novel, *Jane Eyre*—though any other text, "literary" or otherwise, would do here—may be thought of, accordingly, as any of the multiple, diverse kinds and forms of positivity that may have emerged out of various people's engagement with it at various times: the money its sale may have fetched in various markets, its effectiveness in implementing and sustaining various individual and communal projects, its occasioning of various sorts of sensory/perceptual pleasures and excitements, its communication to various people of various reassurances and/or revelations, its eliciting of both memories of such effects in the past and expectations of them in the future, and so forth. Any selection of these effects, or the abstract notion of all of them taken together, may be what someone indicates as the text's "value" in framing a judgment or assessment of it at some particular time.

EVALUATION

In relation to literature, evaluations are commonly thought of as the specific acts of individual people, either journalistic reviewers or others—primarily teachers and academically situated readers—in their role as critics of other people's writings. Acts of evaluation are also typically conceived as taking the form of overt verbal statements, such as "It is among the greatest lyrics in English" or "His first book was more forceful, though this one is perhaps more imaginatively realized." Such statements are usually thought to be of interest insofar as they are more or less valid, and valid insofar as they correctly identify the objective value of a piece of writing or accurately describe those features of it that are self-evidently related to its value. And the most valid judgments are commonly thought to be made by persons with certain appropriate qualifications, including acute literary sensitivities, wide literary experience, an adequate understanding of the meaning of the work, and freedom from the biases of personal interest or ideology. Just about every aspect of this familiar conception of literary evaluation has, however, been questioned in recent critical theory.

To begin with, literary evaluation is no longer thought of as confined to the discrete verbal statements of journalistic and academic "critics." The evaluation of a work is seen, rather, as a continuous process, operating though a wide variety of individual activities and social and institutional practices. Moreover, the relation between "value" and "evaluation" is itself understood differently, with the work's value seen not as something already fixed in it and *indicated* ("accurately" or not) by particular critical judgments but, rather, as numerous different effects continuously *produced and sustained* by those very evaluative activities and practices themselves.

Thus reconceived, literary evaluation would be seen as including the following:

(a) The initial *evaluations of a work by its author:* for example, in the case of *Jane Eyre,* the innumerable, unspoken acts of approval and rejection, preference and assessment, trial and revision, that constituted the entire process of Charlotte Brontë's writing—in the sense of conceiving, composing and editing—the text. This suggests, in turn, that literary "criticism" should be seen not as distinct from and opposed to literary "creation" but as a central and inevitable aspect of it.

(b) The countless *covert, usually nonverbal, evaluations* of a text that someone may make "for herself" when, for example, she chooses it (usually, of course, to read, but not necessarily) in preference to other texts (or other things), or when she continues to read it rather than setting it aside, or when she keeps it rather than discarding or selling it—or, of course, if some occasion elicits such an act, when she specifically articulates (that is, "gives verbal expression to") her general sense of its "value": either how the work figures for *her* in relation to other texts (or to anything else at all) and/or how she thinks it is likely to figure for other people.

(c) The many diverse acts of *implicit evaluation* of a work performed by the various people and institutions who, as may happen, publish it or purchase, preserve, display, quote, cite, translate, perform, parody, allude to, imitate, or, as in the case of *Jane Eyre,* make a film version of it, and so forth. All these acts are significant in staging—and, indeed, making possible—various positive effects of a work for numbers of people and, therefore, in producing, transmitting, and maintaining its value within some community or culture.

(d) The more explicit, but still relatively casual, *overt verbal judgments* of a work made, debated, and negotiated in informal social contexts by readers and by all those other people for whom, in some way, it may figure. Like the implicit and largely nonverbal acts mentioned above in (c), these informal "expressions of personal preference," tips and recommendations, and defenses and explanations of specific judgments are also part of the systems of cultural activity and social interaction through which the value of texts is continuously sustained and, of course, also continuously challenged and transformed.

(e) The highly specialized *institutionalized forms of evaluation* exhibited in the more or less professional activities of scholars, teachers, and academic or journalistic critics: not only their full-dress reviews and explicit rank-orderings; evaluations, and revaluations, but also such activities as the awarding of literary prizes, the commissioning and publishing of articles *about* certain works, the compiling of anthologies, the writing of introductions, the construction of department curricula, and the drawing up of class reading-lists.

Although our experience of the value—in the sense here of positive effects—of literary works is not a simple product of "social forces" or "cultural influences," nevertheless texts, like all the other objects we engage with, bear the marks and signs of their prior valuings and evaluations by our fellow creatures and are thus, we might say, always to some extent pre-evaluated for us. *Classification* is itself a form of pre-evaluation, for the labels under which we encounter objects are very significant in shaping our experience of their value, often foregrounding certain of their possible effects and operating as signs—in effect, as culturally certified endorsements—of their performance of certain functions.

The labels "art" and "literature" are, of course, commonly signs of membership in distinctly honorific categories. The particular functions those labels may endorse, however, are not readily specifiable but, on the contrary, exceptionally various, mutable, and elusive. To the extent—always limited—that the relation between a label such as "work of literature" and a particular set of expected and desired effects is stabilized within some community, it is largely through the sorts of *normative* (that is, value-maintaining and value-transmitting) activities described above. Although, as the list indicates, textual evaluation is by no means confined to academic criticism, nevertheless the normative practices of scholastic institutions form a central part of the transmission and indeed *definition* of literary value within contemporary Western culture.

As indicated, "evaluation" can be understood as embracing a wide range of *forms* of practice, not all of them public or overt, not all of them individual, and certainly not all of them verbal. Once the range is granted, however, we may recognize the particular interest commonly directed toward those individual acts that *are* over and verbal: that is, explicit value judgments. Current conceptions of literary evaluation emphasize two important features of those judgments obscured in traditional analyses. The first is that, when we offer a verbal judgment of a text, we are always doing so in some *social and/or institutional context:* for example, among family members, to a casual acquaintance, in a classroom, or in the columns of some newspaper or journal. The second is that the "force" of our judgments in every sense—that is, their meaning and interest for other people and their power to affect them—will always depend on, among other things, the nature of that context and *our relationship to the people we address.* Thus an explicit statement concerning the value of *Jane Eyre* will have a certain kind of interest and effect when delivered in the midst of a tense family conversation about the corruption of taste by the mass media, and a rather different interest and effect when affirmed at a meeting of the curriculum-review committee of the English department of some university; it will be different also when offered by a student to his or her teacher, or a teacher to his or her students, or by one student to another, perhaps his or her roommate; and whether it happens to be "his" or "her" may very well itself make a difference in such cases.

Current conceptions of evaluation also emphasize the significance of the *tacit assumptions* evaluators make when producing value judgments. Thus, when someone says *"Jane Eyre* is great," it is always possible for someone else to ask, "Great at doing what?…compared to what?… for whom?" If the answers to such questions were spelled out, the conditional nature both of the evaluation and also of the value of the work itself would be apparent: that is, it would be clear that the judgment implies (and could be rephrased as) *"Jane Eyre* is great, and certainly much better than many other texts, at doing certain things ("doing things" here includes having effects on people) for certain people," which, of course, also implies that it may not be as good as some *other* texts at doing *other* things and/or at doing them for *other* people.

In thus recognizing the tacit assumptions built into value judgments, we can also recognize that, when we frame an explicit verbal evaluation of a text, we are usually not expressing only how we feel about it "personally" but, rather, observing its effects on ourselves and estimating—in effect, predicting—its value for other people: not *all* other people, however, but a limited set of people with certain relevant characteristics—usually, though not necessarily, characteristics that they share with *us.* Though the limits of the set and the nature of those characteristics are usually only implicit, they may be obvious enough to all concerned from the context of the evaluation (as in the informal exchanges of value judgments among colleagues and companions, or in the book reviews published in such magazines as *Art*

News or *Scientific American*) and may, in fact, be quite explicitly described, as in, "This is a challenging work for specialists in neuroanatomy, but is not recommended as an introductory text for first-year medical students."

It should be noted that, in describing, above, how any judgement *could* be rephrased to make explicit certain of its tacit assumptions, the conclusion was not drawn that all judgements, *should be* thus rephrased. Indeed, what follows from the preceding discussion is not that "critics should always make their criteria explicit" but rather, a number of somewhat different points. One is that there is no reason for us to spell out our assumptions when we are pretty sure that they are understood in more or less the same ways by those whom we are addressing—which is why we usually do not spell them out. (By "criteria" in such formulas, what is usually meant, it seems, are the positive effects someone looks for and expects from works of that kind and/or the features of such works that he or she believes produce those effects.)

A second point is that someone's value judgment is likely to be interesting and useful to his or her audience precisely to the extent that the latter (a) *do* take its assumptions for granted in the same ways as the evaluator (that is, look for and want the same sorts of effects) and also (b) think that they are among the set of people for whom the judgment is implicitly framed and whose characteristics are implicitly defined in it—or, of course, are interested in being among such people.

An earlier allusion to the significance of gender for literary evaluation may, accordingly, be amplified here. The *appropriability* of one's judgments for other people (that is, how readily they can use those judgments for themselves) always depends on the extent to which they share one's particular perspective, which is itself always a function of one's relevant characteristics; and, of course, gender—like other characteristics such as age, economic class, and regional background—is sometimes highly relevant to one's perspective as a reader of literature. We may thus imagine the following sort of question as always implicitly put to a literary evaluator by his or her listeners: "Yes, given who you and various of your associates are (among other things, men/women), this work tends to be valuable for all of *you* the way you claim; but, given who *we* (e.g., the readers of your book review; your students) are, and that a number of us are, among other things, women/men, how well does that predict whether it will operate in just that way for *us*?"

It should also be noted here that, because literary authority, like any other normative authority, tends to be vested differentially along lines of general social and cultural dominance (that is, the people whose judgments have institutional power are usually those who have social and cultural power otherwise) and because, in our own communities, general social and cultural dominance follows, among other lines, gender lines, institutionalized literary norms (academic canons, high-culture critical standards, and so on) tend to have, among other biases, those of gender perspectives.

A third related point is that, to the extent that someone's predictions and recommendations of value reflect highly specialized, perhaps even idiosyncratic, assumptions and interests, the use and value of his or her judgments for other people will be limited accordingly. They may be informative to, and appropriable by, *some* people, but will obviously be pointless and useless to those with quite different assumptions, expectations, and interests—and, depending on the context of the evaluation and the evaluator's relation to those people, they may also be (as in exhibitions of class snobbery or acts of state censorship) socially and/or politically arrogant or oppressive.

It is sometimes suggested that, before we can evaluate a work, we must understand its meaning(s). The relation between interpretation and evaluation is, however, more complex than such a formulation indicates. Different aspects of a text—including such aspects as we call its "meaning(s)"—will become more visible and more significant for us in accord with our different interests and perspectives, and the value of the text will vary for us accordingly. But we are also more likely to engage with a text in ways that yield certain meanings—say, broadly philosophical or specifically historical or ideological ones—if its value has already been marked for us in certain ways (as, for example, "a masterpiece of world literature" or, differently, as "a document of English colonialism"), and our expectations of its effects are directed and limited accordingly. As this suggests, our interpretation of a text and our experience of its value are to some extent mutually dependent, and *both* depend upon the particular assumptions, expectations, and interests with which we approach the work.

For those who conceive of interpretation and evaluation as the identification of, respectively, determinate meaning and intrinsic value, the latter—that is, our individual interests, expectations, assumptions, and other personal tendencies and desires with regard to a work—would be seen as our "biases" or "prejudices" and, accordingly, as what would prevent us from being "ideal critics," the sort of people who can frame and deliver "objectively valid" interpretations and judgments of the work. To be sure, as already indicated above, a critic who judges out of narrowly specialized interests and highly idiosyncratic assumptions will not gain much of an audience, since his or her predictions and recommendations will be pointless and useless to most other people. It must be added, however, that, if we could exclude *all* assumptions, expectations, interests, and other individualizing characteristics from our engagements with texts, the result would not be that we would become perfect critics but, rather, that there would be no reason for us to approach any text to begin with and nothing in relation to which we could find any work of literature meaningful or valuable at all.

INTRODUCTION: OR HOW I STOPPED WORRYING AND LEARNED TO LOVE INTERPRETATION (1980)

STANLEY FISH

In this introduction to Is There a Text in This Class?, *a collection of his influential essays in reader response theory, Fish reviews the evolving sequence of his ideas from essay to essay and in the process reviews the most influential concepts in Anglo-American reader response theory.*

What interests me about many of the essays collected here is the fact that I could not write them today. I could not write them today because both the form of their arguments and the form of the problems those arguments address are a function of assumptions I no longer hold. It is often assumed that literary theory presents a set of problems whose shape remains unchanging and in relation to which our critical procedures are found to be more or less adequate; that is, the field of inquiry stands always ready to be interrogated by questions it itself constrains. It seems to me, however, that the relationship is exactly the reverse: the field of inquiry is *constituted* by the questions we are able to ask because the entities that populate it come into being as the presuppositions—they are discourse-specific entities—of those questions. In 1970 I was asking the question "Is the reader or the text the source of meaning?" and the entities presupposed by the question *were* the text and the reader whose independence and stability were thus assumed. Without that assumption—the assumption that the text and the reader can be distinguished from one another and that they will hold still—the merits for their rival claims could not have been debated and an argument for one or the other could not have been made. The fact that I was making such an argument was a direct consequence of the fact that it had already been made, and the position I proceeded to take was dictated by the position that had already been taken. That position was best represented, perhaps, by William Wimsatt and Monroe Beardsley's essays on the affective and intentional fallacies (so called), essays that pled a successful case for the text by arguing, on the one hand, that the intentions of the author were unavailable and, on the other, that the responses of the reader were too variable. Only the text was both indisputably there and stable. To have recourse either to the causes of a poem or to its effects is to exchange objectivity for "impressionism and relativism." "The outcome of either Fallacy, the Intentional or the Affective, is that the poem itself, as an object of specifically critical judgment, tends to disappear."

To the degree that this argument was influential (and it was enormously so) it constrained in advance the form any counterargument might take. In order to dislodge the affective fallacy, for example, one would have to show first that the text was *not* the self-sufficient repository of meaning and, second, that something else was, at the very least, contributory. This was exactly my strategy in the first of the articles presented in this book. I challenged the self-sufficiency of the text by pointing out that its (apparently) spatial form belied the temporal dimension in which its meanings were actualized, and I argued that it was the developing shape of that actualization, rather than the static shape of the printed page, that should be the object of critical description. In short, I substituted the structure of the reader's experience for the formal structures of the text on the grounds that while the latter were the more visible, they acquired significance only in the context of the former. This general position had many consequences. First of all, the activities of the reader were given a prominence and importance they did not have before: if meaning is embedded in the text, the reader's responsibilities are limited to the job of getting it out; but if meaning develops, and if it develops in a dynamic relationship with the reader's expectations, projections, conclusions, judgments, and assumptions, these activities (the things the reader *does*) are not merely instrumental, or mechanical, but essential, and the act of description must both begin and end with them. In practice, this resulted in the replacing of one question—what does this mean?—by another—what does this do?—with "do" equivocating between a reference to the action of the text *on* a reader and the actions performed *by* a reader as he negotiates (and, in some sense, actualizes) the text. This equivocation allowed me to retain the text as a stable entity at the same time that I was dislodging it as the privileged container of meaning. The reader was now given joint responsibility for the production of a meaning that was itself redefined as an event rather than an entity. That is, one could not point to this meaning as one could if it were the property of the text; rather, one could observe or follow its gradual emergence in the interaction between the text, conceived of as a succession of words, and the developing response of the reader.

In this formulation, the reader's response is not *to* the meaning; it *is* the meaning, or at least the medium in which what I wanted to call the meaning comes into being, and therefore to ignore or discount it is, or so I claimed, to risk missing a great deal of what is going on. In order to support this claim I performed analyses designed to demonstrate both the richness of literary experience and the extent to which that experience was unavailable to (because it was flattened out by) a formalist reading. I did not make use of it at the time, but the following passage from *Paradise Lost* might well have been the basis of such a demonstration:

> Satan, now first inflam'd with rage came down,
> The Tempter ere th' Accuser of man-kind,
> To wreck on innocent frail man his loss
> Of that first Battle, and his flight to Hell. (IV, 9–12)

My contention was that in formalist readings meaning is identified with what a reader understands at the *end* of a unit of sense (a line, a sentence, a paragraph, a poem) and that therefore any understandings preliminary to that one are to be disregarded as an unfortunate consequence of the fact that reading proceeds in time. The only making of sense that counts in a formalist reading is the last one, and I wanted to say that everything a reader does, even if he later undoes it, is a part of the "meaning experience" and should not be discarded. One of the things a reader does in the course of negotiating these lines is to assume that the referent of "his" in line 11 is "innocent frail man." Within this assumption the passage would seem to be assigning the responsibility for the Fall to Satan: Satan, inflamed with rage, comes down to inflict the loss of Eden on a couple unable to defend themselves because they are innocent and frail. This understanding, however, must be revised when the reader enters line 12 and discovers that the loss in question is Satan's loss of Heaven, sustained in "that first battle" with the loyal angels. It is that loss of which Adam and Eve are innocent, and the issue of the Fall is not being raised at all. But of course it has been raised, if only in the reader's mind, and in the kind of analysis I am performing, that would be just the point. The understanding that the reader must give up is one that is particularly attractive to him because it asserts the innocence of his first parents, which is, by extension, his innocence too. By first encouraging that understanding and then correcting it, Milton (so my argument would go) makes the reader aware of his tendency, inherited from those same parents, to reach for interpretations that are, in the basic theological sense, self-serving. This passage would then take its place in a general strategy by means of which the reader comes to know that his experience of the poem is a part of its subject; and the conclusion would be that this pattern, essential to the poem's operation, would go undetected by a formalist analysis.

That claim would be attached to the more general claim I was making, that I had escaped formalism by displacing attention from the text, in its spatial configurations, to the reader and his temporal experience. In order to maintain this claim it was necessary to remove the chief objection to talking about the experience of the reader, to wit, that there are (at least potentially) as many experiences as there are readers, and that therefore the decision to focus on the reader is tantamount to giving up the possibility of saying anything that would be of general interest. I met that objection by positing a level of experience which all readers share, independently of differences in education and culture. This level was conceived more or less syntactically, as an extension of the Chomskian notion of linguistic competence, a linguistic system that every native speaker shares. I reasoned that if the speakers of a language share a system of rules that each of them has somehow internalized, understanding will, in some sense, be uniform. The fact that the understandings of so many readers and critics were not uniform was accounted for by superimposing on this primary or basic level (identified more or less with perception itself) a secondary or after-the-fact level at which the differences between individuals make themselves manifest. At times I characterized this secondary level as an emotional reaction to the experience of the first (whether the reader likes or dislikes the experience of Faulkner's delays, he will, in common with every other reader, experience them); and at other times I spoke of it as an act of intellection, more or less equivalent with what we usually call interpretation. In either case the assertion was that this subsequent and distorting activity was the source of the apparent variation in the response of readers to literary texts: "It is only when readers become literary critics and the passing of judgment takes precedence over the reading experience that opinions begin to diverge. The act of interpretation is often so removed from the act of reading that the latter (in time the former) is hardly remembered."

The distinction then was between the actual reading experience and whatever one might feel or say about it in retrospect. It was also a distinction between something that was objective and shared (the basic data of the meaning experience) and something that was subjective and idiosyncratic. From this it followed that the proper practice of literary criticism demanded the suppressing of what is subjective and idiosyncratic in favor of the level of response that everyone shares. In terms of my own criticism this provided me with a strategy for dealing with my predecessors. I treated their accounts of literary works as disguised reports of the normative experience that all informed readers have. These reports are disguised, I reasoned, because a reader who is also a critic will feel compelled to translate his experience into the vocabulary of the critical principles he self-consciously holds. He will, that is, be reporting not on his immediate or basic response to a work but on his response (as dictated by his theoretical persuasion) to that response. In relation to such critics I performed the service of revealing to them what their actual experience of a work was before it was obscured by their after-the-fact (interpretive) reflections.

In short, I was practicing a brand of criticism whose most distinctive claim was not to be criticism at all but a means of undoing the damage that follows in criticism's wake. This is particularly true of the essay on Milton's *L'Allegro*, where the argument is that as a poem whose parts are arranged in such a way as to exert no interpretive pressures it is unavailable to criticism insofar as interpretation is its only mode. It follows then that since others who have written on the poem have to a man sought to interpret it, they are necessarily wrong. They are wrong, however, in ways that point inadvertently to my description of its experience; for it is in response to the curious discreteness that characterizes a reading of *L'Allegro* that the critics are moved to fault the poem for a lack of unity or to supply the unity by supplying connections more firm and delimiting than the connections available in the text. Thus, the very efforts of my predecessors testify to their involuntary recognition of the truth of what I am telling them: their reading experience is finally exactly like mine; it is just that their critical preconceptions lead them either to ignore or devalue it. Not only did this strategy enable me to turn opposing positions into versions of my own, but it also gave me a way of answering the question most often asked in the classroom and in public meetings: How is it that readers who are at least as informed as you are (in the sense of having "literary competence") do not experience literature as you say they should? I simply said that they do, even though they may not (consciously) know it, and that if they will only listen to me they will learn how to recognize the configurations of the experience they have always had. In this way I was able to account for the (apparent) differences in literary response without having to give up the claim of generality.

Like any other polemical success, however, this one had its price; for by thus preserving generality I left myself vulnerable to the most persistent objection to the method, that in essence it was no different from the formalism to which it was rhetorically opposed. In order to argue for a common reading experience, I felt obliged to posit an object in relation to which readers' activities could be declared uniform, and that object was the text (at least insofar as it was a temporal structure of ordered items); but this meant that the integrity of the text was as basic to my position as it was to the position of the New Critics. And, indeed, from the very first I was much more dependent on new critical principles than I was willing to admit. The argument in "Literature in the Reader" is mounted (or so it is announced) on behalf of the reader and against the self-sufficiency of the text, but in the course of it the text becomes more and more powerful, and rather than being liberated, the reader finds himself more constrained in his new prominence than he was before. Although his standard is raised in opposition to formalism, he is made into an extension of formalist principles, as his every operation is said to be strictly controlled by the features of the text. The last paragraph of the essay urges a method of classroom teaching in which students are trained first to recognize and then to "discount" whatever was unique and personal in their response so that there would be nothing between them and the exertion of the text's control.

What I didn't see was that I could not consistently make the two arguments at the same time. That is, I could not both declare my opposition to new critical principles and retain the most basic of those principles—the integrity of the text—in order to be able to claim universality and objectivity for my method. I kept this knowledge from myself by never putting the two arguments together but marshaling each of them only to rebut specific points. When someone would charge that an emphasis on the reader leads directly to solipsism and anarchy, I would reply by insisting on the constraints imposed on readers by the text; and when someone would characterize my position as nothing more than the most recent turn of the new-critical screw, I would reply by saying that in my model the reader was freed from the tyranny of the text and given the central role in the production of meaning.

In short, I was moving in two (incompatible) directions at once: in the one the hegemony of formalism was confirmed and even extended by making the text responsible for the activities of its readers; in the other those same activities were given a larger and larger role to the extent that at times the very existence of the text was called into question. The tension between these two directions is particularly obvious in the second of these essays, "What Is Stylistics and Why Are They Saying Such Terrible Things About It?" The argument of this piece is largely a negative one, directed at those practitioners of stylistics who wish to go directly from the description of formal features to a specification of their meaning. My thesis was that such a move, because it is unconstrained by any principle, produces interpretations that are always arbitrary. I did not, however, deny either the possibility or the relevance of cataloguing formal features; I merely insisted that the value of those features could only be determined by determining their function in the developing experience of the reader. Linguistic facts, I conceded, do have meaning, but the explanation for that meaning is not the capacity of syntax to express it but the ability of a reader to confer it.

Thus I retained the distinction between description and interpretation and by so doing affirmed the integrity and objectivity of the text. In the second part of the essay, however, the argument is much more adventurous and (potentially, at least) subversive. Objecting to the formalist assumption that the reader's job is to extract the meanings that formal patterns possess prior to, and independently of, his activities, I proceed to give an account of those activities that greatly expanded their scope:

> In my view, these same activities are constitutive to a structure of concerns which is necessarily prior to any examination of formal patterns because it is itself the occasion of their coming into being. The stylisticians proceed as if there were observable facts that could first be described and then interpreted. What I am suggesting is that an interpreting entity, endowed with purposes and concerns, is, by virtue of its very operation, determining what counts as the facts to be observed.

This clearly weakens, if it does not wholly blur, the distinction between description and interpretation, and it goes a long way toward suggesting that linguistic and textual facts, rather than being the objects of interpretation, are its products. Typically, however, there is a loophole, a space for equivocation which allows me to avoid the more unsettling implications of my argument. The phrase "determining what counts as the facts" is capable of two readings: in one reading it is a radical assertion of the unavailability of facts apart from interpretation; in the other it merely means that of all the specifiable linguistic facts, only some are relevant to the act of interpretation, and these can only be picked out in the context of the reader's activities. (This is more or less the position taken by Michael Riffaterre in his critique of the Jakobson–Levi-Strauss analysis of "Les Chats.") That is, in one reading the status of the text is put into radical question, while in the other it is a matter of selecting from the text, which is still assumed to be stable and objective, those components that will be regarded as significant. The equivocation finally rests on the key word "interpretation." In the first statement of the position (in "Literature in the Reader") interpretation is characterized as a second-level response that prevents us from recognizing the shape of our immediate experience; but in this essay interpretation is identified with that experience when I declare that the reader's activities *are* interpretive. Again, however, this is a statement that points in two directions: it can either mean that a reader's activities are constitutive of what can be formally described or that formal features are prior to those activities and act in relation to them as promptings or cues. The article trades on these meanings and ends without confronting the contradiction that exists at its center.

The source of this contradiction was my unthinking acceptance of another formalist assumption, the assumption that subjectivity is an ever present danger and that any critical procedure must include a mechanism for holding it in check. Indeed, it was the absence of such a mechanism in the procedures of the stylisticians that was the basis of my attack on their work. It is not, I complained, that what they do can't be done, but that it can be done all too easily and in any direction one likes. Behind the phrase "any direction one likes" is the Arnoldian fear that, in the absence of impersonal and universal constraints, interpreters will be free to impose their idiosyncratic meanings on texts. So long as I subscribed to this fear and even used it as a polemical weapon, it was unlikely that I would ever see my way to abandoning the chief stay against it, the stability and integrity of the text. As it turned out, the removal of that fear depended on my reconceiving of the reader in such a way as to eliminate the category of "the subjective" altogether, and although I didn't know it at the time, that process had already begun in "How Ordinary Is Ordinary Language?" written in 1972. In that essay I challenge the opposition between a basic or neutral language that is responsible to or reflects the world of objective fact and a language that reflects the uniqueness of individual or subjective perception. This distinction in turn is attached to another, between the language we ordinarily use in managing the business of everyday life and the language of literature, and as a result "ordinary language" is detached from the realm of perspective and values (now the province of subjectivity and literature) and turned into a purely formal structure that exists apart from any particular purpose or situation. My strategy in the essay is to rescue ordinary language from this impoverishing characterization by arguing that at its heart is precisely the realm of values, intentions, and purposes which is often assumed to be the exclusive property of literature.

This, of course, has the effect of blurring the distinction between ordinary language and literature, and leaves me with the problem of explaining how, in the absence of formal criteria, literary texts come to be identified. I solved this problem in a way that was to have great consequences for the position I was developing. Literature, I argue, is a conventional category. What will, at any time, be recognized as literature is a function of a communal decision as to what will count as literature. All texts have the potential of so counting, in that it is possible to regard any stretch of language in such a way that it will display those properties presently understood to be literary. In other words, it is not that literature exhibits certain formal properties that compel a certain kind of attention; rather, paying a certain kind of attention (as defined by what literature is understood to be) results in the emergence into noticeability of the properties we know in advance to be literary. The conclusion is that while literature is still a category, it is an open category, not definable by fictionality, or by a disregard of propositional truth, or by a predominance of tropes and figures, but simply by what we decide to put into it. And the conclusion to that conclusion is that it is the reader who "makes" literature. This sounds like the rankest subjectivism, but it is qualified almost immediately when the reader is identified not as a free agent, making literature in any old way, but as a member of a community whose assumptions about literature determine the kind of attention he pays and thus the kind of literature "he" "makes." (The quotation marks indicate that "he" and "makes" are *not* being understood as they would be under a theory of autonomous individual agency.) Thus the act of recognizing literature is not constrained by something in the text, nor does it issue from an independent and arbitrary will; rather, it proceeds from a collective decision as to what will count as literature, a decision that will be in force only so long as a community of readers or believers continues to abide by it.

This statement is not without its equivocations, and they are familiar. The notion of a decision by which persons do or do not abide implies that what one believes is a matter of choice. On this reading, the free and autonomous subject is not eliminated but granted the considerable power of determining the beliefs that determine his world. The stronger reading would be one in which the subject's consciousness was wholly informed by conventional notions, with the result that any "decision" to affirm this or that belief would itself be enabled by beliefs that he did not choose. But that reading has not quite surfaced and the argument remains poised between two characterizations of the self: in one the self is constituted, no less than the texts it constitutes in turn, by conventional ways of thinking; in the other the self stands in a place of its own from the vantage point of which it surveys conventional ways of thinking and chooses among them.

The same hesitation also informs the conception of the text. When I say that literature is made by "a decision to regard with a particular self-consciousness the resources language has always possessed," the integrity of the text is still preserved because the "decision" (to pay a certain kind of attention, to put on one's literary perceiving set) merely brings out, in the sense of highlighting, properties the text has always had. This stops quite a bit short of the stronger assertion that the properties of the text (whether they be literary or "ordinary" properties) are the product of certain ways of paying attention. The symmetry between my position on the text and my position on the self reflects my continuing commitment to the assumption (shared by the formalists) that the text and the reader are independent and competing entities whose spheres of influence and responsibility must be defined and controlled. The crucial step will be to see that the claims of neither the text nor the reader can be upheld, because neither has the independent status that would make its claim possible.

That step is taken in "Interpreting the *Variorum*," in which the text and the reader fall together. The text goes first in response to an objection that I myself raise: If the content of the reader's experience is the succession of acts he performs, and if he performs those acts at the bidding of the text, does not the text then contain everything and have I not compromised my antiformalist position? My answer to this question indicates that for the first time I was directly confronting my relation to formalism rather than simply reacting to the accusation that I was a closet formalist. This objection will have force, I declared, only if the formal patterns of the text are assumed to exist independently of the reader's experience. This, of course, was the enabling assumption of my reader-oriented analyses and the basis for my claim of generality. I now proceeded to give it up by demonstrating that in my own analyses the formal features with which I began are the *product* of the interpretive principles for which they are supposedly evidence:

> I did what critics always do: I "saw" what my interpretive principles permitted or directed me to see and then I turned around and attributed what I had "seen" to a text and an intention. What my principles direct me to "see" are readers performing acts; the points at which I find (or to be more precise, declare) those acts to have been performed become (by a sleight of hand) demarcations *in* the text; those demarcations are then available for the designation "formal features," and as formal features they can be (illegitimately) assigned the responsibility for producing the interpretation which in fact produced them.

This would mean, for example, that the moment crucial to my analysis of *Paradise Lost*, IV, 9–12, the moment when the reader mistakenly thinks that it is the loss of Eden of which Adam and Eve are declared innocent, is not discovered by the analytical method but produced by it. The "units of sense" that mark the points at which my readers "do things" are only units within the assumption that reading is an activity of a particular kind, a succession of deliberative acts in the course of which sense is continually being made and then made again. That assumption cannot be "proved out" or proven wrong by the analysis since it will be responsible for the shape the analysis necessarily has (a description of a succession of deliberative acts, each of which revises or modifies a previous understanding).

The extent to which this is a decisive break from formalism is evident in my unqualified conclusion that formal units are always a function of the interpretive model one brings to bear (they are not "in the text"). Indeed, the text as an entity independent of interpretation and (ideally) responsible for its career drops out and is replaced by the texts that emerge as the consequence of our interpretive activities. There are still formal patterns, but they do not lie innocently in the world; rather, they are themselves constituted by an interpretive act. The facts one points to are still there (in a sense that would not be consoling to an objectivist) but only as a consequence of the interpretive (man-made) model that has called them into being. The relationship between interpretation and text is thus reversed: interpretive strategies are not put into execution after reading; they are the shape of reading, and because they are the shape of reading, they give texts their shape, making them rather than, as is usually assumed, arising from them.

At this point it looks as if the text is about to be dislodged as a center of authority in favor of the reader whose interpretive strategies make it; but I forestall this conclusion by arguing that the strategies in question are not his in the sense that would make him an independent agent. Rather, they proceed not from him but from the interpretive community of which he is a member; they are, in effect, community property, and insofar as they at once enable and limit the operations of his consciousness, he is too. The notion of "interpretive communities," which had surfaced occasionally in my discourse before, now becomes central to it. Indeed, it is interpretive communities, rather than either the text or the reader, that produce meanings and are responsible for the emergence of formal features. Interpretive communities are made up of those who share interpretive strategies not for reading but for writing texts, for constituting their properties. In other words these strategies exist prior to the act of reading and therefore determine the shape of what is read rather than, as is usually assumed, the other way around.

Even this formulation is not quite correct. The phrase "those who share interpretive strategies" suggests that individuals stand apart from the communities to which they now and then belong. In later essays I will make the point that since the thoughts an individual can think and the mental operations he can perform have their source in some or other interpretive community, he is as much a product of that community (acting as an extension of it) as the meanings it enabled him to produce. At a stroke the dilemma that gave rise to the debate between the champions of the text and the champions of the reader (of whom I had certainly been one) is dissolved because the competing entities are no longer perceived as independent. To put it another way, the claims of objectivity and subjectivity can no longer be debated because the authorizing agency, the center of interpretive authority, is at once both and neither. An interpretive community is not objective because as a bundle of interests, of particular purposes and goals, its perspective is interested rather than neutral; but by the very same reasoning, the meanings and texts produced by an interpretive community are not subjective because they do not proceed from an isolated individual but from a public and conventional point of view.

Once the subject–object dichotomy was eliminated as the only framework within which critical debate could occur, problems that had once seemed so troublesome did not seem to be problems at all. As an advocate of the rights of the reader, I could explain agreement only by positing an ideal (or informed) reader in relation to whom other readers were less informed or otherwise deficient. That is, agreement was secured by making disagreement aberrant (a position that was difficult to defend since the experience with which one had to agree was mine). But given the notion of interpretive communities, agreement more or less explained itself: members of the same community will necessarily agree because they will see (and by seeing, make) everything in relation to that community's assumed purposes and goals; and conversely, members of different communities will disagree because from each of their respective positions the other "simply" cannot see what is obviously and inescapably there: This, then, is the explanation for the stability of interpretation among different readers (they belong to the same community). It also explains why there are disagreements and why they can be debated in a principled way: not because of a stability in texts, but because of a stability in the makeup of interpretive communities and therefore in the opposing positions they make possible.

It followed then that what I had been doing in essays like "What It's Like To Read *L'Allegro* and *Il Penseroso*" was not revealing what readers had always done but trying to persuade them to a set of community assumptions so that when they read they would do what I did. As soon as I realized this, I realized that I was assenting to a characterization of my position that I had always resisted: you're not telling us how we've always read: you're trying to persuade us to a new way of reading. I resisted that characterization because I wanted to be able to claim generality. That is, I wanted to put my accounts of *the* reader's experience on as firm a ground as the ground claimed by the champions of the text by identifying the *real* reading experience in relation to which others were deviations or distortions. What I finally came to see was that the identification of what was real and normative occurred within interpretive communities and what was normative for the members of one community would be seen as strange (if it could be seen at all) by the members of another. In other words, there is no single way of reading that is correct or natural, only "ways of reading" that are extensions of community perspectives. Once I saw this, the judgment that I was trying to persuade people to a new way of reading was no longer heard as an accusation because what I was trying to persuade them *from* was not a fundamental or natural way but a way no less conventional than mine and one to which they had similarly been persuaded, if not by open polemics then by the pervasiveness of the assumptions within which they had learned how to read in the first place. This meant that the business of criticism was not (as I had previously thought) to determine a correct way of reading but to determine from which of a number of possible perspectives reading will proceed. This determination will not be made once and for all by a neutral mechanism of adjudication, but will be made and remade again whenever the interests and tacitly understood goals of one interpretive community replace or dislodge the interests and goals of another. The business of criticism, in other words, was not to decide between interpretations by subjecting them to the test of disinterested evidence but to establish by political and persuasive means (they are the same thing) the set of interpretive assumptions from the vantage of which the evidence (and the facts and the intentions and everything else) will hereafter be specifiable. In the end I both gave up generality and reclaimed it: I gave it up because I gave up the project of trying to identify the one true way of reading, but I reclaimed it because I claimed the right, along with everyone else, to argue for a way of reading, which, if it became accepted, would be, for a time at least, the true one. In short, I preserved generality by rhetoricizing it.

The distance I have traveled can be seen in the changed status of interpretation. Whereas I had once agreed with my predecessors on the need to control interpretation lest it overwhelm and obscure texts, facts, authors, and intentions, I now believe that interpretation is the source of texts, facts, authors, and intentions. Or to put it another way, the entities that were once seen as competing for the right to constrain interpretation (text, reader, author) are now all seen to be the *products* of interpretation. A polemic that was mounted in the name of the reader and against the text has ended by the subsuming of both the text and reader under the larger category of interpretation. What one finds waiting at the "end," however, is a whole new set of problems. Having redefined the activity of criticism so that it was no longer a matter of demonstration but a matter (endlessly negotiated) of persuasion, I am faced with the task of accounting, within the new model, for everything that had been recognized under the old model as being constitutive of the literary institution: texts, authors, periods, genres, canons, standards, agreements, disputes, values, changes, and so on. That task is begun in some of the essays that follow, and especially in those written after "Interpreting the *Variorum*," but if the rehearsing of this personal history has taught me anything, it is that the prosecution of that task will also be, in ways that I cannot now see, its transformation.

TOWARDS A POETICS OF VISION, SPACE, AND THE BODY: SIGN LANGUAGE AND LITERARY THEORY[1] (1997)

H-DIRKSEN L. BAUMAN

Thoughtfully and sometimes critically connecting to Derridean deconstruction, feminism, postcolonial studies, race studies, disability studies, and reader response, Bauman proposes a theory and a series of questions for the study of Sign literature (the visual literature of Sign language) and for what Sign and Sign literature can help us consider for theory and literary studies in general.

Suppose that we had no voice or tongue, and wanted to communicate with one another, should we not, like the deaf… make signs with the hands and head and the rest of the body?

—Plato, *The Cratylus* (212)

An exchange between literary theory and sign languages is long overdue. Centuries overdue: for as early as Plato's *Cratylus,* Western "hearing" intellectuals have been aware of the manual languages of Deaf[2] communities, but twenty-five centuries since Plato, we remain largely ignorant that our concepts of language and literature have evolved within a false dualism of speech and writing. Only as recently as William Stokoe's linguistic research in the 1960s, have we realized that Sign[3] is an "official" human language with the capacity to generate a nearly infinite number of propositions from a vast lexicon. Yet, while linguists have been exploring this revolution in language, literary critics remain largely unaware that Sign is a natural linguistic mode capable of producing a body of literature.[4] This body of literature is, rather, a literature of the body that transforms the linear model of speech and writing into an open linguistic field of vision, time, space, and the body.

As Sign literature emerges in the late twentieth century, we can only wonder how its absence has helped to shape our ideas about language, literature, and the world. We must wonder if Sign's absence has lead to hidden limits and desires in our relationship to language. One could, perhaps, argue that speech and writing have been searching for their visual/spatial counterpart since Simonides of Keos' formulation that "poetry is speaking painting" while "painting is mute poetry," and extending through, among others, Horace's dictum *ut pictura poesis,* centuries of religious "pattern poetry,"[5] Blake's illustrations, Stein's cubism, Pound's ideograms, Olson's hieroglyphics, concrete poetry, performance poetry, ethnopoetics, video-texts, and virtual texts. These experiments have, in their various ways, sought to imbue speech and writing with the visual and spatial dimensions of images and the body. Have these experiments emerged out of a phantom-limb phenomenon where writers have sensed language's severed visual-spatial mode and went groping after it?[6] If the Deaf poet had been mythologized as the blind poet has been, would literature have developed differently? Would the map which draws the historical relation between visual and literary arts have to be redrawn? What sorts of genres would have emerged? Would our metaphysical heritage have been different if we were not only the speaking but also the "signing animal"?

While these questions are beyond the scope of the present essay, they lead toward its general purpose: to show that what many scholars would consider the marginal literary practices (if you can even call them "literary") of "disabled" persons is, on the contrary, of central importance to any one, hearing or Deaf, who is interested in the relations of language and literature to culture, identity, and being. In order to recognize Sign as a medium for literature, we must open an exchange between Sign and theory by exploring ways that theory enhances our understanding of Sign and ways that Sign enhances—and challenges— our understanding of theory and literature. This opening exchange will ask numerous questions that will gesture toward a more in-depth study of Sign literature.

The following dialogue between Sign and theory is more like a conference call between Sign and interconnected and contradictory areas of criticism: deconstruction, cultural studies (at the intersection of feminism/postcolonialism/multiculturalism), semiotics, and phenomenology. Rather than applying a monolithic paradigm, I hope to assemble a collection of perspectives that will offer the best vantage points from which to explore a nonwritten, spatial form of literature. This eclectic approach is especially important as the small body of criticism of Sign literature remains rooted in one-dimensional approaches. The formalist analyses of Clayton Valli and Edward Klima and Ursula Bellugi and the semiotic approaches of Jim Cohn and Heidi Rose are much needed contributions to their field, but are unable to place Sign literature in its proper historical, political, metaphysical perspective—which is the goal of this present study. My intent, though, is ultimately not to feed Sign poems through a convoluted critical machine to produce insightful "readings" or rather, "viewings"; instead, one hopes these concepts and connections will eventually develop dialogically with Sign poetic practices themselves.

DECONSTRUCTION AND DEAFNESS: PHONOCENTRISM, AUDISM, AND SIGN LANGUAGE

The exchange between theory and Sign should open, appropriately, with Jacques Derrida, for it is he who has brought the importance of nonphonetic linguistic modalities to the forefront of twentieth-century thought by severing the "natural" connection between the voice and language. The voice, Derrida believes, is more than a means of communicating—it is the source for Western ideas of truth, being, and presence. The system of "hearing-oneself-speak," Derrida contends, "has necessarily dominated the history of the world during an entire epoch, and has even produced the idea of the world, the idea of world-origin" (8). This constitutive role of the voice results from the self-presence created by hearing-oneself-speak. One's own voice is completely interior, fully present to the speaker; it is the source of self-identity, of self-presence. Meaning constituted within this full-presence then becomes the standard for notions of identity, precipitating a metaphysics based on the full-presence of self, meaning, and identity. The privileging of the voice, which Derrida calls "phono-centrism," is the linguistic phenomenon that leads toward "logocentrism," the Western metaphysical orientation which perceives meaning to be anchored by the self-presence of identity. Against this tradition, Derrida recognizes that the voice has no natural primacy over nonphonetic forms of language and that the metaphysics of presence is infused with the free-play and undecidability of language. Seeking to deconstruct phonocentric metaphysics, Derrida explores nonphonetic forms of language—hieroglyphics, ideograms, algebraic nota-tions, and nonlinear writing. His explorations lead beyond phonocentric linguistics toward "grammatology," a science of writing and textuality.

When seen through deconstructive lenses, Sign dilates its sphere of influence from the sociopolitical site of the Deaf community to the entire history of Western "hearing" meta-physics. With its deconstruction of the voice-centered tradition, grammatology, one might say, initiates a "Deaf philosophy"—if it weren't for the fact that Derrida fails to engage theo-retical issues of deafness or signing to any significant degree. The exchange between Sign and deconstruction, then, recognizes the metaphysical implications of Sign while Sign, in turn, extends the project of deconstruction beyond its own limitations drawn by the exclusion of Sign and Deaf history.

The theoretical significance of "deafness," in this sense, takes on new historical and metaphysical importance that pathologized "deafness" cannot. If nonphonetic writing inter-rupts the primacy of the voice, deafness signifies the consummate moment of disruption. Deafness exiles the voice from the body, from meaning, from being; it sabotages its interior-ity from within, corrupting the system which has produced the "hearing" idea of the world. Deafness, then, occupies a consummate moment in the deconstruction of Western ontology. Further, deafness does more than disrupt the system of "hearing-oneself-speak"; it creates an embodied linguistic system which, unlike speech, is not fully present to itself. Signers, unless gazing into the mirror, do not fully see themselves signify. While they may see their hands, they cannot see their own face perform much of Sign's grammatical nuances. The eye, unlike the ear in the system of "hearing-oneself-speak," can only partially "see-oneself-sign." There is always a trace of nonpresence in the system of signing.

One wonders, then, if Derrida had engaged the theoretical implications of deafness and Sign further, might he have expanded the term "Sign" as he did "Writing" to signify *differ-ance*, Derrida's neologism that cannot be spoken but only seen, signifying that phonetic writing is not simply a copy of speech. At this point, we can only begin to conjecture what sort of different philosophical resonance would occur by re-reading deconstruction with regards to Sign in the place of—or in addition to—writing.

While Derrida does not engage the theoretical implications of deafness or Sign in any depth, he does entertain Rousseau's contradictory relation to the language of gesture, which Rousseau attributes to Deaf persons on occasion. Early in the *Essay on the Origin of Human Languages* when Rousseau imagines that a society could develop arts, commerce, govern-ment—all without recourse to speech. After all, Rousseau writes, "The mutes of great nobles understand each other and understand everything that is said to them by means of signs, just as well as one can understand anything said in discourse" (*Essay* 9). This observation leads Rousseau to muse that "the art of communicating our ideas depends less upon the organs we use in such communication than it does upon a power proper to man, according to which he uses his organs in this way, and which, if he lacked these, would lead him to use others to the same end" (10). Derrida seizes on this nonphonocentric moment in Rousseau to destabilize the primacy of the voice in Western philosophy. "It is once again the power of substituting one organ for another," Derrida writes, "of articulating space and time, sign and voice, hand and spirit, it is this faculty of supplementarity which is the true origin—or nonorigin—of languages" (241). As the condition leading toward the supplement, deafness could be read, ironically, as that which makes the origin of language possible. Deafness summonses up the visual-spatial dimension of language to supplant the voice from within. It sets *differance* in motion.

This inversion of deafness—from linguistic isolation to the precondition of language itself—has political implications for the Deaf community's difficult task of depathologizing Deaf identity within the culture of academia. After considering deafness in relation to deconstruction, one may begin to see the Deaf community—not as a group defined by its pathological relation to language—but rather as an example of a culture flourishing beyond the reaches of logocentrism. The possibility of such a community raises questions. Is resisting phonocentrism tantamount to resisting logocentrism? What are the phenomenological differences between "being-in-the deaf-world" and "being-in-the-hearing-world"? Are Deaf persons—over ninety percent of whom are born in hearing families—really out of reach of logocentrism? By raising issues surrounding Sign to the metaphysical level, could the argument for a Deaf cultural identity be expanded beyond the anthropological and socio-linguistic identifications of distinctly "Deaf" cultural acts—such as Deaf folklore, jokes, attention getting strategies, and social organizations—to encompass a deeper level: a level that Sign and "not-hearing-oneself-speak" creates outside of hearing-dominated metaphysics?

Given the relevance of these questions to grammatology, it is surprising that Derrida never engages signing and deafness as theoretically and historically significant issues.[7] When he does mention deafness it is through the "voices" of others: Hegel, Leibniz, Rousseau, and Saussure. Making others speak about deafness is a strange ventriloquism which demonstrates that Derrida is aware, obviously, of Sign and Deaf communities. One may link this critical oversight as being symptomatic of not really *seeing* Deaf people, of tacitly acknowledging their absence from being. If this is so, this audist oversight reinscribes the very phonocentrism Derrida sets out to deconstruct. At the very least, one may accuse Derrida's grammatology of suffering from an undertheorized sociopolitical site because he neglects Deaf history. While he considers logocentrism to be "the most original and powerful ethnocentrism," (3) he does not follow this statement to its most severe sociopolitical manifestation: audism.

Audism is the most extreme deployment of phonocentrism ranging from incarcerating Deaf persons in mental institutions, to eugenics movements (one sponsored by Alexander Graham Bell in America, another curred practiced in China), to the oppression of sign language in the education of Deaf persons. Many Deaf adults today tell of their violent experiences growing up in oralist schools—their hands slapped or tied behind their backs if they were caught signing.[8] Further, early Deaf schools offered a collection of subjugated bodies on which doctors could develop the science of otology. Acids, needles, and hammers all violated the ears and skulls of Deaf children so that they could be returned to "normal."[9]

While he could have made many relevant connections between phonocentrism and oralist educational practices, Derrida instead labels the condemnation of Leibniz's desire for a nonphonetic, universal script as "the most energetic eighteenth-century *reaction* organizing the defense of phonologism and of logocentric metaphysics" (99). I propose, instead, that the history of deaf education, as it is marked by violent oppression of sign and the subjugation of Deaf persons, is a more "energetic reaction" to phonocentrism. It is where phonocentrism meets social and educational policy. Indeed, nowhere will one find a more vehement declaration of voice-as-presence than by reading the words of oralist educators. Consider, for example, the following declaration from the father of deaf education in German-speaking lands:

> The breath of life resides in the voice....The voice is a living emanation of that spirit that God breathed into man when he created him a living soul....What stupidity we find in most of these unfortunate deaf....How little they differ from animals. (Lane, 107)

This all too common association between Deaf persons and animals offers arguably the most vivid illustration of Derrida's central connection between voice and human presence. As Douglas Baynton, Harlan Lane, and others have shown, Deaf identity has been publicly constructed through metaphorics of animality, darkness, imprisonment, and isolation, resulting in a relay of hierarchized binary oppositions which divide along the axis of absence and presence: animal/human; prisoner/property owner; foreigner/citizen; darkness/light; normality/pathology. Just as the Deaf voice is exiled from its own body, Deaf persons have been exiled from the phonocentric body-politic.

One hopes these initial ideas point toward a future critical project of exploring a grammatology of Sign that recognizes Sign's historical and metaphysical context while also documenting phonocentrism's political legacy. Such a project, however, would require a broader theoretical base than grammatology itself offers. If Sign criticism is to be an instrumental means of spreading the recognition of Sign literature and Deaf culture, it needs to articulate itself as an oppositional discourse alongside others which oppose oppression in its various forms. For this reason, Sign criticism would benefit from exploring its relation with feminism, postcolonialism, and multiculturalism, in addition to deconstruction.

FEMINISM/POSTCOLONIALISM/MULTICULTURALISM AND SIGN LITERATURE

Inviting feminism, postcolonialism, and multiculturalism into a dialogue with deconstruction brings together an uneasy alliance. It has become a critical cliche, for example, to accuse deconstruction of decentering the human subject just as disempowered groups were gaining empowered subjectivities. Despite important differences, however, deconstruction may find its greatest alliance with these oppositional discourses in its dismantling of phonocentrism and audism. Instead of exhuming well-documented contentions, therefore, it seems more advantageous to draw together overlapping concerns in order to form a broad textual, social, and political context for the emergence of Deaf/Sign literature.

Forming such a coalition of ideas is based on Audre Lorde's belief that sexism, homophobia, and racism are "particular manifestations of the same disease" (137)—as are ethnocentrism, colonialism, ableism, and audism. "Can any one here," Lorde asks, "still afford to believe that the pursuit of liberation can be the sole and particular province of any one particular race, or sex, or age, or religion, or sexuality, or class?" (140). Indeed, we cannot—nor can we continue to neglect the commonly elided category of "ability" from this "pursuit of liberation."

In clearing a space to talk about Deaf culture and Sign literature, a number of questions arise in the initial dialogue between Deaf studies and each area: feminism, postcolonialism, and multiculturalism; and from those questions, a few overlapping concerns may be identified that will form ways of talking about Sign literature in a political and cultural context. This exchange will, one hopes, begin to build for Deaf studies a strong sociopolitical foundation while Deaf studies, in turn, may expand the "pursuit of liberation" to include ableism and audism which are frequently overlooked by an overdetermination of racism and sexism.

The project of recognizing Deaf identity bears similarities to the feminist project of regaining a "body of one's own" through linguistic and literary practices. Sign, in a more graphic way, perhaps, than *l'écriture feminine* is a "writing of/on the body." The relation between Sign and *l'écriture feminine* raises questions that could have interesting implications for feminist performance. Does the antiphonocentric nature of Sign offer a means of averting the essentializing tendency of *l'écriture feminine?* Does the four-dimensional space of performance offer ways of deconstructing phallogocentric linear discourse? How does the gender of the signer influence the reading/viewing of the "text" itself? How does the male gaze construct the female body/text? Can gender ever be bracketed out of a reading of a Sign performance?

Many of these feminist issues anticipate those of postcolonial discourse. At first glance, though, one would not think of Deaf persons as being "colonized"—disciplined, yes, but colonized? However, as Harlan Lane shows, audism is homologous with colonialism, including "the physical subjugation of a disempowered people, the imposition of alien language and mores, and the regulation of education in behalf of the colonizers goals" (32). How accurate is Lane's position? Could one consider medicine's often brutal experimentation on the ears of Deaf children a form of physical subjugation? Could the controversial surgical procedure used to restore hearing—the cochlear implant—be considered a form of colonizing the Deaf body and eradicating a Deaf culture? Is the effort to impose English-only in Deaf residential schools similar, say, to forcing Native Americans to adopt a nationalized language and identity in residential schools? Is the fact that oral-based pedagogies exclude Deaf persons from deaf education a means of securing hearing dominance over the Deaf community? How does a postcolonial writer/signer resist the hegemony of dominant literature while working within the field of literature?

In addition, if Sign literature is to be considered as an "ethnic" literature, it should inquire into its relation to other minority literatures and their ethnic origins. The very claim that Deaf identity is cultural rather than pathological provokes an interrogation of our assumed "natural" categories of cultural identity. How can Deaf persons share a cultural identity if they do not have a common religion, nationality, race, or ethnicity? Do predominantly "Deaf spaces," such as Deaf residential schools and Deaf clubs, constitute a type of national "homeland"? How does Deaf identity intersect with other simultaneous subject positions—gender, race, nationality, class? Would a Deaf American feel more "at home" with, say, a Deaf Japanese than a hearing American from around the block? Is it possible to acknowledge the strength of Deaf identity but not fall into the trap of hierarchizing identities? Is Deaf culture, as it crosses national, racial, and economic borders, an emblematic postmodern culture? And finally, how does a postmodern theory of Deaf culture influence a theory of Sign literature?

This initial meeting of Deaf studies, Sign literature, and cultural studies helps to identify a few underlying concepts—anti-essentialism, hybridity, and border consciousness—that will be helpful in providing a political context for discussing Sign literature. Because of the relay between logocentrism, phonocentrism, and audism, any critical practice of Sign literature needs to move beyond logocentric ways of looking at identity—that is, basing one's identity on essentialized definitions such as "speech is an *essential* human trait" or "whites are *essentially* more intelligent than other races." Instead, we need to recognize identities as constantly being constructed within a complex network of social, political, and linguistic influences. Such anti-essentialist thinking is important, for, as Edward Said comments, "essentialisms have the power to turn human beings against one another" by allowing us to slide into "an unthinking acceptance of stereotypes, myths, animosities, and traditions encouraged by imperialism" (229). If audism is itself a form of essentialist thinking, then Deaf resistance to it should not be a reinscription of it. We need to recognize, then, that a person cannot be *purely* Deaf apart from the confluence of multiple subject positions—nationality, race, gender, class, disability, sexual preference—just as one cannot be *purely* Female, Mexican, or Asian. Avoiding an essentialist view of Deaf identity would be the equivalent of avoiding what Frantz Fanon calls "the pitfalls of national consciousness" that reinscribes the oppressive essentialism of colonialism.

As opposed to an essentialized "national" or "audist" consciousness, Sign literature might be more effectively approached through a "border consciousness" that recognizes the uniqueness of Deaf culture and Sign literature, but that also acknowledges their social construction. Indeed, the institutional patterns of Deaf cultural transmission offer a particularly postmodern example of the constructed rather than essential nature of identity. Over ninety percent of Deaf persons do not form their cultural identity through their family but through social organizations and institutions. As Carol Padden and Tom Humphries explain, one learns to be Deaf, not through an essential "presence of a common physical condition," but by gaining "access to a certain cultural history, the culture of Deaf people in America" (25). To paraphrase Simone de Beauvoir's famous statement about female identity: one is not born but rather becomes Deaf. Such a perspective of Deaf identity has bearing on the ways we discuss Sign literature; for, as Edward Said reminds us, we need to recognize that all "cultural forms are hybrid, mixed, impure, and the time has come in cultural analysis to reconnect their analysis with their actuality" (14).

In fact, the notion of "Sign literature" is itself a product of hearing/Deaf borderlands. As the term "literature" derives from the Latin *litere*, or "letter," "Sign literature" is oxymoronic in the same sense as "oral literature." Because of the inaccuracy of the label, Heidi Rose has proposed that creative use of American Sign Language be known as "ASL ART" which "should be studied as a distinct phenomenon, not as some sort of hybrid between the written and oral form" ("Critical Methodology," 15). Rose's re-definition raises interesting ontological questions regarding the definition of Sign literature. Yet, rather than establishing a wholesale re-definition, it may be wise to let the question of ASL "literature" remain just that, a question. The desire to define whether creative use of ASL is or is not "literature," I feel, unnecessarily limits the discussion to an essentialized either/or opposition. The issues involved in making such a distinction are far too complex and important to both hearing and Deaf communities to be reduced to such a dichotomy. Rather than offering a totalizing answer, it may be wise to tolerate the ambiguity that ASL "art" both *is* and *is not* "literature," that it is akin to hearing literary practices, but also cannot be contained by those practices.[10]

There are too many political and analytical benefits of discussing creative Sign as literature to banish it from the curricular domain of literature. These benefits have been demonstrated best, perhaps, by Clayton Valli who has defined such techniques as "lines" and "rhymes" in Sign poetry. In his essay, "The Nature of a Line in ASL Poetry," Valli explains how an ASL poet creates signed "lines" through visual rhyme patterns. A signed rhyme is made through a repetition of particular handshapes, movement paths, sign locations, or nonmanual markers such as facial expressions or body postures. For example, in his poem, "Snowflake" Valli employs visual rhyme by repeating the same "five" handshape (palm open, all fingers extended) to sign TREE, then to draw the outline of the leaves on the tree, and then to show the leaves falling to the ground. In addition, Valli and others accept the same genre distinctions for Sign as for hearing literature. Identifying such hearing-centered literary analogues demonstrates that Sign can be explored creatively to produce as linguistically complex "texts" as can speech and writing. That Sign can partake in the literary traditions of the West is an indispensable argument in convincing universities to recognize Sign literature, a move which would continue to depathologize Deaf identity in the minds of hearing persons.

However, uncritically adopting the signifier of "literature" dismisses the fact that literature has been formed within exclusive practices of spoken and written languages. As the linear model is the structural embodiment of hearing forms of literature, Valli's concept of the "line" places Sign literature directly within a phonocentric/audist tradition. Why even concern ourselves with the discussions of "lines" and "rhymes"? What sort of political, historical, and metaphysical baggage do those terms carry? How well can the terms of an aural/temporal art be applied to a visual-spatial art? In order to discuss Sign as literature, then, one must proceed through the lexicon of hearing criticism and interrogate the terms for their imbedded audist ideologies and their critical accuracy. In some instances, terminology can take on new dimensions when it crosses the inter-semiotic gap to visual/spatial language—or old dimensions, as with "rhythm" which originated, not in the musical arts, but in dance.[11] Within Sign criticism, the concept of rhythm may be restored to its original connection with the movements of the body in time and space.

In fact, there is no reason to confine a lexicon for Sign literature to the literary arts. As a visual performance art, Sign literature may bear more similarity to painting, dance, drama, film, and video than to poetry or fiction. A "line" in Sign poetry, for example, might be more accurately modeled after the concept of the "line" in painting or a choreographed "phrase" in dance. Instead of moving from left to right, the Sign poet draws lines through space in all directions. In addition, given the cinematic nature of ASL,[12] the Sign lexicon must be expanded to include such concepts as "editing," "montage," "panning," "close-up," and "slow-motion." Indeed, why not go so far as to invent a new vocabulary in Sign and then translate that lexicon into written glosses for ASL signs?

This "border theory" asks us to consider ways to avert a reductive either/or response to Sign literature; it asks us how we may refer to it in such a way that always already implies resistance to being called "*literature*"; it asks us to see Sign literature as a hybrid creation, at once unique to Deaf cultural experience, but also crossing over a multitude of national, economic, racial, ethnic, gendered, sexual, linguistic, artistic, and textual borders. Identifying the borders that a particular poem, narrative, or performer crosses over, invites critical dialogue about the relations between minority and dominant literatures, between Deaf and hearing worlds, and between Deaf identity and Sign literature.

One hopes that, as Trinh Minh-ha writes, "this shuttling in-between frontiers is a working out of and an appeal to another sensibility, another consciousness of the condition of marginality: that in which marginality is the condition of the center" (216). The ultimate scope of this project, then, is to recognize the previously marginalized body of Sign literature, and in so doing to expose the false dualism of speech and writing that has helped to structure the hearing "center" of Western civilization.

TOWARD A "POETICS OF SPACE": FROM SEMIOTICS TO PHENOMENOLOGY

If Sign literature offers a rare opportunity to reconsider what literature is, then Sign criticism needs to amass the critical breadth for such an undertaking. The first step is to move beyond Sign criticism's preoccupation with formalist linguistic analysis. The writings of Clayton Valli, Edward Klima, and Ursula Bellugi offer a useful vocabulary for describing a Sign's physical and linguistic characteristics, but they are unable to explore the wider metaphysical, sociopolitical, and phenomenological dimensions of Sign literature. As linguists, these writers are more concerned with demonstrating ASL's depth and flexibility than with exploring a fundamental rethinking of the way that literature is produced and perceived.

Heidi Rose is one of the first persons to break away from linguistic formalism to discuss Sign literature in the context of a more contemporary criticism—semiotics. In her essay, "A Semiotic Analysis of Artistic American Sign Language and a Performance of Poetry," Rose makes a significant contribution toward a theory of Sign literature by applying C. S. Peirce's semiotics to a reading of a signed poem. According to Peirce, signs (not ASL "signs," but rather anything that produces meaning) can take three different forms: icon (representation by likeness, e.g., portrait, onomatopoeia), index (representation by relation, e.g., smoke to fire, temperature to fever), and symbol (representation by arbitrary signifiers, e.g., conventional words). Unlike speech and writing, Sign is most often associated with iconic signification. Rose agrees that Sign's unique character is its iconicity, but only after demonstrating that a Sign poem is more complex than a series of manual pictures in the air. During the course of a performance, Rose explains, the hands may sign on the iconic or symbolic levels while the non-manual markers (i.e., facial expressions) tend to produce indexical meaning. In the end, though, the noniconic elements of the poem "flesh out the manual signs and complete the message with the final effect highlighting the iconic means of communication" (154). The body signifies differently throughout the course of a poem, though its ultimate goal, according to Rose, is to embody iconic images, to move closer to the thing-itself.

Underlying Rose's analysis (and the existing body of Sign criticism), however, is the assumption that iconicity is an inherent and constant element within the text, independent of the viewer's relationship to the poem. This assumption is closely allied with another: that Peirce's semiotic taxonomy is mutually exclusive and stable. Deaf critic Joseph Grigely, however, demonstrates that semiotics cannot, in the end, produce the predictable science of language that it had hoped. "Peirce's taxonomy of signs," Grigely writes, "is essentially an unstable ontology, and that the attribution of sign values—iconicity, indexicality, and arbitrariness—is part of a dynamic process by which a reader circumscribes frames of reference as part of the act of reading" (243). While Grigely discusses but does not focus on Sign poetry, he helps Sign criticism to move beyond its preoccupation with iconicity to engage the larger process of how iconicity is itself produced and received. In "The Implosion of Iconicity," Grigely writes:

> Every time we claim to discover an iconic presence—be it an onomatope like "moo-cow" or in a visual analogue like the ASL sign for TREE—our discovery is actually a hermeneutic act, an interpretation of certain textual relations....An interpretive model of iconicity does not require a factual similarity between a sign and its referent, but merely an impression that similitude of some kind or form exists—whether or not it actually does. (246)

Iconicity, therefore, is less an element of the poem itself than a form of perception, less an absolute value than, as Charles Morris has remarked, "a matter of degree" (quoted in Grigely, 246). Taking into account the role of the reader or viewer in the production of meaning, Grigely moves away from the formalized "text-as-object" toward the "text-as-an-event" that takes place somewhere between the poet and the audience. This move is liberating, especially to oral and sigh poetics, for it recognizes the inescapable performative nature of literature.

Once we expand our criticism to accommodate the viewer's active role in creating the poem, we are no longer limited to discussing poems as if they took place in objectifiable, linguistic space, for we do not *perceive* that space. Such linguistic space is based on a Newtonian constancy of spatial relations. The poetic space we perceive, however, is of a different nature. Calculating and recording the positions of the hands in relation to the body, for instance, may help to describe the physical properties of text, but leaves us unable to explain our perceptions of embodied images that appear, dissolve, enlarge, shrink, transform, as they shift from close-up to far-away, wide-angle, slow-motion, fast-forward, and freeze-frame. While these spatio-temporal techniques have their basis in Sign's unique linguistic use of four-dimensions, their effect can only be articulated within a theory that remains rooted in the perceptions of the body. For this reason any linguistic or semiotic analysis is incomplete without considering viewer-oriented phenomenological criticism.

Phenomenology takes as its starting point Edmund Husserl's questioning of the "natural attitude" that objects exist independently from our consciousness of them. Human consciousness, according to Husserl and other phenomenologists, is not formed through a passive reception of the ready-made world, but through active constitution of that world. Phenomenological or "reader-response" criticism, then, inquires into the ways that readers are themselves producers of literary texts. Any "viewer-response" criticism of Sign poetry must begin by taking into account the embodied perception of space, vision, and time, and then by considering these in relation to phenomenologies of language and the literary imagination. This confluence of phenomenologies leads toward what may be called the "poetics of space," intentionally borrowing from Gaston Bachelard's book by the same title.

A starting point for the understanding of the poetics of space is Merleau-Ponty's phenomenology of language which applies to Sign as well as to speaking and writing. "The word and speech," Merleau-Ponty writes,

> must somehow cease to be a way of designating things or thoughts, and become the presence of that thought in the phenomenal world, and, moreover, not its clothing, but its token or *its body*.…[W]e find there, beneath the conceptual meaning of the words, an existential meaning which is not only rendered by them, but which inhabits them. (*Phenomenology of Perception*, 182)

In taking on a phenomenal, embodied presence of its own, language is not condemned to the perpetual task of mimesis and referentiality; language is itself the body, flesh, and bone of meaning. When audiences watch Clayton Valli's poem, "Dew on Spiderweb," for example, they may witness the linguistic spinning of a spiderweb as real as any spiderweb seen before. Of course, this is an image of a spiderweb, but as Gaston Bachelard asks, "why should the actions of the imagination not be as real as those of perception?" (158). Valli's image does not so much iconically *refer* to a spiderweb "out-there," but rather brings what Merleau-Ponty has called "a diagram of the life of the actual" ("Eye and Mind," 126) into *being*. As witnesses of this poetic incarnation, we inhabit the poem's four-dimensional topography and find ourselves in the intimate physical and phenomenal presence of image-things.[13]

Such an experience cannot be measured. We do not so much see the text as an object "out there" as we "see according to, or with it" (Merleau-Ponty, 126). We do not so much see a stable volume of linguistic space, but rather a much more volatile volume of poetic space. For "everything, even size, is a human value," Bachelard writes. Just as "miniature can accumulate size… [and become] *vast* in its own way," "the dialectics of inside and outside can no longer be taken in their simple reciprocity" (216). In the poetics of space, the "duality of subject and object is iridescent, shimmering, unceasingly active in its inversions" (xv). Indeed, it would even be difficult to say exactly where any given image *is*; in the "text-as-event," the borders between viewer and text, subject and object, inside and outside, become porous.

We now enter into a whole new field of questions about the nature of perception, body, space, time, Sign, and literature. A few beginning questions must be asked, even if there is not time to answer them: How is (or isn't) "poetic space" different from "everyday" space? How is spatial perception in Sign different from that of speech and writing? Does Sign structure the world differently? What are the poetic and cultural implications of this different "structure"? How would a phenomenology of Sign change the ways we talk about relations between the viewer and the text, the subject and the object?

In order to demonstrate briefly how the poetics of space may help us to approach Sign poetry, I return to the notion of the poetic "line." As Valli chooses the rhymed line break as the exclusive model for the signed line, this analogy precludes ASL from more contemporary types of line breaks, such as those of free verse. One wonders why Sign criticism would want to coerce ASL's most unique quality—its four dimensions—into the one-dimensional model of the line. Not only is this an inaccurate analogy, it also places ASL literature as a derivative form of poetry.

Instead of forcing the linear model of oral and written poetics on Sign, it may be more beneficial to inquire into the phenomenological reception of a "line." A viewer does not actually perceive line division rhyme as such—for it is a linguistic analogy. What the viewer sees, rather, is a complex assemblage of lines drawn through space by fingers, hand movements, arm movements, or whole body movements. If the afterimage of all the lines were recorded on video throughout the course of a poem, the visual effect would be more like that of a Susan Howe poem than a sonnet.

Take, for example, the opening of Flying Word Project's "Poetry," where performer Peter Cook gestures shooting a gun. He begins the "line" by tracing the direction of the bullet with the index finger. Cook repeats the motion quickly, conveying the speed of the bullet. This line drawn through space then extends and curves as it transforms into signifying a moon circling a planet.

This radical transformation from human to cosmic scale, from straight to circular, threaded together through the same handshape, moves the reader through vastly different experiences of space. From the intimacy of a mid-range shot to the immensity of the distance shot of a whole planet, the producer/viewer's body not only shifts perspectives, but in so doing, *inhabits a new kind of space*. This perceived "line," in other words, cannot be measured as a constant volume, but only in its ability to generate *poetic volume*.

Seeing the line within the full space and time of the body leads Sign literature away from the phonocentric literary model, and toward concepts more akin to the visual and performative arts. Indeed, at the hands of Sign poets, the poetic line may resemble a Klee more than a Keats; and like the lines in a Klee, Sign is "a matter of freeing the line, of revivifying its constituting power" (Merleau-Ponty, "Eye and Mind," 143). Such a liberation of the prosaic line may provide an example of the margin freeing the center from its own constraints.

Further phenomenological study of Sign poetry will, one hopes, explore other literary concepts in their visual-spatial quality, as opposed to their linguistic quantity. This approach will keep Sign criticism close to the original site of poetic creation: the meeting of body, time, space, and language. In the end, we may arrive at a viewing practice in which Sign poems are not so much "read" or "seen" as they are *lived* in from the inside.

CONCLUSION

Drawing out all the possible connections, contradictions, and ambiguities between deconstruction, cultural studies, semiotics, and phenomenology as they apply to Sign literature will be a major critical task. To begin, a few key critical concepts may be isolated:

while Sign literature is a minority cultural practice, it nonetheless has profound implications for the dominant group's understanding of language, literature, and culture. These implications manifest at the metaphysical site (the breaking of the hegemony of speech-writing); the sociopolitical site (the emergence of a postmodern culture outside of phonocentrism); the textual site (the practice of a postmodern bardic tradition recorded only through video-text); and the phenomenological site (the performance of an alternative visual-spatial means of being-in-the-world). Through the performance of a signed text, all these sites operate simultaneously, each within the other. Boundaries give way and become openings. "A narrow gate," Bachelard writes, "opens up an entire world" (185). One hopes the narrow gate of Sign literature and criticism will open up the entire world of experience previously foreclosed by the dominance of speech and writing. If the figure of the blind poet inhabits the origins of poetry, then we may look toward the Deaf poet to explore the future of poetry as it becomes increasingly visual, spatial, and embodied.

NOTES

1. Deaf persons, I believe, are first and foremost members of a cultural and linguistic community, bearing more similarity, say, to Hispanics than to persons with cerebral palsy. My publishing this article in a disability studies reader, however, highlights what I feel may be a coalition formed between Deaf studies and disability studies. This coalition must be aware that Deaf persons form a unique linguistic and cultural group, but that both groups may strive in tandem to resist the pathologization of the body by the abled body-politic. Deaf and disability studies, for example, could collaborate to resist China's present eugenics practice of sterilizing "disabled" persons. Only by joining forces and resources may the Deaf and persons with disabilities gain a larger political voice to denounce China's human rights violations as well as America's policy to China.
2. In keeping with conventions within Deaf studies, I use the capitalized *Deaf* to refer to the cultural group of ASL-users while lower case *deaf* and *deafness* refer to the physical phenomena of not hearing.
3. I refer to sign languages collectively as "Sign." Sign includes all native sign languages—British Sign Language, American Sign Language, French Sign Language, Chinese Sign Language, etc. but does not include manual versions of dominant languages such as Signed Exact English. The distinctions between manual versions of dominant languages and the native languages of Deaf communities presents an interesting field of study which may illuminate the constitutive nature of vision in Sign grammar that is at odds with the logic of spoken languages.
4. Since the advent of video publications, a number of Deaf poets and storytellers have achieved national recognition within the Deaf community: Ella Mae Lentz, Dorothy Miles, Bernard Bragg, Debbie Rennie, Patrick Graybill, Gilbert Eastman, Ben Bahan, Sam Supalla and Flying Words Project (Peter Cook and Kenny Lerner). The most accessible videos are produced by Dawn Sign Press which has published the *Poetry in Motion* series featuring Debbie Rennie, Patrick Graybill, and Clayton Valli, the ASL *Literature* series featuring narratives by Ben Bahan and Sam Supalla, and more recently, Clayton Valli's *Selected Works*. In Motion Press has also published a collection of poems by Ella Mae Lentz entitled *The Treasure*.
5. See Dick Higgins's *Pattern Poetry: Guide to an Unknown Literature.*

6. Indeed, some writers tread so close to the poetics of Sign, that it is only their inability to see through the label of disability (and the oppression of Sign in the early part of this century) that precluded recognition of Sign as a medium for literature. Ernest Fenollosa's *The Chinese Written Character as a Medium for Poetry* might have been more accurate had he written about ASL rather than the Chinese ideogram. In addition, Artaud's *The Theater and Its Double* praises sign language without ever connecting the language of gesture to the Deaf community. No doubt, Artaud, Fenollosa, and Pound would have been enthralled with the experimental poetics of avant-garde Deaf poets. More recently, only a scattering of contemporary poets and critics have recognized Sign poetry. Jerome and Diane Rothenberg include an article on Sign poetry by Edward Klima and Ursula Bellugi in *Symposium of the Whole: A Range of Discourse Toward an Ethnopoetics*; in 1984, Allen Ginsberg visited the National Technical Institute for the Deaf in Rochester, New York where he met with Deaf poets (cf. Cohn's "Visible Poetics" essay); and in the *MLA Newsletter*, critic W.J.T. Mitchell wrote that "The poetry of the deaf stages for us in the most vivid possible form the basic shift in literary understanding that has been occurring in the last decade: the movement from a 'textual' model (based in the narrowly defined circuit of writing and speech) to a 'performance' model" (14).

7. In the thirty years since the publication of *De la Grammatologie*, Derrida continued to overlook deafness and Sign. In those years, Europe and the United States have witnessed the most important years in Deaf history. With the 1988 Gallaudet Revolution, Deaf culture has become recognized in the international media. And yet, Derrida continues to avoid the questions raised by deafness even though he, along with Paul de Man has explored the metaphorics of blindness. Derrida, however, is not the only deconstructionist to miss the metaphysical implications of deafness. In *The Telephone Book*, Avital Ronnell is an audist tourist in her brief foray into Deaf culture. In fact, she treats the audist, Alexander Graham Bell, so sympathetically that she fails to see the strong arm of logocentrism reaching through Bell's call for a eugenics movement to eradicate "a deaf variety of the human race." When discussing the work of Bell, Ronell writes, "We are still talking art, and of the poetry diverting a child from the isolation of deafness, saving the child in language, bringing him to the proximity of speech with his father. AGB did this—an act of genuine *poiesis*…" (329–30). Is this not, rather, an act of coercing a deaf child into phonocentrism?; is it not a form of violence to deny a child a natural visual language when he cannot hear speech? Would it not be more of an act of genuine *poeisis* to teach the Father to sign? Further, Ronell's worst kind of tourism is evident as she does not bother to understand basic cultural literacy of Deaf persons. She calls the Abbé de l'Epée the "first literate deaf-mute"; the Abbé, however, was a hearing man in his fifties who stumbled upon two deaf women in Paris and subsequently became interested in deaf education.

8. See Bernard Bragg's *Lessons in Laughter: The Autobiography of a Deaf Actor* as signed to Eugene Bergman. Bragg recounts his childhood experiences being taught how to laugh like hearing persons because his teacher was annoyed that his pupils sounded like animals when they laughed.

9. See Harlan Lane, *The Mask of Benevolence* for further discussion, especially p. 212–16. Lane is the first to use the work of Michel Foucault as it applies to deafness. As with Derrida, Foucault's work may be enormously beneficial to Deaf Studies, even though he overlooks the question of Deaf Culture. In fact, the discursive "birth of deafness" is so closely allied to the births of the asylum, the clinic and prisons, it is quite surprising to find no mention of deafness in Foucault. The same years that witnessed the rise of Pinel's asylums for the insane also witnessed Pinel's methods of observation and classification deployed by his student, Jean-Marc Itard, within the newly founded "Asylums for the Deaf and the Dumb"; when the medical gaze penetrated the surface of the body in the age of Bichat, otologists probed the workings of the ear; when *écoles normales* produced disciplinary pedagogies, "oralist" teachers (some of whom were also teachers at *écoles normales*) developed pedagogies

to discipline the deaf body into normative language practices. In short, the Asylum for the Deaf and Dumb served as a point of convergence of discourses which, as Foucault demonstrates, all work toward the same goal: to separate the normal from the abnormal, the hearing from the deaf, in order to normalize the transgressive Other, to eradicate all differences—while ironically exacerbating them, perpetuating the subjugation of the abnormal body.

10. The inability to define ASL literature is not unique to ASL; rather, I believe hearing literature itself cannot be defined with any consistency and accuracy. The term *define* originates from the Latin *definare,* meaning to limit; I believe that it is unwise to be overly concerned with limiting the boundaries of creative practices—whether Deaf or hearing.

11. As J. J. Pollitt notes, "[rhythmos] were originally the 'positions' that the human body was to assume in the course of a dance in other words the patterns or *schemata* that the body made. In the course of a dance certain obvious patterns or positions, like the raising or lowering of a foot, were naturally repeated, thus marking intervals in the dance. Since music and singing were synchronized with dancing, the recurrent positions taken by the dancer in the course of his movements also marked distinct intervals in the music….This explains why the basic component of music and poetry was called a…foot" (quoted in Mitchell 280–81).

12. Linguist William Stokoe describes the cinematic properties of ASL, a concept originally developed by Deaf artists Bernard Bragg and Gil Eastman: "In a signed language…narrative is no longer linear and prosaic. Instead, the essence of sign language is to cut from a normal view to a close-up to a distant shot to a close up again, and so on, even including flashback and flash-forward scenes, exactly as a movie editor works….Not only is signing itself arranged more like edited film than like written narration, but also each signer is placed very much as a camera: the field of vision and angle of view are directed but variable. Not only the signer signing but also the signer watching is aware at all times of the signer's visual orientation to what is being signed about" (quoted in Sacks, 90).

13. While this phenomenology of language could lead toward a type of logocentric self-presence, Merleau-Ponty recognizes the ambiguity of absence/presence which underlies all perception. "The perceived thing exists only insofar as I perceive it, and yet its being is never exhausted by the view I have of it. It is this simultaneous presence and absence that is required for 'something to be perceived at all'" (*Logos and Eidos: The Concept in Phenomenology,* 10). For this reason, Merleau-Ponty refers to the realm of language and the imaginary to be "quasi-present."

WORKS CITED

Artaud, Antonin. 1958. *The Theater and Its Double.* Trans. Mary Richards. New York: Grove Press.

ASL Literature Series. 1994. *Video with Ben Behan and Sam Supalla.* Pro. Joe Dannis. Dir. James. R. DeBee. San Diego: DawnSignPress.

Bachelard, Gaston. 1969. *The Poetics of Space.* Trans. Maria Jolas. Boston: Beacon Press.

Baynton, Douglas. 1992. "'Silent Exile on This Earth': The Metaphorical Construction of Deafness in the Nineteenth Century." *American Quarterly* 44.2: 216–43.

Cohn, Jim. 1986. "The New Deaf Poetics: Visible Poetry." *Sign Language Studies* 52: 263–77.

Derrida, Jacques. 1976. *Of Grammatology.* Trans. Gayatri Spivak. Baltimore: The Johns Hopkins Press.

Fanon, Frantz. 1968. *The Wretched of the Earth.* Trans. Constance Farrington. New York: Grove Press.

Fenollosa, Ernest. 1968. *The Chinese Written Character as a Medium for Poetry.* Ed. Ezra Pound. San Francisco: City Lights Books.

Graybill, Patrick. 1990. *Patrick Graybill.* Video. Series *Poetry in Motion: Original Works in ASL.* Burtonsville, MD: Sign Media.

Grigely, Joseph. 1993. "The Implosion of Iconicity." *Word and Image Interactions: A Selection of Papers Given at the Second International conference on Word and Image.* Ed. Martin Housser. Wiese Verlay Basel.

Higgins, Dick. 1987. *Pattern Poetry: Guide to an Unknown Literature.* Albany: SUNY Press.

Klima, Edward and Ursula Bellugi. 1983. "Poetry Without Sound." *Symposium of the Whole: A Range of Discourse Toward an Ethnopoetics.* Eds. Jerome and Diane Rothenberg. Berkeley: University of California Press.

Lane, Harlan. 1992. *The Mask of Benevolence.* New York: Alfred Knopf.

Lentz, Ella Mae. 1995. *The Treasure.* Video. In Berkeley, CA: Motion Press.

Lorde, Audre. 1984. "Learning From the 60s." *Sister Outsider.* Freedom, CA: The Crossing Press.

Merleau-Ponty. 1989. *The Phenomenology of Perception.* Trans. Colin Smith. London: Routledge.

———. "Eye and Mind." 1993. *The Merleau-Ponty Aesthetics Reader: Philosophy and Painting.* Ed. Galen Johnson. Evanston, Ill: Northwestern University Press.

Mitchell, W. J. T. 1989. "Gesture, Sign, and Play: ASL Poetry and Deaf Community." *MLA Newsletter.* Summer (1989): 13–14.

———. 1974, "Spatial Form in Literature: Toward a General Theory." *The Language of Images.* Ed. W. J. T. Mitchell. Chicago: University of Chicago Press.

Padden, Carol and Humphries, Tom. 1988. *Deaf in America: Voices from a Culture.* Cambridge: Harvard University Press.

Plato. 1937. *The Dialogues of Plato.* Vol. 2 Trans. Benjamin Jowett. New York: Random House.

Rennie, Debbie. 1990. *Debbie Rennie.* Video. Poetry in Motion: Original Works in ASL. Burtonsville, MD: Sign Media.

Ronell, Avital. 1989. *The Telephone Book: Technology—Schizophrenia—Electric Speech.* Lincoln: University of Nebraska Press.

Rose, Heidi. 1993. "A Critical Methodology for Analyzing American Sign Language Literature." Dissertation, Arizona State University.

———. 1992. "A Semiotic Analysis of Artistic American Sign Language and a Performance of Poetry." *Text and Performance Quarterly* 12.2: 146–59.

Rothenberg, Jerome and Rothenberg, Diane, eds. 1983. *Symposium of the Whole: A Range of Discourse Toward an Ethnopoetics.* Berkeley: University of California Press.

Sacks, Oliver. 1990. *Seeing Voices: A Journey into the World of the Deaf.* New York: HarperPerennial.

Said, Edward. 1994. *Culture and Imperialism.* New York: Vintage.

Trinh, Minh-ha. 1995. "No Master Territories." *The Post-Colonial Studies Reader.* Eds. Ashcroft, Bill, Griffiths, Gareth, Tiffin Helen. London: Routledge.

Valli, Clayton. 1995. *ASL Poetry: Selected Works of Clayton Valli.* Video. Pro. Joe Dannis. Dir. Clayton Valli. San Diego DawnSignPress,1995.

———.1990. *Clayton Valli.* Video. Series *Poetry in Motion: Original Works in ASL.* Burtonsville, MD: Sign Media.

———. 1990. "The Nature of the Line in ASL Poetry." *SLR'87 Papers from The Fourth International Symposium on Sign Language Research.* Eds. W.H. Edmondson and F. Karlsson. Hamburg: Signum Press.

THEORY OF MIND AND EXPERIMENTAL REPRESENTATIONS OF FICTIONAL CONSCIOUSNESS (2003)

LISA ZUNSHINE

Zunshine introduces the argument for interpreting the process of reading fiction in light of recent developments in cognitive science and the theory of mind, particularly studies of how people think that other people think. She sees the process of thinking about how people think as overlapping with what readers do as they read about fictional characters and seek out the pleasure of thinking about how characters think. For characters, as Zunshine notes, resemble people but are not people. She argues, therefore, that the literary study of reading fiction and the scientific study of how people think that other people think can illuminate each other. For an expanded version of Zunshine's argument, see many of her later publications, including Why We Read Fiction: Theory of Mind and the Novel *(2006).*

Let me begin with a seemingly nonsensical question. When Peter Walsh unexpectedly comes to see Clarissa Dalloway "at eleven o'clock on the morning of the day she [is] giving a party," and, "positively trembling," asks her how she is, "taking both her hands; kissing both her hands," thinking that "she's grown older," and deciding that he "shan't tell her anything about it...for she's grown older" (40), how do we know that his "trembling" is to be accounted for by his excitement at seeing his Clarissa again after all these years, and not, for instance, by his progressing Parkinson's disease?

Assuming that you are a particularly good-natured reader of *Mrs. Dalloway,* you could patiently explain to me that if Walsh's trembling were occasioned by an illness, Woolf would tell us so. She wouldn't leave us long under the impression that Walsh's body language betrays his agitation, his joy, and his embarrassment, and that the meeting has instantaneously and miraculously brought back the old days when Clarissa and Peter had "this queer power of communicating without words" because, reflecting Walsh's "trembling," Clarissa herself is "so surprised,...so glad, so shy, so utterly taken aback to have [him] come to her unexpectedly in the morning!" (40). Too much, you would point out, hinges on our getting the emotional undertones of the scene right for Woolf to withhold from us a crucial piece of information about Walsh's health.

I then would ask you why it is that were Walsh's trembling caused by an illness, Woolf would have to explicitly tell us so, but as it is not, she can simply take for granted that we will interpret it as being caused by his emotions. In other words, what allows Woolf to assume that we will automatically read a character's body language as indicative of his thoughts and feelings?

She assumes this because of our collective past history as readers, you perhaps would say. Writers have been using descriptions of their characters' behaviors to inform us about their feelings since time immemorial, and we expect authors to do so when we open the book. We all learn, whether consciously or not, that the default interpretation of behavior reflects the character's state of mind, and every fictional story that we read reinforces our tendency to make that kind of interpretation first.[1]

Had this imaginary conversation about readers' automatic assumptions taken place twenty years ago, it would have ended here. Or it would have never happened—not even in this hypothetical form—because the answers to my naïve questions would have seemed so obvious. Today, however, this conversation has to go on because recent research in cognitive psychology and anthropology has shown that not *every* reader can learn that the default meaning of a character's behavior lies with the character's mental state. To understand what enables most of us to constrain the range of possible interpretations, we may have to go beyond the explanation that evokes our personal reading histories and admit some evidence from our evolutionary history.

In what follows, then, I attempt to make a broader case for introducing the recent findings of cognitive scientists into literary studies by showing how their research into our ability to explain behavior in terms of the underlying states of mind—or our *mind-reading* ability—can furnish us with a series of surprising insights into our interaction with literary texts. I begin by discussing the research on autism that alerted cognitive psychologists to the existence of the cognitive capacity that enables us to narrow the range of interpretations of people's behavior down to their mental states, and that makes literature, as we know it, possible. I then consider the potentially controversial issue of the "effortlessness" with which we thus read other people's—including literary characters'—minds. To explore one specific aspect of the role played by such mind-reading in fictional representations of consciousness, I then return to *Mrs. Dalloway.* Here I describe a series of recent experiments exploring our capacity for imagining serially embedded representations of mental states (that is, "representations of representations of representations" of mental states)[2] and suggest that Woolf's prose pushes this particular capacity beyond its everyday "zone of comfort," a realization that may account partially for the trepidation that Woolf's writing tends to provoke in some of her readers. I conclude by addressing two issues concerning the interdisciplinary potential of the new field of cognitive approaches to literature. First, I discuss the relationship between cognitive analysis and the more traditional literary-historical analysis of Woolf. Second, I suggest that literary critics should take a more proactive stand toward cognitive scientists' increasing tendency to use literature in their study of human cognition.

I. THEORY OF MIND AND AUTISM

Mind-reading is a term used by cognitive psychologists to describe our ability to explain people's behavior in terms of their thoughts, feelings, beliefs, and desires; for example, "Lucy *reached* for the chocolate because she *wanted* something sweet," or "Peter Walsh was *trembling* because he was *excited* to see Clarissa again." They also call this ability our Theory of Mind (ToM), and I will use the two terms interchangeably throughout this essay.

This proliferation of fancy terminology adds extra urgency to the question of why we need this newfangled concept of mind-reading or ToM to explain what appears so obvious. Our ability to interpret the behavior of real-life people—*and, by extension,* of literary characters[3]—in terms of their underlying states of mind seems to be such an integral part of being human that we could be understandably reluctant to dignify it with a fancy term and elevate it into a separate object of study. Indeed, the main reason that ToM has received the sustained attention of cognitive psychologists over the last twenty years is that they had come across people whose ability to "see bodies as animated by minds" (Brook and Ross 81) was drastically impaired—people with autism. By studying autism and a related constellation of cognitive deficits (such as Asperger syndrome), cognitive scientists and philosophers of mind began to appreciate our mind-reading ability as a special cognitive endowment, structuring in suggestive ways our everyday communication and cultural representations.

Most scholars working with ToM agree that this adaptation must have developed during the "massive neurocognitive evolution" which took place during the Pleistocene, when our brain increased threefold in size. The determining factor behind the increase in brain size was the social nature of our species (which we share with other primates).[4] The emergence of a ToM "module" was evolution's answer to the "staggeringly complex" challenge faced by our ancestors, who needed to make sense of the behavior of other people in their group, which could include up to two hundred individuals. In his influential 1995 study, *Mindblindness: An Essay on Autism and a Theory of Mind*, Simon Baron-Cohen points out that "attributing mental states to a complex system (such as a human being) is by far the easiest way of understanding it," that is, of "coming up with an explanation of the complex system's behavior and predicting what it will do next" (21).[5] Thus our tendency to explain observed behavior in terms of underlying mental states seems to be so effortless and automatic because our evolved cognitive architecture "prods" us toward learning and practicing mind-reading daily, from the beginning of awareness. (This is not to say, however, that our actual interpretations of other people's mental states are always correct—far from it!)

Baron-Cohen describes autism as the "most severe of all childhood psychiatric conditions," one that affects between approximately four to fifteen children per ten thousand and that "occurs in every country in which it has been looked for and across social classes" (60). Although "mind-reading is not an all-or-none affair [since]….[p]eople with autism lack the ability to a greater or lesser degree" (Origgi and Sperber 163), and although the condition may be somewhat alleviated if the child receives a range of "educational and therapeutic interventions," autism presently remains "a lifelong disorder" (Baron-Cohen 60). Autism is highly heritable,[6] and its key symptoms, which manifest themselves in the first years of life, include the profound impairment of social and communicative development and the "lack of the usual flexibility, imagination, and pretence" (Baron-Cohen 60). It is also characterized—crucially for our present discussion—by a lack of interest in fiction and storytelling, differing in degree, though not in kind, across the wide spectrum of autism cases.

In his book *An Anthropologist on Mars*, Oliver Sacks describes one remarkable case of autism, remarkable because the afflicted woman, Temple Grandin, has been able to overcome her handicap to some degree. She has a doctorate in agricultural science, teaches at the University of Arizona, and can speak about her perceptions, thus giving us a unique insight into what it means not to be able to read other people's minds. Sacks reports Grandin's school experience: "Something was going on between the other kids, something swift, subtle, constantly changing—an exchange of meanings, a negotiation, a swiftness of understanding so remarkable that sometimes she wondered if they were all telepathic. She is now aware of the existence of those social signals. She can infer them, she says, but she herself cannot perceive them, cannot participate in this magical communication directly, or conceive of the many-leveled, kaleidoscopic states of mind behind it" (272).

Predictably, Grandin comments on having a difficult time understanding fictional narratives. She remembers being "bewildered by *Romeo and Juliet*: 'I never knew what they were up to'" (259). Fiction presents a challenge to people with autism because in many ways it calls for the same kind of mind-reading as is necessary in regular human communication—that is, the inference of the mental state from the behavior.

To compensate for her inability to interpret facial expressions, which at first left her a "target of tricks and exploitation," Grandin has built up over the years something resembling a "library of videotapes, which she could play in her mind and inspect at any time—'videos' of how people behaved in different circumstances. She would play these over and over again, and learn, by degrees, to correlate what she saw, so that she could then predict how people in similar circumstances might act" (259–60). This account of Grandin's "library" suggests that we do not just "learn" how to communicate with people and read their emotions (or how to read the minds of fictional characters based on their behavior)—Grandin, after all, has had as many opportunities to "learn" these things as you and me—but that we also have evolved cognitive architecture that makes this particular kind of learning possible. If this architecture is damaged, as in the case of autism, a wealth of experience would never fully make up for the damage.

Whereas the correlation between the impaired ToM and the lack of interest in fiction and storytelling is highly suggestive, the jury is still out on the exact nature of the connection between the two. It could be argued, for example, that the cognitive mechanisms that evolved to process information about human thoughts and feelings are constantly on the alert, checking out their environment for cues that fit their input conditions.[7] On some level, then, works of fiction manage to "cheat" these mechanisms into "believing" that they are in the presence of material that they were "designed" to process, i.e., that they are in the presence of agents endowed with a potential for a rich array of intentional stances. Literature pervasively capitalizes on and stimulates ToM mechanisms that evolved to deal with real people, even as readers remain aware on some level that fictive characters are not real people at all.[8]

Thus one preliminary implication of applying what we know about ToM to our study of fiction is that ToM makes literature as we know it possible. The very process of making sense of what we read appears to be grounded in our ability to invest the flimsy verbal constructions that we generously call "characters" with a potential for a variety of thoughts, feelings, and desires, and then to look for the "cues" that allow us to guess at their feelings and thus to predict their actions.[9] (The illusion is complete: like Erich Auerbach, we are convinced that "the people whose story the author is telling experience much more than [the author] can ever hope to tell" [549].)

II. "EFFORTLESS" MIND-READING

As we discuss mind-reading as an evolved cognitive capacity enabling both our interaction with each other and our ability to make sense of fiction, we have to be aware of the definitional differences between the terminology used by cognitive scientists and literary critics. Cognitive psychologists and philosophers of mind investigating our ToM ask such questions as: what is the evolutionary history of this adaptation, i.e., in response to what environmental challenges did it evolve? At what age and in what forms does it begin to manifest itself? What are its neurological foundations? They focus on the ways "in which mind-reading [plays] an essential part in *successful* communication" (Baron-Cohen 29 emphasis mine). When cognitive scientists turn to literary (or, as in the case below, cinematic) examples to illustrate our ability for investing fictional characters with minds of their own and reading those minds, they stress the "effortlessness" with which we do so. As Dennett observes, "watching a film with a highly original and unstereotyped plot, we see the hero smile at the villain and we all swiftly and effortlessly arrive at the same complex theoretical diagnosis: 'Aha!' we conclude (but perhaps not consciously), 'He wants her to think he doesn't know she intends to defraud her brother!' " (48).

Readers outside the cognitive science community may find this emphasis on "effortlessness" and "success" unhelpful. Literary critics, in particular, know that the process of attributing thoughts, beliefs, and desires to other people may lead to *misinterpreting* those thoughts, beliefs, and desires. Thus, they would rightly resist any notion that we could effortlessly—that is, correctly and unambiguously, nearly telepathically—figure out what the person whose behavior we are trying to explain is thinking. It is important to underscore here that cognitive scientists and lay readers (here including literary critics) bring very different frames of reference to measuring the relative "success" of mind-reading. For the lay reader, the example of a glaring failure in mind-reading and communication might be a person's interpreting her friend's tears of joy as tears of grief and reacting accordingly. For a cognitive psychologist, a glaring failure in mind-reading would be a person's not even knowing that the water coursing down her friend's face is supposed to be somehow indicative of his feelings at that moment. If you find the latter possibility absurd, recall that this is how (many) people with autism experience the world, perhaps because of neurological deficits that prevent their cognitive architecture from narrowing the range of interpretive possibilities and restricting them, in this particular case, to the domain of emotions.

Consequently, one of the crucial insights offered by cognitive psychologists is that by thus parsing the world and narrowing the scope of relevant interpretations of a given phenomenon, our cognitive adaptations enable us to contemplate an infinitely rich array of interpretations *within* that scope. As Nancy Easterlin puts it, "without the inborn tendency to organize information in specific ways, we would not be able to experience choice in our responses" ("Making Knowledge" 137).[10] "Constraints," N. Katherine Hayles observes in a different context, "operate constructively by restricting the sphere of possibilities" (145).[11] In other words, our ToM allows us to connect Peter Walsh's trembling to his emotional state (in the absence of any additional information that could account for his body language in a different way), thus usefully constraining our interpretive domain and enabling us to start considering endlessly nuanced choices *within that domain*. The context of the episode would then constrain our interpretation even further; we could decide, for instance, that it is unlikely that Peter is trembling because of a barely concealed hatred and begin to explore the complicated gamut of his bittersweet feelings. Any additional information that we would bring to bear upon our reading of the passage—biographical, sociohistorical, literary-historical—would alert us to new shades in its meaning, and could, in principle, lead us to some startling conjectures about Walsh's state of mind. Note too, that the description of Walsh's "trembling" may connect to something in my personal experience that will induce me to give significantly more weight to one detail of the text and to ignore others, which means that you and I may wind up with wildly different readings of Peter's and Clarissa's emotions "at eleven o'clock on the morning of the day she [is] giving a party." None of this can happen, however, before we have first eliminated a whole range of other explanations, such as explanations evoking various physical forces (for instance, a disease) acting upon the body, and have focused instead solely on the mind of the character.

This elimination of irrelevant interpretations can happen so fast as to be practically imperceptible. Consider an example from Stanley Fish's famous essay, "How to Recognize a Poem." To demonstrate his point that our mental operations are "limited by institutions in which we are already embedded," Fish reports the following classroom experiment:

> While I was in the course of vigorously making a point, one of my students, William Newlin by name, was just as vigorously waving his hand. When I asked the other members of the class what it was that [he] was doing, they all answered that he was seeking permission to speak. I then asked them how they knew that. The immediate reply was that it was obvious; what else could he be thought of doing? The meaning of his gesture, in other words, was right there on its surface, available for reading by anyone who had the eyes to see. That meaning, however, would not have been available to someone without any knowledge of what was involved in being a student. Such a person might have thought that Mr. Newlin was pointing to the fluorescent lights hanging from the ceiling, or calling our attention to some object that was about to fall ("the sky is falling," "the sky is falling"). And if the someone in question were a child of elementary or middle-school age, Mr. Newlin might well have been seen as seeking permission not to speak but to go to the bathroom, an interpretation or reading that would never have occurred to a student at Johns Hopkins or any other institution of "higher learning." (110–11)

Fish's point that "it is only by inhabiting…the institutions [that] precede us [here, the college setting] that we have access to the public and conventional senses they make [here, the raised hand means the person seeks permission to speak]" (110) is well taken. Yet note that all of his patently "wrong" explanations (e.g., Mr. Newlin thought that the sky was falling; he wanted to go to the bathroom, etc.) are "correct" in the sense that they call on a ToM; that is, they explain the student's behavior in terms of his underlying thoughts, beliefs, and desires. As Fish puts it, "what else could he be *thought* of doing?" (emphasis mine). Nobody ventured to suggest, for example, that there was a thin, practically invisible string threaded through the loop in the classroom's ceiling, one end of which was attached to Mr. Newlin's sleeve and another held by a person sitting behind him who could pull the string any time and produce the corresponding movement of Mr. Newlin's hand. Absurd, we should say, especially since nobody could observe any string hovering over Mr. Newlin's head. Is it not equally absurd, however, to explain a behavior in terms of a mental state that is completely unobservable? Yet we do it automatically, and the only reason that no "normal" (i.e., non-autistic) person would think of a "mechanistic" explanation (such as the string pulling on the sleeve) is that we have cognitive adaptations that prompt us to "see bodies as animated by minds."

But then, by the very logic of Fish's essay, which urges us not to take for granted our complex *institutional* embedment that allows us to make sense of the world, shouldn't we inquire with equal vigor into our *cognitive* embedment that—as I hope I have demonstrated in the example above—profoundly informs the institutional one? Given the suggestively constrained range of the "wrong" interpretations offered by Fish (that is, all his interpretations connect the behavior to a mental state), shouldn't we qualify his assertion that unless we read Mr. Newlin's raised hand in the context of his being a student, "there is nothing *in the form* of [his] gesture that tells his fellow students how to determine its significance" (112)? Surely the *form* of the gesture—staying with the word that Fish himself has emphasized—is quite informative because its very deliberateness seems to delimit the range of possible "wrong" interpretations. That is, had Mr. Newlin unexpectedly jerked his hand instead of "waving" it "vigorously," some mechanical explanation such as a physiological spasm or someone pushing his elbow, perhaps even a wire attached to his sleeve, would seem far less absurd.

To return, then, to the potentially problematic issue of the effortlessness with which we "read" minds: a flagrantly "wrong," from lay readers' perspective, interpretation, such as taking tears of grief for tears of joy or thinking that Mr. Newlin raises his hand to point out that the sky is falling, is still "effortless" from the point of view of cognitive psychologists because of the ease with which we correlate tears with an emotional state or the raised hand with a certain underlying desire/intention. Mind-reading is thus effortless in the sense that we "intuitively" connect people's behavior to their mental states—as in the example involving Walsh's "trembling"—although our subsequent description of their mental states could run a broad gamut of mistaken or disputed meanings. For any description is, as Fish reminds us on a different occasion, "always and already interpretation," a "text," a story reflecting the personal history, biases, and desires of the reader.[12]

III. CAN COGNITIVE SCIENCE TELL US WHY WE ARE AFRAID OF *MRS. DALLOWAY?*

How much prompting do we need to begin to attribute a mind of her own to a fictional character? Very little, it seems, since any indication that we are dealing with a self-propelled entity (e.g., "Peter Walsh has come back") leads us to assume that this entity possesses thoughts, feelings, and desires, at least some of which we could intuit, interpret, and, frequently, misinterpret. Writers exploit our constant readiness to posit a mind whenever we observe behavior when they experiment with the amount and kind of interpretation of the characters' mental states that they supply themselves and that they expect their readers to supply. When Woolf shows Clarissa observing Peter's body language (Clarissa notices that he is "positively trembling"), she has an option of providing us with a representation of either Clarissa's mind that would make sense of Peter's physical action (something to the effect of "how excited must he be to see her again!") or of Peter's own mind (as in "so excited was he to see his Clarissa again!"). Instead she tells us, first, that Peter is thinking that Clarissa has grown older and, second, that Clarissa is thinking that Peter looks "exactly the same;…the same queer look; the same check suit" (40). Peter's "trembling" still feels like an integral part of this scene, but make no mistake: we, the readers, are called on to supply the missing bit of information (such as "he must be excited to see her again") that makes the narrative emotionally cohesive.

Hemingway famously made it his trademark to underrepresent his protagonists' feelings by forcing the majority of his characters' physical actions to stand in for mental states (for example, as in the ending of *A Farewell to Arms:* "After a while I went out and left the hospital and walked back to the hotel in the rain" [314]). Hemingway could afford such a deliberate, and in its own way highly elaborate, undertelling for the same reason that Woolf could afford to let Peter's trembling "speak for itself": our evolved cognitive tendency to assume that there *must be* a mental stance behind each physical action and our striving to represent to ourselves that possible mental stance even when the author has left us with the absolute minimum of necessary cues for constructing such a representation.

It is thus when we start to inquire into how writers of fiction *experiment* with our mind-reading ability, and perhaps even push it further, that the insights offered by cognitive scientists become particularly pertinent. Although cognitive scientists' investigation of ToM is very much a project-in-progress, literary scholars have enough carefully documented research already available to them to begin asking such questions as: is it possible that literary narrative trains our capacity for mind-reading and also tests its limits? How do different cultural-historical milieus encourage different literary explorations of this capacity? How do different genres? Speculative and tentative as the answers to these questions could only be at this point, they mark the possibility of a genuine interaction between cognitive psychology and literary studies, with both fields having much to offer to each other.

This section's tongue-in-cheek title refers to my attempt to apply a series of recent experiments conducted by cognitive psychologists studying ToM to *Mrs. Dalloway.* I find the results of such an application both exciting and unnerving. On the one hand, I can argue now with a reasonable degree of confidence that certain aspects of Woolf's prose do place extraordinarily high demands on our mind-reading ability and that this could account, *at least in part,* for the fact that many readers feel challenged by that novel. On the other hand, I have come to be "afraid" of *Mrs. Dalloway*—and, indeed, other novels—in a different fashion, realizing that any initial inquiry into the ways fiction teases our ToM immediately raises more questions about ToM and fiction than we are currently able to answer. My ambivalence, in other words, stems from the realization that ToM underlies our interaction with literary texts in such profound and complex ways that any endeavor to isolate one particular aspect of such an interaction feels like carving the text at joints that are fundamentally, paradigmatically absent.

This proviso should be kept in mind as we turn to the experiments investigating one particular aspect of ToM, namely, our ability to navigate multiple levels of intentionality present in a narrative. Although ToM is formally defined as a second-order intentionality, as in the statements "I believe that you desire X" or "Peter Walsh thinks that Clarissa 'would think [him] a failure'" (43), the levels of intentionality can "recurse" further back, for example, to the fourth level, as in a statement like "I believe that you think that she believes that he thinks that X." Dennett, who first discussed this recursiveness of the levels of intentionality in 1983, thought it could be, in principle, infinite. A recent series of striking experiments reported by Robin Dunbar and his colleagues have suggested, however, that our cognitive architecture may discourage the proliferation of cultural narratives that involve "infinite" levels of intentionality.

In those experiments, subjects were given two types of stories—one that involved a "simple account of a sequence of events in which 'A gave rise to B, which resulted in C, which in turn caused D, etc.'" and another that introduced "short vignettes on everyday experiences (someone wanting to date another person, someone wanting to persuade her boss to award a pay rise),…[all of which] contained between three and five levels of embedded intentionality." Subjects were then asked to complete a "series of questions graded by the levels of intentionality present in the story," including some factual questions "designed to check that any failures of intentionality questions were not simply due to failure to remember the material facts of the story." The results of the study were revealing: "Subjects had little problem with the factual causal reasoning story: error rates were approximately 5% across six levels of causal sequencing. Error rates on the mind-reading tasks were similar (5–10%) up to and including fourth-level intentionality, but rose dramatically to nearly 60% on fifth-order tasks." Cognitive scientists knew that this "failure on the mind-reading tasks [was] not simply a consequence of forgetting what happened, because subjects performed well on the memory-for-facts tasks embedded into the mind-reading questions" (Dunbar 241). The results thus suggest that people have marked difficulties processing stories that involve mind-reading above the fourth level.

An important point that should not be lost in the discussion of these experiments is that it is the *content* of the information in question that makes the navigation of multiply-embedded data either relatively easy or difficult. Cognitive evolutionary psychologists suggest the following reason for the relative ease with which we can process long sequences such as "A gave rise to B, which resulted in C, which in turn caused D, which led to E, which made possible F, which eventually brought about G, etc.," as opposed to similarly long sequences that require attribution of states of mind, such as "A wants B to believe that C thinks that D wanted E to consider F's feelings about G." It is likely that cognitive adaptations that underwrite the attribution of states of mind differ in functionally important ways from the adaptations that underwrite reasoning that does not involve such an attribution, a difference possibly predicated on the respective evolutionary histories of both types of adaptations.[13] A representation of a mind as represented by a mind as represented by yet another mind will thus be supported by cognitive processes distinct (to a degree which remains a subject of debate) from cognitive processes supporting a mental representation, for example, of events related to each other as a series of causes and effects or of a representation of a Russian doll nested within another doll nested within another doll. The cognitive process of representing depends crucially on *what* is being represented.

Consider now a randomly selected passage roughly halfway into Woolf's *Mrs. Dalloway*, in which Richard Dalloway and Hugh Whitbread come to Lady Bruton to write a letter to the *Times*, and in which, to understand what is going on, we have to confront a series of multiply embedded states of mind:

> And Miss Brush went out, came back; laid papers on the table; and Hugh produced his fountain pen; his silver fountain pen, which had done twenty years' service, he said, unscrewing the cap. It was still in perfect order; he had shown it to the makers; there was no reason, they said, why it should ever wear out; which was somehow to Hugh's credit, and to the credit of the sentiments which his pen expressed (so Richard Dalloway felt) as Hugh began carefully writing capital letters with rings round them in the margin, and thus marvelously reduced Lady Bruton's tangles to sense, to grammar such as the editor of the *Times*, Lady Bruton felt, watching the marvelous transformation, must respect. (110)

What is going on in this passage? We are seemingly invited to deduce the excellence of Millicent Bruton's civic ideas—put on paper by Hugh—first from the resilience of the pen that he uses, and then from the beauty of his "capital letters with rings around them on the margins." Of course, this reduction of lofty sentiments and superior analytic skills to mere artifacts, such as writing utensils and calligraphy, achieves just the opposite effect. By the end of the paragraph, we are ready to accept Richard Dalloway's view of the resulting epistle as "all stuffing and bunkum," but a harmless bunkum at that. Its inoffensiveness and futility are underscored by the tongue-in-cheek phallic description of the silver pen (should "silver" bring to our mind "gray"?) that has served Hugh for twenty years but that is still "in perfect order"—or so Hugh thinks—once he's done "unscrewing the cap."

There are several ways to map this passage out in terms of the nested levels of intentionality. I will start by listing the smallest irreducible units of embedded intentionally and gradually move up to those that capture as much of the whole narrative gestalt of the described scene as possible:

1. The makers of the pen *think* that it will never wear out. (First level)
2. Hugh *says* that the makers of the pen *think* it will never wear out. (Second level)
3. Lady Bruton *wants* the editor of the *Times* to *respect* and publish her ideas. (Second level)
4. Hugh *wants* Lady Bruton and Richard to *believe* that because the makers of the pen *think* that it will never wear out, the editor of the *Times* will *respect* and publish the ideas recorded by this pen. (Fourth level)
5. Richard *is aware* that Hugh *wants* Lady Bruton and Richard Dalloway to *believe* that because the makers of the pen *think* that it will never wear out, the editor of the *Times* will *respect* and publish the ideas recorded by this pen. (Fifth level)
6. Richard *suspects* that Lady Bruton indeed *believes* that because, as Hugh *says*, the makers of the pen *think* that it will never wear out, the editor of the *Times* will *respect* and publish the ideas recorded by this pen. (Fifth level)
7. By inserting a parenthetical observation ("so Richard Dalloway felt"), Woolf *intends us to recognize* that Richard *is aware* that Hugh *wants* Lady Bruton and Richard to *think* that because the makers of the pen *believe* that it will never wear out, the editor of the *Times* will *respect* and publish the ideas recorded by this pen. (Sixth level)

It could be argued, of course, that in the process of reading we automatically cut through Woolf's stylistic pyrotechnics to come up with a series of more comprehensible, first-, second-, and third-level attributions of states of mind, such as "Richard does not particularly like Hugh"; "Lady Bruton thinks that Hugh is writing a marvelous letter"; "Richard feels that Lady Bruton thinks that Hugh is writing a marvelous letter, but he is skeptical about the whole enterprise"; and so on. Such abbreviated attributions may seem destructive since the effect that they have on Woolf's prose is equivalent to the effect of paraphrasing on poetry, but they do, in fact, convey some general sense of what is going on in the paragraph. The main problem with them, however, is that to arrive at such simplified descriptions of Richard's and Lady Bruton's states of mind, we have to grasp the full meaning of this passage, and to do that, we first have to process several sequences that embed at least five levels of intentionality. Moreover, we have to do it on the spot, unaided by pen and paper and not forewarned that the number of levels of intentionality that we are about to encounter is considered by cognitive scientists to create "a very significant load on most people's cognitive abilities" (Dunbar 240).

Note that in this particular passage, Woolf not only "demands" that we process a string of fifth- and sixth-level intentionalities but she also introduces such embedded intentionalities through descriptions of body language that in some ways approach those of Hemingway in their emotional blandness. No more telling "trembling," as in the earlier scene featuring Peter and Clarissa. Instead, we get Richard watching Lady Bruton watching Hugh producing his pen, unscrewing the cap, and beginning to write. True, Woolf offers us two emotionally colored words ("carefully" and "marvelously"), but what they signal is that Hugh cares a great deal about his writing and that Lady Bruton admires the letter that he produces—two snapshots of the states of mind that only skim the surface of the complex affective undertow of this episode.

Because Woolf has depicted physical actions relatively lacking in immediate emotional content, here, in striking contrast to the scene in Clarissa's drawing-room, she hastens to provide an authoritative interpretation of each character's mental state. We are told what Lady Bruton feels as she watches Hugh (she feels that the editor of the *Times* will respect so beautifully written a letter); we are told what Hugh thinks as he unscrews the cap (he thinks that the pen will never wear out and that its longevity contributes to the worth of the sentiments it produces); we are told what Richard feels as he watches Hugh, his capital letters, and Lady Bruton (he is amused both by Hugh's exalted view of himself and by Lady Bruton's readiness to take Hugh's self-importance at its face value). The apparently unswerving linear hierarchy of the scene—Richard can represent the minds of both Hugh and Lady Bruton, but Hugh and Lady Bruton cannot represent Richard's representations of their minds—seems to enforce the impression that each mind is represented fully and correctly.

Of course, Woolf is able to imply that her representations of Hugh's, Lady Bruton's, and Richard's minds are exhaustive and correct because, creatures with a ToM that we are, we *just know* that there *must be* mental states behind the emotionally opaque body language of the protagonists. The paucity of textual cues that could allow us to imagine those mental states ourselves leaves us no choice but to accept the representations provided by the author. We have to work hard for them, of course, for sifting through all those levels of embedded intentionality tends to push the boundaries of our mind-reading ability to its furthest limits.

When we try to articulate our perception of the cognitive challenge induced by this task of processing fifth- and sixth-level intentionality, we may say that Woolf's writing is difficult or even refuse to continue reading her novels. The personal aesthetics of individual readers thus could be grounded *at least in part* in the nuances of their individual mind-reading capacities. By saying this I do not mean to imply that if somebody "loves" or "hates" Woolf, it should tell us something about that person's general mind-reading "sophistication"—a cognitive literary analysis does not support such misguided value judgments. The nuances of each person's mind-reading profile are unique to that person, just as, for example, we all have the capacity for developing memories (unless that capacity has been clinically impaired), but each individual's actual memories are unique. My combination of memories serves me, and it would be meaningless to claim that it somehow serves me "better" than my friend's combination of memories serves her. At the same time, I see no particular value in celebrating the person's dislike of Woolf as the manifestation of his or her individual cognitive make-up. My teaching experience has shown that if we alert our students to the fact that Woolf tends to play this particular kind of cognitive "mind game" with her readers, it significantly eases their anxiety about "not getting" her prose and actually helps them to start enjoying her style.[14]

IV. COGNITIVE LITERARY ANALYSIS OF *MRS. DALLOWAY*

It is now time to return to the imaginary conversation that opened my essay. Some versions of that exchange did take place at several scholarly forums where I have presented my research on ToM and literature. Once, for instance, after I described the immediate pedagogical payoffs of counting the levels of intentionality in *Mrs. Dalloway* with my undergraduates, I was asked if I could foresee the time when such a cognitive reading would supersede and render redundant the majority of other, more traditional approaches to Woolf.[15] My immediate answer was, and still remains, an unqualified no, but since then I have had the opportunity to consider several of that question's implications that are important for those of us wishing cognitive approaches to literature to thrive.

First of all, counting the levels of intentionality in *Mrs. Dalloway* does not constitute *the* cognitive approach to Woolf. It merely begins to explore one particular way—among numerous others—in which Woolf builds on and experiments with our ToM, and—to cast the net broader—in which fiction builds on and experiments with our cognitive propensities.[16] Many of these propensities, I feel safe saying in spite of remarkable advances in the cognitive sciences during the last two decades, still remain unknown to us.

However, the current state of cognitive approaches to literature already testifies to the spectacular diversity of venues offered by the parent fields of cognitive neuroscience, artificial intelligence, philosophy of mind, cognitive linguistics, evolutionary biology, cognitive psychology, and cognitive anthropology. Literary critics have begun to investigate the ways in which recent research in these areas opens new avenues in gender studies (F. Elizabeth Hart); feminism (Elizabeth Grosz); cultural materialism (Mary Thomas Crane, Alan Richardson); deconstruction (Ellen Spolsky); literary aesthetics (Elaine Scarry, Gabrielle Starr); history of moral philosophy (Blakey Vermeule); ecocriticism (Nancy Easterlin); and narrative theory (Porter Abbott, David Herman, Paul Hernadi). What these scholars' publications show is that far from displacing the traditional approaches or rendering them redundant, a cognitive approach ensures their viability as it builds on, strengthens, and develops their insights.

Second, the ongoing dialogue with, for instance, cultural historicism or feminism is not simply a matter of choice for scholars of literature interested in cognitive approaches. There is no such thing as a cognitive ability, such as ToM, free-floating "out there" in isolation from its human embodiment and its historically and culturally concrete expression. Evolved cognitive predispositions, to borrow Patrick Colm Hogan's characterization of literary universals, "are instantiated variously, particularized in specific circumstances" (226).[17] *Everything* that we learn about Woolf's life and about the literary, cultural, and sociohistorical contexts of *Mrs. Dalloway* is thus potentially crucial for understanding why this particular woman, at this particular historical juncture, seeing herself as working both within and against a particular set of literary traditions, began to push beyond the boundaries of her readers' cognitive "zone of comfort" (that is, beyond the fourth level of intentionality).

At the same time, to paraphrase David Herman ("Regrounding"), the particular combination of these personal, literary, and historical contexts, in all their untold complexity, is a "necessary though not a sufficient condition" for understanding why Woolf wrote the way she did. No matter how much we learn about the writer herself and her multiple environments, and no matter how much we find out about the cognitive endowments of our species that, "particularized in specific circumstances," make fictional narratives possible, we can only go so far in our cause-and-effect analysis. As George Butte puts it, "accounts of material circumstances can describe changes in gender systems and economic privileges, but they cannot explain why *this* bankrupt merchant wrote *Moll Flanders*, or why *this* genteely-impoverished clergyman's daughter wrote *Jane Eyre*." There will always remain a gap between our ever-increasing store of knowledge and the phenomenon of Woolf's prose—or, for that matter, Defoe's, Austen's, Brontë's, and Hemingway's prose.

Yet to consider just one example of how crucial our "other" knowledges are for our cognitive inquiry into *Mrs. Dalloway*, let us situate Woolf's experimentation with multiple levels of intentionality within the history of the evolution of the means of textual reproduction. It appears that a written culture is, on the whole, more able than an oral culture to support elaborately nested intentionality simply because a paragraph with six levels of intentional embedment does not yield itself easily to memorization and subsequent oral transmission. It is thus highly unlikely that we would find many (or any) passages that require us to go beyond the fourth level of intentionality in oral epics such as *Gilgamesh* or *The Iliad*. Walter Benjamin captures the broad point of this difference when he observes that the "listener's naïve relationship to the storyteller is controlled by his interest in retaining what he is told. The cardinal point for the unaffected listener is to assure himself of the possibility of reproducing the story" (97). The availability of the means of written transmission, such as print, enables the writer "to carry the incommensurable to extremes in representations of human life,"[18] and by so doing, to explore (or shall we actually say "develop," thus drawing upon Paul Hernadi's recent argument about the evolutionary origins of literature?)[19] the hitherto quiescent cognitive spaces.

Of course, for a variety of aesthetic, personal, and financial reasons, not every author writing under the conditions of print will venture into such cognitive unknown. Even a cursory look through the best-selling mainstream fiction, from Belva Plain to Danielle Steel, confirms the continuous broad popular appeal of narratives dwelling under the fourth level of intentional embedment. It is, then, the personal histories of individuals (here, individual writers and their audiences) that insure that, as Alan Richardson and Francis Steen observe, the history of cognitive structures "is neither identical to nor separate from the culture they make possible" (3).

In the case of Woolf, scholars agree that severing ties with the Duckworth—the press that had brought forth her first two novels and was geared toward an audience that was "Victorian, conventional, anti-experimentation" (*Diary* 1:261)—"liberated [her] experimentalism" (Whitworth 150). Having her own publishing house, the Hogarth Press, meant that she was "able to do what" she "like[d]—no editors, or publishers, and only people to read who more or less like that sort of thing" (*Letters* 167). Another factor possibly informing the cognitive extremes of *Mrs. Dalloway* was Woolf's acute awareness of the passing of time: "my theory is that at 40 one either increases the pace or slows down" (*Diary* 2:259). Woolf wanted to *increase* the pace of her explorations, to be able to "embody, at last," as she would write several years later, "the exact shapes my brain holds" (*Diary* 4:53). Having struggled in her previous novels with the narrator "chocked with observations" (*Jacob's Room* 67), she discovered in the process of working on *Mrs. Dalloway* how to "dig out beautiful caves behind [her] characters;…The idea is that the caves shall connect, and each comes to daylight at the present moment" (*Diary* 2:263). Embodying the "exact shapes" of Woolf's brain thus meant, among other things, shifting "the focus from the mind of the narrator to the minds of the characters" and "from the external world to the minds of the characters perceiving it" (Dick 51, 52), a technique that would eventually prompt Auerbach to inquire in exasperation, "Who is speaking in this paragraph?" (531).[20]

Woolf's meditations on her writing remind us of yet another reason that simply counting levels of intentionality in *Mrs. Dalloway* will never supersede other forms of critical inquiry into the novel. When Woolf explains that she wants to construct a "present moment" as a delicate "connection" among the "caves" dug behind each character, the emerging image overlaps suggestively with Dennett's image of the infinitely recursive levels of intentionality. ("Aha," concludes the delighted cognitive literary critic. "Woolf had some sort of proto-theory of recursive mind-reading!") But with her vivid description of the catacomb-like subjectivity of the shared present moment,[21] Woolf also manages to do something else—and that "something else" proceeds to quietly burrow into our (and her) cognitive theorizing.

This brings us to a seemingly counterintuitive but important point underlying cognitive literary analysis. Even as I map the passage featuring Richard Dalloway and Hugh Whitbread at Lady Bruton's as a linear series of embedded intentionalities, I expect that something else present in that passage will complicate that linearity and re-pose Auerbach's question, albeit with a difference. Will it be the phallic overtones of the description of Hugh's pen? Or the intrusion of rhetoric of economic exchange—"credit," "makers," "produce," "capital," "margin"? Or the vexed gender contexts of the "ventriloquism" implied by the image of Millicent Bruton spouting political platitudes in Hugh's voice?[22] Or the equally vexed social class contexts of the "seating arrangements" that hierarchize the mind-reading that goes on in the passage? (After all, Woolf must have "seated" Lady Bruton's secretary, Miss Brush, too far from the desk to be able to see the shape of Hugh's letters so as not to add yet another level of mental embedment by having Miss Brush watch Richard watching Lady Bruton watching Hugh.) Cognitive *literary* analysis thus continues beyond the line drawn by cognitive scientists—with the reintroduction of something else, a "noise," if you will, that is usually carefully controlled for and excised, whenever possible, from the laboratory settings.

V. WOOLF, PINKER, AND THE PROJECT OF INTERDISCIPLINARITY

Woolf's prose, fundamentally rooted in and tirelessly stimulating our cognitive capacities, represents such a tantalizing subject for a cognitive literary analysis that one is startled to learn that a cognitive scientist has recently characterized Woolf as having inaugurated an aesthetic movement whose "philosophy did not acknowledge the ways in which it was appealing to human pleasure" (Pinker 413). Although Steven Pinker admits that "modernism comprises many styles and artists,...not [all of which] rejected beauty and other human sensibilities" and that modernist "fiction and poetry offered invigorating intellectual workouts" (404), here is what he has to say about modernism as a whole and Woolf in particular:

> The giveaway [explanation for the current crisis in the arts and humanities] may be found in a famous statement from Virginia Woolf: "[On] or about December 1910, human [character] changed." She was referring to the new philosophy of modernism that would dominate the elite arts and criticism for much of the twentieth century, and whose denial of human nature was carried over with a vengeance to postmodernism, which seized control in its later decades....Modernism certainly proeeeded *as if* human nature had changed. All the tricks that artists had used for millennia to please the human palate were cast aside.... In literature, omniscient narration, structured plots, the orderly introduction of characters, and general readability were replaced by a stream of consciousness, events presented out of order, baffling characters and causal sequences, subjective and disjointed narration, and difficult prose. (409–10)[23]

As literary critics, we have several ways of responding to Pinker's claims about Woolf. We can hope that not "many students, teachers, theorists, and critics of literature will take [him] seriously as an authority on literature or the aesthetics more generally, especially since he misrepresents both Woolf and modernism."[24] At first sight, this is a comfortable stance. It assumes a certain cultural detachment of literary studies and implies that cognitive scientists should just leave literature alone, acknowledging it as an exclusive playing field for properly trained professionals—us. The problem with this view is that it disregards two facts: first, that more people read Pinker (who "misrepresents" Woolf) rather than, say, *PMLA* (which could set the matter straight), and, second, that as a very special, richly concentrated cognitive artifact, literature already is fair game for scientists, including Pinker, Daniel Dennett, Paul Harris, Robin Dunbar, and others, and it will become even more so as cognitive inquiry spreads further across cultural domains.

I suggest that instead of simply ignoring Pinker's assertion that the modernist writers' generally "difficult" prose cannot, by and large, "please the human palate," we should engage his argument, incorporating both the insights from our own field and those offered by cognitive scientists. By taking seriously the idea that our cognitive evolutionary heritage structures the ways in which we make sense of fictional narrative, we can gain a better understanding of why and how different "human palates" in different historical milieus can be "pleased" by quite different literary fare. Furthermore, we can show that it is by paying attention to the elite, to the exceptional, to the cognitively challenging, such as Woolf's experimentation with the levels of intentional embedment, that we can develop, for instance, a more sophisticated perspective on the workings of our ToM. As James Phelan observes, would not Pinker himself and "those in his audience who view modernist literature as he does be more likely to be persuaded to change their dismissive view of it, if literary critics show that [Woolf's] representations of consciousness, though initially challenging to a reader, are highly intelligible because they capture in their own ways insights that Pinker and other cognitive scientists have been offering (and popularizing)?"[25] And what exactly are the epistemological and ethical grounds on which we stand when we mock Pinker's claim to being an "authority on literature" if we have not yet made this kind of good-faith effort to meet Pinker halfway and offer our literary-historical expertise to develop a more sophisticated cognitive perspective on modernist representations of fictional consciousness?

Consider again the above-discussed insights of Robin Dunbar and his colleagues. As I hope to have demonstrated in this essay, Dunbar's research into our processing of stories that involve mind-reading above the fourth level can have far-reaching consequences for literary analysis. Yet there is no reason why, based on our knowledge of literary history, we should not ask him to qualify some of his arguments (and, indeed, would not Dunbar himself appreciate precisely this kind of response?), even if at this point, given how new the whole field is, we may have to settle for less-than-definitive answers to our criticism.

For example, Dunbar offers a fascinating speculation about the significance of his findings for our understanding of why there are generally more good readers than good writers:

> The fact that people seem to experience considerable difficulty with fifth-order intentional statements, but not fourth-order ones, may explain why writing fiction is much harder than reading it, and may thus in part explain why good writers are [much] less common than good readers....A novelist writing about relationship between three people has to "*intend* that the reader *think* that character A *supposes* that character B *wants* character C to *believe* that..."—five orders of intentionality. The reader, in contrast, has a much easier task: he or she merely has to "*think* that A *supposes* that B *wants* C to *believe* that..."—four orders of intentionality. (241)

Dunbar's argument has interesting implications for our theorizing the figure of the unreliable narrator as well as the relationship between the author and the narrator. For instance, our frequently ambivalent reaction to a suddenly perceived split of the narratorial presence—we may react to it by feeling excited, intrigued, and yet unsettled—could be related, among other things, to our semiconscious realization that we must factor in yet another level of intentionality, thus adding to the cognitive challenge already presented by the text.

At the same time, as Phelan notes, Dunbar's speculation that the difficulty that we have with processing fifth-order intentional statements may provide insight into why good writers are less common than good readers is "unpersuasive" because it "would predict that until we get to fictions with five or more levels of intentionality"—which happened relatively recently in our literary history and was predicated on, among other things, the evolution of the means of textual reproduction—"the number of good writers and good readers should be approximately the same." Since the latter is clearly not the case, and since the marked paucity of literary texts going beyond the fourth level of embedded intentionality, say, in the Middle Ages, would not lead us to assume that the number of good writers and good readers in that period was approximately the same, Dunbar may want to consider how this historical dimension complicates his provocative argument.

These examples support my claim that there is now the possibility of a genuine interaction between cognitive science and literary studies, one that does not just pay obligatory lip service to interdisciplinarity while quietly assuming the superiority of science. Paradoxically, it is only while we refuse to "take seriously" the research of cognitive scientists who dare to pronounce "on literature or…aesthetics more generally," that we can be made to feel that our contribution to this interdisciplinary exchange would represent little or nothing of value. Once we enter the conversation and engage with respect the arguments of Dunbar, Pinker, Dennett, and others, we realize that because of their ever-increasing—and well-warranted—interest in how the human mind processes literary narratives, our expertise could make a crucial difference for the future shape of the whole field of cognitive science.

NOTES

1. Like Hermione Lee, we could ground it in Woolf's position as a "pioneer of reader-response theory." Woolf, she writes, "was extremely interested in the two-way dialogue between readers and writers. Books change their readers; they teach you how to read them. But readers also change books. 'Undoubtedly,' Woolf herself had written, 'all writers are immensely influenced by the people who read them'" ("Virginia Woolf's Essays" 91).
2. For a related analysis of "representations of representations" or "metarepresentations," see Zunshine, "Eighteenth-Century Print Culture."
3. An important tenet of a cognitive approach to literature is that, as Paul Hernadi puts it, "there is no clear division between literary and nonliterary signification.…Literary experience is not triggered in a cognitive or emotive vacuum: modern readers, listeners, and spectators mentally process the virtual comings and goings of imagined characters as if they were analogous to remembered actual events" (60, 62). For a related discussion, see Mark Turner, *The Literary Mind.*
4. On the social intelligence of nonhuman primates, see Byrne and Whiten, *Machiavellian Intelligence* and "The Emergence of Metarepresentation"; Gomez, "Visual Behavior"; Premack and Dasser, "Perceptual Origins."
5. For a discussion of alternatives to the Theory of Mind approach, see Dennett, *The Intentional Stance.*
6. Leo Kanner first described autism in 1943. For more than twenty years after that, autism was "mistakenly thought to be caused by a cold family environment." In 1977, however, "a landmark

twin study showed that the incidence of autism is strongly influenced by genetic factors," and, since then, "numerous other investigations have since confirmed that autism is a highly heritable disorder" (Hughes and Plomin 48). For the "pre-history" of the term autism, particularly as introduced by Eugen Bleuler in 1911 and developed by Piaget in 1923, see Harris 3.

7. By using the word "mechanism," I am not trying to smuggle the outdated "body as a machine" metaphor into literary studies. Tainted as this word is by its previous history, it can still function as a convenient shorthand designation for extremely complex cognitive processes.

8. For a discussion, see Leslie 120–25; Carruthers, "Autism as Mind-Blindness" 262–63; Hernadi 58; and Spolsky, "Why and How."

9. The scale of such investment emerges as truly staggering if we attempt to spell out the host of unspoken assumptions that make it possible (for a discussion, see Zunshine, "Richardson's *Clarissa*"). This realization lends new support to what theorists of narrative view as the essential underdetermination or "undertelling" of fiction, its "interior nonrepresentation" (Sternberg 119).

10. For a qualification of the term "inborn" in relation to the processing of incoming data, see Spolsky, *Satisfying Skepticism* 164.

11. For an important recent discussion of "constraints," see Spolsky, "Cognitive Literary Historicism."

12. For a discussion, see Fish, *Is There a Text in this Class?*

13. For a discussion, see Carey and Spelke and Cosmides and Tooby on domain specificity. For a recent application of the theory of domain specificity to the study of literature, see Zunshine, "Rhetoric, Cognition, and Ideology."

14. Thus bringing the findings of cognitive scientists to bear upon the literary text does not diminish its aesthetic value. As Scarry has argued in response to the fear that science would "unweave the rainbow" of artistic creation, "the fact of the matter is that when we actually look at the nature of artistic creation and composition, understanding it does not mean doing it less well. To become a dancer, for example, one must do the small steps again and again and understand them, if one is to achieve virtuosity. Right now we need virtuosity, not only within each discipline, but across the disciplines as well" ("Panel Discussion" 253).

15. For a discussion, see Easterlin, "Voyages in the Verbal Universe."

16. As a friend working with cognitive/evolutionary approaches to fiction observed recently, "literature-fiction-writing is so powerful because it eats theories for breakfast, including cognitive/evolutionary approaches" (Blakey Vermeule, personal communication, 20 November 2002).

17. For a discussion of embodied cognition, see also Hart.

18. For a related discussion, see Hogan 242–43.

19. Hernadi argues that "literature, whether encountered in live performance or in textual and electronic recording, can challenge and thus enhance our brains' vital capacities for expression, communication, representation, and signification." He further connects the fictional text's capacity for developing our minds to the evolutionary history of the literary endeavor. He points our that, "the protoliterary experiences of some early humans could, other things being equal, enable them to outdo their less imaginative rivals in the biological competition for becoming the ancestors of later men and women" (56).

20. Strictly speaking, Auerbach's question refers to *To the Lighthouse,* but it is equally pertinent for our discussion of *Mrs. Dalloway.*

21. A remarkable new study by George Butte, *I Know That You Know That I Know: Narrating Subjects from* Moll Flanders *to* Marnie, offers a fascinating perspective on a writer's interest in constructing a "present moment" as a delicate "connection" among the characters' subjectivities. Applying Maurice Merleau-Ponty's analysis of interlocking consciousnesses *(Phenomenology of Perception)*

to a broad selection of eighteenth- and nineteenth-century novels, as well as to the films of Hitcheock, Hawks, and Woody Allen, Butte argues compellingly that something had changed in the narrative representation of consciousness at the time of Jane Austen: writers became able to represent the "deep intersubjectivity" of their characters, portraying them as aware of each other's perceptions of themselves and as responding to such perceptions with body language observable by their interlocutors, which generated a further series of mutual perceptions and reactions. Although Butte does not refer in his work to cognitive science or the Theory of Mind, his argument is in many respe cts compatible with the literary criticism that does.

22. On Woolf's definition of narrative ventriloquism, see DiBattista 132.
23. Pinker actually misquotes Woolf in his book to make his point stronger. According to Pinker, Woolf wrote that "In or about December 1910, human nature changed."
24. I quote here an anonymous reader for *PMLA*.
25. The quotations of Phelan are from a personal communication from 17 April 2003.

WORKS CITED

Abbott, Porter. "Humanists, Scientists and Cultural Surplus." *Substance* 94/95: 30 (2001): 203–17.

Auerbach, Erich. *Mimesis*. Princeton: Princeton Univ. Press. 1991.

Baron-Cohen, Simon. *Mindblindness: An Essay on Aution and Theory of Mind*. Cambridge: MIT Press, 1995.

Benjamin, Walter. *Illuminations*. New York: Harcourt, Brace & World, 1955.

Brook, Andrew, and Don Ross. *Daniel Dennett*. Cambridge: Cambridge Univ. Press, 2002.

Butte, George. *I know That You Know That I Know: Narrating Subjects from* Moll Flanders *to* Marnie. Columbus: The Ohio State University Press, forthcoming.

Byrne, Richard W., and Andrew Whiten. "The Emergence of Metarepresentation in Human Ontogeny and Primate Phylogeny," In *Natural Theories of Mind: Evolution, Development, and Simulation of Everyday Mindreading*, edited by Andrew Whiten, 267–82. Oxford: Basil Blackwell, 1991.

———. *Machiavellian Intelligence: Social Expertise and the Evolution of Intellect in Monkeys, Apes, and Humans*. Oxford: Oxford Univ. Press. 1988.

Carey, Susan, and Elizabeth Spelke. "Domain-Specific Knowledge and Conceptual Change." In *Mapping the Mind: Domain Specificity in Cognition and Culture*. edited by Lawrence A. Hirschfeld and Susan A. Gelman, 169–200. New York: Cambridge Univ. Press, 1994.

Carruthers, Perter. "Autism as Mind-Blindness: An Elaboration and Partial Defense." In *Theories of Theories of Mind*, edited by Peter Carruthers and Peter K Smith. 257–73. Cambridge Univ. Press, 1996

Cosmides, Leda, and John Tooby. "Origins of Domain Specificity: The Evolution of Functional Organization." In *Mapping the Mind: Domain Specificity in Cognition and Culture*, edited by Lawrence A. Hirschfeld and Susan A. Gelman, 85–116. New York: Cambridge Univ. Press, 1994.

Crane, Mary Thomas. *Shakespeare's Brain: Reading with Cognitive Theory*. Princeton: Princeton Univ. Press. 2001.

Dennett, Daniel. *The Intentional Stance*. Cambridge: MIT Press, 1987.

DiBattista, Maria. "Virginia Woolf and the Language of Authorship." In *The Cambridge Companion to Virginia Woolf*, edited by Sue Roe and Susan Sellers, 127–45. Cambridge: Cambridge Univ. Press, 2000.

Dick, Susan. "Literary Realism in *Mrs. Dalloway, To the Lighthouse, Orlando* and *The Waves.*" In *The Cambridge Companion to Virginia Woolf*, edited by Sue Roe and Susan Sellers, 50–71. Cambridge: Cambridge Univ. Press. 2000.

Dunbar, Robin. "On the Origin of the Human Mind." In *Evolution and the Human Mind: Modularity, Language, and Meta-Cognition,* edited by Peter Carruthers and Andrew Chamberlain, 238–53. Cambridge: Cambridge Univ. Press, 2000.

Easterlin, Nancy. "Making Knowledge: Bioepistemology and the Foundations of Literary Theory." *Mosaic* 32 (1999): 131–47.

———. "Voyages in the Verbal Universe: The Role of Speculation in Darwinian Literary Criticism." *Interdisciplinary Literary Studies: A Journal of Criticism and Theory* 2, no. 2 (Spring 2001): 59–73.

Fish, Stanley. "How to Recognize a Poem When You See One." In *American Criticism in the Poststructuralist Age,* edited by Ira Konigsberg, 102–15. Ann Arbor: Univ. of Michigan Press, 1981.

———. *Is There a Text in this Class?* Cambridge: Cambridge Univ. Press, 1980.

Gomez, Juan C. "Visual Behavior as a Window for Reading the Mind of Others in Primates." In *Natural Theories of Mind: Evolution, Development, and Simulation of Everyday Mindreading,* edited by Andrew Whiten, 195–208. Oxford: Basil Blackwell, 1991.

Grosz, Elizabeth. "Feminist Futures?" *Tulsa Studies in Women's Literature* 21, no. 1 (Spring 2002): 13–20.

Harris, Paul L. *The Work of Imagination.* Oxford: Blackwell Publishers, 2001.

Hart, F. Elizabeth. "The Epistemology of Cognitive Literary Studies." *Philosophy and Literature* 25 (2002): 314–34.

Hayles, N. Katherine. "Desiring Agency: Limiting Metaphors and Enabling Constraints in Dawkins and Deleuze/Guattari." *Substance* 94/95: 30 (2001): 144–59.

Hemingway, Ernest. *A Farewell to Arms.* New York: Charles Scribner's Sons, 1929.

Herman, David. "Regrounding Narratology: The Study of Narratively Organized Systems for Thinking." In *What Is Narratology?* edited by Jan-Christoph Meister, Tom Kindt, and Hans-Harald Müller. Berlin: de Gruyter, forthcoming.

———. "Scripts, Sequences, and Stories: Elements of a Postclassical Narratology." *PMLA* 112 (1997): 1046–59.

Hernadi, Paul. "Literature and Evolution." *Substance* 94/95: 30 (2001): 55–71.

Hogan, Patrick Colm. "Literary Universals." *Poetics Today* 18 (1997): 223–49.

Hughes, Claire, and Robert Plomin. "Individual Differences in Early Understanding of Mind: Genes, Non-Shared Environment and Modularity." In *Evolution and the Human Mind: Modularity, Language, and Meta-Cognition,* edited by Peter Carruthers and Andrew Chamberlain, 47–61. Cambridge: Cambridge Univ. Press, 2000.

Kanner, Leo. "Austistic Disturbances of Affective Contact." *Nervous Children* 2 (1943): 217–50.

Lee, Hermione. *Virginia Woolf.* New York: Alfred A. Knopf, 1997.

———. "Virginia Woolf's Essays." In The *Cambridge Companion to Virginia Woolf,* edited by Sue Roe and Susan Sellers, 91–108. Cambridge: Cambridge Univ. Press, 2000.

Leslie, Alan. "ToMM, ToBY, and Agency: Core Architecture and Domain Specificity." In *Mapping the Mind: Domain Specificity in Cognition and Culture,* edited by Lawrence Hirschfeld and Susan Gelman, 119–48. New York: Cambridge Univ. Press, 1994.

Origgi, Gloria, and Dan Sperber. "Evolution, Communication and the Proper Function of Language." In *Evolution and the Human Mind: Modularity, Language, and Meta-Cognition,* edited by Peter Carruthers and Andrew Chamberlain, 140–69. Cambridge: Cambridge Univ. Press, 2000.

Pinker, Steven. *The Blank Slate: The Modern Denial of Human Nature.* New York: Viking, 2002.

Premack, David, and Verena Dasser. "Perceptual Origins and Conceptual Evidence for Theory of Mind in Apes and Children." In *Natural Theories of Mind: Evolution, Development, and Simulation of Everyday Mindreading,* edited by Andrew Whiten, 253–66. Oxford: Basil Blackwell, 1991.

Richardson, Alan. *British Romanticism and the Science of Mind.* Cambridge: Cambridge Univ. Press, 2001.

Richardson, Alan, and Francis Steen. "Literature and the Cognitive Revolution: An Introduction." *Poetics Today* 23 (2002): 1–8.

Sacks, Oliver. *An Anthropologist on Mars.* New York: Alfred A. Knopf, 1995.

Scarry, Elaine. *Dreaming by the Book.* New York: Farrar, Straus, Giroux, 1999.

———. "Panel Discussion: Science, Culture, Meaning Values." In *Unity of Knowledge: The Convergence of Natural and Human Science,* 233–57. New York: The New York Academy of Sciences, 2001.

Spolsky, Ellen. "Cognitive Literary Historicism: A Response to Adler and Gross." *Poetics Today,* forth-coming.

———. *Satisfying Skepticism: Embodied Knowledge in the Early Modern World.* Aldershot: Ashgate, 2001.

———. "Why and How to Take the Wheat and Leave the Chaff." *Substance* 94/95 30, nos. 1–2(2001): 178–98.

Starr, Gabrielle G. "Ethics, Meaning, and the Work of Beauty." *Eighteenth-Century Studies* 35 (2002): 361–78.

Sternberg, Meir. "How Narrativity Makes a Difference." *Narrative* 9 (2001): 115–22.

Turner, Mark. *The Literary Mind.* New York: Oxford Univ. Press, 1996.

Vermeule, Blakey. *The Party of Humanity: Writing Moral Psychology in Eighteenth-Century Britain.* Baltimore: The Johns Hopkins Univ. Press, 2000.

Whitworth, Michael. "Virginia Woolf and Modernism." In *The Cambridge Companion to Virginia Woolf,* edited by Sue Roe and Susan Sellers, 146–63. Cambridge: Cambridge Univ. Press, 2000.

Woolf, Virginia. *The Diary of Virginia Woolf.* 5 vols. Edited by Anne Olivier Bell. London: Penguin, 1977–84.

———. *Jacob's Room.* London: Hogarth, 1976.

———. *The Letters of Virginia Woolf.* Vol. 2. Edited by Nigel Nicholson. London: Hogarth Press, 1975–80.

———. *Mrs. Dalloway.* San Diego: Harcourt Brace, 1981.

Zunshine, Lisa. "Eighteenth-Century Print Culture and the 'Truth' of Fictional Narrative." *Philosophy and Literature* 25 (2001): 215–32.

———. "Rhetoric, Cognition, and Ideology in Anna Laetitia Barbauld's 1781 *Hymns in Prose for Children.*" *Poetics Today* 23 (2001): 231–59.

———. "Richardson's *Clarissa* and a Theory of Mind." In *The Work of Fiction: Cognition, Culture, and Complexity,* edited by Ellen Spolsky and Alan Richardson. Aldershot: Ashgate Press, forthcoming.

GLOSSARY

This glossary provides concise definitions for many key terms from the essays in this book. It does not attempt to cover every term that someone might want addressed, and it does not pretend to exhaust the meaning of the terms. It only aims to give readers enough to prove useful, and perhaps to encourage them to read more elsewhere. Many of the terms receive more extended discussion in *How to Interpret Literature: Critical Theory for Literary and Cultural Studies,* the companion to this volume. Terms not included in the glossary can usually be understood in context or with a web search or a dictionary. Terms crucial for individual essays are addressed in the headnotes to the essays.

APORIA an undecidable impasse, a question that cannot be answered.

BASE economics, including the conditions of production, labor, and property. In classical Marxism, the base produces the superstructure, the rest of culture. (See *superstructure.*)

CULTURAL STUDIES a movement to study contemporary culture, especially popular culture, especially in light of Marxism and structuralism, and, eventually, psychoanalysis, feminism, race studies, and postcolonial studies.

DECONSTRUCTION the philosophical movement led by Jacques Derrida, focusing on the playful multiplicity and instability of language, as opposed to the stability of language that Derrida found in the structuralist linguistics of Ferdinand de Saussure.

DIACHRONIC having to do with time. (See *synchronic.*)

ESSENTIALISM the belief in an underlying truth that remains consistent across time for all instances of a given category. Such categories often include modes of human identity (gender, race, nationality, and so on), meaning that an essentialist believes that all people belonging to a given category share certain characteristics across otherwise changing times and places.

FALSE CONSCIOUSNESS in Marxist thinking, the way that people, under the unconscious sway of capitalism, often believe that something works in their interest when actually it works against their interest.

FEMINISM a movement that calls for taking women seriously and respectfully, reversing a deeply ingrained cultural pattern that makes not taking women seriously and respectfully seem natural, like mere truth.

HEGEMONY cultural power, including the dominant cultural patterns that achieve and sustain their dominance by encouraging—but not forcing—people to believe in them.

HYBRID mixed, multiple, combined, boundary crossing.

IDEOLOGY in Louis Althusser's influential definition (from the essay included in this volume), the unconscious assumptions of the dominant culture that shape people's thinking without their realizing it, even against their best interests.

INTERPELLATION the process of being passively, unconsciously absorbed into the assumptions (the ideology) of the dominant culture. (See *ideology*.)

MARXISM the political and interpretive thinking based on the ideas of Karl Marx. Marx gave special weight to materialism (as opposed to idealism), economics, and class struggle.

METONYMY the rhetorical figure that describes substituting one term for another term that is connected to or next to it, as when we call soldiers *boots on the ground* or call a train a *choo-choo*. Synecdoche (using a part to refer to a whole) is a kind of metonymy, as when people call a person with red hair *Red* or call a detective a *private eye*. (See the headnote to Jakobson's "The Metaphoric and Metonymic Poles.")

NEW CRITICISM the first systematic movement in American literary criticism. The new critics focused on interpreting individual literary texts. They called for the interpretation of a literary work to rest primarily on the work's intrinsic qualities, the actual words in the text, giving less weight to historical and social or extrinsic qualities.

NEW HISTORICISM a movement to integrate the study of literature with the study of history. For new historicists, literature does not just passively reflect history and culture. It actively influences history and culture.

NORMATIVE based on standards (also called norms). (Normative does not mean normal.)

POSTCOLONIAL STUDIES the study of culture and history, often including literature, in light of colonialism and postcolonialism.

POSTSTRUCTURALISM critical movements that come after structuralism, especially deconstruction, but sometimes associated with a combination of deconstruction and other movements.

PSYCHOANALYSIS the tradition of clinical treatment and cultural interpretation begun by Sigmund Freud and extended by Jacques Lacan, including Freud's focus on the unconscious and on repression, drives, and defenses and Lacan's focus on bringing Freud's ideas together with Saussurean linguistics.

QUEER STUDIES a way of interpreting culture that takes queer acts, life, and thought seriously and treats them respectfully. Queer studies often works in dialogue with a deconstructive sense of multiplicity and instability that evokes the variety of queerness, as opposed to essentializing queerness.

RACE STUDIES the study of race, often with a focus on seeing race in non essentialist ways, as a cultural rather than as a biological phenomenon.

READER RESPONSE a way of studying literature and culture that focuses on its readers and audiences.

REIFICATION when commodification reduces social relations, ideas, and even people to things (Latin *res*), thus intensifying alienation.

RUSSIAN FORMALISM an early- to mid-twentieth century movement of Russian critics who based the study of literature in the study of literary form. Russian formalism eventually influenced structuralism.

STRUCTURALISM patterns of thinking that derive from the structuralist linguistics of Ferdinand de Saussure. Structuralists see language as a construction of signs, linked pairs of signifieds and signifiers. They also see language as constructing what we use it to describe.

SUBJECT agent, doer, like the grammatical subject of a sentence.

SUPERSTRUCTURE In classical Marxism, the base produces the superstructure. The base is the economy. The superstructure is the culture at large: politics, institutions, the arts, and so on. Many contemporary Marxists, especially those who study the arts, see a less direct cause-and-effect relation between the base and the superstructure, but most Marxists and Marxist-influenced critics still see economics as crucially influencing culture. (See *base.*)

SYNCHRONIC literally at one time, though in practice often used to mean without regard to time, as opposed to diachronic. (See *diachronic.*)

TROPE an instance of figurative language (as a noun); also to trope (as a verb), meaning to use figurative language.

INDEX

CPSIA information can be obtained
at www.ICGtesting.com
Printed in the USA
BVHW01s2053080518
515390BV00006B/4/P